Tech Talk

Chapter 1:	Practicing Courteous and Responsible Cell Phone Use
	Tips for Controlling the E-Mail Monster
Chapter 2:	Techniques for Staying Connected in Virtual Teams
Chapter 4:	Being Interculturally Correct on the Web
Chapter 5:	Using Technology to Edit and Revise Collaborative Documents
Chapter 6:	Seven Ways Computers Can Help You Create Better Written Messages, Oral Presentations, and Web Pages
Chapter 7:	Using Spell Checkers and Grammar/Style Checkers Wisely
Chapter 8:	Your Internet Use Could Get You Fired
Chapter 10:	What Successful Online Sales Messages Have in Common
Chapter 11:	Using Technology to Personalize Form Letters
Chapter 12:	Managing Your Electronic Research Data Like a Pro
Chapter 15:	Making Effective Conference Calls

Spotlight on Communicators

Chapter 1:	Oren Harari
	Elaine Chao
Chapter 2:	Dave Thomas
	Roy Richards Jr.
	Peter Drucker
Chapter 3:	Ellen Fowler
	Oprah Winfrey
	Diane Sawyer
	Robert Rosen
Chapter 4:	Jason Rubin
	J. T. (Ted) Childs Jr.
	Andrea Jung
Chapter 5:	Danny O'Neill
	Condoleezza Rice
	Warren Buffett
	John H. Johnson
	Katie Couric
	Jane Bryant Quinn
Chapter 6:	Gerry Laybourne
	Max Messmer
	Arthur Levitt
Chapter 7:	Colin Powell
	Sam Walton
	William Raspberry
	Susan Schott Karr
Chapter 8:	Michael Eisner
	Marco Scibora
	Liz Hughes
	Barbara Hemphill
Chapter 9:	Peggy Foran
	Andrew S. Grove
Chapter 10:	Margaret "Meg" Whitman
	Herb Kelleher
	John W. Thompson
Chapter 11:	Estee Lauder
	Malcolm Forbes
Chapter 12:	Peggy Laun
	Tom Peters
Chapter 13:	Anthony Miranda
Chapter 14:	Tom Sant
Chapter 15:	Patricia F. Russo
	Sandra Day O'Connor
	Dianna Booher
	Nancy Friedman
Chapter 16:	Michael Dell
	Yana Parker
	Daisy Wright

Business Communication

PROCESS & PRODUCT

Mary Ellen Guffey

Professor of Business Emerita
Los Angeles Pierce College

5th edition

THOMSON
SOUTH-WESTERN

Australia · Canada · Mexico · Singapore · Spain · United Kingdom · United States

Business Communication: Process and Product, **5e**
Mary Ellen Guffey

VP/Editorial Director:
Jack W. Calhoun

Acquisitions Editor:
Keith Chasse

Developmental Editor:
Mary Draper

Sr. Marketing Manager:
Larry Qualls

Sr. Production Editor:
Deanna Quinn

Technology Project Editor:
Kelly Reid

Web Coordinator:
Scott Cook

Manufacturing Coordinator:
Diane Lohman

Production House:
WordCrafters Editorial Services, Inc.

Compositor:
GGS Information Services

Printer:
R.R. Donnelley
Willard, OH

Art Director:
Michelle Kunkler

Cover and Internal Designer:
Imbue Design/Kim Torbeck,
Cincinnati

Cover and Feature Illustrations:
Brian Jensen

Photography Manager:
Deanna Ettinger

Photo Researcher:
Terri Miller

Printed in the United States of America
1 2 3 4 5 08 07 06 05

Student Edition Package:
ISBN 0-324-22304-8
Student Edition Book:
ISBN 0-324-31190-7
Instructor's Edition Package:
ISBN 0-324-31223-7
Instructor's Edition Book:
ISBN 0-324-31223-7

Library of Congress Control Number:
2004114398

For more information about our products, contact us at:
Thomson Learning Academic Resource Center
1-800-423-0563

Thomson Higher Education
5191 Natorp Boulevard
Mason, OH 45040
USA

Asia (including India)
Thomson Learning
5 Shenton Way
#01-01 UIC Building
Singapore 068808

Australia/New Zealand
Thomson Learning Australia
102 Dodds Street
Southbank, Victoria 3006
Australia

Canada
Thomson Nelson
1120 Birchmount Road
Toronto, Ontario
M1K 5G4
Canada

Latin America
Thomson Learning
Seneca, 53
Colonia Polanco
11560 Mexico
D.F.Mexico

UK/Europe/Middle East/Africa
Thomson Learning
High Holborn House
50/51 Bedford Row
London WC1R 4LR
United Kingdom

Spain (including Portugal)
Thomson Paraninfo
Calle Magallanes, 25
28015 Madrid, Spain

Dr. Mary Ellen Guffey
Thomson South-Western

Dear Business Communication Students and Instructors:

As we release the Fifth Edition of *Business Communication: Process and Product*, I am proud to bring you an updated version of the award-winning textbook that has won the loyal support of professors and the enthusiastic acceptance of students throughout the world.

Working to make the No. 1 business communication textbook an even better teaching and learning tool, I have added content and resources in several critical areas:

- **Strengthened coverage of communication technology** prepares students for the constant evolution of the digital workplace. New Tech Talk boxes and over 100 new references build student knowledge, skills, and confidence.
- **Renewed emphasis on Guffey's signature 3-x-3 writing process** provides even more instruction and illustration to guide students in applying a simple 3-step plan to solve communication problems.
- **Amplified e-mail instruction** includes new sections devoted to reading and responding to e-mail as well as coverage of increasingly common e-mail uses such as sending résumés and cover letters.
- **Expanded coverage of business plans** gives budding entrepreneurs instruction on how to write successful plans—more treatment than any other mainstream book. In addition, we provide a complete business plan teaching module for instructors.
- **Five new high-quality videos**, made specifically for the Fifth Edition, emphasize key chapter topics, reinforce lectures, and provide critical-thinking discussion questions.

Other features in the Fifth Edition are revised end-of-chapter activities (about 70 percent are new) including a new consumer-oriented assignment in each chapter, revised test bank questions (about 75 percent are new), a revised Student Study Guide, and an exciting self-teaching grammar/mechanics digital program called "Your Personal Language Trainer." Students may purchase access to Guffey Xtra!, an online study assistant that offers Trainer, Speak Right!, Spell Right!, bonus online chapters, documents for analysis, PowerPoint® slides, and much more.

In the preface that follows, we illustrate key features of the Fifth Edition to introduce you to the process of successful business communication and the conversion of that process into powerful products. As always, I welcome your comments and suggestions as you use the No. 1 book in the field, *Business Communication: Process and Product, 5e*.

Cordially,

Mary Ellen Guffey

E-mail: meguffey@westwords.com • Student Web Site: http://guffey.swlearning.com • Guffey Xtra!: http://guffeyxtra.swlearning.com

Partner. Mentor. Resource.

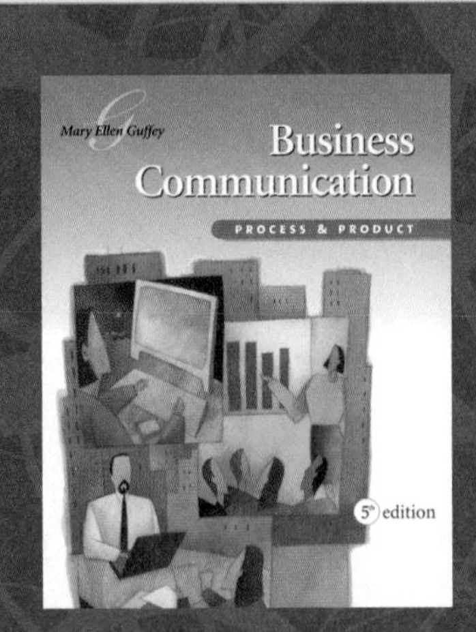

"Whenever I have asked questions via e-mail, I have received prompt responses with clear explanations. As an instructor, I appreciate the vast supply of 'quick find' information that I can use in my classroom. It takes forever to do that kind of research from scratch, time I do not have."

—Judy Dorn

Fox Valley Technical College, Appleton, Wisconsin

Guffey Gives Unparalleled Author Support

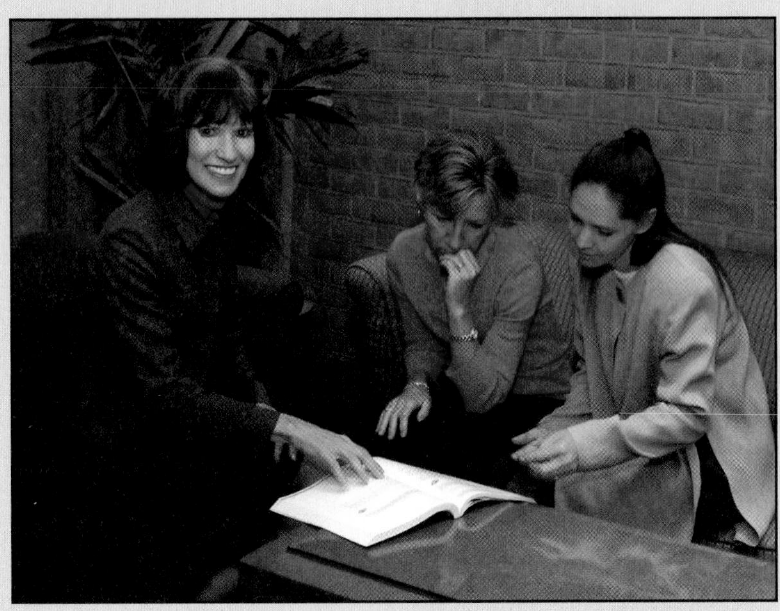

Mary Ellen Guffey is committed to providing instructors with innovative teaching ideas through newsletters, Web sites, and customized teaching materials. Dedicated to her role as a partner in the classroom, Mary Ellen Guffey is shown here (at left) conferring with Diana McKowen, Indiana University, and Rolanda P. Pollard, San Jose State University, at the Association for Business Communication meeting.

Mary Ellen Guffey has earned her status as the world's leading business communication author through her determination to stay at the top of her field and her dedication to the instructors and students who use her textbooks.

Dr. Guffey keeps up-to-date on all issues and innovations in business communication through her intensive research and her active participation at workshops, seminars, and conferences across the country and around the world.

With more than thirty years of classroom experience, Dr. Guffey has developed unique teaching techniques that she generously shares through her newsletters, Web sites, teleconferences, and customized teaching materials. She serves as both partner and mentor to hundreds of business communication instructors who rely on her texts.

Award-Winning. Highly Respected. Used Worldwide.

Simply the Best Business Communication Text

Recognized by the Text and Academic Author's Association as the top book in its field, *Business Communication: Process and Product* remains the No. 1 text on the market, used by more students in the United States and around the world than any other.

Hallmarked by completely up-to-date content and a time-tested, interactive learning system, this text effectively covers all the basic goals recommended by the Association of Collegiate Business Schools and Programs and the American Assembly of Collegiate Schools of Business, including coverage of intercultural communication, diversity, ethics, and evolving communication technologies.

"When I began using Guffey's Business Communication: Process and Product, *the energy level of class discussion was noticeably higher. After 20 years of teaching and consulting experience, I could almost teach without a textbook, but who would want to when one as comprehensive and smart as Guffey's is available? It energizes students with its juicy insider info and rapid-fire style, virtually doing all of my work for me."*

—Eve Dobkins Ash

Oklahoma State University, Tulsa

Practical. Visual. Effective.

The 3-x-3 Writing Process

FIGURE 5.1 *Guffey's 3-x-3 Writing Process*

1 Prewriting	2 Writing	3 Revising
ANALYZE: Decide on your purpose. What do you want the receiver to do or believe? What channel is best?	**RESEARCH:** Gather data to provide facts. Search company files, previous correspondence, and the Internet. What do you need to know to write this message?	**REVISE:** Edit your message to be sure it is clear, conversational, concise, and readable.
ANTICIPATE: Profile the audience. What does the receiver already know? Will the receiver's response be neutral, positive, or negative?	**ORGANIZE:** Group similar facts together. Decide how to organize your information. Outline your plan and make notes.	**PROOFREAD:** Read carefully to find errors in spelling, grammar, punctuation, names, numbers, and format.
ADAPT: What techniques can you use to adapt your message to its audience and anticipated reaction?	**COMPOSE.** Prepare a first draft, usually writing quickly.	**EVALUATE:** Will this message achieve your purpose? Have you thought enough about the audience to be sure this message is appropriate and appealing?

Mary Ellen Guffey's signature 3-x-3 writing process demystifies writing by giving students a solid, universally applicable strategy for developing effective communication.

"I appreciate your comprehensive learning and support system. Great to see so many best practices employed systematically!"

—Dan Doherty

Camosun College, Victoria, British Columbia, Canada

Expanded. Updated. Enhanced

The Features You Value, the Content You Need

Responding to changes in the workplace, Dr. Guffey has expanded and updated coverage in four key areas.

"BC:PP's currency in dealing with business communication issues is just one of the book's many fine features. Its completeness is perhaps its greatest asset as a teaching tool: I don't have to hunt for collateral or supplemental materials because everything I need appears between the covers of your book."

—Richard Dean Hovey

Pima Community College, Tucson, Arizona

1 *Communication Technology*

Business Communication: Process and Product, 5e prepares the business communicator for electronic communication challenges by providing cutting edge communication technology coverage.

- **E-mail coverage** has been expanded. Chapter 8 applies the 3-x-3 writing process to e-mails and memos, and includes sections on reading, replying to, and managing e-mail efficiently and appropriately.
- **Collaboration technology** discussion includes timely coverage of conferencing (audio, video, desktop, media) as well as Internet relay chat, webcasting, and other meeting tools.
- **Instant messaging, wireless networking, and mobile communication**, vital new communication tools, are integrated throughout the text.
- **Employment communication,** covered in Chapter 16, now offers the latest techniques, model documents, and advice for successful job searching, résumé writing, and interviewing in a digital age.

2 *E-mail, Web, and InfoTrac*

E-mail, Web, and InfoTrac assignments help students learn to use technology effectively to communicate.

position. If some jobs are found to be overly demanding, your boss may redistribute job tasks or hire additional employees. Based on your own work or personal experience, write a well-organized message describing your duties, the time you spend on each task, and the skills needed for what you do. Provide enough details to make a clear record of your job. Use actual names and describe actual tasks. Report to the head of the organization. The organization could be a campus club or committee on which you serve. Don't make your message a list of complaints. Just describe what you do in an objective tone. By the way, your boss appreciates brevity. Keep your message under one page.

8.10 Information E-Mail or Memo: Party Time (Obj. 4)

E-MAIL

Staff members in your office were disappointed that no holiday party was given last year. They don't care what kind of party it is, but they do want some kind of celebration this year.
Your Task. You have been asked to draft a message to the office staff about the upcoming December holiday party. Decide what kind of party you would like. Include information about where the party will be held, when it is, what the cost will be, what kind of food will be served, whether guests are allowed, and with whom to make reservations.

8.11 Information E-Mail or Memo: Planning for Important Milestone (Obj. 4)

E-MAIL | TEAM

Your company hired a writing consultant to help employees improve their communication skills.
Your Task. The following message was assigned as an exercise to train your team in recognizing good and bad writing. In small groups discuss its weaknesses and then compose, either individually or as a team, an improved version.

DATE: Current
TO: All Employees
FROM: Margaret Tilly, Coordinator, Employee Resources
SUBJECT: An Important Milestone in Your Life

We know that retirement is an important milestone in anyone's life, and we are aware that many employees do not have sufficient information that relates to the prospect of their retirement. Many employees who are approaching retirement age have come to this office wanting to talk about health, financial needs, family responsibilities, and income from outside sources and how these all relate to their retirement. It would be much easier for us to answer all these questions at once, and that is what we will try to do.

We would like to answer your questions at a series of retirement planning sessions in the company cafeteria. The first meeting is November 17. We will start at 4 p.m., which means that the company is giving you one hour of released time to attend this important session. We will meet from 4 to 6 p.m. when we will stop for dinner. We will begin again at 7 p.m. and finish at 8 p.m.

We have arranged for three speakers. They are: our company benefits supervisor, a financial planner, and a psychologist who treats retirees who have mental problems. The three sessions are planned for: November 17, November 30, and December 7.

8.12 Procedure E-Mail or Memo: Rules for Wireless Phone Use in Sales Reps' Cars (Obj. 4)

E-MAIL | INFOTRAC | TEAM | WEB

As one of the managers of LaReve, a hair care and skin products company, you are alarmed at a newspaper article you just saw. A stockbroker for Smith Barney was making cold calls on his personal phone while driving. His car hit and killed a motorcyclist. The brokerage firm was sued and accused of contributing to an accident by encouraging employees to use cell phones while driving. To avoid the risk of paying huge damages awarded by an emotional jury, the brokerage firm offered the victim's family a $500,000 settlement.

You begin to worry, knowing that your company has provided its 75 sales representatives with wireless phones to help them keep in touch with the home base while they are in the field. At the next management meeting, other members agreed that you should draft a message detailing some wireless phone safety rules for your sales reps. On the Web you learned that anyone with a wireless phone should get to know its features, including speed dial, automatic memory, and redial. Another suggestion involved using a hands-free device. Management members decided to purchase these for every sales rep and have the devices available within one month. In positioning the wireless phone in a car, it should be within easy reach. It should be where you can grab it without removing your eyes from the road. If you get an incoming call at an inconvenient time, your voice mail should be allowed to pick up the call. You should never talk, of course, during hazardous driving conditions, such as rain, sleet, snow, and ice.

Taking notes or looking up phone numbers is dangerous when driving. You want to warn sales reps not to get into dangerous situations by reading (such as an address book) or writing (such as taking notes) while driving.

The more you think about it, the more you think that sales reps should not use their wireless phones while the car is moving. They really should pull over. But you know that would be hard to enforce.

244

Rich chapter resources are available on the Web sites.

3 *Listening and Speaking Skills*

In business communication it's not just what you say but how you say it that counts. New and expanded sections on oral presentations teach students to become careful listeners and dynamic speakers.

- Chapter 3 features a new section on strategies and tips for listening to colleagues and teammates.
- New end-of-chapter activities develop both speaking and listening skills.
- Chapter 15 expands coverage of mutimedia presentation techniques.

4 *Business Plans*

The Fifth Edition of *Business Communication: Process and Product* includes more coverage of business plans than any other mainstream business communication book.

Current Cases and Activities for Every Chapter

Dr. Guffey's commitment to excellence extends to the end-of-chapter materials.

- Over 70 percent of the activities and cases are new or revised with high quality, fully formatted solutions.
- New consumer education cases expand student knowledge, build practical consumer skills, and sharpen language skills.
- Real-world end-of-chapter activities involve actual communication issues and strategies at companies such as Krispy Kreme, Target, Gap Inc., and McDonald's.

Updated Content and Favorite Features

The information students need and the teaching tools instructors rely on are updated and retained in the Fifth Edition.

- **Small Groups and Teams** – The dynamics of team communication are explored through tips, techniques, and strategies that prepare students for effective collaboration, including identifying team and group roles, dealing with dysfunctional members, and managing meetings.
- **Cross-Cultural Workforce Diversity** – Dr. Guffey offers practical skills for achieving successful communication in the global environment and promoting intercultural sensitivity, awareness, tolerance, and accommodation in the workplace.
- **WebThink Activities** – Extending the text into the World Wide Web, each chapter provides references to relevant Web sites and WebThink activities on the Guffey student Web site, along with critical-thinking questions to direct the students' learning.

"Every week when I am teaching a night class until 11 p.m., I am so glad to have the various exercises and case studies you provide. Could not survive without you!"

—Mike Gamble

New York Institute of Technology, Manhattan

"At our initial meetings with new instructors, we recommend they use Guffey because it makes teaching the course easy. She provides everything and anything you might need. Very comprehensive."

—Professor Linda Landis

University of Illinois, Chicago

Real. Useful. Proven.

Features that Promote Learning and Comprehension

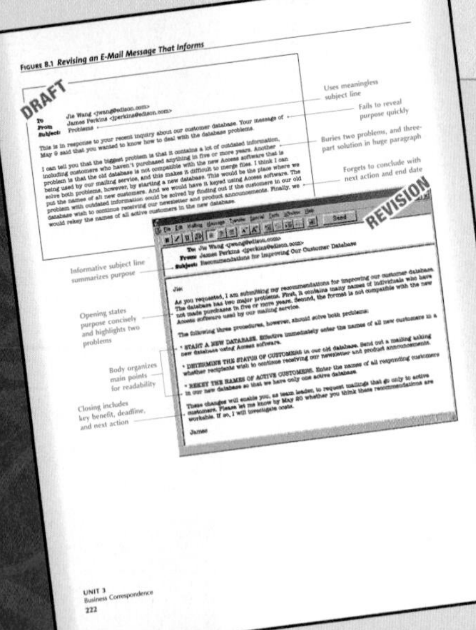

Figure 8.1 *Revising an E-Mail Message That Informs*

DRAFT

To: Jie Wang <jwang@edison.com>
From: James Perkins <jperkins@edison.com>
Subject: Problems

This is in response to your recent inquiry about our customer database. Your message of May 9 said that you wanted to know how to deal with the database problems.

I can tell you that the biggest problem is that it contains a lot of outdated information, including customers who haven't purchased anything in five or more years. Another problem is that the old database is not compatible with the new Access software that is being used by our mailing service, and this makes it difficult to merge files. I think I can solve both problems, however, by starting a new database. This would be the place where we put the names of all new customers. And we would have it keyed using Access software. The problem with outdated information could be solved by finding out if the customers in our old database wish to continue receiving our newsletter and product announcements. Finally, we would rekey the names of all active customers in the new database.

Uses meaningless subject line

Fails to reveal purpose quickly

Buries two problems, and three-part solution in huge paragraph

Forgets to conclude with next action and end date

REVISION

To: Jie Wang <jwang@edison.com>
From: James Perkins <jperkins@edison.com>
Subject: Recommendations for Improving Our Customer Database

Jie:

As you requested, I am submitting my recommendations for improving our customer database. The database has two major problems. First, it contains many names of individuals who have not made purchases in five or more years. Second, the format is not compatible with the new Access software used by our mailing service.

The following three procedures, however, should solve both problems:

- START A NEW DATABASE. Effective immediately enter the names of all new customers in a new database using Access software.
- DETERMINE THE STATUS OF CUSTOMERS in our old database. Send out a mailing asking whether recipients wish to continue receiving our newsletter and product announcements.
- REKEY THE NAMES OF ACTIVE CUSTOMERS. Enter the names of all responding customers in our new database so that we have only one active database.

These changes will enable you, as team leader, to request mailings that go only to active customers. Please let me know by May 20 whether you think these recommendations are workable. If so, I will investigate costs.

James

Informative subject line summarizes purpose

Opening states purpose concisely and highlights two problems

Body organizes main points for readability

Closing includes key benefit, deadline, and next action

UNIT 3
Business Correspondence
222

Model Documents

Fully formatted model documents—letters, e-mail messages, memos, and reports—demonstrate communication concepts in action. "Before and after" messages help students visualize the writing process and revision techniques.

"The diversity of teaching and student supplements appears to be the most detailed I've seen with any business communication textbook. The Career Coach, Ethical Insight, and Tech Talk boxes in each chapter are unique as a way to superimpose themes throughout the text."

—Professor Ron Weidenfeller

Grand Rapids Community College, Grand Rapids, Michigan

Three-Part Real Case Studies

Students learn best from real-world examples—and the unique, three-part case studies from high-profile companies such as Disney, Procter & Gamble, and Amazon.com that run through each chapter reinforce that learning.

COMMUNICATION IN PROCESS

Old Navy Struggles to Help Gap Get Its Groove Back

AFTER SPECTACULAR GROWTH to become the nation's largest specialty apparel retailer in the 1990s, Gap fell from favor in the early 2000s. Critics accused it of making every bad move a retailer could. Besides major misses in fashion, the company failed to differentiate among its three brands—Banana Republic, Gap, and Old Navy—and it opened too many stores.[1]

The company that had pioneered the casual cool look with fitted jeans, khakis, and simple T-shirts suddenly lost its fashion compass. Once-loyal customers were turned off by trendy rhinestone-encrusted pink jeans and other far-out novelties.[2] Under new management, Gap is now working to improve its merchandise mix, reduce inventories, and halt capital spending. Ultimately, though, Gap must find a way to get its customers back.

Perhaps the brightest spot in Gap's comeback has been the company's Old Navy discount division. With 800 big-box stores selling lower-priced apparel, Old Navy now accounts for 41 percent of Gap's total sales.[3] A division of Gap Inc., the Old Navy brand was created in 1994 as a fun fashion label with broad appeal and a casual attitude. Emphasizing humor and mass appeal, Old Navy gave shoppers music and bright colors while promoting a quirky image.[4]

From the beginning Old Navy's president Jenny Ming was intent on building a fun brand that delivered fashion at low prices. But over the years, she began to recognize that the fashion business was changing. Both Gap and Old Navy once chased fickle teenagers too hard, offering super-low-cut jeans and edgy styles that flattered only the young and slender.[5] In rebuilding Old Navy, Ming returned to its tradition of blue jeans, simple tops, and basics as a strategy to regain leadership in the casual-dress business. Ming says that in the past designers dictated what people wore. Now the power is shifting to the consumer. It's more about what individuals want to wear and are comfortable with rather than what designers choose.[6]

In learning to please customers, Old Navy collects ideas from product managers, focus groups, field researchers, and designers, while always keeping an eye on the competition. Color and concept inspiration may come from people-watching on the streets of Tokyo, a flash from a dream, or a visit to a local art gallery.[7]

Old Navy president Jenny Ming helped pull Gap out of a prolonged slump.

Critical Thinking

- In what ways would research (gathering information) be important to Jenny Ming at Old Navy and to other businesspeople?
- Why is it important for Jenny Ming and other business communicators to gather all necessary information before making management decisions?
- What techniques can business communicators at Old Navy and other companies use to generate ideas for new products as well as for business processes?

http://www.oldnavy.com

CONTINUED ON PAGE 173

case study

163

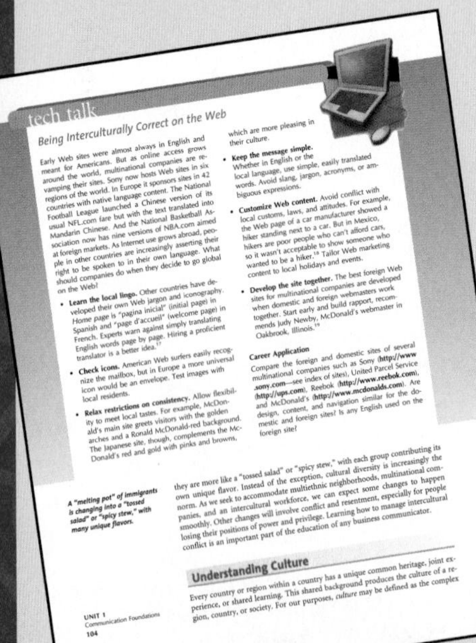

tech talk

Being Interculturally Correct on the Web

Early Web sites were almost always in English and meant for Americans. But as online access grows around the world, multinational companies are revamping their sites. Sony now hosts Web sites in six regions of the world. In Europe it sponsors sites in 42 countries with native language content. The National Football League launched a Chinese version of its usual NFL.com fare but with the text translated into Mandarin Chinese. And the National Basketball Association now has nine versions of NBA.com aimed at foreign markets. As Internet use grows abroad, people in other countries are increasingly asserting their right to be spoken to in their own language. What should companies do when they decide to go global on the Web?

- **Learn the local lingo.** Other countries have developed their own Web jargon and iconography. *Home page* is "pagina inicial" (initial page) in Spanish and "page d'accueil" (welcome page) in French. Experts warn against simply translating English words page by page. Hiring a proficient translator is a better idea.[17]
- **Check icons.** American Web surfers easily recognize the mailbox, but in Europe a more universal icon would be an envelope. Test images with local residents.
- **Relax restrictions on consistency.** Allow flexibility to meet local tastes. For example, McDonald's main site greets visitors with the golden arches and a Ronald McDonald-red background. The Japanese site, though, complements the McDonald's red and gold with pinks and browns, which are more pleasing in their culture.
- **Keep the message simple.** Whether in English or the local language, use simple, easily translated words. Avoid slang, jargon, acronyms, or ambiguous expressions.
- **Customize Web content.** Avoid conflict with local customs, laws, and attitudes. For example, the Web page of a car manufacturer showed a hiker standing next to a car. But in Mexico, hikers are poor people who can't afford cars, so it wasn't acceptable to show someone who wanted to be a hiker.[18] Tailor Web marketing content to local holidays and events.
- **Develop the site together.** The best foreign Web sites for multinational companies are developed when domestic and foreign webmasters work together. Start early and build rapport, recommends Judy Newby, McDonald's webmaster in Oakbrook, Illinois.[19]

Career Application

Compare the foreign and domestic sites of several multinational companies such as Sony (**http://www.sony.com**—see index of sites), United Parcel Service (**http://ups.com**), Reebok (**http://www.reebok.com**), and McDonald's (**http://www.mcdonalds.com**). Are design, content, and navigation similar for the domestic and foreign sites? Is any English used on the foreign site?

they are more like a "tossed salad" or "spicy stew," with each group contributing its own unique flavor. Instead of the exception, cultural diversity is increasingly the norm. As we seek to accommodate multiethnic neighborhoods, multinational companies, and an intercultural workforce, we can expect some changes to happen smoothly. Other changes will involve conflict and resentment, especially for people losing their positions of power and privilege. Learning how to manage intercultural conflict is an important part of the education of any business communicator.

A "melting pot" of immigrants is changing into a "tossed salad" or "spicy stew," with many unique flavors.

Understanding Culture

Every country or region within a country has a unique common heritage, joint experience, or shared learning. This shared background produces the culture of a region, country, or society. For our purposes, *culture* may be defined as the complex

UNIT 1
Communication Foundations
104

TechTalk

Tech Talk boxes throughout the text provide important information bites on the technology tools and issues common in today's workplace.

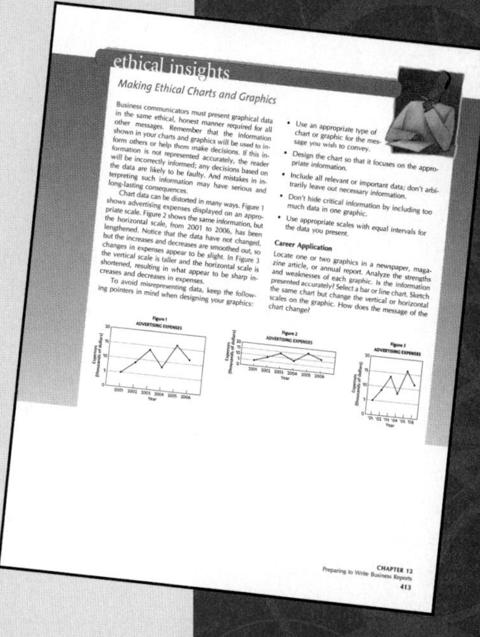

ethical insights

Making Ethical Charts and Graphics

Business communicators must present graphical data in the same ethical, honest manner required for all other messages. Remember that the information shown in your charts and graphics will be used to inform others or help them make decisions. If this information is not represented accurately, the reader will be incorrectly informed; any decisions based on the data are likely to be faulty. And mistakes in interpreting such information may have serious and long-lasting consequences.

Chart data can be distorted in many ways. Figure 1 shows advertising expenses displayed on an appropriate scale. Figure 2 shows the same information, but the horizontal scale, from 2001 to 2006, has been lengthened. Notice that the data have not changed, but the increases and decreases are smoothed out, so changes in expenses appear to be slight. In Figure 3 the vertical scale is taller and the horizontal scale is shortened, resulting in what appear to be sharp increases and decreases in expenses.

To avoid misrepresenting data, keep the following pointers in mind when designing your graphics:

- Use an appropriate type of chart or graphic for the message you wish to convey.
- Design the chart so that it focuses on the appropriate information.
- Include all relevant or important data; don't arbitrarily leave out necessary information.
- Don't hide critical information by including too much data in one graphic.
- Use appropriate scales with equal intervals for the data you present.

Career Application

Locate one or two graphics in a newspaper, magazine article, or annual report. Analyze the strengths and weaknesses of each graphic. Is the information presented accurately? Select a bar or line chart. Sketch the same chart but change the vertical or horizontal scales on the graphic. How does the message of the chart change?

CHAPTER 12
Preparing to Write Business Reports
413

Ethics in the Workplace

To stress the importance of ethical considerations in all communication settings, Dr. Guffey introduces ethical challenges and the tools for doing the right thing in Chapter 1 and then integrates these tools throughout the text to present ethical conduct in context.

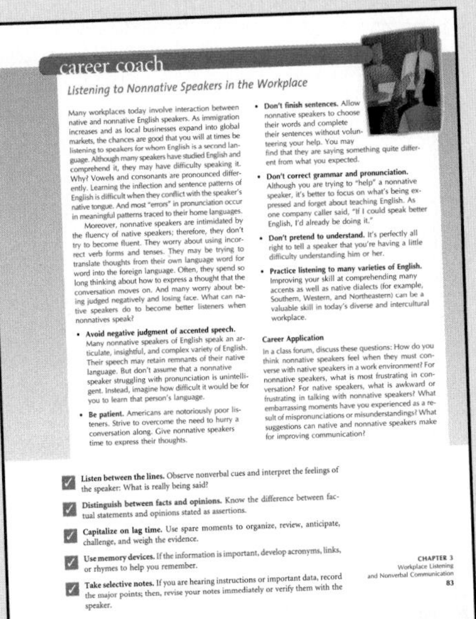

career coach

Listening to Nonnative Speakers in the Workplace

Many workplaces today involve interaction between native and nonnative English speakers. As immigration increases and as local businesses expand into global markets, the chances are good that you will at times be listening to speakers for whom English is a second language. Although many speakers have studied English and comprehend it, they may have difficulty speaking it. Why? Vowels and consonants are pronounced differently. Learning the inflection and sentence patterns of English is difficult when they conflict with the speaker's native tongue. And most "errors" in pronunciation occur in meaningful patterns traced to their home languages.

Moreover, nonnative speakers are intimidated by the fluency of native speakers; therefore, they don't try to become fluent. They worry about using incorrect verb forms and tenses. They may be trying to translate thoughts from their own language word for word into the foreign language. Often, they spend so long thinking about how to express a thought that the conversation moves on. And many worry about being judged negatively and losing face. What can native speakers do to become better listeners when nonnatives speak?

- **Avoid negative judgment of accented speech.** Many nonnative speakers of English speak an articulate, insightful, and complex variety of English. Their speech may retain remnants of their native language. But don't assume that a nonnative speaker struggling with pronunciation is unintelligent. Instead, imagine how difficult it would be for you to learn that person's language.
- **Be patient.** Americans are notoriously poor listeners. Strive to overcome the need to hurry a conversation along. Give nonnative speakers time to express their thoughts.
- **Don't finish sentences.** Allow nonnative speakers to choose their words and complete their sentences without volunteering your help. You may find that they are saying something quite different from what you expected.
- **Don't correct grammar and pronunciation.** Although you are trying to "help" a nonnative speaker, it's better to focus on what's being expressed and forget about teaching English. As one company caller said, "If I could speak better English, I'd already be doing it."
- **Don't pretend to understand.** It's perfectly all right to tell a speaker that you're having a little difficulty understanding him or her.
- **Practice listening to many varieties of English.** Improving your skill at comprehending many accents as well as native dialects (for example, Southern, Western, and Northeastern) can be a valuable skill in today's diverse and intercultural workplace.

Career Application

In a class forum, discuss these questions: How do you think nonnative speakers feel when they must converse with native speakers in a work environment? For nonnative speakers, what is most frustrating in conversation? For native speakers, what is awkward or frustrating in talking with nonnative speakers? What embarrassing moments have you experienced as a result of mispronunciations or misunderstandings? What suggestions can native and nonnative speakers make for improving communication?

- ☑ **Listen between the lines.** Observe nonverbal cues and interpret the feelings of the speaker: What is really being said?
- ☑ **Distinguish between facts and opinions.** Know the difference between factual statements and opinions stated as assertions.
- ☑ **Capitalize on lag time.** Use spare moments to organize, review, anticipate, challenge, and weigh the evidence.
- ☑ **Use memory devices.** If the information is important, develop acronyms, links, or rhymes to help you remember.
- ☑ **Take selective notes.** If you are hearing instructions or important data, record the major points; then, revise your notes immediately or verify them with the speaker.

CHAPTER 3
Workplace Listening
and Nonverbal Communication
83

Applied Career Skills

Career Coach boxes offer practical advice and information on translating communication skills to future careers.

Spotlight on Communicators boxes highlight successful communication strategies of well-known professionals and other business leaders—such as Colin Powell, Meg Whitman, and Oprah Winfrey.

charged, whether angry or extremely happy, it's a good idea to postpone any serious listening.

2. Become Actively Involved. Show that you are listening closely by leaning forward and maintaining eye contact with the speaker. Don't fidget or try to complete another task at the same time you are listening. Listen to more than the spoken words. How are they said? What implied meaning, reasoning, and feelings do you hear behind the spoken words? Does the speaker's body language (eye contact, posture, movements) support or contradict the main message?

You listen better when you control distractions, become actively involved, separate facts from opinion, and identify important facts.

3. Separate Facts From Opinions. Facts are truths known to exist; for example, *Microsoft is located in Redmond, Washington.* Opinions are statements of personal judgments or preferences; for example, *Microsoft stock is always a good investment.* Some opinions are easy to recognize because speakers preface them with statements such as *I think, It seems to me,* and *As far as I'm concerned.*[18] Often, however, listeners must evaluate assertions to decide their validity. Good listeners consider whether speakers are credible and speaking within their areas of competence. They don't automatically accept assertions as facts.

spotlight on communicators

Celebrated talk show host Oprah Winfrey owes much of her success to the artful application of the simple process of listening and responding. "Communicating with people is how I always developed any kind of value about myself," says the most successful female entertainer in the world. On her show she is able to block out external distractions, become actively involved, listen empathically without interrupting, paraphrase her guests' ideas, and ask clarifying questions to draw out deep meanings and issues that underlie their everyday lives.

4. Identify Important Facts. Speakers on the job often intersperse critical information with casual conversation. Unrelated topics pop up—ball scores, a customer's weird request, a computer glitch, the boss's extravagant new SUV. Your task is to select what's important and register it mentally. What step is next in your project? Who does what? What is your role?

5. Don't Interrupt. While someone else has the floor, don't interrupt with a quick reply or opinion. And don't show nonverbal disagreement such as negative head shaking, rolling eyes, sarcastic snorting, or audible sighs. Good listeners let speakers have their say. Interruptions are not only impolite, but they also prevent you from hearing the speaker's complete thought. Listeners who interrupt with their opinions sidetrack discussions and cause hard feelings.

You listen better when you refrain from interrupting, ask clarifying questions, paraphrase, capitalize on lag time, take notes, and observe gender differences.

6. Ask Clarifying Questions. Good listeners wait for the proper moment and then ask questions that do not attack the speaker. Instead of saying, "But I don't understand how you can say that," a good listener seeks clarification with questions such as, "Please help me understand by explaining more about . . . ." Because questions can put you in the driver's seat, think about them in advance. Use open questions (those without set answers) to draw out feelings, motivations, ideas, and suggestions. Use closed fact-finding questions to identify key factors in a discussion.[19] And, by the way, don't ask a question unless you are ready to be quiet and listen to the answer.

7. Paraphrase to Increase Understanding. To make sure you understand a speaker, rephrase and summarize a message in your own words. Be objective and nonjudgmental. Remember, your goal is to understand what the speaker has said—not to show how mindless the speaker's words sound when parroted. Remember, too, that other workplace listeners will also benefit from a clear summary of what was said.

CHAPTER 3
Workplace Listening
and Nonverbal Communication
81

C.L.U.E.

Competent Language Usage Essentials, a condensed business writer's handbook included as an appendix to the text, summarizes key grammar and language principles. Totally revised C.L.U.E. exercises at the end of each chapter encourage students to build their skills with self-teaching checkpoints. Answers to all C.L.U.E. exercises appear at the end of the book.

Powerful. Productive. Provided.

"I have used BC:PP for many years in our Professional Writing course. The book is absolutely wonderful. It contains all the most up-to-date business case studies and examples. Students, both traditional and nontraditional, have consistently remarked that the text is a valuable reference manual. The ancillaries are super and the videos have stimulated great class discussion."

—Carol L. Woods

Nichols College, Dudley, Massachusetts

Technology for Instructors

The book is just the beginning. Extend the classroom, expand learning opportunities, and experience all that education can be with online resources and technology supports that inform, educate, and entertain.

InSite—an online solution for both instructors and students

InSite is a powerful, all-in-one tool that allows instructors the opportunity to manage the flow of homework assignments online. With one integrated program, students can submit business documents and improve writing and grammar skills.

Instructors using InSite can assign, view, and grade student papers while tracking grades with a built-in course management system. InSite also allows instructors to insert editing notes on students' assigned documents. In addition, InSite tracks the total number of times certain types of corrections are made on a student's document.

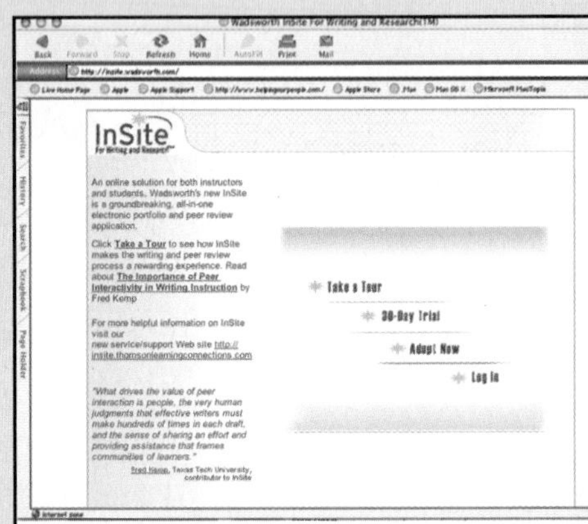

http://insite.swlearning.com

New Videos to Support Teaching

Thomson South-Western offers a new video series called "Building Workplace Communication Skills," developed specifically for Guffey's *Business Communication: Process and Product, 5e.*

- Career Success Starts With Communication Foundations
- Guffey's 3-x-3 Writing Process Develops Fluent Workplace Skills
- Smart E-Mails and Memos Advance Your Career
- Effective On-the-Job Oral Presentations
- Sharpening Your Interview Skills

Additionally, the "Bridging the Gap" video activities complement and enrich the text. Featuring real companies and real communication issues that managers and employees face, these videos require student analysis, problem-solving skills, and application of concepts from the text. The "Bridging the Gap" videos cover these topics:

Erasing Stereotypes • Innovation, Learning and Communication • Social Responsibility and Communication • Routine Business Letters • Persuasion and Profitability • Negative News

Instructor's Resource CD-ROM

This all-on-one handy disk provides a digital version of the Instructor's Manual, plus PowerPoint® chapter review slides, ExamView® software, printed test banks, and transparency masters as Word documents.

WebTUTOR™ Advantage

Taking full advantage of the latest educational technology, Mary Ellen Guffey has developed customized content for WebTutor™ Advantage, available for both Blackboard® and WebCT®. WebTutor™ Advantage offers powerful class management, customization, and communication tools that ensure maximum support for your campus or distance-learning students. Specialized features in Dr. Guffey's WebTutor™ Advantage include:

InSite • Narrated chapter previews • E-lectures • Chapter review quizzes • Demonstration problems • Writing improvement exercises and tutorials • Flash Cards • Critical Thinking Cases • Building Workplace Communication Skills and Bridging the Gap videos

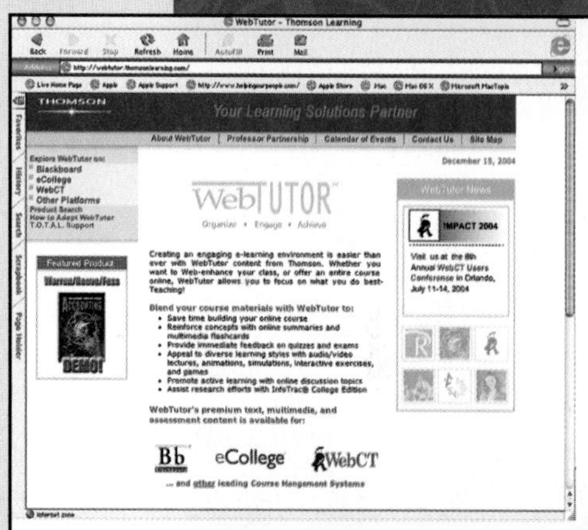

WebTUTOR™ ToolBox

Online learning is growing at a rapid pace. Whether you are planning to offer courses at a distance or offer a Web-enhanced classroom, Thomson South-Western offers you a solution with WebTutor™ ToolBox. It provides links to content at the Guffey Student Web site and rich communication tools to instructors and students including a course calendar, chat, and e-mail.

Instructor Web Site

www.westwords.com/instructor.html

Unrivaled author support! Mary Ellen Guffey develops and maintains all the materials on her Web sites. All inquiries come directly to her and are answered personally—you get a direct line to a knowledgeable, accessible, and concerned author. The Web site includes instructor comments, selected solutions, News Nuggets that summarize relevant current events and offer stimulating classroom discussion questions, a newsletter, and unique teaching materials such as comprehensive instructional modules with handouts, assignment sheets, goals, and teaching tips.

Technology for Students

Guffey Xtra!

Xtra! Passports are an OPTIONAL FREE bundle with NEW textbooks, giving students access to the Guffey Xtra! online study assistant which includes the following features:

- **Your Personal Language Trainer**, a self-teaching grammar/mechanics review, enhances English language skills and offers constructive feedback on student answers.
- **Student version PowerPoint® Slides** provide a visual explanation of the concepts presented in each chapter of the text.
- **Bonus Chapters include these topics:** Managing Communication Technology, Employment and Other Interviewing, and How to Write Instructions.
- **Speak Right!** and **Spell Right!** help students refine their speaking and spelling skills.
- **Sentence Competency Exercises** provide structured writing practice.
- **Documents for Analysis** make revision of select end-of-chapter activities simple.
- **Business Report Topics** provide nearly 100 ideas to stimulate report research.

Students who do not receive an Xtra! Passport with their textbooks should visit http://guffeyxtra.swlearning.com.

InfoTrac® College Edition

InfoTrac® gives students 24-hour-a-day access to full-text articles from hundreds of academic journals and popular periodicals such as *Newsweek*, *BusinessWeek*, *HR Magazine*, and *Computerworld.* Hundreds of thousands of articles are accessible from any computer with Internet access.

Student Web Site

http://guffey.swlearning.com

Unparalleled resources for students! The Guffey Student Web site enriches the learning experience through several interactive learning tools such as chapter review quizzes, WebThink activities, *Dr. Guffey's Guide to Business Etiquette and Workplace Manners*, Dr. Guffey's Listening Quiz, Electronic Documentation Formats for MLA and APA, and updated chapter URLs.

"Your Web site for students is wonderful. Our night classes are four hours long, and I break up the class by using WebThink assignments that integrate and extend the chapter content with technology and critical thinking."

—Sara K. Paris

Indiana Business College, Fort Wayne, Indiana

Business & Company Resource Center

The Business & Company Resource Center provides online access to a wide variety of global business information including competitive intelligence, career and investment opportunities, business rankings, and company histories. This comprehensive database offers ever-changing research results, providing accurate and up-to-date company and industry intelligence for thousands of companies.

Supported. Innovative. Expected.

Instructor Resources

Instructor's Manual

The Instructor's Manual includes course planning tips, sample course schedules, evaluation/grading methods, content summary and technology focus for every chapter, answers to textbook questions, solutions for nearly every correspondence writing assignment, and teaching suggestions.

Instructor's Resource CD-ROM

The Instructor's Resource CD includes the PowerPoint® chapter review slides, test banks, ExamView® Testing Software, the Instructor's Manual, and transparency masters as Word documents.

Test Banks

- **The Printed Test Bank**—The Test Bank provides carefully written questions to review chapter concepts. For this edition at least 75 percent of the questions are new, and every question has been scrutinized to ensure that it is stated as positively and clearly as possible.
- **The Electronic Test Bank - ExamView®**—All items from the printed test banks are available on the Instructor Resource CD with ExamView® Testing Software. This automated testing program allows instructors to create exams by selecting provided questions, modifying existing questions, and adding questions.

PowerPoint® Presentation Slides

Important chapter concepts are professionally presented in PowerPoint. These colorful PowerPoint slides, written by the author, capture attention, create lively lectures, and improve learning and retention. A simplified version of the slides is provided to students on Guffey Xtra!

Teaching Transparency Masters and Acetates

Written by the author, the transparency packet contains acetates and masters with chapter outlines, selected text figures, enrichment material, and solutions to nearly all letter- and memo-writing activities.

Video Library

"Building Workplace Communication Skills" and "Bridging the Gap" videos help emphasize key topic areas and reinforce lectures while encouraging students to apply problem-solving skills from the text.

Leading Web Site for Instructors

www.westwords.com/instructor.html

"I am very impressed with the overall business communication package (BC:PP). The text itself is interesting and relevant to today's workplace needs. The supplemental materials are insightful and comprehensive! This is the first semester I have taught business communication in fourteen years. I appreciate your effort to make my job easier. You are a true 'partner in the classroom'!"

—Susan White

Southeastern Oklahoma State University, Durant, Oklahoma

Student Resources

Student Study Guide

Students benefit from this hands-on workbook because it provides a variety of exercises and sample test questions that review chapter concepts and key terms. The Study Guide also helps students enrich their vocabularies, master frequently misspelled words, and develop language competency with bonus C.L.U.E. (Competent Language Usage Essentials) exercises. Nearly all exercises are self-checked so that students receive immediate feedback.

Guffey Xtra!

Xtra! Passports open the door to amazing student resources including PowerPoint® chapter review slides, online bonus chapters and supplements (which no other textbook offers), Personal Language Trainer, Speak Right!, Spell Right!, Sentence Competency Exercises, and other resources.

Student Web Site

The Student Web site (http://guffey.swlearning.com) offers an interactive learning experience where students test their understanding of chapter topics, explore business communication issues in the real world with WebThink activities, and prepare for successful careers.

brief contents

detailed contents

L.L.Bean
L.L.Bean Factor

SALE
SALE
88
¥1480

kinkos.
FedEx
Federal Express
ShipSite

75
YEARS
MICKEY

EPSI PE

STARBUCKS
COFFEE

appreciation for support

Probably no other book has had as great a level of professional support in its development as *Business Communication: Process and Product.* I am exceedingly grateful to the reviewers and other experts who contributed their pedagogic and academic expertise in shaping this book.

In addition to these friends and colleagues, sincere thanks go to PWS Kent and Wadsworth for propelling the first edition to its No. 1 position. In helping us maintain that top position with subsequent editions, I extend sincere thanks to many professionals at Thomson/South-Western, including Ed Moura, president, Thomson Business and Professional Publishing; Keith Chasse, acquisitions editor; Larry Qualls, senior marketing manager; Deanna Quinn, senior production editor; and especially to Mary Draper, my exceptional and highly valued developmental editor.

My heartfelt appreciation also goes to Carolyn M. Seefer, Diablo Valley College; James Dubinsky, Virginia Technical University; and Corinne Livesay, Bryan College, for sharing their expertise in developing specific topics and outstanding support materials.

Finally, I express profound gratitude to my husband, Dr. George R. Guffey, emeritus professor of English, University of California, Los Angeles, for supplying extraordinary computer and language expertise, as well as love, strength, and wisdom.

Mary Ellen Guffey
meguffey@westwords.com

Deepest Thanks to Reviewers of This Edition

Janet G. Adams, Minnesota State University, Mankato
Charles P. Bretan, Northwood University
Vivian R. Brown, Loredo Community College
Linda W. Cooper, Macon State College
Guy Devitt, Herkimer County Community College
Jim Dubinsky, Virginia Tech
Kay Durden, University of Tennessee
Susan A. Heller, Reading Area Community College
Kenneth Hoffman, Emporia State University
Glen J. Jenewein, Portland Community College
Kathy Lynn Lewis-Adler, University of North Alabama
Thomas A. Marshall II, Robert Morris University
Susan Smith McClaren, Mt. Hood Community College
Matt Newby, Heald College
Jeanne E. Newhall, Middlesex Community College
Melinda L. Phillabaum, Indiana University
Janice Rowan, Rowan University
Betty L. Schroeder, Northern Illinois University
Lori M. Townsend, Niagara County Community College
Beverly A. Westbrook, Delta College

Grateful Thanks to Previous Reviewers

Leslie Adams, Houston Baptist University
Kehinde A. Adesina, Contra Costa College
Asberine Parnell Alford, Suffolk Community College
Virginia Allen, Joliet Junior College
Cynthia Anderson, Youngstown State University
Linda Landis Andrews, University of Illinois, Chicago
Vanessa D. Arnold, University of Mississippi
Lois J. Bachman, Community College of Philadelphia
Rebecca Barksdale, University of Central Florida
Sandra Berill, Arkansas State University
Teresa L. Beyer, Sinclair Community College
Cathie Bishop, Parkland College
Randi Blank, Indiana University
Martha E. Bradshaw, Southeastern Louisiana Univ.
Bernadine Branchaw, Western Michigan University
Maryanne Brandenburg, Indiana University of Pennsylvania

Paula E. Brown, Northern Illinois University
Phyllis C. Bunn, Delta State University
Mary Ann Burris, Pueblo Community College
Roosevelt D. Butler, College of New Jersey
Jane Campanizzi-Mook, Franklin University
James F. Carey, Onondaga Community College
Leila Chambers, Cuesta College
Patricia H. Chapman, University of South Carolina
Judie C. Cochran, Grand Canyon Unviersity
Randy E. Cone, University of New Orleans
James Conley, Eastern Michigan University
Billie Miller Cooper, Cosumnes River College
Jane G. Corbly, Sinclair Community College
Martha Cross, Delta State University
Linda Cunningham, Salt Lake Community College
Dorothy Drayton, Texas Southern University
Bertha Du-Babcock, University of San Francisco
Anna Easton, Indiana University
Lorena B. Edwards, Belmont University
Donald E. English, Texas A&M University
Margaret Erthal, Southern Illinois University
Terry M. Frame, University of South Carolina
Kerry J. Gambrill, Florida Community College
Judith L. Graham, Holyoke Community College
Carolyn G. Gray, The University of Texas, Austin
Diane Gruber, Arizona State University West
David Hamilton, Bemidji State University
Paul Hegele, Elgin Community College
Rovena L. Hillsman, California State Univ., Sacramento
Shirley Houston, University of Nebraska
Warren B. Humphrey, University of Central Florida
Robert G. Insley, University of North Texas
Edna Jellesed, Lane Community College
Carolyn Spillers Jewell, Pembroke State University
Pamela R. Johnson, California State University, Chico
Eric Johnstone, Montana State University
Diana K. Kanoy, Central Florida Community College
Tina S. Kazan, University of Illinois, Chicago
Margaret S. Kilcoyne, Northwestern State University
G. Scott King, Sinclair Community College
Suzanne P. Krissler, Orange County Com. College
Linda L. Labin, Husson College
Richard Lacy, California State University, Fresno
Suzanne Lambert, Broward Community College
Marilyn L. Lammers, California State University, Northridge
Lorita S. Langdon, Columbus State Community College
Joyce N. Larsen, Front Range Community College
Barbara Lea, West Valley College
Claire E. Legowski, North Dakota State University
Mary E. Leslie, Grossmont College
Mary Jean Lush, Delta State University
Sonia Maasik, University of California, Los Angeles
Bruce MacBeth, Clarion University of Pennsylvania
Georgia E. Mackh, Cabrillo College
Andrew Madson, Milwaukee Area Technical College
Maureen L. Margolies, University of Cincinnati
Thomas A. Marshall II, Robert Morris College
Jeanette Martin, University of Mississippi
John F. Mastriani, El Paso Community College
Diana McKowen, Indiana University
Mary C. Miller, Ashland University
Marci Mitchell, South Texas Community College
Nancy B. Moody, Sinclair Community College
Danne Moore, Shawnee State University
Wayne A. Moore, Indiana University of Pennsylvania
Paul W. Murphey, Southwest Wisconsin Technical College
Ed Nagelhout, University of Nevada
Lin Nassar, Oakland Community College
Beverly H. Nelson, University of New Orleans
John P. Nightingale, Eastern Michigan University
Alexa B. North, State University of West Georgia
Rosemary Olds, Des Moines Area Community College
James S. O'Rourke IV, University of Notre Dame
Calvin R. Parks, Northern Illinois University
Pamela A. Patey, Riverside Community College
William Peirce, Prince George's Community College and University of Maryland University College
Joan Policano, Onondaga Community College
Paula J. Pomerenke, Illinois State University
Karen Sterkel Powell, Colorado State University
Gloria Power, Delgado Community College
Richard P. Profozich, Prince George's Community College
Carolyn Mae Rainey, Southeast Missouri State University
Richard G. Raspen, Wilkes University
Virginia L. Reynolds, Cleveland State University
Ruth D. Richardson, University of North Alabama
Joseph H. Roach, Middlesex County College
Terry D. Roach, Arkansas State University
Betty Jane Robbins, University of Oklahoma
Linda Sarlo, Rock Valley College
Christine A. Saxild, Mt. Senario College
Joseph Schaffner, State University of New York at Alfred
Annette Schley, North Seattle Community College
Betty L. Schroeder, Northern Illinois University
Carolyn M. Seefer, Diablo Valley College
Marilyn Simonson, Lakewood Community College
Sue C. Smith, Palm Beach Community Collage
Charles L. Snowden, Sinclair Community College
Gayle A. Sobolik, California State University, Fresno
Kathleen M. Sole, University of Phoenix
Jeanette Spender, Arkansas State University
Judy Steiner-Williams, Indiana University
Ted D. Stoddard, Brigham Young University
Susan Switzer, Central Michigan University
Roni Szeliga, Gateway Technical College
Leslie S. Talley, University of Central Florida
Barbara P. Thompson, Columbus State Community College
Sally J. Tiffany, Milwaukee Area Technical College
Mary L. Tucker, Ohio University
Richard F. Tyler, Anne Arundel Community College
Deborah Valentine, Emory University
Doris A. Van Horn Christopher, California State University, Los Angeles
David Victor, Eastern Michigan University
Lois Ann Wagner, Southwest Wisconsin Technical College
John L. Waltman, Eastern Michigan University
Marion Webb, Cleveland State University
Carol M. Williams, Pima County Community College
Jane D. Williams, J. Sargeant Reynolds Community College
Rosemary B. Wilson, Washtenaw Community College
Beverly C. Wise, State University of New York, Morrisville
William E. Worth, Georgia State University
Myron D. Yeager, Chapman University

about the author

A dedicated professional, Mary Ellen Guffey has taught business communication and business English topics for over thirty years. She received a bachelor's degree, *summa cum laude*, from Bowling Green State University; a master's degree from the University of Illinois, and a doctorate in business and economic education from the University of California, Los Angeles (UCLA). She has taught at the University of Illinois, Santa Monica College, and Los Angeles Pierce College.

Now recognized as the world's leading business communication author, Dr. Guffey corresponds with instructors around the globe who are using her books. She is the author of the award-winning *Business Communication: Process and Product*, the leading business communication textbook in this country and abroad. She has also written *Business English*, which serves more students than any other book in its field; *Essentials of College English*, (with Carolyn M. Seefer), and *Essentials of Business Communication*, the leading text/workbook in its market. The Canadian editions of her books are bestsellers in that country, and one was recently named Book of the Year by Nelson Canada. In addition, Dr. Guffey is active professionally, serving on the review board of the *Business Communication Quarterly* of the Association for Business Communication, participating in all national meetings, and sponsoring awards in business communication.

A teacher's teacher and leader in the field, Dr. Guffey acts as a partner and mentor to hundreds of business communication instructors nationally and internationally. Her workshops, seminars, teleconferences, newsletters, articles, teaching materials, and Web sites help novice and veteran business communication instructors achieve effective results in their courses. She maintains comprehensive Web sites for students and instructors. Her print and online newsletters are used by thousands of instructors in this country and around the world.

unit 1

Communication Foundations

chapter 1

Communicating at Work

chapter 2

Communicating in Small Groups and Teams

chapter 3

Workplace Listening and Nonverbal Communication

chapter 4

Communicating Across Cultures

chapter 1

Communicating at Work

objectives

1 Identify changes in the workplace and explain the importance of communication skills.

2 Describe the process of communication.

3 Discuss barriers to interpersonal communication and the means of overcoming those barriers.

4 Analyze the functions and procedures of communication in organizations.

5 Assess the flow of communication in organizations including barriers and methods for overcoming those barriers.

6 List the goals of ethical business communication and describe important tools for doing the right thing.

COMMUNICATION IN PROCESS

Stodgy Procter & Gamble Stumbles in Reinventing Itself

FOR DECADES PROCTER & Gamble was lionized as the world's smartest and best marketer. But in the late 1990s, the Cincinnati-based consumer-products giant underwent a brutal restructuring that shook it to its very laundry-detergent roots. With more than 100,000 employees, it markets 300 brands in 140 countries and takes in more than $43 billion in annual sales. To promote its brands, it pioneered many mass marketing techniques and even created a new medium—the soap opera.

Many of its products are household names—Tide detergent, Pampers diapers, Crest toothpaste, Cover Girl makeup, and so on. Nearly every American has one or more P & G products tucked under the kitchen or bathroom sink. Despite its well-known brands, however, P & G suffered from a lack of innovation in new products, declining profit share, and a rigid, bureaucratic company culture. Moreover, it was fundamentally a U.S. company.

To make itself over from a stodgy, old-economy dinosaur into a nimble, Net-savvy twenty-first-century innovator, the company instituted a huge makeover plan. This long-range plan set out to speed up the introduction of new products while going global. The workforce was to be cut by 15,000, and chains of command were rearranged, grouping employees by products in five "global business units." For example, food and beverage managers, who were mostly in Cincinnati, reported to a president in Caracas, Venezuela.

Instead of bringing amazing results, however, the radical restructuring created unhappy, confused employees. According to many, the reorganization was too quick and too crude. It was performed with too little consideration for the people responsible for implementing the changes.

In any organization, when employees fear that their jobs will change or even disappear, morale plummets. Rumors fly, and productivity sinks. Excessive caution and mistrust prevail. That's why in times of upheaval, communication—and lots of it—becomes paramount.[1]

Famous for popular brands such as Pampers for babies and little folks, Procter & Gamble faced upheaval after a radical restructuring.

Photo: © Mary Ellen Guffey

Critical Thinking

- How is Procter & Gamble similar to many organizations today? What kinds of changes are other companies undergoing?
- Why is communication within an organization especially important in times of change?
- How could improved communication have helped Procter & Gamble implement its restructuring plan?

http://pg.com

CONTINUED ON PAGE 23

case study

Ensuring That You Succeed in the New Workplace

learning objective 1

Employees around the country and the world are experiencing the kind of change and upheaval felt at Procter & Gamble. In fact, the entire work world you are about to enter is changing dramatically. The kind of work you'll do, the tools you'll use, the form of management, the environment where you'll work, the people with whom you'll interact—all are undergoing a profound transformation. Many of the changes

Figure 1.1 ***Succeeding in Today's Dynamic and Demanding Workplace***

This business communication book and this course will help you

- Apply a universal process that enables you to solve communication problems now and throughout your entire career
- Learn specific writing techniques and organizational strategies to compose clear, concise, and purposeful business messages
- Master effective speaking skills for getting your ideas across to small and large groups
- Learn to be a valuable team player
- Work productively with the Internet and other rapidly evolving communication technologies
- Recognize the importance of nonverbal communication cues
- Value diversity so that you can function with sensitivity in intercultural work environments
- Develop tools for meeting ethically challenging situations
- Feel confident that you will always have excellent document models to follow now and on the job
- Land the job of your dreams by providing invaluable job-search, résumé-writing, and interviewing tips

in this dynamic workplace revolve around processing and communicating information. As a result, the most successful players in this new world of work will be those with highly developed communication skills.

Succeeding in today's world of work demands that you read, listen, speak, and write effectively.

The abilities to read, listen, speak, and write effectively, of course, are not inborn. Thriving in the dynamic and demanding work world depends on many factors, some of which you cannot control. But one factor that you do control is how well you communicate. The goals of this book and this course are to teach you basic business communication skills, such as how to write a memo or letter and how to make a presentation. You will also learn additional powerful communication skills, as summarized in Figure 1.1. Because they will equip you with the skills most needed in today's dynamic workplace, *this book and this course may well be the most important in your entire college curriculum.*

This book and your instructor provide you with the principles, processes, products, and practice that you need to succeed.

The book provides you with not only the process but also the products of effective communication. You'll be able to use it throughout your training for its many models of successful business and professional documents. When you are ready to enter the job market, you'll find it to be an invaluable source of excellent résumés and cover letters. On the job you'll refer to it for examples of business letters, e-mail messages, reports, and other documents. That's why many students decide that this is one book they will keep.

To become an effective communicator, though, you need more than a good book. You also need practice—with meaningful feedback. You need someone such as your instructor to tell you how to modify your responses so that you can improve. We've designed this book and its supplements to provide you and your instructor with principles, processes, products, and practice—everything necessary to make you a successful business communicator in today's dynamic workplace.

Yes, the workplace is undergoing profound changes. As a businessperson and especially as a business communicator, you will undoubtedly be affected by many transformations. Some of the most significant changes include global competition, flattened management hierarchies, and team-based projects. Other changes reflect our constantly evolving information technology, new work environments, a diverse workforce, and the emergence of a knowledge-based economy. The following brief look at this new world of work reveals how directly your success in it will be tied to possessing excellent communication skills.

Kids dressed as Colonel Sanders promote egg tarts in a Kentucky Fried Chicken restaurant in Shanghai, China. Although KFC strives to retain its signature branding image, its restaurants and products, among the most popular in China, are still localized to fit consumers' tastes, cultural practices, and lifestyles.

Photo: © AP / Wide World Photos

Heightened Global Competition

Small, medium, and large companies increasingly find themselves competing in global rather than local markets. Improved systems of telecommunication, advanced forms of transportation, and saturated local markets—all of these developments have encouraged companies to move beyond familiar territories to emerging markets around the world. Wal-Mart invades Japan, one of the world's quirkiest and most difficult retail markets.[2] PepsiCo fights Coca-Cola for new customers in India. FedEx learns the ropes in South America. Burger King challenges McDonald's for fast-food supremacy in Europe,[3] and Kentucky Fried Chicken is the most famous international brand in China.[4]

Communication is more complicated with people who have different religions, customs, and lifestyles.

Doing business in far-flung countries means dealing with people who are very different from you. They have different religions, engage in different customs, live different lifestyles, and rely on different approaches in business. Now add the complications of multiple time zones, vast distances between offices, and different languages. No wonder global communicators can blunder.[5] Take, for example, FedEx's offer of a money-back guarantee in South America. The concept was so unfamiliar to the culture that people automatically thought something must be wrong with the service.[6] FedEx quickly withdrew the offer.

Successful communication in these new markets requires developing new skills and attitudes. These include cultural knowledge and sensitivity, flexibility, patience, and tolerance. Because these are skills and attitudes that most of us need to polish, you will receive special communication training to help you deal with intercultural business transactions.

Flattened Management Hierarchies

In response to intense global competition and other pressures, businesses have for years been cutting costs and flattening their management hierarchies. This flattening means that fewer layers of managers separate decision makers from line workers. In traditional companies, information flows through many levels of managers. In flat organizations, however, where the lines of communication are shorter, decision makers can react more quickly to market changes. Toymaker Mattel transformed itself from an "out-of-control money loser" into a healthy money maker by tightening its organization and cutting six layers from its organizational hierarchy. As a result, when its Matchbox developers came up with a smashing idea for a toy firehouse that required no assembly, the idea could be rushed into production. It didn't languish in the pipeline, drowning in multiple layers of management.[7]

Flatter organizations demand that every employee be a skilled communicator.

Progressive organizations are in the midst of changing from "command and control" to "coordination and cultivation" management styles. This means that work is organized to let people use their own talents more wisely.[8] But today's flatter organizations also bring greater communication challenges. In the past, authoritarian and hierarchical management structures did not require that every employee be a skilled communicator. Managers simply passed along messages to the next level. Today, however, front-line employees as well as managers participate in decision making. Their input and commitment are necessary for their organizations to be successful in global markets. What's more, everyone has become a writer and a communicator.[9] Nearly all employees have computers and write their own messages. Secretaries no longer "clean up" their bosses' writing.

Expanded Team-Based Management

Along with flatter chains of command, companies are also expanding team-based operations. Nearly 80 percent of employees in all industries have adopted some form of quality circles or self-directed teams. At the Frito-Lay plant in Lubbock, Texas, workers formerly loaded bags of potato chips into cartons. Now organized into work teams, they are responsible for everything from potato processing to equipment maintenance. They even interview new hires and make quality control decisions.[10] At Cigna Corporation, a huge national insurance company, three organizational layers were flattened and teams were formed to reduce backups in processing customer claims. The formation of these teams forced technology specialists to communicate constantly with business specialists. Suddenly, computer programmers had to do more than code and debug; they had to listen, interpret, and explain. All members of the team had to analyze problems and negotiate solutions.[11]

When companies form cross-functional teams, individuals must work together and share information. What's tough is that these individuals often don't share the same background, knowledge, or training. Some companies must hire communication coaches to help existing teams get along. They work to develop interpersonal, negotiation, and collaboration techniques. But companies would prefer to hire new workers who already possess these skills. That's why so many advertisements for new employees say "must possess good communication skills."

Innovative Communication Technologies

E-mail, instant messaging, fax, voice mail, wireless networking, cell phones, and other devices are revolutionizing the way we exchange information.

Because technology has completely revolutionized the way we communicate, recruiters are also looking for people with good computer skills. We now exchange information and stay in touch through e-mail, instant messaging, text messaging, fax, voice mail, wireless networking, cell phones, powerful laptop computers, and satellite communications.[12] Through teleconferencing and videoconferencing, we can conduct meetings with associates around the world. Interactive software enables dozens or even hundreds of users to collaborate on projects. And no self-respecting businessperson today would make a presentation without using sophisticated presentation software. We now make tremendous use of the Internet and the Web for collecting information, serving customers, and selling products and services.

Just as companies are scrambling to use the Web most effectively, individual businesspeople are eagerly embracing the new technologies and revamping the way they communicate. E-mail is now the most popular communication channel; it's even replacing face-to-face talk.[13]

To use these new resources most effectively, you, as a skilled business communicator, must develop a tool kit of new communication skills. For example, you will want to know how to select the best communication channel, how to use each channel and medium most effectively, and how to use online search tools efficiently.

New Work Environments

As a result of globalization, restructuring, and the Internet, it's no surprise that we are also seeing dramatic changes in work environments. Thanks to advances in communication and mobile technologies, millions of Americans now *telecommute.* They have flexible working arrangements so that they can work at home or on the road. At first telecommuting was rare, but now working at home or in remote locations is widely embraced, thanks largely to broadband high-speed connections.[14] Tools such as instant and text messaging, file sharing, and wireless networking make it easy for employees to collaborate.[15] But instead of strolling to a colleague's desk to chat, telecommuters generally must send written messages.

Global competition, restructuring, the Internet, and mobile technologies are encouraging flexible working arrangements such as telecommuting and hoteling.

Because they have many employees who work elsewhere, some major accounting firms are instituting the practices of *hoteling* and *hot-desking. Hoteling* involves an open office with unassigned desks.[16] Instead of having personal work spaces, employees must reserve a desk for the days or hours they will be in the office. *Hot-desking* refers to a desk that's still warm from its previous occupant. This is similar to *hot-bunking* for sailors on crowded ships. Hoteling makes sense for companies with staffs that spend most of their time outside the office, such as accountants who work at clients' businesses. Why should a company rent offices for empty desks gathering dust in expensive office buildings?

Amazing wireless and mobile technologies are changing where, when, and how we communicate and work. Although some workers can complete their tasks in attractive remote locations, less fortunate workers may be squeezed into cubicles in large, open offices.

Although hoteling and hot-desking are rare, many office workers face tighter quarters and greater stress. As companies strive to cut rental and real estate costs, they are squeezing more workers into smaller spaces.[17] A trend toward open offices divided into small work *cubicles* results in the need for new rules of office etiquette and civility. For example, instead of wandering into a cubicle, visitors should knock on the frame (they have no doors) to ask permission to enter.[18]

Tight quarters, intense cost-cutting measures, demands for increased productivity, and round-the-clock workdays—all are creating stress for today's workers. In addition, mergers, layoffs, and outsourcing have many employees wondering who's next. Combined with new responsibilities of team problem solving, business communicators can expect to need interpersonal skills that deal with heightened levels of emotion. Especially important are listening to and empathizing with fellow employees. Equally significant is respecting others' periodic need for uninterrupted, focused work time.[19] And employees in remote locations face added communication challenges since staying connected with the office often requires exchanging more written messages than if they were face to face with their colleagues.[20]

Increasingly Diverse Workforce

Changes in today's work environments include more than innovative technology, team management, and different work environments. You can also expect to see hordes of new faces. No longer, say the experts, will the workplace be overwhelmingly male or

FIGURE 1.2 ***Racial and Ethnic Makeup of U.S. Workforce Projected to 2020***

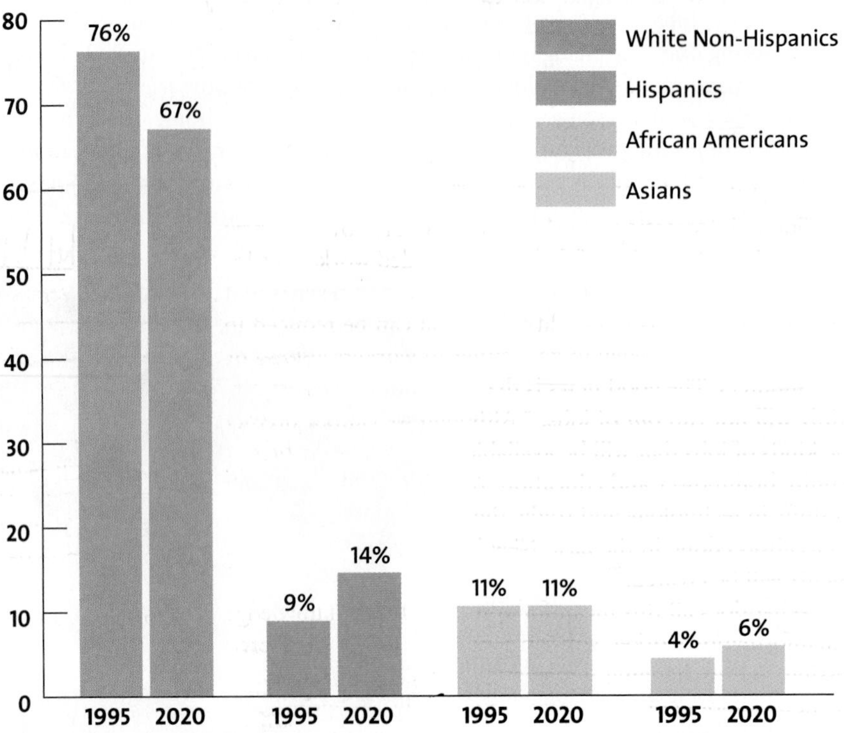

Anglo oriented. By 2005 women and minority men will make up 62 percent of the workforce.[21] By 2020, as shown in Figure 1.2, white non-Hispanics are expected to drop from 76 percent to 67 percent of the overall workforce. Hispanics will climb from 9 percent to 14 percent, African Americans will stay about the same at 11 percent, and Asians will rise from 4 percent to 6 percent.[22] In addition to increasing numbers of minorities, the workforce will see a big jump in older workers. By 2008, 40 percent of America's workers will be 45 years old or older.[23] As a result of these and other demographic trends, you can count on interacting with many coworkers who differ from you in race, ethnicity, gender, age, and many other ways.

Communicating with workers who differ in race, ethnicity, gender, and age requires new attitudes and skills.

Communicating in this diverse work environment requires new attitudes and skills. Acquiring these new employment skills is certainly worth the effort because of the benefits diversity brings to consumers, work teams, and business organizations. A diverse staff is better able to read trends and respond to the increasingly diverse customer base in local and world markets. In the workplace, diversity also makes good business sense. Teams made up of different people with different experiences are more likely to create the different products that consumers demand. Customers also want to deal with companies that respect their values. They are more likely to say, "If you're a company whose ads don't include me, or whose workforce doesn't include me, I won't buy from you."[24] Learning to cooperate and communicate successfully with diverse coworkers should be a major priority for all businesspeople.

Thriving in the Age of Knowledge

We're now witnessing the emergence of an economy based on information and knowledge. Physical labor, raw materials, and capital are no longer the key ingredients in the creation of wealth. Now, the vital raw material in our economy, say futurists Alvin Toffler and Oren Harari, is knowledge.[25] Tomorrow's wealth depends on the development and exchange of knowledge. And individuals entering the workforce offer their knowledge, not their muscles. *Knowledge workers*, says management guru Peter Drucker, get paid for their education and their ability to learn.[26] Microsoft uses the term *information worker* to describe anyone who works with technology.[27] Regardless of the terminology, knowledge and information workers engage in mind work. They deal with symbols: words, figures, and data. And information workers now represent 70 percent of the entire U.S. workforce.[28]

Knowledge workers deal with symbols, such as words, figures, and data.

spotlight *on communicators*

"We are entering an age where intangible assets like expertise, intelligence, speed, agility, imagination, maneuverability, networks, passion, responsiveness and innovation—all facets of 'knowledge'—become more important than the tangibles of traditional balance-sheet perspectives," contends Oren Harari, management expert and futurist. The emerging knowledge economy, he asserts, is "brain-based."

Photo: Professor of Management, University of San Francisco

Some information workers now worry over a new threat—the outsourcing of their jobs to skilled workers in India, China, and other countries abroad. The bad news is that outsourcing overseas is a reality. Jobs that can be reduced to a series of rules are likely to go—either to workers abroad or to computers. The good news is that this country almost certainly will not run out of jobs.[29] Although we cannot predict the kinds of jobs that will be available, they will undoubtedly require brainpower and education. As existing jobs succumb to shifts in technology and trade, the economy will adjust, as it has always done in the past. New jobs using new skills and talents will be created.[30]

What does all this mean for you? As a future knowledge and information worker, you can expect to be generating, processing, and exchanging information. Whether you work in the new economy of *e-commerce* (Internet-based businesses) or the old economy of *bricks and mortar* companies, nearly three out of four jobs will involve some form of mind work. Jobs that require thinking, brainpower, and decision-making skills are likely to remain plentiful. To be successful in these jobs, you must be able to think critically, make decisions, and communicate those decisions.

Learning to Think Critically. Management and employees will be working together in such areas as product development, quality control, and customer satisfaction. You will be asked to think critically. This means having opinions that are backed by reasons and evidence. When your boss or team leader says, "What do you think we ought to do?" you want to be able to supply good ideas. The accompanying Career Coach box provides a five-point critical thinking plan to help you solve problems and make decisions. But having a plan is not enough. You also need chances to try the plan out and get feedback from colleagues and your boss (your instructor, for the time being). At the end of each chapter, you'll find activities and problems that will help you develop and apply your critical thinking skills.

Taking Charge of Your Career. In the new world of work, you can look forward to being in constant training to acquire new skills that will help you keep up with improved technologies and procedures. You can also expect to be exercising greater control over your career. Many workers today will not find nine-to-five jobs, lifetime security, predictable promotions, and even conventional workplaces, as you have learned earlier. Don't presume that companies will provide you with a clearly defined career path or planned developmental experiences. And don't wait for someone to "empower" you. You have to empower yourself.[31] To thrive in the new decentralized work world, you must be flexible and continually willing to learn new skills that supplement the strong foundation of basic skills you acquire in college.

Constantly changing technologies and work procedures mean continual training for employees.

Learning to Communicate. Probably the most important foundation skill for knowledge workers in the new environment is the ability to communicate. In making

career coach

Sharpening Your Skills for Critical Thinking, Problem Solving, and Decision Making

Gone are the days when management expected workers to check their brains at the door and do only as told. As a knowledge worker, you'll be expected to use your brains in thinking critically. You'll be solving problems and making decisions. Much of this book is devoted to helping you learn to solve problems and communicate those decisions to management, fellow workers, clients, the government, and the public.

Faced with a problem or an issue, most of us do a lot of worrying before separating the issues or making a decision. All that worrying can become directed thinking by channeling it into the following procedure.

1. **Identify and clarify the problem.** Your first task is to recognize that a problem exists. Some problems are big and unmistakable, such as failure of an air-freight delivery service to get packages to customers on time. Other problems may be continuing annoyances, such as regularly running out of toner for an office copy machine. The first step in reaching a solution is pinpointing the problem area.

2. **Gather information.** Learn more about the problem situation. Look for possible causes and solutions. This step may mean checking files, calling suppliers, or brainstorming with fellow workers. For example, the air-freight delivery service would investigate the tracking systems of the commercial airlines carrying its packages to determine what went wrong.

3. **Evaluate the evidence.** Where did the information come from? Does it represent various points of view? What biases could be expected from each source? How accurate is the information gathered? Is it fact or opinion? For example, it is a fact that packages are missing; it is an opinion that they are merely lost and will turn up eventually.

4. **Consider alternatives and implications.** Draw conclusions from the gathered evidence and pose solutions. Then weigh the advantages and disadvantages of each alternative. What are the costs, benefits, and consequences? What are the obstacles, and how can they be handled? Most important, what solution best serves your goals and those of your organization? Here's where your creativity is especially important.

5. **Choose and implement the best alternative.** Select an alternative and put it into action. Then, follow through on your decision by monitoring the results of implementing your plan. The freight company decided to give its unhappy customers free delivery service to make up for the lost packages and downtime. Be sure to continue monitoring and adjusting the solution to ensure its effectiveness over time.

Career Application

As the owner of a popular local McDonald's franchise, you recognize a problem. Customers are unhappy with the multiple lines for service. They don't seem to know where to stand to be next served. Tempers flare when aggressive customers cut in line, and other customers spend so much time protecting their places in line that they fail to study the menu. Then they don't know what to order when they approach the counter. As a franchise owner, you would like to solve this problem. How would the steps discussed here be helpful in approaching this problem?

hiring decisions, employers often rank communication skills among the most-requested competencies.[32] This means being able to listen as well as to express your ideas effectively in writing and in speech. As you advance in your career, communication skills become even more important. A primary requirement for promotion to management is the ability to communicate. Corporate president Ben Ordover explained how he makes executive choices: "Many people climbing the corporate ladder are very good. When faced with a hard choice between candidates, I use writing ability as the deciding factor. Sometimes a candidate's writing is the only skill that separates him or her from the competition."[33]

Examining the Process of Communication

learning objective

2

Since communication is a central factor in the emerging knowledge economy and a major consideration for anyone entering today's workforce, we need to look more closely at the total process of communication. Just what is communication? For our purposes communication is the *transmission of information and meaning from one individual or group to another.* The crucial element in this definition is *meaning.* Communication has as its central objective the transmission of meaning. The process of communication is successful only when the receiver understands an idea as the sender intended it. Both parties must agree not only on the information transmitted but also on the meaning of that information. This entire book is devoted to one objective: teaching you the skills of communication so that you can transmit meaning along with information. How does an idea travel from one person to another? Despite what you may have seen in futuristic science fiction movies, we can't just glance at another person and transfer meaning directly from mind to mind. We engage in a sensitive process of communication that generally involves five steps, discussed here and depicted in Figure 1.3.

Sender Has Idea

The communication process has five steps: idea formation, message encoding, message transmission, message decoding, and feedback.

The process of communication begins when the person with whom the message originates—the *sender*—has an idea. The form of the idea will be influenced by complex factors surrounding the sender: mood, frame of reference, background, culture, and physical makeup, as well as the context of the situation and many other factors. The way you greet people on campus or on the job, for example, depends a lot on

FIGURE 1.3 ***The Communication Process***

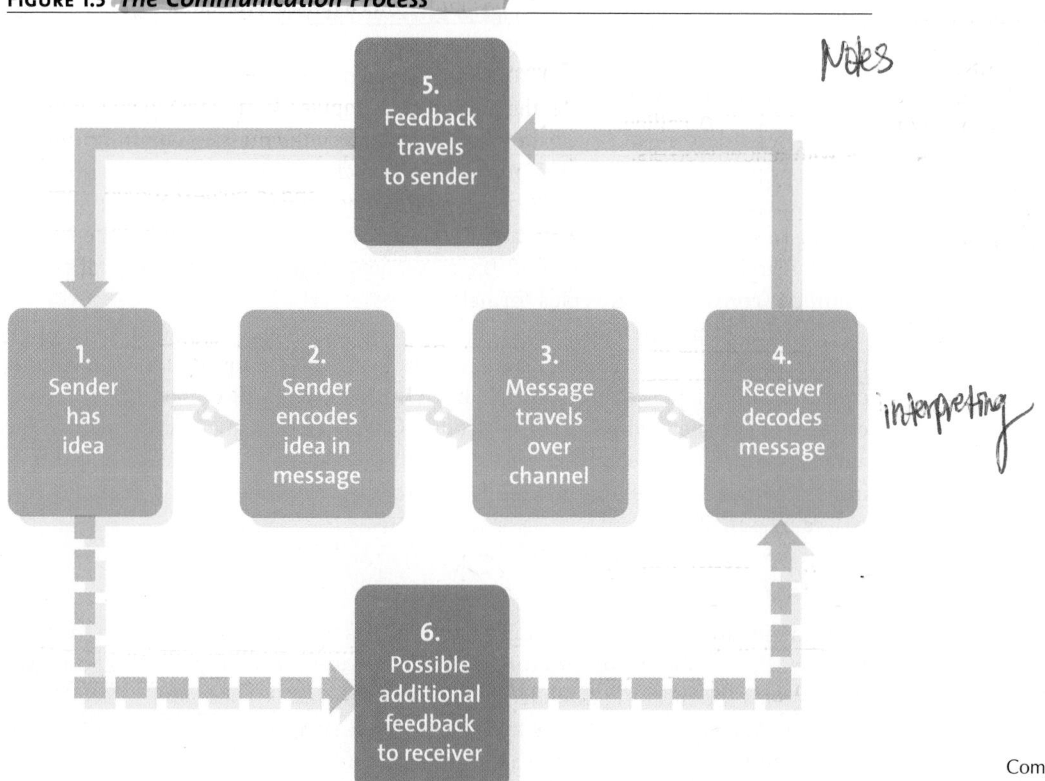

how you feel, whom you are addressing (a classmate, a professor, a colleague, or your boss), and what your culture has trained you to say ("Good morning," "Hey," "Hi," "Howdy," or "How ya doing?").

Predicting the effect of a message and adapting the message to a receiver are key factors in successful communication.

The form of the idea, whether a simple greeting or a complex idea, is shaped by assumptions based on the sender's experiences. A manager sending an e-mail announcement to employees assumes they will be receptive, whereas direct-mail advertisers assume that receivers will give only a quick glance to their message. The ability to accurately predict how a message will affect its receiver and skill in adapting that message to its receiver are key factors in successful communication.

Sender Encodes Idea in Message

The next step in the communication process involves *encoding*. This means converting the idea into words or gestures that will convey meaning. A major problem in communicating any message verbally is that words have different meanings for different people. When misunderstandings result from missed meanings, it's called *bypassing*. Recognizing how easy it is to be misunderstood, skilled communicators choose familiar words with concrete meanings on which both senders and receivers agree. In selecting proper symbols, senders must be alert to the receiver's communication skills, attitudes, background, experiences, and culture: How will the selected words affect the receiver? For example, a Dr. Pepper cola promotion failed miserably in Great Britain because American managers had not done their homework. They had to change their "I'm a Pepper" slogan after learning that *pepper* is British slang for *prostitute*.[34] Because the sender initiates a communication transaction, he or she has primary responsibility for its success or failure. Choosing appropriate words or symbols is the first step.

Message Travels Over Channel

Channels are the media—computer, telephone, cell phone, letter, report, and so on—that transmit messages.

The medium over which the message is physically transmitted is the *channel*. Messages may be delivered by computer, telephone, cell phone, letter, memorandum, report, announcement, picture, spoken word, fax, pager, Web page, or through some other channel. Because communication channels deliver both verbal and nonverbal messages, senders must choose the channel and shape the message carefully. A company may use its annual report, for example, as a channel to deliver many messages to stockholders. The verbal message lies in the report's financial and organizational news. Nonverbal messages, though, are conveyed by the report's appearance (showy versus bland), layout (ample white space versus tightly packed columns of print), and tone (conversational versus formal).

Anything that interrupts the transmission of a message in the communication process is called *noise*. Channel noise ranges from static that disrupts a telephone conversation to typographical and spelling errors in a letter or e-mail message. Such errors damage the credibility of the sender. Channel noise might even include the annoyance a receiver feels when the sender chooses an improper medium for sending a message, such as announcing a loan rejection via postcard or firing an employee by e-mail.

Receiver Decodes Message

The individual for whom the message is intended is the *receiver*. Translating the message from its symbol form into meaning involves *decoding*. Only when the receiver understands the meaning intended by the sender—that is, successfully decodes the message—does communication take place. Such success, however, is difficult to achieve because no two people share the same life experiences and because many barriers can disrupt the process.

Decoding can be disrupted internally by the receiver's lack of attention to or bias against the sender. It can be disrupted externally by loud sounds or illegible words. Decoding can also be sidetracked by semantic obstacles, such as misunderstood words or emotional reactions to certain terms. A memo that refers to all the women in an office as "girls" or "chicks," for example, may disturb its receivers so much that they fail to comprehend the total message.

Feedback Travels to Sender

The verbal and nonverbal responses of the receiver create *feedback*, a vital part of the communication process. Feedback helps the sender know that the message was received and understood. If, as a receiver, you hear the message "How are you," your feedback might consist of words ("I'm fine") or body language (a smile or a wave of the hand). Although the receiver may respond with additional feedback to the sender (thus creating a new act of communication), we'll concentrate here on the initial message flowing to the receiver and the resulting feedback.

Asking questions encourages feedback that clarifies communication.

Senders can encourage feedback by asking questions such as, *Am I making myself clear?* and *Is there anything you don't understand?* Senders can further improve feedback by timing the delivery appropriately and by providing only as much information as the receiver can handle. Receivers can improve the process by paraphrasing the sender's message with comments, such as, *Let me try to explain that in my own words.* The best feedback is descriptive rather than evaluative. For example, here's a descriptive response: *I understand you want to launch a used golf ball business.* Here's an evaluative response: *Your business ideas are always weird.* An evaluative response is judgmental and doesn't tell the sender whether the receiver actually understood the message.

Overcoming Interpersonal Communication Barriers

learning objective

3

The communication process is successful only when the receiver understands the message as intended by the sender. It sounds quite simple. Yet, it's not. How many times have you thought that you delivered a clear message, only to learn later that your intentions were totally misunderstood? Most messages that we send reach their destination, but many are only partially understood.

Obstacles That Create Misunderstanding

Barriers to successful communication include bypassing, differing frames of reference, lack of language or listening skills, emotional interference, and physical distractions.

You can improve your chances of communicating successfully by learning to recognize barriers that are known to disrupt the process. The most significant barriers for individuals are bypassing, frames of reference, lack of language skill, and distractions.

Bypassing. One of the biggest barriers to clear communication involves words. Each of us attaches a little bundle of meanings to every word, and these meanings are not always similar. *Bypassing* happens when people miss each other with their meanings.[35] Let's say your boss asks you to "help" with a large customer mailing. When you arrive to do your share, you learn that you are expected to do the whole mailing yourself. You and your boss attached different meanings to the word *help.* Bypassing can lead to major miscommunication because people assume that meanings are contained in words. Actually, meanings are in people. For communication to be successful, the receiver and sender must attach the same symbolic meanings to their words.

Miscommunication often results when the sender's frame of reference differs markedly from the receiver's.

Differing Frames of Reference. Another barrier to clear communication is your *frame of reference*. Everything you see and feel in the world is translated through your individual frame of reference. Your unique frame is formed by a combination of your experiences, education, culture, expectations, personality, and many other elements. As a result, you bring your own biases and expectations to any communication situation. Because your frame of reference is totally different from everyone else's, you will never see things exactly as others do. American owners attempting to modernize a Mexican assembly plant, for example, perceived failure when they saw a report indicating a slow pace of change. The Mexican managers, on the other hand, saw the report and congratulated themselves on their splendid progress. Wise business communicators strive to prevent communication failure by being alert to both their own frames of reference and those of others.

Lack of Language Skill. No matter how extraordinary the idea, it won't be understood or fully appreciated unless the communicators involved have good language skills. Each individual needs an adequate vocabulary, a command of basic punctuation and grammar, and skill in written and oral expression. Moreover, poor listening skills can prevent us from hearing oral messages clearly and thus responding properly.

Distractions. Other barriers include emotional interference and physical distractions. Shaping an intelligent message is difficult when you're feeling joy, fear, resentment, hostility, sadness, or some other strong emotion. To reduce the influence of emotions on communication, both senders and receivers should focus on the content of the message and try to remain objective. Physical distractions such as faulty acoustics, noisy surroundings, or a poor cell phone connection can disrupt oral communication. Similarly, sloppy appearance, poor printing, careless formatting, and typographical or spelling errors can disrupt written messages.

spotlight *on communicators*

Secretary of Labor Elaine Chao spoke not a word of English when she arrived in this country with her four sisters from her native Taiwan at the age of eight. Mastering the language and conquering other barriers, she became the first Asian American woman ever to serve in a president's cabinet. In this role she makes frequent speeches before groups that may be supportive or hostile. She must adapt her message logically and use words precisely to prevent miscommunication. Whether addressing antagonistic union members or cheering female entrepreneurs, the personable yet fearless Chao overcomes communication obstacles by anticipating reactions, shaping her remarks to the audience, and being prepared to respond.

Photo: © Alex Wong / Getty Images

Overcoming the Obstacles

To overcome obstacles, communicators must anticipate problems in encoding, transmitting, and decoding.

Careful communicators can conquer barriers in a number of ways. Half the battle in communicating successfully is recognizing that the entire process is sensitive and susceptible to breakdown. Like a defensive driver anticipating problems on the road, a good communicator anticipates problems in encoding, transmitting, and decoding a message. Effective communicators also focus on the receiver's environment and frame of reference. They ask themselves questions such as, *How is that individual likely to react to my message?* or *Does the receiver know as much about the subject as I do?*

Misunderstandings are less likely if you arrange your ideas logically and use words precisely. Mark Twain was right when he said, "The difference between an almost-right word and the right word is like the difference between lightning and the lightning bug." But communicating is more than expressing yourself well. A large part of successful communication is listening. Management advisor Peter Drucker observed that "too many executives think they are wonderful with people because they talk well. They don't realize that being wonderful with people means listening well."[36]

Overcoming interpersonal barriers often involves questioning your preconceptions. Successful communicators continually examine their personal assumptions, biases, and prejudices. The more you pay attention to subtleties and know "where you're coming from" when you encode and decode messages, the better you'll communicate. A U.S. software company, for example, failed unnecessarily in Japan because it simply translated its glossy brochure from English into Japanese. The Americans didn't realize that in Japan such brochures are associated with low-priced consumer products. The software producer wrongly assumed that because glossy is considered upscale here, it would be perceived similarly in Japan.

Finally, effective communicators create an environment for useful feedback. In oral communication this means asking questions such as, *Do you understand?* and *What questions do you have?* as well as encouraging listeners to repeat instructions or paraphrase ideas. As a listener it means providing feedback that describes rather than evaluates. And in written communication it means asking questions and providing access: *Do you have my phone numbers in case you have questions?* or *Here's my e-mail address so that you can give me your response immediately.*

Good communicators ask questions to stimulate feedback.

Communicating in Organizations

learning objective

4

Until now, you've probably been thinking about the communication you do personally. But business communicators must also be concerned with the bigger picture, and that involves sharing information in organizations. Creating and exchanging knowledge are critical to fostering innovation, the key challenge in today's knowledge economy. On the job you'll be exchanging information by communicating internally and externally.

Internal and External Functions

Internal communication includes sharing ideas and messages with superiors, coworkers, and subordinates. When those messages must be written, you'll probably choose e-mail or a printed memorandum, such as the memo shown in Figure 1.4. When you are communicating externally with customers, suppliers, the government, and the public, you will generally send letters on company stationery, such as American Airlines' letter also shown in Figure 1.4.

Internal communication often consists of e-mail, memos, and voice messages; external communication generally consists of letters.

Some of the functions of internal communication are to issue and clarify procedures and policies, inform management of progress, develop new products and services, persuade employees or management to make changes or improvements, coordinate activities, and evaluate and reward employees. External functions are to answer inquiries about products or services, persuade customers to buy products or services, clarify supplier specifications, issue credit, collect bills, respond to government agencies, and promote a positive image of the organization.

In all of these tasks, employees and managers use a number of communication skills: reading, listening, speaking, and writing. As college students and workers, you probably realize that you need to improve these skills to the proficiency level required for success in today's knowledge society. This book and this course will provide you with practical advice on how to do just that.

Organizational communication has three basic functions: to inform, to persuade, and/or to promote goodwill.

Now look back over the preceding discussion of internal and external functions of communication in organizations. Although there appear to be a large number of diverse business communication functions, they can be summarized in three simple categories, as Figure 1.5 shows: (1) to inform, (2) to persuade, and/or (3) to promote goodwill.

FIGURE 1.4 ***Internal and External Forms of Communication***

AmericanAirlines®

EXECUTIVE OFFICE

March 4, 2006

Ms. Christie Bonner
1792 Southern Avenue
Mesa, AZ 85202

Dear Ms. Bonner:

Congratulations for taking steps to overcome your fear of flying! Your eloquent words are testimony to the effectiveness of our AAir Born program; and more important, they underline how liberating the experience can be. I know the door is now open for you to enjoy many satisfying travel experiences.

Probably the most pleasant part of my responsibilities at American is receiving compliments from our customers about the service provided by our employees. I have passed along your kind words about those individuals who made such a difference to you in realizing your dream of flight. We appreciate the opportunity to recognize their fine performance.

On behalf of all of us associated with the AAir Born program, thank you very much, Ms. Bonner. We look forward to welcoming you aboard again soon.

Sincerely,

Janice Moore

Janice Moore
Staff Supervisor

Letters on company stationery communicate with outsiders. Notice how this one builds a solid relationship between American Airlines and a satisfied customer.

Eudora Pro - [Bob Markum, NEWS RELEASE ABOUT NASHVILLE C]

File Edit Mailbox Message Transfer Special Tools Window Help

Send

To: Bob Markum <bmarkum@aa.com>
From: Tim Smith <tsmith@aa.com>
Subject: NEWS RELEASE ABOUT NASHVILLE CREW BASE
Cc:
Bcc:
Attached: News_Release.txt

As an attachment, Bob, I'm sending a draft of the news release announcing the Nashville crew base. Please look it over and make any changes you like. We've tried to keep it short and to the point. Captain Bill Baker has agreed to do the media conference late Tuesday morning since your schedule is so tight.

Because *Flagship News* is close to its deadline and would like to run a brief story on the announcement, I'll need your response by August 12. Thanks for your help.

Tim

E-mail messages and printed memorandums typically deliver messages within organizations. They use a standardized format and are direct and concise.

FIGURE 1.5 ***Functions of Business Communication***

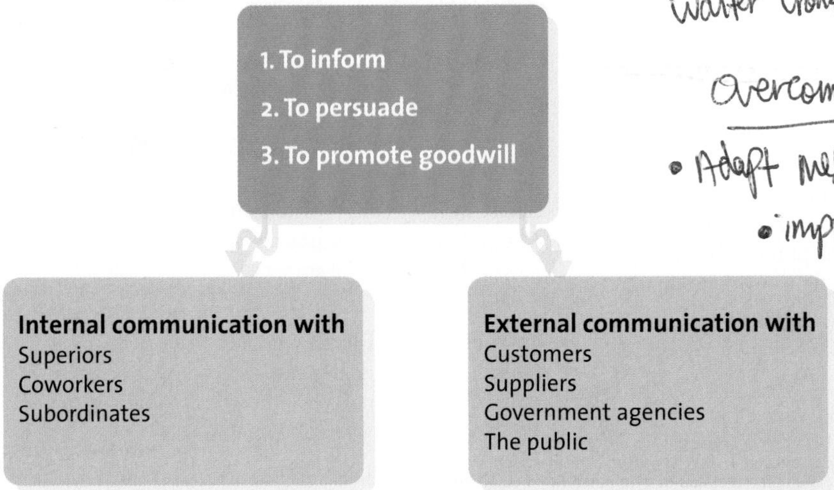

1. To inform
2. To persuade
3. To promote goodwill

Internal communication with
Superiors
Coworkers
Subordinates

External communication with
Customers
Suppliers
Government agencies
The public

New Emphasis on Interactive, Mobile, and Instant Communication

The flattening of organizations coupled with the development of sophisticated information technology has greatly changed the way we communicate internally and externally. We're seeing a major shift away from one-sided and rather slow forms of communication, such as memos and letters, to more interactive, fast-results communication. Speeding up the flow of communication are technologies such as e-mail, instant messaging (IM), text messaging, voice mail, cell phones, and wireless fidelity ("Wi-Fi") networks. Wi-Fi lets mobile workers connect to the Internet at ultrafast speeds without cables. For example, Steve S. can't imagine his life without instant messenging. An employee at a New York brokerage firm, Steve uses IM to talk simultaneously with clients, colleagues, and friends. With IM, he can carry on six conversations at once, which he says allows him to get his job done and serve clients better.[37] Steve can also use text messaging on his cell phone, laptop, or handheld hardware when he needs to send or receive messages quietly.

Like Steve's dependence on IM, many businesspeople can't get along without their cell phones. But cell phones have proliferated so rapidly that their careless use has become an annoyance in many public places. See the accompanying Tech Talk box for tips on using this technological privilege courteously and responsibly.

Other forms of interactive communication include intranets (company versions of the Internet), Web sites, video transmission, and videoconferencing. You'll be learning more about these forms of communication in subsequent chapters. Despite the range of interactive technologies, communicators are still working with two basic forms of communication: oral and written. Each has advantages and disadvantages.

Oral communication minimizes miscommunication but provides no written record.

Oral Communication. Nearly everyone agrees that the best way to exchange information is orally in face-to-face conversations or meetings. Oral communication has many advantages. For one thing, it minimizes misunderstandings because communicators can immediately ask questions to clarify uncertainties. For another, it enables communicators to see each other's facial expressions and hear voice inflections, further improving the process. Oral communication is also an efficient way to develop consensus when many people must be consulted. Finally, most of us

tech talk

Practicing Courteous and Responsible Cell Phone Use

Business communicators find cell phones to be enormously convenient and real time-savers. But rude users have generated a backlash of sorts. Most of us have experienced thoughtless and offensive cell phone behavior. Although the cell phone industry vigorously opposes restrictive legislation, many major manufacturers admonish users to be courteous. Here are specific suggestions for using cell phones safely and responsibly:

- **Be courteous to those around you.** Don't force those near you to hear your business. Think first of those in close proximity instead of those on the other end of the phone. Apologize and make amends gracefully for occasional cell phone blunders.
- **Observe wireless-free quiet areas.** Don't allow your cell phone to ring in theaters, restaurants, museums, classrooms, important meetings, and similar places. Use the cell phone's silent/vibrating ring option. A majority of travelers prefer that cell phone conversations not be held on most forms of public transportation.
- **Speak in low, conversational tones.** Microphones on cell phones are quite sensitive, thus making it unnecessary to talk loudly. Avoid "cell yell."
- **Take only urgent calls.** Make full use of your cell phone's caller ID feature to screen incoming calls. Let voice mail take those calls that are not pressing.
- **Drive now, talk later.** Pull over if you must make a call. Talking while driving increases the chance of accidents fourfold, about the same as driving while intoxicated.

Career Application

How do you feel when you must listen to nearby cell phone conversations? Should cell phone use in cars be prohibited? During business meetings, how should participants react if their cell phones ring?

enjoy face-to-face interpersonal communication because it's easy, feels warm and natural, and promotes friendships.

The main disadvantages of oral communication are that it produces no written record, sometimes wastes time, and may be inconvenient. When individuals meet face to face or speak on the telephone, someone's work has to be interrupted. And how many of us are able to limit a conversation to just business? Nevertheless, oral communication has many advantages. The forms and advantages of both oral and written communication are summarized in Figure 1.6.

Written communication provides a permanent record but lacks immediate feedback.

Written Communication. Written communication is impersonal in the sense that two communicators cannot see or hear each other and cannot provide immediate feedback. Most forms of business communication—including e-mail, announcements, memos, faxes, letters, newsletters, reports, proposals, and manuals—fall into this category.

Organizations rely on written communication for many reasons. It provides a permanent record, a necessity in these times of increasing litigation and extensive government regulation. Writing out an idea instead of delivering it orally enables communicators to develop an organized, well-considered message. Written documents are also convenient. They can be composed and read when the schedules of both communicators permit, and they can be reviewed if necessary.

Written messages have drawbacks, of course. They require careful preparation and sensitivity to audience and anticipated effects. Words spoken in conversation may soon be forgotten, but words committed to hard or soft copy become a public record—and sometimes an embarrassing or dangerous one. E-mail records, even

Figure 1.6 ***Forms of Organizational Communication***

Oral Communication	Written Communication
Form	**Form**
Phone call	Announcement
Conversation	Memo, e-mail, fax
Interview	Letter
Meeting	Report, proposal
Conference	Newsletter
Advantages	**Advantages**
Immediate feedback	Permanent record
Nonverbal clues	Convenience
Warm feeling	Economy
Forceful impact	Careful message
Multiple input	Easy distribution

deleted ones, have often become "smoking guns" in court cases, revealing insider information that was never meant for public consumption.[38]

Written messages demand good writing skills, which can be developed through training.

Another drawback to written messages is that they are more difficult to prepare. They demand good writing skills, and such skills are not inborn. But writing proficiency can be learned. Because as much as 90 percent of all business transactions may involve written messages and because writing skills are so important to your business success, you will be receiving special instruction in becoming a good writer.

Avoiding Information Overload and Productivity Meltdown

The large volume of messages and communication channel choices overwhelms many workers.

Although technology provides a myriad of communication channel choices, the sheer volume of messages is overwhelming many employees. Many U.S. workers are sending or receiving between 50 and 200 messages daily, and it is not unusual for them to spend one or two hours a day just answering e-mail. As faster and more powerful information pathways deliver increasing torrents of data to our computers, wireless devices, telephones, and desks, it's frighteningly easy to become bogged down or overwhelmed. Workers often feel that they're getting no work done because interruptions average once every ten minutes.

Information overload and resulting productivity meltdown are becoming serious problems for workers and their employers. One midlevel manager at a global company solved his overload problem by deleting all the messages in his e-mail inbox when it got too full. "If it's important," he reasoned, "people will get back to me."[39] That technique, however, flirts with disaster. One communication specialist admonishes us to put our inboxes on a diet. We must wean ourselves from spending too much time on *noise* e-mails—those that act as a distraction and diminish productivity.[40] But how can we do that? Suggestions for controlling the e-mail monster are shown in the accompanying Tech Talk box.

Improving the Flow of Information in Organizations

learning objective

5

Information within organizations flows through formal and informal communication channels. A free exchange of information helps organizations respond rapidly to

tech talk

Tips for Controlling the E-Mail Monster

In an amazingly short time, e-mail has become one of the most powerful and useful communication channels in the workplace. But it has also produced information overload for many workers. The following techniques can help you control the e-mail monster:

- Send only business messages that you would have sent in a memo format. If a quick phone call or a short in-person chat could solve the problem immediately, avoid sending an e-mail.
- Check your e-mail inbox only at specific times each day, say at 9 a.m. and again at 4 p.m.
- Deal with a message only once. Answer it, delegate it to someone else, or move it to a project-specific folder for later action.
- Block unwanted incoming messages. Learn to use the filters on your mail program.
- Practice e-mail triage. Focus on the most urgent messages first. Be ruthless in deleting e-mail messages based on their headers.
- Use an alternative address when registering for anything on the Web. Avoid giving out your primary e-mail address.
- Subscribe only to mailing lists in which you are really interested.

Career Application

Discuss methods you have used or have heard about for controlling incoming e-mail. Use InfoTrac or Google (**www.google.com**) to search for additional tips for controlling e-mail overload.

changing markets, increase efficiency and productivity, build employee morale, serve the public, and take full advantage of the ideas of today's knowledge workers. Barriers, however, can obstruct the flow of communication, as summarized in Figure 1.7.

Formal Channels

Formal communication channels follow an organization's chain of command.

Formal channels of communication generally follow an organization's hierarchy of command, as shown in Figure 1.8. Information about policies and procedures orig-

FIGURE 1.7 ***Barriers Block the Flow of Communication in Organizations***

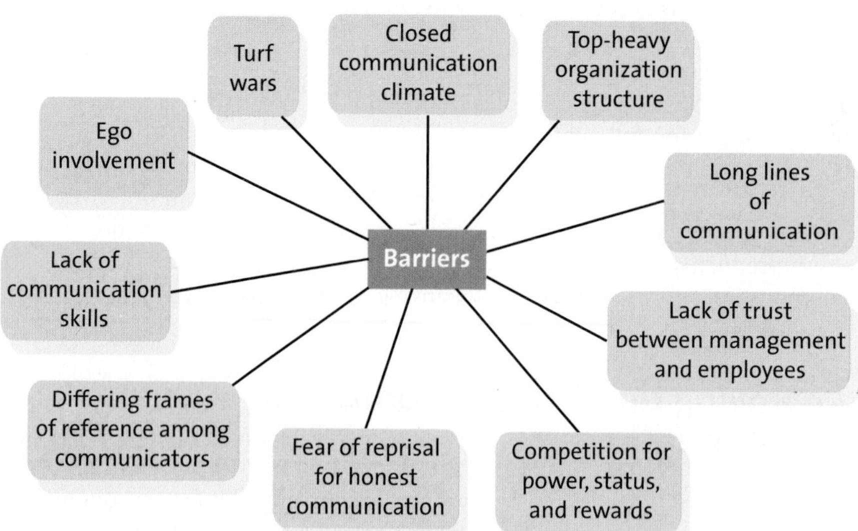

FIGURE 1.8 *Formal Communication Channels*

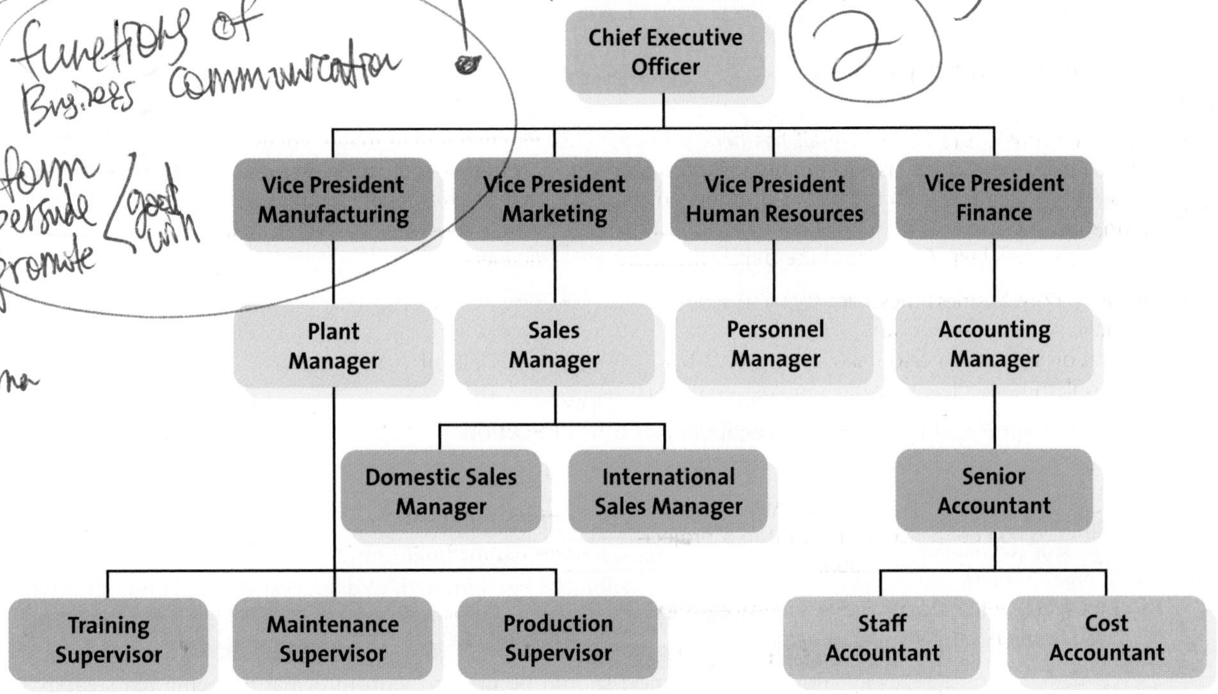

Chief Executive Officer

Vice President Manufacturing | Vice President Marketing | Vice President Human Resources | Vice President Finance

Plant Manager | Sales Manager | Personnel Manager | Accounting Manager

Domestic Sales Manager | International Sales Manager | Senior Accountant

Training Supervisor | Maintenance Supervisor | Production Supervisor | Staff Accountant | Cost Accountant

inates with executives and flows down through managers to supervisors and finally to lower-level employees. Many organizations have formulated official communication policies that encourage regular open communication, suggest means for achieving it, and spell out responsibilities. As summarized in Figure 1.9, official information among workers typically flows through formal channels in three directions: downward, upward, and horizontally.

Downward Flow. Information flowing downward generally moves from decision makers, including the CEO and managers, through the chain of command to workers. This information includes job plans, policies, and procedures. Managers also provide feedback about employee performance and instill a sense of mission in achieving the organization's goals.

Job plans, policies, instructions, feedback, and procedures flow downward from managers to employees.

One obstacle that can impede the downward flow of information is distortion resulting from long lines of communication. If, for example, the CEO in Figure 1.8 wanted to change an accounting procedure, she or he would probably not send a memo directly to the staff or cost accountants who would implement the change. Instead, the CEO would relay the idea through proper formal channels—from the vice president for finance, to the accounting manager, to the senior accountant, and so on—until the message reached the affected employees. Obviously, the longer the lines of communication, the greater the chance that a message will be distorted.

To improve communication and to compete more effectively, many of today's companies have "reengineered" themselves into smaller operating units and work teams. Rather than being bogged down with long communication chains, management speaks directly to team leaders, thus speeding up the entire process. Management is also improving the downward flow of information through newsletters, announcements, meetings, videos, and company intranets. Instead of hoarding information at the top, today's managers recognize the importance of letting workers know how well the company is doing and what new projects are planned.

FIGURE 1.9 ***Communication Flow Serves Organizations***

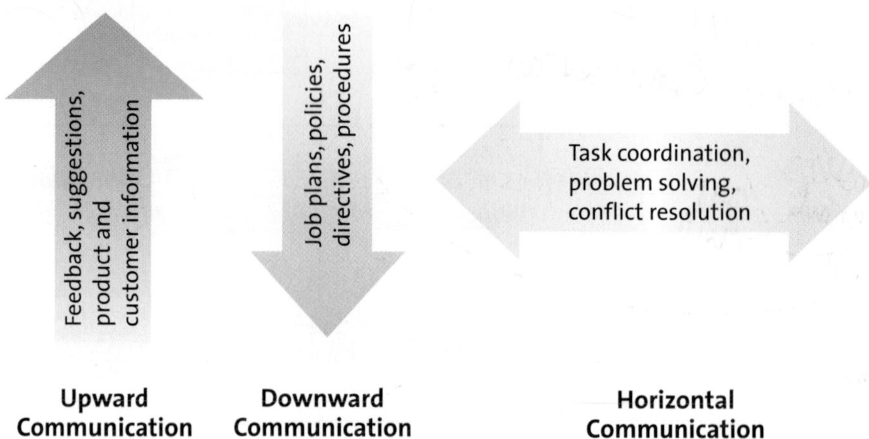

Feedback from employees forms the upward flow of communication in most organizations.

Upward Flow. Information flowing upward provides feedback from nonmanagement employees to management. Subordinate employees describe progress in completing tasks, report roadblocks encountered, and suggest methods for improving efficiency. Channels for upward communication include phone messages, e-mail, memos, reports, departmental meetings, and suggestion systems. Ideally, the heaviest flow of information should be upward with information being fed steadily to decision makers.

A number of obstacles, however, can interrupt the upward flow of communication. Employees who distrust their employers are less likely to communicate openly. Employees cease trusting managers if they feel they are being tricked, manipulated, criticized, or treated unfairly. Unfortunately, some employees today no longer have a strong trusting attitude toward employers. Downsizing, cost-cutting measures, the tremendous influx of temporary workers, discrimination and harassment suits, outrageous compensation packages for chief executives, and many other factors have eroded the feelings of trust and pride that employees once felt toward their employers and their jobs. Other obstacles include fear of reprisal for honest communication, lack of adequate communication skills, and differing frames of reference. Imperfect communication results when individuals are not using words or symbols with similar meanings, when they cannot express their ideas clearly, or when they come from different backgrounds.

Information flows upward more readily when companies provide a nonthreatening, supportive environment.

To improve the upward flow of communication, some companies are (1) hiring communication coaches to train employees, (2) asking employees to report customer complaints, (3) encouraging regular meetings with staff, (4) providing a trusting, nonthreatening environment in which employees can comfortably share their observations and ideas with management, and (5) offering incentive programs that encourage employees to collect and share valuable feedback. Companies are also building trust by setting up hotlines for anonymous feedback to management and by installing *ombudsman* programs. An *ombudsman* is a mediator who hears employee complaints, investigates, and seeks to resolve problems fairly.

To encourage the free flow of information each month, a manager at the Mirage Hotel in Las Vegas asks staff members for one thing that she can do better for each of them. In return, she tells them one thing they can do better for her. This two-way communication helps the hotel improve guest services month after month.[41]

Horizontal Flow. Lateral channels transmit information horizontally among workers at the same level, such as between the training supervisor and maintenance supervisor in Figure 1.8. These channels enable individuals to coordinate tasks, share

PROCESS IN PROGRESS

Procter & Gamble Revisited

LONG ADMIRED AS one of the country's best-managed companies, Procter & Gamble fell upon bad times when it launched a plan to reinvent itself. Durk Jager, the CEO in charge of the restructuring, lasted only 17 months before he was "coached out," which is P & G lingo for being fired. The company's stock price plunged to half of its former value, a startling drop for a company widely regarded as the world's preeminent marketer.

Critics say that a major reason for the CEO's departure was that he did not bring the managers of P & G's brands with him on the changes. This means that he was unable to communicate to them his vision for reorganizing the company, and he did not get their support or "buy-in." Within 18 months 80 percent of the most senior managers were performing different jobs from those they had done earlier. Jager himself was described as a "fearsome character, more than willing to shoot the messenger who brought him bad news."[42] Naturally, managers who were having trouble achieving the reorganization goals were reluctant to reveal their problems to him. As a result, problems were not resolved. Although Jager's job was "to give P & G a serious kick in the pants,"[43] many felt that the reorganization could have been executed less brutally. His brusque, noncommunicative style alienated managers.

Critical Thinking

- How could Procter & Gamble have improved the downward flow of information regarding its reorganization plans?
- How could Procter & Gamble have improved its upward flow of information? What are typical obstacles? What part does a manager's personality play in encouraging or discouraging upward communication?
- Is horizontal communication important in an organization such as Procter & Gamble? What are typical obstacles? How could horizontal communication be improved?

CONTINUED ON PAGE 30

case study

information, solve problems, and resolve conflicts. Horizontal communication takes place through personal contact, telephone, e-mail, memos, voice mail, and meetings. Most traditional organizations have few established regular channels for the horizontal exchange of information. Restructured companies with flattened hierarchies and team-based management, however, have discovered that when employees combine their knowledge with that of other employees, they can do their jobs better. Much of the information in these organizations is traveling horizontally among team members.[44]

Workers coordinate tasks, share information, solve problems, and resolve conflicts through horizontal communication.

Obstacles to the horizontal flow of communication, as well as to upward and downward flow, include poor communication skills, prejudice, ego involvement, and turf wars. Some employees avoid sharing information if doing so might endanger their status or chances for promotion within the organization. Competition within units and an uneven reward system may also prevent workers from freely sharing information.

To improve horizontal communication, companies are (1) training employees in teamwork and communication techniques, (2) establishing reward systems based on team achievement rather than individual achievement, and (3) encouraging full participation in team functions. However, employees must also realize that they are personally responsible for making themselves heard, for really understanding what other people say, and for getting the information they need. Developing those business communication skills is exactly what this book and this course will do for you.

To improve horizontal communication, companies are training and rewarding employees as well as encouraging team functions.

Informal Channels

An informal communication channel, the grapevine carries organizationally relevant gossip.

Not all information within an organization travels through formal channels. The *grapevine* is an informal channel of communication that carries organizationally relevant gossip.[45] This informal channel functions through social relationships in which individuals talk about work when they are having lunch, meeting at the water cooler, working out, golfing, or carpooling to work. Alert managers find the grapevine an excellent source of information about employee morale and problems. They have also used the grapevine as a "break it to them gently" device, planting "rumors," for example, of future layoffs or other changes.

Researchers studying communication flow within organizations know that the grapevine can be a major source of information. In some organizations it can account for as much as two thirds of an employee's information. Is this bad? Well, yes and no. The grapevine can be a fairly accurate and speedy source of organization information. However, grapevine information is often incomplete because it travels in headlines: "Robinson Canned" or "Jerk on the Fourth Floor Promoted."[46] When employees obtain most of their company news from the grapevine, it's a pretty sure bet that management is not releasing sufficient information through formal channels.

Employees prefer to receive vital company information through formal channels.

The truth is that most employees want to know what's going on. In fact, one study found that regardless of how much information organization members reported receiving, they wanted more.[47] Many companies today have moved away from a rigid authoritarian management structure in which only managers were privy to vital information, such as product success and profit figures. Employees who know the latest buzz feel like important members of the team.[48] Through formal lines of communication, smart companies are keeping employees informed. Thus, the grapevine is reduced to carrying gossip about who's dating whom and what restaurant is cool for lunch.

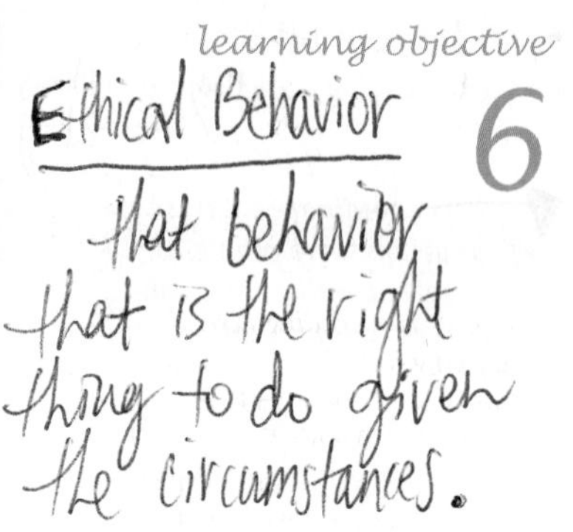

learning objective 6

Facing Increasing Ethical Challenges

The work world is indeed changing. One of the most remarkable changes involves ethics in the workplace. At one time the expression "business ethics" drew a big laugh. Many considered it an *oxymoron,* a combination of contradictory words. How could a business, which is obviously governed by profits, also be ethical? Yet, corporations made a remarkable turnabout in the 1990s. Following the "greed is good" era of the 1980s, businesspeople became increasingly concerned with ethics. In a study of Fortune 1000 companies, 98 percent of the respondents addressed ethics and conduct issues in policy manuals, codes of ethics, or some other formal document.[49]

Ethical awareness grows as companies recognize that ethical practices make good business sense.

What caused this explosion of ethical awareness? According to one poll, many companies were primarily interested in incorporating ethics into their organizations because they wished to be more socially responsible.[50] Actually, however, many businesses simply recognized that ethical practices make good business sense. Ethical companies endure less litigation, less resentment, and less government regulation.[51] As a result, companies are adding ethics officers, hotlines, workshops, training programs, and codes of conduct. If you go to work for a large company, chances are good that you'll be asked to comply with its code of conduct.

Violating Business Ethics

Despite this trend, however, the business world continues to be plagued by unethical behavior and a poor public image. In recent years business in general, and CEOs in particular, have plummeted in public opinion. One survey showed that Americans trusted CEOs about as much as they trusted used car salesmen.[52] Why this drop in credibility?

The business world suffers from a poor public image resulting from unethical behavior by some organizations.

Almost every day we read of new scandals involving corporate malfeasance, accounting fraud, business conflicts of interest, and CEO excesses. Enron, the seventh-largest company in the United States, collapsed in bankruptcy after admitting inflated earnings, misuse of reserve accounts, concealment of losses, inflation of asset values, and deliberate use of improper accounting methods. Many Enron officials await criminal prosecution.[53] At ImClone, CEO Dr. Samuel Waksal was sentenced to 87 months in prison after pleading guilty to charges including securities fraud. Rite Aid CEO Martin Grass admitted lining his pockets with millions and was sentenced to eight years in prison. Four top executives at Xerox agreed to pay a total of $22 million in fines to settle civil fraud charges.[54] And one of the most egregious cases centers on Dennis Kozlowski, former CEO of Tyco, who is accused of looting the conglomerate of hundreds of millions of dollars. A $6,000 shower curtain and $15,000 umbrella stand for his Manhattan corporate apartment plus a $2 million birthday party on Sardinia for his wife were all funded from company coffers.

But it's not just executives who are tempted. One study revealed that 56 percent of the employees surveyed felt some pressure to act unethically or illegally. Another 48 percent admitted they had engaged in one or more unethical and/or illegal actions during the past year. The most common violations follow:[55]

- Cutting corners on quality
- Covering up incidents
- Abusing or lying about sick days
- Deceiving customers
- Lying to a supervisor or underling
- Taking credit for a colleague's ideas

Charged with evading taxes as well as dipping into Tyco's corporate funds to the tune of $600 million, former CEO Dennis Koslowski is led away. Although his attorneys argued to the contrary, newspaper stories reveal years of alleged corruption, malfeasance, and all-around bad behavior. His unethical actions destroyed his reputation and nearly ruined a major American company.

Photo: © AP / Wide World Photos

Achieving Ethical Behavior

With downsized staffs and fewer resources, employees feel pressure to increase productivity—by whatever means. Knowingly or not, managers under pressure to make profit quotas may send the message to workers that it's OK to lie, cheat, or steal to achieve company goals.[56] Couple these pressures with a breakdown in the traditional attitudes of trust and loyalty toward employers, and it's easy to see why ethical lapses are causing concern in the workplace.

Just what is ethical behavior? Ethics author Mary E. Guy defines ethics as "that behavior which is the *right* thing to do, given the circumstances."[57] Ethical behavior involves four principles: honesty, integrity, fairness, and concern for others. "These four principles are like the four legs of a stool," explains ethics authority Michael Josephson. "If even one leg is missing, the stool wobbles, and if two are missing, the stool falls. It's not enough to pride oneself on your honesty and integrity if you're not fair or caring."[58] Consider a manager who would never dream of behaving dishonestly on the job or off. Yet this same manager forces a key employee to choose between losing her job and staying home with a sick child. The manager's lack of caring and failure to consider the circumstances create a shaky ethical position that would be difficult to justify.

Five Common Ethical Traps

Recognizing five ethical traps can help communicators avoid them.

In making ethical decisions, business communicators commonly face five traps that can make arriving at the right decision difficult.[59]

The False Necessity Trap. People act from the belief that they're doing what they must do. They convince themselves that they have no other choice, when in fact it's generally a matter of convenience or comfort. Consider the Beech-Nut Corporation's actions when it discovered that its supplier was providing artificial apple juice. Beech-Nut canceled its contracts but continued to advertise and sell the adulterated "apple" juice as a 100 percent natural product in its baby food line. Apparently falling into the false necessity trap, Beech-Nut felt it had no choice but to continue the deception.

The Doctrine-of-Relative-Filth Trap. Unethical actions sometimes look good when compared with the worse behavior of others. What's a little fudging on an expense account compared with the pleasure cruise the boss took and charged as a business trip? Or how about using your PC at work to send a little personal e-mail (just a few quick notes) and perhaps do some much-needed research on an SUV you are considering buying. After all, the fellows in Engineering told you that they spend hours on their PCs checking sports scores, playing games, and conducting recreational Web surfing. They even have bookmarked "Don's Boss Page" so that they can look busy while cruising the Internet.[60] Your minor infraction is insignificant compared with what's happening regularly in Engineering.

The Rationalization Trap. In falling into the rationalization trap, people try to explain away unethical actions by justifying them with excuses. Consider employees who "steal" time from their employers by taking long lunch and coffee breaks, claiming sick leave when not ill, and completing their own tasks on company time. It's easy to rationalize such actions: "I deserve an extra-long lunch break because I can't get all my shopping done on such a short lunch hour" or "I'll just write my class report at the office because the computer printer is much better than mine, and they aren't paying me what I'm worth anyway."

Explaining unethical actions by justifying them with excuses is a form of rationalization.

The Self-Deception Trap. Applicants for jobs often fall into the self-deception trap. They are all too willing to inflate grade-point averages or exaggerate past accomplishments to impress prospective employers. One applicant, for example, claimed experience as a broker's assistant at a prestigious securities firm. A background check revealed that he had interviewed for the securities job but was never offered it. Another applicant claimed that in his summer job he was "responsible for cross-corporate transferal of multidimensional client receivables." In other words, he moved boxes from sales to shipping. Self-deception can lead to unethical and possibly illegal behavior.

The Ends-Justify-the-Means Trap. Taking unethical actions to accomplish a desirable goal is a common trap. Consider a manager in a Medicare claims division of a large health insurance company who coerced clerical staff into working overtime without pay. The goal was the reduction of a backlog of unprocessed claims. Despite the worthy goal, the means of reaching it was unethical.

Goals of Ethical Business Communication

Business communicators can minimize the danger of falling into ethical traps by setting specific ethical goals. Although the following goals hardly constitute a formal code of conduct, they will help business writers maintain a high ethical standard.

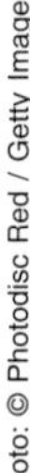

Telling the Truth. Ethical business communicators do not intentionally make statements that are untrue or deceptive. We become aware of dishonesty in business when violators break laws, notably in advertising, packaging, and marketing. The Federal Trade Commission, for example, ordered Kraft Foods to cancel a deceptive advertisement claiming that each Kraft Singles processed cheese slice contained as much calcium as five ounces of milk, an untrue statement.[61] In a similar case, the FTC charged Stouffer Foods with misrepresentation for its claim that Lean Cuisine entrees always contain less than 1 gram of sodium. In a fine-print footnote, careful consumers learn that 1 gram is equivalent to 1,000 milligrams, which is the commonly used unit of measurement for sodium.[62] The FTC also has cracked down on the makers of exercise equipment, such as Abflex, because three minutes a day on the "ab" machine doesn't come close to producing a "washboard stomach," as the manufacturer claimed.[63]

Goals of ethical communicators include telling the truth, labeling opinions, being objective, communicating clearly, and giving credit.

Half-truths, exaggerations, and deceptions constitute unethical communication. But conflicting loyalties in the workplace sometimes blur the line between right and wrong. Let's say you helped the marketing director, who is both your boss and your friend, conduct consumer research about a new company product. When you see the final report, you are astonished at how the findings have been distorted to show a highly favorable product approval rating. You are torn between loyalty to your boss (and friend) and loyalty to the company. Tools for helping you solve such ethical dilemmas will be discussed shortly.

Labeling Opinions. Sensitive communicators know the difference between facts and opinions. Facts are verifiable and often are quantifiable; opinions are beliefs held with confidence but without substantiation. It's a fact, for example, that women in the last decade started new businesses twice as fast as men.[64] It's an opinion, though, that the so-called "glass ceiling" is the cause for the increase in the number of female entrepreneurs. It's a fact that many companies are developing teams as tools to achieve management objectives. It's an opinion that teams are more effective in solving problems than individuals. Stating opinions as if they were facts is unethical.

Facts ***are verifiable;*** **opinions** ***are*** ***beliefs held with conviction.***

Being Objective. Ethical business communicators recognize their own biases and strive to keep them from distorting a message. Suppose you are asked to investigate desktop computers and write a report recommending a brand for your office. As you visit stores and watch computer demonstrations, you discover that an old high school friend is selling Brand X. Because you always liked this individual and have faith in his judgment, you may be inclined to tilt your recommendation in his direction. However, it's unethical to misrepresent the facts in your report or to put a spin on your arguments based on friendship. To be ethical, you could note in your report that you have known the person for ten years and that you respect his opinion. In this way, you have disclosed your relationship as well as the reasons for your decision. Honest reporting means presenting the whole picture and relating all facts fairly.

"Plain English" laws require simple, understandable language in policies, contracts, warranties, and other documents.

Communicating Clearly. Ethical business communicators feel an obligation to write clearly so that receivers understand easily and quickly. Some states have even passed "Plain English" laws that require businesses to write policies, warranties, and contracts in language comprehensible to average readers. Plain English means short sentences, simple words, and clear organization. Communicators who intentionally obscure the meaning with long sentences and difficult words are being unethical. A thin line, however, separates unethical communication from ethical communication. Some might argue that writers and speakers who deliver wordy, imprecise messages requiring additional correspondence or inquiry to clarify the meaning are acting unethically. However, the problem may be one of experience and skill rather than ethics. Such messages waste the time and resources of both senders and receivers. However, they are not unethical unless the intent is to deceive.

Giving Credit. As you probably know, using the written ideas of others without credit is called plagiarism. Ethical communicators give credit for ideas by (1) referring to originators' names within the text; (2) using quotation marks; and (3) documenting sources with endnotes, footnotes, or internal references. (You'll learn how to do this in Chapter 12 and Appendix C.) One student writer explained his reasons for plagiarizing material in his report by rationalizing, "But the encyclopedia said it so much better than I could!" This may be so, yet such an argument is no justification for appropriating the words of others. Quotation marks and footnotes could have saved the student. In school or on the job, stealing ideas or words from others is unethical.

Tools for Doing the Right Thing

Acting ethically means doing the right thing—given the situation.

In composing messages or engaging in other activities on the job, business communicators can't help being torn by conflicting loyalties. Do we tell the truth and risk our jobs? Do we show loyalty to friends even if it means bending the rules? Should we be tactful or totally honest? Is it our duty to make a profit or to be socially responsible? Acting ethically means doing the right thing given the circumstances. Each set of circumstances requires analyzing issues, evaluating choices, and acting responsibly.

Resolving ethical issues is never easy, but the task can be made less difficult if you know how to identify key issues. The following questions may be helpful.

- **Is the action you are considering legal?** No matter who asks you to do it or how important you feel the result will be, avoid anything that is prohibited by law. Giving a kickback to a buyer for a large order is illegal, even if you suspect that others in your field do it and you know that without the kickback you will lose the sale.

Business communicators can help resolve ethical issues through self-examination.

- **How would you see the problem if you were on the opposite side?** Looking at all sides of an issue helps you gain perspective. Consider the issue of mandatory drug testing among employees. From management's viewpoint such testing could stop drug abuse, improve job performance, and lower health insurance premiums. From the employees' viewpoint mandatory testing reflects a lack of trust of employees and constitutes an invasion of privacy. By weighing both sides of the issue, you can arrive at a more equitable solution.
- **What are alternate solutions?** Consider all dimensions of other options. Would the alternative be more ethical? Under the circumstances, is the alternative feasible? Can an alternate solution be implemented with a minimum of disruption and with a good possibility of success? In the situation involving your boss's distortion of consumer product research, you could go to the head of the company and tell what you know. A more tactful alternative, however, would be to approach your boss and ask whether you misunderstood the report's findings or whether an error might have been made.

Discussing an ethical problem with a coworker or colleague might lead to helpful alternatives.

- **Can you discuss the problem with someone whose advice you trust?** Suppose you feel ethically bound to report accurate information to a client even though your boss has ordered you not to do so. Talking about your dilemma with a coworker or with a colleague in your field might give you helpful insights and lead to possible alternatives.

- **How would you feel if your family, friends, employer, or coworkers learned of your action?** If the thought of revealing your action publicly produces cold sweats, your choice is probably unwise. Losing the faith of your friends or the confidence of your customers is not worth whatever short-term gains might be realized.

Perhaps the best advice in ethical matters is contained in the Golden Rule: Do unto others as you would have others do unto you. The ultimate solution to all ethics problems is treating others fairly and doing what is right to achieve what is good. In succeeding chapters you will find additional discussions of ethical questions as they relate to relevant topics.

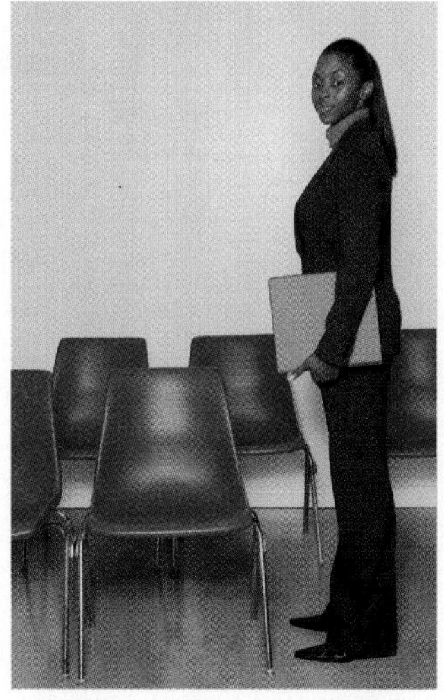

You can improve your communication skills by making use of the model documents, practice exercises, procedures, tips, strategies, summaries, and checklists in this book.

Strengthening Your Communication Skills

You've just taken a brief look at the changing workplace, the process of communication, the flow of communication in organizations, and ethical challenges facing business communicators today. Each topic provided you not only with the latest information about an issue but also with tips and suggestions that will help you function successfully in the changing workplace. After all, it's not enough to know the problems; you also need to know some of the solutions. Our goal is to help you recognize the problems and also to equip you with techniques for overcoming the obstacles that others have faced. This book is crammed with model documents, practice exercises, procedures, tips, strategies, suggestions, summaries, and checklists—all meant to ensure that you develop the superior communication skills that are so vital to your success as a businessperson today.

Remember, communication skills are not inherent; they must be learned. Remember, too, to take advantage of the unique opportunity you now have. You have an expert who is willing to work with you to help improve your writing, speaking, and other communication skills. Many organizations pay thousands of dollars to communication coaches and trainers to teach employees the very skills that you are learning in this course. Your coach is your instructor. Get your money's worth! Pick his or her brains. With this book as your guide and your instructor as your coach, you will find that this course, as we mentioned earlier, could very well be the most important in your entire college curriculum.

Summary of Learning Objectives

1 **Identify changes in the workplace and explain the importance of communication skills.** The workplace has undergone profound changes, such as the emergence of heightened global competition, flattened management hierarchies, expanded team-based management, innovative communication technologies, new work environments, and an increasingly diverse workforce. In this dynamic workplace you can expect to be a knowledge worker; that is, you will deal with words, figures, and data. The most important foundation skill for knowledge workers is the ability to communicate. You can improve your skills by studying the principles, processes, and products of communication provided in this book and in this course.

2 **Describe the process of communication.** The sender encodes (selects) words or symbols to express an idea. The message is sent verbally over a

PROCESS TO PRODUCT

Applying Your Skills at Procter & Gamble

WHEN the flamboyant Jager was pressured to resign, A. G. Lafley took over as Procter & Gamble CEO, and he began a quiet, yet sweeping transformation. The soft-spoken Lafley uses persuasion instead of intimidation; he listens more than he talks. "I'm not a screamer, not a yeller," he confesses. "But don't get confused by my style. I can be very decisive." A favorite form of communication for Lafley is the slogan. In a company famously resistant to new ideas, he patiently communicates how he wants P & G to change. When he felt that P & G was too engrossed in using technology to develop new products and not paying enough attention to what consumers wanted, he said, "The consumer is boss." To young marketing managers, he observed, "We are the voice of the consumer within P & G."

- As a communication tool, how effective are slogans? What functions do they serve in a large organization such as P & G? What obstacles could they create to understanding?
- In turning around P & G, Lafley avoided saying that P & G people were bad. Instead, he said, "I enrolled them in change." Analyze this statement as a communication strategy.
- At meetings with managers, Lafley occasionally joins in the discussion, but he feels that his real role is that of coach. What are the advantages and disadvantages of this communication style?

Your Task

In teams of three to five, discuss your responses to the preceding questions. Summarize your conclusions and (a) appoint one team representative to report to the class or (b) write individual memos or e-mails describing your conclusions. (See Chapter 8 and Appendix B for tips on writing memos.) ■

case study

channel (such as a letter, e-mail message, or telephone call) or is expressed nonverbally, perhaps with gestures or body language. "Noise"—such as loud sounds, misspelled words, or other distractions—may interfere with the transmission. The receiver decodes (interprets) the message and attempts to make sense of it. The receiver responds with feedback, informing the sender of the effectiveness of the message. The objective of communication is the transmission of meaning so that a receiver understands a message as intended by the sender.

3 **Discuss barriers to interpersonal communication and the means of overcoming those barriers.** *Bypassing* causes miscommunication because people have different meanings for the words they use. One's *frame of reference* creates a filter through which all ideas are screened, sometimes causing distortion and lack of objectivity. *Weak language skills* as well as *poor listening skills* impair communication efforts. *Emotional interference*—joy, fear, anger, and so forth—hampers the sending and receiving of messages. *Physical distractions*—noisy surroundings, faulty acoustics, and so forth—can disrupt oral communication. You can reduce or overcome many interpersonal communication barriers if you (a) realize that the communication process is imperfect, (b) adapt your message to the receiver, (c) improve your language and listening skills, (d) question your preconceptions, and (e) plan for feedback.

4 **Analyze the functions and procedures of communication in organizations.** Internal functions of communication include issuing and clarifying procedures and policies, informing management of progress, persuading others to make changes or improvements, and interacting with employees. External functions of communication include answering inquiries about products or services, persuading customers to buy products or services, clarifying supplier specifications, and so forth. Oral, face-to-face communication is most effective, but written communication is often more expedient. The volume of messages today is overwhelming many employees, who must institute techniques to control information overload and productivity meltdown.

As its new CEO, A. J. Lafley restored Procter & Gamble's equilibrium and staff morale by using many skillful communication techniques including one that he calls "peeling the onion." Instead of imposing his ideas, he asks a series of keen questions that help shape decisions. Each question peels back another layer of perspective. His wise questioning and supportive listening build confidence and empower managers to recognize alternatives, goals, and outcomes in their decision making.

5 **Assess the flow of communication in organizations including barriers and methods for overcoming those barriers.** Formal channels of communication follow an organization's hierarchy of command. Information flows downward from management to workers. Long lines of communication tend to distort information. Many organizations are improving the downward flow of communication through newsletters, announcements, meetings, videos, and company intranets. Information flows upward from employees to management, thus providing vital feedback for decision makers. Obstacles include mistrust, fear of reprisal for honest communication, lack of adequate communication skills, and differing frames of reference. To improve upward flow, companies are improving relations with staff, offering incentive programs that encourage employees to share valuable feedback, and investing in communication training programs. Horizontal communication is among workers at the same level. Obstacles include poor communication skills, prejudice, ego involvement, competition, and turf wars. Techniques for overcoming the obstacles include (a) training employees in communication and teamwork techniques, (b) establishing reward systems, and (c) encouraging full participation in team functions. Informal channels of communication, such as the grapevine, deliver unofficial news—both personal and organizational—among friends and coworkers.

6 **List the goals of ethical business communication and describe important tools for doing the right thing.** Ethical business communicators strive to (a) tell the truth, (b) label opinions so that they are not confused with facts, (c) be objective and avoid distorting a message, (d) write clearly and avoid obscure language, and (e) give credit when using the ideas of others. When you face a difficult decision, the following questions serve as valuable tools in guiding you to do the right thing: (a) Is the action you are considering legal? (b) How would you see the problem if you were on the opposite side? (c) What are alternate solutions? (d) Can you discuss the problem with someone whose advice you trust? (e) How would you feel if your family, friends, employer, or coworkers learned of your action?

Photo: © AP / Wide World Photos

chapter review

1. How are business communicators affected by the emergence of global competition, flattened management hierarchies, and expanded team-based management? (Obj. 1)
2. How are business communicators affected by the emergence of innovative communication technologies, new work environments, and an increasingly diverse workforce? (Obj. 1)
3. What are knowledge workers? Why are they hired? (Obj. 1)
4. Define *communication* and explain its most critical factor. (Obj. 2)
5. Describe the five steps in the process of communication. (Obj. 2)
6. List four barriers to interpersonal communication. Be prepared to discuss each. (Obj. 3)
7. Name five specific ways you can personally reduce barriers in your communication. (Obj. 3)
8. What are the three main functions of organizational communication? (Obj. 4)
9. What are the advantages of oral, face-to-face communication? (Obj. 4)
10. What are the advantages of written communication? (Obj. 4)
11. How do formal and informal channels of communication differ within organizations? (Obj. 5)
12. Describe three directions in which communication flows within organizations and what barriers can obstruct each. (Obj. 5)
13. How can barriers to the free flow of information in organizations be reduced? (Obj. 5)
14. Discuss five thinking traps that block ethical behavior. (Obj. 6)
15. When faced with a difficult ethical decision, what questions should you ask yourself? (Obj. 6)

critical thinking

1. Why should you, as a business student and communicator, strive to improve your communication skills; and why is it difficult or impossible to do so on your own? (Obj. 1)
2. Recall a time when you experienced a problem as a result of poor communication. What were the causes of and possible remedies for the problem? (Objs. 2 and 3)
3. Some companies say that the more information provided to employees, the more employees want. How would you respond to this complaint? (Objs. 4 and 5)
4. As a channel of organizational communication, what are the advantages and disadvantages of e-mail? (Objs. 4 and 5)
5. How are the rules of ethical behavior that govern businesses different from those that govern your personal behavior? (Obj. 6)
6. **Ethical Issue:** Suppose your superior asked you to alter year-end financial data, and you knew that if you didn't you might lose your job. What would you do if it were a small amount? A large amount?

INFOTRAC COLLEGE EDITION

Building Knowledge and Research Skills

To excel as a knowledge worker in today's digital workplace, you must know how to find and evaluate information on the Internet. As a student purchasing a new copy of Guffey's *Business Communication: Process and Product*, 5e, you have an extraordinary opportunity to develop these research skills. For four months you have special access to College Edition, a comprehensive Web-based collection with millions of journal, magazine, encyclopedia, and newspaper articles. You'll find many activities and study questions in this book that help you build knowledge and develop research skills using InfoTrac. Watch for the InfoTrac icons. InfoTrac is available only with NEW copies of your textbook.

Building Knowledge and Research Skills

With your Web browser on your computer screen, key the following URL: **www.infotrac-college.com.** Click *Register New Account.* Establish your logon name and password. (You may wish to read Thomson's Privacy Policy.) When you feel confident, go to the *Keyword Search* page and enter your search term. If you need a little help, click *InfoTrac Demo.*

Rich chapter resources are available on the Web sites.

activities

1.1 Communication Assessment: How Do You Stack Up? (Objs. 1–3)

You know more about yourself than anyone else. That makes you the best person to assess your present communication skills. Take an honest look at your current skills and rank them using the following chart. How well you communicate will be an important factor in your future career—particularly if you are promoted into management, as many college graduates are. For each skill, circle the number from 1 (indicating low ability) to 5 (indicating high ability) that best reflects your perception of yourself.

THREE GREAT RESOURCES FOR YOU!

1. ***Guffey Student Web Site***
   http://guffey.swlearning.com

   Your companion Web site offers chapter review quizzes, WebThink activities, updated chapter URLs, and many additional resources.

2. ***Guffey XTRA!***
   http://guffeyxtra.swlearning.com

   This online study assistant includes Your Personal Language Trainer, Speak Right!, Spell Right!, bonus online chapters, Documents for Analysis, PowerPoint slides, and much more.

3. ***Student Study Guide***

   Self-checked workbook activities and applications review chapter concepts and develop career skills.

		Low				*High*
Writing Skills						
1.	Possess basic spelling, grammar, and punctuation skills	1	2	3	4	5
2.	Am familiar with proper memo, letter, and report formats for business documents	1	2	3	4	5
3.	Can analyze a writing problem and quickly outline a plan for solving the problem	1	2	3	4	5
4.	Am able to organize data coherently and logically	1	2	3	4	5
5.	Can evaluate a document to determine its probable success	1	2	3	4	5
Reading Skills						
1.	Am familiar with specialized vocabulary in my field as well as general vocabulary	1	2	3	4	5
2.	Can concentrate despite distractions	1	2	3	4	5
3.	Am willing to look up definitions whenever necessary	1	2	3	4	5
4.	Am able to move from recreational to serious reading	1	2	3	4	5
5.	Can read and comprehend college-level material	1	2	3	4	5
Speaking Skills						
1.	Feel at ease in speaking with friends	1	2	3	4	5
2.	Feel at ease in speaking before a group of people	1	2	3	4	5
3.	Can adapt my presentation to the audience	1	2	3	4	5
4.	Am confident in pronouncing and using words correctly	1	2	3	4	5
5.	Sense that I have credibility when I make a presentation	1	2	3	4	5
Listening Skills						
1.	Spend at least half the time listening during conversations	1	2	3	4	5
2.	Am able to concentrate on a speaker's words despite distractions	1	2	3	4	5
3.	Can summarize a speaker's ideas and anticipate what's coming during pauses	1	2	3	4	5
4.	Provide feedback, such as nodding, paraphrasing, and asking questions	1	2	3	4	5
5.	Listen with the expectation of gaining new ideas and information	1	2	3	4	5

Now analyze your scores. Where are you strongest? Weakest? How do you think outsiders would rate you on these skills and traits? Are you satisfied with your present skills? The first step to improvement is recognition of a need. Put check marks next to the five traits you feel you should begin working on immediately.

1.2 Pumping Up Your Basic Language Muscles: Dr. Guffey as Your Personal Trainer (Obj. 1)

You can enlist the aid of the author to help you pump up your basic language skills. As your personal trainer, Dr. Guffey provides a three-step workout plan and hundreds of interactive questions to help you improve your grammar and mechanics skills. You receive immediate feedback in the warm-up sessions, and when you finish a complete workout you can take a short test to assess what you learned. These workouts are completely self-teaching, which means you can review at your own pace and repeat as often as you need. *Your Personal Language Trainer* is available at your online study assistant **Xtra! (http://guffeyxtra.swlearning.com)**. In addition to pumping up your basic language muscles, you can also use *Spell Right!* and *Speak Right!* to improve your spelling and pronunciation skills.

Your Task. Begin using *Your Personal Language Trainer* to brush up on your basic grammar and mechanics skills by completing one to three workouts per week or as many as your instructor advises. Be prepared to submit a printout of your "fitness" (completion) certificate when you finish a workout module. If your instructor directs, complete the spelling exercises in *Spell Right!* and submit a certificate of completion for the spelling final exam.

1.3 Collaborating on the Opening Case Study (Objs. 1–5)

LISTENING | TEAM | SPEAKING

Each chapter opens with a three-part case study of a well-known company. To help you develop collaboration and speaking skills as well as to learn about the target company and apply the chapter concepts, your instructor may ask you to do the following.

Your Task. As part of a three-student team during your course, work on one of the 16 case studies in the textbook. Answer the questions posed in all parts of the case study, look for additional information in articles or Web sites, complete the application assignment, and then make a 5- to 10-minute presentation to the class with your findings.

1.4 Getting to Know You (Objs. 1 and 2)

E-MAIL

Your instructor wants to know more about you, your motivation for taking this course, your career goals, and your writing skills.

Your Task. Send an e-mail or write a memo of introduction to your instructor. See Appendix B for memo formats and Chapter 8 for tips on preparing an e-mail message. In your message include the following:

a. Your reasons for taking this class
b. Your career goals (both temporary and long-term)
c. A brief description of your employment, if any, and your favorite activities
d. An assessment and discussion of your current communication skills, including your strengths and weaknesses

1.5 Small-Group Presentation: Getting to Know Each Other (Objs. 1 and 2)

LISTENING | TEAM | SPEAKING

Many business organizations today use teams to accomplish their goals. To help you develop speaking, listening, and teamwork skills, your instructor may assign team projects. One of the first jobs in any team is selecting members and becoming acquainted.

Your Task. Your instructor will divide your class into small groups or teams. At your instructor's direction, either (a) interview another group member and introduce that person to the group or (b) introduce yourself to the group. Think of this as an informal interview for a team assignment or for a job. You'll want to make notes from which to speak. Your introduction should include information such as the following:

a. Where did you grow up?
b. What work and extracurricular activities have you engaged in?
c. What are your interests and talents? What are you good at doing?
d. What have you achieved?
e. How familiar are you with various computer technologies?
f. What are your professional and personal goals? Where do you expect to be five years from now?

To develop listening skills, team members should practice good listening techniques (see Chapter 2) and take notes. They should be prepared to discuss three important facts as well as remember details about each speaker.

WEB RESOURCES THE EASY WAY

In the text of *Business Communication: Process and Product*, 5e, you will find many Web references, activities, and resources that help you build the Internet skills you will need in today's digital workplace. To make it easy for you to access our Web resources, go to your student Web site **(http://guffey.swlearning.com)** and click *Chapter URLs.* This list will be updated with new addresses or alternative Web links as needed. Use this list to avoid wasting time with mistyped addresses or dead links.

1.6 Communication Skills: What Do Employers Really Want? (Obj. 1)

TEAM WEB

What do employers request when they list job openings in your field?

Your Task. To learn what employers request in classified ads, check out the listings at an online job board. Visit a job board such as Monster, College Recruiter, Career Builder, or Career Journal. Use your favorite search engine to locate their sites. Follow the instructions to search job categories and locations. Study the jobs listed. Find five or more job listings in your field. If possible, print the results of your search. If you cannot print, make notes on what you find. Study the skills requested. How often do the ads mention communication, teamwork, and computer skills? What tasks do the ads mention? Discuss your findings with your team members. Prepare a list of the most frequently requested skills. Your instructor may ask you to submit your findings and/or report to the class. If you are not satisfied with the job selection at this site, choose another job board.

1.7 Workplace Writing: Separating Myths From Facts (Obj. 1)

Today's knowledge workers are doing more writing on the job than ever before. Flattened management hierarchies, heightened global competition, expanded team-based management, and heavy reliance on e-mail have all contributed to more written messages.

Your Task. In teams or in class, discuss the following statements. Are they myths or facts?

- **a.** Because I'm in a technical field, I'll work with numbers, not words.
- **b.** Secretaries will clean up my writing problems.
- **c.** Technical writers do most of the real writing on the job.
- **d.** Computers can fix any of my writing mistakes.
- **e.** I can use form letters for most messages.

1.8 Communication Process: Analyzing the Process at CompUSA (Obj. 2)

TEAM

"One misspelled word and customers begin to doubt the validity of the information they are getting," warns Mary Jo Lichtenberg. She's director of training, quality, and career development at CompUSA, in Plano, Texas. One of her big problems is training service agents with weak communication skills. "Just because agents understand technically how to troubleshoot computers or pieces of software and can walk customers through solutions extremely well over the telephone doesn't mean they can do the same in writing," she complains. "The skill set for phone does not necessarily translate to the skill set needed for writing e-mail." With more than 200 superstores, CompUSA is a leading retailer and reseller of computer hardware and software. As more and more of its customers choose e-mail and Web chat sessions to obtain service and support, CompUSA service reps are doing more writing. Lichtenberg's solution to this problem is to introduce writing classes in its training programs.[65]

Your Task. As an intern in the training program at CompUSA, you and other interns have been asked to brainstorm the communication process with Mary Jo Lichtenberg. How can she best communicate her proposal to her boss? Review the entire communication process from sender to feedback. What is involved in encoding the proposal to her boss? What assumptions might she make about her audience? What communication channel should she choose and why? What noise might she expect in the transmission process and how could she overcome it? Individually or in teams, discuss your analysis in class or in a memo to your instructor.

1.9 Communication Process: Avoiding Misunderstanding (Obj. 2)

Communication is not successful unless the receiver understands the message as the sender meant it.

Your Task. Analyze the following examples of communication failures. What went wrong?

- **a.** A manager said to his assistant, "I'd sure appreciate your help in preparing a roster of volunteers." Later, the assistant was resentful when she found that she had to complete the task herself.
- **b.** A supervisor issued the following announcement: "Effective immediately the charge for copying services in Repro will be raised 1/2 to 2 cents each." Receivers scratched their heads.
- **c.** The pilot of a military airplane about to land decided that the runway was too short. He shouted to his engineer, "Takeoff power!" The engineer turned off the engines; the plane crashed.
- **d.** A China Airways flight, operating in zero visibility, crashed into the side of a mountain shortly after takeoff. The pilot's last words were "What does *pull up* mean?" The official term is *climb.*
- **e.** The following statements actually appeared in letters of application for an advertised job opening. One applicant wrote, "Enclosed is my résumé in response to Sunday's New York Times." Another wrote, "Enclosed is my résumé in response to my search for an editorial/creative position." Still another wrote, "My experience in the production of newsletters, magazines, directories, and on-line data bases puts me head and shoulders above the crowd of applicants you have no doubtedly been inundated with."
- **f.** Skiers in an Austrian hotel saw the following sign in English: "Not to perambulate the corridors in the hours of repose in the boots of ascension."

g. The editor of Salt Lake City's *Deseret News* told his staff to "change the picture" of film icon James Dean, who had a cigarette dangling from his lips. The staff thought that the editor wanted the cigarette digitally removed from the picture, which they did. When published, the altered picture drew considerable criticism. The editor later explained that he had expected the staff to find a new picture.

1.10 Communication Channels: Informed Workers Are Happier (Obj. 5)

INFOTRAC

Within organizations, communication flow is more than merely theoretical. Information flowing from management down to employees is thought to make a difference in employee attitudes, loyalty, and productivity.

Your Task. Using InfoTrac, locate an article titled "Randstad Survey Shows Importance of Communication" (*Long Island Business News,* 19 April 2002, 4D). After reading the article, answer the following questions. Be prepared to discuss your responses in class or in a memo to your instructor:

a. What happens when businesses regularly give employees performance reviews and information about how the company is doing?
b. What evidence did the Randstad survey provide to support its statement that better communication can help companies reduce high employee turnover?
c. How do you think businesses can improve the way they communicate with employees? Discuss at least five channels of communication.

1.11 Document for Analysis: Barriers to Communication (Objs. 3, 4, and 5)

The following memo is from an exasperated manager to his staff. Obviously, this manager has no secretary to clean up his writing.

Your Task. Comment on the memo's effectiveness, tone, and potential barriers to communication. Your instructor may ask you to revise the memo improving its tone, grammar, and organization.

DATE: Current

TO: All Employees

FROM: Harold Robinson, Operations Manager

SUBJECT: Cleanup!

You were all suppose to clean up your work areas last Friday, but that didn't happen. A few people cleaned their desks, but no one pitched in to clean the common areas, and you all seen what a mess they were in!

So we're going to try again. As you know, we don't hardly have a big enough custodial budget anymore. Everyone must clean up himself. This Friday I want to see action in the copy machine area, things like emptying waste baskets and you should organize paper and toner supplies. The lunch room is a disaster area. You must do something about the counters, the refrigerator, the sinks, and the coffee machine. And any food left in the refrigerator on Friday afternoon should be throwed out because it stinks by Monday. Finally, the office supply shelves should be straightened.

If you can't do a better job this Friday, I will have to assign individuals to a specific cleaning schedule. Which I don't want to do, but you may force me to.

1.12 Communicating in Organizations: Controlling the E-Mail Monster (Obj. 4)

Brad M. has been working at CoolDog Software for six months. He loved e-mail when he first joined CoolDog, but now it's overwhelming him. Every day he receives between 200 and 300 messages, some important and some junk. To keep caught up, Brad checks his e-mail every hour—sometimes more often if he's expecting a response. He joined five mailing lists because they sounded interesting and helpful. But when a topic really excites the subscribers, Brad's e-mail box is jammed with 50 or 60 postings at once. Reading all his messages prevents him from getting his real work done. If he ignores his e-mail, though, he may miss something important. What really frustrates him is what to do with messages that he must retain until he gathers the necessary information to respond.

Your Task. What suggestions can you make to lessen Brad's e-mail overload?

1.13 Information Flow: What's the Latest Buzz? (Obj. 5)

All organizations provide information to the public and to members through official channels. But information also flows through unofficial channels.

Your Task. Consider an organization to which you belong or a business where you've worked. How did members learn what was going on in the organization? What kind of information flowed through formal channels? What were those channels? What kind of information was delivered through informal channels? Was the grapevine as accurate as official channels? What barriers obstructed the flow of information? How could the flow be improved?

1.14 Workplace Ethics: Where Do You Stand? (Obj. 6)

How do your ethics compare with those of workers across the country?

Your Task. Answer *yes* or *no* to each item in the following *Wall Street Journal Workplace Ethics Quiz.*[66] Be prepared to discuss your responses in class. At the end of this chapter you can see how others responded to this quiz.

1. Is it wrong to use company e-mail for personal reasons?
2. Is it wrong to use office equipment to help your children or spouse do schoolwork?
3. Is it wrong to play computer games on office equipment during the workday?
4. Is it wrong to use office equipment to do Internet shopping?
5. Is it unethical to blame an error you made on a technological glitch?
6. Is it unethical to visit pornographic Web sites using office equipment?
7. Is a $50 gift to a boss unacceptable?
8. Is a $50 gift FROM the boss unacceptable?
9. Is it OK to take a $200 pair of football tickets from a supplier?
10. Is it OK to accept a $75 prize won at a raffle at a supplier's conference?

1.15 Ethics: Does White-Collar Crime Pay? (Obj. 6)

INFOTRAC

You've been asked to participate in a panel discussing white-collar crime. Some people argue that executives seldom serve prison time for white-collar crime. You think that high-profile people have actually been sentenced to prison.

Your Task. Using InfoTrac, look for ammunition for your position. Try to find at least five examples of individuals who have been sentenced for corporate wrongdoing. What did they do, and what penalty did they receive? Be sure to document your sources, including author, title, publication, date, and page. If you wish to expand your topic, examine companies that have paid fines, suffered bad press, or been forced into bankruptcy for corporate malfeasance. Remember that InfoTrac requires good search terms to return good results. Try "white collar crime" and "corporate scandals," along with other search terms. Discuss your findings in class or in a memo to your instructor. Can you draw any conclusions from your findings?

Photo: © Photodisc Red / Getty Images

1.16 Developing Critical Thinking and Consumer Skills: A Victim of Identity Theft Wants Your Help (Obj. 1)

CRITICAL THINKING | **CONSUMER**

Your friend Lisa Williams, whose banking experience consisted mainly of ATM use, knew something was wrong when a Citibank debt consolidation representative called her. Lisa was astounded to learn that she had an overdue credit card balance of $4,600. Impossible! she thought. She didn't even own a Citibank credit card! Unfortunately, Lisa is one of more than 27 million Americans who have been victimized by fraud or identity theft in the past five years.[67]

Your Task. Lisa asks you to help her through this mess. Using the critical thinking steps outlined in this chapter and listed here, decide on a problem-solving strategy. At the same time, learn more about identity theft for your own protection. To find information, use InfoTrac or your favorite Internet search engine (such as **www.google.com**). Answer the following questions in a class discussion or in a memo to your instructor. (See Chapter 8 and Appendix B for information about writing memos.)

1. **Identify and clarify the problem.** How do banks issue credit cards? What information is needed? How is it verified? How do identity thieves get your personal information?
2. **Gather information.** Should Lisa ask Citibank for its application record for this fraudulent card? How can you learn more about identity theft in general?
3. **Evaluate the evidence.** Should Lisa investigate this herself or involve the police? Should she go to credit bureaus (Experian, Equifax, and TransUnion) and ask for their help in clearing her credit record?
4. **Consider alternatives and implications.** What actions can a victim of identity theft take?

5. **Choose and implement the best alternative.** What should Lisa do first and what follow-up actions should she take? How can people reduce the chances of identity theft?

WebThink

To further develop your Internet research and critical thinking skills, explore the special Web sites we've selected for this chapter. You'll find links that enrich your learning with real-world applications. Your instructor may assign the critical thinking questions to help you focus on key ideas.

Responses to *The Wall Street Journal Workplace Ethics Quiz* in Activity 1.14.

1. Thirty-four percent said using company e-mail for personal reasons is wrong.
2. Thirty-seven percent said using office equipment to help your children or spouse do schoolwork is wrong.
3. Forty-nine percent said playing computer games at work is wrong.
4. Fifty-four percent said using office equipment to do Internet shopping is wrong.
5. Sixty-one percent said blaming your own error on faulty technology is unethical.
6. Eighty-seven percent said visiting pornographic Web sites using office equipment is unethical.
7. Thirty-five percent said making a $50 gift to a boss is unacceptable.
8. Thirty-five percent said accepting a $50 gift from the boss is unacceptable.
9. Seventy percent said accepting a $200 pair of football tickets from a supplier is unacceptable.
10. Forty percent said accepting a $75 prize won at a raffle at a supplier's conference is unacceptable.

video resources

Two special sets of videos accompany Guffey's *Business Communication: Process and Product*, 5e. These videos take you beyond the classroom to build the communication skills you will need to succeed in today's rapidly changing workplace.

Video Library 1 *Building Workplace Skills* presents five new videos that introduce and reinforce concepts in selected chapters. These excellent tools ease the learning load by demonstrating chapter-specific material to strengthen your comprehension and retention of key ideas.

Video Library 2 *Bridging the Gap* presents five videos taking you inside high-profile companies such as Yahoo!, Ben & Jerry's, and World Gym. You'll be able to apply your new skills in structured applications aimed at bridging the gap between the classroom and the real world of work.

The recommended video for this chapter is *Career Success Starts with Communication Foundations*, which illustrates how strong communication skills can help you advance your career in today's challenging world of work. Be prepared to discuss critical-thinking questions provided.

C.L.U.E. review 1

Each chapter includes an exercise based on Appendix A, *Competent Language Usage Essentials (C.L.U.E.)*. This appendix is a business communicator's condensed guide to language usage, covering 50 of the most used, and abused, language elements. It also includes a list of frequently misspelled words and a quick review of selected confusing words. If you are rusty on these language essentials (and who isn't?), you need to do two things:

a. Study the guidelines and examples in Appendix A.
b. Complete the grammar and mechanics interactive workouts in *Your Personal Language Trainer*, which is available at **Xtra! (http://guffeyxtra.swlearning.com)**. You can also brush up on your spelling and pronunciation skills with Spell Right! and Speak Right! on your student CD.

The following ten sentences are packed with errors based on concepts and spelling words from Appendix A and *Your Personal Language Trainer*. You will find the corrections for these exercises at the end of Appendix A. On a separate sheet, edit the following sentences to correct faults in grammar, capitalization, punctuation, numbers, spelling, and word use.

1. To sucede in todays high-tech busness world you need highly-developed communication skills.
2. You especially need writting and grammer skills, because employes spend 60% of there time processing documents.
3. One organization paid three thousand dollars each for twelve employes to attend a 1 week work shop in communication training.
4. My coworker and me was serprised to learn that more information has been produced in the last thirty years then in the previous five thousand years.
5. If you work in a office with open cubicles its rude to listen to web radio streaming audio or other multimedia, without headphones.

6. When making a decision you should gather information, and than weigh the advantages and disadvantage of each alternative.
7. If you are defining communication for example, a principle element are the transmission of information and meaning.
8. Ms Johnson had 3 messages to send immediately, consequently she choose e-mail because it was definitly the most fastest comunication channel.
9. 5 elements that make up your frame of reference are the following, Experience, Education, Culture, Expectations and Personality.
10. Just between you and I; I'm sure our company President thinks that honesty and integrity is more important then increase profits.

chapter 2

Communicating in Small Groups and Teams

objectives

1 Discuss why groups and teams are formed and how they are different.

2 Describe team development, team and group roles, dealing with conflict, and methods for reaching group decisions.

3 Identify the characteristics of successful teams including an emphasis on workplace etiquette.

4 List techniques for organizing team-based written and oral presentations.

5 Discuss how to plan and participate in productive meetings.

6 Describe collaboration technologies used to facilitate meetings, manage projects, and make decisions.

COMMUNICATION IN PROCESS

Harley-Davidson Cruises Toward Team-Based Management

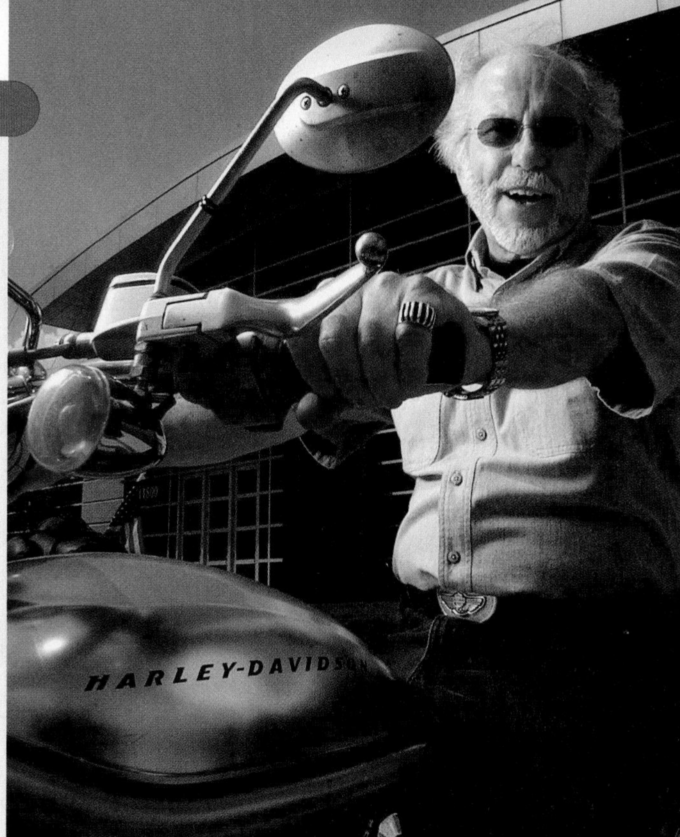

Vice President Willie Davidson on a V-Rod model outside the Willie G. Davidson Product Development Center helped revitalize Harley styling.

FOR NEARLY A century Harley-Davidson motorcycles cruised the open road, the ultimate symbol of free-wheeling joy and machismo. But though the Harley-Davidson Motor Company is wallowing in "hog heaven" profits now, the company was near death's door in the early 1980s. Poor quality was a major problem. Bikers took perverse joy in pointing to any oil puddle on the road and speculating that a Harley had recently been parked there. Plagued with reliability and other problems, the company lost significant market share to Honda, Suzuki, Kawasaki, and Yamaha.

Under new ownership, however, Harley-Davidson narrowly averted bankruptcy to emerge as a classic American Cinderella story. Its remarkable turnaround resulted from a number of factors, including a fanatical brand of customer loyalty. Many customers actually have the company logo tattooed on their bodies. More relevant to its comeback, though, were extensive changes in organization and management.

With new owners the Harley-Davidson Motor Company created a flatter, more interdependent organizational structure. It moved away from the traditional model of independent leaders issuing orders to dependent followers. New managers emphasized empowered work teams called "circles," leading to greater employee involvement in decision making.

Although new leadership and a flatter organization boosted Harley-Davidson to its current position as the leading global supplier of premium heavyweight motorcycles, it's facing new threats. Upstart companies with new factories want to cash in on the world's robust appetite for cruising and touring machines. And the aging of its core market has forced Harley to pour money into new models such as its youth-oriented Harley V-Rod, shown here with Vice President of Styling Willie G. Davidson. This high-powered, low-slung number is nicknamed the "crotch rocket." To appeal to women, Harley has converted grimy bike shops into sparkling retail showrooms. Some advertisements even attempt to soften the company image with less testosterone and leather and more "poetry" of the open road.

Meeting local and global competition, appealing to a younger audience without alienating its core market, and maintaining quality are continuing challenges for Harley-Davidson. Its move away from a strong hierarchical organization to management by collaborating teams has enabled it to meet these challenges, but not always smoothly.[1]

Critical Thinking

- Why are companies such as Harley-Davidson switching to team-based management?
- How can smaller operating units be helpful in responding to competition?
- What kinds of problems would you expect work groups or teams to experience when they form to make decisions?

www.harley-davidson.com

CONTINUED ON PAGE 56

case study

learning objective

1

Preparing to Work With Groups and Teams

Like employees at the Harley-Davidson Motor Company, you will probably find yourself working with small groups or in a team-oriented environment. You may already be part of one or more groups or teams. That's good, because experience on a team has become one of the top requests among recruiters looking over job candidates. To participate most effectively on a team, however, you need to learn about groups and teams. In this chapter you'll study why groups and teams are formed, how they differ and develop, typical roles members play, and how to resolve conflicts. In addition, you'll learn about workplace etiquette, how to collaborate in team-based presentations, uses of collaboration technologies, and how to plan and participate in productive meetings.

Why Form Groups and Teams?

Organizations are forming teams for better decisions, faster response, increased productivity, greater "buy-in," less resistance to change, improved morale, and reduced risks.

As organizations in the past decade were downsized, restructured, and reengineered, one reality became increasingly clear. Companies were expected to compete globally, meet higher standards, and increase profits—but often with fewer people and fewer resources.[2] Striving to meet these seemingly impossible goals, organizations began developing groups and teams for the following specific reasons:[3]

- ***Better decisions.*** Decisions are generally more accurate and effective because group and team members contribute different expertise and perspectives.
- ***Faster response.*** When action is necessary to respond to competition or to solve a problem, small groups and teams can act rapidly.
- ***Increased productivity.*** Because they are often closer to the action and to the customer, team members can see opportunities for improving efficiencies.
- ***Greater "buy-in."*** Decisions derived jointly are usually better received because members are committed to the solution and are more willing to support it.
- ***Less resistance to change.*** People who have input into making decisions are less hostile, aggressive, and resistant to change.
- ***Improved employee morale.*** Personal satisfaction and job morale increase when teams are successful.
- ***Reduced risks.*** Responsibility for a decision is diffused, thus carrying less risk for any individual.

Teams can be very effective in solving problems and in developing new products. Take, for example, the creation of Red Baron's "Stuffed Pizza Slices." Featuring a one-of-a-kind triangular, vented design, the product delivers taste, convenience, and style. But coming up with an innovative new hit required a cross-functional team with representatives from product development, packaging, purchasing, and operations. The entire team worked to shape an idea into a hit product using existing machinery.[4]

Some companies rejected teams because they slowed decisions, shielded workers from responsibility, and reduced productivity.

Despite the current popularity of teams, however, they are not a panacea for all workplace problems. Some critics complain that they are the latest in a succession of management fads. Others charge that they are a screen behind which management intensifies its control over labor.[5] Companies such as Ford, Levi-Strauss, Honda, and GM's Saturn plant retreated from teams, finding that they slowed decision making, shielded workers from responsibility, and created morale and productivity problems.[6] Yet, in most models of future organizations, teams, not individuals, function as the primary performance unit.[7]

Some organizations are even creating *virtual teams,* which are defined as groups of people who work interdependently with a shared purpose across space, time, and organization boundaries using technology.[8] For example, the CEO of Valent Software lived in Massachusetts, the president worked from Utah, the engineering team was based in Ohio, and other team members worked from their homes.[9] People who work together usually see each other and can talk face to face, but virtual teams must stay connected through technology. To learn more about how to communicate effectively in digital groups, see the accompanying Tech Talk box.

spotlight *on communicators*

"Teamwork is the starting point for treating people right," said Dave Thomas, founder of Wendy's Old Fashioned Hamburgers. "Most people think that teamwork is only important when competing against other teams. But competition is only part of the picture. In most things we do in life, people have to work with rather than against each other to get something done. Win-win situations and partnerships are the most important results of teamwork. The best teams in the world are the ones that help people become better and achieve more than they ever thought they could on their own."

Comparing Groups and Teams

Although teams and groups are similar, they are not identical. A *group* is a collection of three or more individuals who perceive themselves as a group but who may work independently to achieve organization goals. For example, members of an advertising department within a company are a group. Members of the department often complete their tasks independently, and their leader is a manager. A *team* is a group of individuals who interact over time to achieve a purpose. Members recognize a need for each other's expertise, talents, and commitment to achieve their goals. For example, a task force established to increase sales in a given territory is a team. Although the word *team* is used loosely to describe many combinations of workers, no one would dispute that the workplace trend today is definitely toward teams. Estimates suggest that between 54 and 80 percent of U.S. organizations use teams in some way.[10]

A group may work independently, but a team must interact.

Much of the emphasis today is on *self-directed teams.* They are different from single-leader work groups in a number of dimensions, as shown in Figure 2.1. Self-directed teams are most useful for solving problems that require people with different skills working together. Single-leader work groups are most useful for solving problems quickly when the leader already knows how to proceed. Ideally, the most successful self-directed teams will have many of the following characteristics:

Self-directed teams are best for solving problems that require people with different skills.

- **Clearly stated goals.** They are able to state their purpose and assess progress toward it.
- **Autonomy.** They can hire, fire, and discipline their own members. They complete jobs on their own with little or no supervision.
- **Decision-making authority.** They do not require a manager's approval for decisions.
- **Frequent communication.** They meet often or exchange messages to coordinate activities, avoid duplication, and make decisions.
- **Ongoing training.** They emphasize improving their skills to meet their goals.

Understanding Team Development, Roles, and Conflict

learning objective

2

Small groups and teams may be formed to complete single tasks or to function as permanent ongoing bodies. Regardless of their purpose, successful teams normally go through predictable phases as they develop. In this section you'll learn about the four phases of team development. You'll see how team members can perform in

tech talk

Techniques for Staying Connected in Virtual Teams

When Roger Rodriguez goes to work at BakBone Software in San Diego, he connects with a team of customer support people in Maryland, the United Kingdom, and Japan. He has never met these people and probably never will. Rodriguez is one of many workers and managers who belong to *virtual* teams. These are teams with members in remote locations who communicate electronically. With networked computers, desktop teleconferencing, e-mail, cell phones, fax, and collaborative software, it's possible for teams to complete projects no matter where they are geographically based.

Rodriguez and others working on virtual teams must overcome many obstacles not faced by intact groups. Because team members may be separated by geography, time zones, and cultures, they must work especially hard to develop understanding, commitment, and trust. Virtual team managers offer the following recommendations to help members work together.

- **Select team members carefully.** Choose team members who are self-starters, good communicators, flexible, trusting, and experts in areas needed by the team.
- **Invest in beginnings.** Team processes are expedited by spending time initially in reaching consensus about goals, tasks, and procedures. If possible, meet face to face to work out procedures and to bond.
- **Redefine "we."** Team members should be present in one another's thoughts even when not in their physical presence. Encourage behavior that reflects unity, such as including one another in decisions and sharing information. Consider having a team photograph taken and made into something used frequently such as a mouse pad or computer wallpaper.
- **Get the maximum benefit from technology.** Make use of speaker phones, collaborative software, e-mail, teleconferencing, and videoconferencing. But be sure that members are well-trained in their use.
- **Concentrate on building credibility and trust.** Team members should pay close attention to the way that others perceive them. Acting consistently, fulfilling promises, considering other member's schedules, and responding promptly to e-mail and voice messages help build credibility and trust.
- **Put communication on the agenda.** Members should discuss how and when it is appropriate to communicate with one another. They should establish clear expectations about response times.
- **Avoid misinterpreting messages.** Because it's so easy to misunderstand e-mail messages, one virtual manager advises team members to always doubt their first instinct about another team member if the response is negative. Always take time to question your reactions.

Career Application

Why do you think increasing numbers of employees are joining virtual teams? What are the advantages and disadvantages for employees and for employers?

functional and dysfunctional roles. You'll also study the role of conflict and how to apply a six-step plan for resolving conflict.

Four Phases of Team Development

Successful teams generally go through four phases: forming, storming, norming, and performing.

When groups are formed, they generally evolve through four phases, as identified by psychologist B. A. Tuckman. These phases include **forming**, **storming**, **norming**, and **performing**.[11] Some groups get lucky and move quickly from forming to performing. But most struggle through disruptive, although ultimately constructive, team-building stages.

Forming. During the first stage individuals get to know each other. They often are overly polite and feel a bit awkward. As they search for similarities and attempt to

Figure 2.1 ***Comparing Self-Directed Teams and Single-Leader Work Groups***

Dimension	Self-Directed Team	Single-Leader Work Group
Best business use	Most useful for solving problems that require people with various skill sets working together	Most useful for solving problems in which time is of the essence and the leader already knows how to proceed
Leadership	Shifts to member best suited to lead tasks at hand	Formally assigned to one person, usually the senior member
Goals and agenda	Set by group, based on dialogue about purpose	Set by leader, often in consultation with sponsoring executive
Conflict	Recognized as constructive	Avoided by members
Work style	Determined by members	Determined by leader
Success	Defined by members' aspirations	Defined by leader's aspirations
Speed and efficiency	Low until group learns to function as a team; afterward, as fast as a single-leader group	Higher at first because members need no time to develop commitment or to learn to work as a team
End products	Best produced by collective group working together	Best produced by individuals working on their own
Accountability	Set by team members who hold one another mutually accountable	Set by leader who holds individuals accountable for their output

bond, they begin to develop trust in each other. Members will discuss fundamental topics such as why the team is necessary, who "owns" the team, whether membership is mandatory, how large it should be, and what talents members can contribute. A leader functions primarily as a traffic director. Groups and teams should resist the efforts of some members to sprint through the first stages and vault to the performing stage. Moving slowly through the stages is necessary in building a cohesive, productive unit.

Storming. During the second phase, members define their roles and responsibilities, decide how to reach their goals, and iron out the rules governing how they interact. Unfortunately, this stage often produces conflict, resulting in *storming.* A good leader, however, should step in to set limits, control the chaos, and offer suggestions. The leader will be most successful if she or he acts like a coach rather than a cop. Teams composed of dissimilar personality types may take longer to progress through the storming phase. Tempers may flare, sleep may be lost, leaders may be deposed. But most often the storm passes, and a cohesive group emerges.

Norming. Once the sun returns to the sky, teams and groups enter the *norming* stage. Tension subsides, roles clarify, and information begins to flow among members. The group periodically checks its agenda to remind itself of its progress toward its goals. People are careful not to shake the hard-won camaraderie and formation of a single-minded purpose. Formal leadership is unnecessary since everyone takes on leadership functions. Important data is shared with the entire group, and mutual interdependence becomes typical. The group or team begins to move smoothly in one direction. Members make sure that procedures are in place to resolve future conflicts.

In the norming stage, tensions subside, roles clarify, and information flows among team members.

Performing. In Tuckman's team growth model, some groups never reach the final stage of *performing.* Problems that may cause them to fail are shown in Figure 2.2.

FIGURE 2.2 ***Why Teams Fail: Typical Problems, Symptoms, and Solutions***

Problems	Symptoms	Solutions
Confused goals	People don't know what they're supposed to do	Clarify team purpose and expected outcomes
Mismatched needs	People with private agendas working at cross-purposes	Get hidden agendas on table by asking what people personally want from team
Unresolved roles	Team members are uncertain what their jobs are	Inform team members what is expected of them
Senseless procedures	Team is at the mercy of an employee handbook from hell	Throw away the book and develop procedures that make sense
Bad leadership	Leader is tentative, inconsistent, or foolish	Leader must learn to serve the team and keep its vision alive or give up role
Antiteam culture	Organization is not committed to the idea of teams	Team for the right reasons or don't team at all; never force people onto a team
Poor feedback	Performance is not being measured; team members are groping in the dark	Create system of free flow of useful information from all team members

For those that survive the first three phases, however, the final stage is gratifying. Group members have established a pace and a shared language. They develop loyalty and a willingness to resolve all problems. A "can-do" mentality pervades as they progress toward their goal. Fights are clean, and members continue working together without grudges. Best of all, information flows freely, deadlines are met, and production exceeds expectations.

Typical Team and Group Roles

Team members play different roles when they work together in groups. These roles can be grouped into three categories. *Task roles* are those that help the group meet its goals. *Relationship roles* facilitate the smooth functioning of the group. *Dysfunctional roles* are those that hinder a group from moving forward to achieve its purpose.[12]

Members who assume positive task roles help a team achieve its purpose.

Group Task Roles. Group members who are committed to achieving the group's purpose contribute to the group in a number of positive roles. You can be a better group member if you assume one or more of the following task roles.

- **Initiator.** Defines problems, sets rules, contributes ideas (e.g., "I think the problem is not lack of funds but rather lack of support from upper management").
- **Information seeker/information giver.** Asks for or supplies relevant information (e.g., "Didn't we have a similar situation two years ago?").
- **Opinion giver/opinion seeker.** Asks for and offers personal opinions, attitudes, and beliefs (e.g., "Matt, I think your position needs more facts to support it").
- **Direction giver.** Tells how to perform the task at hand.
- **Summarizer.** Reviews significant points, synthesizing points of agreement and the group's progress toward the goal.
- **Diagnoser.** Analyzes the task and discussion. Tells what is needed to reach the goal.
- **Energizer.** Exhorts members to stay on task; offers encouraging remarks.

- **Gatekeeper.** Controls participants, drawing in nontalkers and cutting off monopolizers (e.g., "You've described your plan, Eric, but now I'd like to hear what Karen thinks").
- **Reality tester.** Compares the group's ideas with the feasibility of real-world implementation.

At Yahoo, marketing team members must generate ideas and work harmoniously in promoting programs such as one in which advertisers pay a flat rate or cost-per-click fee to have their Web pages included in Yahoo's index. Team members assume many task and relationship roles ranging from initiator to energizer to reality tester.

Group Relationship Roles. In addition to contributing to task functions, effective members of groups perform relationship functions. When you assume these roles, you are helping to build harmony and strong relationships among group members.

- **Participation encourager.** Seeks to involve silent members (e.g., "Matt, what do you think about Lisa's ideas?").
- **Harmonizer/tension reliever.** Resolves differences, relaxes atmosphere, reduces tension—sometimes with the use of humor or informality.
- **Evaluator of emotional climate.** Reflects the feelings of the group (e.g., "I sense that we're becoming destructive instead of constructive. Does anyone else feel that way?").
- **Praise giver.** Encourages a warm, supportive climate by praising and agreeing with others (e.g., "I really like Lisa's idea; let's build on it").
- **Empathic listener.** Shows interest by listening actively without interrupting or evaluating.

Members who carry out relationship roles help a team achieve harmony and strong bonds.

Dysfunctional Group Roles. When group members perform the following roles, they disrupt the group and slow progress toward its goal. As you study the following list, think about groups you know and individuals who may have played these self-serving roles.

- **Blocker.** Constantly puts down the ideas and suggestions of others.
- **Attacker.** Insults, criticizes, and aggresses against others (e.g., "Why should we listen to your ideas when you've been wrong so many times in the past?").
- **Recognition seeker.** Wastes the group's time with unnecessary and irrelevant recounting of personal achievements and successes.
- **Joker.** Distracts the group with excessive joke-telling, inappropriate comments, and disruptive antics.
- **Withdrawer.** Participates very little or not at all. Refuses to be drawn out or to offer opinions.

Members who play dysfunctional roles disrupt the group's progress toward its goal.

Resolving Workplace Conflicts

Conflict is a normal part of every workplace and every team. Although the word alone is enough to make your heart go into overdrive, conflict is not always negative. When managed properly, conflict can improve decision making, clarify values, increase group cohesiveness, stimulate creativity, decrease tensions, and undermine dissatisfaction. Unresolved conflict, however, can destroy productivity and seriously undermine morale. You will be better prepared to resolve workplace conflict if you know the five most common response patterns as well as study a six-step procedure for dealing with conflict.

Common Conflict Response Patterns. Recall a time when you were very upset with a workplace colleague, boss, or teammate. How did you respond? Experts who have studied conflict say that most of us deal with conflict in one of the following predictable patterns:[13]

Although avoidance does not solve conflicts, it may be the best response to some situations such as when the issue is trivial.

- **Avoidance/withdrawal.** Instead of trying to resolve the conflict, one person or the other simply withdraws. Avoidance of conflict generally results in a "lose–lose" situation because the problem festers and no attempt is made to understand the issues causing the conflict. On the other hand, avoidance may be the best response when the issue is trivial, when potential losses from an open conflict outweigh potential gains, or when insufficient time is available to work through the issue adequately.
- **Accommodation/smoothing.** When one person gives in quickly, the conflict is smoothed over and surface harmony results. This accommodation/smoothing strategy may be the best method when the issue is minor, when damage to the relationship would harm both parties, and when tempers are too hot for productive discussion.
- **Compromise.** When both people give up something of lesser importance to gain something more important, a compromise results. This may be the best approach when both parties stand to gain, when a predetermined "ideal" solution is not required, and when time is short.
- **Competition/forcing.** In some contests, one person comes out on top, leaving the other with a sense of failure. This method forces the end of the conflict, but it may result in hurt feelings and potential future problems from the loser. This competition/forcing strategy is appropriate when a decision or action must be immediate. It also works when the parties recognize the power relationship between themselves.

Resolving conflict through the collaboration/problem-solving method is best, but this technique requires training and commitment.

- **Collaboration/problem solving.** If both parties are willing to collaborate to reach consensus, the problem may be solved. This approach works when the involved people have common goals, but they disagree over how to reach them. Conflict may arise from misunderstanding or a communication breakdown. Collaboration works best when all parties are trained in problem-solving techniques.

Six-Step Procedure for Dealing With Conflict. Probably the best pattern for resolving conflicts entails collaboration and problem-solving procedures. But this method requires a certain amount of training. Fortunately, experts in the field of negotiation have developed a six-step pattern that you can try the next time you need to resolve a conflict.[14]

Following an effective six-step procedure can help you resolve conflicts through collaboration and cooperation.

1. **Listen.** To be sure you understand the problem, listen carefully. If the other person doesn't seem to be listening to you, you need to set the example and be the first to listen.
2. **Understand the other point of view.** Once you listen, it's much easier to understand the other's position. Show your understanding by asking questions and paraphrasing. This will also verify what you think the other person means.

3. **Show a concern for the relationship.** By focusing on the problem, not the person, you can build, maintain, and even improve relationships. Show an understanding of the other person's situation and needs. Show an overall willingness to come to an agreement.
4. **Look for common ground.** Identify your interests and help the other side identify its interests. Learn what you have in common, and look for a solution to which both sides can agree.
5. **Invent new problem-solving options.** Spend time identifying the interests of both sides. Then brainstorm to invent new ways to solve the problem. Be open to new options.
6. **Reach an agreement based on what's fair.** Seek to determine a standard of fairness that is acceptable to both sides. Then weigh the possible solutions, and choose the best option.

Avoiding Groupthink

Groupthink means that team members agree without examining alternatives or considering contingency plans.

Conflict is normal in team interactions, and successful teams are able to resolve it using methods you just learned. But some teams avoid conflict. They smooth things over and in doing so may fall victim to *groupthink.* This is a term coined by theorist Irving Janis to describe faulty decision-making processes by team members who are overly eager to agree with one another. Several conditions can lead to groupthink: team members with similar backgrounds, a lack of methodical procedures, a demand for a quick decision, and a strong leader who favors a specific decision. Symptoms of groupthink include pressures placed on a member who argues against the group's shared beliefs, self-censorship of thoughts that deviate from the group consensus, collective efforts to rationalize, and an unquestioned belief in the group's inherent morality. Teams suffering from groupthink fail to examine alternatives, are biased in collecting and evaluating information, and ignore the risks of the preferred choice. They may also forget to work out a contingency plan in case the preferred choice fails.[15]

Effective teams avoid groupthink by striving for team diversity—in age, gender, backgrounds, experience, and training. They encourage open discussion, search for relevant information, evaluate many alternatives, consider how a decision will be implemented, and plan for contingencies in case the decision doesn't work out.

Reaching Group Decisions

Groups may reach decisions by majority vote, consensus, minority vote, averaging of votes, or authority rule.

The way teams reach decisions greatly affects the morale and commitment of the team, as well as the implementation of any team decision. In U.S. culture the majority usually rules, but other methods, five of which are discussed here, may be more effective. As you study these methods, think about which methods would be best for routine decisions and which methods would be best for dealing with emergencies.

- **Majority.** Group members vote and a majority wins. This method results in a quick decision but may leave an alienated minority uncommitted to implementation.
- **Consensus.** Discussion continues until all team members air their opinions and, ultimately, agree. This method is time consuming; but it produces creative, high-quality discussion and generally elicits commitment by all members to implement the decision.

Although time consuming, consensus decisions generally produce the most team commitment.

- **Minority.** Typically, a subcommittee investigates and makes a recommendation for action. This method is useful when the full group cannot get together to make a decision or when time is short.

- **Averaging.** Members haggle, bargain, cajole, and negotiate to reach a middle position, which often requires compromise. With this method, the opinions of the least knowledgeable members may cancel the opinions of the most knowledgeable.
- **Authority rule with discussion.** The leader, boss, or manager listens to team members' ideas, but the final decision is his or hers. This method encourages lively discussion and results in participatory decision making. However, team members must have good communication skills. This method also requires a leader who is willing to make decisions.

learning objective 3

Characteristics of Successful Teams

The use of teams has been called the solution to many ills in the current workplace.[16] Someone even observed that as an acronym TEAM means "Together, Everyone Achieves More."[17] Yet, many teams do not work well together. In fact, some teams can actually increase frustration, lower productivity, and create employee dissatisfaction. Experts who have studied team workings and decisions have discovered that effective teams share some or all of the following characteristics.

Small, diverse teams often produce more creative solutions with broader applications than homogeneous teams.

Small Size, Diverse Makeup. For most functions the best teams range from 2 to 25 members, although 4 or 5 is optimum for many projects. Larger groups have trouble interacting constructively, much less agreeing on actions.[18] For the most creative decisions, teams generally have male and female members who differ in age, social background, training, and experience. Members should bring complementary skills to a team. Paul Fireman, founder of sports shoe manufacturer Reebok, wisely remarked, "If you put five centers on the basketball court, you're going to lose the game. You need, we all need, people of different strengths and talents—and that means, among other things, people of different backgrounds."[19] Diverse teams can produce innovative solutions with broader applications than homogeneous teams can.

spotlight *on communicators*

"Teamwork is absolutely essential," says community and industry leader Roy Richards Jr., who was CEO of Southwire Company, North America's largest producer of aluminum and copper rod, wire, and cable. "Two heads are better than one and 200 are better than 10. The greatest bulk of ideas is at the bottom of the organization and not at the top, and therefore the empowerment of all our employees and the networking of all their ideas is necessary for us to move forward and upward and to always improve."

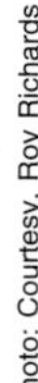

Photo: Courtesy, Roy Richards

Agreement on Purpose. An effective team begins with a purpose. For example, when Magic Johnson Theatres was developing its first theater, it hired a team whose sole purpose was to help his company move rapidly through the arduous state permit application process. Even the task of obtaining a license for the site's popcorn machine was surprisingly difficult.[20] Xerox scientists who invented personal computing developed their team purpose after the chairman of Xerox called for an "architecture of information." A team at Sealed Air Corporation developed its purpose when management instructed it to cut waste and reduce downtime.[21] Working from a general purpose to specific goals typically requires a huge investment of time and effort. Meaningful discussions, however, motivate team members to "buy into" the project.

Agreement on Procedures. The best teams develop procedures to guide them. They set up intermediate goals with deadlines. They assign roles and tasks, requiring all members to contribute equivalent amounts of real work. They decide how they will reach decisions using one of the strategies discussed earlier. Procedures are continually evaluated to ensure movement toward the attainment of the team's goals.

Ability to Confront Conflict. Poorly functioning teams avoid conflict, preferring sulking, gossip, or backstabbing. A better plan is to acknowledge conflict and address the root of the problem openly using the six-step plan outlined earlier. Although it may feel emotionally risky, direct confrontation saves time and enhances team commitment in the long run. To be constructive, however, confrontation must be task oriented, not person oriented. An open airing of differences, in which all team members have a chance to speak their minds, should center on strengths and weaknesses of the different positions and ideas—not on personalities. After hearing all sides, team members must negotiate a fair settlement, no matter how long it takes. Good decisions are based on consensus: all members agree.

Use of Good Communication Techniques. The best teams exchange information and contribute ideas freely in an informal environment. Team members speak clearly and concisely, avoiding generalities. They encourage feedback. Listeners become actively involved, read body language, and ask clarifying questions before responding. Tactful, constructive disagreement is encouraged. Although a team's task is taken seriously, successful teams are able to inject humor into their interactions.

Good teams exchange information freely and collaborate rather than compete.

Ability to Collaborate Rather Than Compete. Effective team members are genuinely interested in achieving team goals instead of receiving individual recognition. They contribute ideas and feedback unselfishly. They monitor team progress, including what's going right, what's going wrong, and what to do about it. They celebrate individual and team accomplishments.

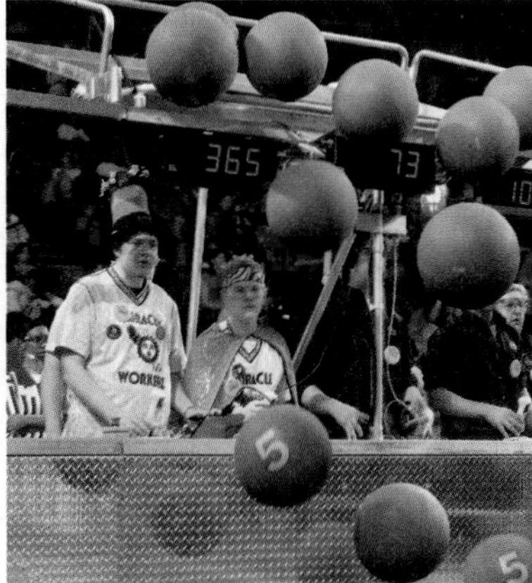

To win the FIRST (For Inspiration and Recognition of Science and Technology) robotics competition, this New Jersey high school team had to design and build a robot that could grab bouncing balls, climb stairs, and complete other tasks. "The secret of a successful team," said FIRST founder Dean Kamen, "is not to assemble the largest team possible, but rather to assemble a team that can work well together."

Acceptance of Ethical Responsibilities. Teams as a whole have ethical responsibilities to their members, to their larger organizations, and to society. Members have a number of specific responsibilities to each other, as described in the accompanying Ethical Insights box. As a whole, groups have a responsibility to represent the organization's view and respect its privileged information. They should not discuss with outsiders any sensitive issues without permission. In addition, groups have a broader obligation to avoid advocating actions that would endanger members of society at large.

Shared Leadership. Effective teams often have no formal leader. Instead, leadership rotates to those with the appropriate expertise as the team evolves and moves from one phase to another. Many teams operate under a democratic approach. This approach can achieve buy-in to team decisions, boost morale, and create fewer hurt feelings and less resentment. But in times of crisis, a strong team member may need to step up as leader.

Demonstration of Good Workplace Manners. Rudeness and bad manners have become alarmingly common in the American workplace. One surveyed showed that 71 percent of workers said they had been insulted, demeaned, ignored, or otherwise treated discourteously by their coworkers and superiors.[22] Successful team members treat each other and colleagues politely and respectfully. This may involve a few more *pleases* and *thank yous,* as well as showing consideration for others. Good team members are aware of noise levels when colleagues are trying to concentrate. They offer support to colleagues with heavy workloads. They respect others' boundaries and need for privacy. They value others' time. Look for *Dr. Guffey's Guide to Business Etiquette and Workplace Manners* at your student Web site (**http://guffey.swlearning.com**). You'll find the author's tips on topics such as networking manners, coping with cubicles, managers' manners, business gifts, dealing with angry customers, and gender-free etiquette.

ethical insights

Ethical Responsibilities of Group Members and Leaders

When people form a group or a team to achieve a purpose, they agree to give up some of their individual sovereignty for the good of the group. They become interdependent and assume responsibilities to one another and to the group. Here are important ethical responsibilities for members to follow:

- **Determine to do your best.** When you commit to the group process, you are obligated to offer your skills freely. Don't hold back, perhaps fearing that you will be repeatedly targeted because you have skills to offer. If the group project is worth doing, it's worth the best effort you can offer.
- **Decide to behave with the group's good in mind.** You may find it necessary to set aside your personal goals in favor of the group's goals. Decide to keep an open mind and to listen to evidence and arguments objectively. Strive to evaluate information carefully, even though it may contradict your own views or thwart your personal agendas.
- **Make a commitment to fair play.** Group problem solving is a cooperative, not a competitive, event. Decide that you cannot grind your private ax at the expense of the group project.
- **Expect to give and receive a fair hearing.** When you speak, others should give you a fair hearing. You have a right to expect them to listen carefully, provide you with candid feedback, strive to understand what you say, and treat your ideas seriously. Listeners do not have to agree with you, of course. However, all speakers have a right to a fair hearing.
- **Be willing to take on a participant/analyst role.** As a group member, it is your responsibility to pay attention, evaluate what is happening, analyze what you learn, and help make decisions.
- **As a leader, be ready to model appropriate team behavior.** It is a leader's responsibility to coach team members in skills and teamwork, to acknowledge achievement and effort, to share knowledge, and to periodically remind members of the team's missions and goals.

Career Application

Assume you're a member of a campus committee to organize a celebrity auction to raise funds for a local homeless shelter. Your friend Eric is committee chair, but he is carrying a heavy course load and is also working part time. As a result, he has taken no action. You call him, but he is evasive when you try to pin him down about committee plans. What should you do?

Checklist for Developing Team Effectiveness

✓ **Establish small teams.** Smaller teams are thought to function more efficiently and more effectively than larger teams.

✓ **Encourage diversity.** Innovative teams typically include members who differ in age, gender, and background. Team members should possess technical expertise, problem-solving skills, and interpersonal skills.

✓ **Determine the purpose, procedures, and roles.** Members must understand the task at hand and what is expected of them. Teams function best when operating procedures are ironed out early on and each member has a specific role.

✓ **Acknowledge and manage conflict.** Conflict is productive when it motivates a team to search for new ideas, increase participation, delay premature decisions, or discuss disagreements. Keep conflict centered on issues rather than on people.

✓ **Cultivate good communication skills.** Effective team members are willing and able to articulate ideas clearly and concisely, recognize nonverbal cues, and listen actively.

- ✓ **Advance an environment of open communication.** Teams are most productive when members trust each other and feel free to discuss all viewpoints openly in an informal atmosphere.
- ✓ **Encourage collaboration and discourage competition.** Sharing information in a cooperative effort to achieve the team purpose must be more important than competing with other members for individual achievement.
- ✓ **Share leadership.** Members with the most expertise should lead at various times during the project's evolution.
- ✓ **Create a sense of fairness in making decisions.** Effective teams resolve issues without forcing members into a win–lose situation.
- ✓ **Lighten up.** The most successful teams take their task seriously, but they are also able to laugh at themselves and interject humor to enliven team proceedings.
- ✓ **Continually assess performance.** Teams should establish checkpoints along the way to determine whether they are meeting their objectives and adjust procedures if progress is unsatisfactory.

Organizing Team-Based Written and Oral Presentations

learning objective

4

Companies form teams for many reasons. The goal of some teams is an oral presentation to pitch a new product or to win a high-stakes contract. Before Bill Gates and his Microsoft team roll out their latest software product, you can bet that team members spend months preparing the presentation so that everything flows smoothly. The goal of other teams is to investigate a problem and submit recommendations to decision makers in a report. At Kodak, for example, the "Zebra Team" advised management regarding the development and marketing of all black-and-white film products. The end product of any team is often a written report or an oral presentation.

Guidelines for Team Writing and Oral Presentations

Team projects proceed more smoothly when members agree on ground rules.

Whether your team's project produces written reports or oral presentations, you generally have considerable control over how the project is organized and completed. If you've been part of any team efforts before, you also know that such projects can be very frustrating—particularly when some team members don't carry their weight or when members cannot resolve conflict. On the other hand, team projects can be harmonious and productive when members establish ground rules and follow guidelines related to preparing, planning, collecting information for, organizing, rehearsing, and evaluating team projects.

Teams must decide whether they will be governed by consensus, by majority rule, or by some other method.

Preparing to Work Together. Before you begin talking about a specific project, it's best to discuss some of the following issues in regard to how your group will function.

- Name a meeting leader to plan and conduct meetings, a recorder to keep a record of group decisions, and an evaluator to determine whether the group is on target and meeting its goals.
- Decide whether your team will be governed by consensus (everyone must agree), by majority rule, or by some other method.

spotlight *on communicators*

Peter Drucker, this country's most influential management thinker and business intellectual, recognized early on that working together on team projects demanded that everyone put the team's goal ahead of self-recognition. "[Team members] . . . who work most effectively, it seems to me, never say I. *And that's not because they have trained themselves not to say* I. *They don't think* I. *They think* we; *they think* team. *They understand their job to be to make the team function. They accept responsibility and don't sidestep it, but* we *gets the credit . . . . This is what creates trust, what enables you to get the task done."*

- Compare schedules of team members in order to set up the best meeting times. Plan to meet often. Make team meetings a top priority. Avoid other responsibilities that might cause disruption during these meetings.
- Discuss the value of conflict. By bringing conflict into the open and encouraging confrontation, your team can prevent personal resentment and group dysfunction. Confrontation can actually create better final products by promoting new ideas and avoiding groupthink. Conflict is most beneficial when team members are allowed to air their views fully.
- Discuss how you will deal with team members who are not pulling their share of the load.

Planning the Document or Presentation. Once you've established ground rules, you're ready to discuss the final document or presentation. Be sure to keep a record of the following decisions your team makes.

- Establish the specific purpose for the document or presentation. Identify the main issues involved.
- Decide on the final format. For a report determine what parts it will include, such as an executive summary, figures, and an appendix. For a presentation, decide on its parts, length, and graphics.
- Discuss the audience(s) for the product and what questions it would want answered in your report or oral presentation. If your report is persuasive, consider what appeals might achieve its purpose.

In planning a team document or presentation, develop a work plan, assign jobs, and set deadlines.

- Develop a work plan (see Chapter 12). Assign jobs. Set deadlines. If time is short, work backward from the due date. For oral presentations build in time for content and creative development as well as for a series of rehearsals.
- For oral presentations give each team member a written assignment that details his or her responsibilities for researching content, producing visuals, developing handout materials, building transitions between segments, and showing up for rehearsals.
- For written reports decide how the final document will be composed: individuals working separately on assigned portions, one person writing the first draft, the entire group writing the complete document together, or some other method.

Unless facts are accurate, reports and presentations will fail.

Collecting Information. The following suggestions help teams generate and gather accurate information. Unless facts are accurate, the most beautiful report or the best high-powered presentation will fail.

- Brainstorm for ideas; consider cluster diagramming (see Figure 6.2 in Chapter 6).
- Assign topics. Decide who will be responsible for gathering what information.
- Establish deadlines for collecting information.
- Discuss ways to ensure the accuracy of the information collected.

Organizing, Writing, and Revising. As the project progresses, your team may wish to modify some of its earlier decisions.

- Review the proposed organization of your final document or presentation and adjust it if necessary.

Photo: Courtesy of Peter F. Drucker Research Library and Archive

- Compose the first draft of a written report or presentation. If separate team members are writing segments, they should use the same word processing and/or presentation graphics program to facilitate combining files.
- Meet to discuss and revise the draft(s) or rehearse the presentation.
- If individuals are working on separate parts of a written report, appoint one person (probably the best writer) to coordinate all the parts, striving for consistent style and format. Work for a uniform look and feel to the final product.
- For oral presentations be sure each member builds a bridge to the next presenter's topic and launches it smoothly. Strive for logical connections between segments.

For team reports assign one person to coordinate all the parts and make the style consistent.

Editing, Rehearsing, and Evaluating. Before the presentation is made or the final document is submitted, complete the following steps.

- For a written report give one person responsibility for finding and correcting grammatical and mechanical errors.
- For a written report meet as a group to evaluate the final document. Does it fulfill its purpose and meet the needs of the audience? Successful group documents emerge from thoughtful preparation, clear definition of contributors' roles, commitment to a group-approved plan, and willingness to take responsibility for the final product.
- For oral presentations assign one person the task of merging the various files; running a spell checker; and examining the entire presentation for consistency of design, format, and vocabulary.
- Schedule at least five rehearsals, say the experts.[23] Consider videotaping one of the rehearsals so that each presenter can critique his or her own performance.
- Schedule a dress rehearsal with an audience at least two days before the actual presentation. Practice fielding questions.

Schedule at least five rehearsals for a team presentation.

More information about writing business reports and making individual presentations appears in subsequent chapters of this book.

Planning and Participating in Productive Meetings

learning objective

5

As businesses become more team oriented and management becomes more participatory, people are attending more meetings than ever. One survey of managers found that they were devoting as many as two days a week to various gatherings.[24] Yet, meetings are almost universally disliked. Typical comments include, "We have too many of them," "They don't accomplish anything," and "What a waste of time!" In spite of employee reluctance and despite terrific advances in communication and team technology, face-to-face meetings are not going to disappear. In discussing the future of meetings, Akio Morita, former chairman of the Sony Corporation, said that he expects "face-to-face meetings will still be the number one form of communication in the twenty-first century."[25] So, get used to them. Meetings are here to stay. Our task, then, as business communicators is to learn how to make them efficient, satisfying, and productive.

Because you can expect to attend many meetings, learn to make them efficient, satisfying, and productive.

Meetings, by the way, consist of three or more individuals who gather to pool information, solicit feedback, clarify policy, seek consensus, and solve problems. But meetings have another important purpose for you. They represent opportunities. Because they are a prime tool for developing staff, they are career-critical. "If you

PROCESS IN PROGRESS

Harley-Davidson Revisited

BLITZING country curves or cruising highway straight stretches, Harley bikers own the road. And the Harley-Davidson Motor Company wants to keep it that way. Staying ahead of ever-growing local and global competition is a major concern. After surviving serious quality problems and competition from Japanese motorcycles, the company now commands 56 percent of the U.S. heavyweight or "hog" market. Much of its current success, say managers, results from its switch to team-based management.

But the switch has been difficult. When he served as vice president for business development, Clyde Fessler admitted as much when he said, "We would probably all agree that the shift from hierarchy to circles has not been easy—practicing consensus decision-making never is. However, defining the roles and responsibilities of each functional circle and each circle member has brought clarity, which in turn stimulates dialogue, trust, and eventually, nonthreatening confrontation."

Collaborative, interdependent teams work more slowly than a single, decisive leader in a hierarchy. "But," said Fessler, "they can be more innovative and resourceful and, ultimately, more effective in today's complex business climate."[26]

Critical Thinking

- What stages of development could Harley-Davidson teams have expected to pass through as they were formed?
- Why are decisions by consensus harder to achieve than those from a majority vote or from an authoritative leader?
- Given that team-based management is slower and more painful than management from a strong leader and line managers, why would a company such as Harley-Davidson adopt this strategy?

CONTINUED ON PAGE 66

case study

can't orchestrate a meeting, you're of little use to the corporation," says Morris Schechtman, head of a leadership training firm.[27] At meetings judgments are formed and careers are made. Therefore, instead of treating them as thieves of your valuable time, try to see them as golden opportunities to demonstrate your leadership, communication, and problem-solving skills. So that you can make the most of these opportunities, here are techniques for planning and conducting successful meetings.

Deciding Whether a Meeting Is Necessary

Call meetings only when necessary, and invite only key people.

No meeting should be called unless the topic is important, can't wait, and requires an exchange of ideas. If the flow of information is strictly one way and no immediate feedback will result, then don't schedule a meeting. For example, if people are merely being advised or informed, send an e-mail, memo, or letter. Leave a telephone or voice mail message, but don't call a costly meeting. Remember, the real expense of a meeting is the lost productivity of all the people attending. To decide whether the purpose of the meeting is valid, it's a good idea to consult the key people who will be attending. Ask them what outcomes are desired and how to achieve those goals. This consultation also sets a collaborative tone and encourages full participation.

Selecting Participants

The number of meeting participants is determined by the purpose of the meeting, as shown in Figure 2.3. If the meeting purpose is motivational, such as an awards ceremony for sales reps of Mary Kay Cosmetics, then the number of participants is unlimited. But to make decisions, according to studies at 3-M Corporation, the best number is five or fewer participants.[28] Ideally, those attending should be people who will make the decision and people with information necessary to make the decision. Also attending should be people who will be responsible for implementing the decision and representatives of groups who will benefit from the decision. Let's say, for example, that the CEO of sportswear manufacturer Timberland is strongly committed to community service. He wants his company to participate more fully in community service. So he might meet with managers, employee representatives, and community leaders to decide how his employees could volunteer to refurbish a school, build affordable housing, or volunteer at a clinic.[29]

Problem-solving meetings should involve five or fewer people.

Distributing Advance Information

At least two days in advance of a meeting, distribute an agenda of topics to be discussed. Also include any reports or materials that participants should read in advance. For continuing groups, you might also include a copy of the minutes of the previous meeting. To keep meetings productive, limit the number of agenda items. Remember, the narrower the focus, the greater the chances for success. A good agenda, as illustrated in Figure 2.4, covers the following information:

Pass out a meeting agenda showing topics to be discussed and other information.

- Date and place of meeting
- Start time and end time
- Brief description of each topic, in order of priority, including the names of individuals who are responsible for performing some action
- Proposed allotment of time for each topic
- Any premeeting preparation expected of participants

Getting the Meeting Started

To avoid wasting time and irritating attendees, always start meetings on time—even if some participants are missing. Waiting for latecomers causes resentment and sets a bad precedent. For the same reasons, don't give a quick recap to anyone who arrives late. At the appointed time, open the meeting with a three- to five-minute introduction that includes the following:

Start meetings on time and open with a brief introduction.

- Goal and length of the meeting
- Background of topics or problems

FIGURE 2.3 ***Meeting Purpose and Number of Participants***

Purpose	Ideal Size
Intensive problem solving	5 or fewer
Problem identification	10 or fewer
Information reviews and presentations	30 or fewer
Motivational	Unlimited

FIGURE 2.4 ***Typical Meeting Agenda***

AGENDA

Quantum Travel International
Staff Meeting September 4, 2006
10 to 11 a.m.
Conference Room

I. Call to order; roll call

II. Approval of agenda

III. Approval of minutes from previous meeting

	Person	Proposed Time
IV. Committee reports		
A. Web site update	Kevin	5 minutes
B. Tour packages	Lisa	10 minutes
V. Old business		
A. Equipment maintenance	John	5 minutes
B. Client escrow accounts	Alicia	5 minutes
C. Internal newsletter	Adrienne	5 minutes
VI. New business		
A. New accounts	Sarah	5 minutes
B. Pricing policy for trips	Marcus	15 minutes

VII. Announcements

VIII. Chair's summary, adjournment

- Possible solutions and constraints
- Tentative agenda
- Ground rules to be followed

A typical set of ground rules might include arriving on time, communicating openly, being supportive, listening carefully, participating fully, confronting conflict frankly, and following the agenda. More formal groups follow parliamentary procedures based on Robert's Rules. After establishing basic ground rules, the leader should ask if participants agree thus far. The next step is to assign one attendee to take minutes and one to act as a recorder. The recorder stands at a flipchart or whiteboard and lists the main ideas being discussed and agreements reached.

Moving the Meeting Along

After the preliminaries, the leader should say as little as possible. Like a talk show host, an effective leader makes "sure that each panel member gets some air time while no one member steals the show."[30] Remember that the purpose of a meeting is to exchange views, not to hear one person, even the leader, do all the talking. If the group has one member who monopolizes, the leader might say, "Thanks, Kurt, for that perspective, but please hold your next point while we hear how Ann would respond to that." This technique also encourages quieter participants to speak up.

Keep the meeting moving by avoiding issues that sidetrack the group.

To avoid allowing digressions to sidetrack the group, try generating a "Parking Lot" list. This is a list of important but divergent issues that should be discussed at a later time. Another way to handle digressions is to say, "Folks, we are getting off track here. Forgive me for pressing on, but I need to bring us back to the central issue of . . . ."[31] It's important to adhere to the agenda and the time schedule. Equally important, when the group seems to have reached a consensus, is to summarize the group's position and check to see whether everyone agrees.

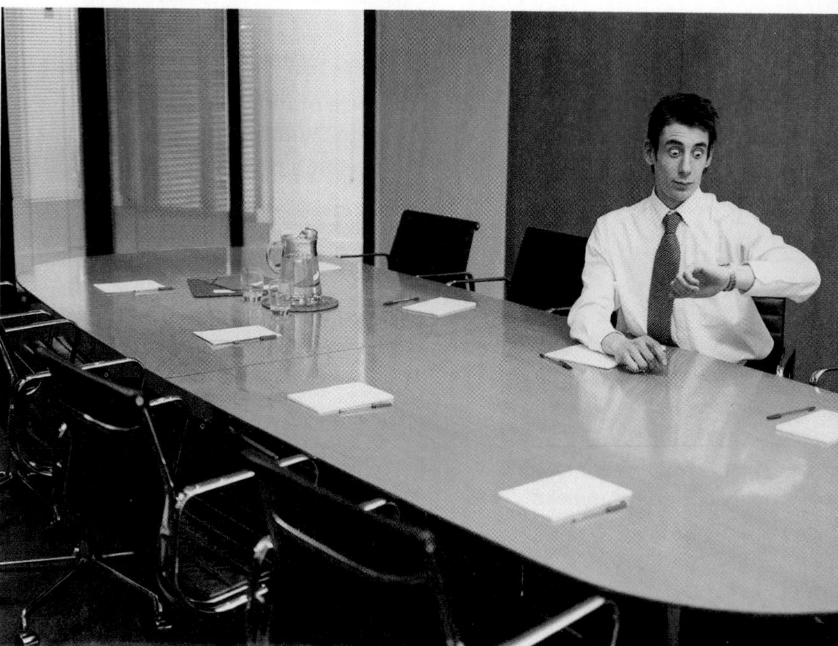

To prevent meeting attendees from habitually arriving late, consider implementing a rule that everyone must arrive at least five minutes before the start of the meeting. Then start the meeting on time with no catching up for latecomers.

Handling Conflict in Meetings

As you learned earlier, conflict is natural and even desirable. But it can cause awkwardness and uneasiness. In meetings, conflict typically develops when people feel unheard or misunderstood. If two people are in conflict, the best approach is to encourage each to make a complete case while group members give their full attention. Let each one question the other. Then, the leader should summarize what was said, and the group should offer comments. The group may modify a recommendation or suggest alternatives before reaching consensus on a direction to follow.

When a conflict develops between two members, allow each to make a complete case before the group.

Managing Dysfunctional Group Members

When individuals are performing in any of the dysfunctional roles described earlier (such as blocker, attacker, joker, and withdrawer), they should be handled with care and tact. The following specific techniques can help a leader or gatekeeper control some group members and draw others out.[32]

To control dysfunctional behavior, team leaders should establish rules and seat problem team members strategically.

- **Lay down the rules in an opening statement.** Give a specific overall summary of topics, time allotment, and expected behavior. Warn that speakers who digress will be interrupted.
- **Seat potentially dysfunctional members strategically.** Experts suggest seating a difficult group member immediately next to the leader. It's easier to bypass a person in this position. Make sure the person with dysfunctional behavior is not seated in a power point, such as at the end of table or across from the leader.

- **Avoid direct eye contact.** In American society direct eye contact is a nonverbal signal that encourages talking. Thus, when asking a question of the group, look only at those whom you wish to answer.
- **Assign dysfunctional members specific tasks.** Ask a potentially disruptive person, for example, to be the group recorder.
- **Ask members to speak in a specific order.** Ordering comments creates an artificial, rigid climate and should be done only when absolutely necessary. But such a regimen ensures that everyone gets a chance to participate.
- **Interrupt monopolizers.** If a difficult member dominates a discussion, wait for a pause and then break in. Summarize briefly the previous comments or ask someone else for an opinion.
- **Encourage nontalkers.** Give only positive feedback to the comments of reticent members. Ask them direct questions about which you know they have information or opinions.
- **Give praise and encouragement** to those who seem to need it, including the distracters, the blockers, and the withdrawn.

Ending With a Plan

End the meeting with a summary of accomplishments.

End the meeting at the agreed time. The leader should summarize what has been decided, who is going to do what, and by what time. It may be necessary to ask people to volunteer to take responsibility for completing action items agreed to in the meeting. No one should leave the meeting without a full understanding of what was accomplished. One effective technique that encourages full participation is "once around the table." Everyone is asked to summarize briefly his or her interpretation of what was decided and what happens next. Of course, this closure technique works best with smaller groups. The leader should conclude by asking the group to set a time for the next meeting. He or she should also assure the group that a report will follow and thank participants for attending.

Following Up Actively

Follow up by reminding participants of their assigned tasks.

If minutes were taken, they should be distributed within a couple of days after the meeting. It is up to the leader to see that what was decided at the meeting is accomplished. The leader may need to call people to remind them of their assignments and also to volunteer to help them if necessary.

Meetings are a necessary evil for today's team-oriented workplace. The following checklist can help you use them effectively and perhaps accelerate your career.

Checklist for Planning and Participating in Productive Meetings

Before the Meeting

Consider alternatives. Unless a topic is important and pressing, avoid calling a meeting. Perhaps an e-mail message, telephone call, or announcement would serve the purpose as well.

Invite the right people. To make decisions, invite those people who have information and authority to make the decision and implement it.

- **Distribute an agenda.** Prepare and distribute an agenda that includes the date and place of meeting, the starting and ending time, a brief description of each topic, the names of people responsible for any action, and a proposed time allotment for each topic.

During the Meeting

- **Start on time and introduce the agenda.** Discuss the goal and length of the meeting, provide background of topics for discussion, suggest possible solutions and constraints, propose a tentative agenda, and clarify the ground rules for the meeting.
- **Appoint a secretary and a recorder.** Ask one attendee to make a record of the proceedings, and ask another person to record discussion topics on a flipchart or whiteboard.
- **Encourage balanced participation.** Strive to be sure that all participants' views are heard and that no one monopolizes the discussion. Avoid digressions by steering the group back to the topics on the agenda.
- **Confront conflict frankly.** Encourage people who disagree to explain their positions completely. Then restate each position and ask for group comments. The group may modify a recommendation or suggest alternatives before agreeing on a plan of action.
- **Summarize along the way.** When the group seems to reach a consensus, summarize and see whether everyone agrees.

Ending the Meeting and Following Up

- **Review meeting decisions.** At the end of the meeting, summarize what has been decided, discuss action items, and establish a schedule for completion.
- **Distribute minutes of meeting.** A few days after the meeting, arrange to have the secretary distribute the minutes.
- **Remind people of action items.** Follow up by calling people to see if they are completing the actions recommended at the meeting.

Using Collaboration Technology to Facilitate Meetings, Manage Projects, and Make Decisions

learning objective 6

Collaboration technology *(sometimes called* groupware*) facilitates group activities.*

Collaboration technology (sometimes called *groupware*) refers to software designed to facilitate group activities. The term relates to a number of constantly evolving technologies that help groups exchange information, collaborate in team projects, and make decisions. New technologies are continually appearing, resulting in significant cost savings, greater efficiency, and more intuitive equipment.

Collaboration tools that you may use on the job include teleconferencing, Web conferencing, screen sharing, chat servers, instant messaging, folder sharing, intranets, message boards, and e-mail, to name a few. These tools are increasingly important when members of organizations must work together to solve problems, develop products, forecast future performance, and complete other team projects.

The tools are equally useful whether team members are just down the hall, across the country, or around the world.

Let's say, for example, that a Harley-Davidson team is working to solve a gear-making problem. The team's goal is to reduce gear noise, which is perceived as poor quality, and to give customers more exhaust noise (the cherished "potato, potato" Harley exhaust sound). The project manager is in Milwaukee; two engineers are in York, Pennsylvania; and the production staff is in Kansas City. Rather than travel to meet face to face, they gather in a private online room using a Web-based conferencing tool. They work with an online whiteboard using different colored markers until they reach agreement on the gear design. Then the manager assigns action items, and the meeting is over. And no one had to travel farther than the PC on his or her desk!

The latest tools help companies, team members, and customers exchange information efficiently using the Web.

First-generation collaboration tools involved expensive, cumbersome, and complex software systems. Many required local area networks with well-trained technical staffs to keep them functioning. The latest tools, however, enable companies, team members, and customers to exchange information more efficiently, often using the Web. Today's collaboration tools are most often employed to help teams with three important functions: meeting facilitation, project management, and decision support.

Meeting Facilitation

The most commonly used meeting tool is* teleconferencing, *which connects speakers by telephones.

Everyone agrees that the best meetings are face to face. But when distance or other factors prevent face-to-face gatherings, numerous collaboration tools enable far-flung colleagues to meet. One of the simplest tools is *teleconferencing* (sometimes called *audioconferencing*). It involves one or two people who confer with others by telephone. Phone "bridges" may be engaged to allow a limitless number of people to share the same call. Teleconferences may involve several people in a room with an enhanced speakerphone that enables people at both ends to speak and be heard simultaneously. Thanks to cellular service, you can even participate in a conference call from an airplane or your home. Although teleconferencing is not as glitzy as other collaboration tools, it is really the "bread and butter" of the entire teleconferencing industry.[33] More people use it than any other of the collaboration meeting tools.

Videoconferencing *enables real-time collaboration by combining video, audio, and networking technologies.*

If team members need to see each other, they use *videoconferencing*. This collaboration tool combines video, audio, and communications networking technologies for real-time interaction. Generally, participants meet in special conference rooms equipped with cameras and television screens for transmitting images and documents. Because participants do not have to journey to distant meetings, organizations can reduce travel expenses, travel time, and employee fatigue. But first-generation videoconferencing equipment was expensive, and only large organizations could afford it.

Desktop videoconferencing *combines personal computing with audio, video, and networking technologies.*

More recently companies have turned to *desktop videoconferencing*. It combines personal computing with audio, video, and networking technologies to provide real-time interaction from desktop computers.

Media conferencing *combines PC functionality with media features that emulate face-to-face meetings.*

The latest technologies use a *media conferencing* approach. Relying heavily on the Web, it facilitates meetings by incorporating PC functionality with media features that emulate "real-life" meetings. The media conferencing approach enables participants to present PowerPoint slides or share spreadsheets, just as they might do in a face-to-face meeting. They can even demonstrate products and make changes in real time during a meeting without having to interrupt the flow of the presentation. Companies are now able to turn instant messenger sessions into interactive WebEx meetings.

Microsoft features Live Meeting™, which requires only a phone, a PC, and an Internet connection. The service allows groups of two to thousands to share applications, mark up documents, illustrate ideas, and create flowcharts—all in real time without the cost and hassle of business travel.

Team members who merely want to chat find *Internet relay chat* (IRC) a simple alternative to other forms of conferencing. The cyber equivalent of CB radio, IRC gives ordinary folks the ability to chat in real time. Team members prearrange a time and enter a chat room where everyone can "hear" what everyone else is saying. It's more efficient than individual e-mails with copies to other participants.

Internet relay chat ***allows people to exchange comments in a chat room at a prearranged time.***

Webcasting involves the delivery of one-way live audio and video programs to large groups via the Internet. Webcasts are rapidly replacing conference calls and press meetings as a cheaper, more convenient way to reach a large number of people when limited interactivity is necessary. For example, let's say Harley-Davidson wants all dealers to see the launching of its flashy sales promotion for Electra Glide, a top-of-the-line archetypal hog. Harley could webcast the launching with live audio and video, thus enabling dealers to experience the hype without leaving their desks.

Webcasting ***involves sending audio and video programs to large groups over the Internet.***

Driven by a number of factors, from the grassroots adoption of instant messaging to frustration with e-mail's limitations, richer kinds of technology-enabled meeting and collaboration tools will continue to evolve. The most sophisticated companies want to embed *presence awareness*. This is the ability to detect the online status of others so that employees can find available experts, project team members, and managers without even looking away from their screens.

Although Bernd Pischetsrider speaks at a Volkswagen press conference in Wolfsburg, Germany, his presentation can be broadcast to dealerships around the world by means of webcasting.

Project Management

Completing a project successfully generally requires unrestricted sharing of information. Project management software can allow remote team members, suppliers, partners, and others with an interest in the project's successful completion to view the project and modify their own tasks via the Web. For example, users can input time sheet information, submit status reports, and delegate tasks. Some programs provide guides that help managers identify project phases, clarify goals, establish deadlines, and anticipate obstacles. Executives can create a portfolio view to determine the status of all projects under way as well as search more deeply for detailed descriptions of key events. Team members can work together more easily by using software features such as shared calendaring, scheduling, and shared folders.

Project management software helps distant team members, suppliers, partners, and others clarify project goals, set deadlines, and anticipate obstacles.

Decision Support

Another group of software products helps teams and organizations analyze information and make decisions based on solid data. Sometimes called *business intelligence* software or, more fashionably, *digital dashboards*, these tools bring together data from internal and external sources. Equipped with a "digital dashboard," team members and managers can check actual performance and make adjustments. Harley-Davidson, for instance, can study sales figures on a regional, product, or customer basis. Harley's biggest problem is one of pace. During its centennial celebration, it ramped up production of centennial-year bikes. But now it's the morning after, and sales have slumped.[34] What products should it produce, and how many

Business intelligence software, **including digital dashboards,** ***helps people analyze information and make rapid decisions.***

of them will sell and in what parts of the country? Using sophisticated business intelligence tools, Harley and other companies can find answers to sales trends even in the middle of a promotion. They can also play "what if" scenarios to test plans before implementing them.

Connected to live sources, digital dashboards help teams explain and forecast future performance.

As decision support tools continue to evolve, they become more useful in gathering, analyzing, and manipulating data to assist in planning and decision making. Today's tools are more scalable, which means that they can run on multiprocessor servers. This makes it possible to gather more data and crunch more information in shorter periods of time. Team members are able to develop their own queries and report on information relevant to their jobs. Most of the time, they receive answers in near real time. Connected to live data sources, such as sales transactions, digital dashboards enable team members to create reports with information that can help forecast or explain shifts in business performance. Every business welcomes tools that help it analyze performance and make decisions regarding the future.

Strengthening Your Teamwork Skills Now

At one time or another in your current or future job and certainly in your college career, you will be working on a team. It may be a temporary team created to complete one specific task, such as developing a new product or completing a project. It could be a permanent team with a continuing function, such as overseeing a complete line of products. In your personal life you could be a committee member or part of the governing body for your church, a social group, or a housing group. Most assuredly, however, in your professional life you will be part of a team effort. You may be thinking, "Yeah, down the road a bit I might need some of these skills, but why worry about them now?"

Developing effective teamwork skills requires study, modeling, nurturing, and practice.

The truth is that you need to start developing teamwork skills now. You can't just turn them on when you want them. They need to be studied, modeled, nurtured, and practiced. You've just taken a look at the inner workings of teams, including the four phases of team development, the role of conflict, the characteristics of successful teams, functional and dysfunctional team roles, participating in productive meetings, and using collaboration technology. In this book, in this course, and throughout your college career, you will have opportunities to work with teams. Begin to analyze their dynamics. Who has the power and why? Who are the most successful team members and why? What would make a team function more effectively? How can you improve your teamwork skills?

Remember, job recruiters consider team skills among the most important requirements for many of today's jobs. You can become the number one candidate for your dream job by developing team skills and acquiring experience now.

Summary of Learning Objectives

1 **Discuss why groups and teams are formed and how they are different.** Many organizations have found that groups and teams are more effective than individuals because groups make better decisions, respond faster, increase productivity, achieve greater buy-in, reduce resistance to change, improve employee morale, and result in reduced risk for individuals. A *group* is a collection of three or more individuals who perceive themselves as a group but who may complete their tasks independently. A *team* is a group that interacts over time to achieve a purpose. Businesses are increas-

ingly turning to *self-directed teams*, which are characterized by clearly stated goals, autonomy, decision-making authority, frequent communication, and ongoing training.

2 **Describe team development, team and group roles, dealing with conflict, and methods for reaching group decisions.** Teams typically go through four stages of development: forming, storming, norming, and performing. Team members may play functional or dysfunctional roles. Common conflict response patterns include avoidance/withdrawal, accommodation/smoothing, compromise, competition/forcing, and collaboration/problem solving. To resolve conflict, team members should listen, understand the other's point of view, show a concern for the relationship, look for common ground, invent new problem-solving options, and reach an agreement based on what is fair. Open discussion of conflict prevents *groupthink*, a condition that leads to faulty decisions. Methods for reaching group decisions include majority, consensus, minority, averaging, and authority rule with discussion.

3 **Identify the characteristics of successful teams including an emphasis on workplace etiquette.** The most effective teams are usually small and diverse; that is, they are made up of people representing different ages, genders, and backgrounds. Successful teams agree on their purpose and procedures. They are able to channel conflict into constructive discussion and reach consensus. They accept their ethical responsibilities, encourage open communication, listen actively, provide feedback, and have fun. Members are able to collaborate rather than compete, and leadership is often a shared responsibility depending on the situation and expertise required. Successful team members are polite and courteous. They are aware of noise levels, they value others' time, and they respect coworkers' boundaries. They freely use *please* and *thank you*, and they praise team members for work well done.

4 **List techniques for organizing team-based written and oral presentations.** In preparing to work together, teams should limit their size; name a meeting leader; and decide whether they wish to make decisions by consensus, majority rule, or some other method. They should work out their schedules, discuss the value of conflict, and decide how to deal with team members who do not do their share. They should decide on the purpose, form, and procedures for preparing the final document or presentation. They must brainstorm for ideas, assign topics, establish deadlines, and discuss how to ensure information accuracy. In composing the first draft of a report or presentation, they should use the same software and meet to discuss drafts and rehearsals. For written reports one person should probably compose the final draft, and the group should evaluate it. For group presentations they need to work for consistency of design, format, and vocabulary. At least five rehearsals, one of which should be videotaped, will enhance the final presentation.

5 **Discuss how to plan and participate in productive meetings.** Call a meeting only when urgent two-way communication is necessary. Limit participants to those directly involved. Distribute an agenda in advance, start the meeting on time, and keep the discussion on track. Confront conflict openly by letting each person present his or her views fully before having the group decide which direction to take. Summarize what was said and end the meeting on time. Follow up by distributing minutes of the meeting and verifying that action items are being accomplished.

Process to Product

Applying Your Skills at Harley-Davidson

IN TURNING AROUND its fortunes, Harley-Davidson was able to expand its market share, eliminate its debt, and, most important, regain the respect of its customers. Keys to its success were establishing team-based management techniques and gaining employee involvement. As employees were moved to work groups, team members would set their own schedules and be cross-trained.

One critical need was training employees in the techniques of how to run meetings and how consensus decision making works. According to training manager Darlene Rindo, "the basic idea is that while not everyone in the group will agree with a decision, they have to be able to go out and support it on the factory floor. That means never moving on to another agenda item without reaching closure."[35]

Your Task

As an assistant to the training manager at Harley-Davidson, you have been asked to prepare a summary of suggestions for developing effective meetings. Discuss how to prepare for meetings, how to conduct meetings, and how to follow up after meetings. Your suggestions will eventually become part of a training video called "Meetings Harley Style." Suggest ways to illustrate your points in a video. Present your ideas in an oral report (with chalkboard, flipchart, transparency, or electronic graphics) or submit your ideas in a memo with descriptive side headings. ■

case study

6 **Describe collaboration technologies used to facilitate meetings, manage projects, and make decisions.** Today's collaboration tools help team members exchange information, work together in team projects, and make decisions. To facilitate meetings, teams may take part in *teleconferencing* using telephones or *videoconferencing*, which combines video, audio, and networking technologies. *Desktop videoconferencing* provides real-time interaction from personal computers. *Media conferencing* incorporates features that emulate face-to-face meetings such as PowerPoint and spreadsheets. *Internet relay chat* enables individuals to exchange ideas in an Internet chat room. *Webcasting* involves the delivery of one-way audio and video programs to large groups via the Internet. Project management software enables remote team members, suppliers, partners, and others to work together in clarifying goals, establishing deadlines, and completing other project tasks. Decision support software, sometimes called *business intelligence software* or *digital dashboards*, helps teams and organizations analyze information and make decisions based on solid data.

chapter review

1. List seven reasons that explain why organizations are forming groups and teams. (Obj. 1)
2. How are virtual teams different from face-to-face teams? (Obj. 1)
3. To be most successful, self-directed teams need to have what characteristics? (Obj. 1)
4. What are the four phases of team development? Is it best to move through the stages quickly? Why or why not? (Obj. 2)
5. Name five team roles that relate to tasks and five roles that relate to developing relationships. Which roles do you think are most important and why? (Obj. 2)
6. Name five dysfunctional team roles. (Obj. 2)
7. Name five common patterns for resolving conflict. Which pattern works best in solving problems? (Obj. 2)
8. What is *groupthink*? (Obj.2)
9. Why can diverse teams be more effective than homogeneous teams? (Obj. 3)
10. Why are team decisions based on consensus generally better than decisions reached by majority rule? (Obj. 3)
11. What is the best way to set team deadlines when time is short to complete a project? (Obj. 4)
12. In completing a team-written report, should all team members work together to write the report? Why or why not? (Obj. 4)
13. When groups or teams meet, what are seven ground rules they should begin with? (Obj. 5)
14. Name five techniques for handling dysfunctional group members. (Obj. 5)
15. Name three important functions that collaboration technology serves. Describe six tools available to facilitate team or group meetings. (Obj. 6)

critical thinking

1. Compare the advantages and disadvantages of using teams in today's workplace. (Objs. 1, 2, and 3)
2. What kinds of conflict could erupt during the "storming" phase of team development? Should conflict be avoided? (Obj. 2)
3. How would you comment on this statement made by an executive? "If you can't orchestrate a meeting, then you are of little use to an organization." (Obj. 5)
4. Compare the advantages and disadvantages of face-to-face meetings with virtual meetings using teleconferencing and videoconferencing. (Obj. 5)
5. **Ethical issue:** You're disturbed that Randy, one member of your team, is selling Amway products to other members of the team. He shows catalogs and takes orders at lunch, and he distributes products after work and during lunch. He also leaves an order form on the table during team meetings. What should you do? What if Randy were selling Girl Scout cookies?

THREE GREAT RESOURCES FOR YOU!

1. Guffey Student Web Site
http://guffey.swlearning.com

Your companion Web site offers chapter review quizzes, WebThink activities, updated chapter URLs, and many additional resources.

2. Guffey XTRA!
http://guffeyxtra.swlearning.com

This online study assistant includes Your Personal Language Trainer, Speak Right!, Spell Right!, bonus online chapters, Documents for Analysis, PowerPoint slides, and much more.

3. Student Study Guide

Self-checked workbook activities and applications review chapter concepts and develop career skills.

activities

2.1 Team or Individual? Timberland Wants You (Obj. 1)

He introduces himself as a New Hampshire bootmaker, but Timberland CEO Jeffrey B. Swartz is much more. Although he heads a fast-rising company that produces boots and sportswear, he is strongly committed to civic responsibility and employee involvement. *Fortune* magazine consistently ranks Timberland as one of the 100 best companies to work for in America. With the zeal of a missionary, the enthusiastic, fast-talking Swartz travels extensively, preaching the power of volunteerism among the 200 Timberland stores and factories.[36]

Your Task. Let's say that you work for Timberland, and Swartz asks you to organize an extensive volunteer program using Timberland employees. The program involves much planning and cooperation to be successful. You are flattered that he respects you and thinks that you are capable of completing the task. But you think that a team could do a better job than an individual. What arguments would you use to convince him that a team could work better than a single person?

2.2 Responding to Workplace Conflicts (Obj. 2)

TEAM

Experts say that we generally respond to conflict in one of the following patterns: avoidance/withdrawal, accommodation/smoothing, compromise, competition/forcing, or collaboration/problem solving.

Your Task. For each of the following conflict situations, name an appropriate response pattern(s) and be prepared to explain your choice.

a. A company policy manual is posted and updated at an internal Web page. Employees must sign that they have read and understand the manual. A conflict arises when one manager insists that employees should sign electronically. Another manager thinks that a paper form should be signed by employees so that better records may be kept. What conflict response pattern is most appropriate?

b. Jeff and Mark work together but frequently disagree. Today they disagree on what computer disks to purchase for an order that must be submitted immediately. Jeff insists on buying Brand X computer disks. Mark knows that Brand X is made by a company that markets an identical disk at a slightly lower price. However, Mark doesn't have stock numbers for the cheaper disks at his fingertips. How should Mark respond?

c. A manager and his assistant plan to attend a conference together at a resort location. Six weeks before the conference, the company announces a cutback and limits conference support to only one person. The assistant, who has developed a presentation specifically for the conference, feels that he should be the one to attend. Travel arrangements must be made immediately. What conflict response pattern will most likely result?

d. Two vice presidents disagree on a company e-mail policy. One wants to ban personal e-mail totally. The other thinks that an outright ban is impossible to implement. He is more concerned with limiting Internet misuse, including visits to online game, porn, and shopping sites. The vice presidents agree that they need an e-mail policy, but they disagree on what to allow and what to prohibit. What conflict response pattern is appropriate?

e. Customer service rep Jackie comes to work one morning and finds Alexa sitting at Workstation 2. Although the customer service reps have no special workstation assigned to them, Jackie has the longest seniority and has always assumed that Workstation 2 was hers. Other workstations were available, but the supervisor told Alexa to use Workstation 2 that morning because she didn't know that Jackie would be coming in. When Jackie arrives and sees her workstation occupied, she becomes angry and demands that Alexa vacate "her" station. What conflict response pattern might be most appropriate for Alexa and the supervisor?

2.3 Reaching Group Decisions: Which Method? (Objs. 1 and 2)

TEAM

Your Task. In small groups decide which decision strategy is best for the following situations:

a. Union employees numbering 600 or more must decide whether to strike or remain on the job.

b. Appointed by management, an employee team is charged with making recommendations regarding casual Fridays. Management feels that too many employees are abusing the privilege.

c. The owner of your company is meeting with all managers to decide which departments will be allowed to move into a new facility.

d. Members of a homeowners' association must decide which members will become directors.

e. An employee committee of three members (two supervisors and the manager) must decide on promotions within a department.

f. The human resources department of a large company must work with employees to hammer out a new benefits package within its budget.

g. A group of town officials and volunteers must decide how to organize a town Web site. Only a few members have technical expertise.

2.4 Analyzing Team Formation, Decision Making, and Group Roles (Objs. 1, 2, and 3)

TEAM

Members of small groups play a number of different roles as their groups are formed and decisions are made. To better understand the dynamics of group formation, decision making, and group roles, you will form small groups to discuss one of the following topics.

Your Task. Decide on a team leader and a recorder. Discuss a topic for ten minutes (or as long as your instructor directs). As the discussion progresses, analyze the comments made and the group roles they represent. Then, as a group, draft an outline of the major points discussed, your team decision, and the specific roles played in the discussion. Your instructor may ask you to report to the class or prepare a group memo summarizing your discussion.

a. Should an employee be allowed to sell products such as Amway items or Girl Scout cookies at work? (See Critical Thinking Question 5 for more details.)

b. Should an employee be allowed to send personal e-mail messages during breaks or lunch hours? How

about using company computers after hours to prepare a college report? What if your supervisor gives her permission but asks you to keep quiet about it?

c. Should companies have the right to monitor e-mail messages sent by employees? If so, is it necessary for an organization to inform the employees of its policy?

2.5 Group Roles: Observing a Group in Action (Obj. 1, 2, 3, and 5)

Watching a company, school board, city council, campus organization, or other meeting in which problems and solutions are discussed can be useful in understanding group actions and roles.

Your Task. Attend or watch on TV the meeting of an organized group. Analyze the roles played by participants. What roles related to completing the task at hand? What roles related to developing group relationships? Did any participants play dysfunctional roles? How was conflict resolved?

2.6 Group Roles: Revealing Comments (Obj. 2)

In teams or in class discussion, analyze the following statements in relation to the group roles presented in this chapter. What group role does each statement represent? Is it a positive or negative contribution to the team?

a. "I think we can accomplish more if we each talk without being interrupted."

b. "I don't think the two of you are as far apart as you think. Mark, are you saying . . . . And Nathan, you seem to be saying . . . . Is that what you mean?"

c. "We've looked at the downside of this proposal. Does anyone have a more positive take on the situation?"

d. "Hey, did you all hear the one about the . . . ."

e. "Don't we all need a break about now? I'm tired and confused. How about the rest of you?

f. "What a great idea! Stacy, you're really on to something. We need more input like this."

g. "I know it's a little off the subject, but you're going to love this. Wait till I tell you about what happened to me today."

h. "I think we should . . . . When I was in charge of . . . , I was able to . . . . Don't you think I'm right?" (Don't you think I'm wonderful?)

i. "Emma, you've been awfully quiet. What do you think about this?"

j. "Well, let's see what we have here. Thus far, we seem to be agreed on these points: . . . Does everyone think this is a fair synopsis?"

k. "That's about the dumbest thing I ever heard. Why don't you come out from under your rock and see what's happening in the real world?"

l. "Before we go down that road, does anyone know how this method has worked with other groups?"

m. "It sounds as if you think we're all against you, Ethan."

n. "Based on what you have all said, I think our next step is to . . . ."

2.7 Workplace Etiquette: Avoiding Shooting Yourself in the Foot (Obj. 2)

INFOTRAC

When the economy slows down, business interactions seem to become more formal, according to two etiquette experts. Dining manners, greeting etiquette, and body language awareness become more important in tough times. You can learn how to avoid "shooting yourself in the foot" by reading an interview about how to gain a competitive edge.

Your Task. Using InfoTrac, search for "Manners Matter" by Andy Cohen (Article No. A108838323) and answer the following questions.

a. According to the two etiquette experts, how have business interactions changed in the last few years?

b. When is profanity appropriate?

c. In what ways are people misusing e-mail and cell phones?

2.8 Guide to Business Etiquette and Workplace Manners: Sharpening Your Skills (Obj. 2)

Business communicators feel more confident and make better impressions when they are aware of current business etiquette and proper workplace manners. But how do you know what's the right thing to do? You can gauge your current level of knowledge and sharpen your etiquette skills with a little effort.

Your Task. At your student Web site (**http://guffey.swlearning.com**), find the *Guide to Business Etiquette and Workplace Manners.* Take the preview test and then study the 17 business etiquette topics presented. Your instructor may give you one or more posttests to learn whether you fully understand the implications of the workplace manners discussed.

2.9 Group Roles: How Do You Function in Groups? (Obj. 2)

Chances are that you belong to one or more social groups or work groups. You will probably be assigned to a team in this class.

Your Task. Think about a work group, class team, or social group in which you have interacted with others. Based on the discussion in this chapter, what group role do you usually play? Do you play more than one role? What roles could you adopt to improve the functioning of your group? In a memo or an e-mail to your instructor, identify a group and answer these questions in relation to that group.

2.10 Groupthink: Are We A Bit Overeager? (Obj. 2)

You are a member of the Community Service Committee, which is part of the Business Newcomers Club in your town. Your committee must decide what local cause to support with funds earned at the Newcomers' annual celebrity auction. Matt, the committee chair, suggested that the group support a local literacy program. His aunt is literacy coordinator at the Davis Outreach Center, and he knows that the group would be delighted with any contribution. Heather said that she favored any cause that was educational. Eric announced that he had to leave for an appointment in five minutes. Mona described an article she read in the newspaper about surprisingly large numbers of people who were functionally illiterate. Kevin said that he thought they ought to consider other causes such as the homeless center, but Matt dismissed the idea saying, "The homeless already receive lots of funding. Besides, our contribution could make a real difference with the literacy program." The other members of the committee persuaded Kevin to agree with them. The committee voted unanimously to support the literacy program.

Your Task. In class discussion, answer the following questions:

a. What aspects of groupthink were at work in this committee?
b. What conditions contribute to groupthink?
c. What can groups do to avoid groupthink?

2.11 Characteristics of Successful Teams: A Tale of Teamwork and Turnaround (Obj. 3)

INFOTRAC

Ceridian, a Minneapolis-based provider of outsourced human resources services, desperately needed a makeover. Chief Revenue Officer Pat Goebel complained that Ceridian suffered from underperformance, inertia, and a severe lack of communication. "We were talking too much about what we do, rather than about what customers need and how we can help. That had to change fast," he said. To turn the company around rapidly, Goebel brought together a cross-functional team of employees. He locked the team of 20 staffers in a room for three days and gave them a specific purpose.

Your Task. Using InfoTrac, search for "Turn Around Artist" by Andy Cohen appearing in *Sales & Marketing Management* (Article No. A104551391). After reading about Ceridian's turnaround, answer these questions:

a. What was the specific purpose of this cross-functional team?
b. What characteristics of successful teams did you recognize in this group?
c. Why was it better to bring together a cross-functional staff team rather than hire an outside consultant to solve the company's problem?

2.12 Team Presentations: Oh, No, Not Me! (Obj. 4)

WEB

You have just been named to a class team that must research a topic, produce a report, and make a class presentation. Alternatively, assume that you have been asked to head a team that is to produce an organizational five-year plan for your company. You know this assignment will end with a written report and a presentation to management and stockholders. Your first reaction is dismay. But you decide that if you must take on this task, you want to make sure you know what you are doing. And you always feel more comfortable after you've poked around the Web a bit.

Your Task. Using your favorite search tool (such as **www.google.com**), see what you can find that might be helpful in preparing a team report or oral presentation. Use search terms such as "team writing" or "team presentation." Surrounding your term with quotation marks ensures that it will be searched as a unit. Ignore commercial sites trying to sell you services or software. Focus on finding practical advice. In a class discussion or in a memo to your instructor, name at least five good tips that were not discussed in this chapter. Identify and evaluate the Web sites where you find the best information.

2.13 Planning a Meeting: Spring Campus Event (Obj. 5)

Assume that the next meeting of your campus associated students organization will discuss preparations for a careers day in the spring. The group will hear reports from committees working on speakers, business recruiters, publicity, reservation of campus space, setup of booths, and any other matters you can think of.

Your Task. As president of your ASO, prepare an agenda for the meeting. Compose your introductory remarks to open the meeting. Your instructor may ask you to submit these two documents or use them in staging an actual meeting in class.

2.14 Evaluating Meetings: Effective or Ineffective? (Obj. 5)

Attend a structured meeting of a college, social, business, or other organization. Compare the way the meeting is conducted with the suggestions presented in this chapter. Why did the meeting succeed or fail? In a class discussion or in a memo to your instructor, discuss your analysis.

2.15 Lessons in Teamwork: What We Can Learn From Geese (Objs. 1–6)

TEAM

When geese fly in formation, we can't help but look up and marvel at their beauty. But their behavior also represents successful teamwork patterns that have evolved over the ages.
Your Task. In small groups discuss what teamwork lesson might be learned from each of the following:

- **a.** The V formation helps each follower goose derive energy from the flowfield generated by the goose immediately ahead. Every bird experiences lower drag and needs less energy to maintain its speed.
- **b.** Whenever a goose gets out of formation, it tries to get back into formation.
- **c.** When the lead goose gets tired, it rotates back into formation and another goose flies at the head.
- **d.** The geese flying in the rear of the formation honk, apparently to encourage those up front to keep up their speed.
- **e.** When a goose gets sick or wounded and falls, two geese fall out and stay with it until it revives or dies. Then they catch up or join another flock.[37]

2.16 Videoconferencing: Getting Straight Talk for the Boss (Obj. 6)

CRITICAL THINKING | WEB

Your boss wants to learn more about workplace videoconferencing because many company meetings require traveling. She thinks that the company may be able to save money and reduce employee fatigue if it could find a way to cut back traveling to meetings. Because she is a busy executive and a Web novice, she asks you to do research. She wants you to find three Web sites that will help her learn more about the terminology, functions, and costs involved in videoconferencing.

Your Task. Use a search engine such as Google (**www.google.com**) to locate three helpful sites describing videoconferencing. For this purpose you should definitely consider commercial sites including some "sponsored" sites. This means that a company paid the search engine to be listed prominently. Watch any demonstrations and evaluate what you see. In an e-mail or memo to your instructor, submit a list of the three best sites that you find. Provide a short description of each site and why you think your boss should see it.

2.17 Webcasting: Who's Doing It? (Obj. 6)

INFOTRAC | WEB

Your company will be launching a new product shortly, and it is wondering whether webcasting is a possibility for announcing it.
Your Task. Your boss asks you to use the Web or InfoTrac to find examples of three organizations that have used webcasting recently. In a class discussion or in an e-mail to your instructor, list three webcasts and explain briefly who announced what.

2.18 Team Reports and Presentations: Learning More About Credit Counseling and Repair Services (Objs. 2, 4, and 5)

CONSUMER | TEAM | WEB

With personal bankruptcies at record highs, government and private organizations are increasingly concerned with credit counseling scams and so-called "credit repair" schemes. Your company sponsors occasional lunchtime in-service training and educational sessions for employees. You and a few other employees have been asked to outline a 30-minute program providing solid consumer credit information.
Your Task. Working with a team of three to five fellow students, decide how to approach this assignment. Should you use the Web, InfoTrac, or both to gather information? Should each of you work individually to search for information? Since this is a large topic and you have limited presentation time, you will probably want to divide it into four or five subtopics. Consider assigning each team member specific tasks, such as investigating (a) credit repair scams, (b) the cost of credit consolidation programs, (c) questions to ask a credit counseling agency, and (d) how to repair credit yourself. Learn as much as you can so that you can help others as well as educate yourself. Remember, though, that you don't have to prepare the entire presentation—just an outline. Present your findings in class or in a memo to your instructor.

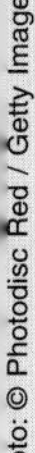
Photo: © Photodisc Red / Getty Images

C.L.U.E. review 2

On a separate sheet edit the following sentences to correct faults in grammar, punctuation, spelling, numbers, proofreading, and word use.

1. Our companies management counsel had all ready decided to apoint a investigative team, however, they acted to slow.
2. Organization's are forming teams for at least 3 good reasons; better decisions, more faster response times and increase productivity.
3. Most teams go through 4 development phases, Forming, Storming, Norming, and Performing.
4. Some group members play dysfunctional rolls and they disrupt the groups progress toward it's goal.
5. Successful self directed teams are autonomous, that is they can hire fire and discipline there own member.
6. Although we tried to reach a consensus several Managers and even the Vice President opposed the hole proposal.
7. At last months Staff meeting the CEO and him complemented the teams efforts and made warm supportive comments.
8. Rather then schedule many face to face meetings the team decided to investigate a three thousand dollar desk top videoconferencing system.
9. When conflict erupted at our teams january meeting we made a conscience effort to confront the under-lying issues.
10. 55 people are expected to attend the Training Session on April 15th consequently her and I must find a more larger room.

chapter 3

Workplace Listening and Nonverbal Communication

objectives

1 Explain the importance of listening in the workplace and describe three types of workplace listening.

2 Discuss the listening process and its barriers.

3 Enumerate ten techniques for improving workplace listening.

4 Define nonverbal communication and explain its functions.

5 Describe the forms of nonverbal communication and how they can be used positively in your career.

6 List specific techniques for improving nonverbal communication skills in the workplace.

COMMUNICATION IN PROCESS

L. L. Bean's Success Secret Is Listening to Customers

ONE OF THIS country's biggest listeners is L. L. Bean, Inc. During its peak holiday season, the giant cataloger employs nearly 4,000 telephone representatives in three different call centers. They listen to customers seeking product information and placing orders. Listening to customers and fulfilling promises are probably the most important keys to L. L. Bean's remarkable 90 years of success in selling outdoor apparel and accessories.

In 1917 Leon Leonwood Bean created the now-famous Maine hunting boot, which he personally guaranteed. Orders poured in, but when 90 of the first 100 pairs of boots had to be replaced, L. L. Bean, Inc., nearly folded. True to his word, Bean refunded the purchase price for every pair of failed boots. Although his company nearly went bankrupt, it eventually earned a reputation as a trusted source for reliable outdoor equipment and expert advice.[1]

L. L. Bean, Inc., has now become an American icon, representing Yankee prudence, thrift, and integrity as well as premier personalized customer service around the clock. Whether a customer is looking for information about choosing the right outdoor gear for a backpacking trip or registering for an upcoming wedding, L. L. Bean's customer satisfaction representatives are on hand to help 24 hours a day, 365 days a year.

Far beyond mere customer service, L. L. Bean strives to develop lasting customer loyalty. Ellen Fowler, former manager for Customer Satisfaction Learning and Communication, said, "Customers can be satisfied with a transaction, but that doesn't mean they will return. We want to truly delight and amaze customers so that we ensure their continued business."[2]

More than 3.5 million customers annually visit L. L. Bean's flagship retail store in Freeport, Maine. However, most of its sales come from 15 million telephone orders generated by its 50 separate catalogs.[3] Telephone representatives take the time to understand and meet the needs of all callers. They are trained to listen carefully, be polite, use professional language, and let the customer establish the progression of the call.

L L. Bean attracts customers to its flagship store in Maine and especially to its catalog call centers by perfecting the art of customer listening.

L. L. Bean has made listening to customers an art, thus earning their loyalty. Such loyalty is especially remarkable in an age of "here today, gone tomorrow" retailers and "disposable transient brands."[4] Maintaining its position as a top American brand with legendary customer service requires constant attention to listening to customers and treating them as valued individuals.

Critical Thinking

- What do you think really influences long-term customer retention and loyalty? Products? Promotions? Prices? Staff? Convenience? Reward programs?
- How could feedback from telephone representatives be helpful to companies such as L. L. Bean?
- In what ways is listening to customers similar to listening to friends and colleagues?

www.llbean.com

CONTINUED ON PAGE 84

case study

Listening in the Workplace

learning objective

1

"No one ever listened himself out of a job," observed President Calvin Coolidge many years ago. His words are even more significant today as employers become increasingly aware that listening is a critical employee and management skill. In addition, listening to customers, such as those calling L. L. Bean, takes on increasing importance as our economy becomes ever more service oriented.

But, you may be thinking, everyone knows how to listen. Most of us believe that listening is an automatic response to noise. We do it without thinking. Perhaps that explains why so many of us are poor listeners. You can develop good listening habits by learning more about the process and by studying specific techniques. In this chapter we'll explore the importance of listening, the kinds of listening required in the workplace, the listening process, listening barriers, and how to become a better listener. You'll also study the powerful effect of nonverbal messages. These include all unwritten and unspoken messages. Although many of the tips for improving your listening and nonverbal skills will be effective in your personal life, our discussion centers primarily on workplace and employment needs.

spotlight *on communicators*

At L. L. Bean Ellen Fowler taught customer service representatives to listen as if the speaker were the only person in the world. She advised focusing totally on what the person is saying instead of thinking about what you will say when it is your turn. "Know that you'll have plenty of time to formulate a response once the person has finished."

As you learned earlier, workers are doing more communicating than ever before, largely because of the Internet, team environments, global competition, and an increasing emphasis on customer service. A vital ingredient in every successful workplace is high-quality communication. And three quarters of high-quality communication involves listening.[5]

Listening skills are critical for career success, organization effectiveness, and worker satisfaction.

Listening skills are important for career success, organization effectiveness, and worker satisfaction. Numerous studies report that good listeners make good managers and that good listeners advance more rapidly in their organizations.[6] Studies of Fortune 500 companies report that soft skills such as listening, writing, and speaking are most likely to determine hiring and career success.[7] Other studies show that listening skills are an important part of customer service. The enduring success of companies such as L. L. Bean is largely a result of listening to customers. Such attention to customers is becoming increasingly feasible and a major cause of marketing effectiveness.[8] Listening is equally significant within organizations. Workers are most satisfied when they feel that management listens to their concerns.

Listening is especially important in the workplace because we spend so much time doing it. Most workers spend 30 to 45 percent of their communication time listening,[9] whereas executives spend 60 to 70 percent of their communication time listening.[10]

Poor Listening Habits

Most of us listen at only 25 percent efficiency.

Although executives and workers devote the bulk of their communication time to listening, research suggests that they're not very good at it. In fact, most of us are poor listeners. Some estimates indicate that only half of the oral messages heard in a day are completely understood.[11] Experts say that we listen at only 25 percent efficiency. In other words, we ignore, forget, distort, or misunderstand 75 percent of everything we hear.

Poor listening habits may result from several factors. Lack of training is one significant reason. Few schools give as much emphasis to listening as they do to the development of reading, speaking, and writing skills. In addition, our listening skills may be less than perfect because of the large number of competing sounds and stimuli in our lives that interfere with concentration. Finally, we are inefficient listeners

Photo: Courtesy Eileen Fowler / L. L. Bean

We are inefficient listeners because of lack of training, competing sounds, slowness of speech, and daydreaming.

because we are able to process speech much faster than others can speak. While most speakers talk at about 125 to 250 words per minute, listeners can think at 1,000 to 3,000 words per minute.[12] The resulting lag time fosters daydreaming, which clearly reduces listening efficiency.

Types of Workplace Listening

In an employment environment, you can expect to be involved in many types of listening. These include listening to superiors, listening to fellow colleagues and team members, and listening to customers. As an entry-level employee, you will probably be most concerned with listening to superiors. But you also must develop skills for listening to colleagues and team members. As you advance in your career and enter the ranks of management, you will need skills for listening to subordinates. Finally, the entire organization must listen to customers to compete in today's service-oriented economy.

Listening to superiors involves hearing instructions, assignments, and explanations of work procedures.

Listening to Superiors. On the job one of your most important tasks will be listening to instructions, assignments, and explanations about how to do your work. You will be listening to learn and to comprehend. To focus totally on the speaker, be sure you are not distracted by noisy surroundings or other tasks. Don't take phone calls, and don't try to complete another job while listening with one ear. Show your interest by leaning forward and striving for good eye contact.

Listen carefully, take selective notes, and don't interrupt.

Above all, take notes. Don't rely on your memory. Details are easy to forget. Taking selective notes also conveys to the speaker your seriousness about hearing accurately and completely. Don't interrupt. When the speaker finishes, paraphrase the instructions in your own words. Ask pertinent questions in a nonthreatening manner. And don't be afraid to ask "dumb" questions, if it means you won't have to do a job twice. Avoid criticizing or arguing when you are listening to a superior. Your goals should be to hear accurately and to convey an image of competence.

Listening to colleagues and teammates involves critical listening and discriminative listening.

Listening to Colleagues and Teammates. Much of your listening will result from interactions with fellow workers and teammates. In these exchanges two kinds of listening are important. *Critical listening* enables you to judge and evaluate what you are hearing. You will be listening to decide whether the speaker's message is fact, fiction, or opinion. You will also be listening to decide whether an argument is based on logic or emotion. Critical listening requires an effort on your part. You must remain objective, particularly when you disagree with what you are hearing. Control your tendency to prejudge. Let the speaker have a chance to complete the message before you evaluate it. *Discriminative listening* is necessary when you must understand and remember. It means you must identify main ideas, understand a logical argument, and recognize the purpose of the message.

Dampening means listening with minimal response and maximum acceptance; redirecting involves restating the message, and reflecting clarifies content and feeling.

Three listening strategies will be especially useful to you in team and group interactions: *dampening, redirecting,* and *reflecting.*[13] *Dampening* involves listening with minimal response and maximum acceptance. It is particularly necessary when group members are in conflict. If one team member is unhappy about something, it is often best to let that person vent without interrupting. Dampening is also appropriate in situations requiring politeness. You listen courteously, for example, when team members are introducing themselves or when a valued employee describes a stressful encounter with a customer. *Redirecting* involves asking questions, restating the message, and getting the speaker back on track. For example, "I believe, Jeff, that our goal is to find a way to reduce travel expenses. Although your comments on airport delays are interesting, do you have specific suggestions for cutting back travel expenses?"

Reflecting is useful to clarify both content and feeling. By reflecting emotions, you are better able to interpret a message in the proper context. Reflecting is a helpful tool in managing conflict. A wise strategy, for instance, is to repeat the speaker's message and acknowledge the feeling that goes with it. Paraphrase what has been said and check with the speaker to make sure you understand. For example, "I understand, Holly, that you were upset and inconvenienced because we changed the meeting date without consulting you. Is that correct?"

Although dampening, redirecting, and reflecting are listening techniques that work well in group interactions, they are equally effective in listening to customers.

Listening to Customers. As the U.S. economy becomes increasingly service oriented, the new management mantra has become "customers rule." Yet, despite 50 years of talk about customer service, the concept of "customer-centric" business is still in its infancy.[14] Many organizations are just learning that listening to customers results in increased sales and profitability as well as improved customer acquisition and retention. The simple truth is that consumers just feel better about companies that value their opinions. Listening is an acknowledgment of caring and is a potent retention tool. Customers want to be cared about; by doing so, companies fulfill a powerful human need.

Organizations that listen to customers improve sales and profitability.

FIGURE 3.1 ***Listening to Customers: Comparing Trained and Untrained Listeners***

Untrained Listeners	Trained Listeners
You tune out some of what the customer is saying because you know what the answer is.	You defer judgment. You listen for the customer's feelings and assess the situation.
You are quick to mentally criticize grammar, voice tone, and speaking style. You focus on style.	You pay most attention to content, not to appearances, form, or other surface issues.
You tend to listen mainly for facts and specific bits of information.	You listen completely, trying to really understand every nuance. This enthralls speakers.
You attempt to take in everything the customer is saying, including exaggerations and errors (referred to as "fogging") so that you can refute each comment.	You listen primarily for the main idea and avoid replying to everything, especially sidetracking issues.
You divide your attention among two or more tasks because listening is automatic.	You do one thing at a time, realizing that listening is a full-time job.
You tend to become distracted by emotional words and have difficulty controlling your angry responses.	You control your anger, refusing to allow your emotions to govern.
You interrupt the customer.	You are silent for a few seconds after a customer finishes to be sure the thought is completed.
You give few, if any, verbal responses.	You give affirming statements and invite additional comments.

How can organizations improve their customer listening techniques? Since employees are the eyes and ears of the organization, smart companies begin by hiring employees who genuinely care about customers. Listening organizations also train their employees to listen actively and to ask gentle, probing questions to ensure clear understanding. As you can see in Figure 3.1, employees trained in listening techniques are far more likely to elicit customer feedback and promote goodwill than untrained employees are.

Many organizations today stay in touch with customers through *call centers* that process hundreds of thousands of telephone calls daily. For example, if you

Call centers are an important customer access channel and a major source of customer-related information.

call American Airlines or Carnival Cruise Lines to make a reservation, you will doubtless speak to a call center representative. Similarly, if you need help with your new computer or your satellite cable service, the help desk you reach is probably a call center. As service expands to the Web, call centers and voice communications are rapidly evolving into key, integrated components of new customer relation management programs. Call centers have become an important customer access channel as well as a significant source of customer-related information. In call centers and in all contacts with customers, effective listening is an essential business skill.

learning objective 2

The Listening Process and Its Barriers

Skillful listening to superiors, colleagues, and customers can mean the difference between workplace success and failure. To help you build effective listening skills, we'll begin by examining the process of listening, as well as its barriers.

Listening takes place in four stages—perception, interpretation, evaluation, and action, as illustrated in Figure 3.2. Barriers, however, can obstruct the listening process. These barriers may be mental or physical.

Perception

The four stages of listening are perception, interpretation, evaluation, and action.

The listening process begins when you hear sounds and concentrate on them. Stop reading for a moment and become conscious of the sounds around you. Do you notice the hum of your computer or printer, background sounds from a TV program, muffled traffic noise, or the murmur of distant voices? Until you "tuned in" to them, these sounds went unnoticed. The conscious act of listening begins when you focus on the sounds around you and select those you choose to hear. You tune in when you (1) sense that the message is important, (2) are interested in the topic, or (3) are in the mood to listen. Perception is reduced by impaired hearing, noisy surroundings, inattention, and pseudolistening. *Pseudolistening* occurs when listeners "fake" it. They look as though they are listening, but their minds are wandering far off.

FIGURE 3.2 ***The Listening Process and Its Barriers***

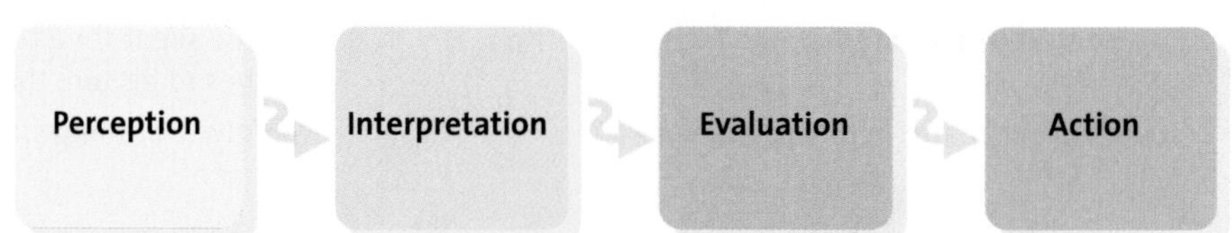

COMMON LISTENING BARRIERS

Mental Barriers	Physical and Other Barriers
Inattention	Hearing impairment
Prejudgment	Noisy surroundings
Frame of reference	Speaker's appearance
Closed-mindedness	Speaker's mannerisms
Pseudolistening	Lag time

Interpretation

Once you have focused your attention on a sound or message, you begin to interpret, or decode, it. As described in Chapter 1, interpretation of a message is colored by your cultural, educational, and social frames of reference. The meanings you attach to the speaker's words are filtered through your expectations and total life experiences. Thus, your interpretation of the speaker's meaning may be quite different from what the speaker intended because your frame of reference is different.

Evaluation

Evaluation involves separating fact from opinion and judging messages objectively.

After interpreting the meaning of a message, you analyze its merit and draw conclusions. To do this, you attempt to separate fact from opinion. Good listeners try to be objective, and they avoid prejudging the message. In a study of college students, one researcher determined that closed-mindedness and opinionated attitudes functioned as major barriers to listening. Certain students were not good listeners because their prejudices prevented them from opening up to a speaker's ideas.[15] The appearance and mannerisms of the speaker can also affect a listener's evaluation of a message. A juror, for example, might jump to the conclusion that an accused man is guilty because of his fierce expression or his substandard English. Thus, to evaluate a message accurately and objectively, you should (1) consider all the information, (2) be aware of your own biases, and (3) avoid jumping to hasty conclusions.

Action

Action involves storing a message in memory, reacting, or supplying feedback.

Responding to a message may involve storing the message in memory for future use, reacting with a physical response (a frown, a smile, a laugh), or supplying feedback to the speaker. Listener feedback is essential because it helps clarify the message so that it can be decoded accurately. Feedback also helps the speaker to find out whether the message is getting through clearly. In one-to-one conversation, of course, no clear distinction exists between the roles of listener and speaker—you give or receive feedback as your role alternates.

Enhancing Retention

Unfortunately, most of us are able to recall only 50 percent of the information we heard a day earlier and only 20 percent after two days, as shown in Figure 3.3.[16] How can we improve our retention?

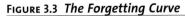

FIGURE 3.3 ***The Forgetting Curve***

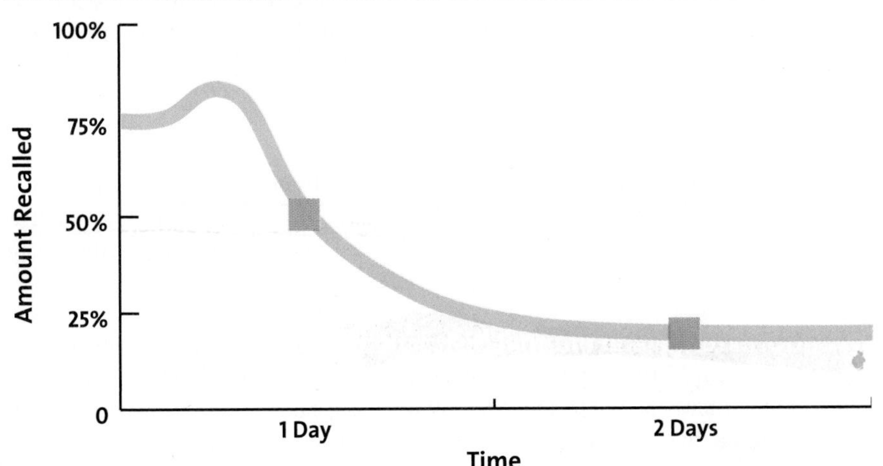

Retention can be improved by deciding to remember, structuring incoming information to form relationships, and reviewing.

Memory training specialists say that effective remembering involves three factors: (1) deciding to remember, (2) structuring the incoming information to form relationships, and (3) reviewing. In the first step you determine what information is worth remembering. Once you have established a positive mind-set, you look for a means of organizing the incoming information to form relationships. Chain links can help you associate the unfamiliar with something familiar. For instance, make an acronym of the first letters of the item to be remembered. To recall the names of the Great Lakes—Huron, Ontario, Michigan, Erie, and Superior—remember the word "HOMES." To remember the listening process—perception, interpretation, evaluation, action—think "PIE-A." Rhyming is another helpful chain-link tool. To remember how to spell words with "EI" combinations, think "I before E except after C."

The world memory champion uses a device called *loci.* To remember the sequence of a pack of 52 playing cards, for example, he associates each card with a character. The queen of diamonds he might imagine covered head to foot in diamonds. Then he places each character in a location (hence, *loci*), say around the local golf course, which has 52 stages.[17]

To further improve retention, take notes and rewrite them immediately after listening.

One of the most reliable ways to improve retention is to take notes of the important ideas to be remembered. Rewriting within ten minutes of completing listening improves your notes and takes advantage of peak recall time, which immediately follows listening.

learning objective 3

The final step in improving retention is reviewing your notes, repeating your acronym, or saying your rhyme to move the targeted information into long-term memory. Frequent reviews help strengthen your memory connections.

Improving Workplace Listening

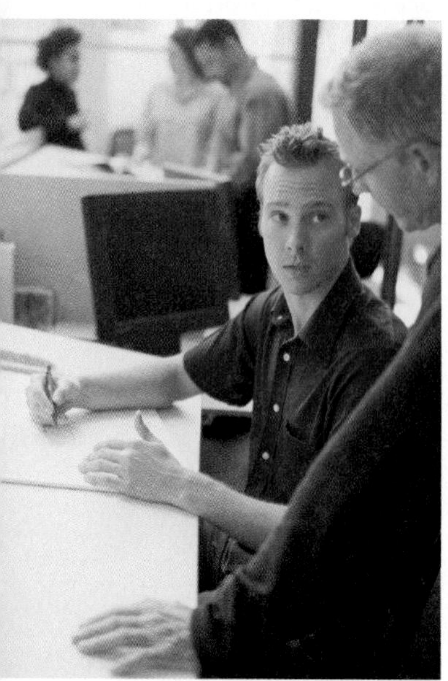

Listening on the job involves controlling external and internal distractions, becoming actively involved, identifying important facts, and taking notes. When listening to your boss, ask clarifying questions, but wait for the right moment.

Photo: © Photodisc Green / Photo Edit

Listening on the job is more difficult than listening in college classes where experienced professors present well-organized lectures and repeat important points. Workplace listening is more challenging because information is often exchanged casually. It may be disorganized, unclear, and cluttered with extraneous facts. Moreover, your fellow workers are usually friends. Because they are familiar with one another, they may not be as polite and respectful as they are with strangers. Friends tend to interrupt, jump to conclusions, and take each other for granted.

Listening in groups or listening to nonnative speakers further complicates the listening process. In groups, more than one person talks at once, and topics change rapidly. Group members are monitoring both verbal and nonverbal messages to learn what relates to their group roles. Listening to nonnative speakers often creates special challenges. The accompanying Career Coach box offers suggestions for improving communication between native and nonnative speakers. You'll find more suggestions for communicating across cultures in Chapter 4.

Ten Keys to Building Powerful Listening Skills

Despite the complexities and challenges of workplace listening, good listeners on the job must remember that their goal is to listen carefully and to *understand* what is being said so that they can do their work well. The following recommendations can help you improve your workplace listening effectiveness.

1. Control External and Internal Distractions. Move to an area where you can hear without conflicting noises or conversations. Block out surrounding physical distractions. Internally, try to focus totally on the speaker. If other projects are on your mind, put them on the back burner temporarily. When you are emotionally charged, whether angry or extremely happy, it's a good idea to postpone any serious listening.

You listen better when you control distractions, become actively involved, separate facts from opinion, and identify important facts.

2. Become Actively Involved. Show that you are listening closely by leaning forward and maintaining eye contact with the speaker. Don't fidget or try to complete another task at the same time you are listening. Listen to more than the spoken words. How are they said? What implied meaning, reasoning, and feelings do you hear behind the spoken words? Does the speaker's body language (eye contact, posture, movements) support or contradict the main message?

3. Separate Facts From Opinions. Facts are truths known to exist; for example, *Microsoft is located in Redmond, Washington.* Opinions are statements of personal judgments or preferences; for example, *Microsoft stock is always a good investment.* Some opinions are easy to recognize because speakers preface them with statements such as *I think, It seems to me*, and *As far as I'm concerned.*[18] Often, however, listeners must evaluate assertions to decide their validity. Good listeners consider whether speakers are credible and speaking within their areas of competence. They don't automatically accept assertions as facts.

spotlight *on communicators*

Celebrated talk show host Oprah Winfrey owes much of her success to the artful application of the simple process of listening and responding. "Communicating with people is how I always developed any kind of value about myself," says the most successful female entertainer in the world. On her show she is able to block out external distractions, become actively involved, listen empathically without interrupting, paraphrase her guests' ideas, and ask clarifying questions to draw out deep meanings and issues that underlie their everyday lives.

4. Identify Important Facts. Speakers on the job often intersperse critical information with casual conversation. Unrelated topics pop up—ball scores, a customer's weird request, a computer glitch, the boss's extravagant new SUV. Your task is to select what's important and register it mentally. What step is next in your project? Who does what? What is your role?

You listen better when you refrain from interrupting, ask clarifying questions, paraphrase, capitalize on lag time, take notes, and observe gender differences.

5. Don't Interrupt. While someone else has the floor, don't interrupt with a quick reply or opinion. And don't show nonverbal disagreement such as negative head shaking, rolling eyes, sarcastic snorting, or audible sighs. Good listeners let speakers have their say. Interruptions are not only impolite, but they also prevent you from hearing the speaker's complete thought. Listeners who interrupt with their opinions sidetrack discussions and cause hard feelings.

6. Ask Clarifying Questions. Good listeners wait for the proper moment and then ask questions that do not attack the speaker. Instead of saying, "But I don't understand how you can say that," a good listener seeks clarification with questions such as, "Please help me understand by explaining more about . . . ." Because questions can put you in the driver's seat, think about them in advance. Use open questions (those without set answers) to draw out feelings, motivations, ideas, and suggestions. Use closed fact-finding questions to identify key factors in a discussion.[19] And, by the way, don't ask a question unless you are ready to be quiet and listen to the answer.

7. Paraphrase to Increase Understanding. To make sure you understand a speaker, rephrase and summarize a message in your own words. Be objective and nonjudgmental. Remember, your goal is to understand what the speaker has said—not to show how mindless the speaker's words sound when parroted. Remember, too, that other workplace listeners will also benefit from a clear summary of what was said.

8. Capitalize on Lag Time. While you are waiting for a speaker's next idea, use the time to review what the speaker is saying. Separate the central idea, key points, and details. Sometimes you may have to supply the organization. Use lag time to silently rephrase and summarize the speaker's message. Another effective trick for keeping your mind from drifting is to try to guess what a speaker's next point will be. Most important, keep your mind focused on the speaker and his or her ideas—not on all the other work waiting for you.

spotlight *on communicators*

Television interviewer, commentator, and talk show host Diane Sawyer, star of ABC's Primetime, *says that the key to her success is active and empathic listening. "You listen, ready to move in any direction. You listen without self-consciousness and without self-importance. You listen as a human being first. And as a pursuer of facts second. And as a television personality never."*

9. Take Notes to Ensure Retention. Don't trust your memory. A wise person once said that he'd rather have a short pencil than a long memory. If you have a hallway conversation with a colleague and don't have a pencil handy, make a mental note of the important items. Then write them down as soon as possible. Even with seemingly easily remembered facts or instructions, jot them down to ease your mind and also to be sure you understand them correctly. Two weeks later you'll be glad you did. Be sure you have a good place to store notes of various projects, such as file folders, notebooks, or computer files.

10. Be Aware of Gender Differences. Men tend to listen for facts, whereas women tend to perceive listening as an opportunity to connect with the other person on a personal level.[20] Men tend to use interrupting behavior to control conversations, whereas women generally interrupt to communicate assent, to elaborate on an idea of another group member, or to participate in the topic of conversation.[21] Women listeners tend to be attentive, provide steady eye contact, remain stationary, and nod their heads.[22] Male listeners are less attentive, provide sporadic eye contact, and move around. Being aware of these tendencies will make you a more sensitive and knowledgeable listener. To learn more about gender differences in communication, see the Career Coach box in Chapter 4.

Checklist for Improving Listening

- ✓ **Stop talking.** Accept the role of listener by concentrating on the speaker's words, not on what your response will be.
- ✓ **Work hard at listening.** Become actively involved; expect to learn something.
- ✓ **Block out competing thoughts.** Concentrate on the message. Don't allow yourself to daydream during lag time.
- ✓ **Control the listening environment.** Move to a quiet area where you won't be interrupted by telephone calls or visitors. Check to be certain that listeners can hear speakers.
- ✓ **Maintain an open mind.** Know your biases and try to correct for them. Be tolerant of less-abled and different-looking speakers. Provide verbal and nonverbal feedback. Encourage the speaker with comments such as "Yes," "I see," "OK," and "Uh huh," and ask polite questions. Look alert by leaning forward.
- ✓ **Paraphrase the speaker's ideas.** Silently repeat the message in your own words, sort out the main points, and identify supporting details. In conversation sum up the main points to confirm what was said.

career coach

Listening to Nonnative Speakers in the Workplace

Many workplaces today involve interaction between native and nonnative English speakers. As immigration increases and as local businesses expand into global markets, the chances are good that you will at times be listening to speakers for whom English is a second language. Although many speakers have studied English and comprehend it, they may have difficulty speaking it. Why? Vowels and consonants are pronounced differently. Learning the inflection and sentence patterns of English is difficult when they conflict with the speaker's native tongue. And most "errors" in pronunciation occur in meaningful patterns traced to their home languages.

Moreover, nonnative speakers are intimidated by the fluency of native speakers; therefore, they don't try to become fluent. They worry about using incorrect verb forms and tenses. They may be trying to translate thoughts from their own language word for word into the foreign language. Often, they spend so long thinking about how to express a thought that the conversation moves on. And many worry about being judged negatively and losing face. What can native speakers do to become better listeners when nonnatives speak?

- **Avoid negative judgment of accented speech.** Many nonnative speakers of English speak an articulate, insightful, and complex variety of English. Their speech may retain remnants of their native language. But don't assume that a nonnative speaker struggling with pronunciation is unintelligent. Instead, imagine how difficult it would be for you to learn that person's language.
- **Be patient.** Americans are notoriously poor listeners. Strive to overcome the need to hurry a conversation along. Give nonnative speakers time to express their thoughts.
- **Don't finish sentences.** Allow nonnative speakers to choose their words and complete their sentences without volunteering your help. You may find that they are saying something quite different from what you expected.
- **Don't correct grammar and pronunciation.** Although you are trying to "help" a nonnative speaker, it's better to focus on what's being expressed and forget about teaching English. As one company caller said, "If I could speak better English, I'd already be doing it."
- **Don't pretend to understand.** It's perfectly all right to tell a speaker that you're having a little difficulty understanding him or her.
- **Practice listening to many varieties of English.** Improving your skill at comprehending many accents as well as native dialects (for example, Southern, Western, and Northeastern) can be a valuable skill in today's diverse and intercultural workplace.

Career Application

In a class forum, discuss these questions: How do you think nonnative speakers feel when they must converse with native speakers in a work environment? For nonnative speakers, what is most frustrating in conversation? For native speakers, what is awkward or frustrating in talking with nonnative speakers? What embarrassing moments have you experienced as a result of mispronunciations or misunderstandings? What suggestions can native and nonnative speakers make for improving communication?

- ✓ **Listen between the lines.** Observe nonverbal cues and interpret the feelings of the speaker: What is really being said?
- ✓ **Distinguish between facts and opinions.** Know the difference between factual statements and opinions stated as assertions.
- ✓ **Capitalize on lag time.** Use spare moments to organize, review, anticipate, challenge, and weigh the evidence.
- ✓ **Use memory devices.** If the information is important, develop acronyms, links, or rhymes to help you remember.
- ✓ **Take selective notes.** If you are hearing instructions or important data, record the major points; then, revise your notes immediately or verify them with the speaker.

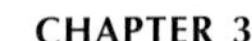

PROCESS IN PROGRESS

L. L. Bean Revisited

THE MANAGER OF Customer Satisfaction Learning and Communication at L. L. Bean recognizes that telephone customer service can be pretty boring and repetitive work. Yet, L. L. Bean call center reps manage to sound enthusiastic, cheerful, and responsive. To practice developing their listening skills, new hires engage in role-playing with different scenarios. They are taught to be courteous, use professional language, and establish rapport with a customer. In addressing customers, they are encouraged to use "Mr." and "Mrs." unless customers specifically request first names. Those reps who handle customer service problems are given authority to achieve "one-call" solutions whenever possible. In the rare instances when something goes wrong and customers are really upset, reps are encouraged to acknowledge the emotions they hear and to let people feel hurt. Then they try to solve the problem to the customer's satisfaction.

Critical Thinking

- What listening skills are important in establishing rapport with customers?
- What are the advantages of "one-call" solutions to customers and to companies?
- How might you respond to a customer who is frustrated and angry? What listening skills are appropriate?

CONTINUED ON PAGE 91

case study

learning objective 4

Communicating Through Nonverbal Messages

Understanding messages often involves more than merely listening to spoken words. Nonverbal clues also carry powerful meanings. Nonverbal communication includes all unwritten and unspoken messages, both intentional and unintentional. Eye contact, facial expression, body movements, space, time, distance, appearance—all of these nonverbal cues influence the way a message is interpreted, or decoded, by the receiver. Many of the nonverbal messages that we send are used intentionally to accompany spoken words. When Stacy pounds her desk and shouts "This computer just crashed again!" we interpret the loudness of her voice and the act of slamming her fist as intentional emphasis of her words. But people can also communicate nonverbally even when they don't intend to. And not all messages accompany words. When Jeff hangs on to the rostrum and barely looks at the audience, he sends a nonverbal message of fear and lack of confidence.

Because nonverbal communication can be an important tool for you to use and control in the workplace, you need to learn more about its functions and forms.

spotlight *on communicators*

Some cultures are better at listening and interpreting nonverbal messages than others, says Robert Rosen, psychologist, cross-cultural consultant, and author of Global Literacies. *In their high-context nonverbal culture, the Japanese, for example, have developed a special skill for listening deeply. Germans, on the other hand, are better at verbal clues. Westerners in general, Rosen contends, are good verbal communicators. Easterners are good at the nonverbal. The challenge is to learn the skill of the other.*

Photo: Courtesy of Healthy Companies International

Functions of Nonverbal Communication

Nonverbal communication functions, illustrated in Figure 3.4, help to convey meaning in at least five ways. As you become more aware of the following functions of nonverbal communication, you will be better able to use these silent codes to your advantage in the workplace.

Figure 3.4 ***How We Use Nonverbal Communication***

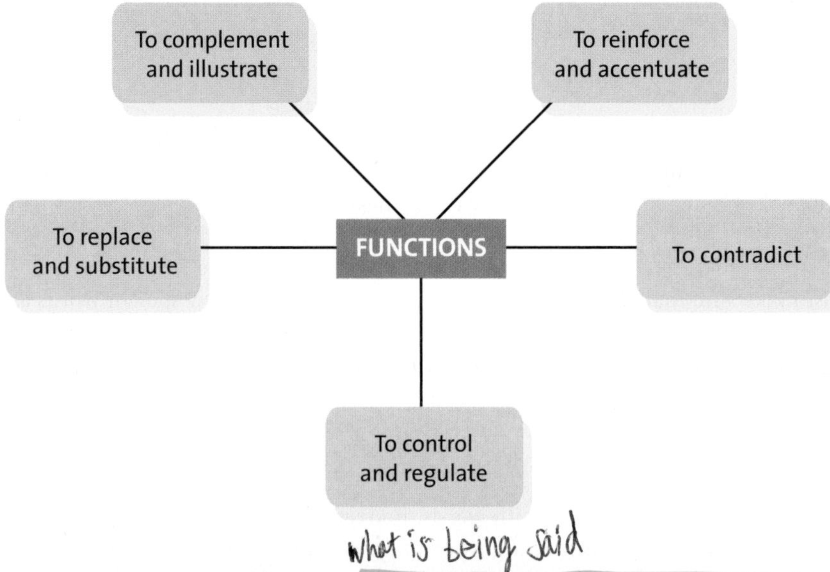

- **To complement and illustrate.** Nonverbal messages can amplify, modify, or provide details for a verbal message. For example, in describing the size of a cell phone, a speaker holds his fingers apart 5 inches. In pumping up sales reps, the manager jams his fist into the opposite hand to indicate the strong effort required.
- **To reinforce and accentuate.** Skilled speakers raise their voices to convey important ideas, but they whisper to suggest secrecy. A grimace forecasts painful news, whereas a big smile intensifies good news. A neat, well-equipped office reinforces a message of professionalism.
- **To replace and substitute.** Many gestures substitute for words: nodding your head for "yes," giving a *V* for victory, making a thumbs-up sign for approval, and shrugging your shoulders for "I don't know" or "I don't care." In fact, a complex set of gestures totally replaces spoken words in sign language.
- **To control and regulate.** Nonverbal messages are important regulators in conversation. Shifts in eye contact, slight head movements, changes in posture, raising of eyebrows, nodding of the head, and voice inflection—all of these cues tell speakers when to continue, to repeat, to elaborate, to hurry up, or to finish.
- **To contradict.** To be sarcastic, a speaker might hold his nose while stating that your new perfume is wonderful. During one presidential debate, a candidate was seriously attacking his opponent's "fuzzy" math. The other candidate smiled and winked at the audience. His body language contradicted the attack being made by his opponent. In the workplace, individuals may send contradictory messages with words or actions. The boss, for example, says he wants to promote Kevin, but he fails to submit the necessary recommendation.

Most of us cannot talk without gestures. Almost instinctively, we use the body language of gestures to illustrate, reinforce, accentuate, and even replace words.

Photo: © Photodisc Blue / Getty Images

In the workplace people may not be aware that they are sending contradictory messages. Researchers have found that when verbal and nonverbal messages contradict each other, listeners tend to believe and act on the nonverbal message. How would you interpret the following?

- Brenda assures her boss that she has enough time to complete her assigned research, but she misses two deadlines.

- Tyler protests that he's not really angry but slams the door when he leaves a group meeting.
- Kyoko claims she's not nervous about a team presentation, but her brow is furrowed and she perspires profusely.

Because nonverbal messages may speak louder than words, make sure that your nonverbal cues reinforce your spoken words.

The nonverbal messages in these situations speak louder than the words uttered. In one experiment speakers delivered a positive message but averted their eyes as they spoke. Listeners perceived the overall message to be negative. Moreover, listeners thought that gaze aversion suggested nonaffection, superficiality, lack of trust, and nonreceptivity.[23] The lesson to be learned here is that effective communicators must make sure that all their nonverbal messages reinforce their spoken words and their professional goals. To make sure that you're on the right track to nonverbal communication competency, let's look more carefully at the specific forms of nonverbal communication.

learning objective 5

Forms of Nonverbal Communication

Instead of conveying meaning with words, nonverbal messages carry their meaning in a number of different forms ranging from facial expressions to body language and even clothes. Each of us sends and receives thousands of nonverbal messages daily in our business and personal lives. Although the following discussion covers all forms of nonverbal communication, we will be especially concerned with workplace applications. As you learn about the messages sent by eye contact, facial expressions, posture, gestures, as well as the use of time, space, territory, and appearance—think about how you can use these nonverbal cues positively in your career.

The eyes are thought to be the most accurate predictor of a speaker's true feelings.

Eye Contact. The eyes have been called the "windows to the soul." Even if communicators can't look directly into the soul, they consider the eyes to be the most accurate predictor of a speaker's true feelings and attitudes. Most of us cannot look another person straight in the eyes and lie. As a result, we tend to believe people who look directly at us. We have less confidence in and actually distrust those who cannot maintain eye contact. Sustained eye contact suggests trust and admiration; brief eye contact signifies fear or stress. Prolonged eye contact, however, can be intrusive and intimidating. One successful CEO says that he can tell from people's eyes whether they are focused, receptive, or distant. He also notes the frequency of eye blinks when judging a person's honesty.[24]

Good eye contact enables the message sender to determine whether a receiver is paying attention, showing respect, responding favorably, or feeling distress. From the receiver's perspective good eye contact reveals the speaker's sincerity, confidence, and truthfulness. Since eye contact is a learned skill, however, you must be respectful of people who do not maintain it. You must also remember that nonverbal cues, including eye contact, have different meanings in various cultures. You'll learn more about the cultural influence of nonverbal cues in Chapter 4.

Facial Expression. The expression on a communicator's face can be almost as revealing of emotion as the eyes. Researchers estimate that the human face can display over 250,000 different expressions.[25] Although a few people can control these expressions and maintain a "poker face" when they want to hide their feelings, most of us display our emotions openly. Raising or lowering the eyebrows, squinting the eyes, swallowing nervously, clenching the jaw, smiling broadly—these voluntary and involuntary facial expressions supplement or entirely replace verbal messages. In the workplace, maintaining a pleasant expression with frequent smiles promotes harmony.

Posture and Gestures. An individual's general posture can convey anything from high status and self-confidence to shyness and submissiveness. Leaning toward a speaker suggests attraction and interest; pulling away or shrinking back denotes fear, distrust, anxiety, or disgust. Similarly, gestures can communicate entire thoughts via simple movements. But remember that these nonverbal cues may have vastly different meanings in different cultures. An individual who signals success by forming the thumb and forefinger into a circle would be in deep trouble in Germany or parts of South America. The harmless OK sign is actually an obscene reference in those areas.[26]

Erect posture sends a message of confidence, competence, diligence, and strength.

In the workplace you can make a good impression by controlling your posture and gestures. When speaking, make sure your upper body is aligned with the person to whom you're talking. Former President Nixon was famous for talking to someone while his body was facing another direction, thus giving the impression that his heart wasn't in the conversation. Erect posture sends a message of confidence, competence, diligence, and strength. Using an upward palm gesture can help you immediately establish rapport, either across a meeting room or one on one. This trust-generating gesture shows that you are friendly without being too aggressive. Women are advised to avoid tilting their heads to the side when making an important point. This gesture diminishes the main thrust of the message.[27]

Time. How we structure and use time tells observers about our personality and attitudes. For example, when Maritza Perez, a banking executive, gives a visitor a prolonged interview, she signals her respect for, interest in, and approval of the visitor or the topic being discussed. By sharing her valuable time, she sends a clear nonverbal message. Likewise, when David Ing twice arrives late for a meeting, it could mean that the meeting has low priority to David, that he is a self-centered person, or that he has little self-discipline. These are assumptions that typical Americans might make. In other cultures and regions, though, punctuality is viewed differently. In the workplace you can send positive nonverbal messages by being on time for meetings and appointments, staying on task during meetings, and giving ample time to appropriate projects and individuals.

Being on time sends a positive nonverbal message in American workplaces.

Space. How we arrange things in the space around us tells something about ourselves and our objectives. Whether the space is a dorm room, an office, or a department, people reveal themselves in the design and grouping of furniture within that space. Generally, the more formal the arrangement, the more formal and closed the communication environment. An executive who seats visitors in a row of chairs across from his desk sends a message of aloofness and desire for separation. A team leader who arranges chairs informally in a circle rather than in straight rows or a rectangular pattern conveys her desire for a more open, egalitarian exchange of ideas. A manager who creates an open office space with few partitions separating workers' desks seeks to encourage an unrestricted flow of communication and work among areas.

The way an office is arranged can send nonverbal messages about the openness of its occupant.

Territory. Each of us has certain areas that we feel are our own territory, whether it's a specific spot or just the space around us. Your father may have a favorite chair in which he is most comfortable, a cook might not tolerate intruders in his or her kitchen, and veteran employees may feel that certain work areas and tools belong to them. We all maintain zones of privacy in which we feel comfortable. Figure 3.5 categorizes the four zones of social interaction among Americans, as formulated by anthropologist Edward T. Hall. Notice that we North Americans are a bit standoffish; only intimate friends and family may stand closer than about 1½ feet. If someone violates that territory, we feel uncomfortable and defensive and may step back to

Figure 3.5 ***Four Space Zones for Social Interaction***

Intimate Zone
(1 to 1 1/2 feet)

Personal Zone
(1 1/2 to 4 feet)

Social Zone
(4 to 12 feet)

Public Zone
(12 or more feet)

reestablish our space. A classic episode in the *Seinfeld* TV program aptly described a close-talker as a "space invader."[28] In the workplace be aware of the territorial needs of others and don't invade their space.

Your appearance and the appearance of your documents convey nonverbal messages.

Appearance of Business Documents. The way a letter, memo, or report looks can have either a positive or a negative effect on the receiver. Envelopes through their postage, stationery, and printing can suggest routine, important, or junk mail. Letters and reports can look neat, professional, well organized, and attractive—or just the opposite. Sloppy, hurriedly written documents convey negative nonverbal messages regarding both the content and the sender. Among the worse offenders are e-mail messages.

Although they seem like conversation, e-mails are business documents that create a permanent record and often a bad impression. Sending an e-mail message full of errors conveys a damaging nonverbal message. It says that the writer doesn't care enough about this message to take the time to make it read well or look good. The sender immediately doubts the credibility of the sender. How much faith can you put in someone who can't spell, capitalize, or punctuate and won't make the effort to communicate clearly?

In succeeding chapters you'll learn how to create documents that send positive nonverbal messages through their appearance, format, organization, readability, and correctness.

Figure 3.6 ***Sending Positive Nonverbal Signals in the Workplace***

Eye contact	Maintain direct but not prolonged eye contact.
Facial expression	Express warmth with frequent smiles.
Posture	Convey self-confidence with erect stance.
Gestures	Suggest accessibility with open-palm gestures.
Time	Be on time; use time judiciously.
Space	Maintain neat, functional work areas.
Territory	Use closeness to show warmth and to reduce status differences.
Business documents	Produce careful, neat, professional, well-organized messages.
Appearance	Be well groomed, neat, and appropriately dressed.

career coach

The Perils of Casual Apparel in the Workplace

Your choice of work clothes sends a strong nonverbal message about you. It also affects the way you work. That's why many employers have mixed feelings about the current trend toward increasingly casual business attire.

What Critics Are Saying

Some employers oppose casual dress because, in their opinion, too many workers push the boundaries of what is acceptable. They contend that absenteeism, tardiness, and flirtatious behavior have increased since dress-down policies began to be implemented. Relaxed dress codes also lead to reduced productivity and lax behavior. Image counselor Judith Rasband claims that the general casualization of America has resulted in an overall decline in civility. "Manners break down, you begin to feel down, and you're not as effective," she says.[29] Others fear that the authority and credibility of casually attired executives, particularly females and minorities, are undermined.[30] Moreover, customers are often turned off by casually attired employees.[31]

What Supporters Are Saying

Regardless of what the critics are saying, employees love casual dress policies. As a result, nine out of ten employers have adopted casual dress days for at least part of the workweek—even if it's just on Fridays during the summer. Supporters argue that comfortable clothes and relaxed working environments lift employee morale, increase employee creativity, and improve internal communication. Employees appreciate reduced clothing-related expenses, while employers use casual dress as a recruitment and retention tool.

Advice for Employees

The following suggestions, gleaned from surveys and articles about casual dress trends in the workplace, can help future and current employees avoid casual dress blunders.

- For job interviews, dress conservatively or call ahead to ask the interviewer or the receptionist what is appropriate.
- Find out what your company allows. Ask whether a dress-down policy is available. Observe what others are wearing on casual dress days.
- If your company has no casual dress policy, volunteer to work with management to develop relevant guidelines, including illustrations of suitable casual attire.
- Avoid wearing the following items (which 80 percent of executives find unacceptable): sweatsuits, spandex, shorts, T-shirts with slogans, bared-midriff outfits, halter tops, tank tops, and flip-flops.[32]
- When meeting customers, dress as well as or better than they do.

Career Application

In small groups or in your full class, debate the following proposition: Resolved: That business casual dress be made the dress standard throughout the United States. Think of arguments beyond those presented here. Your instructor will provide details for arranging the debate.

Appearance of People. The way you look—your clothing, grooming, and posture—telegraphs an instant nonverbal message about you. Based on what they see, viewers make quick judgments about your status, credibility, personality, and potential. Business communicators who look the part are more likely to be successful in working with superiors, colleagues, and customers. Because appearance is such a powerful force in business, some aspiring professionals are turning for help to image consultants (who charge up to $500 an hour!).

What do image consultants say? They suggest investing in appropriate, professional-looking clothing and accessories; quality is more important than quantity. Avoid flashy garments, clunky jewelry, garish makeup, and overpowering colognes. Pay attention to good grooming, including a neat hairstyle, body cleanliness, polished shoes, and clean nails. Project confidence in your posture, both standing and sitting.

The current trend is toward one or more days per week of casual dress at work. Be aware, though, that casual clothes change the image you project and also may affect your work style. See the accompanying Career Coach box regarding the pros and cons of casual apparel.

In the preceding discussion of nonverbal communication, you have learned that each of us gives and responds to thousands of nonverbal messages daily in our personal and work lives. You can harness the power of silent messages by reviewing Figure 3.6 and by studying the tips in the following checklist.

learning objective 6

Checklist of Techniques for Improving Nonverbal Communication Skills in the Workplace

- ✓ **Establish and maintain eye contact.** Remember that in America appropriate eye contact signals interest, attentiveness, strength, and credibility.
- ✓ **Use posture to show interest.** Encourage communication interaction by leaning forward, sitting or standing erect, and looking alert.
- ✓ **Reduce or eliminate physical barriers.** Move out from behind a desk or lectern; shorten lines of communication; arrange meeting chairs in a circle.
- ✓ **Improve your decoding skills.** Watch facial expressions and body language to understand the complete verbal and nonverbal message being communicated.
- ✓ **Probe for more information.** When you perceive nonverbal cues that contradict verbal meanings, politely seek additional clues (*I'm not sure I understand, Please tell me more about . . .*, or *Do you mean that . . .*).
- ✓ **Avoid assigning nonverbal meanings out of context.** Make nonverbal assessments only when you understand a situation or a culture.
- ✓ **Associate with people from diverse cultures.** Learn about other cultures to widen your knowledge and tolerance of intercultural nonverbal messages.
- ✓ **Appreciate the power of appearance.** Keep in mind that the appearance of your business documents, your business space, and yourself send immediate positive or negative messages to receivers.
- ✓ **Observe yourself on videotape.** Ensure that your verbal and nonverbal messages are in sync by taping and evaluating yourself making a presentation.
- ✓ **Enlist friends and family.** Ask them to monitor your conscious and unconscious body movements and gestures to help you become a more effective communicator.

PROCESS TO PRODUCT

Applying Your Skills at L. L. Bean, Inc.

ALTHOUGH MOST OF L. L. Bean's orders used to come from telephone callers, more and more customers are responding online. In praising its Web site, *Forbes* magazine said that "this $1 billion preppy catalog company had successfully made the leap to the Net."[33] Its Web site enables customers to send e-mail to customer satisfaction representatives with questions about their accounts, shopping choices, returns and repairs, international questions, and Outdoor Discovery Schools. With a shift in order volume from the telephone to the Internet and with declining prices in retail apparel, L. L. Bean realized it had to find ways to become more efficient.[34] Layoffs and budget cuts became necessary.

Your Task

Assume that the manager of Customer Satisfaction Learning and Communication faces a big cut in her training budget. She asks you, her assistant, to help her decide what to do. Should she recommend reducing the training budget for telephone reps? Reduce the training budget for online reps? Combine the training programs? In teams or individually, discuss the skills needed by the online reps answering e-mail inquiries. How are these skills similar to those needed by telephone sales reps? Do you think the training programs for each could be combined? In an e-mail message to the manager of Customer Satisfaction Learning and Communication, make a recommendation and provide reasons for your choice. Then, outline six to eight skillful techniques that are equally appropriate for telephone and online sales reps. ■

case study

Summary of Learning Objectives

1 **Explain the importance of listening in the workplace and describe three types of workplace listening.** A large part of the communication process involves listening. Good listeners advance more rapidly in their careers, and listening skills are increasingly important in our economy with its emphasis on customer service. Workers spend 30 to 45 percent of their communication time listening, whereas executives spend 60 to 70 percent. However, most of us listen at only 25 percent efficiency. Workplace listening involves listening to superiors, to colleagues, and to customers. When listening to superiors, take selective notes, don't interrupt, ask pertinent questions, and paraphrase what you hear. When listening to colleagues and teammates, listen critically to recognize facts and listen discriminatingly to identify main ideas and to understand logical arguments. Three listening strategies that are helpful are *dampening, redirecting,* and *reflecting.* When listening to customers, employees should defer judgment, pay attention to content rather than form, listen completely, control emotions, give affirming statements, and invite additional comments.

2 **Discuss the listening process and its barriers.** The listening process involves (a) perception of sounds, (b) interpretation of those sounds, (c) evaluation of meaning, and (d) action, which might involve a physical response or storage of the message in memory for future use. Mental barriers to listening include inattention, prejudgments, differing frames of reference, closed-mindedness, and pseudolistening. Physical and other barriers include hearing impairment, noisy surroundings, speaker's appearance, speaker's

mannerisms, and lag time. Retention can be improved by developing a positive mind-set, structuring the incoming information to form relationships, and reviewing.

3 **Enumerate ten techniques for improving workplace listening.** Listeners can improve their skills by controlling external and internal distractions, becoming actively involved, separating facts from opinions, identifying important facts, refraining from interrupting, asking clarifying questions, paraphrasing, taking advantage of lag time, taking notes to ensure retention, and being aware of gender differences.

4 **Define nonverbal communication and explain its functions.** Nonverbal communication includes all unwritten and unspoken messages, both intentional and unintentional. Its primary functions are to complement and illustrate, to reinforce and accentuate, to replace and substitute, to control and regulate, and to contradict. When verbal and nonverbal messages contradict each other, listeners tend to believe the nonverbal message.

5 **Describe the forms of nonverbal communication and how they can be used positively in your career.** Nonverbal communication takes many forms including eye contact, facial expressions, posture and gestures, as well as the use of time, space, and territory. Appearance of business documents and of people also sends silent messages. Eye contact should be direct but not prolonged; facial expression should express warmth with frequent smiles. Posture should convey self-confidence, and gestures should suggest accessibility. Being on time and maintaining neat, functional work areas send positive nonverbal messages. Use closeness to show warmth and to reduce status differences. Strive for neat, professional, well-organized business messages; and be well groomed, neat, and appropriately dressed.

6 **List specific techniques for improving nonverbal communication skills in the workplace.** To improve your nonverbal skills, establish and maintain eye contact, use posture to show interest, reduce or eliminate physical barriers, improve your decoding skills, probe for more information, avoid assigning nonverbal meanings out of context, associate with people from diverse cultures, appreciate the power of appearance, observe yourself on videotape, and enlist friends and family to monitor your conscious and unconscious body movements and gestures.

chapter review

1. According to experts, we ignore, forget, distort, or misunderstand 75 percent of everything we hear. Why are we such poor listeners? (Obj. 1)
2. How can you improve your listening when superiors are giving instructions, assignments, and explanations? (Obj. 1)
3. What are three strategies that help you listen in team and group interactions? (Obj. 1)
4. How can employees do a better job of listening to customers? (Obj. 1)
5. Describe the four elements in the listening process. (Obj. 2).
6. How can listeners improve retention? (Obj. 2)
7. What are ten techniques for improving workplace listening? Be prepared to explain each. (Obj. 3)
8. Define *nonverbal communication.* (Obj. 4)
9. List five functions of nonverbal communication. Give an original example of each. (Obj. 4)
10. When verbal and nonverbal messages disagree, which message does the receiver consider more truthful? Give an example. (Obj. 4)
11. North Americans are said to be a little "standoffish." What does this mean? (Obj. 5)
12. How can posture send nonverbal messages? (Obj. 5)
13. How can the use of space send nonverbal messages? (Obj. 5)
14. What nonverbal messages are sent by organizations with casual dress codes? (Obj. 5)
15. List ten techniques for improving nonverbal communication skills in the workplace. (Obj. 6)

critical thinking

1. Why do executives and managers spend more time listening than do workers? (Obj. 1)
2. Americans are said to have the world's worst listening skills.[35] Why do you think Americans get such a bad rap? (Objs. 1–3)
3. Why can two 280-pound professional football players slap each other on the rear end during a game, whereas two business associates in a meeting cannot? What principle of nonverbal communication can you extract from this example? (Obj. 4)
4. What arguments could you give for or against the idea that body language is a science with principles that can be interpreted accurately by specialists? (Obj. 4)
5. **Ethical Issue:** Tim, a member of your workplace team, talks too much, hogs the limelight, and frequently strays from the target topic. In an important meeting he announces, "Hey, I want you all to listen up. I've got this cool new idea, and you're gonna love it!" Is it unethical for you to tune Tim out based on your past experience with his digressions? You want to sigh deeply and shout "Not again!" You're inclined to slump in your chair, slam your pencil down on the table, and stop taking notes. What is your ethical responsibility? What nonverbal message should you send?

THREE GREAT RESOURCES FOR YOU!

1. Guffey Student Web Site

http://guffey.swlearning.com

Your companion Web site offers chapter review quizzes, WebThink activities, updated chapter URLs, and many additional resources.

2. Guffey XTRA!

http://guffeyxtra.swlearning.com

This online study assistant includes Your Personal Language Trainer, Speak Right!, Spell Right!, bonus online chapters, Documents for Analysis, PowerPoint slides, and much more.

3. Student Study Guide

Self-checked workbook activities and applications review chapter concepts and develop career skills.

activities

3.1 Observing Listening Behavior (Objs. 1–3)

LISTENING

You've probably never paid much attention to listening. But now that you have studied it, you have become more conscious of both good and bad listening behavior.

Your Task. For one week focus on the listening behavior of people around you—at work, at school, at home. Make a list of five good listening habits that you see and five bad habits. Identify the situation and participants for each item on your list. Who is the best listener you know? What makes that person a good listener? Be prepared to discuss your responses in class, with your team, or in a memo to your instructor.

3.2 Listening in the Workplace (Objs. 1 and 5)

TEAM

Do the listening skills and behaviors of individuals differ depending on their careers?

Your Task. Your instructor will divide you into teams and give each team a role to discuss, such as business executive, teacher, physician, police officer, attorney, accountant, administrative assistant, mentor, or team leader. Create a list of verbal and nonverbal cues that a member of this profession would display to indicate that he or she is listening. Would the cues and behavior change if the person were trying to listen discriminatively versus critically? How?

3.3 Active Listening (Objs. 2 and 3)

"Just because you're talking doesn't mean I'm listening," asserts communication consultant Harvey McChesney III.[36] You decide to use his quotation as the opening in a talk about "Active Listening" that you must give before your Toastmasters group.

Your Task. Prepare a list of eight to ten active listening tips appropriate for someone going into your field (such as management, marketing, law enforcement, accounting, corporate communication, and so forth). Include sentences that could serve as a transition from the opening quotation to your list.

3.4 Overcoming Listening Barriers: Attending a Boring Lecture (Obj. 2)

Companies often get into a bind when they must sell the homes of employees who are transferred. At one time the Wilmington, Delaware-based DuPont Company had 800 unsold homes valued at $275 million in its inventory. Your boss, the manager of relocation for DuPont, asks you to learn more about mortgage subsidies and other techniques for reducing the company's excessive relocation costs for transferred employees.[37]

Your Task. You must attend a lecture and training session sponsored by GMAC Global Relocation Services. You expect this to be hugely boring because you know nothing about mortgages. What mental and physical listening barriers could you anticipate for this assignment? How could you overcome these barriers?

3.5 Listening and Retention: How Much Can You Remember? (Objs. 2 and 3)

LISTENING

After studying the suggestions in this chapter for improving listening, you should be able to conduct a before-and-after study.

Your Task. Listen to a 30-minute segment of TV news using your normal listening habits. When you finish, make a list of the major items you remember, recording names, places, and figures. A day later watch the same 30-minute segment but put to use the good listening tips in this chapter, including taking selective notes and possibly using memory devices. When the segment is completed, make a list of the major items you remember. Which experience provided more information? What made a major difference for you?

3.6 Rating Your Listening Skills (Objs. 1–3)

You can learn whether your listening skills are excellent or deficient by completing a brief quiz.

Your Task. Take *Dr. Guffey's Listening Quiz* at **http://guffey.swlearning.com**. What two listening behaviors do you think you need to work on the most?

3.7 Evaluating Trained and Untrained Listeners (Objs. 1–3)

Play the part of a training consultant hired to help improve customer service at a high-volume travel agency. During one training session, you hear the following comments from current customer service representatives.

Your Task. Based on what you learned in this chapter (and especially Figure 3.1), would you characterize the speaker as a trained or an untrained listener, and what advice would you give to improve the speaker's listening skills?

a. "You know what I can't stand? Those customers who call to complain but distort and exaggerate what happened. I nail them on every point that I know can't be true."

b. "It's pretty hard to take seriously a customer whose accent and grammar are so bad that you know she could never afford the trip to Hawaii that she's asking about."

c. "My biggest gripe are those people who want to complain about something that went wrong—but they can't stick to the facts. They insist on telling you every little detail."

d. "When I have a customer who wants to tell a long story, I cut her off and get the conversation under control with my questions."

e. "I think the best way to handle unhappy customers is silence. I try not to encourage them."

f. "When the caller is upset, I try to listen carefully and occasionally give affirming comments."

g. "You know all the forms we have to fill out? The best time to do that is while you're listening to customers. I save a lot of time that way."

h. "When someone gets snippy with me, I come right back with more of the same. Works every time."

i. "I don't waste time with customers who ramble. After the first few words, I can always tell what they want."

3.8 Listening to Nonnative Speakers (Objs. 1–3)

LISTENING

In our increasingly multicultural workplace and global economy, you will probably have occasion to listen to nonnative speakers. To improve your skills and widen your perspective, your instructor will present a video, audiotape, or person speaking a nonnative variety of English (preferably on a topic with "real" content). You should have a copy of the pronunciation guide from a college-level dictionary showing how vowels and consonants are pronounced in standard English.
Your Task. As you listen to the presentation, focus on any differences in the pronunciation of vowels and consonants. Study your chart. Then list the differences and similarities between the pronunciation you heard and that on your dictionary chart. Do you hear any patterns, such as the substitution of *b*'s for *p*'s, *v*'s for *w*'s, and *r*'s for *l*'s? If you recognize a pattern, how can that help you improve your listening comprehension? Also, summarize the content of the presentation. Did any misunderstandings result from mispronunciation? Submit your written observations to your instructor or discuss them in class.

3.9 Distinguishing Facts From Opinions (Obj. 3)

TEAM

Good listeners make an effort to distinguish facts from opinions. Facts can be checked and verified through objective evidence. Opinions express beliefs, feelings, or judgments that cannot be proven.
Your Task. In teams, discuss the following statements. Decide whether they are facts or opinions. Be prepared to justify your choices.

- **a.** Most workers spend 30 to 40 percent of their communication time listening, whereas executives spend 60 to 70 percent of their communication time listening.
- **b.** Because they have been promoted, managers have better listening skills than subordinates do.
- **c.** Feedback helps a receiver know whether the message got through clearly.
- **d.** Women are good listeners.
- **e.** Most people who learn how to listen more accurately are amazed when they find out what they have been missing.
- **f.** Oprah Winfrey hosts a syndicated TV talk show.
- **g.** One reason Oprah Winfrey is so successful is that she is a good listener.
- **h.** Capital punishment is legalized murder.

3.10 Listening Too Fast: Avoiding Miscommunication (Objs. 1–3)

INFOTRAC

Many physicians think they are good communicators. They're intelligent, educated, and articulate. Yet, many have bad listening habits, according to Jeffrey J. Denning.
Your Task. Using InfoTrac, locate "How to Improve Your Listening Skills, Avoid Mixups" by Jeffrey J. Denning (*Opthamology Times*). In this article the author names a number of bad listening habits attributed to physicians. But are these bad habits limited to physicians? Read the article and then answer the following questions:

- **a.** What are four bad listening habits of physicians? Give an example of each.
- **b.** What are six good listening habits that appear as a checklist accompanying the article?
- **c.** Are the bad habits described in the article restricted to physicians? Are the good techniques equally appropriate for all communicators? Explain.

3.11 Nonverbal Communication: Recognizing Functions (Obj. 4)

Most of us use nonverbal cues and react to them unconsciously. We seldom think about the functions they serve.
Your Task. To become more aware of the functions of nonverbal communication, keep a log for one week. Observe how nonverbal communication is used by friends, family, instructors, coworkers, managers, politicians, newsmakers, businesses, and others. For each of the five functions of nonverbal communication identified in this chapter, list examples illustrating that function. For example, under "To reinforce and accentuate," you might list a friend who whispers a message to you, thus suggesting that it is a secret. Under "To control and regulate," you might list the steady gaze of your instructor who has targeted a student not paying attention. Train yourself to become more observant, and begin making notes in your log. How many examples can you name for each of the five functions? Be prepared to submit your list or discuss it in class.

3.12 Nonverbal Communication: How to Be More Influential (Obj. 6)

Assume you've just been hired into a prestigious job and you want to make a good impression. You also want very much to become influential in the organization.
Your Task. When you attend meetings, what nonverbal behaviors and signals can you send that will make a good impression as well as improve your influence? In interacting with colleagues, what nonverbal behavior will make you more impressive and influential?

3.13 Nonverbal Communication: Document Appearance (Objs. 5 and 6)

How does the appearance of a document send a nonverbal message?
Your Task. Select several business letters and envelopes that you have received at home or work. Analyze the appearance

and nonverbal message the letters and envelopes send. Consider the amount of postage, method of delivery, correctness of address, kind of stationery, typeface(s), format, and neatness. What assumptions did you make when you saw the envelopes and letters?

3.14 Body Language (Objs. 5 and 6)

What attitudes do the following body movements suggest to you? Do these movements always mean the same thing? What part does context play in your interpretations?

- **a.** Whistling, wringing hands
- **b.** Bowed posture, twiddling thumbs
- **c.** Steepled hands, sprawling position
- **d.** Rubbing hand through hair
- **e.** Open hands, unbuttoned coat
- **f.** Wringing hands, tugging ears

3.15 Nonverbal Communication: Universal Sign for "I Goofed" (Objs. 4–6)

CRITICAL THINKING | TEAM

In an effort to promote tranquility on the highways and reduce road rage, motorists submitted the following suggestions. They were sent to a newspaper columnist who asked for a universal nonverbal signal admitting that a driver "goofed."[38]

Your Task. In small groups consider the pros and cons for each of the following gestures intended as an apology when a driver makes a mistake. Why would some fail?

- **a.** Lower your head slightly and bonk yourself on the forehead with the side of your closed fist. The message is clear: "I'm stupid. I shouldn't have done that."
- **b.** Make a temple with your hands, as if you were praying.
- **c.** Move the index finger of your right hand back and forth across your neck—as if you are cutting your throat.
- **d.** Flash the well-known peace sign. Hold up the index and middle fingers of one hand, making a *V*, as in Victory.
- **e.** Place the flat of your hands against your cheeks, as children do when they've made a mistake.
- **f.** Clasp your hand over your mouth, raise your brows, and shrug your shoulders.
- **g.** Use your knuckles to knock on the side of your head. Translation: "Oops! Engage brain."
- **h.** Place your right hand high on your chest and pat a few times, like a basketball player who drops a pass or a football player who makes a bad throw. This says, "I'll take the blame."
- **i.** Place your right fist over the middle of your chest and move it in a circular motion. This is universal sign language for "I'm sorry."
- **j.** Open your window and tap the top of your car roof with your hand.
- **k.** Smile and raise both arms, palms outward, which is a universal gesture for surrender or forgiveness.
- **l.** Use the military salute, which is simple and shows respect.
- **m.** Flash your biggest smile, point at yourself with your right thumb and move your head from left to right, as if to say, "I can't believe I did that."

3.16 Verbal vs. Nonverbal Signals (Objs. 4–6)

To show the power of nonverbal cues, the president of a large East Coast consulting company uses the following demonstration with new employees. Raising his right hand, he touches his pointer finger to his thumb to form a circle. Then he asks new employees in the session to do likewise. When everyone has a finger-thumb circle formed, the president tells each to touch that circle to the chin. But as he says this, he touches his own finger-thumb circle to his cheek. What happens? You guessed it! About 80 percent of the group follow what they see the president do rather than following what they hear.[39]

Your Task. Try this same demonstration with several of your friends, family members, or work colleagues. Which is more effective—verbal or nonverbal signals? What conclusion could you draw from this demonstration? Do you think that nonverbal signals are always more meaningful than verbal ones? What other factors in the communication process might determine whether verbal or nonverbal signals were more important?

3.17 Nonverbal Signals Sent by Business Casual Dress (Objs. 5 and 6)

LISTENING | SPEAKING | TEAM

Although many employers are beginning to allow casual dress, not all employers and customers are happy with the results. To learn more about the implementation, acceptance, and effects of casual dress programs, select one of the following activities. All of the following activities involve some form of interviewing. You can learn how to become a good interviewer by checking out the online chapter, "Interviewing," at **Xtra!** (**http://guffeyxtra.swlearning.com**). Click *Asking Good Questions* and *Checklist for Conducting Informational and Other Interviews.*

Your Task

- **a.** In teams, gather information from human resource directors to determine which companies allow business casual dress, how often, and under what specific conditions. The information may be collected by personal interviews, by e-mail, or by telephone.
- **b.** In teams, conduct inquiring-reporter interviews. Ask individuals in the community how they react to casual dress in the workplace. Develop a set of standard interview questions.

c. In teams, visit local businesses on both business casual days and on traditional business dress days. Compare and contrast the effects of different business dress standards on such factors as the projected image of the company, the nature of the interactions with customers and with fellow employees, the morale of employees, and the productivity of employees. What generalizations can you draw from your findings?

3.18 Role-Playing Business Casual Dress-Related Guidance (Objs. 5 and 6)

LISTENING | SPEAKING

Supervisors in the workplace must occasionally deliver dress-related guidance to workers who may have dressed inappropriately for work. The following situations, written by Dr. James Calvert Scott, provide excellent opportunities for you to develop skills in applying diplomatic, positive feedback in realistic workplace contexts.[40]

Your Task. Volunteer (or be assigned) the role of supervisor. Assume your organization has an existing business casual dress policy. Your job is to encourage an employee to comply with the dress code in the following situations:

a. A 35-year-old male systems analyst is working in his glass-walled private office wearing a T-shirt that has an obscene slogan printed on the back.

b. A 21-year-old secretary working in an open-office area is wearing a tight-fitting cropped top and hip-hugger pants that expose her pierced navel.

c. A 17-year-old high school marketing intern is wearing low-riding baggy pants that expose the top three inches of his underwear as he works in the public area assigned to the marketing division.

d. A 43-year-old custodian is wearing loose-fitting sandals as he tries to move a 55-gallon drum of carpet-cleaning solution from the loading dock to his supply room.

e. A 54-year-old obese female customer service representative who always wears tight-fitting pantsuits and frequently works with offsite clients in their offices shakes uncontrollably every time she moves, causing those around her to smirk and chuckle behind her back—and occasionally to her face.

3.19 Defining "Business Casual" (Objs. 5 and 6)

TEAM | WEB

Although many business organizations are adopting business casual dress, most people cannot define the term. Your boss asks your internship team to use the Web to find out exactly what "business casual" means.

Your Task. Using a good search engine (such as **www.google.com**), explore the Web for "business casual dress code." A few Web sites actually try to define the term and give examples of appropriate clothing. Visit several sites and decide whether they are reliable enough to use as sources of accurate information. Print several relevant pages. Get together with your team and compare notes. Then write a memo to your boss explaining what men and women should and shouldn't wear on business casual days.

3.20 Consumer Rebate Ripoffs: Making Sure You Get Yours

CONSUMER | TEAM | WEB

Recently you bought a new cell phone, motivated in part by the lure of a $50 mail-in rebate. You filled out all the paperwork and submitted your rebate application. But three months passed and you were getting worried that you would never see that $50 rebate check. Finally, it did arrive and you sighed in relief. While you were sweating out the wait for the check, you told some of your friends at work that you were totally turned off by rebates in general. Andy Miller, editor of the company newsletter, heard your complaint and asked you to help him collect information for a newsletter article. He wants to call the article "Ripoff Rebates: Tips for Making Sure Your Rebate Arrives."

Your Task. In teams or individually, collect information about rebates. First, interview friends and colleagues and listen to their stories. Have they been successful in obtaining rebates? Employ some of the listening techniques you learned in this chapter. Then use a search engine such as Google (**www.google.com**) to look for Web articles or discussions regarding consumer rebates. Find at least four examples of people who have had trouble getting promised rebates. Compile a list of five or six suggestions that can help people get the rebates to which they are entitled. Discuss your findings with your team and submit your information individually or as a group to Andy Miller in a memo or in a class discussion.

Photo: © Photodisc Red / Getty Images

C.L.U.E. review 3

On a separate sheet edit the following sentences to correct faults in grammar, capitalization, punctuation, numbers, spelling, proofreading, and word use.

1. Every one knows how to listen but many of us listen at only twenty-five per cent effecency.
2. Its wise to avoid arguing or criticizing, when listening to a superior.
3. The 4 stages of listening are: Perception, Interpretation, Evaluation and Action.
4. To improve retention you should take notes, and rewrite it immediatley after listening.
5. While waiting for the speakers next idea you should review what was all ready spoke.
6. High-status and self-confidence is conveyed by erect posture.
7. On May 12th, the company President awarded bonuses to Tyler and I, however we didn't recieve our checks until June first.
8. In a poll of nearly three thousand employees only 1/3 felt that there companys' valued there opinions and suggestion.
9. The appearance and mannerisms of a speaker effects a listeners evaluation of a message.
10. A list of suggestions for improving retention of a speakers ideas are found in an article titled Best Listening Habits which appeared in Fortune.

chapter 4

Communicating Across Cultures

objectives

1 Discuss three significant trends related to the increasing importance of intercultural communication.

2 Define *culture*. Describe five significant characteristics of culture, and compare and contrast five key dimensions of culture.

3 Explain the effects of ethnocentrism, tolerance, and patience in achieving intercultural proficiency.

4 Illustrate how to improve nonverbal and oral communication in intercultural environments.

5 Illustrate how to improve written messages in intercultural environments.

6 Discuss intercultural ethics, including ethics abroad, bribery, prevailing customs, and methods for coping.

7 Explain the challenge of capitalizing on workforce diversity, including its dividends and its divisiveness. List tips for improving harmony and communication among diverse workplace audiences.

COMMUNICATION IN PROCESS

Mighty Wal-Mart Eyes Famously Finicky Japanese Consumers

IT'S 8:15 a.m. and 50 managers of the Seiyu supermarket in Japan are performing the Wal-Mart morning ritual. "Give me an S!" shouts a Japanese boss. The resounding "S!" reverberates through the second floor headquarters. The chant is repeated until the group spells "S-E-I-Y-U." "Who's No. 1?" barks the cheerleading boss. "Customers!" boom the Japanese managers as they punch the air with their fists.[1]

Routines like this boost employee morale in the United States. And if they work here, they must work in Japan, figures Wal-Mart. Seiyu employees are learning Wal-Mart routines because Wal-Mart is purchasing and revamping the Seiyu food and clothing chain to gain a foothold in Japan. Wal-Mart is betting big that it can succeed in a country where countless other foreign companies have failed.

Why expand into Japan, where consumers are notoriously fickle?[2] Expanding its international market is a primary push for Wal-Mart because sales growth is declining at home. With fewer new stores opening in the United States, global expansion is a must for Wal-Mart. The Japanese market is especially attractive because it is the second largest economy in the world, and its consumers are Asia's richest.[3] What's more, Japanese consumers are becoming more price conscious, and discounting is increasingly appealing.

Although hugely successful in the United States, Wal-Mart must overcome significant distribution, location, and cultural barriers to become profitable in Japan. Costly real estate and cramped space make it difficult to build the big stores common in the United States. In addition to restricted space, its hallmark "everyday low prices" strategy is confusing to local shoppers accustomed to poring over newspaper ads and scurrying around town for the best buys.

Equally disturbing is the resistance of employees to sell the Wal-Mart way. For one thing, they balk at the "10-foot rule," which encourages them to offer assistance to any customer within 10 feet. To overcome these hurdles, workers are receiving a heavy dose of "culture training." They're being taught to be more outspoken, upbeat, and goal oriented.

Wary shoppers, unfamiliar with English "sale" signs, shop tentatively as Wal-Mart expands into Japanese markets.

Photo: © AP / Wide World Photos

Critical Thinking

- What domestic and global changes are taking place that encourage the international expansion of companies such as Wal-Mart?
- What other U.S. businesses can you name that have merged with foreign companies or expanded to become multinational in scope? Have you heard of any notable successes or failures?
- Should multinational companies impose their local culture on employees in other countries?

www.wal-mart.com

CONTINUED ON PAGE 113

case study

The Increasing Importance of Intercultural Communication

learning objective

1

The "global village" predicted many years ago is increasingly becoming a reality. National and even local businesses push products across borders and seek customers in diverse foreign markets. Especially in North America, this movement toward a global economy has swelled to a torrent. To better compete, many organizations form multinational alliances, such as that between Wal-Mart, the U.S. super discounter, and Seiyu, Japan's fifth-largest food and retail chain. But many expanding companies stumble when they are forced to confront obstacles never before encountered.

Learning more about how culture affects behavior helps you reduce friction and misunderstandings.

Significant obstacles involve misunderstandings and contrary views resulting from intercultural differences. You may face such intercultural differences in your current or future jobs. Your employers, fellow workers, or clients could very well be from other countries. You may travel abroad for your employer or on your own. Learning more about the powerful effect that culture has on behavior will help you reduce friction and misunderstanding in your dealings with people from other cultures. Before examining strategies for helping you surmount intercultural obstacles, let's take a closer look at three significant trends: (1) the globalization of markets, (2) technological advancements, and (3) an intercultural workforce.

Globalization of Markets

National boundaries mean less as businesses expand through mergers, alliances, and acquisitions.

Doing business beyond our borders is now commonplace. Procter & Gamble is selling disposable diapers in Asia; Rubbermaid would like to see its plastic products in all European kitchens; and McDonald's and Starbucks have establishments around the world. Not only are market borders blurring, but acquisitions, mergers, and alliances are obscuring the nationality of many companies. Firestone is owned by Japan's Bridgestone; Sylvania is controlled by German lighting giant OSARM; and Chrysler has merged with Daimler-Benz, makers of Mercedes luxury cars. After acquiring a 49-store department chain in Brazil, J. C. Penney is growing faster there than in this country.[4] Two thirds of Colgate-Palmolive's employees work outside North America, and Nike is raking in more revenue overseas than in the United States.

American companies in global markets must adapt to other cultures.

To be successful in this interdependent global village, American companies are increasingly finding it necessary to adapt to other cultures. In China and Korea, Procter & Gamble learned to promote unisex white diapers. Although Americans preferred pink for girls and blue for boys, Korean and Chinese housewives balked at pink diapers. In a society where intense sexism favors boys, shoppers preferred white diapers that did not signal their child's sex.[5] In promoting its shoes and apparel to kids from Rome to Rio De Janeiro, Nike ads feature Brazilian soccer star Ronaldo, rather than a U.S. basketball star.[6] To sell its laundry products in Europe, Unilever learned that Germans demand a product that's gentle on lakes and rivers. Spaniards wanted cheaper products that get shirts white and soft. And Greeks preferred small packages that were cheap and easy to carry home.[7] To sell ketchup in Japan, H. J. Heinz had to overcome a cultural resistance to sweet flavors. Thus, it offered Japanese homemakers cooking lessons instructing them how to use the sugary red sauce on omelets, sausages, and pasta.[8] Domino's Pizza also catered to the Japanese by adding squid to its pizza toppings.[9]

Favorable trade agreements, declining domestic markets, and the growth of the middle class fuel the expansion of global markets.

What's caused this rush toward globalization of markets and blurring of national identities? Many companies, such as Wal-Mart, are increasingly looking overseas as domestic markets mature. They can no longer expect double-digit sales growth at home. Another significant factor is the passage of favorable trade agreements. The

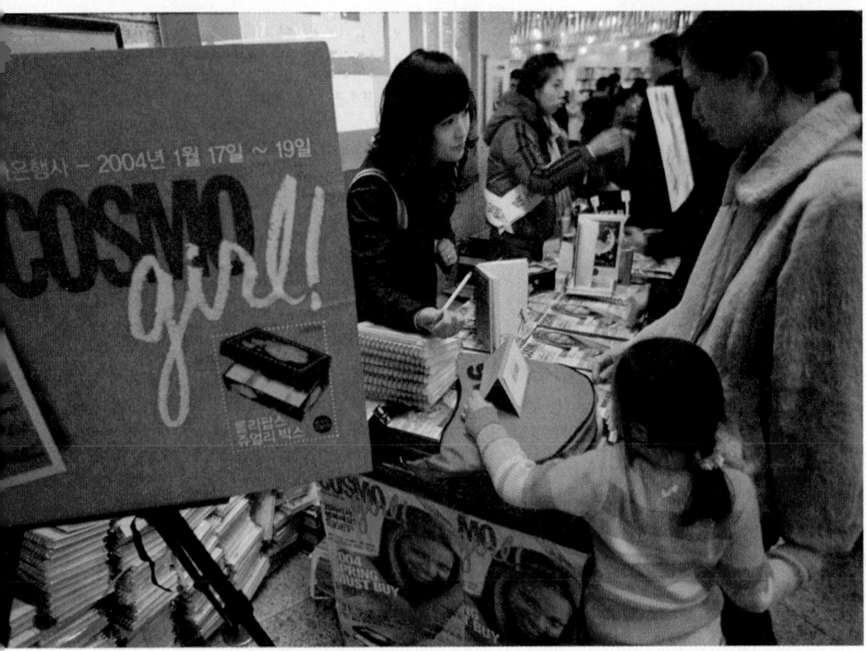

Driven by global brands in need of advertising vehicles in new markets, a dizzying array of Western magazines, such as Cosmo Girl*, compete for new customers around the world. In adapting to the Seoul market, the Korean version of* Cosmo Girl *enticed new customers with a gift bonanza including a shoulder bag, calendar, makeup box, and money-saving coupon. U.S. companies and brands are increasingly operating on a global basis.*

General Agreement on Tariffs and Trade (GATT) promotes open trade globally, and the North American Free Trade Agreement (NAFTA) expands free trade among Canada, the United States, and Mexico. NAFTA created the largest and richest free-trade region on earth.[10] The opening of Eastern Europe and the shift away from communism in Russia have also fueled the progress toward expanding world markets. And China's admission to the World Trade Organization opens its skyrocketing economy to world markets.[11]

Equally important to expanding global markets is the explosive growth of the middle class. Parts of the world formerly considered underdeveloped now boast robust middle classes. And these consumers crave everything from cola to cell phones. But probably the most important factor in the rise of the global market is the development of new transportation and information technologies.

Technological Advancements

Advancements in transportation and information technologies contribute to global interconnectivity.

Amazing new transportation and information technologies are major contributors to the development of our global interconnectivity. Supersonic planes now carry goods and passengers to other continents overnight. As a result, produce shoppers in Japan can choose from the finest apples, artichokes, avocados, and pears only hours after they were picked in California. Americans enjoy bouquets of tulips, roses, and exotic lilies soon after harvesting in Holland and Colombia. In fact, 70 percent of the cut flowers in the United States now come from Colombia in South America. Continent-hopping planes are so fast and reliable that most of the world is rapidly becoming an open market.

Along with transportation progress, the global economy is being fueled by incredible advancements in communication technologies. The Internet now permits instantaneous oral and written communication across time zones and continents. Managers in Miami or Milwaukee can use high-speed data systems to swap marketing plans instantly with their counterparts in Milan or Munich. IBM now relies on 5,000 programmers in India to solve intricate computer problems and return the solutions overnight via digital transmission.[12] Employees at Procter & Gamble send their payroll questions to back-office service centers in England, Costa Rica, or Manila.[13] Fashion designers at Liz Claiborne can snap a digital photo of a garment and immediately transmit the image to manufacturers in Hong Kong and Djakarta, Indonesia.[14] They can even include a video clip to show a tricky alteration.

Companies use the Web to sell products, provide support, offer service, investigate the competition, and link to suppliers.

Moreover, the growth of electronic commerce (e-commerce) has made every marketer with a Web site a global company. Companies depend on the Web to sell products, provide technical support, offer customer service, investigate the competition, and link directly to suppliers. Many multinational companies are now establishing country-specific Web sites, as discussed in the accompanying Tech Talk box and illustrated by the NBA China Web site shown in Figure 4.1.

FIGURE 4.1 *Screen Capture of China Web site for NBA*

To capitalize on the growing number of Internet users overseas, more U.S. Web sites are speaking their language. The National Basketball Association now has nine versions of NBA.com aimed at foreign markets. Interest is particularly high at the China NBA site, written entirely in Chinese characters, since Yao Ming became a superstar for the Houston Rockets.

Internal networks called *intranets* streamline business processes and improve access to critical company information. Through intranets employees have access to information that formerly had to be printed, such as a company phone book, training manuals, job postings, employee newsletters, sales figures, price lists, and even confidential reports, which can be password-protected. The Internet and the Web are changing the way we do business and the way we communicate. These advancements in communication and transportation have made markets and jobs more accessible. They've also made the world of business more efficient and more globally interdependent. You can learn more about intranets and other communication technologies in an online chapter called "Managing Communication Technology" available with **Xtra! (http://guffeyxtra.swlearning.com)**.

Intercultural Workforce

As world commerce mingles more and more, another trend gives intercultural communication increasing importance: people are on the move. Lured by the prospects of peace, prosperity, education, or a fresh start, persons from many cultures are moving to countries promising to fulfill their dreams. For generations the two most popular destinations have been the United States and Canada.

Because of increases in immigration, foreign-born persons are an ever-growing portion of the total U.S. population. Over the next 50 years, the population of the United States is expected to grow by nearly 50 percent, from about 275 million in the year 2000 to an estimated 394 million people in 2050. And two thirds of the increase will be due to net immigration.[15] Estimates also suggest that immigrants will account for half of all new U.S. workers in the years ahead.[16]

Immigration makes intercultural communication skills increasingly necessary.

This influx of immigrants is reshaping American and Canadian societies. Earlier immigrants were thought to be part of a "melting pot" of ethnic groups. Today,

tech talk

Being Interculturally Correct on the Web

Early Web sites were almost always in English and meant for Americans. But as online access grows around the world, multinational companies are revamping their sites. Sony now hosts Web sites in six regions of the world. In Europe it sponsors sites in 42 countries with native language content. The National Football League launched a Chinese version of its usual NFL.com fare but with the text translated into Mandarin Chinese. And the National Basketball Association now has nine versions of NBA.com aimed at foreign markets. As Internet use grows abroad, people in other countries are increasingly asserting their right to be spoken to in their own language. What should companies do when they decide to go global on the Web?

- **Learn the local lingo.** Other countries have developed their own Web jargon and iconography. *Home page* is "pagina inicial" (initial page) in Spanish and "page d'accueil" (welcome page) in French. Experts warn against simply translating English words page by page. Hiring a proficient translator is a better idea.[17]
- **Check icons.** American Web surfers easily recognize the mailbox, but in Europe a more universal icon would be an envelope. Test images with local residents.
- **Relax restrictions on consistency.** Allow flexibility to meet local tastes. For example, McDonald's main site greets visitors with the golden arches and a Ronald McDonald-red background. The Japanese site, though, complements the McDonald's red and gold with pinks and browns, which are more pleasing in their culture.
- **Keep the message simple.** Whether in English or the local language, use simple, easily translated words. Avoid slang, jargon, acronyms, or ambiguous expressions.
- **Customize Web content.** Avoid conflict with local customs, laws, and attitudes. For example, the Web page of a car manufacturer showed a hiker standing next to a car. But in Mexico, hikers are poor people who can't afford cars, so it wasn't acceptable to show someone who wanted to be a hiker.[18] Tailor Web marketing content to local holidays and events.
- **Develop the site together.** The best foreign Web sites for multinational companies are developed when domestic and foreign webmasters work together. Start early and build rapport, recommends Judy Newby, McDonald's webmaster in Oakbrook, Illinois.[19]

Career Application

Compare the foreign and domestic sites of several multinational companies such as Sony (**http://www.sony.com**—see index of sites), United Parcel Service (**http://ups.com**), Reebok (**http://www.reebok.com**), and McDonald's (**http://www.mcdonalds.com**). Are design, content, and navigation similar for the domestic and foreign sites? Is any English used on the foreign site?

A "melting pot" of immigrants is changing into a "tossed salad" or "spicy stew," with many unique flavors.

they are more like a "tossed salad" or "spicy stew," with each group contributing its own unique flavor. Instead of the exception, cultural diversity is increasingly the norm. As we seek to accommodate multiethnic neighborhoods, multinational companies, and an intercultural workforce, we can expect some changes to happen smoothly. Other changes will involve conflict and resentment, especially for people losing their positions of power and privilege. Learning how to manage intercultural conflict is an important part of the education of any business communicator.

Understanding Culture

Every country or region within a country has a unique common heritage, joint experience, or shared learning. This shared background produces the culture of a region, country, or society. For our purposes, *culture* may be defined as the complex system of values, traits, morals, and customs shared by a society. Culture teaches people how to behave, and it conditions their reactions.

learning objective

2

The Computer as Cultural Metaphor

People are like computers who are controlled by operating systems—their cultures.

In some respects we are like computers that are controlled by operating systems—our cultures. Anthropologists Edward T. Hall and Mildred Reed Hall suggested that culture is "a system for creating, sending, storing, and processing information." Sounds rather like the standard definition for a computer, doesn't it? This useful metaphor helps us better understand how culture operates. Think of your body as the hardware of a computer. Computers are controlled by specific operating systems, such as Unix, Linux, and Windows. They also have software that controls specific applications, such as word processing, spreadsheets, and presentations. When you are functioning under one operating system, say as a European North American, you behave like others in that group. But at times you may be controlled by another operating system, say, when you are in a situation where you are functioning as a female. Society programs men and women to act differently. Gender, race, age, religion, and many other factors affect our behavior. These factors are like operating systems that program us to behave in certain patterns.

Just as computers with differing operating systems have difficulty communicating, so do people from differing cultures.

Just as you cannot run a Unix program on a Windows machine, so do people from one culture have difficulty getting through to those from another culture. Because individuals have more than one operating system, they do not always behave as expected. And just as operating systems can control many software applications, people are further differentiated by the software application that may be operating at any given time. For example, work cultures differ remarkably from one organization to another. When people conditioned to work in casual surroundings are placed in work cultures that are more formal and regimented, they may experience culture shock.

The important thing to remember is that culture is a powerful operating force that conditions the way we think and behave. And yet, we are not truly computers. As thinking individuals, we are extraordinarily flexible and are capable of phenomenal change. The purpose of this chapter is to broaden your view of culture and open your mind to flexible attitudes so that you can avoid frustration when cultural adjustment is necessary.

Characteristics of Culture

Understanding basic characteristics of culture helps us make adjustments and accommodations.

Culture is shaped by attitudes learned in childhood and later internalized in adulthood. As we enter this current period of globalization and interculturalism, we should expect to make adjustments and adopt new attitudes. Adjustment and accommodation will be easier if we understand some basic characteristics of culture.

Culture Is Learned. Rules, values, and attitudes of a culture are not inherent. They are learned and passed down from generation to generation. For example, in many Middle Eastern and some Asian cultures, same-sex people may walk hand-in-hand in the street, but opposite-sex people may not do so. In Arab cultures conversations are often held in close proximity, sometimes nose to nose. But in Western cultures if a person stands too close, one may react as if violated: "He was all over me like a rash." Cultural rules of behavior learned from your family and society are conditioned from early childhood.

Cultures Are Inherently Logical. The rules in any culture originated to reinforce that culture's values and beliefs. They act as normative forces. For example, in Japan the original Barbie doll was a failure for many reasons, one of which was her toothy smile.[20] This is a country where women cover their mouths with their hands when they laugh so as not to expose their teeth. Exposing one's teeth is not only immodest but also aggressive. Although current cultural behavior may sometimes seem silly and illogical, nearly all serious rules and values originate in deep-seated beliefs. Rules about exposing teeth or how close to stand are linked to values about sexuality, aggression, modesty, and respect. Acknowledging the inherent logic of a culture is extremely important when learning to accept behavior that differs from one's own cultural behavior.

Skateboard virtuoso Tony Hawk was part of an extremely effective campaign promoting milk. Sports stars, movie celebrities, singers, and others posed with milk mustaches; and each ad said, "Got milk?" To many Hispanics, though, the "Got Milk" theme was offensive. Its literal translation became an off-color expression meaning "Are you lactating?" What's more, Hispanics didn't see anything funny in running out of milk. To appeal to Hispanic cultural values, a different campaign, shown on the opposite page, was developed.

Photo: Courtesy of LOWE WORLDWIDE, INC. AS AGENT FOR NATIONAL FLUID MILK PROCESSOR PROMOTION BOARD

Culture Is the Basis of Self-Identity and Community. Culture is the basis for how we tell the world who we are and what we believe. People build their identities through cultural overlays to their primary culture. North Americans, for example, make choices in education, career, place of employment, and life partner. Each of these choices brings with it a set of rules, manners, ceremonies, beliefs, language, and values. They add to one's total cultural outlook, and they represent major expressions of a person's self-identity.

Culture Combines the Visible and Invisible. To outsiders, the way we act—those things that we do in daily life and work—are the most visible parts of our culture. In Japan, for instance, harmony with the environment is important. Thus, when attending a flower show, a woman would wear a dress with pastel rather than primary colors to avoid detracting from the beauty of the flowers. And in India people avoid stepping on ants or insects because they believe in reincarnation and are careful about all forms of life.[21] These practices are outward symbols of deeper values that are invisible but that pervade everything we think and do.

Culture Is Dynamic. Over time, cultures will change. Changes are caused by advancements in technology and communication, as discussed earlier. Change is also caused by events such as migration, natural disasters, and wars. The American Civil War, for instance, produced far-reaching cultural changes for both the North and the South. Another major event in this country has been the exodus of people living on farms. When families moved to cities, major changes occurred in the way family members interacted. Attitudes, behaviors, and beliefs change in open societies more quickly than in closed societies.

About Stereotypes, Prototypes, Prejudices, and Generalizations

Stereotypes *are oversimplified behavioral patterns applied uncritically to groups;* prototypes *describe general characteristics that are dynamic and may change.*

Most experts recognize that it is impossible to talk about cultures without using mental categories, representations, and generalizations to describe groups. These categories are sometimes considered *stereotypes.* Because the term *stereotype* has a negative meaning, intercultural authors Varner and Beamer suggest that we distinguish between *stereotype* and *prototype.*

A *stereotype* is an oversimplified behavioral pattern applied uncritically to groups. The term was used originally by printers to describe identical type set in two frames, hence *stereo type.* Stereotypes are fixed and rigid. Although they may be exaggerated and overgeneralized beliefs when applied to groups of people, stereotypes are not always entirely false.[22] Often they contain a grain of truth. When a stereotype develops into a rigid attitude and when it's based on erroneous beliefs or preconceptions, then it should be called a *prejudice*.

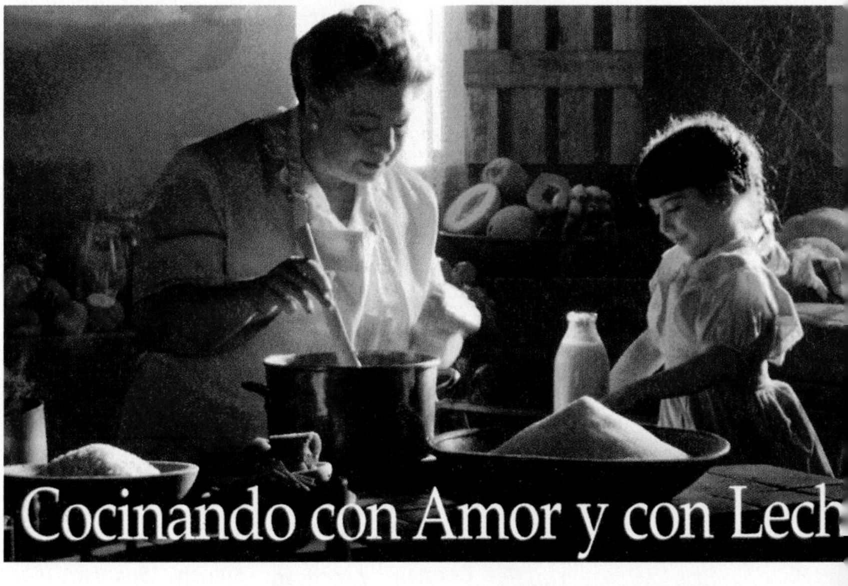

Varner and Beamer recommend the use of the term *prototype* to describe "mental representations based on general characteristics that are not fixed and rigid, but rather are open to new definitions."[23] Prototypes, then, are dynamic and change with fresh experience. Prototypes based on objective observations usually have a considerable amount of truth in them. That's why they can be helpful in studying culture. For example, Latin businesspeople often talk about their families before getting down to business. This prototype is generally accurate, but it may not universally apply and it may change over time.

Instead of using the English-language "Got Milk" ad, which was enormously successful in U.S. markets, a new ad aimed at Hispanic markets featured a "Generations" campaign. The new tagline, "Cooking with love and with milk," reflected the Hispanic cultural emphasis on families. The Spanish-language campaign, showing milk-based recipes being handed down over three generations, was just as successful as its English-language counterpart in persuading people to consume more milk.

Some people object to making any generalizations about cultures whatever. Yet, it is wise to remember that whenever we are confronted with something new and unfamiliar, we naturally strive to categorize the data in order to make sense out of it. In categorizing these new data, we are making generalizations. Significant intellectual discourse is impossible without generalizations. In fact, science itself would be impossible without generalizations, for what are scientific laws but valid generalizations? Much of what we teach in college courses could be called generalizations. Being able to draw generalizations from masses of data is a sign of intelligence and learning. Unfounded generalizations about people and cultures, of course, can lead to bias and prejudice. But for our purposes, when we discuss cultures, it's important to be able to make generalizations and describe cultural prototypes.

Dimensions of Culture

Being able to draw valid generalizations is necessary for learning and education.

The more you know about culture in general and your own culture in particular, the better able you will be to adapt to an intercultural perspective. A typical North American has habits and beliefs similar to those of other members of Western, technologically advanced societies. In our limited space in this book, it's impossible to cover fully the infinite facets of culture. But we can outline some key dimensions of culture and look at them from different views.

So that you will better understand your culture and how it contrasts with other cultures, we will describe five key dimensions of culture: context, individualism, formality, communication style, and time orientation.

Low-context cultures (such as those in North America and Western Europe) depend less on the environment of a situation to convey meaning than do high-context cultures (such as those in Japan, China, and Arab countries).

Context. Context is probably the most important cultural dimension and also the most difficult to define. It's a concept developed by cultural anthropologist Edward T. Hall. In his model, context refers to the stimuli, environment, or ambience surrounding an event. Communicators in low-context cultures (such as those in North America, Scandinavia, and Germany) depend little on the context of a situation to convey their meaning. They assume that listeners know very little and must be told practically everything. In high-context cultures (such as those in Japan, China, and Arab countries), the listener is already "contexted" and does not need to be given

Figure 4.2 ***Comparing Low- and High-Context Cultures***

Low Context	High Context
Tends to prefer direct verbal interaction	Tends to prefer indirect verbal interaction
Tends to understand meaning at one level only	Tends to understand meanings embedded at many sociocultural levels
Is generally less proficient in reading nonverbal cues	Is generally more proficient in reading nonverbal cues
Values individualism	Values group membership
Relies more on logic	Relies more on context and feeling
Employs linear logic	Employs spiral logic
Says *no* directly	Talks around point; avoids saying *no*
Communicates in highly structured (contexted) messages, provides details, stresses literal meanings, gives authority to written information	Communicates in simple, ambiguous, noncontexted messages; understands visual messages readily

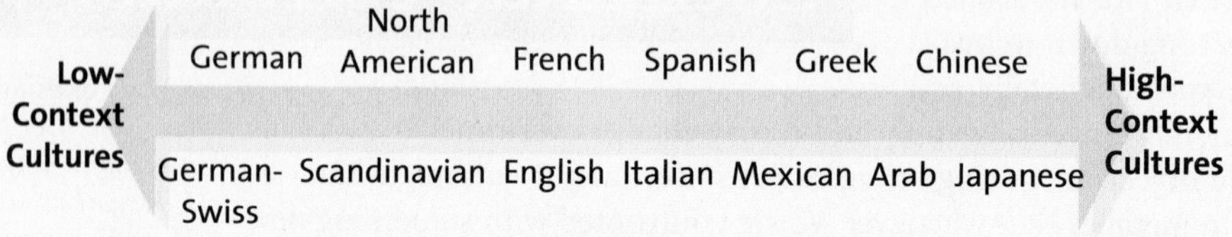

Low-Context Cultures ← German-Swiss, German, Scandinavian, North American, English, French, Italian, Spanish, Mexican, Greek, Arab, Chinese, Japanese → **High-Context Cultures**

much background information.[24] To identify low- and high-context countries, Hall arranged them on a continuum, as shown in Figure 4.2.

People in low-context cultures tend to be logical, analytical, and action oriented.

Low-context cultures tend to be logical, analytical, and action oriented. Business communicators stress clearly articulated messages that they consider to be objective, professional, and efficient. High-context cultures are more likely to be intuitive and contemplative. Communicators in high-context cultures pay attention to more than the words spoken. They emphasize interpersonal relationships, nonverbal expression, physical setting, and social setting. They are more aware of the communicator's history, status, and position. Communication cues are transmitted by posture, voice inflection, gestures, and facial expression. Establishing relationships is an important part of communicating and interacting.

In terms of thinking patterns, low-context communicators tend to use *linear logic*. They proceed from Point A to Point B to Point C and finally arrive at a conclusion. High-context communicators, however, may use *spiral logic*, circling around a topic indirectly and looking at it from many tangential or divergent viewpoints. A conclusion may be implied but not argued directly. For a concise summary of important differences between low- and high-context cultures, see Figure 4.2.

Members of many low-context cultures value independence and freedom from control.

Individualism. An attitude of independence and freedom from control characterizes individualism. Members of low-context cultures, particularly Americans, tend to value individualism. They believe that initiative and self-assertion result in personal achievement. They believe in individual action and personal responsibility, and they desire a large degree of freedom in their personal lives.

Members of high-context cultures are more collectivist. They emphasize membership in organizations, groups, and teams; they encourage acceptance of group values, duties, and decisions. They typically resist independence because it fosters competition and confrontation instead of consensus. In group-oriented cultures like many Asian societies, for example, self-assertion and individual decision making are discouraged. "The nail that sticks up gets pounded down" is a common Japanese saying.[25] Business decisions are often made by all who have competence in the matter under discussion. Similarly, in China managers also focus on the group rather than on the individual, preferring a "consultative" management style over an autocratic style.[26]

Many cultures, of course, are quite complex and cannot be characterized as totally individualistic or group oriented. For example, European Americans are generally quite individualistic, whereas African Americans are less so, and Latin Americans are closer to the group-centered dimension.[27]

Formality. People in some cultures place less emphasis on tradition, ceremony, and social rules than do members of other cultures. Americans, for example, dress casually and are soon on a first-name basis with others. Their lack of formality is often characterized by directness. In business dealings Americans come to the point immediately; indirectness, they feel, wastes time, a valuable commodity in American culture.

Tradition, ceremony, and social rules are more important in some cultures.

This informality and directness may be confusing abroad. In Mexico, for instance, a typical business meeting begins with handshakes, coffee, and an expansive conversation about the weather, sports, and other light topics. An invitation to "get down to business" might offend a Mexican executive.[28] In Japan signing documents and exchanging business cards are important rituals. In Europe first names are never used without invitation. In Arab, South American, and Asian cultures, a feeling of friendship and kinship must be established before business can be transacted.

In Western cultures people are more relaxed about social status and the appearance of power.[29] Deference is not generally paid to individuals merely because of their wealth, position, seniority, or age. In many Asian cultures, however, these characteristics are important and must be respected. Wal-Mart, facing many hurdles in breaking into the Japanese market, admits having difficulty training local employees to speak up to their bosses. In their culture lower-level employees do not question management. Deference and respect are paid to authority and power. Recognizing this cultural pattern, Marriott Hotel managers learned to avoid placing a lower-level Japanese employee on a floor above a higher-level executive from the same company.

Communication Style. People in low- and high-context cultures tend to communicate differently with words. To Americans and Germans, words are very important, especially in contracts and negotiations. People in high-context cultures, on the other hand, place more emphasis on the surrounding context than on the words describing a negotiation. A Greek may see a contract as a formal statement announcing the intention to build a business for the future. The Japanese may treat contracts as statements of intention, and they assume changes will be made as a project develops. Mexicans may treat contracts as artistic exercises of what might be accomplished in an ideal world. They do not necessarily expect contracts to apply consistently in the real world. An Arab may be insulted by merely mentioning a contract; a person's word is more binding.[30]

Words are used differently by people in low- and high-context cultures.

Americans tend to take words literally, whereas Latins enjoy plays on words; and Arabs and South Americans sometimes speak with extravagant or poetic figures of speech that may be misinterpreted if taken literally. Nigerians prefer a quiet, clear form of expression; and Germans tend to be direct but understated.[31]

In communication style Americans value straightforwardness, are suspicious of evasiveness, and distrust people who might have a "hidden agenda" or who "play their cards too close to the chest."[32] Americans also tend to be uncomfortable with silence and impatient with delays. Some Asian businesspeople have learned that the longer they drag out negotiations, the more concessions impatient Americans are likely to make.

Americans value a direct, straightforward communication style.

Western cultures have developed languages that use letters describing the *sounds* of words. But Asian languages are based on pictographical characters representing the *meanings* of words. Asian language characters are much more complex than the Western alphabet; therefore, Asians are said to have a higher competence in the discrimination of visual patterns.

North Americans tend to correlate time with productivity, efficiency, and money.

Time Orientation. North Americans consider time a precious commodity to be conserved. They correlate time with productivity, efficiency, and money. Keeping people waiting for business appointments wastes time and is also rude.

In other cultures time may be perceived as an unlimited and never-ending resource to be enjoyed. An American businessperson, for example, was kept waiting two hours past a scheduled appointment time in South America. She wasn't offended, though, because she was familiar with Hispanics' more relaxed concept of time.

Asians tend to need time for deliberation and contemplation.

Although Asians are punctual, their need for deliberation and contemplation sometimes clashes with our desire for speedy decisions. They do not like to be rushed. A Japanese businessperson considering the purchase of American appliances, for example, asked for five minutes to consider the seller's proposal. The potential buyer crossed his arms, sat back, and closed his eyes in concentration. A scant 18 seconds later, the American resumed his sales pitch to the obvious bewilderment of the Japanese buyer.[33]

learning objective

3

Achieving Intercultural Proficiency

Being aware of your own culture and how it contrasts with others is an important first step in achieving intercultural proficiency. Another step involves recognizing barriers to intercultural accommodation and striving to overcome them. Some of these barriers occur quite naturally and require conscious effort to surmount. You might be thinking, why bother? Probably the most important reasons for becoming interculturally competent are that your personal life will be more satisfying and your work life will be more productive, gratifying, and effective.

Avoiding Ethnocentrism

Ethnocentrism, ***the belief in the superiority of one's own race, tends to cause us to judge others by our own values.***

The belief in the superiority of one's own race is known as *ethnocentrism*, a natural attitude inherent in all cultures. If you were raised in North America, many of the dimensions of culture described previously probably seem "right" to you. For example, it's only logical to think that time is money and you should not waste it. Everyone knows that, right? That's why an American businessperson in an Arab or Asian country might feel irritated at time spent over coffee or other social rituals before any "real" business is transacted. In these cultures, however, time is viewed differently. And personal relationships must be established and nurtured before credible negotiations may proceed.

Ethnocentrism causes us to judge others by our own values. We expect others to react as we would, and they expect us to behave as they would. Misunderstandings naturally result. A North American who wants to set a deadline for completion of negotiations is considered pushy by an Arab. That same Arab, who prefers a handshake to a written contract, is seen as naïve and possibly untrustworthy by a North American. These ethnocentric reactions can be reduced through knowledge of other cultures and development of increased intercultural sensitivity.

Consider the dilemma of the international consulting firm of Burns & McCallister, described in the accompanying Ethical Insights box. In refusing to send women to negotiate in certain countries, the company enraged some women's rights groups. But was Burns & McCallister actually respecting the cultures of those countries?

ethical insights

Firm Lands in Hot Water for Caving in to Cultural Prejudices

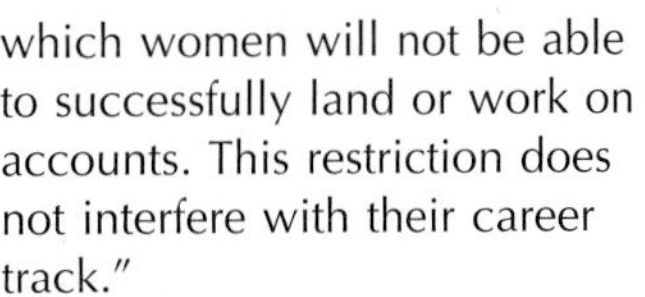

At one time the international management consulting firm of Burns & McCallister found itself in cultural hot water. The problem? Although the company had earned kudos for its fair treatment of women in this country, it declined to send female partners to negotiate contracts in certain countries.

Silent Women. In some cultures women may work in clerical positions, but they are not allowed to speak in a meeting of men. Contacts with clients must be through male partners or account executives. Japan, for example, has a two-track hiring system with women represented in only 3 percent of all professional positions. Other women in the workforce are uniformed office ladies who do the filing and serve tea. One American businesswoman said that when she finished a presentation in Japan, the men in the audience would ask who her boss was. She eventually hired a man to go along with her because merely having a man by her side, even a virtual dummy, increased her sales significantly.[34]

Company Justification. In defense of its ban on sending women to negotiate in certain cultures, the head of Burns & McCallister said: "Look, we're about as progressive a firm as you'll find. But the reality of international business is that if we try to use women, we don't get the job. It's not a policy on all foreign accounts. We've just identified certain cultures in which women will not be able to successfully land or work on accounts. This restriction does not interfere with their career track."

Women's Rights. The National Organization for Women (NOW) argued that Burns & McCallister should apply its American standards throughout the world. Since women are not restricted here, they should not be restricted abroad. Our culture treats women fairly, and other cultures should recognize and respect that treatment. Unless Burns & McCallister stands up for its principles, change can never be expected.

Career Application

Organize a debate or class discussion focused on these questions. On what grounds do you support or oppose the position of Burns & McCallister to prohibit women from negotiating contracts in certain cultures? Should U.S. businesses impose their cultural values abroad? Should Burns & McCallister sacrifice potential business to advance a high moral position? If the career advancement of women within the firm is not affected by the policy, should women care? Do you agree with NOW that change cannot occur unless Burns & McCallister takes a stand?

Bridging the Gap

Developing cultural competence often involves changing attitudes. Remember that culture is learned. Through exposure to other cultures and through training, such as you are receiving in this course, you can learn new attitudes and behaviors that help bridge gaps between cultures.

Because culture is learned, you can learn new attitudes and behaviors through training.

Tolerance. One desirable attitude in achieving intercultural proficiency is that of *tolerance.* Closed-minded people cannot look beyond their own ethnocentrism. But as global markets expand and as our own society becomes increasingly multiethnic, tolerance becomes especially significant. Some job descriptions now include statements such as, "Must be able to interact with ethnically diverse personnel."

Empathy, *which means trying to see the world through another's eyes, helps you be more tolerant and less judgmental.*

To improve tolerance, you'll want to practice *empathy.* This means trying to see the world through another's eyes. It means being less judgmental and more eager to seek common ground. For example, one of the most ambitious cross-cultural business projects ever attempted joined Siemens AG, the giant German technology firm, with Toshiba Corporation of Japan and IBM. Scientists from each country worked at the IBM facility on the Hudson River in New York State to develop a revolutionary computer memory chip. All sides devoted extra effort to overcome communication and other problems. The Siemens employees had been briefed on America's "hamburger style of management." When American managers must criticize subordinates, they generally start with small talk, such as "How's the family?" That, according to the Germans, is the bun on the top of the hamburger. Then they slip in the meat, which is the criticism. They end with encouraging words, which is the bun on the bottom. "With Germans," said a Siemens cross-cultural trainer, "all you get is the meat. And with the Japanese, it's all the soft stuff—you have to *smell* the meat."[35] Along the continuum of high-context, low-context cultures, you can see that the Germans are more direct, the Americans are less direct, and the Japanese are very subtle.

Recognizing these cultural differences enabled the scientists to work together with greater tolerance. They also sought common ground when trying to solve disagreements, such as one involving workspace. The Toshiba researchers were accustomed to working in big crowded areas like classrooms where constant supervision and interaction took place. But IBMers worked in small isolated offices. The solution was to knock out some walls for cooperative work areas while also retaining smaller offices for those who wanted them. Instead of passing judgment and telling the Japanese that solitary workspaces are the best way for serious thinkers to concentrate, the Americans acknowledged the difference in work cultures and sought common ground. Accepting cultural differences and adapting to them with tolerance and empathy often results in a harmonious compromise.

Saving face ***may require indirectness to respect the feelings and dignity of others.***

Saving Face. In business transactions North Americans often assume that economic factors are the primary motivators of people. It's wise to remember, though, that strong cultural influences are also at work. *Saving face*, for example, is important in many parts of the world. *Face* refers to the image a person holds in his or her social network. Positive comments raise a person's social standing, but negative comments lower it. People in low-context cultures are less concerned with face. Germans and North Americans, for instance, value honesty and directness; they generally come right to the point and "tell it like it is." Mexicans, Asians, and members of other high-context cultures, on the other hand, are more concerned with preserving social harmony and saving face. They are indirect and go to great lengths to avoid giving offense by saying *no*. The Japanese, in fact, have 16 different ways to avoid an outright *no*. The empathic listener recognizes the language of refusal and pushes no further.

Tolerance sometimes involves being patient and silent.

Patience. Being tolerant also involves patience. If a foreigner is struggling to express an idea in English, Americans must avoid the temptation to finish the sentence and provide the word that they presume is wanted. When we put words into their mouths, our foreign friends often smile and agree out of politeness, but our words may in fact not express their thoughts. Remaining silent is another means of exhibiting tolerance. Instead of filling every lapse in conversation, North Americans, for example, should recognize that in Asian cultures people deliberately use periods of silence for reflection and contemplation.

learning objective 4

Improving Communication With Intercultural Audiences

Thus far we've discussed the increasing importance of intercultural proficiency as a result of globalization of markets, increasing migration, and technological advancements. We've described characteristics and dimensions of cultures, and we've talked about avoiding ethnocentrism. Our goal was to motivate you to unlock the oppor-

PROCESS IN PROGRESS

Wal-Mart Revisited

AS PART OF its audacious expansion plan, Wal-Mart seeks to introduce discounting strategies in Japan. It has joined with Seiyu, Japan's fifth-largest supermarket chain. This local partner promises to help Wal-Mart navigate Japan's dense supplier network as well as provide expensive real estate. But cultural differences may thwart Wal-Mart's expansion hopes.

"Our biggest challenge," said Seiyu President Masao Kiuchi, "is that Japanese people think if it's too cheap, the quality is bad."[36] What's more, they don't understand Wal-Mart's everyday low prices. Most Japanese shoppers are accustomed to weekly advertised bargains. Housewives are addicted to scouring the newspapers for sales and then scurrying around town for the best deals. Wal-Mart, on the other hand, shuns so-called "sales" and features overall low prices every day. Shoppers are also having trouble understanding some of Wal-Mart's jargon, such as "rollbacks."[37]

Teaching employees to sell the Wal-Mart way presents another hurdle. Instead of relying on their hunches, store managers must learn to use laptop computers and spreadsheets to analyze sales and inventory. Company trainers are also trying to teach employees to be more aggressive about approaching customers. One manager explained that the 10-foot rule is difficult for Japanese to apply because they are a very restrained people. In regard to directing employees, Japanese managers balk at the Wal-Mart practice of continually praising coworkers. As one reporter remarked, "Back-slapping compliments are rare in a country where workers are taught to be humble and bosses often command respect through intimidation."[38] Unlike American employees, Japanese workers are timid in speaking up to managers and supervisors.

Critical Thinking

- How do Japanese and Americans differ on key dimensions of culture as described in this chapter?
- Is it realistic for Wal-Mart's trainers to expect Japanese managers and employees to perform exactly like American workers? Why or why not?
- How can Wal-Mart and other multinational companies overcome the cultural barriers they face when expanding into other countries?

CONTINUED ON PAGE 125

case study

tunities offered by intercultural proficiency. Remember, the key to future business success may very well lie in finding ways to work harmoniously with people from different cultures.

Adapting Messages to Intercultural Audiences

As business communicators, we need to pay special attention to specific areas of communication to enhance the effectiveness of intercultural messages. To minimize the chance of misunderstanding, we'll look more closely at nonverbal communication, oral messages, and written messages.

Understanding nonverbal messages is particularly difficult when cultures differ.

Nonverbal Communication. Verbal skills in another culture can generally be mastered if one studies hard enough. But nonverbal skills are much more difficult to learn. Nonverbal behavior includes the areas described in Chapter 3, such as eye contact, facial expression, posture, gestures, and the use of time, space, and territory. The messages sent by body language and the way we arrange time and space have always been open to interpretation. Does a raised eyebrow mean that your boss doubts your statement or just that she is seriously considering it? Does that closed

spotlight *on communicators*

Breaking sales records around the globe, Naughty Dog's software, featured on Sony's PlayStation 2, uses cutting-edge technology and graphics to create wholesome, nonviolent computer games such as Crash Bandicoot and Jak & Daxter for international audiences. As cofounder Jason Rubin learned, appealing to intercultural audiences requires careful preplanning by test groups in target territories as well as reliance on locals for translation and feedback. Even wacky wisecracking cartoon characters should not violate local cultural taboos. Rubin, however, foresees a decline in international differences as a dominant culture begins to pervade the planet.

door to an office mean that your coworker is angry or just that he is working on a project that requires concentration? Deciphering nonverbal communication is difficult for people who are culturally similar, and it is even more troublesome when cultures differ.

In Western cultures, for example, people perceive silence as a negative trait. It suggests rejection, unhappiness, depression, regret, embarrassment, or ignorance. The English expression, "The silence was deafening,"conveys its feeling of oppression. However, the Japanese admire silence and consider it a key to success. A Japanese proverb says, "Those who know do not speak; those who speak do not know." Over 60 percent of Japanese businesswomen said that they would prefer to marry silent men.[39] Silence is equated with wisdom.

Although nonverbal behavior is ambiguous within cultures and even more problematic between cultures, it nevertheless conveys meaning. If you've ever had to talk with someone who does not share your language, you probably learned quickly to use gestures to convey basic messages. Since gestures can create very different reactions in different cultures, one must be careful in using and interpreting them. In some societies it is extremely bad form to point one's finger, as in giving directions. Other hand gestures can also cause trouble. The thumbs-up symbol may be used to indicate approval in North America, but in Iran and Ghana it is a vulgar gesture.[40]

Gestures can create different reactions in intercultural environments.

As businesspeople increasingly interact with their counterparts from other cultures, they will become more aware of these differences. Some behaviors are easy to warn against, such as touching people from the Middle East with the left hand (because it is considered unclean and is used for personal hygiene). We're also warned not to touch anyone's head (even children) in Thailand, as the head is considered sacred. Numerous lists of cultural dos and don'ts have been compiled. However, learning all the nuances of nonverbal behavior in other cultures is impossible, and such lists are merely the tip of the cultural iceberg.

Becoming more aware of your own use of nonverbal cues can make you more sensitive to variations in other cultures.

Although we can't ever hope to understand fully the nuances of meaning transmitted by nonverbal behavior in various cultures, we can grow more tolerant, more flexible, and eventually, more competent. An important part of achieving nonverbal competence is becoming more aware of our own nonverbal behaviors and their meanings. Much of our nonverbal behavior is learned in early childhood from our families and from society, and it is largely unconscious. Once we become more aware of the meaning of our own gestures, posture, eye gaze, and so on, we will become more alert and more sensitive to variations in other cultures. Striving to associate with people from different cultures can further broaden our intercultural competence.

Descriptiveness, nonjudgmentalism, and supportiveness all help you broaden your intercultural competence.

In achieving competence, one intercultural expert, M. R. Hammer, suggests that three processes or attitudes are effective. *Descriptiveness* refers to the use of concrete and specific feedback. As you learned in Chapter 1 in regard to the process of communication, descriptive feedback is more effective than judgmental feedback. For example, using objective terms to describe the modest attire of Muslim women is more effective than describing it as unfeminine or motivated by oppressive and unequal treatment of females. A second attitude is what Hammer calls *nonjudgmentalism.* This attitude goes a long way in preventing defensive reactions from communicators. Most important in achieving effective communication is *supportiveness.* This attitude requires us to support others positively with head nods, eye contact, facial expression, and physical proximity.[41]

From a practical standpoint, when interacting with businesspeople in other cultures, it's always wise to follow their lead. If they avoid intense eye contact, don't stare. If no one is putting his or her elbows on a table, don't be the first to do so. Until you are knowledgeable about the meaning of gestures, it's probably a good idea to keep yours to a minimum. Learning the words for *please*, *yes*, and *thank you*, some of which are shown in Figure 4.3, is even better than relying on gestures.[42] Achieving intercultural competence in regard to nonverbal behavior may never be totally attained, but sensitivity, nonjudgmentalism, and tolerance go a long way toward improving interactions.

Keep your gestures to a minimum or follow the lead of native businesspeople.

FIGURE 4.3 ***Basic Expressions in Other Languages***

Country	Good Morning	Please	Thank You	Yes	No	Goodbye
Arabic	saBAH al-khayr	minFUDlak	shookRAAN	NAA-am	LAA	MAA-a salAAMuh
French	Bonjour [bohnzhoor]	S'il vous plaît [see voo pleh]	Merci (beaucoup) [mare-see (bo-coo)]	Oui [weeh]	Non [nonh]	Au revoir [oh vwar]
German	Guten morgen [Goo-ten more-gen]	Bitte [Bitt-eh]	Danke [Dahnk-eh]	Ja [Yah]	Nein [Nine]	Auf Wiedersehen [auwf vee-dur-zain]
Italian	Buon giorno	Per favore/per piacere	Grazie (tante)	Si	No	Arrivederia (Arrivederci, informal)
Japanese	Ohayoo [Ohio (go-ZAI-mahss) or simply Ohio]	oh-NEH-ga-ee she-mahss (when requesting)	Arigato [Ah-ree-GAH-tow (go-ZAI-mahss)]	High, so-dess	Ee-yeh	Sayonara
Norwegian	God morgen	Vaer sa snill [var so snill]	Takk [tahk]	Ja [yah]	Nei [nay]	Adjo [adieu]
Russian	Do'braye oo-tra	Pa-JAH-loos-tah	Spa-SEE-bah	Dah	N'yet	DasviDANya
Spanish	Buenos días [BWEH-nos DEE-ahs]	Con permiso [Con pair-ME-soh], Por favor [Pohr fah-VOHR]	Gracias [GRAH-seeahs]	Sí [SEEH]	No [NOH]	Adiós

Oral Messages. Although it's best to speak a foreign language fluently, many of us lack that skill. Fortunately, global business transactions are increasingly conducted in English. English has become the language of technology, the language of Hollywood, and the language to know in global business even for traditionally non-English-speaking countries. English is so dominant in business that when Koreans go to China, English is the language they use to conduct business.[43] However, the level of proficiency may be limited among those for whom it is a second language. Americans abroad make a big mistake in thinking that people who speak English always understand what is being said. Comprehension can be fairly superficial. The following suggestions are helpful for situations in which one or both communicators may be using English as a second language.

Don't assume that speakers of English as a second language understand everything you say.

- **Learn foreign phrases.** In conversations, even when English is used, foreign nationals appreciate it when you learn greetings and a few phrases in their language. See Figure 4.3 for a list of basic expressions in some of the world's major languages. Practice the phrases phonetically so that you will be understood.

Use simple English and avoid puns, sports references, slang, and jargon when communicating with people for whom English is a second language.

- **Use simple English.** Speak in short sentences (under 15 words), and try to stick to the 3,000 to 4,000 most common English words. For example, use *old* rather than *obsolete* and *rich* rather than *luxurious* or *sumptuous*. Eliminate puns, sports and military references, slang, and jargon (special business terms). Be especially alert to idiomatic expressions that can't be translated, such as *burn the midnight oil* and *under the weather*.
- **Speak slowly and enunciate clearly.** Avoid fast speech, but don't raise your voice. Overpunctuate with pauses and full stops. Always write numbers for all to see.

To improve communication with those for whom English is a second language, speak slowly, enunciate clearly, observe eye messages, encourage feedback, check for comprehension, accept blame, don't interrupt, remember to smile, and follow up important conversations in writing.

- **Observe eye messages.** Be alert to a glazed expression or wandering eyes—these tell you the listener is lost.
- **Encourage accurate feedback.** Ask probing questions, and encourage the listener to paraphrase what you say. Don't assume that a *yes*, a nod, or a smile indicates comprehension.
- **Check frequently for comprehension.** Avoid waiting until you finish a long explanation to request feedback. Instead, make one point at a time, pausing to check for comprehension. Don't proceed to B until A has been grasped.
- **Accept blame.** If a misunderstanding results, graciously accept the blame for not making your meaning clear.
- **Listen without interrupting.** Curb your desire to finish sentences or to fill out ideas for the speaker. Keep in mind that North Americans abroad are often accused of listening too little and talking too much.
- **Remember to smile!** Roger Axtell, international behavior expert, calls the smile the single most understood and most useful form of communication in either personal or business transactions.[44]
- **Follow up in writing.** After conversations or oral negotiations, confirm the results and agreements with follow-up letters. For proposals and contracts, engage a translator to prepare copies in the local language.

learning objective

5

To improve written messages, adopt local formats, use short sentences and short paragraphs, avoid ambiguous expressions, strive for clarity, use correct grammar, cite numbers carefully, and accommodate readers in organization, tone, and style.

Written Messages. In sending letters and other documents to businesspeople in other cultures, try to adapt your writing style and tone appropriately. For example, in cultures where formality and tradition are important, be scrupulously polite. Don't even think of sharing the latest joke. Humor translates very poorly and can cause misunderstanding and negative reactions. Familiarize yourself with accepted channels of communication. Are letters, e-mail, and faxes common? Would a direct or indirect organizational pattern be more effective? And forget about trying to cut through "red tape." In some cultures "red tape" is appreciated. The following suggestions, coupled with the earlier guidelines, can help you prepare successful written messages for intercultural audiences.

- **Adopt local formats.** Learn how documents are formatted and addressed in the intended reader's country. Use local formats and styles.
- **Observe titles and rank.** Use last names, titles, and other signals of rank and status. Send messages to higher-status people and avoid sending copies to lower-rank people.
- **Use short sentences and short paragraphs.** Sentences with fewer than 15 words and paragraphs with fewer than 7 lines are most readable.
- **Avoid ambiguous expressions.** Include relative pronouns (*that, which, who*) for clarity in introducing clauses. Stay away from contractions (especially ones like *Here's the problem*). Avoid idioms (*once in a blue moon*), slang (*my presen-*

FIGURE 4.4 *Typical Data Formats*

	United States	United Kingdom	France	Germany	Portugal
Dates	May 15, 2006 5/15/06	15th May 2006 15/5/06	15 mai 2006 15.05.06	15. Mai 2006 15.5.06	06.05.15
Time	10:32 p.m.	10:32 pm	22.32 22 h 32	22:32 Uhr 22.32	22H32m
Currency	$123.45 US$123.45	£123.45 GB£123.45	123F45 123,45F 123.45 euros	DM 123,45 123,45 DM 123.45 euros	123$45 ESC 123.45 123.45 euros
Large numbers	1,234,567.89	1,234,567.89	1.234.567,89 1 234 567	1.234.567,89	1.234.567,89
Phone numbers	(205) 555-1234	(081) 987 1234 0255 876543	(15) 61-87-34-02 (15) 61.87.34.02	(089) 2 61 39 12	056-244 33 056 45 45 45

tation really bombed), acronyms (*ASAP,* for *as soon as possible*), abbreviations (*DBA,* for *doing business as*) jargon (*input, bottom line*), and sports references (*play ball, slam dunk, ballpark figure*). Use action-specific verbs (*purchase a printer* rather than *get a printer*).

- **Strive for clarity.** Avoid words that have many meanings (the word *light* has 18 different meanings!). If necessary, clarify words that may be confusing. Replace two-word verbs with clear single words (*return* instead of *bring back*; *delay* instead of *put off*; *maintain* instead of *keep up*).
- **Use correct grammar.** Be careful of misplaced modifiers, dangling participles, and sentence fragments. Use conventional punctuation.
- **Cite numbers carefully.** For international trade it's a good idea to learn and use the metric system. In citing numbers use figures (*15*) instead of spelling them out (*fifteen*). Always convert dollar figures into local currency. Avoid using figures to express the month of the year. See Figure 4.4 for additional guidelines on data formats.
- **Accommodate the reader in organization, tone, and style.** Organize your message to appeal to the reader. If flowery tone, formal salutations, indirectness, references to family and the seasons, or unconditional apologies are expected, strive to accommodate.

Making the effort to communicate with sensitivity across cultures pays big dividends. "Much of the world wants to like us," says businessman and international consultant Kevin Chambers. "When we take the time to learn about others, many will bend over backward to do business with us."[45] The following checklist summarizes suggestions for improving communication with intercultural audiences.

Checklist for Improving Intercultural Proficiency and Communication

Study your own culture. Learn about your customs, biases, and views and how they differ from those in other societies. This knowledge can help you better understand, appreciate, and accept the values and behavior of other cultures.

- ✓ **Learn about other cultures.** Education can help you alter cultural misconceptions, reduce fears, and minimize misunderstandings. Knowledge of other cultures opens your eyes and teaches you to expect differences. Such knowledge also enriches your life.
- ✓ **Curb ethnocentrism.** Avoid judging others by your personal views. Get over the view that the other cultures are incorrect, defective, or primitive. Try to develop an open mind-set.
- ✓ **Avoid judgmentalism.** Strive to accept other behavior as different, rather than as right or wrong. Try not to be defensive in justifying your culture. Strive for objectivity.
- ✓ **Seek common ground.** When cultures clash, look for solutions that respect both cultures. Be flexible in developing compromises.
- ✓ **Observe nonverbal cues in your culture.** Become more alert to the meanings of eye contact, facial expression, posture, gestures, and the use of time, space, and territory. How do they differ in other cultures?
- ✓ **Use plain English.** Speak and write in short sentences using simple words and standard English. Eliminate puns, slang, jargon, acronyms, abbreviations, and any words that cannot be easily translated.
- ✓ **Encourage accurate feedback.** In conversations ask probing questions and listen attentively without interrupting. Don't assume that a yes or a smile indicates assent or comprehension.
- ✓ **Adapt to local preferences.** Shape your writing to reflect the reader's document styles, if appropriate. Express currency in local figures. Write out months of the year for clarity.

learning objective

6

Coping With Intercultural Ethics

A perplexing problem faces conscientious organizations and individuals who do business around the world. Whose values, culture, and, ultimately, laws do you follow? Do you heed the customs of your country or those of the country where you are engaged in business? Some observers claim that when American businesspeople venture abroad, they're wandering into an "ethical no-man's land, where each encounter holds forth a fresh demand for a 'gratuity,' or baksheesh."[46]

Business Practices Abroad

When Americans conduct business abroad, their ethics are put to the test.

As companies do more and more business around the globe, their assumptions about ethics are put to the test. Businesspeople may face simple questions regarding the appropriate amount of money to spend on a business gift or the legitimacy of payments to agents and distributors to "expedite" business. Or they may encounter out-and-out bribery, child-labor abuse, environment mistreatment, and unscrupulous business practices. In the post-Enron era, the ethics of U.S. businesses are increasingly being scrutinized. Those who violate company policy or the law land in big trouble. But what ethical standards do these companies follow when they do business abroad?

Today most companies that are active in global markets have ethical codes of conduct. These codes are public documents and can usually be found on company Web sites. They are an accepted part of governance. The growing sophistication of these codes results in ethics training programs that often include complicated hypothetical questions. Ethics trainers teach employees how to solve problems by reconciling legal requirements, company policies, and conflicting cultural norms.[47]

Businesses in other countries are also adopting ethics codes and helping employees live up to the standards. In Mexico, where the World Bank estimates that corruption costs nearly 10 percent of the nation's gross domestic product, one food processing company cracked down on "mordidas" (bribes). The company adopted an ethics code forbidding drivers to pay bribes when their trucks were impounded—even though perishable food would go bad. Federal police officers eventually learned that they would receive no bribes, and they stopped impounding the company's trucks. Over time, the company saved more than $100 million because it was no longer paying off officials.[48]

The least corrupt countries are Finland, Denmark, New Zealand, Sweden, and Canada.

All countries, of course, are not corrupt. Transparency International, a Berlin-based watchdog group, compiled a ranking of corruption in many countries. Based on polls and surveys of businesspeople and journalists, the index shown in Figure 4.5 presents a look at the perceptions of corruption. Gauging corruption precisely

FIGURE 4.5 ***Corruption Perceptions Index***

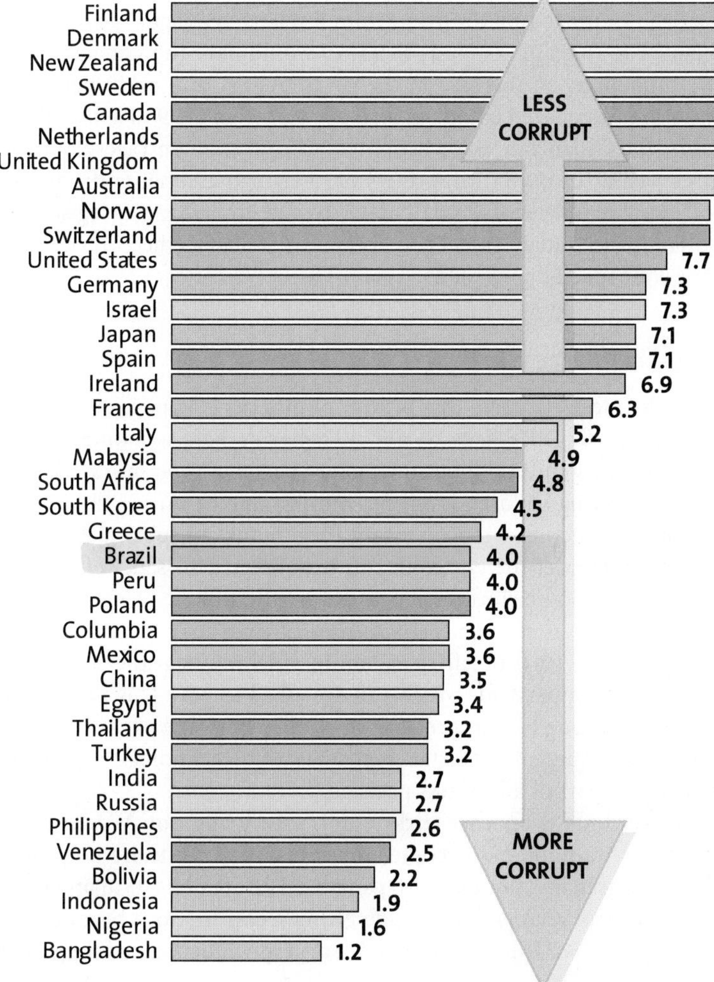

This index of selected countries represents a compilation of polls and surveys put together by Transparency International. The purpose of this Berlin-based watchdog organization is curbing the corruption that is stunting the development of poor countries. The index relates to perceptions of the degree of corruption as seen by businesspeople, risk analysts, and the general public. It ranges between 10 (highly clean) and 0 (highly corrupt).

is impossible. But this graph reflects the feelings of individuals doing business in the countries shown. Of the countries selected for this graph, the least corrupt are Finland, Denmark, New Zealand, Sweden, and Canada. The most corrupt were Bolivia, Indonesia, Nigeria, and Bangladesh. The United States ranked between Switzerland and Germany, in the upper third.

Laws Forbidding Bribery

The United States leads the global fight against corruption.

The United States is not highest on the index of least corruptible countries. Yet, it has taken the global lead in fighting corruption. Nearly three decades ago the U.S. government passed the Foreign Corrupt Practices Act of 1977. It prohibits payments to foreign officials for the purpose of obtaining or retaining business. But the law applied only to U.S. companies. Thus, they were at a decided disadvantage when competing against less scrupulous companies from other nations. U.S. companies complained that they lost billions of dollars in contracts every year because they refused to bribe their way to success.

Most other industrialized countries looked the other way when their corporations used bribes. They considered the "greasing of palms" just a cost of doing business in certain cultures. Until 1999 German corporations were even allowed to deduct bribes as a business expense—as long as they got receipts! But in this country, bribery is a criminal offense; and corporate officials found guilty are fined and sent to jail.

More attention is now being paid to the problem of global corruption. With increased global interdependence, corruption is increasingly seen as costly as well as unethical. It has been estimated that moving from a relatively "clean" government like that of Singapore to one as corrupt as Mexico's would have the same effect on foreign direct investment as an increase in the corporate tax rate of 50 percent.[49] Many of the world's industrialized countries formally agreed in 1999 to a new global treaty promoted by the Organization for Economic Cooperation and Development (OECD). This treaty bans the practice of bribery of foreign government officials. Although 29 countries signed the treaty, only 21 have passed implementing legislation, and recent negotiations to outlaw global corruption are stalled as the United States and Europe battle over specific provisions.[50]

Whose Ethics Should Prevail?

Although world leaders agree that bribery of officials is wrong, they do not agree on other ethical behavior.

Although world leaders seem to agree that bribery of officials is wrong, many other shady areas persist. Drawing the lines of ethical behavior here at home is hard enough. When faced with a cultural filter, the picture becomes even murkier. Most people agree that mistreating children is wrong. But in some countries, child labor is not only condoned, it is considered necessary for a family to subsist. Although most countries want to respect the environment, they might also sanction the use of DDT because crops would be consumed by insects without it.

In some cultures "grease" payments to customs officials may be part of their earnings—not blackmail. In parts of Africa a "family" celebration at the conclusion of a business deal includes a party for which you are asked to pay. This payment is a sign of friendship and lasting business relationship, not a personal payoff. In some Third World countries, requests for assistance in developing technologies or reducing hunger may become part of a business package.[51]

Gifts may be a sign of gratitude and hospitality, but they also suggest future obligation.

The exchanging of gifts is another tricky subject. In many non-Western cultures, the gift exchange tradition has become a business ritual. Gifts are not only a sign of gratitude and hospitality, but they also generate a future obligation and trust. Americans, of course, become uneasy when gift-giving seems to move beyond normal courtesy and friendliness. If it even remotely suggests influence-peddling, they back off.[52]

Whose ethics should prevail across borders? Unfortunately, no clear-cut answers can be found. Americans are sometimes criticized for being ethical "fanatics," wishing to impose their "moralistic" views on the world. Also criticized are ethical "relativists" who contend that no absolute values exist.[53]

Making Ethical Decisions Across Borders

Instead of trying to distinguish "good ethics" and "bad ethics," perhaps the best plan is to look for practical solutions to the cultural challenges of global business interaction. Following are suggestions that acknowledge different values but also respect the need for moral initiative.[54]

Finding practical solutions to ethical problems is most important.

- **Broaden your view.** Become more sensitive to the values and customs of other cultures. Look especially at what they consider moral, traditional, practical, and effective.
- **Avoid reflex judgments.** Don't automatically judge the business customs of others as immoral, corrupt, or unworkable. Assume they are legitimate and workable until proved otherwise.
- **Find alternatives.** Instead of caving in to government payoffs, perhaps offer nonmonetary public service benefits, technical expertise, or additional customer service.
- **Refuse business if options violate your basic values.** If an action seriously breaches your own code of ethics or that of your firm, give up the transaction.
- **Work in the fresh air.** Conduct all relations and negotiations as openly as possible.
- **Don't rationalize shady decisions.** Avoid agreeing to actions that cause you to say, "This isn't *really* illegal or immoral," "This is in the company's best interest," or "No one will find out."
- **Resist legalistic strategies.** Don't use tactics that are legally safe but ethically questionable. For example, don't call "agents" (who are accountable to employers) "distributors" (who are not).

Businesspeople abroad can choose many alternatives that acknowledge different values but also respect the need for moral initiative.

When faced with an intercultural ethical dilemma, you can apply the same five-question test you learned in Chapter 1. Even in another culture, these questions can guide you to the best decision.

1. Is the action you are considering legal?
2. How would you see the problem if you were on the opposite side?
3. What are alternate solutions?
4. Can you discuss the problem with someone whose advice you trust?
5. How would you feel if your family, friends, employer, or coworkers learned of your action?

Capitalizing on Workforce Diversity

learning objective

7

At the same time that North American businesspeople are interacting with people from around the world, the domestic workforce is becoming more diverse. This diversity has many dimensions—race, ethnicity, age, religion, gender, national origin, physical ability, and countless other qualities. No longer, say the experts, will the workplace be predominantly Anglo oriented or male. By 2050 many groups now considered minorities (African Americans, Hispanics, Asians, Native Americans) are

spotlight *on communicators*

"In the past five years, I've realized that customers are the most powerful arbiters of workplace diversity," says J. T. (Ted) Childs Jr. In his position as vice president, global workforce diversity for IBM Corp, Childs wants to shift the conversation away from affirmative action and toward the marketplace. Ultimately, he says, promoting diversity is good for business. "More than ever, your customers need to be able to look into your company and see people like themselves."

Photo: Courtesy of J. T. Childs Jr.—IBM Corporation

projected to become 47 percent of the U.S. population.[55] Women are projected to become nearly 50 percent of the workforce. Moreover, it is estimated that the share of the population over 65 will jump dramatically from 13 percent now to 20 percent in 2050. Trends suggest that many of these older people will remain in the workforce. And because of technological advances, more physically challenged people are also joining the workforce.

Dividends of Diversity

As society and the workforce become more diverse, successful interaction and communication among the various identity groups brings distinct challenges and dividends in three areas.

A diverse workforce benefits consumers, work teams, and business organizations.

Consumers. A diverse staff is better able to read trends and respond to the increasingly diverse customer base in local and world markets. Diverse consumers now want specialized goods and services tailored to their needs. Teams made up of different people with different experiences are better able to create the different products that these markets require. Consumers also want to deal with companies that respect their values and reflect themselves. "We find that more and more of our clients are demanding that our partners and staff—involved in securing new business as well as delivering the work—reflect the diversity within their organizations," says Toni Riccardi. She represents PricewaterhouseCoopers, the world largest accounting firm.[56]

Work Teams. As you learned in Chapter 2, employees today work in teams. Team members with different backgrounds may come up with more creative and effective problem-solving techniques than homogeneous teams. At Procter & Gamble a senior marketing executive hit the nail on the head when he said, "I don't know how you can effectively market to the melting pot that this country represents without a workforce and vendors who have a gut-level understanding of the needs and wants of all of these market segments. . . . When we started getting a more diverse workforce, we started getting richer [marketing] plans, because they came up with things that white males were simply not going to come up with on their own."[57]

Business Organizations. Companies that set aside time and resources to cultivate and capitalize on diversity will suffer fewer discrimination lawsuits, fewer union clashes, and less government regulatory action. Most important, though, is the growing realization among organizations that diversity is a critical bottom-line business strategy to improve employee relationships and to increase productivity. Developing a diverse staff that can work together cooperatively is one of the biggest challenges facing business organizations today.

Divisiveness of Diversity

Diversity can cause divisiveness, discontent, and clashes.

Diversity can be a positive force within organizations. But all too often it can also cause divisiveness, discontent, and clashes. Many of the identity groups, the so-called workforce "disenfranchised," have legitimate gripes.

Women complain of the *glass ceiling*, that invisible barrier of attitudes, prejudices, and "old boy networks" blocking them from reaching important corporate positions. Some women feel that they are the victims of sexual harassment, unequal wages, sexism, and even their style of communication. See the accompanying

career coach

He Said, She Said: Gender Talk and Gender Tension

Has the infiltration of gender rhetoric done great damage to the workplace? Are men and women throwing rotten tomatoes at each other as a result of misunderstandings caused by stereotypes of "masculine" and "feminine" attitudes? Deborah Tannen's book *You Just Don't Understand: Women and Men in Conversation,* as well as John Grey's *Men Are From Mars, Women Are From Venus,* caused an avalanche of discussion (and some hostility) by comparing the communication styles of men and women. Here are some of their observations (greatly simplified):[58]

	Women	Men
Object of talk	Establish rapport, make connections, negotiate inclusive relationships	Preserve independence, maintain status, exhibit skill and knowledge
Listening behavior	Attentive, steady eye contact; remain stationary; nod head	Less attentive, sporadic eye contact; move around
Pauses	Frequent pauses, giving chance for others to take turns	Infrequent pauses; interrupt each other to take turns
Small talk	Personal disclosure	Impersonal topics
Focus	Details first, pulled together at end	Big picture
Gestures	Small, confined	Expansive
Method	Questions, apologies; "we" statements; hesitant, indirect, soft speech	Assertions; "I" statements; clear, loud, take-charge speech

Gender theorists suggest that one reason women can't climb above the glass ceiling is that their communication style is less authoritative than that of men.

Career Application

In small groups or in a class discussion, consider these questions: Do men and women have different communication styles? Which style is more appropriate for today's team-based management? Do we need a kind of communicative affirmative action to give more recognition to women's ways of talking? Should training be given to men and women encouraging the interchangeable use of these styles depending on the situation?

Career Coach box to learn more about gender talk and gender tension. On the other hand, men, too, have gender issues. One manager described gender discrimination in his office: "My boss was a woman and was very verbal about the opportunities for women to advance in my company. I have often felt she gave much more attention to the women in the office than the men."[59]

***The glass ceiling** is an invisible barrier of attitudes, prejudices, and "old boy networks" that blocks women from reaching important positions.*

Older employees feel that the deck is stacked in favor of younger employees. Minorities complain that they are discriminated against in hiring, retention, wages, and promotions. Physically challenged individuals feel that their limitations should not hold them back, and they fear that their potential is often prejudged. Individuals with different religions feel uncomfortable working alongside each other. A Jew, for example, may be stressed if he has to help train a Palestinian. Similarly, a manager confessed, "I am half Jewish on my father's side. Very often someone will make a comment about Jews and I am always faced with the decision of speaking up or not."[60]

Tips for Improving Communication Among Diverse Workplace Audiences

A diverse workforce may reduce productivity unless trained to value differences.

Integrating all this diversity into one seamless workforce is a formidable task and a vital one. Harnessed effectively, diversity can enhance productivity and propel a company to success well into the twenty-first century. Mismanaged, it can become a tremendous drain on a company's time and resources. How companies deal with diversity will make all the difference in how they compete in an increasingly global environment. And that means that organizations must do more than just pay lip service to these issues. Harmony and acceptance do not happen automatically when people who are dissimilar work together. The following suggestions can help you and your organization find ways to improve communication and interaction.

- **Seek training.** Especially if an organization is experiencing diversity problems, awareness-raising sessions may be helpful. Spend time reading and learning about workforce diversity and how it can benefit organizations. Look upon diversity as an opportunity, not a threat. Intercultural communication, team building, and conflict resolution are skills that can be learned in diversity training programs.
- **Understand the value of differences.** Diversity makes an organization innovative and creative. Sameness fosters an absence of critical thinking called "groupthink," which you learned about in Chapter 2. Case studies, for example, of the *Challenger* shuttle disaster suggest that groupthink prevented alternatives from being considered. Even smart people working collectively can make dumb decisions if they do not see different perspectives.[61] Diversity in problem-solving groups encourages independent and creative thinking.
- **Don't expect conformity.** Gone are the days when businesses could say, "This is our culture. Conform or leave."[62] Paul Fireman, CEO of Reebok, stresses seeking people who have new and different stories to tell. "And then you have to make real room for them, you have to learn to listen, to listen closely, to their stories. It accomplishes next to nothing to employ those who are different from us if the condition of their employment is that they become the same as us. For it is their differences that enrich us, expand us, provide us the competitive edge."[63]
- **Learn about your cultural self.** Begin to think of yourself as a product of your culture, and understand that your culture is just one among many. Try to stand outside and look at yourself. Do you see any reflex reactions and automatic thought patterns that are a result of your upbringing? These may be invisible to you until challenged by difference. Remember, your culture was designed to help you succeed and survive in a certain environment. Be sure to keep what works and yet be ready to adapt as environments change.
- **Make fewer assumptions.** Be careful of seemingly insignificant, innocent workplace assumptions. For example, don't assume that everyone wants to observe the holidays with a Christmas party and a decorated tree. Celebrating only Christian holidays in December and January excludes those who honor Hanukkah, Kwanzaa, and the Chinese New Year. Moreover, in work-

spotlight *on communicators*

Sleek, stylishly turned out, confident, and assertive, Andrea Jung completely transformed staid and stodgy Avon Products. As CEO, she modernized and enlivened the products, packaging, advertising, research, and marketing procedures, while doubling Avon's stock price. Named one of the most powerful women in U.S. business, Jung understands how important it is to encourage diversity in Avon's global expansion as well as to avoid groupthink in management decisions. "I have to work harder to bring out the conflict in people because it's my tendency to get everyone to agree. But sometimes conflict is good," she confesses. "You lose a lot of time thinking that people agree and then the issues don't come up. It's important to get them out on the table and work through them."

Don't expect all workers to think or act alike.

Photo: © Mario Tama / Getty Images

Process to Product

Applying Your Skills at Wal-Mart

AS PART OF the U.S. team working with Wal-Mart's Seiyu supermarket chain, you face a big problem. At home Wal-Mart refuses to advertise sales or bargains on specific items. Everyday low prices at Wal-Mart already undercut competitors' prices on nearly all items. After all, the concept of everyday low prices is the bedrock of Wal-Mart's success. In Japan, however, Seiyu's managers contend that Wal-Mart must follow the lead of other local supermarkets and promote sales so that housewives will be enticed to shop at Seiyu. Some members of your team are adamant in demanding that Seiyu discontinue the practice of stuffing mailboxes with circulars publicizing twice-a-week sales.

Although the American management team holds the power and ultimately makes decisions, it resists imposing its will on Seiyu's managers. It is concerned with saving face for them. Yet, the American managers feel strongly that they should implement the same selling strategies that have worked so well at home.

Your Task

Within your team, discuss and evaluate possible options regarding the promotion of "sales" and distributing circulars twice a week. Select the best option. Your team may be asked to explain its decision to the class or to write an individual summary of the pros and cons of each option. Be prepared to support your choice. ■

case study

place discussions don't assume that everyone is married or wants to be or is even heterosexual, for that matter. For invitations, avoid phrases such as *managers and their wives. Spouses* or *partners* is more inclusive. Valuing diversity means making fewer assumptions that everyone is like you or wants to be like you.

- **Build on similarities.** Look for areas in which you and others not like you can agree or at least share opinions. Be prepared to consider issues from many perspectives, all of which may be valid. Accept that there is room for different points of view to coexist peacefully. Although you can always find differences, it's much harder to find similarities. Look for common ground in shared experiences, mutual goals, and similar values. Concentrate on your objective even when you may disagree on how to reach it.[64]

In times of conflict, look for areas of agreement and build on similarities.

Summary of Learning Objectives

1 **Discuss three significant trends related to the increasing importance of intercultural communication.** Three trends are working together to crystallize the growing need for developing intercultural proficiencies and improved communication techniques. First, the globalization of markets means that you can expect to be doing business with people from around the world. Second, technological advancements in transportation and information are making the world smaller and more intertwined. Third, more and more immigrants from other cultures are settling in North America, thus changing the complexion of the workforce. Successful interaction requires awareness, tolerance, and accommodation.

2 **Define *culture*. Describe five significant characteristics of culture, and compare and contrast five key dimensions of culture.** *Culture* is the complex system of values, traits, morals, and customs shared by a society. Like a computer, each of us is shaped by the operating system of our culture. Some of the significant characteristics of culture include the following: (1) culture is learned, (2) cultures are inherently logical, (3) culture is the basis of self-identity and community, (4) culture combines the visible and invisible, and (5) culture is dynamic. Members of low-context cultures (such as those in North America, Scandinavia, and Germany) depend on words to express meaning, whereas members of high-context cultures (such as those in Japan, China, and Arab countries) rely more on context (social setting, a person's history, status, and position) to communicate meaning. Other key dimensions of culture include individualism, degree of formality, communication style, and time orientation.

3 **Explain the effects of ethnocentrism, tolerance, and patience in achieving intercultural proficiency.** *Ethnocentrism* refers to an individual's feeling that the culture you belong to is superior to all others and holds all truths. To function effectively in a global economy, we must acquire knowledge of other cultures and be willing to change attitudes. Developing tolerance often involves practicing *empathy*, which means trying to see the world through another's eyes. Saving face and promoting social harmony are important in many parts of the world. Moving beyond narrow ethnocentric views often requires tolerance and patience.

4 **Illustrate how to improve nonverbal and oral communication in intercultural environments.** We can minimize nonverbal miscommunication by recognizing that meanings conveyed by eye contact, posture, and gestures are largely culture dependent. Nonverbal messages are also sent by the use of time, space, and territory. Becoming aware of your own nonverbal behavior and what it conveys is the first step in broadening your intercultural competence. In improving oral messages, you can learn foreign phrases, use simple English, speak slowly and enunciate clearly, observe eye messages, encourage accurate feedback, check for comprehension, accept blame, listen without interrupting, smile, and follow up important conversations in writing.

5 **Illustrate how to improve written messages in intercultural environments.** To improve written messages, adopt local formats, observe titles and rank, use short sentences and short paragraphs, avoid ambiguous expressions, strive for clarity, use correct grammar, and cite numbers carefully. Also try to accommodate the reader in organization, tone, and style.

6 **Discuss intercultural ethics, including ethics abroad, bribery, prevailing customs, and methods for coping.** In doing business abroad, businesspeople should expect to find differing views about ethical practices. Although deciding whose ethics should prevail is tricky, the following techniques are helpful. Broaden your understanding of values and customs in other cultures, and avoid reflex judgments regarding the morality or corruptness of actions. Look for alternative solutions, refuse business if the options violate your basic values, and conduct all relations as openly as possible. Don't rationalize shady decisions, resist legalistic strategies, and apply a five-question ethics test when faced with a perplexing ethical dilemma.

7 **Explain the challenge of capitalizing on workforce diversity, including its dividends and its divisiveness. List tips for improving harmony and communication among diverse workplace audiences.** Having a diverse work-

force can benefit consumers, work teams, and business organizations. However, diversity can also cause divisiveness among various identity groups. To promote harmony and communication, many organizations develop diversity training programs. As an individual, you must understand and accept the value of differences. Don't expect conformity, and create zero tolerance for bias and prejudice. Learn about your cultural self, make fewer assumptions, and seek common ground when disagreements arise.

chapter review

1. Why are domestic companies such as Wal-Mart expanding into overseas markets, and what developments have made such globalization possible? (Obj. 1)
2. In what ways is the Web used to promote e-commerce? (Obj. 1)
3. What is culture and how is culture learned? (Obj. 2)
4. Describe five major dimensions of culture. (Obj. 2)
5. Briefly, contrast high- and low-context cultures. (Obj. 2)
6. What is *ethnocentrism*? (Obj. 3)
7. How is a *stereotype* different from a *prototype*? (Obj. 3)
8. Why is nonverbal communication more difficult to study and learn than verbal communication? (Obj. 4)
9. Name three processes that are effective in achieving competence in dealing with nonverbal messages in other cultures. (Obj. 4)
10. Describe five specific ways you can improve oral communication with a foreigner. (Obj. 4)
11. Describe five specific ways you can improve written communication with a foreigner. (Obj. 5)
12. Why is giving business gifts problematic for Americans? (Obj. 6)
13. List seven techniques for making ethical decisions across borders. (Obj. 6)
14. Name three groups who benefit from workforce diversity and explain why. (Obj. 7)
15. Describe six tips for improving communication among diverse workplace audiences. (Obj. 7)

critical thinking

1. Because English is becoming the world's business language and because the United States is a dominant military and trading force, why should Americans bother to learn about other cultures? (Objs. 1, 2, and 7)
2. If the rules, values, and attitudes of a culture are learned, can they be unlearned? Explain. (Obj. 2)
3. An international business consultant quipped that Asians spend money on entertainment, whereas Americans spend money on attorneys. What are the implications of this statement for business communicators? (Objs. 2, 3, and 6)
4. Some economists and management scholars argue that statements such as "diversity is an economic asset" or "diversity is a new strategic imperative"are unproved and perhaps unprovable assertions. Should social responsibility or market forces determine whether an organization strives to create a diverse workforce? Why? (Obj. 7)
5. **Ethical Issue:** In many countries government officials are not well paid, and "tips" (called "bribes" in the United States) are a way of compensating them. If such payments are not considered wrong in those countries, should you pay them as a means of accomplishing your business? (Objs. 2 and 6)

THREE GREAT RESOURCES FOR YOU!

1. ***Guffey Student Web Site***
   http://guffey.swlearning.com

   Your companion Web site offers chapter review quizzes, WebThink activities, updated chapter URLs, and many additional resources.

2. ***Guffey XTRA!***
   http://guffeyxtra.swlearning.com

   This online study assistant includes Your Personal Language Trainer, Speak Right!, Spell Right!, bonus online chapters, Documents for Analysis, PowerPoint slides, and much more.

3. ***Student Study Guide***

   Self-checked workbook activities and applications review chapter concepts and develop career skills.

activities

4.1 Global Interactions: What We Can Learn When Things Go Wrong (Objs. 1–3)

As business organizations become increasingly global in their structure and marketing, they face communication problems resulting from cultural misunderstandings. The following situations really happened.

Your Task. Based on what you have learned in this chapter, describe several broad principles that could be applied in helping the individuals involved understand what went wrong in the following events. What suggestions could you make for remedying the problems involved?

a. When Wal-Mart opened a store in Germany, shoppers were annoyed by the door greeters, and they regarded the ever-helpful clerks as an intrusion on their private space. They also were suspicious and wary when clerks tried to help customers carry their purchases outside.[65]
b. The employees of a large U.S. pharmaceutical firm became angry over the e-mail messages they received from

the firm's employees in Spain. The messages weren't offensive. Generally, these routine messages just explained ongoing projects. What riled the Americans was this: every Spanish message was copied to the hierarchy within its division. The Americans could not understand why e-mail messages had to be sent to people who had little or nothing to do with the issues being discussed. But this was accepted practice in Spain.[66]

c. J. Bernard van Lierop, a businessperson from Salem, New Hampshire, guided a group of Japanese to a Wisconsin hospital on a business trip. The hospital director threw a handful of his business cards on a table for the Japanese to pick up. "It's so American to dispense with this formality," said Mr. van Lierop.[67] Why might the Japanese be offended?

d. A U.S. T-shirt maker in Miami printed shirts for the Spanish market that promoted the pope's visit. Instead of the desired "I Saw the Pope" in Spanish, the shirts proclaimed "I Saw the Potato."

4.2 Cross-Cultural Gap at Resort Hotel in Thailand (Objs. 1–4)

TEAM

The Laguna Beach Resort Hotel in Phuket, Thailand, nestled between a tropical lagoon and the sparkling Andaman Sea, is one of the most beautiful resorts in the world. (You can take a virtual tour by using Google and searching for "Laguna Beach Resort Phuket.") When Brett Peel arrived as the director of the hotel's kitchen, he thought he had landed in paradise. Only on the job six weeks, he began wondering why his Thai staff would answer *yes* even when they didn't understand what he had said. Other foreign managers discovered that junior staff managers rarely spoke up and never expressed an opinion contrary to those of senior executives. And guests with a complaint thought that Thai employees were not taking them seriously because the Thais smiled at even the worst complaints. Thais also did not seem to understand deadlines or urgent requests.[68]

Your Task. In teams decide how you would respond to the following. If you were the director of this hotel, would you implement a training program for employees? If so, would you train only foreign managers, or would you include local Thai employees as well? What topics should a training program include? Would your goal be to introduce Western ways to the Thais? At least 90 percent of the hotel guests are non-Thai.

4.3 From Waterloo, Wisconsin, Trek Bicycles Goes Global (Objs. 1, 3, and 7)

The small town of Waterloo, Wisconsin (population 2,888), is about the last place you would expect to find the world's largest specialty bicycle maker. But Trek Bicycles started its global business in a red barn smack in the middle of Wisconsin farm country. Nearly 40 percent of the sales of the high-tech, Y-frame bicycles come from international markets. And future sales abroad look promising. Europeans buy 15 million bikes a year, whereas Americans and Canadians together purchase only 10 million. In Asia bicycles are a major means of transportation. To accommodate domestic and international consumers, Trek maintains a busy Web site at **www.trekbikes.com**.

Like many companies, Trek encountered problems in conducting intercultural transactions. For example, in Mexico, cargo was often pilfered while awaiting customs clearance. Distributors in Germany were offended by catalogs featuring pictures of Betty Boop, a cartoon character that decorated Allied bombers during World War II. In Singapore, a buyer balked at a green bike helmet, explaining that when a man wears green on his head it means his wife is unfaithful. In Germany, Trek had to redesign its packaging to reduce waste and meet environmental requirements. Actually, the changes required in Germany helped to bolster the company's overall image of environmental sensitivity.

Your Task. Based on principles you studied in this chapter, name several lessons that other entrepreneurs can learn from Trek's international experiences.[69]

4.4 Interpreting Intercultural Proverbs (Objs. 2 and 3)

Proverbs, which tell truths with metaphors and simplicity, often reveal fundamental values held by a culture.

Your Task. Discuss the following proverbs and explain how they relate to some of the cultural values you studied in this chapter. What additional proverbs can you cite, and what do they mean?

North American proverbs

An ounce of prevention is worth a pound of cure.
The squeaking wheel gets the grease.
A bird in the hand is worth two in the bush.
He who holds the gold makes the rules.

Japanese proverbs

A wise man hears one and understands ten.
The pheasant would have lived but for its cry.
The nail that sticks up gets pounded down.

German proverbs

No one is either rich or poor who has not helped himself to be so.
He who is afraid of doing too much always does too little.

4.5 Negotiating Traps (Objs. 2, 3, 4, and 5)

Businesspeople often have difficulty reaching agreement on the terms of contracts, proposals, and anything that involves bargaining. They have even more difficulty when the negotiators are from different cultures.

Your Task. Discuss the causes and implications of the following common mistakes made by North Americans in their negotiations with foreigners.

a. Assuming that a final agreement is set in stone
b. Lacking patience and insisting that matters progress more quickly than the pace preferred by the locals
c. Thinking that an interpreter is always completely accurate
d. Believing that individuals who speak English understand every nuance of your meaning
e. Ignoring or misunderstanding the significance of rank

4.6 Global Economy (Obj. 1)

Fred Smith, CEO of Federal Express, said, "It is an inescapable fact that the U.S. economy is becoming much more like the European and Asian economies, entirely tied to global trade."

Your Task. Read your local newspapers for a week and peruse national news magazines (*Time, Newsweek, BusinessWeek, U.S. News*, and so forth) for articles that support this assertion. Your instructor may ask you to (a) report on many articles or (b) select one article to summarize. Report your findings orally or in a memo to your instructor. This topic could be expanded into a long report for Chapters 13 or 14.

4.7 Fighting Anti-Americanism Abroad (Objs. 2 and 3)

INFOTRAC

International advertising executive Tim Love urges U.S. corporations to address the issue of rising anti-Americanism in a fresh way.

Your Task. Use InfoTrac to locate "Old Ideas Fail Brand America," *Advertising Age*, Article No. A104987112. After reading the article, answer these questions:

a. What does the author believe to be the responsibility of global corporations today?
b. What are five keys to a new mind-set that can combat the significant resentment toward and misunderstanding of the United States abroad? Briefly explain each.
c. Which of these keys do you think could be implemented by U.S. corporations?

4.8 Analyzing a Problem International Letter (Obj. 5)

American writers sometimes forget that people in other countries, even if they understand English, are not aware of the meanings of certain words and phrases.

Your Task. Study the following letter[70] to be sent by a U.S. firm to a potential supplier in another country. Identify specific weaknesses that may cause troubles for intercultural readers.

Dear Hoshi:

Because of the on-again/off-again haggling with one of our subcontractors, we have been putting off writing to you. We were royally turned off by their shoddy merchandise, the excuses they made up, and the way they put down some of our customers. Since we have our good name to keep up, we have decided to take the bull by the horns and see if you would be interested in bidding on the contract for spare parts.

By playing ball with us, your products are sure to score big. So please give it your best shot and fire off your price list ASAP. We'll need it by 3/8 if you are to be in the running.

Yours,

4.9 Talking Turkey: Avoiding Ambiguous Expressions (Obj. 5)

When a German firm received a message from a U.S. firm saying that it was "time to talk turkey," it was puzzled but decided to reply in Turkish, as requested.

Your Task. Assume you are a businessperson engaged in exporting and importing. As such, you are in constant communication with suppliers and customers around the world. In messages sent abroad, what kinds of ambiguous expressions should you avoid? In teams or individually, list three to five original examples of idioms, slang, acronyms, sports references, abbreviations, jargon, and two-word verbs.

4.10 Making Grease Payments Abroad (Obj. 6)

CRITICAL THINKING

The Foreign Corrupt Practices Act prohibits giving anything of value to a foreign official in an effort to win or retain business. However, the FCPA does allow payments that may be necessary to expedite or secure "routine governmental action." For instance, a company could make "grease" payments to obtain permits and licenses or to process visas or work orders. Also allowed are payments to secure telephone service and power and water supplies, as well as payments for the loading and unloading of cargo.

Your Task. In light of what you have learned in this chapter, how should you act in the following situations? Are the actions legal or illegal?[71]

a. Your company is moving toward final agreement on a contract in Pakistan to sell farm equipment. As the contract is prepared, officials ask that a large amount be included to enable the government to update its agriculture research. The extra amount is to be paid in cash to the three officials you have worked with. Should your company pay?
b. You have been negotiating with a government official in Niger regarding an airplane maintenance contract. The official asks to use your Diner's Club card to charge $2,028 in airplane tickets as a honeymoon present. Should you do it to win the contract?
c. You are trying to collect an overdue payment of $163,000 on a shipment of milk powder to the Dominican Republic. A senior government official asks for $20,000 as a collection service fee. Should you pay?

- **d.** Your company is in the business of arranging hunting trips to East Africa. You are encouraged to give guns and travel allowances to officials in a wildlife agency that has authority to issue licenses to hunt big game. The officials have agreed to keep the gifts quiet. Should you make the gifts?
- **e.** Your firm has just moved you to Malaysia, and your furniture is sitting on the dock. Cargo handlers won't unload it until you or your company pays off each local dock worker. Should you pay?
- **f.** In Mexico your firm has been working hard to earn lucrative contracts with the national oil company, Pemex. One government official has hinted elaborately that his son would like to do marketing studies for your company. Should you hire the son?

4.11 Enforcing the Foreign Corrupt Practices Act (Obj. 6)

INFOTRAC

The Foreign Corrupt Practices Act was passed in 1977 and updated in 1988 and 1998. Any domestic and foreign companies involved in international commercial transactions must understand and appreciate their obligations under this act.
Your Task. Using InfoTrac, search for recent information regarding the Foreign Corrupt Practices Act. Find articles describing at least two recent violations of the act. Who did what, and what punishment was given? In a class discussion or in a memo to your instructor, summarize the act and describe two violations.

4.12 Diversity Role-Playing: Hey, We're All Clones! (Obj. 7)

LISTENING | SPEAKING

Reebok International, the athletic footwear and apparel company, swelled from a $12-million-a-year company to a $3 billion footwear powerhouse in less than a decade. "When we were growing very, very fast, all we did was bring another friend into work the next day," recalls Sharon Cohen, Reebok vice president. "Everybody hired nine of their friends. Well, it happened that nine white people hired nine of their friends, so guess what? They were white, all about the same age. And then we looked up and said, 'Wait a minute. We don't like the way it looks here.'"[72] Assume you are a manager for a successful, fast-growing company like Reebok. One day you look around and notice that everyone looks alike.
Your Task. Pair off with a classmate to role-play a discussion in which you strive to convince another manager that your organization would be better if it were more diverse. The other manager (your classmate), however, is satisfied with the status quo. Suggest advantages for diversifying the staff. The opposing manager argues for homogeneity.

4.13 What Makes a "Best" Company for Minorities? (Obj. 7)

SPEAKING

Each year *Fortune* publishes its rankings for the "50 Best Companies for Minorities." A recent edition includes the following suggestions for fostering diversity:[73]

- Make an effort to hire, retain, and promote minorities.
- Interact with outside minority communities.
- Hold management accountable for diversity efforts.
- Create a culture where people of color and other minorities feel that they belong.
- Match a diverse workforce with diversity in an organization's management ranks and on its board.

Your Task. Assume you are the individual in Activity 4.12 who believes your organization would be better if it were more diverse. Because of your interest in this area, your boss says he'd like you to give a 3- to 5-minute informational presentation at the next board meeting. Your assignment is to provide insights on what the leading companies for minority employees are doing. You decide to prepare your comments based on *Fortune* magazine's list of the 50 best companies for minorities, using as your outline the above bulleted list. You plan to provide examples of each means of fostering diversity. Your instructor may ask you to give your presentation (a) to the entire class or (b) to small groups.

4.14 Culture Clash: Hiring a New Supervisor Was Not the Answer (Obj. 7)

INFOTRAC

A new manager from the Midwest was hired for a troubled New York apparel contractor. The firm had many workers from the Caribbean, primarily Puerto Rico and Haiti, and a poor productivity record. Full of vim and vigor, the new manager jumped into his new job enthusiastically.
Your Task. Read about his experiences in the InfoTrac article titled "The Hispanic Work Force: How to Deal With Diversity" by Woodruff Imberman and Mariah de Forest (Article No. A112411096). Then answer these questions:

- **a.** Why did the new manager fail in his attempts to correct the workers and improve plant performance?
- **b.** What did the largely Hispanic workforce expect from supervisors?
- **c.** How do Hispanic workplace values differ from those of Anglos, according to the author?

4.15 Locating Diversity Training Consultants (Obj. 7)

E-MAIL | WEB

Management thought it was doing the right thing in diversifying its staff. But now signs of friction are appearing. Staff meetings are longer, and conflicts have arisen in solving problems. Some of the new people say they aren't taken seriously and that they are expected to blend in and become just like everybody else. A discrimination suit was filed in one department.

Your Task. CEO William Somers asks you, a human resources officer, to present suggestions for overcoming this staff problem. Make a list of several suggestions, based on what you have learned in this chapter. In addition, go to the Web and locate three individuals, teams, or firms who you think might be possibilities for developing a diversity training program for your company. Prepare a memo or an e-mail to Mr. Somers outlining your suggestions and listing your recommendations for possible diversity training consultants. Describe the areas of expertise of each potential consultant.

4.16 Consumer: Could You Become a Victim to Cross-Border Fraud?

CONSUMER | E-MAIL | TEAM | WEB

Exciting advancements in trade and technology have given consumers unprecedented access to new products, services, information, and markets. But they have also exposed large numbers of consumers to scams and fraud. Pyramid and lottery schemes, travel- and credit-related ploys, and high-tech scams such as modem and Web-page hijacking now plague consumers. Business communicators must be especially alert to cross-border fraud because operators strike quickly and then disappear.

Your Task. To arm yourself against cross-border fraud, use the Web or InfoTrac to learn about the latest scams and what you can do if victimized. Individually, search for answers to the questions listed here. Then in teams discuss your findings. Individually or in teams, use e-mail to report your findings to your instructor.

a. What are six kinds of cross-border fraud that have been reported? Explain each.
b. What should you do before ordering from a Web site?
c. What should you do to resolve your complaint if something goes wrong?

video resources

Bridging the Gap Video Library 2

Erasing Stereotypes: Zubi Advertising

Two sets of videos accompany Guffey's *Business Communication: Process and Product*, 5e. **Video Library 1**, *Building Workplace Skills*, presents five videos that introduce and reinforce concepts in selected chapters. **Video Library 2**, *Bridging the Gap*, presents six videos that focus on real companies with chapter-specific learning activities. The recommended video for this chapter is "Erasing Stereotypes: Zubi Advertising."

Your Task. After watching the video, in class discussion or in a memo to your instructor, answer the following questions:

a. Why is it necessary for big companies such as Ford to hire a company such as Zubi Advertising to develop special ad campaigns aimed at Hispanic markets? What role does culture play in the development of such campaigns?
b. Why is it important for all businesspeople to think about how their products, services, and organizations are perceived in other cultures?
c. What does the phrase "erasing stereotypes" mean at Zubi Advertising? Could advertising that targets specific cultural groups enforce rather than erase stereotypes? Based on what you learned in this chapter, how is a stereotype different from a prototype?
d. Is stereotyping always inaccurate?

C.L.U.E. review 4

Edit the following sentences to correct faults in grammar, capitalization, punctuation, spelling, and word use.

1. The President of MainStreet Enterprises, along with other executives of local companys are considering overseas' sales.
2. International business was all ready common among big companys however even small bussinesses are now seeking global markets.
3. 3 different employees asked the Supervisor and I whether we should give gifts to our chinese business guests?
4. Gifts for the children of an arab are welcome however gifts for an arabs wife are not advisible.
5. In latin america knifes are not proper gifts, they signify cutting off an relationship.
6. When it opened it's one hundred and twenty million dollar plant in Beijing Motorola had to offer housing too attract qualety applicants.
7. On May 12th a article titled The chinese puzzle which appeared in the magazine Workforce Management described the difficultys of managing employees' world wide.
8. We invited seventy-five employees to hear the cross cultural talk that begins at four p.m..
9. The u.s. census bureau reports that 1/3 of the foreign born population of the united states are from: central america, the caribbean, and south america.
10. By 2,050 many groups now considered minorities African Americans, hispanics, asians, and native americans are projected to constitute forty-seven percent of the U.S. population.

unit 2

Guffey's 3-x-3 Writing Process

chapter 5

Writing Process Phase 1: Analyze, Anticipate, Adapt

chapter 6

Writing Process Phase 2: Research, Organize, Compose

chapter 7

Writing Process Phase 3: Revise, Proofread, Evaluate

chapter 5

Writing Process Phase 1: Analyze, Anticipate, Adapt

objectives

1 Identify three basics of business writing, summarize Guffey's 3-x-3 writing process, and explain how a writing process helps a writer.

2 Explain how the writing process may be altered and how it is affected by team projects.

3 Clarify what is involved in analyzing a writing task and selecting a communication channel.

4 Describe anticipating and profiling the audience for a message.

5 Specify six writing techniques that help communicators adapt messages to the task and audience.

6 Explain why communicators must adapt their writing in four high-risk areas.

COMMUNICATION IN PROCESS

Kinko's Trades Its Quirky Campus Image As FedEx Moves In

IF YOU STILL think of Kinko's as those quirky self-serve copy shops, "you're stuck in the Seventies, man," says *Fortune* magazine.[1] Recently purchased by FedEx, Kinko's has become a strategic acquisition for the huge delivery company. Kinko's already employs over 20,000 "coworkers" in 1,200 locations worldwide and now enjoys entrée into Fortune 500 corporations through its well-financed parent.

Kinko's has come a long way from the days when its founder Paul ("Kinko") Orfalea began hawking school supplies from an oversized knapsack to students in dormitories at the University of California, Santa Barbara. He is fond of telling stories about his lackluster college career. After attending his first philosophy class, he said, "God, I don't understand any of that. . . . I'm never going to make it in this world." Orfalea did indeed have a problem. He suffered from such severe dyslexia that as a child he was barely able to read or write. "Some people say they have dyslexia," he confided, rolling his eyes. "I got the real thing!"[2] Although not particularly gifted as a student, he was definitely talented as a businessperson.

While finishing his degree, Orfalea (whose nickname comes from his kinky red hair) noticed a copy machine in the university library. Seeing its potential, he leased one and set up business in a tiny vacated hamburger stand near campus. His cheap prices drew in the students, and before long he expanded his copy store concept to other campuses. Kinko's now combines printer, publisher, high-volume duplicating, color copying, faxing, and computer access for "mobile professionals"—salespeople and executives on the road. Quick to respond to the home office trend, Kinko's became "your branch office," supplying increasing numbers of self-employed people with quality services.

More recently Kinko's set out to capture another branch of consumers: corporate types that occupy Fortune 500 offices. Under FedEx's wing, Kinko's now has easier access to corporate outsourcing jobs. Its goal is to produce a professional sales force that can convince big companies that Kinko's can give better reprographic service than their own in-house departments. And that requires a change in image. Revamping its college image and adapting to a new audience demand special communication talents and procedures.

Photo: © AP/Wide World Photos

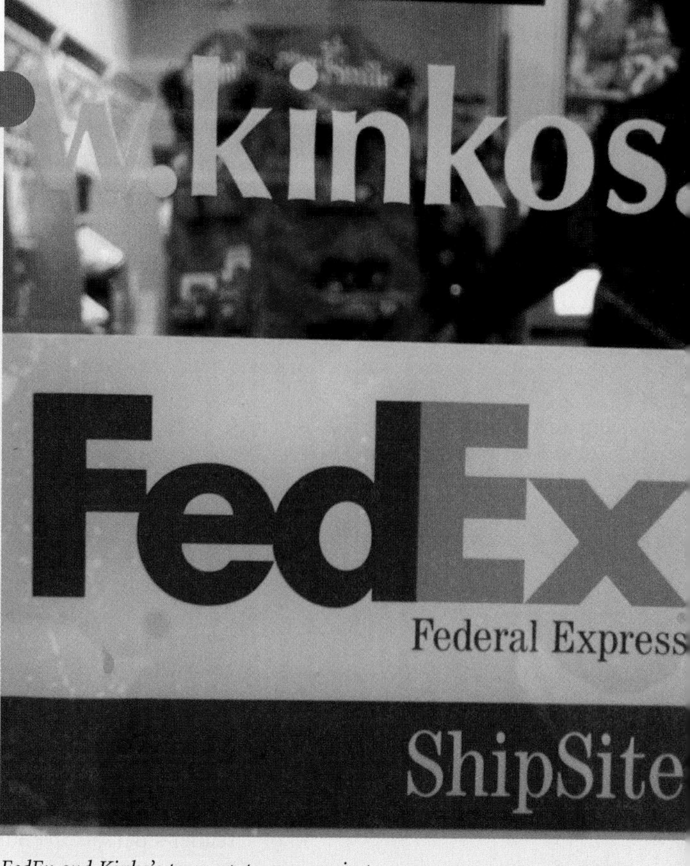

FedEx and Kinko's team up to communicate a new message to consumers.

Critical Thinking

- How could a company like Kinko's go about changing its image?
- In the messages it sends to customers, how can Kinko's present a new image?
- What communication skills will be important to Kinko's marketing representatives?

http://www.kinkos.com

CONTINUED ON PAGE 148

case study

learning objective 1

Approaching the Writing Process Systematically

As Kinko's moves into a new marketing arena under FedEx ownership, its representatives must finely tune their communication skills to project a new image and capture new clients. Preparing and writing any business message—whether a letter, e-mail memo, or a Kinko's sales presentation—is easier when the writer or presenter has a systematic plan to follow.

Business Writing Basics

Business writing is purposeful, economical, and reader oriented.

Business writing differs from other writing you may have done. In writing high school or college compositions and term papers, you probably focused on discussing your feelings or displaying your knowledge. Professors wanted to see your thought processes, and they wanted assurance that you had internalized the subject matter. You may have had to meet a minimum word count. Business writers, however, have different goals. In preparing business messages and oral presentations, you'll find that your writing needs to be:

- **Purposeful.** You will be writing to solve problems and convey information. You will have a definite purpose to fulfill in each message.
- **Economical.** You will try to present ideas clearly but concisely. Length is not rewarded.
- **Reader oriented.** You will concentrate on looking at a problem from the reader's perspective instead of seeing it from your own.

***Business writers seek to* express *rather than* impress.**

These distinctions actually ease the writer's task. In writing most business documents, you won't be searching your imagination for creative topic ideas. You won't be stretching your ideas to make them appear longer. One writing consultant complained that newly hired graduates entering industry seem to think that quantity enhances quality.[3] Wrong! Get over the notion that longer is better. Conciseness is what counts in business. Furthermore, you won't be trying to dazzle readers with your extensive knowledge, powerful vocabulary, or graceful phrasing. The goal in business writing is to *express* rather than *impress*. You will be striving to get your ideas across naturally, simply, and clearly.

In many ways business writing is easier than academic writing, yet it still requires hard work, especially from beginners. However, following a process, studying models, and practicing the craft can make nearly anyone a successful business writer and speaker. This book provides all three components: process, products (models), and practice. First, you'll focus on the process of writing business messages.

Guffey's 3-x-3 Writing Process for Business Messages and Oral Presentations

The phases of the 3-x-3 writing process are prewriting, writing, and revising.

In the first edition of this book, the author set forth an innovative and original process for writing business messages and making presentations. Unlike past business communication books, this one developed a special plan to help beginning writers understand the entire writing process. Guffey's 3-x-3 writing process and its unique illustrations proved so successful that more students used this book to learn to write than any other business communication book. Students quickly understood the writing process because it was divided into three easy-to-use phases: prewriting, writing, and revising. More important, Guffey's 3-x-3 writing process explains exactly what to do in each of the three phases, as shown in Figure 5.1

FIGURE 5.1 ***Guffey's 3-x-3 Writing Process***

1 Prewriting

ANALYZE: Decide on your purpose. What do you want the receiver to do or believe? What channel is best?

ANTICIPATE: Profile the audience. What does the receiver already know? Will the receiver's response be neutral, positive, or negative?

ADAPT: What techniques can you use to adapt your message to its audience and anticipated reaction?

2 Writing

RESEARCH: Gather data to provide facts. Search company files, previous correspondence, and the Internet. What do you need to know to write this message?

ORGANIZE: Group similar facts together. Decide how to organize your information. Outline your plan and make notes.

COMPOSE. Prepare a first draft, usually writing quickly.

3 Revising

REVISE: Edit your message to be sure it is clear, conversational, concise, and readable.

PROOFREAD: Read carefully to find errors in spelling, grammar, punctuation, names, numbers, and format.

EVALUATE: Will this message achieve your purpose? Have you thought enough about the audience to be sure this message is appropriate and appealing?

How can this process help you? Guffey's 3-x-3 writing process provides you with a systematic plan for developing all your business communications from simple memos and informational reports to corporate proposals and oral presentations. You'll learn how to apply the process in Chapters 5, 6, and 7. In all the writing chapters that follow, you will find examples of documents illustrated with Guffey's "process visualizers." These three-box illustrations, which have appeared in this book since the first edition, help you quickly see how a document was conceived, organized, and written.

Let's watch Guffey's 3-x-3 writing process being applied in a typical business situation. Kinko's received an inquiry at its Web site from a prospective customer of its videoconferencing services. Kinko's product manager, Kevin Matthews, quickly recognized that this was an opportunity to promote its services. In the first phase of the writing process, Kevin analyzed the situation. His purpose was to gain a new Kinko's customer. To do that, he must make a good impression in telling the customer about Kinko's services. The customer is the president of his company, and Kevin anticipated that he would be receptive to this message since he had inquired about the services. But company presidents are busy people. Kevin knew that he would have to adapt techniques to ensure that his message was concise and easily scanned. In choosing a communication channel, Kevin decided that a letter on company stationery would be more impressive than an e-mail message or a telephone call. A letter would also allow him to be systematic, concise, and professional in presenting considerable information about videoconferencing services. After analyzing, anticipating, and adapting, he moved to the second phase.

Collecting data, organizing it, and composing a first draft make up the second phase of the writing process.

In the second phase, Kevin gathered information. He collected all of the promotional material that had been written about videoconferencing services. But he found that way too much data existed. He needed to condense and organize it into a bulleted format that would be more appealing to an executive in a hurry. He also knew that he should emphasize the benefits to the customer. How would videoconferencing solve the customer's problems? After writing many paragraphs, Kevin decided to condense all that information into a bulleted list. He decided on an organizational format and then wrote a first draft at his computer.

In the last phase of the 3-x-3 writing process, Kevin edited his letter. He liked his opening, but his bulleted list needed work. He revised it until each item began with a verb, thus achieving the parallelism he sought. As he revised, he found many ways to make his writing clearer and more concise. When he had a final copy, he

FIGURE 5.2 ***Applying Guffey's 3-x-3 Writing Process at Kinko's***

1 Prewriting

ANALYZE: The purpose of this letter is to develop goodwill while persuading a customer to use Kinko's services.

ANTICIPATE: The receiver is a busy company president who will probably be receptive to the message.

ADAPT: Describe benefits from the reader's point of view. Be sure the message is concise, conversational, readable, and professional.

2 Writing

RESEARCH: Collect information about videoconferencing. Ask experts how it can help small business owners.

ORGANIZE: Prepare a list or outline of ideas. Open directly and cordially. Explain the advantages of videoconferencing. Close with an invitation to visit plus a reference to ease of use and special cameras.

COMPOSE: Write first draft at a computer. Compose quickly.

3 Revising

REVISE: Look for ways to improve clarity and conciseness. Revise the bulleted list so that all items begin with verbs.

PROOFREAD: Look for typos and spelling errors. Check punctuation and placement. Consider asking someone else to read the letter.

EVALUATE: Is this message conversational? Will the letter (especially the closing) prompt the receiver to act?

kinko's

Three Galleria Tower
13155 Noel Road
Suite 1600
Dallas, TX 75240

February 7, 2006

Mr. Peter M. Manchester, President
Manchester & Associates
3420 North Capital Boulevard
Raleigh, NC 27604

Dear Mr. Manchester:

We appreciate your recent inquiry about Kinko's videoconferencing services. Because today's business moves at a fast pace and often requires face-to-face meetings, we'd like to tell you how you can conduct those meetings worldwide—without ever leaving town!

Kinko's videoconferencing services can help you launch a product, complete a project on time, or hire a prized job candidate. These and many other tasks demand swift action. Instead of sending employees to remote locations, you can use Kinko's videoconferencing, available in 150 locations, to conduct effective meetings, make presentations to clients, and meet new business prospects. Other benefits of Kinko's videoconferencing include the following:

- Conduct several meetings in one day instead of traveling to attend just one
- Express your ideas clearly with slides and other visual aids
- Present graphs or other documents right from your laptop
- Access Internet information during your videoconference
- Videotape your conference for future viewing
- Schedule and check room availability 24 hours a day, seven days a week

Videoconferencing reduces staff fatigue, eliminates travel expenses, and cuts meeting time. Just think of it—you can actually complete a one-hour meeting in one hour! At the same time, you can boost the impact and results of your presentation.

If you already have your own videoconferencing equipment, you can extend your network with direct links to Kinko's 150 videoconferencing sites without incremental equipment costs.

For more information, visit www.kinkos.com or call 1-800-669-1235. Better yet, come in for a demonstration of our easy-to-use equipment including voice-activated cameras that track all the action.

Sincerely,

Kevin Matthews

Kevin Matthews
Account Manager

More than 1,100 Kinko's locations worldwide. For the location nearest you, call 1-800-2-KINKOS or visit our web site at www.kinkos.com

100% post-consumer recycled.

Promotes videoconferencing by showing benefits to reader

Opens directly with appreciation for customer's inquiry

Uses bulleted list to improve readability and produce high "skim value"

Explains advantages from perspective of reader

Uses conversational tone in building interest

Makes it easy to respond

Closes with contact information and motivation to act

printed it and read it once again. Then he asked himself whether this letter would achieve its purpose—gaining a new customer for Kinko's. You can see his final version in Figure 5.2.

Adapting and Altering the Writing Process

learning objective 2

Although the diagrams in Figures 5.1 and 5.2 show the three phases equally, the time you spend on each varies. Moreover, the process is not always linear.

In the writing process revising takes the most time.

Scheduling the Process. One expert gives these rough estimates for scheduling a project: 25 percent worrying and planning (Phase 1), 25 percent writing (Phase 2), 45 percent revising, and 5 percent proofreading (Phase 3). These are rough guides, yet you can see that good writers spend most of their time revising. Much depends, of course, on your project, its importance, and your familiarity with it. What's critical to remember, though, is that revising is a major component of the writing process.

This process may seem a bit complicated for the daily messages and oral presentations that many businesspeople prepare. Does this same process apply to memos and short letters? And how do collaborators and modern computer technologies affect the process?

Steps in the writing process may be rearranged, shortened, or repeated.

Although good writers proceed through each phase of the writing process, some steps may be compressed for short, routine messages. Brief, everyday documents enlist Guffey's 3-x-3 process, but many of the steps are performed quickly, without prolonged deliberation. For example, prewriting may take the form of a few moments of reflection. The writing phase may consist of looking in the files quickly, jotting a few notes in the margin of the original document, and composing at your computer. Revising might consist of reading a printout, double-checking the spelling and grammar, and making a few changes. Longer, more involved documents—such as persuasive memos, sales letters, management reports, proposals, and résumés—require more attention to all parts of the process.

Recursive Nature of the Process. One other point about the 3-x-3 writing process needs clarification. It may appear that you perform one step and progress to the next, always following a linear order. Most business writing, however, is not that rigid. Although writers perform the tasks described, the steps may be rearranged, abbreviated, or repeated. Some writers revise every sentence and paragraph as they go. Many find that new ideas occur after they've begun to write, causing them to back up, alter the organization, and rethink their plan. Thus, the 3-x-3 writing process is more nearly recursive than linear. It sometimes curves backward before moving forward.

You should expect to follow the 3-x-3 process closely as you begin developing your business communication skills. With experience, though, you'll become like other good writers and presenters who alter, compress, and rearrange the steps as needed.

Team-written projects are necessary for big tasks, jobs with short deadlines, and projects that require the expertise or consensus of many people. Team members generally work together to brainstorm and make assignments, but they work separately to do the writing.

Photo: © Photodisc Blue/Getty Images

Working With Teams

As you learned in Chapter 2, many of today's workers will work with teams to deliver services, develop products, and complete projects. It's almost assumed that today's progressive organizations will employ teams in some capacity to achieve their objectives.[4] Because much of a team's work involves writing, you can expect to be putting your writing skills to work as part of a team.

When is writing collaboration necessary? It is especially important for (1) big tasks, (2) items with short deadlines, and (3) team projects that require the expertise

tech talk

Using Technology to Edit and Revise Collaborative Documents

Collaborative writing and editing projects are challenging. Fortunately, Microsoft Word offers many useful tools to help team members edit and share documents electronically. Two simple but useful editing tools are *Highlight* and *Font Color.* These tools, which are found on the **Formatting** toolbar, enable reviewers to point out errors and explain problematic passages through the use of contrast. However, some projects may require more advanced editing tools such as *Track Changes* and *Insert Comments.*

Track Changes. To suggest specific editing changes to other team members, *Track Changes* is handy. The revised wording is visible on-screen, and deletions show up in call-out balloons that appear in the right-hand margin (see Figure 5.3). Suggested revisions offered by different team members are identified and dated. The original writer may accept or reject these changes. In recent versions of Word, you'll find *Track Changes* on the **Tools** menu.

Insert Comments. Probably the most useful editing tool is *Insert Comments,* also shown in Figure 5.3. This tool allows users to point out problematic passages or errors, ask or answer questions, and share ideas without changing or adding text. When more than one person adds comments, the comments appear in different colors and are identified by the individual writer's name and a date/time stamp. To use this tool in newer versions of Word, each reviewer must click **Tools, Options,** and fill in the **User Information** section. In older versions of Word, this collaborative tool was called *Annotation.* To facilitate adding, reviewing, editing, or deleting comments, Word now provides a special toolbar. You can activate it by using the **View** pull-down menu (click **Toolbars** and **Reviewing**). On the **Reviewing** toolbar, click **New Comment**. Then type your comment, which can be seen in the web or print layout view (click **View** and **Print Layout** or **Web Layout**).

Career Application

Organize into groups of three. Using the latest version of Word, copy and respond to the Document for Analysis in Activity 5.1. Set up a round-robin e-mail file exchange so that each member responds to the other group members' documents by using the **Comment** feature of Word to offer advice or suggestions for improvement. Submit a printout of the document with group comments, as well as a final edited document.

or consensus of many people. Businesspeople sometimes collaborate on short documents, such as memos, letters, information briefs, procedures, and policies. But more often, teams work together on big documents and presentations. For example, let's say that a team of Kinko's specialists is writing a proposal to submit to Bank of America. The proposal offers a wide range of services from business cards and stationery to signs, banners, and online printing. The task requires different members of the Kinko's team to conduct research and write different sections of the proposal.

Team-written documents and presentations produce better products.

Team-written documents and presentations are standard in most organizations because collaboration has many advantages. Most important, collaboration produces a better product. Many heads are better than one. In addition, team members and organizations benefit from team processes. Working together helps socialize members. They learn more about the organization's values and procedures. They are able to break down functional barriers, and they improve both formal and informal chains of communication. Additionally, they "buy into" a project when they are part of its development. Members of effective teams are eager to implement their recommendations.

In preparing big projects, teams may not actually function together for each phase of the writing process. Typically, team members gather at the beginning to brainstorm. They iron out answers to questions about purpose, audience, content, organization, and design of their document or presentation. They develop procedures for team functioning, as you learned in Chapter 2. Then, they often assign seg-

FIGURE 5.3 ***Team-Written Document Showing MS Word Collaboration Tools***

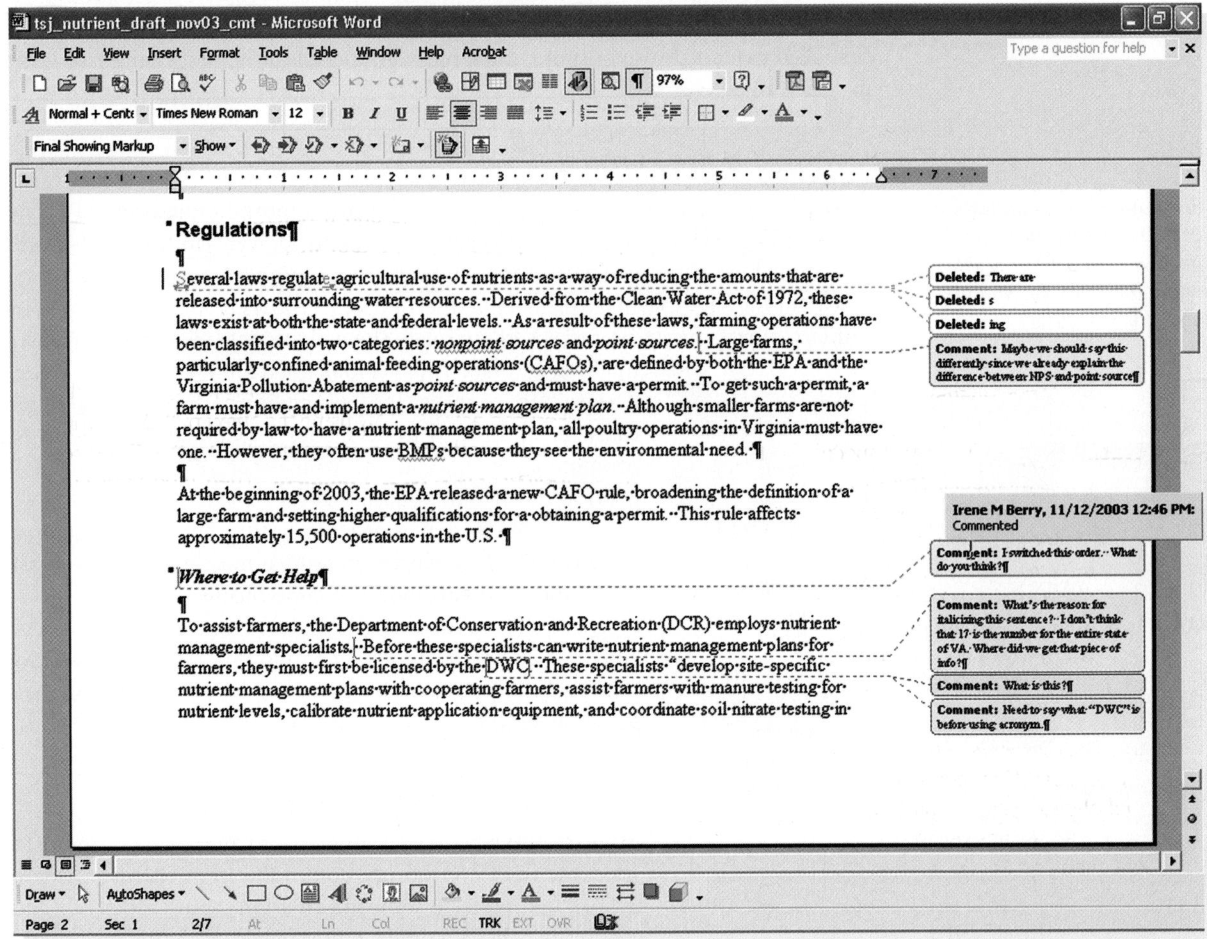

ments of the project to individual members. Thus, teams work together closely in Phase 1 (prewriting) of the writing process. However, members generally work separately in Phase 2 (writing), when they conduct research, organize their findings, and compose a first draft. During Phase 3 (revising) teams may work together to synthesize their drafts and offer suggestions for revision. They might assign one person the task of preparing the final document and another the job of proofreading. The revision and evaluation phase might be repeated several times before the final product is ready for presentation.

Teams generally work closely in Phase 1, work separately in Phase 2, and synthesize their drafts in Phase 3.

One of the most frustrating tasks for teams is writing shared documents. Keeping the different versions straight and recognizing who made what comment can be confusing. Microsoft Word, however, provides a number of wonderful tools that enable team members to track changes and insert comments while editing one team document. The accompanying Tech Talk box presents these tools, and Figure 5.3 illustrates how they work.

Writing Process Phase 1: Analyze

learning objective 3

Whether you're working with a team, composing by yourself, or preparing an oral presentation, the end result of your efforts can be greatly improved by following the steps outlined in Guffey's 3-x-3 writing process. Not only are you more likely to get your message across, but you'll also feel less anxious and your writing will progress more quickly. The remainder of this chapter focuses on the prewriting phase of composition: analyzing, anticipating, and adapting. In this phase you'll first need to identify the purpose of the message and select the best channel or form in which to deliver it.

Identifying the Purpose

Most business communication has both primary purposes (to inform or persuade) and secondary purposes (to promote goodwill).

As you begin to compose a message, ask yourself two important questions: (1) Why am I sending this message? and (2) What do I hope to achieve? Your responses will determine how you organize and present your information.

Your message may have primary and secondary purposes. For college work your primary purpose may be merely to complete the assignment; secondary purposes might be to make yourself look good and to get a good grade. The primary purposes for sending business messages are typically to inform and to persuade. A secondary purpose is to promote goodwill: you and your organization want to look good in the eyes of your audience.

Most business messages do nothing more than *inform.* They explain procedures, announce meetings, answer questions, and transmit findings. Some business messages, however, are meant to *persuade.* These messages sell products, convince managers, motivate employees, and win over customers. Informative messages are developed differently than persuasive messages.

spotlight *on communicators*

Danny O'Neill, president of The Roasterie, a Kansas City coffee retailer, begins each writing session by analyzing his task and thinking about his audience. "Half of my preparation when writing memos is anticipating hurdles and predicting how my employees will react." For example, in a memo on the importance of collecting accounts receivable, he anticipated that some employees might not make this their top priority. Thus, his memo clearly stated that "if we don't collect the money, nothing else matters."

Selecting the Best Channel

After identifying the purpose of your message, you need to select the most appropriate communication channel. As you learned in Chapter 1, some information is most efficiently and effectively delivered orally. Other messages should be written, and still others are best delivered electronically. Whether to set up a meeting, send a message by e-mail, or write a report depends on some of the following factors:

- Importance of the message
- Amount and speed of feedback required
- Necessity of a permanent record
- Cost of the channel
- Degree of formality desired

The foregoing factors could help you decide which of the channels shown in Figure 5.4 is most appropriate for delivering a message. Kinko's account managers, for example, would probably choose face-to-face conversations or group meetings as the most effective communication channel in delivering their changed-image message.

learning objective

4

Writing Process Phase 1: Anticipate

Some messages miss the mark. Consider this message that responds to a nine-year-old boy who requested a toy rocket launcher from a breakfast cereal company: "Due to the overwhelming response this promotion has generated, we have unfortunately depleted our stock temporarily. We are, therefore, holding your request pending

Photo: Courtesy of Danny O'Neill

Figure 5.4 ***Choosing Communication Channels***

Channel	Best Use
Face-to-face conversation	When you want to be persuasive, deliver bad news, or share a personal message.
Telephone call	When you need to deliver or gather information quickly, when nonverbal cues are unimportant, and when you cannot meet in person.
Voice mail message	When you wish to leave important or routine information that the receiver can respond to when convenient.
Fax	When your message must cross time zones or international boundaries, when a written record is significant, or when speed is important.
E-mail	When you need feedback but not immediately. Insecurity makes it problematic for personal, emotional, or private messages. Effective for communicating with a large, dispersed audience.
Face-to-face group meeting	When group decisions and consensus are important. Inefficient for merely distributing information.
Video- or teleconference	When group consensus and interaction are important but members are geographically dispersed.
Memo	When you want a written record to clearly explain policies, discuss procedures, or collect information within an organization.
Letter	When you need a written record of correspondence with customers, the government, suppliers, or others outside an organization.
Report or proposal	When you are delivering complex data internally or externally.

Choosing the best channel to deliver a message depends on the importance of the message, the feedback required, the need for a permanent record, the cost, and the degree of formality needed.

stock replenishment." The breakfast cereal company's representative had no sense of audience; as a result, the language was largely inappropriate.

A good writer anticipates the audience for a message: What is the reader like? How will that reader react to the message? Although you can't always know exactly who the reader is, you can imagine some characteristics of the reader. The breakfast cereal company writer could have pictured a typical young boy and imagined the vocabulary and expectations he might have. Even writers of direct mail sales letters have a general idea of the audience they wish to target. Picturing a typical reader is important in guiding what you write. One copywriter at Lands' End, the catalog company, pictures his sister-in-law whenever he writes product descriptions for the catalog. By profiling your audience and shaping a message to respond to that profile, you are more likely to achieve your communication goals.

Profiling the Audience

By profiling your audience before you write, you can identify the appropriate tone, language, and channel.

Visualizing your audience is a pivotal step in the writing process. The questions in Figure 5.5 will help you profile your audience. How much time you devote to answering these questions depends greatly on your message and its context. An analytical report that you compose for management or an oral presentation before a big group would, of course, demand considerable audience anticipation. On the other hand, an e-mail to a coworker or a letter to a familiar supplier might require only a few moments of planning. No matter how short your message, though, spend some time thinking about the audience so that you can tailor your words to your readers or listeners.

spotlight *on communicators*

Described as brilliant and unflappable, Condoleezza Rice became the first female, first nonwhite, and youngest provost in the history of Stanford University. Admirers have called her one of the country's best and brightest as well as the president's secret weapon. When she served as National Security Adviser to President Bush, she put great thought into the words she used as she sharpened and presented the arguments of the administration's often rambunctious National Security Council. Analyzing the task and adapting to the audience enabled her to hold her own whether she was persuading older colleagues at Stanford, fielding reporters' questions, or translating the president's instincts into policy.

Photo: © AP/Wide World Photos

Responding to the Profile

Anticipating your audience helps you make decisions about shaping the message. You'll discover what kind of language is appropriate, whether you're free to use specialized technical terms, whether you should explain everything, and so on. You'll decide whether your tone should be formal or informal, and you'll select the most desirable channel. Imagining whether the receiver is likely to be neutral, positive, or negative will help you determine how to organize your message.

Another result of profiling your audience will be recognizing whether a secondary audience is possible. For example, let's say you start to write an e-mail message to your supervisor describing a problem you're having. Halfway through the message you realize that your supervisor will probably forward this message to her boss, the vice president. She will not want to summarize what you said; instead she will take the easy route and merely forward your e-mail. When you realize that the vice president will probably see your message, you decide to back up and use a more formal tone. You remove

FIGURE 5.5 ***Asking the Right Questions to Profile Your Audience***

Primary Audience	Secondary Audience
Who is my primary reader or listener?	Who might see or hear this message after the primary audience?
What is my personal and professional relationship with that person?	How do these people differ from the primary audience?
What position does the individual hold in the organization?	How must I reshape my message to make it understandable and acceptable to others to whom it might be forwarded?
How much does that person know about the subject?	
What do I know about that person's education, beliefs, culture, and attitudes?	
Should I expect a neutral, positive, or negative response to my message?	

your inquiry about your supervisor's family, you reduce your complaints, and you tone down your language about why things went wrong. Instead, you provide more background information, and you are more specific in identifying items that the vice president might not recognize. Analyzing the task and anticipating the audience assists you in adapting your message so that it will accomplish what you intend.

spotlight *on communicators*

Warren Buffett, the second richest man in the U.S. and one of the most successful investors of all time, offers advice on how to improve your messages by profiling your audience and responding to that profile. When writing annual reports, he pretends that he's talking to his sisters. "I have no trouble picturing them. Though highly intelligent, they are not experts in accounting or finance. They will understand plain English but jargon may puzzle them . . . . No sisters to write to? Borrow mine: Just begin with 'Dear Doris and Bertie,'" he suggests.

Writing Process Phase 1: Adapt

After analyzing your purpose and anticipating your audience, you must convey your purpose to that audience. Adaptation is the process of creating a message that suits your audience.

One important aspect of adaptation is *tone.* Conveyed largely by the words in a message, tone reflects how a receiver feels upon reading or hearing a message. For example, think how you would react to these statements:

You must return the form by 5 p.m.

Would you please return the form by 5 p.m.

learning objective

5

The wording of the first message establishes an aggressive or negative tone—no one likes being told what to do. The second message is reworded in a friendlier, more positive manner. Poorly chosen words may sound demeaning, condescending, discourteous, pretentious, or demanding. Notice in the Lands' End letter in Figure 5.6 that the writer achieves a courteous and warm tone. The letter responds to a customer's concern about the changing merchandise mix available in Lands' End catalogs. The customer also wanted to receive fewer catalogs. The writer explains the company's expanded merchandise line and reassures the customer that Lands' End has not abandoned its emphasis on classic styles.

Skilled communicators create a positive tone in their messages by using a number of adaptive techniques, some of which are unconscious. These include spotlighting receiver benefits; cultivating a "you" view; and avoiding gender, racial, age, and disability bias. Additional adaptive techniques include being courteous, using familiar words, and choosing precise words.

Ways to adapt to the audience include choosing the right words and tone; spotlighting reader benefits; cultivating a "you" view; and using sensitive, courteous language.

Spotlighting Receiver Benefits

Focusing on the audience sounds like a modern idea, but actually one of America's early statesmen and authors recognized this fundamental writing principle over 200 years ago. In describing effective writing, Ben Franklin observed, "To be good, it ought to have a tendency to benefit the reader."[5] These wise words have become a fundamental guideline for today's business communicators. Expanding on Franklin's counsel, a contemporary communication consultant gives this solid advice to his business clients: "Always stress the benefit to the readers of whatever it is you're trying to get them to do. If you can show them how you're going to save them frustration or help them meet their goals, you have the makings of a powerful message."[6]

Empathic communicators envision the receiver and focus on benefits to that person.

Adapting your message to the receiver's needs means putting yourself in that person's shoes. It's called *empathy.* Empathic senders think about how a receiver will decode a message. They try to give something to the receiver, solve the receiver's problems, save the receiver's money, or just understand the feelings and position of that person. Which of the following messages are more appealing to the receiver?

Empathy ***means being able to understand another's situation, feelings, and motives.***

Photo: © AP/Wide World Photos

FIGURE 5.6 ***Customer Response Letter***

February 23, 2006

Mrs. Elaine Hough
9403 Farwest Drive SW
Tacoma, WA 98498

Dear Mrs. Hough:

Your letter was a strong endorsement of our belief that we made the right choice when we devoted our company to traditional, classic styles—and that it's still the right choice.

Opens response to inquiry by agreeing with customer

Explains evolving merchandise line from company's and reader's view

It's true we've made changes. In the past few years, with the markets soft and tastes changing, we reexamined our merchandise, with a view to continuing to serve valued customers while introducing ourselves to new ones. We decided that our styles needed freshening and that we would offer clothes that didn't chase after trends but did have a feel for what was current.

Our commitment to the classics hasn't weakened, as I hope you'd agree, having seen recent catalogs. But we've defined "classic" more inclusively than in the past. We're using new fabrics, new colors, a more relaxed fit. There's more imagination in our product mix now, but the sweaters, rugbys, blouses, button-downs, and other basics for which you've relied on us are still here. You may not find each one in every catalog, and you may notice the new products more than those you've seen before. The classics are still here, and the selection will be growing.

Uses conversational language to convey warmth and sincerity

Emphasizes areas of agreement

I've arranged to send you just the four catalogs a year you wanted. I hope you'll keep an eye on them. I think that, more and more, you'll be able to come to us for the styles you want.

Concludes by giving customer what she wants and promoting future business

Sincerely,

Brian Finnegan
Customer Relations

LANDS' END, INC.
1 LANDS' END LANE DODGEVILLE, WI 53595
(608)935-9341

Sender-Focused	**Receiver-Focused**
To enable us to update our stockholder records, we ask that the enclosed card be returned.	So that you may promptly receive dividend checks and information related to your shares, please return the enclosed card.
Our warranty becomes effective only when we receive an owner's registration.	Your warranty begins working for you as soon as you return your owner's registration.
We offer a CD language course that we have complete faith in.	The sooner you order the CD language program, the sooner the rewards will be yours.
The Human Resources Department requires that every employee complete an online questionnaire immediately so that we can allocate our training resource funds.	You can be one of the first employees to sign up for the new career development program. Complete the online questionnaire and send it immediately.

Cultivating the "You" View

Notice how many of the previous receiver-focused messages included the word *you*. In concentrating on receiver benefits, skilled communicators naturally develop the "you" view. They emphasize second-person pronouns (*you, your*) instead of first-person pronouns (*I/we, us, our*). Whether your goal is to inform, persuade, or promote goodwill, the catchiest words you can use are *you* and *your*. Compare the following examples.

Effective communicators develop the "you" view in a sincere, not manipulative or critical, tone.

"I/We" View	**"You" View**
I have granted you permission to attend the communication seminar.	You may attend the seminar to improve your communication skills.
We have shipped your order by UPS, and we are sure it will arrive in time for the sales promotion January 15.	Your order will be delivered by UPS in time for your sales promotion January 15.
I'm asking all of our employees to respond to the attached survey regarding working conditions.	Because your ideas count, please complete the attached survey regarding working conditions.

Your goal is to focus on the reader. But second-person pronouns can be overused and misused. Readers appreciate genuine interest; on the other hand, they resent obvious attempts at manipulation. Some sales messages, for example, are guilty of overkill when they include *you* dozens of times in a direct mail promotion. Furthermore, the word can sometimes create the wrong impression. Consider this statement: *You cannot return merchandise until you receive written approval. You* appears twice, but the reader feels singled out for criticism. In the following version the message is less personal and more positive: *Customers may return merchandise with written approval.* In short, avoid using *you* for general statements that suggest blame and could cause ill will.

In recognizing the value of the "you" view, however, writers do not have to sterilize their writing and avoid any first-person pronouns or words that show their feelings. Skilled communicators are able to convey sincerity, warmth, and enthusiasm by the words they choose. Don't be afraid to use phrases such as *I'm happy* or *We're delighted*, if you truly are.

spotlight *on communicators*

John H. Johnson always concentrates on what customers want rather than on what he wants. His focus on the "you" view helped him build Ebony *and* Jet *magazines, along with* Fashion Fair Cosmetics, *into multimillion-dollar businesses. Recently voted as the greatest minority entrepreneur in U.S. history, Johnson is a master at profiling potential customers and cultivating the "you" view. "I want to know where they came from, what are their interests, [and] what can I talk to them about." He works to establish rapport with people by having mutual interests.*

When speaking face to face, communicators show sincerity and warmth with nonverbal cues such as a smile and pleasant voice tone. In letters, memos, and e-mail messages, however, only expressive words and phrases can show these feelings. These phrases suggest hidden messages that say to readers and customers "You are important, I hear you, and I'm honestly trying to please you." Mary Kay Ash, one of the most successful cosmetics entrepreneurs of all times, gave her salespeople wise advice. She had them imagine that any person they were addressing wore a sign saying "Make me feel important."

Using Bias-Free Language

In adapting a message to its audience, be sure your language is sensitive and bias-free. Few writers set out to be offensive. Sometimes, though, we all say things that we never thought might be hurtful. The real problem is that we don't think about the words that stereotype groups of people, such as *the boys in the mail room* or *the*

Photo: Courtesy Johnson Publishing Company, Inc.

PROCESS IN PROGRESS

Kinko's Revisited

KINKO'S FAMOUSLY eccentric founder Paul Orfalea built a hugely successful copy services chain by following a simple marketing strategy. Build a store, keep it open 24 hours a day, and customers will come. Just walk into a Kinko's any time of the day or night. Chances are you'll find college students using computers, businesspeople copying proposals, and job seekers printing résumés. More recently, though, Kinko's began to cultivate a new kind of market—Fortune 500 corporations who are more accustomed to having the office brought to them.

These potential customers required a totally new strategy. Instead of waiting for customers to pop in the door, Kinko's now has to solicit business actively, preferably from multibillion-dollar companies. Many of these companies have their own in-house business services departments, which Kinko's hopes to shut down. Convincing big companies that duplicating work can be done better at Kinko's is no easy task. Kinko's 550 salespeople, called account managers, do a lot of "cold-calling" to generate business. Although they often get the cold shoulder, occasionally they hit pay dirt. For example, in Seattle, after knocking on 50 doors, one account manager knocked on the door of a consulting company. Inside, employees were frantically preparing training packets for a Monday morning course, and they were behind schedule on Friday afternoon. Kinko's came to the rescue and gained a new client.

A major challenge for the growing platoon of account managers is learning about Kinko's new corporate audience and communicating successfully Kinko's new image. The goal of Kinko's management is to increase corporate sales to 30 percent of the company's total revenue.

Critical Thinking

- In planning a presentation or proposal for a potential customer, why is analyzing the task and anticipating the audience such an important part of preparation?
- If a Kinko's account manager is working on a presentation or a proposal for a potential customer, such as Bank of America, what kinds of questions should he or she ask to profile the audience?
- How important is it to consider receiver benefits before communicating a message, particularly the kinds of sales messages that Kinko's account managers must send?

CONTINUED ON PAGE 154

case study

girls in the front office. Be cautious about expressions that might be biased in terms of gender, race, ethnicity, age, and disability.[7]

Avoiding Gender Bias. You can defuse gender time bombs by replacing words that exclude or stereotype women (sometimes called *sexist language*) with neutral, inclusive expressions. The following examples show how sexist terms and phrases can be replaced with neutral ones.

Gender-Biased	Improved
female doctor, woman attorney, cleaning woman	doctor, attorney, cleaner
waiter/waitress, authoress, stewardess	server, author, cabin attendant
mankind, man-hour, man-made	humanity, working hours, artificial
office girls	office workers
the doctor . . . he	doctors . . . they
the teacher . . . she	teachers . . . they

Gender-Biased	Improved
executives and their wives	executives and their spouses
foreman, flagman, workman	lead workers, flagger, worker
businessman, salesman	businessperson, sales representative
Each worker had his picture taken.	Each worker had a picture taken.
	All workers had their pictures taken.
	Each worker had his or her picture taken.

Sensitive communicators avoid gender, racial or ethnic, and disability biases.

Generally, you can avoid gender-biased language by leaving out the words *man* or *woman*, by using plural nouns and pronouns, or by changing to a gender-free word (*person* or *representative*). Avoid the "his or her" option whenever possible. It's wordy and conspicuous. With a little effort, you can usually find a construction that is graceful, grammatical, and unself-conscious.

Avoiding Racial or Ethnic Bias. You need indicate racial or ethnic identification only if the context demands it.

Racially or Ethnically Biased	Improved
An Indian accountant was hired.	An accountant was hired.
James Lee, an African American, applied.	James Lee applied.

Avoiding Age Bias. Specify age only if it is relevant, and avoid expressions that are demeaning or subjective.

Age Biased	Improved
The law applied to old people.	The law applied to people over 65.
Sally Kay, 55, was transferred.	Sally Kay was transferred.
a spry old gentleman	a man
a little old lady	a woman

Avoiding Disability Bias. Unless relevant, do not refer to an individual's disability. When necessary, use terms that do not stigmatize disabled individuals.

Disability Biased	Improved
afflicted with, suffering from, crippled by	has
defect, disease	condition
confined to a wheelchair	uses a wheelchair

The preceding examples give you a quick look at a few problem expressions. The real key to bias-free communication, though, lies in your awareness and commitment. Be on the lookout to be sure that your messages do not exclude, stereotype, or offend people.

Expressing Yourself Positively

Positive language creates goodwill and gives more options to readers.

Certain negative words create ill will because they appear to blame or accuse readers. For example, opening a letter to a customer with *You claim that* suggests that you don't believe the customer. Other loaded words that can get you in trouble are *complaint, criticism, defective, failed, mistake,* and *neglected.* Often the writer is unconscious of the effect of these words. To avoid angry reactions, restrict negative words and try to find positive ways to express ideas. You provide more options to the reader when you tell what can be done instead of what can't be done.

Negative expressions can often be rephrased to sound positive.

Negative	Positive
You failed to include your credit card number so we can't mail your order.	We'll mail your order as soon as we receive your credit card number.
Your letter of May 2 claims that you returned a defective headset.	Your May 2 letter describes a headset you returned.
You cannot park in Lot H until April 1.	You may park in Lot H starting April 1.
You won't be sorry that . . .	You will be happy that . . .
Without the aid of top management, the problem can't be solved.	With the aid of top management, the problem can be solved.
Do you have any complaints?	Can you suggest ways for us to improve?

Being Courteous

Even when you are justifiably angry, courteous language is the best way to achieve your objectives.

Maintaining a courteous tone involves not just guarding against rudeness but also avoiding words that sound demanding or preachy. Expressions like *you should, you must,* and *you have to* cause people to instinctively react with *Oh, yeah?* One remedy is to turn these demands into rhetorical questions that begin with *Will you please. . . .* Giving reasons for a request also softens the tone.

spotlight *on communicators*

Katie Couric, co-host of NBC's popular Today *show and former Pentagon reporter, does her homework before she conducts interviews. Disarmingly cheerful and chummy, she can also be hard-hitting and uncompromising in her blunt questioning of newsmakers. Yet she always strives to be positive, courteous, and fair—important characteristics of every good communicator.*

Photo: © Kevin Winter/Getty Images

Less Courteous	More Courteous
You must complete this report before Friday.	Will you please complete the report by Friday.
You should organize a car pool in this department.	Organizing a car pool will reduce your transportation costs and help preserve the environment.

Even when you feel justified in displaying anger, remember that losing your temper or being sarcastic will seldom accomplish your goals as a business communicator to inform, to persuade, and to create goodwill. When you are irritated, frustrated, or infuriated, keep cool and try to defuse the situation. Concentrate on the real problem. What must be done to solve it?

You May Be Thinking This	Better to Say This
This is the second time I've written. Can't you get anything right?	Please credit my account for $843. My latest statement shows that the error noted in my letter of June 2 has not been corrected.
Am I the only one who can read the operating manual?	Let's review the operating manual together so that you can get your documents to print correctly next time.
Hey, don't blame me! I'm not the promoter who took off with the funds.	Please accept our sincere apologies and two complimentary tickets to our next event. Let me try to explain why we had to substitute performers.

Simplifying Your Language

The simpler the language, the better.

In adapting your message to your audience, whenever possible use short, familiar words that you think they will recognize. Don't, however, avoid a big word that conveys your idea efficiently and is appropriate for the audience. Your goal is to shun pompous and pretentious language. Instead, use "GO" words. If you mean *begin*, don't say *commence* or *initiate*. If you mean *give*, don't write *render*.[8] By substituting everyday, familiar words for unfamiliar ones, as shown here, you help your audience comprehend your ideas quickly.

Unfamiliar	**Familiar**
commensurate	equal
interrogate	question
materialize	appear
obfuscate	confuse
remuneration	pay, salary
terminate	end

spotlight *on communicators*

The hardest part of her job is making complicated financial information easy to read and understand, admits Newsweek *columnist and financial advisor Jane Bryant Quinn. Diligent revision helps her clarify her thinking and her language. Whether writing about borrowing, investing, or insuring, she constantly adapts to her audience and looks for familiar language. "I'm always asking myself, 'Will the reader understand this word, this phrase?'"*

Photo: Courtesy Jane Bryant Quinn

At the same time, be selective in your use of jargon. *Jargon* describes technical or specialized terms within a field. These terms enable insiders to communicate complex ideas briefly, but to outsiders they mean nothing. Human resources professionals, for example, know precisely what's meant by *cafeteria plan* (a benefits option program), but most of us would be thinking about lunch. Geologists refer to *plate tectonics*, and physicians discuss *metastatic carcinomas*. These terms mean little to most of us. Use specialized language only when the audience will understand it. And don't forget to consider secondary audiences: Will those potential readers understand any technical terms used?

Using Precise, Vigorous Words

Using familiar but precise language helps receivers understand.

Strong verbs and concrete nouns give readers more information and keep them interested. Don't overlook the thesaurus (or the thesaurus program on your computer) for expanding your word choices and vocabulary. Whenever possible, use specific words as shown here.

Imprecise, Dull	**More Precise**
a change in profits	a 25 percent hike in profits a 10 percent plunge in profits
to say	to promise, confess, understand to allege, assert, assume, judge
to think about	to identify, diagnose, analyze to probe, examine, inspect

By reviewing the tips in the following checklist, you can master the steps of writing preparation. As you review these tips, remember the three basics of prewriting: analyzing, anticipating, and adapting.

Checklist for Adapting a Message to Its Audience

- ✓ **Identify the message purpose.** Ask yourself why you are communicating and what you hope to achieve. Look for primary and secondary purposes.

- ✓ **Select the most appropriate form.** Determine whether you need a permanent record or whether the message is too sensitive to put in writing.

- ✓ **Profile the audience.** Identify your relationship with the reader and your knowledge about that individual or group. Assess how much the receiver knows about the subject.

- ✓ **Focus on reader benefits.** Phrase your statements from the readers' viewpoint, not the writer's. Concentrate on the "you" view (*Your order will arrive, You can enjoy, Your ideas count*).

- ✓ **Avoid gender and racial bias.** Use bias-free words (*businessperson* instead of *businessman*; *working hours* instead of *man-hours*). Omit ethnic identification unless the context demands it.

- ✓ **Avoid age and disability bias.** Include age only if relevant. Avoid potentially demeaning expressions (*spry old gentleman*), and use terms that do not stigmatize disabled people (*he is disabled* instead of *he is a cripple* or *he has a handicap*).

- ✓ **Express ideas positively rather than negatively.** Instead of *Your order can't be shipped before June 1*, say *Your order can be shipped June 1.*

- ✓ **Use short, familiar words.** Use technical terms and big words only if they are appropriate for the audience (*end* not *terminate, required* not *mandatory*).

- ✓ **Search for precise, vigorous words.** Use a thesaurus if necessary to find strong verbs and concrete nouns (*announces* instead of *says, brokerage* instead of *business*).

learning objective

6

Adapting to Legal Responsibilities

Careful communicators should familiarize themselves with information in four information areas: investments, safety, marketing, and human resources.

One of your primary responsibilities in writing for an organization or for yourself is to avoid language that may land you in court. In our current business environment, lawsuits abound, many of which center on the use and abuse of language. You can protect yourself and avoid litigation by knowing what's legal and by adapting your language accordingly. Be especially careful when communicating in the following four areas: investments, safety, marketing, and human resources. Because these information areas generate the most lawsuits, we will examine them more closely.

Investment Information

Writers describing the sale of stocks or financial services must follow specific laws written to protect investors. Any messages—including e-mails, letters, newsletters, and pamphlets—must be free from misleading information, exaggerations, or half-truths. One company in Massachusetts inadvertently violated the law by declaring that it was "recession-proof." After going bankrupt, the company was sued by angry stockholders claiming that they had been deceived. A software company caused a flurry of lawsuits by withholding information that revealed problems in a new version of one of its most popular programs. Stockholders sued, charging that managers had deliberately concealed the bad news, thus keeping stock prices artificially high. Experienced financial writers know that careless language and even poor timing may provoke litigation.

Safety Information

Warnings on dangerous products must be written especially clearly.

Writers describing potentially dangerous products worry not only about protecting people from physical harm but also about being sued. During the past three decades, litigation arising from product liability has been the most active area of tort law (tort law involves wrongful civil acts other than breach of contract).[9] Manufacturers are obligated to warn consumers of any risks in their products. These warnings must do more than suggest danger; they must also clearly tell people how to use the product safely. In writing warnings, concentrate on major points. Omit anything that is not critical. In the work area describe a potential problem and tell how to solve it. For example, *Lead dust is harmful and gets on your clothes. Change your clothes before leaving work.*

Clearly written safety messages use easy-to-understand words, such as *doctor* instead of *physician, clean* instead of *sanitary,* and *burn* instead of *incinerate.* Technical terms are defined. For example *Asbestos is a carcinogen (something that causes cancer).*[10] Effective safety messages also include highlighting techniques, such as using headings and bullets. In coming chapters you'll learn more about these techniques for improving readability.

Marketing Information

(Know the product - don't misrepresent)

Sales and marketing messages must not make claims that can't be verified.

Sales and marketing messages are illegal if they falsely advertise prices, performance capability, quality, or other product characteristics. Marketing messages must not deceive the buyer in any way. A Southern California entrepreneur, for example, promoted a Band-Aid-like device, Le Patch, as "a dramatic breakthrough in weight control technology." When worn around the waist, Le Patch was supposed to reduce appetite. The claims, however, could not be proved; and the promoter was charged with misrepresenting the product. Sellers of services must also be cautious about the language they use to describe what they will do. Letters, reports, and proposals that describe services to be performed are interpreted as contracts in court. Therefore, language must not promise more than intended. Here are some dangerous words (and recommended alternatives) that have created misunderstandings leading to lawsuits.[11]

(Notes)

Dangerous Word	Court Interpretation	Recommended Alternative
inspect	to examine critically, to investigate and test officially, to scrutinize	to review, to study, to tour the facility
determine	to come to a decision, to decide; to resolve	to evaluate, to assess, to analyze
assure	to render safe, to make secure, to give confidence, to cause to feel certain	to facilitate, to provide further confidence, to enhance the reliability of

PROCESS TO PRODUCT

Applying Your Skills at Kinko's

A NEW MARKETING strategy at Kinko's is to attract corporate clients with such services as high-speed duplicating for big jobs, color and graphics printing using the best equipment available, creating proposal and brochure packets, and videoconferencing. Kinko's has even installed its own network called "Kinkonet." This service enables clients to use digital technologies and modems to compose reports or other materials and have them printed wherever they are needed, say, for instance, in Amsterdam.

Your Task

You have been hired as a communication trainer to assist Matt Rivers, vice president of sales for Kinko's. He realizes that his newly hired product managers do not always think in terms of adapting a message to its audience. He asks you to give the new hires some pointers on specific techniques for improving their presentations and proposals. Before the training session, though, Rivers asks you to submit a list of points you will emphasize in your talk. Individually or in small groups, review suggestions in this chapter for adapting a message to its audience. Prepare a list of at least six points to submit to Vice President Rivers. For each point, try to supply an example from a case in which Kinko's is trying to convince Bank of America to have its next set of color brochures printed by Kinko's instead of having them prepared in-house. ■

case study

Human Resources Information

The safest employment recommendations contain positive, job-related information.

The vast number of lawsuits relating to employment makes this a treacherous area for business communicators. In evaluating employees in the workplace, avoid making unsubstantiated negative comments. It's also unwise to assess traits (*she is unreliable*) because they require subjective judgment. Concentrate instead on specific incidents (*in the last month she missed four work days and was late three times*). Defamation lawsuits have become so common that some companies no longer provide letters of recommendation for former employees. To be safe, give recommendations only when the former employee authorizes the recommendation and when you can say something positive. Stick to job-related information.

Statements in employee handbooks also require careful wording because a court might rule that such statements are "implied contracts." Consider the following handbook remark: "We at Hotstuff, Inc., show our appreciation for hard work and team spirit by rewarding everyone who performs well." This seemingly harmless statement could make it difficult to fire an employee because of the implied employment promise.[12] Companies are warned to avoid promissory phrases in writing job advertisements, application forms, and offer letters. Phrases that suggest permanent employment and guaranteed job security can be interpreted as contracts.[13]

In statements to existing and prospective employees, companies must recognize that oral comments may trigger lawsuits. A Minnesota television news anchor won damages when she gave up her job search because her station manager promised to extensively market her in a leading role. But he failed to follow through. A Vermont engineer won his case of negligent misrepresentation when he was not told that the defense project for which he was hired faced a potential cutback. Companies are warned to require employees to sign employment agreements indicating that all terms of employment orally agreed upon must be made in writing to be valid.[14]

In adapting messages to meet today's litigious business environment, be sensitive to the rights of others and to your own rights. The key elements in this adaptation process are awareness of laws, sensitivity to interpretations, and careful use of language.

Summary of Learning Objectives

1 **Identify three basics of business writing, summarize Guffey's 3-x-3 writing process, and explain how a writing process helps a writer.** Business writing differs from academic writing in that it strives to solve business problems, it is economical, and it is reader oriented. Phase 1 of Guffey's 3-x-3 writing process (prewriting) involves analyzing the message, anticipating the audience, and considering ways to adapt the message to the audience. Phase 2 (writing) involves researching the topic, organizing the material, and composing the message. Phase 3 (revising) includes proofreading and evaluating the message. A writing process helps a writer by providing a systematic plan describing what to do in creating messages.

2 **Explain how the writing process may be altered and how it is affected by team projects.** The writing process may be compressed for short messages; steps in the process may be rearranged. Team writing, which is necessary for large projects or when wide expertise is necessary, alters the writing process. Teams often work together in brainstorming and working out their procedures and assignments. Then individual members write their portions of the report or presentation during Phase 2. During Phase 3 (revising) teams may work together to combine their drafts. Collaboration software helps teams working on shared documents.

3 **Clarify what is involved in analyzing a writing task and selecting a communication channel.** Communicators must decide why they are delivering a message and what they hope to achieve. Although many messages only inform, some must also persuade. After identifying the purpose of a message, communicators must choose the most appropriate channel. That choice depends on the importance of the message, the amount and speed of feedback required, the need for a permanent record, the cost of the channel, and the degree of formality desired.

4 **Describe anticipating and profiling the audience for a message.** A good communicator tries to envision the audience for a message. What does the receiver know about the topic? How well does the receiver know the sender? What is known about the receiver's education, beliefs, culture, and attitudes? Will the response to the message be positive, neutral, or negative? Is the secondary audience different from the primary audience? How should a document be changed if it will be read by additional readers?

5 **Specify six writing techniques that help communicators adapt messages to the task and audience.** Skilled communicators strive to (a) spotlight reader benefits; (b) look at a message from the receiver's perspective (the "you" view); (c) use sensitive language that avoids gender, racial, ethnic, and disability biases; (d) state ideas positively; (e) show courtesy; and (f) use short, familiar, and precise words.

6 **Explain why communicators must adapt their writing in four high-risk areas.** Actions and language in four information areas generate the most lawsuits: investments, safety, marketing, and human resources. In writing

about investments, communicators must avoid misleading information, exaggerations, and half-truths. Safety information, including warnings, must tell people clearly how to use a product safely and motivate them to do so. In addition to being honest, marketing information must not promise more than intended. Communicators in the area of human resources must use careful wording (particularly in employment recommendations and employee handbooks) to avoid potential lawsuits. They must also avoid oral promises that can result in lawsuits.

chapter review

1. Explain how writing business messages differs from writing college compositions and term papers. (Obj. 1)
2. Describe the components in each stage of Guffey's 3-x-3 writing process. (Obj. 1)
3. Name three instances in which collaborative writing is necessary. (Obj. 2)
4. Why is writing shared documents frustrating, and what software tools make the editing task easier? (Obj. 2)
5. List five factors to consider when selecting a communication channel. (Obj. 3)
6. Why should you "profile" your audience before composing a message? (Obj. 4)
7. How can a writer emphasize "reader benefits"? (Obj. 5)
8. When is the "you" view appropriate, and when is it inappropriate? (Obj. 5)
9. What is bias-free language? Give original examples. (Obj. 5)
10. Name replacements for the following gender-biased terms: *waitress, stewardess, foreman* (Obj. 5)
11. Revise the following expression to show more courtesy: *For the last time I'm warning all staff members that they must use virus-protection software—or else!* (Obj. 5)
12. What is *jargon*, and when is it appropriate for business writing? (Obj. 5)
13. What's wrong with using words such as *commence, mandate,* and *interrogate*? (Obj. 5)
14. What four information areas generate the most lawsuits? (Obj. 6)
15. How can business communicators protect themselves against litigation? (Obj. 6)

critical thinking

1. Business communicators are encouraged to profile or "visualize" the audience for their messages. How is this possible if you don't really know the people who will receive a sales letter or who will hear your business presentation? (Obj. 4)
2. How can Guffey's 3-x-3 writing process help the writer of a business report as well as the writer of an oral presentation? (Obj. 1)
3. If adapting your tone to the receiving audience and developing reader benefits are so important, why do we see so much writing that does not reflect these suggestions? (Objs. 3–5)
4. Discuss the following statement: "The English language is a landmine—it is filled with terms that are easily misinterpreted as derogatory and others that are blatantly insulting. . . . Being fair and objective is not enough; employers must also appear to be so."[15] (Obj. 5)
5. **Ethical Issue:** Wall Street traders, corporations, and knowledgeable consumers hang on every word from Alan Greenspan, chairman of the Federal Reserve Board. His pronouncements have great influence on the economy, particularly in relation to whether the Fed will raise or lower interest rates. But Mr. Greenspan is not exactly plainspoken. Delighting in tortuous sentences and his ability to obfuscate, he once quipped, "I know you believe you understand what you think I said, but I am not sure you realize that what you heard is not what I meant." He rarely speaks in simple sentences, even when he intends to convey a clear message. He avoids getting pinned down, perhaps because even he realizes that he can't precisely forecast the future. Is it unethical for a public official to present reports that few listeners or readers can understand?[16]

THREE GREAT RESOURCES FOR YOU!

1. ***Guffey Student Web Site***
http://guffey.swlearning.com

Your companion Web site offers chapter review quizzes, WebThink activities, updated chapter URLs, and many additional resources.

2. ***Guffey XTRA!***
http://guffeyxtra.swlearning.com

This online study assistant includes Your Personal Language Trainer, Speak Right!, Spell Right!, bonus online chapters, Documents for Analysis, PowerPoint slides, and much more.

3. ***Student Study Guide***

Self-checked workbook activities and applications review chapter concepts and develop career skills.

activities

5.1 Document for Analysis (Obj. 5)

TEAM

Your Task. Study the following memo, which is based on an actual document sent to employees. How can you apply what you learned in this chapter to improving this memo? Revise the memo to make it more courteous, positive, and precise. Focus on developing the "you" view and using familiar language. Remove any gender-biased references. Consider revising this memo as a collaboration project using Word's **Comment** feature.

TO: All Employees Using HP 5000 Computers

It has recently come to my attention that a computer security problem exists within our organization. I understand that the problem is twofold in nature:

a. You have been sharing computer passwords.
b. You are using automatic logon procedures.

Henceforth, you are prohibited from sharing passwords for security reasons that should be axiomatic. We also must forbid you to use automatic logon files because they empower anyone to have access to our entire computer system and all company data.

Enclosed please find a form that you must sign and return to the aforementioned individual, indicating your acknowledgment of and acquiescence to the procedures described here. Any computer user whose signed form is not returned will have his personal password invalidated.

5.2 Selecting Communication Channels (Obj. 3)

Your Task. Using Figure 5.4, suggest the best communication channels for the following messages. Assume that all channels shown are available. Be prepared to explain your choices.

a. You need to know whether Elizabeth in Reprographics can produce a special brochure for your department within two days.
b. A prospective client in Italy wants price quotes for a number of your products—pronto!
c. As assistant to the vice president, you are to investigate the possibility of developing internship programs with several nearby colleges and universities.
d. You must respond to a notice from the Internal Revenue Service insisting that you did not pay the correct amount for last quarter's employer's taxes.
e. As manager, you must inform an employee that continued tardiness is jeopardizing her job.
f. Members of your task force must meet to discuss ways to improve communication among 5,000 employees at 32 branches of your large company. Task force members are from Los Angeles, Orlando, San Antonio, White Plains, and Columbus (Ohio).
g. As department manager, you need to inform nine staff members of a safety training session scheduled for the following month.

5.3 Analyzing Audiences (Obj. 4)

Your Task. Using the questions in Figure 5.5, write a brief analysis of the audience for each of the following communication tasks.

a. An e-mail memo to your district sales manager describing your visit to a new customer who demands special discounts.
b. A letter of application for a job advertised in your local newspaper. Your qualifications match the job description.
c. An e-mail memo to your boss persuading her to allow you to attend a computer class that will require you to leave work early two days a week for ten weeks.
d. An unsolicited sales letter promoting life insurance to a targeted group of executives.
e. A letter from the municipal water department explaining that the tap water may taste and smell bad; however, it poses no threats to health.
f. A letter from a credit card organization refusing credit to an applicant.

5.4 Adapting Your Management Message to Fit Your Employees' Needs (Obj. 5)

SPEAKING

Jay Conger is ranked number five on *BusinessWeek*'s list of the world's top ten management gurus. He is professor of organizational behavior at the London Business School and senior research scientist at the Center for Effective Organizations at the University of Southern California in Los Angeles.[17] Conger offers the following excellent management advice regarding what leaders should give to their followers:

- Employees want to know that their manager values them.
- Employees want to feel a sense of community—that they belong to special place.
- Employees want to feel a sense of purpose and meaning communicated to them in ways that energize and excite them.[18]

Messages from effective managers will reflect these needs. The best way to achieve the desired result is for managers to try to put themselves in the shoes of their employees and adapt messages accordingly.

Your Task. Form class discussion groups of three to five students. Put yourself in the shoes of employees at one of the Yum! Brands restaurants (Pizza Hut, KFC, Long John Silver's, A&W, or Taco Bell). Discuss how the profile of an hourly employee at a Yum! restaurant would differ from the profile of a scientist working in the research laboratory at a

Rich chapter resources are available on the Web sites. 

pharmaceutical company such as Pfizer or Abbott Laboratories. Next, discuss ways that the manager at a fast-food restaurant might meet the three needs mentioned above. How would the manager of a research lab meet these needs? Be prepared to share the results of your group's discussion with the rest of the class.

5.5 Reader Benefits and the "You" View (Obj. 5)

Your Task. Revise the following sentences to emphasize the reader's perspective and the "you" view.

- **a.** To help us expand and grow our business, we are proud to announce that videoconferencing is now available at 125 of our branches.
- **b.** To prevent us from possibly losing large sums of money, our bank now requires verification of any large check presented for immediate payment.
- **c.** So that we may bring our customer records up-to-date and eliminate the expense of duplicate mailings, we are asking you to complete the enclosed card.
- **d.** For just $300 per person, we have arranged a three-day trip to Las Vegas that includes deluxe accommodations, the "City Lights" show, and selected meals.
- **e.** I give my permission for you to attend the two-day workshop.
- **f.** We're requesting all employees to complete the enclosed questionnaire so that we may develop a master schedule for summer vacations.
- **g.** I think my background and my education match the description of the manager trainee position you advertised.
- **h.** We are presenting an in-house training program for employees who want to improve their writing skills.
- **i.** We are pleased to announce an arrangement with Compaq that allows us to offer discounted computers in the student bookstore.
- **j.** Our safety policy forbids us from renting power equipment to anyone who cannot demonstrate proficiency in its use.

5.6 Language Bias (Obj. 5)

Your Task. Revise the following sentences to eliminate gender, racial, age, and disability stereotypes.

- **a.** A skilled assistant proofreads her boss's documents and catches any errors he makes.
- **b.** CyberSystems hired Jamal Alexander, an African American, for the position of project manager.
- **c.** Because Kevin is confined to a wheelchair, we look for restaurants without stairs.
- **d.** Every employee must wear his ID badge on the job.
- **e.** Some restaurants offer special discounts for old people.
- **f.** How many man-hours will the project require?
- **g.** James is afflicted with arthritis, but his crippling rarely interferes with his work.
- **h.** Debbie Sanchez, 24, was hired; and Tony Morris, 57, was promoted.
- **i.** Representing the community are a businessman, a lady attorney, and a female doctor.
- **j.** Every attorney has ten minutes for his summation.

5.7 Positive Expression (Obj. 5)

Your Task. Revise the following statements to make them more positive.

- **a.** If you fail to follow each requirement, you will not receive your $50 rebate.
- **b.** In the message you left at our Web site, you claim that you returned a printer.
- **c.** Although you apparently failed to read the operator's manual, we are sending you a replacement blade for your food processor. Next time read page 18 carefully so that you will know how to attach this blade.
- **d.** We can't process your application because you neglected to insert your social security number.
- **e.** Construction cannot begin until the building plans are approved.
- **f.** Because of a mistake in its address, your letter did not arrive until January 3.
- **g.** In response to your e-mail complaint, we are investigating our agent's poor behavior.
- **h.** It is impossible to move forward without community support.
- **i.** Customers are ineligible for the 10 percent discount unless they show their membership cards.
- **j.** You won't be disappointed with your new smart phone.

5.8 Courteous Expression (Obj. 5)

Your Task. Revise the following messages to show greater courtesy.

- **a.** We will be forced to deactivate your debit card if you don't call this 800 number immediately to activate it.
- **b.** This is the last time I'm writing to try to get you to record my January 6 payment of $500 to my account. Anyone who can read can see from the attached documents that I've tried to explain this to you before.
- **c.** As departmental manager, you must organize a car pool if you expect to help us reduce air pollution.
- **d.** To the Staff: Can't anyone around here read instructions? Page 12 of the operating manual for our copy machine very clearly describes how to remove jammed paper. But I'm the only one who ever does it, and I've had it! No more copies will be made until you learn how to remove jammed paper!
- **e.** If you had listened to our agent more carefully, you would know that your policy does not cover accidents outside the United States.

5.9 Familiar Words (Obj. 5)

Your Task. Revise the following sentences to avoid unfamiliar words.

- **a.** The salary we are offering is commensurate with other managers' remuneration.
- **b.** To expedite ratification of this agreement, we urge you to vote in the affirmative.
- **c.** In a dialogue with the manager, I learned that you plan to terminate our agreement.
- **d.** Did the steering problem materialize subsequent to our recall effort?
- **e.** Pursuant to your invitation, we will interrogate our agent.

5.10 Precise Words (Obj. 5)

Your Task. From the choices in parentheses, select the most precise, vigorous words.

- **a.** When replying to e-mail, (*bring in, include, put*), enough of the old message for (*someone, the person, the recipient*) to recognize the original note.
- **b.** For a (*hard, long, complicated*) e-mail message, (*make, create, have*) the note in your word processing program.
- **c.** If an e-mail (*thing, catch, glitch*) interferes while writing, you can easily (*get, have, retrieve*) your message.
- **d.** We plan to (*acknowledge, publicize, applaud*) the work of exemplary employees.
- **e.** Ryan's excellent report has (*a lot of, many, a warehouse of*) relevant facts.

For the following sentences provide more precise alternatives for the italicized words.

- **f.** In her e-mail memo she said that she would (a) *change* overtime hours in order to (b) *fix* the budget.
- **g.** Our new manager (a) *said* that only (b) *the right kind of* applicants should apply.
- **h.** After (a) *reading* the report, I decided it was (b) *bad.*
- **i.** Rebecca said the movie was (a) *different*, but her remarks weren't very (b) *clear* to us.
- **j.** I'm (a) *going* to Phoenix tomorrow, and I plan to (b) *find out* the real problem.

5.11 Legal Language (Obj. 6)

Your Task. To avoid possible litigation, revise the italicized words in the following sentences taken from proposals.

- **a.** We have *inspected* the septic system and will send a complete report.
- **b.** Our goal is to *assure* completion of the project on schedule.
- **c.** We will *determine* the amount of stress for each supporting column.

5.12 Clear Writing

INFOTRAC

Your boss has always been a stickler for clear business writing. He has preached on the subject so much that a local business organization asked him to address its members. They want him to discuss how to write clearly. He asks you to help research the topic. He desperately needs examples and tips.

Your Task. Using InfoTrac, search for "clear business writing." Read one or two fairly recent articles that you consider effective. In a memo to your boss (your instructor) or in a class discussion, answer the following questions:

- **a.** What one or two InfoTrac articles provide effective information about clear business writing?
- **b.** What are the advantages of clear writing? Supply specific examples of organizations that benefited from clear writing.
- **c.** How can people learn to write more clearly? What specific tips can you list?

Photo: © Photodisc Blue/Getty Images

5.13 Communicating Mortgage Information: Tired of Paying Rent

CONSUMER WEB

Your best friends, Suzy and Mark, are definitely tired of paying rent. One Sunday they saw an "Open House" sign and stopped to see the home that was for sale. They fell in love with the tree-shaded home, but they quickly realized that purchasing a home required more cash and more knowledge than they had. They knew nothing about home mortgages. Because they think you are a whiz at computer searching, they ask you to help them get educated.

Your Task. Using a search tool such as **www.google.com**, locate Web sites with home mortgage tips. Sort through the commercial clutter until you find answers to these questions:

- **a.** What are the advantages and disadvantages of the main types of mortgages?

b. What does a mortgage payment consist of? Explain PITI.

c. How much down payment will Suzy and Mark need?

d. What is prequalification?

e. What are some general tips for new home buyers seeking a mortgage?

After collecting the information, think about the best way to present it to Suzy and Mark. How much do they already know about this subject? How detailed should you make your explanations? What channel of communication would be best? Will they want a written record? Be prepared to discuss your findings and analysis in class, in teams, or in a memo to your instructor.

video resource

Building Workplace Skills Video Library 1

Guffey's 3-x-3 Writing Process Develops Fluent Workplace Skills

Your instructor may show you a video that steps you through the writing process in a workplace environment. It shows all three phases of the writing process so that you can see how it guides the development of a complete message. This video illustrates concepts in Chapters 5, 6, and 7.

C.L.U.E. review 5

On a separate sheet edit the following sentences to correct faults in grammar, capitalization, punctuation, spelling, and word use.

1. In this class my friend and I learned that business writing should be: Purposeful, Economical and Reader Oriented.
2. 5 or 6 members of our team will probly attend the writers workshop therefore be sure they recieve notices.
3. If I was you I would learn the following 3 parts of the writing process, prewriting writing and revising.
4. Experts' suggest that you spend twenty-five percent of your time planning; twenty-five percent writing; forty-five percent revising and five percent proofreading.
5. Although one of the employees are not available we proceded to schedule the meeting at three o'clock p.m. on Wednesday October 12th.
6. The Vice President was supprised to learn that a 2 day writing workshop for our companies employees would cost one thousand two hundred dollars each.
7. Were not asking the seller to altar it's proposal we are asking team members to check the proposals figures.
8. There wondering whether a list of all our customers names and addresses were inadvertently released?
9. As you begin to write you should analyse the task, and identity the purpose.
10. By replacing unfamiliar words with every day familiar ones you can make you audience comprehend your ideas more quicker.

chapter 6

Writing Process Phase 2: Research, Organize, Compose

objectives

1. Apply Phase 2 of the 3-x-3 writing process, which begins with formal and informal methods for researching data and generating ideas.
2. Specify how to organize data into lists and alphanumeric or decimal outlines.
3. Compare direct and indirect patterns for organizing ideas.
4. Discuss composing the first draft of a message, focusing on techniques for creating effective sentences.
5. Define a paragraph and describe three classic paragraph plans and techniques for composing meaningful paragraphs.

COMMUNICATION IN PROCESS

Old Navy Struggles to Help Gap Get Its Groove Back

AFTER SPECTACULAR GROWTH to become the nation's largest specialty apparel retailer in the 1990s, Gap fell from favor in the early 2000s. Critics accused it of making every bad move a retailer could. Besides major misses in fashion, the company failed to differentiate among its three brands—Banana Republic, Gap, and Old Navy—and it opened too many stores.[1]

The company that had pioneered the casual cool look with fitted jeans, khakis, and simple T-shirts suddenly lost its fashion compass. Once-loyal customers were turned off by trendy rhinestone-encrusted pink jeans and other far-out novelties.[2] Under new management, Gap is now working to improve its merchandise mix, reduce inventories, and halt capital spending. Ultimately, though, Gap must find a way to get its customers back.

Perhaps the brightest spot in Gap's comeback has been the company's Old Navy discount division. With 800 big-box stores selling lower-priced apparel, Old Navy now accounts for 41 percent of Gap's total sales.[3] A division of Gap Inc., the Old Navy brand was created in 1994 as a fun fashion label with broad appeal and a casual attitude. Emphasizing humor and mass appeal, Old Navy gave shoppers music and bright colors while promoting a quirky image.[4]

From the beginning Old Navy's president Jenny Ming was intent on building a fun brand that delivered fashion at low prices. But over the years, she began to recognize that the fashion business was changing. Both Gap and Old Navy once chased fickle teenagers too hard, offering super-low-cut jeans and edgy styles that flattered only the young and slender.[5] In rebuilding Old Navy, Ming returned to its tradition of blue jeans, simple tops, and basics as a strategy to regain leadership in the casual-dress business. Ming says that in the past designers dictated what people wore. Now the power is shifting to the consumer. It's more about what individuals want to wear and are comfortable with rather than what designers choose.[6]

In learning to please customers, Old Navy collects ideas from product managers, focus groups, field researchers, and designers, while always keeping an eye on the competition. Color and concept inspiration may come from people-watching on the streets of Tokyo, a flash from a dream, or a visit to a local art gallery.[7]

Old Navy president Jenny Ming helped pull Gap out of a prolonged slump.

Critical Thinking

- In what ways would research (gathering information) be important to Jenny Ming at Old Navy and to other businesspeople?
- Why is it important for Jenny Ming and other business communicators to gather all necessary information before making management decisions?
- What techniques can business communicators at Old Navy and other companies use to generate ideas for new products as well as for business processes?

http://www.oldnavy.com

CONTINUED ON PAGE 173

case study

Photo: Photographer Evan Kafka

learning objective

1

Writing Process Phase 2: Research

Before writing, conduct formal or informal research to collect or generate necessary data.

Business communicators at Old Navy and Gap face daily challenges that require data collection, idea generation, and concept organization. Before they can make decisions and convey those decisions in written messages or presentations, they must gather information and organize that information. These activities are part of the second phase of Guffey's 3-x-3 writing process. You will recall that the 3-x-3 writing process, as reviewed in Figure 6.1, involves three phases. This chapter focuses on the second phase of the process: researching, organizing, and composing.

No smart businessperson would begin writing a message before collecting all the needed information. We call this collection process *research*, a rather formal-sounding term. For simple documents, though, the procedure can be quite informal. Research is necessary before beginning to write because the information you collect helps shape the message. Discovering significant data after a message is half completed often means starting over and reorganizing. To avoid frustration and inaccurate messages, collect information that answers a primary question:

- *What does the receiver need to know about this topic?*

When the message involves action, search for answers to secondary questions:

- *What is the receiver to do?*
- *How is the receiver to do it?*
- *When must the receiver do it?*
- *What will happen if the receiver doesn't do it?*

Whenever your communication problem requires more information than you have in your head or at your fingertips, you must conduct research. This research may be formal or informal.

Formal Research Methods

Formal research may involve searching electronic databases and libraries or investigating primary sources (interviews, surveys, and experimentation).

Long reports and complex business problems generally require some use of formal research methods. Let's say you are part of the management team at Gap Inc. and you want to evaluate several locations for the placement of a new Old Navy store. In a similar task, let's assume you must write a term paper for a college class. Both tasks require more data than you have in your head or at your fingertips. To conduct formal research, you could:

- **Access electronically.** Like other facets of life, the research process has been changed considerably by the computer. Most businesspeople begin any research process by seeing what they can find electronically. Much of the current printed material in libraries is available from the Internet, databases, or CDs that can be accessed by computer. Database providers, such as the InfoTrac service that comes with this textbook, enable you to search millions of magazine, newspaper, and journal articles. The Internet also provides a wealth of information from public records, public and private organizations, and many other sources. You'll learn more about using the Internet and other electronic information resources in Unit 4.
- **Search manually.** If you need background or supplementary information, you will probably conduct manual research in public or college libraries. These traditional resources include periodical indexes for lists of newspaper, magazine, and journal articles, along with the card catalog for books. Other manual

FIGURE 6.1 ***Guffey's 3-x-3 Writing Process***

1 Prewriting	2 Writing	3 Revising
Analyze	Research	Revise
Anticipate	Organize	Proofread
Adapt	Compose	Evaluate

sources are book indexes, encyclopedias, reference books, handbooks, dictionaries, directories, and almanacs.

- **Investigate primary sources.** To develop firsthand, primary information for a project, go directly to the source. In searching for locations for Old Navy stores, you might travel to possible sites and check them out. If you need information about how many shoppers pass by a location or visit a shopping center, you might conduct a traffic count. To learn more about specific shoppers who might become Old Navy customers, you could use questionnaires, interviews, or focus groups. Formal research includes scientific sampling methods that enable investigators to make accurate judgments and valid predictions.
- **Experiment scientifically.** Another source of primary data is experimentation. Instead of merely asking for the target audience's opinion, scientific researchers present choices with controlled variables. Assume, for example, that the management team at Gap wants to know at what price and under what circumstances consumers would purchase khakis or jeans from Old Navy instead of Abercrombie & Fitch. In another example, let's say that management wants to study the time of year and type of weather conditions that motivate consumers to begin purchasing sweaters, jackets, and cold-weather gear. The results of such experimentation would provide valuable data for managerial decision making.

Because formal research techniques are particularly necessary for reports, you'll study resources and techniques more extensively in Unit 4.

Informal Research Methods

Informal research may involve looking in the files, talking with your boss, interviewing the audience, and conducting an informal survey.

Most routine tasks—such as composing e-mail messages, memos, letters, informational reports, and oral presentations—require data that you can collect informally. For some projects, though, you rely more on your own ideas instead of—or in addition to—researching existing facts. Here are some techniques for collecting informal data and for generating ideas:

- **Look in the files.** Before asking others for help, see what you can find yourself. For many routine messages you can often find previous documents to help you with content and format.
- **Talk with your boss.** Get information from the individual making the assignment. What does that person know about the topic? What slant should you take? What other sources would he or she suggest?
- **Interview the target audience.** Consider talking with individuals at whom the message is aimed. They can provide clarifying information that tells you what they want to know and how you should shape your remarks.

- **Conduct an informal survey.** Gather unscientific but helpful information via questionnaires or telephone surveys. In preparing a memo report predicting the success of a proposed fitness center, for example, circulate a questionnaire asking for employee reactions.

The most productive group brainstorming sessions begin with defining the problem and creating an agenda.

Generating Ideas by Brainstorming

One popular method for generating ideas is brainstorming. We should point out, however, that some critics argue that brainstorming groups "produce fewer and poorer quality ideas than the same number of individuals working alone."[8] Proponents say that if "you've had bad luck with brainstorming, you're just not doing it right."[9] Here are suggestions for productive group brainstorming:

- Define the problem and create an agenda that outlines the topics to be covered.
- Establish time limits, remembering that short sessions are best.
- Set a quota, such as a minimum of 100 ideas. The goal is quantity, not quality.
- Require every participant to contribute ideas, accept the ideas of others, or improve on ideas.
- Encourage wild, "out of the box" thinking. Allow no one to criticize or evaluate ideas.
- Write ideas on flipcharts or on sheets of paper hung around the room.
- Organize and classify the ideas, retaining the best. Consider using cluster diagrams, discussed shortly.

spotlight *on communicators*

Generating ideas takes top priority for Gerry Laybourne, who, after serving as president of cable network's Nickelodeon/Nick at Nite and president of Disney/ABC Cable network, started her own media company. Three techniques work for her: being unafraid of making mistakes or looking silly, refusing to censor ideas, and brainstorming with her staff. Energizing a flagging group, she challenged managers at her new company to a brainstorming word-association game. To pinpoint the tone of new cable shows, they came up with words such as irreverent, introspective, brassy, sexy, *and so forth.*

Photo: © AP/Wide World Photos

Collecting Information and Generating Ideas on the Job

Assume you work in the corporate offices of Gap Inc. and you have been given the task of developing a college recruiting brochure for all Gap stores. You think this is a great idea because many college students don't know about exciting career opportunities and benefits at Old Navy and Gap. You know right away that you want the brochure to be colorful, exciting, concise, youthfully oriented, lightweight (because it has to be carried to college campuses), and easily updated. Beyond that, you realize that you need ideas from others on how to develop this recruiting brochure.

To develop ideas for a recruiting brochure, use both formal and informal research.

To collect data for this project, you decide to use both formal and informal research methods. You study recruiting brochures from other companies. You talk with college students about information they would like to see in a brochure. You conduct more formal research among recently hired employees and among Gap division presidents and executives to learn what they think a recruiting brochure should include. Working with an outside consultant, you prepare a questionnaire to use in personal interviews with employees and executives. The interviews include some open-ended questions, such as *How did you start with the company?* It also asks specific questions about career paths, degree requirements, personality traits desired, and so forth.

Next you ask five or six fellow employees and team members to help brainstorm ideas for the brochure. In a spirited session, your team comes up the cluster diagram shown in Figure 6.2. The ideas range from the cost of the brochure to career development programs and your company's appealing location in the San Francisco Bay area.

FIGURE 6.2 *Creating Cluster Diagram to Generate Ideas for Old Navy/Gap Recruiting Brochure*

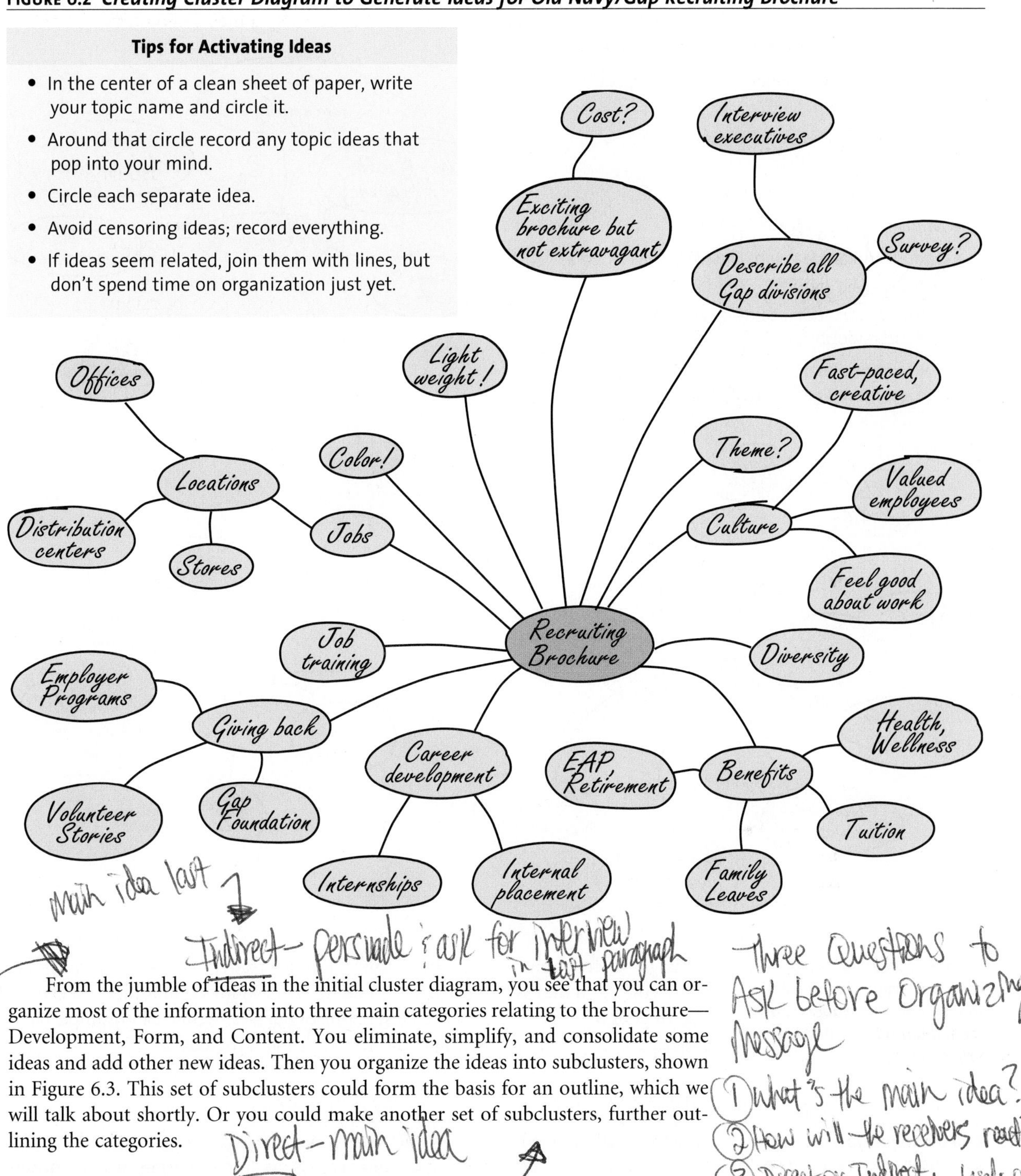

From the jumble of ideas in the initial cluster diagram, you see that you can organize most of the information into three main categories relating to the brochure—Development, Form, and Content. You eliminate, simplify, and consolidate some ideas and add other new ideas. Then you organize the ideas into subclusters, shown in Figure 6.3. This set of subclusters could form the basis for an outline, which we will talk about shortly. Or you could make another set of subclusters, further outlining the categories.

Writing Process Phase 2: Organize

learning objective 2

Well-organized messages group similar ideas together. These groups of ideas are then sequenced in a way that helps the reader understand relationships and accept the writer's views. Unorganized messages proceed free-form, jumping from one thought to another. They look like the jumbled ideas in our Figure 6.2 cluster diagram. Such

Figure 6.3 ***Organizing Ideas From Cluster Diagram Into Subclusters***

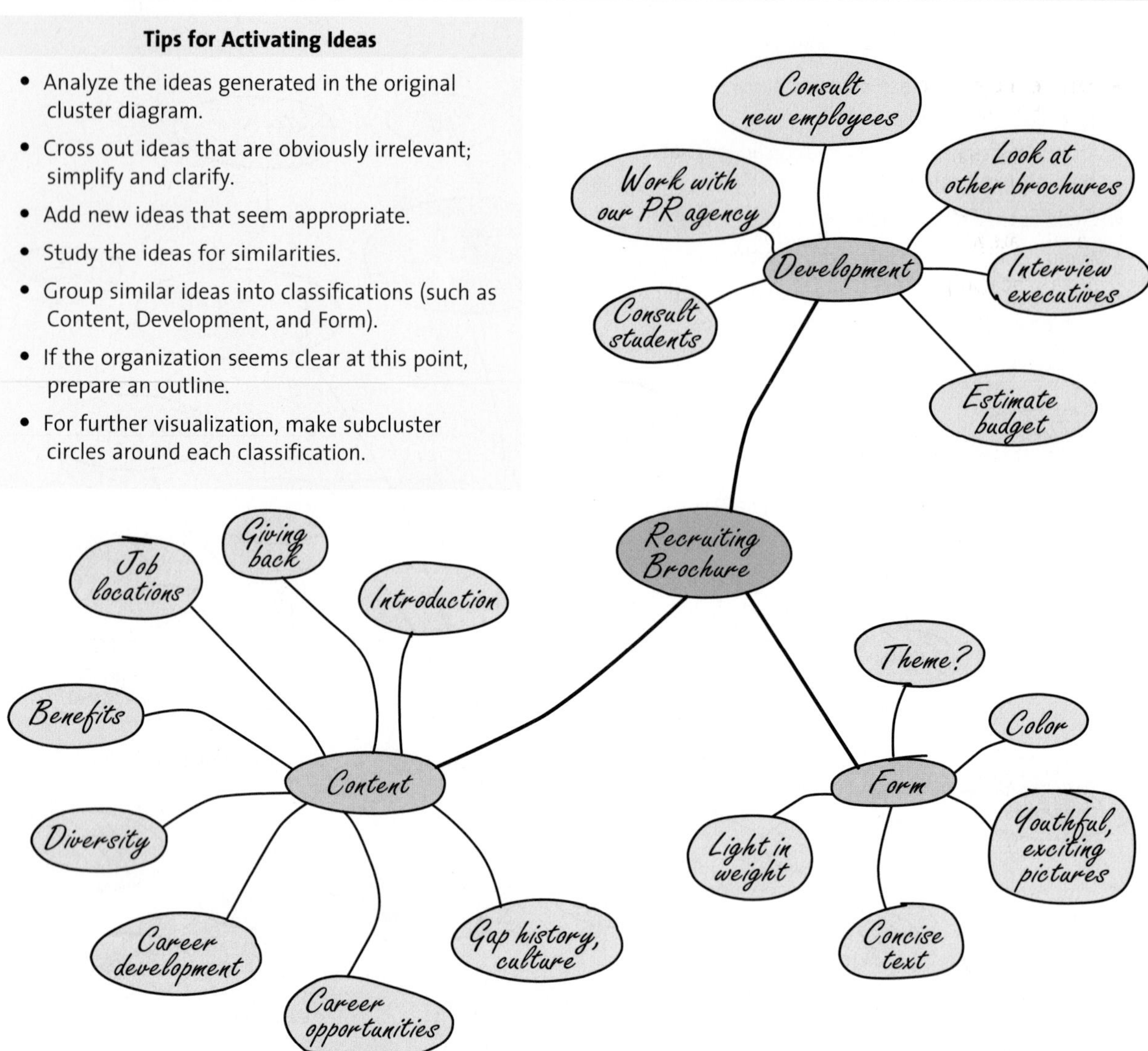
Tips for Activating Ideas
• Analyze the ideas generated in the original cluster diagram.
• Cross out ideas that are obviously irrelevant; simplify and clarify.
• Add new ideas that seem appropriate.
• Study the ideas for similarities.
• Group similar ideas into classifications (such as Content, Development, and Form).
• If the organization seems clear at this point, prepare an outline.
• For further visualization, make subcluster circles around each classification.
Recruiting Brochure
Development
Consult new employees
Work with our PR agency
Look at other brochures
Interview executives
Consult students
Estimate budget
Content
Job locations
Giving back
Introduction
Benefits
Diversity
Career development
Career opportunities
Gap history, culture
Form
Theme?
Color
Youthful, exciting pictures
Light in weight
Concise text

Writers of well-organized messages group similar ideas together so that readers can see relationships and follow arguments.

messages fail to emphasize important points. Puzzled readers can't see how the pieces fit together, and they become frustrated and irritated. Many communication experts regard poor organization as the greatest failing of business writers. Two simple techniques can help you organize data: the scratch list and the outline.

Using Lists and Outlines to Organize Ideas

Two techniques for organizing data are a scratch list and an outline.

In developing simple messages, some writers make a quick scratch list of the topics they wish to cover. Writers often jot this scratch list in the margin of the letter or memo to which they are responding (the majority of business messages are written in response to other documents). These writers then compose a message at their computers directly from the scratch list.

Most writers, though, need to organize their ideas—especially if the project is complex—into a hierarchy, such as an outline. The beauty of preparing an outline is that it gives you a chance to organize your thinking before you get bogged down in word choice and sentence structure.[10] Figure 6.4 shows two outline formats:

Figure 6.4 ***Two Outlining Formats***

Tips for Making Outlines

- Define the main topic (purpose of message) in the title.
- Divide the main topic into major components or classifications (preferably three to five). If necessary, combine small components into one larger category.
- Break the components into subpoints.
- Don't put a single item under a major component; if you have only one subpoint, integrate it with the main item above it or reorganize.
- Strive to make each component exclusive (no overlapping).
- Use details, illustrations, and evidence to support subpoints.

Format for Alphanumeric Outline	Format for Decimal Outline
Title: Major Idea, Purpose	Title: Major Idea, Purpose
I. First major component	1.0. First major component
A. First subpoint	1.1. First subpoint
1. Detail, illustration, evidence	1.1.1. Detail, illustration, evidence
2. Detail, illustration, evidence	1.1.2. Detail, illustration, evidence
B. Second subpoint	1.2. Second subpoint
1.	1.2.1.
2.	1.2.2.
II. Second major component	2.0. Second major component
A. First subpoint	2.1. First subpoint
1.	2.1.1.
2.	2.1.2.
B. Second subpoint	2.2. Second subpoint
1.	2.2.1.
2.	2.2.2.
III. Third major component	3.0. Third major component
A.	3.1.
1.	3.1.1.
2.	3.1.2.
B.	3.2.
1.	3.2.1.
2.	3.2.2.
(This method is simple and familiar.)	*(This method relates every item to the overall outline.)*

alphanumeric and decimal. The familiar alphanumeric format uses Roman numerals, letters, and numbers to show major and minor ideas. The decimal format, which takes a little getting used to, has the advantage of showing how every item at every level relates to the whole. Both outlining formats force you to focus on the topic, identify major ideas, and support those ideas with details, illustrations, or evidence. Many computer outlining programs now on the market make the mechanics of the process a real breeze.

Grouping ideas into categories is the hardest part of outlining.

The hardest part of outlining is grouping ideas into components or categories—ideally three to five in number. By the way, these major categories will become the major headings in your report. If you have more than five components, look for ways to combine smaller segments into broader topics. The following example shows how a portion of the Gap recruiting brochure subclusters (Figure 6.3) can be organized into an alphanumeric outline.[11]

Alphanumeric outlines show major and minor ideas; decimal outlines show how ideas relate to one another.

An alphanumeric outline divides items into major and minor categories.

I. Introduction
   A. Brief history of Gap Inc.
      1. Founding
      2. Milestones
   B. Corporate culture
      1. Fast-paced, creative, feel good about work
      2. Valuing diversity, employees
      3. Social responsibility
II. Careers
   A. Opportunities
      1. Internships
      2. Management trainee programs
      3. M.B.A. programs
   B. Development
      1. Internal promotion
      2. Job training

Every major category in an outline should have at least two subcategories.

spotlight *on communicators*

"Writing skills in the business world are no longer simply an advantage—they are a necessity," says Max Messmer, CEO of Robert Half International, the world's largest specialized staffing firm. At the heart of effective writing, he contends, is the ability to organize a series of thoughts. Diving blindly into a writing project is a recipe for disaster. He advises taking the time to prioritize and record the key points you want to make, using either a formal outline or an informal list.

Notice that each major category is divided into at least two subcategories. These categories are then fleshed out with examples, details, statistics, case histories, and other data. In moving from major point to subpoint, you are progressing from large abstract concepts to small concrete ideas. And each subpoint could be further subdivided with more specific illustrations if you desired. You can determine the appropriate amount of detail by considering what your audience (primary and secondary) already knows about the topic and how much persuading you must do.

How you group ideas into components depends on your topic and your channel of communication. Business documents usually contain typical components arranged in traditional patterns, as shown in Figure 6.5.

Thus far, you've seen how to collect information, generate ideas, and prepare an outline. How you order the information in your outline, though, depends on what pattern or strategy you choose.

FIGURE 6.5 ***Typical Major Components in Business Outlines***

Letter or Memo
I. Opening
II. Body
III. Closing

Procedure
I. Step 1
II. Step 2
III. Step 3
IV. Step 4

Informational Report
I. Introduction
II. Facts
III. Summary

Analytical Report
I. Introduction/problem
II. Facts/findings
III. Conclusions
IV. Recommendations (if requested)

Proposal
I. Introduction
II. Proposed solution
III. Staffing
IV. Schedule, cost
V. Authorization

Photo: Courtesy of Robert Half International Inc.

Organizing Ideas Into Patterns

Two organizational patterns provide plans of action for typical business messages: the direct pattern and the indirect pattern. The primary difference between the two patterns is where the main idea is placed. In the direct pattern the main idea comes first, followed by details, explanation, or evidence. In the indirect pattern the main idea follows the details, explanation, and evidence. The pattern you select is determined by how you expect the audience to react to the message, as shown in Figure 6.6.

learning objective

3

Business messages typically follow either the (1) direct pattern, with the main idea first, or (2) the indirect pattern, with the main idea following explanation and evidence.

Direct Pattern for Receptive Audiences

In preparing to write any message, you need to anticipate the audience's reaction to your ideas and frame your message accordingly. When you expect the reader to be pleased, mildly interested, or, at worst, neutral—use the direct pattern. That is, put your main point—the purpose of your message—in the first or second sentence. Dianna Booher, renowned writing consultant, points out that typical readers begin any message by saying, "So what am I supposed to do with this information?" In business writing you have to say, "Reader, here is my point!"[12] As quickly as possible, tell why you are writing. Compare the direct and indirect patterns in the following memo openings. Notice how long it takes to get to the main idea in the indirect opening.

Indirect Opening
Our company has been concerned with attracting better-qualified prospective job candidates. For this reason, the Management Council has been gathering information about an internship program for college students. After considerable investigation, we have voted to begin a pilot program starting next fall.

Direct Opening
The Management Council has voted to begin a college internship pilot program next fall.

FIGURE 6.6 ***Audience Response Determines Pattern of Organization***

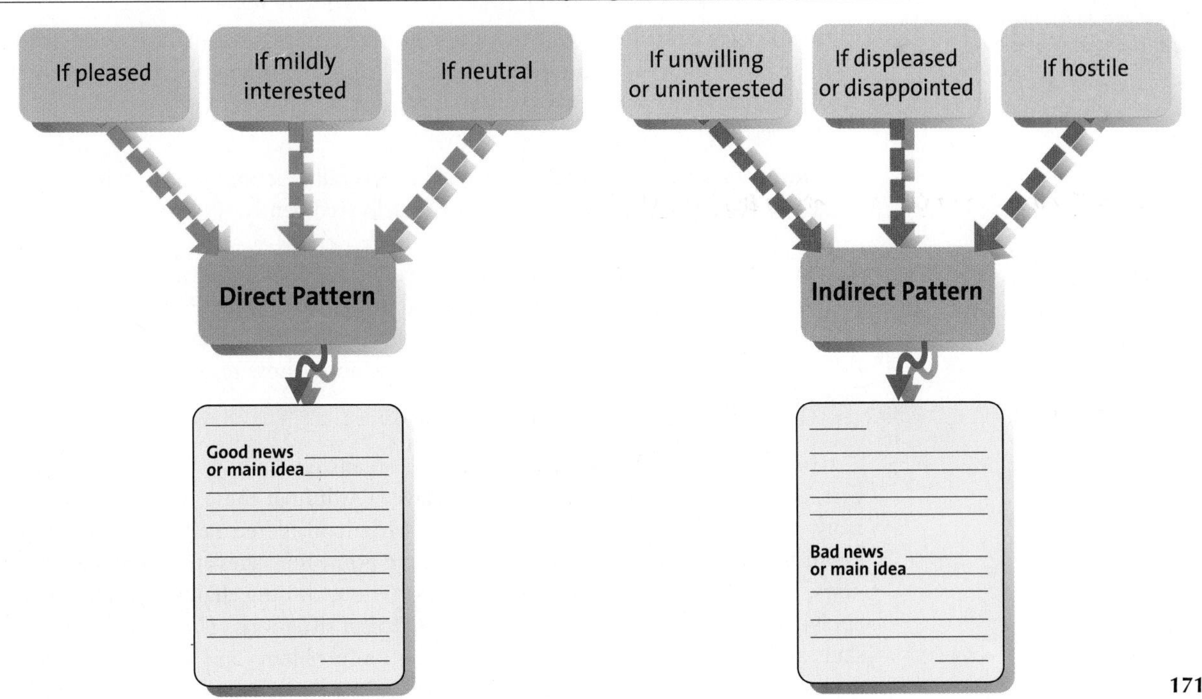

Frontloading saves the reader's time, establishes the proper frame of mind, and prevents frustration.

Explanations and details should follow the direct opening. What's important is getting to the main idea quickly. This direct method, also called *frontloading*, has at least three advantages:

- **Saves the reader's time.** Many of today's businesspeople can devote only a few moments to each message. Messages that take too long to get to the point may lose their readers along the way.
- **Sets a proper frame of mind.** Learning the purpose up front helps the reader put the subsequent details and explanations in perspective. Without a clear opening, the reader may be thinking, "Why am I being told this?"
- **Prevents frustration.** Readers forced to struggle through excessive verbiage before reaching the main idea become frustrated. They resent the writer. Poorly organized messages create a negative impression of the writer.

This frontloading technique works best with audiences that are likely to be receptive to or at least not disagree with what you have to say. Typical business messages that follow the direct pattern include routine requests and responses, orders and acknowledgments, nonsensitive memos, e-mail messages, informational reports, and informational oral presentations. All these tasks have one element in common: none has a sensitive subject that will upset the reader.

Indirect Pattern for Unreceptive Audiences

When you expect the audience to be uninterested, unwilling, displeased, or perhaps even hostile, the indirect pattern is more appropriate. In this pattern you don't reveal the main idea until after you have offered explanation and evidence. This approach works well with three kinds of messages: (1) bad news, (2) ideas that require persuasion, and (3) sensitive news, especially when being transmitted to superiors. The indirect pattern has these benefits:

The indirect pattern respects the feelings of the audience, facilitates a fair hearing, and minimizes a negative reaction.

- **Respects the feelings of the audience.** Bad news is always painful, but the trauma can be lessened when the receiver is prepared for it.
- **Encourages a fair hearing.** Messages that may upset the reader are more likely to be read when the main idea is delayed. Beginning immediately with a piece of bad news or a persuasive request, for example, may cause the receiver to stop reading or listening.
- **Minimizes a negative reaction.** A reader's overall reaction to a negative message is generally improved if the news is delivered gently.

Typical business messages that could be developed indirectly include letters and memos that refuse requests, deny claims, and disapprove credit. Persuasive requests, sales letters, sensitive messages, and some reports and oral presentations also benefit from the indirect strategy. You'll learn more about how to use the indirect pattern in Chapters 10 and 11.

In summary, business messages may be organized directly, with the main idea first, or indirectly, with the main idea delayed. Although these two patterns cover many communication problems, they should be considered neither universal nor inviolate. Every business transaction is distinct. Some messages are mixed: part good news, part bad; part goodwill, part persuasion. In upcoming chapters you'll practice applying the direct and indirect patterns in typical situations. Then, you'll have the skills and confidence to evaluate communication problems and vary these patterns depending on the goals you wish to achieve.

PROCESS IN PROGRESS

Old Navy Revisited

REBUILDING ITS CUSTOMER base and correcting its fashion missteps are major initiatives at Old Navy and its parent Gap. At the same time the stores must be ever watchful that their garments are not made in sweatshops. Stiff competition and consumer demand for low prices have forced many U.S. apparel manufacturers to shift production offshore. And some of that production ends up in sweatshops, such as those found in Cambodia, Bangladesh, and Honduras. The worst sweatshops use child labor and demand 80-hour workweeks without overtime pay. Bosses routinely shout at workers and may send them home for talking on the job. Workers earn as little as 29 cents an hour.

Like other major apparel manufacturers, Old Navy and Gap strive to control working conditions with factory-monitoring and labor-standards programs. Around the world Gap Inc. has more than 90 employees whose sole focus is working to improve conditions in the factories that make its clothing. In one year these employees conducted more than 13,000 inspections at 3,000 factories.[13] When a problem is found, Gap takes action. It works with contractors and factories to improve practices and conditions. If conditions don't improve, it stops using errant contractors.[14] Enforcing its standards worldwide requires an ongoing effort. When complaints from human rights activists and others arrive, Old Navy and Gap must investigate and respond to each inquiry.

Critical Thinking

- When a business communicator responds to an inquiry, such as a letter about human rights violations among contractors, is "research" necessary?
- What are the differences between formal and informal research?
- What are the advantages and disadvantages of brainstorming with groups?

CONTINUED ON PAGE 183

case study

Writing Process Phase 2: Compose

learning objective 4

Once you've researched your topic, organized the data, and selected a pattern of organization, you're ready to begin composing. Most writers expect to use their computers for composition, but many are unaware of all the ways a computer can help create better written messages, oral presentations, and Web pages. See the accompanying Tech Talk box to learn how you can take full advantage of your computer.

Even with a computer, some writers have trouble getting started, especially if they haven't completed the preparatory work. Organizing your ideas and working from an outline are very helpful in overcoming writer's block. Composition is also easier if you have a quiet environment in which to concentrate. Businesspeople with messages to compose set aside a given time and allow no calls, visitors, or other interruptions. This is a good technique for students as well.

When composing the first draft, write quickly and save revision for later.

As you begin composing, keep in mind that you are writing the first draft, not the final copy. Experts suggest that you write quickly (*sprint writing*). Get your thoughts down now and refine them in later versions.[15] As you take up each idea, imagine that you are talking to the reader. Don't let yourself get bogged down. If you can't think of the right word, insert a substitute or type "find perfect word later." Sprint writing works especially well for those composing on a computer because it's simple to make changes at any point of the composition process. If you are handwriting the first draft, double-space so that you have room for changes.

tech talk

Seven Ways Computers Can Help You Create Better Written Messages, Oral Presentations, and Web Pages

Although computers can't actually do the writing for you, they provide powerful tools that make the composition process easier and the results more professional. Here are seven ways your computer can help you improve your written documents, oral presentations, and even Web pages.

1. **Fighting writer's block.** Because word processors enable ideas to flow almost effortlessly from your brain to a screen, you can expect fewer delays resulting from writer's block. You can compose rapidly, and you can experiment with structure and phrasing, later retaining and polishing your most promising thoughts.

2. **Collecting information electronically.** As a knowledge worker in an information economy, you will need to find information quickly. Much of the world's information is now accessible in databases or on the Web. You'll learn more about these exciting electronic resources in Unit 4.

3. **Outlining and organizing ideas.** Most word processors include some form of "outliner," a feature that enables you to divide a topic into a hierarchical order with main points and subpoints. Your computer keeps track of the levels of ideas automatically so that you can easily add, cut, or rearrange points in the outline.

4. **Improving correctness and precision.** Nearly all word processing programs today provide features that catch and correct spelling and typographical errors. Grammar checkers detect many errors in capitalization, word use (such as *it's, its*), double negatives, verb use, subject–verb agreement, sentence structure, number agreement, number style, and other writing faults. But the errors are merely highlighted—not corrected. You have to do that.

5. **Adding graphics for emphasis.** Your letters, memos, and reports may be improved by the addition of graphs and artwork to clarify and illustrate data. You can import charts, diagrams, and illustrations created in database, spreadsheet, graphics, or draw-and-paint programs. Ready-made pictures, called clip art, can be used to symbolize or illustrate ideas.

6. **Designing and producing professional-looking documents, presentations, and Web pages.** Most software now includes a large selection of scalable fonts (for different character sizes and styles), italics, boldface, symbols, and styling techniques to aid you in producing consistent formatting and professional-looking results. Presentation software enables you to incorporate showy slide effects, color, sound, pictures, and even movies into your talks for management or customers. Web document builders also help you design and construct Web pages.

7. **Using collaborative software for team writing.** Special programs with commenting and revision features, described in Chapter 5, allow you to make changes and to identify each team member's editing.

Career Application

Individually or in teams, identify specific software programs that perform the tasks described here. Prepare a table naming each program, its major functions, and its advantages and disadvantages for business writers in your field.

Creating Effective Sentences

Sentences must have subjects and verbs and must make sense.

As you create your first draft, you'll be working at the sentence level of composition. Although you've used sentences all your life, you may be unaware of how they can be shaped and arranged to express your ideas most effectively. First, let's review some basic sentence elements.

Complete sentences have subjects and verbs and make sense.

SUBJECT (manager) — VERB (sent)

The manager of Information Technology sent an e-mail to all employees.

Clauses and phrases, the key building blocks of sentences, are related groups of words. Clauses have subjects and verbs; phrases do not.

Clauses have subjects and verbs, but phrases do not.

The manager [of Information Technology]PHRASE sent an e-mail [to all employees.]PHRASE

[By reading carefully,]PHRASE we learned [about the latest computer viruses.]PHRASE

[Because he is experienced,]CLAUSE [Adam knows how to repair most computer problems.]CLAUSE

[When we have technology problems,]CLAUSE [we call a technician in our support group.]CLAUSE

Clauses may be divided into two groups: independent and dependent. Independent clauses are grammatically complete. Dependent clauses depend for their meaning on independent clauses. In the two preceding examples the clauses beginning with *Because* and *When* are dependent. Dependent clauses are often introduced by words such as *if, when, because,* and *as.*

Independent clauses may stand alone; dependent clauses may not.

[Adam solves our technology problems.]INDEPENDENT CLAUSE

[When employees need help,]DEPENDENT CLAUSE [Adam solves our technology problems.]INDEPENDENT CLAUSE

By learning to distinguish phrases, independent clauses, and dependent clauses, you'll be able to punctuate sentences correctly and avoid three basic sentence faults: the fragment, the run-on sentence, and the comma splice. In Guide 1, Appendix A, we examine these writing problems in greater detail. For now, however, let's look at some ways to make your sentences more readable.

Preferring Short Sentences. Because your goal is to communicate clearly, you're better off limiting your sentences to about 20 or fewer words. The American Press Institute reports that reader comprehension drops off markedly as sentences become longer.[16] Thus, in crafting your sentences, think about the relationship between sentence length and comprehension:

Effective sentences are short and stress important ideas.

Sentence Length	Comprehension Rate
8 words	100%
15 words	90%
19 words	80%
28 words	50%

Sentences of 20 or fewer words have the most impact.

Instead of stringing together clauses with *and, but,* and *however,* break some of those complex sentences into separate segments. Business readers want to grasp ideas immediately. They can do that best when thoughts are separated into short sentences. On the other hand, too many monotonous short sentences will sound

Eager to return home, these U.S. infantry soldiers will doubtlessly begin to receive many Veterans Bureau messages, which in the past were not always well written. Now VBA writers have improved the readability of their messages by shortening sentences, emphasizing important ideas with graphic highlighting, and using active-voice verbs.

"grammar schoolish" and may bore or even annoy the reader. Strive for a balance between longer sentences and shorter ones. Your computer probably can point out long sentences and give you an average sentence length.

Emphasizing Important Ideas. You can stress prominent ideas mechanically by underscoring, italicizing, or boldfacing. You'll learn more about these graphic highlighting devices shortly. You can also emphasize important ideas with five stylistic devices. In the bulleted items that follow, notice that each of these suggestions involves the choice of words or attention to the placement of an important idea.

- **Use vivid words.** Vivid words are emphatic because the reader can picture ideas clearly.

General	**Vivid**
One business uses personal selling techniques.	Avon uses face-to-face selling techniques.

- **Label the main idea.** If an idea is significant, tell the reader:

Unlabeled	**Labeled**
Explore the possibility of leasing a site, but also hire a consultant.	Explore the possibility of leasing a site; but, *most important,* hire a consultant.

Emphasize an important idea by using vivid words, labeling the main idea, placing the idea first or last in a sentence, and making it the sentence subject.

- **Place the important idea first or last in the sentence.** Ideas have less competition from surrounding words when they appear first or last in a sentence. Observe how the date of the meeting can be emphasized:

Unemphatic	**Emphatic**
All production and administrative personnel will meet on May 23, at which time we will announce a new plan of salary incentives.	On May 23 all personnel will meet to learn about salary incentives.

- **Place the important idea in a simple sentence or in an independent clause.** Don't dilute the effect of the idea by making it share the spotlight with other words and clauses.

Unemphatic	**Emphatic**
Although you are the first trainee that we have hired for this program, we have interviewed many candidates and expect to expand the program in the future. (Main idea lost in introductory dependent clause.)	You are the first trainee that we have hired for this program. (Simple sentence contains main idea.)

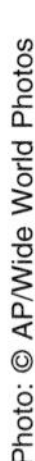
Photo: © AP/Wide World Photos

- **Make sure the important idea is the sentence subject.** You'll learn more about active and passive voice shortly, but at this point just focus on making the important idea the subject.

Unemphatic	**Emphatic**
The environmental report was written by Michelle. (Deemphasizes *Michelle*; emphasizes the report.)	Michelle wrote the environmental report. (Emphasizes *Michelle*.)

Managing Active and Passive Voice. In sentences with active-voice verbs, the subject is the doer of the action. In passive-voice sentences, the subject is acted upon.

In active-voice sentences the subject is the doer; in passive-voice sentences the subject is acted upon.

Passive verb	**Active verb**
The tax return *was completed* before the April 15 deadline. (The subject, *tax return*, is acted upon.)	Brandon *completed* his tax return before the April 1 deadline. (The subject, *Brandon*, is the doer of the action.)

In the first sentence, the passive-voice verb emphasizes the tax return. In the second sentence, the active-voice verb emphasizes Brandon. Active-voice sentences are more direct because they reveal the performer immediately. They're easier to understand and shorter. Most business writing should be in the active voice.

Yet, passive verbs are useful in certain instances. In sentences with passive-voice verbs, the doer of the action may be revealed or left unknown. In business writing, as well as in personal interactions, some situations demand tact and sensitivity. Instead of using a direct approach with active verbs, we may prefer the indirectness that passive verbs allow. Rather than making a blunt announcement with an active verb (*Tyler made a major error in the estimate*), we can soften the sentence with a passive construction (*A major error was made in the estimate*).

Here's a summary of the best uses of active- and passive-voice verbs:

spotlight *on communicators*

Arthur Levitt, former chair of the U.S. Securities and Exchange Commission, is said to have been the most activist chair in the SEC's history. As a champion of "plain English," he was instrumental in requiring that disclosure documents written for investors be readable. To improve their readability, he advocated using the active voice, familiar words, and a conversational tone. He also recommended emphasizing important ideas with boldface, graphics, headings, and color. All of these techniques can vastly improve the readability of business writing.

- **Use the active voice for most business writing.** *Our company gives drug tests to all applicants.*
- **Use the passive voice to emphasize an action or the recipient of the action.** *Drug tests are given to all applicants.*
- **Use the passive voice to deemphasize negative news.** *Your monitor cannot be repaired.*
- **Use the passive voice to conceal the doer of an action.** *A major error was made in the estimate.*

Passive-voice sentences are useful for tact and to direct attention to actions instead of people.

How can you tell whether a verb is active or passive? Identify the subject of the sentence and decide whether the subject is doing the acting or whether it is being acted upon. For example, in the sentence *An appointment was made for January 1*, the subject is *appointment.* The subject is being acted upon; therefore, the verb (*was made*) is passive. Another clue in identifying passive-voice verbs is that they generally include a *to be* helping verb, such as *is, are, was, were, being,* or *been.*

Modifiers must be close to the words they describe or limit.

Avoiding Dangling and Misplaced Modifiers. For clarity, modifiers must be close to the words they describe or limit. A dangling modifier describes or limits a word or words that are missing from the sentence. A misplaced modifier occurs when the word or phrase it describes is not close enough to be clear. In both instances, the solution is to move the modifier closer to the word(s) it describes or limits. Introductory verbal phrases are particularly dangerous; be sure to follow them immediately with the words they can logically describe or modify.

Dangling Modifier	**Improved**
To win the lottery, a ticket must be purchased. (*The introductory verbal phrase must be followed by a logical subject.*)	To win the lottery, you must purchase a ticket.
Driving through Malibu Canyon, the ocean suddenly came into view. (*Is the ocean driving through Malibu Canyon?*)	As we drove through Malibu Canyon, the ocean suddenly came into view.
Speaking before the large audience, Lisa's knees began to knock. (*Are Lisa's knees making a speech?*)	Speaking before the large audience, Lisa felt her knees begin to knock.

Try this trick for detecting and remedying these dangling modifiers. Ask the question *who?* or *what?* after any introductory phrase. The words immediately following should tell the reader *who* or *what* is performing the action. Try the *who?* test on the previous danglers and on the following misplaced modifiers.

A modifier is misplaced when the word or phrase it describes is not close enough to be clear.

Misplaced Modifier	**Improved**
Seeing his error too late, the envelope was immediately resealed by Mark. (*Did the envelope see the error?*)	Seeing his error too late, Mark immediately resealed the envelope.
A wart appeared on my left hand that I want removed. (*Is the left hand to be removed?*)	A wart that I want removed appeared on my left hand.
The busy personnel director interviewed only candidates who had excellent computer skills in the morning. (*Were the candidates skilled only in the morning?*)	In the morning the busy personnel director interviewed only candidates who had excellent computer skills.

learning objective

5

Effective paragraphs focus on one topic, link ideas to build coherence, and use transitional devices to enhance coherence.

Drafting Meaningful Paragraphs

From composing sentences, we progress to paragraphs. A paragraph is one or more sentences designated as a separate thought group. To avoid muddled paragraphs, writers must recognize basic paragraph elements, conventional sentence patterns, and ways to organize sentences into one of three classic paragraph patterns. They must also be able to polish their paragraphs by linking sentences and using transitional expressions.

Well-constructed paragraphs discuss only one topic. They reveal the primary idea in a main sentence that usually, but not always, appears first. Paragraphs are generally composed of three kinds of sentences:[17]

Main sentence: expresses the primary idea of the paragraph.

Supporting sentence: illustrates, explains, or strengthens the primary idea.

Limiting sentence: opposes the primary idea by suggesting a negative or contrasting thought; may precede or follow the main sentence.

These sentences may be arranged in three classic paragraph plans: direct, pivoting, and indirect.

Using the Direct Paragraph Plan to Define, Classify, Illustrate, or Describe

Paragraphs arranged in the direct plan begin with the main sentence, followed by supporting sentences. Most business messages use this paragraph plan because it clarifies the subject immediately. This plan is useful whenever you must define (a new product or procedure), classify (parts of a whole), illustrate (an idea), or describe (a process). Simply start with the main sentence; then strengthen and amplify that idea with supporting ideas, as shown here:

The direct paragraph pattern is appropriate when defining, classifying, illustrating, or describing.

Main Sentence	A social audit is a report on the social performance of a company.
Supporting Sentences	Such an audit may be conducted by the company itself or by outsiders who evaluate the company's efforts to produce safe products, engage in socially responsible activities, and protect the environment. Many companies publish the results of their social audits in their annual reports. Ben & Jerry's Homemade, for example, devotes a major portion of its annual report to its social audit. The report discusses Ben & Jerry's efforts to support environmental restoration. Moreover, it describes workplace safety, employment equality, and peace programs.

You can alter the direct plan by adding a limiting sentence if necessary. Be sure, though, that you follow with sentences that return to the main idea and support it, as shown here:

Main Sentence	Flexible work scheduling could immediately increase productivity and enhance employee satisfaction in our entire organization.
Limiting Sentence	Such scheduling, however, is impossible for all employees.
Supporting Sentences	Managers would be required to maintain their regular hours. For many other employees, though, flexible scheduling permits extra time to manage family responsibilities. Feeling less stress, employees are able to focus their attention better at work; hence they become more relaxed and more productive.

Using the Pivoting Paragraph Plan to Compare and Contrast

Paragraphs arranged in the pivoting plan start with a limiting sentence that offers a contrasting or negative idea before delivering the main sentence. Notice in the following example how two limiting sentences about drawbacks to foreign service

The pivoting paragraph pattern is appropriate when comparing and contrasting.

careers open the paragraph; only then do the main and supporting sentences describing rewards in foreign service appear. The pivoting plan is especially useful for comparing and contrasting ideas. In using the pivoting plan, be sure you emphasize the turn in direction with an obvious *but* or *however*.

Limiting Sentences	Foreign service careers are certainly not for everyone. Many are in remote countries where harsh climates, health hazards, security risks, and other discomforts exist.
Main Sentence	However, careers in the foreign service offer special rewards for the special people who qualify.
Supporting Sentences	Foreign service employees enjoy the pride and satisfaction of representing the United States abroad. They enjoy frequent travel, enriching cultural and social experiences in living abroad, and action-oriented work.

Using the Indirect Paragraph Plan to Explain and Persuade

The indirect paragraph pattern is appropriate when delivering bad news.

Paragraphs arranged in the indirect plan start with the supporting sentences and conclude with the main sentence. This useful plan enables you to build a rationale, a foundation of reasons, before hitting the audience with a big idea—possibly one that is bad news. It enables you to explain your reasons and then in the final sentence draw a conclusion from them. In the following example the vice president of a large accounting firm begins by describing the trend toward casual dress and concludes with a recommendation that his firm change its dress code. This indirect plan works well for describing causes followed by an effect.

Supporting Sentences	According to a recent poll, more than half of all white-collar workers are now dressing casually at work. Many high-tech engineers and professional specialists have given up suits and ties, favoring khakis and sweaters instead. In our own business our consultants say they stand out like "sore thumbs" because they are attired in traditional buttoned-down styles, while the businesspeople they visit are usually wearing comfortable, casual clothing.
Main Sentence	Therefore, I recommend that we establish an optional "business casual" policy allowing consultants to dress casually, if they wish, as they perform their duties both in and out of the office.

You'll learn more techniques for implementing direct and indirect writing strategies when you prepare letters, memos, e-mail messages, reports, and oral presentations in subsequent chapters.

Linking Ideas to Build Coherence

Coherent paragraphs link ideas by sustaining the main idea, using pronouns, dovetailing sentences, and using transitional expressions.

Paragraphs are coherent when ideas are linked, that is, when one idea leads logically to the next. Well-written paragraphs take the reader through a number of steps. When the author skips from Step 1 to Step 3 and forgets Step 2, the reader is lost. You can use several techniques to keep the reader in step with your ideas.

Sustaining the Key Idea. This involves simply repeating a key expression or using a similar one. For example:

Our philosophy holds that every customer is really a *guest*. All new employees to our theme parks are trained to treat *guests* as *VIPs*. These *VIPs* are never told what they can or cannot do.

Notice how the repetition of *guest* and *VIP* connects ideas.

Using Pronouns. Familiar pronouns, such as *we*, *they*, *he*, *she*, and *it*, help build continuity, as do demonstrative pronouns, such as *this*, *that*, *these*, and *those*. These words confirm that something under discussion is still being discussed. For example:

Using pronouns strategically helps build coherence and continuity.

All new park employees receive a two-week orientation. They learn that every staffer has a vital role in preparing for the show. This training includes how to maintain enthusiasm.

Be careful with *this*, *that*, *these*, and *those*, however. These words usually need a noun with them to make their meaning absolutely clear. In the last example notice how confusing *this* becomes if the word *training* is omitted.

Dovetailing Sentences. Sentences are "dovetailed" when an idea at the end of one connects with an idea at the beginning of the next. For example:

Dovetailing sentences means connecting ending and beginning ideas.

New hosts and hostesses learn about the theme park and its *facilities*. These *facilities* include telephones, food services, bathrooms, and attractions, as well as the location of *offices*. Knowledge of administrative *offices* and internal workings of the company, such as who's who in administration, ensures that staffers will be able to *serve guests* fully. *Serving guests*, of course, is our No. 1 priority.

Dovetailing of sentences is especially helpful with dense, difficult topics. This technique, however, should not be overused.

Showing Connections With Transitional Expressions. Transitional expressions are another excellent device for showing connections and achieving paragraph coherence. These words, some of which are shown in Figure 6.7, act as verbal road signs to readers and listeners. Transitional expressions enable the receiver to anticipate what's coming, to reduce uncertainty, and to speed up comprehension. They signal that a train of thought is moving forward, being developed, possibly detouring, or ending. Transitions are especially helpful in persuasive writing.

Transitional expressions help readers anticipate what's coming, reduce uncertainty, and speed comprehension.

As Figure 6.7 shows, transitions can add or strengthen a thought, show time or order, clarify ideas, show cause and effect, contradict thoughts, and contrast ideas. Thus, you must be careful to select the best transition for your purpose. Look back at the examples of direct, pivoting, and indirect paragraphs to see how transitional expressions and other devices build paragraph coherence. Remember that coherence in communication rarely happens spontaneously; it requires effort and skill.

Composing Short Paragraphs for Readability

Although no rule regulates the length of paragraphs, business writers recognize that short paragraphs are more attractive and readable than longer ones. Paragraphs with eight or fewer lines look inviting, whereas long, solid chunks of print appear formidable. If a topic can't be covered in eight or fewer printed lines (not sentences), consider breaking it up into smaller segments.

Paragraphs with eight or fewer lines are inviting and readable.

FIGURE 6.7 ***Transitional Expressions to Build Coherence***

To Add or Strengthen	To Show Time or Order	To Clarify	To Show Cause and Effect	To Contradict	To Contrast
additionally	after	for example	accordingly	actually	as opposed to
again	before	for instance	as a result	but	at the same time
also	earlier	I mean	consequently	however	by contrast
besides	finally	in other words	for this reason	in fact	conversely
likewise	first	that is	so	instead	on the contrary
moreover	meanwhile	this means	therefore	rather	on the other hand
further	next	thus	thus	still	
furthermore	now	to put it another way	under the circumstances	though	
	previously			yet	

The following checklist summarizes the key points of composing a first draft.

Checklist for Composing Sentences and Paragraphs

For Effective Sentences

- ✓ **Control sentence length.** Use longer sentences occasionally, but rely primarily on short and medium-length sentences.
- ✓ **Emphasize important ideas.** Place main ideas at the beginning of short sentences for emphasis.
- ✓ **Apply active and passive verbs carefully.** Use active verbs (*She sent the e-mail* instead of *The e-mail was sent by her*) most frequently; they immediately identify the doer. Use passive verbs to be tactful, to emphasize an action, or to conceal the performer.
- ✓ **Eliminate misplaced modifiers.** Be sure that introductory verbal phrases are followed by the words that can logically be modified. To check the placement of modifiers, ask *who?* or *what?* after such phrases.

For Meaningful Paragraphs

- ✓ **Develop one idea.** Use main, supporting, and limiting sentences to develop a single idea within each paragraph.
- ✓ **Use the direct plan.** Start most paragraphs with the main sentence followed by supporting sentences. This direct plan is useful in defining, classifying, illustrating, and describing.
- ✓ **Use the pivoting plan.** To compare and contrast ideas, start with a limiting sentence; then, present the main sentence followed by supporting sentences.
- ✓ **Use the indirect plan.** To explain reasons or causes first, start with supporting sentences. Build to the conclusion with the main sentence at the end of the paragraph.

PROCESS TO PRODUCT

Applying Your Skills at Old Navy

THE MANAGEMENT team at Old Navy is often occupied by major issues such as rebuilding its fashion image, maintaining quality, and controlling overseas working conditions to avoid human rights violations. But smaller problems also require attention. One perplexing issue involves returned goods. After years of cheerfully accepting returned items anytime, many stores, including Gap and Old Navy, have tightened their return policies. About 6 percent of all retail purchases are returned every year, and some stores say a growing proportion of those are from customers involved in some kind of scam.[18] But perhaps Gap has gone too far. It received a complaint from Dana Moses, a loyal shopper, who was given many unneeded gifts for her newborn son. After returning about a dozen items to Gap, Moses received a series of letters from the company informing her that she would no longer receive refunds unless she had original receipts. Old Navy heard about this and wants to consider revamping its exchange policy.[19]

Your Task

Your group of Old Navy interns has been given the task of researching exchange policies. First study Old Navy's policy at its Web site. Compare it with those at three other major retailers such as Target, L. L. Bean, Wal-Mart, or Home Depot. As a team, compare your findings. Then brainstorm to determine the major categories of a recommended return policy for Old Navy. Make a cluster diagram. Then organize your findings into an outline summarizing what you think should be included in a return policy. Submit your outline to your intern advisor (your instructor). ■

case study

- ✓ **Build coherence by linking sentences.** Hold ideas together by repeating key words, using pronouns, and dovetailing sentences (beginning one sentence with an idea from the end of the previous sentence).

- ✓ **Provide road signs with transitional expressions.** Use verbal signals to help the audience know where the idea is going. Words such as *moreover, accordingly, as a result,* and *thus* function as idea pointers.

- ✓ **Limit paragraph length.** Remember that paragraphs with eight or fewer printed lines look inviting. Consider breaking up longer paragraphs if necessary.

Summary of Learning Objectives

1 **Apply Phase 2 of the 3-x-3 writing process, which begins with formal and informal methods for researching data and generating ideas.** The second phase of the writing process includes researching, organizing, and writing. Researching means collecting information using formal or informal techniques. Formal research for long reports and complex problems may involve searching electronically or manually, as well as conducting interviews, surveys, focus groups, and experiments. Informal research for routine tasks may include looking in company files, talking with your boss, interviewing

the target audience, conducting informal surveys, brainstorming for ideas, and cluster diagramming.

2 **Specify how to organize data into lists and alphanumeric or decimal outlines.** One method for organizing data in simple messages is to list the main topics to be discussed. Organizing more complex messages usually requires an outline. To prepare an outline, divide the main topic into three to five major components. Break the components into subpoints consisting of details, illustrations, and evidence. For an alphanumeric outline arrange items using Roman numerals (I, II), capital letters (A, B), and numbers (1, 2). For a decimal outline show the ordering of ideas with decimals (1., 1.1, 1.1.1).

3 **Compare direct and indirect patterns for organizing ideas.** The direct pattern places the main idea first. This pattern is useful when audiences will be pleased, mildly interested, or neutral. It saves the reader's time, sets the proper frame of mind, and prevents reader frustration. The indirect pattern places the main idea after explanations. This pattern is useful for audiences that will be unwilling, displeased, or hostile. It respects the feelings of the audience, encourages a fair hearing, and minimizes negative reactions.

4 **Discuss composing the first draft of a message, focusing on techniques for creating effective sentences.** Compose the first draft of a message in a quiet environment where you won't be interrupted. Compose quickly, preferably at a computer. Plan to revise. As you compose, remember that sentences are most effective when they are short (under 20 words). A main idea may be emphasized by making it the sentence subject, placing it first, and removing competing ideas. Effective sentences use active verbs, although passive verbs may be necessary for tact or de-emphasis. Effective sentences avoid dangling and misplaced modifiers.

5 **Define a paragraph and describe three classic paragraph plans and techniques for composing meaningful paragraphs.** A paragraph consists of one or more sentences designated as a separate thought group. Typical paragraphs follow one of three plans. Direct paragraphs (main sentence followed by supporting sentences) are useful to define, classify, illustrate, and describe. Pivoting paragraphs (limiting sentence followed by main sentence and supporting sentences) are useful to compare and contrast. Indirect paragraphs (supporting sentences followed by main sentence) build a rationale and foundation of ideas before presenting the main idea. Paragraphs may be improved through the use of coherence techniques and transitional expressions.

chapter review

1. What are the three main activities involved in the second phase of Guffey's 3-x-3 writing process? (Obj. 1)
2. Name seven specific techniques for a productive group "brainstorming" session. (Obj. 1)
3. What is a cluster diagram, and when might it be useful? (Obj. 1)
4. Describe an alphanumeric outline. (Obj. 2)
5. What is the relationship between the major categories in an outline and those in a report written from the outline? (Obj. 2)
6. Distinguish between the direct and indirect patterns of organization for typical business messages. (Obj. 3)
7. Why should most messages be "frontloaded"? (Obj. 3)
8. List some business messages that should be frontloaded and some that should not be frontloaded. (Obj. 3)
9. Why should writers plan for revision? How can they do it? (Obj. 4)
10. Name three ways to emphasize important ideas in sentences. (Obj. 4)
11. Distinguish between active-voice sentences and passive-voice sentences. Give examples. (Obj. 4)
12. Give an original example of a dangling or misplaced modifier. Why are introductory verbal phrases dangerous? (Obj. 4)
13. Describe three kinds of sentences used to develop ideas in paragraphs. (Obj. 5)
14. Describe three paragraph plans. Identify the uses for each. (Obj. 5)
15. What is coherence, and how is it achieved? (Obj. 5)

critical thinking

1. Why is cluster diagramming considered an intuitive process whereas outlining is considered an analytical process? (Obj. 1)
2. Why is audience analysis so important in choosing the direct or indirect pattern of organization for a business message? (Obj. 3)
3. In what ways do you imagine that writing on the job differs from the writing you do in your academic studies? Consider process as well as product. (Obj. 1)
4. Why are short sentences and short paragraphs appropriate for business communication? (Objs. 4 and 5)
5. **Ethical Issue:** Discuss the ethics of the indirect pattern of organization. Is it manipulative to delay the presentation of the main idea in a message?

THREE GREAT RESOURCES FOR YOU!

1. ***Guffey Student Web Site***
   http://guffey.swlearning.com

   Your companion Web site offers chapter review quizzes, WebThink activities, updated chapter URLs, and many additional resources.

2. ***Guffey XTRA!***
   http://guffeyxtra.swlearning.com

   This online study assistant includes Your Personal Language Trainer, Speak Right!, Spell Right!, bonus online chapters, Documents for Analysis, PowerPoint slides, and much more.

3. ***Student Study Guide***

   Self-checked workbook activities and applications review chapter concepts and develop career skills.

activities

6.1 Document for Analysis (Objs. 3, 4, and 5)

The following interoffice memo is hard to read. It suffers from numerous writing faults discussed in this chapter.

Your Task. First, read the memo to see whether you can understand what the writer requests from all Southeast Division employees. Then, discuss why this memo is so hard to read. How long are the sentences? How many passive-voice constructions can you locate? How effective is the paragraphing? Can you spot four dangling or misplaced modifiers? In the next activity you'll improve the organization of this message. (Superscript numbers in the following sentences are provided to help you identify problem sentences.)

TO: All Southeast Division Employees

[1]Personal computers and all the software to support these computers are appearing on many desks of Southeast Division employees. [2]After giving the matter considerable attention, it has been determined by the Systems Development Department (SDD) that more control should be exerted in coordinating the purchase of hardware and software to improve compatibility throughout the division so that a library of resources may be developed. [3]Therefore, a plan has been developed by SDD that should be followed in making all future equipment selections and purchases. [4]To make the best possible choice, SDD should be contacted as you begin your search because questions about personal computers, word processing programs, hardware, and software can be answered by our knowledgeable staff, who can also provide you with invaluable assistance in making the best choice for your needs at the best possible cost.

[5]After your computer and its software arrive, all your future software purchases should be channeled through SDD. [6]To actually make your initial purchase, a written proposal and a purchase request form must be presented to SDD for approval. [7]A need for the purchase must be established; benefits that you expect to derive resulting from its purchase must be analyzed and presented, and an itemized statement of all costs must be submitted. [8]By following these new procedures, coordinated purchasing benefits will be realized by all employees. [9]I may be reached at X466 if you have any questions.

6.2 Organizing Data (Obj. 2)

The interoffice memo in Activity 6.1 is hard to read and hard to follow. One of its biggest problems is organization.

Your Task. Use either a cluster diagram or an outline to organize the garbled message in Activity 6.1. Beyond the opening and closing of the message, what are the three main points the writer is trying to make? Should this message use the direct pattern or the indirect pattern? Your instructor may ask you to discuss how this entire message could be revised or to actually rewrite it.

6.3 Collaborative Brainstorming (Obj. 1)

SPEAKING TEAM

Brainstorming can be a productive method for generating problem-solving ideas. You can improve your brainstorming skills through practice.

Your Task. In teams of four or five, analyze a problem on your campus such as the following: unavailable classes, unrealistic degree requirements, lack of student intern programs, poor parking facilities, inadequate registration process, lack of diversity among students on campus, and so forth. Use brainstorming techniques to generate ideas that clarify the problem and explore its solutions. Each team member should prepare a cluster diagram to record the ideas generated. Either individually or as a team, organize the ideas into an outline with three to five main points and numerous subpoints. Assume that your ideas will become part of a letter to be sent to an appropriate campus official or to your campus newspaper discussing the problem and your solution. Remember, however, your role as a student. Be polite, positive, and constructive—not negative, hostile, or aggressive.

6.4 Individual Brainstorming (Objs. 1 and 2)

E-MAIL

Brainstorming techniques can work for individuals as well as groups. Assume that your boss or department chair wants you to submit a short report analyzing a problem.

Your Task. Analyze a problem that exists where you work or go to school, such as long lines at the copy or fax machines, overuse of express mail services, understaffing during peak customer service hours, poor scheduling of employees, inappropriate cell phone use, an inferior or inflexible benefits package, outdated office or other equipment, or one of the campus problems discussed in Activity 6.3. Select a problem about which you have some knowledge. Prepare a cluster diagram to develop ideas. Then, organize the ideas into an outline with three to five main points and numerous subpoints. Be polite, positive, and constructive. Send the outline to your boss (your instructor). Include an introduction (such as, *Here is the outline you requested in regard to . . .*). Include a closing that offers to share your cluster diagram if your boss would like to see it.

6.5 Researching and Outlining "How-to" Techniques for Productive Brainstorming (Obj. 1)

INFOTRAC

Casandra M., your supervisor at Old Navy, has been asked to lead a brainstorming group in an effort to generate new ideas for the company's product line. Although Casandra knows a great deal about the company and its products, she doesn't know much about brainstorming. She asks you to research the topic quickly and give her a concise guide on how to brainstorm. One other thing—Casandra doesn't want to read an entire article. She wants you to outline it.

Your Task. Conduct an InfoTrac keyword search for "brainstorming." Locate an article with specific instructions for running a productive brainstorming session. Prepare an outline that tells how to (a) prepare for a brainstorming session, (b) conduct the session, and (c) follow up after the meeting. Submit your outline in a memo or an e-mail message to your supervisor (your instructor).

6.6 Research Interviews (Obj. 1)

SPEAKING

In your follow-up meeting with Casandra M. from Activity 6.5, she asks you to complete one more task in preparation for the brainstorming session. She needs further insight in defining the problem and creating an agenda for the outline of topics to be covered in the brainstorming session. She asks you to conduct informal interviews of Old Navy shoppers.

Your Task. Form five-member class groups. Two members of each group, if possible, should be familiar with Old Navy. Decide who will role-play the interviewer and the two interviewees (those most familiar with Old Navy), and who will act as recorder and group spokesperson. If your group has fewer than five members, some will have to fill more than one role. The interviewer asks both interviewees the same three questions outlined below. The recorder takes notes, and the group spokesperson summarizes the group's research results during the class discussion. Use the following interview questions:

a. During your last two visits to Old Navy, were there any products you expected Old Navy to carry but couldn't find? If yes, describe the products.

b. Can you think of any seasonal products you would like Old Navy to carry? Specifically, identify products for winter, spring, summer, and fall.

c. If you were in charge of Old Navy's product lines, what three changes would you make to Old Navy's existing product lines? What three totally new product lines would you want to create?

6.7 Using the Web to Compare Brainstorming Resources (Objs. 1 and 2)

CRITICAL THINKING | TEAM | WEB

You are part of an internship program at a large company, such as Gap Inc. Ron W., the manager in charge of interns, wants your group to use the Web to research two topics: (a) group brainstorming and (b) brainstorming software. Ron wants to know the two best Web sites that provide free advice about brainstorming, but he also wants your group to recommend two software products that teach people how to brainstorm.

Your Task. Using one or more search tools (such as Google), locate a few good Web sites that provide free advice on how to conduct brainstorming sessions. Then locate sites that sell software teaching individuals how to brainstorm. As a team, discuss which sites seemed most useful and trustworthy. How can you judge a Web software product if you have not seen it? In an e-mail or a memo to Ron, tell him what two sites you thought were best for free advice and what two software products you would recommend. Explain and defend your choices.

6.8 Outlining (Obj. 2)

Web designers at Gap Inc. are complaining about their assignment to develop Web pages describing Gap's employment benefits. Although Gap Inc. offers one of the most comprehensive benefits packages around, the jumble of information has the Web designers totally confused.

The benefits programs include health and wellness benefits covering medical, dental, and vision care. To promote peace of mind among employees and their eligible dependents, Gap offers life insurance, disability insurance, accidental death and dismemberment insurance, and protection against business travel accidents. Another health benefit is a special health care flexible spending account.

Gap Inc. also offers a service that allows employees to speak with a registered nurse 24 hours a day, seven days a week. It's called NurseLine. To prepare for the future, Gap offers a 401(k) plan plus a separate employee stock purchase option. As a "helping hand" to employees, it provides an Employee Assistance Program (EAP) called Life Resources. This is a confidential service that provides counseling resources to help employees and their families cope with personal problems. Gap also offers home loans, moving and relocation assistance, and travel assistance. One special benefit aimed at career development is the tuition reimbursement plan. Gap also encourages employees to develop their careers through its internal placement program.

Your Task. As part of the human resources staff at Gap Inc., you've been asked to make sense of the preceding information so that your Web designers can build it into a coherent presentation. Arrange the benefits information into a simple outline with about five major headings and a title.

6.9 Collaborative Letter (Objs. 3–5)

TEAM

One of the best ways to learn about the skills required in your field is to interview individuals working in that field.

Your Task. Divide into teams of three to five people who have similar majors. Work together to compose an inquiry letter requesting career information from someone in your field. Include questions about technical and general courses to take, possible starting salaries, good companies to apply to, technical skills required, necessary interpersonal skills, computer tools currently used, and tips for getting started in the field. Although this is a small project, your team can work more harmoniously if you apply some of the suggestions from Chapter 2. For example, appoint a meeting leader, recorder, and evaluator.

6.10 Sentence Elements (Obj. 4)

Your Task. In the following sentences underscore and identify dependent clauses (DC), independent clauses (IC), and phrases (P). Circle subjects and verbs in clauses.

a. We hire talented undergraduates in our intern program.

b. If you qualify, you should send an application to us.

c. In the summer, interns appreciate a program if it offers a learning experience.

6.11 Sentence Length (Obj. 4)

Your Task. Break the following sentences into shorter sentences. Use appropriate transitional expressions.

a. If firms have a substantial investment in original research or development of new products, they should consider protecting those products with patents, although all patents eventually expire and what were once trade secrets can become common knowledge in the industry.

b. As soon as consumers recognize a name associated with a product or service, that name is entitled to legal protection as a trademark; in fact, consumers may

even create a trademark where none existed or create a second trademark by using a nickname as a source indicator, such as the name "Coke," which was legally protected even before it had ever been used by the company.

c. Although no magic formula exists for picking a good trademark name, firms should avoid picking the first name that pops into someone's head; moreover, they should be aware that unique and arbitrary marks are best, whereas descriptive terms such as "car" or "TV repair" are useless, and surnames and geographic names are weak because they lack distinction and exclusivity.

6.12 Active and Passive Voice (Obj. 4)

Your Task. In the following sentences convert passive-voice verbs to active-voice verbs. Add subjects if necessary. Be prepared to discuss which sentence version is more effective.

a. Programs were created by our board so that employees could become volunteers.
b. Employees are encouraged to take up to five hours a month of paid time to volunteer.
c. Café-style restaurants are provided for employees in our corporate buildings.
d. When it was realized that transportation was a problem, interoffice shuttles were established.
e. Our company was named in *Fortune* magazine's "100 Best Places to Work."

Now convert active-voice verbs to passive-voice verbs, and be prepared to discuss which sentence version is more effective.

f. We cannot authorize repair of your DVD because you have allowed the warranty period to expire.
g. I cannot give you a cash refund for merchandise that you purchased 90 or more days ago.
h. ValleyView Hospital does not accept patients who are uninsured.
i. You must submit your résumé and cover letter by e-mail.
j. Jennifer added the two columns instead of subtracting them, thus producing the incorrect total.

6.13 Dangling and Misplaced Modifiers (Obj. 4)

Your Task. Remedy any dangling or misplaced modifiers in the following sentences. Add subjects as needed, but retain the introductory phrases. Mark *C* if correct.

a. Ignoring the warning prompt on the screen, the computer was turned off resulting in the loss of data.
b. Using a number of creative search terms, the Web site was finally found.
c. By working as a summer intern, your chance of permanent employment is greatly improved.
d. Acting as team leader, the meeting was organized and led by Matt.
e. To prevent head injuries, wear a helmet when cycling. *(Tricky!)*
f. It's hard to understand why employees would not go to our technical support staff with software problems.
g. Having found the misplaced file, the search was ended.
h. The presidential candidate announced his intention to run for national office in his hometown of Blue Bell, Pennsylvania.

6.14 Transitional Expressions (Obj. 5)

Your Task. Add transitional expressions to the following sentences to improve the flow of ideas (coherence).

a. We recognize that giving your time to important causes is just as important as giving your money. We've created several programs that make it easy and rewarding for our employees to get involved.
b. Our computerized file includes all customer data. It provides space for name, address, and other vital information. It has an area for comments, a feature that comes in handy and helps us keep our records up-to-date.
c. No one likes to turn out poor products. We began highlighting recurring problems. Employees make a special effort to be more careful in doing their work right the first time. It doesn't have to be returned to them for corrections.
d. In-depth employment interviews may be structured or unstructured. Structured interviews have little flexibility. All candidates are asked the same questions in the same order. Unstructured interviews allow a free-flowing conversation. Topics are prepared for discussion by the interviewer.
e. Fringe benefits consist of life, health, and dental insurance. Some fringe benefits might include paid vacations and sick pay. Other fringe benefits include holidays, funeral leave, and emergency leave. Paid lunch, rest periods, tuition reimbursement, and child care are also sometimes provided.

6.15 Paragraph Organization (Obj. 5)

Your Task. The following poorly written paragraphs follow the indirect plan. Locate the main sentence in each paragraph. Then revise each paragraph so that it is organized directly. Improve coherence by using the techniques described in this chapter.

a. Many of our customers limp through their business despite problems with their disk drives, printers, and peripherals. We cannot service their disk drives, printers, and peripherals. These customers are unable to go without this equipment long enough for the repair. We've learned that there are two times when we can get to that equipment. We can do our repairs in the middle of the night or on Sunday. All of our staff of technicians now work every Sunday. Please authorize additional budget for my department to hire technicians for night and weekend service hours.

b. Air express is one of the ways SturdyBilt power mowers and chain saws may be delivered. Air express promises two-day delivery but at a considerable cost. The cheapest method is for retailers to pick up shipments themselves at our nearest distribution center. We have distribution centers in St. Louis, Phoenix, and Los Angeles. Another option involves having our trucks deliver the shipment from our distribution center to the retailer's door for an additional fee. These are the options SturdyBilt provides for the retailers purchasing our products.

6.16 Researching, Brainstorming, and Organizing: Student Loans (Objs. 1–3)

CONSUMER WEB | INFOTRAC | TEAM

Sarah was all smiles when she graduated and got that degree in her hand. Soon, however, she began to worry about her student loans. Student debt has risen 58 percent in the last decade, according to the College Board, a New York-based college testing and information firm. One study showed that about one third of all recent graduates are unprepared to make their first student loan payment.[20]

Your Task. In teams collect information about student debt. Who has it? How much debt does an average student carry? How do most students repay their loans? What strategies are proposed for helping students avoid, reduce, and repay educational loans? As a group, discuss your findings. Brainstorm for additional strategies. Then organize your findings into an outline with a title, an introduction, and recommendations for helping current students avoid, reduce, and repay their student loans. Submit your outline to your instructor.

Photo: © Photodisc Green/Getty Images

video resource

Building Workplace Skills Video Library 1
Mastering Guffey's 3-x-3 Writing Process

If you didn't see the video, "Mastering Guffey's 3-x-3 Writing Process," when you studied Chapter 5, your instructor may show it with this chapter. It shows all three phases of the writing process so that you can see how it guides the development of a complete message. This video illustrates concepts in Chapters 5, 6, and 7.

C.L.U.E. review 6

Edit the following sentences to correct faults in grammar, punctuation, spelling, and word use.

1. When our Marketing Manager had to write a twenty page report she started by collecting information, and organizing it.
2. A business writers biggest problem is usually poor organization according to experts.
3. The company Vice President came to the President and I asking for help with 2 complex but seperate advertising problems.
4. Because neither of us were particularly creative we decided to organize a brainstorming session rather then work by ourself.
5. Our brain storming session included: Amanda, Rory, Rashid and Cynthia.
6. One of our principle goals were to create one hundred ideas in thirty minutes however we were prepared to meet up to 1 hour.
7. Although we knew the principals of outlining we had trouble grouping our ideas into 3 to 5 major headings.
8. Robyn Clarkes article titled A Better way to brainstorm which appeared in the magazine Black Enterprise was helpful to the President and I.
9. Frontloading a message saves a readers time therefore its worth making the effort to put the main idea first.
10. By learning to distinguish phases from clauses youll be better able to avoid 3 basic sentence faults, the fragment, the run on sentence and the comma splice.

chapter 7

Writing Process Phase 3: Revise, Proofread, Evaluate

objectives

1 Apply Phase 3 of the 3-x-3 writing process, which begins with techniques to make a message clear and conversational.

2 Describe specific revision tactics that make a message concise.

3 Describe revision techniques that make a message vigorous and direct.

4 Discuss revision strategies that improve readability.

5 Recognize proofreading problem areas, and be able to list techniques for proofreading both routine and complex documents.

6 Evaluate a message to judge its success.

COMMUNICATION IN PROCESS

Thinking Outside the Bun, Taco Bell Seeks Fresh Menu

TIRED OF THE burger-and-fries routine, many fast-food customers are looking for healthful alternatives with more exotic flavors. Can Mexican fast-food favorite Taco Bell meet the challenge? Although it is the most successful of the three fast-food chains owned by Yum! Brands Inc.,[1] Taco Bell must compete for customers with McDonald's, Burger King, and Wendy's, as well as with trendy upstarts Baja Fresh Mexican Grill and Qdoba Mexican Grill.

Taco Bell holds a 78 percent share of the Mexican fast-food market. Yet Yum! Brand's CEO characterized overall U.S. operations as "mediocre."[2] The company worries that its value meal position is being co-opted by burger and chicken fast-food rivals. It's also concerned about customers' new emphasis on low-fat, healthful meals.

On the bright side, Taco Bell is in a good position to capitalize on an increasing awareness of Mexican food. Some restaurant experts have credited Taco Bell's high-profile ad campaigns with increasing customer awareness of Mexican food as an alternative to burgers and chicken. One food industry executive said, "Burgers are your dad's food, and Mexican is the choice of the new generation."[3]

In the increasingly crowded fast-food market, customers are slowly but surely shifting away from the traditional burger and chicken fast foods.[4] Poised to capitalize on this movement, Taco Bell remains keenly aware that (1) it sells a quasi-Mexican food, and (2) its customers are mainstream Americans. This means that its products cannot veer too far from what appeals to the masses. But it must also compete with new Mexican restaurants emphasizing low-fat items and fresh ingredients.

A recently hired culinary product manager is charged with the task of coming up with menu suggestions and communicating them to management.

Communicating menu ideas to management is a task facing a newly hired Taco Bell culinary product manager.

Photo: © John Neubauer/Photo Edit

Critical Thinking

- If Taco Bell sales are improving, why should it make any attempt to change its menu?
- How could Taco Bell entice customers to try healthful, innovative items?
- Is it dangerous for Taco Bell to tamper with its signature menu items, such as offering low-calorie freshly made salsa to replace high-calorie cheese and sauces?

www.tacobell.com

CONTINUED ON PAGE 201

case study

Writing Process Phase 3: Revise

learning objective 1

The final phase of the 3-x-3 writing process focuses on revising, proofreading, and evaluating. Revising means improving the content and sentence structure of your message. Proofreading involves correcting its grammar, spelling, punctuation, format, and mechanics. Evaluating is the process of analyzing whether your message achieved its purpose. One would not expect people in the restaurant business to require these kinds of skills. Yet, the new culinary product manager at Taco Bell—and many other similar businesspeople—realize that bright ideas are worth little unless they can be communicated effectively to fellow workers and to management. In the communication process the techniques of revision can often mean the difference between the acceptance or rejection of ideas.

Although the composition process differs for individuals and situations, this final phase should occupy a significant share of the total time you spend on a message. As you learned earlier, some experts recommend devoting about half the total composition time to revising and proofreading.[5]

Because few writers can produce a satisfactory copy on the first attempt, revision is an important step in the writing process.

Rarely is the first or even second version of a message satisfactory. Only amateurs expect writing perfection on the first try. The revision stage is your chance to make sure your message says what you mean. Many professional writers compose the first draft quickly without worrying about language, precision, or correctness. Then they revise and polish extensively. Other writers, however, prefer to revise as they go—particularly for shorter business documents.

Important messages—such as those you send to management or to customers or turn in to instructors for grades—deserve careful revision and proofreading. When you finish a first draft, plan for a cooling-off period. Put the document aside and return to it after a break, preferably after 24 hours or longer.

Whether you revise immediately or after a break, you'll want to examine your message critically. You should be especially concerned with ways to improve its clarity, conciseness, vigor, and readability.

Revising for Clarity

The goal of business writing is to express rather than impress.

One of the first revision tasks is assessing the clarity of your message. A clear message is one that is immediately understood. To achieve clarity, resist the urge to show off or be fancy. Remember that your goal is not to impress an instructor. Instead, the goal of business writing is to *express*, not *impress*. This involves two simple rules: (1) keep it simple and (2) keep it conversational.

Why do some communicators fail to craft simple, direct messages? Following are several reasons:

- Untrained executives and professionals worry that plain messages don't sound important.
- Subordinates fear that plain talk won't impress the boss.
- Unskilled writers create foggy messages because they haven't learned how to communicate clearly.
- Unethical writers intentionally obscure a message to hide the truth.

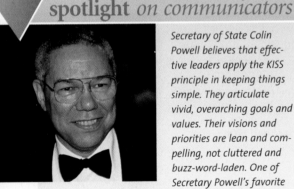

spotlight *on communicators*

Secretary of State Colin Powell believes that effective leaders apply the KISS principle in keeping things simple. They articulate vivid, overarching goals and values. Their visions and priorities are lean and compelling, not cluttered and buzz-word-laden. One of Secretary Powell's favorite quotations illustrates his conviction: "Great leaders are almost always great simplifiers, who can cut through argument, debate and doubt, to offer a solution everybody can understand."

Photo: © Rufus F. Folkks/CORBIS

Whatever the cause, you can eliminate the fog by applying the familiar KISS formula: Keep It Short and Simple! One way to achieve clear writing is to use active-voice sentences that avoid foggy, indirect, and pompous language.

To achieve clarity, remember to KISS: Keep It Short and Simple!

Foggy	**Clear**
Employees have not been made sufficiently aware of the potentially adverse consequences involved regarding these chemicals.	Warn your employees about these chemicals.

Foggy	Clear
To be sure of obtaining optimal results, it is essential that you give your employees the implements that are necessary for completion of the job.	To get the best results, give employees the tools they need to do the job.

Revising for Conversational Tone

To achieve a conversational tone, sound professional but not stilted.

Clarity is further enhanced by language that sounds like conversation. This doesn't mean that your letters and memos should be chatty or familiar. Rather, you should strive to sound professional, yet not artificial or formal. This means avoiding legal terminology, technical words, and third-person constructions (*the undersigned, the writer*). Business messages should sound warm, friendly, and conversational—not stuffy and formal. To sound friendly, include occasional contractions (*can't, doesn't*) and first-person pronouns (*I/we*). This warmth is appropriate in all but the most formal business reports. You can determine whether your writing is conversational by trying the kitchen test. If it wouldn't sound natural in your kitchen, it probably needs revision. Note how the following formal sentences were revised to pass the kitchen test.

Formal	Conversational
As per your verbal instruction, steps will be undertaken immediately to investigate your billing problem.	At your suggestion I'm investigating your billing immediately.
Our organization takes this opportunity to inform you that your account is being credited in the aforementioned sum.	We're crediting your account for $78.

Revising for Conciseness

learning objective 2

In revising, be certain that a message makes its point in the fewest possible words. One of the shortest and most effective business letters ever written contained only 19 words. Composed by business tycoon Cornelius Vanderbilt, the following masterpiece in brevity was sent to a pair of business associates who tried to swindle him while he vacationed in Europe:

> Gentlemen:
>
> You have undertaken to cheat me. I won't sue you, for the law is too slow. I'll ruin you.
>
> Yours truly,
>
> Cornelius Vanderbilt

Messages without flabby phrases and redundancies are easier to comprehend and more emphatic because main points stand out, as Vanderbilt's letter proves. Efficient messages also save the reader valuable time.

Many busy executives today won't read wordy reports. Chairman Martin Kallen, of Monsanto Europe, "flipped" because too much paper was clogging the company. He complained that reports were too long, too frequent, and too unread. He then decreed that all writing be more concise, and he refused to read any report that was not summarized in two or fewer pages.[6] Similarly, Procter & Gamble, the giant household products manufacturer, for years required all memos to be limited to one page. The president returned long messages, urging writers to "boil it down to something I can grasp." And Microsoft Chairman Bill Gates is said to stop reading e-mail messages after three screens.

Short messages require more effort than long, flabby ones.

But concise writing is not easy. As one expert copyeditor observed, "Trim sentences, like trim bodies, usually require far more effort than flabby ones."[7] To turn out slim sentences and lean messages, you do not have to be brusque, rude, or simple-minded. Instead, you must take time in the revision stage to "trim the fat." And before you can do that, you must learn to recognize it. Locating and excising wordiness involves eliminating (1) fillers, (2) long lead-ins, (3) redundancies, (4) compound prepositions, and (5) empty words.

Removing Fillers

Avoid fillers that fatten sentences with excess words. Beginning an idea with *There is* usually indicates that writers are spinning their wheels until they decide where the sentence is going. Used correctly, *there* indicates a specific place (*I placed the box there*). Used as fillers, *there* and occasionally *it* merely take up space. Most, but not all, sentences can be revised so that these fillers are unnecessary.

Wordy	**Concise**
There are three vice presidents who report directly to the president.	Three vice presidents report directly to the president.
It is the client who should make application for a license.	The client should apply for a license.

Deleting Long Lead-Ins

Long lead-ins delay getting to the "meat" of the sentence.

Delete unnecessary introductory words. The meat of the sentence often follows the words *that* and *because.* In addition, many long lead-ins say what is obvious.

Wordy	**Concise**
I am sending this announcement to let you all know that the office will be closed Monday.	The office will be closed Monday.
This is to inform you that you can redeem travel awards at our Web site.	You can redeem travel awards at our Web site.
I am writing this letter because Dr. Marcia Howard suggested that your organization was hiring trainees.	Dr. Marcia Howard suggested that your organization was hiring trainees.

Eliminating Redundancies

Redundancies convey the same meaning more than once.

Expressions that repeat meaning or include unnecessary words are redundant. To say *unexpected surprise* is like saying "surprise surprise" because *unexpected* carries the same meaning as *surprise.* Excessive adjectives, adverbs, and phrases often create redundancies and wordiness. The following list represents a tiny segment of the large number of redundancies appearing in business writing today. What word in each expression creates the redundancy?

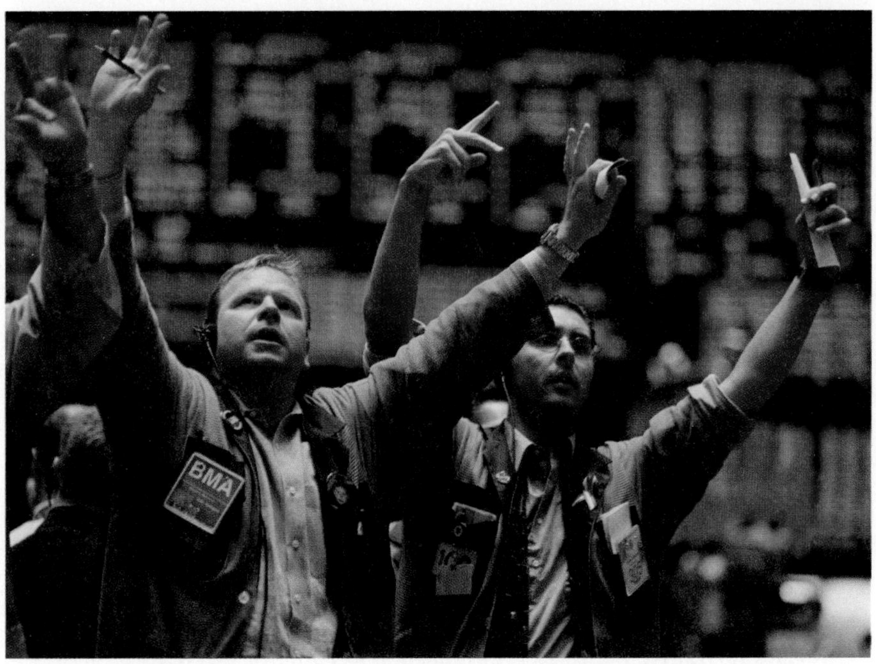

Although traders understand the meaning of their finger gestures in buying and selling stocks, investors were often confused by the language appearing in investment literature. That's why the S.E.C. published The Plain English Handbook *explaining how to avoid redundancies, long sentences, wordy phrases, passive voice, and abstract words. These techniques are helpful to all business communicators.*

Redundancies to Avoid

advance warning	exactly identical	perfectly clear
alter or change	few in number	personal opinion
assemble together	free and clear	potential opportunity
basic fundamentals	grateful thanks	positively certain
collect together	great majority	proposed plan
consensus of opinion	integral part	serious interest
contributing factor	last and final	refer back
dollar amount	midway between	true facts
each and every	new changes	visible to the eye
end result	past history	unexpected surprise

Reducing Compound Prepositions

Single words can often replace wordy prepositional phrases. In the following examples notice how the shorter forms say the same thing but more efficiently.

Wordy prepositional phrases can be shortened to single words.

Wordy Compound Preposition	Shorter Form
as to whether	whether
at a later date	later
at this point in time	now
at such time, at which time	when
by means of, in accordance with	by
despite the fact that	although
due to the fact that, inasmuch as, in view of the fact that	because
for the amount of	for
in advance of, prior to	before
subsequent to	after
the manner in which	how
until such time as	until

Purging Empty Words

Familiar phrases roll off the tongue easily, but many contain expendable parts. Be alert to these empty words and phrases: *case, degree, the fact that, factor, instance, nature*, and *quality*. Notice how much better the following sentences sound when we remove all the empty words:

> ~~In the case of~~ *USA Today* ~~the newspaper~~ improved its readability.
>
> Because of ~~the degree of~~ active participation by our sales reps, profits soared.
>
> We are aware ~~of the fact~~ that many managers need assistance.
>
> Except for ~~the instance of~~ Toyota, Japanese imports sagged.
>
> She chose a career in a field that was analytical ~~in nature~~. (Or, *She chose a career in an analytical field.*)
>
> Student writing in that class is excellent ~~in quality~~.

Good writers avoid saying what is obvious.

Also avoid saying the obvious. In the following examples notice how many unnecessary words we can omit through revision:

> ~~When it arrived~~, I cashed your check immediately. (*Announcing the check's arrival is unnecessary. That fact is assumed in its cashing.*)
>
> ~~We need printer cartridges; therefore~~, please send me two dozen laser cartridges. (*The first clause is obvious.*)
>
> ~~This is to inform you that~~ the meeting will start at 2 p.m. (*Avoid unnecessary lead-ins.*)

Finally, look carefully at clauses beginning with *that, which*, and *who*. They can often be shortened without loss of clarity. Search for phrases, such as *it appears that*. Such phrases can be reduced to a single adjective or adverb, such as *apparently*.

> Changing the name of a ^successful company ~~that is successful~~ is always risky.
>
> All employees ~~who are among those~~ completing the course will be reimbursed.
>
> Our ^final proposal, which was slightly altered ~~in its final form~~, won approval.
>
> We plan to schedule ^weekly meetings ~~on a weekly basis~~.

learning objective 3

Revising for Vigor and Directness

Much business writing is plagued by wordiness and triteness.

Much business writing has been criticized as lifeless, cautious, and "really, really boring."[8] This boredom results not so much from content as from wordiness and dull, trite expressions. You've already studied ways to improve clarity and conciseness. You can also reduce wordiness and improve vigor by (1) kicking the noun habit and (2) dumping trite business phrases.

Kicking the Noun Habit

Some writers become addicted to nouns, needlessly transforming verbs into nouns (*we make a recommendation of* instead of *we recommend*). This bad habit increases sentence length, drains verb strength, slows the reader, and muddies the thought. Notice how efficient, clean, and forceful the following verbs sound compared with their noun phrase counterparts.

Wordy Noun Phrase	Verb
conduct a discussion of	discuss
create a reduction in	reduce
engage in the preparation of	prepare
give consideration to	consider
make an assumption of	assume
make a discovery of	discover
perform an analysis of	analyze
reach a conclusion about	conclude
take action on	act

spotlight *on communicators*

Sam Walton, one of America's most successful merchants, said, "If you had to boil down the Wal-Mart system to one single idea, it would probably be communication, because it is one of the real keys to our success." His brand of communication meant sharing management strategies with sales associates in direct, vigorous, and simple talk, as in his sales plan: "Buy it low, stack it high, sell it cheap."

Dumping Trite Business Phrases

To sound "businesslike," many writers repeat the same stale expressions that other writers have used over the years. Your writing will sound fresher and more vigorous if you eliminate these phrases or find more original ways to convey the idea.

Avoid trite expressions that are overused in business writing.

Trite Phrase	Improved Version
as per your request	as you request
pursuant to your request	at your request
enclosed please find	enclosed is
every effort will be made	we'll try
in accordance with your wishes	as you wish
in receipt of	have received
please do not hesitate to	please
thank you in advance	thank you
under separate cover	separately
with reference to	about

Revising for Readability

learning objective 4

To help receivers anticipate and comprehend ideas quickly, a number of graphic highlighting techniques are helpful. You can use (1) parallelism, which involves balanced writing; (2) lists and bullets, which facilitate quick comprehension; (3) headings, which make important points more visible; and (4) other highlighting techniques to improve readability.

Developing Parallelism for Balance

As you revise, be certain that you express similar ideas in balanced or parallel construction. For example, the phrase *clearly, concisely, and correctly* is parallel because all the words end in *-ly*. To express the list as *clearly, concisely, and with correctness* is jarring because the last item is not what the receiver expects. Instead of an adverb, the series ends with a noun. To achieve parallelism, match nouns with nouns, verbs with verbs, phrases with phrases, and clauses with clauses. Avoid mixing active-voice verbs with passive-voice verbs.

Parallelism means matching nouns with nouns, verbs with verbs, phrases with phrases, and so on.

Not Parallel	Improved
The policy affected all vendors, suppliers, and those involved with consulting.	The policy affected all vendors, suppliers, and consultants. (*Series matches nouns.*)
Good managers analyze a problem, collect data, and alternatives are evaluated.	Good managers analyze a problem, collect data, and evaluate alternatives. (*Series matches verb forms.*)

Numbered and bulleted lists improve readability by making important ideas stand out.

Struggling to merge cultures and regions as different as Holland, with its lighted canal bridges, and contemporary Paris and London, the European Union recently drafted a complex constitution. It was such a dense document that a reader-friendly version was posted online. Underlined sections along with marginal comments, such as those used in this textbook, improved readability and "skim value," a goal of the European Union Parliament.

Photo: © Digital Vision/Getty Images

Using Numbered and Bulleted Lists for Quick Comprehension

One of the best ways to ensure rapid comprehension of ideas is through the use of numbered or bulleted lists. Ideas formerly buried within sentences or paragraphs stand out when listed. Readers not only understand your message more rapidly and easily but also consider you efficient and well organized. Lists provide high "skim value." This means that readers use lists to read quickly and grasp main ideas. By breaking up complex information into smaller chunks, lists improve readability, comprehension, and retention. They also force the writer to organize ideas and write efficiently. Use numbered lists for items that represent a sequence or reflect a numbering system. Use bulleted lists to highlight items that don't necessarily show a chronology.

Numbered List

Our recruiters follow these steps in hiring applicants:

1. Examine the application.
2. Interview the applicant.
3. Check the applicant's references.

Bulleted List

To attract upscale customers, we feature the following:

- Quality fashions
- Personalized service
- A generous return policy

Improve the skim value of a message by adding high-visibility vertical lists.

In listing items vertically, capitalize the word at the beginning of each line. Add end punctuation only if the statements are complete sentences, and be sure to use parallel construction. Notice in the numbered list that each item begins with a verb. In the bulleted list each item follows an adjective/noun sequence. In Chapter 8 you'll learn more about using lists to improve readability in e-mail messages and memos. In Chapter 15 you'll learn how to convert a paragraph into bulleted items for a PowerPoint presentation.

Be careful, however, not to overuse the list format. One writing expert warns that too many lists make messages look like grocery lists.[9]

Adding Headings for Visual Impact

Headings help writers to organize information and enable readers to absorb important ideas.

Headings are an important tool for highlighting information and improving readability. They encourage the writer to organize carefully so that similar material is grouped together. They help the reader separate major ideas from details. Moreover, headings enable a busy reader to skim familiar or less important information. They also provide a quick preview or review. Headings appear most often in reports, which you'll study in greater detail in Unit 4. But main headings, subheadings, and category headings can also improve readability in e-mail messages, memos, and letters. Here, they are used with bullets to summarize categories:

Category Headings
Our company focuses on the following areas in the employment process:

- **Attracting applicants.** We advertise for qualified applicants, and we also encourage current employees to recommend good people.
- **Interviewing applicants.** Our specialized interviews include simulated customer encounters as well as scrutiny by supervisors.
- **Checking references.** We investigate every applicant thoroughly, including conversations with former employers and all listed references.

Improving Readability With Other Graphic Techniques

Graphic techniques such as capital letters, underlining, bold type, italics, and blank space spotlight ideas.

Vertical lists and headings are favorite tools for improving readability, but other graphic techniques can also focus attention.

To highlight individual words, use CAPITAL letters, underlining, **bold** type, or *italics.* Be careful with these techniques, though, because readers may feel they are being shouted at.

One final technique to enhance comprehension is blank space. Space is especially important in e-mail messages when formatting techniques don't always work. Grouping ideas under capitalized headings with blank space preceding the heading can greatly improve readability.

The following chapters supply additional ideas for grouping and spotlighting data. Although highlighting techniques can improve readability, they can also clutter a message if overdone. Many of these techniques, such as listing items vertically, also require more space, so use them judiciously.

Measuring Readability

Too much graphic highlighting can clutter a document and reduce comprehension.

Formulas can measure how easy or difficult a message is to read. Two well-known formulas are Robert Gunning's Fog Index and the Flesch-Kincaid Index. Both measure word and sentence length to determine readability. The longer a sentence, the more difficult it is to read. If you are using a current version of Microsoft Word, the software will calculate a readability score for any passage you highlight.* Word shows a "reading ease" score as well as the Flesch-Kincaid grade level score. A score of 10, for example, means that the passage can be easily read by a person with 10 years of schooling.

Your goal should be to keep your writing between the levels of 8 and 12. Magazines and newspapers that strive for wide readership keep their readability between

* On the **Tools** menu, click **Options,** and then click the **Spelling & Grammar** tab. Select the **Check grammar with spelling** check box. Select the **Show readability statistics** check box, and then click **OK.** When Microsoft Word finishes checking spelling and grammar, it displays information about the reading level of the highlighted passage.

Pulitzer Prize-winning Washington Post *columnist William Raspberry frequently promotes the value of language skills: "Misused words, haphazard sentences, failed subject-verb agreement can distract people from our ideas and get them concentrating on our inadequacies. Good English, carefully spoken and written, can open more doors than a college degree. Bad English can slam doors we don't even know about."*

these grade levels. (*USA Today* is 10.6, *The New York Times* is 12.6, and *People* magazine ranges between 8.4 and 11.2.)

Readability formulas, however, don't always tell the full story. Although they provide a rough estimate, those based solely on word and sentence counts fail to measure meaningfulness. Even short words (such as *skew*, *onus*, and *wane*) can cause trouble if readers don't recognize them. More important than length are a word's familiarity and meaningfulness to the reader. In Chapter 5 you learned to adapt your writing to the audience by selecting familiar words. Other techniques that can improve readability include well-organized paragraphs, transitions to connect ideas, lists, and headings.

Improving readability is one of the goals of revision. As you will see in the following checklist, the task of revision has many goals, and they aren't always easy to achieve. Revision demands objectivity and a willingness to cut, cut, cut. Though painful, the process is also gratifying. It's a great feeling when you realize your finished message is clear, concise, and readable.

Readability formulas based on word and sentence lengths do not always measure meaningfulness.

Checklist for Revising Messages

✓ **Keep the message simple.** Express ideas directly. Don't show off or use fancy language.

✓ **Be conversational.** Include occasional contractions (*hasn't, don't*) and first-person pronouns (*I/we*). Use natural-sounding language.

✓ **Avoid opening fillers and long lead-ins.** Omit sentence fillers such as *there is* and long lead-ins such as *this is to inform you that.*

✓ **Shun redundancies.** Eliminate words that repeat meanings, such as *mutual cooperation.* Watch for repetitious adjectives, adverbs, and phrases.

✓ **Tighten your writing.** Check phrases that include *case, degree, the fact that, factor*, and other words and phrases that unnecessarily increase wordiness. Avoid saying the obvious.

✓ **Don't convert verbs to nouns.** Keep your writing vigorous by avoiding the noun habit (*analyze* not *make an analysis of*).

✓ **Avoid trite phrases.** Keep your writing fresh, direct, and contemporary by skipping such expressions as *enclosed please find* and *pursuant to your request.*

✓ **Strive for parallelism.** Help receivers anticipate and comprehend your message by using balanced writing (*planning, drafting, and constructing* not *planning, drafting, and construction*).

✓ **Highlight important ideas.** Use bullets, lists, headings, capital letters, underlining, boldface, italics, and blank space to spotlight ideas and organization.

✓ **Consider readability.** Strive to keep the reading level of a message between Grades 8 and 12. Remember that short, familiar words and short sentences help readers comprehend.

Photo: Courtesy of The Washington Post Writers Group—*www.washpost.com*

PROCESS IN PROGRESS

Taco Bell Revisited

THE NEWLY HIRED culinary product manager at Taco Bell has her job cut out for her. Management expects her to anticipate trends in Mexican foods and improve restaurant menus. Part of the challenge is recognizing trends that consumers haven't even picked up yet and then working these trends into restaurant products. In her words, "We want to kick it up a notch, but we still have to deliver to mainstream America." She needs to read the market and then create innovative menu ideas. The new chef is eager to incorporate some of the rich, complex flavors of authentic Mexican cuisine. But she must do it in ways that are acceptable to mainstream America. Although she has excellent culinary references, the new chef has not been trained in communication. She has plenty of ideas to put into a memo or a presentation. Her job now depends on how well she can communicate these ideas to management.

Critical Thinking

- Based on what you learned in this chapter, what specific advice can you give about keeping a message clear? Should a business message be conversational? How is a conversational tone achieved?
- Why is conciseness important, and what techniques can be used to achieve it?
- Would you advise the culinary chef to be direct with her ideas? What advice can you give for improving the directness and readability of a business message?

CONTINUED ON PAGE 204

case study

Writing Process Phase 3: Proofread

learning objective

5

Proofreading before a document is completed is generally a waste of time.

Once you have the message in its final form, it's time to proofread. Don't proofread earlier because you may waste time checking items that eventually are changed or omitted. Proofreading is especially difficult because most of us read what we thought we wrote. That's why it's important to look for specific problem areas.

What to Watch for in Proofreading

Careful proofreaders check for problems in these areas:

- **Spelling.** Now's the time to consult the dictionary. Is *recommend* spelled with one or two *c*'s? Do you mean *affect* or *effect*? Use your computer spell checker, but don't rely on it totally.
- **Grammar.** Locate sentence subjects; do their verbs agree with them? Do pronouns agree with their antecedents? Review the C.L.U.E. principles in Appendix A if necessary. Use your computer's grammar checker, but be suspicious, as explained in the accompanying Tech Talk box.
- **Punctuation.** Make sure that introductory clauses are followed by commas. In compound sentences put commas before coordinating conjunctions (*and, or, but, nor*). Double-check your use of semicolons and colons.
- **Names and numbers.** Compare all names and numbers with their sources because inaccuracies are not always

spotlight *on communicators*

Mistakes in messages take the reader's mind off the subject, says writing coach Susan Schott Karr. She advises proofreading from a printed copy because you can do a better job of catching mistakes. To hear how your message will sound to someone else, read it aloud. You'll hear whether a sentence or paragraph seems vague or awkward. You'll notice words and phrases you've overused, and you'll recognize when to vary your word choice.

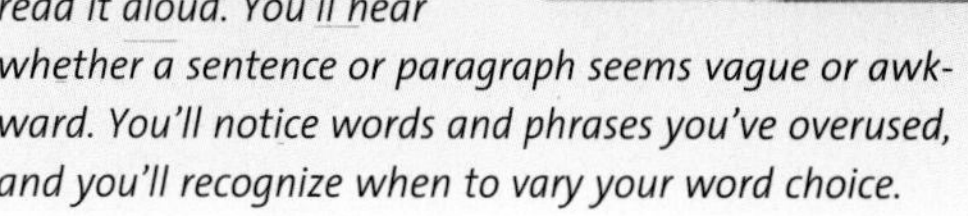

Photo: Courtesy, Susan Schott Karr

visible. Especially verify the spelling of the names of individuals receiving the message. Most of us immediately dislike someone who misspells our name.

- **Format.** Be sure that your document looks balanced on the page. Compare its parts and format with those of standard documents shown in Appendix B. If you indent paragraphs, be certain that all are indented.

How to Proofread Routine Documents

Routine documents need a light proofreading.

Most routine documents require a light proofreading. You may be working with a handwritten or a printed copy or on your computer screen. If you wish to print a copy, make it a rough draft (don't print it on good stationery). In time, you may be able to produce a "first-time-final" message, but beginning writers seldom do.

For handwritten or printed messages, read the entire document. Watch for all of the items just described. Use standard proofreading marks, shown in Figure 7.1, to indicate changes.

For both routine and complex documents, it's best to proofread from a printed copy, not on a computer screen.

You can read computer messages on the screen using the down arrow to reveal one line at a time. This focuses your attention at the bottom of the screen. A safer proofreading method, however, is reading from a printed copy. You're more likely to find errors and to observe the tone. "Things really look different on paper," observes veteran writer Louise Lague at *People* magazine. "Don't just pull a letter out of the printer and stick it in an envelope. Read every sentence again. You'll catch bad line endings, strange page breaks, and weird spacing. You can also get a totally different feeling about what you've said when you see it in print. Sometimes you can say something with a smile on your face; but if you put the same thing in print, it won't work."[10]

FIGURE 7.1 ***Proofreading Marks***

Most proofreaders use these standard marks to indicate revisions.

ℊ	Delete	∧	Insert
≡	Capitalize	# ∧	Insert space
/lc	Lowercase (don't capitalize)	∧	Insert punctuation
∩∪	Transpose	⊙	Insert period
⁀‿	Close up	¶	Start paragraph

Marked Copy

~~This is to inform you that~~ beginning september 1 the doors leading to the Westside of the building will have alarms. Because ~~of the fact that~~ these ~~exits~~ doors also function as fire exits they can not ~~actually~~ be locked consequently we are instaling alrams. Please ~~utilize~~ use the east side exists to avoid setting off the ear piercing alarms.

tech talk

Using Spell Checkers and Grammar/Style Checkers Wisely

Spell-checking and grammar-checking software are two useful tools that can save you from many embarrassing errors. They can also greatly enhance your revision techniques—if you know how to use them wisely.

Spell Checkers

Although some writers dismiss spell checkers as an annoyance, most of us are only too happy to have our typos and misspelled words detected. If you are using Microsoft Word, you need to set the options to "check spelling as you type." (Use the **Tools** menu, click **Options.** On the **Spelling & Grammar** tab choose *Check spelling as you type* and *Always suggest corrections.*) When you see a wavy red line under a word, you are being notified that the highlighted word is not in the computer's dictionary. Right click for a list of suggested replacements and other actions.

Spell checkers are indeed wonderful, but they are far from perfect. If you mistype a word, the spell checker is not sure what you meant and the suggested replacements may be way off target. What's more, a spell checker cannot know when you type *form* that you meant *from.* Lesson: Don't rely totally on spell checkers to find all typos and spelling errors.

Grammar and Style Checkers

Like spell checkers, today's grammar and style checkers are amazingly sophisticated. Microsoft Word marks faults in capitalization, fragments, misused words, double negatives, possessives, plurals, punctuation, subject–verb agreement, gender-specific words, wordiness, and many other problems.

How does a grammar checker work? Let's say you typed the sentence, *The office and its equipment is for sale.* You would see a wavy green line appear under *is.* Right click and a box identifies the subject–verb agreement error and suggests the verb *are* as a correction. When you click *are*, the error is corrected. Pretty nifty, eh? You can set grammar and style options in the **Grammar Settings** dialog box (**Tools** menu, **Options** command, **Spelling & Grammar** tab, and **Settings**).

Before you decide that a grammar checker will solve all your writing problems, think again. Even Word's highly developed software misses plenty of errors, and it also mismarks some correct expressions.

Career Application

Study the spelling and grammar/style settings on your computer. Decide which settings are most useful to you. As you prepare written messages for this class, analyze the suggestions made by your spell checker and grammar checker. For one or two documents, list the spelling, grammar, and style corrections suggested by Word. How many were valid?

How to Proofread Complex Documents

Computer programs can help analyze writing, calculate readability, and locate some grammar and punctuation errors.

Long, complex, or important documents demand more careful proofreading using the following techniques:

- Print a copy, preferably double-spaced, and set it aside for at least a day. You'll be more alert after a breather.
- Allow adequate time to proofread carefully. A common excuse for sloppy proofreading is lack of time.
- Be prepared to find errors. One student confessed, "I can find other people's errors, but I can't seem to locate my own." Psychologically, we don't expect to find errors, and we don't want to find them. You can overcome this obstacle by anticipating errors and congratulating, not criticizing, yourself each time you find one.
- Read the message at least twice—once for word meanings and once for grammar/mechanics. For very long documents (book chapters and long articles or reports), read a third time to verify consistency in formatting.
- Reduce your reading speed. Concentrate on individual words rather than ideas.

Complex documents should be proofread at least twice.

(NOTES)

PROCESS TO PRODUCT

Applying Your Skills at Taco Bell

UPGRADING THE MENU at Taco Bell is an exciting challenge for the new culinary product manager. In response to management's request, she comes up with terrific ideas for capitalizing on eating trends and converting them to mainstream tastes. She has been asked to submit a memo summarizing her longer report, which will be presented at a management meeting next week.

Although the new culinary product manager has exceptional talent in the field of cuisine, she realizes that her writing skills are not as well developed as her cooking skills. She comes to the corporate communications department and shows your boss the first draft of her memo. Your boss is a nice guy; and, as a favor, he revises the first two paragraphs, as shown in Figure 7.3.

Your Task

Your boss, the head of corporate communications, has many important tasks to oversee. Thus, he hands the product manager's memo to you, his assistant, and tells you to finish cleaning it up. He adds, "Her ideas are right on target, but the main points are totally lost in wordy sentences and solid paragraphs. Revise this and concentrate on conciseness, parallelism, and readability. Don't you think some bulleted lists would help this memo a lot?" Revise the remaining four paragraphs of the memo using the techniques you learned in this chapter. Type a copy of the complete memo to submit to your boss (your instructor). ■

case study

- For documents that must be perfect, enlist a proofreading buddy. Have someone read the message aloud. Spell names and difficult words, note capitalization, and read punctuation.
- Use standard proofreading marks, shown in Figure 7.1, to indicate changes.

learning objective

6

Writing Process Phase 3: Evaluate

As part of applying finishing touches, take a moment to evaluate your writing. How successful will this message be? Does it say what you want it to? Will it achieve your purpose? How will you know if it succeeds?

A good way to evaluate messages is through feedback.

As you learned in Chapter 1, the best way to judge the success of your communication is through feedback. Thus, you should encourage the receiver to respond to your message. This feedback will tell you how to modify future efforts to improve your communication technique.

Your instructor will also be evaluating some of your writing. Although any criticism is painful, try not to be defensive. Look on these comments as valuable advice tailored to your specific writing weaknesses—and strengths. Many businesses today spend thousands of dollars bringing in communication consultants to improve employee writing skills. You're getting the same training in this course. Take advantage of this chance—one of the few you may have—to improve your skills. The best way to improve your skills, of course, is through instruction, practice, and evaluation.

In this class you have all three elements: instruction in the writing process (summarized in Figure 7.2), practice materials, and someone willing to guide and evaluate your efforts. Those three elements are the reasons that this book and this course may be the most valuable in your entire curriculum. Because it's almost impossible to improve your communication skills alone, grab this chance!

FIGURE 7.2 ***The Complete 3-x-3 Writing Process***

1 Prewriting	2 Writing	3 Revising
ANALYZE Define your purpose. Select the most appropriate form (channel). Visualize the audience.	**RESEARCH** Collect data formally and informally. Generate ideas by brainstorming and clustering.	**REVISE** Revise for clarity, tone, conciseness, and vigor. Revise to improve readability.
ANTICIPATE Put yourself in the reader's position and predict his or her reaction to this message.	**ORGANIZE** Group ideas into a list or an outline. Decide whether to arrange ideas using a direct or indirect strategy.	**PROOFREAD** Proofread to verify spelling, grammar, punctuation, and format. Check for overall appearance.
ADAPT Consider ways to shape the message to benefit the reader, using his or her language.	**COMPOSE** In quiet surroundings, compose quickly (sprint writing), recognizing that this is a first draft.	**EVALUATE** Ask yourself whether the final product will achieve its purpose.

FIGURE 7.3 ***Partially Revised First Draft***

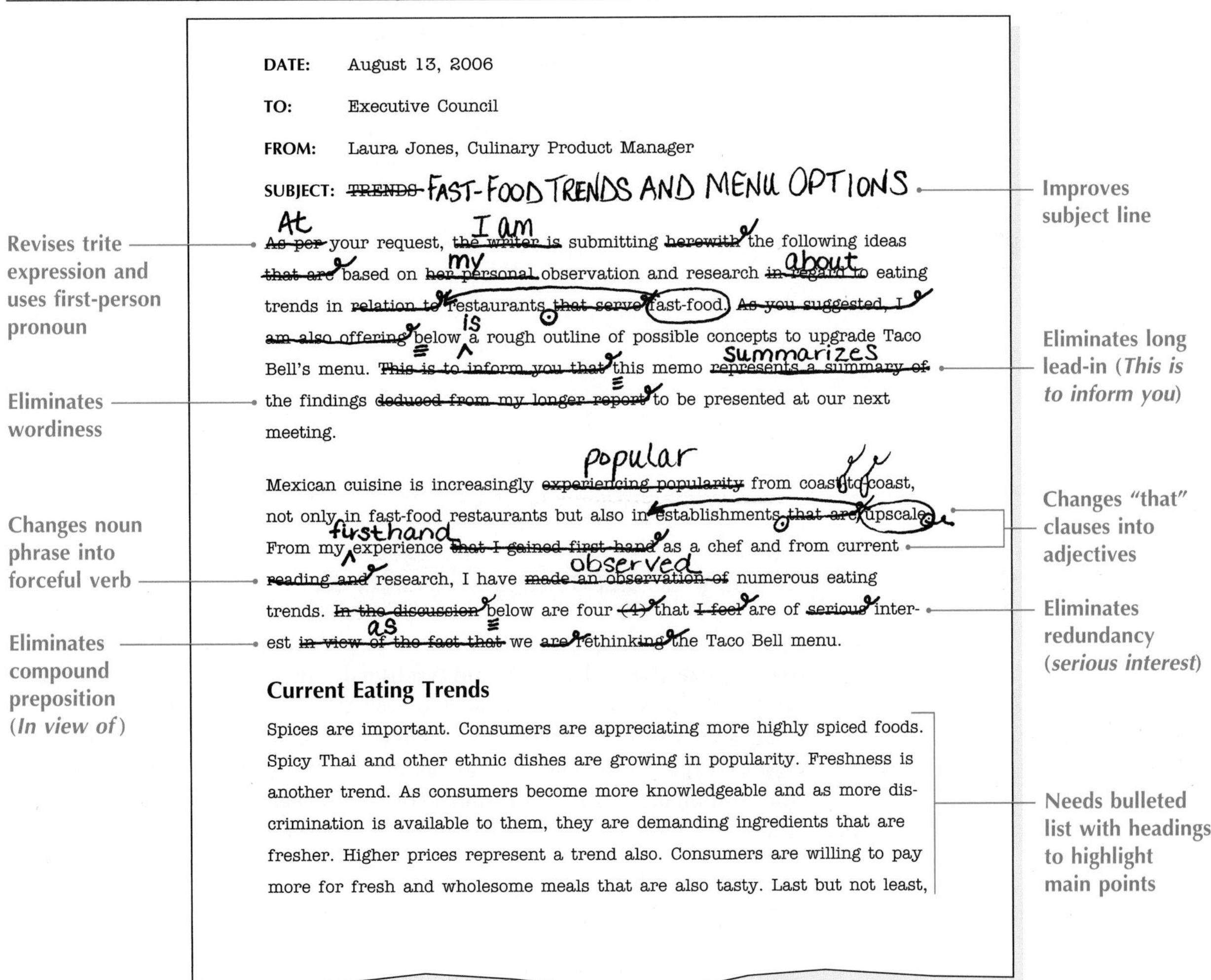

DATE: August 13, 2006

TO: Executive Council

FROM: Laura Jones, Culinary Product Manager

SUBJECT: ~~TRENDS~~ FAST-FOOD TRENDS AND MENU OPTIONS

~~As per~~ At your request, ~~the writer is~~ I am submitting ~~herewith~~ the following ideas ~~that are~~ based on ~~her personal~~ my observation and research ~~in regard to~~ about eating trends in ~~relation to~~ restaurants ~~that serve~~ fast-food. ~~As you suggested, I am also offering~~ below is a rough outline of possible concepts to upgrade Taco Bell's menu. ~~This is to inform you that~~ this memo ~~represents a summary of~~ summarizes the findings ~~deduced from my longer report~~ to be presented at our next meeting.

Mexican cuisine is increasingly ~~experiencing popularity~~ popular from coast to coast, not only in fast-food restaurants but also in establishments ~~that are~~ upscale. From my firsthand experience ~~that I gained first-hand~~ as a chef and from current ~~reading and~~ research, I have ~~made an observation of~~ observed numerous eating trends. ~~In the discussion~~ below are four ~~(4)~~ that ~~I feel~~ are of ~~serious~~ interest ~~in view of the fact that~~ as we ~~are~~ rethink~~ing~~ the Taco Bell menu.

Current Eating Trends

Spices are important. Consumers are appreciating more highly spiced foods. Spicy Thai and other ethnic dishes are growing in popularity. Freshness is another trend. As consumers become more knowledgeable and as more discrimination is available to them, they are demanding ingredients that are fresher. Higher prices represent a trend also. Consumers are willing to pay more for fresh and wholesome meals that are also tasty. Last but not least, a final trend includes big appetites. Other fast-food restaurants are cashing in on sandwiches that are satisfying, such as the Whopper, the Big Mac, and the Big Jack. In this respect, teenagers are our prime targets.

Given the increasing degree of acceptance of Mexican cuisine and the rich array of flavors and textures in Mexican cuisine, we find that we have many possibilities for the expansion of our menu. Despite the fact that my full report contains a number of additional trends and menu ideas, I will concentrate below on four significant concepts.

Needs to reduce wordy phrases

New Menu Concepts

First, I am of the opinion that we should add **More Grilled Items**. Offer spicy chicken marinated in lime juice or chipotle-rubbed ahi tuna served with cranberry mango salsa. A second idea involves **Larger-Portion Sandwiches**. Consider a "Machaca Taco," an oversized taco featuring shredded beef. Another possibility is "Mad Mex," a wild burrito served with a smoky rojo sauce. Third, concentrate on Higher Quality, More Expensive Dishes. Consider churrascos, made with prime beef tenderloin basted with a South American pesto sauce. Lastly, we should consider a Self-Serve Salsa Bar. In relation to this, we could offer exotic fresh salsas with bold flavors and textures.

Needs bulleted list with headings to improve readability

Must revise for conciseness

I would be more than happy to have a discussion of these ideas with you in greater detail and to have a demonstration of them in the kitchen. Thanks for this opportunity to work with you in the expansion of our menu in a move to ensure that Taco Bell remains tops in Mexican cuisine.

Needs to eliminate empty words

Must convert noun phrases to verbs

Summary of Learning Objectives

1 **Apply Phase 3 of the 3-x-3 writing process, which begins with techniques to make a message clear and conversational.** The final phase of the writing process involves editing, revising, and evaluating. Revising for clarity means using active-voice sentences and simple words while avoiding confusing negative expressions. Clarity is further enhanced by language that sounds conversational, including occasional contractions and first-person pronouns (*I/we*).

2 **Describe specific revision tactics that make a message concise.** Concise messages make their points in the fewest possible words. Revising for conciseness involves excluding opening fillers (*There are*), redundancies (*basic essentials*), and compound prepositions (*by means of, due to the fact that*).

3 **Describe revision techniques that make a message vigorous and direct.** Writers can achieve vigor in messages by revising wordy phrases that needlessly convert verbs into nouns. For example, instead of *we conducted a discussion of,* write *we discussed.* To make writing more direct, good writers replace trite business phrases, such as *please do not hesitate to,* with similar expressions, such as *please.*

4 **Discuss revision strategies that improve readability.** One revision technique that improves readability is the use of balanced constructions (*parallelism*). For example, *collecting, analyzing, and illustrating data* is balanced and easy to read. *Collecting, analysis of, and illustration of data* is more difficult to read because it is unbalanced. Parallelism involves matching nouns with nouns, verbs with verbs, phrases with phrases, and clauses with clauses. Other techniques that improve readability are bullets and lists for quick comprehension, headings for visual impact, and graphic techniques such as capital letters, underlining, italics, and bold print to highlight and order ideas. Readability can be measured by formulas that count long words and sentence length.

5 **Recognize proofreading problem areas, and be able to list techniques for proofreading both routine and complex documents.** Proofreaders must be especially alert to spelling, grammar, punctuation, names, numbers, and document format. Routine documents may be proofread immediately after completion. They may be read line by line on the computer screen or, better yet, from a printed draft copy. More complex documents, however, should be proofread after a breather. To do a good job, you must read from a printed copy, allow adequate time, reduce your reading speed, and read the document at least three times—for word meanings, for grammar/mechanics, and for formatting.

6 **Evaluate a message to judge its success.** Encourage feedback from the receiver so that you can determine whether your communication achieved its goal. Try to welcome any advice from your instructor on how to improve your writing skills. Both techniques contribute to helping you evaluate the success of a message.

chapter review

1. Approximately how much of the total composition time should be spent revising, proofreading, and evaluating? (Obj. 1) ½ of the total time
2. What is the KISS method? In what three ways can it apply to business writing? (Obj. 1)
3. What is a redundancy? Give an example. Why should writers avoid redundancies? (Obj. 2)
4. Why should communicators avoid openings such as *there is*? (Obj. 2)
5. What shorter forms could be substituted for the expressions *at this point in time*, *for the amount of*, and *in advance of*? (Obj. 2)
6. Why should a writer avoid the opening *I am sending this e-mail because we have just hired a new manager, and I would like to introduce her.* (Obj. 2)
7. Why should a writer avoid an expression such as *We expect the executive committee to give authorization to the merger*? (Obj. 3)
8. What's wrong with businesslike expressions such as *enclosed please find* and *as per your request*? (Obj. 3)
9. What is parallelism, and how can you achieve it? (Obj. 4)
10. What is "high skim value," and how can you achieve it? (Obj. 4)
11. What factors determine whether you should use bulleted or numbered items in a list? (Obj. 4)
12. Name five specific items to check in proofreading. Be ready to discuss methods you find useful in spotting these errors. (Obj. 5)
13. In proofreading, what major psychological problem do you face in finding errors? How can you overcome this barrier? (Obj. 5)
14. List four or more effective techniques for proofreading complex documents. (Obj. 5)
15. How can you overcome defensiveness when your writing is criticized constructively? (Obj. 6)

critical thinking

1. Why is it difficult to recommend a specific process that all writers can follow in composition? (Obj. 1)
2. Would you agree or disagree with the following statement by writing expert William Zinsser? "Plain talk will not be easily achieved in corporate America. Too much vanity is on the line." (Objs. 1 and 2)
3. Since business writing should have high "skim value," why not write everything in bulleted lists? (Objs. 2 and 4)
4. Why should the proofreading process for routine documents differ from that for complex documents? (Objs. 4 and 5)
5. **Ethical Issue:** What advice would you give in this ethical dilemma? Lisa is serving as interim editor of the company newsletter. She receives an article written by the company president describing, in abstract and pompous language, the company's goals for the coming year. Lisa thinks the article will need considerable revising to make it readable. Attached to the president's article are complimentary comments by two of the company vice presidents. What action should Lisa take?

THREE GREAT RESOURCES FOR YOU!

1. ***Guffey Student Web Site***
http://guffey.swlearning.com
Your companion Web site offers chapter review quizzes, WebThink activities, updated chapter URLs, and many additional resources.

2. ***Guffey XTRA!***
http://guffeyxtra.swlearning.com
This online study assistant includes Your Personal Language Trainer, Speak Right!, Spell Right!, bonus online chapters, Documents for Analysis, PowerPoint slides, and much more.

3. ***Student Study Guide***
Self-checked workbook activities and applications review chapter concepts and develop career skills.

activities

7.1 Document for Analysis: Poorly Written Letter (Objs. 1–5)

The following letter suffers from a number of weaknesses discussed in this chapter.

Your Task. Study the letter and analyze its weaknesses. In teams or in a class discussion, list at least five specific weaknesses. Then, revise for clarity, tone, conciseness, readability, and correctness. As your instructor directs, use standard proofreading marks to show corrections or revise at a computer.

Current date
Mr. Gene Gorsky
406 DeKalb Pike
Blue Bell, PA 19422
Dear Mr. Gorsky:

As per your request, the undersigned is transmitting to you the attached documents with regard to the improvement of security in your business. To ensure the improvement of your after-hours security, you should initially make a decision with regard to exactly what you contemplate must have protection. You are, in all probability, apprehensive not only about your electronic equipment and paraphernalia but also about your company records, information, and data.

Due to the fact that we feel you will want to obtain protection for both your equipment and data, we will make suggestions for taking a number of judicious steps to inhibit crime. First and foremost, we make a recommendation that you install defensive lighting. A consultant for lighting, currently on our staff, can design both outside and inside lighting, which brings me to my second point. Exhibit security signs, because of the fact that nonprofessional thieves are often as not deterred by posted signs on windows and doors. As my last and final recommendation, you should install space alarms, which are sensors that look down over the areas that are to receive protection, and activate bells or additional lights, thus scaring off intruders.

After reading the materials that are attached, please call me to initiate a verbal discussion regarding protection of your business.

Sincerely,

7.2 Document for Analysis: Poorly Written Letter (Objs. 1–5)

The following letter suffers from a number of weaknesses discussed in this chapter.

Your Task. Study the letter and analyze its weaknesses. In teams or in a class discussion, list at least five specific weaknesses. Then, revise for clarity, tone, conciseness, readability, and correctness. As your instructor directs, use standard proof reading marks to show corrections or revise at a computer.

Current date
Ms. Jeanne Griffin
Wilkes Data Service Center
P.O. Box 443
Wilkesboro, NC 28697
Dear Ms. Griffith,

We appreciate you interest in employe leasing through Enterprise Staffing Services. Our programs and our service has proved to be powerful management tools for business owners, like you. Our 20 year history, Ms. Griffen provide the local service and national strength neccesary to offer the best employee leasing programs available. Due to the fact that we have many years of experience the undersigned as well as our entire staff is certain that we can assemble together a plan that will save you time and money as well as protect you from employee hassles and employer liability.

When you commence a program with us, your employees' will receive health care benifits, retirement plan choices and a national credit union. As a small business owner we are certain that we can also eliminate personel administration for you. Which involves at this point in time alot of goverment paperwork.

Whether you have 10 or 1,000 employees and offer no benefits to a full-benefits package Enterprise Staffing Services can make an analysis of your needs and get you back to the basics of running your business and improvement in profits. I will call you to arrange a time to meet, and talk about your specific needs.

Cordially,

7.3 Document for Analysis: Weak E-Mail Message (Objs. 1–5)

The following e-mail message suffers from a number of weaknesses discussed in this chapter.

Your Task. Study the message and analyze its weaknesses. In teams or in a class discussion, list at least five specific weaknesses. Then, revise for clarity, tone, conciseness, readability, and correctness. In this message consider using two bulleted lists and headings to improve readability. As your instructor directs, use standard proofreading marks to show corrections or revise at a computer.

TO: Keisha Love, Sales and Marketing Manager <klove@ricco.com>
FROM: Arthur Pentilla, CEO <apentilla@ricco.com>
DATE: Current
SUBJECT: IMPROVING SAFETY AND SECURITY FOR TELECOMMUTERS

This e-mail is to inform you that due to the fact that telecommuting is becoming increasingly popular, we feel that it's important and necessary for us to be more careful in planning for information security as well as for the health and personal safety of our employees.

In view of the fact that many of our employees may be considering telecommuting, we have prepared a complete guide for managers. There are structured agreements in the guide that specify space, equipment, and how you should schedule employees. Please discuss the recommendations that follow for a home workspace as well as recommendations for security with any of your staff members who may be making a consideration of telecommuting.

Preparation of a Home Workspace

In regard to the home workspace, employees should create a space that is free and clear of traffic and distractions. They should make the home workspace as comfortable as possible but also provide sufficient space for computer, printer, and for a fax. For security reasons the home workspace should be off limits to family and also to friends. Be sure to provide proper lighting and telephone service.

In regard to the matter of information security and personal security, tell your telecommuters that they should remember that a home office is an extension of the company office. They must be careful and vigilant about avoiding computer viruses and the protection of company information. On the same topic of information security, they should positively be sure to back up information that is important and it should be stored in a safe place that is off site. We do not recommend at-home meetings for telecommuters. By the same token, postal boxes are suggested rather than giving out home addresses. Smoke detectors should be installed in home work areas.

These are just a few of our recommendations. At this point in time you will find a complete guide for telecommuters at our Web site for our company. We urge you to read it carefully as soon as possible. Please do not hesitate to call Human Resources if you have questions.

7.4 Learning About Writing Techniques in Your Field (Objs. 1–6)

SPEAKING

How much writing is required by people working in your career area? The best way to learn about on-the-job writing is to talk with someone who has a job similar to the one you hope to have one day.

Your Task. Interview someone in your field of study. Your instructor may ask you to present your findings orally or in a written report. Ask questions such as these: *What kind of writing do you do? What kind of planning do you do before writing? Where do you get information? Do you brainstorm? Make lists? Do you compose with pen and paper, a computer, or a dictating machine? How many e-mail messages do you typically write in a day? How long does it take you to compose a routine one- or two-page memo or letter? Do you revise? How often? Do you have a preferred method for proofreading? When you have questions about grammar and mechanics, what or whom do you consult? Does anyone read your drafts and make suggestions? Can you describe your entire composition process? Do you ever work with others to produce a document? How does this process work? What makes writing easier or harder for you? Have your writing methods and skills changed since you left school?*

Note: You can find excellent tips on how to conduct an interview such as this one by studying the information and tips at the online chapter, "Employment and Other Interviewing." Locate this chapter at **Xtra! (http://guffeyxtra.swlearning.com)**. Look for "Conducting Successful Interviews," and be sure to find the tips checklist.

7.5 Writing Surpasses Guns as a Law Enforcement Weapon (Objs 1–6)

CRITICAL THINKING | INFOTRAC

Even law enforcement officers need to know how to write. As one student at the FBI National Academy said, "In law enforcement, there is a point where the gun becomes less of a weapon and writing becomes more of one." How do law enforcement officers and civilian employees learn to improve their writing at the FBI?

Your Task. Using InfoTrac, locate Julie R. Linkins' article titled "The Pen and the Sword: How to Make the Writing Process Work for You" (Article No. A98253658). After reading the article, answer these questions:

- **a.** As employees advance through an agency, how does the nature of their writing change? Is this true of employees in most organizations?
- **b.** How does the writing process described in this article compare and contrast with Guffey's 3-x-3 writing process?
- **c.** What is the author's position on spell-checking and grammar-checking software? Do you agree? Why or why not?

7.6 Searching for Deadwood (Obj. 2)

TEAM | WEB

Many writers and speakers are unaware of "deadwood" phrases they use. Some of these are redundancies, compound prepositions, or trite business phrases.

Your Task. Using your favorite Web browser, locate two or three sites devoted to deadwood phrases. Your instructor may ask you to (a) submit a list of ten deadwood phrases (and their preferred substitutes) not mentioned in this textbook, or (b) work in teams to prepare a comprehensive "Dictionary of Deadwood Phrases," including as many as you can find. Be sure to include a preferred substitute.

7.7 Clarity (Objs. 1 and 2)

Your Task. Revise the following sentences to make them direct, simple, and conversational.

- **a.** In response to your verbal suggestion on the telephone, action will be undertaken immediately by the undersigned to make an assessment of your account with us.
- **b.** A recommendation that we are making to supervisors is that they not spend all their time in their own departments and instead visit other departments one hour a month.

c. There is an e-mail policy within our organization that makes a statement that management may access and monitor the e-mail activity of each and every employee.
d. Due to the fact that e-mail is a valuable tool in business, we in management are pleased to make e-mail available to all employees who are authorized to use it.
e. Please be advised that it is our intention to make every effort to deliver your order by the date of your request, December 1.
f. Enclosed herewith please find the proposal which we have the honor to submit to your esteemed organization in regard to the acquisition and purchase of laptop computers.
g. It has been established that the incontestable key to the future success of QuadCam is a deep and firm commitment to quality.
h. It is our suggestion that you do not attempt to move forward until you seek and obtain approval of the plan from the team leader prior to beginning this project.

7.8 Conciseness (Obj. 2)

Your Task. Suggest shorter forms for the following expressions.

a. in view of the fact that
b. in reference to
c. subsequent to
d. without further delay
e. on a monthly basis
f. in the event that
g. a policy for which we have no use
h. a supervisor who was diligent
i. arranged according to chronological dates
j. a program that is intended to save time

7.9 Conciseness (Obj. 2)

Your Task. Revise and shorten the following sentences.

a. There are only two applicants among all who applied who we think are qualified.
b. As per your recommendation, we will not attempt to make alterations or changes in the proposal at this point in time.
c. Because of the fact that his visit was an unexpected surprise, we were totally unprepared to make a presentation of profit and loss figures.
d. It is perfectly clear that meetings held on a monthly basis are most effective.
e. Despite our supposition that the bill appeared erroneous, we sent a check in the amount of $250.
f. We have received your press release, and we will be making a decision soon about whether to use it.
g. A great majority of companies are unaware of the fact that college interns cannot displace regular employees.
h. There are numerous benefits that can result from a good program that focuses on customer service.

i. Because of the degree of active employee participation, we are of the opinion that our team management program will be successful.
j. At this point in time in the program, I wish to extend my grateful thanks to all the support staff who helped make this occasion possible.

7.10 Conciseness Is Hard Work (Obj. 2)

LISTENING SPEAKING

Just as most people are unmotivated to read wordy documents, most are unmotivated to listen to wordy speakers. Effective communicators work to eliminate "rambling" in both their written and spoken words.

Abraham Lincoln expressed the relationship between conciseness and hard work with his reply to the question, "How long does it take you to prepare a speech?" "Two weeks for a 20-minute speech," he replied. "One week for a 40-minute speech; and I can give a rambling, two-hour talk right now." Rambling takes little thought and effort; conciseness takes a great deal of both.

Your Task. For a 24-hour period, apply the conciseness principles to the spoken word by carefully listening and recording conciseness violations. Try to find one violation in the five areas you studied in the chapter: (1) remove fillers, (2) delete long lead-ins, (3) eliminate redundancies, (4) reduce compound prepositions, and (5) purge empty words. Identify the *source* of the violation using descriptors such as friend, family member, coworker, boss, instructor, actor in TV sitcom, interviewer or interviewee on a radio or TV talk show, and so forth. Include the *communication medium* for each example (telephone, conversation, radio, television, etc.). Be prepared to share the results of this activity during a class discussion.

7.11 Vigor (Obj. 3)

Your Task. Revise the following sentences to reduce noun conversions, trite expressions, and other wordiness.

a. It is my understanding that your team shows a preference for bringing its investigation to an end.
b. Please give consideration to our latest proposal, despite the fact that it comes into conflict with the original plan.
c. Our assessment of the damages in the amount of $500 caused us to make a reduction in the amount of the claim.
d. Please give authorization to Human Resources for the conduct of an investigation of employee turnover for the period of January through August.
e. After we engage in the preparation of a report, our recommendations will be presented in their final form before the Executive Committee.
f. There are three members of our staff who are making every effort to locate your lost order.

g. Whether or not we make a continuation of the sales campaign is dependent upon its success in the city of Houston.
h. Please do not hesitate to call me if you have any questions.

7.12 Parallelism (Obj. 3)

Your Task. Revise the following sentences to improve parallelism. If elements cannot be balanced fluently, use appropriate subordination.

a. Your goal should be to write business messages that are concise, clear, and written with courteousness.
b. Ensuring equal opportunities, the removal of barriers, and elimination of age discrimination are our objectives.
c. The market for industrial goods includes manufacturers, contractors, wholesalers, and those concerned with the retail function.
d. Last year Amanda Thomas wrote letters and was giving presentations to promote investment in her business.
e. Because this office has air-conditioning and since it is light and attractive, I prefer this office.
f. For this position we assess oral and written communication skills, how well individuals solve problems, whether they can work with teams, and we're also interested in interpersonal skills, such as cultural awareness and sensitivity.
g. We have three objectives: increase the frequency of product use, introduce complementary products, and the enhancement of our corporate image.

7.13 Lists, Bullets, and Headings (Obj. 4)

Your Task. Revise the following sentences and paragraphs using techniques presented in this chapter. Improve parallel construction and reduce wordiness if necessary.

a. Revise using a bulleted list.
HR Plus specializes in pre-employment background reports. Among our background reports are ones that include professional reference interviews, criminal reports, driving records, employment verification, and credit reports.
b. Revise using a numbered list.
In writing to customers granting approval for loans, you should follow four steps that include announcing that loan approval has been granted. Then you should specify the terms and limits. Next you should remind the reader of the importance of making payments that are timely. Finally, a phone number should be provided for assistance.
c. Revise using a bulleted list.
The American Automobile Association makes a provision of the following tips for safe driving. You should start your drive well rested. You should wear sunglasses in bright sunshine. To provide exercise breaks, plan to stop every two hours. Be sure not to drink alcohol or take cold and allergy medications before you drive.
d. Revise using bulleted items with category headings.
Our attorney made a recommendation that we consider several things to avoid litigation in regard to sexual harassment. The first thing he suggested was that we should take steps regarding the establishment of an unequivocal written policy prohibiting sexual harassment within our organization. The second thing we should do is make sure training sessions are held for supervisors regarding a proper work environment. Finally, some kind of official procedure for employees to lodge complaints is necessary. This procedure should include investigation of complaints.

7.14 Proofreading (Obj. 5)

Your Task. Use proofreading marks to mark spelling, grammar, punctuation, capitalization, and other errors in the following sentences.

a. One of the beautyes of e-mail, is that it enables you to comunicate quick and easy with colleagues, and customers around theGlobe.
b. English maybe the International Language of commerce but that does not mean that every readr will have a trouble-free experience with message writen in english.
c. Be especially carful with dates. For example A message that reads "Our video conference begins at 6 p.m. on 7/8/06" would mean July 8, 2006, to americans.
d. To europeans the time and date would be written as follows: "The video conference will begin at 18:00 on 7 July 2006.
e. Because europeans use a twenty-four-hour military clock be sure to write int'l messages in that format.
f. To avoid confusion give metric measurments followed by there american equivalents. For Example, "The office is 10 kilometers (6.2 miles from the TrainStation.

7.15 How Plain Is the English in Your Apartment Lease? (Objs. 1–4)

E-MAIL | CONSUMER | CRITICAL THINKING | TEAM

Have you read your apartment lease carefully? Did you understand it? Many students—and their friends and family members—are intimidated, frustrated, or just plain lost when they try to comprehend an apartment lease.

Your Task. Locate an apartment lease—yours, a friend's, or a family member's. In teams, analyze its format and readability. What size is the paper? How large are the margins? Is the type large or small? How much white space appears on the page? Are paragraphs and sentences long or short? Does the lease contain legalese or obscure language? What makes it

difficult to understand? In an e-mail message to your instructor, summarize your team's reaction to the lease. Your instructor may ask you to revise sections or the entire lease to make it more readable. In class discuss how ethical it is for an apartment owner to expect a renter to read and comprehend a lease while sitting in the rental office.

C.L.U.E. review 7

Edit the following sentences to correct faults in grammar, punctuation, spelling, and word use.

1. My manager tole my colleague and I that we had to be more conscience of our proofreading because our reports had to many errors.
2. Readers want to scan messages quick therefore we should use every day language and be concise.
3. Even in europe and canada company executives are disapointed by messages that are to long an to difficult to read.
4. One managers report contained so many redundancys that it's main principals requesting State and Federal funding was lost.
5. You're writing will sound more fresher, if you eliminate trite business phases such as "pursuant to you're request.
6. All 3 of our companys recruiters: Angelica Santos, Kirk Adams, and David Toms—critisized there poorly-written procedures.
7. To help recievers anticipate and comprehend ideas quick 2 special writing techniques is helpful, parallalism which involves balanced writing and bulleting which make important points more visible.
8. When I proof read a important document I all ways work with a buddy, and read from a printed copy.
9. Read a message once for word meanings, read it again for grammer and mechanics.
10. Its all most impossible to improve ones communication skills alone, therefore every one should take advantage of this educational oppertunity.

unit 3

Business Correspondence

chapter 8

Routine E-Mail Messages and Memos

objectives

1 Discuss how Guffey's 3-x-3 writing process helps you produce effective e-mail messages and memos.

2 Analyze the structure and formatting of e-mail messages and memos.

3 Describe smart e-mail practices, including getting started; content, tone, and correctness; netiquette; reading and replying to e-mail; personal use; and other practices.

4 Write information and procedure e-mail messages and memos.

5 Write request and reply e-mail messages and memos.

6 Write confirmation e-mail messages and memos.

COMMUNICATION IN PROCESS

Disney's Michael Eisner Finds E-Mail Powerful but Dangerous

HE STARTED AS an usher at NBC. But eventually Michael Eisner became the driving force behind a dramatic transformation of the Walt Disney Company. Once famous only for its vintage animated films for children and its aging theme parks, Disney became an entertainment powerhouse. In addition to its animation business, Disney owns movie studios, the ABC television network, ESPN cable television network, renovated and innovative theme parks, and cruise ships that ply the Bahamas.[1]

Described as creative, domineering, and energetic, Eisner is one of the entertainment world's great survivors. Now serving as Disney's chief executive, the sometimes-controversial Eisner has been instrumental in guiding Disney for two decades.[2]

One of the prime requirements for effective leadership, says Eisner, is keeping in touch with employees. He focuses on the 40 or so members of his management team with whom he deals daily. If necessary, he also communicates with all 110,000 "cast members," as Disney calls its employees. For example, when Walt Disney World had to be closed for a hurricane, he sent an e-mail explaining this first-time-ever closing. "They want[ed] to know what we did to protect our cast members and our guests down there. . . . It's a great way to stay connected."[3]

Eisner recognizes both the power and the dangers of e-mail. "E-mail is changing our behavior, our way of interacting with people, our institutions. And it is happening incredibly fast," he says. E-mail has democratized communication. People can communicate between remote corners of the globe for virtually no cost.

But e-mail is not perfect. "Because it's spread so fast," he notes, "it has raced ahead of our abilities to fully adapt to this new form of communication." He points out that "it took years to learn that there is a way to talk to your peers that differs from talking to your boss or your parents or your teachers or a policeman or a judge. And now here suddenly comes e-mail . . . and, to a frightening extent, we're unprepared."[4]

Photo: © AP/Wide World Photos

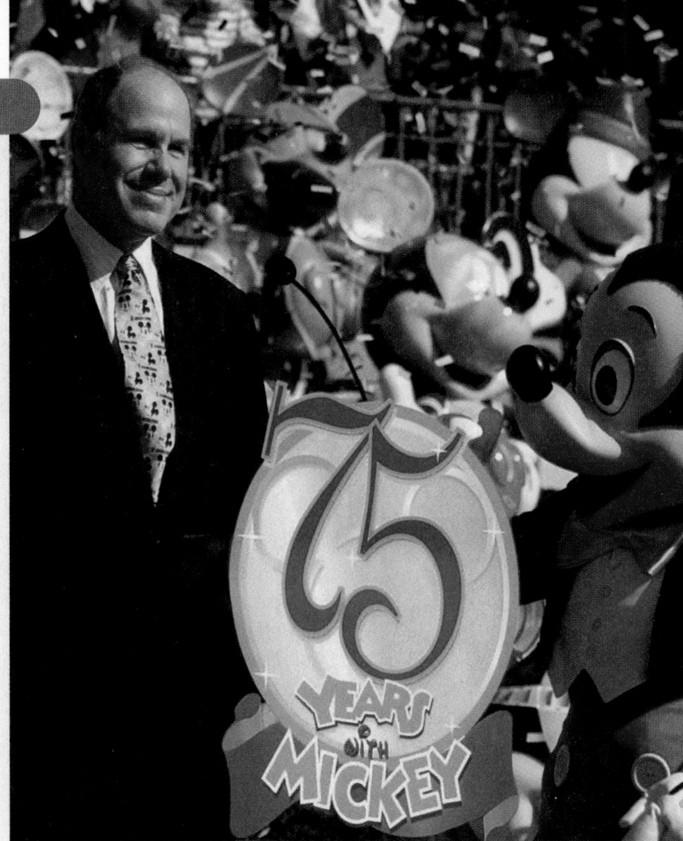

Michael Eisner clowns it up with Mickey Mouse, but he's serious about using e-mail carefully.

Critical Thinking

- In what ways has e-mail changed our behavior, our way of interacting with people, and our institutions?
- How has e-mail democratized communication in general and workplace communication in particular?
- Will it take years for us to learn to adapt to this new form of communication? What adaptation or preparation is necessary?

http://www.disney.com

CONTINUED ON PAGE 230

case study

learning objective 1

Applying the Writing Process to Produce Effective E-Mail Messages and Memos

E-mail has become the primary communication channel for internal communication.

In most organizations today, an amazing change has taken place in internal communication. In the past, written messages from insiders took the form of hard-copy memorandums. But e-mail is now the communication channel of choice not only in this country but abroad. Estimates suggest that the volume of e-mail worldwide will increase from 9.7 billion e-mails in 2000 to 35 billion in 2005.[5] As you learned from the opening case study, cautious leaders such as Michael Eisner at Disney recognize the functions and benefits but also the potential dangers of e-mail.

spotlight *on communicators*

Michael Eisner, CEO of the vast Disney entertainment empire, recommends a cooling-off period before firing off angry messages. "I learned early in the hard paper world of the '70s that when I was annoyed with someone, I should write it all down in a memo. I would then put the memo in my desk drawer and leave it there until the next day." By the next morning, his anger had passed; and he realized that telephoning or seeing the other person was the best way to respond.

A primary function of e-mail is exchanging messages within organizations. Such internal communication has taken on increasing importance today. Organizations are downsizing, flattening chains of command, forming work teams, and empowering rank-and-file employees. Given more power in making decisions, employees find that they need more information. They must collect, exchange, and evaluate information about the products and services they offer. Management also needs input from employees to respond rapidly to local and global market changes. This growing demand for information means an increasing use of e-mail, although hard-copy memos are still written.

Developing skill in writing e-mail messages and memos brings you two important benefits. First, well-written documents are likely to achieve their goals. They create goodwill by being cautious, caring, and clear. They do not intentionally or unintentionally foment ill feelings. Second, well-written internal messages enhance your image within the organization. Individuals identified as competent, professional writers are noticed and rewarded; most often, they are the ones promoted into management positions.

This chapter concentrates on routine e-mail messages and memos. These straightforward messages open with the main idea because their topics are not sensitive and require little persuasion. You'll study the writing process as well as the structure and format of e-mail messages and memos. Because e-mail is such a new and powerful channel of communication, we'll devote special attention to composing smart e-mail messages and reading and responding to e-mail professionally. Finally, you'll learn to write procedure, information, request, reply, and confirmation memos.

Careful writing takes time—especially at first. By following a systematic plan and practicing your skill, however, you can speed up your efforts and greatly improve the product. Bear in mind, moreover, that the effort you make to improve your communication skills can pay big dividends. Frequently, your speaking and writing abilities determine how much influence you'll have in your organization. As with other writing tasks, e-mail and memo writing follow Guffey's 3-x-3 writing process.

Phase 1: Analysis, Anticipation, and Adaptation

Before writing, ask questions that help you analyze, anticipate, and adapt your message.

In Phase 1, prewriting, you'll need to spend some time analyzing your task. It's amazing how many of us are ready to put our pens or computers into gear before engaging our minds. Before writing, ask yourself these important questions:

- **Do I really need to write this e-mail or memo?** A phone call or a quick visit to a nearby coworker might solve the problem—and save the time and expense of a written message. On the other hand, some written messages are needed to provide a permanent record.

- **Should I send an e-mail or a hard-copy memo?** It's tempting to use e-mail for all your correspondence. But a phone call or face-to-face visit is a better channel choice if you need to (a) convey enthusiasm, warmth, or other emotion; (b) supply a context; or (c) smooth over disagreements.
- **Why am I writing?** Know why you are writing and what you hope to achieve. This will help you recognize what the important points are and where to place them.
- **How will the reader react?** Visualize the reader and the effect your message will have. In writing e-mail messages, imagine that you are sitting and talking with your reader. Avoid speaking bluntly, failing to explain, or ignoring your reader's needs. Consider ways to shape the message to benefit the reader. Also remember that your message may very well be forwarded to someone else.
- **How can I save my reader's time?** Think of ways that you can make your message easier to comprehend at a glance. Use bullets, asterisks, lists, headings, and white space, discussed in Chapter 7, to improve readability.

Phase 2: Research, Organization, and Composition

Gather background information; organize it into an outline; compose your message; and revise for clarity, correctness, and feedback.

In Phase 2, writing, you'll first want to check the files, gather documentation, and prepare your message. Make an outline of the points you wish to cover. For short messages jot down notes on the document you are answering or make a scratch list at your computer. As you compose your message, avoid amassing huge blocks of text. No one wants to read endless lines of type. Instead, group related information into paragraphs, preferably short ones. Paragraphs separated by white space look inviting. Be sure each paragraph begins with the main point and is backed up by details. If you bury your main point in the middle of a paragraph, it may be missed. Be sure to prepare for revision, because excellence is rarely achieved on the first effort.

Phase 3: Revision, Proofreading, and Evaluation

Phase 3, revising, involves putting the final touches on your message. Careful and caring writers will ask a number of questions as they do the following:

- **Revise for clarity.** Viewed from the receiver's perspective, are the ideas clear? Do they need more explanation? If the memo is passed on to others, will they need further explanation? Consider having a colleague critique your message if it is an important one.
- **Proofread for correctness.** Are the sentences complete and punctuated properly? Did you overlook any typos or misspelled words? Remember to use your spell checker and grammar checker to proofread your message before sending it.
- **Plan for feedback.** How will you know whether this message is successful? You can improve feedback by asking questions (such as *Are you comfortable with these suggestions?* or *What do you think?*). Remember to make it easy for the receiver to respond.

spotlight on communicators

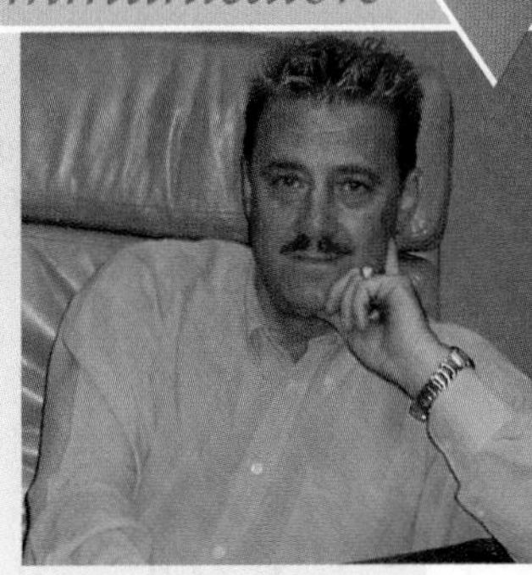

As the busy head of Advanced Communication Design Inc., a small technology company in Minnesota, Marco Scibora scans his incoming messages with the efficient eye of an editor looking for the crux of the story. "For me, time is of the essence. Keep it short, official, and to the point," he says. If he doesn't get the information he needs out of the first three sentences, he moves on to the next message, postponing the reading of wordy messages until later. He has little tolerance for smiley faces, acronyms, and sloppy phrases.

learning objective

2

E-mail messages and memos inform employees, request data, give responses, confirm decisions, and provide directions.

Analyzing the Structure and Format of E-Mail Messages and Memos

Because e-mail messages and memos are standard forms of communication within organizations, they will probably become your most common business communication channel. These messages perform critical tasks such as informing employees, requesting data, supplying responses, confirming decisions, and giving directions. They generally follow similar structure and formatting.

Structuring E-Mail Messages and Memos

Whether electronic or hard copy, routine memos generally contain four parts: (1) an informative subject line that summarizes the message, (2) an opening that reveals the main idea immediately, (3) a body that explains and justifies the main idea, and (4) an appropriate closing. Remember that routine messages deliver good news or standard information.

Subject lines summarize the purpose of the message in abbreviated form.

Subject Line. In e-mails and memos an informative subject line is mandatory. It summarizes the central idea, thus providing quick identification for reading and for filing. In e-mail messages, subject lines are essential. Busy readers glance at a subject line and decide when and whether to read the message. Those without subject lines are automatically deleted.

What does it take to get your message read? For one thing, stay away from meaningless or dangerous words. A sure way to get your message deleted or ignored is to use a one-word heading such as *Issue, Problem, Important,* or *Help.* Including a word such as *Free* is dangerous because it may trigger spam filters. Try to make your subject line *talk* by including a verb. Explain the purpose of the message and how it relates to the reader (*Need You to Showcase Two Items at Our Next Trade Show* rather than *Trade Show*). Finally, update your subject line to reflect the current message (*Staff Meeting Rescheduled for May 12* rather than *Re: Re: Staff Meeting*). Remember that a subject line is usually written in an abbreviated style, often without articles (*a, an, the*). It need not be a complete sentence, and it does not end with a period.

Routine e-mails and memos open directly by revealing the main idea immediately.

Opening. Most e-mails and memos cover nonsensitive information that can be handled in a straightforward manner. Begin by frontloading; that is, reveal the main idea immediately. Even though the purpose of the memo or e-mail is summarized in the subject line, that purpose should be restated—and amplified—in the first sentence. As you learned in Chapters 5 and 6, busy readers want to know immediately why they are reading a message. Notice how the following indirect opener can be improved by frontloading.

Indirect Opening	**Direct Opening**
For the past six months the Human Resources Development Department has been considering changes in our employees' benefit plan.	Please review the following proposal regarding employees' benefits, and let me know by May 20 if you approve these changes.

The body explains one topic and is designed for easy comprehension.

Body. The body provides more information about the reason for writing. It explains and discusses the subject logically. Good e-mail messages and memos generally discuss only one topic. Limiting the topic helps the receiver act on the subject and file it appropriately. A writer who, for example, describes a computer printer problem and also requests permission to attend a conference runs a 50 percent failure risk. The reader may respond to the printer problem but delay or forget about the conference request.

Design your data for easy comprehension by using numbered lists, headings, tables, and other graphic highlighting techniques, as introduced in Chapter 6. Compare the following versions of the same message. Notice how the graphic devices of bullets, columns, headings, and white space make the main points easier to comprehend.

make your writing easy on the reader!

Hard-to-Read Paragraph Version

Effective immediately are the following air travel guidelines. Between now and December 31, only account executives may take company-approved trips. These individuals will be allowed to take a maximum of two trips, and they are to travel economy or budget class only.

Improved Version With Graphic Highlighting

Effective immediately are the following air travel guidelines:

- Who may travel: Account executives only
- How many trips: A maximum of two trips
- By when: Between now and December 31
- Air class: Economy or budget class only

Messages should close with (1) action information including dates and deadlines, (2) a summary, or (3) a closing thought.

Closing. Generally end with (1) action information, dates, or deadlines; (2) a summary of the message; or (3) a closing thought. Here again the value of thinking through the message before actually writing it becomes apparent. The closing is where readers look for deadlines and action language. An effective memo or e-mail closing might be, *Please submit your report by June 15 so that we can have your data before our July planning session.*

In more complex messages a summary of main points may be an appropriate closing. If no action request is made and a closing summary is unnecessary, you might end with a simple concluding thought (*I'm glad to answer your questions* or *This sounds like a useful project*). You needn't close messages to coworkers with goodwill statements such as those found in letters to customers or clients. However, some closing thought is often necessary to prevent a feeling of abruptness. Closings can show gratitude or encourage feedback with remarks such as *I sincerely appreciate your help* or *What are your ideas on this proposal?* Other closings look forward to what's next, such as *How would you like to proceed?* Avoid closing with overused expressions such as *Please let me know if I may be of further assistance.* This ending sounds mechanical and insincere.

Revision helps you think through a problem, clarify a solution, and express it clearly.

Putting It All Together. Now let's follow the development of an e-mail message to see how we can apply the ideas just discussed. Figure 8.1 shows the first draft of an e-mail message James Perkins, marketing manager, wrote to his boss, Jie Wang. Although it contained solid information, the message was so wordy and dense that the main points were submerged.

After writing the first draft, James realized that he needed to reorganize his message into an opening, body, and closing. And he desperately needed to improve the readability. In studying what he had written, he realized that he was talking about two main problems. He also discovered that he could present a three-part solution. These ideas didn't occur to him until he had written the first draft. Only in the revision stage was he able to see in his own mind that he was talking about two separate problems as well as a three-part solution. The revision process can help you think through a problem and clarify a solution.

In the revised version, James was more aware of the subject line, opening, body, and closing. He used an informative subject line and opened directly by explaining why he was writing. His opening also outlined the two main problems so that his reader understood the background of the following recommendations. In the body

FIGURE 8.1 ***Revising an E-Mail Message That Informs***

1 Prewriting

Analyze: The purpose of this memo is to describe database problems and recommend solutions.

Anticipate: The audience is the writer's boss, who is familiar with the topic and who appreciates brevity.

Adapt: Because the reader requested this message, the direct pattern is most appropriate.

2 Writing

Research: Gather data documenting the customer database and how to use Access software.

Organize: Announce recommendations and summarize problems. In the body, list the three actions for solving the problem. In the closing, describe reader benefits, provide a deadline, and specify the next action.

Compose: Prepare the first draft.

3 Revising

Revise: Highlight the two main problems and the three recommendations. Use asterisks, caps, and headings to improve readability. Make the bulleted ideas parallel.

Proofread: Double-check to see whether *database* is one word or two. Use spell checker.

Evaluate: Does this e-mail supply concise information the boss wants in an easy-to-read form?

DRAFT

To Jie Wang <jwang@edison.com>
From James Perkins <jperkins@edison.com>
Subject: Problems

This is in response to your recent inquiry about our customer database. Your message of May 9 said that you wanted to know how to deal with the database problems.

I can tell you that the biggest problem is that it contains a lot of outdated information, including customers who haven't purchased anything in five or more years. Another problem is that the old database is not compatible with the new Access software that is being used by our mailing service, and this makes it difficult to merge files. I think I can solve both problems, however, by starting a new database. This would be the place where we put the names of all new customers. And we would have it keyed using Access software. The problem with outdated information could be solved by finding out if the customers in our old database wish to continue receiving our newsletter and product announcements. Finally, we would rekey the names of all active customers in the new database.

Uses meaningless subject line

Fails to reveal purpose quickly

Buries two problems and three-part solution in huge paragraph

Forgets to conclude with next action and end date

REVISION

File Edit Mailbox Message Transfer Special Tools Window Help

Send

To: Jie Wang <jwang@edison.com>
From: James Perkins <jperkins@edison.com>
Subject: Recommendations for Improving Our Customer Database

Jie:

As you requested, I am submitting my recommendations for improving our customer database. The database has two major problems. First, it contains many names of individuals who have not made purchases in five or more years. Second, the format is not compatible with the new Access software used by our mailing service.

The following three procedures, however, should solve both problems:

* START A NEW DATABASE. Effective immediately enter the names of all new customers in a new database using Access software.

* DETERMINE THE STATUS OF CUSTOMERS in our old database. Send out a mailing asking whether recipients wish to continue receiving our newsletter and product announcements.

* REKEY THE NAMES OF ACTIVE CUSTOMERS. Enter the names of all responding customers in our new database so that we have only one active database.

These changes will enable you, as team leader, to request mailings that go only to active customers. Please let me know by May 20 whether you think these recommendations are workable. If so, I will investigate costs.

James

Informative subject line summarizes purpose

Opening states purpose concisely and highlights two problems

Body organizes main points for readability

Closing includes key benefit, deadline, and next action

of his message, James identified three corrective actions, and he highlighted them for improved readability. Notice that he listed his three recommendations using asterisks (bullets don't always transmit well in e-mail messages) with capitalized headings. Asterisks, white space, and capitalized letters work well in e-mail messages to highlight important points. Notice, too, that James closed his message with a deadline and a reference to the next action to be taken.

Formatting E-Mail Messages

Because e-mail is a developing communication channel, its formatting and usage conventions are still fluid. Users and authorities, for instance, do not always agree on what's appropriate for salutations and closings. The following suggestions, however, can guide you in formatting most e-mail messages, but always check with your organization to observe its practices.

E-mails contain guide words, optional salutations, and a concise and easy-to-read message.

Guide Words. Following the guide word *To*, some writers insert just the recipient's electronic address, such as *mphilly@accountpro.com.* Other writers prefer to include the receiver's full name plus the electronic address, as shown in Figure 8.2. By including full names in the *To* and *From* slots, both receivers and senders are better able to identify the message. By the way, the order of *Date, To, From, Subject,* and other guide words varies depending on your e-mail program and whether you are sending or receiving the message.

Most e-mail programs automatically add the current date after *Date.* On the *Cc* line (which stands for *carbon* or *courtesy copy*) you can type the address of anyone who is to receive a copy of the message. Remember, though, to send copies only to those people directly involved with the message. Most e-mail programs also include a line for *Bcc* (*blind carbon copy*). This sends a copy without the addressee's knowledge. Many savvy writers today use *Bcc* for the names and addresses of a list of receivers, a technique that avoids revealing the addresses to the entire group. On the subject line, identify the subject of the memo. Be sure to include enough information to be clear and compelling.

On messages to outsiders, salutations are important to show friendliness and to indicate the beginning of the message.

Salutation. How to treat the salutation is a problem. Many writers omit a salutation because they consider the message a memo. In the past, hard-copy memos were sent only to company insiders, and salutations were omitted. However, when e-mail messages travel to outsiders, omitting a salutation seems curt and unfriendly. Because the message is more like a letter, a salutation is appropriate (such as *Dear Jake; Hi, Jake; Greetings;* or just *Jake*). Including a salutation is also a visual cue to where the message begins. Many messages are transmitted or forwarded with such long headers that finding the beginning of the message can be difficult. A salutation helps, as shown in Figure 8.2. Other writers do not use a salutation; instead, they use the name of the recipient in the first sentence.

Body. When typing the body of an e-mail message, use standard caps and lowercase characters—never all uppercase or all lowercase characters. Cover just one topic, and try to keep the total message under three screens in length. To assist you, many e-mail programs have basic text-editing features, such as cut, copy, paste, and wordwrap. However, avoid graphics, font changes, boldface, and italics unless your reader's system can handle them. Some e-mail writers use _Book Title_ to show underlining and *emphasized word* to show italics.

Closing Lines. Writers of e-mail messages sent within organizations may omit closings and even skip their names at the end of messages. They can omit these items

FIGURE 8.2 ***Formatting an E-Mail Request***

Tips for E-Mail Formatting

- After *To,* type the receiver's electronic address. If you include the receiver's name, enclose the address in angle brackets.
- After *From,* type your name and electronic address, if your program does not insert it automatically.
- After *Subject,* present a clear description of the message. Use all caps or uppercase for the initial letters of principal words.
- Insert the addresses of anyone receiving courtesy or blind copies.
- Include a salutation (such as *Dear Melinda; Hi, Melinda; Greetings*) or weave the receiver's name into the first line (see Figure 8.6). Some writers omit a salutation.
- Double-space (press *Enter*) between paragraphs.
- Do not type in all caps or in all lowercase letters.
- Include a complimentary close, your name, and your address if appropriate.

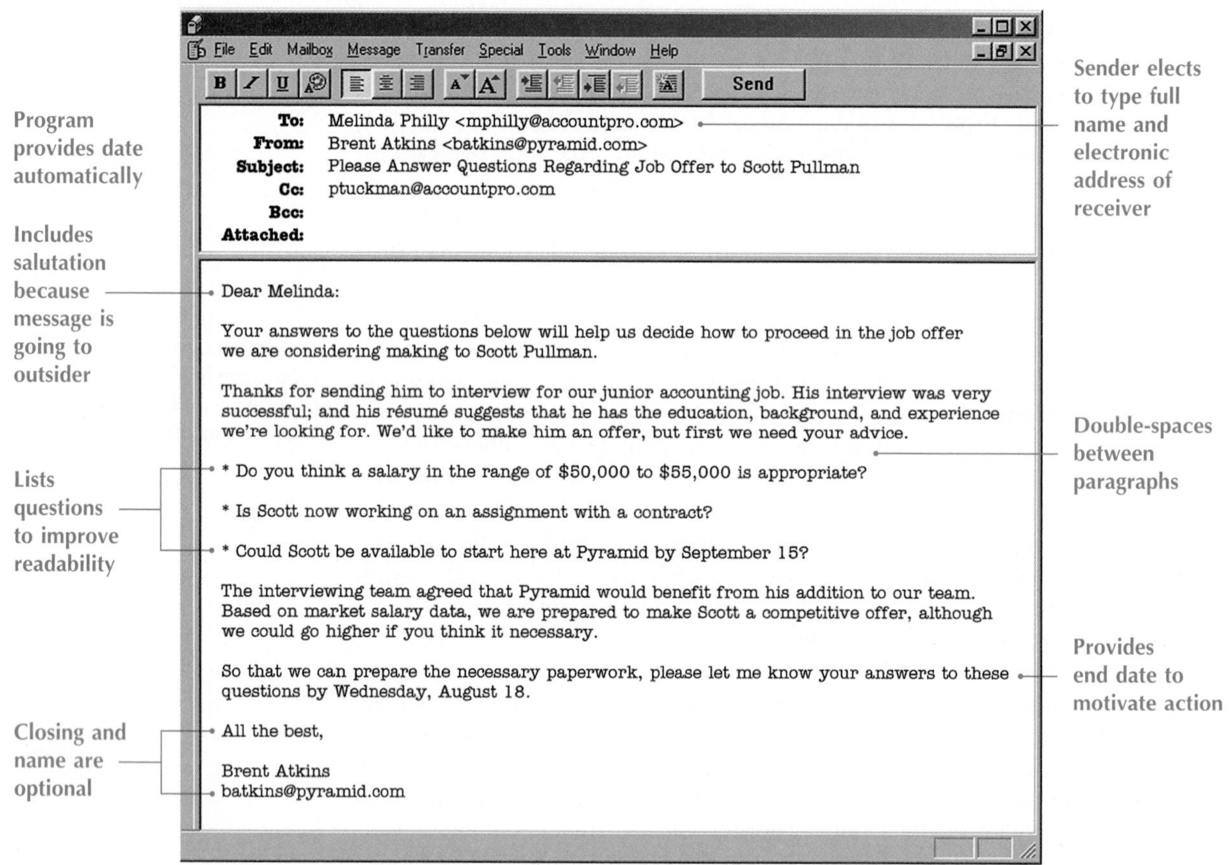
File Edit Mailbox Message Transfer Special Tools Window Help
Send
To: Melinda Philly <mphilly@accountpro.com>
From: Brent Atkins <batkins@pyramid.com>
Subject: Please Answer Questions Regarding Job Offer to Scott Pullman
Cc: ptuckman@accountpro.com
Bcc:
Attached:
Dear Melinda:
Your answers to the questions below will help us decide how to proceed in the job offer we are considering making to Scott Pullman.
Thanks for sending him to interview for our junior accounting job. His interview was very successful; and his résumé suggests that he has the education, background, and experience we're looking for. We'd like to make him an offer, but first we need your advice.
* Do you think a salary in the range of $50,000 to $55,000 is appropriate?
* Is Scott now working on an assignment with a contract?
* Could Scott be available to start here at Pyramid by September 15?
The interviewing team agreed that Pyramid would benefit from his addition to our team. Based on market salary data, we are prepared to make Scott a competitive offer, although we could go higher if you think it necessary.
So that we can prepare the necessary paperwork, please let me know your answers to these questions by Wednesday, August 18.
All the best,
Brent Atkins
batkins@pyramid.com
Program provides date automatically
Includes salutation because message is going to outsider
Lists questions to improve readability
Closing and name are optional
Sender elects to type full name and electronic address of receiver
Double-spaces between paragraphs
Provides end date to motivate action

because receivers recognize them from identification in the opening lines. But for outside messages, a writer might include a closing such as *Cheers* or *All the best* followed by the writer's name and e-mail address (because some systems do not transmit your address automatically). If the recipient is unlikely to know you, it's wise to include your title and organization. Some veteran e-mail users include a *signature file* with identifying information embellished with keyboard art. Use restraint, however, because signature files take up precious bandwidth (Internet capacity).

E-mail messages to outsiders should include the writer's name and identification.

Formatting Hard-Copy Memos

Hard-copy memorandums deliver information within organizations. Although e-mail is more often used, hard-copy memos are still useful for important internal messages that require a permanent record or formality. For example, changes in procedures, official instructions, and organization reports are often prepared as hard-copy memos. Because e-mail is new and still evolving, we examined its formatting carefully in the previous paragraphs.

Hard-copy memos require less instruction because formatting is fairly standardized. Some offices use memo forms imprinted with the organization name and, optionally, the department or division names. Although the design and arrangement of memo forms vary, they usually include the basic elements of *Date*, *To*, *From*, and *Subject*. Large organizations may include other identifying headings, such as *File Number*, *Floor*, *Extension*, *Location*, and *Distribution*. Because of the difficulty of aligning computer printers with preprinted forms, many business writers store memo formats in their computers and call them up when preparing memos. The guide words are then printed with the message, thus eliminating alignment problems.

Hard-copy memos are typed with guide words but no salutation or closing lines.

If no printed or stored computer forms are available, memos may be typed on company letterhead, as shown in Figure 8.3, or typed on plain paper. On a full sheet of paper, start the guide words 2 inches from the top; on a half sheet, start 1 inch from the top. Double-space and type in all caps the guide words. Align all the fill-in information 2 spaces after the longest guide word (usually *Subject:*). Leave 2 blank lines between the last line of the heading and the first line of the memo. Single-space within paragraphs and double-space between paragraphs. Memos are generally formatted with side margins of 1 to 1.25 inches, or they may conform to the printed memo form. Do not justify the right margins. Research has shown that "ragged-right" margins in printed messages are easier to read.

Using E-Mail Smartly and Safely

learning objective

3

Early e-mail users were encouraged to ignore stylistic and grammatical considerations. They thought that "words on the fly" required little editing or proofing. Correspondents used emoticons (such as sideways happy faces) to express their emotions. Some e-mail today is still quick and dirty. As this communication channel continues to mature, however, messages are becoming more proper and more professional. Today more than 31 billion e-mails are sent each day worldwide. E-mail is twice as likely as the telephone to be used to communicate at work. We have become so dependent on e-mail that 53 percent of people using it at work say that their productivity drops when they are away from it.[6]

E-mail messages are becoming more proper and more professional.

Wise e-mail business communicators are aware of the importance as well as the dangers of e-mail as a communication channel. Like Disney's Michael Eisner, they know that thoughtless messages can cause irreparable harm. They know that their messages can travel (intentionally or unintentionally) long distances. A quickly drafted note may end up in the boss's mailbox or be forwarded to an adversary's

FIGURE 8.3 ***Hard-Copy Memo That Responds to Request***

Tips for Formatting Hard-Copy Memos

- Set one tab to align entries evenly after *Subject*.
- Type the subject line in all caps or capitalize the initial letters of principal words.
- Leave one or two blank lines after the subject line.
- Single-space all but the shortest memos. Double-space between paragraphs.
- For full-page memos on plain paper, leave a 2-inch top margin.
- For half-page memos, leave a 1-inch top margin.
- Use 1.25-inch side margins.
- For a two-page memo, use a second-page heading with the addressee's name, page number, and date.
- Handwrite your initials after your typed name.
- Place bulleted or numbered lists flush left or indent them 0.5 inches.

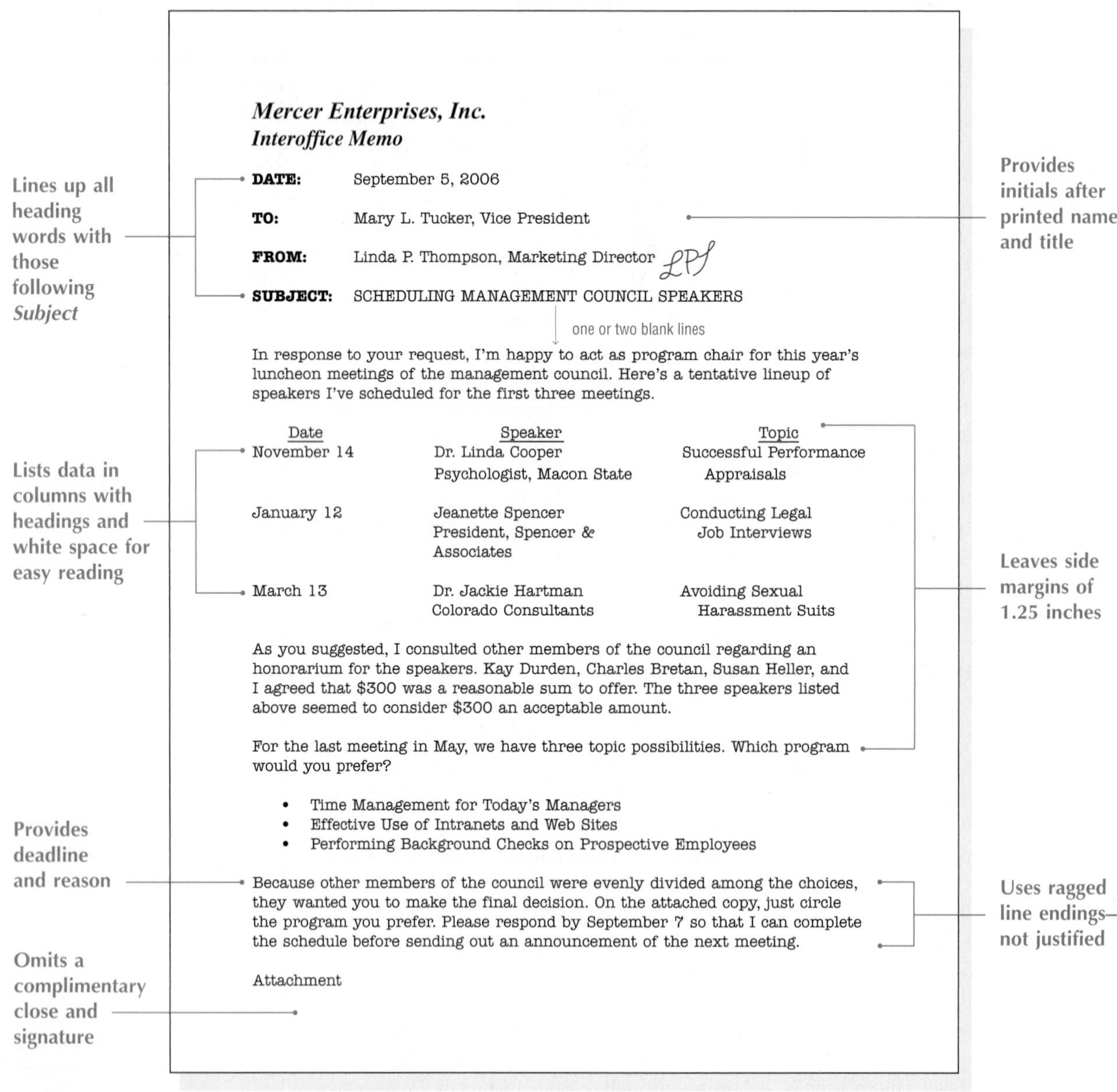

Lines up all heading words with those following *Subject*
Provides initials after printed name and title
one or two blank lines
Lists data in columns with headings and white space for easy reading
Leaves side margins of 1.25 inches
Provides deadline and reason
Uses ragged line endings—not justified
Omits a complimentary close and signature

Mercer Enterprises, Inc.
Interoffice Memo

DATE: September 5, 2006

TO: Mary L. Tucker, Vice President

FROM: Linda P. Thompson, Marketing Director *LPT*

SUBJECT: SCHEDULING MANAGEMENT COUNCIL SPEAKERS

In response to your request, I'm happy to act as program chair for this year's luncheon meetings of the management council. Here's a tentative lineup of speakers I've scheduled for the first three meetings.

Date	Speaker	Topic
November 14	Dr. Linda Cooper Psychologist, Macon State	Successful Performance Appraisals
January 12	Jeanette Spencer President, Spencer & Associates	Conducting Legal Job Interviews
March 13	Dr. Jackie Hartman Colorado Consultants	Avoiding Sexual Harassment Suits

As you suggested, I consulted other members of the council regarding an honorarium for the speakers. Kay Durden, Charles Bretan, Susan Heller, and I agreed that $300 was a reasonable sum to offer. The three speakers listed above seemed to consider $300 an acceptable amount.

For the last meeting in May, we have three topic possibilities. Which program would you prefer?

- Time Management for Today's Managers
- Effective Use of Intranets and Web Sites
- Performing Background Checks on Prospective Employees

Because other members of the council were evenly divided among the choices, they wanted you to make the final decision. On the attached copy, just circle the program you prefer. Please respond by September 7 so that I can complete the schedule before sending out an announcement of the next meeting.

Attachment

box. Making matters worse, computers—like elephants and spurned lovers—never forget. Even erased messages can remain on disk drives. Increasingly, e-mail has turned into the "smoking gun" uncovered by prosecutors to prove indelicate or even illegal intentions.[7]

E-mail messages may be dangerous because they travel long distances and are difficult to erase.

E-mail has become the corporate equivalent of DNA evidence. Like "forgotten landmines," damaging e-mails have been dug up to prove a prosecutor's case. For example, in the antitrust suit against Microsoft, Bill Gates squirmed when the court heard his e-mail in which he asked, "How much do we need to pay you to screw Netscape?" In another case banker Frank Quattrone was found guilty of obstructing justice based on an e-mail message in which he instructed employees to "clean up" their e-mail files after he learned that he was being investigated for securities irregularities.[8] More often, e-mail writers simply forget that their message is a permanent record. "It's as if people put their brains on hold when they write e-mail," said one expert. "They think that e-mail is a substitute for a phone call, and that's the danger."[9] Another observer noted that e-mail is like an electronic truth serum.[10] Writers blurt out thoughts without thinking. For these reasons, e-mail represents a number of dangers, both to employees and to employers, as discussed in the accompanying Tech Talk box.

Getting Started

Despite its dangers and limitations, e-mail has definitely become a mainstream channel of communication. That's why it's important to take the time to organize your thoughts, compose carefully, and be concerned with correct grammar and punctuation. The following pointers will help you get off to a good start in using e-mail smartly and safely.

Because e-mail is now a mainstream communication channel, messages should be well organized, carefully composed, and grammatically correct.

- **Consider composing offline.** Especially for important messages, think about using your word processing program to write offline. Then upload your message to the e-mail network. This avoids "self-destructing" (losing all your writing through some glitch or pressing the wrong key) when working online.
- **Get the address right.** E-mail addresses are sometimes complex, often illogical, and always unforgiving. Omit one character or misread the letter *l* for the number 1, and your message bounces. Solution: Use your electronic address book for people you write to frequently. And double-check every address that you key in manually. Also be sure that you don't reply to a group of receivers when you intend to answer only one.
- **Avoid misleading subject lines.** As discussed earlier, make sure your subject line is relevant and helpful. Generic tags such as *Hi!* and *Important!* may cause your message to be deleted before it is opened.
- **Apply the top-of-screen test.** When readers open your message and look at the first screen, will they see what is most significant? Your subject line and first paragraph should convey your purpose.

spotlight *on communicators*

"To avoid misunderstandings when sending e-mail messages, consider how the recipient will react to your message," says Liz Hughes, executive director of Office Team, the nation's leading staffing service. "If you use terse or abbreviated language, for example, you may appear angry. If your style is too informal, you may seem unprofessional," says Hughes. Written communication is particularly dangerous because you are not present to correct misunderstanding. Hughes points out that written communication tends to amplify emotions, so be sure to reread the message and listen to its tone before you send it. Never compose any message while you are upset.

Photo: Courtesy of Elizabeth Hughes

Content, Tone, and Correctness

Although e-mail seems as casual as a telephone call, it's not. Because it produces a permanent record, think carefully about what you say and how you say it.

tech talk

Your Internet Use Could Get You Fired

As communication technologies continue to change the way we work, Internet use has become a danger zone for employees and employers. Misuse costs employers millions of dollars in lost productivity and litigation, and it can cost employees their jobs. Chevron, Dow Chemical, Xerox, and the New York Times are among the many companies that have fired or disciplined employees for online shopping, gambling, gossiping, and pursuing various nonbusiness activities. Current surveys reveal that e-mail and Internet misuse by staff has become the biggest disciplinary problem for employers.[11] Intentional activities, as well as unintentional but careless miscues, can gobble up precious network resources and waste valuable work time. It's no wonder that companies are increasingly monitoring and restricting employee Internet use. Here are some Internet problems you'll face on the job:

- **Personal use on company time.** Just as employees once ran up phone bills making personal calls, they now spend company time surfing, chatting, shopping, or exchanging e-mails that have little to do with their jobs. One observer noted that in addition to being a channel for commercial exchange, the Web also provides employees access to the world's biggest playground for work and life."[12]
- **Sexual harassment.** Companies must maintain a workplace free of harassment. If employees download pornography, transmit sexually explicit jokes, or use inappropriate screen savers, the work environment can become "poisoned" and employers are liable.
- **Copyright infringement.** Employees may copy or distribute graphics, pictures, logos, cartoons, and so forth without permission. For example, a report writer may cut and paste a picture into a report, thus violating copyright laws.
- **Viruses.** Employees frequently forget to scan incoming attachments or files for viruses. Attachments with executable files or video files are especially vulnerable. Many of these files are personal, making the sting of viruses even worse.
- **Confidential information.** Sensitive organizational information may find its way into the wrong hands when transmitted electronically.
- **Defamation.** Employees can defame other individuals or organizations in e-mail messages, bulletin boards, or in chat rooms. One college lab technician was terminated for distributing a lengthy e-mail to his coworkers claiming gross incompetence, favoritism, and mismanagement of funds in his department.[13]

Career Application

Based on what you learned in this chapter, what can employees do to avoid jeopardizing their jobs because of Internet misuse? Do employees deserve access to the Internet if they are responsible? Should employers block access to Web sites in these categories: adult content, gambling, illegal activities, racism, abortion or antiabortion advocacy, activist groups, cultural institutions (including galleries and museums), educational institutions, gay and lesbian issues, health information, hobbies, job search, news, personals, political groups, religion, restaurants, search engines, sex education, shopping, sports, and travel?

Avoid sending sensitive, confidential, inflammatory, or potentially embarrassing messages because e-mail is not private.

- **Be concise.** Don't burden readers with unnecessary information. Remember that monitors are small and typefaces are often difficult to read. Organize your ideas tightly.
- **Don't send anything you wouldn't want published.** Because e-mail seems like a telephone call or a person-to-person conversation, writers sometimes send sensitive, confidential, inflammatory, or potentially embarrassing messages. Beware! E-mail creates a permanent record that does not go away even when deleted. And every message is a corporate communication that can be used against you or your employer. Don't write anything that you wouldn't want your boss, your family, or a judge to read.

- **Don't use e-mail to avoid contact.** E-mail is inappropriate for breaking bad news or for resolving arguments. For example, it's improper to fire a person by e-mail. It's also not a good channel for dealing with conflict with supervisors, subordinates, or others. If there's any possibility of hurt feelings, pick up the telephone or pay the person a visit.
- **Care about correctness.** People are still judged by their writing, whether electronic or paper-based. Sloppy e-mail messages (with missing apostrophes, haphazard spelling, and stream-of-consciousness writing) make readers work too hard. They resent not only the information but also the writer.
- **Care about tone.** Your words and writing style affect the reader. Avoid sounding curt, negative, or domineering.
- **Resist humor and tongue-in-cheek comments.** Without the nonverbal cues conveyed by your face and your voice, humor can easily be misunderstood.

Netiquette

Although e-mail is a new communication channel, a number of rules of polite online interaction are emerging.

- **Limit any tendency to send blanket copies.** Send copies only to people who really need to see a message. It is unnecessary to document every business decision and action with an electronic paper trail.
- **Never send "spam."** Sending unsolicited advertisements ("spam") either by fax or e-mail is illegal in the United States.
- **Consider using identifying labels.** When appropriate, add one of the following labels to the subject line: *Action* (action required, please respond); *FYI* (for your information, no response needed); *Re* (this is a reply to another message); *Urgent* (please respond immediately).
- **Use capital letters only for emphasis or for titles.** Avoid writing entire messages in all caps, which is like SHOUTING.
- **Don't forward without permission.** Obtain approval before forwarding a message.
- **Reduce attachments.** Because attachments may carry viruses, some receivers won't open them. Consider including short attachments within an e-mail message. If you must send a longer attachment, explain it.

spotlight *on communicators*

Barbara Hemphill, author of Taming the Paper Tiger at Work, *helps major corporations increase their productivity and efficiency. When it comes to reading and replying to e-mail, she recommends the FAT™ System: F stands for* File, *A for* Act, *and T for* Toss. *If you need more than two minutes to reply,* File *the message in a folder with a reminder in your calendar system. If you can reply in two minutes, then* Act. *If you aren't sure you need the message,* Toss *it. Unlike using a paper wastebasket, you can retrieve deleted messages in most e-mail systems. Her Web site with more efficiency tips is at* ***www.productiveenvironment.com****.*

Reading and Replying to E-Mail

The following tips can save you time and frustration when reading and answering messages:

- **Scan all messages in your inbox before replying to each individually.** Because subsequent messages often affect the way you respond, skim all messages first (especially all those from the same individual).
- **Print only when necessary.** Generally, read and answer most messages online without saving or printing. Use folders to archive messages on special topics. Print only those messages that are complex, controversial, or involve significant decisions and follow-up.

Photo: Courtesy of Barbara Hemphill

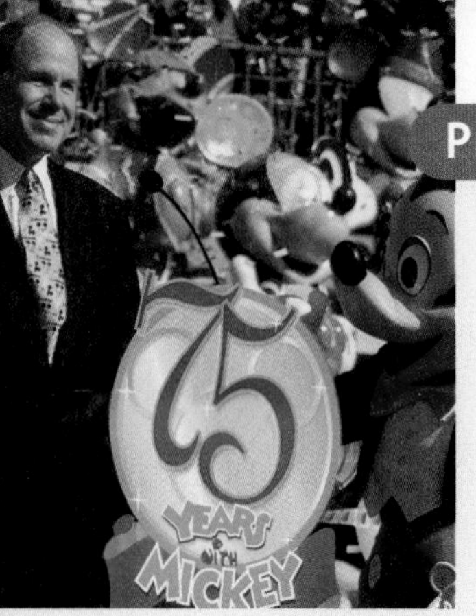

Process in Progress

The Walt Disney Company Revisited

TODAY, THE SUN never sets on the Disney entertainment empire. CEO Michael Eisner is in charge of managing all of Disney's divisions, including ABC, three movie studios, the Mighty Ducks professional hockey team, numerous Internet ventures, and Disney's amusement parks scattered throughout the world. Eisner, like many of today's executives, relies on e-mail to communicate with his far-flung cast of employees. Although he touts its many benefits, Eisner also recognizes the dark side of e-mail. "E-mail's very virtues," says Eisner, "also make it dangerous—it's instant, it's global, it's quick, and it's easy. It becomes easy to be rude, easy to use language incorrectly, easy to make stupid mistakes, and easy to do irreparable harm."[14]

Eisner warns that thoughtless e-mails can be dangerous to organizations. By its nature, the creative work going on at Disney generates strong feelings, candid critiques, and positive competition. But the intensity of emotions at Disney, Eisner believes, is "higher than usual" because of e-mail. He is convinced that "every fight that goes on seems to start with a misunderstanding over an e-mail." A sarcastic remark, such as saying "you dope" with a smile over the dinner table, he suggests, can be endearing. In an e-mail message, however, that same expression can start a war of words. He notes that words carry more impact when they are transmitted in writing. "I'm afraid that spell check does not check for anger, emotion, inflection, or subtext," admonishes Eisner. "Only we can do that."[15]

As Eisner wisely observes, "E-mail isn't just about speed and efficiency and information. It's also about unscreened emotions, about opinions untempered by body language, about thoughts unrefined by reflection, about hostility and provocation . . . ." E-mail should be the ultimate tool of communication and openness. But, ironically, if used thoughtlessly, warns Eisner, e-mail can foment mistrust, secrecy, and havoc in an organization.[16]

Critical Thinking

- What do you think Eisner means when he says that e-mail is about "opinions untempered by body language"? Why are written and spoken words interpreted differently?
- What does Eisner mean by "thoughts unrefined by reflection"? How does this statement relate to e-mail?
- What practices can you suggest to prevent the kind of "thoughtless" e-mail messages Eisner condemns?

CONTINUED ON PAGE 238

case study

Skim all messages before responding, paste in relevant sections, revise the subject if the topic changes, provide a clear first sentence, and never respond when angry.

- **Acknowledge receipt.** If you can't reply immediately, tell when you can (*Will respond Friday*).
- **Don't automatically return the sender's message.** When replying, cut and paste the relevant parts. Avoid irritating your recipients by returning the entire "thread" (sequence of messages) on a topic.
- **Revise the subject line if the topic changes.** When replying or continuing an e-mail exchange, revise the subject line as the topic changes.
- **Provide a clear, complete first sentence.** Avoid fragments such as *That's fine with me* or *Sounds good!* Busy respondents forget what was said in earlier messages, so be sure to fill in the context and your perspective when responding.
- **Never respond when you're angry.** Always allow some time to cool off before shooting off a response to an upsetting message. You often come up with different and better alternatives after thinking about what was said. If possible, iron out differences in person.

Personal Use

Remember that office computers are meant for work-related communication.

- **Don't use company computers for personal matters.** Unless your company specifically allows it, never use your employer's computers for personal messages, personal shopping, or entertainment.
- **Assume that all e-mail is monitored.** Employers legally have the right to monitor e-mail, and many do.

Other Smart E-Mail Practices

Depending on your messages and audience, the following tips promote effective electronic communication.

Design your messages to enhance readability, and double-check before sending.

- **Use design to improve the readability of longer messages.** When a message requires several screens, help the reader with headings, bulleted listings, side headings, and perhaps an introductory summary that describes what will follow. Although these techniques lengthen a message, they shorten reading time.
- **Consider cultural differences.** When using this borderless tool, be especially clear and precise in your language. Remember that figurative clichés (*pull up stakes, playing second fiddle*), sports references (*hit a home run, play by the rules*), and slang (*cool, stoked*) cause confusion abroad.
- **Double-check before hitting the Send button.** Have you included everything? Avoid the necessity of sending a second message, which makes you look careless. Use spell-check and reread for fluency before sending. It's also a good idea to check your incoming messages before sending, especially if several people are involved in a rapid-fire exchange. This helps avoid "passing"—sending out a message that might be altered depending on an incoming note.

Writing Information and Procedure E-Mail Messages and Memos

learning objective 4

Thus far in this chapter we've reviewed the writing process, analyzed the structure and format of e-mail messages and memos, and presented a number of techniques for using e-mail smartly and safely. Now we're going to apply those techniques to three categories of messages that you can expect to be writing as a business communicator: (1) information and procedure messages, (2) request and reply messages, and (3) confirmation messages.

Information and procedure messages generally flow downward from management to employees.

Let's focus first on techniques that will help you write information and procedure messages quickly and efficiently. These messages distribute standard information, describe procedures, and deliver instructions. They typically flow downward from management to employees and relate to the daily operation of an organization. In writing these messages, you have one primary function: conveying your idea so clearly that no further explanation (return message, telephone call, or personal visit) is necessary.

As you compose information and procedure messages, follow the writing process and organization plan outlined earlier. That includes an informative subject line, a direct opening, a body that explains, and an appropriate closing.

When writing messages that describe procedures, be particularly careful about clarity and readability. Figure 8.4 shows the first draft of a hard-copy memo

FIGURE 8.4 ***Memo That Describes a New Procedure***

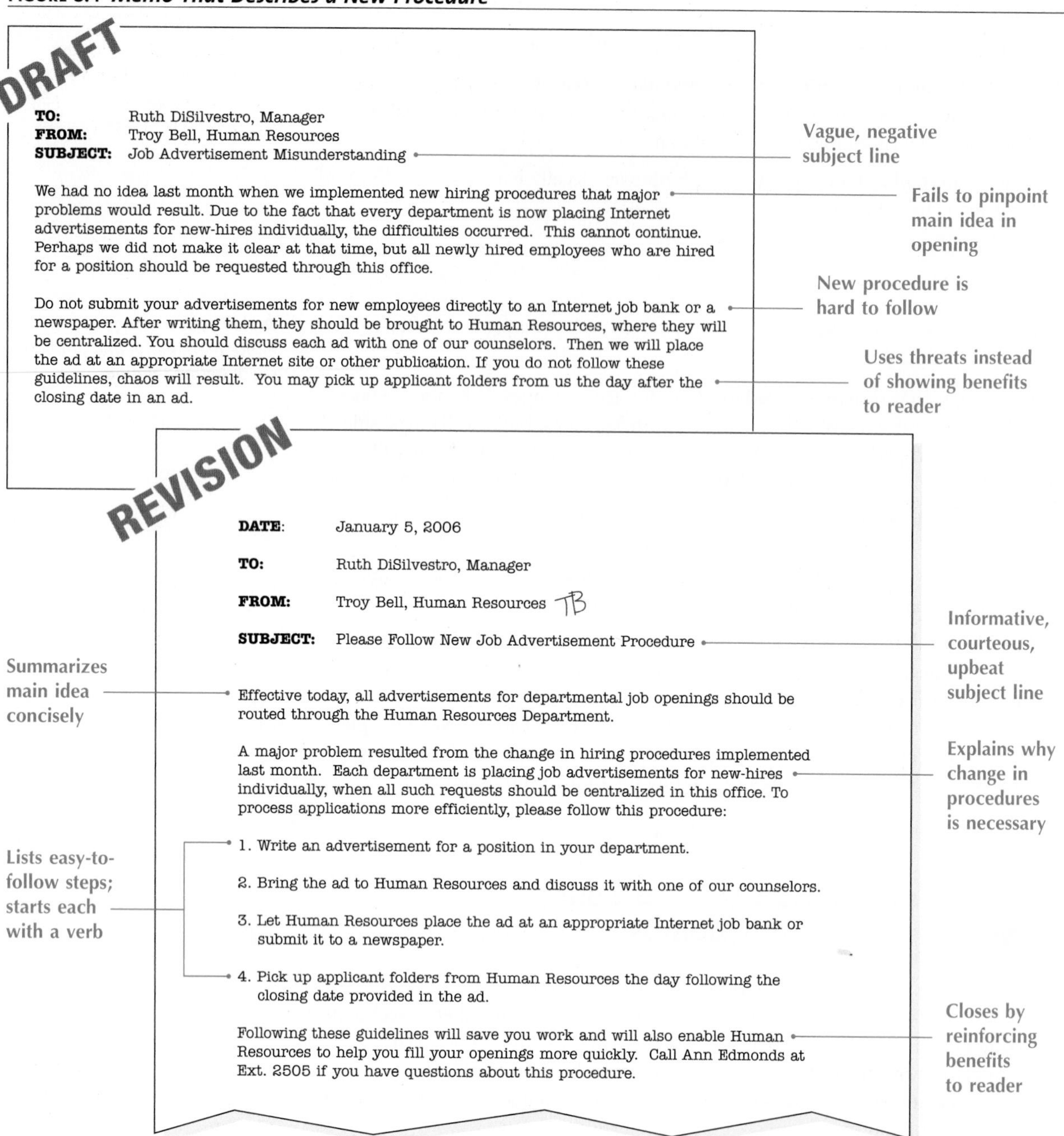
DRAFT

TO: Ruth DiSilvestro, Manager
FROM: Troy Bell, Human Resources
SUBJECT: Job Advertisement Misunderstanding

We had no idea last month when we implemented new hiring procedures that major problems would result. Due to the fact that every department is now placing Internet advertisements for new-hires individually, the difficulties occurred. This cannot continue. Perhaps we did not make it clear at that time, but all newly hired employees who are hired for a position should be requested through this office.

Do not submit your advertisements for new employees directly to an Internet job bank or a newspaper. After writing them, they should be brought to Human Resources, where they will be centralized. You should discuss each ad with one of our counselors. Then we will place the ad at an appropriate Internet site or other publication. If you do not follow these guidelines, chaos will result. You may pick up applicant folders from us the day after the closing date in an ad.

Vague, negative subject line
Fails to pinpoint main idea in opening
New procedure is hard to follow
Uses threats instead of showing benefits to reader

REVISION

DATE: January 5, 2006

TO: Ruth DiSilvestro, Manager

FROM: Troy Bell, Human Resources TB

SUBJECT: Please Follow New Job Advertisement Procedure

Effective today, all advertisements for departmental job openings should be routed through the Human Resources Department.

A major problem resulted from the change in hiring procedures implemented last month. Each department is placing job advertisements for new-hires individually, when all such requests should be centralized in this office. To process applications more efficiently, please follow this procedure:

1. Write an advertisement for a position in your department.
2. Bring the ad to Human Resources and discuss it with one of our counselors.
3. Let Human Resources place the ad at an appropriate Internet job bank or submit it to a newspaper.
4. Pick up applicant folders from Human Resources the day following the closing date provided in the ad.

Following these guidelines will save you work and will also enable Human Resources to help you fill your openings more quickly. Call Ann Edmonds at Ext. 2505 if you have questions about this procedure.

Informative, courteous, upbeat subject line
Summarizes main idea concisely
Explains why change in procedures is necessary
Lists easy-to-follow steps; starts each with a verb
Closes by reinforcing benefits to reader

written by Troy Bell. His memo was meant to announce a new procedure for employees to follow in advertising open positions. However, the tone was negative, the explanation of the problem rambled, and the new procedure was unclear. Notice, too, that Troy's first draft told readers what they *shouldn't* do *(Do not submit advertisements for new employees directly to an Internet job bank or a newspaper)*. It's more helpful to tell readers what they *should* do. Finally, Troy's memos closed with a threat instead of showing readers how this new procedure will help them.

In the revision Troy improved the tone considerably. The subject line contains a *please*, which is always pleasant to see even if one is giving an order. The subject line also includes a verb and specifies the purpose of the memo. Instead of expressing his ideas with negative words and threats, Troy revised his message to explain objectively and concisely what went wrong.

Troy realized that his original explanation of the new procedure was vague. Messages explaining procedures are most readable when the instructions are broken down into numbered steps listed chronologically. Each step should begin with an action verb in the command mode. Notice in Troy's revision in Figure 8.4 that numbered items begin with *Write, Bring, Let,* and *Pick up.* It's sometimes difficult to force all the steps in a procedure into this kind of command language. Troy struggled, but by trying out different wording, he finally found verbs that worked.

***Procedures and instructions are often written in numbered steps using command language* (Do this, don't do that).**

Why should you go to so much trouble to make lists and achieve parallelism? Because readers can comprehend what you have said much more quickly. Parallel language also makes you look professional and efficient.

In writing information and procedure messages, be careful of tone. Today's managers and team leaders seek employee participation and cooperation. These goals can't be achieved, though, if the writer sounds like a dictator or an autocrat. Avoid making accusations and fixing blame. Rather, explain changes, give reasons, and suggest benefits to the reader. Assume that employees want to contribute to the success of the organization and to their own achievement. Notice in the Figure 8.4 revision that Troy tells readers that they will save time and have their open positions filled more quickly if they follow the new procedures.

The writing of instructions and procedures is so important that we have developed a special bonus online supplement providing you with more examples and information. This online supplement extends your textbook with in-depth material including links to real businesses to show you examples of well-written procedures and instructions. To use this free supplement, go to **Xtra! (http://guffeyxtra.swlearning.com)** and locate *Supplement: How to Write Instructions.*

Special online supplement at Xtra! teaches you how to write instructions and provides hot links to real companies.

Writing Request and Reply E-Mail Messages and Memos

learning objective 5

Business organizations require information as their fuel. To make operations run smoothly, managers and employees request information from each other and then respond to those requests. Knowing how to write those requests and responses efficiently and effectively can save you time and make you look good.

Making Requests

If you are requesting routine information or action within an organization, the direct approach works best. Generally, this means asking for information or making the request without first providing elaborate explanations and justifications. Remember that readers are usually thinking, "Why me? Why am I receiving this?" Readers can understand the explanation better once they know what you are requesting.

Use the direct approach in routine requests for information or action, opening with the most important question, a polite command, or a brief introductory statement.

If you are seeking answers to questions, you have three options for opening the message: (1) ask the most important question first, followed by an explanation and then the other questions, (2) use a polite command (*Please answer the following questions regarding*), or (3) introduce the questions with a brief statement (*Your answers to the following questions will help us. . .*).

In the body of the memo, you can explain and justify your request or reply. When you must ask many questions, list them, being careful to phrase them similarly. Be courteous and friendly. In the closing include an end date (with a reason, if possible) to promote a quick response. For simple requests some writers encourage their readers to jot responses directly on the request memo.

FIGURE 8.5 ***E-Mail Message That Makes a Request***

1 Prewriting

Analyze: The purpose of this e-mail is to solicit feedback regarding a casual-dress policy.

Anticipate: The message is going to a subordinate who is busy but probably eager to be consulted in this policy matter.

Adapt: Use a direct approach beginning with the most important question. Strive for a positive, professional tone rather than an autocratic, authoritative tone.

2 Writing

Research: Collect secondary information about dress-down days in other organizations. Collect primary information by talking with company managers.

Organize: Begin with the main idea followed by a brief explanation and questions. Conclude with an end date and a reason.

Compose: Prepare the first draft remembering that the receiver is busy and appreciates brevity.

3 Revising

Revise: Rewrite questions to ensure that they are parallel and readable.

Proofread: Decide whether to hyphenate *casual-dress policy* and *dress-down days.* Be sure commas follow introductory clauses. Check question marks.

Evaluate: Does this memo encourage participatory management? Will the receiver be able to answer the questions and respond easily?

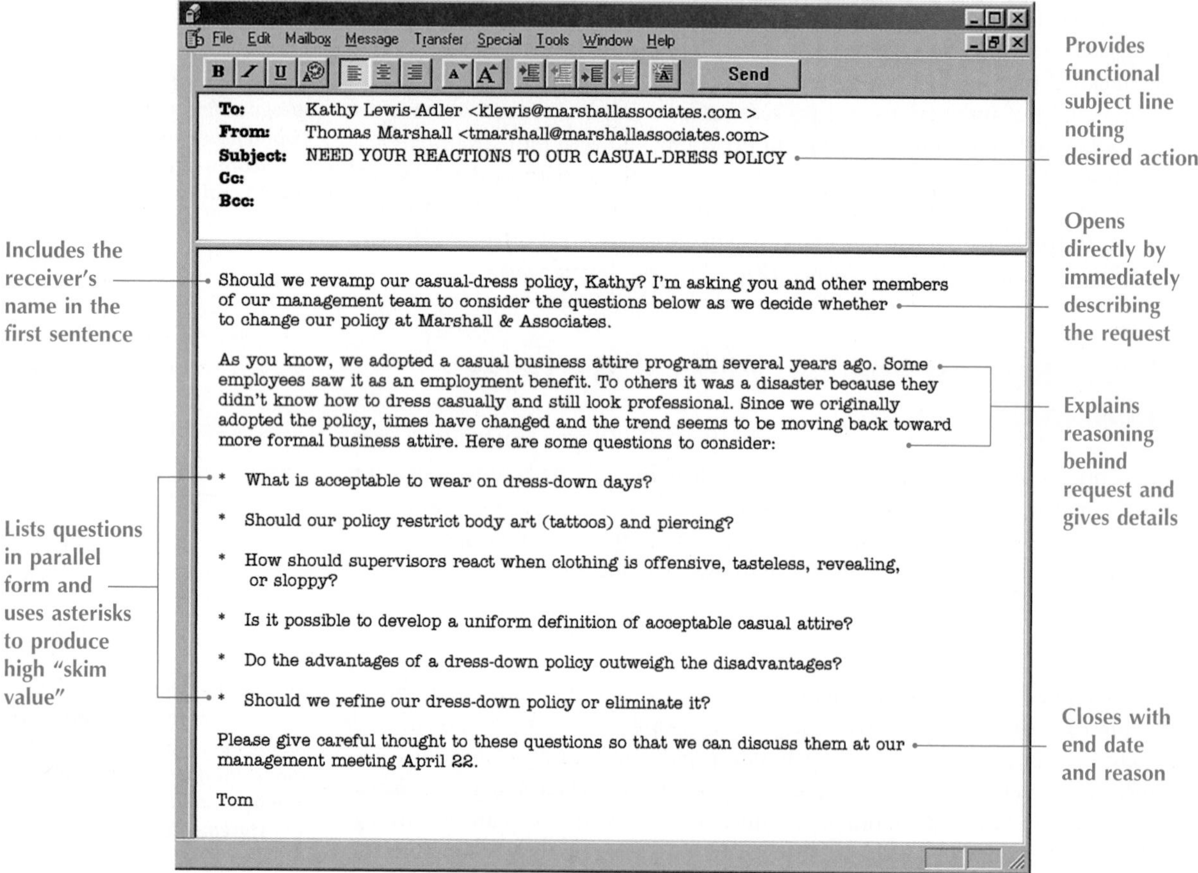

File Edit Mailbox Message Transfer Special Tools Window Help
Send
To: Kathy Lewis-Adler <klewis@marshallassociates.com >
From: Thomas Marshall <tmarshall@marshallassociates.com>
Subject: NEED YOUR REACTIONS TO OUR CASUAL-DRESS POLICY
Cc:
Bcc:
Should we revamp our casual-dress policy, Kathy? I'm asking you and other members of our management team to consider the questions below as we decide whether to change our policy at Marshall & Associates.
As you know, we adopted a casual business attire program several years ago. Some employees saw it as an employment benefit. To others it was a disaster because they didn't know how to dress casually and still look professional. Since we originally adopted the policy, times have changed and the trend seems to be moving back toward more formal business attire. Here are some questions to consider:
* What is acceptable to wear on dress-down days?
* Should our policy restrict body art (tattoos) and piercing?
* How should supervisors react when clothing is offensive, tasteless, revealing, or sloppy?
* Is it possible to develop a uniform definition of acceptable casual attire?
* Do the advantages of a dress-down policy outweigh the disadvantages?
* Should we refine our dress-down policy or eliminate it?
Please give careful thought to these questions so that we can discuss them at our management meeting April 22.
Tom
Provides functional subject line noting desired action
Includes the receiver's name in the first sentence
Opens directly by immediately describing the request
Explains reasoning behind request and gives details
Lists questions in parallel form and uses asterisks to produce high "skim value"
Closes with end date and reason

The e-mail message shown in Figure 8.5 requests information. It opens with a polite command followed by a brief explanation. Notice that the questions are highlighted with asterisks to provide the high "skim value" that is important in business messages. The reader can quickly see what is being asked. The message concludes with an end date and a reason. Providing an end date helps the reader know how to plan a response so that action is completed by the date given. Expressions such as *do it whenever you can* or *complete it as soon as possible* make little impression on procrastinators or very busy people. It's always wise to provide a specific date for completion. Dates can be entered on calendars to serve as reminders.

Replying to Requests

Much business correspondence reacts or responds to previous messages. When responding to an e-mail, memo, or other document, be sure to follow the 3-x-3 writing process. Analyze your purpose and audience, collect whatever information is necessary, and organize your thoughts. Make a brief outline of the points you plan to cover.

Overused and long-winded openers bore readers and waste their time.

Writers sometimes fall into bad habits in replying to messages. Here are some trite and long-winded openers that are best avoided:

In response to your message of the 15th . . . (*States the obvious.*)

Thank you for your memo of the 15th in which you . . . (*Suggests the writer can think of nothing more original.*)

I have before me your memo of the 15th in which you . . . (*Unnecessarily identifies the location of the previous message.*)

Pursuant to your request of the 15th . . . (*Sounds old-fashioned.*)

This is to inform you that . . . (*Delays getting to the point.*)

Instead of falling into the trap of using one of the preceding shopworn openings, start directly by responding to the writer's request. If you agree to the request, show your cheerful compliance immediately. Consider these good-news openers:

Direct opening statements can also be cheerful and empathic.

Yes, we will be glad to . . . (*Sends message of approval by opening with "Yes."*)

Here are answers to the questions you asked about . . . (*Sounds straightforward, businesslike, and professional.*)

You're right in seeking advice about . . . (*Opens with two words that every reader enjoys seeing and hearing.*)

We are happy to assist you in . . . (*Shows writer's helpful nature and goodwill.*)

As you requested, I am submitting . . . (*Gets right to the point.*)

After a direct and empathic opener, provide the information requested in a logical and coherent order. If you are answering a number of questions, arrange your answers in the order of the questions. In the hard-copy memo response shown in Figure 8.3, information describing dates, speakers, and topics was listed in columns with headings. Although listing format requires more space than paragraph format, listing vastly improves readability and comprehension.

In providing additional data, use familiar words, short sentences, short paragraphs, and active-voice verbs. When alternatives exist, make them clear. Consider using graphic highlighting techniques, as shown in Figure 8.3, for both the speakers' schedules and the three program choices offered further along in the message. Imagine how much more effort would be required to read and understand the memo without the speaker list or the bulleted choices.

If further action is required, be specific in spelling it out. What may be crystal clear to you (because you have been thinking about the problem) is not always immediately apparent to a reader with limited time and interest.

learning objective

6

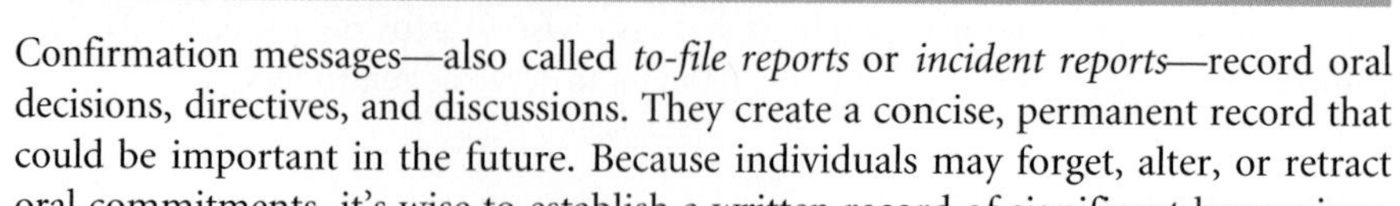

Writing Confirmation E-Mail Messages and Memos

Confirmation messages provide a permanent record of oral discussions, decisions, and directives.

Confirmation messages—also called *to-file reports* or *incident reports*—record oral decisions, directives, and discussions. They create a concise, permanent record that could be important in the future. Because individuals may forget, alter, or retract oral commitments, it's wise to establish a written record of significant happenings. Such records are unnecessary, of course, for minor events. The confirmation e-mail message shown in Figure 8.6 reviews the significant points of a sales agreement discussed in a telephone conversation. When you write to confirm an oral agreement, remember these tips:

- Include the names and titles of involved individuals.
- Itemize major issues or points concisely.
- Request feedback regarding unclear or inaccurate points.

Confirmation messages can save employees from being misunderstood or blamed unfairly.

Another type of confirmation message simply verifies the receipt of materials or a change of schedule. It is brief and often kept on file to explain your role in a project. For example, suppose you are coordinating an interdepartmental budget report. Carla Ramey from Human Resources calls to let you know that her portion of the report will be a week late. To confirm, you would send Carla the following one-sentence message: *This message verifies our telephone conversation of November 5 in which you said that your portion of the budget report will be submitted November 14 instead of November 7.* Be sure to print a copy if you are using e-mail. Notice that the tone is objective, not accusatory. However, if you are later asked why your project is running late (and you probably will be), you'll have a record of the explanation. In fact, you should probably send a copy to your superior so that he or she can intervene if necessary.

Business discussions may take place casually in hotel lobbies, in office hallways, or over coffee in the lunch room. When significant oral decisions and commitments are made, it's always a good idea to write a confirmation memo that creates a permanent record of the facts.

Photo: © Royalty-Free/CORBIS

Some critics complain that too many "cover-your-tail" messages are written, thus creating excessive and unnecessary paperwork.[17] However, legitimate messages that confirm and clarify events have saved many thoughtful workers from being misunderstood or blamed unfairly.

Sometimes taken lightly, e-mail messages and office memos, like other business documents, should be written carefully. Once they leave the author's hands, they are essentially published. They can't be retrieved, corrected, or revised. Review the following checklist for tips in writing memos that accomplish what you intend.

Checklist for Writing Routine E-Mail Messages and Memos

Subject Line

 **Summarize the central idea.** Express concisely what the message is about and how it relates to the reader.

 **Make the subject line *talk*.** Particularly if action is involved, include a verb.

FIGURE 8.6 ***Confirmation E-Mail***

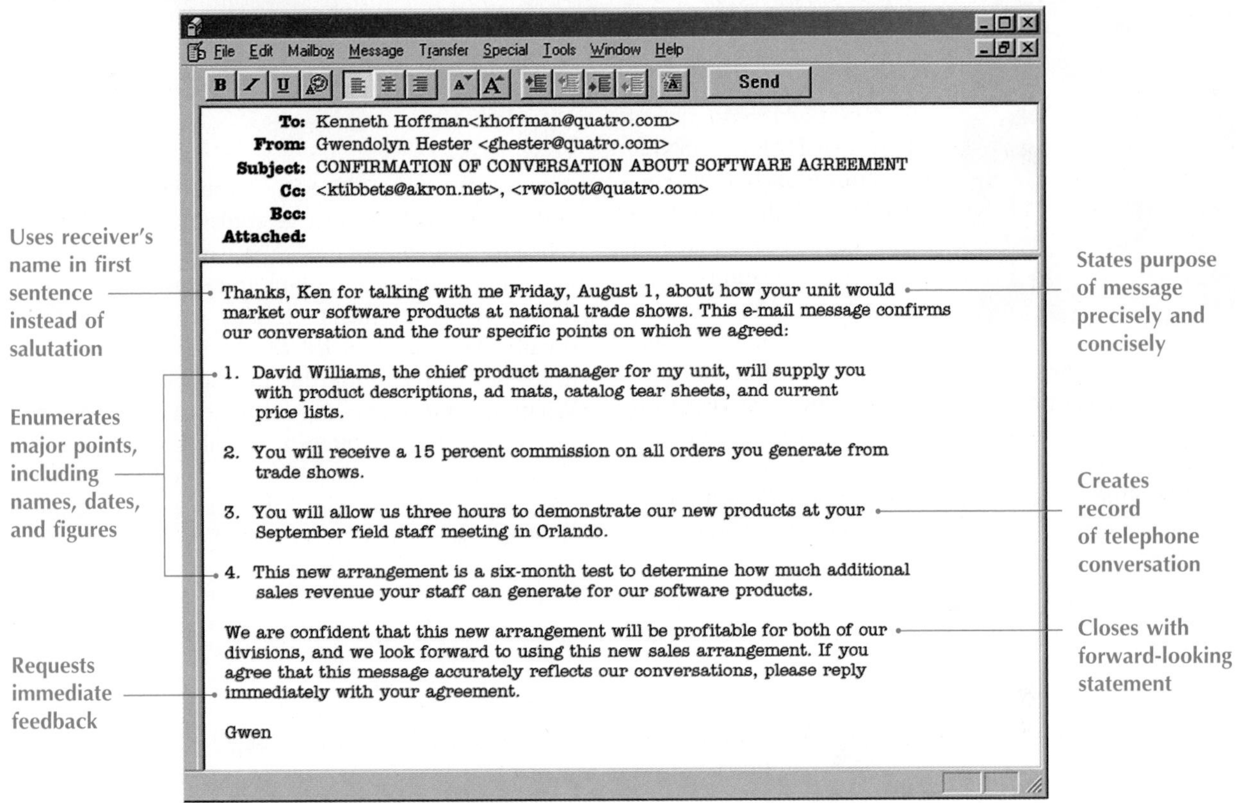

✓ **Avoid empty or dangerous words.** Don't write one-word subject lines such as *Help*, *Problem*, or *Free*.

Opening

✓ **State the purpose for writing.** Include the same information that's in the subject line, but expand it.

✓ **Highlight questions.** If you are requesting information, begin with the most important question, use a polite command (*Please answer the following questions about . . .*), or introduce your request courteously.

✓ **Supply information directly.** If responding to a request, give the reader the requested information immediately in the opening. Explain later.

Body

✓ **Explain details.** Arrange information logically. For complex topics use separate paragraphs developed coherently.

✓ **Enhance readability.** Use short sentences, short paragraphs, and parallel construction for similar ideas.

✓ **Supply graphic highlighting.** Provide bulleted and/or numbered lists, tables, or other graphic devices to improve readability and comprehension.

Process to Product

Applying Your Skills at the Walt Disney Company

CEO MICHAEL EISNER feels strongly about the harmful effects of thoughtless e-mails. He has been asked to make a graduation commencement address at the University of Southern California, and he's decided to talk about the powers and the dangers of e-mail. He's had his own troubles with e-mail, such as sending a confidential message to the wrong person because he mistyped the address. And he's witnessed the harmful effects of sarcasm within his organization. Now he needs more data and anecdotes for his speech.

Your Task

Assume you are working with a group of interns at Disney. Because you are college students, Michael Eisner wants to pick your brains in preparation for his commencement address. Working in teams, make a list of the ways you use e-mail both in the workplace and personally. Then make a list of "horror" stories you've heard or experienced in the use and misuse of e-mail. What can go wrong? Finally, make a list of smart e-mail practices that might prevent mistakes and misunderstandings. Use your imagination to add to the list in this chapter. Submit your lists in an e-mail memo to your instructor. ■

case study

✓ **Be cautious.** Remember that memos and e-mail messages often travel far beyond their intended audiences.

Closing

✓ **Request action.** If appropriate, state specifically what you want the reader to do. Include a deadline, with reasons, if possible.

✓ **Summarize the memo or provide a closing thought.** For long memos provide a summary of the important points. If neither an action request nor a summary is necessary, end with a closing thought.

✓ **Avoid cliché endings.** Use fresh remarks rather than overused expressions such as *If you have additional questions, please do not hesitate to call* or *Thank you for your cooperation.*

Summary of Learning Objectives

1 **Discuss how Guffey's 3-x-3 writing process helps you produce effective e-mail messages and memos.** Guffey's 3-x-3 writing process helps you analyze your purpose and audience before writing. E-mail and memos are appropriate for routine business messages, but they shouldn't be used if you need to convey enthusiasm, warmth, or some other emotion; if you need to supply a context; or if you need to smooth over a disagreement. The 3-x-3 process helps you decide how the reader will react and makes you consider how you can save the reader's time. Before writing routine e-mails and memos, collect information and organize your thoughts into a brief outline. After com-

posing the first draft, revise for clarity, proofread for correctness, and plan for feedback.

2 **Analyze the structure and formatting of e-mail messages and memos.** Routine e-mails and memos begin with a subject line that summarizes the central idea. The opening repeats that idea and amplifies it. The body explains and provides more information. The closing includes (1) action information, dates, and deadlines; (2) a summary of the memo; and/or (3) a closing thought. E-mail messages should be formatted with a meaningful subject line, an optional salutation, a single-spaced body that is typed with a combination of upper- and lowercase letters, and optional closing lines. Hard-copy memos are formatted similarly but without a salutation or closing. Writers place their initials next to their names on the *From* line.

3 **Describe smart e-mail practices, including getting started; content, tone, and correctness; netiquette; reading and replying to e-mail; personal use; and other practices.** Careful e-mail users compose offline, get the address right, avoid misleading subject lines, and apply the top-of-the-screen test. They write concisely and don't send anything they wouldn't want published. They don't use e-mail to avoid contact. They care about correctness, resist humor, never send spam, use identifying labels when appropriate, and use attachments sparingly. In reading and responding, they employ a number of efficient practices such as scanning all incoming messages, limiting printing, and revising the subject line as the message thread changes. They don't use company computers for personal use unless specifically allowed to do so, and they realize that e-mail may be monitored. They strive to improve readability through design, they consider cultural differences, and they double-check before hitting the *Send* button.

4 **Write information and procedure e-mail messages and memos.** Messages delivering information or outlining procedures follow the direct plan with the main idea stated immediately. Ideas must be explained so clearly that no further explanation is necessary. The tone of the memo or e-mail message should be positive and encourage cooperation. Procedures should enumerate steps in command language (*Do this, don't do that*) and should be written in parallel form.

5 **Write request and reply e-mail messages and memos.** Messages requesting action or information open with a specific request, followed by details. Messages that reply to requests open with information the reader most wants to learn. The body contains details, and the closing may summarize the important points or look forward to a subsequent event or action.

6 **Write confirmation e-mail messages and memos.** Sometimes called "to-file reports" or "incident reports," confirmation messages create a permanent record of oral decisions, directives, and discussions. They should include the names and titles of involved individuals, the major issues discussed, and a request for approval by the receiver.

chapter review

1. List five questions you should ask yourself before writing an e-mail or memo. (Obj. 1)
2. Briefly describe the standard structure of e-mail messages and memos. (Obj. 2)
3. What can writers do to improve the readability and comprehension of e-mails and memos? (Obj. 2)
4. What are three ways in which a routine e-mail or memo may be closed? (Obj. 2)
5. How are the structure and formatting of e-mail messages and memos similar and different? (Obj. 2)
6. What are some of the dangers of e-mail in the workplace? (Obj. 3)
7. Suggest at least ten pointers that you could give to a first-time e-mail user. (Obj. 3)
8. Name at least five rules of e-mail etiquette that show respect for others. (Obj. 3)
9. What are three possibilities in handling the salutation for an e-mail message? (Obj. 3)
10. What tone should managers avoid in writing procedure or information e-mail messages and memos? (Obj. 4)
11. Why should writers of information e-mail messages and memos strive to express ideas positively instead of negatively? (Obj. 4)
12. Should a request e-mail message or memo open immediately with the request or with an explanation? Why? (Obj. 5)
13. What's wrong with a message opener such as *This is to inform you that . . .*? (Obj. 5)
14. What is a confirmation e-mail message or memo? What other names could be given? (Obj. 6)
15. What three elements should most confirmation e-mail messages and memos include? (Obj. 6)

critical thinking

1. How can the writer of a business e-mail message or memo develop a conversational tone and still be professional? Why do e-mail writers sometimes forget to be professional? (Objs. 1–3)
2. What factors would help you decide whether to write a memo, send an e-mail, make a telephone call, leave a voice mail message, or deliver a message in person? (Objs. 1 and 2)
3. Why are lawyers and technology experts warning companies to store, organize, and manage computer data, including e-mail, with sharper diligence? (Obj. 3)
4. Discuss the ramifications of the following statement: Once a memo or any other document leaves your hands, you have essentially published it. (Objs. 2–6)
5. **Ethical Issue:** Should employers have the right to monitor all e-mail messages of employees? Present the employer's position and then the employees' position.

THREE GREAT RESOURCES FOR YOU!

1. ***Guffey Student Web Site***
http://guffey.swlearning.com
Your companion Web site offers chapter review quizzes, WebThink activities, updated chapter URLs, and many additional resources.

2. ***Guffey XTRA!***
http://guffeyxtra.swlearning.com
This online study assistant includes Your Personal Language Trainer, Speak Right!, Spell Right!, bonus online chapters, Documents for Analysis, PowerPoint slides, and much more.

3. ***Student Study Guide***
Self-checked workbook activities and applications review chapter concepts and develop career skills.

activities

8.1 Document for Analysis: Information E-Mail (Objs. 1–4)

Your Task. Analyze the following e-mail message. It suffers from many writing faults. List its specific weaknesses. If your instructor directs, revise it.

To: Ceresa Rothery <crothery@rancho.com>
From: Paul Rouse <prouse@rancho.com>
Subject: REPORT
Cc:

Ceresa:

I went to the Workplace Issues conference on November 3, as you suggested. The topic was how to prevent workplace violence, and I found it very fascinating. Although we have been fortunate to avoid serious incidents at our company, it's better to be safe than sorry. Since I was the representative from our company and you asked for a report, here it is. Susan Sloan was the presenter, and she made suggestions in three categories, which I will summarize here.

Ms. Sloan cautioned organizations to prescreen job applicants. As a matter of fact, wise companies do not offer employment until after a candidate's background has been checked. Just the mention of a background check is enough to make some candidates withdraw. These candidates, of course, are the ones with something to hide.

A second suggestion was that companies should prepare a good employee handbook that outlines what employees should do when they suspect potential workplace violence. This handbook should include a way for informers to be anonymous.

A third recommendation had to do with recognizing red-flag behavior. This involves having companies train managers to recognize signs of potential workplace violence. What are some of the red flags? One sign is an increasing number of arguments (most of them petty) with coworkers. Another sign is extreme changes in behavior or statements indicating depression over family or financial problems. Another sign is bullying or harassing behavior. Bringing a firearm to work or displaying an extreme fascination with firearms is another sign.

By the way, the next Workplace Issues conference is in January, and the topic is the employee e-mail monitoring.

I think that the best recommendation is prescreening job candidates. This is because it is most feasible. If you want me to do more research on prescreening techniques, do not hesitate to let me know. Let me know by November 18 if you want me to make a report at our management meeting, which is scheduled for December 3.

Paul

8.2 Document for Analysis: Request Memo (Objs. 1–5)

Your Task. Analyze the following memo. List its weaknesses. If your instructor directs, revise it.

DATE: Current
TO: All Employees
FROM: Kim Albano, Human Resources
SUBJECT: NEW PLAN

In the past we've offered all employees 11 holidays (starting with New Year's Day in January and proceeding through Christmas Day the following December). Other companies offer similar holiday schedules.

In addition, we've given all employees one floating holiday. As you know, we've determined that day by a companywide vote. As a result, all employees had the same day off. Now, however, management is considering a new plan that we feel would be better. This new plan involves a floating holiday that each individual employee may decide for herself or himself. We've given it considerable thought and decided that such a plan could definitely work. We would allow each employee to choose a day that he or she wants. Of course, we would have to issue certain restrictions. Selections would have to be subject to our staffing needs within individual departments. For example, if everyone wanted the same day, we could not allow everyone to take it. In that case, we would allow the employee with the most seniority to have the day off.

Before we institute the new plan, though, we wanted to see what employees thought about this. Is it better to continue our current companywide uniform floating holiday? Or should we try an individual floating holiday? Please let us know what you think as soon as possible.

8.3 Document for Analysis: Confirmation E-Mail (Objs. 1–6)

Your Task. Analyze the following e-mail message. List its weaknesses. If your instructor directs, revise it.

To: David Ricci <dricci@commercial.com>
From: Jillian Ann Brody <JillianAnnBrody@aol.com>
Subject: OUR RECENT TALK
Cc:

Dear Mr. Ricci:

It was good to talk to you on the telephone yesterday (December 2) after exchanging letters with you and after reading so much about Bermuda. I was very interested in learning about the commercials you want me to write. As I understand it, Mr. Ricci, you want a total of 240 one-minute radio commercials. These commercials are intended to rejuvenate the slumping tourist industry in Bermuda. You said that these commercials would be broadcast from March 30 through June 30. You said these commercials would be played on three radio stations. These stations are in five major cities on the East Coast. The commercials would be aimed at morning and evening drive time, for drivers who are listening to their radios, and the campaign would be called "Radio Bermuda."

I am sure I can do as you suggested in reminding listeners that Bermuda is less than two hours away. You expect me to bring to these commercials the color and character of the island. You want me to highlight the attractions and the civility of Bermuda, at least as much as can be done in one-minute radio commercials. In my notes I wrote that you also mentioned that I should include references to tree frogs and royal palm trees. Another item you suggested that I include in some of the commercials was special Bermuda food, such as delicacies like shark on toast, conch fritters, and mussel stew.

I wanted to be sure to write these points down so that we both agreed on what we said in our telephone conversation. I am eager to begin working on these commercials immediately, but I would feel better if you looked over these points to see if I have it right. I look forward to working with you.

Jillian Ann Brody

8.4 Openers for E-Mail Messages and Memos (Objs. 1–3)

Your Task. Revise the following e-mail and memo openers so that they are more direct.

a. I enjoyed talking with you at our last committee meeting. I told you that I didn't believe in electronic monitoring of employees, but just yesterday we discovered that one of our employees printed out several pages from a porn site and forgot to retrieve them from the printer. Now we realize that we need to crack down. You said you were pleased with your organization's written Internet policy and that you would be willing to share it. I would be very happy if you would send me a copy of that policy.[18]

b. I appreciate your asking me for my ideas on selling soft drinks in schools. Some local school officials and consumer groups say that guidelines established by the Coca-Cola Company and other bottlers do not go far enough to combat childhood obesity and commercialism in schools. I've worked out six suggestions for school boards to consider in regard to practices for all current and future deals regarding vending machine sales. My suggestions are described below.

c. I have before me your memo of the 16th in which you request permission to attend the Web Site Design Seminar sponsored by Presentation Planners. As I understand it, this is a two-day seminar scheduled for February 25 and 26. Your reasons for attending were well stated and convincing. You have my permission to attend.

d. As you are aware, the document specialists in our department have been unhappy about their chairs and their inability to adjust the back height. The chairs are uncomfortable and cause back fatigue. As a result, I looked into the possibility of purchasing new adjustable chairs that I think will be just right for these employees. New chairs have been ordered for all these employees. The new chairs should be arriving in about three weeks.

8.5 Subject Lines (Objs. 1–3)

Your Task. Write effective subject lines for the messages represented by the openings in Activity 8.4.

8.6 Graphic Highlighting Techniques (Objs. 1 and 3)

Your Task. Revise the following hard-to-read paragraphs. Include an introductory statement or a title before presenting the data in bulleted or numbered lists.

a. The personal computer has become indispensable for many workers. A recent survey revealed interesting information about how the computer is used. Of the 72.3 million workers who use a computer on the job, 72 percent said that they used the computer to connect to the Internet or to their e-mail. At the lowest end of the scale were 32 percent who used it for graphics and design, while 15 percent reported using computers for programming. A fairly large number (67 percent) said that they used the computer for word processing. Close to that number were 62 percent who worked with spreadsheets or databases. Slightly more than half (53 percent) said they used the computer in calendar-related or scheduling activities.

b. Our employee leasing program has proven to be an efficient management tool for business owners because we take care of everything. Our program will handle your payroll preparation. Moreover, benefits for employees are covered. We also know what a chore calculating workers' compensation premiums can be, so we do that for you. And we make all the necessary state and federal reports that are required today.

c. We are concerned about your safety in using our automated teller machines (ATMs) at night, so we think you should consider the following tips. Users of ATMs are encouraged to look around—especially at night—before using the service. If you notice anything suspicious, the use of another ATM is recommended. Or you could come back later. Another suggestion that we give our customers involves counting your cash. Be sure that the cash you receive is put away quickly. Don't count it as soon as you get it. It's better to check it in the safety of your car or at home. Also, why not take a friend with you if you must use an ATM at night? We also suggest that you park in a well-lighted area as close to the actual location of the ATM as possible.

8.7 Information Memo or E-Mail: Alone in the Office at Night (Obj. 4)

E-MAIL WEB

After a recent frightening experience, your boss, Beth Meggison, realized that she must draft a memo about office security. Here's why she's concerned. A senior associate, Lisa Taylor, was working overtime cleaning up overdue reports. At about 9 p.m. she heard the office door open, but the intruder quickly left when he found that someone was in the office. Your boss hurriedly put together the following memo to be distributed to office managers in five branch offices.

Rich chapter resources are available on the Web sites. 

But she was on her way out of town, and she asked you to revise her draft and have it ready for her approval when she returns. One other thing—she wondered whether you would do some research (InfoTrac? Google?) to find other helpful suggestions. Your boss trusts you to totally revise, if necessary.

Your Task. Conduct an InfoTrac or Google search to look for reasonable office security suggestions. Then improve the memo's organization, clarity, conciseness, correctness, and readability. Don't be afraid to do a total overhaul! Bulleted points are a must, and check the correctness, too. Your boss is no Ms. Grammar! Be sure to add an appropriate closing.

DATE: Current
TO: Branch Managers
FROM: Beth Meggison, Vice President
SUBJECT: TERRIFYING EXPERIENCE!

Office security is a topic we have not talked enough about. I was totally terrified recently when a senior associate, who was working late, told me she heard the front door of the branch office open and she thought she heard a person enter. When she called out, the person apparently left. This frightening experience reminded me there are several things that each branch can do to improve it's office security. The following are a few simple things, but we will talk more about this at our next quarterly meeting (June 8?). Please come with additional ideas.

If an office worker is here early or late, then it is your responsibility to talk with them about before and after hours security. When someone comes in early it is not smart to open the doors until most of the rest of the staff arrive. Needless to say, employees working overtime should make sure the door is locked and they should not open there office doors after hours to people they don't know, especially if you are in the office alone. Dark offices are especially attractive to thieves with valuable equipment.

Many branches are turning off lights at points of entry and parking areas to conserve energy. Consider changing this policy or installing lights connected to motion detectors, which is an inexpensive (and easy!) way to discourage burglars and intruders. I also think that "cash-free" decals are a good idea because they make thieves realize that not much is in this office to take. These signs may discourage breaking and entering. On the topic of lighting, we want to be sure that doors and windows that are secluded and not visible to neighbors or passersby is illuminated.

We should also beware of displaying any valuable equipment or other things. When people walk by, they should not be able to look in and see expensive equipment. Notebook computers and small portable equipment is particularly vulnerable at night. It should be locked up. In spite of the fact that most of our branches are guarded by FirstAlert, I'm not sure all branches are displaying the decals prominently—especially on windows and doors. We want people to know that our premises are electronically protected.

8.8 Information E-Mail or Memo: Driving Less and Breathing Easier (Obj. 4)

E-MAIL

The air in your city has been getting progressively worse over the years. Your company, Mercer Enterprises, just received another announcement from the Air Quality Management District (AQMD). To reduce air pollution, the AQMD is requiring all big employers to offer incentives that encourage employees to participate in the AQMD's Trip Reduction Plan. If your company can't get a significant number of employees to share rides, take the bus, or ride a bicycle to work, it faces huge fines.

After studying what other large companies were doing, Mercer developed a number of incentives to entice employees to leave their cars at home. One incentive offers employees who maintain a 75 percent rate of participation in the ride-share program for a period of six months one full workday off with pay. This incentive begins May 1. Other incentives include preferential parking near building entrances. These special parking places are for car pools only, and a parking pass is required. Another incentive involves bus passes. Employees who use public transportation will receive a subsidy of $25 per month. Employees will also get a free round-trip transit pass for the first month. This pass applies only to workplace commuting, of course.

Employees receiving this memo might want more information about the program. They may also want to sign up for the incentives mentioned here. If so, they should contact Jennifer O'Toole (Jennifer.Otoole@mercer.com) before June 1.

Another incentive is the provision of a subsidy for van pools. The company will help obtain a van and will provide a $150 per month subsidy to the van pool. What's even more terrific is that the van-pool driver will have unlimited personal use of the vehicle off company time. A final subsidy involves bicycles. Employees who bicycle to work will receive $25 per month as a subsidy. And Mercer Enterprises will provide bicycle racks, locks, and chains.

Your Task. As employee transportation coordinator for your company, send an e-mail or memo to all employees describing the incentives offered by Mercer to comply with the Air Quality Management District's Trip Reduction Plan. You can improve readability of your message by using graphic highlighting for the incentives.

8.9 Information E-Mail or Memo: What I Do on the Job (Obj. 4)

E-MAIL

Some employees have remarked to the boss that they are working more than other employees. Your boss has decided to study the matter by collecting information from everyone.

Your Task. He asks you to write an e-mail or memo describing your current duties and the skills required for your position. If some jobs are found to be overly demanding, your boss may redistribute job tasks or hire additional employees. Based on your own work or personal experience, write a well-organized message describing your duties, the time you spend on each task, and the skills needed for what you do. Provide enough details to make a clear record of your job. Use actual names and describe actual tasks. Report to the head of the organization. The organization could be a campus club or committee on which you serve. Don't make your message a list of complaints. Just describe what you do in an objective tone. By the way, your boss appreciates brevity. Keep your message under one page.

8.10 Information E-Mail or Memo: Party Time (Obj. 4)

E-MAIL

Staff members in your office were disappointed that no holiday party was given last year. They don't care what kind of party it is, but they do want some kind of celebration this year.

Your Task. You have been asked to draft a message to the office staff about the upcoming December holiday party. Decide what kind of party you would like. Include information about where the party will be held, when it is, what the cost will be, what kind of food will be served, whether guests are allowed, and with whom to make reservations.

8.11 Information E-Mail or Memo: Planning for Important Milestone (Obj. 4)

E-MAIL | TEAM

Your company hired a writing consultant to help employees improve their communication skills.

Your Task. The following message was assigned as an exercise to train your team in recognizing good and bad writing. In small groups discuss its weaknesses and then compose, either individually or as a team, an improved version.

DATE: Current
TO: All Employees
FROM: Margaret Tilly, Coordinator, Employee Resources
SUBJECT: An Important Milestone in Your Life

We know that retirement is an important milestone in anyone's life, and we are aware that many employees do not have sufficient information that relates to the prospect of their retirement. Many employees who are approaching retirement age have come to this office wanting to talk about health, financial needs, family responsibilities, and income from outside sources and how these all relate to their retirement. It would be much easier for us to answer all these questions at once, and that is what we will try to do.

We would like to answer your questions at a series of retirement planning sessions in the company cafeteria. The first meeting is November 17. We will start at 4 p.m., which means that the company is giving you one hour of released time to attend this important session. We will meet from 4 to 6 p.m. when we will stop for dinner. We will begin again at 7 p.m. and finish at 8 p.m.

We have arranged for three speakers. They are: our company benefits supervisor, a financial planner, and a psychologist who treats retirees who have mental problems. The three sessions are planned for: November 17, November 30, and December 7.

8.12 Procedure E-Mail or Memo: Rules for Wireless Phone Use in Sales Reps' Cars (Obj. 4)

E-MAIL | INFOTRAC | TEAM | WEB

As one of the managers of LaReve, a hair care and skin products company, you are alarmed at a newspaper article you just saw. A stockbroker for Smith Barney was making cold calls on his personal phone while driving. His car hit and killed a motorcyclist. The brokerage firm was sued and accused of contributing to an accident by encouraging employees to use cell phones while driving. To avoid the risk of paying huge damages awarded by an emotional jury, the brokerage firm offered the victim's family a $500,000 settlement.

You begin to worry, knowing that your company has provided its 75 sales representatives with wireless phones to help them keep in touch with the home base while they are in the field. At the next management meeting, other members agreed that you should draft a message detailing some wireless phone safety rules for your sales reps. On the Web you learned that anyone with a wireless phone should get to know its features, including speed dial, automatic memory, and redial. Another suggestion involved using a hands-free device. Management members decided to purchase these for every sales rep and have the devices available within one month. In positioning the wireless phone in a car, it should be within easy reach. It should be where you can grab it without removing your eyes from the road. If you get an incoming call at an inconvenient time, your voice mail should be allowed to pick up the call. You should never talk, of course, during hazardous driving conditions, such as rain, sleet, snow, and ice.

Taking notes or looking up phone numbers is dangerous when driving. You want to warn sales reps not to get into dangerous situations by reading (such as an address book) or writing (such as taking notes) while driving.

The more you think about it, the more you think that sales reps should not use their wireless phones while the car is moving. They really should pull over. But you know that would be hard to enforce.

Your Task. Individually or in teams write a memo or e-mail to LaReve sales reps outlining company suggestions (or should they be rules?) for safe wireless phone use in cars. You may wish to check the Web or InfoTrac for additional safety ideas. Try to suggest receiver benefits in this message. How is safety beneficial to the reader? The message is from you acting as operations manager.

8.13 Procedure E-Mail or Memo: Parking Guidelines With a Smile (Obj. 4)

E-MAIL

As Adelle Justice, director of Human Resources, you must remind both day-shift and swing-shift employees of the company's parking guidelines. Day-shift employees must park in Lots A and B in their assigned spaces. If they have not registered their cars and received their white stickers, the cars will be ticketed.

Day-shift employees are forbidden to park at the curb. Swing-shift employees may park at the curb before 3:30 p.m. Moreover, after 3:30 p.m., swing-shift employees may park in any empty space—except those marked Tandem, Handicapped, Van Pool, Car Pool, or Management. Day-shift employees may loan their spaces to other employees if they know they will not be using them.

One serious problem is lack of registration (as evidenced by white stickers). Registration is done by Employee Relations. Any car without a sticker will be ticketed. To encourage registration, Employee Relations will be in the cafeteria May 12 and 13 from 11:30 a.m. to 1:30 p.m. and from 3 p.m. to 5 p.m. to take applications and issue white parking stickers.

Your Task. Write a procedure e-mail or memo to employees that reviews the parking guidelines and encourages them to get their cars registered. Use itemization techniques, and strive for a tone that fosters a sense of cooperation rather than resentment.

8.14 Procedure E-Mail or Memo: Countdown to Performance Appraisal Deadline (Obj. 4)

E-MAIL WEB

It's time to remind all supervisory personnel that they must complete employee performance appraisals by April 15. Your boss, James Robinson, director, Human Resources, asks you to draft a procedure memo or e-mail announcing the deadline. In talking with Jim, you learn that he wants you to summarize some of the main steps in writing these appraisals. Jim says that the appraisals are really important this year because of changes in work and jobs. Many offices are installing new technologies, and some offices are undergoing reorganization. It's been a hectic year.

Jim also mentions that some supervisors will want to attend a training workshop on February 20 where they can update their skills. Supervisors who want to reserve a space at the training workshop should contact Lynn Jeffers at *ljeffers@rainco.com.* When you ask him what procedures you should include in the memo, he tells you to consult the employee handbook and pick out the most important steps.

In the handbook you find suggestions that say each employee should have a performance plan with three or four main objectives. In the appraisal the supervisor should mention three strengths the employee has, as well as three areas for improvement. One interesting comment in the handbook indicated that improvements should focus on skills, such as time management, rather than on things like being late frequently. Supervisors are supposed to use a scale of 1 to 5 to assess employees: 1 = consistently exceeds requirements; 5 = does not meet requirements at all. You think to yourself that this scale is screwy; it's certainly not like grades in school. But you can't change the scale. Finally, supervisors should meet with employees to discuss the appraisal. The completed appraisal should be sent to your office.

Your Task. Draft a memo or e-mail from James Robinson, Director, Human Resources, to all department heads, managers, and supervisors. Announce the April 15 deadline for performance appraisals. List five or six steps to be taken by supervisors in completing performance appraisals. If you need more information about writing performance appraisals, search that term on the Web. You'll find many sites with helpful advice.

8.15 Procedure Memo: Managing Your Time More Wisely (Obj. 4)

INFOTRAC

You work with a group of engineers who are constantly putting in 60- and 70-hour workweeks. The vice president worries that major burnout will occur. Personally, he believes that some of the engineers simply manage their time poorly. He asks you to look into the topic of time management and put together a list of procedures that might help these professionals use their time more wisely. Your suggestions may become the basis for an in-service training program.

Your Task. Using InfoTrac, conduct a keyword search for articles about time management. Read several articles. Summarize five or six procedures that might be helpful to employees. Write a memo to Thomas Sawicky, vice president, with your suggestions.

8.16 Request E-Mail: Learning About Team Retreats (Obj. 5)

E-MAIL

Tiptoeing gingerly across a wobbling jerrybuilt bridge of slender planks stretched between two boxes, the chief financial officer of Wells Fargo completed his task. Cheers greeted Howard Atkins as he reached the other side with a final lunge. His team of senior financial executives applauded their leader who made it across the bridge without falling off.

Atkins had pulled together a group of 73 financial executives, risk managers, accountants, and group presidents for team-building exercises on the sun-drenched lawns of a luxury hotel in Sonoma, California. The three-day retreat also provided conventional business meetings with reports and presentations. Atkins described the attendees as "very high-powered, very capable, very technically skilled, very competitive people." Yet, he was striving for an even higher level of performance. "They are very individualistic in their approach to their work," he said. "What I have been trying to do is get them to see the power of acting more like a team." And by the end of the day, he was clearly pleased with what he saw. He credits double-digit gains in Wells Fargo income and earnings in large part to the bank's people programs. "Success is more often than not a function of execution, and execution is really about people, so we invest pretty heavily in our people."

For his company's team-building exercises, Atkins chose low-stress challenges such as balancing on planks, building tents blindfolded, and stepping through complex webs of ropes. But other companies use whitewater rafting, rock walls, treetop rope bridges, and even fire pits as metaphors for the business world.

Your boss at BancFirst saw the news about Wells Fargo and is intrigued. He is understandably dubious about the value of team building that could result from a retreat. Yet, he is interested because he believes that the widespread use of electronic technology is reducing personal contact. He asks you to have the Human Resources Department investigate.[19]

Your Task. As assistant to the president, draft an e-mail to Charlotte Evers, manager, Human Resources. Ask her to investigate the possibility of a retreat for BancFirst. Your message should include many questions for her to answer. Include an end date and a reason.

8.17 Request Memo or E-Mail: Smokers vs. Nonsmokers (Obj. 5)

CRITICAL THINKING | E-MAIL

The city of Milwaukee has mandated that employers "shall adopt, implement, and maintain a written smoking policy which shall contain a prohibition against smoking in restrooms and infirmaries." Employers must also "maintain a nonsmoking area of not less than two thirds of the seating capacity in cafeterias, lunchrooms, and employee lounges, and make efforts to work out disputes between smokers and nonsmokers."

Your Task. As Lindsay English, director of Human Resources, write an e-mail or memo to all department managers of General Wheat, a large foods company. Announce the new restriction, and tell the managers that you want them to set up departmental committees to mediate any smoking conflicts before the complaints surface. Explain why this is a good policy.

8.18 Reply Memo or E-Mail: Enforcing Smoking Ban (Obj. 5)

CRITICAL THINKING | E-MAIL

As Bruni Comenic, manager of Accounting Services for General Wheat, you want to respond to Ms. English's memo in the preceding activity. You could have called Ms. English, but you prefer to have a permanent record of this message. You are having difficulty enforcing the smoking ban in restrooms. Only one men's room serves your floor, and 9 of your 27 male employees are smokers. You have already received complaints, and you see no way to enforce the ban in the restrooms. You have also noticed that smokers are taking longer breaks than other employees. Smokers complain that they need more time because they must walk to an outside area. Smokers are especially unhappy when the weather is cold, rainy, or snowy. Moreover, smokers huddle near the building entrances, thus creating a negative impression for customers and visitors. Your committee members can find no solutions; in fact, they have become polarized in their meetings to date. You need help from a higher authority.

Your Task. Write an e-mail or memo to Ms. English appealing for solutions. Perhaps she should visit your department.

8.19 Reply Memo or E-Mail: Office Romances Off Limits? (Obj. 5)

CRITICAL THINKING | E-MAIL
INFOTRAC | TEAM

Where can you find the hottest singles scene today? Some would say in your workplace. Because people are working long hours and have little time for outside contacts, relationships often develop at work. Estimates suggest that one third to one half of all romances start at work. Your boss is concerned about possible problems resulting from relationships at work. What happens if a relationship between a superior and subordinate results in perceived favoritism? What happens if a relationship results in a nasty breakup? Your boss would like to simply ban all relationships among employees. But that's not likely to work. He asks you, his assistant, to learn what guidelines could be established regarding office romances.

Your Task. Using InfoTrac, read Timothy Bland's "Romance in the Workplace: Good Thing or Bad?" (Article No. A66460590). From this article select four or five suggestions that you could make to your boss in regard to protecting an employer. Why is it necessary for a company to protect itself? Discuss your findings and reactions with your team. Individually or as a group, submit your findings and reactions in a well-organized, easy-to-read e-mail or memo to your boss (your instructor). You may list main points from the article, but use your own words to write the message.

8.20 Reply Memo or E-Mail: One Sick Day Too Many (Obj. 5)

CRITICAL THINKING | E-MAIL | TEAM

As director of Human Resources at a midsized insurance company, you received an inquiry from Suzette Chase, who is supervisor of Legal Support. It seems that one of Suzette's veteran employees recently implemented a four-day workweek for herself. On the fifth morning, the employee calls in with some crisis or sickness that makes it impossible for her to get to work. Suzette asks for your advice in how to handle this situation.

In the past you've told supervisors to keep a written record (a log) of each absence. This record should include the financial and productive impact of the absence. It should include a space where the employee can include her comments and signature. You've found that a written document always increases the significance of the event. You've also told supervisors that they must be objective and professional. It's difficult, but they should not personalize the situation.

Occasionally, of course, an absence is legitimate. Supervisors must know what is unavoidable and what is a lame excuse. In other words, they must know how to separate reasons from excuses. Another thing to consider is how the employee reacts when approached. Is her attitude sincere, or does she automatically become defensive?

You also tell supervisors that "if they talk the talk, they must walk the walk." In other words, they must follow the same policies that are enforced. The best plan, of course, is to clearly define what is and is not acceptable attendance policy and make sure every new hire is informed.

Your Task. In teams discuss what advice to give to Suzette Chase regarding her habitually absent worker. Why is a log important? What other suggestions can you make? How should you conclude this message? Individually or in teams, write a well-organized reply memo or e-mail message to Suzette Chase, supervisor of Legal Support. Remember that bulleted items improve readability.

8.21 Reply E-Mail: Escaping the Mountains of E-Mail (Objs. 1–5)

E-MAIL | INFOTRAC | TEAM

E-mail has become an essential part of our business lives. Yet workers throughout the country may be losing hours from each business day because of it. Some are distracted from work and waste valuable time on meaningless communications, says Dr. Mark Langemo, records management author and expert. In an article titled "11 Practical Strategies for Managing E-Mail" (InfoTrac Article No. A111112220), Dr. Langemo tells how companies can manage e-mail more efficiently and reduce their legal vulnerability. The vice president of your company has been complaining that e-mail is out of control. He asks you to be on the lookout for any ideas he should present to management for dealing with the problem.

Your Task. Using InfoTrac, study the article. You believe that some of the suggestions would certainly work for your company. You decide to discuss them with your team. Decide which of the suggestions are most appropriate, and organize them into a set of procedures. What should be done first? Some of the suggestions could be combined with others. Once your team agrees on a set of procedures, write an e-mail to Vice President Stanton Childress (or your instructor). In your own words, list the most significant strategies and explain each briefly.

8.22 Reply E-Mail or Memo: Cross-Cultural Dilemma (Obj. 5)

E-MAIL | TEAM | WEB

The Air Force's highest ranking female fighter pilot, Lt. Col. Martha McSally, is unhappy about being required to wear neck-to-toe robes in Saudi Arabia when she's off base. She filed a federal lawsuit seeking to overturn the policy that requires female servicewomen to wear such conservative clothing even when they are off base.

After seeing an article about this in the newspaper, your boss began to worry about sending female engineers to Saudi Arabia. Your company has been asked to submit a proposal to develop telecommunications within that country, and some of the company's best staff members are female. If your company wins the contract, it will undoubtedly need women to be in Saudi Arabia to complete the project. Because your boss knows little about the country, he asks you, his assistant, to do some research to find out what is appropriate business dress.

Your Task. Visit two or three Web sites and learn about dress expectations in Saudi Arabia. Is Western-style clothing acceptable for men? For women? Are there any clothing taboos? Should guest workers be expected to dress like natives? In teams discuss your findings. Individually or collectively, prepare a memo or e-mail addressed to J. E. Rivers, your boss. Summarize your most significant findings.

8.23 Reply Memo or E-Mail: Scheduling Appointments to Interview a New Project Manager (Obj. 5)

E-MAIL

You're frustrated! Your boss, Paul Rosenberg, has scheduled three appointments to interview applicants for the position of project manager. All of these appointments are for Thursday, May 5. However, he now must travel to Atlanta on that weekend. He asks you to reschedule all the appointments for one week later. He also wants a brief summary of the background of each candidate.

Despite your frustration, you call each person and are lucky to arrange these times. Carol Chastain, who has been a project manager for nine years with Piedmont Corporation, agrees to come at 10:30 a.m. Richard Emanuel, who is a systems analyst and a consultant to many companies, will come at 11:30. Lara Lee, who has an M.A. degree and six years of experience as senior project coordinator at High Point Industries, will come at 9:30 a.m. You're wondering whether Mr. Rosenberg forgot to include Hilary Iwu, operations personnel officer, in these interviews. Ms. Iwu usually is part of the selection process.

Your Task. Write an e-mail or memo to Mr. Rosenberg including all the vital information he needs.

8.24 Reply E-Mail: Reaching Consensus Regarding Casual-Dress Policy (Obj. 5)

CRITICAL THINKING	E-MAIL
INFOTRAC	TEAM

Casual dress in professional offices has been coming under attack. Your boss, Kathy Lewis-Adler, received the e-mail shown in Figure 8.5. She thinks it would be a good assignment for her group of management trainees to help her respond to that message. She asks your team to research answers to the first five questions in CEO Thomas Marshall's message. She doesn't expect you to answer the final question, but any information you can supply to the first questions would help her shape a response.

Marshall & Associates is a public CPA firm with a staff of 120 CPAs, bookkeepers, managers, and support personnel. Located in downtown Pittsburgh, the plush offices in One Oxford Center overlook the Allegheny River and the North Shore. The firm performs general accounting and audit services as well as tax planning and preparation. Accountants visit clients in the field and also entertain them in the downtown office.

Your Task. Decide whether the entire team will research each question in Figure 8.5 or whether team members will be assigned certain questions. Collect information, discuss it, and reach consensus on what you will report to Ms. Lewis-Adler. Write a concise, one-page response from your team. Your goal is to inform, not persuade. Remember that you represent management, not students or employees.

8.25 Reply Memo: Squawking About a Company E-Mail Policy (Obj. 5)

INFOTRAC	TEAM	WEB

At first, he couldn't figure it out. The IS (Information Systems) network manager at Lionel Trains in Chesterfield, Michigan, worried that his company would have to upgrade its Internet connection because operations were noticeably slower than in the past. Upon checking, however, he discovered that extensive recreational Web surfing among employees was the real reason for the slowdown. Since the company needed a good policy regulating the use of e-mail and the Internet, he assigned your team the task of investigating existing policies. Your team leader, Rick Rodriquez, who has quite a sense of humor, said, "Adopting an Internet policy is a lot like hosting a convention of pigeons. Both will result in a lot of squawking, ruffled feathers, and someone getting dumped on." Right! No one is going to like having e-mail and Internet use restricted. It is, indeed, a dirty job, but someone has to do it.

Your Task. Working individually, locate examples or models of company e-mail and Internet policies. Use InfoTrac and the Web trying variations of the search term "Company E-Mail Policy." Print any helpful material. Then meet as a group and select six to eight major topics that you think should be covered in a company policy. Your investigation will act as a starting point in the long process of developing a policy that provides safeguards but is not overly restrictive. You are not expected to write the policy at this time. But you could attach copies of anything interesting. Your boss would especially like to know where he could see or purchase model company policies. Send a reply memo to Rick Rodriquez, your team leader.

8.26 Confirmation Memo or E-Mail: Did I Hear This Correctly? (Obj. 6)

E-MAIL

At lunch one day you had a stimulating discussion with Jayne Moneysmith, an attorney specializing in employment risk management. You are a manager with a growing brokerage firm that employs more than 250 employees. All employees except top managers are "at will" employees without employment contracts. Your company has an extensive set of procedures and policies regarding sexual harassment. But it has no e-mail policies.

Ms. Moneysmith told you that in certain instances e-mail transmissions can constitute hostile-environment sexual harassment. Although an e-mail message is not a "verbal statement" uttered by an alleged harasser face to face, it can cross the legal line. If the message is severe and adversely affects the receiver's work environment, the message could constitute actionable sexual harassment. Even deleted messages can come back to haunt the company in employment discrimination cases. E-mails leave a "meta data" trail revealing attachments, dates and times of edits and transmissions, file size, conversation threads, and document file paths. These attributes ensure that any inappropriate behavior conducted via an employer's digital technology will leave a permanent record. She said that "at will" employees who send inappropriate messages or pornographic materials can legally be terminated if the circumstances suggest an outright dismissal is appropriate.[20]

Your Task. You would like to report Ms. Moneysmith's remarks at the next management council meeting. Before you do, however, you want to be sure that you heard her accurately. Write a memo or e-mail to Ms. Moneysmith condensing and confirming the major points she covered.

8.27 Confirmation Memo: Off to See the Dogwoods in Atlanta (Obj. 6)

As Paul Paggi, senior marketing coordinator, you had a vacation planned for May 1 through May 15. But yesterday your wife suggested changing the dates to April 1 through April 15 so that you and she could visit the Dogwood Festival in Atlanta. You're not wild about dogwoods, but you would like to visit Atlanta and perhaps keep on going for a quick trip to Florida. Perhaps you could change your vacation dates. Unfortunately, you remember that you are scheduled to represent your company at a Boston trade show April 5 through April 8. But maybe Alicia Noriega would fill in for you and make the presentation of the company's newest product, FlexiStand, a device to support notebook computers. You see your boss, Connor Romanski, in the hall and decide to ask whether you can change your vacation to April 1 through April 15. To your surprise, he agrees to the new dates. He also assures you that he will ask Alicia Noriega to make the presentation and encourage her to give a special trade show demonstration to Mercer Corporation, which you believe should be targeted.

Your Task. Back in your office, you begin to worry. What if Mr. Romanski forgets about your conversation? You can't afford to take that chance. Write a confirmation memo to Connor Romanski, vice president in Marketing. Because you want your note to show your gratitude, send a hard-copy memo. Summarize the necessary facts and also convey your appreciation. Establish an end date and provide a reason.

8.28 Confirmation Memo: Verifying a Job Severance Package (Obj. 6)

You're congratulating yourself on landing a fantastic job. Terrific title. Terrific salary. Terrific boss. You were even smart enough to talk about an exit package during your interview. You had read an article in *The Wall Street Journal* suggesting that the best time to win a generous departure deal is before you accept a position.

Because you knew your skills were in high demand for this position and because you would be giving up a good position, you wanted to know what the typical severance package involved. What would you receive if this job disappeared through a merger or downturn in the economy or similar unforeseen event? The hiring manager told you that the standard severance package includes one week's salary for every year of service, outplacement counseling for up to six months, accrued but unused vacation pay, and extended medical coverage. After a little bargaining, you were able to increase the severance pay to two weeks' salary for each year of service and medical insurance for you and your family up to one year or until you found another position.

Then you begin to worry. You didn't get any of this in writing.

Your Task. You decide to write a confirmation memo outlining the severance package discussed in your interview. *The Wall Street Journal* says that your memo becomes an enforceable contract.[21] Write a hard-copy memo to Jefferson Walker, operations manager, describing your understanding of what you were promised. If Mr. Walker doesn't agree with any of the details, ask him to respond immediately. Show your enthusiasm for the job and keep the tone of your message upbeat. Add any necessary details.

8.29 How to Write Clear Instructions (Obj. 4)

At the student Web site for this book, you will find a supplement devoted to writing instructions. It includes colorful examples and hot links to Web sites with relevant examples of real sets of instructions from business Web sites.

Your Task. At **Xtra! (http://guffeyxtra.swlearning.com)**, find the bonus supplement, "How to Write Instructions." Study all of the sections of this supplement. Then choose one of the following application activities: A-5, Revising the Instructions for an Imported Fax Machine, A-6, Evaluation: Catnix Basic Cat Playground; or A-7, Instructions for Dealing With Car Emergencies. Complete the assignment and submit it to your instructor. If any of the links fail, be sure to check the list of updated URLs at your student Web site (**http://guffeyswlearning.com**) for replacements.

8.30 What to Do About the Junk E-Mail Epidemic? (Obj. 3)

SPEAKING

The modern-day epidemic of unsolicited electronic messages sent over the Internet, popularly known as "spam," is estimated to cost $25 billion a year worldwide and is expected to soon represent as much as 86 percent of electronic messaging traffic. Hundreds of millions of junk e-mails sent each day cause problems for communications systems and rack up financial losses and productivity losses for both companies and individual users.

In Geneva, Switzerland, the International Telecommunication Union (ITU) organized a meeting to discuss ways to combat the epidemic in Geneva, Switzerland. Representatives from 60 countries—mostly officials from telecommunication regulatory agencies and industry executives—discussed four response avenues:

- Legislation
- Public education
- Industry actions by Internet service providers
- Software solutions[22]

Your Task. As a member in your group of three to five students, assume the role of one of the delegates at the Geneva meeting. Discuss specific strategies you would suggest under each of the four methods for combating the junk e-mail epidemic. Submit the results of your group's discussion either in a written format specified by your instructor or during a class discussion.

8.31 Reply Memo or E-Mail: What Is a FICO Credit Rating Score? (Obj. 5)

CONSUMER | E-MAIL | WEB

For years the credit industry hushed up a consumer's credit score. Credit bureaus would reveal a consumer's credit rating only to a lender when an applicant wanted a loan. Customers could not learn their scores unless credit was denied. Now, all that has changed. Using the Internet, consumers can check their credit files and even obtain specific credit scores, which are key factors in obtaining loans, renting property, and protecting against identity theft. Although the three national credit bureaus (Equifax, Experian, and TransUnion) may use different scoring systems, many lenders now mention FICO scores as the favored ranking to estimate the risk involved in an individual's loan application.

Your Task. As an intern in architect Eric Larson's office, you must do some Internet research. Mr. Larson recently had to reject two potentially lucrative house construction jobs because the clients received low FICO scores from their credit bureaus. They could not qualify for construction loans. He wants you to learn exactly what "FICO" means and how this score is determined. Mr. Larson also wants to know how consumers can raise their FICO scores. Go to **http://www.myfico.com** and study its information. (Use a search engine with the term "My Fico" if this URL fails.) Summarize your findings in your own words in a well-organized, concise memo or e-mail addressed to Eric Larson at *elarson@arnet.com.* Use bulleted lists for some of the information.

video resources

This important chapter offers two learning videos.

Building Workplace Skills Video Library 1

Smart E-Mail Messages and Memos Advance Your Career

Watch this chapter-specific video for a demonstration of how to use e-mail skillfully and safely. You'll better understand the writing process in relation to composing messages. You'll also pick up tips for writing messages that advance your career instead of sinking it.

Bridging the Gap Video Library 2

Innovation, Learning, and Communication: A Study of Yahoo!

This video familiarizes you with managers and inside operating strategies at the Internet company Yahoo! After watching the film, assume the role of assistant to John Briggs, senior producer, who appeared in the video. John has just received a letter asking for permission from another film company to use Yahoo offices and personnel in an educational video, similar to the one you just saw.

John wants you to draft a message for him to send to the operations manager, Ceci Lang, asking for permission for VX Studios to film. VX says it needs about 15 hours of filming time and would like to interview four or five managers as well as founders David Filo and Jerry Yang. VX would need to set up its mobile studio van in the parking lot and would need permission to use advertising film clips. Although VX hopes to film in May, it is flexible about the date. John Briggs reminds you that Yahoo has participated in a number of films in the past two years, and some managers are complaining that they can't get their work done.

Your Task. After watching the video, write a persuasive memo or e-mail message to Ceci Lang, operations manager, asking her to allow VX Studios to film at Yahoo. Your message should probably emphasize the value of these projects in enhancing Yahoo's image among future users. Provide any other details you think are necessary to create a convincing request memo that will win authorization from Ceci Lang to schedule this filming.

C.L.U.E. review 8

Edit the following sentences to correct all language faults, including grammar, punctuation, spelling, and word use.

1. More then ninety percent of companys now use e-mail therefore employees must become more knowlegable about it's dangers.
2. Most e-mails and memos delivery straight-forward information that is not sensitive, and require little persuasion.
3. If I was you I would check all in coming e-mail and attachments that was sent to you and he.
4. Memos typically contain 4 nesessary parts; subject line, opening, body and action closing.
5. Fear of inappropriate e-mail use, and the need to boost productivity, has spurred employee monitoring programs.
6. When you respond too a e-mail message you should not automaticly return the senders message.
7. Wasnt it Dr Rivers and Ms Johnson who allways wrote there e-mails in all capitol letters.
8. A list of the names' and addresses' of e-mail recipients were sent using the "bcc" function.
9. Our information technology department which was formerally in room 35 has moved it's offices to room 5.
10. The Evening news press our local newspaper featured as its principle article a story entitled, Cyber-slacking is killing productivity!

chapter 9

Routine Letters and Goodwill Messages

objectives

1 Explain why business letters are written and how the three phases of Guffey's 3-x-3 writing process relate to creating successful business letters.

2 Analyze the structure and characteristics of good business letters.

3 Write direct letters that request information and action as well as place orders for products and services.

4 Write letters that make direct claims.

5 Write letters that comply with requests.

6 Write letters that make adjustments.

7 Write letters of recommendation.

8 Write messages that generate goodwill.

9 Modify international letters to accommodate other cultures.

Ben & Jerry's Uses Routine Letters to Sweeten Relations With Customers

AMERICA'S LOVE AFFAIR with numbingly rich ice cream may have finally plateaued. Health and weight worries have apparently cut the breakneck growth of superpremium ice creams. Yet, Ben & Jerry's Homemade, premier purveyor of the superpremiums, remains one of the country's most visible ice cream companies.

In growing from a 12-flavor miniparlor in Burlington, Vermont, into a Fortune 500 company called a "national treasure," Ben & Jerry's has been showered with publicity. The flood of press notices flowed partly from its rapid ascent and its funky flavor hits such as "Chubby Hubby," "Half Baked Carb Karma," "New York Super Fudge Chunk," "Phish Food," and "Dilbert's World Totally Nuts" (butter almond ice cream with roasted hazelnuts, praline pecans, and white fudge-coated almonds). Of even greater media interest was the New Age business philosophy of founders Ben Cohen and Jerry Greenfield. Unlike most entrepreneurs, their aim was to build a successful business but, at the same time, be a force for social change.

Some time ago Ben and Jerry resigned their symbolic positions as brand icons after the company was purchased by the Anglo-Dutch mega-conglomerate Unilever. Before the change in ownership, Ben & Jerry's tried to operate in a way that improved local and global quality of life. The company donates $1.1 million of pretax profits to philanthropic causes. It also strives to create career opportunities, financial rewards, and a fun-filled work environment for employees.

Although no longer locally owned, Ben & Jerry's is a visible company with a popular national product and a strong social image. It naturally generates a good deal of correspondence. Customer letters typically fall into three categories: (1) "fan" mail, (2) information requests, and (3) claims. Fan mail contains praise and testimonials: "Tried the new Cherry Garcia Frozen Yogurt and . . . I want to go to Vermont and shake your sticky hands." Information requests may involve questions about ingredients or food processing, and some letters comment on Ben & Jerry's social positions. Claim letters generally contain a complaint and require immediate response. Responding to customer letters in all three categories is a critical element in maintaining customer goodwill and market position for Ben & Jerry's.[1]

Scrumptious cones satisfy customers, but excellent communication builds long-time loyalty.

Critical Thinking

- Have you ever written a letter or sent an e-mail to a company? What might motivate you to do so? Would you expect a response?
- If a company such as Ben & Jerry's receives a fan letter complimenting products or service, is it necessary to respond?
- Why is it important for companies to answer claim (complaint) letters immediately?

http://www.benjerry.com

CONTINUED ON PAGE 275

case study

Applying Guffey's 3-x-3 Writing Process to Create Successful Letters

learning objective

1

Letters, such as those sent by Ben & Jerry's to its customers, are a primary channel of communication for delivering messages *outside* an organization. Although e-mail is incredibly successful for both internal and external communication, many important messages still call for letters. Business letters are important when a permanent record is required, when formality is necessary, and when a message is sensitive and requires an organized, well-considered presentation. In this book we'll divide letters into three groups: (1) routine letters communicating straightforward requests, replies, and goodwill messages, covered in Chapter 9; (2) persuasive messages including sales pitches, covered in Chapter 10; and (3) negative messages delivering refusals and bad news, covered in Chapter 11.

Business letters are necessary (a) when a permanent record is required, (b) when formality is important, and (c) when a message is sensitive and requires an organized, well-considered presentation.

This chapter concentrates on routine, straightforward letters through which we conduct everyday business and convey goodwill to outsiders. Such letters go to suppliers, government agencies, other businesses, and, most important, customers. The letters to customers receive a high priority because these messages encourage product feedback, project a favorable image of the company, and promote future business.

Routine letters to outsiders encourage product feedback, project a favorable company image, and promote future business.

Publisher Malcolm Forbes understood the power of business letters when he said, "A good business letter can get you a job interview, get you off the hook, or get you money. It's totally asinine to blow your chances of getting *whatever* you want—with a business letter that turns people off instead of turning them on."[2] This chapter teaches you what turns readers on. We'll begin by reviewing the writing process for business letters and analyzing the structure and characteristics of letters. Then you'll learn to apply this information in writing routine letters that request information, require action, place orders, and make straightforward claims. You'll also learn to grant claims, comply with requests, write letters of recommendation, and compose goodwill messages. Finally, you'll study how to modify your letters to accommodate other cultures.

Although routine letters may be short and straightforward, they benefit from attention to the composition process. "At the heart of effective writing is the ability to organize a series of thoughts," says writing expert and executive Max Messmer. Taking the time to think through what you want to achieve and how the audience will react makes writing much easier.[3] Here's a quick review of Guffey's 3-x-3 writing process to help you think through its application to routine letters.

Phase 1: Analysis, Anticipation, and Adaptation

Before writing, spend a few moments analyzing your task and audience. Your key goals here are (1) determining your purpose, (2) visualizing the audience, and (3) anticipating the reaction to your message. Too often, letter writers start a message without enough preparation.

In Phase 1 of the writing process, analyze your purpose, visualize the audience, and anticipate the response.

Alice Blachly, a veteran letter writer at Ben & Jerry's, realizes the problem. She says, "If I'm having trouble with a letter and it's not coming out right, it's almost always because I haven't thought through exactly what I want to say."[4] In the Ben & Jerry's letter shown in Figure 9.1, Blachly responds to a request from a young Ben & Jerry's customer. Before writing the letter, she thought about the receiver and tried to find a way to personalize what could have been a form letter.

Phase 2: Research, Organization, and Composition

In the second phase, collect information and make a list of the points you wish to cover. For short messages such as an answer to a customer's inquiry, you might jot

Figure 9.1 *Ben & Jerry's Reply to Customer Inquiry*

1 Prewriting

Analyze: The purpose of this letter is to build goodwill and promote Ben & Jerry's products.

Anticipate: The reader is young, enthusiastic, and eager to hear from Ben & Jerry's. She will appreciate personalized comments.

Adapt: Use short sentences, cheerful thoughts, and plenty of references to the reader and to her club, school, and request.

2 Writing

Research: Reread the customer's letter. Decide on which items to enclose and locate them.

Organize: Open directly with a positive response. Explain the enclosed items. Find ways to make the reader feel a special connection with Ben & Jerry's.

Compose: Write the first draft quickly. Realize that revision will improve it.

3 Revising

Revise: Revise the message striving for a warm tone. Use the receiver's name. Edit long paragraphs and add bulleted items.

Proofread: Check the address of the receiver. Decide whether to hyphenate *cofounder* and how to punctuate quotations.

Evaluate: Consider how you would feel if you received this letter.

BEN & JERRY'S®
VERMONT'S FINEST • ICE CREAM & FROZEN YOGURT™

January 18, 2006

Ms. Jennifer Ball
1401 Churchville Lane
Bel Air, MD 21014

Dear Jennifer:

We're delighted to hear of your Ben & Jerry's Club at Franklin Middle School and to send the items you request! — *Opens directly with response to customer's request*

Personalizes reply and builds goodwill with reference to writer's letter — Your club sounds as though it resembles its parent in many ways. We, too, can't seem to control our growth; and we, too, get a little out of control on Friday afternoons. Moreover, the simplicity of your club rules mirrors the philosophy of our cofounder, who says, "If it's not fun, why do it?"

Enclosed are the following items:

- A list of all flavors available in pints. If you can't find these flavors at your grocer's, I'm sending you some "ballots" for your club's use in encouraging your grocer to stock your favorites.
- The latest issue of Ben & Jerry's "Chunk Mail." We're also putting you on our mailing list so that your club will receive our Chunk Mail newsletter regularly.

Itemizes and explains enclosures requested by customer

Uses receiver's name to make letter sound conversational and personal — We hope, Jennifer, that you'll soon tour our plant here in Vermont. Then, you can be on an equal footing with your prez and sport one of our tour buttons. This seems only appropriate for the consensus-building, decision-making model you are pioneering in your Ben & Jerry's Club! — *Ties in cordial closing with more references to customer's letter*

Sincerely,

Alice

Alice Blachly
Consumer Affairs

Enc: Flavor list, ballots, Chunk Mail

P.O. BOX 240, WATERBURY, VERMONT 05676 (802) 244-6957 FAX (802) 244-5944
100% Post-Consumer Recycled Paper

your notes down on the document you are answering. For longer documents that require formal research, use a cluster diagram or the outlining techniques discussed in Chapter 6. When business letters carry information that won't upset the receiver, you can organize them in the direct manner with the main idea expressed immediately. In Alice Blachly's letter shown in Figure 9.1, she made a scratch outline of the points she wanted to cover before writing.

In Phase 2 of the writing process, gather information, make notes or prepare an outline, and compose the first draft.

Phase 3: Revision, Proofreading, and Evaluation

When you finish the first draft, revise for clarity. The receiver should not have to read the message twice to grasp its meaning. Proofread for correctness. Check for punctuation irregularities, typos, misspelled words, or other mechanical problems. Also be sure to look for ways to create high "skim value." In Figure 9.1 Alice Blachly saw that she could use bullets to highlight two items instead of burying them inside a paragraph. Although a good speller, she wouldn't dream of sending out a letter without using her spell checker. The last step in the 3-x-3 writing process is evaluating the product. Before any letter leaves her desk at Ben & Jerry's, Blachly always rereads it and puts herself in the shoes of the reader: "How would I feel if I were receiving it?"

In Phase 3 of the writing process, revise for clarity, add graphic highlighting if possible, and proofread for correctness.

Analyzing the Structure and Characteristics of Business Letters

learning objective

2

The everyday transactions of a business consist mainly of routine requests and responses. Because you expect the reader's response to be positive or neutral, you won't need special techniques to be convincing, to soften bad news, or to be tactful. Use the direct strategy, outlined in Chapter 6. In composing routine letters, you can structure your message, as shown in Figure 9.2, into three parts:

- **Opening:** a statement that announces the purpose immediately
- **Body:** details that explain the purpose
- **Closing:** a request for action or a courteous conclusion

Frontload in the Opening

You should use the direct strategy for routine, everyday messages. This means developing ideas in a straightforward manner and frontloading the main idea. State immediately why you are writing so that the reader can anticipate and comprehend what follows. Remember, every time a reader begins a message, he or she is thinking, "Why was this sent to me?" "What am I to do?"

Everyday business messages "frontload" by presenting the main idea or purpose immediately.

Some writers make the mistake of organizing a message as if they were telling a story or solving a problem. They start at the beginning and follow the same sequence in which they thought through the problem. This means reviewing the background, discussing the reasons for action, and then requesting an action. Most business letters, though, are better written "backward." Start with the action desired or the main idea. Don't get bogged down in introductory material, history, justifications, or old-fashioned "business" language.[5] Instead, reveal your purpose immediately. Compare the following indirect and direct openers to see the differences:

Indirect Opening
Our company is experiencing difficulty in retaining employees. We also need help in screening job applicants. Our current testing program is unsatisfactory.

FIGURE 9.2 ***Three-Part Structure for Routine Requests and Responses***

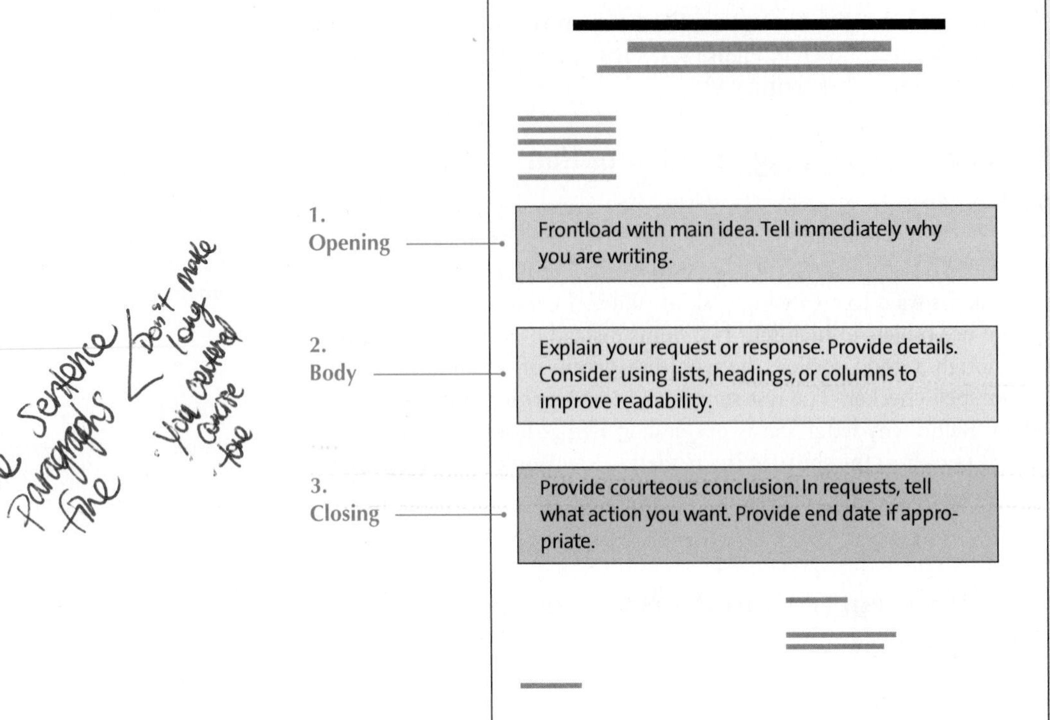

I understand that you offer employee testing materials, and I have a number of questions to ask.

Direct Opening
Please answer the following questions about your personnel testing materials.

Most simple requests should open immediately with a statement of purpose (*Please answer these questions about . . .*). Occasionally, however, requests may require a sentence or two of explanation or background before the purpose is revealed. What you want to avoid, though, is delaying the purpose of the letter beyond the first paragraph.

Explain in the Body

The body explains the purpose for writing, perhaps using graphic devices to highlight important ideas.

After a direct opening that tells the reader why you are writing, present details that explain your request or response. This is where your planning pays off, allowing you to structure the information for maximum clarity and readability. Here you should consider using some graphic devices to highlight the details: a numbered or bulleted list, headings, columns, or boldface or italic type.

If you have considerable information, you'll want to develop each idea in a separate paragraph with effective transitions to connect them. The important thing to remember is to keep similar ideas together. The biggest problem in business writing is poor organization, and the body of a letter is where that failure becomes apparent.

Be Specific and Courteous in the Closing

In the last paragraph of direct letters, readers look for action information: schedules, deadlines, activities to be completed. Thus, at this point, you should specify what you want the reader to do. If appropriate, include an end date—a date for completion of the action. If possible, give reasons for establishing the deadline. Research shows that people want to know why they should do something—even if the reasons seem obvious. Moreover, people want to be treated courteously (*Please answer these questions before April 1, when we must make a final decision*), not bossed around (*Send this information immediately*).

The closing courteously specifies what the receiver is to do.

Characteristics of Good Letters

Although routine letters deliver straightforward facts, they don't have to sound and look dull or mechanical. At least three characteristics distinguish good business letters: clear content, a tone of goodwill, and correct form.

Clear Content. A clearly written letter separates ideas into paragraphs, uses short sentences and paragraphs, and guides the reader through the ideas with transitional expressions. Moreover, a clear letter uses familiar words and active-voice verbs. In other words, it incorporates the writing techniques you studied in Chapters 5, 6, and 7.

Clear letters feature short sentences and paragraphs, transitional expressions, familiar words, and active-voice verbs.

Many business letters, however, are not written well. As many as one third of business letters do nothing more than seek clarification of earlier correspondence. Clear letters avoid this problem by answering all the reader's questions or concerns so that no further correspondence is necessary. Clear letters also speak the language of the receiver. One expert says, "The only sure-fire way to avoid miscommunication is to determine your audience's characteristics" and write in his or her language.[6] This doesn't mean "dumbing down" your remarks. It means taking into consideration what your reader knows about the subject and using appropriate words.

spotlight *on communicators*

Peggy Foran, a vice president at pharmaceutical giant Pfizer Corporation, is known for "pushing the envelope" in practicing good communication with investors. In correspondence, news releases, and proxy statements, Foran insists on clear, basic English. Although accustomed to the dense language of her industry, she admits to confusion. "I do this for a living, and I can't understand a lot of [corporate material] on the first read." She demands clear expression in Pfizer messages. "Transparency is part of our culture. We believe in plain English." To be sure their communication is clear, Pfizer writers are encouraged to put themselves in the shoes of readers, which is good advice for all business communicators.

Goodwill Tone. Good letters, however, have to do more than deliver clear messages; they also must build goodwill. Goodwill is a positive feeling the reader has toward an individual or an organization. By analyzing your audience and adapting your message to the reader, your letters can establish an overall tone of goodwill.

To achieve goodwill, look for ways to present the message from the reader's perspective. In other words, emphasize the "you" view and point out benefits to the reader. In addition, be sensitive to words that might suggest gender, racial, age, or disability bias. Finally, frame your ideas positively because they will sound more pleasing and will give more information than negative constructions. For example, which sounds better and gives more information? *We cannot send your order until April 1* or *We can send your order April 1.*

Correct Form. A business letter conveys silent messages beyond that of its printed words. The letter's appearance and format reflect the writer's carefulness and experience. A short letter bunched at the top of a sheet of paper, for example, looks as though it were prepared in a hurry or by an amateur.

Appropriate letter formats send silent but positive messages.

For your letters to make a good impression, you need to select an appropriate format. The block style shown in Figure 9.3 is a popular format. Other letter formats are illustrated later in this chapter and shown in Appendix B. In the block style

FIGURE 9.3 ***Business Letter Formatting—Block Style***

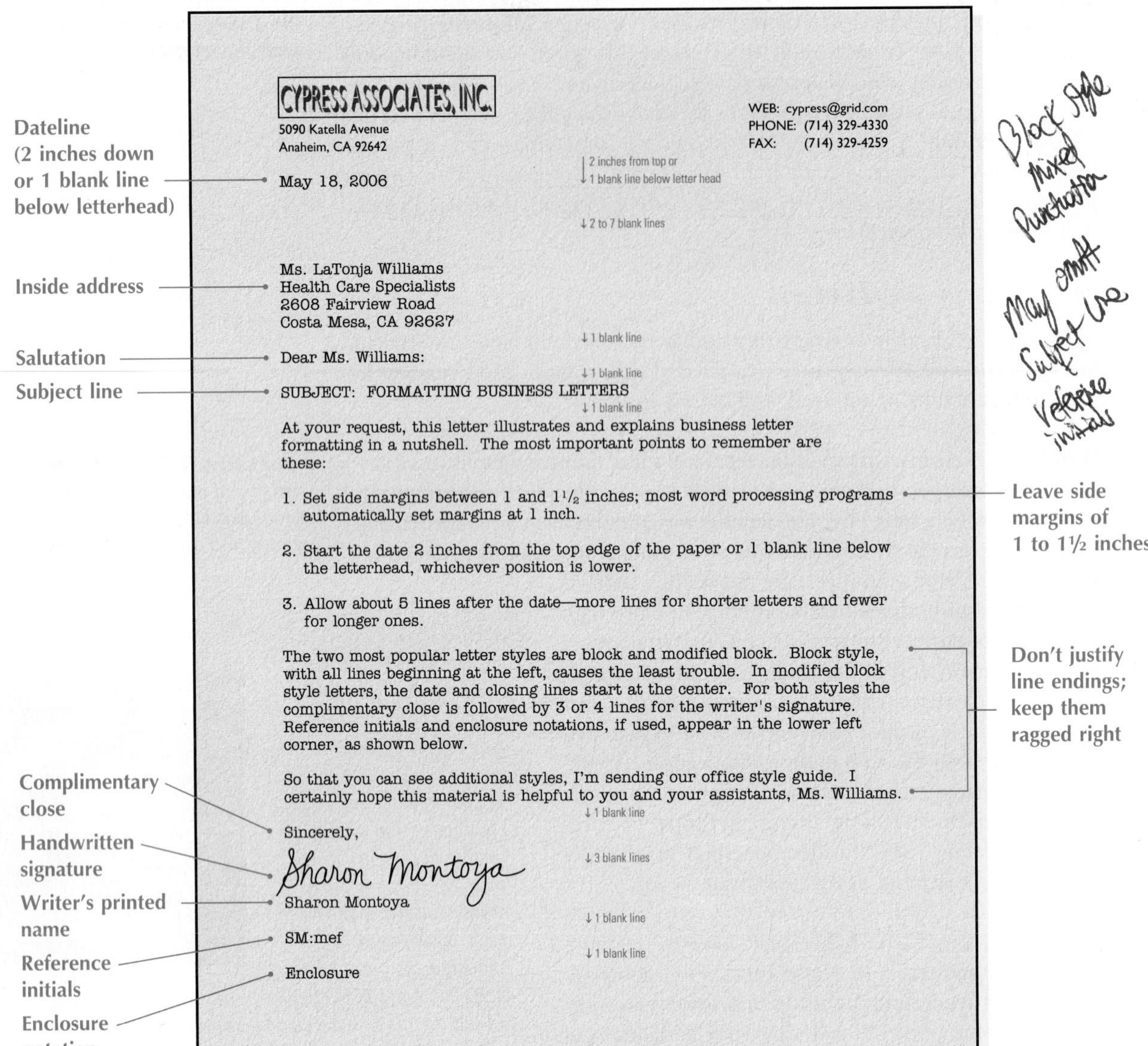

CYPRESS ASSOCIATES, INC.

5090 Katella Avenue
Anaheim, CA 92642

WEB: cypress@grid.com
PHONE: (714) 329-4330
FAX: (714) 329-4259

May 18, 2006

Ms. LaTonja Williams
Health Care Specialists
2608 Fairview Road
Costa Mesa, CA 92627

Dear Ms. Williams:

SUBJECT: FORMATTING BUSINESS LETTERS

At your request, this letter illustrates and explains business letter formatting in a nutshell. The most important points to remember are these:

1. Set side margins between 1 and 1½ inches; most word processing programs automatically set margins at 1 inch.

2. Start the date 2 inches from the top edge of the paper or 1 blank line below the letterhead, whichever position is lower.

3. Allow about 5 lines after the date—more lines for shorter letters and fewer for longer ones.

The two most popular letter styles are block and modified block. Block style, with all lines beginning at the left, causes the least trouble. In modified block style letters, the date and closing lines start at the center. For both styles the complimentary close is followed by 3 or 4 lines for the writer's signature. Reference initials and enclosure notations, if used, appear in the lower left corner, as shown below.

So that you can see additional styles, I'm sending our office style guide. I certainly hope this material is helpful to you and your assistants, Ms. Williams.

Sincerely,

Sharon Montoya

Sharon Montoya

SM:mef

Enclosure

the parts of your letter—dateline, inside address, body, and so on—are set flush left on the page. Also, the letter is formatted so that it is centered on the page and framed by white space. Most letters will have margins of 1 to 1½ inches.

Finally, be sure to use ragged-right margins; that is, don't allow your computer to justify the right margin and make all lines end evenly. Unjustified margins improve readability, say experts, by providing visual stops and by making it easier to tell where the next line begins. Although book publishers use justified right margins, as you see on this page, your letters should be ragged right. Study Figure 9.3 for more tips on making your letters look professional.

learning objective 3

Direct Requests for Information or Action

The majority of your business letters will involve routine messages organized directly. Before you write any letter, though, consider its costs in terms of your time and workload. Whenever possible, don't write! Instead of asking for information, could you find it yourself? Would a telephone call, an e-mail message, or a brief visit to a coworker solve the problem quickly? If not, use the direct pattern to present your request efficiently.

Because business letters are costly, don't write if a phone call or e-mail message might solve the problem.

Many of your messages will request information or action. Suppose you have questions about a payroll accounting service your company is considering or you need to ask a customer to supply missing data from an order. If your request involves several questions, you could open with a polite request, such as *Will you please answer the following questions about your payroll service.* Note that although this request sounds like a question, it's actually a disguised command. Because you expect an action rather than a reply, punctuate this polite command with a period instead of a question mark. To avoid this punctuation problem, just omit *Will you* and start with *Please answer.*

Clarify Requests

A direct letter may open with a question or a polite request.

In the body of your letter, explain your purpose and provide details. If you have questions, express them in parallel form so that you balance them grammatically. To elicit the most information, pose open-ended questions (*What computer lock-down device can you recommend?*) instead of yes-or-no questions (*Do you carry computer lock-down devices?*). If you are asking someone to do something, be sure your tone is polite and undemanding. Remember that your written words cannot be softened by a smile. When possible, focus on benefits to the reader (*To ensure that you receive the exact sweater you want, send us your color choice*). In the closing tell the reader courteously what is to be done. If a date is important, set an end date to take action and explain why. Some careless writers end request letters simply with *Thank you,* forcing the reader to review the contents to determine what is expected and when. You can save the reader time by spelling out the action to be taken. Avoid other overused endings such as *Thank you for your cooperation* (trite), *Thank you in advance for . . .* (trite and presumptuous), and *If you have any questions, do not hesitate to call me* (suggests that you didn't make yourself clear).

Show Appreciation

Request letters maintain a courteous tone, spell out what needs to be done, and focus on reader benefits.

It's always appropriate to show appreciation, but try to do so in a fresh and efficient manner. For example, you could hook your thanks to the end date (*Thanks for returning the questionnaire before May 5, when we will begin tabulation*). You might connect your appreciation to a statement developing reader benefits (*We are grateful for the information you will provide because it will help us serve you better*). You could also describe briefly how the information will help you (*I appreciate this information that will enable me to . . .*). When possible, make it easy for the reader to comply with your request (*Note your answers on this sheet and return it in the postage-paid envelope* or *Here's my e-mail address so that you can reach me quickly*).

Let's now analyze the first draft of a direct request letter written by office manager Deana Gomez. She wants information about computer security devices, but the first version of her letter, shown in Figure 9.4 on page 260, is confusing and inefficient. Deana makes a common mistake: starting the message with a description of the problem instead of starting with the main idea. Deana's revision on page 261 begins more directly. The opening sentence introduces the purpose immediately so that the reader quickly knows why the letter was sent. Deana then provides background information. Most important, she organizes all her requests into specific questions, which are sure to bring a better result than her previous diffuse request. Study the 3-x-3 writing process outlined in Figure 9.4 to see the plan Deana followed in improving her letter.

FIGURE 9.4 *Direct Request Letter*

1 Prewriting	2 Writing	3 Revising
ANALYZE: The purpose of this letter is to ask specific questions about computer devices. **ANTICIPATE:** The audience is expected to be a busy but receptive service representative. **ADAPT:** Because the reader will react positively, the direct pattern is best.	**RESEARCH:** Determine equipment needs and what questions must be answered. **ORGANIZE:** Open with a general inquiry. In the body give details; arrange any questions logically. Close by courteously providing a specific deadline. **COMPOSE:** Write the first draft.	**REVISE:** Improve the clarity by grouping similar ideas. Improve readability by numbering questions. **PROOFREAD:** Look for typos and spelling errors. Check punctuation, placement, and format. **EVALUATE:** Is this message attractive and easily comprehended?

DRAFT

Opens with background information instead of request

Our insurance rates will be increased soon if we don't install security devices on our computer equipment. We have considered some local suppliers, but none had exactly what we wanted.

Fails to organize information logically

We need a device that can be used to secure separate computer components at a workstation including a computer, keyboard, and monitor. We currently own 18 computers, keyboards, and monitors, along with six printers.

Ends with cliché; fails to reveal what to do and when

We wonder if professionals are needed to install your security devices. We're also interested in whether the devices can be easily removed when we need to move equipment around. We are, of course, very interested in prices and quantity discounts, if you offer them. Thank you for your attention to this matter.

Order Letters

Letters placing orders specify items or services, quantities, dates, prices, and payment method.

You may occasionally need to write a letter that orders supplies, merchandise, or services. Generally, such purchases are made by Web page, telephone, catalog order form, or fax. Sometimes, however, you may not have a telephone number, order form, or Web address—only a street address. Other times you may want to have a written record of your order. To order items by letter, supply the same information that an order blank would require. In the opening let the reader know immediately that this is a purchase authorization and not merely an information inquiry. Instead of *I saw a number of interesting items in your catalog*, begin directly with order language such as *Please send me by UPS the following items from your fall merchandise catalog*.

If you're ordering many items, list them vertically in the body of your letter. Include as much specific data as possible: quantity, order number, complete description, unit price, and total price. Show the total amount, and figure the tax and shipping costs if possible. The more information you provide, the less likely that a mistake will be made.

In the closing tell how you plan to pay for the merchandise. Enclose a check, provide a credit card number, or ask to be billed. Many business organizations have credit agreements with their regular suppliers that enable them to send goods without prior payment. In addition to payment information, tell when the merchandise should be sent and express appreciation. The order letter from Michael Walker of Wilkenson Industries, shown in Figure 9.5, illustrates the pattern of an order letter.

REVISION

EARTH SYSTEMS
Geotechnical Engineers
4439 Hitchcock Way

www.earthsystems.com
Ventura, CA 93105

(805) 558-8791

January 28, 2006

Mr. Jeff Lee, Customer Service
Micro Supplies and Software
P.O. Box 648
Fort Atkinson, WI 53538

Dear Mr. Lee:

Please provide information and recommendations regarding security equipment to prevent theft of office computers and peripherals.

Our office now has 18 computer workstations and 6 printers that we must secure to desks or counters. Answers to the following questions will help us select the best devices for our purposes:

1. What device would you recommend that can secure a workstation consisting of a computer, monitor, and keyboard?

2. What expertise and equipment are required to install and remove the security device?

3. How much is each device? Do you offer quantity discounts, and if so, how much?

Your response before February 15 will help us meet an April 1 deadline from our insurance carrier for locking down this equipment.

Sincerely,

Deana Gomez

Deana Gomez
Office Manager

Addresses receiver by name

Introduces purpose immediately

Explains need for information

Groups open-ended questions into list for quick comprehension and best feedback

Courteously provides end date and reason

Direct Claims

learning objective

4

Claim letters are written by customers to identify or correct a wrong.

In business many things can go wrong—promised shipments are late, warrantied goods fail, or service is disappointing. When you as a customer must write to identify or correct a wrong, the letter is called a *claim*. Straightforward claims are those to which you expect the receiver to agree readily. But even these claims often require a letter. Your first action may be a telephone call or a visit to submit your claim, but you may not be satisfied with the result. Written claims are often taken more seriously, and they also establish a record of what happened. Straightforward claims use a direct approach. Claims that require persuasion are presented in Chapter 10.

Figure 9.5 ***Order Letter***

WILKENSON INDUSTRIES

2359 Colorado Boulevard Pasadena, CA 91106	www.wilkenson.com mewalker@wilkenson.com	Phone: (626) 430-8721 Fax: (626) 430-2360

June 9, 2006

Omni Marketing Direct
350 Commerce Street
P.O. Box 410
Oshkosh, WI 54902-0320

Dear Omni Marketing:

Identifies method of delivery and catalog source

Please send by express mail the following items from your spring catalog:

Opens directly with authorization for purchase

Uses columns to make quantity, catalog number, description, unit price, and total stand out

Quantity	Catalog No.	Item	Unit Price	Total
75	87018	Apothecary Candy Jar	$ 5.39	$404.25
25	50416	Deluxe Beach Towel	19.99	499.75
100	38190	Business Card Tape Measure	2.19	219.00
75	25918	3M Post-It Cube	3.59	269.25
	Subtotal			$1,392.25
	Tax at 7%			97.46
	Shipping			34.25
	Total			$1,523.96

Calculates totals to prevent possible mistakes

Expresses appreciation and tells when items are expected

My company would appreciate receiving these items immediately because we plan to use them as promotional items at a number of trade shows, the first of which is August 15. Enclosed is our check for $1,523.96. If additional charges are necessary, please bill my company.

Identifies method of payment

Sincerely,

WILKENSON INDUSTRIES

Michael E. Walker

Michael E. Walker, Manager
Marketing and Sales Promotions

Enclosure

Open With a Clear Statement (Request)

Claim letters open with a clear problem statement or with an explanation of the action necessary to solve the problem.

When you, as a customer, have a legitimate claim, you can expect a positive response from a company. Smart businesses want to hear from their customers. They know that retaining a customer is far less costly than recruiting a new customer. That's why you should open a claim letter with a clear statement of the problem or with the action you want the receiver to take. You might expect a replacement, a refund, a new order, credit to your account, correction of a billing error, free repairs, free inspection, or cancellation of an order. When the remedy is obvious, state it immediately (*Please send us 25 Sanyo digital travel alarm clocks to replace the Sanyo analog travel alarm clocks sent in error with our order shipped January 4*). When the remedy is less obvious, you might ask for a change in policy or procedure or simply for an explanation (*Because three of our employees with confirmed reservations were refused rooms September 16 in your hotel, would you please clarify your policy regarding reservations and late arrivals*).

Explain and Justify

In the body of a claim letter, explain the problem and justify your request. Provide the necessary details so that the difficulty can be corrected without further correspondence. Avoid becoming angry or trying to fix blame. Bear in mind that the person reading your letter is seldom responsible for the problem. Instead, state the facts logically, objectively, and unemotionally; let the reader decide on the causes. Include copies of all pertinent documents such as invoices, sales slips, catalog descriptions, and repair records. (By the way, be sure to send copies and NOT your originals, which could be lost.) When service is involved, cite names of individuals spoken to and dates of calls. Assume that a company honestly wants to satisfy its customers—because most do. When an alternative remedy exists, spell it out (*If you are unable to send 25 Sanyo digital travel alarm clocks immediately, please credit our account now and notify us when they become available*).

Customers who call to complain may not reach the right person at the best time. To register a serious claim, always write a letter. A letter creates a paper trail and is taken more seriously than a telephone call. Use the direct strategy for straightforward claims.

Conclude With an Action Request

End a claim letter with a courteous statement that promotes goodwill and summarizes your action request. If appropriate, include an end date (*We realize that mistakes in ordering and shipping sometimes occur. Because we've enjoyed your prompt service in the past, we hope that you will be able to send us the Sanyo digital travel alarm clocks by January 15*). Finally, in making claims, act promptly. Delaying claims makes them appear less important. Delayed claims are also more difficult to verify. By taking the time to put your claim in writing, you indicate your seriousness. A written claim starts a record of the problem, should later action be necessary. Be sure to keep a copy of your letter.

Close a claim letter with a summary of the action requested and a courteous goodwill statement.

When Keith Krahnke received a statement showing a charge for a three-year service warranty that he did not purchase, he was furious. He called the store but failed to get satisfaction to his complaint. Then he decided to write. You can see the first draft of his direct claim letter in Figure 9.6. This draft gave him a chance to vent his anger, but it accomplished little else. The tone was belligerent, and it assumed that the company intentionally mischarged him. Furthermore, it failed to tell the reader how to remedy the problem. The revision, also shown in Figure 9.6, tempered the tone, described the problem objectively, and provided facts and figures. Most important, it specified exactly what Keith wanted to be done.

Written claims submitted promptly are taken more seriously than delayed ones.

Notice in Figure 9.6 that Keith used the personal business letter style, which is appropriate for you to use in writing personal messages. Your return address, but not your name, appears above the date. Keith used modified block style, in which the return address, date, and closing lines start at the center. Full block style, however, is also appropriate for personal business letters.

To sum up, use the direct pattern with the main idea first when you expect little resistance to letters making requests. The following checklist reviews the direct strategy for information and action requests, orders, and claim letters.

FIGURE 9.6 ***Direct Claim Letter***

DRAFT

Dear Good Vibes:

You call yourselves Good Vibes, but all I'm getting from your service is bad vibes! I'm furious that you have your salespeople slip in unwanted service warranties to boost your sales.

Sounds angry; jumps to conclusions

When I bought my Panatronic DVR from Good Vibes, Inc., in August, I specifically told the salesperson that I did NOT want a three-year service warranty. But there it is on my Visa statement this month! You people have obviously billed me for a service I did not authorize. I refuse to pay this charge.

Forgets that mistakes happen

How can you hope to stay in business with such fraudulent practices? I was expecting to return this month and look at MP3 players, but you can be sure I'll find an honest dealer this time.

Fails to suggest solution

Sincerely,

REVISION

1201 Lantana Court
Lake Worth, FL 33461
September 3, 2006

Personal business letter style

Mr. Sam Lee, Customer Service
Good Vibes, Inc.
2003 53rd Street
West Palm Beach, FL 33407

Dear Mr. Lee:

Please credit my Visa account, No. 0000-0046-2198-9421, to correct an erroneous charge of $299.

States simply and clearly what to do

On August 1 I purchased a Panatronic DVR from Good Vibes, Inc. Although the salesperson discussed a three-year extended warranty with me, I decided against purchasing that service for $299. However, when my credit card statement arrived this month, I noticed an extra $299 charge from Good Vibes, Inc. I suspect that this charge represents the warranty I declined. Enclosed is a copy of my sales invoice along with my Visa statement on which I circled the charge.

Explains objectively what went wrong

Doesn't blame or accuse

Documents facts

Please authorize a credit immediately and send a copy of the transaction to me at the above address. I'm enjoying all the features of my Panatronic DVR and would like to be shopping at Good Vibes for an MP3 player shortly.

Summarizes request and courteously suggests continued business once problem is resolved

Sincerely,

Keith Krahnke

Keith Krahnke

Enclosure

Checklist for Writing Direct Requests

Information or Action Request Letters

- ✓ **Open by stating the main idea.** To elicit information, ask a question or issue a polite command (*Will you please answer the following questions . . .*).
- ✓ **Explain and justify the request.** In seeking information, use open-ended questions structured in parallel, balanced form.
- ✓ **Request action in the closing.** Express appreciation, and set an end date if appropriate. Avoid clichés (*Thank you for your cooperation*).

Order Letters

- ✓ **Open by authorizing the purchase.** Use order language (*Please send me . . .*), designate the delivery method, and state your information source (such as a catalog, advertisement, or magazine article).
- ✓ **List items in the body.** Include quantity, order number, description, unit price, total price, tax, shipping, and total costs.
- ✓ **Close with the payment data.** Tell how you are paying and when you expect delivery. Express appreciation.

Direct Claim Letters

- ✓ **Begin with the purpose.** Present a clear statement of the problem or the action requested—such as a refund, replacement, credit, explanation, or correction of error.
- ✓ **Explain objectively.** In the body tell the specifics of the claim. Provide copies of necessary documents.
- ✓ **End by requesting action.** Include an end date if important. Add a pleasant, forward-looking statement. Keep a copy of the letter.

Direct Replies

learning objective

5

Often, your messages will reply directly and favorably to requests for information or action. A customer wants information about a product. A supplier asks to arrange a meeting. Another business inquires about one of your procedures or about a former employee. In complying with such requests, you'll want to apply the same direct pattern you used in making requests.

Letters responding to requests may open with a subject line to identify the topic immediately.

The opening of a customer reply letter might contain a subject line, as shown in Figure 9.7. A subject line helps the reader recognize the topic immediately. Usually appearing two lines below the salutation, the subject line refers in abbreviated form to previous correspondence and/or summarizes a message (*Subject: Your July 12 Inquiry About WorkZone Software*). It often omits articles (*a, an, the*), is not a complete sentence, and does not end with a period. Knowledgeable business communicators use a subject line to refer to earlier correspondence so that in the first sentence, the most emphatic spot in a letter, they are free to emphasize the main idea.

FIGURE 9.7 *Customer Reply Letter*

The Three Phases of the Writing Process

1 Prewriting

ANALYZE: The purpose of this letter is to provide helpful information and to promote company products.

ANTICIPATE: The reader is the intelligent owner of a small business who needs help with personnel administration.

ADAPT: Because the reader requested this data, she will be receptive to the letter. Use the direct pattern.

2 Writing

RESEARCH: Gather facts to answer the business owner's questions. Consult brochures and pamphlets.

ORGANIZE: Prepare a scratch outline. Plan for a fast, direct opening. Use numbered answers to the business owner's three questions.

COMPOSE: Write the first draft on a computer. Strive for short sentences and paragraphs.

3 Revising

REVISE: Eliminate jargon and wordiness. Look for ways to explain how the product fits the reader's needs. Revise for "you" view.

PROOFREAD: Double-check the form of numbers (*July 12, page 6, 8 to 5 PST*).

EVALUATE: Does this letter answer the customer's questions and encourage an order?

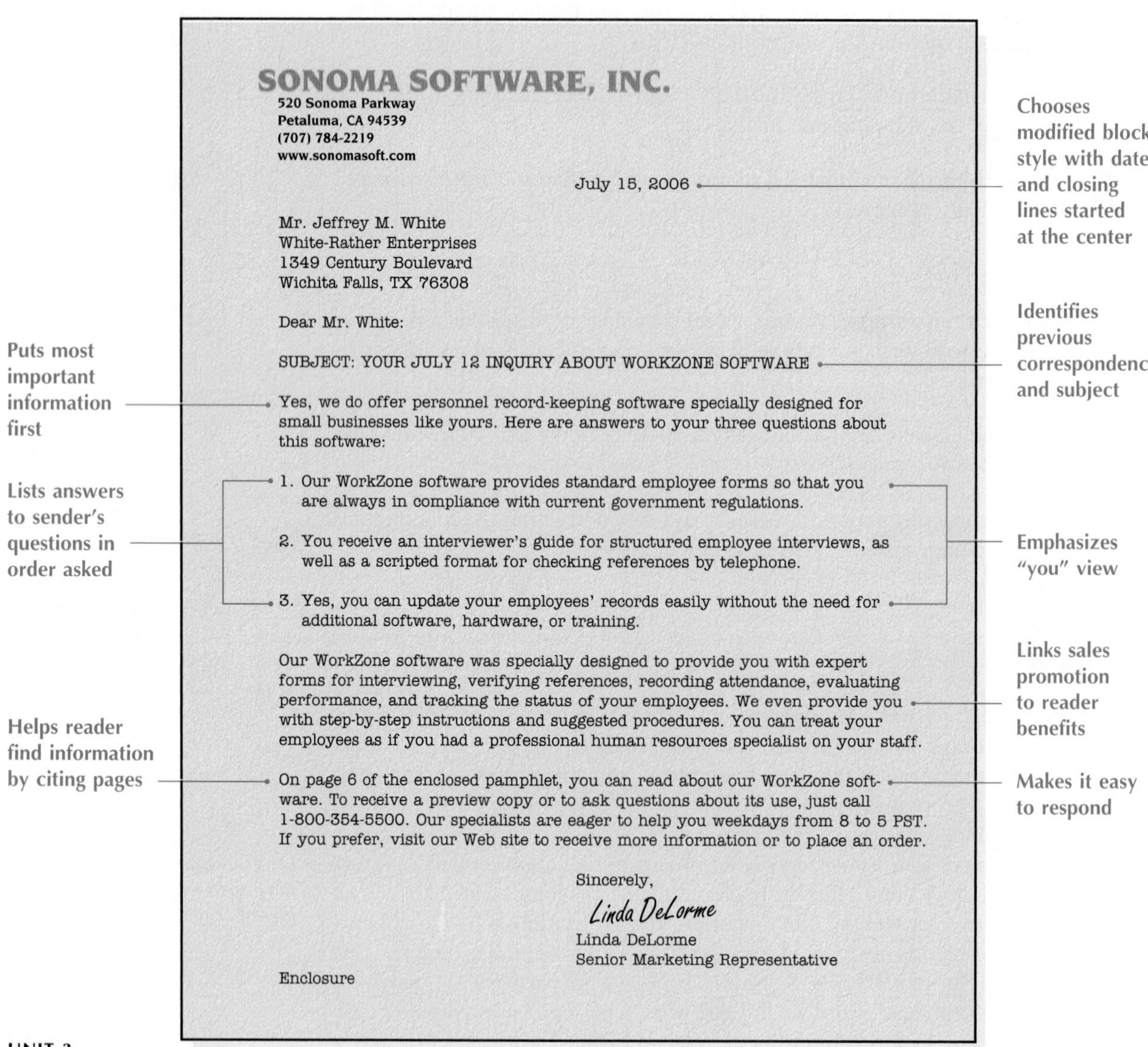

SONOMA SOFTWARE, INC.
520 Sonoma Parkway
Petaluma, CA 94539
(707) 784-2219
www.sonomasoft.com

July 15, 2006

Mr. Jeffrey M. White
White-Rather Enterprises
1349 Century Boulevard
Wichita Falls, TX 76308

Dear Mr. White:

SUBJECT: YOUR JULY 12 INQUIRY ABOUT WORKZONE SOFTWARE

Yes, we do offer personnel record-keeping software specially designed for small businesses like yours. Here are answers to your three questions about this software:

1. Our WorkZone software provides standard employee forms so that you are always in compliance with current government regulations.

2. You receive an interviewer's guide for structured employee interviews, as well as a scripted format for checking references by telephone.

3. Yes, you can update your employees' records easily without the need for additional software, hardware, or training.

Our WorkZone software was specially designed to provide you with expert forms for interviewing, verifying references, recording attendance, evaluating performance, and tracking the status of your employees. We even provide you with step-by-step instructions and suggested procedures. You can treat your employees as if you had a professional human resources specialist on your staff.

On page 6 of the enclosed pamphlet, you can read about our WorkZone software. To receive a preview copy or to ask questions about its use, just call 1-800-354-5500. Our specialists are eager to help you weekdays from 8 to 5 PST. If you prefer, visit our Web site to receive more information or to place an order.

Sincerely,

Linda DeLorme

Linda DeLorme
Senior Marketing Representative

Enclosure

Chooses modified block style with date and closing lines started at the center
Identifies previous correspondence and subject
Puts most important information first
Lists answers to sender's questions in order asked
Emphasizes "you" view
Links sales promotion to reader benefits
Helps reader find information by citing pages
Makes it easy to respond

Open Directly

In the first sentence of a direct reply letter, deliver the information the reader wants. Avoid wordy, drawn-out openings such as *I have before me your letter of August 5, in which you request information about* . . . . More forceful and more efficient is an opener that answers the inquiry (*Here is the information you wanted about* . . .). When agreeing to a request for action, announce the good news promptly (*Yes, I will be happy to speak to your business communication class on the topic of* . . .).

Announce the good news promptly.

In the body of your reply, supply explanations and additional information. Because a letter written on company stationery is considered a legally binding contract, be sure to check facts and figures carefully. If a policy or procedure needs authorization, seek approval from a supervisor or executive before writing the letter.

Arrange Information Logically

When answering a group of questions or providing considerable data, arrange the information logically and make it readable by using lists, tables, headings, boldface, italics, or other graphic devices. When customers or prospective customers inquire about products or services, your response should do more than merely supply answers. You'll also want to promote your organization and products. Often, companies have particular products and services they want to spotlight. Thus, when a customer writes about one product, provide helpful information that satisfies the inquiry, but consider using the opportunity to introduce another product as well. Be sure to present the promotional material with attention to the "you" view and to reader benefits (*You can use our standardized tests to free you from time-consuming employment screening*). You'll learn more about special techniques for developing sales and persuasive messages in Chapter 10.

Responding to customer inquiries provides a good opportunity to promote your business.

In concluding, make sure you are cordial and personal. Refer to the information provided or to its use (*The enclosed list summarizes our recommendations. We wish you all the best in redesigning your Web site.*) If further action is required, describe the procedure and help the reader with specifics (*The Small Business Administration publishes a number of helpful booklets. Its Web address is* . . .).

Emphasize the Positive in Mixed Messages

The direct pattern is also appropriate for messages that are mostly good news but may have some negative elements. For example, a return policy has time limits; an airfare may contain holiday restrictions; a speaker can come but not at the time requested; an appliance can be repaired but not replaced. When the message is mixed, emphasize the good news by presenting it first (*Yes, I would be happy to address your marketing class on the topic of* . . .). Then, explain why a problem exists (*My schedule for the week of October 10, however, takes me to Washington and Philadelphia, where I am* . . .). Present the bad news in the middle (*Although I cannot meet with your class during the week of October 10, perhaps we can schedule a date during the week of* . . .). End the message cordially by returning to the good news (*Thanks for the invitation. I'm looking forward to arranging a date in October when I can talk with your students about careers in marketing*).

In mixed-news messages the good news should precede the bad.

Your goal is to present the negative news clearly without letting it become the focus of the message. Thus, you want to spend more time talking about the good news; and by placing the bad news in the middle of the letter, you deemphasize it. You'll learn other techniques for presenting bad news in Chapter 11.

learning objective

6

When a company responds favorably to a customer's claim, the response is called an adjustment.

Adjustments

Even the best-run and best-loved businesses occasionally receive claims or complaints from consumers. When a company receives a claim and decides to respond favorably, the letter is called an *adjustment letter.* Most businesses make adjustments promptly—they replace merchandise, refund money, extend discounts, send coupons, and repair goods. Businesses make favorable adjustments to legitimate claims for two reasons. First, consumers are protected by contractual and tort law for recovery of damages.[7] If, for example, you find an insect in a package of frozen peas, the food processor of that package is bound by contractual law to replace it. And if you suffer injury, the processor may be liable for damages. Second, and more obviously, most organizations genuinely want to satisfy their customers and retain their business.

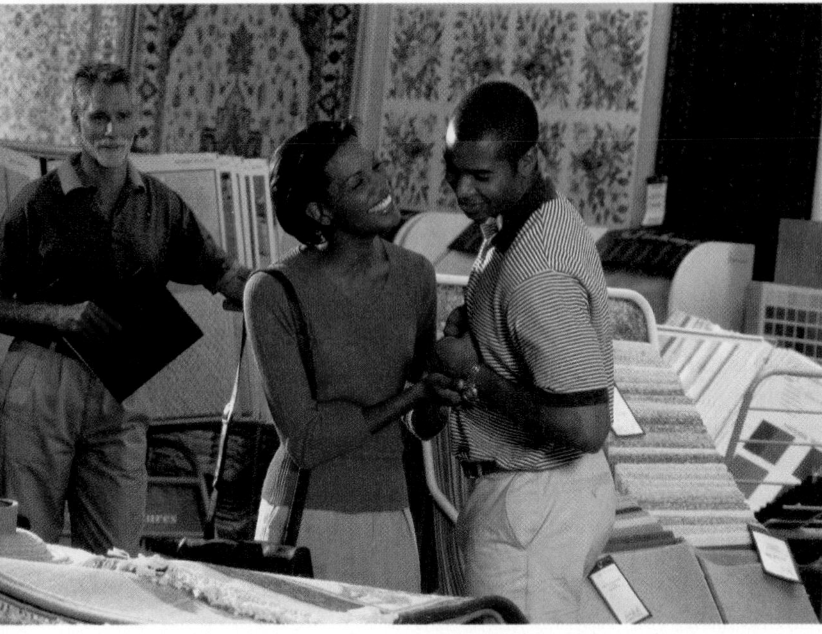

Whether selling carpets, computers, or cars, businesses want happy customers. When something goes wrong, most companies try their best to satisfy their customers. Research shows that 7 of 10 customers who complain will do business with the company again so long as their concern is handled properly. Adjustment letters respond to customer complaints.

Photo: © Comstock Images/Getty Images

Most businesses today honestly want to please their customers. To compete globally and to pump up local markets, American industry is particularly sold on the idea of improving the quality of its service. Retaining current customers is enormously important. In a recent survey of financial services companies, the average cost to retain a customer was $57. The cost to recruit a new customer was a whopping $279![8]

One way to retain customers is to listen to what they have to say—even when it's a complaint. One industry expert observed, "You're most likely to hear from customers when they have a complaint, and that's a good thing. They're not only giving you a chance to help them, but they're initiating a dialogue, which is exactly what you want to have with your best customers."[9] When customers are unhappy, they don't return. A staggering 91 percent of disgruntled customers swear they will never do business again with a company that does not resolve their complaint.[10]

Favorable responses to customer claims follow the direct pattern; unfavorable responses follow the indirect pattern.

In responding to customer claims, you must first decide whether to grant the claim. Unless the claim is obviously fraudulent or represents an excessive sum, you'll probably grant it. When you say *yes*, your adjustment letter will be good news to the reader, so you'll want to use the direct pattern. When your response is *no*, the indirect pattern might be more appropriate. Chapter 11 discusses the indirect pattern for conveying negative news.

You'll have three goals in adjustment letters:

- Rectifying the wrong, if one exists
- Regaining the confidence of the customer
- Promoting further business

Open With the Good News

The opening of a positive adjustment letter should approve the customer's claim immediately. Notice how quickly the following openers announce the good news:

> You're right! We agree that the warranty on your American Standard Model UC600 dishwasher should be extended for six months.
>
> The enclosed $250 refund check demonstrates our desire to satisfy our customers and earn their confidence.
>
> You will be receiving shortly a new slim Nokia 8860 cell phone to replace the one that shattered when dropped recently.
>
> Please take your portable Admiral microwave oven to A-1 Appliance Service, 220 Orange Street, Pasadena, where it will be repaired at no cost to you.

Adjustment letters seek to right wrongs, regain customer confidence, and promote further business.

Opening sentences reveal the good news quickly.

Occasionally, customers merely want to lodge a complaint and know that something is being done about it. Here's the opening from a bank responding to such a complaint:

> We agree with you completely. Some of our customers have recently spent too much time "on hold" while waiting to speak to a customer service representative. These delays are unacceptable, and we are taking strong measures to eliminate such delays.

In making an adjustment, avoid sounding resentful or grudging. Once you decide to grant a claim, do so willingly. Remember that a primary goal in adjustments is retaining customer loyalty. Statements that sound reluctant (*Although we generally refuse to extend warranties, we're willing to make an exception in this case*) may cause greater dissatisfaction than no response at all.

Explain the Reasons

In the body of an adjustment letter, your goal is to win back the confidence of the customer. You can do this by explaining what caused the problem (if you know) or by describing the measures you are taking to avoid recurrences of the problem, such as in the following:

Explain what caused the problem and the measures taken to avoid future recurrence.

> In preparing our products, we take special care to see that they are wholesome and free of foreign matter. Approved spraying procedures in the field control insects when necessary during the growing season. Our processing plants use screens, air curtains, ultraviolet lights, and other devices to exclude insects. Moreover, we inspect and clean every product to ensure that insects are not present.

Notice that this explanation does not admit error. Many companies sidestep the issue of responsibility because they feel that such an admission damages their credibility or might even encourage legal action. Others admit errors indirectly (*Oversights may sometimes occur*) or even directly (*Once in a while a product that is less than perfect goes out*). The major focus of attention, however, should be on explaining how you are working to prevent the recurrence of the problem, as illustrated in the following:

> Waiting "on hold" is as unacceptable to us as it is to you. This delay was brought about when we installed a new automated system. Unfortunately, it took longer than we expected to implement the system and to train our people in their new roles. We are now taking strong measures to eliminate the problem. We have made a significant investment in new technology that will free our customer representatives from routine calls so that they can help you with those banking needs that require personal attention. We are also rerouting calls and modifying the way they are handled.

Explain what went wrong without admitting liability or making excuses.

When an explanation poses no threat of admitting liability, provide details. But don't make your explanation sound like an excuse. Customers resent it when organizations don't take responsibility or try to put the blame elsewhere. When Intel Corp. was swamped with a flood of unfavorable responses regarding a flawed Pentium chip, President Andy Grove posted a letter to the Internet. His letter said, "I'd like to comment a bit on the conversations that have been taking place here. First of all, I'm truly sorry for the anxiety created among you by our floating-point issue." He went on to explain how Intel had tested the chip and appointed a group of mathematicians and scientists to study the problem. Eventually, Intel decided to replace all flawed chips. His letter concluded, "Please don't be concerned that the passing of time will deprive you of the opportunity to get your problem resolved. We will stand behind these chips for the life of your computer."[11] The tone of a response is extremely important, and Grove sounded sincere in his explanation.

Decide Whether to Apologize

Apologize if it seems natural and appropriate.

Another sticky issue is whether to apologize. Notice that Andy Grove of Intel apologized in his Internet letter. Studies of adjustment letters received by consumers show that a majority do contain apologies, either in the opening or in the closing.[12] Attorneys generally discourage apologies fearing that they admit responsibility and will trigger lawsuits. But an analysis of case outcomes indicates that both judges and juries tend to look on apologies favorably. And a few states are even passing laws that protect those who apologize.[13] Some business writing experts advise against apologies, contending that they are counterproductive and merely remind the customer of unpleasantness related to the claim. If, however, it seems natural to you to apologize, do so. People like to hear apologies. It raises their self-esteem, shows the humility of the writer, and acts as a form of "psychological compensation."[14] Don't, however, fall back on the familiar phrase, *I'm sorry for any inconvenience we may have caused.* It sounds mechanical and totally insincere. Instead try something like this: *We understand the frustration our delay has caused you. We're sorry you didn't receive better service,* or *You're right to be disappointed.* If you feel that an apology is appropriate, do it early and briefly, as Andy Grove did in his Internet response. Remember that the primary focus of your letter is on (1) how you are complying with the request, (2) how the problem occurred, and (3) how you are working to prevent its recurrence.

Use Sensitive Language

Focus on complying with the request, explaining reasons, and preventing recurrence.

The language of adjustment letters must be particularly sensitive, since customers are already upset. Here are some don'ts:

- Don't use negative words (*trouble, regret, misunderstanding, fault, error, inconvenience, you claim*).
- Don't blame customers—even when they may be at fault.
- Don't blame individuals or departments within your organization; it's unprofessional.
- Don't make unrealistic promises; you can't guarantee that the situation will never recur.

To regain the confidence of your reader, consider including resale information. Describe a product's features and any special applications that might appeal to the reader. Promote a new product if it seems appropriate.

Be Fair but Don't Give Away the Farm

If the complaint is justified, offer to solve the problem. Be careful, though, not to "give away the farm." In some instances, all the customer wants is an explanation or an apology. Depending on the product or the damage, consumers might prefer repair or replacement rather than refund. Companies will want to do what is fair. And, within reason, they strive to comply with customers' expectations. Solving a problem, even at a loss to the company, may pay valuable rewards in the form of future sales saved.[15] But, as one researcher points out, "it seems ill advised to think that we can 'buy' more satisfaction by increasing the compensation."[16] What is important is responding to complaints sincerely and appropriately.

Companies strive to offer fair, but not excessive, adjustments.

Close Positively

To close an adjustment letter, assume that the problem has been resolved and that future business will continue. You might express appreciation that the reader wrote, extend thanks for past business, refer to your desire to be of service, or mention a new product. Here are some effective adjustment letter closings for various purposes:

Close an adjustment letter with appreciation, thanks for past business, a desire to be of service, or the promotion of a new product.

> You were most helpful in informing us of this situation and permitting us to correct it. We appreciate your thoughtfulness in writing to us.
>
> Thanks for writing. Your satisfaction is important to us. We hope that this refund check convinces you that service to our customers is our No. 1 priority. Our goals are to earn your confidence and continue to justify that confidence with quality products and excellent service.
>
> Your Nokia 8860 cell phone will come in handy when you're playing and working outside this summer. For additional summer enjoyment take a look at the portable CD player on page 37 of the enclosed catalog. We value your business and look forward to your future orders.

The adjustment letter in Figure 9.8 offers to replace dead rose bushes. It's very possible that grower error caused the plants to die, yet the letter doesn't blame the customer. Notice, too, how resale information and sales promotion material are introduced without seeming pushy. Most important, the tone of the letter suggests that the company is in the customer's corner and wants to do what is fair and right.

Although the direct pattern works for many requests and replies, it obviously won't work for every situation. With more practice and experience, you'll be able to alter the pattern and apply the writing process to other communication problems.

Letters of Recommendation

learning objective 7

Letters of recommendation may be written to nominate people for awards and for membership in organizations. More frequently, though, they are written to evaluate present or former employees. The central concern in these messages is honesty. Thus, you should avoid exaggerating or distorting a candidate's qualifications to cover up weaknesses or to destroy the person's chances. Ethically and legally, you have a duty to the candidate as well as to other employers to describe that person truthfully and objectively. You don't, however, have to endorse everyone who asks. Because recommendations are generally voluntary, you can—and should—resist writing letters for individuals you can't truthfully support. Ask these people to find other recommenders who know them better.

Letters of recommendation present honest, objective evaluations of individuals and help match candidates to jobs.

FIGURE 9.8 ***Adjustment Letter***

FLOWER FIELDS NURSERIES AND ROSES
304 Litchfield Lane
Bakersfield, CA 92501
www.flowerfields.com
(661) 650 3591

June 3, 2006

Mr. James Bronski
1390 Moorpark Avenue
San Jose, CA 95127

Dear Mr. Bronski:

You may choose six rose bushes as replacements, or you may have a full cash refund for the roses you purchased last year. — *Approves customer's claim immediately*

The quality of our plants and the careful handing they receive assure you of healthy, viable roses for your garden. Even so, plants sometimes fail without apparent cause. That's why every plant carries a guarantee to grow and to establish itself in your garden. — *Tactfully skirts the issue of what caused plant failure*; *Avoids blaming customer*

Along with this letter is a copy of our current catalog for you to select six new roses or reorder the favorites you chose last year. Two of your previous selections—Red Velvet and Rose Princess—were last season's best-selling roses. For fragrance and old-rose charm, you might like to try the new David Austin English Roses. These enormously popular hybrids resulted from crossing full-petaled old garden roses with modern repeat-flowering shrub roses. — *Offers resale information to assure customer of a wise choice*; *Includes some sales promotion without overkill*

To help you enjoy your roses to the fullest, you'll also receive a copy of our authoritative *Home Gardener's Guide to Roses*. This comprehensive booklet provides easy-to-follow planting tips as well as sound advice about sun, soil, and drainage requirements for roses. — *Projects personal, conversational tone*

To receive your free replacement order, just fill out the order form inside the catalog and attach the enclosed certificate. Or return the certificate, and you will receive a full refund of the purchase price. — *Tells reader clearly what to do next*

The quality of Flower Fields' plants reflects the expertise of over a century of hybridizing, growing, harvesting, and shipping top-quality garden stock. Your complete satisfaction is our primary goal. If you're not happy, Mr.Bronski, we're not happy. To ensure your satisfaction and your respect, we maintain our 100 percent guarantee policy. — *Shows pride in the company's products and concern for its customers*; *Strives to regain customer's confidence in both products and service*

Sincerely,

Michael Vanderer

Michael Vanderer
General Manager

mv:meg

Enclosures

Some businesspeople today refuse to write recommendations for former employees because they fear lawsuits. See the accompanying Ethical Insights box for tips on using caution in these letters. Other businesspeople argue that recommendations are useless because they're always positive. Despite the general avoidance of negatives, well-written recommendations do help match candidates with jobs. Hiring companies learn more about a candidate's skills and potential. As a result, they are able to place a candidate properly. Therefore, you should learn to write such letters because you will surely be expected to do so in your future career.

Open With Identification

Begin an employment recommendation by identifying the candidate and the position sought, if you know it. State that your remarks are confidential, and suggest

ethical insights

Using Caution in Writing Letters of Recommendation

Fearing lawsuits, many companies prohibit their managers from recommending ex-employees. Instead, they provide only the essentials, such as date of employment and position held. But nearly three fourths of the states have enacted job-reference shield statues. These laws generally protect employers from liability—so long as the reference information is job-related, is truthful, and does not disclose anything prohibited.[17] Regardless of the problems involved, most ethical and conscientious businesspeople recognize that references serve a valuable purpose in conveying personnel data. Yet, they are cautious in writing them. Here are six guidelines that a careful writer can follow in writing recommendations:

- **Respond only to written requests.** Moreover, don't volunteer information, particularly if it's negative.
- **State that your remarks are confidential.** Although such a statement does not prevent legal review, it does suggest the intentions of the writer.
- **Provide only job-related information.** Avoid commenting on behavior or activities away from the job.
- **Avoid vague or ambiguous statements.** Keep in mind that imprecise, poorly explained remarks (*she left the job suddenly*) may be made innocently but could be interpreted quite differently.
- **Supply specific evidence for any negatives.** Support any damaging information with verifiable facts.
- **Stick to the truth.** Avoid making any doubtful statements. Truth is always a valid defense against accusations of libel or slander.

Career Application

As manager of productions at a midsized graphic design company, you have been asked by a well-regarded former employee to write a recommendation. You want to write. However, your boss has recently prohibited the writing of any letters of recommendation. You feel strongly that you should write this recommendation. What should you do?

that you are writing at the request of the applicant. Describe your relationship with the candidate, as shown in the first paragraph of the employment recommendation letter in Figure 9.9. Letters that recommend individuals for awards may open with more supportive statements, such as, *I'm very pleased to nominate Robert Walsh for the Employee-of-the-Month award. For the past sixteen months, Mr. Walsh served as staff accountant in my division. During that time he distinguished himself by. . . .*

Provide Evidence in the Body

The body of a letter of recommendation should describe the candidate's job performance and potential in specific terms.

The body of an employment recommendation should describe the applicant's job performance and potential. Employers are particularly interested in such traits as communication skills, organizational skills, people skills, the ability to work with a team, the ability to work independently, honesty, dependability, ambition, loyalty, and initiative. In describing these traits, be sure to back them up with evidence. One of the biggest weaknesses in letters of recommendation is that writers tend to make global, nonspecific statements (*He was careful and accurate* versus *He completed eight financial statements monthly with about 99 percent accuracy*). Employers prefer definite, task-related descriptions, as shown in the second and third paragraphs of Figure 9.9.

Be especially careful to support any negative comments with verification (not *He was slower than other customer service reps* but *He answered 18 calls an hour, whereas most service reps average 30 calls an hour*). In reporting deficiencies, be sure to describe behavior (*her last two reports were late and had to be rewritten by her supervisor*) rather than evaluate it (*she is unreliable and her reports are careless*).

FIGURE 9.9 ***Employment Recommendation Letter***

Tips for Writing Letters of Recommendation

- Identify the purpose and confidentiality of the message.
- Establish your relationship with the applicant.
- Describe the length of employment and job duties, if relevant.
- Provide specific examples of the applicant's professional and personal skills.
- Compare the applicant with others in his or her field.
- Offer an overall rating of the applicant.
- Summarize the significant attributes of the applicant.
- Draw a conclusion regarding the recommendation.

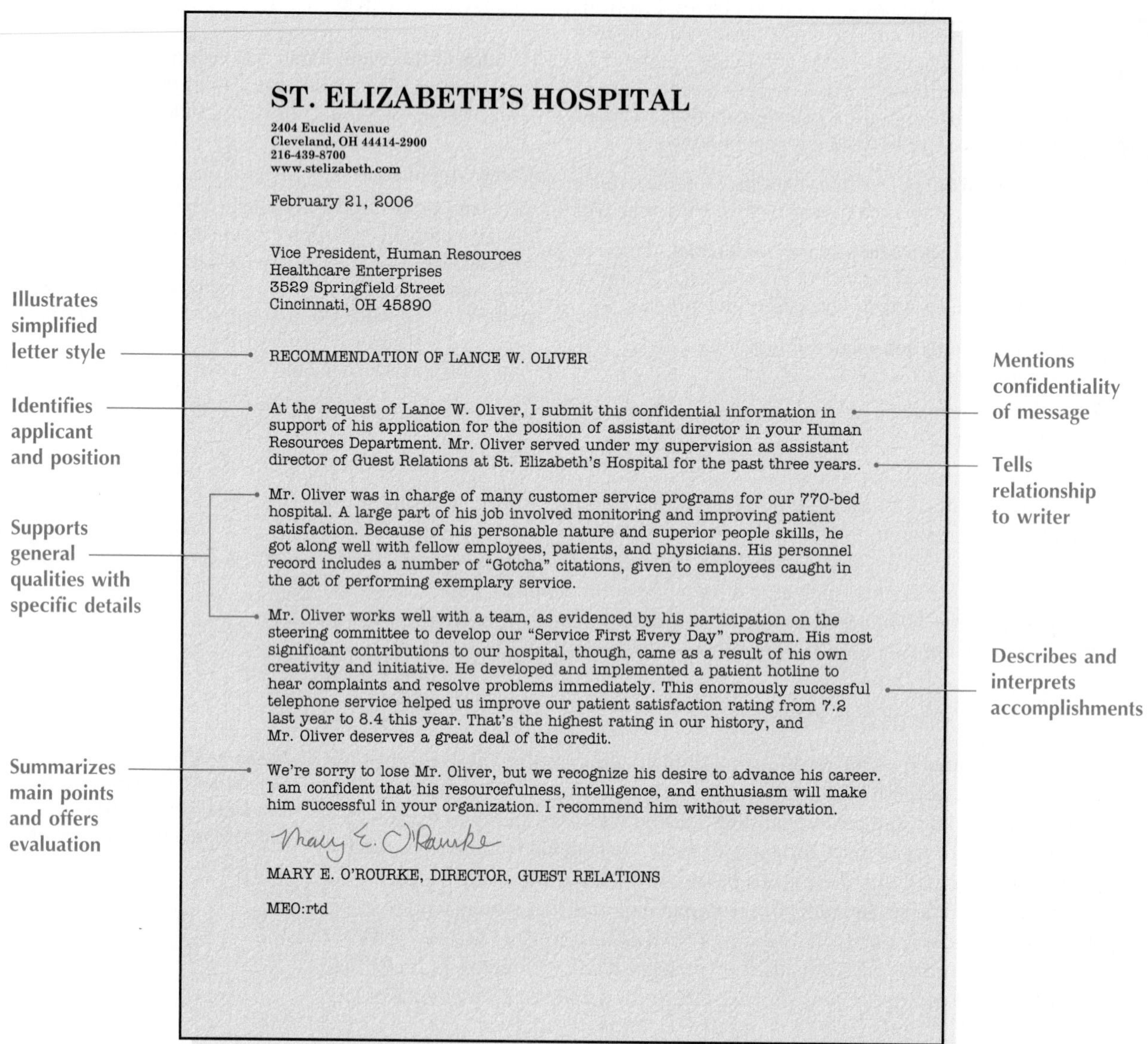

ST. ELIZABETH'S HOSPITAL

2404 Euclid Avenue
Cleveland, OH 44414-2900
216-439-8700
www.stelizabeth.com

February 21, 2006

Vice President, Human Resources
Healthcare Enterprises
3529 Springfield Street
Cincinnati, OH 45890

RECOMMENDATION OF LANCE W. OLIVER

At the request of Lance W. Oliver, I submit this confidential information in support of his application for the position of assistant director in your Human Resources Department. Mr. Oliver served under my supervision as assistant director of Guest Relations at St. Elizabeth's Hospital for the past three years.

Mr. Oliver was in charge of many customer service programs for our 770-bed hospital. A large part of his job involved monitoring and improving patient satisfaction. Because of his personable nature and superior people skills, he got along well with fellow employees, patients, and physicians. His personnel record includes a number of "Gotcha" citations, given to employees caught in the act of performing exemplary service.

Mr. Oliver works well with a team, as evidenced by his participation on the steering committee to develop our "Service First Every Day" program. His most significant contributions to our hospital, though, came as a result of his own creativity and initiative. He developed and implemented a patient hotline to hear complaints and resolve problems immediately. This enormously successful telephone service helped us improve our patient satisfaction rating from 7.2 last year to 8.4 this year. That's the highest rating in our history, and Mr. Oliver deserves a great deal of the credit.

We're sorry to lose Mr. Oliver, but we recognize his desire to advance his career. I am confident that his resourcefulness, intelligence, and enthusiasm will make him successful in your organization. I recommend him without reservation.

Mary E. O'Rourke

MARY E. O'ROURKE, DIRECTOR, GUEST RELATIONS

MEO:rtd

Illustrates simplified letter style
Identifies applicant and position
Supports general qualities with specific details
Summarizes main points and offers evaluation
Mentions confidentiality of message
Tells relationship to writer
Describes and interprets accomplishments

Process in Progress

Ben & Jerry's Revisited

CUSTOMER LETTERS ARRIVING at Ben & Jerry's get special attention from Alice Blachly, one of the consumer affairs coordinators. In responding to fan letters, Blachly prepares handwritten cards or printed letters that promote good feelings and cement a long-lasting bond between Ben & Jerry's and its satisfied consumers. To letters with questions, Blachly locates the information and responds. For example, a consumer worried that cottonseed oil, formerly contained in one of the nut-butter portions of an exotic ice cream, might be contaminated by pesticides. Blachly checked with company quality assurance experts and also investigated articles about cottonseed oil before responding. Other consumers might wonder about Ben & Jerry's position on the treatment of cows by Vermont dairy farmers.

However, letters with consumer complaints, such as *My pint didn't have quite enough cookie dough*, get top priority. "We have trained our consumers to expect the best," says Blachly, "so they are disappointed when something goes wrong. And we are disappointed, too. We refund the purchase price, and we explain what caused the problem, if we know."

Critical Thinking

- When customers write to Ben & Jerry's for information and the response must contain both positive and negative news, what strategy should the respondent follow?
- If a customer writes to complain about something for which Ben & Jerry's is not responsible (such as ice in frozen yogurt), should the response letter contain an apology? Why or why not?
- Why is letter-writing an important function for a company like Ben & Jerry's?

CONTINUED ON PAGE 283

case study

Evaluate in the Closing

In the final paragraph of a recommendation, you should offer an overall evaluation. Indicate how you would rank this person in relation to others in similar positions. Many managers add a statement indicating whether they would rehire the applicant, given the chance. If you are strongly supportive, summarize the candidate's best qualities. In the closing you might also offer to answer questions by telephone. Such a statement, though, could suggest that the candidate has weak skills and that you will make damaging statements orally but not in print.

General letters of recommendation, written when the candidate has no specific position in mind, often begin with the salutation TO PROSPECTIVE EMPLOYERS. More specific recommendations, to support applications to known positions, address an individual. When the addressee's name is unknown, consider using the simplified letter format, shown in Figure 9.9, which avoids a salutation.

In writing letters of recommendation and other positive reply messages, follow Guffey's 3-x-3 writing process along with the specific tips suggested in the following checklist.

Checklist for Writing Positive Reply Letters

Letters That Comply With Requests

✓ **Use a subject line.** Identify previous correspondence and the topic of this letter.

- ✓ **Open directly.** In the first sentence deliver the information the reader wants (*Yes, I can meet with your class* or *Here is the information you requested*). If the message is mixed, present the best news first.
- ✓ **In the body provide explanations and additional information.** Arrange this information logically, perhaps using a bulleted list, headings, or columns. For prospective customers build your company image and promote your products.
- ✓ **End with a cordial, personalized statement.** If further action is required, tell the reader how to proceed and give helpful details.

Letters That Make Adjustments

- ✓ **Open with approval.** Comply with the customer's claim immediately. Avoid sounding grudging or reluctant.
- ✓ **In the body win back the customer's confidence.** Explain the cause of the problem or describe your ongoing efforts to avoid such difficulties. Focus on your efforts to satisfy customers. Apologize if you feel that you should, but do so early and quickly. Avoid negative words, accusations, and unrealistic promises. Consider including resale and sales promotion information.
- ✓ **Close positively.** Express appreciation to the customer for writing, extend thanks for past business, anticipate continued patronage, refer to your desire to be of service, and/or mention a new product if it seems appropriate.

Letters of Recommendation

- ✓ **Open with identifying information.** Name the candidate, identify the position, and explain your relationship. State that you are writing at the request of the candidate and that the letter is confidential.
- ✓ **In the body add supporting statements.** Describe the applicant's present duties, job performance, skills, and potential. Back up general qualities with specific evidence. Verify any negative statements.
- ✓ **Close with an overall ranking of the candidate.** (*Of all the people I have known in this position, Jim ranks. . . .*) Offer to supply more information by telephone.

learning objective

8

Goodwill Messages

Written goodwill messages carry more meaning than ready-made cards.

Many communicators are intimidated when they must write messages expressing thanks, recognition, and sympathy. Finding the right words to express feelings is often more difficult than writing ordinary business documents. That's why writers tend to procrastinate when it comes to goodwill messages. It's easier to send a ready-made card or pick up the telephone. Remember, though, that the personal sentiments of the sender are always more expressive and more meaningful to readers than are printed cards or oral messages. Taking the time to write gives more importance to our well-wishing. Personal notes also provide a record that can be reread, savored, and treasured.

In expressing thanks, recognition, or sympathy, you should always do so promptly. These messages are easier to write when the situation is fresh in your mind. They also mean more to the recipient. And don't forget that a prompt thank-you note carries the hidden message that you care and that you consider the event to be important. The best goodwill messages—whether thanks, congratulations, praise, or sympathy—concentrate on the five *S*'s. These goodwill messages are

- **Selfless.** Be sure to focus the message solely on the receiver not the sender. Don't talk about yourself; avoid such comments as *I remember when I . . . .*
- **Specific.** Personalize the message by mentioning specific incidents or characteristics of the receiver. Telling a colleague *Great speech* is much less effective than *Great story about McDonald's marketing in Moscow.* Take care to verify names and other facts.
- **Sincere.** Let your words show genuine feelings. Rehearse in your mind how you would express the message to the receiver orally. Then transform that conversational language to your written message. Avoid pretentious, formal, or flowery language (*It gives me great pleasure to extend felicitations on the occasion of your firm's twentieth anniversary*).
- **Spontaneous.** Keep the message fresh and enthusiastic. Avoid canned phrases (*Congratulations on your promotion, Good luck in the future*). Strive for directness and naturalness, not creative brilliance.
- **Short.** Although goodwill messages can be as long as needed, try to accomplish your purpose in only a few sentences. What is most important is remembering an individual. Such caring does not require documentation or wordiness. Individuals and business organizations often use special note cards or stationery for brief messages.

spotlight *on communicators*

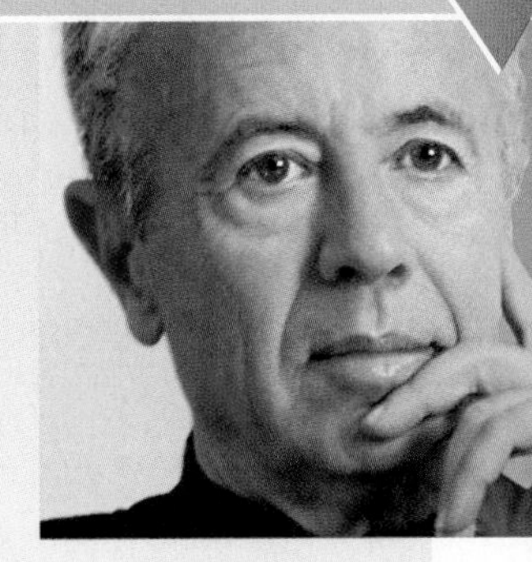

Andrew S. Grove, cofounder and chairman of Intel, the nation's principal computer chip maker, is best known as an information age leader and a technology visionary. But he also recognizes the value of promoting personal relationships through goodwill messages. A mere thank-you followed by general comments is rather hollow, he says. Instead, when sending thanks or good wishes, Grove suggests making the thanks match the deed. Ask yourself what was special, unusual, extraordinary, or over and above the call of duty—and then describe it. Being specific, warm, and sincere are as important as the difference between a personal note and a computerized form letter.

Thanks

When someone has done you a favor or when an action merits praise, you need to extend thanks or show appreciation. Letters of appreciation may be written to customers for their orders, to hosts and hostesses for their hospitality, to individuals for kindnesses performed, and especially to customers who complain. After all, complainers are actually providing you with "free consulting reports from the field." Complainers who feel that they were listened to often become the greatest promoters of an organization.[18]

Because the receiver will be pleased to hear from you, you can open directly with the purpose of your message. The letter in Figure 9.10 thanks a speaker who addressed a group of marketing professionals. Although such thank-you notes can be quite short, this one is a little longer because the writer wants to lend importance to the receiver's efforts. Notice that every sentence relates to the receiver and offers enthusiastic praise. By using the receiver's name along with contractions and positive words, the writer makes the letter sound warm and conversational.

Written notes that show appreciation and express thanks are significant to their receivers. In expressing thanks, you generally write a short note on special notepaper or heavy card stock. The following messages provide models for expressing thanks for a gift, for a favor, and for hospitality.

A bouquet of flowers is a safe, easy way to express thanks or appreciation, especially for women. But a written message, which takes more effort, provides a record that can be reread, savored, and treasured.

FIGURE 9.10 ***Thank-You Letter for a Favor***

1 Prewriting

Analyze: The purpose of this letter is to express appreciation to a business executive for presenting a talk before professionals.

Anticipate: The reader will be more interested in personalized comments than in general statements showing gratitude.

Adapt: Because the reader will be pleased, use the direct pattern.

2 Writing

Research: Consult notes taken during the talk.

Organize: Open directly by giving the reason for writing. Express enthusiastic and sincere thanks. In the body provide specifics. Refer to facts and highlights in the talk. Supply sufficient detail to support your sincere compliments. Conclude with appreciation. Be warm and friendly.

Compose: Write the first draft.

3 Revising

Revise: Revise for tone and warmth. Use the reader's name. Include concrete detail but do it concisely. Avoid sounding gushy or phony.

Proofread: Check the spelling of the receiver's name; verify facts. Check the spelling of *gratitude, patience, advice, persistence,* and *grateful.*

Evaluate: Does this letter convey sincere thanks?

International Marketing Association

225 West 17th Street
New York, New York 10029
http://www.ima.com

February 26, 2006

Mr. Michael T. Reese
Marketing Manager, Eastern Division
Toys "R" Us, Inc.
One Geoffrey Way
Wayne, NJ 07470-2030

Dear Michael:

You have our sincere gratitude for providing the Manhattan chapter of the IMA with one of the best presentations our group has ever heard. — *Tells purpose and delivers praise*

Personalizes the message by using specifics rather than generalities — Your description of the battle Toys "R" Us waged to begin marketing products in Japan was a genuine eye-opener for many of us. Nine years of preparation establishing connections and securing permissions seems an eternity, but obviously such persistence and patience pay off. We now understand better the need to learn local customs and nurture relationships when dealing in Japan or other Asian countries.

In addition to your good advice, we particularly enjoyed your sense of humor and jokes—as you must have recognized from the uproarious laughter. What a great routine you do on faulty translations! — *Spotlights the reader's talents*

Concludes with compliments and thanks — We're grateful, Michael, for the entertaining and instructive evening you provided our marking professionals. Thanks!

Cordially

Rosetta H. Johnson

Rosetta H. Johnson
Program Chair, IMA

RHJ:mef

To Express Thanks for a Gift

Thanks, Laura, to you and the other members of the department for honoring me with the elegant Waterford crystal vase at the party celebrating my twentieth anniversary with the company.

The height and shape of the vase are perfect to hold roses and other bouquets from my garden. Each time I fill it, I'll remember your thoughtfulness in choosing this lovely gift for me.

Identify the gift, tell why you appreciate it, and explain how you will use it.

To Send Thanks for a Favor

I sincerely appreciate your filling in for me last week when I was too ill to attend the planning committee meeting for the spring exhibition.

Without your participation much of my preparatory work would have been lost. It's comforting to know that competent and generous individuals like you are part of our team, Mark. Moreover, it's my very good fortune to be able to count you as a friend. I'm grateful to you.

Tell what the favor means using sincere, simple statements.

To Extend Thanks for Hospitality

Jeffrey and I want you to know how much we enjoyed the dinner party for our department that you hosted Saturday evening. Your charming home and warm hospitality, along with the lovely dinner and sinfully delicious chocolate dessert, combined to create a truly memorable evening.

Most of all, though, we appreciate your kindness in cultivating togetherness in our department. Thanks, Jennifer, for being such a special person.

Compliment the fine food, charming surroundings, warm hospitality, excellent host and hostess, and/or good company.

Response

Should you respond when you receive a congratulatory note or a written pat on the back? By all means! These messages are attempts to connect personally; they are efforts to reach out, to form professional and/or personal bonds. Failing to respond to notes of congratulations and most other goodwill messages is like failing to say "You're welcome" when someone says "Thank you." Responding to such messages is simply the right thing to do. Do avoid, though, minimizing your achievements with comments that suggest you don't really deserve the praise or that the sender is exaggerating your good qualities.

Take the time to respond to any goodwill message you may receive.

To Answer a Congratulatory Note

Thanks for your kind words regarding my award, and thanks, too, for sending me the newspaper clipping. I truly appreciate your thoughtfulness and warm wishes.

To Respond to a Pat on the Back

Your note about my work made me feel good. I'm grateful for your thoughtfulness.

Sympathy

Most of us can bear misfortune and grief more easily when we know that others care. Notes expressing sympathy, though, are probably more difficult to write than any other kind of message. Commercial "In sympathy" cards make the task easier—but they are far less meaningful. Grieving friends want to know what you think—not what Hallmark's card writers think. To help you get started, you can always glance through cards expressing sympathy. They will supply ideas about the kinds of thoughts you might wish to convey in your own words. In writing a sympathy note, (1) refer to the death or misfortune sensitively, using words that show you understand what a crushing blow it is; (2) in the case of a death, praise the deceased

Sympathy notes should refer to the misfortune sensitively and offer assistance.

in a personal way; (3) offer assistance without going into excessive detail; and (4) end on a reassuring, forward-looking note. Sympathy messages may be typed, although handwriting seems more personal. In either case, use notepaper or personal stationery.

Mention the loss tactfully; recognize good qualities of the deceased; assure the receiver of your concern; offer assistance; and conclude on a positive, reassuring note.

To Express Condolences

We are deeply saddened, Gayle, to learn of the death of your husband. Warren's kind nature and friendly spirit endeared him to all who knew him. He will be missed.

Although words seem empty in expressing our grief, we want you to know that your friends at QuadCom extend their profound sympathy to you. If we may help you or lighten your load in any way, you have but to call.

We know that the treasured memories of your many happy years together, along with the support of your family and many friends, will provide strength and comfort in the months ahead.

Checklist for Writing Goodwill Messages

General Guidelines: The Five Ss

- ✓ **Be selfless.** Discuss the receiver, not the sender.
- ✓ **Be specific.** Instead of generic statements (*You did a good job*), include special details (*Your marketing strategy to target key customers proved to be outstanding*).
- ✓ **Be sincere.** Show your honest feelings with conversational, unpretentious language (*We're all very proud of your award*).
- ✓ **Be spontaneous.** Strive to make the message natural, fresh, and direct. Avoid canned phrases (*If I may be of service, please do not hesitate . . .*).
- ✓ **Keep the message short.** Remember that, although they may be as long as needed, most goodwill messages are fairly short.

Giving Thanks

- ✓ **Cover three points in gift thank-yous.** (1) Identify the gift, (2) tell why you appreciate it, and (3) explain how you will use it.
- ✓ **Be sincere in sending thanks for a favor.** Tell what the favor means to you. Avoid superlatives and gushiness. Maintain credibility with sincere, simple statements.
- ✓ **Offer praise in expressing thanks for hospitality.** Compliment, as appropriate, the (1) fine food, (2) charming surroundings, (3) warm hospitality, (4) excellent host and hostess, and (5) good company.

Answering Congratulatory Messages

- ✓ **Respond to congratulations.** Send a brief note expressing your appreciation. Tell how good the message made you feel.
- ✓ **Accept praise gracefully.** Don't make belittling comments (*I'm not really all that good!*) to reduce awkwardness or embarrassment.

Extending Sympathy

- ✓ **Refer to the loss or tragedy directly but sensitively.** In the first sentence mention the loss and your personal reaction.
- ✓ **For deaths, praise the deceased.** Describe positive personal characteristics (*Howard was a forceful but caring leader*).
- ✓ **Offer assistance.** Suggest your availability, especially if you can do something specific.
- ✓ **End on a reassuring, positive note.** Perhaps refer to the strength the receiver finds in friends, family, colleagues, or religion.

International Messages

learning objective 9

International letters should conform to the organizational, format, and cultural conventions of the receiver's country.

The letter-writing suggestions you've just studied work well for correspondence in this country. You may wish, however, to modify the organization, format, and tone of letters going abroad.

American businesspeople appreciate efficiency, straightforwardness, and conciseness in letters. Moreover, American business letters tend to be informal and conversational. Foreign correspondents, however, may look upon such directness and informality as inappropriate, insensitive, and abrasive. Letters in Japan, for example, may begin with deference, humility, and references to nature:

> The season for cherry blossoms is here with us and everybody is beginning to feel refreshed. We sincerely congratulate you on becoming more prosperous in your business.[19]

Chinese letters strive to build relationships. A sales letter might begin with the salutation *Honored Company*, indicating a high level of respect. While American business writers use direct requests, Chinese writers are more tentative. For example, a Chinese sales letter might say, *I hope you'll take a moment to complete and mail the enclosed application.* The verb *hope* reduces the imposition of a direct request. Avoiding pressure tactics results from the cultural need to show respect and preserve harmony. A typical closing in Chinese letters is, *wishing good health*, which emphasizes the importance of showing respect and developing reciprocal relationships.[20]

Letters in Germany commonly start with a long, formal lead-in, such as, *Referring to your kind inquiry from the 31st of the month, we take the liberty to remind you with this letter . . . .*[21] Italian business letters may refer to the receiver's family and children. And French correspondents would consider it rude to begin a letter with a request before it is explained. French letters typically include an ending with this phrase (or a variation of it): *I wish to assure you* [insert reader's most formal title] *of my most respectful wishes* [followed by the writer's title and signature].[22] Foreign letters are also more likely to include passive-voice constructions (*your letter has been received*), exaggerated courtesy (*great pleasure, esteemed favor*), and obvious flattery (*your eminent firm*).[23]

Foreign letters may use different formatting techniques. Whereas American business letters are typewritten and single-spaced, in other countries they may be handwritten and single- or double-spaced. Address arrangements vary as well, as shown in the following:

German	Japanese
Herr [title, Mr., on first line]	Ms. Atsuko Takagi [title, name]
Deiter Woerner [name]	5-12 Koyo-cho 4 chome [street, house number]
Fritz-Kalle-Strasse 4 [street, house number]	Higashinada-ku [city]
6200 Wiesbaden [postal district, city]	Tokyo 194 [prefecture, postal district]
Germany [country]	Japan [country]

Dates and numbers can be particularly confusing, as shown here:

United States	Some European Countries
June 3, 2006	3rd of June 2006
6/3/06	3.6.06
$5,320.00 U.S.	$5.320,00 U.S.

To be safe, spell out the names of months instead of using figures. Verify sums of money and identify the currency unit.

Always learn about local preferences before sending letters abroad.

Because the placement and arrangement of letter addresses and closing lines vary greatly, you should always research local preferences before writing. For important letters going abroad, it's also wise to have someone familiar with local customs read and revise the message. An American graduate student learned this lesson when she wrote a letter, in French, to a Paris museum asking for permission to do research. She received no response. Before writing a second time, she took the letter to her French tutor. "No, no, mademoiselle! It will never do! It must be more respectful. You must be very careful of individuals' titles. Let me show you!" The second letter won the desired permission.

Summary of Learning Objectives

1 **Explain why business letters are written and how the three phases of Guffey's 3-x-3 writing process relate to creating successful business letters.** Although many e-mail messages are written today, business letters are important when a permanent record is necessary, when formality is required, and when a message is sensitive and needs an organized, well-considered presentation. In Phase 1 of the writing process for straightforward letters, you should determine your purpose, visualize the audience, and anticipate the reaction of the reader to your message. In Phase 2 you should collect information, make an outline of the points to cover, and write the first draft. In Phase 3 you should revise for clarity, proofread for correctness, and look for ways to apply graphic highlighting techniques so that the message has high "skim value." Finally, you should decide whether the message accomplishes its goal.

2 **Analyze the structure and characteristics of good business letters.** Most straightforward business letters are structured into three parts: (a) an opening that announces the purpose immediately, (b) a body with details explaining the purpose, and (c) a closing that includes a request for action or a courteous conclusion. Letters that make requests close by telling what ac-

Process to Product

Applying Your Skills at Ben & Jerry's

ALICE BLACHLY, CUSTOMER affairs coordinator at Ben & Jerry's, is overloaded with work. She asks you, her assistant, to help out and hands you a stack of letters. The top one is from a customer who complains that she didn't get quite enough cookie and chocolate chunks in her last pint. She also wants to know whether Ben & Jerry's has ever considered a sugar-free ice cream, and she concludes by saying that she agrees with Ben & Jerry's stand on peace.

Blachly tells you to explain that, although we work hard and long at it, the chunking equipment for nuts, chocolate, and cookies is not always as consistent as B & J would like and that you will report the problem of cookie and chocolate chunks to production. She tells you to refund the estimated purchase price for one pint of ice cream. As she walks away, she says that B & J experimented with a sugar-free ice cream, but it was so far below its taste standards that it never got beyond lab tests.

Your Task

Respond to all three of the comments in the letter of Diane Gruber, 1968 West Griswold Road, Phoenix, AZ 85051. Although her complaint was gentle, it is, nevertheless, a complaint that warrants an adjustment. In your response strive to maintain her goodwill and favorable opinion of Ben & Jerry's. ■

case study

tion is desired and establishing a deadline (end date) for that action. Good letters are characterized by clear content, a tone of goodwill, and correct form. Letters carrying positive or neutral messages should be organized directly. That means introducing the main idea (the purpose for writing) immediately in the opening.

3 **Write letters that request information and action as well as place orders for products and services.** In a letter requesting information and action, the opening immediately states the purpose of the letter, perhaps asking a question. The body explains and justifies the request. The closing tells the reader courteously what to do and shows appreciation. In letters that place orders, the opening introduces the order and authorizes a purchase (*Please send me the following items . . .*). The body lists the desired items including quantity, order number, description, unit price, and total price. The closing describes the method of payment, tells when the merchandise should be sent, and expresses appreciation.

4 **Write letters that make direct claims.** When a customer writes to identify and correct a wrong, the message is called a *claim.* A direct claim is one in which the receiver is expected to readily agree. A well-written claim begins by describing the problem clearly or telling what action is to be taken. The body explains and justifies the request without anger or emotion. The closing summarizes the request or action to be taken. It includes an end date if appropriate and courteously looks forward to continued business if the problem is resolved. Copies of relevant documents should be enclosed.

5 **Write letters that comply with requests.** In a letter that complies with a request, a subject line identifies previous correspondence, and the opening immediately delivers the good news. If the message is mixed, the best news

comes first. The body explains and provides additional information. The closing is cordial and personalized. If action is necessary, the ending tells the reader how to proceed and gives helpful details.

6 **Write letters that make adjustments.** When a company grants a customer's claim, it is called an *adjustment.* An adjustment letter has three goals: (1) rectifying the wrong, if one exists; (2) regaining the confidence of the customer; and (3) promoting further business. The opening immediately grants the claim without sounding grudging. To regain the confidence of the customer, the body may explain what went wrong and how the problem will be rectified. However, it may avoid accepting responsibility for any problems. The closing expresses appreciation, extends thanks for past business, refers to a desire to be of service, and/or mentions a new product. If an apology is offered, it should be presented early and briefly. A good adjustment letter is fair but doesn't promise more than can be fulfilled and doesn't "give away the farm."

7 **Write letters of recommendation.** In a letter of recommendation, the opening identifies the candidate, the position, the writer's relationship, and the confidentiality of the letter. The body describes the candidate's job duties, performance, skills, and potential. The closing provides an overall ranking of the candidate and offers to give additional information by telephone.

8 **Write messages that generate goodwill.** Goodwill messages deliver thanks, praise, or sympathy. They should be selfless, specific, sincere, spontaneous, and short. Gift thank-yous should identify the gift, tell why you appreciate it, and explain how you will use it. Thank-yous for favors should tell, without gushing, what they mean to you. Expressions of sympathy should mention the loss tactfully; recognize good qualities in the deceased (in the case of a death); offer assistance; and conclude on a positive, reassuring note.

9 **Modify international letters to accommodate other cultures.** Letters going to individuals in some areas, such as Japan and Europe, should probably use a less direct organizational pattern and be more formal in tone. They should also be adapted to appropriate regional letter formats.

~~I understand that you offer a prod~~

chapter review

1. Under what conditions is it important to send business letters rather than e-mail messages? (Obj. 1)
2. What three activities should you perform in Phase 1 of the writing process for a business letter? (Obj. 1)
3. Describe the three-part structure of a routine business letter. (Obj. 2)
4. What is "frontloading," and why is it useful in routine business letters? (Obj. 2)
5. Why is it best to write most business letters "backward"? (Obj. 2)
6. What is goodwill? Briefly describe five ways to develop goodwill in a letter. (Obj. 2)
7. For order letters what information goes in the opening? In the body? In the closing? (Obj. 3)
8. What is a claim? When is it straightforward? (Obj. 4)
9. In complying with requests, why is it especially important that all facts are correct on letters written on company stationery? (Obj. 5)
10. What is an adjustment letter, and what are a writer's three goals in writing adjustment letters? (Obj. 6)
11. Name four things to avoid in adjustment letters. (Obj. 6)
12. What are six guidelines to follow in writing recommendations? (Obj. 7)
13. What salutation is appropriate for recommendation letters when candidates have no specific position in mind? (Obj. 7)
14. Name five characteristics of goodwill messages. (Obj. 8)
15. Describe three elements of business letters going abroad that might be modified to accommodate readers from other cultures. (Obj. 9)

critical thinking

1. A recent article in a professional magazine carried this headline: "Is Letter Writing Dead?"[24] How would you respond to such a question? (Obj. 1)
2. Is it insensitive to include resale or sales promotion information in an adjustment letter? (Obj. 6)
3. Why is it important to regain the confidence of a customer in an adjustment letter? How can it be done? (Obj. 6)
4. How are American business letters different from those written in other countries? Why do you suppose this is so? (Obj. 9)
5. **Ethical Issue:** Let's say you've drafted a letter to a customer in which you apologize for the way the customer's account was fouled up by the Accounting Department. You show the letter to your boss, and she instructs you to remove the apology. It admits responsibility, she says, and the company cannot allow itself to be held liable. You're not an attorney, but you can't see the harm in a simple apology. What should you do? Refer to the section "Tools for Doing the Right Thing" in Chapter 1 to review the five questions you might ask yourself in trying to do the right thing.

THREE GREAT RESOURCES FOR YOU!

1. *Guffey Student Web Site*
http://guffey.swlearning.com

Your companion Web site offers chapter review quizzes, WebThink activities, updated chapter URLs, and many additional resources.

2. *Guffey XTRA!*
http://guffeyxtra.swlearning.com

This online study assistant includes Your Personal Language Trainer, Speak Right!, Spell Right!, bonus online chapters, Documents for Analysis, PowerPoint slides, and much more.

3. *Student Study Guide*

Self-checked workbook activities and applications review chapter concepts and develop career skills.

activities

main idea (1st sentence) subject line

9.1 Direct Openings (Objs. 1–8)

Your Task. Revise the following openings so that they are more direct. Add information if necessary.

a. My name is Brandon Brockway, and I am assistant to the manager of Information Services & Technology at HealthCentral, Inc. Our company needs to do a better job of integrating human resources and payroll functions. I understand that you have a software product called "HRFocus" that might do this, and I need to ask you some questions about it.

request for info about HR focus

b. I seem to have lost your order blank, so I have to write this letter. I hope that it is acceptable to place an order this way. I am interested in ordering a number of items from your winter catalog, which I still have although the order blank is missing.

c. Your letter of March 4 has been referred to me. Pursuant to your inquiry, I have researched your question in regard to whether or not we offer our European-style patio umbrella in colors. This unique umbrella is one of our most popular items. Its 10-foot canopy protects you when the sun is directly overhead, but it also swivels and tilts to virtually any angle for continuous sun protection all day long. It comes in two colors: cream and forest green.

d. Pursuant to your inquiry of June 14, which was originally sent to *Classic Motorcycle Magazine*, I am happy to respond to you. In your letter you ask about the tire choices for the Superbike and Superstock teams competing at the Honda Superbike Classic in Alabama. As you noted, the track temperatures reached above 125 degrees, and the new asphalt surface had an abrasive effect on tires. With the added heat and reduced grip, nearly all of the riders in the competition selected Dunlop Blue Groove hard compound front and rear tires.

e. I am pleased to receive your inquiry regarding the possibility of my acting as a speaker at the final semester meeting of your business management club on May 2. The topic of online résumés interests me and is one on which I think I could impart helpful information to your members. Therefore, I am responding in the affirmative to your kind invitation.

f. Thank you for your recent order of February 4. We are sure your customers and employees will love the high-quality Color-Block Sweatshirts with an 80/20 cotton/polyester blend that you ordered from our spring catalog. Your order is currently being processed and should leave our warehouse in Iowa in mid-February. We use UPS for all deliveries in southern California. Because you ordered sweatshirts with your logo embroidered in a two-tone combination, your order cannot be shipped until February 18. You should not expect it until about February 20.

g. We have just received your letter of October 3 regarding the unfortunate troubles you are having with your Premier DVD. In your letter you ask if you may send the flawed DVD to us for inspection. It is our normal practice to handle all service requests through our local dealers. However, in your circumstance we are willing to take a look at your unit here at our Columbus plant. Therefore, please send it to us so that we may determine what's wrong.

9.2 Subject Lines (Objs. 1–8)

Your Task. Write efficient subject lines for each of the messages in Activity 9.1. Add dates and other information if necessary.

9.3 Letter Formatting (Obj. 2)

Your Task. On a sheet of paper draw two rectangles about 4 by 6 inches. Within these rectangles show where the major parts of letters go: letterhead, dateline, inside address, salutation, body, complimentary close, signature, and author's name. Use lines to show how much space each part would occupy. Illustrate two different letter formats, such as block and modified-block style. Be prepared to discuss your drawings. Consult Appendix B for format guidelines.

9.4 Document for Analysis: Information Request (Obj. 3)

Your Task. Analyze the following letter. It suffers from many writing faults. List its weaknesses. If your instructor directs, revise the letter.

Current date

Meeting Manager
The Venetian
3355 Las Vegas Boulevard
Las Vegas, NV 89109

Dear Sir:

As a recently hired member of the Marketing and Special Events Division of my company, Cynergy, I have been given the assignment of making initial inquiries in regard to our next marketing meeting. Pursuant to this assignment, I am writing to you. We would like to find a resort hotel with conference facilities, and we have heard wonderful things about The Venetian.

Our marketing meeting will require banquet facilities where we can all be together, but we will also need at least four smaller meeting rooms. Each of these rooms should accommodate about 75. We hope to arrange our conference October 23–27, and we expect about 250 sales associates. Most of our associates will be flying in, so I'm interested in transportation to and from the airport.

Does The Venetian have public address systems in the meeting rooms? How about audio-visual equipment and computer facilities for presentations? I am also interested in learning whether the Sands Convention Center is part of The Venetian. Thank you for your cooperation.

Sincerely,

9.5 Document for Analysis: Direct Claim (Obj. 4)

Your Task. Analyze the following letter. List its weaknesses. If your instructor directs, revise the letter.

Current date

Ms. Deborah M. Griffin
Manager, Customer Response Center
Hurst Car Rentals
2259 Weatherford Boulevard
Dallas, TX 74091

Dear Deborah Griffin, Customer Response Center:

This is to inform you that you can't have it both ways. Either you provide customers with cars with full gas tanks or you don't. And if you don't, you shouldn't charge them when they return with empty tanks!

In view of the fact that I picked up a car at the Dallas-Ft. Worth International Airport on June 23 with an empty tank, I had to fill it immediately. Then I drove it until June 27. When I returned the car to Houston, as previously planned, I naturally let the tank go nearly empty, since that is the way I received the car in Dallas-Ft. Worth.

But your attendant in Houston charged me to fill the tank—$39.43 (premium gasoline at premium prices)! Although I explained to her that I had received it with an empty tank, she kept telling me that company policy required that she charge for a fill-up. My total bill came to $416.50, which, you must agree, is a lot of money for a rental period of only four days. I have the signed rental agreement and a receipt showing that I paid the full amount and that it included $39.43 for a gas fill-up when I returned the car.

Inasmuch as my company is a new customer and inasmuch as we had hoped to use your agency for our future car rentals because of your competitive rates, I trust that you will give this matter your prompt attention.

Your unhappy customer,

9.6 Document for Analysis: Adjustment (Obj. 6)

Your Task. Analyze the following letter. It suffers from many writing faults. List its weaknesses. If your instructor directs, revise the letter.

Current date

Mr. Joseph M. Thomas
2321 Columbia Circle
Orlando, FL 33204

Dear Mr. Thomas:

Your letter has been referred to me for reply. You claim that the painting recently sent by Central Park Gallery arrived with sags in the canvas and that you are unwilling to hang it in your executive offices.

I have examined your complaint carefully, and, frankly, I find it difficult to believe because we are so careful about shipping, but if what you say is true, I suspect that the shipper may be the source of your problem. We give explicit instructions to our shippers that large paintings must be shipped standing up, not lying down. We also wrap every painting in two layers of convoluted foam and one layer of Perf-Pack foam, which we think should be sufficient to withstand any bumps and scrapes that negligent shipping may cause. We will certainly look into this.

Although it is against our policy, we will in this instance allow you to take this painting to a local framing shop for restretching. We are proud that we can offer fine works of original art at incredibly low prices, and you can be sure that we do not send out sagging canvases.

Sincerely,

9.7 Direct Request: Going to the Source (Obj. 3)

You feel fortunate to have found a manager in your field who is willing to talk to you about careers. Your purpose is to learn more about your career area so that you can train for the occupation and also find a job when you finish your schooling. The manager you selected is a busy person, and he will try to work a personal interview into his schedule. But in case he can't meet you in person, he would like to have your questions in letter form so that he could answer them in a telephone conversation if necessary. Seeing the questions arranged in a logical order will also help him be best prepared.

Your Task. Write an information request to a real or hypothetical person in a company where you would like to work. If you want to start your own business, write to someone who has done it. Assume that the person has agreed to talk with you, but you haven't set a date. Use your imagination in creating five to eight interview questions. Be sure to show appreciation!

9.8 Direct Request: Beach Bike Rentals Seeks Web Exposure (Obj. 3)

TEAM

As the successful co-owner of Beach Bike Rentals, you and your partner decide that you need a Web site to attract even more business to your resort location. Primarily you rent bicycles and surreys to tourists visiting hotels along the beach. In addition, you carry tandems, pedal go-carts, mountain bikes, slingshot and chopper trikes, and other unique bikes, as well as inline skates. Business is good at your sunny beachside location, but a Web site would provide 24-hour information and attract a wider audience. The trouble is that you don't know anything about creating, hosting, or maintaining a Web site. Your partner has heard of a local company called Spiderside Web Production, and you decide to inquire about creating a Web site. You and he prefer to write

a letter so that you can work on your questions together and present a unified, orderly presentation.

Your Task. In teams of two or three, prepare an information request with logical questions about designing, hosting, and maintaining a Web site for a small business. You are not expected to create the content of the site. That will come later. Instead you want to ask questions about how a Web site is developed. You know for sure that you want a page that invites resort and hotel operators to feature your fun-filled facilities at their sites, but you don't know how to go about it. Address your letter to Richard Wolziac, Spiderside Web Production, 927 El Fuerte Boulevard, Carlsbad, CA 92008. Be sure to include an end date and a reason.

9.9 Information Request: Krispy Kreme Bake Sale (Obj. 3)

You've always loved Krispy Kreme doughnuts, so you were delighted to learn that they are now being sold in a nearby shopping center. You also heard that they can be used in fund-raising events. As chair of the spring fund-raising committee for Noah's Ark Children's Center, you need to find out more about how Krispy Kreme's fund-raising partnership works. Do you hold a traditional bake sale or what? How do you make any money if you sell the doughnuts at their regular retail price? You looked at the company's Web site and got basic information. You're still unclear about how certificates work in fund-raising. And what about Krispy Kreme partnership cards? You left a brief note at the Krispy Kreme Web site, but you didn't get a response. Now you decide to write.

Your Task. Compose a letter asking specific questions about how you can partner with Krispy Kreme in raising funds. Use your return address in a personal business letter style (see Figure 9.6). Send your letter to Customer Relations, Krispy Kreme Doughnut Corporation, P.O. Box 83, Winston-Salem, NC 27103. You need feedback by March 1 if you are to use Krispy Kreme in your spring fund-raising event. How do you want Krispy Kreme to respond?

9.10 Direct Request: Conference at the Fabulous Paris Las Vegas (Obj. 3)

Your company, Vortex Enterprises, has just had an enormously successful two-year sales period. CEO Kenneth Richardson has asked you, as marketing manager, to arrange a fabulous conference/retreat. "This will be a giant thank-you gift for all 75 of our engineers, product managers, and salespeople," he says. Warming up to the idea, he says, "I want the company to host a four-day combination sales conference/vacation/retreat at some spectacular location. Let's begin by inquiring at Paris Las Vegas. I hear it's awesome!" You check its Web site and find some general information. However, you decide to write a letter so that you can have a permanent, formal record of all the resorts you investigate. You estimate that your company will require about 75 rooms—preferably with a view of the Strip. You'll also need about three conference rooms for one and a half days. You want to know room rates, conference facilities, and entertainment possibilities for families. The CEO gave you two possible times: July 8–12 or August 18–22. You know that these are off-peak times, and you wonder whether you can get a good room rate. What entertainment will be showing at Paris Las Vegas during these times? One evening the CEO will want to host a banquet for about 140 people. Oh yes, he wants a report from you by March 1.

Your Task. Write a well-organized information request to Ms. Nancy Mercado, Manager, Convention Services, Paris Las Vegas, 281 Paris Drive, Las Vegas, NV 87551. Spell out your needs and conclude with a logical end date.

9.11 Direct Request: Computer Code of Conduct (Obj. 3)

WEB

As an assistant in the campus computer laboratory, you have been asked by your boss to help write a code of conduct for use of the laboratory facilities. This code will spell out what behavior and activities are allowed in your lab. The first thing you are to do is conduct a search of the Internet to see what other college or university computing labs have written as conduct codes.

Your Task. Using at least two search engines, search the Web employing variations of the keywords "computer code of conduct." Print two or three codes that seem appropriate. Write a letter (or an e-mail message, if your instructor agrees) to the director of an educational computer laboratory asking for further information about its code and its effectiveness. Include at least five significant questions. Attach your printouts to your letter.

9.12 Direct Request: Checking on Fats and Carbs (Obj. 3)

As Patrick Clark, manager of a health spa and also an ardent backpacker, you are organizing a group of hikers for a

wilderness trip to Alaska. One item that must be provided is freeze-dried food for the three-week trip. You are unhappy with the taste and quality of the backpacking food products currently available. You expect to have a group of hikers who are older, affluent, and natural-food enthusiasts. Some are concerned about products containing preservatives, sugar, and additives. Others are on diets restricting carbohydrates, cholesterol, fat, and salt. It's a rather finicky group!

You heard that Malibu Outfitters offers a new line of freeze-dried products. You want to know what they offer and whether they have sufficient variety to serve all the needs of your group. You need to know where their products can be purchased and what the cost range is. You'd also like to try a few of their items before placing a large order. You are interested in how they produce the food products and what kinds of ingredients they use. If you have any items left over, you wonder how long they can be kept and still be usable.

Your Task. Write an information request letter to Robin Smith, Malibu Outfitters, 24389 Pacific Coast Highway, Malibu, CA 90265.

9.13 Order Letter: Office Supply Jumble (Obj. 3)

Your Task. Study the following poorly written request for merchandise. Revise the letter and place your return address above the date. Address the letter to Office Central, 3814 Macon Cove, Memphis, TN 38134. Add any necessary information.

Dear Sir:

A number of office supplies items in your winter catalog interested me for my home office. I've lost the catalog order form, so I hope I can submit my order by letter. Please send me 5 stackable letter trays, No. 648291-J4. They cost $3.39 each. Also send 3 Premier recycled easel pads, Item No. 247411-J4. Each one costs 24.49. I could also use a box (100 to the box) of your Top-load sheet protectors at $14.95 for the box of 100. The item number is 489130-J4. And I need a box of Avery self-laminating sheets (Item 262981-J4) at the price of $21.99, with 50 to a box.

I am interested in having these items charged to my credit card. Please send them quickly because I'm about to run out.

Sincerely,

9.14 Direct Claim: Headaches From "No Surprise" Offer (Obj. 4)

As vice president of Breakaway Travel Service, you are upset with Virtuoso Enterprises. Virtuoso is a catalog company that provides imprinted promotional products for companies. Your travel service was looking for something special to offer in promoting its cruise ship travel packages. Virtuoso offered free samples of its promotional merchandise, under its "No Surprise" policy.

You figured, what could you lose? So on February 5 you placed a telephone order for a number of samples. These included an insulated lunch sack, an AM-FM travel radio, a square-ended barrel bag with fanny pack, as well as a deluxe canvas attaché case and two colors of garment-dyed sweatshirts. All items were supposed to be free. You did think it odd that you were asked for your company's MasterCard credit number, but Virtuoso promised to bill you only if you kept the samples.

When the items arrived, you were not pleased, and you returned them all on February 11 (you have a postal receipt showing the return). But your March credit statement showed a charge of $229.13 for the sample items. You called Virtuoso in March and spoke to Rachel, who assured you that a credit would be made on your next statement. However, your April statement showed no credit. You called again and received a similar promise. It's now May and no credit has been made. You decide to write and demand action.

Your Task. Write a claim letter that documents the problem and states the action that you want taken. Add any information you feel is necessary. Address your letter to Ms. Paula Loveday, Customer Services, Virtuoso Enterprises, 420 Ninth Street South, LaCrosse, WI 54602.

9.15 Direct Claim: This Desk Is Going Back (Obj. 4)

As the founder and president of a successful consulting firm, you decided to splurge and purchase a fine executive desk for your own office. You ordered an expensive desk described as "North American white oak embellished with hand-inlaid walnut cross-banding." Although you would not ordinarily purchase large, expensive items by mail, you were impressed by the description of this desk and by the money-back guarantee promised in the catalog.

When the desk arrived, you knew that you had made a mistake. The wood finish was rough, the grain looked splotchy, and many of the drawers would not pull out easily. The advertisement had promised "full suspension, silent ball-bearing drawer slides."

Your Task. Because you are disappointed with the desk, you decide to send it back, taking advantage of the money-back guarantee. Write a claim letter to Patrick Dwiggens, Operations Manager, Premier Wood Products, P.O. Box 528, High Point, NC 27261, asking for your money back. You're not sure whether the freight charges can be refunded, but it's worth a try. Supply any details needed.

9.16 Direct Claim: Backing Out of Project Management Seminar (Obj. 4)

Ace Executive Training Institute offered a seminar titled "Enterprise Project Management Protocol" that sounded terrific. It promised to teach project managers how to estimate work, report status, write work packages, and cope with project conflicts. Because your company often is engaged in large cross-functional projects, it decided to send four key managers to the seminar to be held June 1–2 at the Ace headquarters in Pittsburgh. The fee was $2,200 each, and it was paid in advance. About six weeks before the seminar, you learned that three of the managers would be tied up in projects that would not be completed in time for them to attend.

Your Task. On your company letterhead, write a claim letter to Addison O'Neill, Registrar, Ace Executive Training Institute, 5000 Forbes Avenue, Pittsburgh, PA 15244. Ask that the seminar fees for three employees be returned because they cannot attend. Give yourself a title and supply any details necessary.

9.17 Direct Claim: A Matter of Mismeasurement (Obj. 4)

As the owner of Custom Designs, you recently completed a living room remodel that required double-glazed, made-to-order oak French doors. You ordered them, by telephone, on April 14 from Capitol Lumber and Hardware. When they arrived on May 18, your carpenter gave you the bad news: the doors were cut too small. Instead of measuring a total of 11 feet 8 inches, the doors measured 11 feet 4 inches. In your carpenter's words, "No way can I stretch those doors to fit these openings!" You waited nearly five weeks for these doors, and your clients wanted them installed immediately. Your carpenter said, "I can rebuild this opening for you, but I'm going to have to charge you for my time." His extra charge came to $376.

You feel that the people at Capitol Lumber should reimburse you for this amount because it was their error. In fact, you actually saved them a bundle of money by not returning the doors. You decide to write to Capitol Lumber and enclose a copy of your carpenter's bill. You wonder whether you should also include a copy of Capitol Lumber's invoice, even though it does not show the exact door measurements. You are a good customer of Capitol Lumber and Hardware, having used their quality doors, windows, and hardware on many other remodeling jobs. You're confident that it will grant this claim.

Your Task. Write a claim letter to Sal Rodriguez, Sales Manager, Capitol Lumber and Hardware, 3568 East Washington Avenue, Indianapolis, IN 46204.

9.18 Direct Claim: The Real Thing (Obj. 4)

Let's face it. Like most consumers, you've probably occasionally been unhappy with service or with products you have used.

Your Task. Select a product or service that has disappointed you. Write a claim letter requesting a refund, replacement, explanation, or whatever seems reasonable. Generally, such letters are addressed to customer service departments. For claims about food products, be sure to include bar-code identification from the package, if possible. Your instructor may ask you to actually mail this letter. Remember that smart companies want to know what their customers think, especially if a product could be improved. Give your ideas for improvement. When you receive a response, share it with your class.

9.19 Direct Reply: So You Want an Internship at the Gap? (Obj. 5)

WEB

The Gap Inc. headquarters in the San Francisco Bay area is a popular place to work. Many students inquire about summer internships. Although it supplies oodles of information about internships at its Web site, Gap Inc. still receives letters requesting this information. As one of its current summer interns, you have been given a task by your supervisor. She wants you to write a general letter that she can use to reply to requests from college students seeking summer internships. She doesn't have time to answer each one individually, and she doesn't want to tell them all to just go to the Web site. She feels responsible to reply in a way that builds goodwill for Gap, which also operates Old Navy and Banana Republic.

Your Task. Draft a reply to students seeking summer intern information. Go to the Gap Web site and study its offerings. Prepare a letter that describes the summer intern program, its requirements, and how to apply. Summarize some of the lengthy descriptions from the Web site. Use bulleted lists where appropriate. Since the letter may involve two pages, group similar information under side headings that improve its readability. Although your letter may become a form letter, address your draft to Lisa M. Hernandez, 493 Cesar Court, Walnut Creek, CA 94598.

9.20 Direct Reply: River Rafting on the Web (Obj. 5)

WEB

As the program chair for the campus Ski Club, you have been asked by the president to investigate river rafting. The Ski Club is an active organization, and its members want to schedule a summer activity. A majority favored rafting. Use a browser to search the Web for relevant information. Select five of the most promising Web sites offering rafting. If possible, print a copy of your findings.

Your Task. Summarize your findings in a letter to Brian Krauss, Ski Club president. The next meeting of the Ski Club is May 8, but you think it would be a good idea if you could discuss your findings with Brian before the meeting. Write to Brian Krauss, SIU Ski Club, 303 Founders Hall, Carbondale, IL 62901.

Photo: Courtesy of Krispy Kreme

9.21 Direct Reply: Krispy Kreme Helps Raise Funds (Obj. 5)

WEB

Despite low-carb diet fads, people still crave yummy doughnuts—especially the oh-so-light yet rich and scrumptious Krispy Kreme creations. As a customer service representative at Krispy Kreme in Winston-Salem, you have received a letter from a customer interested in using your doughnuts as a fund-raising activity for Noah's Ark Children's Center (see Activity 9.9). Although much of the information is at the Web site, you must answer this customer's letter personally.

Your Task. Respond to Mrs. Tiffany Lane, Noah's Ark Children's Center, 4359 Blue Creek Road, Austin, TX 78746. You need to explain the three ways that Krispy Kreme helps organizations raise funds. Use the Krispy Kreme Web site to gather information, but summarize and paraphrase what you find. Compose a letter that not only provides information but also promotes your product. Consider using bullet points and paragraph headings to set off the major points.

9.22 Direct Reply: McDonald's Recycles and Reduces Waste (Obj. 5)

TEAM

Danielle Turner, director of Customer Service for McDonald's Corporation, has received a letter from Nedra Lowe, an environmentalist. Ms. Lowe wants to know what McDonald's is doing to reduce the huge amounts of waste products that its restaurants generate. She argues that these wastes not only deplete world resources but also clog our already overburdened landfills. Danielle Turner thinks that this is a good opportunity for her student interns to sharpen their reasoning and writing skills on the job. She asks you and the other interns to draft a response to the inquiry telling how McDonald's is cleaning up its act. Here are some of the facts that your boss supplies your group.

Actually, McDonald's has been quite active in its environmental efforts. Working with the Environmental Defense Fund, McDonald's has initiated a series of 42 resolutions that are cutting by more than 80 percent the huge waste stream from its 12,000 restaurants. McDonald's efforts meant making changes in packaging, increasing their recycling campaign, trying more composting, and retraining employees.

McDonald's was one of the food industry leaders in abandoning the polystyrene "clamshell" box for hamburgers and sandwiches. Formerly using an average of 20 pounds of polystyrene a day per restaurant, McDonald's now uses only 10 percent of that figure. Moreover, McDonald's is increasing the postconsumer recycled content of its napkins and using lighter-weight paperboard for its fry cartons. Other environmental efforts include testing a starch-based material in consumer cutlery to replace plastic forks, knives, and spoons. Many restaurants have also begun trial composting of eggshells, coffee grounds, and food scraps. McDonald's is also starting a nationwide program for recycling corrugated boxes. In addition, the company is testing reusable salad lids and shipping pallets, pump-style bulk dispensers for condiments, and refillable coffee mugs.

McDonald's has retrained its restaurant crews to give waste reduction equal weight with other priorities, such as quickness, cleanliness, and quality service. The company is trying to reduce the waste both behind the counter (which accounts for 80 percent of the total waste) and over the counter.[25]

Your Task. Prepare a letter that can be used for inquiries. To promote goodwill, you might wish to throw in a few coupons for free sandwiches. Send this letter to Nedra Lowe, 2591 Green Valley Parkway, Huntington, WV 25755.

9.23 Direct Reply: Explaining How to Send Résumés (Obj. 5)

CRITICAL THINKING | SPEAKING | TEAM | WEB

You've worked at CyberSoft in the Silicon Valley for a couple of years. It's a great place to work, and it receives many letters from job applicants. Some of them inquire about the company's résumé-scanning techniques. You generally send out the following form letter that has been in the files for some time.

Dear Sir or Madam:

Your letter of April 11 has been referred to me for a response. We are pleased to learn that you are considering employment here at CyberSoft, and we look forward to receiving your résumé, should you decide to send same to us.

You ask if we scan incoming résumés. Yes, we certainly do. Actually, we use SmartTrack, an automated résumé-tracking system. SmartTrack is incredible! We sometimes receive as many as 300 résumés a day, and SmartTrack helps us sort, screen, filter, and separate the résumés. It also processes them, helps us organize them, and keeps a record of all of these résumés. Some of the résumés, however, cannot be scanned, so we have to return those—if we have time.

The reasons that résumés won't scan may surprise you. Some applicants send photocopies or faxed copies, and these can cause misreading, so don't do it. The best plan is to send an original copy. Some people use colored paper. Big mistake! White paper (8 1/2 x 11-inch) printed on one side is the best bet. Another big problem is unusual type fonts, such as script or fancy gothic or antique fonts. They don't seem to realize that scanners do best with plain, readable fonts such as Arial or Universe in a 10- to 14-point size.

Other problems occur when applicants use graphics, shading, italics, underlining, horizontal and vertical lines, parentheses, and brackets. Scanners like plain "vanilla" résumés! Oh yes, staples can cause misreading. And folding of a résumé can also cause the scanners to foul up. To be safe, don't staple or fold, and be sure to use wide margins and a quality printer.

When a hiring manager within CyberSoft wants to look for an appropriate candidate, he is told to submit keywords to describe the candidate he has in mind for his opening. We tell him (or sometimes her) to zero in on nouns and phrases that best describe what they want. Thus, my advice to you is to try to include those words that highlight your technical and professional areas of expertise.

If you do decide to submit your résumé to CyberSoft, be sure you don't make any of the mistakes described herein that would cause the scanner to misread it.

Sincerely,

Your Task. Your boss saw this letter one day and thought it was miserable. She asks you and your team to produce an informative and effective letter that can be sent to anyone who inquires. As a team, (1) discuss how this letter could be improved; (2) decide what information is necessary to send to potential job applicants; (3) search the Web for additional information that might be helpful; and (4) develop a better letter. Address your first letter to Mr. Octavio Chavez, 259 East Plaza Drive, Santa Maria, CA 93454.

9.24 Direct Reply: Tell Me About Your Major (Obj. 5)

A friend in a distant city is considering moving to your area for more education and training in your field. This individual wants to know about your program of study.

Your Task. Write a letter describing a program in your field (or any field you wish to describe). What courses must be taken? Toward what degree, certificate, or employment position does this program lead? Why did you choose it? Would you recommend this program to your friend? How long does it take? Add any information you feel would be helpful.

9.25 Direct Reply: Backpacking Meals for Fussy Eaters (Obj. 5)

As Robin Smith, owner of Malibu Outfitters, which produces freeze-dried backpacking foods, you must respond to Patrick Clark (see Activity 9.12). You are eager to have Mr. Clark sample your new all-natural line of products containing no preservatives, sugar, or additives. You want him to know that you started this company two years ago after you found yourself making custom meals for discerning backpackers who rejected typical camping fare. Some of your menu items are excellent for individuals on restricted diets. Some dinners are cholesterol-, fat-, and salt-free. Others feature low carbs, but he'll have to look at your list to see for himself.

You will send him your complete list of dinner items and the suggested retail prices. You will also send him a sample "Saturday Night on the Trail," a four-course meal that comes with fruit candies and elegant appetizers. All your food products are made from choice ingredients in sanitary kitchens that you personally supervise. They are flash frozen in a new vacuum process that you patented. Although your dried foods are meant to last for years, you don't recommend that they be kept beyond 18 months because they may deteriorate. This could happen if a package were punctured or if the products became overheated.

Your Task. Your products are currently available at Malibu Outfitters, 19605 Pacific Coast Highway, Malibu, CA 90265. Large orders may be placed directly with you. You offer a 5 percent discount on direct orders. Write a response to Patrick Clark, 425 Washington Parkway, Milpitas, CA 95035.

9.26 Direct Reply: Sharing Customer Information (Obj. 5)

CRITICAL THINKING | TEAM

You work as an assistant to the vice president of First Bank (P.O. Box 70899, Baton Rouge, LA 70866), a medium-size bank with six branches. With so many recent news stories about companies revealing private customer information, some of the bank's customers are beginning to inquire about its privacy policy. Like many financial organizations (including insurance companies and brokerage firms), First Bank does share some customer information within the First Bank family of branches. It also shares customer information with selected subsidiaries outside the First Bank family. Companies are legally allowed to share information such as names, addresses, social security numbers, account balances, and spending habits of individuals—unless the customer specifically asks them to stop. But at First Bank, privacy is one of its highest priorities.

First Bank has a privacy policy based on three principles. First, information security is extremely important. The bank regularly reviews its security standards and practices to protect customers from any unauthorized access to information. But the bank also feels that privacy is a shared responsibility. This is the second point. Customers trust the bank to take care of their financial needs. They should feel confident

that the bank is managing customers' accounts responsibly. However, customers also have a responsibility. They can help the bank protect their privacy by knowing what information is on their credit reports, understanding the choices they have about the use of their information, and protecting their passwords. Finally, the bank feels that responsible use of information is beneficial. Information is important for meeting customer needs and providing consistent service quality. The more the bank understands about customers and their needs, the better the bank can suggest products and services, create new opportunities, and help customers manage their financial assets. By being able to share information, banks are better able to service accounts and protect against fraud.

First Bank's privacy policy provides for "opting out." If customers don't want any of their information shared within the bank or with selected companies outside the bank, customers should call 1-800-848-7632.

Your Task. The vice president wants you to draft a response letter to customers who inquire about First Bank's privacy policy. In teams, discuss the content of the letter. Should it reveal that First Bank already shares customer information? Would it be smarter business practice to emphasize the privacy policy and not say anything about the "opt out" toll-free line? The bank has prepared a booklet that provides helpful tips on how to protect privacy. You'll probably want to include it. Address your first letter to Valeria MacCammon, 4529 Evergreen Drive, Fort Wayne, IN 46805. Be sure that your letter could also be sent to other customers who inquire.

9.27 Direct Reply: And You Want Us to Pay to Move Your Dogs Too? (Obj. 5)

INFOTRAC

At a recent professional meeting, your friend Jason Jackson told you about his company's dismay when it hired a strong candidate. To entice the candidate to the company's Milwaukee location, the company paid for house-hunting trips, temporary living, mortgage prepayment, and even costs for transporting the family's two Labrador retrievers. After a month on the job, the new-hire quit. Your friend Jason wonders how your company avoids the problems involved in relocation of newly hired employees. Because you're in a hurry, you tell Jason that you will send him a letter outlining some of the ways your company handles relocation issues for new employees.

Your Task. Using InfoTrac, read several articles about employee relocation. Two particularly good articles are "Words to Move By" (*HR Magazine*, May 2004) and "Cafeteria-Style Relocation Policies Gain in Popularity" (*Plants Sites & Parks*, March 2003). Assume that your company uses the three-tier plan outlined in one article. Your company also employs other effective relocation policies. You don't have all the answers, but you can certainly make some general suggestions that would prevent the experience Jason described. You might include a copy of the three-tier plan as an attachment. Address your letter to Mr. Jason Jackson, Vortex International, 3420 Northern Lakes Drive, Milwaukee, WI 53201.

9.28 Adjustment: A Matter of Mismeasurement (Obj. 6)

CRITICAL THINKING

As Sal Rodriguez, sales manager of Capitol Lumber and Hardware, you have a problem. Your firm manufactures quality precut and custom-built doors and frames. You have received a letter dated May 25 from Candace Olmstead (described in Activity 9.17). Ms. Olmstead is an interior designer, and she complains that the oak French doors she recently ordered for a client were made to the wrong dimensions.

Although they were the wrong size, she kept the doors and had them installed because her clients were without outside doors. However, her carpenter charged an extra $376 to install them. She claims that you should reimburse her for this amount, because your company was responsible for the error. You check her June 9 order and find that the order was filled correctly. In a telephone order, Ms. Olmstead requested doors that measured 11 feet 4 inches, and that's what you sent. Now she says that the doors should have been 11 feet 8 inches. Your policy forbids refunds or returns on custom orders. Yet, you remember that in the early part of June you had two new people working the phones taking orders. It's possible that they did not hear or record the measurements correctly. You don't know whether to grant this claim or refuse it. But you do know that you must look into the training of telephone order takers and be sure that they verify all custom order measurements. It might also be a good idea to have your craftsmen call a second time to confirm custom measurements.

Ms. Olmstead is a successful interior designer and has provided Capitol Lumber and Hardware with a number of orders. You value her business but aren't sure how to respond.

Your Task. Decide how to treat this claim and then write to Candace Olmstead, Custom Designs, 903 Hazel Dell Parkway, Carmel, IN 46033. In your letter remind her that Capitol Lumber and Hardware has earned a reputation as the manufacturer of the finest wood doors and frames on the market. Your doors feature prime woods, and the craftsmanship is meticulous. The designs of your doors have won awards, and the engineering is ingenious. You have a new line of greenhouse windows that are available in three sizes. Include a brochure describing these windows.

9.29 Adjustment: Backing Out of Project Management Seminar (Obj. 6)

Ace Executive Training Institute offered a seminar titled "Enterprise Project Management Protocol" for June 1–2 and was delighted to receive reservations for four attendees (see Activity 9.16). But six weeks before the seminar, Ace received a letter from Raintree Manufacturing asking for a refund because three of the four cannot attend. Ace has already hired the instructor and made arrangements for the seminar based on the projected attendance, so it is disappointed to see this cancellation. Yet, it wants to retain good relations with Raintree in anticipation of future business. It will return the registration fees of $6,600. Because Raintree is having difficulty allowing its employees to get away for training, it may be interested in Ace's AccuVision Training Series with on-site training modules. These modules bring the seminar to the client. They teach team building, situational interaction style, initiative, and analysis/problem solving—right on the client's premises. Your Web site provides all the details.

Your Task. As assistant to Addison O'Neill, registrar, write an adjustment letter to Kit Adkins, Raintree Manufacturing, 491 South Emerald Road, Greenwood, SC 29647. Take advantage of this opportunity to promote your company's on-site programs.

9.30 Adjustment: This Desk Came Back (Obj. 6)

As Patrick Dwiggens, Premier Wood Products, you reply to customer claims, and today you must respond to Stephanie Ahlfeldt (described in Activity 9.15). You are unhappy that she is returning the executive desk (Invoice No. T-2873), but your policy is to comply with customer wishes. If she doesn't want to keep the desk, you will certainly return the purchase price plus shipping charges. On occasion, desks are damaged in shipping, and this may explain the marred finish and the sticking drawers.

You want Ms. Ahlfeldt to give Premier Wood Products another chance. After all, your office furniture and other wood products are made from the finest hand-selected woods by master artisans. Because she is apparently furnishing her office, send her another catalog and invite her to look at the traditional conference desk on page 5. This is available with a matching credenza, file cabinets, and accessories.

Your Task. Write an adjustment letter granting the claim of Stephanie Ahlfeldt, President, Ahlfeldt Consulting Services, 258 Mountain View Drive, Fargo, ND 58105. She might be interested in your furniture-leasing plan, which can produce substantial savings. Be sure to promise that you will personally examine any furniture she may order in the future. Add any necessary details.

9.31 Adjustment: No Birds Will Be Harmed (Obj. 6)

You didn't want to do it. But guests were complaining about the pigeons that roost on the Scottsdale Hilton's upper floors and tower. Pigeon droppings splattered sidewalks, furniture, and people. As the hotel manager, you had to take action. You called an exterminator, who recommended Avitrol. This drug, he promised, would disorient the birds, preventing them from finding their way back to the Hilton. The drugging, however, produced a result you didn't expect: pigeons began dying.

After a story hit the local newspapers, you began to receive complaints. The most vocal came from the Avian Affairs Coalition, a local bird-advocacy group. It said that the pigeons are really Mediterranean rock doves, the original "Dove of Peace" in European history and the same species the Bible said Noah originally released from his ark during the great flood. Activists claimed that Avitrol is a lethal drug causing birds, animals, and even people who ingest as little as 1/600th of a teaspoon to convulse and die lingering deaths of up to two hours.

Repulsed at the pigeon deaths and the bad publicity, you stopped the use of Avitrol immediately. You are now considering installing wires that offer a mild, nonlethal electrical shock. These wires, installed at the Maricopa County Jail in downtown Phoenix for $50,000, keep thousands of pigeons from alighting and could save $1 million in extermination and cleanup costs over the life of the building. You are also considering installing netting that forms a transparent barrier, sealing areas against entry by birds.

Your Task. Respond to Mrs. Deborah Leverette, 24 Canyon Lake Shore Drive, Spring Branch, TX 52319, a recent Scottsdale Hilton guest. She sent a letter condemning the pigeon poisoning and threatening to never return to the hotel unless it changed its policy. Try to regain the confidence of Mrs. Leverette and promote further business.[26]

9.32 Adjustment: Cure for "No Surprise" Headache (Obj. 6)

Virtuoso Enterprises prides itself on its "No Surprise" offer. This means that anything ordered from its catalog of promotional products may be returned for a full refund within two weeks of purchase. The claim from Breakaway Travel Service (see Activity 9.14) describes an order placed February 5 and returned February 11. As assistant to Paula Loveday, manager, Customer Services, you check the return files and see that items were received February 16. You speak with service agent Rachel, who agrees with you—the credit of $229.13 should have been granted to Breakaway Travel. She reminds you that a new system for handling credits was implemented in March. Perhaps the Breakaway return slipped through the cracks. Regardless of the reason, you decide to tell accounting to issue the credit immediately.

Your Task. In an adjustment letter, try to regain the confidence and the business of Breakaway Travel Service, 350 Valle Vista Drive, San Luis Obispo, CA 93403. Include a sample imprinted travel mug in a gift box and a Coleman 8-quart jug cooler. You know that you are the most reliable source for the lowest-priced imprinted promotional products in the field, and this travel agency should be able to find something suitable in your catalog. Address your letter to Leila Chambers.

9.33 Letter of Recommendation: Recommending Yourself (Obj. 7)

You are about to leave your present job. When you ask your boss for a letter of recommendation, to your surprise he tells you to write it yourself and then have him sign it. [Actually, this is not an unusual practice today. Many businesspeople find that employees are very perceptive and accurate when they evaluate themselves.]

Your Task. Use specifics from a current or previous job. Describe your duties and skills. Be sure to support general characteristics with specific examples.

9.34 Thanks for a Favor: Got the Job! (Obj. 8)

Congratulations! You completed your degree and got a terrific job in your field. One of your instructors was especially helpful to you when you were a student. This instructor also wrote an effective letter of recommendation that was instrumental in helping you obtain your job.

Your Task. Write a letter thanking your instructor.

9.35 Thanks for a Favor: Electronic Résumé Revolution (Obj. 8)

TEAM

Your business communication class was fortunate to have author Joyce Lain Kennedy speak to you. She has written many books including *Electronic Job Search Revolution; Hook Up, Get Hired!;* and *Electronic Résumé Revolution.* Ms. Kennedy talked about writing a scannable résumé, using keywords to help employers hire you, protecting your information on the Internet, and searching company Web sites. The class especially liked hearing the many examples of how real people had found their jobs. Ms. Kennedy shared many suggestions from human resources people, and she described how large and small employers are using computers to read résumés and track employees. You know that she did not come to plug her books, but when she left, most class members wanted to head straight for a bookstore to get some of them. Her talk was a big hit.

Your Task. Individually or in groups, draft a thank-you letter to Joyce Lain Kennedy, P.O. Box 3502, Carlsbad, CA 92009.

9.36 Thanks for the Hospitality: Holiday Entertaining (Obj. 8)

You and other members of your staff or organization were entertained at an elegant dinner during the winter holiday season.

Your Task. Write a thank-you letter to your boss (supervisor, manager, vice president, president, or chief executive officer) or to the head of an organization to which you belong. Include specific details that will make your letter personal and sincere.

9.37 Sending Good Wishes: Personalizing Group Greeting Cards (Obj. 8)

TEAM | WEB

When a work colleague has a birthday, gets promoted, or retires, someone generally circulates a group greeting card. In the past it wasn't a big deal. Office colleagues just signed their names and passed the store-bought card along to others. But the current trend is toward personalization with witty, oh-so-clever quips. And that presents a problem. What should you say—or not say? You know that people value special handwritten quips, but you realize that you're not particularly original and you don't have a store of "bon mots" (clever sayings, witticisms). You're tired of the old standbys, such as "This place won't be the same without you" and "You're only as old as you feel."

Your Task. To be prepared for the next greeting card that lands on your desk at work, you decide to work with some friends to make a list of remarks appropriate for business occasions. Use the Web to research witty sayings appropriate for promotions, birthdays, births, weddings, illnesses, or personal losses. Use a search term such as "birthday sayings," "retirement quotes," or "cool sayings." You may decide to assign each category (birthday, retirement, promotion, and so forth) to a separate team. Submit the best sayings in a memo to your instructor.

9.38 Responding to Good Wishes: Saying Thank You (Obj. 8)

Your Task. Write a short note thanking a friend who sent you good wishes when you recently completed your degree.

9.39 Extending Sympathy: To a Spouse (Obj. 8)

Your Task. Imagine that a coworker was killed in an automobile accident. Write a letter of sympathy to his or her spouse.

9.40 Consumer Claim: The Check in the Mail Is a Bill (Obj. 4)

CONSUMER | CRITICAL THINKING | TEAM

Houston chiropractor Brett Downey cashed a $2.50 check last December from Yellow Pages Inc. of Anaheim, California. And that's when his troubles began. He thought the check was some kind of refund for overpaying his company's ad in the Southwestern Bell's local telephone book. Like many small business owners and professional people, he takes care of his own bills and does not have time to read everything carefully.

In January he was flabbergasted to receive a bill for $179 from the Anaheim company for registering his Fairview

Health Center in its Yellow Pages directory. He called and discovered that by cashing the check, he unknowingly had signed up for a one-year listing on the Internet. Fine print on the back of the check apparently authorized the listing. Representatives of the company insisted that by signing the check, Dr. Downey had accepted their promotional incentive, which starts the billing process. He did, after all, sign the check.[27]

Your Task. In teams or individually, analyze what happened. How many companies do you think have "Yellow Pages" in their names? Does this "Yellow Pages" check offer sound like a scam? What other scams do you know about that involve small businesspeople? Should Dr. Downey contact the Better Business Bureau? Assume that Dr. Downey has received several billings, and he wants them to stop. He asks you to help him write an appropriate letter to Yellow Pages Inc., P.O. Box 4298, Anaheim, CA 95091. Should he send back the $2.50 from the check he cashed? Use the simplified letter style to avoid a salutation.

video resources

Bridging the Gap Video Library 2

Social Responsibility and Communication: Ben & Jerry's

In an exciting inside look, you see managers discussing six factors that determine Ben & Jerry's continuing success. Toward the end of the video, you'll listen in on a discussion of a new packaging material made with unbleached paper. As a socially responsible company, Ben & Jerry's wanted to move away from ice cream packages made from bleached papers. Bleaching requires chlorine, a substance that contains dioxin, which is known to cause cancer, genetic and reproductive defects, and learning disabilities. In producing paper, pulp mills using chlorine are also adding to dioxin contamination of waterways. After much research, Ben & Jerry's found a chlorine-free, unbleached paper board for its packages. That was the good news. The bad news is that the inside of the package is now brown.

Assume you've been hired at Ben & Jerry's to help answer incoming letters. Although you're fairly new, your boss gives you a letter from an unhappy customer. This customer opened a pint of Ben & Jerry's "World's Best Vanilla" and then threw it out. After seeing the brown inner lid, he decided that his pint must have been used for chocolate before it was used for vanilla. Or, he said, "the entire pint has gone bad and somehow turned the sides brown." Whatever the reason, he wasn't taking any chances. He wanted his money back.

Your Task. Write a letter that explains the brown carton, justifies the reason for using it, and retains the customer's business. Address the letter to Mr. Cecil Hamm, 1608 South McKenna, Poteau, OK 74954.

Bridging the Gap Video Library 2

MeetingsAmerica

In Salt Lake City, MeetingsAmerica arranges conferences and conventions for visitors to the city. Businesses planning big conferences often outsource arrangements such as registration, ground transportation, special events, and other details. In this video you'll learn how MeetingsAmerica operates as a destination meeting organization. Your instructor may provide a special writing activity after you see this video.

C.L.U.E. review 9

Edit the following sentences to correct faults in grammar, punctuation, spelling, and word use.

1. Business letters, despite the enormous popularity of e-mail must still be wrote when a permenent record is neccessary.
2. If you follow a writing process organizing the content and composing the first draft is easier.
3. Chelsea acts as if she was the only person who ever received a complement about their business writting.
4. Chelseas letter which she sent to the manager and I was distinguished by 3 characteristics. Clear content, a goodwill tone, and correct form.
5. Davonne Jordan whom I think is our newly-appointed Vice President wants everyone in the Company to beware of computer viruses.
6. When the Office Manager writes business letters or memos he allways ends it with the same "Do not hesitate" phrase.
7. The manager and myself realized an item was missing from the April 1st shipment consequently we sent a claim letter for one hundred thirty-one dollars.
8. After our supervisor and her returned from there meeting at two P.M. we were able to sort the customers names and addresses more quick.
9. If you must write an order letter be sure to include: the quantity order number description unit price tax shipping and total costs.
10. Matthew enclosed a check for two hundred dollars, however he worried that it was insufficient to regain the confidence of the customer.

chapter 10

Persuasive and Sales Messages

objectives

1. Apply the 3-x-3 writing process to persuasive messages.
2. Explain the components in a persuasive message and how to blend them effectively.
3. Write successful persuasive messages including requesting favors and actions, persuading within organizations, and writing complaint letters.
4. Plan and compose outstanding sales messages.
5. Describe the basic elements in persuasive press releases.

COMMUNICATION IN PROCESS

Amazon.com Solidifies Its Status as the Top E-Marketer Through Personalized Persuasion

BOASTING A PRODUCT line that staggers the imagination, Amazon.com ballooned from "Earth's biggest bookstore" into the earth's biggest marketplace for just about every merchandise category under the sun. When Jeff Bezos founded Amazon over a decade ago, he chose the name for its image of colossal size as well as for its alphabetical advantage. Living up to its name, Amazon eventually became the undisputed leader in providing a superior online shopping experience.

Bezos' original plan was to give customers access to an enormous selection of books—many more than any single bricks-and-mortar bookstore could hold. His success in selling books soon extended into music, movies, electronics, and technology services. A pioneer in e-commerce, Jeff Bezos abandoned conventional business models. His use of technology created an entirely new way of doing business.

Many dot-coms have flopped, but Amazon's popularity among Internet users is unmatched. It enjoys unsurpassed brand-name recognition and has armies of customers who adore it. People especially love its low prices, convenience, and personalized one-to-one marketing. It was the first company to really take advantage of the Internet's capacity to keep track of customers. Previously, only small-time merchants could know all of their customers personally. Amazon developed technology that enables it to remember all customers' names and what they are interested in.

From the beginning Bezos was intent on building a customer-oriented culture. "Customers come first," he said. "If you focus on what customers want and build a relationship, they will allow you to make money." No one knows more about its online shoppers than Amazon, and no one is more adept at using that information to market products. One happy shopper said, "No other outfit comes close to tracking what its customers do and using that information to make its customers happy. The result: As time goes by, I find myself buying more and more stuff from Amazon.com and feeling good about it."[1]

Amazon founder Jeff Bezos pioneered e-commerce and continues to innovate personalized e-marketing strategies.

Photo: © AP/Wide World Photos

Critical Thinking

- Amazon.com has amassed a great deal of information about its customers. Should it share this information with other companies or with its affiliates?
- Why is it important for a seller to have information about a potential buyer?
- In what ways does Amazon.com have to be persuasive with its customers? How often do you use persuasion in your daily life?

http://www.amazon.com

CONTINUED ON PAGE 307

case study

Strategies for Making Persuasive Requests

The ability to persuade is one of life's important skills. Persuading means using argument or discussion to change an individual's beliefs or actions. Persuasion, of course, is a very important part of any business that sells goods or services. Selling online, such as Jeff Bezos must do with Amazon.com, is even more challenging than other forms of persuasion because of the technology barrier that must be overcome. However, many of the techniques that Bezos uses at Amazon.com are similar to those you will use in persuasion at home, at school, and on the job.

Doubtless you've had to be persuasive to convert others to your views or to motivate them to do what you want. The outcome of such efforts depends largely on the reasonableness of your request, your credibility, and the ability to make your request attractive to the receiver. In this chapter you will learn many techniques and strategies to help you be successful in any persuasive effort.

Successful persuasion results from a reasonable request, a credible source, and a well-presented argument.

When you think that your listener or reader is inclined to agree with your request, you can start directly with the main idea. But when the receiver is likely to resist, don't reveal the purpose too quickly. Ideas that require persuasion benefit from a slow approach that includes ample preparation.

Let's say you want to replace your outdated office PC with a new, powerful laptop with built-in wireless networking. It could travel with you and also replace your desktop computer. In a memo to your boss Laura, who is likely to resist this request because of budget constraints and other reasons, you wisely decide not to open with a direct request. Instead, you gain her attention and move to logical reasons supporting your request. This indirect pattern is effective when you must persuade people to grant you favors, accept your recommendations, make adjustments in your favor, or grant your claims.

The same is true for sales messages. Instead of making a sales pitch immediately, smart communicators prepare a foundation by developing credibility and hooking their requests to benefits for the receiver. In persuasive messages other than sales, you must know precisely what you want the receiver to think or do. You must also anticipate what appeals to make or "buttons to push" to motivate action. Achieving these goals in both written and oral messages requires special attention to the initial steps in the process.

Effective sales messages reflect thorough product knowledge, writer credibility, and specific reader benefits.

Applying Guffey's 3-x-3 Writing Process to Persuasive Messages

learning objective 1

Persuasion means changing people's views, and that's a difficult task. Pulling it off demands planning and perception. Guffey's 3-x-3 writing process provides you with a helpful structure for laying a foundation for persuasion. Of particular importance here are (1) analyzing the purpose, (2) adapting to the audience, (3) collecting information, and (4) organizing the message.

Analyzing the Purpose. The purpose of a persuasive message is to convert the receiver to your ideas or to motivate action. A message without a clear purpose is doomed. Not only must you know what your purpose is and what response you want, but you must know these things when you start writing a letter or planning a presentation. Too often, ineffective communicators reach the end of a message before discovering exactly what they want the receiver to do. Then they must start over, giving the request a different "spin" or emphasis. Because your purpose establishes the strategy of the message, determine it first.

Persuasive messages require careful analysis of the purpose for writing.

Let's return to your memo requesting a new laptop. What exactly do you want your boss to do? Which of these actions do you expect Laura to take? (1) Meet with you so that you can show her how much computer time is lost with slow software

career coach

Seven Rules Every Persuader Should Know

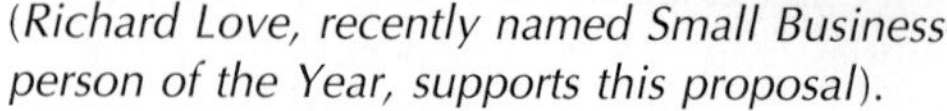

Successful businesspeople create persuasive memos, letters, reports, and presentations that get the results they want. Yet, their approaches are all different. Some persuaders are gentle, leading readers by the hand to the targeted recommendation. Others are brisk and authoritative. Some are objective, examining both sides of an issue like a judge deciding a difficult case. Some move slowly and carefully toward a proposal, whereas others erupt like a volcano in their eagerness to announce a recommendation. Different situations and different goals require different techniques. The following seven rules suggest various strategies—depending on your individual need.

- **RULE 1: Consider whether your views will create problems for your audience.** A student engineer submitted a report recommending a simple change at a waste-treatment facility. His recommendation would save $200,000 a year, but the report met with a cool reception. Why? His supervisors would have to explain to management why they had allowed a waste of $200,000 a year! If your views make trouble for the audience, think of ways to include the receivers in your recommendation if possible. Whatever your strategy, be tactful and empathic.
- **RULE 2: Don't offer new ideas, directives, or recommendations for change until your audience is prepared for them.** Receivers are threatened by anything that upsets their values or interests. The greater the change you suggest, the more slowly you should proceed. For example, if your boss is enthusiastic about a new marketing scheme (that would cost $50,000 to develop), naturally you will go slowly in shooting it down. If, on the other hand, your boss has little personal investment in the scheme, you could be more direct in your attack.
- **RULE 3: Select a strategy that supports your credibility.** If you have great credibility with your audience, you can proceed directly. If not, you need to establish that credibility. *Given* credibility results from position or reputation, such as that of the head of an organization or a highly regarded scientist. *Acquired* credibility is earned. To acquire credibility, successful persuaders often identify themselves, early in the message, with the goals and interests of the audience (*As a small business owner myself . . .*). Another way to acquire credibility is to mention evidence or ideas that support the audience's existing views (*We agree that small business owners need more government assistance*). Finally, you can acquire credibility by citing authorities who rate highly with your audience (*Richard Love, recently named Small Businessperson of the Year, supports this proposal*).
- **RULE 4: If your audience disagrees with your ideas or is uncertain about them, present both sides of the argument.** You might think that you would be most successful by revealing only one side of an issue—your side, of course. But persuasion doesn't work that way. You'll be more successful—particularly if the audience is unfriendly or uncertain—by disclosing *all* sides of an argument. This approach suggests that you are objective. It also helps the receiver remember your view by showing the pros and cons in relation to one another. Thus, if you want to convince the owner of a realty firm to invest in personal digital assistants (PDAs) for all agents, be truthful about any shortcomings, weaknesses, and limitations.
- **RULE 5: Win respect by making your opinion or recommendation clear.** Although you should be truthful in presenting both sides of an argument, don't be shy in supporting your conclusions or final proposals. You will, naturally, have definite views and should persuade your audience to accept them. The two-sided strategy is a means to an end, but it does not mean compromising your argument. One executive criticized reports from his managers because they presented much data and concluded, in effect, with "Here is what I found out and maybe we should do this or maybe we should do that." Be decisive and make specific recommendations.
- **RULE 6: Place your strongest points strategically.** Some experts argue that if your audience is deeply concerned with your subject, you can afford to begin with your weakest points. Because of its commitment, the audience will stay with you until you reach the strongest points at the end. For an unmotivated audience, begin with your strongest points to get them interested. Other experts feel that a supportive audience should receive the main ideas or recommendations immediately, to avoid wasting time. Whichever position you choose, don't bury your recommendation, strongest facts, or main idea in the middle of your argument.

- **RULE 7: Don't count on changing attitudes by offering information alone.** "If customers knew the truth about our costs, they would not object to our prices," some companies reason. Well, don't bet on it. Companies have pumped huge sums into advertising and public relations campaigns that provided facts alone. Such efforts often fail because learning something new (that is, increasing the knowledge of the audience) is rarely an effective way to change attitudes. Researchers have found that presentations of facts alone may strengthen opinions—but primarily for people who already agree with the persuader. The added information reassures them and provides ammunition for defending themselves in discussions with others. But to change attitudes, you must connect facts with emotional and rational appeals, as discussed in this chapter.

Career Application

Consider a career-oriented problem in a current or past job: customer service must be improved, workers need better training, inventory procedures are inefficient, equipment is outdated, worker scheduling is arbitrary, and so forth. Devise a plan to solve the problem. How could the preceding rules help you persuade a decision maker to adopt your plan? In a memo to your instructor or in a class discussion, outline the problem and your plan for solving it. Describe your persuasive strategy.

and poor Internet connections? (2) Purchase a Brand X laptop for you now? (3) Include your laptop request in the department's five-year equipment forecast? By identifying your purpose up front, you can shape the message to point toward it. This planning effort saves considerable rewriting time and produces the most successful persuasive messages.

Effective persuasive messages focus on audience needs or goals.

Adapting to the Audience. While you're considering the purpose of a persuasive message, you also need to concentrate on the receiver. How can you adapt your request to that individual so that your message is heard? Zorba the Greek wisely observed, "You can knock forever on a deaf man's door." A persuasive message is equally futile unless it meets the needs of its audience. In a broad sense, you'll be seeking to show how your request helps the receiver achieve some of life's major goals or fulfills key needs: money, power, comfort, confidence, importance, friends, peace of mind, and recognition, to name a few.

On a more practical level, you want to show how your request solves a problem, achieves a personal or work objective, or just makes life easier for your audience. In your request for a new laptop, for example, you could appeal to your boss's expressed concern for increasing productivity. If you were asking for a four-day work schedule, you could cite the need for improved efficiency and better employee morale.

To adapt your request to the receiver, consider these questions that receivers will very likely be asking themselves:

Why should I?

What's in it for me?

What's in it for you?

Who cares?

Adapting to your audience means being ready to answer these questions. It means learning about audience members and analyzing why they might resist your proposal. It means searching for ways to connect your purpose with their needs. If completed before you begin writing, such analysis goes a long way toward overcoming resistance and achieving your goal. The accompanying Career Coach box presents additional strategies that can make you a successful persuader.

The key components of a persuasive request are gaining attention, showing the worth of the proposal, overcoming resistance, and motivating action.

Researching and Organizing Data. Once you've analyzed the audience and considered how to adapt your message to its needs, you're ready to collect data and organize it. You might brainstorm and prepare cluster diagrams to provide a rough outline of ideas. For your request for a new laptop, your strategy might focus on portability and productivity. You could be more mobile and more productive with better equipment. In this case, you would gather data to show how much time and effort could be saved with the new equipment. To overcome resistance to cost, you would need information about prices. To ensure getting exactly what you want, you would study many laptop models.

The next step is organizing your data. Suppose you have already decided that your request will meet with resistance. Thus, you decide not to open directly with your request. Instead, you use the four-part indirect pattern, listed here and shown graphically in Figure 10.1:

- Gain attention
- Build interest
- Reduce resistance
- Motivate action

learning objective

2

Blending the Components of a Persuasive Message

Although the indirect pattern appears to contain separate steps, successful persuasive messages actually blend these steps into a seamless whole. However, the sequence of the components may change depending on the situation and the emphasis. Regardless of where they are placed, the key elements in persuasive requests are (1) gaining the audience's attention, (2) convincing them that your proposal is worthy, (3) overcoming resistance, and (4) motivating action.

Gaining Attention

Successful openers to persuasive requests should be brief, targeted, and interesting.

To grab attention, the opening statement in a persuasive request should be brief, relevant, and engaging. When only mild persuasion is necessary, the opener can be low-key and factual. If, however, your request is substantial and you anticipate strong resistance, provide a thoughtful, provocative opening. The following examples suggest possibilities.

FIGURE 10.1 ***Four-Part Indirect Pattern for Sales or Persuasion***

Gaining Attention	Building Interest	Reducing Resistance	Motivating Action
Free offer	Rational appeals	Testimonials	Gift
Promise	Emotional appeals	Satisfied users	Incentive
Question	Dual appeals	Guarantee	Limited offer
Quotation	Product description	Free trial	Deadline
Product feature	Reader benefits	Sample	Guarantee
Testimonial	Cold facts mixed with warm feelings	Performance tests	Repetition of selling feature
Action setting		Polls, awards	

- **Problem description.** In a recommendation to hire temporary employees: *Last month legal division staff members were forced to work 120 overtime hours, costing us $6,000 and causing considerable employee unhappiness.* With this opener you've presented a capsule of the problem your proposal will help solve.
- **Unexpected statement.** In a memo to encourage employees to attend an optional sensitivity seminar: *Men and women draw the line at decidedly different places in identifying what behavior constitutes sexual harassment.* Note how this opener gets readers thinking immediately.
- **Reader benefit.** In a letter promoting Clear Card, a service that helps employees make credit card purchases without paying interest: *The average employee carries nearly $9,000 in revolving debt and pays $1,800 in interest and late fees. The Clear Card charges zero percent interest. You can't beat it!* Employers immediately see this offer as a benefit it can offer employees.
- **Compliment.** In a letter inviting a business executive to speak: *Because our members admire your success and value your managerial expertise, they want you to be our speaker.* In offering praise or compliments, however, be careful to avoid obvious flattery.
- **Related fact.** In a message to company executives who are considering restricting cell phone use by employee drivers: *A recent study revealed that employers pay an average of $16,500 each time an employee is in a traffic accident.* This relevant fact sets the scene for the interest-building section that follows.
- **Stimulating question.** In a plea for funds to support environmental causes: *What do golden tortoise beetles, bark spiders, flounders, and Arctic foxes have in common?* Readers will be curious to find the answer to this intriguing question. [They all change color depending on their surroundings.]

When Subway began promoting its low-fat sandwiches as healthier options for takeout-eating Americans, it gained attention by showing Lanette Kovach, its chief nutritionist, with a platter of mouth-watering menu options. The first step in developing a sales or persuasive message is gaining attention and shaping the message to the receiver's interests and benefit.

Photo: © Todd Plitt-Imagebox

Building Interest

After capturing attention, a persuasive request must retain that attention and convince the audience that the request is reasonable. To justify your request, be prepared to invest in a few paragraphs of explanation. Persuasive requests are likely to be longer than direct requests because the audience must be convinced rather than simply instructed. You can build interest and conviction through the use of the following:

The body of a persuasive request may require several paragraphs to build interest and reduce resistance.

- Facts, statistics
- Expert opinion
- Direct benefits
- Examples
- Specific details
- Indirect benefits

Showing how your request can benefit the audience directly or indirectly is a key factor in persuasion. If you were asking alumni to contribute money to a college foundation, for example, you might promote *direct benefits* such as listing the donor's name in the college magazine or sending a sweatshirt with the college logo.

Another direct benefit is a tax write-off for the contribution. An *indirect benefit* comes from feeling good about helping the college and knowing that students will benefit from the gift. Nearly all charities rely in large part on indirect benefits—the selflessness of givers—to promote their causes.

Reducing Resistance

Persuasive requests reduce resistance by addressing* What if? *questions and establishing credibility.

One of the biggest mistakes in persuasive requests is the failure to anticipate and offset audience resistance. How will the receiver object to your request? In brainstorming for clues, try *What if?* scenarios. Let's say you are trying to convince management that the employees' cafeteria should switch from paper and plastic plates and cups to ceramic. What if managers say the change is too expensive? What if they argue that they are careful recyclers of paper and plastic? What if they contend that ceramic dishes would increase cafeteria labor and energy costs tremendously? What if they protest that ceramic is less hygienic? For each of these *What if?* scenarios, you need a counterargument.

Unless you anticipate resistance, you give the receiver an easy opportunity to dismiss your request. Countering this resistance is important, but you must do it with finesse (*Although ceramic dishes cost more at first, they actually save money over time*). You can minimize objections by presenting your counterarguments in sentences that emphasize benefits: *Ceramic dishes may require a little more effort in cleaning, but they bring warmth and graciousness to meals. Most important, they help save the environment by requiring fewer resources and eliminating waste.* However, don't spend too much time on counterarguments, thus making them overly important. Finally, avoid bringing up objections that may never have occurred to the receiver in the first place.

Another factor that reduces resistance is credibility. Receivers are less resistant if your request is reasonable and if you are believable. When the receiver does not know you, you may have to establish your expertise, refer to your credentials, or demonstrate your competence. Even when you are known, you may have to establish your knowledge in a given area. In making your request for a new laptop, you might have to establish your credibility by showing your boss articles you have read about the latest laptops and how much more efficient you could be with better Internet connections. Some charities establish their credibility by displaying on their stationery the names of famous people who serve on their boards. The credibility of speakers making presentations is usually outlined by someone who introduces them.

Motivating Action

Persuasive requests motivate action by specifying exactly what should be done.

After gaining attention, building interest, and reducing resistance, you'll want to inspire the receiver to act. This is where your planning pays dividends. Knowing exactly what action you favor before you start to write enables you to point your arguments toward this important final paragraph. Here you will make your recommendation as specifically and confidently as possible—without seeming pushy. A proposal from one manager to another might conclude with, *So that we can begin using the employment assessment tests by May 1, please send a return e-mail immediately.* In making a request, don't sound apologetic (*I'm sorry to have to ask you this, but . . .*), and don't supply excuses (*If you can spare the time, . . .*). Compare the following closings for a persuasive memo recommending training seminars in communication skills.

Too General

We are certain we can develop a series of training sessions that will improve the communication skills of your employees.

Too Timid
If you agree that our training proposal has merit, perhaps we could begin the series in June.

Too Pushy
Because we're convinced that you will want to begin improving the skills of your employees immediately, we've scheduled your series to begin in June.

Effective
You will see decided improvement in the communication skills of your employees. Please call me at 439-2201 by May 1 to give your approval so that training sessions may start in June, as we discussed.

Note how the last opening suggests a specific and easy-to-follow action. Figure 10.2 summarizes techniques for overcoming resistance and crafting successful persuasive messages.

Being Persuasive but Ethical

Business communicators may be tempted to make their persuasion even more forceful by fudging on the facts, exaggerating a point, omitting something crucial, or providing deceptive emphasis. Consider the case of a manager who sought to persuade employees to accept a change in insurance benefits. His memo emphasized a small perk (easier handling of claims) but deemphasized a major reduction in total coverage. Some readers missed the main point—as the manager intended. Others recognized the deception, however, and before long the manager's credibility was lost. A persuader is effective only when he or she is believable. If receivers suspect that they are being manipulated or misled or if they find any part of the argument untruthful, the total argument fails. Persuaders can also fall into traps of logic without even being aware of it. Take a look at the accompanying Ethical Insights box to learn about common logical fallacies that you will want to avoid.

Ethical business communicators maintain credibility and respect by being honest, fair, and objective.

Persuasion becomes unethical when facts are distorted, overlooked, or manipulated with an intent to deceive. Of course, persuaders naturally want to put forth their strongest case. But that argument must be based on truth, objectivity, and fairness.

In prompting ethical and truthful persuasion, two factors act as powerful motivators. The first is the desire to preserve your reputation and credibility. Once lost, a good name is difficult to regain. An equally important force prompting ethical behavior, though, is your opinion of yourself. One stockbroker admitted that she was

FIGURE 10.2 ***Components of a Persuasive Message***

Gaining Attention	Building Interest	Reducing Resistance	Motivating Action
Summary of problem	Facts, figures	Anticipate objections	Describe specific request
Unexpected statement	Expert opinion	Offer counterarguments	Sound confident
Reader benefit	Examples	Play *What if?* scenarios	Make action easy to take
Compliment	Specific details	Establish credibility	Offer incentive
Related fact	Direct benefits	Demonstrate competence	Don't provide excuses
Stimulating question	Indirect benefits	Show value of proposal	Repeat main benefit

ethical insights

What's Fair in Persuasion? Avoiding Common Logical Fallacies

While being persuasive, we must be careful to remain ethical. In our eagerness to win others over to our views, we may inadvertently overstep the bounds of fair play. Philosophers through the years have pinpointed a number of logical fallacies. Here are three you'll want to avoid in your persuasive messages. For an online discussion of many logical fallacies, use a Web search engine to find "Stephen's Guide to the Logical Fallacies."

- **Circular reasoning.** When the support given for a contention merely restates the contention, the reasoning is circular. For example, *Investing in the stock market is dangerous for short-term investors because it is unsafe.* The evidence (*because it is unsafe*) offers no proof. It merely circles back to the original contention. Revision: *Investing in the stock market is dangerous for short-term investors because stock prices fluctuate widely.*
- **Begging the question.** A statement such as *That dishonest CEO should be replaced* begs the question. Merely asserting that the CEO is dishonest is not enough. Be sure to supply solid evidence for such assertions. Revision: *That CEO is dishonest because he awards contracts only to his friends. A good manager would require open bidding.*
- **Post hoc (after, thus, because).** Although two events may have happened in immediate sequence, the first did not necessarily cause the second. For example, *The company switched to team-based management, and its stock price rose immediately afterward.* Switching to teams probably had no effect on the stock price. Revision: *At about the same time the company switched to team-based management, its stock price began to rise, although the two events are probably unrelated.*

Career Application

In teams or in a class discussion, cite examples of how these fallacies could be used in persuasive messages or sales letters. Provide a logical, ethical revision for each.

in the business to make money, but she realized that she still had to be able to face herself in the mirror each morning. If she were unethical, she confessed, she may make all the money in the world. But she wouldn't retain family, friends, or lasting business relationships.[2]

learning objective

3

The indirect pattern is appropriate when requesting favors and action, persuading within organizations, and writing complaint letters.

Writing Successful Persuasive Requests

Convincing someone to change a belief or to perform an action when that individual is reluctant requires planning and skill—and sometimes a little luck. If the request is in writing, rather than face to face, the task is even more difficult. The indirect pattern, though, can help you shape effective persuasive appeals that (1) request favors and action, (2) persuade within organizations, and (3) write complaints and make claims.

Requesting Favors and Actions

Persuading someone to do something that largely benefits you is not easy. Fortunately, many individuals and companies are willing to grant requests for time, money, information, special privileges, and cooperation. They grant these favors for a variety of reasons. They may just happen to be interested in your project, or they may see goodwill potential for themselves. Often, though, they comply because they

PROCESS IN PROGRESS

Amazon.com Revisited

JEFF BEZOS, FOUNDER and CEO of Amazon.com, knew that persuading customers to buy online was going to be difficult. They had to have computers, they had to be willing to use this technology, and they had to overcome fears about security and loss of privacy. But he also knew that people are time-starved, thrifty, and eager for convenience. As Amazon grew, Bezos learned that its customers have higher-than-average incomes and education. They also tend to be busy, which makes the convenience factor even more important.

In anticipating the fears of his audience, Bezos developed a secure method for giving credit information. Through focus groups, he devised techniques to allow customers to fill their online shopping carts with a minimum of hassle. He overcame people's reluctance to use technology by capitalizing on its possibilities, such as offering a huge selection of products and promising rapid delivery. Repeat customers are immediately greeted by name, and they receive recommendations based on their previous purchases. He also anticipated the needs of his customers by providing easy search functions, reviews, product associations, and sale rankings. This information facilitates quick, easy, and appropriate purchase decisions.

Critical Thinking

- How does knowledge of Amazon.com's customers help shape its persuasive efforts?
- Why is it difficult to change attitudes (such as the fear of giving your credit card number to an online company) by offering information only?
- How is the four-part plan for persuasion effective for sales messages such as Amazon.com might send to its customers?

CONTINUED ON PAGE 321

case study

see that others will benefit from the request. Professionals sometimes feel obligated to contribute their time or expertise to "pay their dues."

You may find that you have few direct benefits to offer in your persuasion. Instead, you'll be focusing on indirect benefits, as the writer does in Figure 10.3. In asking a manager to speak before a restaurant industry meeting, the writer has little to offer as a direct benefit other than a $200 honorarium. But indirectly, the writer offers enticements such as an enthusiastic audience and a chance to help other restaurateurs solve common problems. This persuasive request appeals primarily to the reader's desire to serve her profession—although a receptive audience and an opportunity to function as an expert among one's peers have a certain ego appeal as well. Together, these appeals—professional, egoistic, monetary—make a persuasive argument rich and effective.

An offer to work as an intern, at no cost to a company, would seem to require little persuasion. Many companies, however, hesitate to participate in internship programs because student interns require supervision, desk space, and equipment. They also pose an insurance liability threat.

In Figure 10.4 college student Melanie Harris seeks to persuade Software Enterprises to accept her as an intern. In the analysis process before writing, Melanie thought long and hard about what benefits she could offer the reader and how she could present them strategically. She decided that the offer of a trained college student's free labor was her strongest benefit. Thus, she opens with it, as well as mentioning the same benefit in the letter body and in the closing. After opening with the main audience benefit, she introduces the actual request ("Could you use the part-time services of a college senior . . . ?").

FIGURE 10.3 ***Persuasive Favor Request***

1 Prewriting

ANALYZE: The purpose of this letter is to persuade the reader to speak at a dinner meeting.

ANTICIPATE: Although the reader is busy, she may respond to appeals to her ego (describing her previous excellent presentation) and to her professionalism.

ADAPT: Because the reader may be uninterested at first and require persuasion, use the indirect pattern.

2 Writing

RESEARCH: Study the receiver's interests and find ways to relate this request to her interests.

ORGANIZE: Gain attention by opening with praise or a stimulating remark. Build interest with explanations and facts. Show how compliance benefits the reader and others. Reduce resistance by providing ideas for the dinner talk.

COMPOSE: Prepare a first draft with the intention to revise.

3 Revising

REVISE: Revise to show direct and indirect benefits more clearly.

PROOFREAD: Check spelling of *restaurateur*. In the fourth paragraph, use a semicolon in the compound sentence. Start all lines at the left for a block-style letter.

EVALUATE: Will this letter convince the reader to accept the invitation?

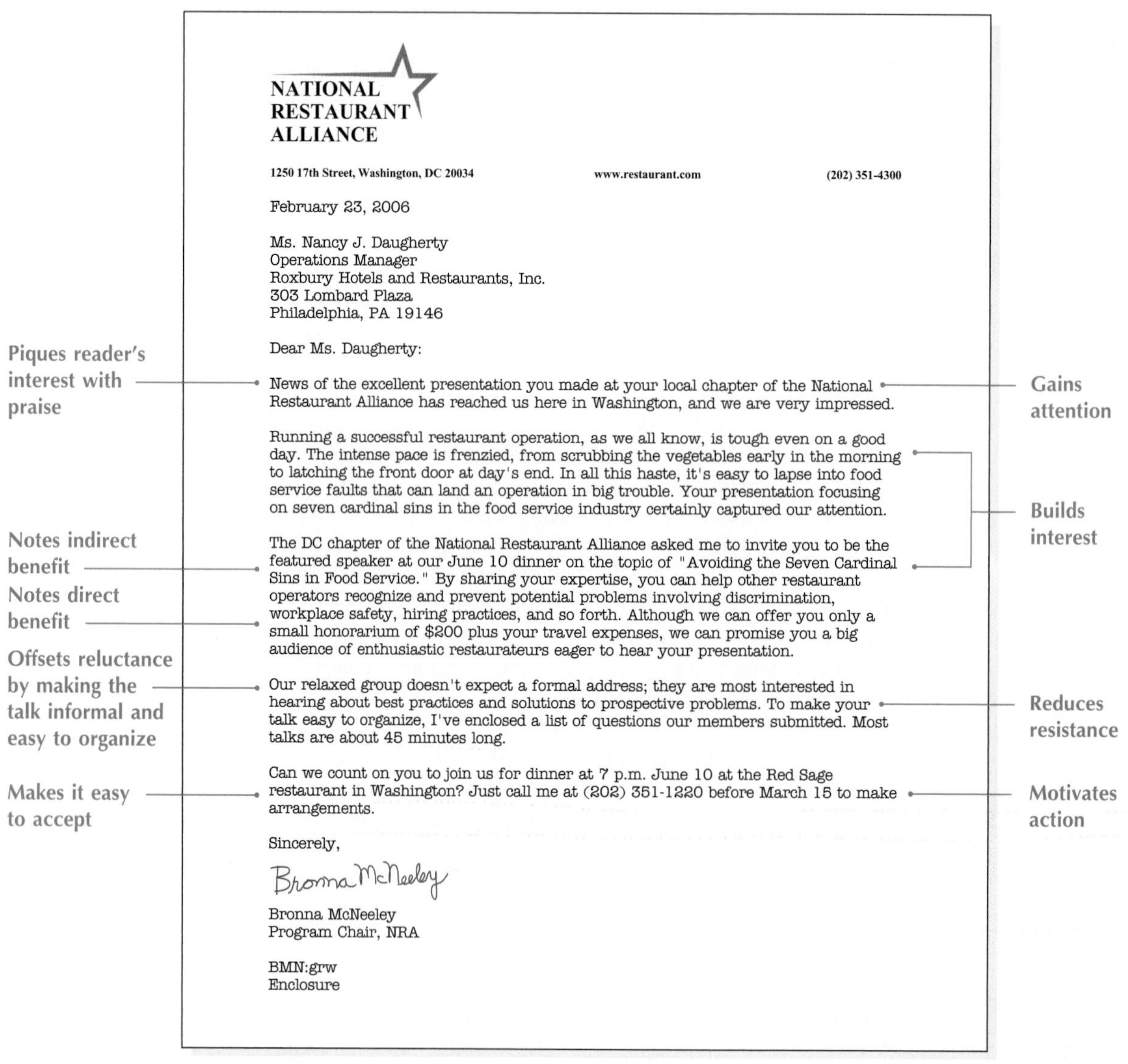

NATIONAL
RESTAURANT
ALLIANCE

1250 17th Street, Washington, DC 20034 www.restaurant.com (202) 351-4300

February 23, 2006

Ms. Nancy J. Daugherty
Operations Manager
Roxbury Hotels and Restaurants, Inc.
303 Lombard Plaza
Philadelphia, PA 19146

Dear Ms. Daugherty:

News of the excellent presentation you made at your local chapter of the National Restaurant Alliance has reached us here in Washington, and we are very impressed.

Running a successful restaurant operation, as we all know, is tough even on a good day. The intense pace is frenzied, from scrubbing the vegetables early in the morning to latching the front door at day's end. In all this haste, it's easy to lapse into food service faults that can land an operation in big trouble. Your presentation focusing on seven cardinal sins in the food service industry certainly captured our attention.

The DC chapter of the National Restaurant Alliance asked me to invite you to be the featured speaker at our June 10 dinner on the topic of "Avoiding the Seven Cardinal Sins in Food Service." By sharing your expertise, you can help other restaurant operators recognize and prevent potential problems involving discrimination, workplace safety, hiring practices, and so forth. Although we can offer you only a small honorarium of $200 plus your travel expenses, we can promise you a big audience of enthusiastic restaurateurs eager to hear your presentation.

Our relaxed group doesn't expect a formal address; they are most interested in hearing about best practices and solutions to prospective problems. To make your talk easy to organize, I've enclosed a list of questions our members submitted. Most talks are about 45 minutes long.

Can we count on you to join us for dinner at 7 p.m. June 10 at the Red Sage restaurant in Washington? Just call me at (202) 351-1220 before March 15 to make arrangements.

Sincerely,

Bronna McNeeley

Bronna McNeeley
Program Chair, NRA

BMN:grw
Enclosure

Piques reader's interest with praise
Gains attention
Builds interest
Notes indirect benefit
Notes direct benefit
Offsets reluctance by making the talk informal and easy to organize
Reduces resistance
Makes it easy to accept
Motivates action

FIGURE 10.4 ***Persuasive Action Request***

4320 Mountlake Terrace Drive
Lynnwood, WA 98250
January 12, 2006

Ms. Nancy Ashley, Director
Human Resources Department
Software Enterprises, Inc.
268 Redmond Avenue
Bellevue, WA 98420

Dear Ms. Ashley:

How often do college-trained specialists offer to work for nothing?

Very infrequently, I imagine. But that's the offer I'm making to Software Enterprises. During the next 14 weeks, could you use the part-time services of a college senior with communication and computer skills?

To gain work experience and to earn three units of credit, I would like to become an intern at Software Enterprises. My skills in Word and Excel, as well as training in letter and report writing, could be put to use in your Customer Service, Human Resources, Legal, Documentation, or other departments.

By granting this internship, your company not only secures the skills of an enthusiastic and well-trained college student, but it also performs a valuable service to Edmonds College. Your cooperation provides an opportunity for students to acquire the kind of job training that college classrooms simply cannot give.

If equipment and desk space at Software Enterprises are limited, you may want me to fill in for employees who can then be freed up for other projects, training, or release time. In regard to supervision you'll find that I require little direction once I start a project. Moreover, you don't need to worry about insurance, as our college provides liability coverage for all students at internship sites.

Although I'm taking classes in the mornings, I'm available to work afternoons for 15 hours a week. Please examine the attached résumé to confirm my preparation and qualifications.

Do you have any questions about my proposal to become an intern? To talk with me about it, please call 893-2155. I could begin working for you as early as February 1. You gain a free employee, and you also provide an appreciative local college student with much-needed job training.

Sincerely,

Melanie E. Harris

Melanie E. Harris

Enclosure

Starts with date and address in personal business style

Introduces request after presenting main benefit

Uses strongest benefit for stimulating opener

Notes direct benefit

Notes indirect benefit

Anticipates three obstacles and answers each

Introduces a negative in a positive way

Refers to enclosure only after presenting main points

Couples action request with reference to direct and indirect benefits

In the interest section, Melanie tells why she is making the request and describes its value in terms of direct and indirect benefits. Notice how she transforms obstacles (lack of equipment or desk space) into helpful suggestions about how her services would free up other staff members to perform more important tasks. She delays mentioning a negative (being able to work only 15 hours a week and only in the afternoon) until she builds interest and reduces resistance. And she closes confidently and motivates action with reference to both direct and indirect benefits.

Persuading Within Organizations

Internal persuasive memos present honest arguments detailing specific reader benefits.

Instructions or directives moving downward from superiors to subordinates usually require little persuasion. Employees expect to be directed in how to perform their jobs. These messages (such as information about procedures, equipment, or customer service) follow the direct pattern, with the purpose immediately stated. However, employees are sometimes asked to perform in a capacity outside their work roles or to accept changes that are not in their best interests—such as pay cuts, job transfers, or reduced benefits. In these instances, a persuasive memo using the indirect pattern may be most effective.

The goal is not to manipulate employees or to seduce them with trickery. Rather, the goal is to present a strong but honest argument, emphasizing points that are important to the receiver. In business, honesty is not just the best policy—it's the *only* policy. Especially within your own organization, people see right through puffery and misrepresentation. For this reason, the indirect pattern is effective only when supported by accurate, honest evidence.

When selling an idea to management, writers often are successful if they make a strong case for saving money.

Another form of persuasion within organizations centers on suggestions made by subordinates. Convincing management to adopt a procedure or invest in a product or new equipment generally requires skillful communication. Managers are just as resistant to change as others. Providing evidence is critical when subordinates submit recommendations to their bosses. Be ready to back up your request with facts, figures, and evidence. When selling an idea to management, strive to make a strong dollars-and-cents case.[3] A request that emphasizes how the proposal saves money or benefits the business is more persuasive than one that simply announces a good deal or tells how a plan works.

In Figure 10.5 you see the draft copy of a persuasive memo that needs revision. Marketing manager Mona Massey wants her boss to authorize the purchase of a second copy machine. She was so excited about a good deal that she wrote her memo quickly and didn't spend much time organizing it. Before sending it, though, she reconsidered. Although she thought that her request was totally reasonable, she realized that her memo failed to present a well-organized "dollar-and-cents" case. She also recognized that, if she spent a little more time developing her persuasive argument, she had a better chance of approval.

Notice that Mona's revision is longer. But it's far more effective. A successful persuasive message will typically take more space than a direct message because proving a case requires evidence. Mona's revised memo includes a subject line that tells the purpose of the memo without disclosing the actual request. By delaying the request until she's had a chance to describe the problem and discuss a solution, Mona prevents the reader's premature rejection.

The strength of this revision, though, is in the clear presentation of comparison figures showing how much money can be saved by purchasing a remanufactured copier. Although the organization pattern is not obvious, the revised memo begins with an attention-getter (frank description of problem), builds interest (with easy-to-read facts and figures), provides benefits, and reduces resistance. Notice that the conclusion tells what action is to be taken, makes it easy to respond, and repeats the main benefit to motivate action.

Complaint Letters: Writing Persuasive Claims

Persuasive claim letters typically involve damaged products, mistaken billing, inaccurate shipments, warranty problems, return policies, insurance snafus, faulty merchandise, and so on. Generally, the direct pattern is best for requesting straightforward adjustments (see Chapter 9). When you feel your request is justified and will be granted, the direct strategy is most efficient. But if a past request has been refused or ignored or if you anticipate reluctance, then the indirect pattern is appropriate.

Effective complaint/adjustment letters make reasonable claims backed by solid evidence.

In a sense, a claim letter is a complaint letter. Someone is complaining about something that went wrong. Some complaint letters just vent anger; the writers are mad, and they want to tell someone about it. But if the goal is to change something (and why bother to write except to motivate change?), then persuasion is necessary. Effective claim letters make a reasonable request, present a logical case with clear facts, and adopt a moderate tone. Anger and emotion are not effective persuaders.

FIGURE 10.5 ***Persuasive Memo***

DRAFT

TO: Kenneth Richardson, Vice President

Although you've opposed the purchase of additional copiers in the past, I think I've found a great deal on a copier that's just too good to pass up but we must act before May 1! Copy City has reconditioned copiers that are practically being given away. If we move fast, they will provide many free incentives—like a free copier stand, free starter supplies, free delivery, and free installation.

We must find a way to reduce copier costs in my department. Our current copier can't keep up with our demand. We're sending secretaries or sales reps to Copy Quick for an average of 10,000 copies a month. These copies cost 7 cents a page and waste a lot of time. We're making at least eight trips a week, adding up to a considerable expense in travel time and copy costs.

Please give this matter your immediate attention and get back to me as soon as possible. We don't want to miss this great deal!

Begins poorly with reminder of past negative feelings

Sounds high-pressured

Fails to compare costs and emphasize savings in logical, coherent presentation

Does not request or motivate specific action

REVISION

DATE: April 18, 2006

TO: Kenneth Richardson, Vice President

FROM: Mona Massey, Marketing

SUBJECT: Saving Time and Money on Copying

Describes topic without revealing request

Summarizes problem

We're losing money on our current copy services and wasting the time of employees as well. Because our Canon copier is in use constantly, we find it increasingly necessary to send major jobs out to Copy Quick. Just take a look at how much we spend each month for outside copy service:

Copy Costs: Outside Service

10,000 copies/month made at Copy Quick	$700.00
Salary costs for assistants to make 32 trips to drop off originals and pick up copies	384.00
Total	$1,084.00

Uses headings and columns for easy comparison

When sales reps make the trips, the costs are even greater. Because this expense must be reduced, I've been considering alternatives. New copiers with collating capability and automatic multidrawer paper feeding are very expensive. But reconditioned copiers with all the features we need are available—and at attractive prices and terms. From Copy City we can get a fully remanufactured copier that is guaranteed to work like new. After we make an initial payment of $219, our monthly costs would look like this:

Proves credibility of request with facts and figures

Copy Costs: Remanufactured Copier

Paper supplies for 10,000 copies	$130.00
Toner and copy supplies	95.00
Labor of assistants to make copies	130.00
Monthly financing charge for copier (purchase price of $1,105 amortized at 10% with 29 payments)	34.52
Total	$389.52

As you can see, **a remanufactured copier saves us nearly $700 per month.**

Highlights most important benefit

Provides more benefits

For a limited time Copy City is offering a free 15-day trial offer, a free copier stand (worth $165), free starter supplies, and free delivery and installation. We have office space available, and my staff is eager to add a second machine.

Counters possible resistance

Makes it easy to grant approval

Call me at Ext. 630 if you have questions. This copier is such a good opportunity that I've attached a purchase requisition authorizing the agreement with Copy City. With your approval before May 1, we can have our machine by May 10 and start saving time and nearly $700 every month. Fast action will also take advantage of Copy City's free start-up incentives.

Repeats main benefit with motivation to act quickly

Attachment

Logical Development. Strive for logical development in a claim letter. You might open with sincere praise, an objective statement of the problem, a point of agreement, or a quick review of what you have done to resolve the problem. Then you can explain precisely what happened or why your claim is legitimate. Don't provide a blow-by-blow chronology of details; just hit the highlights. Be sure to enclose copies of relevant invoices, shipping orders, warranties, and payments. And close with a clear statement of what you want done: refund, replacement, credit to your account, or other action. Be sure to think through the possibilities and make your request reasonable.

Adjustment requests should adopt a moderate tone, appeal to the receiver's sense of responsibility, and specify needed actions.

Moderate Tone. The tone of the letter is important. Don't suggest that the receiver intentionally deceived you or intentionally created the problem. Rather, appeal to the receiver's sense of responsibility and pride in its good name. Calmly express your disappointment in view of your high expectations of the product and of the company. Communicating your feelings, without rancor, is often your strongest appeal.

Janet Walker's letter, shown in Figure 10.6, follows the persuasive pattern as she seeks to return three answering machines. Notice that she uses simplified letter style (skipping the salutation and complimentary close) because she doesn't have a person's name to use in addressing the letter. Note also her positive opening, her calm and well-documented claims, and her request for specific action.

The following checklist reviews pointers for helping you make persuasive requests of all kinds.

Checklist for Making Persuasive Requests

✓ **Gain attention.** In requesting favors, begin with a compliment, statement of agreement, unexpected fact, stimulating question, reader benefit, summary of the problem, or candid plea for help. For claims and complaints, also consider opening with a review of action you have taken to resolve the problem.

✓ **Build interest.** Prove the accuracy and merit of your request with solid evidence, including facts, figures, expert opinion, examples, and details. Suggest direct and indirect benefits for the receiver. Avoid sounding high-pressured, angry, or emotional.

✓ **Reduce resistance.** Identify what factors will be obstacles to the receiver; offer counterarguments. Demonstrate your credibility by being knowledgeable. In requesting favors or making recommendations, show how the receiver or others will benefit. In making claims, appeal to the receiver's sense of fairness and desire for goodwill. Express your disappointment.

✓ **Motivate action.** Confidently ask for specific action. For favors include an end date (if appropriate) and try to repeat a key benefit.

learning objective 4

Planning and Composing Outstanding Sales Messages

Sales messages involve using persuasion to promote specific products and services. In our coverage we will be most concerned with sales messages delivered by mail or e-mail. Many of the concepts you will learn about sales persuasion can be applied to radio, TV, print, online, and wireless media. The best sales messages, whether

Figure 10.6 *Claim (Complaint) Letter*

Tips for Writing Claim Letters and Making Complaints

- Begin with a compliment, point of agreement, statement of the problem, or brief review of action you have taken to resolve the problem.
- Provide identifying data.
- Prove that your claim is valid; explain why the receiver is responsible.
- Enclose document copies supporting your claim.
- Appeal to the receiver's fairness, ethical and legal responsibilities, and desire for customer satisfaction.
- Describe your feelings and your disappointment.
- Avoid sounding angry, emotional, or irrational.
- Close by telling exactly what you want done.

CHAMPION AUTOMOTIVES
309 Porterville Plaza, Lansing, Michigan 48914 (517) 690-3500

November 21, 2006

Customer Service
Raytronic Electronics
594 Stanton Street
Mobile, AL 36617

SUBJECT: CODE-A-PHONE MODEL 100S — *Uses simplified letter style when name of receiver is unknown*

Begins with compliment — Your Code-A-Phone Model 100S answering unit came well recommended. We liked our neighbor's unit so well that we purchased three for different departments in our business.

Describes problem calmly — After the three units were unpacked and installed, we discovered a problem. Apparently our office fluorescent lighting interferes with the electronics in these units. When the lights are on, heavy static interrupts every telephone call. When the lights are off, the static disappears.

We can't replace the fluorescent lights, so we tried to return the Code-A-Phones to the place of purchase (Office Mart, 2560 Haslett Avenue, Lansing, MI 48901). A salesperson inspected the units and said they could not be returned because they were not defective and they had been used.

Suggests responsibility — Because the descriptive literature and instructions for the Code-A-Phones say nothing about avoiding use in rooms with fluorescent lighting, we expected no trouble. We were quite disappointed that this well-engineered unit—with its time/date stamp, room monitor, and auto-dial features—failed to perform as we hoped it would. — *Stresses disappointment*

If you have a model with similar features that would work in our offices, give me a call. Otherwise, please authorize the return of these units and refund the purchase price of $519.45 (see enclosed invoice). — *Tells what action to take* — We're confident that a manufacturer with your reputation for excellent products and service will want to resolve this matter quickly. — *Appeals to company's desire to preserve good reputation*

Janet Walker

JANET WALKER, PRESIDENT

JPW:ett
Enclosure

delivered by e-marketing or direct mail, have much in common. In this section we'll look at the changing world of direct marketing. We'll study how to apply Guffey's 3-x-3 writing process to sales messages. Then you'll learn techniques developed by experts to draft outstanding sales messages, both in print and online.

The Changing World of Direct Marketing

Traditional direct-mail marketing involves messages delivered by land mail.

Traditional direct-mail marketing involves the sale of goods and services through letters, catalogs, brochures, envelope stuffers, and other messages delivered by land mail. But today's powerful communication technologies present advertisers with exciting new ways to reach target audiences. As discussed in Chapter 1, the whole communication infrastructure has changed in the past decade. Companies employing direct marketing may now turn to electronic marketing, which involves sales messages delivered by e-mail, Web sites, and even wireless devices. To some marketers, e-mail sounds like a promised land, guaranteeing instant delivery at pennies per message. However, unsolicited commercial e-mail, or "spam," has generated an incredible backlash from recipients. They want their e-mail addresses to remain private and unviolated.

E-Marketing. Although many consumers object to unsolicited e-mail sales messages, others don't mind receiving helpful information about services or new products they can use. Later in this chapter you'll learn how to write effective "permission-based" e-mails. This kind of e-marketing is rapidly gaining acceptance because it is efficient, cheap, easily tracked, and faster than direct mail.

Effective marketing strategies balance traditional direct mail and e-marketing.

E-marketing, however, is limited to tech-savvy audiences. Smart companies will strive to develop a balanced approach to their overall marketing strategy, including both e-marketing and direct mail when appropriate. "Even when e-commerce is exploding, every marketing plan should include a direct-mail component in order to communicate a company's message," insists marketing expert John R. Graham. To enforce his point, Graham points out that "if you want proof of the power of direct mail, notice how Internet companies rely on direct mail to promote their Web sites."[4] You can learn what successful e-mail marketing messages have in common in the accompanying Tech Talk box.

Direct-Mail Marketing. Our main focus in this chapter will be on writing sales letters as part of direct-mail marketing. Traditional sales letters are a powerful means to make sales, generate leads, boost retail traffic, solicit donations, and direct consumers to Web sites. Mail allows a personalized, tangible, three-dimensional message that is less invasive than telephone solicitations and less reviled than unsolicited e-mail.

Professional direct mailers study the product, target an audience, and prepare a complete package.

Professionals who specialize in traditional direct-mail services have made it a science. They analyze a market, develop an effective mailing list, study the product, prepare a sophisticated campaign aimed at a target audience, and motivate the reader to act. You've probably received many direct-mail packages, often called "junk" mail. These packages typically contain a sales letter, a brochure, a price list, illustrations of the product, testimonials, and other persuasive appeals.

We're most concerned here with the sales letter: its strategy, organization, and evidence. Because sales letters are generally written by specialists, you may never write one on the job. Why, then, learn how to write a sales letter? In many ways, every letter we create is a form of sales letter. We sell our ideas, our organizations, and ourselves. Learning the techniques of sales writing will help you be more successful in any communication that requires persuasion and promotion. Furthermore, you'll recognize sales strategies, thus enabling you to become a more perceptive consumer of ideas, products, and services.

tech talk

What Successful Online Sales Messages Have in Common

To make the best use of limited advertising dollars, many businesses are turning to e-mail marketing campaigns instead of traditional direct mailings. E-mail marketing can attract new customers, keep existing ones, upsell, cross-sell, and cut costs. As consumers feel more comfortable and secure with online advertising, they will be receiving more e-mail sales messages. If your organization requires an online sales message, try using the following techniques gleaned from the best-performing e-mails:

- **Communicate only with those who have given permission!** By sending messages only to "opt-in" folks, you greatly increase your "open rate"—those e-mail messages that will be opened. E-mail users detest spam. However, receivers are surprisingly receptive to offers specifically for them. Remember that today's customer is *somebody*—not *anybody*.
- **Craft a catchy subject line.** Offer discounts or premiums. Promise solutions to everyday work-related problems. Highlight hot new industry topics. Invite readers to scan a top-10 list, such as issues, trends, or people.
- **Keep the main information "above the fold."** E-mail messages should be top heavy. Primary points should appear early in the message so that they capture the reader's attention.
- **Keep the message short, conversational, and focused.** Because on-screen text is taxing to read, be brief. Focus on one or two central selling points only.
- **Convey urgency.** Top-performing e-mail messages state an offer deadline or demonstrate why the state of the industry demands action on the reader's part. Good messages also tie the product to relevant current events.
- **Sprinkle testimonials throughout the copy.** Consumers' own words are the best sales copy. These comments can serve as callouts or be integrated into the copy.
- **Provide a means for opting out.** It's polite and a good business tactic to include a statement that tells receivers how to be removed from the sender's mailing database.

Career Application

In teams or in a class discussion, debate the pros and cons of e-mail marketing. From a business perspective, what are the advantages and disadvantages? Use the Web or InfoTrac to locate evidence to support your views.

Applying Guffey's 3-x-3 Writing Process to Sales Messages

Marketing professionals analyze every aspect of a sales message because consumers reject most direct-mail offers. Like the experts, you'll want to pay close attention to the preparatory steps of analysis and adaptation before writing the actual message.

Successful sales messages require research on the product or service offered and analysis of the purpose for writing.

Analyzing the Product and Purpose. Before sitting down to write a sales letter, you must study the product carefully. What can you learn about its design, construction, raw materials, and manufacturing process? About its ease of use, efficiency, durability, and applications? Be sure to consider warranties, service, price, premiums, exclusivity, and special appeals. At the same time, evaluate the competition so that you can compare your product's strengths against the competitor's weaknesses.

Now you're ready to identify your central selling points. At Amazon.com the central selling points are economy, selection, and convenience. The company has won scores of loyal customers by delivering packages on time, often beating customers' expectations. Another company enjoying enormous customer goodwill is cataloger Lands' End. A central selling point for one Lands' End marketing campaign was economical custom clothing. It used a testimonial from a real customer who said that the $49 Lands' End custom dress shirts he bought were better than

spotlight *on communicators*

As CEO of Internet auction giant eBay, Margaret "Meg" Whitman realizes the enormous benefits of adapting to her audience. In making eBay one of the most powerful economic forces on the Internet, Whitman is constantly "listening, adapting, enabling." She never loses sight of the fans. To know her audience thoroughly, she regularly attends conferences and also brings 10 to 20 of eBay's best customers into its offices each month. Her goal is getting to know them and their shopping habits. Understanding your audience is a major part of every successful sales effort.

Photo: © Kim Kulish/Corbis

the $120 shirts he previously purchased from custom shops.[5] Analyzing your product and studying the competition help you determine what to emphasize in your sales letter.

Equally important is determining the specific purpose of your letter. Do you want the reader to call for a free video and brochure? See a demonstration at your Web site? Fill out an order form? Send a credit card authorization? Before you write the first word of your message, know what response you want and what central selling points you will emphasize to achieve that purpose.

Adapting to the Audience. Blanket mailings sent "cold" to occupants generally produce low responses—typically less than 2 percent. That means that 98 percent of the receivers usually toss direct-mail sales letters directly into the trash. But the response rate can be increased dramatically by targeting the audience through selected database mailing lists. These lists can be purchased or compiled. By directing your message to a selected group, you can make certain assumptions about the receivers. Let's say you're selling fitness equipment. A good mailing list might come from subscribers to fitness or exercise magazines. You would expect similar interests, needs, and demographics (age, income, and other characteristics). With this knowledge you can adapt the sales letter to a specific audience.

Crafting a Winning Sales Message

Your primary goal in writing a sales message is to get someone to devote a few moments of attention to it.[6] You may be promoting a product, a service, an idea, or yourself. In each case the most effective messages will (1) gain attention, (2) build interest, (3) reduce resistance, and (4) motivate action. This is the same recipe we studied earlier, but the ingredients are different.

Openers for sales messages should be brief, honest, relevant, and provocative.

Gaining Attention. One of the most critical elements of a sales letter is its opening paragraph. This opener should be short (one to five lines), honest, relevant, and stimulating. Marketing pros have found that eye-catching typographical arrangements or provocative messages, such as the following, can hook a reader's attention:

- **Offer:** *A free trip to Hawaii is just the beginning!*
- **Promise:** *Now you can raise your sales income by 50 percent or even more with the proven techniques found in . . . .*
- **Question:** *Do you yearn for an honest, fulfilling relationship?*
- **Quotation or proverb:** *Necessity is the mother of invention.*
- **Fact:** *The Greenland Eskimos ate more fat than anyone in the world. And yet . . . they had virtually no heart disease.*
- **Product feature:** *Volvo's snazzy new convertible ensures your safety with a roll bar that pops out when the car tips 40 degrees to the side.*
- **Testimonial:** "The Journal *surprises, amuses, investigates, and most of all educates.*" (*The New Republic* commenting on *The Wall Street Journal.*)
- **Startling statement:** *Let the poor and hungry feed themselves! For just $100 they can.*

- **Personalized action setting:** *It's 4:30 p.m. and you've got to make a decision. You need everybody's opinion, no matter where they are. Before you pick up your phone to call them one at a time, pick up this card: AT&T Teleconference Services.*

Other openings calculated to capture attention might include a solution to a problem, an anecdote, a personalized statement using the receiver's name, or a relevant current event.

Building Interest. In this phase of your sales message, you should describe clearly the product or service. In simple language emphasize the central selling points that you identified during your prewriting analysis. Those selling points can be developed using rational or emotional appeals.

Rational appeals are associated with reason and intellect. They translate selling points into references to making or saving money, increasing efficiency, or making the best use of resources. In general, rational appeals are appropriate when a product is expensive, long-lasting, or important to health, security, and financial success. Emotional appeals relate to status, ego, and sensual feelings. Appealing to the emotions is sometimes effective when a product is inexpensive, short-lived, or nonessential. Many clever sales messages, however, combine emotional and rational strategies for a dual appeal. Consider these examples:

spotlight on communicators

In writing winning sales messages, beware of impossible promises, warns Herb Kelleher, cofounder of Southwest Airlines. He believes his company has the quickest baggage delivery in the industry—only eight minutes from jetway to pickup. But when his marketing staff proposed making such a promise in the Southwest promotions, Kelleher balked. On rare occasions Southwest wouldn't be able to deliver, he reasoned, and broken promises are not easily forgotten.

Rational Appeal
You can buy the things you need and want, pay household bills, and pay off higher-cost loans and credit cards—as soon as you're approved and your Credit-Line account is opened.

Rational appeals reflect reason and intellect.

Emotional Appeal
Leave the urban bustle behind and escape to sun-soaked Bermuda! To recharge your batteries with an injection of sun and surf, all you need are your bathing suit, a little suntan lotion, and your Credit-Line card.

Emotional appeals reflect status, ego, and sensual feelings.

Dual Appeal
New Credit-Line cardholders are immediately eligible for a $200 travel certificate and additional discounts at fun-filled resorts. Save up to 40 percent while lying on a beach in picturesque, sun-soaked Bermuda, the year-round resort island.

Dual appeals combine reason and emotion.

Zig Ziglar, thought by some to be America's greatest salesperson, points out that no matter how well you know your product, no one is persuaded by cold, hard facts alone. In the end, he contends, people buy because of product benefits.[7] Your job is to translate those cold facts into warm feelings and reader benefits. Let's say a sales message promotes a hand cream made with aloe and cocoa butter extracts, along with Vitamin A. Those facts become, *Nature's hand helpers—including soothing aloe and cocoa extracts, along with firming Vitamin A—form invisible gloves that protect your sensitive skin against the hardships of work, harsh detergents, and constant environmental assaults.*

On the next page you will see a happy baby picture, which grabs attention. The caption describes how Procter & Gamble combined emotional and rational appeals in focusing on reader benefits to sell its diapers.

To capture attention in its sales messages for Pampers diapers, Procter & Gamble may show a happy, healthy baby. But the sales copy develops an emotional yet rational appeal as it discusses the development of babies when they get a good night's sleep from having a drier diaper than that sold by the competition. "This is probably the biggest challenge for our advertising—how you move beyond functional advertising to emotional resonance," reports manager Austin Lally.

Reducing Resistance. Marketing pros use a number of techniques to overcome resistance and build desire. When price is an obstacle, consider these suggestions:

- Delay mentioning price until after you've created a desire for the product.
- Show the price in small units, such as the price per issue of a magazine.
- Demonstrate how the reader saves money by, for instance, subscribing for two or three years.
- Compare your prices with those of a competitor.

In addition, you need to anticipate other objections and questions the receiver may have. When possible, translate these objections into selling points (*If you're worried about training your staff members on the new software, remember that our offer includes $1,000 worth of on-site one-on-one instruction*). Other techniques to overcome resistance and prove the credibility of the product include the following:

- **Testimonials:** *"I never stopped eating, yet I lost 107 pounds."—Tina Rivers, Greenwood, South Carolina*
- **Names of satisfied users (with permission, of course):** *Enclosed is a partial list of private pilots who enthusiastically subscribe to our service.*
- **Money-back guarantee or warranty:** *We offer the longest warranties in the business—all parts and service on-site for two years!*
- **Free trial or sample:** *We're so confident that you'll like our new accounting program that we want you to try it absolutely free.*
- **Performance tests, polls, or awards:** *Our TP-3000 was named Best Web Phone, and Etown.com voted it Cell Phone of the Year.*

Motivating Action. All the effort put into a sales message is wasted if the reader fails to act. To make it easy for readers to act, you can provide a reply card, a stamped and preaddressed envelope, a toll-free telephone number, an easy Web site, or a promise of a follow-up call. Because readers often need an extra push, consider including additional motivators, such as the following:

- **Offer a gift:** *You'll receive a free cell phone with the purchase of any new car.*
- **Promise an incentive:** *With every new, paid subscription, we'll plant a tree in one of America's Heritage Forests.*
- **Limit the offer:** *Only the first 100 customers receive free checks.*
- **Set a deadline:** *You must act before June 1 to get these low prices.*
- **Guarantee satisfaction:** *We'll return your full payment if you're not entirely satisfied—no questions asked.*

The final paragraph of the sales letter carries the punch line. This is where you tell readers what you want them to do and give them reasons for doing it. Most sales letters also include postscripts because they make irresistible reading. Even readers who might skim over or bypass paragraphs are drawn to a P.S. Therefore, use a postscript to reveal your strongest motivator, to add a special inducement for a quick response, or to reemphasize a central selling point.

Because direct mail is an expensive way to advertise, messages should present complete information in a personalized tone for specific audiences.

Putting It All Together. Sales letters are a preferred marketing medium because they can be personalized, directed to target audiences, and filled with a more complete message than other advertising media. But direct mail is expensive. That's why the total sales message is crafted so painstakingly.

Let's examine a sales letter, shown in Figure 10.7, addressed to a target group of small business owners. To sell the new magazine *Small Business Monthly*, the letter incorporates all four components of an effective persuasive message. Notice that the personalized action-setting opener places the reader in a familiar situation (getting into an elevator) and draws an analogy between failing to reach the top floor and failing to achieve a business goal. The writer develops a rational central selling point (a magazine that provides valuable information for a growing small business) and repeats this selling point in all the components of the letter. Notice, too, how a testimonial from a small business executive lends support to the sales message, and how the closing pushes for action. Because the price of the magazine is not a selling feature, it's mentioned only on the reply card. This sales letter saves its strongest motivator—a free booklet—for the high-impact P.S. line.

Whether you actually write sales letters on the job or merely receive them, you'll better understand their organization and appeals by reviewing this chapter and the tips in the following checklist.

Checklist for Writing Sales Letters

- ✓ **Gain attention.** Offer something valuable, promise the reader a result, pose a stimulating question, describe a product feature, present a testimonial, make a startling statement, or show the reader in an action setting. Other attention-getters are a solution to a problem, an anecdote, a statement using the receiver's name, and a relevant current event.

- ✓ **Build interest.** Describe the product in terms of what it does for the reader: save or make money, reduce effort, improve health, produce pleasure, boost status. Connect cold facts with warm feelings and needs.

- ✓ **Reduce resistance.** Counter reluctance with testimonials, money-back guarantees, attractive warranties, trial offers, or free samples. Build credibility with results of performance tests, polls, or awards. If price is not a selling feature, describe it in small units (*only 99 cents an issue*), show it as savings, or tell how it compares favorably with the competition.

- ✓ **Motivate action.** Close with a repetition of the central selling point and clear instructions for an easy action to be taken. Prompt the reader to act immediately with a gift, incentive, limited offer, deadline, and/or guarantee of satisfaction. Put the strongest motivator in a postscript.

spotlight *on communicators*

Powerful new viruses and wily hackers are a growing danger to the security of the Internet. But Symantec CEO John W. Thompson gives consumers and corporations a whole arsenal of defenses. Described as a hard-charging but trustworthy leader, Thompson uses both emotional and rational appeals to reduce resistance in crafting Symantec's sales messages. The company makes rational promises assuring users of its real-time analysis by a staff of security experts using cutting-edge technology to monitor cyberintrusion. Emotionally, it assures users that they can rest easy knowing that it will issue alerts within 15 minutes of virus, worm, and other attack trends before major problems arise.

Photo: © Mike Theiler/Getty Images

Developing Persuasive Press Releases

learning objective 5

Press (news) releases announce information about your company to the media: new products, new managers, new facilities, participation in community projects, awards given or received, joint ventures, donations, or seminars and demonstrations. Naturally, you hope that this news will be published and provide good publicity for your company. But this kind of largely self-serving information is not always appealing

FIGURE 10.7 ***Sales Letter***

1 Prewriting

ANALYZE: The purpose of this letter is to persuade the reader to return the reply card and subscribe to *Small Business Monthly.*

ANTICIPATE: The targeted audience consists of small-business owners. The central selling point is providing practical business data that will help their businesses grow.

ADAPT: Because readers will be reluctant, use the indirect pattern.

2 Writing

RESEARCH: Gather facts to promote your product, including testimonials.

ORGANIZE: Gain attention by opening with a personalized action picture. Build interest with an analogy and a description of magazine features. Use a testimonial to reduce resistance. Motivate action with a free booklet and an easy-reply card.

COMPOSE: Prepare first draft for pilot study.

3 Revising

REVISE: Use short paragraphs and short sentences. Replace words like *malfunction* with *glitch*.

PROOFREAD: Indent long quotations on the left and right sides. Italicize or underscore titles of publications. Hyphenate *hard-headed* and *first-of-its-kind*.

EVALUATE: Monitor the response rate to this letter to assess its effectiveness.

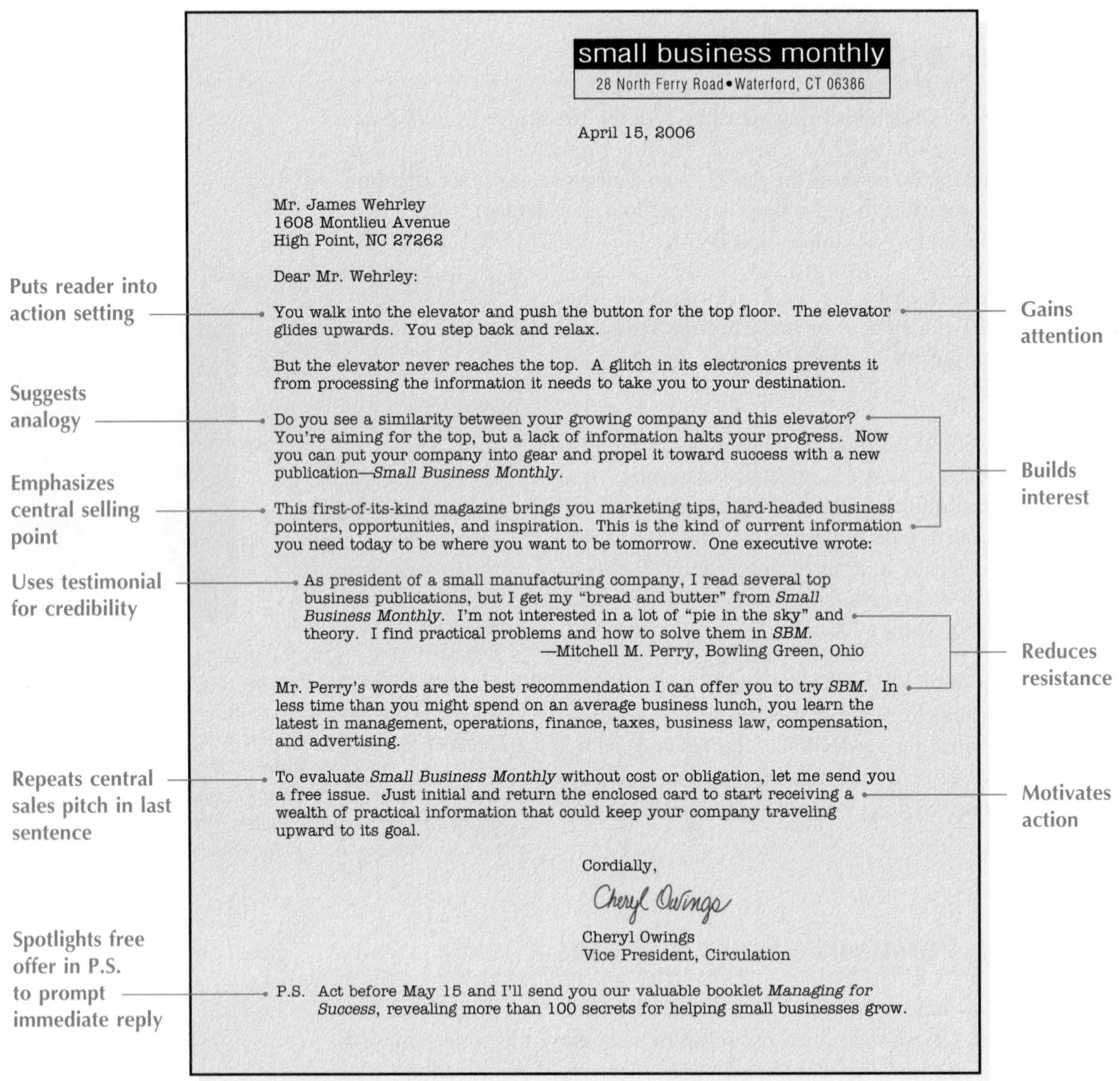

small business monthly
28 North Ferry Road • Waterford, CT 06386

April 15, 2006

Mr. James Wehrley
1608 Montlieu Avenue
High Point, NC 27262

Dear Mr. Wehrley:

You walk into the elevator and push the button for the top floor. The elevator glides upwards. You step back and relax.

But the elevator never reaches the top. A glitch in its electronics prevents it from processing the information it needs to take you to your destination.

Do you see a similarity between your growing company and this elevator? You're aiming for the top, but a lack of information halts your progress. Now you can put your company into gear and propel it toward success with a new publication—*Small Business Monthly.*

This first-of-its-kind magazine brings you marketing tips, hard-headed business pointers, opportunities, and inspiration. This is the kind of current information you need today to be where you want to be tomorrow. One executive wrote:

> As president of a small manufacturing company, I read several top business publications, but I get my "bread and butter" from *Small Business Monthly*. I'm not interested in a lot of "pie in the sky" and theory. I find practical problems and how to solve them in *SBM.*
>
> —Mitchell M. Perry, Bowling Green, Ohio

Mr. Perry's words are the best recommendation I can offer you to try *SBM*. In less time than you might spend on an average business lunch, you learn the latest in management, operations, finance, taxes, business law, compensation, and advertising.

To evaluate *Small Business Monthly* without cost or obligation, let me send you a free issue. Just initial and return the enclosed card to start receiving a wealth of practical information that could keep your company traveling upward to its goal.

Cordially,

Cheryl Owings

Cheryl Owings
Vice President, Circulation

P.S. Act before May 15 and I'll send you our valuable booklet *Managing for Success*, revealing more than 100 secrets for helping small businesses grow.

Puts reader into action setting
Gains attention
Suggests analogy
Builds interest
Emphasizes central selling point
Uses testimonial for credibility
Reduces resistance
Repeats central sales pitch in last sentence
Motivates action
Spotlights free offer in P.S. to prompt immediate reply

PROCESS TO PRODUCT

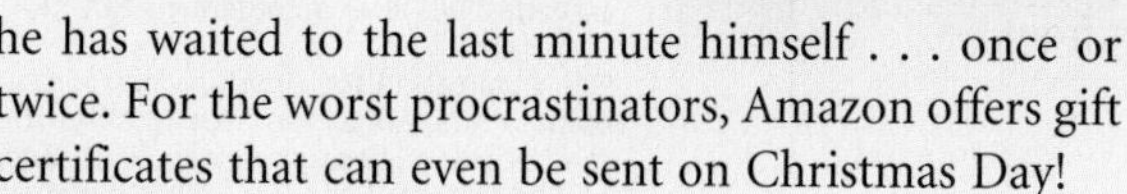

Applying Your Skills at Amazon.com

AS THE DECEMBER gift-giving season approaches, Jeff Bezos decides to send a personal message to Amazon's opt-in customers. Naturally, he'll include holiday greetings, but his primary purpose is to remind shoppers of the gift store and its many conveniences.

Amazon's gift section offers gift certificates, a wish list, gift wrapping, free e-cards, a baby registry, and special-occasion reminders. Check the site to see what is currently highlighted. Bezos' favorite feature is Gift-Click, which enables customers to select a gift while Amazon takes care of everything. Customers just type in the recipient's e-mail address. Amazon finds the mailing address, selects, wraps, and sends the gift. Another terrific feature is Gift Explorer, which prompts shoppers with gift ideas based on a favorite product or interest of the recipient. For example, if you type in *Star Wars, photography, iPod,* or *baseball,* scads of imaginative gift ideas pop up.

He asks you and your corporate communication staff to write the holiday message. He tells you to select gift ideas and features that you think will interest holiday shoppers. Remember to emphasize savings—up to 40 percent off many items. Amazon will gift wrap and ship gifts wherever customers want—right up to the last minute. Bezos confesses that he has waited to the last minute himself . . . once or twice. For the worst procrastinators, Amazon offers gift certificates that can even be sent on Christmas Day!

Your Task

In teams or individually, write a concise online sales letter from Jeff Bezos to Amazon's opt-in customers. Because this is a personal note, use the first-person pronouns *I* and *me.* Should the message contain a salutation and complimentary closing? What central selling points should you emphasize? What could serve as a motivator in a P.S.? ■

Effective press releases feature an attention-getting opener, place key information up front, appeal to the target audience, and maintain visual interest.

to magazine and newspaper editors or to TV producers. To get them to read beyond the first sentence, try these suggestions:

- Open with an attention-getting lead or a summary of the important facts.
- Include answers to the five *W*'s and one *H* (*who, what, when, where, why,* and *how*) in the article—but not all in the first sentence!
- Appeal to the audience of the target media. Emphasize reader benefits written in the style of the focus publication or newscast.
- Present the most important information early, followed by supporting information. Don't put your best ideas last because they may be chopped off or ignored.
- Make the release visually appealing. Limit the text to one or two double-spaced pages with attractive formatting.
- Look and sound credible—no typos, no imaginative spelling or punctuation, no factual errors.

The most important ingredient of a press release, of course, is *news.* Articles that merely plug products end up in the circular file. The Google press release in Figure 10.8 announces a preview version of Gmail. This new Google offering is a Web mail service intended to compete with Yahoo! and HotMail. Naturally, Google hopes to launch a better service, and the press release promotes its features. What's notable about this press release is its conversational tone and readability. By including a personal anecdote and comments from Google founders, the press release becomes a

FIGURE 10.8 ***Press Release***

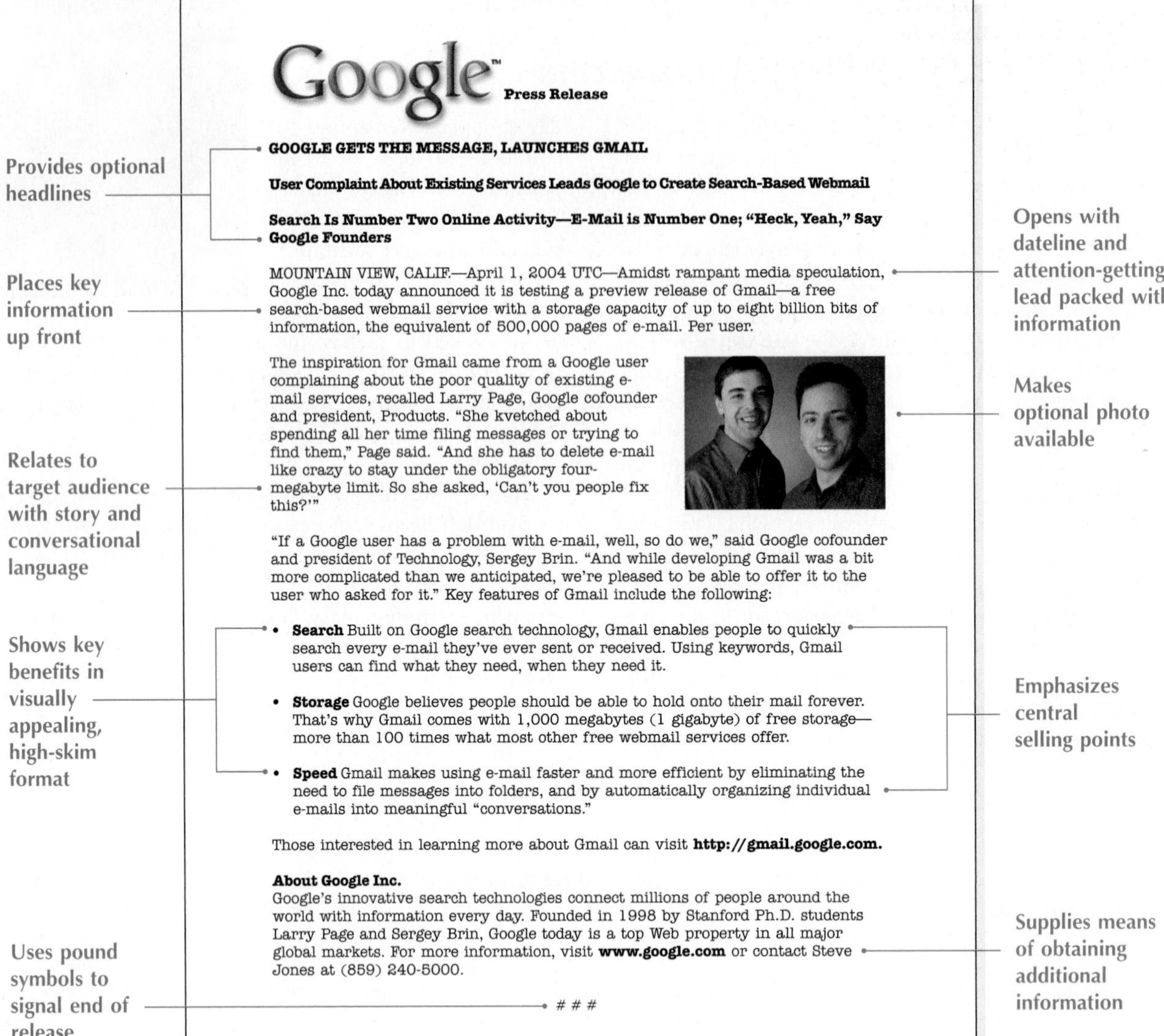

Press Release

GOOGLE GETS THE MESSAGE, LAUNCHES GMAIL

User Complaint About Existing Services Leads Google to Create Search-Based Webmail

Search Is Number Two Online Activity—E-Mail is Number One; "Heck, Yeah," Say Google Founders

MOUNTAIN VIEW, CALIF.—April 1, 2004 UTC—Amidst rampant media speculation, Google Inc. today announced it is testing a preview release of Gmail—a free search-based webmail service with a storage capacity of up to eight billion bits of information, the equivalent of 500,000 pages of e-mail. Per user.

The inspiration for Gmail came from a Google user complaining about the poor quality of existing e-mail services, recalled Larry Page, Google cofounder and president, Products. "She kvetched about spending all her time filing messages or trying to find them," Page said. "And she has to delete e-mail like crazy to stay under the obligatory four-megabyte limit. So she asked, 'Can't you people fix this?'"

"If a Google user has a problem with e-mail, well, so do we," said Google cofounder and president of Technology, Sergey Brin. "And while developing Gmail was a bit more complicated than we anticipated, we're pleased to be able to offer it to the user who asked for it." Key features of Gmail include the following:

- **Search** Built on Google search technology, Gmail enables people to quickly search every e-mail they've ever sent or received. Using keywords, Gmail users can find what they need, when they need it.
- **Storage** Google believes people should be able to hold onto their mail forever. That's why Gmail comes with 1,000 megabytes (1 gigabyte) of free storage—more than 100 times what most other free webmail services offer.
- **Speed** Gmail makes using e-mail faster and more efficient by eliminating the need to file messages into folders, and by automatically organizing individual e-mails into meaningful "conversations."

Those interested in learning more about Gmail can visit **http://gmail.google.com.**

About Google Inc.
Google's innovative search technologies connect millions of people around the world with information every day. Founded in 1998 by Stanford Ph.D. students Larry Page and Sergey Brin, Google today is a top Web property in all major global markets. For more information, visit **www.google.com** or contact Steve Jones at (859) 240-5000.

# # #

Google
Provides optional headlines
Places key information up front
Relates to target audience with story and conversational language
Shows key benefits in visually appealing, high-skim format
Uses pound symbols to signal end of release
Opens with dateline and attention-getting lead packed with information
Makes optional photo available
Emphasizes central selling points
Supplies means of obtaining additional information

real news story. Newspapers and magazines will be eager to publish this release because it is both informative and interesting. Many companies provide readily available press information, including releases and photos, at their Web sites.

Summary of Learning Objectives

1 **Apply the 3-x-3 writing process to persuasive messages.** The first step in the writing process for a persuasive message is analysis of the audience and purpose. Writers must know exactly what they want receivers to do or think. The second step involves thinking of ways to adapt the message to the audience. Particularly important is expressing the request so that it may benefit the reader. Next, the writer must collect data and organize it into an appropriate strategy. An indirect strategy is probably best if the audience will resist the request.

2 **Explain the components of a persuasive message and how to blend them effectively.** The most effective persuasive messages gain attention by opening with a problem, unexpected statement, reader benefit, compliment, related fact, stimulating question, or similar device. They build interest with facts, expert opinions, examples, details, and additional reader benefits. They reduce resistance by anticipating objections and presenting counterarguments. They conclude by motivating a specific action and making it easy for the reader to respond. Skilled communicators avoid distortion, exaggeration, and deception when making persuasive arguments.

3 **Write successful persuasive messages including requesting favors and actions, persuading within organizations, and writing complaint letters.** When you ask for a favor or action, the indirect pattern is appropriate. This means delaying the request until after logical reasons have been presented. Such messages should emphasize, if possible, benefits to the reader. Appeals to professionalism are often a useful technique. Writers should counter any anticipated resistance with explanations and motivate action in the closing. Use the same indirect method when writing internal messages that require persuasion. These messages might begin with a frank discussion of a problem. They build interest by emphasizing points that are important to the readers. They support the request with accurate, honest evidence. When writing about damaged products, mistaken billing, or other complaints and claims, the indirect pattern is appropriate. These messages might begin with a sincere compliment or an objective statement of the problem. They explain concisely why a claim is legitimate. Copies of relevant documents should be enclosed. The message should conclude with a clear statement of the action to be taken.

4 **Plan and compose outstanding sales messages.** Before writing a sales message, it's necessary to analyze the product and purpose carefully. The letter begins with an attention-getting statement that is short, honest, relevant, and stimulating. It builds interest by describing the product or service clearly in simple language, incorporating appropriate appeals. Testimonials, a money-back guarantee, a free trial, or some other device can reduce resistance. A gift, incentive, deadline, or other device can motivate action.

5 **Describe the basic elements in persuasive press releases.** Effective press releases usually open with an attention-getting lead or summary of the important facts. They attempt to answer the questions *who, what, when, where, why,* and *how.* They are written carefully to appeal to the audience of the target media. The best press releases present the most important information early, make the release visually appealing, and look and sound credible.

chapter review

1. List the four key elements in a persuasive request. (Objs. 1 and 2)
2. List six or more techniques for opening a persuasive request for a favor. (Obj. 2)
3. List techniques for building interest in a persuasive request for a favor. (Obj. 3)
4. Describe ways to reduce resistance in persuasive requests. (Obj. 3)
5. How should a persuasive request end? (Objs. 2 and 3)
6. When does persuasion become unethical? (Obj. 2)
7. What are the differences between direct and indirect reader benefits? Give an original example of each (other than those described). (Obj. 3)
8. When would persuasion be necessary in messages moving downward in organizations? (Obj. 3)
9. Why are persuasive messages usually longer than direct messages? (Objs. 1–4)
10. When is it necessary for a subordinate to be persuasive in addressing a superior on the job? (Obj. 3)
11. What is an appropriate tone for a claim letter? (Obj. 3)
12. Name eight or more ways to attract attention in opening a sales message. (Obj. 4)
13. How do rational appeals differ from emotional appeals? Give an original example of each. (Obj. 4)
14. Name five or more ways to motivate action in closing a sales message. (Obj. 5)
15. List five or more topics that an organization might feature in a press release. (Obj. 5)

critical thinking

1. How are requests for action and sales letters similar and how are they different? (Objs. 3 and 4)
2. What are some of the underlying motivations that prompt individuals to agree to requests that do not directly benefit themselves or their organizations? (Objs. 2–4)
3. In view of the burden that "junk" mail places on society (depleted landfills, declining timber supplies, overburdened postal system), how can "junk" mail be justified? (Obj. 4)
4. Why is it important to know your needs and have documentation when you make requests of superiors? (Obj. 3)
5. How can a business use e-mail marketing so that its customers think its messages are valuable? (Obj. 4)
6. **Ethical Issue:** Identify and discuss direct-mail sales messages that you consider unethical.

THREE GREAT RESOURCES FOR YOU!

1. *Guffey Student Web Site*
http://guffey.swlearning.com

Your companion Web site offers chapter review quizzes, WebThink activities, updated chapter URLs, and many additional resources.

2. *Guffey XTRA!*
http://guffeyxtra.swlearning.com

This online study assistant includes Your Personal Language Trainer, Speak Right!, Spell Right!, bonus online chapters, Documents for Analysis, PowerPoint slides, and much more.

3. *Student Study Guide*

Self-checked workbook activities and applications review chapter concepts and develop career skills.

activities

10.1 Document for Analysis: Inviting the Dummies Author (Obj. 3)

Your Task. Analyze the following poorly written invitation. List its weaknesses. If your instructor directs, revise the letter. Add appropriate information if needed.

Current date

Ms. Joyce Lain Kennedy
P. O. Box 3029
Carlsbad, CA 92009

Dear Ms. Kennedy:

Because you are a local author, we thought it would not be too much trouble for you to be the keynote speaker at our SCU Management Society banquet May 5.

Some of us business students here at South California University have read and admired your many newspaper columns and books on careers. One of our professors said that you were the "dean of career columnists." We were surprised, though, to see that you have written a number of "Dummies" books, including *Résumés for Dummies, Cover Letters for Dummies, College Financial Aid for Dummies,* and *Job Interviews for Dummies.* Perhaps you could tell us

why you think that "dummies" is an effective way to address your readers. We are especially interested in learning what a "competency-based" interview is.

Because we have no funds for honoraria, we have to rely on local speakers. We also know that your home in Carlsbad is not too far from our campus in San Diego, so we hoped you could work us into your schedule. Our banquets usually begin at 6:30 with a social hour, followed by dinner at 7:30 and the speaker from 8:30 until 9 or 9:15. We can arrange transportation for you and your husband, if you need it.

We realize that you have a busy schedule, but we hope you'll carve out a space for us. Please let our advisor, Professor Rachel Pierce, have the favor of an early reply.

Cordially,

10.2 Document for Analysis: Weak Persuasive Memo (Obj. 3)

Your Task. Analyze the following memo, which suffers from many writing faults. List its weaknesses. If your instructor directs, revise the letter.

DATE: Current
TO: Candace Daly, Vice President, Marketing
FROM: Robert Forsythe, Exhibit Manager
SUBJECT: TRADE BOOTH

Trade shows are a great way for us to meet customers and sell our Life Fitness equipment. But instead of expanding our visits to these trade shows, we continue to cut back the number that we attend. And we send fewer staff members. I know that you've been asking us to find ways to reduce costs, but perhaps we're not going about it right.

With increased air fares and hotel charges, my staff has tried to find ways to live within our very tight budget. Yet, we're being asked to find other ways to reduce our costs. I'm currently thinking ahead to the big Las Vegas trade show coming up in September.

One area where we could make a change is in the gift that we give away. In the past we have presented booth visitors with a nine-color T-shirt that is silk screened and gorgeous. But it comes at a cost of $15 for each and every one of these beauties from a top-name designer. To save money, I suggest that we try a $4 T-shirt made in China, which is reasonably presentable. It's got our name on it, and, after all, folks just use these shirts for workouts. Who cares if it is a fancy silk-screened T-shirt or a functional Chinese one that has "Life Fitness" plastered on the chest? Since we give away 2,000 T-shirts at our largest show, we could save big bucks by dumping the designer shirt. But we have to act quickly. I've enclosed a cheap one for you to see.

Let me know what you think.

10.3 Document for Analysis: Poor Claim Letter (Obj. 3)

Your Task. Analyze the following poorly written claim letter. List its weaknesses. If your instructor directs, revise it.

Current date

Mr. Kurt Littleton
Lawson Business Products
291 Bostwick Northeast
Grand Rapids, MI 49503

Dear Sir:

Three months ago we purchased four of your E-Studio 120 photocopiers, and we've had nothing but trouble ever since.

Our salesperson, Julia Franks, assured us that the E-Studio 120 could easily handle our volume of 3,000 copies a day. This seemed strange since the sales brochure said that the E-Studio 120 was meant for 500 copies a day. But we believed Ms. Franks. Big mistake! Our four E-Studio 120 copiers are down constantly; we can't go on like this. Because they're still under warranty, they eventually get repaired. But we're losing considerable business in downtime.

Your Ms. Franks has been less than helpful, so I telephoned the district manager, Ron Rivera. I suggested that we trade in our E-Studio 120 copiers (which we got for $2,500 each) on two E-Studio 600 models (at $13,500 each). However, Mr. Rivera said he would have to charge 50 percent depreciation on our E-Studio 120 copiers. What a ripoff! I think that 20 percent depreciation is more reasonable since we've had the machines only three months. Mr. Rivera said he would get back to me, and I haven't heard from him since.

I'm writing to your headquarters because I have no faith in either Ms. Franks or Mr. Rivera, and I need action on these machines. If you understood anything about business, you would see what a sweet deal I'm offering you. I'm willing to stick with your company and purchase your most expensive model—but I can't take such a steep loss on the E-Studio 120 copiers. The E-Studio 120 copiers are relatively new; you should be able to sell them with no trouble. And think of all the money you'll save by not having your repair technicians making constant trips to service our 120 copiers! Please let me hear from you immediately.

Sincerely yours,

10.4 Sales Letter Analysis (Obj. 4)

Your Task. Select a one- or two-page sales letter received by you or a friend. Study the letter and then answer these questions:

a. What techniques capture the reader's attention?
b. Is the opening effective? Explain.

c. What are the central selling points?
d. Does the letter use rational, emotional, or a combination of appeals? Explain.
e. What reader benefits are suggested?
f. How does the letter build interest in the product or service?
g. How is price handled?
h. How does the letter anticipate reader resistance and offer counterarguments?
i. What action is the reader to take? How is the action made easy?
j. What motivators spur the reader to act quickly?

10.5 Persuasive Request: A Helping Hand for College Expenses (Obj. 3)

CRITICAL THINKING | TEAM

After working a few years, you would like to extend your college education on a part-time basis. You know that your education can benefit your employer, but you can't really afford the fees for tuition and books. You've heard that many companies offer reimbursement for fees and books when employees complete approved courses with a grade of C or higher.

Your Task. In teams discuss the best way to approach an employer whom you wish to persuade to start a tuition/books reimbursement program. How could such a program help the employer? Remember that the most successful requests help receivers see what's in it for them. What objections might your employer raise? How can you counter them? After discussing strategies in teams, write a team memo or individual memos to your boss (for a company where you now work or one with which you are familiar). Persuade her or him to act on your action request.

10.6 Persuasive Favor/Action Request: Celebrity Auction (Obj. 3)

CRITICAL THINKING | TEAM

Your professional or school organization (such as the Associated Students Organization) must find ways to raise money. The president of your group appoints a team and asks it to brainstorm for ways to meet your group's pledge to aid the United Way's battle against adult illiteracy in your community. The campaign against adult illiteracy has targeted an estimated 10,000 people in your community who cannot read or write. After considering and discarding a number of silly ideas, your team comes up with the brilliant idea of a celebrity auction. At a spring function, items or services from local and other celebrities would be auctioned. Your organization approves your idea and asks your team to persuade an important person in your professional organization (or your college president) to donate one hour of tutoring in a subject he or she chooses. If you have higher aspirations, write to a movie star or athlete (perhaps one who attended your school) to request an auction item.

Your Task. As a team, discuss the situation and decide what action to take. Then write a persuasive letter to secure an item for the auction. You might wish to ask a star to donate a prop from a recent movie.

10.7 Persuasive Favor/Action Request: Inviting the Diva of Retail (Obj. 3)

As program chair of the National Association of Retail Merchandisers, you must find a speaker for your annual meeting in April. In *Inc.* magazine you saw an impressive article about J'Amy Owens, president of the Retail Group Inc., a Seattle-based strategic retail consulting firm. Owens has become the guru of retail makeovers with a client list of over 400 companies. She believes that the retail economy will increasingly be driven by *experience* as opposed to transactions. "Retail has to feel relevant or it's dead," she says.

Driving the shift in retail focus is Generation Y (those born between 1977 and 1994). They will represent 41 percent of the U.S. population in 10 years. And only 15 percent of this group frequent department stores. Besides being the place where parents shop, department stores specialize in *products* as opposed to *customers*, Owens believes. The store of the future will provide in-store Web access; give environmental controls to customers; furnish lots of sunlight, water, and vegetation; and offer "safe dangers," such as climbing walls and skateboard ramps.

Owens is very much in demand. She has been credited with helping many well-known brands regain lost luster, including McDonald's, Blockbuster Video, Sears, and Starbucks. When Nike lost the devotion of Generation Y, it commissioned her to figure out how to win them back. After her startling redesign of Mega Mart, a consumer electronics firm, it became one of the highest-grossing sellers of consumer electronics in North America. And her work with Seattle's award-winning Pacific Place helped develop the concept of a downtown vertical mall.[8]

Your Task. Write a persuasive letter inviting J'Amy Owens, president, Retail Group Inc., 240 Pacific Avenue, Seattle, WA 98303. You know that she generally earns $5,000 a pop for industry presentations, but your budget allows only $3,000. You hope, however, that she'll be receptive because you expect about 1,500 of the top retailers to attend the April 6 conference in New Orleans.

10.8 Persuasive Favor/Action Request: PDAs Lighten Realtors' Load in Historic Charleston (Obj. 3)

CRITICAL THINKING | SPEAKING
TEAM | WEB

Charleston, South Carolina, one of America's most beautifully preserved architectural and historic treasures, enjoys a booming real estate market. *Forbes* magazine forecasts a 200

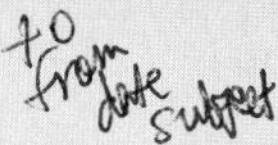

percent appreciation for its properties by the year 2009. The Cooper River Bridge project is America's largest construction project, and the entire regional economy glows. Real estate agents have plenty of work showing off new homes as well as beautifully preserved structures from the colonial and antebellum periods. The problem is that agents have to grapple with telephone directory-size books of multiple listings—or run back and forth to their offices as they show home buyers what's on the market.

As a staffer at one of Charleston's top realty agencies, you recently attended a Association of Realtors meeting and talked with fellow agent Bob Drewisch. He showed you his new personal digital assistant (PDA) and said, "Watch this." He accessed listing after listing of homes for sale by his company and others. You couldn't believe your eyes. You saw island properties, historic homes, beachfront condos—all with pictures and complete listing information. In this little device, which could easily fit into a pocket (or purse), you could carry six months of active, pending, and closed listings, along with contact details for agents and other valuable information.

You thought about the size of your multiple listing books and how often you had to trudge back to the office when a home buyer wanted to see a market listing. "Looks terrific," you said to Bob. "But what about new listings? And how much does this thing cost? And I bet it has a steep learning curve." Eager to show off his new toy, Bob demonstrated its user-friendly interface that follows intuitive prompts such as *price, area,* and *number of bedrooms.* He explained that his agency bought the software for $129. For a monthly fee of $19, he downloads updates as often as he likes. In regard to ease of use, Bob said that even his fellow agent Emily, notoriously computer challenged, loved it. None of the staff found it confusing or difficult to operate.

You decide that the agency where you work should provide this service to all 18 full-time staff agents. Assume that multiple listing software is available for the greater Charleston area.

Your Task. With other staff members (your classmates), decide how to approach the agency owner, who is "old school" and shuns most technology. Decide what you want to request. Do you merely want the owner to talk with you about the service? Should you come right out and ask for PDAs and the service for all 18 staff members? Should you expect staff members to provide the hardware (a basic PDA at about $200) and the agency to purchase the service and individual updates for each full-time agent? Or should you ask for the service plus a top-of-the-line device that combines PDA/phone, GPS (global positioning system), and other capabilities? Learn more about PDA possibilities on the Web. Explore this information with your team. Once you decide on a course of action, what appeals would be most persuasive? Discuss how to handle price in your persuasive argument. Individually or as a group, prepare a persuasive message to George R. Hollings, president, Hollings Carolina Realty. Decide whether you should deliver your persuasive message as a hard-copy memo or an e-mail.[9]

10.9 Persuasive Favor/Action Request: How About Mandatory Tipping? (Obj. 3)

TEAM

Centered in the heart of a 2,400-acre Florida paradise, the Bayside Inn Golf and Beach Resort offers gracious hospitality and beautiful accommodations. Its restaurant, Dolphin Watch, overlooks the scenic Choctawhatchee Bay, a perfect place to spy dolphins. As a server at the Dolphin Watch, you enjoy working in this resort setting—except for one thing. You have occasionally been "stiffed" by a patron who left no tip. You know your service is excellent, but some customers just don't get it. They seem to think that tips are optional, a sign of appreciation. For servers, however, tips are 80 percent of their income.

In a recent *New York Times* article, you learned that some restaurants—like the famous Coach House Restaurant in New York—automatically add a 15 percent tip to the bill. In Santa Monica the Lula restaurant prints "gratuity guidelines" on checks, showing customers what a 15 or 20 percent tip would be. You also know that American Express recently developed a gratuity calculation feature on its terminals. This means that diners don't even have to do the math!

Your Task. Because they know you are studying business communication, your fellow servers have asked you to write a serious letter to Nicholas Ruiz, General Manager, Bayside Inn Golf and Beach Resort, 9300 Emerald Coast Parkway West, Sandestin, FL 32550-7268. Persuade him to adopt mandatory tipping guidelines in the restaurant. Talk with fellow servers (your classmates) to develop logical persuasive arguments.

10.10 Pesuasive Favor/Action Request: Dictionary Definition of *McJobs* Angers McDonald's (Obj. 3)

CRITICAL THINKING

The folks at McDonald's fumed when they heard about the latest edition of a highly regarded dictionary. *Merriam-Webster's Collegiate Dictionary* defined the word *McJob* as "a low-paying job that requires little skill and provides little opportunity for advancement." Naturally, McDonald's was outraged. One executive said, "It's a slap in the face to the 12 million men and women who work hard every day in America's 900,000 restaurants."

The term *McJob* was coined by Canadian novelist Douglas Coupland in his 1991 novel *Generation X.* In this novel the term described a low-prestige, low-dignity, low-benefit, no-future job in the service sector. But McDonald's strongly objects to this corruption of its name. For one thing, the company rejects the notion that its jobs are dead ends. Significant members of top management—including the president, chief operating officer, and CEO—began their McDonald's careers behind the counter. Moreover, when it comes to training, McDonald's trains more young people than the U.S. armed forces.

What's more, McDonald's is especially proud of its "MCJOBS" program for mentally and physically challenged people. Some officers even wonder if the dictionary term *McJob* doesn't come dangerously close to the trademarked name for its special program. Another point that rankles McDonald's is that, according to its records, over 1,000 people who now own McDonald's restaurants received their training while serving customers. Who says that its jobs have no future?

The CEO is burned up about Merriam-Webster's dictionary definition, and he wants to send a complaint letter. But he is busy and asks you, a member of the communication staff, to draft a first version. He's so steamed that he's thinking of sending a copy of the letter to news agencies.

Your Task. Before writing this letter, decide what action, if any, to request. Think about an appropriate tone and also about the two possible audiences. Then write a persuasive letter for the signature of CEO Charlie Bell. Include the "a slap in the face" statement, which he insists on inserting. Address your letter to Frederick C. Mish, editor in chief, Merriam-Webster. Look for a street address on the Web.

10.11 Persuasive Action Request: Appealing to Your Congressional Representative to Listen and Act (Obj. 3)

CRITICAL THINKING | **WEB**

Assume you are upset about an issue, and you want your representative or senator to know your position. Choose a national issue about which you feel strongly: student loans, social security depletion, human rights in other countries, federal safety regulations for employees, environmental protection, affirmative action, gun control, taxation of married couples, finding a cure for obesity, the federal deficit, or some other area regulated by Congress.

Your Task. Use your favorite Web search engine (such as **www.google.com**) to obtain your congressional representative's address. Try the search term "Contacting Congress." You should be able to find e-mail and land addresses, along with fax and telephone numbers. Remember that although e-mail and fax messages are fast, they don't carry as much influence as personal letters. What's more, congressional representatives are having trouble responding to the overload of e-mail messages they receive. Decide whether it's better to send an e-mail message or a letter. For best results, consider these tips: (1) Use the proper form of address (*The Honorable John Smith, Dear Senator Smith* or *The Honorable Joan Doe, Dear Representative Doe*). (2) Identify yourself as a member of his or her state or district. (3) Immediately state your position (*I urge you to support/oppose . . . because . . .*). (4) Present facts and illustrations and how they affect you personally. If legislation were enacted, how would you or your organization be better off or worse off? Avoid generalities. (5) Offer to provide further information. (6) Keep the message polite, constructive, and brief (one page tops).

10.12 Persuasive Favor/Action Request: Vending Machines Are Cash Cows to Schools (Obj. 3)

CRITICAL THINKING | **INFOTRAC** | **TEAM**

"If I start to get huge, then, yeah, I'll cut out the chips and Coke," says 17-year-old Nicole O'Neill, as she munches sour-cream-and-onion potato chips and a cold can of soda fresh from the snack machine. Most days her lunch comes from a vending machine. The trim high school junior, however, isn't too concerned about how junk food affects her weight or overall health. Although she admits she would prefer a granola bar or fruit, few healthful selections are available from school vending machines.

Vending machines loaded with soft drinks and snacks are increasingly under attack in schools and lunchrooms. Some school boards, however, see them as cash cows. In Gresham, Oregon, the school district is considering a lucrative soft drink contract. If it signs an exclusive 12-year agreement with Coca-Cola to allow vending machines at Gresham High School, the school district will receive $75,000 up front. Then it will receive an additional $75,000 three years later. Commission sales on the 75-cent drinks will bring in an additional $322,000 over the 12-year contract, provided the school sells 67,000 cans and bottles every year. In the past the vending machine payments supported student body activities such as sending students to choir concerts and paying athletic participation fees. Vending machine funds also paid for an electronic reader board in front of the school and a sound system for the gym. The latest contract would bring in $150,000, which is already earmarked for new artificial turf on the school athletic field.

Coca-Cola's vending machines would dispense soft drinks, Fruitopia, Minute Maid juices, Powerade, and Dasani water. The hands-down student favorite, of course, is calorie-laden Coke. Because increasing childhood and adolescent obesity across the nation is a major health concern, the Gresham Parent-Teacher Association (PTA) decided to oppose the contract. The PTA realizes that the school board is heavily influenced by the income generated from the Coca-Cola contract. It wonders what other school districts are doing about their vending machine contracts.

Your Task. As part of a PTA committee, you have been given the task of researching and composing a persuasive but concise (no more than one page) letter addressed to the school board. Use InfoTrac or the Web to locate articles that might help you develop arguments, alternatives, and counterarguments. Meet with your team to discuss your findings. Then individually or as a group, write a letter to the Board of Directors, Gresham-Barlow School District, P.O. Box 310, Gresham, OR 97033.

10.13 Persuasive Favor/Action Request: How to Spend $5 Million (Obj. 3)

As you're having your second cup of coffee and reading the morning newspaper, you see an article that blows your mind. One of your school's alums has made a fortune in the software business. Before the dot-com bust, he sold his company for over $70 million. The article says that like many successful people, he wants to give back something to the school that gave him his education and his start. As a result, he has donated $5 million to your school! As you try to fathom how much $5 million would buy, you begin to wonder how your school will use this windfall.

Your Task. Write a persuasive letter to your dean outlining some of the ways you think the money could be spent at your school. From your perspective, how could programs, services, or equipment be improved? How about tutoring in some of your classes? Use specific examples of areas that could be improved.

10.14 Persuasive Internal Memo or E-Mail: Dear Boss (Obj. 3)

CRITICAL THINKING E-MAIL

In your own work or organization experience, identify a problem for which you have a solution. Should a procedure be altered to improve performance? Would a new or different piece of equipment help you perform your work better? Could some tasks be scheduled more efficiently? Are employees being used most effectively? Could customers be better served by changing something? Do you want to work other hours or perform other tasks? Do you deserve a promotion? Do you have a suggestion to improve profitability?

Your Task. Once you have identified a situation requiring persuasion, write a memo or an e-mail to your boss or organization head. Use actual names and facts. Employ the concepts and techniques in this chapter to help you convince your boss that your idea should prevail. Include concrete examples, anticipate objections, emphasize reader benefits, and end with a specific action to be taken.

10.15 Persuasive Internal Request: Reducing Overnight Costs (Obj. 3)

E-MAIL

As office manager of an East Coast software company, write a memo persuading your technicians, engineers, programmers, and other employees to reduce the number of overnight or second-day mail shipments. Your Federal Express and other shipping bills have been sky high, and you feel that staff members are overusing these services.

You think employees should send messages by e-mail or fax. Sending a zipped file as an e-mail attachment costs very little. And a fax costs only about 35 cents a page to most long-distance areas and nothing to local areas. Compare this with $20 to $25 for FedEx service! Whenever possible, staff members should obtain the FedEx account number of the recipient and use it for charging the shipment. If staff members plan ahead and allow enough time, they can use UPS ground service, which takes three to five days and is much cheaper. You wonder whether staff members consider whether the recipient is *really* going to use the message as soon as it arrives. Does it justify an overnight shipment? You'd like to reduce overnight delivery services voluntarily by 50 percent over the next two months. Unless a sizable reduction occurs, the CEO threatens severe restrictions in the future.

Your Task. Address your memo to all employees. What other ways could employees reduce shipping costs?

10.16 Persuasive Internal Request: Supporting Project H.E.L.P. (Obj. 3)

E-MAIL

As employee relations manager of The Prudential Insurance Company, one of your tasks is to promote Project H.E.L.P. (Higher Education Learning Program), an on-the-job learning opportunity. Project H.E.L.P. is a combined effort of major corporations and the Newark Unified School District. You must recruit 12 employees who will volunteer as instructors for 50 or more students. The students will spend four hours a week at the Prudential Newark facility earning an average of five units of credit a semester.

This semester the students will be serving in the Claims, Word Processing, Corporate Media Services, Marketing, Communications, Library, and Administrative Support departments. Your task is to convince employees in these departments to volunteer. They will be expected to supervise and instruct the students. In return, employees will receive two hours of release time per week to work with the students. The program has been very successful thus far. School officials, students, and employees alike express satisfaction with the experience and the outcomes.

Your Task. Write a persuasive memo or e-mail message with convincing appeals that will bring you 12 volunteers to work with Project H.E.L.P.

10.17 Persuasive Internal Request: Revising Miserable Memo (Obj. 3)

The following memo (with names changed) was actually sent.

Your Task. Based on what you have learned in this chapter, improve the memo. Expect the staff to be somewhat resistant because they've never before had meeting restrictions.

TO: All Managers and Employees
FROM: Nancy Nelson, CEO
SUBJECT: SCHEDULING MEETINGS

Please be reminded that travel in the greater Los Angeles area is time consuming. In the future we're asking that you set up meetings that

1. Are of critical importance
2. Consider travel time for the participants
3. Consider phone conferences (or video or e-mail) in lieu of face-to-face meetings
4. should be at the location where most of the participants work and at the most opportune travel times
5. Traveling together is another way to save time and resources.

We all have our traffic stories. A recent one is that a certain manager was asked to attend a one-hour meeting in Burbank. This required one hour travel in advance of the meeting, one hour for the meeting, and two and a half hours of travel through Los Angeles afterward. This meeting was scheduled for 4 p.m. Total time consumed by the manager for the one-hour meeting was four and a half hours.

Thank you for your consideration.

10.18 Persuasive Internal Request: Curbing Profanity on the Job (Obj. 3)

CRITICAL THINKING | E-MAIL | INFOTRAC
LISTENING | SPEAKING

As sales manager for a large irrigation parts manufacturer, you are concerned about the use of profanity by your sales associates. Some defend profanity, claiming that it helps them fit in. Your female sales reps have said that it helps relax listeners, drive home a point, and makes them "one of the boys." You have done some research, however, and learned that courts have ruled that profanity can constitute sexual harassment—whether in person or in print. In addition to causing legal problems, profanity on the job projects a negative image of the individual and of the company. Although foul language is heard increasingly on TV and in the movies, you think it's a bad habit and you want to see it curbed on the job.

Your Task. Use InfoTrac and the Web to locate articles related to the use of profanity and strategies employed by organizations for dealing with it. One good resource is **www.cusscontrol.com**. In small groups or in class, discuss the place of formal and informal language in communication. Prepare a list of reasons why people curse and reasons not to do so. Your instructor may ask you to interview employers to learn their reactions to the issue of workplace profanity. As sales manager at Rain City, compose a persuasive memo or e-mail message to your sales staff that will encourage them to curb their use of profanity.[10]

10.19 Persuasive Internal Request: "Push Me But Don't Leave Me Alone," Say Telecommuters (Obj. 3)

CRITICAL THINKING | E-MAIL
INFOTRAC | TEAM

James Lush arose from bed in his Connecticut home and looked outside to see a heavy snowstorm creating a fairyland of white. But he felt none of the giddiness that usually accompanies a potential snow day. Such days were a gift from heaven when schools closed, businesses shut down, and the world ground to a halt. As an on-and-off telecommuter for many years, he knew that snow days were a thing of the past. These days, work for James Lush and 23.5 million other American employees is no farther than their home office.

More and more employees are becoming telecommuters. They want to work at home, where they feel they can be more productive and avoid the hassle of driving to work. Some need to telecommute only temporarily, while they take care of family obligations, births, illnesses, or personal problems. Others are highly skilled individuals who can do their work at home as easily as in the office. Businesses definitely see advantages to telecommuting. They don't have to supply office space for workers. What's more, as businesses continue to flatten management structures, bosses no longer have time to micromanage employees. Increasingly, they are leaving workers to their own devices.

But the results have not been totally satisfactory. For one thing, in-house workers resent those who work at home. More important are problems of structure and feedback. Telecommuters don't always have the best work habits, and lack of communication is a major issue. Unless the telecommuter is expert at coordinating projects and leaving instructions, productivity can fizzle. Appreciating the freedom but recognizing that they need guidance, employees are saying, "Push me, but don't leave me out there all alone!"

As human resources director at your company, you already have 83 employees who are either full- or part-time telecommuters. With increasing numbers asking to work in remote locations, you decide that workers and their managers must receive training on how to do it effectively. You are considering hiring a consultant to train your prospective telecommuters and their managers. Another possibility is developing an in-house training program.

Your Task. As human resources director, you must convince Victor Vasquez, vice president, that your company needs a training program for all individuals who are currently telecommuting or who plan to do so. Their managers should also receive training. You decide to ask your staff of four to help you gather information. Using InfoTrac, you and your team read several articles on what such training should include. Now you must decide what action you want the vice president to take. Meet with you to discuss a training program? Commit to a budget item for future training? Hire a consultant or agency to come in and conduct training programs? Individually or as a team, write a convincing message that describes the problem, suggests what the training should include, and asks for action by a specific date. Add any reasonable details necessary to build your case.[11]

10.20 Persuasive Claim: Please Remove This "Technology" Fee From My Bill (Obj. 3)

LISTENING SPEAKING

As they check out, hotel guests are increasingly being hit with unexpected charges such as energy surcharges, technology fees, and Internet connection fees. At the Washington Terrace Hotel in Washington, D.C., Jeff Wansley dialed a local number from his computer to check his e-mail and stayed connected for hours. When he checked out, he was handed a bill for more than $200. Nothing on the desk in his room indicated he would be charged by the minute for local phone calls. He did, however, persuade the hotel to halve the bill.

When Anthony Marshall checked out of his hotel recently he was upset by a $3-per-night "technology fee" that popped up on his bill. The technology fee covered wireless access in the atriums and Internet bar, plus free local phone calls. Because Marshall did not bring his laptop on the trip and used his cell phone to place all his calls, he did not use these hotel services. The fee was never mentioned when he was first quoted a room rate. Although receptionists were trained to tell guests about the technology charge at check-in, Marshall's receptionist apparently did not tell him. He noticed later, however, that the fee was explained in fine print on the key envelope he received at check-in.

Anthony Marshall was totally steamed at the charge, and his angry reaction to the extra charge was not motivated by the money involved. Instead, he was upset by the deceptive way the charge was added to his bill. Along with a growing number of other travelers, Marshall believes that hotel room rate quotes should include all mandatory charges. All other charges should be user-based or voluntary.[12]

Your Task. Form groups of three to four students. One will role-play Anthony Marshall; one will role-play the hotel's customer service representative that Anthony calls. The remaining group members are observers. Anthony's goal is removal of the technology fee from his bill. The customer service rep's goal is to keep Anthony's goodwill while supporting the hotel's policy. The hotel will not remove the charge. The goal of the remaining group members is to analyze Anthony's request to determine how well he followed the chapter's persuasive claim principles. As a group, discuss what you learned from this exercise to help you get the results you want the next time you're trying to persuade someone in a spoken claim situation.

10.21 Persuasive Claim: Wounded Buffalo and Pygmy Circus Skip Summertime Slam (Obj. 3)

You and your friend bought $75 tickets to the "Summertime Slam" concert featuring Wounded Buffalo and Pygmy Circus. These two high-energy rock bands were to perform at Five Flags Lake Point Park. But when you arrived for the concert July 4, neither the Buffalos nor the Pigs appeared. Instead, three decidedly not-ready-for-prime-time groups filled in. You had been looking forward to this concert for seven weeks. After the concert started, you and your friend stayed through two acts to see whether the talent might improve. It didn't. You remember seeing newspaper advertisements publicizing the Buffalo/Pygmy performance as recently as the day of the concert. When you left the Five Flags parking lot after your early exit from the concert, you saw a small poster describing a "change in the talent" for the evening's concert.

When you called to demand a refund, you were told that a change had been announced prior to the concert. You were fuming! How could a tiny poster be sufficient to announce a major change in talent! You also learned that Five Flags could not refund your ticket price because you had stayed for the concert. You felt that they should have paid you to sit through the lame performance that was presented! What a scam! They advertised big-name groups and then filled in with three no-name talentless garage bands. Adding insult to injury, they refused to refund the ticket price!

In the heat of your fury, you wrote an angry letter to express your frustration and resentment over your treatment. But, wisely, you didn't mail the letter.

Your Task. Compose a claim letter based on the suggestions in this chapter. Strive for a moderate tone that achieves your goal. Send your letter to Ms. Felicity Meadows, Guest Relations, Five Flags Lake Point Park, P.O. Box 4300, Sandusky, OH 45320.

10.22 Persuasive Claim: Legal Costs for Sharing a Slice of Heaven (Obj. 3)

Originally a shipbuilding village, the town of Mystic, Connecticut, captures the spirit of the nineteenth-century seafaring era. But it is best known for Mystic Pizza, a bustling local pizzeria featured in a movie that launched the film career of Julia Roberts. Today, customers line the sidewalk waiting to taste its pizza, called by some "a slice of Heaven."

Assume that you are the business manager for Mystic Pizza's owners. They were approached by an independent vendor who wants to use the Mystic Pizza name and secret recipes to distribute frozen pizza through grocery and convenience stores. As business manager, you worked with a law firm, Giordano, Murphy, and Associates. This firm was to draw up contracts regarding the use of Mystic Pizza's name and quality standards for the product. When you received the bill from Henry Giordano, you were flabbergasted. It itemized 38 hours of attorney preparation, at $400 per hour, and 55 hours of paralegal assistance, at $100 per hour. The bill also showed $415 for telephone calls, which might be accurate because Mr. Giordano had to talk with the owners, who were vacationing in Italy at the time. You seriously doubt, however, that an experienced attorney would require 38 hours to draw up the contracts in question. When you began checking, you discovered that excellent legal advice could be obtained for $200 an hour.

Your Task. Decide what you want to request, and then write a persuasive request to Henry Giordano, Attorney at Law, Giordano, Murphy, and Associates, 254 Sherborn Street, Boston, MA 02215. Include an end date and a reason for it.

10.23 Persuasive Claim: Kodak Ruins His Round-the-World Trip (Obj. 3)

Pictures of himself in front of the Great Pyramids of Giza, shots of the famous Blue Mosque in Istanbul, and photographs of himself dancing with children around a fire in a Thailand village—all lost because of a faulty shutter mechanism on his camera. Brian P. Coyle, a 27-year-old resident of Orlando, Florida, made a once-in-a-lifetime trip around the world last fall. To record the sights and adventures, he invested in a Kodak Advantix camera. This is the camera featured by Eastman Kodak Company in television ads showing an American tourist snapping a shot of his gorgeous Italian date in Venice. When she is gone, he discovers that he misloaded the film, and he shouts, "I should have had a Kodak Advantix camera!"

In fact, Coyle selected the Advantix because of this easy-load feature, which worked well. But when he returned, he discovered that 12 of the 15 rolls of film he shot were ruined. He learned later that the camera shutter had malfunctioned. Needless to say, Coyle is very unhappy. After all, half of the fun of a trip lies in the memories summoned forth by photographs that can be enjoyed years after one returns. The emotional value of his pictures is far greater than the film on which they are recorded. He decides that he won't settle for 12 rolls of new film and perhaps replacement of the camera. He wants Kodak to send him around the world to repeat his trip. He figures that it is the only way he can recapture and record his lost adventure. He thinks it would cost him about $20,000 to repeat his 27-day trip.

Coyle asks you, who he knows is studying business communication, to help him write a convincing letter to Kodak. You respond that it's highly unlikely that Kodak will grant this claim, and Coyle says, "Hey, what have I got to lose? Kodak ruined my trip, and I think a lot of travelers would be interested in hearing about my troubles with Kodak's Advantix camera."[13]

Your Task. Write a persuasive claim to Mr. Charles Smith, Customer Relations, Eastman Kodak Company, 258 West Main Street, Rochester, NY 14605. Return the defective camera, copies of the purchase papers, and 12 rolls of ruined film. Should you send your package by FedEx or by Certified Mail with a return receipt requested?

10.24 Persuasive Claim: Champagne Breakfast Appears Only on Credit Card (Obj. 3)

As regional manager for an electronics parts manufacturer, you and two other employees attended a conference in Washington, D.C. You stayed at the Harvard House Hotel because your company recommends that employees use this hotel chain. Generally, your employees have liked their accommodations, and the rates have been within your company's budget. The hotel's service has been excellent.

Now, however, you're unhappy with the charges you see on your company's credit statement from Harvard House. When your department's administrative assistant made the reservations, she was assured that you would receive the weekend rates and that a hot breakfast—in the hotel restaurant, the Atrium—would be included in the rate. You hate those cold sweet rolls and instant coffee "continental" breakfasts, especially when you have to leave early and won't get another meal until afternoon. So you and the other two employees went to the restaurant and ordered a hot meal from the menu.

When you received the credit statement, though, you see a charge for $81 for three champagne buffet breakfasts in the Atrium. You hit the ceiling! For one thing, you didn't have a buffet breakfast and certainly no champagne. The three of you got there so early that no buffet had been set up. You ordered pancakes and sausage, and for this you were billed $25 each. You're outraged! What's worse, your company may charge you personally for exceeding the expected rates.

In looking back at this event, you remembered that other guests on your floor were having a "continental" breakfast in a lounge on your floor. Perhaps that's where the hotel expected all guests on the weekend rate to eat. However, your administrative assistant had specifically asked about this matter when she made the reservations, and she was told that you could order breakfast from the menu at the hotel's restaurant.

Your Task. You want to straighten out this matter, and you can't do it by telephone because you suspect that you will need a written record of this entire mess. Write a claim request to Customer Service, Washington Harvard House Hotel, 1221 22nd Street, N.W., Washington, DC 20037. Should you include a copy of the credit statement showing the charge?

10.25 Sales Letter: Getting in Shape at General Foods (Obj. 4)

INFOTRAC | WEB

Obesity in this country is swelling to unprecedented levels with nearly 60 percent of adults overweight. In addition to the risks to individuals, businesses estimate a loss of $5.5 billion in lowered productivity resulting from absenteeism and weight-related chronic disease. Companies from Wall Street

to the Rust Belt are launching or improving programs to help employees lose weight. Union Pacific Railroad is considering giving out pedometers to track workers around the office, as well as dispensing weight-loss drugs. Merrill Lynch sponsors Weight Watchers meetings. Caterpillar instituted the Healthy Balance Program. It promotes long-term behavorial change and healthier lifestyles for Caterpillar workers. Estimates suggest that employers and employees could save $1,200 a year for each person's medical costs if overweight employees shed their excess weight.

As a sales representative for Vector Lifetime Fitness, one of the country's leading fitness operators, you are convinced that your fitness equipment and programs are instrumental in helping people lose weight. With regular exercise at an on-site fitness center, employees lose weight and improve overall health. As employee health improves, absenteeism is reduced and overall productivity increases. And employees love working out before or after work. They make the routine part of their workday, and they often have work buddies who share their fitness regimen.

Although many companies resist spending money to save money, fitness centers need not be large or expensive to be effective. Studies show that moderately sized centers coupled with motivational and training programs yield the greatest success. For just $30,000, Vector Lifetime Fitness will provide exercise equipment including treadmills, elliptical trainers, exercise bikes, multigyms, and weight machines. Their fitness experts will design a fitness room, set up the equipment, and create appropriate programs. Best of all, the one-time cost is usually offset by cost savings within one year of center installation. For additional fees Vector can provide fitness consultants for employee fitness assessments. Vector specialists will also train employees on the proper use of the equipment and clean and manage the facility—for an extra charge, of course.

Your Task. Use InfoTrac or the Web to update your obesity statistics. Then prepare a sales letter addressed to Cheryl O'Berry, Vice President, Human Resources, General Foods, Inc., 2300 Thousand Lakes Blvd., Eagan, MN 65123. Ask for an appointment to meet with her. Send a brochure detailing the products and services that Vector Lifetime Fitness provides. As an incentive, offer a free fitness assessment for all employees if General Foods installs a fitness facility by December 1.

10.26 Sales Letter: Promoting Your Product or Service (Obj. 4)

Identify a situation in your current job or a previous one in which a sales letter is/was needed. Using suggestions from this chapter, write an appropriate sales letter that promotes a product or service. Use actual names, information, and examples. If you have no work experience, imagine a business you'd like to start: word processing, pet grooming, car detailing, tutoring, specialty knitting, balloon decorating, delivery service, child care, gardening, lawn care, or something else. Write a letter selling your product or service to be distributed to your prospective customers. Be sure to tell them how to respond.

10.27 Press Release: Fast-Food Wraps That Decompose Like Grass and Leaves (Obj. 5)

INFOTRAC | WEB

You have been interviewed for a terrific job in corporate communications at EarthShell. It produces biodegradable packaging materials for traditional food service items. Its clamshell sandwich containers and food wraps are made from potato starch, limestone, and other biodegradable materials that actually decompose like leaves and grass. At this writing its newest customer is Hood Packaging, which plans to market EarthShell's food service wraps. These are the papers that cover tacos, burritos, hamburgers, and other take-out sandwiches.

You're excited about the job for many reasons, including EarthShell's location in Santa Barbara, one of California's most beautiful cities. However, EarthShell wants you to submit a press release as a writing sample. EarthShell features some rather long press releases at its Web site. Many articles about its products have also appeared in periodicals. The EarthShell recruiter wants you to submit a press release that would appeal to the publisher of your local newspaper.[14]

Your Task. Using InfoTrac, search for EarthShell information. Read several articles. Also go to its Web site (use a search engine to find it) and look at its current press releases. Select one event or product that you think would be of interest to your local newspaper. Although you can use the information from current EarthShell press releases, don't copy the exact wording because it will be obvious to EarthShell. Use a name from a current EarthShell press release as a contact person.

10.28 Press Release: It's New! (Obj. 5)

Your Task. In a company where you now work or for an organization you belong to, identify a product or service that could be publicized. Consider writing a press release announcing a new course at your college, a new president, new equipment, or a campaign to raise funds. Write the press release for your local newspaper.

10.29 Press Release: Finding the Best (Obj. 5)

INFOTRAC

One of the best ways to learn about press releases is to study them on the Web.

Your Task. Using InfoTrac, search for "news releases." You'll find some that are boring and self-serving and others that are entertaining and instructive. Study many recent releases looking for those that are good enough to appear in your local newspaper. Select the best three. In a message to your instructor or in a class discussion, identify your selections and describe at least six elements that make them outstanding.

10.30 Persuasive Claim: Honolulu Country Club Gets Scammed on Phony Toner Phoner (Obj. 3)

CONSUMER | CRITICAL THINKING

Heather W. was new to her job as administrative assistant at the Waialae Country Club in Honolulu. Alone in the office one morning, she answered a phone call from Rick, who said he was the country club's copier contractor. "Hey, look, babydoll," Rick purred, "the price on the toner you use is about to go way up. I can offer you a great price on this toner if you order right now." Heather knew that the copy machine regularly needed toner, and she thought she should probably go ahead and place the order to save the country club some money. Ten days later two bottles of toner arrived, and Heather was pleased at the perfect timing. The copy machine needed it right away. Three weeks later Maureen, the bookkeeper, called to report a bill from Copy Machine Specialists for $960.43 for two bottles of toner. "What's going on here?" said Maureen. "We don't purchase supplies from this company, and this price is totally off the charts!"[15]

Heather spoke to the manager, Steven Tanaka, who immediately knew what had happened. He blamed himself for not training Heather. "Never, never order anything from a telephone solicitor, no matter how fast-talking or smooth he sounds," warned Steven. He outlined an office policy for future supplies purchases. Only certain people can authorize or finalize a purchase, and purchases require a confirmed price including shipping costs settled in advance. But what to do about this $960.43 bill? The country club had already begun to use the toner, although the current copies were looking faint and streaked.

Your Task. As Steven Tanaka, decide how to respond to this obvious scam. Should you pay the bill? Should you return the unused bottle? Write a persuasive claim to Copy Machine Specialists, 4320 Admiralty Way, Honolulu, HI 96643. Supply any details necessary.

video resource

Bridging the Gap Video Library 2

Persuasion and Profitability: World Gym

World Gym Showplace Square has been rated the best gym in the Bay Area. The physical plant has over 35,000 square feet stocked with free weights, treadmills, lifecycles, Stairmasters, recumbent bikes, and rowing machines. Although business is good, World Gym finds that most of its traffic comes from 4 p.m. to 8 p.m. If it could persuade members to come later and stay until 10 or 11 p.m., it could increase profitability and improve service. The owners, Joe and Robin Talmudge, are thinking of adding video cameras inside and outside to improve security. This might encourage members to stay later. After watching the film, you'll see some of the problems facing the Talmudges.

Your Task. As an assistant to the owners, you have been asked to draft a letter to members that persuades them to fill out a simple questionnaire regarding the addition of security cameras. In the prewriting phase, decide the purpose of your message. Consider the best channel, along with direct and indirect benefits you can suggest. Write a message addressed to "Valued World Gym Members." Your instructor may help you think through this case with specific questions.

C.L.U.E. review 10

Edit the following sentences to correct faults in grammar, punctuation, spelling, and word use.

1. Persuasion requires learning about you're audience, and analysing why they might resist your goal.
2. An especialy effective arguement includes 2 indespensable elements; a reasonable request, and a well presented line of reasoning.
3. If you're goal is to persuade a lending institution to give you fifty thousand dollars you would probably use rational appeal.
4. Our President and Senior Sales Manager decided to send a sales letter to all current customers therefore they analyzed the product, purpose and audience.
5. There sales letter focuses on the following 4 parts (1) Gaining the audiences attention (2) Convincing them that the purpose is worthy (3) Overcoming resistance and (4) Motivating action.
6. Experts agree that one of the biggest mistakes in persuasive request's are the failure to anticipate, and off set audience resistance.
7. Because the Manager and him builded interest with easy to read facts and figures they're letter will undoubtably suceed.
8. A claim letter is a form of complaint consequently its wise to use the indirect strategy.
9. Anger and emotion is not effective in persuasion but many writers can not controll there temper.
10. Our latest press release which was written in our corporate communication department announces the opening of 3 canadian office.

chapter 11

Negative Messages

objectives

1. Describe the goals and strategies of business communicators in delivering bad news, including knowing when to use the direct and indirect patterns, applying the writing process, and avoiding legal problems.
2. Explain techniques for delivering bad news sensitively.
3. Identify routine requests and describe a strategy for refusing such requests.
4. Explain techniques for delivering bad news to customers.
5. Explain techniques for delivering bad news within organizations.
6. Compare strategies for revealing bad news in different cultures.

Communication in Process

Pepsi Sometimes Says No

"IT'S AMAZING HOW a soft drink can become so much a part of people's lives that they feel passionate about it," said Cathy Dial, former manager of Consumer Relations at Pepsi-Cola. Dial's office employed 23 representatives who responded to at least 1,000 telephone calls and 100 letters every day. The majority of the contacts were inquiries about promotions or products, and she could respond with positive information. But sometimes she had to deliver disappointing news or refuse a request.

"The refillable bottle is a really passionate issue for some consumers," said Dial. Although the entire beverage industry moved away from returnable glass bottles, some consumers insisted that Pepsi offer them. Dial received letters saying, "Pepsi just doesn't taste the same in cans or plastic bottles; I want my bottle back!"

Other inquiries were from consumers who thought they had won a prize in a promotion. In one contest a few years ago, the word *Van* appeared under a Pepsi bottle cap. Many consumers saw the word and called or wrote to claim their automobiles. "Actually," explained Dial, "*Van* meant that consumers were entitled to a 10 percent discount at Van's Shoes. In a situation like this, our job is to carefully explain the rules of the promotion to consumers and thank them for participating."

Sometimes people complain about sponsorship of TV shows that have celebrities or messages that they don't like or agree with. Dial's office also received passionate letters from individuals asking Pepsi-Cola to contribute money to their charity, to provide soft drinks for a function, or to sponsor events. Pepsi-Cola's employees give generously of their own time. Additionally, the company has a longtime partnership with the YMCA, which provides substantial funding for local programs for children and families. Other contributions support Save the Children, pediatric AIDS care centers, and national food distribution programs. But it cannot support every request it receives. At times, Cathy Dial at Pepsi-Cola had to deliver disappointing news.[1]

Producing one of the most recognizable brands in the world, PepsiCo receives more requests for contributions than it can grant.

Critical Thinking

- If you had to reveal bad news to your parents or to your spouse (such as denting the fender of that person's car), would you break the bad news quickly or build up to it? Why?
- What are some techniques you could use to soften the blow of bad news?
- When an organization has to reveal disappointing news to customers, employees, or others, what goals should it try to achieve?

http://www.pepsi.com

CONTINUED ON PAGE 357

Photo: © Morton Beebe/CORBIS

case study

learning objective 1

Strategies for Delivering Bad News

Breaking bad news was a fact of business life for Cathy Dial at Pepsi-Cola, as it is for nearly every business communicator. In all businesses, things occasionally go wrong. Goods are not delivered, a product fails to perform as expected, service is poor, billing gets fouled up, or customers are misunderstood. Because bad news disappoints, irritates, and sometimes angers the receiver, such messages must be written carefully. The bad feelings associated with disappointing news can generally be reduced if (1) the reader knows the reasons for the rejection and (2) the bad news is revealed with sensitivity. You've probably heard people say, "It wasn't so much the bad news that I resented. It was the way I was told!"

The sting of bad news can be reduced by giving reasons and communicating sensitively.

The direct strategy, which you learned to apply in earlier chapters, frontloads the main idea, even when it's bad news. This direct strategy appeals to efficiency-oriented writers who don't want to waste time with efforts to soften the effects of bad news.[2] Many business writers, however, prefer to use the indirect pattern in delivering negative messages. The indirect strategy is especially appealing to relationship-oriented writers. They care about how a message will affect its receiver.

In this chapter you'll learn when to use the direct or indirect pattern to deliver bad news. You'll study the goals of business communicators in working with bad news, and you'll examine three causes for legal concerns. The major focus of this chapter, however, is on developing the indirect strategy and applying it to situations in which you must refuse routine requests, decline invitations, and deliver negative news to employees and customers. You'll also learn how bad news is handled in other cultures.

Goals in Communicating Bad News

Delivering bad news is not the happiest writing task you may have, but it can be gratifying if you do it effectively. As a business communicator working with bad news, you will have many goals, the most important of which are these:

In communicating bad news, key goals include getting the receiver to accept it, maintaining goodwill, and avoiding legal liability.

- **Acceptance.** Make sure the reader understands and *accepts* the bad news. The indirect pattern helps in achieving this objective.
- **Positive image.** Promote and maintain a good image of yourself and your organization. Realizing this goal assumes that you will act ethically.
- **Message clarity.** Make the message so clear that additional correspondence is unnecessary.
- **Protection.** Avoid creating legal liability or responsibility for you or your organization.

These are ambitious goals, and we're not always successful in achieving them all. The patterns you're about to learn, however, provide the beginning communicator with strategies and tactics that many writers have found successful in conveying disappointing news sensitively and safely. With experience, you'll be able to vary these patterns and adapt them to your organization's specific writing tasks.

Using the Indirect Pattern to Prepare the Reader

Whereas good news can be revealed quickly, bad news is generally easier to accept when broken gradually. Revealing bad news slowly and indirectly shows sensitivity to your reader. By preparing the reader, you tend to soften the impact. A blunt announcement of disappointing news might cause the receiver to stop reading and toss the message aside. The indirect strategy enables you to keep the reader's attention until you have been able to explain the reasons for the bad news. In fact, the most important part of a bad-news letter is the explanation, which you'll learn about shortly. The indirect plan consists of four parts, as shown in Figure 11.1:

The indirect pattern softens the impact of bad news by giving reasons and explanations first.

- **Buffer.** Offer a neutral but meaningful statement that does not mention the bad news.

FIGURE 11.1 ***Four-Part Indirect Pattern for Bad News***

Buffer	Reasons	Bad News	Closing
Open with a neutral but meaningful statement that does not mention the bad news.	Explain the causes of the bad news before disclosing it.	Reveal the bad news without emphasizing it. Provide an alternative or compromise, if possible.	End with a personalized, forward-looking, pleasant statement. Avoid referring to the bad news.

- **Reasons.** Give an explanation of the causes for the bad news before disclosing it.
- **Bad news.** Provide a clear but understated announcement of the bad news that may include an alternative or compromise.
- **Closing.** Include a personalized, forward-looking, pleasant statement.

When to Use the Direct Pattern

The direct pattern is appropriate when the receiver might overlook the bad news, when directness is preferred, when firmness is necessary, when the bad news is not damaging, or when the goodwill of the receiver is unimportant.

Many bad-news letters are best organized indirectly, beginning with a buffer and reasons. The direct pattern, with the bad news first, may be more effective, though, in situations such as the following:

- **When the receiver may overlook the bad news.** With the crush of mail today, many readers skim messages, looking only at the opening. If they don't find substantive material, they may discard the message. Rate increases, changes in service, new policy requirements—these critical messages may require boldness to ensure attention.
- **When organization policy suggests directness.** Some companies expect all internal messages and announcements—even bad news—to be straightforward and presented without frills.
- **When the receiver prefers directness.** Busy managers may prefer directness. Such shorter messages enable the reader to get in the proper frame of mind immediately. If you suspect that the reader prefers that the facts be presented straightaway, use the direct pattern.
- **When firmness is necessary.** Messages that must demonstrate determination and strength should not use delaying techniques. For example, the last in a series of collection letters that seek payment of overdue accounts may require a direct opener.
- **When the bad news is not damaging.** If the bad news is insignificant (such as a small increase in cost) and doesn't personally affect the receiver, then the direct strategy certainly makes sense.
- **When the receiver's goodwill is not an issue.** Rarely, a business may have to send a message rejecting a customer's business. For instance, Filene's Basement, a chain of bargain retail stores, sent letters to two sisters announcing that their business was no longer welcome. The sisters had a history of returning items and making complaints about service.[3]

Applying Guffey's 3-x-3 Writing Process

The 3-x-3 writing process is especially important in crafting bad-news messages because of the potential consequences of poorly written messages.

Thinking through the entire process is especially important in bad-news letters. Not only do you want the receiver to understand and accept the message, but you want to be careful that your words say only what you intend. Thus, you'll want to apply the familiar 3-x-3 writing process to bad-news letters.

Analysis, Anticipation, and Adaptation. In Phase 1 (prewriting) you need to analyze the bad news so that you can anticipate its effect on the receiver. If the disappointment will be mild, announce it directly. If the bad news is serious or personal, consider techniques to reduce the pain. Adapt your words to protect the receiver's ego. Instead of *You neglected to change the oil, causing severe damage to the engine*, switch to the passive voice: *The oil wasn't changed, causing severe damage to the engine*. Choose words that show you respect the reader as a responsible, valuable person.

Research, Organization, and Composition. In Phase 2 (writing) you can gather information and brainstorm for ideas. Jot down all the reasons you have that explain the bad news. If four or five reasons prompted your negative decision, concentrate on the strongest and safest ones. Avoid presenting any weak reasons; readers may seize on them to reject the entire message. After selecting your best reasons, outline the four parts of the bad-news pattern: buffer, reasons, bad news, closing. Flesh out each section as you compose your first draft.

Revision, Proofreading, and Evaluation. In Phase 3 (revising) you're ready to switch positions and put yourself into the receiver's shoes. Have you looked at the problem from the receiver's perspective? Is your message too blunt? Too subtle? Does the message make the refusal, denial, or bad-news announcement clear? Prepare the final version, and proofread for format, punctuation, and correctness.

Avoiding Three Causes of Legal Problems

Before we examine the components of a bad-news message, let's look more closely at how you can avoid exposing yourself and your employer to legal liability in writing negative messages. Although we can't always anticipate the consequences of our words, we should be alert to three causes of legal difficulties: (1) abusive language, (2) careless language, and (3) the "good-guy syndrome."

spotlight *on communicators*

On the way to developing the world's largest prestige cosmetics firm, Estee Lauder learned valuable lessons for dealing with anger and remaining in control. "When you're angry," she said, "never put it in writing. It's like carving your anger in stone." She preferred face-to-face confrontations or, better yet, cooling off before reacting.

Abusive Language. Calling people names (such as *deadbeat, crook*, or *quack*) can get you into trouble. *Defamation* is the legal term for any false statement that harms an individual's reputation. When the abusive language is written, it's called *libel*; when spoken, it's *slander*.

To be actionable (likely to result in a lawsuit), abusive language must be (1) false, (2) damaging to one's good name, and (3) "published"—that is, spoken within the presence of others or written. Thus, if you were alone with Jane Doe and accused her of accepting bribes and selling company secrets to competitors, she couldn't sue because the defamation wasn't published. Her reputation was not damaged. But if anyone heard the words or if they were written, you might be legally liable.

Abusive language becomes legally actionable when it is false, harmful to the person's good name, and "published."

In a new wrinkle, you may now be prosecuted if you transmit a harassing or libelous message by e-mail or on a bulletin board. Such electronic transmission is considered to be "published." Moreover, a company may incur liability for messages sent through its computer system by employees. That's why many companies are increasing their monitoring of both outgoing and internal messages. "Off-the-cuff, casual e-mail conversations among employees are exactly the type of messages that tend to trigger lawsuits and arm litigators with damaging evidence," says e-mail guru Nancy Flynn.[4] Instant messaging adds another danger for companies. Its use in U.S.

companies doubled in just two years, and it's a largely unmonitored channel.[5] Whether in print or electronically, competent communicators avoid making unproven charges and letting their emotions prompt abusive language.

Careless language includes statements that could be damaging or misinterpreted.

Careless Language. As the marketplace becomes increasingly litigious, we must be certain that our words communicate only what we intend. Take the case of a factory worker injured on the job. His attorney subpoenaed company documents and discovered a seemingly harmless letter sent to a group regarding a plant tour. These words appeared in the letter: "Although we are honored at your interest in our company, we cannot give your group a tour of the plant operations as it would be too noisy and dangerous." The court found in favor of the worker, inferring from the letter that working conditions were indeed hazardous.[6] The letter writer did not intend to convey the impression of dangerous working conditions, but the court accepted that interpretation.

This case points up two important cautions. First, be careful in making statements that are potentially damaging or that could be misinterpreted. Be wary of explanations that convey more information than you intend. Second, be careful about what documents you save. Attorneys may demand, in pursuing a lawsuit, all company files pertaining to a case. Even documents marked "Confidential" or "Personal" may be used.

Remember, too, that e-mail messages are especially risky. You may think that a mere tap of the delete key makes a file disappear. No way! Messages continue to exist on backup storage devices in the files of the sender and the recipient.

Avoid statements that make you feel good but may be misleading or inaccurate.

The Good-Guy Syndrome. Most of us hate to have to reveal bad news—that is, to be the bad guy. To make ourselves look better, to make the receiver feel better, and to maintain good relations, we are tempted to make statements that are legally dangerous. Consider the case of a law firm interviewing job candidates. One of the firm's partners was asked to inform a candidate that she was not selected. The partner's letter said, "Although you were by far the most qualified candidate we interviewed, unfortunately, we have decided we do not have a position for a person of your talents at this time." To show that he personally had no reservations about this candidate and to bolster the candidate, the partner offered his own opinion. But he differed from the majority of the recruiting committee. When the rejected interviewee learned later that the law firm had hired two male attorneys, she sued, charging sexual discrimination. The court found in favor of the rejected candidate. It agreed that a reasonable inference could be made from the partner's letter that she was the "most qualified candidate."[7]

Use organizational stationery for official business only, and beware of making promises that can't be fulfilled.

Two important lessons emerge. First, business communicators act as agents of their organizations. Their words, decisions, and opinions are assumed to represent those of the organization. If you want to communicate your personal feelings or opinions, use your home computer or write on plain paper (rather than company letterhead) and sign your name without title or affiliation. Second, volunteering extra information can lead to trouble. Thus, avoid supplying data that could be misused, and avoid making promises that can't be fulfilled. Don't admit or imply responsibility for conditions that caused damage or injury. Even apologies (*We're sorry that a faulty bottle cap caused damage to your carpet*) may suggest liability.

In Chapter 5 we discussed four information areas that generate the most lawsuits: investments, safety, marketing, and human resources. In this chapter we'll make specific suggestions for avoiding legal liability in writing responses to claim letters, credit letters, and personnel documents. You may find that in the most critical areas (such as collection letters or hiring/firing messages) your organization pro-

FIGURE 11.2 ***Delivering Bad News Sensitively***

Buffer	Reasons	Bad News	Closing
Best news Compliment Appreciation Agreement Facts Understanding Apology	Cautious explanation Reader or other benefits Company policy explanation Positive words Evidence that matter was considered fairly and seriously	Embedded placement Passive voice Implied refusal Compromise Alternative	Forward look Information about alternative Good wishes Freebies Resale Sales promotion

vides language guidelines and form letters approved by legal counsel. As the business environment becomes more perilous, we must not only be sensitive to receivers but also keenly aware of risks to ourselves and to the organizations we represent.

Techniques for Delivering Bad News Sensitively

learning objective

2

Legal matters aside, let's now study specific techniques for using the indirect pattern in sending bad-news messages. In this pattern the bad news is delayed until after explanations have been given. The four components of the indirect pattern, shown in Figure 11.2, include buffer, reasons, bad news, and closing.

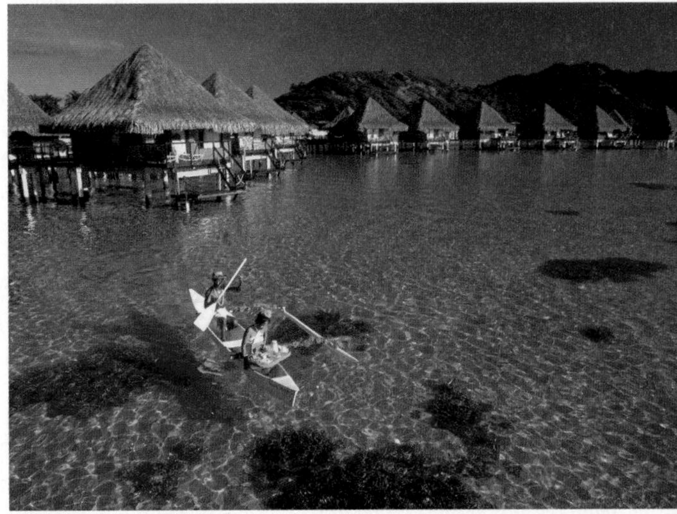

Hotel giant Starwood accidentally listed exclusive bungalows at a Bora Bora resort in the South Pacific for $85 instead of $850 a night over the Internet. The deal was pounced on by 136 people who booked thousands of nights. Honoring the rate, however, would have cost the company $2 million in lost revenue. When companies are forced to deliver bad news, they generally begin with a buffer and reasons before announcing the bad news.

Buffering the Opening

A buffer is a device to reduce shock or pain. To buffer the pain of bad news, begin with a neutral but meaningful statement that makes the reader continue reading. The buffer should be relevant and concise and provide a natural transition to the explanation that follows. The individual situation, of course, will help determine what you should put in the buffer. Avoid trite buffers such as *Thank you for your letter.* Here are some possibilities for opening bad-news messages.

Best News. Start with the part of the message that represents the best news. For example, a message to workers announced new health-plan rules limiting prescriptions to a 34-day supply and increasing copayments. With home delivery, however, employees could save up to $24 on each prescription. To emphasize the good news, you might write, *You can now achieve significant savings and avoid trips to the drug store by having your prescription drugs delivered to your home.*[8]

Compliment. Praise the receiver's accomplishments, organization, or efforts. But do so with honesty and sincerity. For instance, in a letter declining an invitation to speak, you could write, *The Thalians have my sincere admiration for their fund-raising projects on behalf of hungry children. I am honored that you asked me to speak Friday, November 5.*

Openers can buffer the bad news with compliments, appreciation, agreement, relevant facts, and understanding.

Appreciation. Convey thanks to the reader for doing business, for sending something, for conveying confidence in your organization, for expressing feelings, or simply for providing feedback. Suppose you had to draft a letter that refuses employment. You could say, *I appreciated learning about the hospitality management program at Cornell and about your qualifications in our interview last Friday.* Avoid thanking the reader, however, for something you are about to refuse.

Agreement. Make a relevant statement with which both reader and receiver can agree. A letter that rejects a loan application might read, *We both realize how much the export business has been affected by the relative strength of the dollar in the past two years.*

Facts. Provide objective information that introduces the bad news. For example, in a memo announcing cutbacks in the hours of the employees' cafeteria, you might say, *During the past five years the number of employees eating breakfast in our cafeteria has dropped from 32 percent to 12 percent.*

Understanding. Show that you care about the reader. Notice how in this letter to customers announcing a product defect, the writer expresses concern: *We know that you expect superior performance from all the products you purchase from OfficeCity. That's why we're writing personally about the Exell printer cartridges you recently ordered.*

Apology. As you learned in Chapter 9, a carefully worded apology may be appropriate. If you do apologize, do it early, briefly, and sincerely. For example, a manufacturer of superpremium ice cream might respond to a customer's complaint with, *We're genuinely sorry that you were disappointed in the price of the ice cream you recently purchased at one of our scoop shops. Your opinion is important to us, and we appreciate your giving us the opportunity to look into the problem you describe.* In responding to a complaint about poor service, a company might write, *I appreciate the frustration our delay has caused you. I'm sorry you didn't receive better service.* Or, *You're right to be concerned.*

Good buffers avoid revealing the bad news immediately. Moreover, they do not convey a false impression that good news follows. Additionally, they provide a natural transition to the next bad-news letter component—the reasons.

Presenting the Reasons

Bad-news messages should explain reasons before stating the negative news.

The most important part of a bad-news letter is the section that explains why a negative decision is necessary. Without sound reasons for denying a request or refusing a claim, a letter will fail, no matter how cleverly it is organized or written. As part of your planning before writing, you analyzed the problem and decided to refuse a request for specific reasons. Before disclosing the bad news, try to explain those reasons. Providing an explanation reduces feelings of ill will and improves the chances that the reader will accept the bad news.

Being Cautious in Explaining. If the reasons are not confidential and if they will not create legal liability, you can be specific: *Growers supplied us with a limited number of patio roses, and our demand this year was twice that of last year.* In refusing a speaking engagement, tell why the date is impossible: *On January 17 we have a board of directors meeting that I must attend.* Don't, however, make unrealistic or dangerous statements in an effort to be the "good guy."

Citing Reader or Other Benefits if Plausible. Readers are more open to bad news if in some way, even indirectly, it may help them. In refusing a customer's request for free hemming of skirts and slacks, Lands' End wrote: "We tested our ability to hem skirts a few months ago. This process proved to be very time-consuming. We have decided not to offer this service because the additional cost would have increased the selling price of our skirts substantially, and we did not want to impose that cost on all our customers."[9] Readers also accept bad news better if they recognize that someone or something else benefits, such as other workers or the environment: *Although we would like to consider your application, we prefer to fill managerial positions from within.* Avoid trying to show reader benefits, though, if they appear insincere: *To improve our service to you, we're increasing our brokerage fees.*

spotlight *on communicators*

Millionaire publisher Malcolm Forbes recognized that being agreeable while disagreeing is truly an art. He advised being positive and "nice." Contrary to the cliché, genuinely nice people most often finish first or very near it. He suggested using the acid test, particularly for a bad-news message. After you finish, read it out loud. You'll know if it sounds natural, positive, and respectful.

Photo: © Bettmann/CORBIS

Readers accept bad news more readily if they see that someone benefits.

Explaining Company Policy. Readers resent blanket policy statements prohibiting something: *Company policy prevents us from making cash refunds* or *Contract bids may be accepted from local companies only* or *Company policy requires us to promote from within.* Instead of hiding behind company policy, gently explain why the policy makes sense: *We prefer to promote from within because it rewards the loyalty of our employees. In addition, we've found that people familiar with our organization make the quickest contribution to our team effort.* By offering explanations, you demonstrate that you care about readers and are treating them as important individuals.

Choosing Positive Words. Because the words you use can affect a reader's response, choose carefully. Remember that the objective of the indirect pattern is holding the reader's attention until you've had a chance to explain the reasons justifying the bad news. To keep the reader in a receptive mood, avoid expressions with punitive, demoralizing, or otherwise negative connotations. Stay away from such words as *cannot, claim, denied, error, failure, fault, impossible, mistaken, misunderstand, never, regret, rejected, unable, unwilling, unfortunately,* and *violate.*

Showing That the Matter Was Treated Seriously and Fairly. In explaining reasons, demonstrate to the reader that you take the matter seriously, have investigated carefully, and are making an unbiased decision. Consumers are more accepting of disappointing news when they feel that their requests have been heard and that they have been treated fairly. Avoid passing the buck or blaming others within your organization. Such unprofessional behavior makes the reader lose faith in you and your company.

Cushioning the Bad News

Although you can't prevent the disappointment that bad news brings, you can reduce the pain somewhat by breaking the news sensitively. Be especially considerate when the reader will suffer personally from the bad news. A number of thoughtful techniques can cushion the blow.

Techniques for cushioning bad news include positioning it strategically, using the passive voice, implying the refusal, and suggesting alternatives or compromises.

Positioning the Bad News Strategically. Instead of spotlighting it, sandwich the bad news between other sentences, perhaps among your reasons. Don't let the refusal begin or end a paragraph—the reader's eye will linger on these high-visibility spots. Another technique that reduces shock is putting a painful idea in a subordinate clause: *Although another candidate was hired, we appreciate your interest in our organization and wish you every success in your job search.* Subordinate clauses often begin with words such as *although, as, because, if,* and *since.*

Using the Passive Voice. Passive-voice verbs enable you to depersonalize an action. Whereas the active voice focuses attention on a person (*We don't give cash refunds*), the passive voice highlights the action (*Cash refunds are not given because . . .*). Use the passive voice for the bad news. In some instances you can combine passive-voice verbs and a subordinate clause: *Although franchise scoop shop owners cannot be required to lower their ice cream prices, we are happy to pass along your comments for their consideration.*

Accentuating the Positive. As you learned earlier, messages are far more effective when you describe what you can do instead of what you can't do. Rather than *We will no longer allow credit card purchases,* try a more positive appeal: *We are now selling gasoline at discount cash prices.*

Implying the Refusal. It's sometimes possible to avoid a direct statement of refusal. Often, your reasons and explanations leave no doubt that a request has been denied. Explicit refusals may be unnecessary and at times cruel. In this refusal to contribute to a charity, for example, the writer never actually says no: *Because we will soon be moving into new offices in Glendale, all our funds are earmarked for relocation costs. We hope that next year we'll be able to support your worthwhile charity.* The danger of an implied refusal, of course, is that it is so subtle that the reader misses it. Be certain that you make the bad news clear, thus preventing the need for further correspondence.

Suggesting a Compromise or an Alternative. A refusal is not so depressing—for the sender or the receiver—if a suitable compromise, substitute, or alternative is available. In denying permission to a group of students to visit a historical private residence, for instance, this writer softens the bad news by proposing an alternative: *Although private tours of the grounds are not given, we do open the house and its gardens for one charitable event in the fall.* You can further reduce the impact of the bad news by refusing to dwell on it. Present it briefly (or imply it), and move on to your closing.

Closing Pleasantly

Closings to bad-news messages might include a forward look, an alternative, good wishes, freebies, and resale or sales promotion information.

After explaining the bad news sensitively, close the message with a pleasant statement that promotes goodwill. The closing should be personalized and may include a forward look, an alternative, good wishes, freebies, resale information, or an off-the-subject remark.

Forward Look. Anticipate future relations or business. A letter that refuses a contract proposal might read: *Thanks for your bid. We look forward to working with your talented staff when future projects demand your special expertise.*

Alternative. If an alternative exists, end your letter with follow-through advice. For example, in a letter rejecting a customer's demand for replacement of landscaping plants, you might say: *I will be happy to give you a free inspection and consultation. Please call 746-8112 to arrange a date for my visit.*

Good Wishes. A letter rejecting a job candidate might read: *We appreciate your interest in our company, and we extend to you our best wishes in your search to find the perfect match between your skills and job requirements.*

Freebies. When customers complain—primarily about food products or small consumer items—companies often send coupons, samples, or gifts to restore confidence and to promote future business. In response to a customer's complaint about a frozen dinner, you could write, *Your loyalty and your concern about our frozen entrees is genuinely appreciated. Because we want you to continue enjoying our healthful and convenient dinners, we're enclosing a coupon that you can take to your local market to select your next Green Valley entree.*

Resale or Sales Promotion. When the bad news is not devastating or personal, references to resale information or promotion may be appropriate: *The computer workstations you ordered are unusually popular because of their stain-, heat-, and scratch-resistant finishes. To help you locate hard-to-find accessories for these workstations, we invite you to visit our Web site where our online catalog provides a huge selection of surge suppressors, multiple outlet strips, security devices, and PC tool kits.*

Avoid endings that sound canned, insincere, inappropriate, or self-serving. Don't invite further correspondence (*If you have any questions, do not hesitate . . .*), and don't refer to the bad news. To review these suggestions for delivering bad news sensitively, take another look at Figure 11.2.

Refusing Routine Requests

learning objective

3

Every business communicator will occasionally have to say no to a request. Depending on how you think the receiver will react to your refusal, you can use the direct or the indirect pattern. If you have any doubt, use the indirect pattern.

Rejecting Requests for Favors, Money, Information, and Action

Most of us prefer to be let down gently when we're being refused something we want. That's why the reasons-before-refusal pattern works well when you must turn down requests for favors, money, information, action, and so forth.

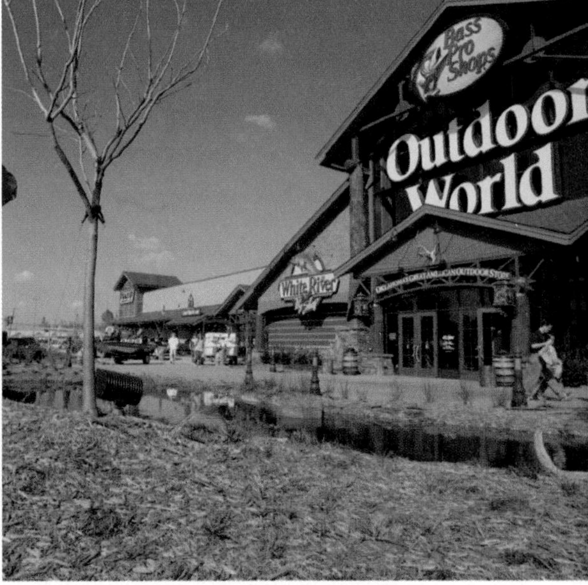

Although Bass Pro takes its social responsibility program seriously and supports numerous charity programs, it must refuse many requests for funds and donations. The indirect pattern with its reasons-before-refusal works well for messages that deliver bad news.

Saying No to Requests From Outsiders. Requests for contributions to charity are common. Many big and small companies receive requests for contributions of money, time, equipment, and support. Although the causes may be worthy, resources are usually limited. In a letter from Forest Financial Services, shown in Figure 11.3, the company must refuse a request for a donation to a charity. Following the indirect strategy, the letter begins with a buffer acknowledging the request. It also praises the good works of the charity and uses those words as a transition to the second paragraph. In the second paragraph the writer explains why the company cannot donate. Notice that the writer reveals the refusal without actually stating it (*Because of sales declines and organizational downsizing, we're forced to take a much harder look at funding requests that we receive this year*). This gentle refusal makes it unnecessary to be more blunt in stating the denial.

In some donation refusal letters, the reasons may not be fully explained: *Although we can't provide financial support at this time, we all unanimously agree that the symphony orchestra contributes much to the community.* The emphasis is on the symphony's attributes rather than on an explanation for the refusal. In the letter shown in Figure 11.3, the writer felt a connection to the charity. Thus, he wanted to give a fuller explanation.

FIGURE 11.3 ***Refusing Donation Request***

1 Prewriting

ANALYZE: The purpose of this letter is to reject the request for a monetary donation without causing bad will.

ANTICIPATE: The reader is proud of his or her organization and the good work it pursues.

ADAPT: The writer should strive to cushion the bad news and explain why it is necessary.

2 Writing

RESEARCH: Collect information about the receiver's organization as well as reasons for the refusal.

ORGANIZE: Use the indirect strategy. Begin with complimentary comments, present reasons, reveal the bad news gently, and close pleasantly.

COMPOSE: Write the message and consider keeping a copy to serve as a form letter.

3 Revising

REVISE: Be sure that the tone of the message is positive and that it suggests that the matter was taken seriously.

PROOFREAD: Check the receiver's name and address to be sure they are accurate. Check the letter's format.

EVALUATE: Will this message retain the goodwill of the receiver despite its bad news?

FOREST FINANCIAL SERVICES
3410 Willow Grove Boulevard
Philadelphia, PA 19137
215.593.4400
www.forestfinancial.com

November 14, 2006

Ms. Rachel Brown, Chair
Montgomery County Chapter
National Reye's Syndrome Foundation
342 DeKalb Pike
Blue Bell, PA 19422

Dear Ms. Brown:

We appreciate your letter describing the good work your Montgomery County chapter of the National Reye's Syndrome Foundation is doing in preventing and treating this serious affliction. Your organization is to be commended for its significant achievements resulting from the efforts of dedicated members.

Supporting the good work of your organization and others, although unrelated to our business, is a luxury we have enjoyed in past years. Because of sales declines and organizational downsizing, we're forced to take a much harder look at funding requests that we receive this year. We feel that we must focus our charitable contributions on areas that relate directly to our business.

We're hopeful that the worst days are behind us and that we'll be able to renew our support for worthwhile projects like yours next year.

Sincerely,

Paul Rosenberg

Paul Rosenberg
Vice President

Opens with praise and compliments

Doesn't say yes or no

Transitions with repetition of key idea (*good work*)

Explains sales decline and cutback in gifts

Reveals refusal without actually stating it

Closes graciously with forward look

If you were required to write frequent refusals, you might prepare a form letter, changing a few variables as needed. See the accompanying Tech Talk box to learn how you can personalize form letters by using word processing equipment. The refusal for a donation shown in Figure 11.3 could be adapted, using word processing equipment, to respond to other charity requests.

The reasons-before-refusal pattern works well when turning down requests for favors, money, information, or action.

Refusing Internal Requests. Just as managers must refuse requests from outsiders, they must also occasionally refuse requests from employees. In Figure 11.4 you see the first draft and revision of a message responding to a request from a key manager, Mark Stevenson. He wants permission to attend a conference. However, he can't attend the conference because the timing is bad; he must be present at budget planning meetings scheduled for the same two weeks. Normally, this matter would be discussed in person. But Mark has been traveling among branch offices, and he just hasn't been in the office recently.

Internal request refusals focus on explanations and praise, maintaining a positive tone, and offering alternatives.

The vice president's first inclination was to send a quickie memo, as shown in Figure 11.4, and "tell it like it is." In revising, the vice president realized that this message was going to hurt and that it had possible danger areas. Moreover, the memo misses a chance to give Mark positive feedback. An improved version of the memo starts with a buffer that delivers honest praise (*pleased with your leadership* and *your genuine professional commitment*). By the way, don't be stingy with compliments; they cost you nothing. As a philosopher once observed, *We don't live by bread alone. We need buttering up once in a while.* The buffer also includes the date of the meeting, used strategically to connect the reasons that follow. You will recall from Chapter 6 that repetition of a key idea is an effective transitional device to provide smooth flow between components of a message.

The middle paragraph provides reasons for the refusal. Notice that they focus on positive elements: Mark is the specialist; the company relies on his expertise; and everyone will benefit if he passes up the conference. In this section it becomes obvious that the request will be refused. The writer is not forced to say, *No, you may not attend.* Although the refusal is implied, the reader gets the message.

Melissa Thomas

The closing suggests a qualified alternative (*if our workloads permit, we'll try to send you then*). It also ends positively with gratitude for Mark's contributions to the organization and with another compliment (*you're a valuable player*). Notice that the improved version focuses on explanations and praise rather than on refusals and apologies.

The success of this message depends on attention to the entire writing process, not just on using a buffer or scattering a few compliments throughout.

Declining Invitations

When we must decline an invitation to speak or attend a program, we generally try to provide a response that says more than *I can't* or *I don't want to.* Unless the reasons are confidential or business secrets, try to explain them. Because responses to invitations are often taken personally, make a special effort to soften the refusal. In the letter shown in Figure 11.5, an accountant must say no to the invitation from a friend's son to speak before the young man's college business club. This refusal starts with conviviality and compliments.

Compliments can help buffer the impact of request refusals.

The writer then explains why she cannot accept. The refusal is embedded in a long paragraph and de-emphasized in a subordinate clause (*Although your invitation must be declined*). The reader naturally concentrates on the main clause that follows (*I would like to recommend . . .*). If no alternative is available, focus on something positive about the situation (*Although I'm not an expert, I commend your organization for selecting this topic*). Overall, the tone of this refusal is warm, upbeat, and positive.

Figure 11.4 ***Refusing an Internal Request***

DRAFT

DATE: July 2, 2006

TO: Mark Stevenson
Manager, Telecommunications

FROM: Ann Wells-Freed *AWF*
VP, Management Information Systems

SUBJECT: CONFERENCE REQUEST

We can't allow you to attend the conference in September, Mark. Perhaps you didn't know that budget-planning meetings are scheduled for that month. — *Announces the bad news too quickly and painfully*

Your expertise is needed here to help keep our telecommunications network on schedule. Without you, the entire system—which is shaky at best—might fall apart. I'm sorry to have to refuse your request to attend the conference. I know this is small thanks for the fine work you have done for us. Please accept our humble apologies. — *Gives reasons, but includes a dangerous statement*

In the spring I'm sure your work schedule will be lighter, and we can release you to attend a conference at that time. — *Makes a promise that might be difficult to keep*

REVISION

DATE: July 2, 2006

TO: Mark Stevenson
Manager, Telecommunications

FROM: Ann Wells-Freed *AWF*
VP, Management Information Systems

SUBJECT: REQUEST TO ATTEND SEPTEMBER CONFERENCE

The Management Council and I are extremely pleased with the leadership you have provided in setting up live video transmission to our regional offices. Because of your genuine professional commitment, Mark, I can understand your desire to attend the conference of the Telecommunication Specialists of America September 23 to 28 in Atlanta. — *Buffer: Includes sincere praise*

Transition: Uses date to move smoothly from buffer to reasons

The last two weeks in September have been set aside for budget planning. As you and I know, we've only scratched the surface of our teleconferencing projects for the next five years. Since you are the specialist and we rely heavily on your expertise, we need you here for those planning sessions. — *Reasons: Tells why refusal is necessary*

Bad news: Implies refusal

If you're able to attend a similar conference in the spring and if our workloads permit, we'll try to send you then. You're a valuable player, Mark, and I'm grateful you're on our MIS team. — *Closing: Contains realistic alternative*

The following checklist reviews the steps in composing a letter refusing a routine request.

Checklist for Refusing Routine Requests

 **Open indirectly with a buffer.** Pay a compliment to the reader, show appreciation for something done, or mention some mutual understanding. Avoid raising false hopes or thanking the reader for something you will refuse.

FIGURE 11.5 ***Refusing an Invitation***

GALLAGHER, BRACIO, CASAGRANDE, L.L.P.
Certified Public Accountants
942 Lafayette Boulevard
Bridgeport, CT 06604
(203) 435-9800

E-mail: cpa@gbcllp.com www.gbcllp.com

April 14, 2006

Mr. Tyler Simpson
4208 Aspetuck Avenue
Fairfield, CT 04519

Dear Tyler:

News of your leadership position in Epsilon Phi Delta, the campus business honorary club, fills me with delight and pride. Your father must be proud also of your educational and extracurricular achievements.

Opens cordially with praise

You honor me by asking me to speak to your group in the spring about codes of ethics in the accounting field. Because our firm has not yet adopted such a code, we have been investigating the codes developed by other accounting firms. I am decidedly not an expert in this area, but I have met others who are. Although your invitation must be declined, I would like to recommend Dr. Carolyn S. Marshall, who is a member of the ethics subcommittee of the Institute of Internal Auditors. Dr. Marshall is a professor who often addresses groups on the subject of ethics in accounting. I spoke with her about your club, and she indicated that she would be happy to consider your invitation.

Reduces impact of refusal by placing it in subordinate clause

Focuses attention on alternative

It's good to learn that you are guiding your organization toward such constructive and timely program topics. Please call Dr. Marshall at (203) 389-2210 if you would like to arrange for her to address your club.

Ends positively with compliments and offer of assistance

Sincerely,

Joan F. Gallagher

Joan F. Gallagher, CPA

JFG:mhr

✓ **Provide reasons.** In the body explain why the request must be denied—without revealing the refusal. Avoid negativity (*unfortunately, unwilling,* and *impossible*) and potentially damaging statements. Show how your decision benefits the reader or others, if possible.

✓ **Soften the bad news.** Reduce the impact of bad news by using (1) a subordinate clause, (2) the passive voice, (3) a long sentence, or (4) a long paragraph. Consider implying the refusal, but be certain it is clear. Suggest an alternative, if a suitable one exists.

✓ **Close pleasantly.** Supply more information about an alternative, look forward to future relations, or offer good wishes and compliments. Maintain a bright, personal tone. Avoid referring to the refusal.

tech talk

Using Technology to Personalize Form Letters

If you had to send the same information to 200 or more customers, would you write a personal letter to each? Probably not! Responding to identical requests can be tedious, expensive, and time-consuming. That's why many businesses turn to form letters for messages like these: announcing upcoming sales, responding to requests for product information, and updating customers' accounts.

But your letters don't have to sound or look as if a computer wrote them. Word processing equipment can help you personalize those messages so that receivers feel they are being treated as individuals. Here's how the process works.

First, create a form letter (main document) with the basic text that is the same in every document. Insert codes or "merge fields" at each point where information will vary, for example, for the customer's name and address, item ordered, balance due, or due date. A database contains the recipient list. The main document is then merged with the recipient list to create a personalized letter for each individual. It's usually wise to minimize the variable information within the body of your message to keep the merging operation as simple as possible.

Form Letter (Main Document)

Current date
<<Title>> <<First_Name>> <<Last_Name>>
<<Address 1>>
<<City>>, <<State>> <<Zip_Code>>

Dear <<Title>> <<Last_Name>>:

Thanks for your recent order from our fall catalog.

One item that you requested, <<Item>>, has proved to be very popular this season. Occasionally, we are able to appeal to our manufacturers to make more of a popular item. In this instance, though, our pleas went unanswered.

More than anything, we hate to disappoint customers like you, <<Title>> <<Last_Name>>. We pledge to do better with your future orders.

Sincerely,

Cindy Scott

List of Variable Information in Data Source

<<Title>> Mr.
<<First_Name>> Drew
<<Last_Name>> Jamison
<<Street>> 17924 Dreyfuss Avenue
<<City>> Evansville
<<State>> IN
<<Zip_Code>> 47401
<<Item>> No. 8765 Ivory Pullover.

Completed Form Letter

Current date
Mr. Drew Jamison
17924 Dreyfuss Avenue
Evansville, IN 47401

Dear Mr. Jamison:

Thanks for your recent order from our fall catalog.

One item that you requested, No. 8765 Ivory Pullover, has proved to be very popular this season. Occasionally, we are able to appeal to our manufacturers to make more of a popular item. In this instance, though, our pleas went unanswered.

More than anything, we hate to disappoint customers like you, Mr. Jamison. We pledge to do better with your future orders.

Sincerely,

Cindy Scott

Career Application

Bring in a business letter that could be adapted as a form letter. Using it as a guide, prepare a rough draft of the same message indicating the exact locations of all necessary variables. Then ask someone from your class or your campus computer center to demonstrate how this letter would be set up and merged using word processing software.

Delivering Bad News to Customers

learning objective 4

Businesses must occasionally respond to disappointed customers. In Chapter 9 you learned to use the direct strategy in granting claims and making adjustments because these were essentially good-news messages. But in some situations you have little good news to share. Sometimes your company is at fault, in which case an apology is generally in order. Other times the problem is with orders you can't fill, claims you must refuse, or credit you must deny. Messages with bad news for customers generally follow the same pattern as other negative messages. Customer letters, though, differ in one major way: they usually include resale or sales promotion emphasis.

Damage Control: Dealing With Disappointed Customers

When a customer problem arises and the company is at fault, many businesspeople call and apologize, explain what happened, and follow up with a goodwill letter.

All companies occasionally disappoint their customers. Merchandise is not delivered on time, a product fails to perform as expected, service is deficient, charges are erroneous, or customers are misunderstood. All businesses offering products or services must sometimes deal with troublesome situations that cause unhappiness to customers. Whenever possible, these problems should be dealt with immediately and personally. A majority of business professionals strive to control the damage and resolve such problems in the following manner:[10]

- Call the individual involved.
- Describe the problem and apologize.
- Explain why the problem occurred, what you are doing to resolve it, and how you will prevent it from happening again.
- Follow up with a letter that documents the phone call and promotes goodwill.

A written follow-up letter is necessary when personal contact is impossible, to establish a record, to formally confirm follow-up procedures, and to promote good relations.

Dealing with problems immediately is very important in resolving conflict and retaining goodwill. Written correspondence is generally too slow for problems that demand immediate attention. But written messages are important (1) when personal contact is impossible, (2) to establish a record of the incident, (3) to formally confirm follow-up procedures, and (4) to promote good relations.

A bad-news follow-up letter is shown in Figure 11.6. Consultant Maris Richfield found herself in the embarrassing position of explaining why she had given out the name of her client to a salesperson. The client, Data.com, Inc., had hired her firm, Richfield Consulting Services, to help find an appropriate service for outsourcing its payroll functions. Without realizing it, Maris had mentioned to a potential vendor (Payroll Services, Inc.) that her client was considering hiring an outside service to handle its payroll. An overeager salesperson from Payroll Services immediately called on Data.com, thus angering the client. The client had hired the consultant to avoid this very kind of intrusion. Data.com did not want to be hounded by vendors selling their payroll services.

When she learned of the problem, the first thing consultant Maris Richfield did was call her client to explain and apologize. She was careful to control her voice and rate of speaking. A low-pitched, deliberate pace gives the impression that you are thinking clearly, logically, and reasonably—not emotionally and certainly not irrationally. But she also followed up with the letter shown in Figure 11.6. The letter not only confirms the telephone conversation but also adds the right touch of formality. It sends the nonverbal message that the matter is being taken seriously and that it is important enough to warrant a written letter.

When situations involve many unhappy customers, companies may need to write personalized form letters. United Airlines found itself in this situation when it

FIGURE 11.6 ***Bad-News Follow-Up Message***

Tips for Resolving Problems and Following Up

- Whenever possible, call or see the individual involved.
- Describe the problem and apologize.
- Explain why the problem occurred.
- Explain what you are doing to resolve it.
- Explain how it will not happen again.
- Follow up with a letter that documents the personal message.
- Look forward to positive future relations

RICHFIELD CONSULTING SERVICES

4023 Rodeo Drive Plaza, Suite 404
Beverly Hills CA 90640

Voice: (310) 499-8224
Web: www.richfieldconsulting.com

October 23, 2006

Ms. Angela Ranier
Vice President, Human Resources
Data.com, Inc.
21067 Pacific Coast Highway
Malibu, CA 90265

Dear Angela:

Opens with agreement and apology

You have every right to expect complete confidentiality in your transactions with an independent consultant. As I explained in yesterday's telephone call, I am very distressed that you were called by a salesperson from Payroll Services, Inc. This should not have happened, and I apologize to you again for inadvertently mentioning your company's name in a conversation with a potential vender, Payroll Services, Inc.

Explains what caused the problem and how it was resolved

Promises to prevent recurrence

All clients of Richfield Consulting are assured that their dealings with our firm are held in the strictest confidence. Because your company's payroll needs are so individual and because you have so many contract workers, I was forced to explain how your employees differed from those of other companies. The name of your company, however, should never have been mentioned. I can assure you that it will not happen again. I have informed Payroll Services that it had no authorization to call you directly and its actions have forced me to reconsider using its services for my future clients.

Closes with forward look

A number of other payroll services offer excellent programs. I'm sure we can find the perfect partner to enable you to outsource your payroll responsibilities, thus allowing your company to focus its financial and human resources on its core business. I look forward to our next appointment when you may choose from a number of excellent payroll outsourcing firms.

Sincerely yours,

Maris Richfield

Maris Richfield

had to delay or cancel many flights because of a pilot slowdown and other factors. To respond to bad publicity and growing customer annoyance, United's CEO wrote a "damage control" letter to its frequent flyers. The letter contains many elements in the indirect strategy, beginning with an apology:

> *Dear Mr. Victor:*
> *I want to tell you how sorry I am about all of the flight delays and cancellations we at United have subjected you to during the past few weeks.*

The letter continued with a no-excuses explanation of the cause of its delays and cancellations and a frank admission that United's service was worse than that of its competitors:

> *While all airlines have been affected by weather, air traffic control problems, and unprecedented load factors, our performance has been noticeably worse than that of our competitors. Let me explain why and, more important, tell you what we are doing about it.*

The letter explained that United had finally reached an agreement with its pilots, which was a "first step in returning our service to the high standards you deserve." The following sentence began by assuming responsibility but quickly shifted the focus to what United is doing for its customers:

When something goes wrong in customer transactions and damage control is necessary, the first thing most businesspeople do is call the individual involved, explain what happened, and apologize. Written messages follow up.

> *We accept the responsibility for our current situation, and we are working on every front—from the negotiating table to the airports—to improve your experience.*

Bullet points then listed the steps United was taking to solve its problems, including tripling the number of extra aircraft ready for use at the airports, reducing its flight schedule, and adding time to its schedule to reflect operational realities. United also promised to waive service fees for changing flights and offered bonus mileage points. Concluding the United letter, the CEO used warm words and personal entreaties to win back lost customers:

> *These actions are only a beginning. We recognize that we need to get our operation back on track to truly regain your loyalty. If you have stayed with us during our recent difficulties, I want to personally thank you for showing more patience than any company has a right to expect. If you have taken your business elsewhere, I assure you that we will do everything possible to win back your confidence.*[11]

As exemplified in United Airlines' letter, the following specific strategies are effective in dealing with unhappy customers:

- Apologize if your organization is to blame.
- Identify the problem and take responsibility.
- Explain the steps being taken to prevent recurrence.
- Offer gifts, benefits, or bonuses to offset disappointment and to reestablish a relationship.
- Thank customers for their past business and patience.
- Look forward to future warm relations.

Handling Problems With Orders

In handling problems with orders, writers use the indirect pattern unless the message has some good-news elements.

Not all customer orders can be filled as received. Suppliers may be able to send only part of an order or none at all. Substitutions may be necessary, or the delivery date may be delayed. Suppliers may suspect that all or part of the order is a mistake; the customer may actually want something else. In writing to customers about problem orders, it's generally wise to use the direct pattern if the message has some good-news elements. But when the message is disappointing, the indirect pattern may be more appropriate.

Let's say you represent Live and Learn Toys, a large West Coast toy manufacturer, and you're scrambling for business in a slow year. A big customer, Child Land, calls in August and asks you to hold a block of your best-selling toy, the Space Station. Like most vendors, you require a deposit on large orders. September rolls around, and you still haven't received any money from Child Land. You must now write a tactful letter asking for the deposit—or else you will release the toy to other buyers. The problem, of course, is delivering the bad news without losing the customer's order and goodwill. Another challenge is making sure the reader understands the bad news. An effective letter might begin with a positive statement that also reveals the facts:

> *You were smart to reserve a block of 500 Space Stations, which we have been holding for you since August. As the holidays approach, the demand for all our learning toys, including the Space Station, is rapidly increasing.*

Next, the letter should explain why the payment is needed and what will happen if it is not received:

> *Toy stores from Florida to California are asking us to ship these Space Stations. One reason the Space Station is moving out of our warehouses so quickly is its assortment of gizmos that children love, including a land rover vehicle, a shuttle craft, a hover craft, astronauts, and even a robotic arm. As soon as we receive your deposit of $4,000, we'll have this popular item on its way to your stores. Without a deposit by September 20, though, we must release this block to other retailers.*

The closing makes it easy to respond and motivates action:

> *Use the enclosed envelope to send us your check immediately. You can begin showing this fascinating Live and Learn toy in your stores by November 1.*

Denying Claims

In denying claims, the reasons-before-refusal pattern sets an empathic tone and buffers the bad news.

Customers occasionally want something they're not entitled to or that you can't grant. They may misunderstand warranties or make unreasonable demands. Because these customers are often unhappy with a product or service, they are emotionally involved. Letters that say no to emotionally involved receivers will probably be your most challenging communication task. As publisher Malcolm Forbes observed, "To be agreeable while disagreeing—that's an art."[12]

Fortunately, the reasons-before-refusal plan helps you be empathic and artful in breaking bad news. Obviously, in denial letters you'll need to adopt the proper tone. Don't blame customers, even if they are at fault. Avoid *you* statements that sound preachy (*You would have known that cash refunds are impossible if you had read your*

FIGURE 11.7 ***Denying a Claim***

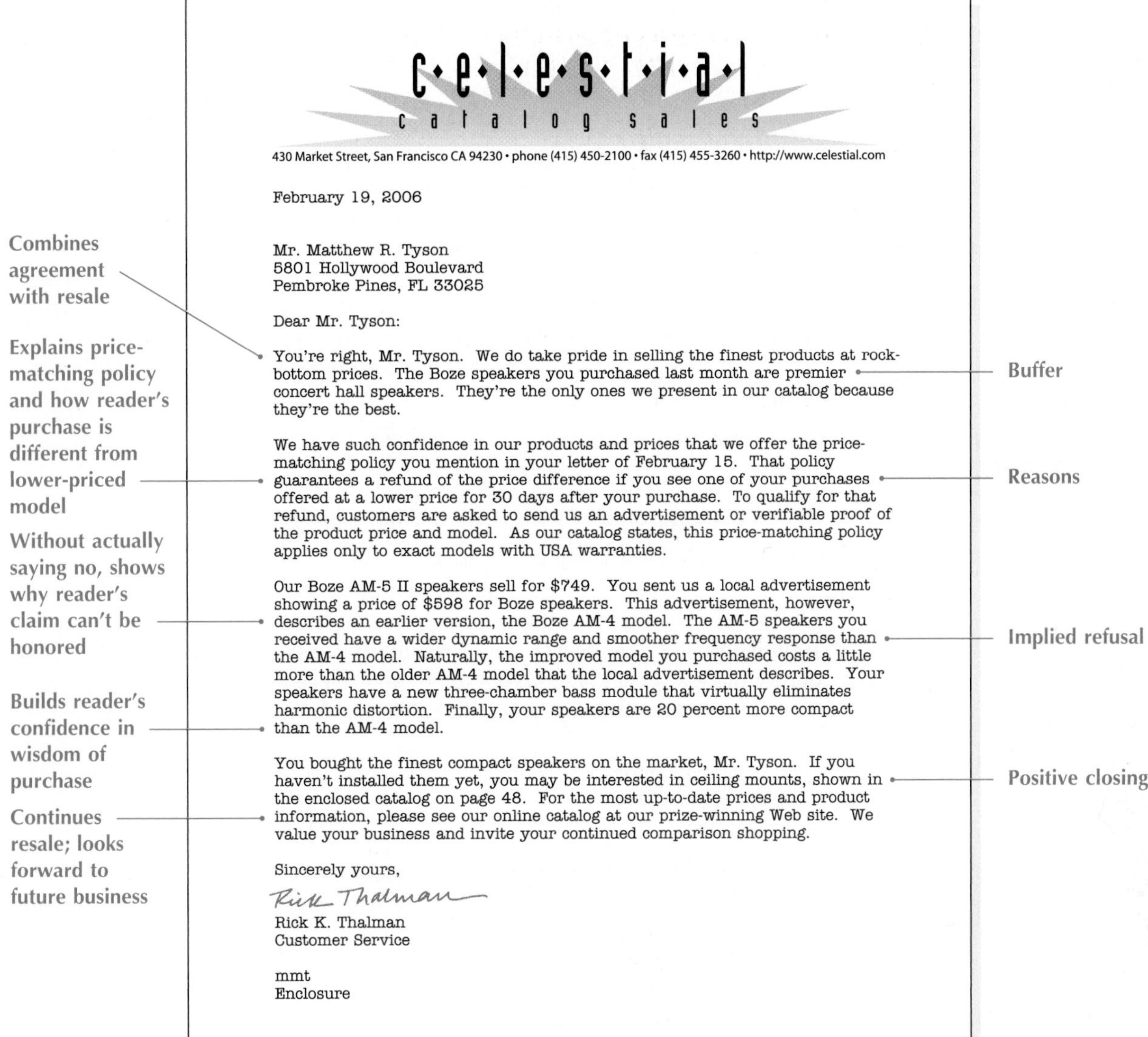

celestial
catalog sales
430 Market Street, San Francisco CA 94230 • phone (415) 450-2100 • fax (415) 455-3260 • http://www.celestial.com

February 19, 2006

Mr. Matthew R. Tyson
5801 Hollywood Boulevard
Pembroke Pines, FL 33025

Dear Mr. Tyson:

You're right, Mr. Tyson. We do take pride in selling the finest products at rock-bottom prices. The Boze speakers you purchased last month are premier concert hall speakers. They're the only ones we present in our catalog because they're the best.

We have such confidence in our products and prices that we offer the price-matching policy you mention in your letter of February 15. That policy guarantees a refund of the price difference if you see one of your purchases offered at a lower price for 30 days after your purchase. To qualify for that refund, customers are asked to send us an advertisement or verifiable proof of the product price and model. As our catalog states, this price-matching policy applies only to exact models with USA warranties.

Our Boze AM-5 II speakers sell for $749. You sent us a local advertisement showing a price of $598 for Boze speakers. This advertisement, however, describes an earlier version, the Boze AM-4 model. The AM-5 speakers you received have a wider dynamic range and smoother frequency response than the AM-4 model. Naturally, the improved model you purchased costs a little more than the older AM-4 model that the local advertisement describes. Your speakers have a new three-chamber bass module that virtually eliminates harmonic distortion. Finally, your speakers are 20 percent more compact than the AM-4 model.

You bought the finest compact speakers on the market, Mr. Tyson. If you haven't installed them yet, you may be interested in ceiling mounts, shown in the enclosed catalog on page 48. For the most up-to-date prices and product information, please see our online catalog at our prize-winning Web site. We value your business and invite your continued comparison shopping.

Sincerely yours,

Rick Thalman

Rick K. Thalman
Customer Service

mmt
Enclosure

Combines agreement with resale
Explains price-matching policy and how reader's purchase is different from lower-priced model
Without actually saying no, shows why reader's claim can't be honored
Builds reader's confidence in wisdom of purchase
Continues resale; looks forward to future business
Buffer
Reasons
Implied refusal
Positive closing

contract). Use neutral, objective language to explain why the claim must be refused. Consider offering resale information to rebuild the customer's confidence in your products or organization. In Figure 11.7 the writer denies a customer's claim for the difference between the price the customer paid for speakers and the price he saw advertised locally (which would have resulted in a cash refund of $151). Although the catalog service does match any advertised lower price, the price-matching policy applies *only* to exact models. This claim must be rejected because the advertisement the customer submitted showed a different, older speaker model.

The letter to Matthew Tyson opens with a buffer that agrees with a statement in the customer's letter. It repeats the key idea of product confidence as a transition to the second paragraph. Next comes an explanation of the price-matching policy. The writer does not assume that the customer is trying to pull a fast one. Nor does he suggest that the customer is a dummy who didn't read or understand the price-matching policy. The safest path is a neutral explanation of the policy along with precise distinctions between the customer's speakers and the older ones. The writer also gets a chance to resell the customer's speakers and demonstrate what a quality product they are. By the end of the third paragraph, it's evident to the reader that his claim is unjustified.

Refusing Credit

As much as companies want business, they can extend credit only when payment is likely to follow. Credit applications, from individuals or from businesses, are generally approved or disapproved on the basis of the applicant's credit history. This record is supplied by a credit-reporting agency, such as Experian, Equifax, or TransUnion. After reviewing the applicant's record, a credit manager applies the organization's guidelines and approves or disapproves the application.

If you must deny credit to prospective customers, you have four goals in conveying the refusal:

Goals when refusing credit include maintaining customer goodwill and avoiding actionable language.

- Avoiding language that causes hard feelings
- Retaining customers on a cash basis
- Preparing for possible future credit without raising false expectations
- Avoiding disclosures that could cause a lawsuit

Because credit applicants are likely to continue to do business with an organization even if they are denied credit, you'll want to do everything possible to encourage that patronage. Thus, keep the refusal respectful, sensitive, and upbeat. A letter to a customer denying her credit application might begin as follows:

> *We genuinely appreciate your application of January 12 for a Fashion Express credit account.*

To avoid possible litigation, many companies offer no explanation of the reasons for a credit refusal. Instead, they provide the name of the credit-reporting agency and suggest that inquiries be directed to it. In the following example notice the use of passive voice (*credit cannot be extended*) and a long sentence to de-emphasize the bad news:

> *After we received a report of your current credit record from Experian, it is apparent that credit cannot be extended at this time. To learn more about your record, you may call an Experian credit counselor at (212) 356-0922.*

The cordial closing looks forward to the possibility of a future reapplication:

> *Thanks, Ms. Love, for the confidence you've shown in Fashion Express. We invite you to continue shopping at our stores, and we look forward to your reapplication in the future.*

Some businesses do provide reasons explaining credit denials (*Credit cannot be granted because your firm's current and long-term credit obligations are nearly twice as great as your firm's total assets*). They may also provide alternatives, such as deferred billing or cash discounts. When the letter denies a credit application that accompanies an order, the message may contain resale information. The writer tries to convert the order from credit to cash. For example, if a big order cannot be filled on a credit basis, perhaps part of the order could be filled on a cash basis.

Process in Progress

Pepsi-Cola Revisited

CATHY DIAL, FORMER manager of Consumer Relations at Pepsi-Cola, knows that delivering disappointing news while retaining goodwill requires tact, empathy, and good communications skills. When things go wrong or requests must be refused, customers are often upset.

When Dial delivered disappointing news to consumers or to the public, she generally began by expressing appreciation. "Any consumer who took the time to call or write us represents many more who did not bother to let us know that something is wrong. And people who take the time to call or write us are usually our most loyal customers. We appreciate their information, and we channel it to our internal partners within the company, such as our buyers, public relations people, marketing managers, quality control experts, and senior management." In her responses Dial explained what went wrong or offered reasons to justify a refusal. In some cases, she was able to offer alternatives to soften the bad news. In one promotion, Dial confessed that they underestimated customer response and ran out of gift merchandise. For these unhappy customers, she offered alternative merchandise.

She closed negative-news letters by expressing appreciation again. If the inquiry was about a product, Dial encouraged customers to give Pepsi-Cola another try and enclosed coupons for free products.

Critical Thinking

- How closely does Cathy Dial's pattern for delivering bad news follow the four-part plan suggested in this chapter?
- Why is the reporting of consumer feedback, even when it is negative, important to an organization?
- When would form letters make sense for a company such as Pepsi-Cola?

CONTINUED ON PAGE 363

case study

Whatever form the bad-news letter takes, it's a good idea to have the message reviewed by legal counsel because of the litigation landmines awaiting unwary communicators in this area. The following checklist provides tips on how to craft effective bad-news letters.

Checklist for Delivering Bad News to Customers

- ✓ **Begin indirectly.** Express appreciation (but don't thank the reader for requesting something you're about to refuse), show agreement on some point, review facts, or show understanding. Consider apologizing if your organization was responsible for disappointing its customers.

- ✓ **Provide reasons.** Except in credit denials, justify the bad news with objective reasons. Use resale, if appropriate, to restore the customer's confidence. Avoid blaming the customer or hiding behind company policy. Look for reader benefits.

- ✓ **Present the bad news.** State the bad news objectively or imply it. Although resale or sales promotion is appropriate in order letters, it may offend in claim or credit refusals.

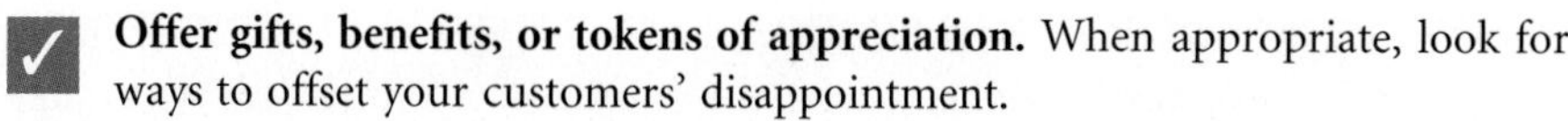

Offer gifts, benefits, or tokens of appreciation. When appropriate, look for ways to offset your customers' disappointment.

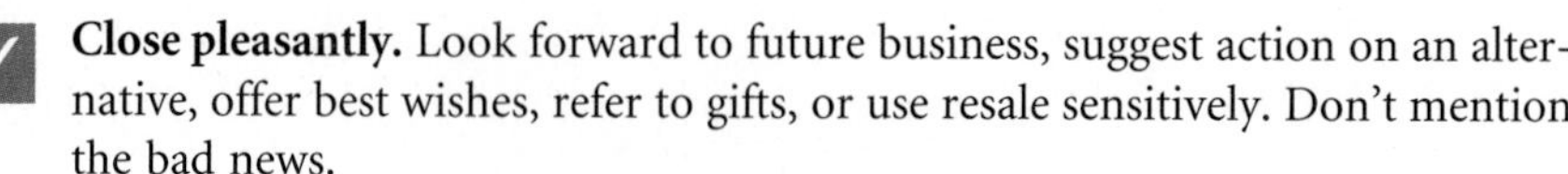

Close pleasantly. Look forward to future business, suggest action on an alternative, offer best wishes, refer to gifts, or use resale sensitively. Don't mention the bad news.

learning objective 5

Delivering Bad News Within Organizations

A tactful tone and a reasons-first approach help preserve friendly relations with customers. These same techniques are useful when delivering bad news within organizations. Interpersonal bad news might involve telling the boss that something went wrong or confronting an employee about poor performance. Organizational bad news might involve declining profits, lost contracts, harmful lawsuits, public relations controversies, and changes in policy. Whether you use a direct or an indirect pattern in delivering that news depends primarily on the anticipated reaction of the audience. Generally, bad news is better received when reasons are given first. Within organizations, you may find yourself giving bad news in person or in writing.

Giving Bad News Personally

Whether you are an employee or a supervisor, you may have the unhappy responsibility of delivering bad news. First, decide whether the negative information is newsworthy. For example, trivial, noncriminal mistakes or one-time bad behaviors are best left alone. But fraudulent travel claims, consistent hostile behavior, or failing projects must be reported.[13] For example, you might have to tell the boss that the team's computer crashed with all its important files. As a team leader or supervisor, you might be required to confront an underperforming employee. If you know that the news will upset the receiver, the reasons-first strategy is most effective. When the bad news involves one person or a small group nearby, you should generally deliver that news in person. Here are pointers on how to do so tactfully, professionally, and safely:[14]

When delivering bad news within organizations, strive to do so tactfully, professionally, and safely.

- **Gather all the information.** Cool down and have all the facts before marching in on the boss or confronting someone. Remember that every story has two sides.
- **Prepare and rehearse.** Outline what you plan to say so that you are confident, coherent, and dispassionate.
- **Explain: past, present, future.** If you are telling the boss about a problem such as the computer crash, explain what caused the crash, the current situation, and how and when you plan to fix it.
- **Consider taking a partner.** If you fear a "shoot the messenger" reaction, especially from your boss, bring a colleague with you. Each person should have a consistent and credible part in the presentation. If possible, take advantage of your organization's internal resources. To lend credibility to your view, call on auditors, inspectors, or human resources experts.
- **Think about timing.** Don't deliver bad news when someone is already stressed or grumpy. Experts also advise against giving bad news on Friday afternoon when people have the weekend to dwell on it.
- **Be patient with the reaction.** Give the receiver time to vent, think, recover, and act wisely.

Delivering Workplace Bad News

Many of the same techniques used to deliver bad news personally are useful when organizations face a crisis or must deliver bad news in the workplace. Smart organizations involved in a crisis prefer to communicate the news openly to employees, customers, and stockholders. A crisis might involve serious performance problems, a major relocation, massive layoffs, a management shakeup, or public controversy. Instead of letting rumors distort the truth, they explain the organization's side of the story honestly and early. Morale can be destroyed when employees learn of major events affecting their jobs through the grapevine or from news accounts—rather than from management.

Organizations can sustain employee morale by communicating bad news openly and honestly.

When routine bad news must be delivered to employees, management may want to deliver the news personally. But with large groups this is generally impossible. Instead, organizations deliver bad news through hard-copy memos. Organizations are experimenting with other delivery channels such as e-mail, videos, webcasts, and voice mail. Still, hard-copy memos seem to function most effectively because they are more formal and make a permanent record.

The draft of the memo shown in Figure 11.8 announces a substantial increase in the cost of employee health care benefits. However, the memo suffers from many problems. It announces jolting news bluntly in the first sentence. Worse, it offers little or no explanation for the steep increase in costs. It also sounds insincere (*We did everything possible . . .*) and arbitrary. In a final miscue, the writer fails to give credit to the company for absorbing previous health cost increases.

The revision of this bad-news memo uses the indirect pattern and improves the tone considerably. Notice that it opens with a relevant, upbeat buffer regarding health care—but says nothing about increasing costs. For a smooth transition, the second paragraph begins with a key idea from the opening (*comprehensive package*). The reasons section discusses rising costs with explanations and figures. The bad news (*you will be paying $119 a month*) is clearly presented but embedded within the paragraph. Throughout, the writer strives to show the fairness of the company's position. The ending, which does not refer to the bad news, emphasizes how much the company is paying and what a wise investment it is. Notice that the entire memo demonstrates a kinder, gentler approach than that shown in the first draft. Of prime importance in breaking bad news to employees is providing clear, convincing reasons that explain the decision.

Saying No to Job Applicants

Being refused a job is one of life's major rejections. The blow is intensified by tactless letters (*Unfortunately, you were not among the candidates selected for . . .*).

Letters that deny applications for employment should be courteous and tactful but free of specifics that could trigger lawsuits.

You can reduce the receiver's disappointment somewhat by using the indirect pattern—with one important variation. In the reasons section it's wise to be vague in explaining why the candidate was not selected. First, giving concrete reasons may be painful to the receiver (*Your grade point average of 2.7 was low compared with the GPAs of other candidates*). Second, and more important, providing extra information may prove fatal in a lawsuit. Hiring and firing decisions generate considerable litigation today. To avoid charges of discrimination or wrongful actions, legal advisors warn organizations to keep employment rejection letters general, simple, and short.

The job refusal letter shown in Figure 11.9 is tactful but intentionally vague. It implies that the applicant's qualifications don't match those needed for the position, but the letter doesn't reveal anything specific.

FIGURE 11.8 ***Announcing Bad News to Employees***

1 Prewriting

ANALYZE: The purpose of this memo is to tell employees that they must share with the company the increasing costs of health care.

ANTICIPATE: The audience will be employees who are unaware of health care costs and, most likely, reluctant to pay more.

ADAPT: Because the readers will probably be unhappy and resentful, use the indirect pattern.

2 Writing

RESEARCH: Collect facts and statistics that document health care costs.

ORGANIZE: Begin with a buffer describing the company's commitment to health benefits. Provide an explanation of health care costs. Announce the bad news. In the closing, focus on the company's major share of the cost.

COMPOSE: Draft the first version on a computer.

3 Revising

REVISE: Remove negativity (*unfortunately, we can't, we were forced, inadvisable, we don't think*). Explain the increase with specifics.

PROOFREAD: Use a semicolon before *however.* Use quotes around *defensive* to show its special sense. Spell out *percent* after *300.*

EVALUATE: Is there any other way to help readers accept this bad news?

DRAFT

Beginning January 1 your monthly payment for health care benefits will be increased to $119 (up from $52 last year).

Every year health care costs go up. Although we considered dropping other benefits, Midland decided that the best plan was to keep the present comprehensive package. Unfortunately, we can't do that unless we pass along some of the extra cost to you. Last year the company was forced to absorb the total increase in health care premiums. However, such a plan this year is inadvisable.

We did everything possible to avoid the sharp increase in costs to you this year. A rate schedule describing the increases in payments for your family and dependents is enclosed.

Hits readers with bad news without any preparation

Offers no explanation

Fails to take credit for absorbing previous increases

REVISION

DATE: October 2, 2006

TO: Fellow Employees

FROM: Lawrence R. Romero, President *LRR*

SUBJECT: Maintaining Quality Health Care

Health care programs have always been an important part of our commitment to employees at Northern, Inc. We're proud that our total benefits package continues to rank among the best in the country.

Such a comprehensive package does not come cheaply. In the last decade health care costs alone have risen over 300 percent. We're told that several factors fuel the cost spiral: inflation, technology improvements, increased cost of outpatient services, and "defensive" medicine practiced by doctors to prevent lawsuits.

Just two years ago our monthly health care cost for each employee was $515. It rose to $569 last year. We were able to absorb that jump without increasing your contribution. But this year's hike to $639 forces us to ask you to share the increase. To maintain your current health care benefits, you will be paying $119 a month. The enclosed rate schedule describes the costs for families and dependents.

Northern continues to pay the major portion of your health care program ($520 each month). We think it's a wise investment.

Enclosure

Begins with positive buffer

Offers reasons explaining why costs are rising

Reveals bad news clearly but embeds it in paragraph

Ends positively by stressing the company's major share of the costs

FIGURE 11.9 ***Saying No to Job Candidates***

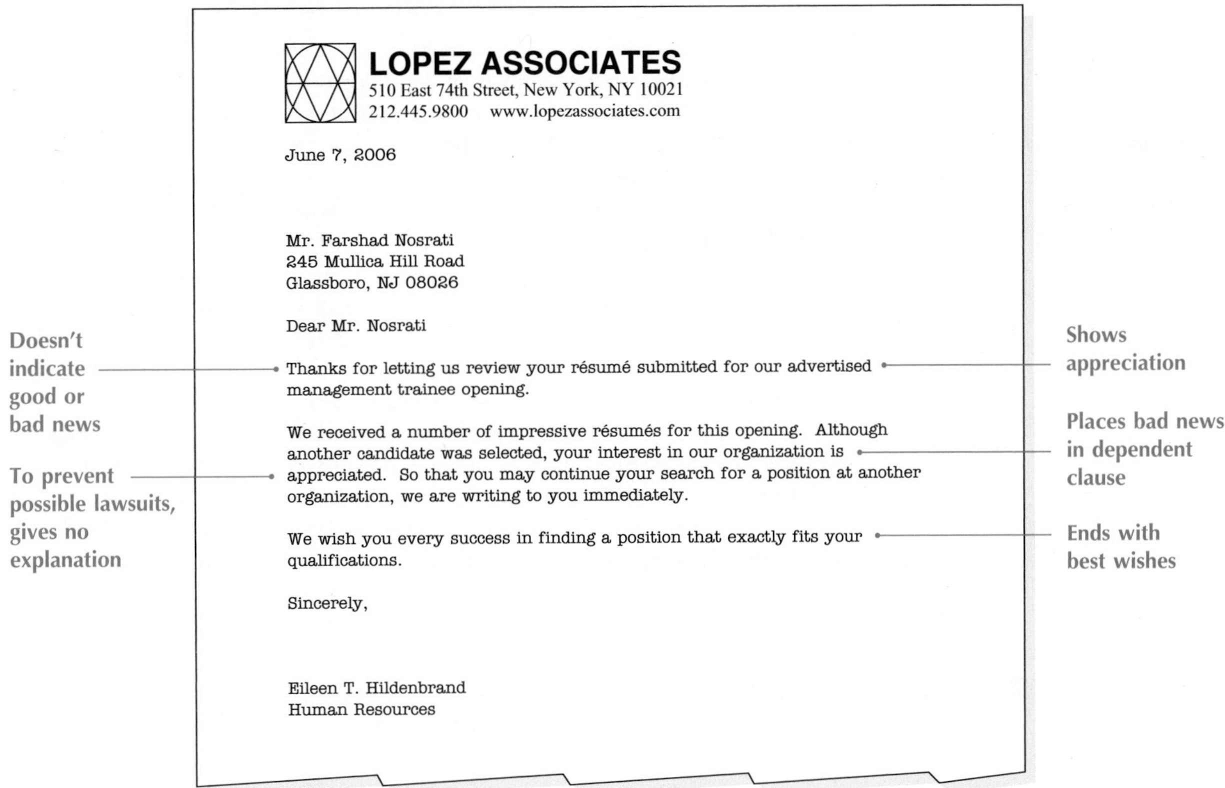

LOPEZ ASSOCIATES
510 East 74th Street, New York, NY 10021
212.445.9800 www.lopezassociates.com

June 7, 2006

Mr. Farshad Nosrati
245 Mullica Hill Road
Glassboro, NJ 08026

Dear Mr. Nosrati

Thanks for letting us review your résumé submitted for our advertised management trainee opening.

We received a number of impressive résumés for this opening. Although another candidate was selected, your interest in our organization is appreciated. So that you may continue your search for a position at another organization, we are writing to you immediately.

We wish you every success in finding a position that exactly fits your qualifications.

Sincerely,

Eileen T. Hildenbrand
Human Resources

Doesn't indicate good or bad news
To prevent possible lawsuits, gives no explanation
Shows appreciation
Places bad news in dependent clause
Ends with best wishes

The following checklist gives tips on how to communicate bad news within organizations.

Checklist for Delivering Bad News Within Organizations

✓ **Start with a relevant, upbeat buffer.** Open with a small bit of good news, praise, appreciation, agreement, understanding, or a discussion of facts leading to the reasons section.

✓ **Discuss reasons.** Except in job refusal letters, explain what caused the decision necessitating the bad news. Use objective, nonjudgmental, and nondiscriminatory language. Show empathy and fairness.

✓ **Reveal the bad news.** Make the bad news clear but don't accentuate it. Avoid negative language.

✓ **Close harmoniously.** End on a positive, friendly note. For job refusals, extend good wishes.

learning objective

6

Communicating bad news in other cultures may require different strategies.

Presenting Bad News in Other Cultures

To minimize disappointment, Americans generally prefer to present negative messages indirectly. Other cultures may treat bad news differently.

In Germany, for example, business communicators occasionally use buffers but tend to present bad news directly. British writers also tend to be straightforward with bad news, seeing no reason to soften its announcement. In Latin countries the question is not how to organize negative messages but whether to present them at all. It's considered disrespectful and impolite to report bad news to superiors. Thus, reluctant employees may fail to report accurately any negative messages to their bosses.

In Asian cultures, harmony and peace are sought in all relationships. Disrupting the harmony with bad news is avoided. To prevent discord, Japanese communicators use a number of techniques to indicate *no*—without being forced to say it. In conversation they may respond with silence or with a counter question, such as "Why do you ask?" They may change the subject or tell a white lie to save face for themselves and for the questioner. Sometimes the answer sounds like a qualified *yes*: "I will do my best, but if I cannot, I hope you will understand," "Yes, but . . . ," or "yes" followed by an apology. All of these responses should be recognized as *no*.

In China, Westerners often have difficulty understanding the "hints" given by communicators.

"I agree" might mean "I agree with 15 percent of what you say."
"We might be able to" could mean "Not a chance."
"We will consider" could mean "WE will, but the real decision maker will not."
"That is a little too much" might equate to "That is outrageous."[15]

In Thailand the negativism represented by a refusal is completely alien; the word *no* does not exist. In many cultures negative news is offered with such subtleness or in such a positive light that it may be overlooked or misunderstood by literal-minded Americans.

In many high-context cultures, saving face is important. A refusal is a potential loss of face for both parties. To save face, a person who must refuse an invitation to dine out with a business associate might say, "You must be very tired and want to have a quiet evening."[16] This subtle refusal avoids putting it in words. To understand the meaning of what's really being communicated, we must look beyond an individual's actual words and consider the communication style, the culture, and especially the context.

You've now studied the indirect method for revealing bad news and analyzed many examples of messages applying this method. As you observed, business writers generally try to soften the blow; however, they do eventually reveal the bad news. No effort is made to sweep it under the carpet or ignore it totally.

Summary of Learning Objectives

1 **Describe the goals and strategies of business communicators in delivering bad news, including knowing when to use the direct and indirect patterns, applying the writing process, and avoiding legal problems.** All businesses will occasionally deal with problems. Good communicators have several goals in delivering bad news: (a) making the reader understand and accept the bad news, (b) promoting and maintaining a good image of themselves and their organizations, (c) making the message so clear that additional cor-

Applying Your Skills at Pepsi-Cola

LARGE ORGANIZATIONS SUCH as Pepsi-Cola receive many inquiries requesting donations to charities, sponsorship of charitable projects, and contribution of free products. Parent company PepsiCo believes that as a corporate citizen, it has a responsibility to contribute to the quality of life in its community. It sponsors local programs and supports employee volunteer activities including contributions of time, talent, and funds. Each division is responsible for its own giving program, but generally corporate giving is focused on activities in which PepsiCo employees can participate.

Assume that a recent request came from Direct Relief, one of the largest nonsectarian health assistance agencies in the world. Specifically, Direct Relief asks Pepsi-Cola to make a major contribution toward purchasing a Mobile Surgical Clinic to aid poor people in remote areas of China. Direct Relief sends volunteer physicians and dentists, medical supplies, and food to aid underserved communities and victims of natural and civil disasters in the United States and abroad. Although the manager of Consumer Relations was impressed by Direct Relief's videotape, literature, and letter appealing for help, she must refuse the request because of Pepsi-Cola's corporate giving policy.

Your Task

As an assistant to the manager of Consumer Relations at Pepsi-Cola, draft a refusal letter to Dr. Melville Haskins, Direct Relief, 27 La Patera Lane, Santa Barbara, CA 93117. Your boss is touched by Dr. Haskin's appeal on behalf of Direct Relief, and she tries to think of some way to help. She asks you to check with Pepsi-Cola's newsletter editor to see if she would like to run an article about Direct Relief and perhaps motivate some employees to volunteer to help in its local health assistance programs. (The newsletter editor agrees and asks you to send her any Direct Relief literature you have.) Decide how to handle the refusal based on what you learned in this chapter. ■

case study

respondence is unnecessary, and (d) avoiding creating legal liability or responsibility. The indirect pattern involves delaying the bad news until reasons have been presented. The direct pattern reveals the main idea immediately. The direct pattern is preferable when the receiver may overlook the bad news, when the organization policy suggests directness, and for other reasons. Careful communicators will avoid careless and abusive language, which is actionable when it is false, damages a person's reputation, and is "published" (spoken within the presence of others or written). Messages written on company stationery represent that company and can be legally binding.

2 **Explain techniques for delivering bad news sensitively.** Begin with a buffer, such as a compliment, appreciation, a point of agreement, objective information, understanding, or some part of the message that represents good news. Then explain the reasons that necessitate the bad news, trying to cite benefits to the reader or others. Choose positive words, and clarify company policy if necessary. Announce the bad news strategically, mentioning a compromise or alternative if possible. Close pleasantly with a forward-looking goodwill statement.

3 **Identify routine requests and describe a strategy for refusing such requests.** Routine requests ask for favors, money, information, action, and other items. When the answer will be disappointing, use the reasons-before-refusal

pattern. Open with a buffer; provide reasons; announce the refusal sensitively; suggest possible alternatives; and end with a positive, forward-looking comment.

4 **Explain techniques for delivering bad news to customers.** When a company disappoints its customers, most organizations (1) call the individual involved, (2) describe the problem and apologize (when the company is to blame), (3) explain why the problem occurred and what is being done to prevent its recurrence, and (4) follow up with a letter that documents the phone call and promotes goodwill. Some organizations also offer gifts or benefits to offset customers' disappointment and to reestablish the business relationship. In denying claims or refusing credit, begin indirectly, provide reasons for the refusal, and close pleasantly, looking forward to future business. When appropriate, resell a product or service.

5 **Explain techniques for delivering bad news within organizations.** When delivering bad news personally to a superior, gather all the information, prepare and rehearse, explain what happened and how the problem will be repaired, consider taking a colleague with you, think about timing, and be patient with the reaction. In delivering workplace bad news, use the indirect pattern but be sure to provide clear, convincing reasons that explain the decision. In refusing job applicants, however, keep letters short, general, and tactful.

6 **Compare strategies for revealing bad news in different cultures.** American communicators often prefer to break bad news slowly and indirectly. In other high-context cultures, such as Germany and Britain, however, bad news is revealed directly. In low-context cultures, straightforwardness is avoided. In Latin cultures bad news may be totally suppressed. In Asian cultures negativism is avoided and hints may suggest bad news. Subtle meanings must be interpreted carefully.

chapter review

1. Why is the indirect strategy appropriate for some bad-news messages? (Obj. 1)
2. What are four goals when a business communicator delivers bad news? (Obj. 1)
3. Describe the four parts of the indirect message pattern. (Obj. 1)
4. Name five situations in which the direct pattern should be used for bad news. (Obj. 1)
5. Name five or more techniques to buffer the opening of a bad-news message. (Obj. 2)
6. Name four or more techniques to de-emphasize bad news when it is presented. (Obj. 2)
7. Name four kinds of routine requests that businesses must frequently refuse. (Obj. 3)
8. Why should you be especially careful in cushioning the refusal to an invitation? (Obj. 3)
9. What is the major difference between bad-news messages for customers and those for other people? (Obj. 4)
10. Identify a process used by a majority of business professionals in resolving problems with disappointed customers. (Obj. 4)
11. List four goals a writer seeks to achieve in writing messages that deny credit to prospective customers. (Obj. 4)
12. Why should a writer be somewhat vague in the reasons section of a letter rejecting a job applicant? (Obj. 4)
13. Why is the reasons-before-refusal strategy appropriate for customers who are unhappy with a product or service? (Obj. 4)
14. What actions are tactful, professional, and safe when a subordinate must personally deliver upsetting news to a superior? (Obj. 5)
15. In Latin countries why may employees sometimes fail to report accurately any negative messages to management? (Obj. 6)

critical thinking

1. Does bad news travel faster and farther than good news? Why? What implications would this have for companies responding to unhappy customers? (Objs. 1–5)
2. Some people feel that all employee news, good or bad, should be announced directly. Do you agree or disagree? Why? (Objs. 1–5)
3. Consider times when you have been aware that others have used the indirect pattern in writing or speaking to you. How did you react? (Objs. 1–5)
4. How effective is the following advice for supervisors? "Most bad news doesn't have to be given to employees. Instead, ask your employee two open-ended questions: How do you think you performed? and How could you do better next time?"[17] (Obj. 5)
5. **Ethical Issue:** You work for a large corporation with headquarters in a small town. Recently you received shoddy repair work and a huge bill from a local garage. Your car's transmission has the same problems that it did before you took it in for repair. You know that a complaint letter written on your corporation's stationery would be much more authoritative than one written on plain stationery. Should you use corporation stationery? (Obj. 1)

THREE GREAT RESOURCES FOR YOU!

1. ***Guffey Student Web Site***
   http://guffey.swlearning.com

   Your companion Web site offers chapter review quizzes, WebThink activities, updated chapter URLs, and many additional resources.

2. ***Guffey XTRA!***
   http://guffeyxtra.swlearning.com

   This online study assistant includes Your Personal Language Trainer, Speak Right!, Spell Right!, bonus online chapters, Documents for Analysis, PowerPoint slides, and much more.

3. ***Student Study Guide***

   Self-checked workbook activities and applications review chapter concepts and develop career skills.

activities

11.1 Organizational Patterns (Objs. 1–5)

Your Task. Identify which organizational pattern you would use for the following messages: direct or indirect.

a. A letter refusing a request by a charitable organization to use your office equipment on the weekend.
b. A memo from the manager denying an employee's request for special parking privileges. The employee works closely with the manager on many projects.
c. An announcement to employees that a financial specialist has canceled a scheduled lunchtime talk and cannot reschedule.

- **d.** A letter from a bank refusing to fund a company's overseas expansion plan.
- **e.** A form letter from an insurance company announcing new policy requirements that many policyholders may resent. If policyholders do not indicate the plan they prefer, they may lose their insurance coverage.
- **f.** A letter from an amusement park refusing the request of a visitor who wants free tickets. The visitor was unhappy that he had to wait in line a very long time to ride a new thrill roller coaster.
- **g.** The last in a series of letters from a collection agency demanding payment of a long-overdue account. The next step will be hiring an attorney.
- **h.** A letter from a computer company refusing to authorize repair of a customer's computer on which the warranty expired six months ago.
- **i.** A memo from an executive refusing a manager's proposal to economize by purchasing reconditioned computers. The executive and the manager both appreciate efficient, straightforward messages.
- **j.** A letter informing a company that the majority of the company's equipment order will not be available for six weeks.

11.2 Passive-Voice Verbs (Obj. 2)

Your Task. Revise the following sentences to present the bad news with passive-voice verbs.

- **a.** We will no longer be accepting credit cards for purchases under $5.
- **b.** Company policy forbids us to give performance reviews until an employee has been on the job for 12 months.
- **c.** Because management now requires more stringent security, we are postponing indefinitely requests for company tours.
- **d.** We do not examine patients until we have verified their insurance coverage.
- **e.** Your car rental insurance coverage does not cover large SUVs.

11.3 Subordinating Bad News (Obj. 2)

Your Task. Revise the following sentences to position the bad news in a subordinate clause. (**Hint:** Consider beginning the clause with *Although.*) Use passive-voice verbs for the bad news.

- **a.** Unfortunately, we no longer print a complete catalog. However, we now offer all of our catalog choices at our Web site, which is always current.
- **b.** We appreciate your interest in our organization, but we are unable to extend an employment offer to you at this time.

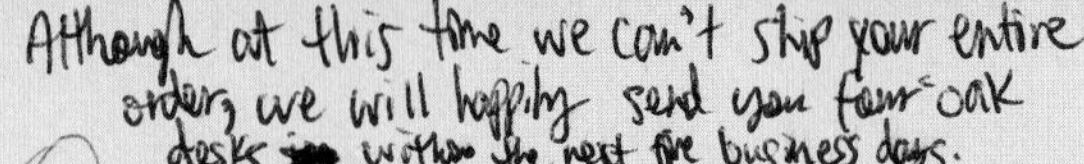

- **c.** It is impossible for us to ship your complete order at this time. However, we are able to send the four oak desks now; you should receive them within five days.
- **d.** State law does not allow smoking within 5 feet of a state building. But the college has set aside 16 outdoor smoking areas.

11.4 Implying Bad News (Obj. 2)

Your Task. Revise the following statements to *imply* the bad news. If possible, use passive-voice verbs and subordinate clauses to further de-emphasize the bad news.

- **a.** Unfortunately, we find it impossible to contribute to the fund-raising campaign this year. At present all the funds of my organization are needed to lease new equipment and offices for our new branch in Richmond. We hope to be able to support this endeavor in the future.
- **b.** Because of the holiday period, all our billboard space was used this month. Therefore, we are sorry to say that we could not give your charitable group free display space. However, next month, after the holidays, we hope to display your message as we promised.
- **c.** We cannot ship our fresh fruit baskets c.o.d. Your order was not accompanied by payment, so we are not shipping it. We have it ready, though, and will rush it to its destination as soon as you call us with your credit card number.

11.5 Evaluating Bad-News Statements (Obj. 2)

Your Task. Discuss the strengths or weaknesses of the following bad-news statements.

- **a.** It's impossible for us to ship your order before May 1.
- **b.** Frankly, we like your résumé, but we were hoping to hire someone a little younger who might be able to stay with us longer.
- **c.** I'm thoroughly disgusted with this entire case, and I will never do business with shyster lawyers like you again.
- **d.** We can assure you that on any return visit to our hotels, you will not be treated so poorly.
- **e.** We must deny your credit application because your record shows a history of late payments, nonpayment, and irregular employment.
- **f.** (*In a confidential company memo:*) I cannot recommend that we promote this young lady into any position where she will meet the public. Her colorful facial decoration, as part of her religion, may offend our customers.

11.6 Negative News in Other Cultures (Obj. 6)

Your Task. Interview fellow students or work colleagues who are from other cultures. How is negative news handled in their cultures? How would typical individuals refuse a re-

quest for a favor, for example? How would a business refuse credit to customers? How would an individual be turned down for a job? Is directness practiced? Report your findings to the class.

11.7 Document for Analysis: Request Refusal (Objs. 1–3)

Your Task. Analyze the following letter. List its weaknesses. If your instructor directs, revise it.

Current date

Ms. Ashley Puckett, Manager
Desert Design and Contracting
202 New Stine Road
N. Las Vegas, NV 89030

Dear Ms. Puckett:

Unfortunately, we cannot allow you to convert the payments you have been making on your Canon X1000 color copier toward its purchase, much as we would love to do so. We understand that you have been making regular payments for the past 14 months.

We operate under a firm company policy prohibiting such conversion of leasing monies. Perhaps you have noticed that we offer extremely low leasing and purchase prices. Obviously, these low prices would never be possible if we agreed to many proposals such as yours. Because we would like to stay in business, we cannot agree to your request asking us to convert all 14 months of rental payments toward the purchase of our popular new equipment.

We understand, Ms. Puckett, that you have had the Canon X1000 color copier for 14 months, and you claim that it has been reliable and versatile. We would like to tell you about another Canon model—one that is perhaps closer to your limited budget.

Sincerely,

11.8 Document for Analysis: Favor Refusal (Objs. 1–3)

Your Task. Analyze the following letter. List its weaknesses. If your instructor directs, revise it.

Current date

Ms. Lindsey Lazarovich
Strategic Marketing
309 Fifth Avenue
New York, NY 10011

Dear Ms. Lazarovich:

I have before me your unusual request inviting my company to participate in your research for a proposed article about "sales stars who are ascending." Unfortunately, your request involves salaries of young salespeople. As must be apparent to any clear-thinking executive, we cannot accept your invitation to release salary information. Exposing the salaries of our salespeople—regardless of how outstanding they are—would violate their privacy, jeopardize their careers, and reveal insider information. Doing so might even violate the law.

We do, however, have many outstanding young salespeople who command top salaries, and we are proud of their success. Unfortunately, during salary negotiations several years ago we reached an agreement. Both sales staff members and management agreed to keep the terms of individual contracts confidential. We could not possibly reveal specific salaries and commission rates.

Since your article is to focus on star performers, you might be interested in our ranked list of top salespeople for the past five years. As I glance over the list, I see that three of our current top salespeople are under the age of 35. We have a fact sheet about all of our top salespeople, and I will include that sheet.

Perhaps you can include some of this information in your article because we would like to see our company represented.

Cordially,

11.9 Document for Analysis: Saying No to a Job Applicant (Objs. 1, 2, and 5)

Your Task. Analyze the following letter. List its weaknesses. If your instructor directs, revise it.

Current date

Mr. Robert W. Margolies
9410 Plainfield Road
Cincinnati, OH 45235

Dear Mr. Margolies:

Ms. Martineau and I wish to thank you for the pleasure of allowing us to interview you last Thursday. We were delighted to learn about your superb academic record, and we also appreciated your attentiveness in listening to our description of the operations of Vortec Enterprises.

However, we had many well-qualified applicants who were interested in the advertised position of human resources assistant. As you may have guessed, we were particularly eager to find a minority individual who could help us fill out our Affirmative Action goals. Although you did not fit one of our goal areas, we enjoyed talking with you. We hired a female graduate of Ohio University who had most of the qualities we sought.

Although we realize that the job market is difficult at this time, you have our heartfelt wishes for good luck in finding precisely what you are looking for.

Sincerely,

11.10 Request Refusal: Dummies Author Declines (Objs. 1–3)

Joyce Lain Kennedy received a request (see **Chapter 10, Activity 10.1**) asking her to speak at the South California University Management Society banquet May 5. She is deluged with work as she strives to complete a new e-marketing book with a June 1 deadline. Although she can't spare the time to make this presentation, she doesn't want to dampen the enthusiasm and goodwill that she enjoys from these potentially influential businesspeople. She wonders if this group might consider a substitute speaker, Anderson B. Andrews. He has been a coauthor on some of her books and helps her with research. He's particularly knowledgeable about technology trends.

Your Task. As her assistant, write a refusal letter for the signature of Joyce Lain Kennedy. Address it to Professor Rachel Pierce, Department of Management, South California University, P.O. Box 286, San Diego, CA 92044. Add appropriate information.

11.11 Request Refusal: Thumbs Down on PDAs for Charleston Agents (Objs. 1–3)

George R. Hollings, president of Hollings Carolina Realty, is not keen on using technology to sell real estate. As you learned in **Chapter 10, Activity 10.8**, he was asked to purchase PDAs plus software plus monthly updates for all 18 staff members of his firm. He did the math, and it figures out to be something like $6,000 for the initial investment plus $4,000 per year for updates. That's a lot of money for technology that he's not convinced is needed. He appreciated the tactful, logical, and persuasive memo that he received from a talented agent requesting this PDA support. He wants to respond in writing because he can control exactly what he says and a written response is more forceful. His memo will also make a permanent record of this decision, in case agents make similar requests in the future. The more he ponders the request, the more Mr. Hollings thinks that this kind of investment in software and hardware should be made by agents themselves—not by the agency.

Your Task. Put yourself in the place of Mr. Hollings and write a refusal that retains the goodwill of the agent yet makes it clear that this request cannot be granted.

11.12 Request Refusal: Carnival Rejects Under-21 Crowd (Objs. 1–3)

The world's largest cruise line finds itself in a difficult position. Carnival climbed to the number one spot by promoting fun at sea and pitching its appeal to younger customers who were drawn to on-board discos, swim-up bars, and hassle-

free partying. But apparently the partying of high school and college students went too far. Roving bands of teens had virtually taken over some cruises in recent years. Travel agents complained of "drunken, loud behavior," as reported by Mike Driscall, editor of *Cruise Week*.

To crack down, Carnival raised the drinking age from 18 to 21 and required more chaperoning of school groups. But young individual travelers were still unruly and disruptive. Thus, Carnival instituted a new policy, effective immediately. No one under 21 may travel unless accompanied by an adult over 25. Says Vicki Freed, Carnival's vice president for marketing, "We will turn them back at the docks, and they will not get refunds." As Eric Rivera, a Carnival marketing manager, you must respond to the inquiry of Sheryl Kiklas of All-World Travel, a New York travel agency that features special spring- and summer-break packages for college and high school students.

All-World Travel has been one of Carnival's best customers. However, Carnival no longer wants to encourage unaccompanied young people. You must refuse the request of Ms. Kiklas to help set up student tour packages. Carnival discourages even chaperoned tours. Its real market is now family packages. You must write to All-World Travel and break the bad news. Try to promote fun-filled, carefree cruises destined for sunny, exotic ports of call that remove guests from the stresses of everyday life. By the way, Carnival attracts more passengers than any other cruise line—over a million people a year from all over the world. Over 98 percent of Carnival's guests say that they were well satisfied.

Your Task. Write your letter to Sheryl Kiklas, All-World Travel Agency, 440 East Broadway, New York, NY 10014. Send her a schedule for spring and summer Caribbean cruises. Tell her you will call during the week of January 5 to help her plan special family tour packages.[18]

11.13 Request Refusal: Excessive Noise Prompts Action (Obj. 4)

CRITICAL THINKING | INFOTRAC | WEB

As the owner of Peachtree Business Plaza, you must respond to the request of Michael Vazquez, one of the tenants in your

Photo: © Andy Newman/EPA/Landov

three-story office building. Mr. Vazquez, a CPA, demands that you immediately evict a neighboring tenant who plays loud music throughout the day, interfering with Mr. Vazquez' conversations with clients and with his concentration. The noisy tenant, Anthony Chomko, seems to operate an entertainment booking agency and spends long hours in his office. You know you can't evict Mr. Chomko because, as a legal commercial tenant, he is entitled to conduct his business. However, you might consider adding soundproofing, an expense that you would prefer to share with Mr. Chomko and Mr. Vazquez. You might also discuss limiting the time of day for noisemaking.

Your Task. Before responding to Mr. Vazquez, you decide to find out more about eviction. Use InfoTrac and the Web to search the keywords "commercial eviction." Then develop a course of action. In writing to Mr. Vazquez, deny his request but retain his goodwill. Tell him how you plan to resolve the problem. Write to Michael Vazquez, CPA, Suite 230, Peachtree Business Plaza, 116 Krog Street, Atlanta, GA 30307.

11.14 Claim Denial: Refusing Wounded Buffalo and Pygmy Circus Refund (Obj. 4)

As manager of Promotions and Advertising, Five Flags Lake Point Park, you must respond to a recent letter. Nataleigh Haggard complained that she was "taken" by Five Flags when the park had to substitute performers for Wounded Buffalo and Pygmy Circus "Summertime Slam" performance Sunday, July 4 (see **Chapter 10, Activity 10.21**). Explain to her that the concert was planned by an independent promoter. Your only obligation was to provide the theater facility and advertising. Three days before the event, the promoter left town, taking with him all advance payments from financial backers. As it turned out, many of the artists he had promised to deliver were not even planning to attend.

Left with a messy situation, you decided on Thursday to go ahead with a modified version of the event since you had been advertising it and many would come expecting some kind of talent. At that time you changed your radio advertising to say that for reasons beyond your control, the Wounded Buffalo and Pygmy Circus bands would not be appearing. You described the new talent and posted signs at the entrance and in the parking lot announcing the change. Contrary to Ms. Haggard's claim, no newspaper advertising featuring Wounded Buffalo or the Pigs appeared on the day of the concert (at least you did not pay for any to appear that day). Somehow she must have missed your corrective radio advertising and signs at the entrance. You feel you made a genuine effort to communicate the changed program. In your opinion, most people who attended the concert thought that Five Flags had done everything possible to salvage a rather unfortunate situation.

Ms. Haggard wants a cash refund of $150 (two tickets at $75 each). Five Flags has a no-money-back policy on concerts after the event takes place. If Ms. Haggard had come to the box office before the event started, you could have returned her money. But she stayed to see the concert. She claims that she didn't know anything about the talent change until after the event was well underway. This sounds unlikely, but you don't quarrel with customers. Nevertheless, you can't give her cash back. You already took a loss on this event. But you can give two complimentary passes to Five Flags Lake Point Park.

Your Task. Write a refusal letter to Ms. Nataleigh Haggard, 9684 Middletown Road, Germantown, OH 45327. Invite her and a friend to return as guests under happier circumstances.

11.15 Claim Denial: No Repeat Round-the-World Trip (Obj. 4)

Kodak Customer Service manager Charlie Smith can't believe what he reads in a letter from Brian P. Coyle (see **Chapter 10, Activity 10.23**). This 27-year-old Orlando resident actually wants Kodak to foot the bill for a repeat round-the-world trip because his Advantix camera malfunctioned and he lost 12 rolls of film! As soon as Smith saw the letter and the returned camera, he knew what was wrong. Of the 2 million Advantix cameras made last year, 20,000 malfunctioned. A supplier squirted too much oil in the shutter mechanism, and the whole lot was recalled. In fact, Kodak spent almost $1 million to remove these cameras from store shelves. Kodak also contacted all customers who could be reached. In addition to the giant recall, the company quickly redesigned the cameras so that they would work even if they had excess oil. But somehow Coyle was not notified of the recall. When Smith checked the warranty files, he learned that this customer had not returned his warranty. Had the customer done so, he would have been notified in August, well before his trip.

Although Customer Service Manager Smith is sorry for the mishap, he thinks that a request for $20,000 to replace "lost memories" is preposterous. Kodak has never assumed any responsibility beyond replacing a camera or film. This customer, however, seems to have suffered more than a routine loss of snapshots. Therefore, Smith decides to sweeten the deal by offering to throw in a digital camera valued at $225, more than double the cost of the Advantix. One of the advantages of a digital camera is that it contains an LCD panel that enables the photographer to view stored images immediately. No chance of losing memories with this camera!

Your Task. As the assistant to Customer Service Manager Charles Smith, you must write a letter that refuses the demand for $20,000 but retains the customer's goodwill. Tell this customer what you will do, and be sure to explain how Kodak reacted immediately when it discovered the Advantix defect. Write a sensitive refusal to Brian P. Coyle, 5942 Bear Crossing Drive, Orlando, FL 32746.[19]

11.16 Bad News to Customers: The StairClimber or the LifeStep? (Obj. 4)

You are delighted to receive a large order from Greg Waller at New Bodies Gym. This order includes two Lifecycle Trainers (at $1,295 each), four Pro Abdominal Boards (at $295 each), three Tunturi Muscle Trainers (at $749 each), and three Dual-Action StairClimbers (at $1,545 each).

You could ship immediately except for one problem. The Dual-Action StairClimber is intended for home use, not for gym or club use. Customers like it because they say it's more like scaling a mountain than climbing a flight of stairs. With each step, users exercise their arms to pull or push themselves up. And its special cylinders absorb shock so that no harmful running impact results. However, this model is not what you would recommend for gym use. You feel Mr. Waller should order your premier stairclimber, the LifeStep (at $2,395 each) This unit has sturdier construction and is meant for heavy use. Its sophisticated electronics provide a selection of customer-pleasing programs that challenge muscles progressively with a choice of workouts. It also quickly multiplies workout gains with computer-controlled interval training. Electronic monitors inform users of step height, calories burned, elapsed time, upcoming levels, and adherence to fitness goals. For gym use the LifeStep is clearly better than the StairClimber. The bad news is that the LifeStep is considerably more expensive.

You get no response when you try to telephone Mr. Waller to discuss the problem. Should you ship what you can, or hold the entire order until you learn whether he wants the StairClimber or the LifeStep? Perhaps you should substitute the LifeStep and send only two of them.

Your Task. Decide what to do and write a letter to Greg Waller, New Bodies Gym, 3402 Copeland Drive, Athens, OH 45701

11.17 Bad News to Customers: Stop Trashing America, Coke and Pepsi! (Obj. 4)

CRITICAL THINKING | TEAM | WEB

In the United States, The Coca-Cola Company and PepsiCo sell an incredible 70 billion or more beverages annually in aluminum cans, plastic containers, and glass bottles. An advertisement in *The New York Times* encouraged stockholders, voters, and taxpayers to send protests to these companies demanding that the bottlers stop trashing America. Protestors urged the companies to take responsibility for their bottle and can litter and waste. These companies, according to activists in the GrassRoots Recycling Network and the Container Recycling Institute, actively oppose bottle deposit legislation. Recycling activists say that the companies have spent millions lobbying the American Beverage Association to block proposed bills requiring deposits on containers. Yet, container deposits produce the most effective litter-reduction tools available—and at almost no cost to taxpayers, according to activists.

Because of current publicity, Coke's public relations offices are receiving many messages from shareholders and consumers accusing the company of "trashing America." Some of the more informed writers want Coke to use at least 25 percent recycled plastic in its container manufacturing process. Actually, Coke claims that one in four PET (polyethylene terephthalate plastic) containers it uses in North America already contains recycled plastic. But when it comes to charging a deposit on soft drink containers, Coke agrees with the rest of the soft drink industry. It argues that narrowly focused programs and mandatory container deposit programs are not reasonable alternatives. These programs provide minimal impact on the waste stream, and their high cost is counterproductive. Moreover, they prevent consideration of better, more comprehensive programs.

Your Task. Assume that you are part of an intern team in a public relations office at The Coca-Cola Company in Atlanta. As a learning experience, your group has been asked to draft a message that can be used in response to the negative incoming mail about container waste and litter. Your intern supervisor tells you to go to the company Web site at **http://www.cocacola.com** and read its environment/waste management statements. She also tells you to check out the soft drink industry's policy on packaging at **http://www.nsda.org/environment/packaging.asp**. Locate other useful articles or information on the Web or with InfoTrac. Discuss an appropriate response based on the information you found and your training in writing bad-news messages. Individually or as a team, draft a message that could be used as a letter or an e-mail responding to inquiries requesting Coke to stop trashing America. You should produce a polite but responsive message, not a long, data-filled defense. For the signature of Newton M. Haynes, prepare a letter draft addressed to Mrs. Dorothy King, 3956 Roosevelt Boulevard, Jacksonville, FL 32205.

11.18 Damage Control for Disappointed Customers: J. Crew Goofs on Cashmere Turtleneck (Obj. 4)

Who wouldn't want a cashmere zip turtleneck sweater for $18? At the J. Crew Web site, many delighted shoppers scrambled to order the bargain cashmere. Unfortunately, the price should have been $218! Before J. Crew officials could correct the mistake, several hundred e-shoppers had bagged the bargain sweater for their digital shopping carts.

When the mistake was discovered, J. Crew immediately sent an e-mail message to the soon-to-be disappointed shoppers. The subject line shouted "Big Mistake!" Emily Woods, chairwoman of J. Crew, began her message with this statement: "I wish we could sell such an amazing sweater for only $18. Our price mistake on your new cashmere zip turtleneck probably went right by you, but rather than charge you such a large difference, I'm writing to alert you that this item has been removed from your recent order."

As an assistant in the communication department at J. Crew, you saw the e-mail message that was sent to cus-

tomers and you tactfully suggested that the bad news might have been broken differently. Your boss says, "OK, hot stuff. Give it your best shot."

Your Task. Although you have only a portion of the message, analyze the customer bad-news message sent by J. Crew. Using the principles suggested in this chapter, write an improved e-mail message. In the end, J. Crew decided to allow customers who ordered the sweater at $18 to reorder it for $118.80 to $130.80, depending on the size. Customers were given a special Web site to reorder (make up an address). Remember that J. Crew customers are youthful and hip. Keep your message upbeat.[20]

11.19 Damage Control for Disappointed Customers: Worms in Her PowerBars!

WEB

In a recent trip to her local grocery store, Kelly Keeler decided for the first time to stock up on PowerBars. These are low-fat, high-carbohydrate energy bars that are touted as a highly nutritious snack food specially formulated to deliver long-lasting energy. Since 1986, PowerBar (**http://www.powerbar.com**) has been dedicated to helping athletes and active people achieve peak performance. It claims to be "the fuel of choice" for top athletes around the world. Kelly is a serious runner and participates in many track meets every year.

On her way to a recent meet, Kelly grabbed a PowerBar and unwrapped it while driving. As she started to take her first bite, she noticed something white and shiny in the corner of the wrapping. An unexpected protein source wriggled out of her energy bar—a worm! Kelly's first inclination was to toss it out the window and never buy another PowerBar. On second thought, though, she decided to tell the company. When she called the toll-free number on the wrapper, Sophie, who answered the phone, was incredibly nice, extremely apologetic, and very informative about what happened. "I'm very sorry you experienced an infested product," said Sophie.

She explained that the infamous Indian meal moth is a pantry pest that causes millions of dollars in damage worldwide. It feeds on grains or grain-based products, such as cereal, flour, dry pasta, crackers, dried fruits, nuts, spices, and pet food. The tiny moth eggs lie dormant for some time or hatch quickly into tiny larvae (worms) that penetrate food wrappers and enter products.

At its manufacturing facilities, PowerBar takes stringent measures to protect against infestation. It inspects incoming grains, supplies proper ventilation, and shields all grain-storage areas with screens to prevent insects from entering. It also uses light traps and electrocuters; these devices eradicate moths with the least environmental impact.

PowerBar President Brian Maxwell makes sure every complaint is followed up immediately with a personal letter. His letters generally tell customers that it is rare for infestations like this to occur. Entomologists say that the worms are not toxic and will not harm humans. Nevertheless, as President Maxwell says, "it is extremely disgusting to find these worms in food."

Your Task. For the signature of Brian Maxwell, PowerBar president, write a bad-news follow-up letter to Kelly Keeler, 932 Opperman Drive, Eagan, MN 55123. Keep the letter informal and personal. Explain how pests get into grain-based products and what you are doing to prevent infestation. You can learn more about the Indian meal moth by searching the Web. In your letter include a brochure titled "Notes About the Indian Meal Moth," along with a kit for Kelly to mail the culprit PowerBar to the company for analysis in Boise, Idaho. Also send a check reimbursing Kelly $26.85 for her purchase.[21]

11.20 Damage Control for Disappointed Customers: Costly SUV Upgrade to a Ford Excursion (Obj. 4)

Steven Chan, a consultant from Oakland, California, was surprised when he picked up his rental car from Budget in Seattle over Easter weekend. He had reserved a full-size car, but the rental agent told him he could upgrade to a Ford Excursion for an additional $25 a day. "She told me it was easy to drive," Mr. Chan reported. "But when I saw it, I realized it was huge—like a tank. You could fit a full-size bed inside."

On his trip Mr. Chan managed to scratch the paint and damage the rear-door step. He didn't worry, though, because he thought the damage would be covered since he had charged the rental on his American Express card. He knew that the company offered backup car rental insurance coverage. To his dismay, he discovered that its car rental coverage excluded large SUVs. "I just assumed they'd cover it," he confessed. He wrote to Budget to complain about not being warned that certain credit cards may not cover damage to large SUVs or luxury cars.

Budget agents always encourage renters to sign up for Budget's own "risk product." But they don't feel that it is their responsibility to study the policies of customers' insurance carriers and explain what may or may not be covered. Moreover, they try to move customers into their rental cars as quickly as possible and avoid lengthy discussions of insurance coverage. Customers who do not purchase insurance are at risk. Mr. Chan does not make any claim against Budget, but he is upset about being "pitched" to upgrade to the larger SUV, which he didn't really want.[22]

Your Task. As a member of the communication staff at Budget, respond to Mr. Chan's complaint. Budget obviously is not going to pay for the SUV repairs, but it does want to salvage his goodwill and future business. Offer him a coupon worth two days' free rental of any full-size sedan. Write to Steven Chan, 5300 Park Ridge, Apt. 4A, Oakland, CA 93578

11.21 Damage Control for Disappointed Customers: McDonald's Squirms Over McAfrika Protests (Obj. 4)

CRITICAL THINKING

The McAfrika burger sounded like a terrific new menu sandwich to fast-food giant McDonald's. Made from an authentic African recipe, the pita bread sandwich combined beef, cheese, tomatoes, and salad. But when launched in Norway, it triggered an avalanche of criticism and bad publicity. McDonald's was accused of "extreme insensitivity" in releasing the new sandwich when 12 million people are facing starvation in southern Africa.

Aid agencies trying to raise funds to avert famine in southern Africa were particularly vociferous in their complaints. They said the McAfrika marketing campaign was "insensitive, crass, and ill considered." Linn Aas-Hansen, of Norwegian Church Aid, complained that it was "inappropriate and distasteful to launch a hamburger called McAfrika when large portions of southern Africa are on the verge of starvation." To punctuate their protest, members of the aid group distributed "catastrophe crackers" outside McDonald's restaurants in Oslo. These crackers are protein-rich biscuits given to starving Africans.

Facing a public relations debacle, McDonald's Norway immediately began a damage-control strategy. Spokeswoman Margaret Brusletto apologized, saying that the name of the product and the timing of its launch were unfortunate. She said the company would consider sharing the proceeds from its sales with aid agencies. McDonald's also offered to allow aid agencies to leave collection boxes and fund-raising posters in its Norwegian restaurants that sold the McAfrika sandwich during its promotional sale.

McDonald's head office issued a statement saying, "All of the involved parties are happy with the solution. We hope this will put a wider focus on the important job that these organizations are doing, and McDonald's in Norway is pleased to be able to support this." Although the McAfrika was launched only in Norway, the protest made headlines in the United States and other countries.[23]

Your Task. As a member of the McDonald's corporate communication staff, you are given the task of drafting a letter to be sent to U.S. customers who have written to protest the McAfrika sandwich in Norway and in the United States. Most of the letters ask McDonald's to withdraw the offending product, a request you must refuse. Address the letter to Mrs. Janice M. Clark, 35 South Washington, Carthage, IL 62325. Prepare your letter so that it can be sent to others.

11.22 Damage Control for Disappointed Customers: Late Delivery of Printing Order (Obj. 4)

LISTENING SPEAKING

Kevin Kearns, a printing company sales manager, must tell one of his clients that the payroll checks his company ordered are not going to be ready by the date Kearns had promised. The printing company's job scheduler overlooked the job and didn't get the checks into production in time to meet the deadline. As a result, Kearns' client, a major insurance company, is going to miss its pay run.

Kearns meets with internal department heads. They decide on the following plan to remedy the situation: (1) move the check order to the front of the production line; (2) make up for the late production date by shipping some of the checks—enough to meet their client's immediate payroll needs—by air freight; (3) deliver the remaining checks by truck.[24]

Your Task. Form groups of three to four students. Discuss the following issues about how to present the bad news to Andrew Tyra, Kearns' contact person at the insurance company.

a. Should Kearns call Tyra directly or delegate the task to his assistant?
b. When should Tyra be informed of the problem?
c. What is the best procedure for delivering the bad news?
d. What follow-up would you recommend to Kearns?

Be prepared to share your group's responses during a class discussion. Your instructor may ask two students to role-play the presentation of the bad news.

11.23 Credit Refusal: Cash Only at Gold's Gym and Fitness Center (Obj. 4)

As manager of Gold's Gym and Fitness Center, you must refuse the application of Becky Peniccia for an Extended Membership. This is strictly a business decision. You liked Becky very much when she applied, and she seems genuinely interested in fitness and a healthful lifestyle. However, your Extended Membership plan qualifies the member for all your testing, exercise, recreation, yoga, and aerobics programs. This multiservice program is expensive for the club to maintain because of the huge staff required. Applicants must have a solid credit rating to join. To your disappointment, you learned that Becky's credit rating is decidedly negative. Her credit report indicates that she is delinquent in payments to four businesses, including Desert Athletic Club, your principal competitor.

You do have other programs, including your Drop In and Work Out plan, which offers the use of available facilities on a cash basis. This plan enables a member to reserve space on the racquetball and handball courts. The member can also sign up for yoga and exercise classes, space permitting. Because Becky is far in debt, you would feel guilty allowing her to plunge in any more deeply.

Your Task. Refuse Becky Peniccia's credit application, but encourage her cash business. Suggest that she make an inquiry to the credit reporting company Experian to learn about her credit report. She is eligible to receive a free credit

report if she mentions this application. Write to Rebecca Peniccia, Box 103, Westgate Hills, 1402 Olive Avenue, Mesa, AZ 85301.

11.24 Credit Refusal: Risky Order for Cool Camera Phones (Obj. 4)

As a CellCity sales manager, you are delighted to land a sizable order for your new T-Mobile Nokia digital video camera phone. This great phone is too cool with its full-color LCD, multimedia player, speaker phone, and voice dialing.

The purchase order comes from Beech Grove Electronics, a retail distributor in Indianapolis. You send the order on to Pat Huckabee, your credit manager, for approval of the credit application attached. To your disappointment, Pat tells you that Beech Grove doesn't qualify for credit. Experian Credit Services reports that credit would be risky for Beech Grove.

Because you think you can be more effective in writing than on the telephone, you decide to write to Beech Grove with the bad news and offer an alternative. Suggest that Beech Grove order a smaller number of the camera phones. If it pays cash, it can receive a 2 percent discount. After Beech Grove has sold these fast-moving units, it can place another cash order through your toll-free order number. With your fast delivery system, its inventory will never be depleted. Beech Grove can get the camera phones it wants now and can replace its inventory almost overnight. Credit Manager Huckabee tells you that your company generally reveals to credit applicants the name of the credit reporting service it used and encourages them to investigate their credit record.

Your Task. Write a credit refusal to Jacob Jackson, Beech Grove Electronics, 3590 Plainfield Road, Indianapolis, IN 46296

11.25 Credit Refusal: No Hawaiian Luaus on the Beach (Obj. 4)

Your Task. Revise the following ineffective letter that refuses credit.

Current date

Mr. Stefano Romano
Creative Catering
3920 Torrey Pines Drive
La Jolla, CA 92037

Dear Mr. Romano:

This is to inform you that we have received your recent order for our fine restaurant supplies. However, we are unable to fill this order because of the bad credit record you have on file at Experian Credit Services.

We understand that at this point in time you are opening a new gourmet catering business called Creative Catering. Our sales rep told us about your plans to serve Hawaiian style barbecue and luaus on the beach. He said your firm will also cater corporate events, box lunches, theme parties, and fund-raising events. I must say that we were all impressed with your plan to provide elegant yet economical catering in the San Diego area. Although we are sure your catering business will be a success, we cannot extend credit because of your current poor credit rating.

You might be interested in investigating what is in your credit file. The Fair Credit Reporting Act guarantees you the right to see the information contained in your file. If you would like to see what prevented you from obtaining credit from us, you should call 1-888-EXPERIAN.

We are truly sorry that we cannot fill your initial order, totaling $1,430, for our superior restaurant supplies. We pride ourselves on serving most of the West Coast's finest restaurants and catering services. We would be proud to add Creative Catering to our list of discerning customers. Perhaps the best way for you to join that select list is with a smaller order to begin with. We would be happy to serve you on a cash basis. If this plan meets with your approval, do let me know.

Sincerely,

11.26 Bad News to Employees: Company Games Are Not Date Nights (Obj. 5)

E-MAIL

As director of Human Resources at Weyerman Paper Company, you received an unusual request. Several employees asked that their spouses or friends be allowed to participate in Weyerman intramural sports teams. Although the teams play only once a week during the season, these employees claim that they can't afford more time away from friends and family. Over 100 employees currently participate in the eight coed volleyball, softball, and tennis teams, which are open to company employees only. The teams were designed

to improve employee friendships and to give employees a regular occasion to have fun together.

If nonemployees were to participate, you're afraid that employee interaction would be limited. And while some team members might have fun if spouses or friends were included, you're not so sure all employees would enjoy it. You're not interested in turning intramural sports into "date night." Furthermore, the company would have to create additional teams if many nonemployees joined, and you don't want the administrative or equipment costs of more teams. Adding teams also would require changes to team rosters and game schedules. This could create a problem for some employees. You do understand the need for social time with friends and families, but guests are welcome as spectators at all intramural games. Besides, the company already sponsors a family holiday party and an annual company picnic.

Your Task. Write an e-mail or hard-copy memo to the staff denying the request of several employees to include nonemployees on Weyerman's intramural sports teams.

11.27 Bad News to Employees: No Go for Tuition Reimbursement (Obj. 5)

TEAM

Ashley Arnett, a hard-working bank teller, has sent a request asking that the company create a program to reimburse the tuition and book expenses for employees taking college courses (see **Chapter 10, Activity 10.5**). Although some companies have such a program, First Federal has not felt that it could indulge in such an expensive employee perk. Moreover, the CEO is not convinced that companies see any direct benefit from such a program. Employees improve their educational credentials and skills, but what is to keep them from moving that education and skill set to another employer? First Federal has over 200 employees. If even a fraction of them started classes, the company could see a huge bill for the cost of tuition and books. Because the bank is facing stiff competition and its profits are sinking, the expense of such a program is out of the question. In addition, it would involve administration—applications, monitoring, and record-keeping. It's just too much of a hassle. When employees were hard to hire and retain, companies had to offer employment perks. But with a soft economy, such inducements are unnecessary.

Your Task. As director of Human Resources, send an individual response to Ashley Arnett. The answer is a definite no, but you want to soften the blow and retain the loyalty of this conscientious employee.

11.28 Bad News to Employees: Suit Up or Ship Out (Obj. 5)

During the feverish dot-com boom days, "business casual" became the workplace norm. Like many other companies, Bear Stearns, the sixth largest securities firm in the United States, loosened its dress policies. It allowed employees to come to work in polo shirts, khaki pants, and loafers for two important reasons: It had to compete with Internet companies in a tight employment market, and it wanted to fit in with its casual dot-com customers. But when the dot-com bubble burst and the economy faltered, the casual workplace environment glorified by failed Internet companies fell out of favor.

Managers at Bear Stearns decided to reverse course and cancel the casual dress code that had been in effect for two years. Company spokesperson Elizabeth Ventura said, "Our employees should reflect the professionalism of our business." Some observers felt that relaxed dress codes carried over into relaxed work attitudes.

Particularly in difficult economic times, Bear Stearns believed that every aspect of the business, including dress, should reflect the serious attitude and commitment it had toward relations with clients. After the securities market plunged, Bear Stearns slashed 830 jobs, amounting to 7.5 percent of its workforce. This was the biggest cut in company history, and officials vowed to get serious about regaining market share.

To put into effect its more serious business tone, Bear Stearns decided to return to a formal dress code. For men, suits and ties would be required. For women, dresses, suits with skirts or slacks, or "equivalent attire" would be expected. Although Bear Stearns decided to continue to allow casual dress on Fridays, sports jackets would be required for men.

Despite the policy reversal, company officials downplayed the return to traditional, more formal attire. Spokesperson Ventura noted that the company's legal, administrative, and private client services departments had never adopted the casual dress code. In addition, she said, "We've always had a formal dress policy for meetings with clients."

To ease the transition, nearby Brooks Brothers Inc., a conservative clothing store, offered a special invitation. On September 20 it would stay open an extra hour to host an evening of wine, cheese, and shopping with discounts of 20 percent for Bear Stearns staffers.[25]

Your Task. As an assistant to John Jones, chairman of the Management and Compensation Committee, you have the challenging task of drafting a message to employees announcing the return to a formal dress code. He realizes that this is going to be a tough sell, but he's hoping that employees will recognize that difficult economic times require serious efforts and sacrifices. In the message to employees, he wants you to tell supervisors that they must speak to employees who fail to adhere to the new guidelines. You ask Mr. Jones whether he wants the message to open directly or indirectly. He says that Bear Stearns generally prefers directness in messages to employees, but he wants you to prepare two versions and he will choose one.

11.29 Bad News to Applicants: Denying Graduate School Applicants (Obj. 5)

Congratulations! You've just finished your undergraduate degree, and you decide to apply to graduate school in the field of communications. You quickly learn that the application process demands serious effort and significant expense. The purpose letter, transcripts, portfolio assembly, letters of recommendation, appropriate admission tests, and the application itself are enough to discourage all but the most persistent and determined candidates. Application fees, postage, telephone bills, testing preparation, and assessment costs can easily run up hundreds of dollars for an application to just one graduate program. And because of competition, you are forced to apply to many programs, multiplying the time and expense.

You didn't expect acceptance from all of your "dream" schools. Still, you can't help but be disappointed when the dreaded "thin letters" of rejection arrive:

1. *Your application for admission to the Graduate School of the University of Texas at Austin has been given careful consideration by the Committee on Graduate Studies in your major department and the Dean of the Graduate School. On the basis of their recommendation, your application has been denied.*
2. *I regret to inform you that the (University of Minnesota) Graduate Faculty of the School of Journalism and Mass Communication was unable to approve your application for admission even though you presented a strong record. Competition for admission to the graduate program in Mass Communication was especially keen this year.*
3. *The Interdepartmental Program in Mass Communication at the University of Michigan receives many more applications than the number of positions available. I regret we must inform you that you have not been approved for admission for the Fall of 2004. We had a large pool of qualified applicants this year. Due to the program's limited size, able students often fail to gain admission because others, whose plans of study or aptitudes are more suited to the program, have applied.*

Your Task. In teams, discuss the strengths and weaknesses of the rejections shown here. Now imagine that you are Dan Drew, admissions director of Indiana University's graduate communications program. Consider how an applicant would want a rejection letter to read. Consider each applicant's expense, time spent, and anticipation of acceptance. Remember, too, that even though the potential customers of your program are rejected, the applicants may represent friends or family of alumni and possible donors to the university's programs and endowment. More is at stake than just rejecting an applicant. Tact and respect become important issues. Individually or in teams, write a form letter that you feel is appropriate for rejecting applicants. Address the first letter to Thad P. Montalban, 4201 Covington Place, Apartment 32, Lake Worth, FL 33462.

11.30 Is Increased Credit Card Security Worth the Inconvenience? (Obj. 4)

CONSUMER

Travel writer Arlene Getz was mystified when the sales clerk at a Paris department store refused her credit card. "Sorry," the clerk said, "your credit card is not being accepted. I don't know why." Getz found out soon enough. Her bank had frozen her account because of an "unusual" spending pattern. The problem? "We've never had a charge from you in France before," a bank official told her. The bank didn't seem to remember that Getz had repeatedly used that card in cities ranging from Boston to Tokyo to Cape Town over the past six years, each time without incident.

Getz was a victim of neural-network technology, a tool that is intended to protect credit cardholders from thieves who steal cards and immediately run up huge purchases. This technology tracks spending patterns. If it detects anything unusual—such as a sudden splurge on easy-to-fence items like jewelry—it sets off an alarm. Robert Boxberger, senior vice president of fraud management at Fleet Credit Card Services, says that the system is "geared toward not declining any travel and entertainment expenses, like hotels, restaurants, or car rentals." But somehow it goofed and did not recognize that Arlene Getz was traveling, although she had used her card earlier to rent a car in Paris, a sure sign that she was traveling.

Getz was what the credit card industry calls a false positive—a legitimate cardholder inconvenienced by the hunt for fraudsters. What particularly riled her was finding out that 75 percent of the transactions caught in the neural network turn out to be legitimate. Yet the technology has been immensely successful for credit card companies. Since Visa started using the program, its fraud rate dropped from 15 cents to 6 cents per $100. To avoid inconveniencing cardholders, the company doesn't automatically suspend a card when it suspects fraud. Instead, it telephones the cardholder to verify purchases. Of course, if the cardholder is traveling, it's impossible to reach her.

Angry at the inconvenience and embarrassment she experienced, Getz sent a letter to Visa demanding an explanation in writing.

Your Task. As an assistant to the vice president in charge of fraud detection at Visa, you have been asked to draft a letter that can be used to respond to Arlene Getz as well as to other unhappy customers whose cards were wrongly refused by your software. You know that the program has been an overwhelming success. It can, however, inconvenience people, especially when they are traveling. You've heard your boss tell travelers that it's a good idea to touch base with your bank before leaving and take along the card's customer service number (1-800-553-0321). Write a letter that explains what happened, retains the goodwill of the customer, and suggests reader benefits. Address your letter to Ms. Arlene Getz, 68 Riverside Drive, Apt. 35, New York, NY 10025.

video resources

Video Library 2: *Bridging the Gap*

Negative News: DawnSign Press

Named Small Business Owner of the Year in the state of California, Joe Dannis is a unique entrepreneur. In this video you'll learn how he started DawnSign Press, but you'll also see American Sign Language in action. Joe and many of his employees are deaf. As business communicators, you'll be exposed to a unique work environment and be inspired by Joe's success story. Notice that both deaf and hearing employees sign to each other. Pay attention to the nature of Joe's business and listen to his reasons for hiring both deaf and hearing employees.

As a staff employee at DawnSign Press, you were surprised but honored when owner Joe Dannis handed you a letter and asked you to answer it for him. The letter was from Melissa Thomas, a customer who had used one of DawnSign Press's books in a class and found it very helpful. However, she said that she was "profoundly disappointed" when she learned that Joe's business was not staffed by deaf people only. Melissa said that, as a deaf person herself, she had experienced great difficulty in finding employment. She felt that DawnSign Press should set an example by hiring an all-deaf staff, thus providing jobs for many deserving people. She wants DawnSign Press to change its hiring policy.

Joe knows that you have studied business communication; that's why he asks you to prepare a letter that responds to this inquiry but that may also be used for any future ones. Because you have heard Joe talk about his employment philosophy, you realize that, in a perfect world, he would hire only deaf employees. But Joe is forced to hire hearing employees as well.

Your Task. For Joe's signature, prepare a bad-news message. Start indirectly, provide reasons, present the bad news (or imply it), and close pleasantly. You might wish to visit the DawnSign Press Web site (**http://www.dawnsign.com**) for more information. Address the draft to Ms. Melissa Thomas, 4752 Monroe Street, Toledo, OH 43623.

C.L.U.E. review 11

Edit the following sentences to correct all language faults, including grammar, punctuation, spelling, and word confusions.

1. Bad news is generaly disapointing, however the negative feelings can be reduced.
2. 2 ways to reduce the disapointment of bad news is to: (1) give reasons first, and (2) reveal the news sensitively.
3. When delivering bad news its important that you make sure the reciever understands and excepts it.
4. The indirect pattern consists of 4 parts, buffer, reasons, bad news, and closing.
5. Although the indirect pattern is not apropriate for every situation it is usualy better then a blunt announcement of bad news.
6. On June 1st, our company President and Vice President revealed a four million dollar drop in profits which was bad news for every one.
7. Because of declining profits and raising Health costs the Director of our Human Resources Department announced a increase in each employees contribution to Health Benefits.
8. Most of us prefer to be let down gentle, when were being refused something, thats why the reasons before refusal pattern is effective.
9. When a well known Tire company recalled 100s of thousands of tires it's President issued a apology to the public, and all injured customers'.
10. If I was you I would begin the bad news message with a complement not a blunt rejection.

unit 4

Reports and Proposals

chapter 12

Preparing to Write Business Reports

chapter 13

Organizing and Writing Typical Business Reports

chapter 14

Proposals and Formal Reports

chapter 12

Preparing to Write Business Reports

objectives

1 Describe business report basics, including functions, patterns, writing style, and formats.

2 Apply Guffey's 3-x-3 writing process to business reports.

3 Understand where to find and how to use print and electronic sources of secondary data.

4 Understand where to find and how to use sources of primary data.

5 Recognize the purposes and techniques of documentation in business reports.

6 Illustrate reports with graphics that create meaning and interest.

Communication in Process

BzzAgent Supports Women's Right to One True Fit

"IMAGINE AN ARMY of unpaid endorsers . . . telling their friends, family and colleagues about [a] product, who in turn tell their friends, family and colleagues."[1] The impact these unpaid endorsers create is known as *buzz*, a marketing phenomenon consisting of word-of-mouth advertising. Dave Balter, CEO for BzzAgent, is a strong advocate of word-of-mouth advertising. He believed that BzzAgent could help Lee Jeans market a new line of jeans called One True Fit by creating buzz.

Managers at Lee Jeans had experimented with word-of-mouth advertising before and had seen the value of creating buzz. They approached Balter and BzzAgent based on the recommendation of one of their agency executives who had actually worked as an unpaid BzzAgent for Balter. Their goal was to reach women in the 22-to-35 age bracket, for whom they had designed the One True Fit line.[2] Lee knew that these women, especially those who had just had children, often were unable to find jeans that fit.[3] Lee also believed that reaching this audience might require supplementing its traditional advertising strategies with a more personal approach.

Based on his experience and recent survey data,[4] Balter believed that his company's proprietary software system, the BzzEngine, and his well-prepared "volunteer brand evangelists" would be an ideal way to supplement Lee's current marketing strategies.[5] He thought that Lee's target audience was ideal for his company's word-of-mouth campaign built on goodwill and honesty.

Armed with his knowledge about word-of-mouth advertising and his belief that women in this target audience liked to share their opinions about products,[6] Balter set out to study the target group's reaction to these jeans. He had three goals. First, he had to determine whether his company could commit to the product. Second, he needed to know whether the One True Fit line lived up to its promises. Third, if it did, he had to show Lee Jeans how his company's system would reach the target audience and add value by generating awareness, delivering credibility, and creating positive buzz about the One True Fit line.

Women want comfortable jeans, and BzzAgent seeks to help Lee Jeans market its One True Fit line.

Photo: © Photodisc Green/Getty Images

Critical Thinking

- In your present workplace or organization, what kinds of reports are you familiar with? What is their purpose and how are they presented?
- Do you think an advertising executive such as Dave Balter, who wants to demonstrate the added value his company can provide, should make his pitch orally or in writing?
- Before funding an expensive advertising campaign, what would most companies require?

http://www.bzzagent.com

CONTINUED ON PAGE 390

case study

learning objective

1

Understanding Report Basics

Reports are common in North American business. In this low-context culture, our values and attitudes seem to prompt us to write reports. We analyze problems, gather and study the facts, and then assess the alternatives. We pride ourselves on being practical and logical as we apply scientific procedures. When we must persuade a client that our services can add value, as Dave Balter of BzzAgent hoped to do, we generally write a report outlining our case.

Management decisions in many organizations are based on information submitted in the form of reports. This chapter examines the functions, patterns, writing style, and formats of typical business reports. It also introduces the report-writing process and discusses methods of collecting, documenting, and illustrating data.

Effective business reports answer questions and solve problems systematically.

Business reports range from informal half-page trip reports to formal 200-page financial forecasts. Reports may be presented orally in front of a group or electronically on a computer screen. Some reports appear as words on paper in the form of memos and letters. Others are primarily numerical data, such as tax reports or profit-and-loss statements. Some provide information only; others analyze and make recommendations. Although reports vary greatly in length, content, form, and formality level, they all have one common purpose: *to answer questions and solve problems.*

Functions

In terms of what they do, most reports fit into two broad categories: informational reports and analytical reports.

Informational reports present data without analysis or recommendations. Analytical reports provide data, analyses, conclusions, and, if requested, recommendations.

Informational Reports. Reports that present data without analysis or recommendations are primarily informational. For such reports, writers collect and organize facts, but they do not analyze the facts for readers. A trip report describing an employee's visit to a trade show, for example, presents information. Other reports that present information without analysis involve routine operations, compliance with regulations, and company policies and procedures.

Analytical Reports. Reports that provide data, analyses, and conclusions are analytical. If requested, writers also supply recommendations. Analytical reports may intend to persuade readers to act or change their beliefs. For example, if you were writing a feasibility report that compares several potential locations for a fast-food restaurant, you might conclude by recommending one site. Your report, an analysis of alternatives and a recommendation, attempts to persuade readers to accept that site.

Organizational Patterns

Like letters and memos, reports may be organized directly or indirectly. The reader's expectations and the content of a report determine its pattern of development, as illustrated in Figure 12.1. In long reports, such as corporate annual reports, some parts may be developed directly whereas other parts are arranged indirectly.

The direct pattern places conclusions and recommendations near the beginning of a report.

Direct Pattern. When the purpose for writing is presented close to the beginning, the organizational pattern is direct. Informational reports, such as the letter report shown in Figure 12.2, are usually arranged directly. They open with an introduction, which is followed by the facts and a summary. In Figure 12.2 the writer explains a legal services plan using a letter report. The report begins with an introduction. The facts, divided into three subtopics and identified by descriptive headings, follow. The report ends with a summary and a complimentary close.

FIGURE 12.1 ***Audience Analysis and Report Organization***

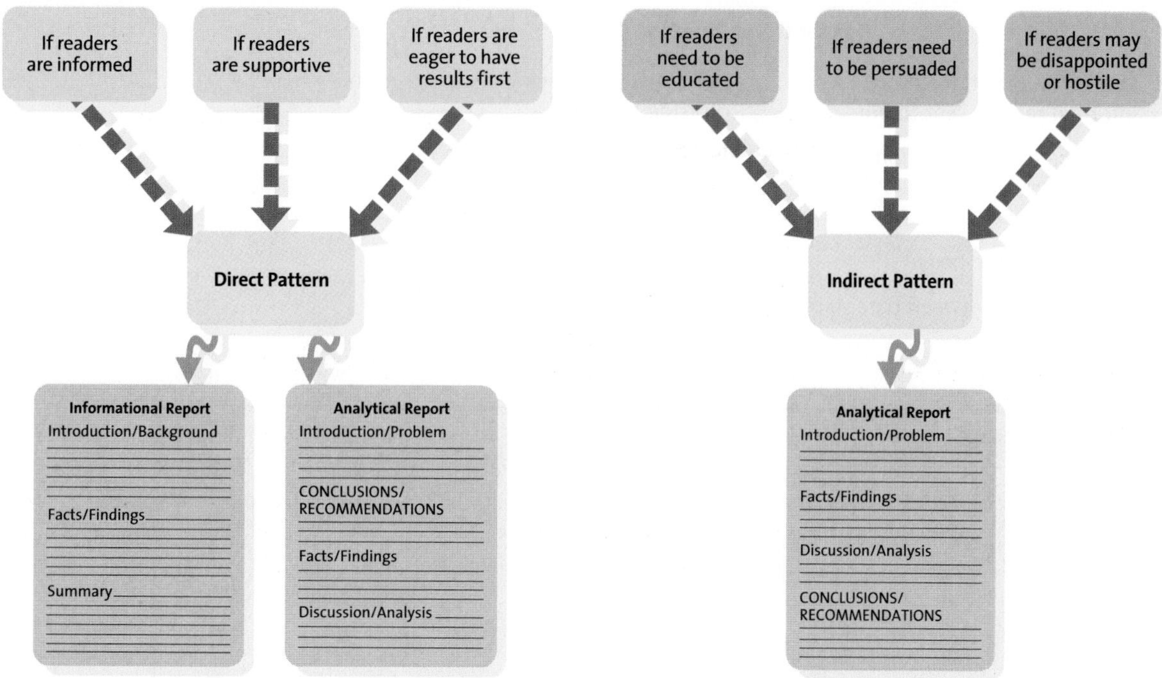

Analytical reports may also be organized directly, especially when readers are supportive of or familiar with the topic. Many busy executives prefer this pattern because it gives them the results of the report immediately. They don't have to spend time wading through the facts, findings, discussion, and analyses to get to the two items they are most interested in—the conclusions and recommendations. Figure 12.3 illustrates such an arrangement. This analytical memo report describes environmental hazards of a property that a realtor has just listed. The realtor is familiar with the investigation and eager to find out the recommendations. Therefore, the memo is organized directly. You should be aware, though, that unless readers are familiar with the topic, they may find the direct pattern confusing. Many readers prefer the indirect pattern because it seems logical and mirrors the way they solve problems.

Indirect Pattern. When the conclusions and recommendations, if requested, appear at the end of the report, the organizational pattern is indirect. Such reports usually begin with an introduction or description of the problem, followed by facts and interpretations from the writer. They end with conclusions and recommendations. This pattern is helpful when readers are unfamiliar with the problem. It's also useful when readers must be persuaded or when they may be disappointed in or hostile toward the report's findings. The writer is more likely to retain the reader's interest by first explaining, justifying, and analyzing the facts and then making recommendations. This pattern also seems most rational to readers because it follows the normal thought process: problem, alternatives (facts), solution.

The indirect pattern is appropriate for analytical reports that seek to persuade or that convey bad news.

Writing Style

Like other business messages, reports can range from informal to formal, depending on their purpose, audience, and setting. Research reports from consultants to their clients tend to be rather formal. Such reports must project an impression of

Reports can be formal or informal depending on the purpose, audience, and setting.

Figure 12.2 ***Informational Report—Letter Format***

Tips for Letter Reports

- Use letter format for short informal reports sent to outsiders.
- Organize the facts section into logical divisions identified by consistent headings.
- Single-space the body.
- Double-space between paragraphs.
- Leave two blank lines above each side heading.
- Create side margins of 1 to 1¼ inches.
- Add a second-page heading, if necessary, consisting of the addressee's name, the date, and the page number.

Center for Consumers of Legal Services

P.O. Box 260
Richmond, VA 23234

(804) 248- 8931
www. cclegalservices.com

Uses letterhead stationery for an informal report addressed to an outsider

September 7, 2006

Ms. Lisa Burgess, Secretary
Lake Austin Homeowners
3902 Oak Hill Drive
Austin, TX 78134

Dear Ms. Burgess:

As executive director of the Center for Consumers of Legal Services, I'm pleased to send you this information describing how your homeowners' association can sponsor a legal services plan for its members. After an introduction with background data, this report will discuss three steps necessary for your group to start its plan.

Presents introduction and facts without analysis or recommendations

Introduction

A legal services plan promotes preventive law by letting members talk to attorneys whenever problems arise. Prompt legal advice often avoids or prevents expensive litigation. Because groups can supply a flow of business to the plan's attorneys, groups can negotiate free consultation, follow-up, and discounts.

Two kinds of plans are commonly available. The first, a free plan, offers free legal consultation along with discounts for services when the participating groups are sufficiently large to generate business for the plan's attorneys. These plans actually act as a substitute for advertising for the attorneys. The second common type is the prepaid plan. Prepaid plans provide more benefits, but members must pay annual fees, usually of $200 or more a year. Over 30 million people are covered by legal services plans today, and a majority belong to free plans.

Since you inquired about a free plan for your homeowners' association, the following information describes how to set up such a program.

Arranges facts of report into section with descriptive headings

Determine the Benefits Your Group Needs

The first step in establishing a free legal services plan is to meet with the members of your group to decide what benefits they want. Typical benefits include the following:

Free consultation. Members may consult a participating attorney—by phone or in the attorney's office—to discuss any matter. The number of consultations is unlimited, provided each is about a separate matter. Consultations are generally limited to 30 minutes, but they include substantive analysis and advice.

Emphasizes benefits in paragraph headings with boldface type

Free document review. Important papers—such as leases, insurance policies, and installment sales contracts—may be reviewed with legal counsel. Members may ask questions and receive an explanation of terms.

Ms. Lisa Burgess Page 2 September 7, 2006

Identifies second and succeeding pages with headings

Discount on additional services. For more complex matters, participating attorneys will charge members 75 percent of the attorney's normal fee. However, some organizations choose to charge a flat fee for commonly needed services.

Select the Attorneys for Your Plan

Groups with geographically concentrated memberships have an advantage in forming legal plans. These groups can limit the number of participating attorneys and yet provide adequate service. Generally, smaller panels of attorneys are advantageous.

Assemble a list of candidates, inviting them to apply. The best way to compare prices is to have candidates submit their fees. Your group can then compare fee schedules and select the lowest bidder, if price is important. Arrange to interview attorneys in their offices.

After selecting an attorney or a panel, sign a contract. The contract should include the reason for the plan, what the attorney agrees to do, what the group agrees to do, how each side can end the contract, and the signatures of both parties. You may also wish to include references to malpractice insurance, assurance that the group will not interfere with the attorney–client relationship, an evaluation form, a grievance procedure, and responsibility for government filings.

Uses parallel side headings for consistency and readability

Publicize the Plan to Your Members

Members won't use a plan if they don't know about it, and a plan will not be successful if it is unused. Publicity must be vocal and ongoing. Announce it in newsletters, meetings, bulletin boards, and flyers.

Persistence is the key. All too frequently, leaders of an organization assume that a single announcement is all that's needed. They expect members to see the value of the plan and remember that it's available. Most organization members, though, are not as involved as the leadership. Therefore, it takes more publicity than the leadership usually expects in order to reach and maintain the desired level of awareness.

Summary

A successful free legal services plan involves designing a program, choosing the attorneys, and publicizing the plan. To learn more about these steps or to order a $25 how-to manual, call me at (804) 355-9901.

Sincerely,

Richard M. Ramos

Richard M. Ramos, Esq.
Executive Director

pas

Includes complimentary close and signature

objectivity, authority, and impartiality. But a report to your boss describing a trip to a conference would probably be informal.

An office worker once called a grammar hot-line service with this problem: "We've just sent a report to our headquarters, and it was returned with this comment, 'Put it in the third person.' What do they mean?" The hot-line experts explained that management apparently wanted a more formal writing style, using third-person constructions (*the company* or *the researcher* instead of *we* and *I*). Figure 12.4, which compares characteristics of formal and informal report-writing styles, can help you decide the writing style that's appropriate for your reports.

FIGURE 12.3 ***Analytical Report—Memo Format***

Tips for Memo Reports

- Use memo format for most short (ten or fewer pages) informal reports within an organization.
- Leave side margins of 1 to 1¼ inches.
- Sign your initials on the *From* line.
- Use an informal, conversational style.
- For direct analytical reports, put recommendations first.
- For indirect analytical reports, put recommendations last.

Atlantic Environmental, Inc.

Interoffice Memo

Applies memo format for short, informal internal report

DATE: March 7, 2006

TO: Kermit Fox, President

FROM: Cynthia M. Rashid, Environmental Engineer CMR

SUBJECT: INVESTIGATION OF MOUNTAIN PARK COMMERCIAL SITE

Uses first paragraph as introduction

For Allegheny Realty, Inc., I've completed a preliminary investigation of its Mountain Park property listing. The following recommendations are based on my physical inspection of the site, official records, and interviews with officials and persons knowledgeable about the site.

Presents recommendations first (direct pattern) because reader is supportive and familiar with topic

Recommendations

To reduce its potential environmental liability, Allegheny Realty should take the following steps in regard to its Mountain Park listing:

- Conduct an immediate asbestos survey at the site, including inspection of ceiling insulation material, floor tiles, and insulation around a gas-fired heater vent pipe at 2539 Mountain View Drive.
- Prepare an environmental audit of the generators of hazardous waste currently operating at the site, including Mountain Technology.
- Obtain lids for the dumpsters situated in the parking areas and ensure that the lids are kept closed.

Combines findings and analyses in short report

Findings and Analyses

My preliminary assessment of the site and its immediate vicinity revealed rooms with damaged floor tiles on the first and second floors of 2539 Mountain View Drive. Apparently, in recent remodeling efforts, these tiles had been cracked and broken. Examination of the ceiling and attic revealed further possible contamination from asbestos. The insulation for the hot-water tank was in poor condition.

Located on the property is Mountain Technology, a possible hazardous waste generator. Although I could not examine its interior, this company has the potential for producing hazardous material contamination.

In the parking area large dumpsters collect trash and debris from several businesses. These dumpsters were uncovered, thus posing a risk to the general public.

In view of the construction date of the structures on this property, asbestos-containing building materials might be present. Moreover, this property is located in an industrial part of the city, further prompting my recommendation for a thorough investigation. Allegheny Realty can act immediately to eliminate one environmental concern: covering the dumpsters in the parking area.

FIGURE 12.4 ***Report-Writing Styles***

	Formal Writing Style	Informal Writing Style
Use	Theses	Short, routine reports
	Research studies	Reports for familiar audiences
	Controversial or complex reports (especially to outsiders)	Noncontroversial reports Most reports for company insiders
Effect	Impression of objectivity, accuracy, professionalism, fairness	Feeling of warmth, personal involvement, closeness
	Distance created between writer and reader	
Characteristics	Absence of first-person pronouns; use of third-person (*the researcher, the writer*)	Use of first-person pronouns (*I, we, me, my, us, our*)
	Absence of contractions (*can't, don't*)	Use of contractions
	Use of passive-voice verbs (*the study was conducted*)	Emphasis on active-voice verbs (*I conducted the study*)
	Complex sentences; long words	Shorter sentences; familiar words
	Absence of humor and figures of speech	Occasional use of humor, metaphors
	Reduced use of colorful adjectives and adverbs	Occasional use of colorful speech
	Elimination of "editorializing" (author's opinions, perceptions)	Acceptance of author's opinions and ideas

Formats

The format of a report is governed by its length, topic, audience, and purpose. After considering these elements, you'll probably choose from among the following four formats.

A report's format depends on its length, audience, topic, and purpose.

Letter Format. Use letter format for short (usually eight or fewer pages) informal reports addressed outside an organization. Prepared on office stationery, a letter report contains a date, inside address, salutation, and complimentary close, as shown in Figure 12.2. Although they may carry information similar to that found in correspondence, letter reports usually are longer and show more careful organization than most letters. They also include headings.

Memo Format. For short informal reports that stay within organizations, the memo format is appropriate. Memo reports begin with essential background information, using standard headings: *Date, To, From,* and *Subject,* as shown in Figure 12.3. Like letter reports, memo reports differ from regular memos in length, use of headings, and deliberate organization.

Manuscript Format. For longer, more formal reports, use the manuscript format. These reports are usually printed on plain paper instead of letterhead stationery or memo forms. They begin with a title followed by systematically displayed headings and subheadings. You will see examples of proposals and formal reports using the manuscript format in Chapter 14.

Printed Forms. Prepared forms are often used for repetitive data, such as monthly sales reports, performance appraisals, merchandise inventories, and personnel and financial reports. Standardized headings on these forms save time for the writer. Preprinted forms also make similar information easy to locate and ensure that all necessary information is provided.

learning objective

2

Applying Guffey's 3-x-3 Writing Process to Reports

Because business reports are systematic attempts to answer questions and solve problems, the best reports are developed methodically. In earlier chapters Guffey's 3-x-3 writing process was helpful in guiding short projects such as e-mails, memos, and letters. That same process is even more necessary in helping you prepare longer projects such as reports and proposals. Let's channel the writing process into seven specific steps:

The best reports grow out of a seven-step process beginning with analysis and ending with proofreading and evaluation.

Step 1: Analyze the problem and purpose.

Step 2: Anticipate the audience and issues.

Step 3: Prepare a work plan.

Step 4: Implement your research strategy.

Step 5: Organize, analyze, interpret, and illustrate the data.

Step 6: Compose the first draft.

Step 7: Revise, proofread, and evaluate.

Managers make major decisions, such as whether to lease vehicles for sales reps, based on reports. The report writer begins by analyzing the problem, determining the purpose of the report, and conducting primary research, such as inspecting possible lease vehicles.

Photo: © Thinkstock/Getty Images

How much time you spend on each step depends on your report task. A short informational report on a familiar topic might require a brief work plan, little research, and no data analysis. A complex analytical report, on the other hand, might demand a comprehensive work plan, extensive research, and careful data analysis. In this section we will consider the first three steps in the process—analyzing the problem and purpose, anticipating the audience and issues, and preparing a work plan.

To illustrate the planning stages of a report, we'll watch Diane Camas develop a report she's preparing for her boss, Mike Rivers, at Mycon Pharmaceutical Laboratories. Mike asked Diane to investigate the problem of transportation for sales representatives. Currently, some Mycon reps visit customers (mostly doctors and hospitals) using company-leased cars. A few reps drive their own cars, receiving reimbursements for use. In three months Mycon's leasing agreement for 14 cars expires, and Mike is considering a major change. Diane's task is to investigate the choices and report her findings to Mike.

Analyzing the Problem and Purpose

Before beginning a report, identify the problem to be solved in a clear statement.

The first step in writing a report is understanding the problem or assignment clearly. For complex reports it's wise to prepare a written problem statement. In analyzing her report task, Diane had many questions: Is the problem that Mycon is spending too much money on leased cars? Does Mycon wish to invest in owning a fleet of cars? Is Mike unhappy with the paperwork involved in reimbursing sales reps when they use their own cars? Does he suspect that reps are submitting inflated mileage figures? Before starting research for the report, Diane talked with Mike to define the problem. She learned several dimensions of the situation and wrote the following statement to clarify the problem—both for herself and for Mike.

Problem Statement: The leases on all company cars will be expiring in three months. Mycon must decide whether to renew them or develop a new policy regarding transportation for sales reps. Expenses and paperwork for employee-owned cars seem excessive.

Diane further defined the problem by writing a specific question that she would try to answer in her report:

Problem Question: What plan should Mycon follow in providing transportation for its sales reps?

Now Diane was ready to concentrate on the purpose of the report. Again, she had questions: Exactly what did Mike expect? Did he want a comparison of costs for buying and leasing cars? Should she conduct research to pinpoint exact reimbursement costs when employees drive their own cars? Did he want her to do all the legwork, present her findings in a report, and let him make a decision? Or did he want her to evaluate the choices and recommend a course of action? After talking with Mike, Diane was ready to write a simple purpose statement for this assignment.

Simple Statement of Purpose: To recommend a plan that provides sales reps with cars to be used in their calls.

A simple purpose statement defines the focus of a report.

Preparing a written purpose statement is a good idea because it defines the focus of a report and provides a standard that keeps the project on target. In writing useful purpose statements, choose action verbs telling what you intend to do: *analyze, choose, investigate, compare, justify, evaluate, explain, establish, determine,* and so on. Notice that Diane's statement begins with the action verb *recommend.*

Some reports require only a simple statement of purpose: to investigate expanded teller hours, to select a manager from among four candidates, to describe the position of accounts supervisor. Many assignments, though, demand additional focus to guide the project. An expanded statement of purpose considers three additional factors: scope, significance, and limitations.

Setting boundaries on a project helps determine its scope.

Scope. What issues or elements will be investigated? To determine the scope, Diane brainstormed with Mike and others to pin down her task. She learned that Mycon currently had enough capital to consider purchasing a fleet of cars outright. Mike also told her that employee satisfaction was almost as important as cost effectiveness. Moreover, he disclosed his suspicion that employee-owned cars were costing Mycon more than leased cars. Diane had many issues to sort out in setting the boundaries of her report.

Significance. Why is the topic worth investigating at this time? Some topics, after initial examination, turn out to be less important than originally thought. Others involve problems that cannot be solved, making a study useless. For Diane and Mike the problem had significance because Mycon's leasing agreement would expire shortly and decisions had to be made about a new policy for transportation of sales reps.

Limitations. What conditions affect the generalizability and utility of a report's findings? For this report Diane realized that her conclusions and recommendations might apply only to reps in her Kansas City sales district. Her findings would probably not be reliable for reps in Seattle, Phoenix, or Atlanta. Another limitation for Diane was time. She had to complete the report in four weeks, thus restricting the thoroughness of her research.

Diane decided to expand her statement of purpose to define the scope, significance, and limitations of the report.

An expanded purpose statement considers scope, significance, and limitations.

Expanded Statement of Purpose: The purpose of this report is to recommend a plan that provides sales reps with cars to be used in their calls. The report will compare costs for three plans: outright ownership, leasing, and compensation for employee-owned cars. It will also measure employee reaction to each plan. The report is significant because Mycon's current leasing agreement expires April 1 and an improved plan could reduce costs and paperwork. The study is limited to costs for sales reps in the Kansas City district.

After preparing a statement of purpose, Diane checked it with Mike Rivers to be sure she was on target.

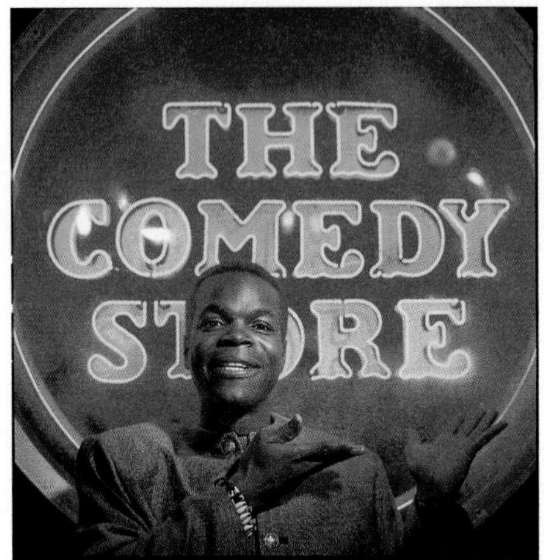

A. J. Jamal, who hosted the Comedy Channel TV show Comic Justice, *attributes his successful career to basic problem-solving skills he learned while working for IBM. "Everybody wonders why I am so businesslike with comedy, and it dawned on me that doing comedy is like troubleshooting a technical problem." Jamal explains that IBM taught its employees to break down a big problem into smaller components and look for solutions to each one. This process, called factoring, is also an important first step in outlining the major issues in any report.*

Anticipating the Audience and Issues

After defining the purpose of a report, a writer must think carefully about who will read it. Concentrating solely on a primary reader is a major mistake. Although one individual may have solicited the report, others within the organization may eventually read it, including upper management and people in other departments. A report to an outside client may first be read by someone who is familiar with the problem and then be distributed to others less familiar with the topic. Moreover, candid statements to one audience may be offensive to another audience. Diane could make a major blunder, for instance, if she mentioned Mike's suspicion that sales reps were padding their mileage statements. If the report were made public—as it probably would be to explain a new policy—the sales reps could feel insulted that their integrity was questioned.

As Diane considered her primary and secondary readers, she asked herself these questions:

- *What do my readers need to know about this topic?*
- *What do they already know?*
- *What is their educational level?*
- *How will they react to this information?*
- *Which sources will they trust?*
- *How can I make this information readable, believable, and memorable?*

Answers to these questions help writers determine how much background material to include, how much detail to add, whether to include jargon, what method of organization and presentation to follow, and what tone to use.

In the planning stages a report writer must also break the major investigative problem into subproblems. This process, sometimes called factoring, identifies issues to be investigated or possible solutions to the main problem. In this case Mycon must figure out the best way to transport sales reps. Each possible "solution" or issue that Diane considers becomes a factor or subproblem to be investigated. Diane came up with three tentative solutions to provide transportation to sales reps: (1) purchase cars outright, (2) lease cars, or (3) compensate employees for using their own cars. These three factors form the outline of Diane's study.

Diane continued to factor these main points into the following subproblems for investigation:

Photo: © Eric Millette

What plan should Mycon use to transport its sales reps?

I. Should Mycon purchase cars outright?
   A. How much capital would be required?
   B. How much would it cost to insure, operate, and maintain company-owned cars?
   C. Do employees prefer using company-owned cars?
II. Should Mycon lease cars?
   A. What is the best lease price available?
   B. How much would it cost to insure, operate, and maintain leased cars?
   C. Do employees prefer using leased cars?
III. Should Mycon compensate employees for using their own cars?
   A. How much has it cost in the past to operate employee-owned cars?
   B. How much paperwork is involved in reporting expenses?
   C. Do employees prefer being compensated for using their own cars?

An outline in question form shows the factoring of a problem and highlights possible solutions.

Each subproblem would probably be further factored into additional subproblems. These issues may be phrased as questions, as Diane's are, or as statements. In factoring a complex problem, prepare an outline showing the initial problem and its breakdown into subproblems. Make sure your divisions are consistent (don't mix issues), exclusive (don't overlap categories), and complete (don't skip significant issues).

Preparing a Work Plan

A good work plan provides an overview of a project: resources, priorities, course of action, and schedule.

After analyzing the problem, anticipating the audience, and factoring the problem, you're ready to prepare a work plan. A good work plan includes the following:

- Statement of the problem (based on key background/contextual information)
- Statement of the purpose including scope, significance, and limitations
- Research strategy including a description of potential sources and methods of collecting data
- Tentative outline that factors the problem into manageable chunks
- Work schedule

spotlight *on communicators*

At Phelps County Bank in Rolla, Missouri, loan processor Peggy Laun helped implement a system of "upward evaluation." She saw a problem, conducted research, collected data, evaluated the results, and then proposed a system that enables employees to review their supervisors. Good research usually begins with a work plan designed to solve a specific problem.

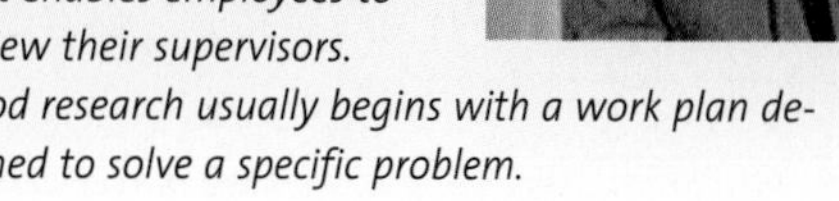

Preparing a plan encourages you to evaluate your resources, set priorities, outline a course of action, and establish a time schedule. Having a plan keeps you on schedule and provides management a means of measuring your progress.

A work plan gives a complete picture of a project. Because the usefulness and quality of any report rest primarily on its data, you'll want to develop a clear research strategy, which includes allocating plenty of time to locate sources of information. For firsthand information you might interview people, prepare a survey, or even conduct a scientific experiment. For secondary information you'll probably search printed materials such as books and magazines as well as electronic materials on the Internet. Your work plan describes how you expect to generate or collect data. Because data collection is a major part of report writing, the next section of this chapter treats the topic more fully.

Figure 12.5 shows a complete work plan for a proposal that Dave Balter will present to Lee Jeans. This work plan is particularly useful because it outlines the

Photo: © Mark Katzman/Ferguson & Kutzman

Process in Progress

BzzAgent Revisited

COMPANIES HAVE LONG understood that word of mouth is a powerful force, but few companies have figured out how to use it effectively. Dave Balter has an answer: turn his network of up to 50,000 agents into "volunteer brand evangelists." However, to achieve the kind of commitment necessary to influence consumer attitudes and affect the distribution cycle positively, Balter believes that his agents, while passionate, must also be honest. The literature the company sends its agents explains that "the personal nature of a BzzAgent campaign requires honesty in order for agents to maintain credibility."[7]

Thus, for the Lee campaign, one of Balter's first tasks was to determine whether he, his marketing team, and his network of BzzAgents believed in the product. He began by asking Lee to send several pairs of jeans to his Boston headquarters. These jeans were shown to women in the company to learn whether this product would fit within their community. In addition, he began polling his network of agents to learn about the word on the street. Only after Balter and his staff recognized the potential for using "volunteer brand evangelism" could he and his company begin work.

In the case of Lee's One True Fit jeans, the response from his staff and agents was extremely favorable, but the campaign still faced obstacles. The marketing team had to take Lee's marketing messages and materials, which focused on sexy models and the tagline of "find your one true fit," and transition them into actual communications that people would generate. This work occurs in what Balter calls a "BzzSession," in which the team breaks down the marketing materials, asking key questions such as, *Who are the targets? What types of people should we talk to about the product?* and *Why would people think this product works?* Balter calls the answers to these questions "BzzHooks" or "BzzFacts." In this campaign, for example, two such BzzFacts were (1) the jeans do not gap in the back when women sit and (2) the leather patch has been eliminated. Following the BzzSession for Lee, Balter and his staff began to put together a proposal that included the segment of agents he recommended (in this case about 1,000), a suggested trial of the product, a reward structure, and key communication components featuring what he calls BzzTargets, BzzActivities, BzzStories, and BzzFacts.

Critical Thinking

- To secure management backing from Lee, should Dave Balter and his team choose an informational or analytical approach to the proposal? Why?
- Should Balter's proposal be developed directly or indirectly? Why? Should it be written formally or informally?
- What are some of the questions that Balter and his team should ask themselves about their audience before making their presentation or writing their proposal?

CONTINUED ON PAGE 414

case study

issues to be investigated. Notice that considerable thought and discussion and even some preliminary research are necessary to be able to develop a useful work plan.

Although this tentative outline guides investigation, it does not determine the content or order of the final report. You may, for example, study five possible solutions to a problem. If two prove to be useless, your report may discuss only the three winners. Moreover, you will organize the report to accomplish your goal and satisfy the audience. Remember that a busy executive who is familiar with a topic may prefer to read the conclusions and recommendations before a discussion of the findings. If someone authorizes the report, be sure to review the work plan with that individual (your manager, client, or professor, for example) before proceeding with the project.

FIGURE 12.5 ***Work Plan for a Formal Report***

Tips for Preparing a Work Plan

- Start early; allow plenty of time for brainstorming and preliminary research.
- Describe the problem motivating the report.
- Write a purpose statement that includes the report's scope, significance, and limitations.
- Describe the research strategy including data collection sources and methods.
- Divide the major problem into subproblems stated as questions to be answered.
- Develop a realistic work schedule citing dates for completion of major tasks.
- Review the work plan with whoever authorized the report.

Statement of Problem

Many women between the ages of 22 and 35 have trouble finding jeans that fit. Lee Jeans hopes to remedy that situation with its One True Fit line. We want to demonstrate to Lee that we can create a word-of-mouth campaign that will help it reach its target audience.

Defines purpose, scope, limits, and significance of report

Statement of Purpose

The purpose of this report is to secure an advertising contract from Lee Jeans. We will examine published accounts about the jeans industry and Lee Jeans in particular. In addition, we will examine published results of Lee's current marketing strategy. We will conduct focus groups of women in our company to generate campaign strategies for our pilot study of 100 BzzAgents. The report will persuade Lee Jeans that word-of-mouth advertising is an effective strategy to reach women in this demographic group and that BzzAgent is the right company to hire. The report is significant because an advertising contract with Lee Jeans would help our company grow significantly in size and stature.

Describes primary and secondary data

Research Strategy (Sources and Methods of Data Collection)

We will gather information about Lee Jeans and the product line by examining published marketing data and conducting focus group surveys of our employees. In addition, we will gather data about the added value of word-of-mouth advertising by examining published accounts and interpreting data from previous marketing campaigns, particularly those with similar age groups. Finally, we will conduct a pilot study of 100 BzzAgents in the target demographic.

Factors problem into manageable chunks

Tentative Outline

I. How effectively has Lee Jeans marketed to the target population (women, ages 22 to 35)?
   A. Historically, who has typically bought Lee Jeans products? How often? Where?
   B. How effective are the current marketing strategies for the One True Fit line?

II. Is this product a good fit for our marketing strategy and our company?
   A. What do our staff members and our sample survey of BzzAgents say about this product?
   B. How well does our pool of BzzAgents correspond to the target demography in terms of age and geographic distribution?

III. Why should Lee Jeans engage BzzAgent to advertise its One True Fit line?
   A. What are the benefits of word of mouth in general and for this demographic in particular?
   B. What previous campaigns have we engaged in that demonstrate our company's credibility?
   C. What are our marketing strategies, and how well did they work in the pilot study?

Estimates time needed to complete report tasks

Work Schedule

Investigate Lee Jeans and the One True Fit line's current marketing strategy	July 15–25
Test product using focus groups	July 15–22
Create campaign materials for BzzAgents	July 18–31
Run a pilot test with a selected pool of 100 BzzAgents	August 1–21
Evaluate and interpret findings	August 22–25
Compose draft of report	August 26–28
Revise draft	August 28–30
Submit final report	September 1

learning objective

3

Gathering Information From Secondary Sources

A report is only as good as its foundation, which is based on data.

One of the most important steps in the process of writing a report is that of gathering information (research). As the philosopher Goethe once said, "The greater part of all mischief in the world arises from the fact that men do not sufficiently understand their own aims. They have undertaken to build a tower, and spend no more labor on the foundation than would be necessary to erect a hut." Think of your report as a tower. Because a report is only as good as its foundation—the questions you ask and the data you gather to answer those questions—the remainder of this chapter describes the foundational work of finding, documenting, and illustrating data.

As you analyze a report's purpose and audience and prepare your research strategy, you'll identify and assess the data you need to support your argument or explain your topic. As you do, you'll answer questions about your objectives and audience: Will the audience need a lot of background or contextual information? Will they value or trust statistics, case studies, or expert opinions? Will they want to see data from interviews or surveys? Will summaries of focus groups be useful? Should you rely on organizational data? Figure 12.6 lists five forms of data and provides questions to guide you in making your research accurate and productive.

Primary data come from firsthand experience and observation; secondary data, from reading.

Data fall into two broad categories, primary and secondary. Primary data result from firsthand experience and observation. Secondary data come from reading what others have experienced and observed. Coca-Cola and Pepsi-Cola, for example, produce primary data when they stage taste tests and record the reactions of consumers. These same sets of data become secondary after they have been published and, let's say, a newspaper reporter uses them in an article about soft drinks. Secondary data are easier and cheaper to develop than primary data, which might involve interviewing large groups or sending out questionnaires.

We're going to discuss secondary data first because that's where nearly every research project should begin. Often, something has already been written about your topic. Reviewing secondary sources can save time and effort and prevent you from "reinventing the wheel." Most secondary material is available either in print or electronically.

Print Resources

Print sources are still the most visible part of libraries.

Although we're seeing a steady movement away from print to electronic data, print sources are still the most visible part of most libraries. Much information is available only in print, and you may want to use some of the following print resources.

By the way, if you are an infrequent library user, begin your research by talking with a reference librarian about your project. These librarians won't do your research for you, but they will steer you in the right direction. And they are very accommodating. Several years ago a *Wall Street Journal* poll revealed that librarians are perceived as among the friendliest, most approachable people in the working world. Many librarians help you understand their computer, cataloging, and retrieval systems by providing advice, brochures, handouts, and workshops.

Books provide historical, in-depth data.

Books. Although quickly outdated, books provide excellent historical, in-depth data on subjects. Books can be located through print or online listings.

- **Card catalogs.** Some libraries still maintain card catalogs with all books indexed on 3-by-5 cards alphabetized by author, title, or subject.
- **Online catalogs.** Most libraries today have computerized their card catalogs. Some systems are fully automated, thus allowing users to learn not only whether a book is located in the library but also whether it is currently available.

FIGURE 12.6 ***Gathering and Selecting Report Data***

Form of Data	Questions to Ask
Background or historical	How much do my readers know about the problem? Has this topic/issue been investigated before? Are those sources current, relevant, and/or credible? Will I need to add to the available data?
Statistical	What or who is the source? How recent are the data? How were the figures derived? Will these data be useful in this form?
Expert opinion	Who are the experts? What are their biases? Are their opinions in print? Are they available for interviewing? Do we have in-house experts?
Individual or group opinion	Whose opinion(s) would the readers value? Have surveys or interviews been conducted on this topic? If not, do questionnaires or surveys exist that I can modify and/or use? Would focus groups provide useful information?
Organizational	What are the proper channels for obtaining in-house data? Are permissions required? How can I learn about public and private companies?

Periodicals. Magazines, pamphlets, and journals are called *periodicals* because of their recurrent or periodic publication. Journals are compilations of scholarly articles. Articles in journals and other periodicals will be extremely useful because they are concise, limited in scope, current, and can supplement information in books.

- **Print indexes.** *The Readers' Guide to Periodical Literature* is a valuable index of general-interest magazine article titles. It includes such magazines as *Time, Newsweek, The New Yorker,* and *U.S. News & World Report.* More useful to business writers, though, will be the titles of articles appearing in business and industrial magazines (such as *Forbes, Fortune,* and *Business Week*). For an index of these publications, consult the *Business Periodicals Index.*

- **Web-based bibliographic and CD-ROM indexes.** Automated indexes similar to the print indexes just described are stored in online and CD-ROM databases. Many libraries now provide such bibliographic databases for computer-aided location of references and abstracts from magazines, journals, and newspapers, such as *The New York Times.* When using Web-based online or CD-ROM indexes, follow the on-screen instructions or ask for assistance from a librarian. It's a good idea to begin with a subject search because it generally turns up more relevant citations than keyword searches (especially when searching for names of people or companies). Once you locate usable references, print a copy of your findings and then check the shelf listings to see whether the publications are available.

Exploration of secondary data includes searching periodicals both in print and electronic forms.

Electronic Databases

As a writer of business reports today, you will probably begin your secondary research with electronic resources. Although some databases are still presented on CD-ROMs, information is increasingly available in online databases. They have become the staple of secondary research. Most writers turn to them first because they are fast and easy to use. This means that you can conduct detailed searches without ever leaving your office, home, or dorm room.

Commercial databases offer articles, reports, and other information online.

A database is a collection of information stored electronically so that it is accessible by computer and is digitally searchable. Databases provide both bibliographic (titles of documents and brief abstracts) and full-text documents. Most researchers today, however, prefer full-text documents. Various databases contain a rich array of magazine, newspaper, and journal articles, as well as newsletters, business reports, company profiles, government data, reviews, and directories. Provided with this textbook is access to InfoTrac, a Web-centered database that is growing rapidly. At this writing, it offers nearly 17 million magazine and journal articles from such publications as *Time, The New York Times*, and *The Wall Street Journal.* Web-based documents are enriched with charts, graphs, bold and italic fonts, color, and pictures. Other well-known databases are Ingenta, ABI/Inform, and LexisNexis.

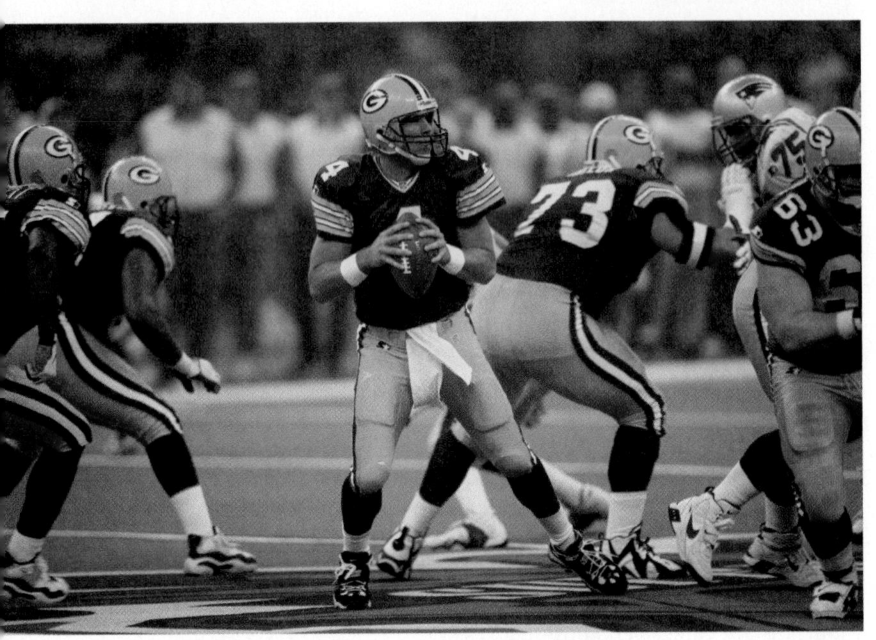

Investors in sports teams, equipment, broadcasting, sponsorship, and marketing require a steady stream of information, much of which comes from electronic databases. For example, the Sports Business Research Network offers a fee-based electronic database with information gathered from various sports governing bodies, magazines, newsletters, and the government. Sports investors and product developers use this electronic database to study leagues and teams, operating results, legal issues, and trends in major market segments, such as youth sports, women's sports, and extreme sports.

Photo: © Wally McNamee/CORBIS

Developing a search strategy and narrowing your search can save time. As you develop your strategy, think about the time frame for your search, the language of publication, and the types of materials you will need. One of the advantages of databases is the ability to focus a search easily. For example, if you were researching the tech bubble that occurred in the late 1990s and wanted to look at articles published between 1995 and 2000, most search engines have features available that enable you to limit your search to that time period. In addition, don't constrain yourself to English language articles only; some Web sites offer translation services, and some of these services are free.

Although well stocked and well organized, specialized commercial databases are indeed expensive to use. Many also involve steep learning curves. While learning how to select *keywords* (or *descriptors*) and how to explore the database, you can run up quite a bill.

The World Wide Web

The Web offers trillions of pages of information.

With nearly two thirds of Americans online[8] and literally trillions of pages of information available on the World Wide Web, odds are that if you have a question, an answer exists online. To a business researcher, the Web offers a wide range of organizational and commercial information. You can expect to find such items as product and service facts, public relations material, mission statements, staff directories, press releases, current company news, government information, selected article reprints, collaborative scientific project reports, and employment information.

Although a wealth of information is available, finding exactly what you need can be frustrating and time-consuming. The constantly changing contents of the Web and its lack of organization make it more problematic for research than searching commercial databases, such as InfoTrac. Moreover, Web content is uneven, and often the quality is questionable. The problem of gathering information is complicated by the fact that the total amount of information on the Web grows daily at the rate of over 7 million pages.[9] In addition, what is now being called the "deep" or "invisible" Web is 400 to 500 times larger than that of the "surface" Web, which is the part of the Web indexed by the most familiar search tools, such as Google.[10] Thus, to succeed in your search for information and answers, you need to understand the search tools. You also need to understand how to evaluate the information you find.

Search Tools. Finding what you are looking for on the Web is hopeless without powerful, specialized search tools, such as Google, AskJeeves, and Yahoo! These search tools can be divided into three types: subject directories, search engines, and search engine partners. Early in the history of the Internet, search tools usually were classified in only one category. Today, larger tools such as Yahoo! are actually search engines and subject directories combined. Subject directories fall into two categories—commercial ones (e.g., Yahoo!) and academic ones (e.g., Infomine). Organized into subject categories, these directories contain a collection of links to Internet resources submitted by site creators or evaluators. The best are excellent; the worst can be misleading or out-of-date.

Search tools such as Google, Yahoo!, and AskJeeves help you locate specific Web sites and information.

Search engines and search engine partners, sometimes referred to as second-generation search tools, are gaining popularity and becoming more sophisticated. Search engines such as Google use automated software "spiders" that crawl through the Web at regular intervals to collect and index the information from each location visited. Search engine partners, such as AskJeeves, use natural language processing technology to enable you to ask questions to gather information. Both tools will help you search for specific information.

Even though search engines such as Google boast about the numbers of items they have indexed (e.g., close to 6 billion),[11] no single search engine or directory can come close to indexing all of the pages on the Internet. In fact, according to the NEC Research Institute, these engines index less than 16 percent of the surface Web, or what we commonly call the World Wide Web, and only about 0.03 percent of the total pages available on the surface and invisible Webs combined.[12]

No search engine or directory indexes all Web pages.

The invisible Web is considerably different from the surface Web. Some researchers claim that it has 500 times more data than the surface Web.[13] Much of that information is dynamic and changing constantly (e.g., data in job banks, flight information, geographical and company information), and some is accessible only through paid subscription sites such as Hoover's. Other information such as that contained in many government databases is free, but often it too is not easily accessed. To help you search for data on both the visible and invisible Webs, consider using the search tools listed in Figure 12.7.

Internet Search Tips and Techniques. To conduct a thorough search for the information you need, build a (re)search strategy by understanding the tools available.

- **Use two or three search tools.** Begin by conducting a topic search. Use a subject directory such as Yahoo! or the UK's BUBL link at **http://bubl.ac.uk/link/**. Once you have narrowed your topic, switch to a search engine or search engine partner.
- **Know your search tool.** When connecting to a search service for the first time, always read the description of its service, including its FAQs (Frequently Asked

Figure 12.7 ***Visible and Invisible Web Search Tools***

Visible Web

Search Engines	**Size and Type**	**Key Features**	**Percent of U.S. Searches**
Google <www.google.com>	Nearly 6 billion pages—over 4 billion fully indexed	Relevance ranking Advanced search options	35%
Yahoo! Search <search.yahoo.com>	Over 3 billion pages fully indexed	Relevance ranking Advanced search options (includes options for different languages)	28%
MSN Search <search.msn.com>	Over 3 billion pages fully indexed	Advanced search options (including international search sites)	15%
Teoma <www.teoma.com>	Over 1 billion pages fully indexed and 1 billion partially indexed	Subject-specific rankings Advanced search options (ten languages) "Refine" feature—suggests topics to explore after initial search	3.1%
AskJeeves <www.ask.com>	Over 1 billion pages fully indexed and 1 billion partially indexed	Natural language questions Relies on Teoma.com's technology Binoculars tool (preview search results)	3.1%
Infospace <www.infospace.com>	N/A; relies on other search engines for data	Metasearch technology: searches Google, FAST, Yahoo!, About, AskJeeves, FindWhat, LookSmart, Inktomi	1.6%
Vivisimo <www.vivisimo.com>	Slightly less than 1 billion pages indexed	Metasearch function clusters results into categories Advanced search options and help	Below 1%
LookSmart <search.looksmart.com>	Over 2.3 billion pages indexed	Primarily a human-compiled directory Articles tab provides access to thousands of periodicals Uses textual analysis of hyperlinks, Web page popularity, and user feedback	Below 1%
HotBot <www.hotbot.com>	N/A; relies on other search engines for data	Quick check of three major search engine databases (Google, Yahoo!, AskJeeves/Teoma) Advanced search options and help	Below 1%
Open Directory Project <http://dmoz.org>	Over 3 billion pages indexed	Comprehensive human-edited directory (59,000+ editors)	Below 1%

Invisible or Deep Web

The Invisible Web Directory <http://www.invisible-web.net/>	Directory of over 1,000 high-quality resources Focuses primarily on information sites that are free Category and subcategory options
InfoMine <http://infomine.ucr.edu>	Directory of nearly 120,000 sites, grouped into nine indexed and annotated categories for scholarly research
About <http://www.about.com>	Directory that organizes content from over 1 million sites with commentary from chosen experts
Librarian's Index to the Internet <http://lii.org/>	Directory of 14,000 well-chosen and annotated sites of use for academic research
Profusion <http://www.profusion.com>	Updated, metasearch engine that offers access to subject categories 21+ categories; option to create new categories
CompletePlanet <http://www.completeplanet.com/>	Directory with over 70,000 searchable databases and specialty search engines

Questions), Help, and How to Search sections. Often there are special features (e.g., the News category on AskJeeves) that can speed up the search process.

- **Understand case sensitivity.** Generally use lowercase for your searches, unless you are searching for a term that is usually written in upper- and lowercase, such as a person's name.

Web research is often time-consuming and frustrating unless you know special techniques.

- **Use nouns as search words and up to six to eight words in a query.** The right key words—and more of them—can narrow the search effectively.
- **Combine keywords into phrases.** Phrases, marked by the use of quotation marks (e.g., "business ethics"), will limit results to specific matches.
- **Omit articles and prepositions.** Known as "stop words," articles and prepositions do not add value to a search. Instead of *request for proposal,* use *proposal request.*
- **Use wild cards.** Most search engines support wild cards, such as asterisks. For example, the search term *cent** will retrieve *cents,* while *cent*** will retrieve both *center* and *centre.*
- **Learn basic Boolean search strategies.** You can save yourself a lot of time and frustration by narrowing your search with the following Boolean operators:

AND	Identifies only documents containing all of the specified words: **employee AND productivity AND morale**
OR	Identifies documents containing at least one of the specified words: **employee OR productivity OR morale**
NOT	Excludes documents containing the specified word: **employee productivity NOT morale**
NEAR	Finds documents containing target words or phrases within a specified distance, for instance, within 10 words: **employee NEAR productivity**

Whether in the library, at home, or at work, you can save yourself countless hours of fruitless and random exploring by mastering techniques such as Boolean searching.

- **Bookmark the best.** To keep track of your favorite Internet sites, save them as bookmarks or favorites.
- **Keep trying.** If a search produces no results, check your spelling. If you are using Boolean operators, check the syntax of your queries. Try synonyms and variations on words. Try to be less specific in your search term. If your search produces too many hits, try to be more specific. Think of words that uniquely identify what you're looking for. Use as many relevant keywords as possible.
- **Repeat your search a week later.** For the best results, return to your search a couple of days or a week later. The same keywords will probably produce additional results. That's because millions of new pages are being added to the Web every day.

Search engines vary in their ability to retrieve data. Learn about their advanced features, and then practice using them.

Remember, subject directories and search engines vary in their contents, features, selectivity, accuracy, and retrieval technologies. Only through clever cybersearching can you uncover the jewels hidden in the Internet.

tech talk

Managing Your Electronic Research Data Like a Pro

In amassing electronic data, you can easily lose track of Web sites and articles you quoted. To document Web data that may change as well as to manage all of your electronic data, you need a specific plan for saving sources. At the very least, you will want to create a *working bibliography* in which you record the URL of each electronic source and its access date. Here are techniques that can help you build your bibliography as well as manage your electronic data like a pro:

- **Saving sources to disk** has advantages, including being able to open the document in a browser even if you don't have access to the Internet. More important, saving sources to disk ensures that you will have access to information that may or may not be available later. Using either the *File* and *Save As* or the *File* and *Save Page As* menu command in your browser, you will be able to store the information permanently. Saving images and other kinds of media can be accomplished with your mouse by either right-clicking or command-clicking on the item, followed by a command such as *Save Picture As* or *Save Image As* from a pop-up window.
- **Copying and pasting** information you find on the Web into word processing documents is an easy way to save and store it. Remember to also copy and paste the URL into the file as well, and record the URL in your working bibliography.
- **Printing** pages is a handy way to gather and store information. Doing so enables you to have copies of important data that you can annotate or highlight. Make sure the URL prints with the document (usually on the bottom of the page). If not, write it on the page.
- **Favorites lists and bookmarks** are options within browsers to enable users to record and store the URLs for important sources. The key to using these options is learning to create folders with names that are relevant and to use names for bookmarks that make sense and are not redundant. Pay attention or the browser will provide the information for you, relying on the name the Web page creator gave it. If no name is provided, the browser will default to the URL.
- **E-mailing** documents, URLs, or messages to yourself is another useful strategy. Many databases and online magazines permit you to e-mail information and sometimes the entire article to your account. If you combine the copy-and-paste function with e-mail, you can send yourself nearly any information you find on the Web.

Career Application

Use **www.excite.com** or another tool that supports Boolean searches to investigate a topic such as business ethics. Explore the same topic using (a) keywords and (b) Boolean operators. Which method produces more relevant hits? Save two relevant sources from each search using two or more of the strategies presented here. Remember to include the URL for each article. In a memo to your instructor, list the bibliographic information from all four sources and explain briefly which method was more productive.

Evaluate the currency, authority, content, and accuracy of Web sites carefully.

Evaluating Web Sources. Most of us using the Web have a tendency to assume that any information turned up via a search engine has somehow been evaluated as part of a valid selection process. Wrong! The truth is that the Internet is rampant with unreliable sites that reside side by side with reputable sites. Anyone with a computer and an Internet connection can publish anything on the Web. Unlike library-based research, information at many sites has not undergone the editing or scrutiny of scholarly publication procedures. The information we read in journals and most reputable magazines is reviewed, authenticated, and evaluated. That's why we have learned to trust these sources as valid and authoritative. But information on the Web is much less reliable. Some sites exist to propagandize; others want to sell you something. To use the Web meaningfully, you must scrutinize what you find. Here are specific questions to ask as you examine a site:

- **Currency.** What is the date of the Web page? When was it last updated? Is some of the information obviously out-of-date? If the information is time sensitive and the site has not been updated recently, the site is probably not reliable.

- **Authority.** Who publishes or sponsors this Web page? What makes the presenter an authority? Is information about the author or creator available? Is a contact address available for the presenter? Learn to be skeptical about data and assertions from individuals whose credentials are not verifiable.
- **Content.** Is the purpose of the page to entertain, inform, convince, or sell? How would you classify this page (e.g., news, personal, advocacy, reference)? Who is the intended audience, based on content, tone, and style? Can you judge the overall value of the content compared with the other resources on this topic? Web presenters with a slanted point of view cannot be counted on for objective data.
- **Accuracy.** Do the facts that are presented seem reliable to you? Do you find errors in spelling, grammar, or usage? Do you see any evidence of bias? Are footnotes provided? If you find numerous errors and if facts are not referenced, you should be alert that the data may be questionable.

Gathering Information From Primary Sources

learning objective 4

Up to this point, we've been talking about secondary data. You should begin nearly every business report assignment by evaluating the available secondary data. However, you'll probably need primary data to give a complete picture. Business reports that solve specific current problems typically rely on primary, firsthand data. If, for example, management wants to discover the cause of increased employee turnover in its Seattle office, it must investigate conditions in Seattle by collecting recent information. Providing answers to business problems often means generating primary data through surveys, interviews, observation, or experimentation.

Business reports often rely on primary data from firsthand experience.

Surveys

Surveys collect data from groups of people. When companies develop new products, for example, they often survey consumers to learn their needs. The advantages of surveys are that they gather data economically and efficiently. Mailed surveys reach

Surveys yield efficient and economical primary data for reports.

Photo: © Jeff Greenberg/Photo Edit

By using primary research, Walt Disney World® learned that customers need assistance planning trips for large groups of friends and families. In response, Disney offers Magical Gatherings™ vacation options that simplify the travel arrangements for large groups who want to vacation together at one of the Disney resorts. Magical Gatherings™ allows members of a travel party to collaborate online to select from a wide variety of shows, dining, and entertainment options.

Although mailed surveys may suffer low response rates, they are still useful in generating primary data.

big groups nearby or at great distances. Moreover, people responding to mailed surveys have time to consider their answers, thus improving the accuracy of the data.

Mailed questionnaires, of course, have disadvantages. Most of us rank them with junk mail, so response rates may be no higher than 5 percent. Furthermore, those who do respond may not represent an accurate sample of the overall population, thus invalidating generalizations from the group. Let's say, for example, that an insurance company sends out a questionnaire asking about provisions in a new policy. If only older people respond, the questionnaire data cannot be used to generalize what people in other age groups might think. A final problem with surveys has to do with truthfulness. Some respondents exaggerate their incomes or distort other facts, thus causing the results to be unreliable. Nevertheless, surveys may be the best way to generate data for business and student reports. In preparing print or electronic surveys, consider these pointers:

- **Select the survey population carefully.** Many surveys question a small group of people (a sample) and project the findings to a larger population. Let's say that a survey of your class reveals that the majority prefer Chicago-style pizza. Can you then say with confidence that all students on your campus (or in the nation) prefer Chicago-style pizza? To be able to generalize from a survey, you need to make the sample as large as possible. In addition, you need to determine whether the sample is like the larger population. For important surveys you will want to consult books on or experts in sampling techniques.

Effective surveys target appropriate samples and ask a limited number of specific questions.

- **Explain why the survey is necessary.** In a cover letter or an opening paragraph, describe the need for the survey. Suggest how someone or something other than you will benefit. If appropriate, offer to send recipients a copy of the findings.
- **Consider incentives.** If the survey is long, persuasive techniques may be necessary. Response rates can be increased by offering money (such as a $1 bill), coupons, gift certificates, free books, or other gifts.
- **Limit the number of questions.** Resist the temptation to ask for too much. Request only information you will use. Don't, for example, include demographic questions (income, gender, age, and so forth) unless the information is necessary to evaluate responses.
- **Use questions that produce quantifiable answers.** Check-off, multiple-choice, yes-no, and scale (or rank-order) questions, illustrated in Figure 12.8, provide quantifiable data that are easily tabulated. Responses to open-ended questions (*What should the bookstore do about plastic bags?*) reveal interesting, but difficult-to-quantify, perceptions.[14] To obtain workable data, give interviewees a list of possible responses, as shown in items 5 through 8 of Figure 12.8. For scale and multiple-choice questions, try to present all the possible answer choices. To be safe, add an "Other" or "Don't know" category in case the choices seem insufficient to the respondent. Many surveys use scale questions because they capture degrees of feelings. Typical scale headings are "agree strongly," "agree somewhat," "neutral," "disagree somewhat," and "disagree strongly."

The way a question is stated influences its response.

- **Avoid leading or ambiguous questions.** The wording of a question can dramatically affect responses to it.[15] When respondents were asked, "Are we spending too much, too little, or about the right amount on *assistance to the poor*?" [emphasis added], 13 percent responded "too much." When the same respondents were asked, "Are we spending too much, too little, or about the right amount on *welfare*?" [emphasis added], 44 percent responded "too much." Because words have different meanings for different people, you must strive to use objective language and pilot test your questions with typical

FIGURE 12.8 ***Preparing a Survey***

1 Prewriting

ANALYZE: The purpose is to help the bookstore decide if it should replace plastic bags with cloth bags for customer purchases.

ANTICIPATE: The audience will be busy students who will be initially uninterested.

ADAPT: Because students will be unwilling to participate, the survey must be short and simple. Its purpose must be significant and clear.

2 Writing

RESEARCH: Ask students how they would react to cloth bags. Use their answers to form question response choices.

ORGANIZE: Open by explaining the survey's purpose and importance. In the body ask clear questions that produce quantifiable answers. Conclude with appreciation and instructions.

COMPOSE: Write the first draft of the questionnaire.

3 Revising

REVISE: Try out the questionnaire with a small, representative group. Revise unclear questions.

PROOFREAD: Read for correctness. Be sure that answer choices do not overlap and that they are complete. Provide "other" category if appropriate (as in No. 9).

EVALUATE: Is the survey clear, attractive, and easy to complete?

North Shore College Bookstore
STUDENT SURVEY

The North Shore College Bookstore wants to do its part in protecting the environment. Each year we give away 45,000 plastic bags for students to carry off their purchases. We are considering changing from plastic to cloth bags or some other alternative, but we need your views.

Explains need for survey (use cover letter for longer surveys)

Please place checks below to indicate your responses.

Uses groupings that do not overlap (not 9 to 15 and 15 or more)

1. How many units are you presently carrying?
   ___ 15 or more units
   ___ 9 to 14 units
   ___ 8 or fewer units

   ___ Male
   ___ Female

2. How many times have you visited the bookstore this semester?
   ___ 0 times ___ 1 time ___ 2 times ___ 3 times ___ 4 or more times

3. Indicate your concern for the environment.
   ___ Very concerned ___ Concerned ___ Unconcerned

4. To protect the environment, would you be willing to change to another type of bag when buying books?
   ___ Yes
   ___ No

Indicate your feeling about the following alternatives.

Uses scale questions to channel responses into quantifiable alternatives, as opposed to open-ended questions

For major purchases the bookstore should	Agree	Undecided	Disagree
5. Continue to provide plastic bags.	___	___	___
6. Provide no bags; encourage students to bring their own bags.	___	___	___
7. Provide no bags; offer cloth bags at reduced price (about $3).	___	___	___
8. Give a cloth bag with each major purchase, the cost to be included in registration fees.	___	___	___

Allows respondent to add an answer in case choices provided seem insufficient

9. Consider another alternative, such as
   ____

Please return the completed survey form to your instructor or to the survey box at the North Shore College Bookstore exit. Your opinion counts.

Tells how to return survey form

Thanks for your help!

respondents. Stay away from questions that suggest an answer (*Don't you agree that the salaries of CEOs are obscenely high?*). Instead, ask neutral questions (*Do CEOs earn too much, too little, or about the right amount?*). Also avoid queries that really ask two or more things (*Should the salaries of CEOs be reduced or regulated by government legislation?*). Instead, break them into separate questions (*Should the salaries of CEOs be reduced by government legislation? Should the salaries of CEOs be regulated by government legislation?*).

- **Make it easy for respondents to return the survey.**
- **Conduct a pilot study.** Try the questionnaire with a small group so that you can remedy any problems. For example, in the survey shown in Figure 12.8, a pilot study revealed that female students generally favored cloth book bags and were willing to pay for them. Male students opposed purchasing cloth bags. By adding a gender category, researchers could verify this finding. The pilot study also revealed the need to ensure an appropriate representation of male and female students in the survey.

Interviews

Interviews with experts yield useful report data, especially when little has been written about a topic.

Some of the best report information, particularly on topics about which little has been written, comes from individuals. These individuals are usually experts or veterans in their fields. Consider both in-house and outside experts for business reports. Tapping these sources will call for in-person, telephone, or online interviews. To elicit the most useful data, try these techniques:

- **Locate an expert.** Ask managers and individuals whom they consider to be most knowledgeable in their areas. Check membership lists of professional organizations, and consult articles about the topic or related topics. Most people enjoy being experts or at least recommending them. You could also post an inquiry to an Internet newsgroup. An easy way to search newsgroups in a topic area is through the browse groups now indexed by the popular search tool Google <**http://groups.google.com**>.
- **Prepare for the interview.** Learn about the individual you're interviewing, and make sure you can pronounce the interviewee's name. Research the background and terminology of the topic. Let's say you're interviewing a corporate communication expert about producing an in-house newsletter. You ought to be familiar with terms such as *font* and software such as QuarkXpress and Adobe InDesign. In addition, be prepared by making a list of questions that pinpoint your focus on the topic. Ask the interviewee if you may record the talk.
- **Maintain a professional attitude.** Call before the interview to confirm the arrangements, and then arrive on time. Be prepared to take notes if your recorder fails (and remember to ask permission beforehand if you want to record). Use your body language to convey respect.
- **Make your questions objective and friendly.** Adopt a courteous and respectful attitude. Don't get into a debating match with the interviewee. And remember that you're there to listen, not to talk! Use open-ended, rather than yes-or-no, questions to draw experts out.
- **Watch the time.** Tell interviewees in advance how much time you expect to need for the interview. Don't overstay your appointment.
- **End graciously.** Conclude the interview with a general question, such as "Is there anything you'd like to add?" Express your appreciation, and ask permission to telephone later if you need to verify points.

Observation and Experimentation

Some kinds of primary data can be obtained only through firsthand observation and investigation. If you determine that the questions you have require observational data, then you need to plan the observations carefully. One of the most important questions is to ask what or whom you're observing and how often those observations are necessary to provide reliable data. For example, if you want to learn more about an organization's customer service on the telephone, you probably need to conduct an observation (along with interviews and perhaps even surveys). You'll want to answer questions such as, "How long does a typical caller wait before a customer service rep answers the call?" and "Is the service consistent?" Recording observations for 60-minute periods at different times throughout a week will give you a better picture than just observing for an hour on a Friday before a holiday.

Some of the best report data come from firsthand observation and investigation.

When you observe, plan ahead. Arrive early enough to introduce yourself and set up whatever equipment you think is necessary. Make sure that you've received permissions beforehand, particularly if you are recording. In addition, take notes, not only of the events or actions but also of the settings. Changes in environment often have an effect on actions.

Experimentation produces data suggesting causes and effects. Informal experimentation might be as simple as a pretest and posttest in a college course. Did students expand their knowledge as a result of the course? More formal experimentation is undertaken by scientists and professional researchers who control variables to test their effects. Assume, for example, that the Hershey Company wants to test the hypothesis (which is a tentative assumption) that chocolate lifts people out of the doldrums. An experiment testing the hypothesis would separate depressed individuals into two groups: those who ate chocolate (the experimental group) and those who did not (the control group). What effect did chocolate have? Such experiments are not done haphazardly, however. Valid experiments require sophisticated research designs and careful attention to matching the experimental and control groups.

spotlight *on communicators*

Premier management consultant and best-selling author Tom Peters recognizes the value of ongoing primary and secondary research. He recommends collecting data not only about the performance of your own company but also about that of the competition. To stay abreast of rivals and their techniques, businesses must (1) collect data, (2) update them regularly, and (3) share them widely within the firm.

Documenting Data

learning objective 5

In writing business and other reports, you will often build on the ideas and words of others. In Western culture, whenever you "borrow" the ideas of others, you must give credit to your information sources. This is called *documentation.*

Purposes of Documentation

As a careful writer, you should take pains to properly document report data for the following reasons:

Documenting data lends credibility, protects the writer from charges of plagiarism, and aids the reader.

- **To strengthen your argument.** Including good data from reputable sources will convince readers of your credibility and the logic of your reasoning.
- **To protect yourself against charges of plagiarism.** Acknowledging your sources keeps you honest. Plagiarism, which is illegal and unethical, is the act of using others' ideas without proper documentation.
- **To instruct the reader.** Citing references enables readers to pursue a topic further and make use of the information themselves.

Academic Documentation vs. Business Documentation

In the academic world, documentation is critical. Especially in the humanities and sciences, students are taught to cite sources by using quotation marks, parenthetical citations, footnotes, and bibliographies. College term papers require full documentation to demonstrate that a student has become familiar with respected sources and can cite them properly in developing an argument. Giving credit to the author is extremely important. Students who plagiarize risk a failing grade in a class and even expulsion from school.

Business writers may not follow the same strict documentation standards as academic writers do.

In the business world, however, documentation is often viewed differently. Business communicators on the job may find that much of what is written does not follow the standards they learned in school.[16] In many instances, individual authorship is unimportant. For example, employees may write for the signature of their bosses. The writer receives no credit. Similarly, team projects turn out documents written by many people, none of whom receives individual credit. Internal business reports, which often include chunks of information from previous reports, also fail to acknowledge sources or give credit. Even information from outside sources may lack proper documentation. Yet, if facts are questioned, business writers must be able to produce their source materials.

Although both internal and external business reports are not as heavily documented as school assignments or term papers, business communication students are well advised to learn proper documentation methods. Your instructor may use a commercial plagiarism detection service, which can cross-reference much of the information on the Web, looking for documents with similar phrasing. The end result, an "originality report," will provide the instructor with a clear idea of whether you've been accurate and honest.

Plagiarism of words or ideas is a serious charge and can lead to loss of a job. Recent stories about the fates of journalists such as Jayson Blair of *The New York Times* illustrate that plagiarism is serious business.[17] You can avoid charges of plagiarism as well as add clarity to your work by knowing what to document and by developing good research habits.

Learning What to Document

When you write reports, especially in college, you are continually dealing with other people's ideas. You are expected to conduct research, synthesize ideas, and build on the work of others. But you are also expected to give proper credit for borrowed material. To avoid plagiarism, you must give credit whenever you use the following:[18]

Give credit when you use another's ideas, when you borrow facts that are not common knowledge, and when you quote or paraphrase another's words.

- Another person's ideas, opinions, examples, or theory
- Any facts, statistics, graphs, and drawings that are not common knowledge
- Quotations of another person's actual spoken or written words
- Paraphrases of another person's spoken or written words

Information that is common knowledge requires no documentation. For example, the statement *The Wall Street Journal is a popular business newspaper* would require no citation. Statements that are not common knowledge, however, must be documented. For example, *Eight of the nation's top 10 fastest growing large cities (100,000 or more population) since Census 2000 lie in the Western states of Arizona, Nevada, and California* would require a citation because most people do not know this fact. Cite sources for proprietary information such as statistics organized and reported by a newspaper or magazine. Also use citations to document direct quotations and ideas that you summarize in your own words.

Developing Good Manual and Electronic Research Habits

Report writers who are gathering information have two methods available for recording the information they find. The time-honored manual method of notetaking works well because information is recorded on separate cards, which can then be arranged in the order needed to develop a thesis or argument. Today, though, writers rely heavily on electronic researching. Traditional notetaking methods may seem antiquated and laborious in comparison. Let's explore both methods.

Manual Notetaking. To make sure you know whose ideas you are using, train yourself to take excellent notes. If possible, know what you intend to find before you begin your research so that you won't waste time on unnecessary notes. Here are some pointers on taking good notes:

Handwritten note cards help writers identify sources and organize ideas.

- Record all major ideas from various sources on separate note cards.
- Include all publication data along with precise quotations.
- Consider using one card color for direct quotes and a different color for your paraphrases and summaries.
- Put the original source material aside when you are summarizing or paraphrasing.

Electronic Notetaking. Instead of recording facts on note cards, savvy researchers today take advantage of electronic tools, as noted in the earlier Tech Talk box. Beware, though, not to cut-and-paste your way into plagiarism. Here are some pointers on taking good electronic notes:

Set up a folder for electronic notes, but be careful not to cut-and-paste excessively in writing reports.

- Begin your research by setting up a folder on your hard drive or on a storage device (Zip disk, USB pen, etc.).
- Create subfolders for major sections, such as introduction, body, and closing.
- When you find facts on the Web or in electronic databases, highlight the material you want to record, copy it, and paste it into a document in an appropriate folder.
- Be sure to include all publication data.
- As discussed in the section on managing research data, consider archiving on a Zip disk those Web pages or articles used in your research in case the data must be verified.

Developing the Fine Art of Paraphrasing

In writing reports and using the ideas of others, you will probably rely heavily on *paraphrasing*, which means restating an original passage in your own words and in your own style. To do a good job of paraphrasing, follow these steps:

Paraphrasing involves putting an original passage into your own words.

- Read the original material intently to comprehend its full meaning.
- Write your own version without looking at the original.
- Do not repeat the grammatical structure of the original, and do not merely replace words with synonyms.
- Reread the original to be sure you covered the main points but did not borrow specific language.

To better understand the difference between plagiarizing and paraphrasing, study the examples on the next page. Notice that the writer of the plagiarized version uses the same grammatical construction as the source and often merely replaces words with synonyms. Even the acceptable version, however, requires a reference to the source author.

Source
The collapse in the cost of computing has made cellular communication economically viable. Worldwide, one in two new phone subscriptions is cellular. The digital revolution in telephony is most advanced in poorer countries because they have been able to skip an outdated technological step relying on land lines.

The plagiarized version uses the same sentence structure as the original and makes few changes other than replacing some words.

Plagiarized version
The drop in computing costs now makes cellular communication affordable around the world. In fact, one out of every two new phones is cellular. The digital revolution in cellular telephones is developing faster in poorer countries because they could skip an outdated technological process using land lines.

The acceptable paraphrase presents ideas from a different perspective and uses a different sentence structure than the original.

Acceptable paraphrase
Cellular phone use around the world is increasing rapidly as a result of decreasing computing costs. Half of all new phones are now wireless. Poorer countries are experiencing the most rapid development because they can move straight to cellular without focusing on outdated technology using land lines (Henderson 44).

Knowing When and How to Quote

On occasion you will want to use the exact words of a source. But beware of overusing quotations. Documents that contain pages of spliced-together quotations suggest that writers have few ideas of their own. Wise writers and speakers use direct quotations for three purposes only:

Use quotations only to provide background data, to cite experts, to repeat precise phrasing, or to duplicate exact wording before criticizing.

- To provide objective background data and establish the severity of a problem as seen by experts
- To repeat identical phrasing because of its precision, clarity, or aptness
- To duplicate exact wording before criticizing

When you must use a long quotation, try to summarize and introduce it in your own words. Readers want to know the gist of a quotation before they tackle it. For example, to introduce a quotation discussing the shrinking staffs of large companies, you could precede it with your words: *In predicting employment trends, Charles Waller believes the corporation of the future will depend on a small core of full-time employees.* To introduce quotations or paraphrases, use wording such as the following:

According to Waller, ...

Waller argues that . . . .

In his recent study, Waller reported . . . .

Use quotation marks to enclose exact quotations, as shown in the following: "The current image," says Charles Waller, "of a big glass-and-steel corporate headquarters on landscaped grounds directing a worldwide army of tens of thousands of employees may soon be a thing of the past."

Using Citation Formats

Guidelines for MLA and APA citation formats may be found in Appendix C; guidelines for electronic citations are at the Guffey student Web site.

You can direct readers to your sources with parenthetical notes inserted into the text and with bibliographies. The most common citation formats are those presented by the Modern Language Association (MLA) and the American Psychological Association (APA). Learn more about how to use these formats in Appendix C. For the most up-to-date citation formats for electronic references, check the Guffey student Web site. You will find model citation formats for online magazine, newspaper, and journal articles, as well as for Web references.

Illustrating Data

learning objective

6

Effective graphics clarify numerical data and simplify complex ideas.

After collecting and interpreting information, you need to consider how best to present it. If your report contains complex data and numbers, you may want to consider using graphics such as tables and charts. These graphics clarify data, create visual interest, and make numerical data meaningful. By simplifying complex ideas and emphasizing key data, well-constructed graphics make key information easier to remember. However, the same data can be shown in many different forms, for example, in a chart, table, or graph. That's why you need to recognize how to match the appropriate graphic with your objective and incorporate it into your report.

Matching Graphics and Objectives

In developing the best graphics, you must decide what data you want to highlight and which graphics are most appropriate to your objectives. Tables? Bar charts? Pie graphs? Line charts? Surface charts? Flow charts? Organization charts? Pictures? Figure 12.9 summarizes appropriate uses for each type of graphic. The following text discusses each visual in more detail.

Tables permit the systematic presentation of large amounts of data, whereas charts and graphs enhance visual comparisons.

Tables. Probably the most frequently used graphic in reports is the table. Because a table presents quantitative or verbal information in systematic columns and rows,

FIGURE 12.9 ***Matching Graphics to Objectives***

Graphic	Objective
Table	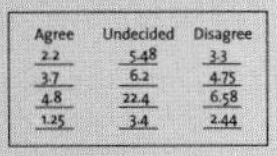 To show exact figures and values
Bar chart	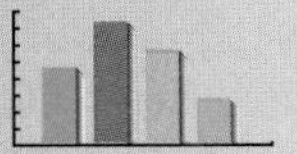 To compare one item with others
Line chart	 To demonstrate changes in quantitative data over time
Pie graph	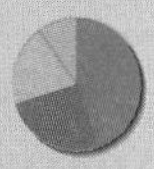 To visualize a whole unit and the proportions of its components
Flow chart	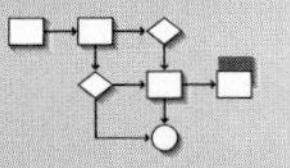 To display a process or procedure
Organization chart	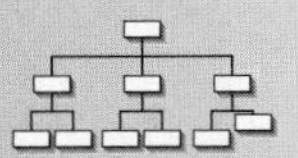 To define a hierarchy of elements
Photograph, map, illustration	 To create authenticity, to spotlight a location, and to show an item in use

it can clarify large quantities of data in small spaces. The disadvantage is that tables do not readily display trends. You may have made rough tables to help you organize the raw data collected from questionnaires or interviews. In preparing tables for your readers or listeners, though, you'll need to pay more attention to clarity and emphasis. Here are tips for making good tables, one of which is provided below in Figure 12.10:

- Place titles and labels at the top of the table.
- Arrange items in a logical order (alphabetical, chronological, geographical, highest to lowest), depending on what you need to emphasize.
- Provide clear headings for the rows and columns.
- Identify the units in which figures are given (percentages, dollars, units per worker hour, and so forth) in the table title, in the column or row heading, with the first item in a column, or in a note at the bottom.
- Use *N/A* (not available) for missing data.
- Make long tables easier to read by shading alternate lines or by leaving a blank line after groups of five.
- Place tables as close as possible to the place where they are mentioned in the text.

Selecting an appropriate graphic depends on the purpose that it serves.

Figure 12.9 shows how various graphics are effective in serving different purposes. Tables, as illustrated in Figure 12.10, are especially suitable in illustrating exact figures in systematic rows and columns. The table in our figure is particularly useful because it presents data about the MPM Entertainment Company over several years, making it easy to compare several different divisions. Figures 12.11 through 12.14 highlight some of the data shown in the MPM Entertainment Company table, illustrating vertical, horizontal, grouped, and segmented bar charts, all of which can achieve different effects.

Bar Charts. Although they lack the precision of tables, bar charts enable you to make emphatic visual comparisons by using horizontal or vertical bars of varying lengths. Bar charts are useful to compare related items, illustrate changes in data over time, and show segments as a part of the whole. Note how the varied bar charts present information in differing ways.

FIGURE 12.10 ***Table Summarizing Precise Data***

Figure 1
MPM ENTERTAINMENT COMPANY
Income by Division (in millions of dollars)

	Theme Parks	Motion Pictures	DVDs & Videos	Total
2002	$15.8	$39.3	$11.2	$66.3
2003	18.1	17.5	15.3	50.9
2004	23.8	21.1	22.7	67.6
2005	32.2	22.0	24.3	78.5
2006 (projected)	35.1	21.0	26.1	82.2

Source: *Industry Profiles* (New York: DataPro, 2005) 225.

FIGURE 12.11 ***Vertical Bar Chart***

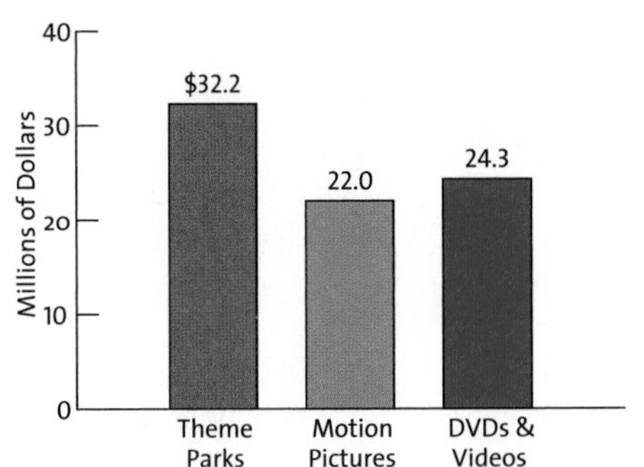

Figure 1
2005 MPM INCOME BY DIVISION
Millions of Dollars
40
30
20
10
0
$32.2
22.0
24.3
Theme Parks
Motion Pictures
DVDs & Videos

Source: *Industry Profiles* (New York: DataPro, 2005), 225.

FIGURE 12.12 ***Horizontal Bar Chart***

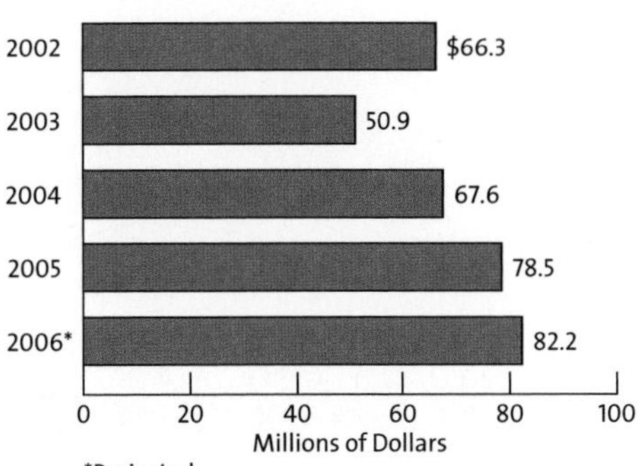

Figure 2
TOTAL MPM INCOME, 2002 TO 2006
2002
2003
2004
2005
2006*
$66.3
50.9
67.6
78.5
82.2
0
20
40
60
80
100
Millions of Dollars
*Projected

Source: *Industry Profiles.*

FIGURE 12.13 ***Grouped Bar Chart***

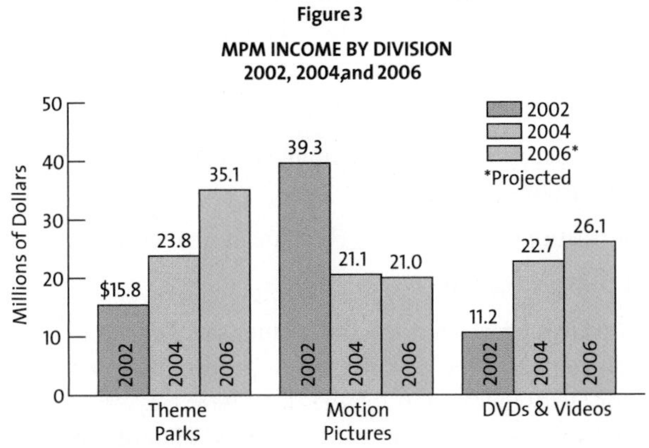

Figure 3
MPM INCOME BY DIVISION
2002, 2004, and 2006
Millions of Dollars
50
40
30
20
10
0
2002
2004
2006*
*Projected
$15.8
23.8
35.1
39.3
21.1
21.0
11.2
22.7
26.1
Theme Parks
Motion Pictures
DVDs & Videos

Source: *Industry Profiles.*

FIGURE 12.14 ***Segmented 100% Bar Chart***

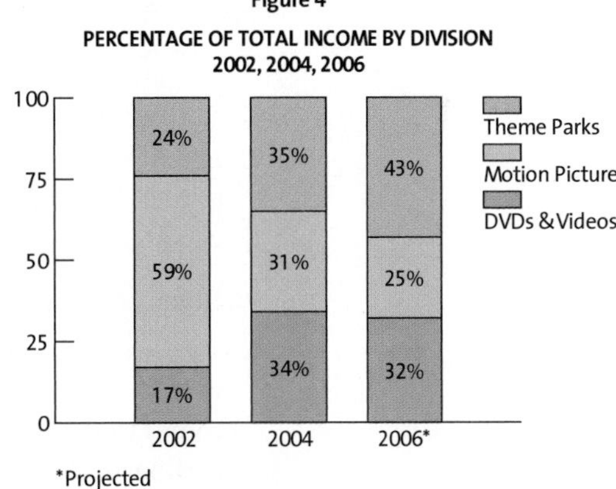

Figure 4
PERCENTAGE OF TOTAL INCOME BY DIVISION
2002, 2004, 2006
100
75
50
25
0
24%
59%
17%
35%
31%
34%
43%
25%
32%
2002
2004
2006*
Theme Parks
Motion Pictures
DVDs & Videos
*Projected

Source: *Industry Profiles.*

Many techniques for constructing tables also hold true for bar charts. Here are a few additional tips:

- Keep the length and width of each bar and segment proportional.
- Include a total figure in the middle of the bar or at its end if the figure helps the reader and does not clutter the chart.
- Start dollar or percentage amounts at zero.
- Place the first bar at some distance (usually half the amount of space between bars) from the *y* axis.
- Avoid showing too much information, thus producing clutter and confusion.
- Place each bar chart as close as possible to the place where it is mentioned in the text.

Line Charts. The major advantage of line charts is that they show changes over time, thus indicating trends. The vertical axis is typically the dependent variable, and the horizontal axis the independent one. Simple line charts (Figure 12.15) show just

FIGURE 12.15 ***Simple Line Chart***

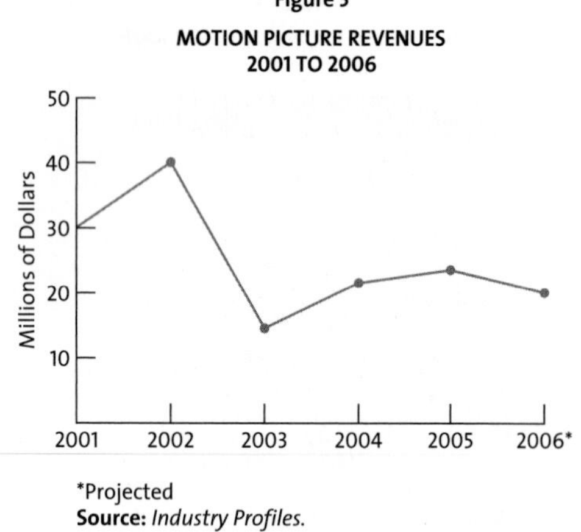

FIGURE 12.16 ***Multiple Line Chart***

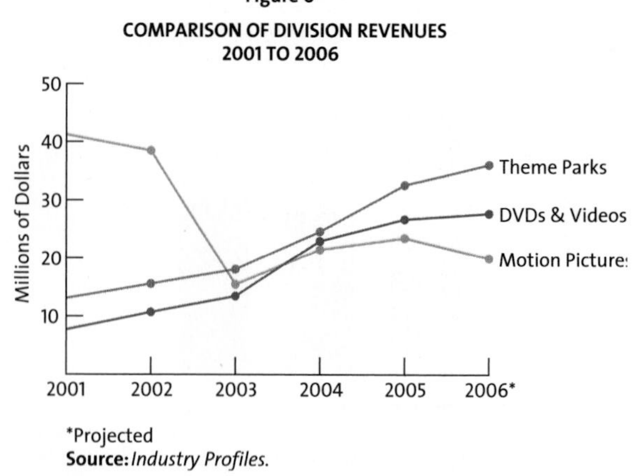

Line charts illustrate trends and changes in data over time.

one variable. Multiple line charts compare items, such as two or more data sets, using the same variable (Figure 12.16). Segmented line charts (Figure 12.17), also called surface charts, illustrate how the components of a whole change over time.

To prepare a line chart, remember these tips:

- Begin with a grid divided into squares.
- Arrange the time component (usually years) horizontally across the bottom; arrange values for the other variable vertically.
- Draw small dots at the intersections to indicate each value at a given year.
- Connect the dots and add color if desired.
- To prepare a segmented (surface) chart, plot the first value (say, DVD and video income) across the bottom; add the next item (say, motion picture income) to the first figures for every increment; for the third item (say, theme park income), add its value to the total for the first two items. The top line indicates the total of the three values.

Pie graphs are most useful in showing the proportion of parts to a whole.

Pie Graphs. Pie, or circle, graphs enable readers to see a whole and the proportion of its components, or wedges. Although less flexible than bar or line charts, pie graphs are useful in showing percentages, as Figure 12.18 illustrates. They are very effective for lay or nonexpert audiences. Notice that a wedge can be "exploded" or popped out for special emphasis, as seen in Figure 12.18.

For the most effective pie graphs, follow these suggestions:

- Begin at the 12 o'clock position, drawing the smallest wedge first and arranging the others in the order of size. Computer software programs don't always observe this practice, but if you're drawing your own graphs, you can.
- Include, if possible, the actual percentage or absolute value for each wedge.
- Use four to six segments for best results; if necessary, group small portions into a wedge called "other."
- Draw radii from the center.
- Distinguish wedges with color, shading, or cross-hatching.
- Keep all the labels horizontal.

FIGURE 12.17 ***Segmented Line (Surface) Chart***

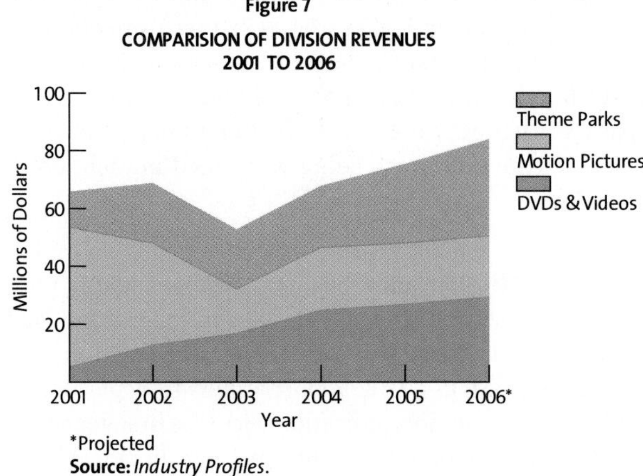

FIGURE 12.18 ***Pie Graph***

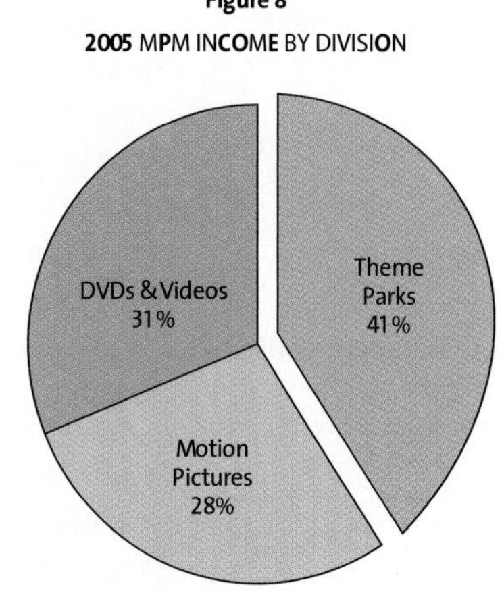

Source: *Industry Profiles.*

Flow Charts. Procedures are simplified and clarified by diagramming them in a flow chart, as shown in Figure 12.19. Whether you need to describe the procedure for handling a customer's purchase order or outline steps in solving a problem, flow charts help the reader visualize the process. Traditional flow charts use the following symbols:

- Ovals to designate the beginning and end of a process
- Diamonds to designate decision points
- Rectangles to represent major activities or steps

FIGURE 12.19 ***Flow Chart***

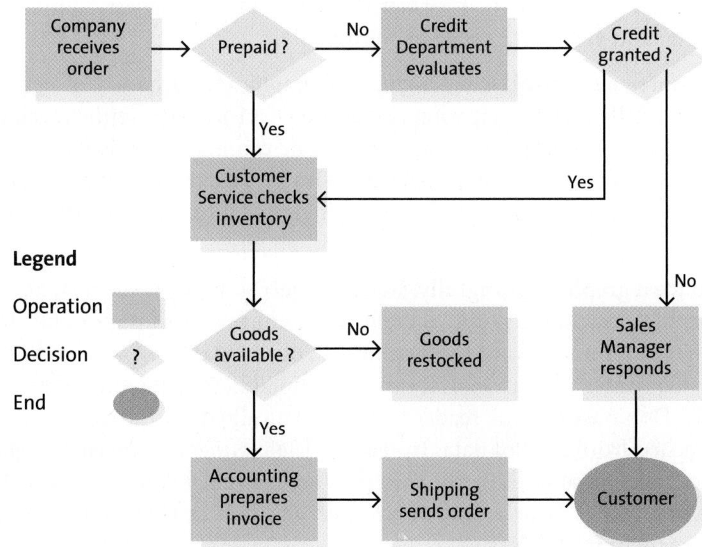

Organization charts show the line of command and thus the flow of official communication from management to employees.

Organization Charts. Many large organizations are so complex that they need charts to show the chain of command, from the boss down to the line managers and employees. Organization charts like the one in Figure 1.8 in Chapter 1 provide such information as who reports to whom, how many subordinates work for each manager (the span of control), and what channels of official communication exist. These charts may illustrate a company's structure, for example, by function, customer, or product. They may also be organized by the work being performed in each job or by the hierarchy of decision making.

Computer technology permits photographs, maps, and illustrations to be scanned directly into reports.

Photographs, Maps, and Illustrations. Some business reports include photographs, maps, and illustrations to serve specific purposes. Photos, for example, add authenticity and provide a visual record. An environmental engineer may use photos to document hazardous waste sites. Maps enable report writers to depict activities or concentrations geographically, such as dots indicating sales reps in states across the country. Illustrations and diagrams are useful in indicating how an object looks or operates. A drawing showing the parts of a printer with labels describing their functions, for example, is more instructive than a photograph or verbal description. With today's computer technology, photographs, maps, and illustrations can be scanned directly into business reports.

Incorporating Graphics in Reports

Effective graphics are accurate and ethical; they do not overuse color or decorations; and they include titles.

Used appropriately, graphics make reports more interesting and easier to understand. In putting graphics into your reports, follow these suggestions for best effects:

- **Evaluate the audience.** Consider the reader, the content, your schedule, and your budget. Graphics take time and money to prepare, so think carefully before deciding how many graphics to use. Six charts in an internal report to an executive may seem like overkill; but in a long technical report to outsiders, six may be too few.
- **Use restraint.** Don't overuse color or decorations. Although color can effectively distinguish bars or segments in charts, too much color can be distracting and confusing. Remember, too, that colors themselves sometimes convey meaning: reds suggest deficits or negative values; blues suggest calmness and authority; and yellow may suggest warning.
- **Be accurate and ethical.** Double-check all graphics for accuracy of figures and calculations. Be certain that your visuals aren't misleading—either accidentally or intentionally. Manipulation of a chart scale can make trends look steeper and more dramatic than they really are. Also be sure to cite sources when you use someone else's facts. The accompanying Ethical Insights box discusses in more detail how to make ethical charts and graphs.

Textual graphics should be introduced by statements that help readers interpret them.

- **Introduce a graph meaningfully.** Refer to every graphic in the text, and place the graphic close to the point where it is mentioned. Most important, though, help the reader understand the significance of the graphic. You can do this by telling the reader what to look for or by summarizing the main point of the graphic. Don't assume the reader will automatically draw the same conclusions you reached from a set of data. Instead of *The findings are shown in Figure 3,* tell the reader what to look for: *Two thirds of the responding employees, as shown in Figure 3, favor a flextime schedule.* The best introductions for graphics interpret them for readers.

ethical insights

Making Ethical Charts and Graphics

Business communicators must present graphical data in the same ethical, honest manner required for all other messages. Remember that the information shown in your charts and graphics will be used to inform others or help them make decisions. If this information is not represented accurately, the reader will be incorrectly informed; any decisions based on the data are likely to be faulty. And mistakes in interpreting such information may have serious and long-lasting consequences.

Chart data can be distorted in many ways. Figure 1 shows advertising expenses displayed on an appropriate scale. Figure 2 shows the same information, but the horizontal scale, from 2001 to 2006, has been lengthened. Notice that the data have not changed, but the increases and decreases are smoothed out, so changes in expenses appear to be slight. In Figure 3 the vertical scale is taller and the horizontal scale is shortened, resulting in what appear to be sharp increases and decreases in expenses.

To avoid misrepresenting data, keep the following pointers in mind when designing your graphics:

- Use an appropriate type of chart or graphic for the message you wish to convey.
- Design the chart so that it focuses on the appropriate information.
- Include all relevant or important data; don't arbitrarily leave out necessary information.
- Don't hide critical information by including too much data in one graphic.
- Use appropriate scales with equal intervals for the data you present.

Career Application

Locate one or two graphics in a newspaper, magazine article, or annual report. Analyze the strengths and weaknesses of each graphic. Is the information presented accurately? Select a bar or line chart. Sketch the same chart but change the vertical or horizontal scales on the graphic. How does the message of the chart change?

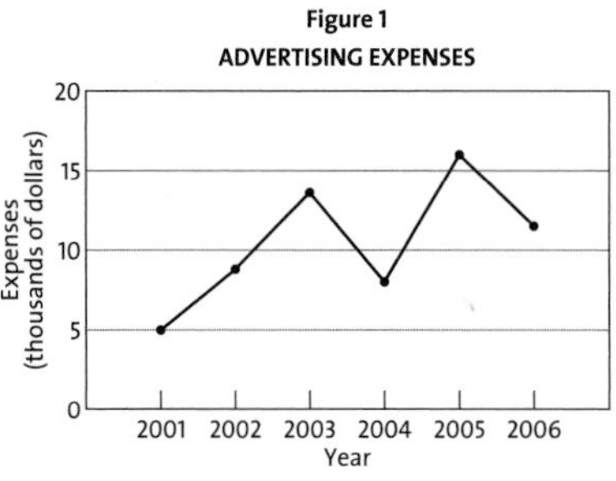

Figure 1
ADVERTISING EXPENSES

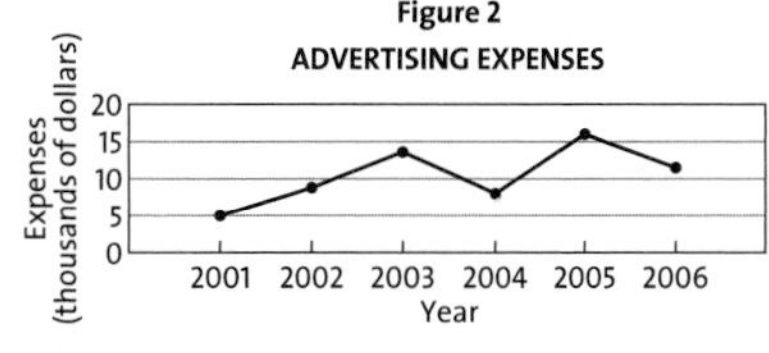

Figure 2
ADVERTISING EXPENSES

Figure 3
ADVERTISING EXPENSES

- **Choose an appropriate caption or title style.** Like reports, graphics may use "talking" titles or generic, descriptive titles. "Talking" titles are more persuasive; they tell the reader what to think. Descriptive titles describe the facts more objectively.

Talking Title	**Descriptive Title**
Average Annual Health Care Costs Per Worker Rise Steeply as Workers Grow Older	Average Annual Health Care Costs per Worker as Shown by Age Groups

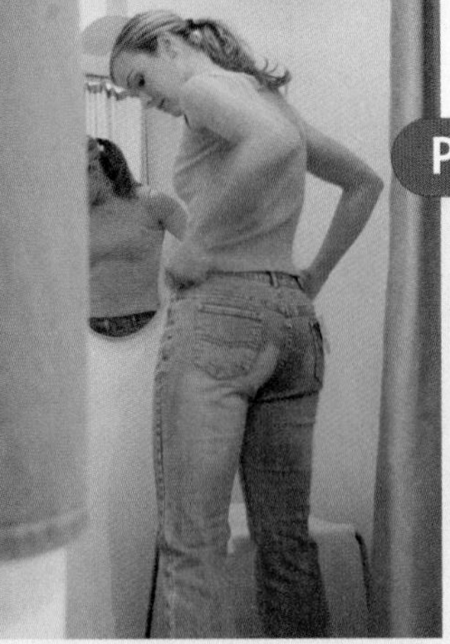

PROCESS TO PRODUCT

Applying Your Skills at BzzAgent

DAVE BALTER AND his colleagues at BzzAgent believed in Lee's new product, and they were convinced that their company's method would produce positive results. Their pilot study that included face-to-face discussions with women in the company, e-mail conversations with their agents, and surveys of those agents demonstrated that the Lee One True Fit jeans were truly different. One True Fit jeans were, in the language of one of the agents, "REALLY comfortable." A friend of another agent wore her new Lee jeans on a Saturday night date and "LOVED" them. She said she couldn't believe she was wearing jeans and didn't want to take them off.[19] However, Balter and his staff now had to convince Lee that their services, which cost approximately $85,000 to deploy 1,000 agents for 12 weeks, were worth the investment.

Balter's task was to write a proposal to Lee Jeans' management that outlined the value of his company's system. To write the proposal, his team planned to gather information (a) from studies about various forms of marketing, with an emphasis on word of mouth; (b) from data generated from previous campaigns, particularly those with similar age groups; and (c) from their pilot study. Potential print sources included *Forbes* and *BusinessWeek*, advertising trade journals, business journals, and interviews with potential customers.

Your Task

As writing consultants, you and several of your colleagues have been asked by Dave's team to help write a persuasive proposal that outlines the strategies and predicts the success of the campaign. You've been assigned the task of researching Lee Jeans and gathering general market information about jeans. Using both the Web and InfoTrac, put together a short report that lists articles that will be useful for the report writers. Add a short summary of your findings as an introduction. Submit your results in a memo or e-mail message to your instructor. ■

case study

Summary of Learning Objectives

1 **Describe business report basics, including functions, patterns, writing style, and formats.** Business reports generally function either as informational reports (without analysis or recommendations) or as analytical reports (with analysis, conclusions, and possibly recommendations). Reports organized directly present the purpose immediately. This pattern is appropriate when the audience is supportive and familiar with the topic. Reports organized indirectly provide the conclusions and recommendations last. This pattern is helpful when the audience is unfamiliar with the problem or when they may be disappointed or hostile. Reports written in a formal style use third-person constructions, avoid contractions, and include many passive-voice verbs, complex sentences, and long words. Reports written informally use first-person constructions, contractions, shorter sentences, familiar words, and active-voice verbs. Reports may be formatted as letters, memos, manuscripts, or prepared forms.

2 **Apply Guffey's 3-x-3 writing process to business reports.** Report writers begin by analyzing a problem and writing a problem statement, which may include the scope, significance, and limitations of the project. Writers then analyze the audience and define major issues. They prepare a work plan, in-

cluding a tentative outline and work schedule. They collect, organize, interpret, and illustrate their data. Then they compose the first draft. Finally, they revise (often many times), proofread, and evaluate.

3 **Understand where to find and how to use print and electronic sources of secondary data.** Secondary data may be located by searching for books, periodicals, and newspapers through print or electronic indexes. Look for information using electronic databases such as InfoTrac and LexisNexis. You may also find information on the Internet, but searching for it requires knowledge of search tools and techniques. Popular search tools such as Google, Yahoo!, and AskJeeves will help you. Once found, however, information obtained on the Internet should be scrutinized for currency, authority, content, and accuracy.

4 **Understand where to find and how to use sources of primary data.** Researchers generate firsthand, primary data through surveys (in-person, print, and online), interviews, observation, and experimentation. Surveys are most economical and efficient for gathering information from large groups of people. Interviews are useful when working with experts in a field. Firsthand observation can produce rich data, but it must be objective. Experimentation produces data suggesting causes and effects. Valid experiments require sophisticated research designs and careful attention to matching the experimental and control groups.

5 **Recognize the purposes and techniques of documentation in business reports.** Documentation means giving credit to information sources. Careful writers document data to strengthen an argument, protect against charges of plagiarism, and instruct readers. Although documentation is less stringent in business reports than in academic reports, business writers should learn proper techniques to be able to verify their sources and to avoid charges of plagiarism. Report writers should document others' ideas, facts that are not common knowledge, quotations, and paraphrases. Good notetaking, either manual or electronic, enables writers to give accurate credit to sources. Paraphrasing involves putting another's ideas into your own words. Quotations may be used to provide objective background data, to repeat identical phrasing, and to duplicate exact wording before criticizing.

6 **Illustrate reports with graphics that create meaning and interest.** Good graphics improve reports by clarifying, simplifying, and emphasizing data. Tables organize precise data into rows and columns. Bar and line charts enable data to be compared visually. Line charts are especially helpful in showing changes over time. Pie graphs show a whole and the proportion of its components. Organization charts, pictures, maps, and illustrations serve specific purposes. In choosing or crafting graphics, effective communicators evaluate their audience, purpose, topic, and budget to determine the number and kind of graphics. They write "talking" titles (telling readers what to think about the graphic) or "descriptive" titles (summarizing the topic objectively).

chapter review

1. What purpose do most reports serve? (Obj. 1)
2. How do informational and analytical reports differ? (Obj. 1)
3. How do the direct and indirect patterns of report development differ? (Obj. 1)
4. Identify four common report formats. (Obj. 1)
5. List the seven steps in the report-writing process. (Obj. 2)
6. What questions should you ask to anticipate your audience's reaction? (Obj. 2)
7. How do primary data differ from secondary data? Give an original example of each. (Obj. 3)
8. What should a research strategy include? (Obj. 3)
9. Discuss five techniques that you think are most useful in enhancing a Web search. (Obj. 3)
10. What are four major sources of primary information? (Obj. 4)
11. Why is a pilot study necessary before conducting a survey? (Obj. 4)
12. What is documentation, and why is it necessary in reports? (Obj. 5)
13. List two strategies for managing your research data. (Obj. 5)
14. Briefly compare the advantages and disadvantages of illustrating data with charts (bar and line) versus tables. (Obj. 6)
15. What is the major advantage of using a pie graph to illustrate data? (Obj. 6)

critical thinking

1. When you are engaged in the planning process of a report, what is the advantage of factoring (the process of breaking problems into subproblems)?
2. For long reports, why is a written work plan a wise idea? (Obj. 2)
3. Is information obtained on the Web as reliable as information obtained from journals, newspapers, and magazines? (Obj. 3)
4. Some people say that business reports never contain footnotes. If you were writing your first report for a business and you did considerable research, what would you do about documenting your sources? (Obj. 5)
5. **Ethical Issue:** Discuss this statement: Let the facts speak for themselves. Are facts always truthful?

THREE GREAT RESOURCES FOR YOU!

1. ***Guffey Student Web Site***
   http://guffey.swlearning.com

   Your companion Web site offers chapter review quizzes, WebThink activities, updated chapter URLs, and many additional resources.

2. ***Guffey XTRA!***
   http://guffeyxtra.swlearning.com

   This online study assistant includes Your Personal Language Trainer, Speak Right!, Spell Right!, bonus online chapters, Documents for Analysis, PowerPoint slides, and much more.

3. ***Student Study Guide***

   Self-checked workbook activities and applications review chapter concepts and develop career skills.

activities

12.1 Report Functions, Writing Styles, and Formats (Obj. 1)

Your Task. For the following reports, (1) name the report's primary function (informational or analytical), (2) recommend a direct or indirect pattern of development, and (3) select a report format (memo, letter, or manuscript).

a. A persuasive proposal from a group of citizens to their town council to turn the old elementary school, which is no longer in use, into a multipurpose building for citizen education, community action meetings, and a low-cost daycare center.
b. A report submitted by a sales rep to her manager describing her attendance at a sports products trade show, including the reactions of visitors to a new noncarbonated sports drink.
c. A recommendation report from a special review team (composed of members of the board of directors and staff) to the executive director of a major nonprofit organization to outline the necessary computer and phone system upgrades for the organization's headquarters building.
d. A progress report from a location manager to a Hollywood production company describing safety, fire, and environmental precautions taken for the shooting of a stunt involving blowing up a boat off Marina del Rey.
e. A report prepared by an outside consultant examining whether a sports franchise should refurbish its stadium or look to relocate to another city.
f. A report from a national moving company telling state authorities how it has improved its safety program so that its trucks now comply with state regulations. The report describes but doesn't interpret the program.

12.2 Collaborative Project: Report Portfolio (Obj. 1)

TEAM

Your Task. In teams of three or four, collect four or more sample business reports illustrating various types of business reports. Don't forget corporate annual reports. For each report identify and discuss the following characteristics:

a. Function (informational or analytical)
b. Pattern (primarily direct or indirect)
c. Writing style (formal or informal)
d. Format (memo, letter, manuscript, preprinted form)
e. Effectiveness (clarity, accuracy, expression)

In an informational memo report to your instructor, describe your findings.

12.3 Data Forms and Questions (Obj. 3)

Your Task. In conducting research for the following reports, name at least one form of data you will need and questions you should ask to determine whether that set of data is appropriate (see Figure 12.6).

a. A report by the Center for Science in the Public Interest investigating the nutritional value of products advertised on afternoon and Saturday television for kids[20]
b. A report by federal investigators analyzing the causes of a massive Midwest power-grid failure[21]
c. A report examining the effectiveness of ethics codes in American businesses

12.4 Problem and Purpose Statements (Obj. 2)

Your Task. The following situations require reports. For each situation write (1) a concise problem question and (2) a simple statement of purpose.

a. Last winter a severe ice storm damaged well over 50 percent of the pear trees lining the main street in the small town of Somerset. The local university's experts believe that well over 70 percent of the damaged trees will die in the next two years and that this variety is not the best one for providing shade (one of the major goals behind planting them eight years ago).
b. New Food and Drug Administration regulations have changed the definitions of common terms such as *fresh*, *fat free*, *low in cholesterol*, and *light*. The Big Deal Bakery worries that it must rewrite all its package labels. Big Deal doesn't know whether to hire a laboratory or a consultant for this project.
c. Customers placing telephone orders for clothing with James River Enterprises typically order only one or two items. JRE wonders whether it can train telephone service reps to motivate customers to increase the number of items ordered per call.

12.5 Problem and Purpose Statements (Obj. 2)

Your Task. Identify a problem in your current job or a previous job, such as inadequate equipment, inefficient procedures, poor customer service, poor product quality, or personnel problems. Assume your boss agrees with your criticism and asks you to prepare a report. Write (a) a two- or three-sentence statement describing the problem, (b) a problem question, and (c) a simple statement of purpose for your report.

12.6 Factoring and Outlining a Problem (Obj. 2)

CRITICAL THINKING

Japan Airlines has asked your company, Connections International, to prepare a proposal for a training school for tour operators. JAL wants to know whether Burbank would be a good spot for its school. Burbank interests JAL but only if nearby entertainment facilities can be used for tour training. JAL also needs an advisory committee consisting, if possible, of representatives of the travel community and perhaps executives of other major airlines. The real problem is how to motivate these people to cooperate with JAL.

You've heard that NBC Studios in Burbank offers training seminars, guest speakers, and other resources for tour operators. You wonder whether Magic Mountain in Valencia would also be willing to cooperate with the proposed school. And you remember that Griffith Park is nearby and might make a good tour training spot. Before JAL will settle on Burbank as its choice, it wants to know if access to air travel is adequate. JAL's management team is also concerned about available school building space. Moreover, JAL wants to know whether city officials in Burbank would be receptive to this tour training school proposal.

Your Task. To guide your thinking and research, factor this problem into an outline with several areas to investigate. Further divide the problem into subproblems, phrasing each entry as a question. For example, *Should the JAL tour training program be located in Burbank?* (See the work plan model in Figure 12.5.)

12.7 Developing a Work Plan (Obj. 2)

Any long report project requires a structured work plan.

Your Task. Select a report topic from those listed at the ends of Chapters 13 and 14 and at the student Web site. For that report prepare a work plan that includes the following:

a. Statement of the problem
b. Expanded statement of purpose (including scope, limitations, and significance)
c. Research strategy to answer the questions
d. Tentative outline of key questions to answer
e. Work schedule (with projected completion dates)

12.8 Using Secondary Sources (Obj. 3)

Secondary sources can provide quite different information depending on your mode of inquiry.

Your Task. Select a topic in your field and conduct research in your school's library. Then research the same topic using the Internet. Write a short memo to your instructor comparing the results, focusing on the strengths and weaknesses of each search strategy.

12.9 Documenting the Best Resources in Your Field (Obj. 3)

Business and professional people should know what publications are most significant in their career fields.

Your Task. Prepare a bibliography of the most important magazines and professional journals in your major field of study. Your instructor may ask you to list the periodicals and briefly describe their content, purpose, and audience. In a cover memo to your instructor, describe your bibliography and your research sources (manual or electronic indexes, Web, databases, CD-ROM, and so on).

12.10 Developing Primary Data: Collaborative Survey (Obj. 4)

TEAM

Parking on campus has always been a problem. Students complain bitterly about the lack of spaces for them, the distance of parking lots from classrooms, and the poor condition of the lots. Some solutions have been proposed: limiting parking to full-time students, using auxiliary parking lots farther away and offering a shuttle bus to campus, encouraging bicycle and moped use, and reducing the number of spaces for visitors.

Your Task. In teams of three to five, design a survey for your associated student body council. The survey seeks student feedback in addressing the parking problem on campus. Discuss these solutions and add at least three other possibilities. Then prepare a questionnaire to be distributed on campus. If possible, pilot test the questionnaire before submitting it to your instructor. Be sure to consider how the results will be tabulated and interpreted.

12.11 Researching Data: Target Wants to Know What's Happening at Wal-Mart (Objs. 3, 4, and 5)

INFOTRAC TEAM

Lauren Bacall and Robert Redford have both promoted it. And Oprah Winfrey thinks it is so chic that she pronounces its name in mock-French ("Tar-jay"). Yet, Target is an American discount retailer that piles it high and sells it cheap, just like Wal-Mart, Sears, and Kmart. Despite its celebrity shoppers, Target still lags behind Wal-Mart, which stands out as the gold standard of retailing. The two companies are similar in net margins and cost structures, but Wal-Mart is way ahead in sales per square foot.

Target is determined to narrow the gap through the sincerest form of flattery: imitation. Gerald Storch, Target's vice chairman, says his company is "the world's premier student of Wal-Mart." If it works well for Wal-Mart, it might work well for Target.[22]

Your Task. As one of several interns working in Target's vice chairman's office, you have been given the task of learning about Wal-Mart's activities and reporting on trends, techniques, procedures, or new marketing plans that might be interesting to Target. For example, Wal-Mart has been experimenting with the idea of adding gas stations to more of its stores. Perhaps Target should consider this. You're not expected to conduct extensive research and write a long report. Your boss just wants you to begin thinking about what's happening at Wal-Mart and whether any policies or practices might be worth imitating at Target. Using InfoTrac, find and read a number of articles about Wal-Mart. Your team should develop three to ten ideas to report to Gerald Storch, vice chairman. Write individual informative memos or one collaborative memo.

Prepare a bibliography of the sources you used. Summarize and paraphrase the key ideas in the two sources you believe are most relevant.

12.12 Gathering and Documenting Data: Biotechnology Alters Foods (Objs. 4 and 5)

INFOTRAC WEB

California is home to the nation's most diverse and valuable agricultural industry. Many of its crops are sold in Japanese and European markets where customers are extremely wary of genetically modified foods. Despite that fact, sources in the state capital are reporting that the biotech industry is actively seeking sponsors for a bill in the state legislature that would preempt the right of counties to ban genetically engineered crops. As an intern working for the Organic Consumers Association, the nation's largest public interest group dedicated to a healthy and sustainable food system, you have been asked to gather data about the dangers of genetically engineered crops. The organization plans to write a report to the state government about this issue.

Your Task. Conduct a keyword search using three different search engines on the Web. Select three articles you think would be most pertinent to the organization's argument. Save them using the strategies for managing data, and create a bibliography. Conduct the same keyword search with InfoTrac. Save the three most pertinent articles, and add these items to your bibliography. In a short memo to your instructor, summarize what you've found and describe its value. Attach the bibliography.

12.13 Selecting Graphics (Obj. 6)

Your Task. Identify the best kind of graphic to illustrate the following data.

a. Figures showing the process of delivering electricity to a metropolitan area
b. Data showing areas in the United States most likely to have earthquakes
c. Figures showing what proportion of every state tax dollar is spent on education, social services, transportation, debt, and other expenses
d. Data showing the academic, administrative, and operation divisions of a college, from the president to department chairs and division managers
e. Figures comparing the sales of PDAs (personal digital assistants), cell phones, and laptop computers over the past five years
f. Figures showing the distribution of West Nile Virus in humans by state
g. Percentages showing the causes of forest fires (lightning, 73 percent; arson, 5 percent; campfires, 9 percent; and so on) in the Rocky Mountains
h. Figures comparing the costs of cable, DSL, and satellite Internet service in ten major metropolitan areas of the United States for the past ten years (for a congressional investigation)

12.14 Evaluating Graphics (Obj. 6)

Your Task. Select four graphics from newspapers or magazines. Look in *The Wall Street Journal, USA Today, BusinessWeek, U.S. News & World Report, Fortune*, or other business news publications. In a memo to your instructor, critique each graphic based on what you have learned in this chapter. What is correctly shown? What is incorrectly shown? How could the graphic be improved?

Photo: © Photodisc Green/Getty Images

12.15 Drawing a Bar Chart (Obj. 6)

Your Task. Prepare a bar chart comparing the tax rates of eight industrial countries in the world: Canada, 34 percent; France, 42 percent; Germany, 39 percent; Japan, 26 percent; Netherlands, 48 percent; Sweden, 49 percent; United Kingdom, 37 percent; United States, 28 percent. These figures represent a percentage of the gross domestic product for each country. The sources of the figures are the International Monetary Fund and the Japanese Ministry of Finance. Arrange the entries logically. Write two titles: a talking title and a descriptive title. What should be emphasized in the chart and title?

12.16 Drawing a Line Chart (Obj. 6)

Your Task. Prepare a line chart showing the sales of Sidekick Athletic Shoes, Inc., for these years: 2005, $6.7 million; 2004, $5.4 million; 2003, $3.2 million; 2002, $2.1 million; 2001, $2.6 million; 2000, $3.6 million. In the chart title, highlight the trend you see in the data.

12.17 Studying Graphics in Annual Reports (Obj. 6)

Your Task. In a memo to your instructor, evaluate the use and effectiveness of graphics in three to five corporation annual reports. Critique their readability, clarity, and effectiveness in visualizing data. How were they introduced in the text? What suggestions would you make to improve them?

12.18 Avoiding Huge Credit Card Debt for College Students

CONSUMER | INFOTRAC | WEB

College students represent a new push for credit card companies. An amazing 54 percent of students carried a credit card in the most recent study of undergraduate card use,[23] and the number undoubtedly continues to skyrocket. Credit cards are a contributing factor when students graduate with an average of $20,402 debt. Because they can't buy cars, rent homes, or purchase insurance, graduates with big credit debt see a bleak future for themselves.

A local newspaper plans to run a self-help story about college credit cards. The editor asks you, a young part-time reporter, to prepare a report with information that could be turned into an article. The article would focus on parents of students who are about to leave for college. What can parents do to help students avoid sinking deeply into credit card debt?

Your Task. Using InfoTrac and the Web, locate basic information about student credit card options. In a memo information report, discuss shared credit cards and other options.

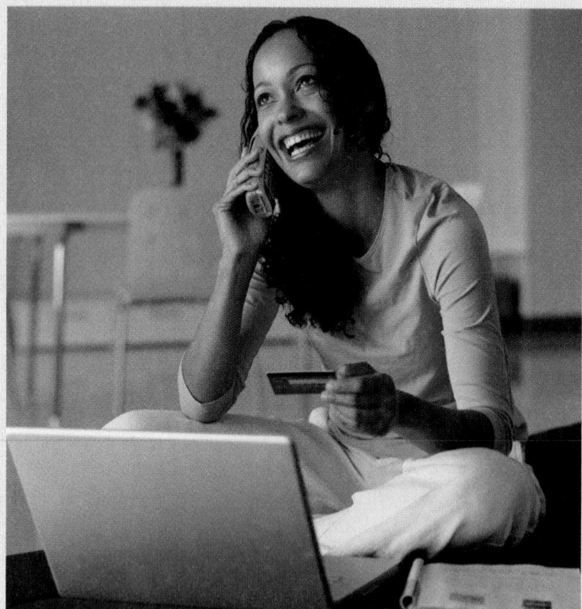

Students are discovering that credit card use during college is a contributing factor to a huge credit debt when they graduate.

Your goal in your memo report on credit card use is to be informative, not to reach conclusions or make recommendations. Use one or more of the techniques discussed in this chapter to track your sources. Address your memo to Barbara Hagler, editor.

C.L.U.E. review 12

On a separate sheet edit the following sentences to correct faults in grammar, punctuation, spelling, numbers, and word use.

1. Reports are a Fact of Life in american business consequently businesswriters must learn to prepare it.
2. Although reports vary in length content form and formality level they all have 1 purpose.
3. The primary purpose of reports, are to answer questions and solve problems systemly.
4. Letter reports usualy have side margins of one to one and a quarter inchs.
5. The format of a report is determined by it's: length topic audience and purpose.
6. The CEO and Manager who had went to a conference in the west delivered a report to Jeff and I when they returned.
7. If you're report is authorized by someone be sure to review it's workplan with them before proceding.
8. Ilia was offerred five hundred dollars to finish Maxs report but she said it was "to little and to late."
9. To search the internet you need a browser such as microsoft internet explorer.
10. If you wish to illustrate report data; you may chose from among the following visual aids, tables, charts, graphs and pictures.

Rich chapter resources are available on the Web sites.

chapter 13

Organizing and Writing Typical Business Reports

objectives

1. Use tabulating and statistical techniques to sort and interpret report data.
2. Draw meaningful conclusions and make practical report recommendations.
3. Organize report data logically and provide cues to aid comprehension.
4. Prepare typical informational reports.
5. Prepare typical analytical reports.

COMMUNICATION IN PROCESS

Something New Is Always Brewing at Starbucks

HOWARD SCHULTZ RETURNED to Seattle from Italy in 1984 impressed by the espresso bars he had visited in Milan. In no time Schultz set up the first U.S. espresso bar in a downtown Seattle Starbucks store, one of only five Starbucks in existence at the time. Until then, Starbucks had sold only coffee beans, not drinks. Today, Starbucks is the world's largest coffee shop chain, with more than 8,000 retail locations in North America, Latin America, Europe, the Middle East, and the Pacific Rim. It serves more than 30 million customers weekly and generates more than $4 billion in annual sales.

Starbucks' customers love such exotic drinks as its Iced Caramel Macchiato and its Espresso Frappuccino blended coffee. Employees also love working there. Who wouldn't, with perks such as health coverage for those who put in 20 or more hours a week and stock options, called "Bean Stock," after one year. Adding to its accolades, Starbucks is the only company to make *Fortune* magazine's "100 Fastest-Growing Companies" six years in a row.

Starbucks is probably best known for bucking traditional retail wisdom. It regularly breaks the retail rule about locating stores so closely that they cannibalize each other's sales. Take Chicago, for example. Starbucks has over 100 shops, and many of them are on the same street. Marshall Fields even has two shops in the same store, one on its lower level and another on its first floor.

This "being everywhere" approach creates several distinct advantages. Clustered storefronts act as billboards, thus allowing Starbucks to keep its advertising budget to a minimum. Its numerous locations mean that Starbucks intercepts consumers on their way to work, home, or anywhere in between. Moreover, ubiquity builds brand awareness.[1]

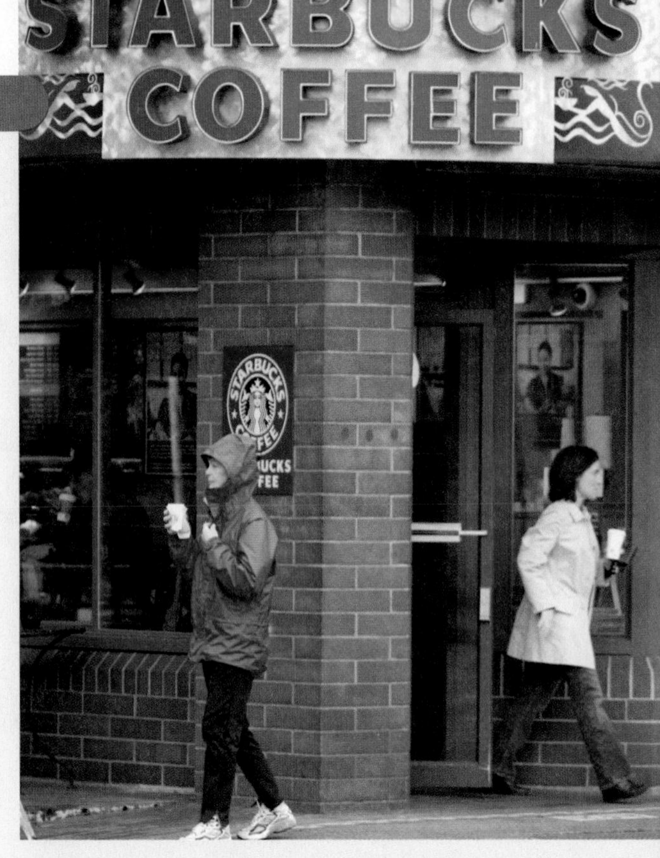

Decision makers at Starbucks rely on demographic and other data to know where to locate new stores.

Photo: © AP/Wide World Photos

Critical Thinking

- What kind of information should Starbucks gather to help it decide how closely to locate its stores?
- How can collected information be transmitted to Starbucks' decision makers?
- How can the organization and presentation of information in reports influence decision makers' reactions?

www.starbucks.com

CONTINUED ON PAGE 444

case study

learning objective 1

Interpreting Data

Starbucks and all other organizations need information to stay abreast of what's happening inside and outside of their firms. Much of that information will be presented to decision makers in the form of reports. This chapter will focus on interpreting and organizing data, drawing conclusions, providing reader cues, and writing typical business reports.

Let's assume you have collected a mass of information for a report. You may feel overwhelmed as you look at a jumble of printouts, note cards, copies of articles, interview notes, questionnaire results, and statistics. It's a little like being a contractor who allowed suppliers to dump all the building materials for a new house in a monstrous pile. Like the contractor you must sort the jumble of raw material into meaningful, usable groups. Unprocessed data become meaningful information through sorting, analysis, combination, and recombination. You'll be examining each item to see what it means by itself and what it means when connected with other data. You're looking for meanings, relationships, and answers to the research questions posed in your work plan.

Interpreting data means sorting, analyzing, combining, and recombining to yield meaningful information.

Tabulating and Analyzing Responses

If you've collected considerable numerical and other information, you must tabulate and analyze it. Fortunately, several tabulating and statistical techniques can help you create order from the chaos. These techniques simplify, summarize, and classify large amounts of data into meaningful terms. From the condensed data you're more likely to be able to draw valid conclusions and make reasoned recommendations. The most helpful summarizing techniques include tables, statistical concepts (mean, median, and mode), correlations, and grids.

Numerical data must be tabulated and analyzed statistically to bring order out of chaos.

Tables. Numerical data from questionnaires or interviews are usually summarized and simplified in tables. Using systematic columns and rows, tables make quantitative information easier to comprehend. After assembling your data, you'll want to prepare preliminary tables to enable you to see what the information means. Here is a table summarizing the response to one question from a campus survey about student parking:

Question: Should student fees be increased to build parking lots?

	Number	Percent	
Strongly agree	76	11.5	To simplify the table, combine these items.
Agree	255	38.5	
No opinion	22	3.3	
Disagree	107	16.1	To simplify the table, combine these items.
Strongly disagree	203	30.6	
Total	**663**	**100.0**	

Notice that this preliminary table includes both a total number of responses and a percentage for each response. (To calculate a percentage, divide the figure for each response by the total number of responses.) To simplify the data and provide a broad overview, you can join categories. For example, combining "strongly agree" (11.5 percent) and "agree" (38.5 percent) reveals that 50 percent of the respondents supported the proposal to finance new parking lots with increased student fees.

Sometimes data become more meaningful when cross-tabulated. This process allows analysis of two or more variables together. By breaking down our student survey data into male/female responses, shown in the following table, we make an interesting discovery.

Question: Should student fees be increased to build parking lots?

	Total		Male		Female	
	Number	Percent	Number	Percent	Number	Percent
Strongly agree	76	11.5	8	2.2	68	22.0
Agree	255	38.5	54	15.3	201	65.0
No opinion	22	3.3	12	3.4	10	3.2
Disagree	107	16.1	89	25.1	18	5.8
Strongly disagree	203	30.6	191	54.0	12	4.0
Total	**663**	**100.0**	**354**	**100.0**	**309**	**100.0**

Although 50 percent of all student respondents supported the proposal, among females the approval rating was much stronger. Notice that 87 percent of female respondents (combining 22 percent "strongly agree" and 65 percent "agree") endorsed the proposal to increase fees for new parking lots. But among male students, only 17 percent agreed with the proposal. You naturally wonder why such a disparity exists. Are female students more unhappy than males with the current parking situation? If so, why? Is safety a reason? Are male students more concerned with increased fees than female students are?

By cross-tabulating the findings, you sometimes uncover data that may help answer your problem question or that may prompt you to explore other possibilities. Don't, however, undertake cross-tabulation unless it serves more than mere curiosity. Tables also help you compare multiple data collected from questionnaires and surveys. Figure 13.1 shows, in raw form, responses to several survey items. To convert these data into a more usable form, you need to calculate percentages for each item. Then you can arrange the responses in some rational sequence, such as largest percentage to smallest.

Once the data are displayed in a table, you can more easily draw conclusions. As Figure 13.1 shows, Midland College students apparently are not interested in public transportation or shuttle buses from satellite lots. They want to park on campus, with restricted visitor parking; and only half are willing to pay for new parking lots.

Three statistical concepts—mean, median, and mode—help you describe data.

The Three Ms: Mean, Median, Mode. Tables help you organize data, and the three Ms help you describe it. These statistical terms—mean, median, and mode—are all occasionally used loosely to mean "average." To be safe, though, you should learn to apply these statistical terms precisely. When people say *average*, they usually intend to indicate the *mean*, or arithmetic average. Let's say that you're studying the estimated starting salaries of graduates from different disciplines, ranging from education to medicine:

Education	$24,000	
Sociology	25,000	
Humanities	27,000	
Biology	30,000	
Health sciences	31,000	*Median (middle point in continuum)*
Engineering	33,000	*Mode (figure occurring most frequently)*
Business	33,000	
Law	35,000	*Mean (arithmetic average)*
Medicine	77,000	

To find the mean, you simply add up all the salaries and divide by the total number of items ($315,000 ÷ 9 = $35,000). Thus, the mean salary is $35,000. Means are very useful to indicate central tendencies of figures, but they have one major flaw:

FIGURE 13.1 ***Converting Survey Data Into Finished Tables***

Tips for Converting Raw Data

- Tabulate the responses on a copy of the survey form.
- Calculate percentages (divide the score for an item by the total for all responses to that item; for example, for item 1, divide 331 by 663).
- Round off figures to one decimal point or to whole numbers.
- Arrange items in a logical order, such as largest to smallest percentage.
- Prepare a table with a title that tells such things as who, what, when, where, and why.
- Include the total number of respondents.

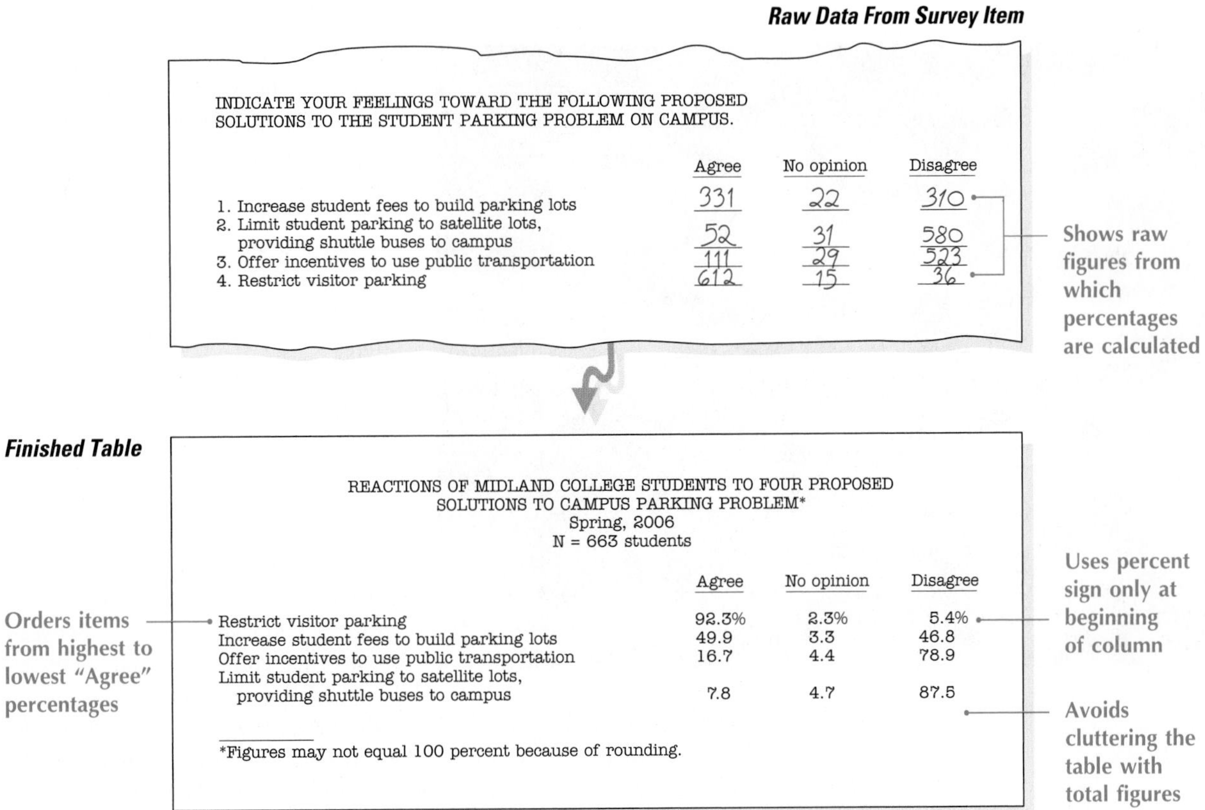

Raw Data From Survey Item

INDICATE YOUR FEELINGS TOWARD THE FOLLOWING PROPOSED SOLUTIONS TO THE STUDENT PARKING PROBLEM ON CAMPUS.

	Agree	No opinion	Disagree
1. Increase student fees to build parking lots	331	22	310
2. Limit student parking to satellite lots, providing shuttle buses to campus	52	31	580
3. Offer incentives to use public transportation	111	29	523
4. Restrict visitor parking	612	15	36

Finished Table

REACTIONS OF MIDLAND COLLEGE STUDENTS TO FOUR PROPOSED SOLUTIONS TO CAMPUS PARKING PROBLEM*
Spring, 2006
N = 663 students

	Agree	No opinion	Disagree
Restrict visitor parking	92.3%	2.3%	5.4%
Increase student fees to build parking lots	49.9	3.3	46.8
Offer incentives to use public transportation	16.7	4.4	78.9
Limit student parking to satellite lots, providing shuttle buses to campus	7.8	4.7	87.5

*Figures may not equal 100 percent because of rounding.

Shows raw figures from which percentages are calculated
Orders items from highest to lowest "Agree" percentages
Uses percent sign only at beginning of column
Avoids cluttering the table with total figures

extremes at either end cause distortion. Notice that the $77,000 figure makes the mean salary of $35,000 deceptively high. It does not represent a valid average for the group. Because means can be misleading, you should use them only when extreme figures do not distort the result.

The mean is the arithmetic average; the median is the midpoint in a group of figures; the mode is the most frequently occurring figure.

The *median* represents the midpoint in a group of figures arranged from lowest to highest (or vice versa). In our list of salaries, the median is $31,000 (health sciences). In other words, half the salaries are above this point and half are below it The median is useful when extreme figures may warp the mean. Whereas salaries for medicine distort the mean, the median, at $31,000, is still a representative figure.

The *mode* is simply the value that occurs most frequently. In our list $33,000 (for engineering and business) represents the mode because it occurs twice. The mode has the advantage of being easily determined—just a quick glance at a list of arranged values reveals it. Although mode is infrequently used by researchers, knowing the mode is useful in some situations. Let's say 7-Eleven sampled its customers to determine what drink size they preferred: 12-ounce, 16-ounce, or Big-Gulp 24-ounce. Finding the mode—the most frequently named figure—makes more sense than calculating the median, which might yield a size that 7-Eleven doesn't even offer. (To remember the meaning of *mode*, think about fashion; the most frequent response, the mode, is the most fashionable.)

Mean, median, and mode figures are especially helpful when the range of values is also known. Range represents the span between the highest and lowest values. To calculate the range, you simply subtract the lowest figure from the highest. In starting salaries for graduates, the range is $53,000 (77,000 − 24,000). Knowing the range enables readers to put mean and median figures into perspective. This knowledge also prompts researchers to wonder why such a range exists, thus stimulating hunches and further investigation to solve problems.

Correlations between variables suggest possible relationships that will explain research findings.

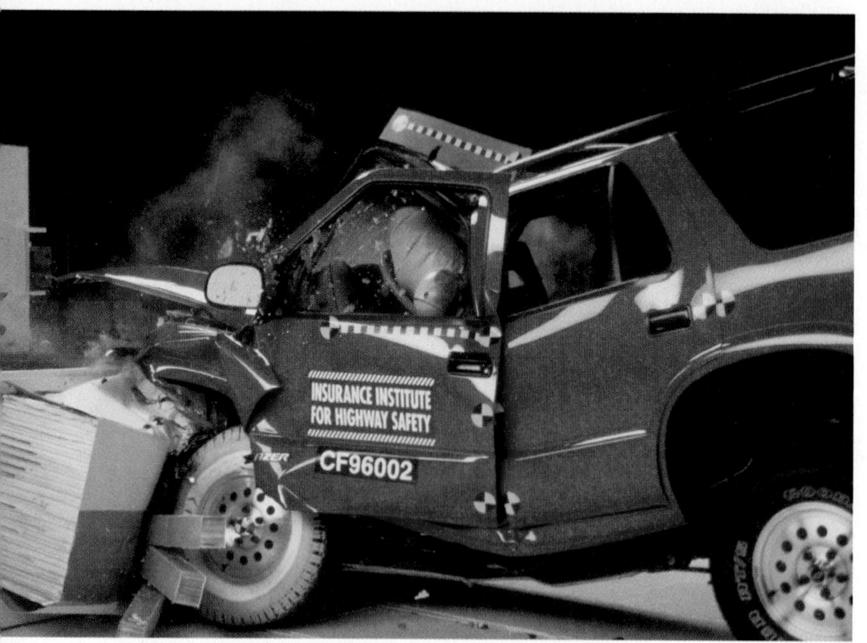

Studies at the Insurance Institute for Highway Safety revealed that simulated tests in its labs correlated well with real-world crashes. This means that vehicles that are safer in the lab, such as the Chevy Blazer, were also safer on the street. Analysis of data helped prove that lab tests can accurately rate the relative safety of vehicles involved in crashes.

Photo: © Insurance Institute for Highway Safety

Correlations. In tabulating and analyzing data, you may see relationships among two or more variables that help explain the findings. If your data for graduates' starting salaries also included years of schooling, you would doubtless notice that graduates with more years of education received higher salaries. For example, beginning teachers, with four years of schooling, earn less than beginning physicians, who have completed nine or more years of education. Thus, a correlation may exist between years of education and starting salary.

Intuition suggests correlations that may or may not prove to be accurate. Is there a relationship between studying and good grades? Between new office computers and increased productivity? Between the rise and fall of hemlines and the rise and fall of the stock market (as some newspaper writers have suggested)? If a correlation seems to exist, can we say that one event caused the other? Does studying cause good grades? Does more schooling guarantee increased salary? Although one event may not be said to cause another, the business researcher who sees a correlation begins to ask why and how the two variables are related. In this way, apparent correlations stimulate investigation and present possible problem solutions to be explored.

In reporting correlations, you should avoid suggesting that a cause-and-effect relationship exists when none can be proved. Only sophisticated research methods can statistically prove correlations. Instead, present a correlation as a possible relationship (*The data suggest that beginning salaries are related to years of education*). Cautious statements followed by explanations gain you credibility and allow readers to make their own decisions.

Grids. Another technique for analyzing raw data—especially verbal data—is the grid. Let's say you've been asked by the CEO to collect opinions from all vice pres-

Figure 13.2 ***Grid to Analyze Complex Verbal Data About Building Cash Reserves***

	Point 1	Point 2	Point 3	Point 4	Overall Reaction
Vice President 1	Disapproves. "Too little, too late."	Strong support. "Best of all points."	Mixed opinion. "Must wait and see market."	Indifferent.	Optimistic, but "hates to delay expansion for six months"
Vice President 2	Disapproves. "Creates credit trap."	Approves.	Strong disapproval.	Approves. "Must improve receivable collections."	Mixed support. "Good self-defense plan."
Vice President 3	Strong disapproval.	Approves. "Key to entire plan."	Indifferent.	Approves, but with "caveats."	"Will work only with sale of unproductive fixed assets."
Vice President 4	Disapproves. "Too risky now."	Strong support. "Start immediately."	Approves, "but may damage image."	Approves. "Benefits far outweigh costs."	Supports plan. Suggests focus on Pacific Rim markets.

idents about the CEO's four-point plan to build cash reserves. The grid shown in Figure 13.2 enables you to summarize the vice presidents' reactions to each point. Notice how this complex verbal information is transformed into concise, manageable data; readers can see immediately which points are supported and which are opposed. Imagine how long you could have struggled to comprehend the meaning of this verbal information before plotting it on a grid.

Grids permit analysis of raw verbal data by grouping and classifying.

Arranging data in a grid also works for projects such as feasibility studies that compare many variables. Assume you must recommend a new printer to your manager. To see how four models compare, you could lay out a grid with the names of printer models across the top. Down the left side, you would list such significant variables as price, warranty, service, capacity, compatibility, and specifications. As you fill in the variables for each model, you can see quickly which model has the lowest price, longest warranty, and so forth. *Consumer Reports* often uses grids to show information.

In addition, grids help classify employment data. For example, suppose your boss asks you to recommend one individual from among many job candidates. You could arrange a grid with names across the top and distinguishing characteristics—experience, skills, education, and other employment interests—down the left side. Summarizing each candidate's points offers a helpful tool for drawing conclusions and writing a report.

Drawing Conclusions and Making Recommendations

learning objective

2

The most widely read portions of a report are the sections devoted to conclusions and recommendations. Knowledgeable readers go straight to the conclusions to see what the report writer thinks the data mean. Because conclusions summarize and explain the findings, they represent the heart of a report. Your value in an organization rises considerably if you can draw conclusions that analyze information logically and show how the data answer questions and solve problems.

Analyzing Data to Arrive at Conclusions

Conclusions summarize and explain the findings in a report.

Any set of data can produce a variety of conclusions. Always bear in mind, though, that the audience for a report wants to know how these data relate to the problem being studied. What do the findings mean in terms of solving the original report problem?

Hired to revive the glory years for the Los Angeles Dodgers, Paul DePodesta is one of the youngest general managers in baseball. A cum laude Harvard graduate, DePodesta challenges conventional wisdom by emphasizing the use of statistical data to arrive at conclusions. Rather than base decisions such as player evaluations on intuition or random observations, he suggests empirical measures. For example, on-base percentage is judged to be three times as important as slugging percentage in determining a player's usefulness and value. Like many contemporary managers, DePodesta aims to blend traditional assessments with quantitative analysis to arrive at conclusions and make recommendations.

Photo: © JON SOOHOO/EPA/Landov

For example, the Marriott Corporation recognized a serious problem among its employees. Conflicting home and work requirements seemed to be causing excessive employee turnover and decreased productivity. To learn the extent of the problem and to consider solutions, Marriott surveyed its staff.[2] It learned, among other things, that nearly 35 percent of its employees had children under age twelve, and 15 percent had children under age five. Other findings, shown in Figure 13.3, indicated that one third of its staff with young children took time off because of child-care difficulties. Moreover, many current employees left previous jobs because of work and family conflicts. The survey also showed that managers did not consider child-care or family problems to be appropriate topics for discussion at work.

A sample of possible conclusions that could be drawn from these findings is shown in Figure 13.3. Notice that each conclusion relates to the initial report problem. Although only a few possible findings and conclusions are shown here, you can see that the conclusions try to explain the causes for the home/work conflict among employees. Many report writers would expand the conclusion section by explaining each item and citing supporting evidence. Even for simplified conclusions, such as those shown in Figure 13.3, you will want to number each item separately and use parallel construction (balanced sentence structure).

Although your goal is to remain objective, drawing conclusions naturally involves a degree of subjectivity. Your goals, background, and frame of reference all color the inferences you make. When Federal Express, for example, initially expanded its next-day delivery service to Europe, it racked up a staggering loss of $1.2 billion in four years of operation.[3] The facts could not be disputed. But what conclusions could be drawn? The CEO might conclude that the competition was greater than anticipated but that FedEx was making inroads; patience was all that was needed. The board of directors and stockholders, however, might conclude that the competition was too well entrenched and that it was time to pull the plug on an ill-fated operation. All writers interpret findings from their own perspectives, but they should not manipulate them to achieve a preconceived purpose.

Effective report conclusions are objective and bias-free.

You can make your report conclusions more objective if you use consistent evaluation criteria. Let's say you are comparing computers for an office equipment purchase. If you evaluate each by the same criteria (such as price, specifications, service, and warranty), your conclusions are more likely to be bias-free.

You also need to avoid the temptation to sensationalize or exaggerate your findings or conclusions. Be careful of words like *many*, *most*, and *all*. Instead of *many of the respondents felt. . .*, you might more accurately write *some of the respondents. . . .* Examine your motives before drawing conclusions. Don't let preconceptions or wishful thinking color your reasoning.

FIGURE 13.3 ***Report Conclusions and Recommendations***

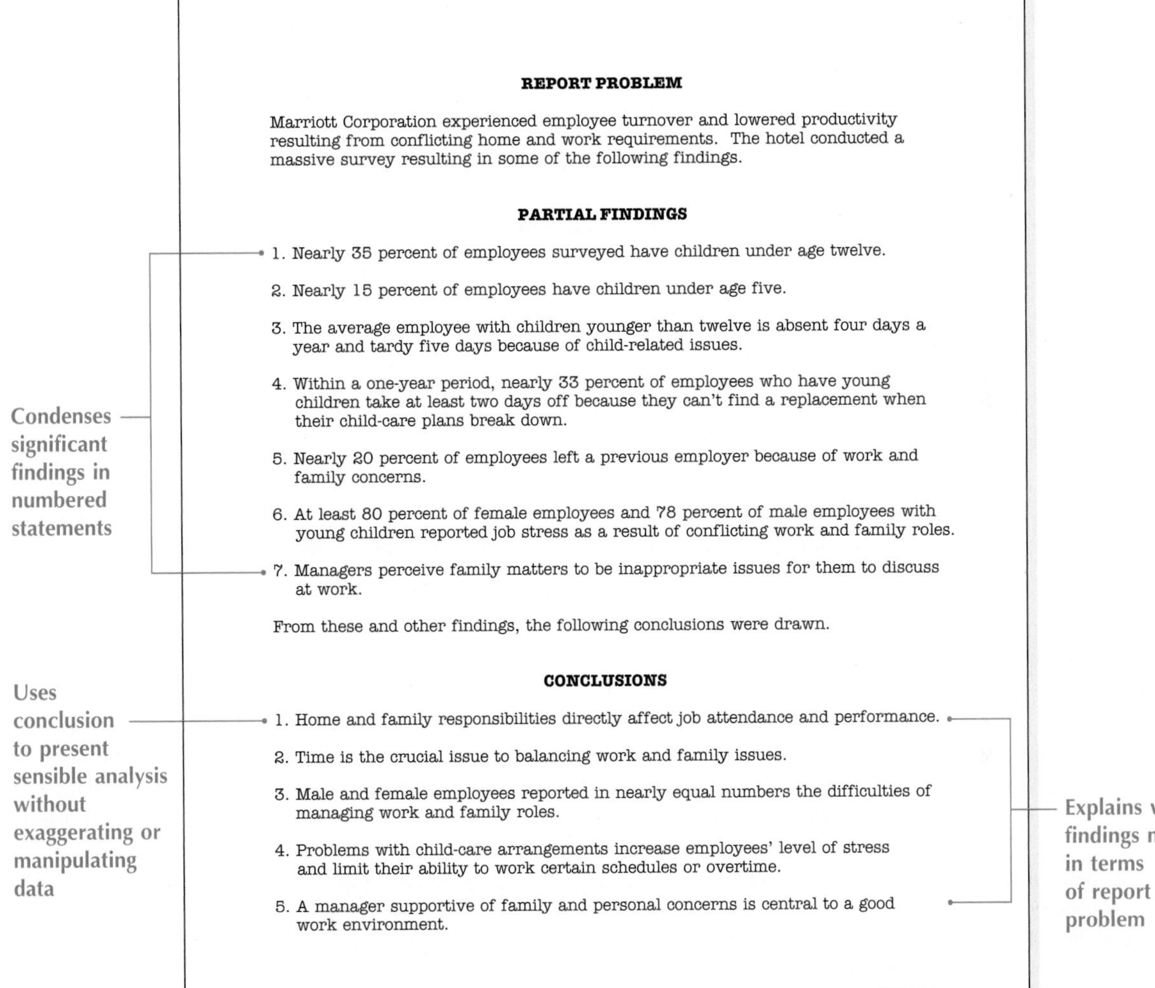

Tips for Writing Conclusions
• Interpret and summarize the findings; tell what they mean.
• Relate the conclusions to the report problem.
• Limit the conclusions to the data presented; do not introduce new material.
• Number the conclusions and present them in parallel form.
• Be objective; avoid exaggerating or manipulating the data.
• Use consistent criteria in evaluating options.
REPORT PROBLEM
Marriott Corporation experienced employee turnover and lowered productivity resulting from conflicting home and work requirements. The hotel conducted a massive survey resulting in some of the following findings.
PARTIAL FINDINGS
1. Nearly 35 percent of employees surveyed have children under age twelve.
2. Nearly 15 percent of employees have children under age five.
3. The average employee with children younger than twelve is absent four days a year and tardy five days because of child-related issues.
4. Within a one-year period, nearly 33 percent of employees who have young children take at least two days off because they can't find a replacement when their child-care plans break down.
5. Nearly 20 percent of employees left a previous employer because of work and family concerns.
6. At least 80 percent of female employees and 78 percent of male employees with young children reported job stress as a result of conflicting work and family roles.
7. Managers perceive family matters to be inappropriate issues for them to discuss at work.
From these and other findings, the following conclusions were drawn.
CONCLUSIONS
1. Home and family responsibilities directly affect job attendance and performance.
2. Time is the crucial issue to balancing work and family issues.
3. Male and female employees reported in nearly equal numbers the difficulties of managing work and family roles.
4. Problems with child-care arrangements increase employees' level of stress and limit their ability to work certain schedules or overtime.
5. A manager supportive of family and personal concerns is central to a good work environment.
Condenses significant findings in numbered statements
Uses conclusion to present sensible analysis without exaggerating or manipulating data
Explains what findings mean in terms of report problem

Preparing Report Recommendations

Conclusions explain what the problem is, whereas the recommendations tell how to solve it. Typically, readers prefer specific recommendations. They want to know exactly how to implement the suggestions. The specificity of your recommendations depends on your authorization. What are you commissioned to do, and what does the reader expect? In the planning stages of your report project, you anticipate what the reader wants in the report. Your intuition and your knowledge of the audience indicate how far your recommendations should be developed.

FIGURE 13.3 *Continued*

Tips for Writing Recommendations

- Make specific suggestions for actions to solve the report problem.
- Prepare practical recommendations that will be agreeable to the audience.
- Avoid conditional words such as *maybe* and *perhaps*.
- Present each suggestion separately as a command beginning with a verb.
- Number the recommendations for improved readability.
- If requested, describe how the recommendations may be implemented.
- When possible, arrange the recommendations in an announced order, such as most important to least important.

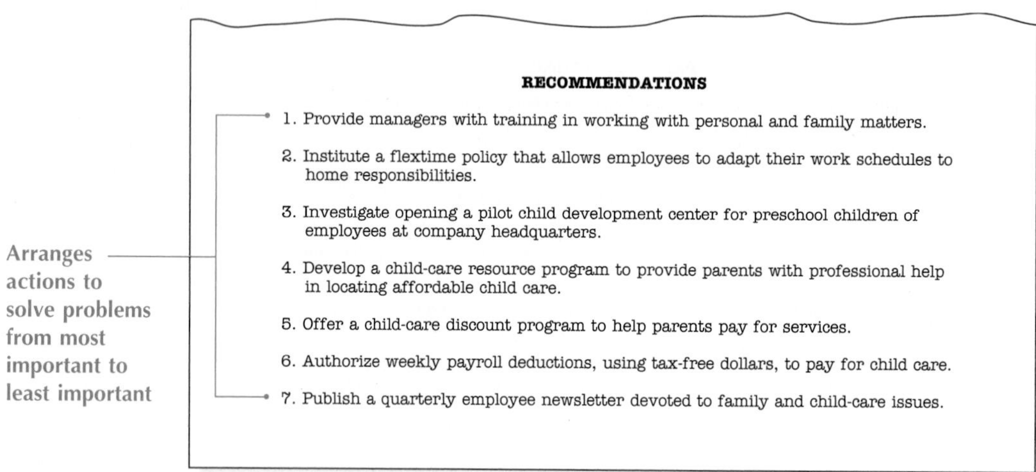

RECOMMENDATIONS

1. Provide managers with training in working with personal and family matters.
2. Institute a flextime policy that allows employees to adapt their work schedules to home responsibilities.
3. Investigate opening a pilot child development center for preschool children of employees at company headquarters.
4. Develop a child-care resource program to provide parents with professional help in locating affordable child care.
5. Offer a child-care discount program to help parents pay for services.
6. Authorize weekly payroll deductions, using tax-free dollars, to pay for child care.
7. Publish a quarterly employee newsletter devoted to family and child-care issues.

Arranges actions to solve problems from most important to least important

In the recommendations section of the Marriott employee survey, shown in Figure 13.3, many of the suggestions are summarized. In the actual report each recommendation could have been backed up with specifics and ideas for implementing them. For example, the child-care resource recommendation would be explained: it provides parents with names of agencies and professionals who specialize in locating child care across the country.

The best recommendations offer practical suggestions that are feasible and agreeable to the audience.

A good report provides practical recommendations that are agreeable to the audience. In the Marriott survey, for example, report researchers knew that the company wanted to help employees cope with conflicts between family and work obligations. Thus, the report's conclusions and recommendations focused on ways to resolve the conflict. If Marriott's goal had been merely to save money by reducing employee absenteeism, the recommendations would have been quite different.

If possible, make each recommendation a command. Note in Figure 13.3 that each recommendation begins with a verb. This structure sounds forceful and confident and helps the reader comprehend the information quickly. Avoid words such as *maybe* and *perhaps*; they suggest conditional statements that reduce the strength of recommendations.

Experienced writers may combine recommendations and conclusions. In short reports writers may omit conclusions and move straight to recommendations. An important point about recommendations is that they include practical suggestions for solving the report problem.

Moving From Findings to Recommendations

Recommendations evolve from interpretation of the findings and conclusions. Consider the following examples from the Marriott survey:

Finding
A majority of managers perceive family matters to be inappropriate issues for them to discuss at work.

Conclusion
Managers are neither willing nor trained to discuss family troubles that may cause employees to miss work.

Conclusions explain a problem; recommendations offer specific suggestions for solving the problem.

Recommendation
Provide managers with training in recognizing and working with personal and family troubles that affect work.

Finding
Within a one-year period, nearly 33 percent of employees who have young children take at least two days off because they can't find a replacement when their child-care plans break down.

Conclusion
Problems with child-care arrangements increase employees' level of stress and create absenteeism.

Recommendation
Develop a child-care resource program to provide parents with professional help in locating affordable child care.

Organizing Data

learning objective

3

After collecting sets of data, interpreting them, drawing conclusions, and thinking about the recommendations you will make, you're ready to organize the parts of the report into a logical framework. Poorly organized reports lead to frustration. Readers will not understand, remember, or be persuaded. Wise writers know that reports rarely "just organize themselves." Instead, organization must be imposed on the data.

The direct pattern is appropriate for informed or receptive readers; the indirect pattern is appropriate when educating or persuading.

Informational reports, as you learned in Chapter 12, generally present data without interpretation. As shown in Figure 13.4, informational reports are typically organized in three parts: (1) introduction/background, (2) facts/findings, and (3) summary/conclusion. Analytical reports, which generally analyze data and draw conclusions, typically contain four parts: (1) introduction/problem, (2) facts/findings, (3) discussion/analysis, and (4) conclusions/recommendations. However, the parts in analytical reports do not always follow the same sequence. For readers who know about the project, are supportive, or are eager to learn the results quickly, the direct method is appropriate. Conclusions and recommendations, if requested, appear up front. For readers who must be educated or persuaded, the indirect method works better. Conclusions/recommendations appear last, after the findings have been presented and analyzed.

Although every report is different, the overall organizational patterns described here typically hold true. The real challenge, though, lies in (1) organizing the facts/findings and discussion/analysis sections and (2) providing reader cues.

FIGURE 13.4 ***Organizational Patterns for Informational and Analytical Reports***

Informational Reports	Analytical Reports	
	Direct Pattern	**Indirect Pattern**
I. Introduction/background	I. Introduction/problem	I. Introduction/problem
II. Facts/findings	II. Conclusions/recommendations	II. Facts/findings
III. Summary/conclusion	III. Facts/findings	III. Discussion/analysis
	IV. Discussion/analysis	IV. Conclusions/recommendations

Ordering Information Logically

Organizing by time, component, importance, criteria, or convention helps readers comprehend data.

Whether you're writing informational or analytical reports, the data you've collected must be structured coherently. Five common organizational methods are by time, component, importance, criteria, or convention. Regardless of the method you choose, be sure that it helps the reader understand the data. Reader comprehension, not writer convenience, should govern organization.

Time. Ordering data by time means establishing a chronology of events. Agendas, minutes of meetings, progress reports, and procedures are usually organized by time. For example, a report describing an eight-week training program would most likely be organized by weeks. A plan for step-by-step improvement of customer service would be organized by each step. A monthly trip report submitted by a sales rep might describe customers visited Week 1, Week 2, and so on. Beware of overusing time chronologies, however. Although this method is easy and often mirrors the way data are collected, chronologies—like the sales rep's trip report—tend to be boring, repetitious, and lacking in emphasis. Readers can't always pick out what's important.

Component. Especially for informational reports, data may be organized by components such as location, geography, division, product, or part. For instance, a report detailing company expansion might divide the plan into West Coast, East Coast, and Midwest expansion. The report could also be organized by divisions: personal products, consumer electronics, and household goods. A report comparing profits among makers of athletic shoes might group the data by company: Nike, Reebok, Adidas, and so forth. Organization by components works best when the classifications already exist.

Organizing by level of importance saves the time of busy readers and increases the odds that key information will be retained.

Importance. Organization by importance involves beginning with the most important item and proceeding to the least important—or vice versa. For example, a report discussing the reasons for declining product sales would present the most important reason first followed by less important ones. The Marriott report describing work/family conflicts might begin by discussing child care, if the writer considered it the most important issue. Using importance to structure findings involves a value judgment. The writer must decide what is most important, always keeping in mind the readers' priorities and expectations. Busy readers appreciate seeing important points first; they may skim or skip other points. On the other hand, building to a climax by moving from least important to most important enables the writer to focus attention at the end. Thus, the reader is more likely to remember the most important item. Of course, the writer also risks losing the attention of the reader along the way.

Criteria. Establishing criteria by which to judge helps writers to treat topics consistently. Let's say your report compares health plans A, B, and C. For each plan you examine the same standards: Criterion 1, cost per employee; Criterion 2, amount of deductible; and Criterion 3, patient benefits. The resulting data could then be organized either by plans or by criteria:

To evaluate choices or plans fairly, apply the same criteria to each.

By Plan	By Criteria
Plan A	Criterion 1
Criterion 1	Plan A
Criterion 2	Plan B
Criterion 3	Plan C
Plan B	Criterion 2
Criterion 1	Plan A
Criterion 2	Plan B
Criterion 3	Plan C
Plan C	Criterion 3
Criterion 1	Plan A
Criterion 2	Plan B
Criterion 3	Plan C

Although you might favor organizing the data by plans (because that's the way you collected the data), the better way is by criteria. When you discuss patient benefits, for example, you would examine all three plans' benefits together. Organizing a report around criteria helps readers make comparisons, instead of forcing them to search through the report for similar data.

Organizing by convention simplifies the organizational task and yields easy-to-follow information.

Convention. Many operational and recurring reports are structured according to convention. That is, they follow a prescribed plan that everyone understands. For example, an automotive parts manufacturer might ask all sales reps to prepare a weekly report with these headings: *Competitive observations* (competitors' price changes, discounts, new products, product problems, distributor changes, product promotions), *Product problems* (quality, performance, needs), and *Customer service problems* (delivery, mailings, correspondence). Management gets exactly the information it needs in an easy-to-read form.

Like operating reports, proposals are often organized conventionally. They might use such groupings as background, problem, proposed solution, staffing, schedule, costs, and authorization. As you might expect, reports following these conventional, prescribed structures greatly simplify the task of organization. (Proposals will be presented in Chapter 14.)

Providing Reader Cues

When you finish organizing a report, you probably see a neat outline in your mind: major points, supported by subpoints and details. Readers, however, don't know the material as well as you do; they cannot see your outline. To guide them through the data, you need to provide the equivalent of a map and road signs. For both formal and informal reports, devices such as introductions, transitions, and headings prevent readers from getting lost.

Good openers tell readers what topics will be covered in what order and why.

Introduction. One of the best ways to point a reader in the right direction is to provide a report introduction that does three things:

- Tells the purpose of the report
- Describes the significance of the topic
- Previews the main points and the order in which they will be developed

The following paragraph includes all three elements in introducing a report on computer security:

> The purpose of this report is to examine the security of our current computer operations and present suggestions for improving security. Lax computer security could mean loss of information, loss of business, and damage to our equipment and systems. Because many former employees released during recent downsizing efforts know our systems, major changes must be made. To improve security, I will present three recommendations: (1) begin using smart cards that limit access to our computer system, (2) alter sign-on and log-off procedures, (3) move central computer operations to a more secure area.

This opener tells the purpose (examining computer security), describes its significance (loss of information and business, damage to equipment and systems), and outlines how the report is organized (three recommendations). Good openers in effect set up a contract with the reader. The writer promises to cover certain topics in a specified order. Readers expect the writer to fulfill the contract. They want the topics to be developed as promised—using the same wording and presented in the order mentioned. For example, if in your introduction you state that you will discuss the use of *smart cards*, don't change the heading for that section to *access cards*. Remember that the introduction provides a map to a report; switching the names on the map will ensure that readers get lost. To maintain consistency, delay writing the introduction until after you have completed the report. Long, complex reports may require introductions for each section.

Like tourists who need a map to understand where they are and to reach their destinations, report readers need the equivalent of a map and road signs to find their way through a report. Introductions, transitions, and headings provide cues so that readers know where they've been and where they are headed.

Transitions. Expressions such as *on the contrary*, *at the same time*, and *however* show relationships and help reveal the logical flow of ideas in a report. These transitional expressions enable writers to tell readers where ideas are headed and how they relate. Notice how abrupt the following two sentences sound without a transition: *American car manufacturers admired Toyota's just-in-time inventory practices. Adopting a JIT system [however] means total restructuring of assembly plants.*

The following expressions (see Chapter 6, Figure 6.7 for a complete list) enable you to show readers how you are developing your ideas.

Transitional expressions inform readers where ideas are headed and how they relate.

To present additional thoughts: additionally, again, also, moreover, furthermore

To suggest cause and effect: accordingly, as a result, consequently, therefore

To contrast ideas: at the same time, but, however, on the contrary, though, yet

To show time and order: after, before, first, finally, now, previously, then, to conclude

To clarify points: for example, for instance, in other words, that is, thus

In using these expressions, recognize that they don't have to sit at the head of a sentence. Listen to the rhythm of the sentence, and place the expression where a natural pause occurs. Used appropriately, transitional expressions serve readers as guides; misused or overused, they can be as distracting and frustrating as too many road signs on a highway.

Headings. Good headings are another structural cue that assist readers in comprehending the organization of a report. They highlight major ideas, allowing busy readers to see the big picture in a glance. Moreover, headings provide resting points for the mind and for the eye, breaking up large chunks of text into manageable and inviting segments.

Good headings provide organizational cues and spotlight key ideas.

Report writers may use functional or talking heads. Functional heads (for example, *Background*, *Findings*, *Personnel*, and *Production Costs*) describe functions or general topics. They show the outline of a report but provide little insight for readers. Functional headings are useful for routine reports. They're also appropriate for sensitive topics that might provoke emotional reactions. By keeping the headings general, experienced writers hope to minimize reader opposition or response to controversial subjects. Talking heads (for example, *Two Sides to Campus Parking Problem* or *Survey Shows Support for Parking Fees*) provide more information and interest. Unless carefully written, however, talking heads can fail to reveal the organization of a report. With some planning, though, headings can be both functional and talking, such as *Parking Recommendations: Shuttle and New Structures.* To create the most effective headings, follow a few basic guidelines:

Headings should be brief, parallel, and ordered in a logical hierarchy.

- **Use appropriate heading levels.** The position and format of a heading indicate its level of importance and relationship to other points. Figure 13.5 both illustrates and discusses a commonly used heading format for business reports.
- **Capitalize and underline carefully.** Most writers use all capital letters (without underlines) for main titles, such as the report, chapter, and unit titles. For first- and second-level headings, they capitalize only the first letter of main words. For additional emphasis, they use a bold font, as shown in Figure 13.5.
- **Balance headings within levels.** All headings at a given level should be grammatically similar. For example, *Developing Product Teams* and *Presenting Plan to Management* are balanced, but *Development of Product Teams* and *Presenting Plan to Management* are not.
- **For short reports use first- or second-level headings.** Many business reports contain only one or two levels of headings. For such reports use first-level headings (centered, bolded) and/or second-level headings (flush left, bolded). See Figure 13.5.
- **Include at least one heading per report page.** Headings increase the readability and attractiveness of report pages. Use at least one per page to break up blocks of text.
- **Keep headings short but clear.** One-word headings are emphatic but not always clear. For example, the heading *Budget* does not adequately describe figures for a summer project involving student interns for an oil company in Texas. Try to keep your headings brief (no more than eight words), but make sure they are understandable. Experiment with headings that concisely tell who, what, when, where, and why.

FIGURE 13.5 ***Levels of Headings in Reports***

2-inch top margin

REPORT, CHAPTER, AND PART TITLES

2 blank lines

The title of a report, chapter heading, or major part (such as CONTENTS or NOTES) should be centered in all caps. If the title requires more than one line, arrange it in an inverted triangle with the longest lines at the top. Begin the text a triple space (two blank lines) below the title, as shown here.

2 blank lines

First-Level Subheading

1 blank line

Headings indicating the first level of division are centered and bolded. Capitalize the first letter of each main word. Whether a report is single-spaced or double-spaced, most typists triple-space (leaving two blank lines) before and double-space (leaving one blank line) after a first-level subheading.

1 blank line

Every level of heading should be followed by some text. For example, we could not jump from "First-Level Subheading," shown above, to "Second-Level Subheading," shown below, without some discussion between.

Good writers strive to develop coherency and fluency by ending most sections with a lead-in that introduces the next section. The lead-in consists of a sentence or two announcing the next topic.

2 blank lines

Second-Level Subheading

Headings that divide topics introduced by first-level subheadings are bolded and begin at the left margin. Use a triple space above and a double space after a second-level subheading. If a report has only one level of heading, use either first- or second-level subheading style.

Always be sure to divide topics into two or more subheadings. If you have only one subheading, eliminate it and absorb the discussion under the previous major heading. Try to make all headings within a level grammatically equal. For example, all second-level headings might use verb forms (*Preparing*, *Organizing*, and *Composing*) or noun forms (*Preparation*, *Organization*, and *Composition*).

1 blank line

Third-level subheading. Because it is part of the paragraph that follows, a third-level subheading is also called a "paragraph subheading." Capitalize only the first word and proper nouns in the subheading. Bold the subheading and end it with a period. Begin typing the paragraph text immediately following the period, as shown here. Double-space before a paragraph subheading. If the entire report is double-spaced, paragraphs would be indented, including this third-level subheading.

Places major headings in the center

Capitalizes initial letters of main words

Does not indent paragraphs because report is single-spaced

Starts at left margin

Makes heading part of paragraph

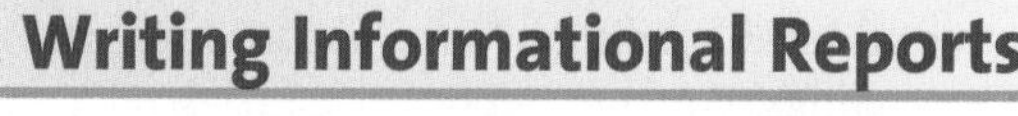

learning objective 4

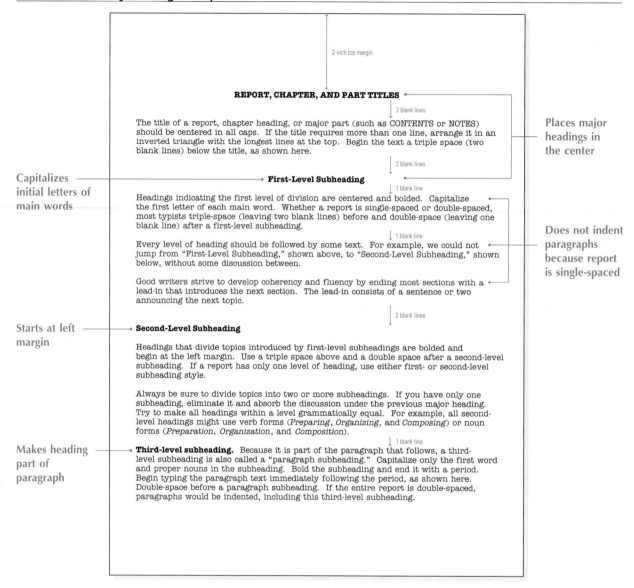

Writing Informational Reports

Informational reports provide data on periodic and situational activities for readers who do not need to be persuaded.

Now that we've covered the basics of gathering, interpreting, and organizing data, we are ready to put it all together into typical informational or analytical reports. Informational reports often describe periodic, recurring activities (such as monthly sales or weekly customer calls) as well as situational, nonrecurring events (such as trips, conferences, and progress on special projects). What they have in common is delivering information to readers who do not have to be persuaded. Informational report readers usually are neutral or receptive.

You can expect to write many informational reports as an entry-level or middle-management employee. Because these reports generally deliver nonsensitive data and thus will not upset the reader, they are organized directly. Often they need little background material or introductory comments because readers are familiar with the topics. Although they're generally conversational and informal, informational reports

career coach

Ten Tips for Designing Better Documents

Desktop publishing packages, high-level word processing programs, and advanced printers now make it possible for you to turn out professional-looking documents and promotional materials. The temptation, though, is to overdo it by incorporating too many features in one document. Here are ten tips for applying good sense and good design principles in "publishing" your documents.

- **Analyze your audience.** Sales brochures and promotional letters can be flashy—with color print, oversized type, and fancy borders—to attract attention. Such effects, however, are out of place for most conservative business documents. Also consider whether your readers will be reading painstakingly or merely browsing. Lists and headings help those readers who are in a hurry.
- **Choose an appropriate type size.** For most business memos, letters, and reports, the body text should be 10 to 12 points tall (a point is 1/72 of an inch). Larger type looks amateurish, and smaller type is hard to read.
- **Use a consistent type font.** Although your software may provide a variety of fonts, stay with a single family of type within one document—at least until you become more expert. The most popular fonts are Times Roman and Arial. For emphasis and contrast, you can vary the font size and weight with **bold**, *italic*, ***bold italic***, and other selections.
- **Generally, don't justify right margins.** Textbooks, novels, newspapers, magazines, and other long works are usually set with justified (even) right margins. However, for shorter works ragged-right margins are recommended because such margins add white space and help readers locate the beginnings of new lines. Slower readers find ragged-right copy more legible.
- **Separate paragraphs and sentences appropriately.** The first line of a paragraph should be indented or preceded by a blank line. To separate sentences, typists have traditionally left two spaces. This spacing is still acceptable, but most writers now follow printers' standards and leave only one space.
- **Design readable headlines.** Presenting headlines and headings in all caps is generally discouraged because solid blocks of capital letters interfere with recognition of word patterns. To further improve readability, select a sans serif typeface (one without cross strokes or embellishment), such as Arial.
- **Strive for an attractive page layout.** In designing title pages or graphics, provide a balance between print and white space. Also consider placing the focal point (something that draws the reader's eye) at the optical center of a page—about three lines above the actual center. Moreover, remember that the average reader scans a page from left to right and top to bottom in a *Z* pattern. Plan your graphics accordingly.
- **Use graphics and clip art with restraint.** Charts, original drawings, photographs, and clip art can be scanned into documents. Use such images, however, only when they are well drawn, relevant, purposeful, and appropriately sized.
- **Avoid amateurish effects.** Many beginning writers, eager to display every graphic device a program offers, produce busy, cluttered documents. Too many typefaces, ruled lines, oversized headlines, and images will overwhelm readers. Strive for simple, clean, and forceful effects.
- **Develop expertise.** Learn to use the desktop publishing features of your current word processing software, or investigate one of the special programs, such as QuarkXPress, Adobe's InDesign, and Corel's Ventura. Although the learning curve for many of these programs is steep, such effort is well spent if you will be producing newsletters, brochures, announcements, visual aids, and promotional literature.

Career Application

Buy or borrow a book or two on designing documents, and select ten tips that you could share with the class. In teams of three or four, analyze the design and layout of three or four annual reports. Evaluate the appropriateness of typeface and type size, white space, headings, and graphics.

should not be so casual that the reader struggles to find the important points. Main points must be immediately visible. Headings, lists, bulleted items, and other graphic highlighting, as well as clear organization, enable readers to grasp major ideas immediately. The Career Coach box on the previous page provides additional pointers on design features and techniques that can improve your reports.

Periodic (Activity) Reports

Periodic reports keep management informed of operations and activities.

Most businesses—especially larger ones—require periodic reports (sometimes called *activity reports*) to keep management informed of operations. These recurring reports are written at regular intervals—weekly, monthly, yearly—so that management can monitor and, if necessary, remedy business strategies. Some periodic reports simply contain figures, such as sales volume, number and kind of customer service calls, shipments delivered, accounts payable, and personnel data. More challenging periodic reports require description and discussion of activities. In preparing a narrative description of their activities, employees writing periodic reports usually do the following:

- Summarize regular activities and events performed during the reporting period
- Describe irregular events deserving the attention of management
- Highlight special needs and problems

spotlight *on communicators*

Regular financial reports keep Protocol Telecommunications squeaky clean. Anthony Miranda, president of Protocol, doesn't wait for his bankers or investors to demand his financials. "I want there to be no question at any time that our financial information was misstated or less than fully disclosed." In addition to periodic financial reports, Protocol employees may submit trip and conference reports describing attendance at trade shows or meetings. Such reports identify the event, summarize relevant information acquired, itemize expenses, and suggest how the information may be applied.

Photo: © Amy Etra

Managers naturally want to know that routine activities are progressing normally. They're often more interested, though, in what the competition is doing and in how operations may be affected by unusual events or problems. In companies with open lines of communication, managers expect to be informed of the bad news along with the good news. Jim Chrisman, sales rep for a West Coast sprinkler manufacturer, worked with a group of fellow sales reps and managers to produce the format for the periodic report shown in Figure 13.6. In Jim's words, "We used to write three- and four-page weekly activity reports that, I hate to admit, rambled all over the place. When our managers complained that they weren't getting the information they wanted, we sat down together and developed a report form with four categories: (1) activity summary, (2) competition update, (3) product problems and comments, and (4) needs. Then one manager wrote several sample reports that we studied. Now, my reports are shorter and more focused. I try to hit the highlights in covering my daily activities, but I really concentrate on product problems and items that I must have to do a better job. Managers tell us that they need this kind of detailed feedback so that they can respond to the competition and also develop new products that our customers want."

Trip, Convention, and Conference Reports

Employees sent on business trips or to conventions and conferences typically must submit reports when they return. Organizations want to know that their money was well spent in funding the travel. These reports inform management about new procedures, equipment, and laws as well as supply information affecting products, operations, and service.

The hardest parts of writing these reports are selecting the most relevant material and organizing it coherently. Generally, it's best not to use chronological

FIGURE 13.6 *Periodic (Activity) Report—Memo Format*

1 Prewriting

ANALYZE: The purpose of this report is to inform management of the week's activities, customer reactions, and the rep's needs.

ANTICIPATE: The audience is a manager who wants to be able to pick out the report highlights quickly. His reaction will probably be neutral or positive.

ADAPT: Introduce the report data in a direct, straightforward manner.

2 Writing

RESEARCH: Verify data for the landscape judging test. Collect facts about competitors. Double-check problems and needs.

ORGANIZE: Make lists of items for each of the four report categories. Be sure to distinguish between problems and needs. Emphasize needs.

COMPOSE: Write and print first draft on a computer.

3 Revising

REVISE: Look for ways to eliminate wordiness. For greater emphasis use a bulleted list for *Competition Update* and for *Needs*. Make all items parallel.

PROOFREAD: Run spell checker. Adjust white space around headings.

EVALUATE: Does this report provide significant data in an easy-to-read format?

Rain Land
Where every drop counts

DATE: March 15, 2006

TO: Steve Schumacher

FROM: Jim Chrisman JC

SUBJECT: Weekly Activity Report

Presents internal informational report in memo format

Activity Summary

Highlights of my activities for the week ending March 14 follow:

Fort Worth. On Thursday and Friday I demonstrated our new Rain Stream drip systems at a vendor fair at Benbrook Farm Supply, where more than 500 people walked through.

Arlington State College. Over the weekend I was a judge for the Texas Landscape Technician test given on the ASC campus. This certification program ensures potential employers that a landscaper is properly trained. Applicants are tested in such areas as irrigation theory, repair, troubleshooting, installation, and controller programming. The event proved to be very productive. I was able to talk to my distributors and to several important contractors whose crews were taking the tests.

Condenses weekly activity report into topics requested by management

Competition Update

- Toronado can't seem to fill its open sales position in the west Texas territory.
- RainCo tried to steal the Trinity Country Club golf course contract from us by waiting until the job was spec'd our way and then submitting a lower bid. Fortunately, the Trinity people saw through this ploy and awarded us the contract nevertheless.
- Atlas has a real warranty problem with its 500 series in this area. One distributor had over 200 controllers returned in a seven-week period.

Uses bulleted list for high "skim value"

Product Problems, Comments

A contractor in Wichita Falls told me that our Rain Stream No. 250 valves do not hold the adjustment screw in the throttled-down position. Are they designed to do so?

Our Remote Streamer S-100 is generating considerable excitement. Every time I mention it, people come out of the woodwork to request demos. I gave four demos last week and have three more scheduled this week. I'm not sure, though, how quickly these demos will translate into sales.

Needs

- More information on xerigation training.
- Spanish training videos showing our products.
- Spray nozzle to service small planter areas, say 6 to 8 feet.

Summarizes needs in abbreviated, easy-to-read form

Trip and conference reports identify the event, summarize three to five main points, itemize expenses separately, and express appreciation or suggest action to be taken.

sequencing (*in the morning we did X, at lunch we heard Y, and in the afternoon we did Z*). Instead, you should focus on three to five topics in which your reader will be interested. These items become the body of the report. Then simply add an introduction and closing, and your report is organized. Here is a general outline for trip, conference, and convention reports:

- Begin by identifying the event (exact date, name, and location) and previewing the topics to be discussed.
- Summarize in the body three to five main points that might benefit the reader.
- Itemize your expenses, if requested, on a separate sheet.
- Close by expressing appreciation, suggesting action to be taken, or synthesizing the value of the trip or event.

Jeff Marchant was recently named employment coordinator in the Human Resources Department of an electronics appliance manufacturer headquartered in central Ohio. Recognizing his lack of experience in interviewing job applicants, he asked permission to attend a one-day conference on the topic. His boss, Angela Taylor, encouraged Jeff to attend, saying, "We all need to brush up on our interviewing techniques. Come back and tell us what you learned." When he returned, Jeff wrote the conference report shown in Figure 13.7. Here's how he describes its preparation: "I know my boss values brevity, so I worked hard to make my report no more than a page and a quarter. The conference saturated me with great ideas, far too many to cover in one brief report. So, I decided to discuss three topics that would be most useful to our staff. Although I had to be brief, I nonetheless wanted to provide as many details—especially about common interviewing mistakes—as possible. By the third draft, I had compressed my ideas into a manageable size without sacrificing any of the meaning."

Progress and Interim Reports

Progress and interim reports describe ongoing projects to both internal and external readers.

Continuing projects often require progress or interim reports to describe their status. These reports may be external (advising customers regarding the headway of their projects) or internal (informing management of the status of activities). Progress reports typically follow this pattern of development:

- Specify in the opening the purpose and nature of the project.
- Provide background information if the audience requires filling in.
- Describe the work completed.
- Explain the work currently in progress, including personnel, activities, methods, and locations.
- Anticipate problems and possible remedies.
- Discuss future activities and provide the expected completion date.

As a location manager for Eagle Video Productions, Gina Genova frequently writes progress reports, such as the one shown in Figure 13.8. Producers want to be informed of what she's doing, and a phone call doesn't provide a permanent record. Here's how she describes the reasoning behind her progress report: "I usually include background information in my reports because a director doesn't always know or remember exactly what specifications I was given for a location search. Then I try to hit the high points of what I've completed and what I plan to do next, without getting bogged down in tiny details. Although it would be easier to skip them, I've learned to be up front with any problems that I anticipate. I don't tell how to solve the problems, but I feel duty-bound to at least mention them."

FIGURE 13.7 ***Conference Report—Memo Format***

Interoffice Memo

DATE: April 22, 2006

TO: Angela Taylor

FROM: Jeff Marchant *JM*

SUBJECT: TRAINING CONFERENCE ON EMPLOYMENT INTERVIEWING

I enjoyed attending the "Interviewing People" training conference sponsored by the National Business Foundation. This one-day meeting, held in Columbus on April 19, provided excellent advice that will help us strengthen our interviewing techniques. Although the conference covered many topics, this report concentrates on three areas: structuring the interview, avoiding common mistakes, and responding to new legislation.

Identifies topic and previews how the report is organized

Structuring the Interview

Job interviews usually have three parts. The opening establishes a friendly rapport with introductions, a few polite questions, and an explanation of the purpose for the interview. The body of the interview consists of questions controlled by the interviewer. The interviewer has three goals: (a) educating the applicant about the job, (b) eliciting information about the applicant's suitability for the job, and (c) promoting goodwill about the organization. In closing, the interviewer should encourage the applicant to ask questions, summarize main points, and indicate what actions will follow.

Sets off major topics with centered headings

Avoiding Common Mistakes

Probably the most interesting and practical part of the conference centered on common mistakes made by interviewers, some of which I summarize here:

1. Not taking notes at each interview. Recording important facts enables you to remember the first candidate as easily as you remember the last—and all those in between.

2. Not testing the candidate's communication skills. To be able to evaluate a candidate's ability to express ideas, ask the individual to explain some technical jargon from his or her current position.

3. Having departing employees conduct the interviews for their replacements. Departing employees may be unreliable as interviewers because they tend to hire candidates not quite as strong as they are.

4. Failing to check references. As many as 15 percent of all résumés may contain falsified data. The best way to check references is to network: ask the person whose name has been given to suggest the name of another person.

Covers facts that will most interest and help reader

Angela Taylor Page 2 April 22, 2006

Responding to New Legislation

Current federal provisions of the Americans With Disabilities Act prohibit interviewers from asking candidates—or even their references—about candidates' disabilities. A question we frequently asked ("Do you have any physical limitations which would prevent you from performing the job for which you are applying?") would now break the law. Interviewers must also avoid asking about medical history; prescription drug use; prior workers' compensation claims; work absenteeism due to illness; and past treatment for alcoholism, drug use, or mental illness.

Concludes with offer to share information

Sharing This Information

This conference provided me with valuable training that I would like to share with other department members at a future staff meeting. Let me know when it can be scheduled.

FIGURE 13.8 ***Progress Report—Letter Format***

Tips for Writing Progress Reports

- Identify the purpose and the nature of the project immediately.
- Supply background information only if the reader must be educated.
- Describe the work completed.
- Discuss the work in progress, including personnel, activities, methods, and locations.
- Identify problems and possible remedies.
- Consider future activities.
- Close by telling the expected date of completion.

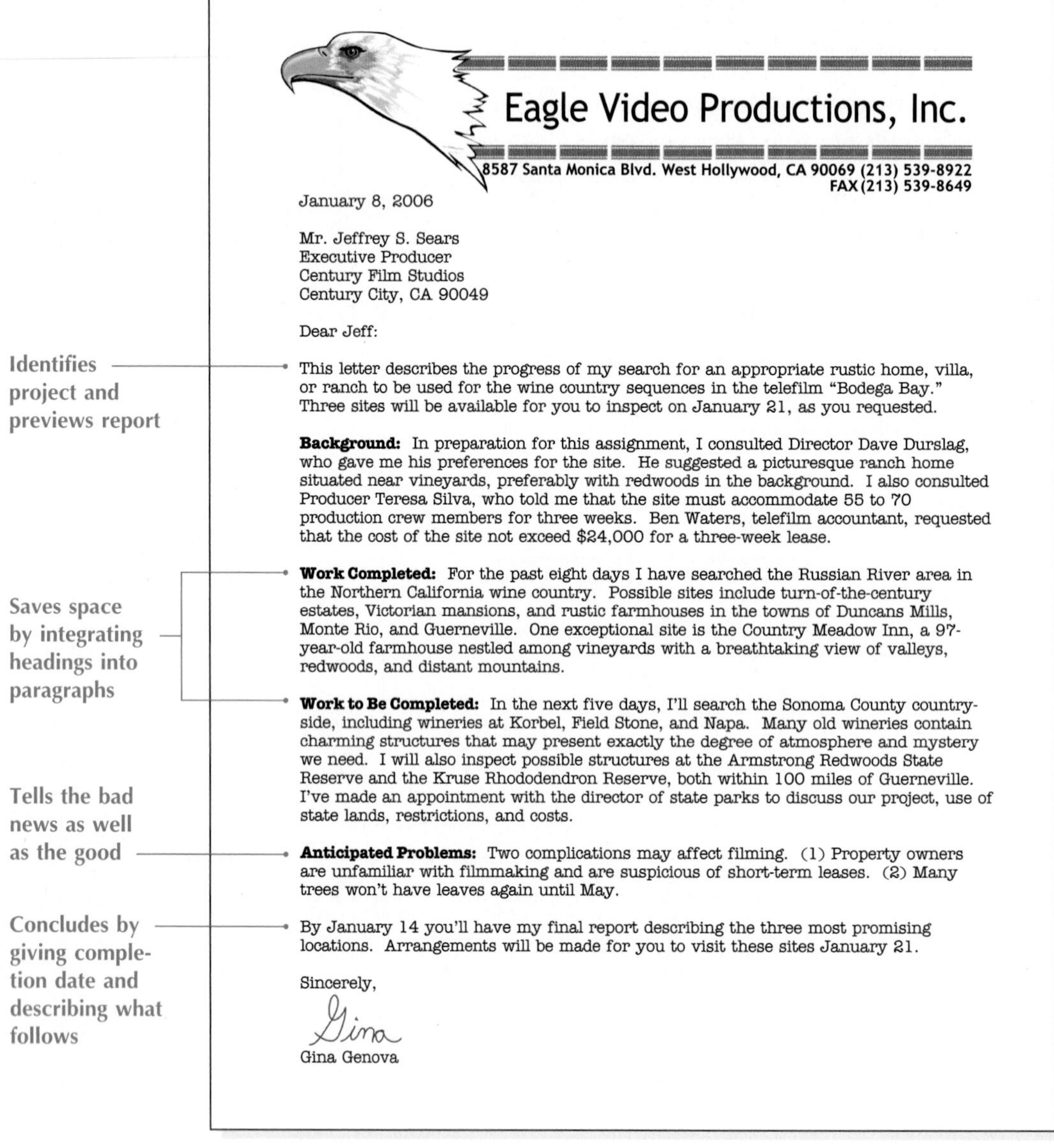

Eagle Video Productions, Inc.
8587 Santa Monica Blvd. West Hollywood, CA 90069 (213) 539-8922
FAX (213) 539-8649

January 8, 2006

Mr. Jeffrey S. Sears
Executive Producer
Century Film Studios
Century City, CA 90049

Dear Jeff:

This letter describes the progress of my search for an appropriate rustic home, villa, or ranch to be used for the wine country sequences in the telefilm "Bodega Bay." Three sites will be available for you to inspect on January 21, as you requested.

Background: In preparation for this assignment, I consulted Director Dave Durslag, who gave me his preferences for the site. He suggested a picturesque ranch home situated near vineyards, preferably with redwoods in the background. I also consulted Producer Teresa Silva, who told me that the site must accommodate 55 to 70 production crew members for three weeks. Ben Waters, telefilm accountant, requested that the cost of the site not exceed $24,000 for a three-week lease.

Work Completed: For the past eight days I have searched the Russian River area in the Northern California wine country. Possible sites include turn-of-the-century estates, Victorian mansions, and rustic farmhouses in the towns of Duncans Mills, Monte Rio, and Guerneville. One exceptional site is the Country Meadow Inn, a 97-year-old farmhouse nestled among vineyards with a breathtaking view of valleys, redwoods, and distant mountains.

Work to Be Completed: In the next five days, I'll search the Sonoma County countryside, including wineries at Korbel, Field Stone, and Napa. Many old wineries contain charming structures that may present exactly the degree of atmosphere and mystery we need. I will also inspect possible structures at the Armstrong Redwoods State Reserve and the Kruse Rhododendron Reserve, both within 100 miles of Guerneville. I've made an appointment with the director of state parks to discuss our project, use of state lands, restrictions, and costs.

Anticipated Problems: Two complications may affect filming. (1) Property owners are unfamiliar with filmmaking and are suspicious of short-term leases. (2) Many trees won't have leaves again until May.

By January 14 you'll have my final report describing the three most promising locations. Arrangements will be made for you to visit these sites January 21.

Sincerely,

Gina

Gina Genova

Identifies project and previews report
Saves space by integrating headings into paragraphs
Tells the bad news as well as the good
Concludes by giving completion date and describing what follows

Investigative Reports

Investigative or informational reports deliver data for a specific situation—without offering interpretation or recommendations. These nonrecurring reports are generally arranged in a direct pattern with three segments: introduction, body, and summary. The body—which includes the facts, findings, or discussion—may be organized by time, component, importance, criteria, or convention. What's important is dividing the topic into logical segments, say, three to five areas that are roughly equal and don't overlap.

Investigative reports provide information without interpretation or recommendations.

The subject matter of the report usually suggests the best way to divide or organize it. Beth Givens, an information specialist for a Minneapolis health care consulting firm, was given the task of researching and writing an investigative report for St. John's Hospital. Her assignment: study the award-winning patient-service program at Good Samaritan Hospital, and report how it improved its patient satisfaction rating from 6.2 to 7.8 in just one year. Beth collected data and then organized her findings into four parts: management training, employee training, patient services, and follow-up program. Although we don't show Beth's complete report here, you can see a similar informational report in Chapter 12, Figure 12.2.

Before Wal-Mart, the world's largest retailer, decided to expand into the famously quirky Japanese market, it studied all aspects of this possibly risky expansion. Wal-Mart decision makers commissioned market studies, projection reports, feasibility studies, investigative reports, and detailed action plans—enough reports to fill rooms the size of three executive offices. Once the decision was made, management continued to need reports to monitor the progress of its expansion move.

Whether you are writing a periodic, trip, conference, progress, or investigative report, you'll want to review the suggestions found in the following checklist.

Checklist for Writing Informational Reports

Introduction

- ✓ **Begin directly.** Identify the report and its purpose.
- ✓ **Provide a preview.** If the report is over a page long, give the reader a brief overview of its organization.
- ✓ **Supply background data selectively.** When readers are unfamiliar with the topic, briefly fill in the necessary details.
- ✓ **Divide the topic.** Strive to group the facts or findings into three to five roughly equal segments that do not overlap.

Body

- ✓ **Arrange the subtopics logically.** Consider organizing by time, component, importance, criteria, or convention.

PROCESS IN PROGRESS

Starbucks Revisited

UNDER THE leadership of chairman and chief global strategist Howard Schultz, Starbucks plans to expand the number of stores and to pursue many other avenues of growth beyond its core coffeehouse business. Rather than striving to make Starbucks the world's biggest coffee shop chain, Schultz is focusing on turning Starbucks into the most recognizable and respected brand in the world. Even as Starbucks grows, however, Schultz and his team must strive to maintain "the intimacy and personalized feel of every Starbucks encounter." He says Starbucks' biggest challenge is "to get big but stay small."[4]

Pursuing the right growth strategy is not easy, and Starbucks has definitely had some flops. *Joe*, the coffeehouse magazine published jointly with *Time*, lasted only three issues. An Internet venture to sell kitchen products online was announced one day, and the next day the stock fell 28 percent. Five Starbucks Café restaurants that opened five years ago no longer exist; and the Mazagran, a carbonated coffee beverage developed with PepsiCo, fizzled out.[5]

Although thousands of copycat coffee shops are springing up around the country, none is positioned to overtake the front-running Starbucks. The market's second-largest player, Diedrich Coffee, Inc., of Irvine, California, has only 473 stores. Interestingly, one of the newest players in the espresso bar market is Wal-Mart. Medina's Kicks Coffee Café, located in a Wal-Mart Supercenter in Plano, Texas, could provide stiff competition down the road.

Critical Thinking

- How important to Starbucks are the collection, organization, and distribution of up-to-date information regarding food and beverage trends, competition, and product development?
- In what ways could Starbucks use the Internet to monitor its competitors, Diedrich Coffee and Kicks Coffee Café?
- What kind of reports might be made to management by individuals assigned the task of monitoring Starbucks' competition?

CONTINUED ON PAGE 455

case study

- ✓ **Use clear headings.** Supply functional or talking heads (at least one per page) that describe each important section.
- ✓ **Determine degree of formality.** Use an informal, conversational writing style unless the audience expects a more formal tone.
- ✓ **Enhance readability with graphic highlighting.** Make liberal use of bullets, numbered and lettered lists, headings, underlined items, and white space.

Summary/Conclusion

- ✓ **When necessary, summarize the report.** Briefly review the main points and discuss what action will follow.
- ✓ **Offer a concluding thought.** If relevant, express appreciation or describe your willingness to provide further information.

Writing Analytical Reports

learning objective

5

Analytical reports differ significantly from informational reports. Although both seek to collect and present data clearly, analytical reports also analyze the data and typically try to persuade the reader to accept the conclusions and act on the recommendations. Informational reports emphasize facts; analytical reports emphasize reasoning and conclusions.

Analytical reports present information but emphasize reasoning, conclusions, and recommendations.

For some readers you may organize analytical reports directly with the conclusions and recommendations near the beginning. Directness is appropriate when the reader has confidence in the writer, based on either experience or credentials. Frontloading the recommendations also works when the topic is routine or familiar and the reader is supportive.

Directness can backfire, though. If you announce the recommendations too quickly, the reader may immediately object to a single idea. You may have had no suspicion that this idea would trigger a negative reaction. Once the reader is opposed, changing an unfavorable mind-set may be difficult or impossible. A reader may also think you have oversimplified or overlooked something significant if you lay out all the recommendations before explaining how you arrived at them. When you must lead the reader through the process of discovering the solution or recommendation, use the indirect method: present conclusions and recommendations last.

Most analytical reports answer questions about specific problems. How can we use a Web site most effectively? Should we close the El Paso plant? Should we buy or lease company cars? How can we improve customer service? Three typical analytical reports answer business questions: justification/recommendation reports, feasibility reports, and yardstick reports. Because these reports all solve problems, the categories are not mutually exclusive. What distinguishes them are their goals and organization.

Justification/Recommendation Reports

Both managers and employees must occasionally write reports that justify or recommend something, such as buying equipment, changing a procedure, hiring an employee, consolidating departments, or investing funds. These reports may also be called *internal proposals* because their persuasive nature is similar to that of external proposals (presented in Chapter 14). Large organizations sometimes prescribe how these reports should be organized; they use forms with conventional headings. When you are free to select an organizational plan yourself, however, let your audience and topic determine your choice of direct or indirect structure.

Justification/recommendation reports follow the direct or indirect pattern depending on the audience and the topic.

Direct Pattern. For nonsensitive topics and recommendations that will be agreeable to readers, you can organize directly according to the following sequence:

The direct pattern is appropriate for justification/recommendation reports on nonsensitive topics and for receptive audiences.

- Identify the problem or need briefly.
- Announce the recommendation, solution, or action concisely and with action verbs.
- Explain more fully the benefits of the recommendation or steps necessary to solve the problem.
- Include a discussion of pros, cons, and costs.
- Conclude with a summary specifying the recommendation and necessary action.

Here's how Justin Brown applied the process in justifying a purchase. Justin is operations manager in charge of a fleet of trucks for a large parcel delivery company

This greenhouse at the popular Keukenhof Gardens in Holland became a key point in the justification report of a tour organizer. In supporting this inclusion of the Keukenhof in a proposed itinerary for an American travel company, the writer argued that tourists can never be rained out. In addition to the 70 acres of outdoor gardens, thousands of flowers bloom under glass. Persuasive justification reports explain fully all the benefits of a recommendation and also anticipate possible reader objections.

in Atlanta. When he heard about a new Goodyear smart tire with an electronic chip, Justin thought his company should give the new tire a try. Because new tires would represent an irregular purchase and because they would require a pilot test, he wrote the justification/recommendation report, shown in Figure 13.9, to his boss. Justin describes his report in this way: "As more and more parcel delivery companies crop up, we have to find ways to cut costs so that we can remain competitive. Although more expensive initially, smart tires may solve many of our problems and save us money in the long run. I knew Bill Montgomery, operations vice president, would be interested in them, especially in view of the huge Firestone tire fiasco.[6] Because Bill would be most interested in what they could do for us, I concentrated on benefits. In my first draft the benefits were lost in a couple of long paragraphs. Only after I read what I had written did I see that I was really talking about four separate benefits. Then I looked for words to summarize each one as a heading. So that Bill would know exactly what he should do, I concluded with specifics. All he had to do was say 'Go.'"

The indirect pattern is appropriate for justification/recommendation reports on sensitive topics and for potentially unreceptive audiences.

Indirect Pattern. When a reader may oppose a recommendation or when circumstances suggest caution, don't be in a hurry to reveal your recommendation. Consider using the following sequence for an indirect approach to your recommendations:

- Make a general reference to the problem, not to your recommendation, in the subject line.
- Describe the problem or need your recommendation addresses. Use specific examples, supporting statistics, and authoritative quotes to lend credibility to the seriousness of the problem.
- Discuss alternative solutions, beginning with the least likely to succeed.
- Present the most promising alternative (your recommendation) last.
- Show how the advantages of your recommendation outweigh its disadvantages.
- Summarize your recommendation. If appropriate, specify the action it requires.
- Ask for authorization to proceed if necessary.

Diane Adams, an executive assistant at a large petroleum and mining company in Grand Prairie, Texas, received a challenging research assignment. Her boss, the director of Human Resources, asked her to investigate ways to persuade employees to quit smoking. Here's how she describes her task: "We banned smoking many years ago inside our buildings, but we never tried very hard to get smokers to actually kick their habits. My job was to gather information about the problem and how other companies have helped workers stop smoking. The report would go to my boss, but I knew he would pass it along to the management council for approval. If the report were just for my boss, I would put my recommendation right up front, because

FIGURE 13.9 *Justification/Recommendation Report: Direct Pattern*

1 Prewriting

ANALYZE: The purpose of this report is to persuade the manager to authorize the purchase and pilot testing of smart tires.

ANTICIPATE: The audience is a manager who is familiar with operations but not with this product. He will probably be receptive to the recommendation.

ADAPT: Present the report data in a direct, straightforward manner.

2 Writing

RESEARCH: Collect data on how smart tires could benefit operations.

ORGANIZE: Discuss the problem briefly. Introduce and justify the recommendation by noting its cost-effectiveness and paperwork benefits. Explain the benefits of smart tires. Describe the action to be taken.

COMPOSE: Write and print first draft.

3 Revising

REVISE: Revise to break up long paragraphs about benefits. Isolate each benefit in an enumerated list with headings.

PROOFREAD: Double-check all figures. Be sure all headings are parallel.

EVALUATE: Does this report make its request concisely but emphatically? Will the reader see immediately what action is required?

DATE: July 19, 2006

TO: Bill Montgomery, Vice President

FROM: Justin Brown, Operations Manager *JB*

SUBJECT: Pilot Testing Smart Tires

Next to fuel, truck tires are our biggest operating cost. Last year we spent $211,000 replacing and retreading tires for 495 trucks. This year the costs will be greater because prices have jumped at least 12 percent and because we've increased our fleet to 550 trucks. Truck tires are an additional burden because they require labor-intensive paperwork to track their warranties, wear, and retread histories. To reduce our long-term costs and to improve our tire tracking system, I recommend that we do the following:

Introduces problem briefly

Presents recommendations immediately

- Purchase 24 Goodyear smart tires.
- Begin a one-year pilot test on six trucks.

How Smart Tires Work

Smart tires have an embedded computer chip that monitors wear, performance, and durability. The chip also creates an electronic fingerprint for positive identification of a tire. By passing a handheld sensor next to the tire, we can learn where and when a tire was made (for warranty and other identification), how much tread it had originally, and its serial number.

Justifies recommendation by explaining product and benefits

How Smart Tires Could Benefit Us

Although smart tires are initially more expensive than other tires, they could help us improve our operations and save us money in four ways:

1. **Retreads.** Goodyear believes that the wear data is so accurate that we should be able to retread every tire three times, instead of our current two times. If that's true, in one year we could save at least $27,000 in new tire costs.
2. **Safety.** Accurate and accessible wear data should reduce the danger of blowouts and flat tires. Last year, drivers reported six blowouts.
3. **Record keeping and maintenance.** Smart tires could reduce our maintenance costs considerably. Currently, we use an electric branding iron to mark serial numbers on new tires. Our biggest headache is manually reading those serial numbers, decoding them, and maintaining records to meet safety regulations. Reading such data electronically could save us thousands of dollars in labor.
4. **Theft protection.** The chip can be used to monitor each tire as it leaves or enters the warehouse or yard, thus discouraging theft.

Enumerates items for maximum impact and readability

Summary and Action

Specifically, I recommend that you do the following:

- Authorize the special purchase of 24 Goodyear smart tires at $450 each, plus one electronic sensor at $1,200.
- Approve a one-year pilot test in our Atlanta territory that equips six trucks with smart tires and tracks their performance.

Explains recommendation in more detail

Specifies action to be taken

FIGURE 13.10 ***Justification/Recommendation Report: Indirect Pattern***

DATE: October 11, 2006

TO: Damon Moore, Director, Human Resources

FROM: Diane Adams, Executive Assistant *DA*

SUBJECT: MEASURES TO HELP EMPLOYEES STOP SMOKING

At your request, I have examined measures that encourage employees to quit smoking. As company records show, approximately 23 percent of our employees still smoke, despite the antismoking and clean-air policies we adopted in 2003. To collect data for this report, I studied professional and government publications; I also inquired at companies and clinics about stop-smoking programs.

Introduces purpose of report, tells method of data collection, and previews organization

Avoids revealing recommendation immediately

This report presents data describing the significance of the problem, three alternative solutions, and a recommendation based on my investigation.

Uses headings that combine function and description

Significance of Problem: Health Care and Productivity Losses

Employees who smoke are costly to any organization. The following statistics show the effects of smoking for workers and for organizations:

- Absenteeism is 40 to 50 percent greater among smoking employees.
- Accidents are two to three times greater among smokers.
- Bronchitis, lung and heart disease, cancer, and early death are more frequent among smokers (Johns, 2004, p. 14).

Documents data sources for credibility; uses APA style citing author, date, and page number in the text

Although our clean-air policy prohibits smoking in the building, shop, and office, we have done little to encourage employees to stop smoking. Many workers still go outside to smoke at lunch and breaks. Other companies have been far more proactive in their attempts to stop employee smoking. Many companies have found that persuading employees to stop smoking was a decisive factor in reducing their health insurance premiums. Below is a discussion of three common stop-smoking measures tried by other companies, along with a projected cost factor for each.

Discusses least effective alternative first

Alternative 1: Literature and Events

The least expensive and easiest stop-smoking measure involves the distribution of literature, such as "The Ten-Step Plan" from Smokefree Enterprises and government pamphlets citing smoking dangers. Some companies have also sponsored events such as the Great American Smoke-Out, a one-day occasion intended to develop group spirit in spurring smokers to quit. "Studies show, however," says one expert, "that literature and company-sponsored events have little permanent effect in helping smokers quit" (Riva, 2005, p. 107).

Cost: Negligible

Footnoting sources lends added credibility to justification/ recommendation reports.

I'm sure he would support it. But the management council is another story. They need persuasion because of the costs involved—and because some of them are smokers. Therefore, I put the alternative I favored last. To gain credibility, I footnoted my sources. I wasn't sure what to do about crediting my sources. In our company not many reports contain footnotes or citation references. However, I checked with my boss, and he said that it was wise for me to do so. He didn't know much about citation formats, but I remembered that we had learned the APA system in some of my college classes, and that's what I decided to use."

Diane had enough material for a ten-page report, but she decided to keep it to two pages in keeping with her company's report policy. She also single-spaced her report, shown in Figure 13.10, because that's her company's preference. Some organizations prefer the readability of double spacing. Be sure to check with your organization for its preference before printing your reports.

Damon Moore Page 2 October 11, 2006

Alternative 2: Stop-Smoking Programs Outside the Workplace

Local clinics provide treatment programs in classes at their centers. Here in Houston we have Smokers' Treatment Center, ACC Motivation Center, and the New-Choice Program for Stopping Smoking. These behavior-modification stop-smoking programs are acknowledged to be more effective than literature distribution or incentive programs. However, studies of companies using off-workplace programs show that many employees fail to attend regularly and do not complete the programs.

Cost: $750 per employee, three-month individual program (New-Choice Program)
$500 per employee, three-month group sessions

Highlights costs for easy comparison

Alternative 3: Stop-Smoking Programs at the Workplace

Many clinics offer workplace programs with counselors meeting employees in company conference rooms. These programs have the advantage of keeping a firm's employees together so that they develop a group spirit and exert pressure on each other to succeed. The most successful programs are on company premises and also on company time. Employees participating in such programs had a 72 percent greater success record than employees attending the same stop-smoking program at an outside clinic (Manley, 2001, p. 35). A disadvantage of this arrangement, of course, is lost work time—amounting to about two hours a week for three months.

Arranges alternatives so that most effective is last

Cost: $500 per employee, three-month program two hours per week release time for three months

Conclusions and Recommendation

Summarizes findings and ends with specific recommendation

Smokers require discipline, counseling, and professional assistance in kicking the nicotine habit, as explained at the University of Michigan Health System Web site ("How to Quit," 2001). Workplace stop-smoking programs on company time are more effective than literature, incentives, and off-workplace programs. If our goal is to reduce health care costs and lead our employees to healthful lives, we should invest in a workplace stop-smoking program with release time for smokers. Although the program temporarily reduces productivity, we can expect to recapture that loss in lower health care premiums and healthier employees.

Therefore, I recommend that we begin a stop-smoking treatment program on company premises with two hours per week of release time for participants for three months.

Reveals recommendation only after discussing all alternatives

3

References

Lists all references in APA style

Magazine — Johns, K. (2004, May). No smoking in your workplace. *Business Times,* 14–16.

Journal — Manley, D. (2001). Up in smoke: A case study of one company's proactive stance against smoking. *Management Review,* 14, 33–37.

Book — Riva, N. A. (2005). *The last gasp*. New York, Field Publishers.

Web — University of Michigan Health System (2001, May). *How to quit smoking*. Retrieved August 28, 2005, from http://www.med.umich.edu/1libr/guides/smoking.htm

This justification/recommendation report analyzes three alternatives for a stop-smoking treatment program. Notice that the writer arranges the report for easy reading and easy comparison. Boldface headings highlight each alternative, and white space makes the cost of each program stand out. By placing the strongest option last, the writer gives it emphasis and persuasive power.

Feasibility Reports

Feasibility reports analyze whether a proposal or plan will work.

Feasibility reports examine the practicality and advisability of following a course of action. They answer this question: Will this plan or proposal work? Feasibility reports typically are internal reports written to advise on matters such as consolidating departments, offering a wellness program to employees, or hiring an outside firm to handle a company's accounting or computing operations. The focus in these reports is on the decision: stopping or proceeding with the proposal. Because your role is not to persuade the reader to accept the decision, you'll want to present the decision immediately. In writing feasibility reports, consider these suggestions:

- Announce your decision immediately.
- Describe the background and the problem necessitating the proposal.
- Discuss the benefits of the proposal, and describe the problems that may result.
- Calculate the costs associated with the proposal, if appropriate.
- Show the time frame necessary for implementation of the proposal.

A typical feasibility report presents the decision, background information, benefits, problems, costs, and a schedule.

Elizabeth Webb, customer service manager for a large insurance company in Omaha, Nebraska, wrote the feasibility report shown in Figure 13.11. She describes the report thus: "We had been losing customer service reps (CSRs) after they were trained and were most valuable to us. When I talked with our vice president about the problem, she didn't want me to take time away from my job to investigate what other companies were doing to retain their CSRs. Instead, we hired a consultant who suggested that we use a CSR career progression schedule. The vice president then wanted to know whether the consultant's plan was feasible. Although my report is only one page long, it provides all necessary information: background, benefits, problems, costs, and time frame."

Yardstick Reports

Yardstick reports consider alternative solutions to a problem by establishing criteria against which to weigh options.

"Yardstick" reports examine problems with two or more solutions. To evaluate the best solution, the writer establishes criteria by which to compare the alternatives. The criteria then act as a yardstick against which all the alternatives are measured. This yardstick approach is effective when companies establish specifications for equipment purchases, and then compare each manufacturer's product with the established specs. The yardstick approach is also effective when exact specifications cannot be established.

For example, when the giant aerospace firm Boeing considered relocating its global headquarters, it evaluated many cities including Dallas, Denver, and Chicago. For each of these sites, Boeing compared geography, economic growth, airline service, training programs for labor, land availability and costs, zoning and environmental regulations, housing costs, and all-important tax breaks. Although Boeing did not set up exact specifications for each category, it compared each city in these various categories.[7] The real advantage to yardstick reports is that alternatives can be measured consistently using the same criteria. Reports using a yardstick approach typically are organized this way:

- Begin by describing the problem or need.
- Explain possible solutions and alternatives.
- Establish criteria for comparing the alternatives; tell how the criteria were selected or developed.
- Discuss and evaluate each alternative in terms of the criteria.
- Draw conclusions and make recommendations.

FIGURE 13.11 *Feasibility Report*

DATE: November 11, 2006

TO: Shauna Clay-Taylor, Vice President

FROM: Elizabeth W. Webb, Customer Service Manager *E.W.W.*

SUBJECT: FEASIBILITY OF PROGRESSION SCHEDULE FOR CSRs

The plan calling for a progression schedule for our customer service representatives is workable, and I think it could be fully implemented by April 1. This report discusses the background, benefits, problems, costs, and time frame involved in executing the plan.

Background: Training and Advancement Problems for CSR Reps. Because of the many insurance policies and agents we service, new customer service representatives require eight weeks of intensive training. Even after this thorough introduction, CSRs are overwhelmed. They take about eight more months before feeling competent on the job. Once they reach their potential, they often look for other positions in the company because they see few advancement possibilities in customer service. These problems were submitted to an outside consultant, who suggested a CSR progression schedule.

Benefits of Plan: Career Progression and Incremental Training. The proposed plan sets up a schedule of career progression, including these levels: (1) CSR trainee, (2) CSR Level I, (3) CSR Level II, (4) CSR Level III, (5) Senior CSR, and (6) CSR supervisor. This program, which includes salary increments with each step, provides a career ladder and incentives for increased levels of expertise and achievement. The plan also facilitates training. Instead of overloading a new trainee with an initial eight-week training program, we would train CSRs slowly with a combination of classroom and on-the-job experiences. Each level requires additional training and expertise.

Problems of Plan: Difficulty in Writing Job Descriptions and Initial Confusion. One of the biggest problems will be distinguishing the job duties at each level. However, I believe that, with the help of our consultant, we can sort out the tasks and expertise required at each level. Another problem will be determining appropriate salary differentials. Attached is a tentative schedule showing proposed wages at each level. We expect to encounter confusion and frustration in implementing this program at first, particularly in placing our current CSRs within the structure.

Costs. Implementing the progression schedule involves two direct costs. The first is the salary of a trainer, at about $40,000 a year. The second cost derives from increased salaries of upper-level CSRs, shown on the attached schedule. I believe, however, that the costs involved are within the estimates planned for this project.

Time Frame. Developing job descriptions should take us about three weeks. Preparing a training program will require another three weeks. Once the program is started, I expect a breaking-in period of at least three months. By April 1 the progression schedule will be fully implemented and showing positive results in improved CSR training, service, and retention.

Enclosure

Reveals decision immediately

Outlines organization of the report

Describes problem and background

Evaluates positive and negative aspects of proposal objectively

Presents costs and schedule; omits unnecessary summary

Kelly Lopez, benefits administrator for computer manufacturer CompuTech, was called on to write a report comparing outplacement agencies. These agencies counsel discharged employees and help them find new positions; fees are paid by the former employer. Kelly knew that times were bad for CompuTech and that extensive downsizing would take place in the next two years. Her task was to compare outplacement agencies and recommend one to CompuTech.

After collecting information, Kelly found that her biggest problem was organizing the data and developing a system for making comparisons. All the outplacement agencies she investigated seemed to offer the same basic package of services. Here's how she described her report, shown in Figure 13.12:

"With the information I gathered about three outplacement agencies, I made a big grid listing the names of the agencies across the top. Down the side I listed general categories—such as services, costs, and reputation. Then I filled in the information for each agency. This grid, which began to look like a table, helped me

FIGURE 13.12 ***Yardstick Report***

DATE: April 28, 2006

TO: George O. Dawes, Vice President

FROM: Kelly Lopez, Benefits Administrator *KL*

SUBJECT: CHOICE OF OUTPLACEMENT SERVICES

Here is the report you requested April 1 investigating the possibility of CompuTech's use of outplacement services. It discusses the problem of counseling services for discharged staff and establishes criteria for selecting an outplacement agency. It then evaluates three prospective agencies and presents a recommendation based on that evaluation.

Introduces purpose and gives overview of report organization

Problem: Counseling Discharged Staff

Discusses background briefly because readers already know the problem

In an effort to reduce costs and increase competitiveness, CompuTech will begin a program of staff reduction that will involve releasing up to 20 percent of our workforce over the next 12 to 24 months. Many of these employees have been with us for ten or more years, and they are not being released for performance faults. These employees deserve a severance package that includes counseling and assistance in finding new careers.

Uses dual headings, giving function and description

Solution and Alternatives: Outplacement Agencies

Numerous outplacement agencies offer discharged employees counseling and assistance in locating new careers. This assistance minimizes not only the negative feelings related to job loss but also the very real possibility of litigation. Potentially expensive lawsuits have been lodged against some companies by unhappy employees who felt they were unfairly released.

In seeking an outplacement agency, we should find one that offers advice to the sponsoring company as well as to dischargees. Frankly, many of our managers need help in conducting termination sessions. The law now requires certain procedures, especially in releasing employees over forty. CompuTech could unwittingly become liable to lawsuits because our managers are uninformed of these procedures. Here in the metropolitan area, I have located three potential outplacement agencies appropriate to serve our needs: Gray & Associates, Right Access, and Careers Plus.

Announces solution and the alternatives it presents

Establishing Criteria for Selecting Agency

Tells how criteria were selected

In order to choose among the three agencies, I established criteria based on professional articles, discussions with officials at other companies using outplacement agencies, and interviews with agencies. Here are the four groups of criteria I used in evaluating the three agencies:

1. Counseling services—including job search advice, résumé help, crisis management, corporate counseling, and availability of full-time counselors
2. Administrative and research assistance—including availability of administrative staff, librarian, and personal computers
3. Reputation—based on a telephone survey of former clients and listing with a professional association
4. Costs—for both group programs and executive services

Creates four criteria to use as yardstick in evaluating alternatives

Grids are a useful way to organize and compare data for a yardstick report.

organize all the bits and pieces of information. After studying the grid, I saw that all the information could be grouped into four categories: counseling services, secretarial and research assistance, reputation, and costs. I made these the criteria I would use to compare agencies. Next, I divided my grid into two parts, which became Table 1 and Table 2. In writing the report, I could have made each agency a separate heading, followed by a discussion of how it measured up to the criteria. Immediately, though, I saw how repetitious that would become. So I used the criteria as headings and discussed how each agency met each criterion—or failed to meet it. Making a recommendation was easy once I had the tables made and could see how the agencies compared."

FIGURE 13.12 *Continued*

Vice President Dawes Page 2 April 28, 2006

Discussion: Evaluating Agencies by Criteria

Each agency was evaluated using the four criteria just described. Data comparing the first three criteria are summarized in Table 1.

Table 1

A COMPARISON OF SERVICES AND REPUTATIONS FOR THREE LOCAL OUTPLACEMENT AGENCIES

Places table close to spot where it is first mentioned

Summarizes complex data in table for easy reading and reference

	Gray & Associates	Right Access	Careers Plus
Counseling services			
Résumé advice	Yes	Yes	Yes
Crisis management	Yes	No	Yes
Corporate counseling	Yes	No	No
Full-time counselors	Yes	No	Yes
Administrative, research assistance			
Administrative staff	Yes	Yes	Yes
Librarian, research library	Yes	No	Yes
Personal computers	Yes	No	Yes
Listed by National Association of Career Consultants	Yes	No	Yes
Reputation (telephone survey of former clients)	Excellent	Good	Excellent

Counseling Services

Highlights the similarities and differences among the alternatives

All three agencies offered similar basic counseling services with job-search and résumé advice. They differed, however, in three significant areas.

Right Access does not offer crisis management, a service that puts the discharged employee in contact with a counselor the same day the employee is released. Experts in the field consider this service especially important to help the dischargee begin "bonding" with the counselor immediately. Immediate counseling also helps the dischargee through the most traumatic moments of one of life's great disappointments and helps him or her learn how to break the news to family members. Crisis management can be instrumental in reducing lawsuits because dischargees immediately begin to focus on career planning instead of concentrating on their pain and need for revenge. Moreover, Right Access does not employ full-time counselors; it hires part-timers according to demand. Industry authorities advise against using agencies whose staff members are inexperienced and employed on an "as-needed" basis.

In addition, neither Right Access nor Careers Plus offers regular corporate counseling, which I feel is critical in training our managers to conduct terminal interviews. Careers Plus, however, suggested that it could schedule special workshops if desired.

Does not repeat obvious data from table

Secretarial and Research Assistance

Both Gray & Associates and Careers Plus offer complete administrative services and personal computers. Dischargees have access to staff and equipment to assist them in their job searches. These agencies also provide research libraries, librarians, and databases of company information to help in securing interviews.

Checklist for Writing Analytical Reports

Introduction

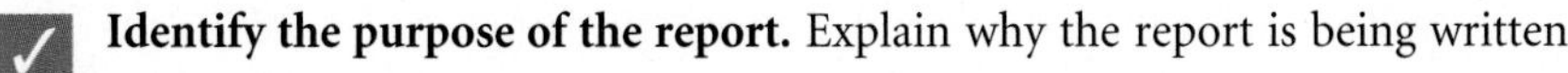

✓ **Identify the purpose of the report.** Explain why the report is being written.

✓ **Preview the organization of the report.** Especially for long reports, explain to the reader how the report will be organized.

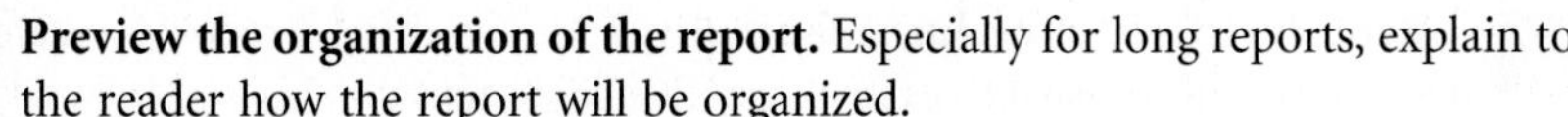

✓ **Summarize the conclusions and recommendations for receptive audiences.** Use the direct pattern only if you have the confidence of the reader.

FIGURE 13.12 *Continued*

Vice President Dawes Page 3 April 28, 2006

Discusses objectively how each agency meets criteria

Reputation

To assess the reputation of each agency, I checked its listing with the National Association of Career Consultants. This is a voluntary organization of outplacement agencies that monitors and polices its members. Gray & Associates and Careers Plus are listed; Right Access is not.

For further evidence I conducted a telephone survey of former agency clients. The three agencies supplied me with names and telephone numbers of companies and individuals they had served. I called four former clients for each agency. Most of the individuals were pleased with the outplacement services they had received. I asked each client the same questions so that I could compare responses.

Costs

All three agencies have two separate fee schedules, summarized in Table 2. The first schedule is for group programs intended for lower-level employees. These include off-site or on-site single-day workshop sessions, and the prices range from $1,000 a session (at Right Access) to $1,500 per session (at Gray & Associates). An additional fee of $40 to $50 is charged for each participant.

Selects most important data from table to discuss

The second fee schedule covers executive services. This counseling is individual and costs from 10 percent to 18 percent of the dischargee's previous year's salary. Since CompuTech will be forced to release numerous managerial staff members, the executive fee schedule is critical. Table 2 shows fees for a hypothetical case involving a manager who earns $60,000 a year.

Table 2

A COMPARISON OF COSTS FOR THREE AGENCIES

	Gray & Associates	Right Access	Careers Plus
Group programs	$1,500/session, $45/participant	$1,000/session, $40/participant	$1,400/session, $50/participant
Executive services	15% of previous year's salary	10% of previous year's salary	18% of previous year's salary plus $1,000 fee
Manager at $60,000/year	$9,000	$6,000	$11,800

Conclusions and Recommendations

Gives reasons for making recommendation

Although Right Access has the lowest fees, it lacks crisis management, corporate counseling, full-time counselors, library facilities, and personal computers. Moreover, it is not listed by the National Association of Career Consultants. Therefore, the choice is between Gray & Associates and Careers Plus. Because they have similar services, the deciding factor is costs. Careers Plus would charge nearly $3,000 more for counseling a manager than would Gray & Associates. Although Gray & Associates has fewer computers available, all other elements of its services seem good. Therefore, I recommend that CompuTech hire Gray & Associates as an outplacement agency to counsel discharged employees.

Narrows choice to final alternative

Findings

- ✓ **Discuss pros and cons.** In recommendation/justification reports evaluate the advantages and disadvantages of each alternative. For unreceptive audiences consider placing the recommended alternative last.
- ✓ **Establish criteria to evaluate alternatives.** In "yardstick" reports, create criteria to use in measuring each alternative consistently.
- ✓ **Support the findings with evidence.** Supply facts, statistics, expert opinion, survey data, and other proof from which you can draw logical conclusions.

PROCESS TO PRODUCT

Applying Your Skills at Starbucks

ONE OF THE most interesting of Starbucks' growth strategies is adding digital music downloading to its outlets. Hear Music, a Starbucks subsidiary, uses technology by Hewlett-Packard for the new concept launched at the Hear Music Coffeehouse in Santa Monica, California. Seventy HP Tablet PC–based listening stations enable customers to sift through 250,000 songs to create their own mixed CD masterpieces.

Customers personalize the listening experience by choosing their own cover art, creating an album title, and selecting their songs. Hanging on the wall is the marketing tagline, "It will be your favorite CD because you picked every song." The first five tracks cost $6.99, and each additional song is $1. In less than five minutes, customers get a beautifully packaged, personalized, and economical CD.

Critics fear that the transformation of Starbucks into a lifestyle-entertainment enterprise will corrupt the brand. They say that customers may feel abused if they perceive this music service as a blatant attempt to extract more dollars from them. In contrast, Schultz sees the music service as the next step along Starbucks' path toward becoming, yes, the world's biggest brand. He believes that "great retailers recognize that they're in the business of constantly surprising and delighting their customers." He expects this move into music to do both.[8]

Your Task

As assistant to Howard Schultz, list at least six criteria to use in evaluating whether the Hear Music Coffeehouse experiment in Santa Monica is successful or unsuccessful. What sources of primary and secondary information would be useful in making a decision? What kind of report would be best for arriving at a decision and reporting the results? How should the report be organized? ■

http://www.starbucks.com

case study

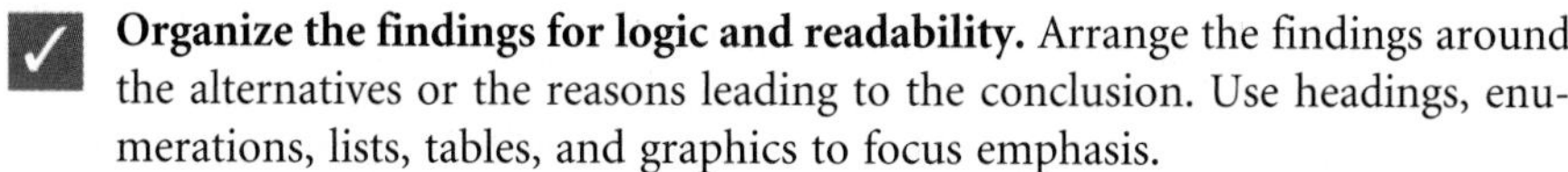

✓ **Organize the findings for logic and readability.** Arrange the findings around the alternatives or the reasons leading to the conclusion. Use headings, enumerations, lists, tables, and graphics to focus emphasis.

Conclusions/Recommendations

✓ **Draw reasonable conclusions from the findings.** Develop conclusions that answer the research question. Justify the conclusions with highlights from the findings.

✓ **Make recommendations, if asked.** For multiple recommendations prepare a list. Use action verbs. Explain needed action.

Summary of Learning Objectives

1 **Use tabulating and statistical techniques to sort and interpret report data.** Report data are more meaningful when sorted into tables or when analyzed by mean (the arithmetic average), median (the midpoint in a group of figures), and mode (the most frequent response). Range represents a span between the highest and lowest figures. Grids help organize complex data into rows and columns.

2 **Draw meaningful conclusions and make practical report recommendations.** Conclusions tell what the survey data mean—especially in relation to the original report problem. They summarize key findings and may attempt to explain what caused the report problem. They are usually enumerated. In reports that call for recommendations, writers make specific suggestions for actions that can solve the report problem. Recommendations should be feasible and potentially agreeable to the audience. They should all relate to the initial problem. Recommendations may be combined with conclusions.

3 **Organize report data logically and provide cues to aid comprehension.** Reports may be organized in many ways, including by (1) time (establishing a chronology or history of events), (2) component (discussing a problem by geography, division, or product), (3) importance (arranging data from most important to least important, or vice versa), (4) criteria (comparing items by standards), or (5) convention (using an already established grouping).

4 **Prepare typical informational reports.** Periodic, trip, convention, progress, and investigative reports are examples of typical informational reports. Such reports include an introduction that may preview the report purpose and supply background data if necessary. The body of the report is generally divided into three to five segments that may be organized by time, component, importance, criteria, or convention. The body should include clear headings and may use an informal, conversational style unless the audience expects a more formal tone. The summary or conclusion reviews the main points and discusses what action will follow. The conclusion may offer a final thought, express appreciation, or express willingness to provide further information.

5 **Prepare typical analytical reports.** Typical analytical reports include justification/recommendation reports, feasibility reports, and yardstick reports. Justification/recommendation reports organized directly identify a problem, immediately announce a recommendation or solution, explain and discuss its merits, and summarize the action to be taken. Justification/recommendation reports organized indirectly describe a problem, discuss alternative solutions, prove the superiority of one solution, and ask for authorization to proceed with that solution. Feasibility reports study the advisability of following a course of action. They generally announce the author's proposal immediately. Then they describe the background, advantages and disadvantages, costs, and time frame for implementing the proposal. Yardstick reports compare two or more solutions to a problem by measuring each against a set of established criteria. They usually describe a problem, explain possible solutions, establish criteria for comparing alternatives, evaluate each alternative in terms of the criteria, draw conclusions, and make recommendations. The advantage to yardstick reports is consistency in comparing various alternatives.

chapter review

1. What is data tabulation? Provide an original example. Why is tabulation necessary for a researcher who has collected large amounts of data? (Obj. 1)
2. What is cross-tabulation? Give an example. (Obj. 1)
3. Calculate the mean, median, and mode for these figures: 3, 4, 4, 4, 10. (Obj. 1)
4. How can a grid help classify material? (Obj. 1)
5. What are the two most widely read sections of a report? (Obj. 2)
6. How do conclusions differ from recommendations? (Obj. 2)
7. When reports have multiple recommendations, how should they be presented? (Obj. 2)
8. Name five methods for organizing report data. Be prepared to discuss each. (Obj. 3)
9. What three devices can report writers use to prevent readers from getting lost in the text? (Obj. 3)
10. Informational reports typically are organized into what three parts? (Obj. 4)
11. Describe periodic reports and what they generally contain. (Obj. 4)
12. What should a progress report include? (Obj. 4)
13. What sequence should a direct justification/ recommendation report follow? (Obj. 5)
14. What is a feasibility report? Are they generally intended for internal or external audiences? (Obj. 5)
15. What is a yardstick report? (Obj. 5)

critical thinking

1. Researchers can draw various conclusions from a set of data. How do you know how to shape conclusions and recommendations? (Obj. 2)
2. Why is audience analysis particularly important in making report recommendations? (Obj. 2)
3. Should all reports be organized so that they follow the sequence of investigation—that is, a description of the initial problem, an analysis of the issues, data collection, data analysis, and conclusions? Why or why not? (Obj. 3)
4. What are the major differences between informational and analytical reports? (Objs. 4 and 5)
5. **Ethical Issue:** Discuss the ethics of using persuasive tactics to convince a report's readers to accept its conclusions. Should you be persuasive only when you believe in the soundness and truth of your conclusions?

THREE GREAT RESOURCES FOR YOU!

1. ***Guffey Student Web Site***
   http://guffey.swlearning.com

   Your companion Web site offers chapter review quizzes, WebThink activities, updated chapter URLs, and many additional resources.

2. ***Guffey XTRA!***
   http://guffeyxtra.swlearning.com

   This online study assistant includes Your Personal Language Trainer, Speak Right!, Spell Right!, bonus online chapters, Documents for Analysis, PowerPoint slides, and much more.

3. ***Student Study Guide***

   Self-checked workbook activities and applications review chapter concepts and develop career skills.

activities

13.1 Tabulation and Interpretation of Survey Results (Obj. 1)

CRITICAL THINKING | LISTENING | SPEAKING | TEAM

Your business communication class at North Shore College was asked by the college bookstore manager, Larry Krause, to conduct a survey (see Figure 12.8). Concerned about the environment, Krause wants to learn students' reactions to eliminating plastic bags, of which 45,000 are given away annually by the bookstore. Students answered questions about a number of proposals, resulting in the following raw data:

For major purchases the bookstore should:

	Agree	Undecided	Disagree
1. Continue to provide plastic bags	132	17	411
2. Provide no bags; encourage students to bring their own bags	414	25	121
3. Provide no bags; offer cloth bags at a reduced price (about $3)	357	19	184
4. Give a cloth bag with each major purchase, the cost to be included in registration fees	63	15	482

Your Task. In groups of four or five, do the following:

a. Convert the data into a table (see Figure 13.1) with a descriptive title. Arrange the items in a logical sequence.
b. How could these survey data be cross-tabulated? Would cross-tabulation serve any purpose?
c. Given the conditions of this survey, name at least three conclusions that could be drawn from the data.
d. Prepare three to five recommendations to be submitted to Mr. Krause. How could they be implemented?
e. Role-play a meeting in which the recommendations and implementation plan are presented to Mr. Krause. One student plays the role of Mr. Krause; the remaining students play the role of the presenters.

13.2 Evaluating Conclusions (Obj. 2)

E-MAIL

Your Task. Read an in-depth article (800 or more words) in *BusinessWeek*, *Fortune*, *Forbes*, or *The Wall Street Journal*. What conclusions does the author draw? Are the conclusions valid, based on the evidence presented? In an e-mail message to your instructor, summarize the main points in the article and analyze the conclusions. What conclusions would you have drawn from the data?

13.3 Distinguishing Between Conclusions and Recommendations (Obj. 2)

A study of red light violations produced the following findings: Red light traffic violations were responsible for more than 25,000 crashes in one state. Crashes from running red lights decreased by 10 percent in areas using camera programs to cite offenders. Two out of seven local governments studied showed a profit from the programs; the others lost money.[9]

Your Task. Based on the preceding facts, indicate whether the following statements are conclusions or recommendations:

a. Red light violations are dangerous offenses.
b. Red light cameras are an effective traffic safety tool.
c. Local governments should be allowed to implement red light camera programs.
d. Although red light camera programs are expensive, they prevent crashes and are, therefore, worthwhile.
e. The city of Centerville should not implement a red light program because of the program's cost.
f. Red light programs are not necessarily profitable for local governments.

13.4 Organizing Data (Obj. 3)

SPEAKING | LISTENING

Your Task. In groups of three to five, discuss how the findings in the following reports could be best organized. Consider these methods: time, component, importance, criteria, and convention.

a. A report comparing three locations for a fast-food company's new restaurant. The report presents data on real estate values, construction costs, traffic patterns, competition, state taxes, labor availability, and population demographics.
b. A report describing the history of the development of dwarf and spur apple trees, starting with the first genetic dwarfs discovered about 100 years ago and progressing to today's grafted varieties on dwarfing rootstocks.
c. An informational brochure for job candidates that describes your company's areas of employment: accounting, finance, information systems, operations management, marketing, production, and computer-aided design.
d. A monthly sales report submitted to the sales manager.
e. A recommendation report to be submitted to management presenting four building plans to improve access to your building, in compliance with federal regulations. The plans range considerably in feasibility and cost.
f. A progress report submitted six months into the process of planning the program for your organization's convention.
g. An informational report describing a company's expansion plans in South America, Europe, Australia, and Southeast Asia.
h. An employee performance appraisal submitted annually.

13.5 Evaluating Headings and Titles (Obj. 3)

Your Task. Identify the following report headings and titles as *functional*, *talking*, or *combination*. Discuss the usefulness and effectiveness of each.

a. Budget
b. Mishandled Baggage Reports Filed by Passengers
c. Upgrades
d. How to Implement Instant Messaging Rules
e. Case History: Focusing on Customer Service
f. Recommendations: Solving Our Applicant Tracking Problem
g. Comparing Costs of Hiring Exempt and Nonexempt Employees
h. Alternatives

13.6 Writing a Survey: Studying Employee Use of Instant Messaging (Obj. 1)

INFOTRAC | WEB

Instant messaging (IM) is a popular way to exchange messages in real time. It offers the convenience of telephone conversations and e-mail. Best of all, it allows employees to contact anyone in the world while retaining a written copy of the conversation—without a whopping telephone bill! But instant messaging is risky for companies. They may lose trade secrets or confidential information over insecure lines. They also may be liable if inappropriate material is exchanged. Moreover, IM opens the door to viruses that can infect a company's entire computer system.

Your boss just read an article stating that 40 percent of companies now use IM for business and up to 90 percent of employees use IM WITHOUT their manager's knowledge or authorization. She asks you to prepare a survey of your 48-member staff to learn how many are using IM. She wants to know what type of IM software they have downloaded, how many hours a day they spend on IM, what are the advantages of IM, and so forth. The goal is not to identify those using or abusing IM. Instead, the goal is to learn when, how, and why it is being used so that appropriate policies can be designed.

Your Task. Use InfoTrac or the Web to learn more about instant messaging. Then prepare a short employee survey (see Figure 12.8). Include an appropriate introduction that explains the survey and encourages a response. Should you ask for names on the survey? How can you encourage return of the forms? Your instructor may wish to expand this survey into a report by having you produce fictitious survey results, analyze the findings, draw conclusions, and make recommendations.

13.7 Periodic Report: Filling in the Boss (Obj. 4)

E-MAIL

You work hard at your job, but you rarely see your boss. Keeping him informed of your activities and accomplishments is difficult.

Your Task. For a job that you currently hold or a previous one, describe your regular activities, discuss irregular events that management should be aware of, and highlight any special needs or problems. Use a memo format in writing a periodic e-mail report to your boss.

13.8 Progress Report: Checking In (Obj. 4)

E-MAIL

Students writing a long report described in Chapter 14 must keep their instructors informed of their progress.

Your Task. Write a progress report informing your instructor of your work. Briefly describe the project (its purpose, scope, limitations, and methodology), work completed, work yet to be completed, problems encountered, future activities, and expected completion date. Address the e-mail memo report to your instructor.

13.9 Investigative Report: Studying the Journals in Your Field (Obj. 4)

Your campus library has limited funds for the purchase of print journals. As a library intern, you have been assigned the task of examining journals in your field. Your report to the head librarian will help the library decide which journals are most helpful to students.

Your Task. Prepare an informational letter or memo report (see Figure 12.2) that identifies three journals in your field. Discuss the format, tone, and readability of each journal. What kinds of articles are presented? Which journals would be most useful to students in your field? Why? Select one article from each journal to critique as part of your report. Address your report to Lisa B. Martin, Head Librarian, College Library, P.O. Box 4230, Greenwood, SC 29649. Remember that your goal is to investigate and inform, not necessarily to promote and recommend.

13.10 Investigative Report: Exploring a Possible Place to Work (Obj. 4)

WEB

You are thinking about taking a job with a Fortune 500 company, and you want to learn as much as possible about the company.

Your Task. Select a Fortune 500 company, and collect information about it on the Web. Visit **www.hoovers.com** for basic facts. Then take a look at the company's Web site; check its background, news releases, and annual report. Learn about its major product, service, or emphasis. Find its Fortune 500 ranking, its current stock price (if listed), and its high and low range for the year. Look up its profit-to-earnings ratio. Track its latest marketing plan, promotion, or product. Identify its home office, major officers, and number of employees. In a memo report to your instructor, summarize your research findings. Explain why this company would be a good or bad employment choice.

13.11 Investigative Report: Marketing Abroad (Obj. 4)

WEB

You have been asked to prepare a training program for U.S. companies doing business outside the country.

Your Task. Select a country to investigate (preferably one for which your library has *Culturgram* materials). Collect data from Culturgram files and from the country's embassy in Washington. Interview on-campus international students. Use the Web to discover data about the country. See **Activity 14.5** and Figure 14.5 in the next chapter for additional ideas

on gathering information on intercultural communication. Collect information about formats for written communication, observance of holidays, customary greetings, business ethics, and other topics of interest to businesspeople. Remember that your report should promote business, not tourism. Prepare a memo report addressed to Kelly Johnson, editor for the training program materials.

13.12 Progress Report: Heading Toward That Degree (Obj. 4)

You have made an agreement with your parents (or spouse, relative, or significant friend) that you would submit a progress report at this time.

Your Task. Prepare a progress report in letter format. Describe your headway toward your educational goal (such as employment, degree, or certificate). List your specific achievements, and outline what you have left to complete.

13.13 Conference or Trip Report: In Your Dreams (Obj. 4)

You have been sent to a meeting, conference, or seminar in an exotic spot at company expense.

Your Task. From a business periodical select an article describing a conference or meeting connected with your major area of study. The article must be at least 500 words long. Assume you attended the meeting. Prepare a memo report to your supervisor.

13.14 Justification/Recommendation Report: Searching for the Best Philanthropic Project (Obj. 5)

WEB

Great news! MegaTech, the start-up company where you work, has become enormously successful. Now the owner wants to support some kind of philanthropic program. He doesn't have time to check out the possibilities, so he asks you, his assistant, to conduct research and report to him and the board of directors.

Your Task. He wants you to investigate the philanthropic projects at 20 high-profile companies of your choice. Visit their Web sites and study programs such as volunteerism, cause-related marketing, matching funds, charitable donations, and so forth. In a recommendation report, discuss five of the best programs and recommend one that can serve as a philanthropic project model for your company.

13.15 Justification/Recommendation Report: Time for a Change (Obj. 5)

CRITICAL THINKING

Your Task. Identify a problem or a procedure that must be changed at your job, such as poor scheduling of employees, outdated equipment, slow order processing, failure to encourage employees to participate fully, restrictive rules, inadequate training, or disappointed customers. Using an indirect pattern, write a recommendation report suggesting one or more ways to solve the problem. Address the memo report to your boss.

13.16 Justification/Recommendation Report: Solving a Campus Problem (Obj. 5)

TEAM

Your Task. In groups of three to five, investigate a problem on your campus, such as inadequate parking, slow registration, poor class schedules, inefficient bookstore, weak job-placement program, unrealistic degree requirements, or lack of internship programs. Within your group develop a solution to the problem. If possible, consult the officials involved to ask for their input in arriving at a feasible solution. Do not attack existing programs; strive for constructive discussion and harmonious improvements. After reviewing persuasive techniques discussed in Chapter 10, write a group or individual justification/recommendation report. Address your report to your instructor.

13.17 Justification/Recommendation Report: Developing an Organizational E-Mail Policy (Obj. 5)

CRITICAL THINKING | INFOTRAC | LISTENING | SPEAKING | TEAM | WEB

As a manager in a midsized engineering firm, you are aware that members of your department frequently use e-mail and the Internet for private messages, shopping, and games. In addition to the strain on computer facilities, you worry about declining productivity as well as security problems. When you walked by one worker's computer and saw what looked like pornography on the screen, you knew you had to do something. Although workplace privacy is a hot-button issue for unions and employee-rights groups, employers have legitimate reasons for wanting to know what is happening on their computers. A high percentage of lawsuits involve the use and abuse of e-mail. You think that the executive council should establish some kind of e-mail policy. The council is generally receptive to sound suggestions, especially if they are inexpensive. At present no e-mail policy exists, and you fear that the executive council is not fully aware of the dangers. You decide to talk with other managers about the problem and write a justification/recommendation report.

Your Task. In teams discuss the need for an e-mail policy. Using InfoTrac and the Web, find information about other firms' use of such policies. Look for examples of companies struggling with lawsuits over e-mail abuse. In your report, should you describe suitable e-mail policies? Should you rec-

ommend computer monitoring and surveillance software? Should the policy cover cell phones, wireless pagers, and instant messaging? Each member of the team should present and support his or her ideas regarding what should be included in the report. Individually or as a team, write a convincing justification/recommendation report to the executive council based on the conclusions you draw from your research and discussion. Decide whether you should be direct or indirect.

13.18 Feasibility Report: International Organization (Obj. 5)

CRITICAL THINKING

To fulfill a senior project in your department, you have been asked to submit a letter report to the dean evaluating the feasibility of starting an organization of international students on campus.

Your Task. Find out how many international students are on your campus, what nations they represent, how one goes about starting an organization, and whether a faculty sponsor is needed. Assume that you conducted an informal survey of international students. Of the 39 who filled out the survey, 31 said they would be interested in joining.

13.19 Feasibility Report: Improving Employee Fitness (Obj. 5)

CRITICAL THINKING

Your company is considering ways to promote employee fitness and morale.

Your Task. Select a possible fitness program that seems reasonable for your company. Consider a softball league, bowling teams, basketball league, lunchtime walks, lunchtime fitness speakers and demos, company-sponsored health club membership, workout room, fitness center, fitness director, and so on. Assume that your boss has tentatively agreed to one of the programs and has asked you to write a memo report investigating its feasibility.

13.20 Yardstick Report: Evaluating Equipment (Obj. 5)

CRITICAL THINKING

You recently complained to your boss that you were unhappy with a piece of equipment that you use (printer, computer, copier, fax, or the like). After some thought, the boss decided you were right and told you to go shopping.

Your Task. Compare at least three different manufacturers' models and recommend one. Because the company will be purchasing ten or more units and because several managers must approve the purchase, write a careful report documenting your findings. Establish at least five criteria for comparing the models. Submit a memo report to your boss.

13.21 Yardstick Report: Measuring the Alternatives (Obj. 5)

CRITICAL THINKING

Your Task. Consider a problem where you work or in an organization you know. Select a problem with several alternative solutions or courses of action (retaining the present status could be one alternative). Develop criteria that could be used to evaluate each alternative. Write a report measuring each alternative by the yardstick you have created. Recommend a course of action to your boss or to the organization head.

13.22 Investigative Report: Check Overdraft Protection—Valuable Service or Consumer Rip-Off? (Obj. 4)

CONSUMER | CRITICAL THINKING
INFOTRAC | WEB

Bounce-protection programs sound like a terrific service to checking account customers. Also called overdraft privilege and courtesy overdraft, these popular banking programs automatically cover bounced checks. Customers can overdraw

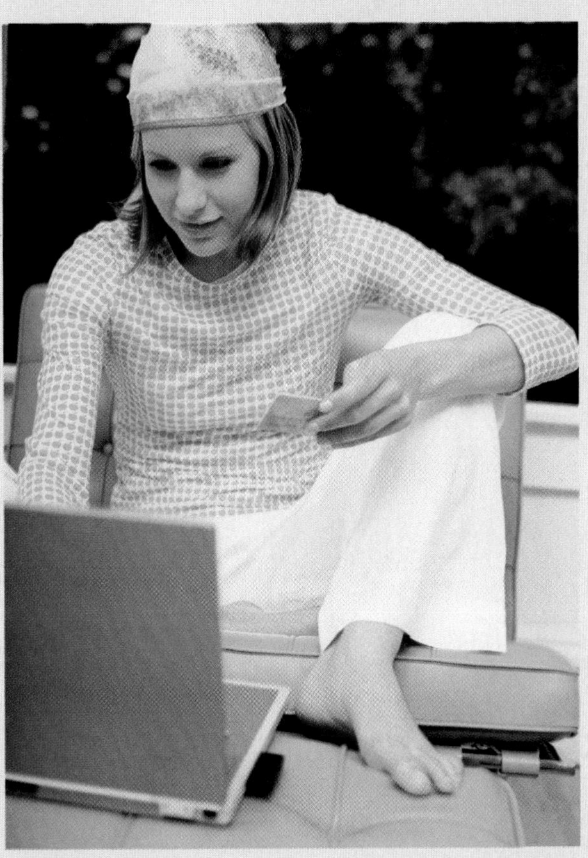

Photo: © Brand X Pictures/Getty Images

up to a certain dollar amount and pay a fee, rather than interest. Commercial banks long ago abandoned the practice of short-term loans. But they are now encouraging fee-based overdrafts, and the effective interest rate is enormous. On an overdraft of $100 that is outstanding for two weeks, you might pay a $20 fee, which amounts to an annual interest rate of 520 percent![10] Consumers receive the equivalent of an unsecured loan, which they can use if they run short of cash between paydays. Critics complain that the programs charge excessive fees and prey on the poor. They also point out that banks exploit customers by processing the largest checks first, thus draining a checking account faster and bouncing several checks at once. Each overdrawn check, no matter how small, is zinged for a separate fee! Yet, fee-based overdraft programs are growing wildly. Banks say that consumers love the service. Critics claim that banks encourage people to overdraw their accounts and then charge them for doing so.[11]

Your Task. First Alert, a consumer advocate organization where you work, had decided to investigate the issue. As a member of its Banking Practices Committee, you are to conduct research and prepare an information report. Use InfoTrac and the Web to collect information about programs that permit customers to overdraft for a fee. In your report discuss the problem and present well-organized pro and con arguments. What stance has the Federal Reserve taken? If your instructor asks you to make this an analytical report, draw conclusions and make recommendations to the Federal Reserve. Should it allow banks to avoid credit laws and continue these programs?

For additional report ideas and topics, go to Guffey Xtra! <http://guffeyxtra.swlearning.com>

C.L.U.E. review 13

On a separate sheet edit the following sentences to correct faults in grammar, punctuation, spelling, numbers, proofreading, and word use.

1. When conducting research for a report you may face an incredable jumble of data including: printouts, disk files, note cards, copys of articles, inter view notes, questionaire results and statistics.
2. The information in tables are usally easier to read then the same information presented in paragraph.
3. When the Company President and myself use the word average we are refering to the mean which is the arithmetic average.
4. The following 3 statistical terms frequently describe data; Mean, Median and Mode.
5. Readers of business' reports often turn frist to the Conclusions and Reccommendations, therefore these section must be written vary carefully.
6. Informational Reports emphasize facts, Analytical Reports however emphasize reasoning and conclusions.
7. Report Conclusions explain what the problem is, Recommendations tell how to solve it.
8. Frontloading the Recommenddations works when the topic is routine, and when the audience is receptive.
9. In writing most business reports you will genrally organize you're data using 1 of the following 5 methods, time, component, importance, criteria or convention.
10. The Introduction to a report should tell it's purpose and significance, it should also preview the main points.

chapter 14

Proposals and Formal Reports

objectives

1 Discuss the components of informal proposals.

2 Discuss the special components in formal proposals.

3 Discuss the components of typical business plans.

4 Identify formal report components that precede the introduction as well as elements to include in the introduction.

5 Describe formal report components that follow the introduction.

6 Specify tips that aid writers of formal reports.

COMMUNICATION IN PROCESS

Proposals From Hewlett-Packard Pave a Path to the Altar

WITH CARLY FIORINA as CEO, Hewlett-Packard completed a controversial merger with Compaq Computer. Critics say that HP has now lost its focus and is being squeezed between two formidable computer rivals, Dell and IBM. HP dominates the market for printers, both laser and inkjet, and it is strong in handheld computers and other consumer electronics items, such as digital camers. It's also a close second to Dell in sales of desktop personal computers and notebooks.[1] But HP would like to transform itself from a traditional hardware and software vendor to a technology services company.[2] Instead of merely selling equipment, it wants to focus on developing relationships with customers. This is particularly true of Fortune 500 companies that desire more than a product. They want a partnership that's almost like a marriage. This partnership begins with a proposal, which is a written offer to sell services and equipment.

At Hewlett-Packard writing good proposals is critical. That's why it has a special department devoted to developing them. Mary Piecewicz, a manager who helped put together many HP proposals, explained why proposals are so important: "Competition today is tough. Customers are shopping around—especially for big purchases. They want to compare apples to apples, and proposals allow them to do that. Big corporations are now going the proposal route simply because money is tight, and they want to get the most for their dollar. Companies are also trying to protect themselves. Since a proposal is a legally binding document, whatever they put down on paper, they have to be able to supply. Proposals allow companies to find the best deal while at the same time giving them protection."[3]

Writing a Hewlett-Packard proposal involves "detective" work. Because customers want to develop a relationship, the HP proposal team must learn all it can about the customer. This means researching such areas as a customer's corporate culture, degree of environmental consciousness, current business strategies, and how it serves its customers. Once the HP proposal team has gathered background information, it is better able to identify the customer's "hot buttons." These are issues that are most important to the customer. Although some customers are interested primarily in low price and high performance, many global customers today are looking for evidence that the two companies are compatible and that a long-lasting partnership will result from the purchase.

HP CEO Carly Fiorina is a persuasive speaker, but it is HP's proposals tha win customers and bind agreements.

Photo: © NOAH BERGER/Bloomberg News/Landov

Critical Thinking

- How can companies use proposals to compare "apples to apples"?
- Why is it important for a seller to know the buyer's "hot buttons"?
- How does a proposal protect a buyer?

http://www.hp.com

CONTINUED ON PAGE 471

case study

Preparing Formal and Informal Proposals

learning objective

1

Proposals are written offers to solve problems, provide services, or sell equipment. Some proposals are internal, often taking the form of justification and recommendation reports. You learned about these reports in Chapter 13. Most proposals, however, are external, such as those written at Hewlett-Packard. They are a critical means of selling equipment and services that generate income for the giant technology company.

Proposals are persuasive offers to solve problems, provide services, or sell equipment.

Because proposals are vital to their success, some businesses hire consultants or maintain specialists, like Piecewicz, who do nothing but write proposals. Such proposals typically tell how a problem can be solved, what procedure will be followed, who will do it, how long it will take, and how much it will cost. As Mary Piecewicz noted, companies today want to be able to compare "apples with apples," and they also want the protection offered by proposals, which are legal contracts.

Proposals may be divided into two categories: solicited and unsolicited. When firms know exactly what they want, they prepare a request for proposal (RFP), specifying their requirements. Government agencies as well as private businesses use RFPs to solicit competitive bids from vendors. Most proposals are solicited, such as that presented by the Kauai Visitors Bureau in Hawaii. Its RFP offered a $500,000 contract for creative print work and Internet exposure that promoted the island's attractions.[4] Enterprising companies looking for work might submit unsolicited proposals. For example, Clean-Up Technology, a U.S. waste disposal company, submitted several unsolicited proposals to government agencies in Mexico offering its expertise in solving environmental problems.[5]

Government agencies and many companies use requests for proposals (RFPs) to solicit competitive bids on projects.

Components of Informal Proposals

Informal proposals may be presented in short (two- to four-page) letters. Sometimes called *letter proposals*, they may contain six principal components: introduction, background, proposal, staffing, budget, and authorization request. As you can see in Figure 14.1, both informal and formal proposals contain these six basic parts. Figure 14.2, an informal letter proposal to a St. Petersburg dentist to improve patient satisfaction, illustrates the six parts of letter proposals.

Introduction. Most proposals begin by briefly explaining the reasons for the proposal and by highlighting the writer's qualifications. To make your introduction more persuasive, you need to provide a "hook," such as the following:

Informal proposals may contain an introduction, background information, the proposal, staffing requirements, a budget, and an authorization request.

- Hint at extraordinary results with details to be revealed shortly.
- Promise low costs or speedy results.
- Mention a remarkable resource (well-known authority, new computer program, well-trained staff) available exclusively to you.
- Identify a serious problem (worry item) and promise a solution, to be explained later.
- Specify a key issue or benefit that you feel is the heart of the proposal.

Although writers may know what goes into the proposal introduction, many face writer's block before they can get started. When she worked as a proposals manager at Hewlett-Packard, Mary Piecewicz recognized that writer's block was a big problem for sales representatives on a proposal team. They simply didn't know how to get started. Piecewicz offered the following advice: "To conquer writer's block, begin with a bulleted list of what the customer is looking for. This list is like a road map; it gets you started and keeps you headed in the right direction."

FIGURE 14.1 *Components of Formal and Informal Proposals*

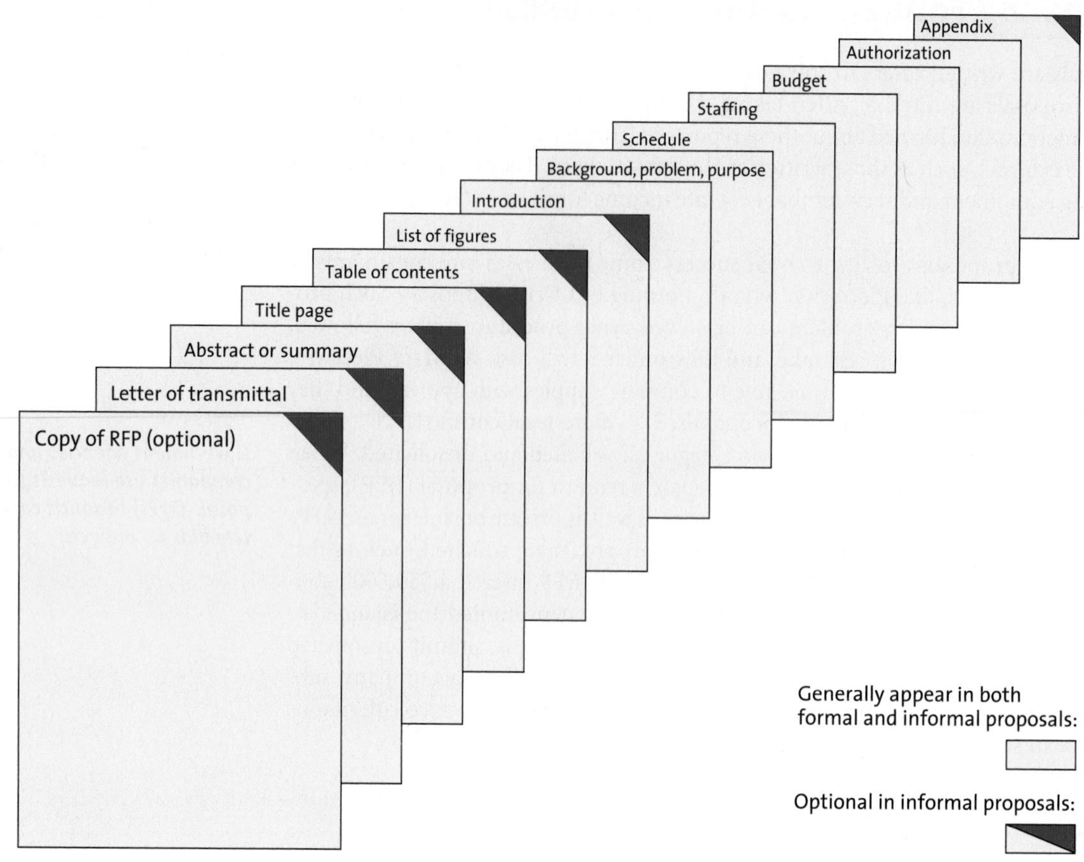

In the proposal introduction shown in Figure 14.2, Elizabeth Metzger focused on what the customer was looking for. She analyzed the request of the St. Petersburg dentist, Dr. Townsend, and decided that he was most interested in specific recommendations for improving service to his patients. But Metzger didn't hit on this hook until she had written a first draft and had come back to it later. Indeed, it's often a good idea to put off writing the proposal introduction until after you have completed other parts. For longer proposals the introduction also describes the scope and limitations of the project, as well as outlining the organization of the material to come.

In the background section of a proposal, the writer discusses the problem and goals of the project.

Background, Problem, Purpose. The background section identifies the problem and discusses the goals or purposes of the project. In an unsolicited proposal your goal is to convince the reader that a problem exists. Thus, you must present the problem in detail, discussing such factors as monetary losses, failure to comply with government regulations, or loss of customers. In a solicited proposal your aim is to persuade the reader that you understand the problem completely. Thus, if you are responding to an RFP, this means repeating its language. For example, if the RFP asks for the *design of a maintenance program for wireless communication equipment,* you would use the same language in explaining the purpose of your proposal. This section might include segments entitled *Basic Requirements, Most Critical Tasks,* and *Most Important Secondary Problems.*

Proposal, Plan, Schedule. In the proposal section itself, you should discuss your plan for solving the problem. In some proposals this is tricky because you want to disclose enough of your plan to secure the contract without giving away so much

FIGURE 14.2 *Informal Proposal*

1 Prewriting

ANALYZE: The purpose is to persuade the reader to accept this proposal.

ANTICIPATE: The reader must be convinced that this survey project is worth its hefty price.

ADAPT: Because the reader will be resistant at first, use a persuasive approach that emphasizes benefits.

2 Writing

RESEARCH: Collect data about the reader's practice and other surveys of patient satisfaction.

ORGANIZE: Identify four specific purposes (benefits) of this proposal. Specify the survey plan. Promote the staff, itemize the budget, and ask for approval.

COMPOSE: Prepare for revision by composing at a word processor.

3 Revising

REVISE: Revise to emphasize benefits. Improve readability with functional headings and lists. Remove jargon and wordiness.

PROOFREAD: Check spelling of client's name. Verify dates and calculation of budget figures. Recheck all punctuation.

EVALUATE: Is this proposal convincing enough to sell the client?

Metzger Research
MARKET RESEARCH CONSULTANTS

One Regal Oaks Plaza
Tampa, FL 33620
813.863.9527
www.metzgerresearch.com

April 6, 2006

Dr. Dale M. Townsend
140 56th Avenue South
St. Petersburg, FL 33705

Dear Dr. Townsend:

Grabs attention with "hook" that focuses on key benefit

Helping you improve your practice is of the highest priority at Metzger Research. That's why we are pleased to submit the following proposal outlining our plan to help you more effectively meet your patients' needs by analyzing their views about your practice.

Uses opening paragraph in place of introduction

Background and Purposes

We understand that you have been incorporating a total quality management system in your practice. Although you have every reason to believe your patients are pleased with the service you provide, you would like to give them an opportunity to discuss what they like and possibly don't like about your service. Specifically, your purposes are to survey your patients to (a) determine the level of their satisfaction with you and your staff, (b) elicit their suggestions for improvement, (c) learn more about how they discovered you, and (d) compare your "preferred" and "standard" patients.

Identifies four purposes of survey

Announces heart of proposal

Proposed Plan

On the basis of our experience in conducting many local and national customer satisfaction surveys, Metzger Research proposes the following plan to you.

Divides total plan into logical segments for easy reading

Describes procedure for solving problem or achieving goals

Survey. We will develop a short but thorough questionnaire probing the data you desire. Although the survey instrument will include both open-ended and closed questions, it will concentrate on the latter. Closed questions enable respondents to answer easily; they also facilitate systematic data analysis. The questionnaire will measure patient reactions to such elements as courtesy, professionalism, accuracy of billing, friendliness, and waiting time. After you approve it, the questionnaire will be sent to a carefully selected sample of 300 patients whom you have separated into groupings of "preferred" and "standard."

Analysis. Data from the survey will be analyzed by demographic segments, such as patient type, age, and gender. Our experienced team of experts, using state-of-the-art computer systems and advanced statistical measures, will study the (a) degree of patient satisfaction, (b) reasons for satisfaction or dissatisfaction, and (c) relationship between responses of your "preferred" and "standard" patients. Moreover, our team will report to you specific suggestions for making patient visits more pleasant.

Report. You will receive a final report with the key findings clearly spelled out, Dr. Townsend. Our expert staff will also draw conclusions based on these findings. The report will include tables summarizing all responses, broken down into groups of preferred and standard clients.

FIGURE 14.2 *Continued*

Dr. Dale M. Townsend Page 2 April 6, 2006

Schedule. With your approval, the following schedule has been arranged for your patient satisfaction survey:

Questionnaire development and mailing	June 1-6
Deadline for returning questionnaire	June 24
Data tabulation and processing	June 24-26
Completion of final report	July 1

Staffing

Metzger Research is a nationally recognized, experienced consulting firm specializing in survey investigation. I have assigned your customer satisfaction survey to Dr. Kelly Miller, our director of research. Dr. Miller was trained at Florida State University and has successfully supervised our research program for the past nine years. Before joining Metzger, she was a marketing analyst with Procter & Gamble Company. Assisting Dr. Miller will be a team headed by James Wilson, our vice president for operations. Mr. Wilson earned a bachelor's degree in computer science and a master's degree in marketing from the University of South Florida, where he was elected to Phi Delta Mu honor society. Within our organization he supervises our computer-aided telephone interviewing (CATI) system and manages our 30-person professional interviewing staff.

Budget

	Estimated Hours	Rate	Total
Professional and administrative time			
Questionnaire development	3	$150/hr.	$ 450
Questionnaire mailing	4	40/hr.	160
Data processing and tabulation	12	40/hr.	480
Analysis of findings	15	150/hr.	2,250
Preparation of final report	5	150/hr.	750
Mailing costs			
300 copies of questionnaire			120
Postage and envelopes			270
Total costs			$4,480

Authorization

We are convinced, Dr. Townsend, that our professionally designed and administered client satisfaction survey will enhance your practice. Metzger Research can have specific results for you by July 1 if you sign the enclosed duplicate copy of this letter and return it to us with a retainer of $2,300. The prices in this offer are in effect only until August 1.

Sincerely,

Elizabeth Metzger

Elizabeth Metzger, Ph.D.
President

EM:pem
Enclosure

Uses past-tense verbs to show that work has already started on the project

Promotes credentials and expertise of key people

Builds credibility by describing outstanding staff and facilities

Itemizes costs carefully because a proposal is a contract offer

Closes by repeating key qualifications and main benefits

Makes response easy

Provides deadline

The actual proposal section must give enough information to secure the contract but not so much detail that the services are no longer needed.

information that your services aren't needed. Without specifics, though, your proposal has little chance, so you must decide how much to reveal. Tell what you propose to do and how it will benefit the reader. Remember, too, that a proposal is a sales presentation. Sell your methods, product, and "deliverables"—items that will be left with the client. In this section some writers specify how the project will be managed and how its progress will be audited. Most writers also include a schedule of activities or timetable showing when events will take place.

The staffing section promotes the credentials and expertise of the project leaders and support staff.

Staffing. The staffing section of a proposal describes the credentials and expertise of the project leaders. It may also identify the size and qualifications of the support staff, along with other resources such as computer facilities and special programs for analyzing statistics. The staffing section is a good place to endorse and promote your staff. Some firms, like Hewlett-Packard, follow industry standards and include staff qualifications in an appendix. HP also uses generic résumés rather than the actual résumés of key people. This ensures privacy for individuals and also protects the company in case the staff changes after a proposal has been submitted to a customer.

Budget. A central item in most proposals is the budget, a list of proposed project costs. You need to prepare this section carefully because it represents a contract; you can't raise the price later—even if your costs increase. You can—and should—protect yourself with a deadline for acceptance. In the budget section some writers itemize hours and costs; others present a total sum only. A proposal to install a complex computer system might, for example, contain a detailed line-by-line budget. Similarly, Elizabeth Metzger felt that she needed to justify the budget for her firm's patient satisfaction survey, so she itemized the costs, as shown in Figure 14.2. But the budget included for a proposal to conduct a one-day seminar to improve employee communication skills might be a lump sum only. Your analysis of the project will help you decide what kind of budget to prepare.

Because a proposal is a legal contract, the budget must be carefully researched.

Authorization Request. Informal proposals often close with a request for approval or authorization. In addition, the closing should remind the reader of key benefits and motivate action. It might also include a deadline date beyond which the offer is invalid. At Hewlett-Packard authorization to proceed is not part of the proposal. Instead, it is usually discussed after the customer has received the proposal. In this way the customer and the sales account manager are able to negotiate terms before a formal agreement is drawn.

Special Components of Formal Proposals

learning objective

2

Formal proposals differ from informal proposals not in style but in size and format. Formal proposals respond to big projects and may range from 5 to 200 or more pages. To facilitate comprehension and reference, they are organized into many parts, as shown in Figure 14.1. In addition to the six basic components just described, formal proposals may contain some or all of the following front and end parts.

Copy of RFP. A copy of the RFP may be included in the opening parts of a formal proposal. Large organizations may have more than one RFP circulating, and identification is necessary.

Formal proposals might also contain a copy of the RFP, a letter of transmittal, an abstract, a title page, a table of contents, a list of figures, and an appendix.

Letter of Transmittal. A letter of transmittal, usually bound inside formal proposals, addresses the person who is designated to receive the proposal or who will make the final decision. The letter describes how you learned about the problem or confirms that the proposal responds to the enclosed RFP. This persuasive letter briefly presents the major features and benefits of your proposal. Here, you should assure the reader that you are authorized to make the bid and mention the time limit for which the bid stands. You may also offer to provide additional information and ask for action, if appropriate.

Abstract or Executive Summary. An abstract is a brief summary (typically one page) of a proposal's highlights intended for specialists or for technical readers. An executive summary also reviews the proposal's highlights, but it is written for managers and so should be less technically oriented. Formal proposals may contain one or both summaries. For more information about writing executive summaries, see page 475.

An abstract summarizes a proposal's highlights for specialists; an executive summary does so for managers.

Title Page. The title page includes the following items, generally in this order: title of proposal, name of client organization, RFP number or other announcement, date of submission, author's name, and/or his or her organization.

Table of Contents. Because most proposals don't contain an index, the table of contents becomes quite important. Tables of contents should include all headings and their beginning page numbers. Items that appear before the contents (copy of RFP, letter of transmittal, abstract, and title page) typically are not listed in the contents. However, any appendixes should be listed.

List of Figures. Proposals with many tables and figures often contain a list of figures. This list includes each figure or table title and its page number. If you have just a few figures or tables, however, you may omit this list.

spotlight *on communicators*

Consultant Tom Sant advises proposal writers to (1) state the client's key need or problem, (2) spell out why the need must be addressed, (3) present a solution in concrete terms, and (4) fill in the details. Above all, he says, be sure a proposal is client focused rather than product focused. If the price tag is hefty, he suggests highlighting long-term savings and cost effectiveness.

Appendix. Ancillary material of interest to some readers goes in appendixes. Appendix A might include résumés of the principal investigators or testimonial letters. Appendix B might include examples or a listing of previous projects. Other appendixes could include audit procedures, technical graphics, or professional papers cited in the body of the proposal.

Proposals in the past were always paper-based and delivered by mail or special messenger. Today, however, companies increasingly prefer *online proposals.* Receiving companies may transmit the electronic proposal to all levels of management without ever printing a page, thus appealing to many environmentally conscious organizations.

Well-written proposals win contracts and business for companies and individuals. Many companies depend entirely on proposals to generate their income, so proposal writing is extremely important. The following checklist summarizes important elements to remember in writing proposals.

Checklist for Writing Proposals

Introduction

- ✓ **Indicate the purpose.** Specify why the proposal is being made.
- ✓ **Develop a persuasive "hook."** Suggest excellent results, low costs, or exclusive resources. Identify a serious problem or name a key issue or benefit.

Background, Problem

- ✓ **Provide necessary background.** Discuss the significance of the proposal and its goals or purposes.
- ✓ **Introduce the problem.** For unsolicited proposals convince the reader that a problem exists. For solicited proposals show that you fully understand the problem and its ramifications.

Proposal, Plan

- ✓ **Explain the proposal.** Present your plan for solving the problem or meeting the need.
- ✓ **Discuss plan management and evaluation.** If appropriate, tell how the plan will be implemented and evaluated.

PROCESS IN PROGRESS

Hewlett-Packard Revisited

STAYING TUNED IN to a customer's concerns is the principal focus of proposal writers at Hewlett-Packard. A proposal today, especially in a global environment, involves more than merely supplying a product. Mary Piecewicz, at Hewlett-Packard, says, "It's more like a marriage between two companies. Before we can write a proposal, we need to be detectives and learn as much as possible about the potential partner." HP begins searching for information. From the customer's annual report, Web site, news releases, industry reports, and other sources, HP detectives search for specifics about its products, strategies, and company culture. What hot buttons is the company likely to respond to?

In organizing proposals, HP always responds to the customer's outline. If the customer doesn't specify a plan, proposals are arranged as follows: Section 1 includes the executive summary, which is the most important part of the proposal. It spotlights the hot buttons and the proposal criteria set forth in the request for proposal (RFP). Section 2 covers specifications and technical descriptions. Section 3 lists costs, terms, and conditions. Section 4 presents supplemental literature, including generic résumés and staff qualifications. Authorization to proceed is usually discussed after receipt of the proposal. In this way customers are able to negotiate the formal agreement with the sales account manager.

Because of its importance, the executive summary gets special attention. It may open with a brief history of HP, but its primary focus is on the customer's needs. "We address every customer issue and specify our 'differentiators,'" explains Piecewicz. "What makes HP stand out from our competitors? The executive summary is really the selling tool in our proposals, and we spend the most time on it.".

Critical Thinking

- Why is it important to become a "detective" before beginning to write a proposal?
- If Hewlett-Packard were preparing a proposal for a Fortune 500 company, what kinds of information should the proposal team investigate and where could it find such information?
- What is the most important part of an HP proposal, and what should it include?

http://www.hp.com

CONTINUED ON PAGE 494

case study

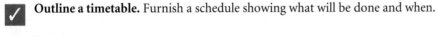

✓ **Outline a timetable.** Furnish a schedule showing what will be done and when.

Staffing

✓ **Promote the qualifications of your staff.** Explain the specific credentials and expertise of the key personnel for the project.

✓ **Mention special resources or equipment.** Show how your support staff and resources are superior to those of the competition.

Budget

✓ **Show project costs.** For most projects itemize costs. Remember, however, that proposals are contracts.

✓ **Include a deadline.** Here or in the conclusion present a date beyond which the bid figures are no longer valid.

Authorization

- ✓ **Ask for approval.** Make it easy for the reader to authorize the project (for example, *Sign and return the duplicate copy*).

learning objective
3

Preparing an Effective Business Plan

Another form of proposal is a business plan. Let's say you want to start your own business. Unless you can count on the Bank of Mom and Dad, you will need financial backing such as a bank loan or venture capital supplied by investors. A business plan is critical for securing financial support of any kind. Such a plan also ensures that you have done your homework and know what you are doing in launching your business. It provides you with a detailed road map to chart a course to success.

Kimberly and Scott Holstein launched a gourmet pretzel business in their studio apartment in Chicago. With exposure on the home-shopping channel QVC, sales of their pizza-flavored and other exotic pretzels skyrocketed. But big sales required a $500,000 investment in equipment, employees, space, and ingredients. Like other entrepreneurs, the Holsteins needed financial assistance. Well-written business plans help entrepreneurs launch or expand their businesses by convincing banks and venture capitalists to take a risk and invest in a promising business.

Photo: © Photo by John Zich/zrlMAGES.com

A good business plan prepared by professionals could cost $24,000 to $30,000 and take about 15 working days to prepare.[6] But many budding entrepreneurs prefer to save the cash and do it themselves.

Components of Typical Business Plans

If you are serious about starting a business, the importance of a comprehensive, thoughtful business plan cannot be overemphasized, says the Small Business Administration. Your business plan is more likely to secure the funds you need if it is carefully written and includes the following elements:

- **Letter of transmittal and/or executive summary with mission statement.** Explain your reason for writing. Provide your name, address, and telephone number, along with contact information for all principals. Include a concise mission statement that describes your business and explains the reasons it will succeed. Because potential investors will be looking for this mission statement, consider highlighting it with a paragraph heading (*Mission statement*) or use bolding or italics. Some consultants say that you should be able to write your mission statement on the back of a business card. Others think that one or two short paragraphs might be more realistic. To give it special treatment, you could make the mission statement a section of its own following the table of contents. Your executive summary should conclude by introducing the parts of the following plan and asking for support.
- **Table of contents.** List the page numbers and topics included in your plan.
- **Company description.** Identify the form of your business (proprietorship, partnership, or corporation) and its business type (merchandising, manufacturing, or service). For existing companies, describe the company's founding, growth, sales, and profit.

- **Product/service description.** In jargon-free language, explain what you are providing, how it will benefit customers, and why it is better than existing products or services. For start-ups, explain why the business will be profitable. Investors aren't always looking for a unique product or service. Instead, they are searching for a concept whose growth potential distinguishes it from other proposals competing for funds.
- **Market analysis.** Discuss market characteristics, trends, projected growth, customer behavior, complementary products and services, and barriers to entry. Identify your customers and how you will attract, hold, and increase your market share. Discuss the strengths and weaknesses of your direct and indirect competitors.
- **Operations and management.** Explain specifically how you will run your business, including location, equipment, personnel, and management. Highlight experienced and well-trained members of the management team and your advisors. Many investors consider this the most important factor in assessing business potential. Can your management team implement this business plan?
- **Financial analysis.** Outline a realistic start-up budget that includes fees for legal/professional services, occupancy, licenses/permits, equipment, insurance, supplies, advertising/promotions, salaries/wages, accounting, income, and utilities. Also present an operating budget that projects costs for personnel, insurance, rent, depreciation, loan payments, salaries, taxes, repairs, and so on. Explain how much money you have, how much you will need to start up, and how much you will need to stay in business.
- **Appendixes.** Provide necessary extras such as managers' résumés, promotional materials, and product photos.

Seeing Sample Business Plans on the Web

Writing a business plan is easier if you can see examples and learn from experts' suggestions. On the Web you will find many sites devoted to business plans. Some sites want to sell you something; others offer free advice. One of the best sites (**www.bplans.com**) does try to sell business plans. But the site also provides 60 free samples of business plans ranging from aircraft rental to wedding consultant businesses. These simple but helpful plans, provided by Palo Alto Software, Inc., illustrate diverse business start-ups.

At the Small Business Administration (SBA) Web site (**http://www.sba.gov/starting_business/**), you will find more business plan advice. In addition to suggestions for writing and using a business plan, the SBA site provides helpful business start-up information about financing, marketing, employees, taxes, and legal matters. The SBA site also links to the 60 business plans provided by Palo Alto Software, Inc.

Writing Formal Reports

learning objective 4

Formal reports are similar to formal proposals in length, organization, and serious tone. Instead of making an offer, however, formal reports represent the end product of thorough investigation and analysis. They present ordered information to decision makers in business, industry, government, and education. In many ways formal reports are extended versions of the analytical business reports presented in Chapter 13. Figure 14.3 shows the components of typical formal reports, their normal sequence, and parts that might be omitted in informal reports.

FIGURE 14.3 ***Components of Formal and Informal Reports***

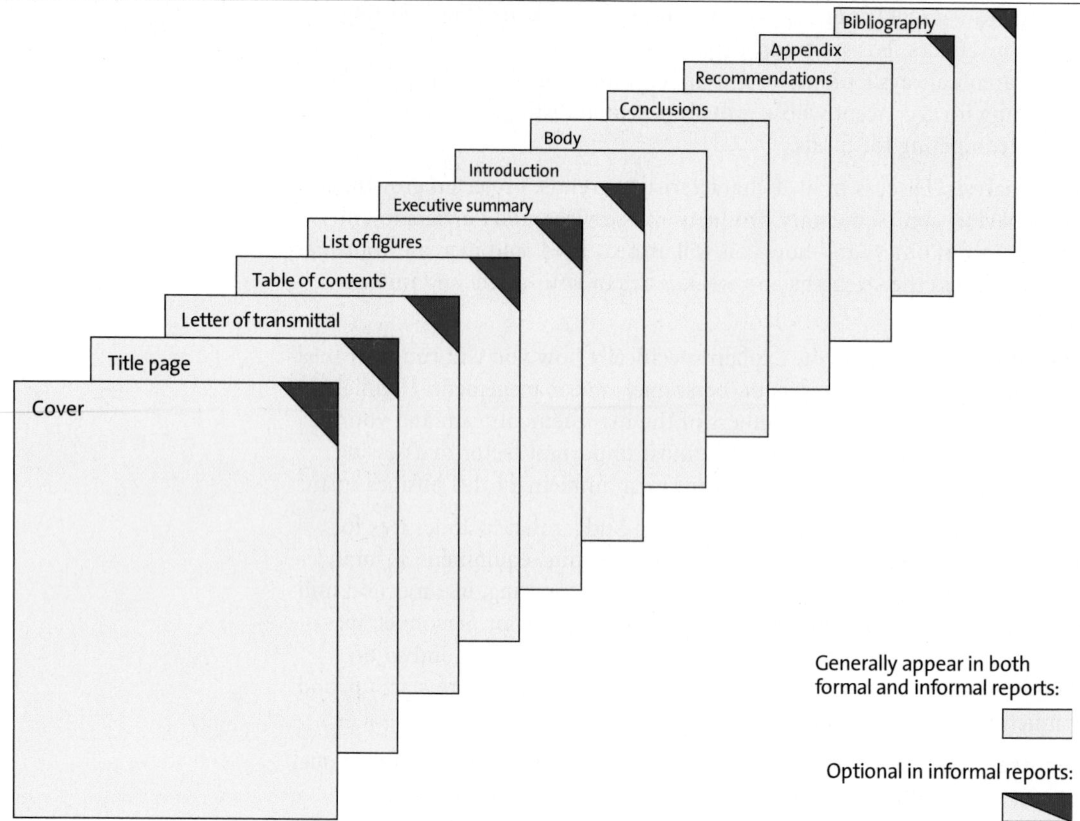

Components of Formal Reports

Formal reports discuss the results of a process of thorough investigation and analysis.

A number of front and end items lengthen formal reports but enhance their professional tone and serve their multiple audiences. Formal reports may be read by many levels of managers, along with technical specialists and financial consultants. Therefore, breaking a long, formal report into small segments makes its information more accessible and easier to understand for all readers. These segments are discussed here and also illustrated in the model report shown later in the chapter (Figure 14.4). This analytical report studies the recycling program at Sun Coast University and makes recommendations for improving its operation.

Like proposals, formal reports are divided into many segments to make information comprehensible and accessible.

Cover. Formal reports are usually enclosed in vinyl or heavy paper binders to protect the pages and to give a professional, finished appearance. Some companies have binders imprinted with their name and logo. The title of the report may appear through a cut-out window or may be applied with an adhesive label. Good stationery and office supply stores usually stock an assortment of report binders and labels.

Title Page. A report title page, as illustrated in the Figure 14.4 model report, begins with the name of the report typed in uppercase letters (no underscore and no quotation marks). Next comes *Presented to* (or *Submitted to*) and the name, title, and organization of the individual receiving the report. Lower on the page is *Prepared by* (or *Submitted by*) and the author's name plus any necessary identification. The last item on the title page is the date of submission. All items after the title are typed in a combination of upper- and lowercase letters.

Letter or Memo of Transmittal. Generally written on organization stationery, a letter or memorandum of transmittal introduces a formal report. You will recall that letters are sent to outsiders and memos to insiders. A transmittal letter or memo follows the direct pattern and is usually less formal than the report itself (for example, the letter or memo may use contractions and the first-person pronouns *I* and *we*). The transmittal letter or memo typically (1) announces the topic of the report and tells how it was authorized; (2) briefly describes the project; (3) highlights the report's findings, conclusions, and recommendations, if the reader is expected to be supportive; and (4) closes with appreciation for the assignment, instruction for the reader's follow-up actions, acknowledgment of help from others, or offers of assistance in answering questions. If a report is going to different readers, a special transmittal letter or memo should be prepared for each, anticipating what each reader needs to know in using the report.

A letter or memo of transmittal gives a personalized overview of a formal report.

Table of Contents. The table of contents shows the headings in a report and their page numbers. It gives an overview of the report topics and helps readers locate them. You should wait to prepare the table of contents until after you've completed the report. For short reports you should include all headings. For longer reports you might want to list only first- and second-level headings. Leaders (spaced or unspaced dots) help guide the eye from the heading to the page number. Items may be indented in outline form or typed flush with the left margin.

List of Figures. For reports with several figures or illustrations, you may wish to include a list of figures to help readers locate them. This list may appear on the same page as the table of contents, space permitting. For each figure or illustration, include a title and page number. Some writers distinguish between tables and all other illustrations, which are called figures. If you make this distinction, you should also prepare separate lists of tables and figures. Because the model report in Figure 14.4 has few illustrations, the writer labeled them all "figures," a method that simplifies numbering.

Executive Summary. The purpose of an executive summary is to present an overview of a longer report to people who may not have time to read the entire document. Generally, an executive summary is prepared by the author who is writing about his or her own report. But occasionally you may be asked to write an executive summary of a published report or article written by someone else. In either case you will probably perform the following activities:

An executive summary supplies an overview of a longer report.

- **Summarize key points.** Your goal is to summarize the important points including the purpose of the report; the problem addressed; and the findings, conclusions, and recommendations. You might also summarize the research methods, if they can be stated concisely.
- **Look for strategic words and sentences.** Read the completed report carefully. Pay special attention to first and last sentences of paragraphs, which often contain summary statements. Look for words that enumerate (*first, next, finally*) and words that express causation (*therefore, as a result*). Also look for words that signal essentials (*basically, central, leading, principal, major*) and words that contrast ideas (*however, consequently*).
- **Prepare an outline with headings.** At a minimum include headings for the purpose, findings, and conclusions/recommendations. What kernels of information would your reader want to know about these topics?
- **Fill in your outline.** Some writers use their computers to cut and paste important parts of the text. Then they condense with careful editing. Others find it most efficient to create new sentences as they prepare the executive summary.

- **Begin with the purpose.** The easiest way to begin an executive summary is with the words "The purpose of this report is to . . . ." Experienced writers may be more creative.
- **Follow the report sequence.** Present all your information in the order in which it is found in the report.
- **Eliminate nonessential details.** Include only main points. Don't include anything not in the original report. Use minimal technical language.
- **Control the length.** An executive summary is usually no longer than 10 percent of the original document. Thus, a 100-page report might require a 10-page summary. A 10-page report might need only a 1-page summary—or no summary at all. The executive summary for a long report may also include graphics to adequately highlight main points.

To see a representative executive summary, look at page 483 of Figure 14.4. Although it is only one page long, this executive summary includes headings to help the reader see the main divisions immediately. Let your organization's practices guide you in determining the length and form of an executive summary.

Introduction. Formal reports begin with an introduction that sets the scene and announces the subject. Because they contain many parts serving different purposes, formal reports have a degree of redundancy. The same information may be included in the letter of transmittal, summary, and introduction. To avoid sounding repetitious, try to present the data slightly differently. But don't skip the introduction because you've included some of its information elsewhere. You can't be sure that your reader saw the information earlier. A good report introduction typically covers the following elements, although not necessarily in this order:

- **Background.** Describe events leading up to the problem or need.
- **Problem or purpose.** Explain the report topic and specify the problem or need that motivated the report.
- **Significance.** Tell why the topic is important. You may wish to quote experts or cite newspapers, journals, books, and other secondary sources to establish the importance of the topic.
- **Scope.** Clarify the boundaries of the report, defining what will be included or excluded.
- **Organization.** Launch readers by giving them a road map that previews the structure of the report.

Beyond these minimal introductory elements, consider adding any of the following information that is relevant for your readers:

- **Authorization.** Identify who commissioned the report. If no letter of transmittal is included, also tell why, when, by whom, and to whom the report was written.
- **Literature review.** Summarize what other authors and researchers have published on this topic, especially for academic and scientific reports.
- **Sources and methods.** Describe your secondary sources (periodicals, books, databases). Also explain how you collected primary data, including survey size, sample design, and statistical programs used.
- **Definitions of key terms.** Define words that may be unfamiliar to the audience. Also define terms with special meanings, such as *small business* when it specifically means businesses with fewer than 30 employees.

learning objective

5

Body. The principal section in a formal report is the body. It discusses, analyzes, interprets, and evaluates the research findings or solution to the initial problem. This is where you show the evidence that justifies your conclusions. Organize the body into main categories following your original outline or using one of the patterns described earlier (such as time, component, importance, criteria, or convention).

Although we refer to this section as the body, it doesn't carry that heading. Instead, it contains clear headings that explain each major section. Headings may be functional or talking. Functional heads (such as *Results of the Survey*, *Analysis of Findings*, or *Discussion*) help readers identify the purpose of the section but don't reveal what's in it. Such headings are useful for routine reports or for sensitive topics that may upset readers. Talking heads (for example, *Recycling Habits of Campus Community*) are more informative and interesting, but they don't help readers see the organization of the report. The model report in Figure 14.4 uses functional heads for organizational sections requiring identification (*Introduction*, *Conclusions*, and *Recommendations*) and talking heads to divide the body.

Conclusions. This important section tells what the findings mean, particularly in terms of solving the original problem. Some writers prefer to intermix their conclusions with the analysis of the findings—instead of presenting the conclusions separately. Other writers place the conclusions before the body so that busy readers can examine the significant information immediately. Still others combine the conclusions and recommendations. Most writers, though, present the conclusions after the body because readers expect this structure. In long reports this section may include a summary of the findings. To improve comprehension, you may present the conclusions in a numbered or bulleted list. See Chapter 13 for more suggestions on drawing conclusions.

The recommendations section of a formal report offers specific suggestions for solving a problem.

Recommendations. When requested, you should submit recommendations that make precise suggestions for actions to solve the report problem. Recommendations are most helpful when they are practical and reasonable. Naturally, they should evolve from the findings and conclusions. Don't introduce new information in the conclusions or recommendations. As with conclusions, the position of recommendations is somewhat flexible. They may be combined with conclusions, or they may be presented before the body, especially when the audience is eager and supportive. Generally, though, in formal reports they come last.

Recommendations require an appropriate introductory sentence, such as *The findings and conclusions in this study support the following recommendations.* When making many recommendations, number them and phrase each as a command, such as *Begin an employee fitness program with a workout room available five days a week.* If appropriate, add information describing how to implement each recommendation. Some reports include a timetable describing the who, what, when, where, and how for putting each recommendation into operation. Chapter 13 provides more information about writing recommendations.

Appendix. Incidental or supporting materials belong in appendixes at the end of a formal report. These materials are relevant to some readers but not to all. Appendixes may include survey forms, copies of other reports, tables of data, computer printouts, and related correspondence. If additional appendixes are necessary, they would be named *Appendix A*, *Appendix B*, and so forth.

Works Cited, References, or Bibliography. Readers look in the bibliography section to locate the sources of ideas mentioned in a report. Your method of report documentation determines how this section is developed. If you use the MLA

The bibliography section of a formal report identifies sources of ideas mentioned in the report.

referencing format, all citations would be listed alphabetically in the "Works Cited." If you use the APA format, your list would be called "References." Regardless of the format, you must include the author, title, publication, date of publication, page number, and other significant data for all ideas or quotations used in your report. For electronic references include the preceding information plus a description of the electronic address or path leading to the citation. Also include the date on which you located the electronic reference. To see electronic and other citations, examine the list of references at the end of Figure 14.4. Appendix C of the text contains additional documentation information.

learning objective

6

Final Writing Tips

Formal reports require careful attention to all phases of the 3-x-3 writing process.

Formal reports are not undertaken lightly. They involve considerable effort in all three phases of writing, beginning with analysis of the problem and anticipation of the audience (as discussed in Chapter 5). Researching the data, organizing it into a logical presentation, and composing the first draft (Chapter 6) make up the second phase of writing. Revising, proofreading, and evaluating (Chapter 7) are completed in the third phase. Although everyone approaches the writing process somewhat differently, the following tips offer advice in problem areas faced by most formal report writers.

- **Allow sufficient time.** The main reason given by writers who are disappointed with their reports is "I just ran out of time." Develop a realistic timetable and stick to it.
- **Finish data collection.** Don't begin writing until you've collected all the data and drawn the primary conclusions. Starting too early often means backtracking. For reports based on survey data, compile the tables and figures first.
- **Work from a good outline.** A big project such as a formal report needs the order and direction provided by a clear outline, even if the outline has to be revised as the project unfolds.

Smart report writers allow themselves plenty of time, research thoroughly, draw up a useful outline, and work on a computer.

- **Provide a proper writing environment.** You'll need a quiet spot where you can spread out your materials and work without interruption. Formal reports demand blocks of concentration time.
- **Use the features of your computer.** Preparing a report on a word processor enables you to keyboard quickly; revise easily; and check spelling, grammar, and synonyms readily. A word of warning, though: save your document often and print occasionally so that you have a hard copy. Take these precautions to guard against the grief caused by lost files, power outages, and computer malfunctions.
- **Write rapidly; revise later.** Some experts advise writers to record their ideas quickly and save revision until after the first draft is completed. They say that quick writing avoids wasted effort spent in polishing sentences or even sections that may be cut later. Moreover, rapid writing encourages fluency and creativity. However, a quick-and-dirty first draft doesn't work for everyone. Many business writers prefer a more deliberate writing style, so consider this advice selectively.
- **Save difficult sections.** If some sections are harder to write than others, save them until you've developed confidence and rhythm working on easier topics.

Effective formal reports maintain parallelism in verb tenses, avoid first-person pronouns, and use the active voice.

- **Be consistent in verb tense.** Use past-tense verbs to describe completed actions (for example, *the respondents said* or *the survey showed*). Use present-tense verbs, however, to explain current actions (*the purpose of the report is, this report examines, the table shows*, and so forth). When citing references, use past-tense verbs (*Jones reported that*). Don't switch back and forth between present- and past-tense verbs in describing related data.

- **Generally avoid *I* and *we*.** To make formal reports seem as objective and credible as possible, most writers omit first-person pronouns. This formal style sometimes results in the overuse of passive-voice verbs (for example, *periodicals were consulted* and *the study was conducted*). Look for alternative constructions (*periodicals indicated* and *the study revealed*). It's also possible that your organization may allow first-person pronouns, so check before starting your report.
- **Let the first draft sit.** After completing the first version, put it aside for a day or two. Return to it with the expectation of revising and improving it. Don't be afraid to make major changes.
- **Revise for clarity, coherence, and conciseness.** Read a printed copy out loud. Do the sentences make sense? Do the ideas flow together naturally? Can wordiness and flabbiness be cut out? Make sure that your writing is so clear that a busy manager does not have to reread any part. See Chapter 7 for specific revision suggestions.
- **Proofread the final copy three times.** First, read a printed copy slowly for word meanings and content. Then read the copy again for spelling, punctuation, grammar, and other mechanical errors. Finally, scan the entire report to check its formatting and consistency (page numbering, indenting, spacing, headings, and so forth).

Putting It All Together

Formal reports in business generally aim to study problems and recommend solutions. Alan Christopher, business senator to the Office of Associated Students (OAS) at Sun Coast University, was given a campus problem to study, resulting in the formal report shown in Figure 14.4.

The campus recycling program, under the direction of Cheryl Bryant and supported by the OAS, was not attracting the anticipated level of participation. As the campus recycling program began its second year of operation, Cheryl and the OAS wondered whether campus community members were sufficiently aware of the program. They also wondered how participation could be increased. Alan volunteered to investigate the problem because of his strong support for environmental causes. He also needed to conduct a research project for one of his business courses, and he had definite ideas for improving the campus OAS recycling program.

Alan's report illustrates many of the points discussed in this chapter. Although it's a good example of typical report format and style, it should not be viewed as the only way to present a report. Wide variation exists in reports.

The checklist on page 493 summarizes the report process and report components in one handy list.

FIGURE 14.4 ***Model Formal Report With MLA Citation Style***

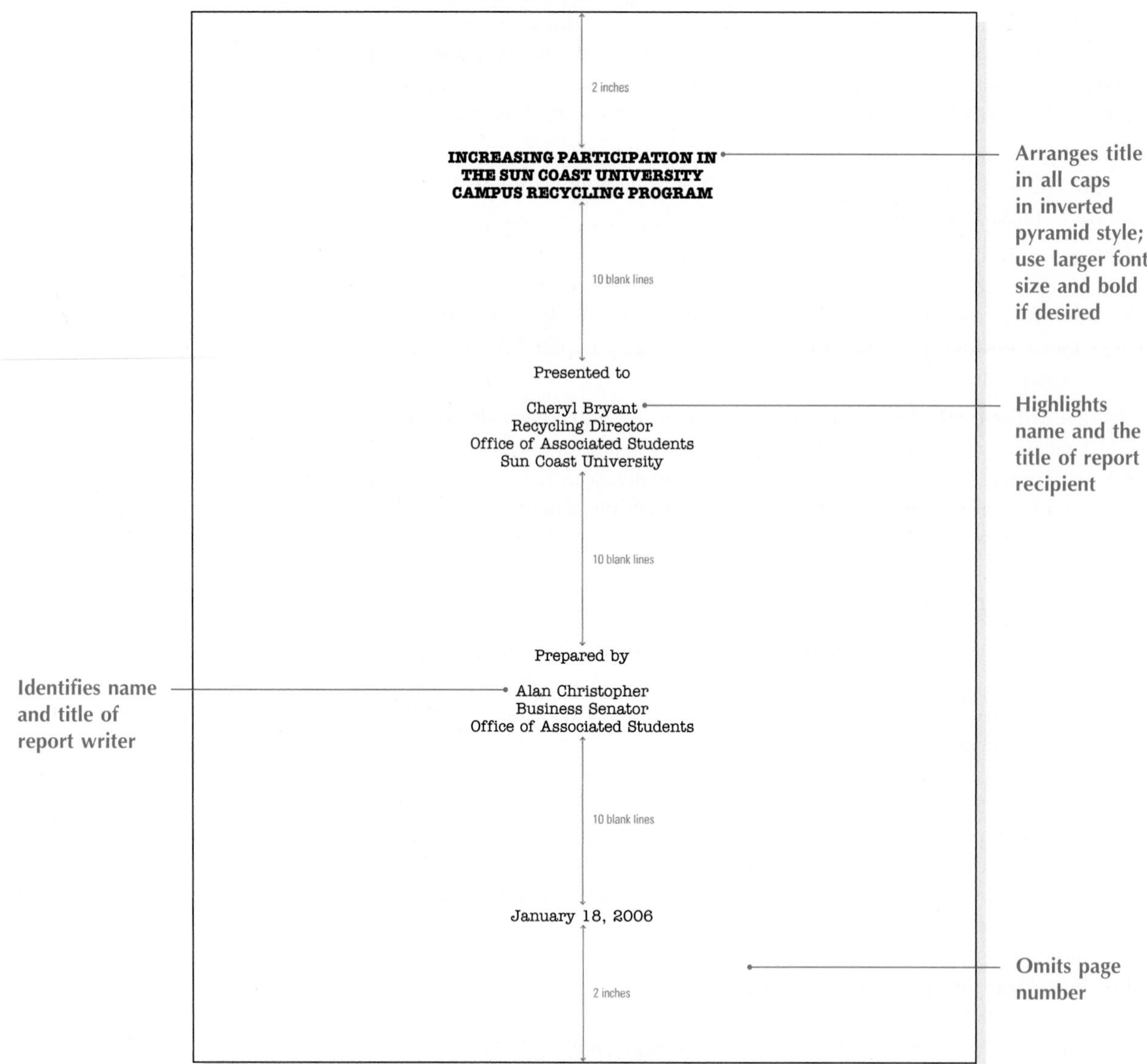

2 inches
INCREASING PARTICIPATION IN
THE SUN COAST UNIVERSITY
CAMPUS RECYCLING PROGRAM
10 blank lines
Presented to
Cheryl Bryant
Recycling Director
Office of Associated Students
Sun Coast University
10 blank lines
Prepared by
Alan Christopher
Business Senator
Office of Associated Students
10 blank lines
January 18, 2006
2 inches
Arranges title in all caps in inverted pyramid style; use larger font size and bold if desired
Highlights name and the title of report recipient
Identifies name and title of report writer
Omits page number

Alan arranges the title page so that the amount of space above the title is equal to the space below the date. If a report is to be bound on the left, move the left margin and center point 1/4 inch to the right. Notice that no page number appears on the title page, although it is counted as page i.

If you use scalable fonts, word processing capabilities, or a laser printer to enhance your report and title page, be careful to avoid anything unprofessional, such as too many type fonts, oversized print, and inappropriate graphics.

FIGURE 14.4 *Continued*

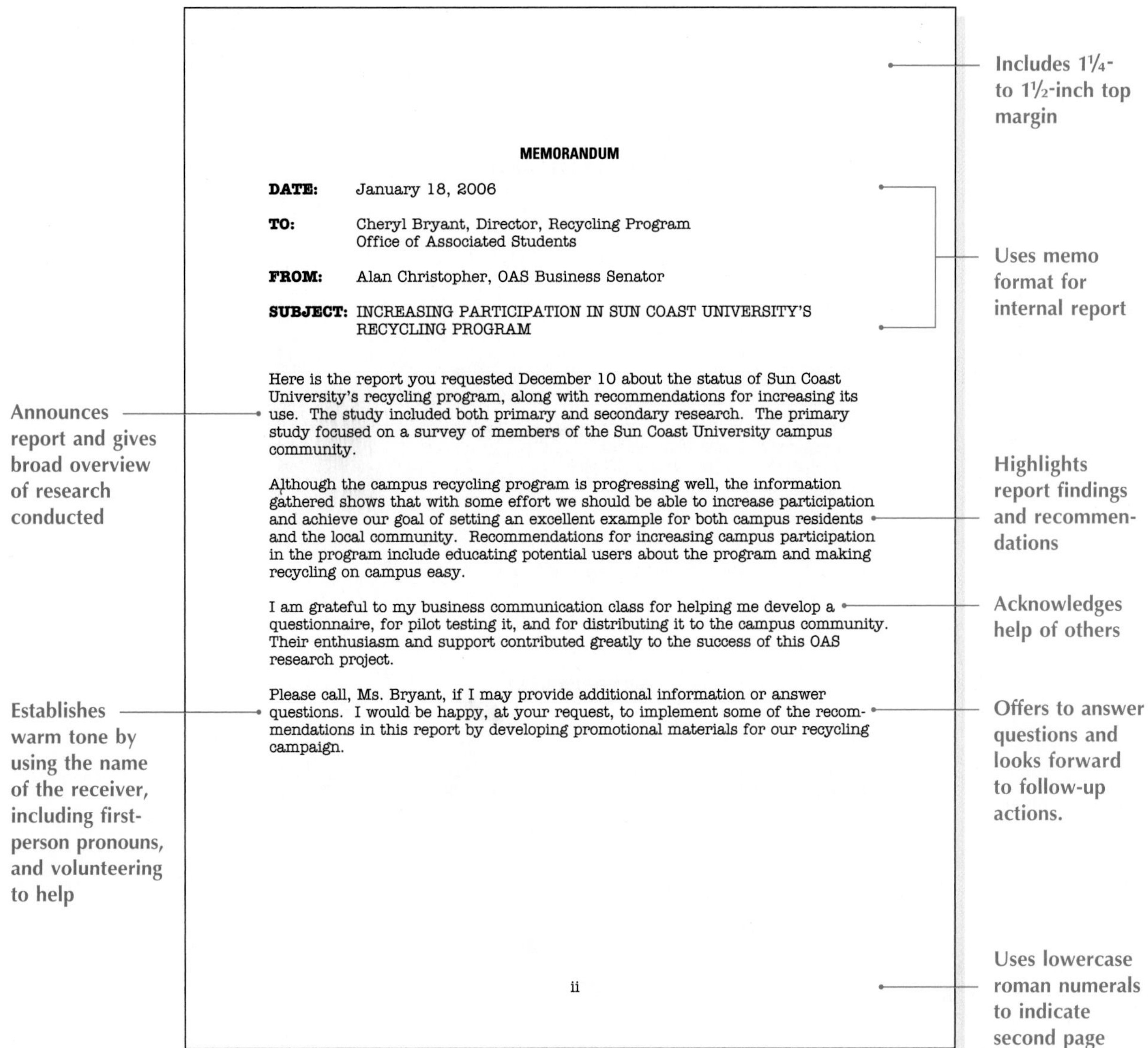

MEMORANDUM

DATE: January 18, 2006

TO: Cheryl Bryant, Director, Recycling Program
Office of Associated Students

FROM: Alan Christopher, OAS Business Senator

SUBJECT: INCREASING PARTICIPATION IN SUN COAST UNIVERSITY'S RECYCLING PROGRAM

Here is the report you requested December 10 about the status of Sun Coast University's recycling program, along with recommendations for increasing its use. The study included both primary and secondary research. The primary study focused on a survey of members of the Sun Coast University campus community.

Although the campus recycling program is progressing well, the information gathered shows that with some effort we should be able to increase participation and achieve our goal of setting an excellent example for both campus residents and the local community. Recommendations for increasing campus participation in the program include educating potential users about the program and making recycling on campus easy.

I am grateful to my business communication class for helping me develop a questionnaire, for pilot testing it, and for distributing it to the campus community. Their enthusiasm and support contributed greatly to the success of this OAS research project.

Please call, Ms. Bryant, if I may provide additional information or answer questions. I would be happy, at your request, to implement some of the recommendations in this report by developing promotional materials for our recycling campaign.

ii

Includes $1^1/_4$- to $1^1/_2$-inch top margin
Uses memo format for internal report
Announces report and gives broad overview of research conducted
Highlights report findings and recommendations
Acknowledges help of others
Establishes warm tone by using the name of the receiver, including first-person pronouns, and volunteering to help
Offers to answer questions and looks forward to follow-up actions.
Uses lowercase roman numerals to indicate second page

Because this report is being submitted within his own organization, Alan uses a memorandum of transmittal. Formal organization reports submitted to outsiders would carry a letter of transmittal printed on company stationery.

The margins for the transmittal should be the same as for the report, about $1^1/_4$ inches on all sides. If a report is to be bound, add an extra $^1/_4$ inch to the left margin. Because the report is single-spaced, the paragraphs are not indented. When a report is double-spaced, paragraphs are indented. A page number is optional.

FIGURE 14.4 ***Continued***

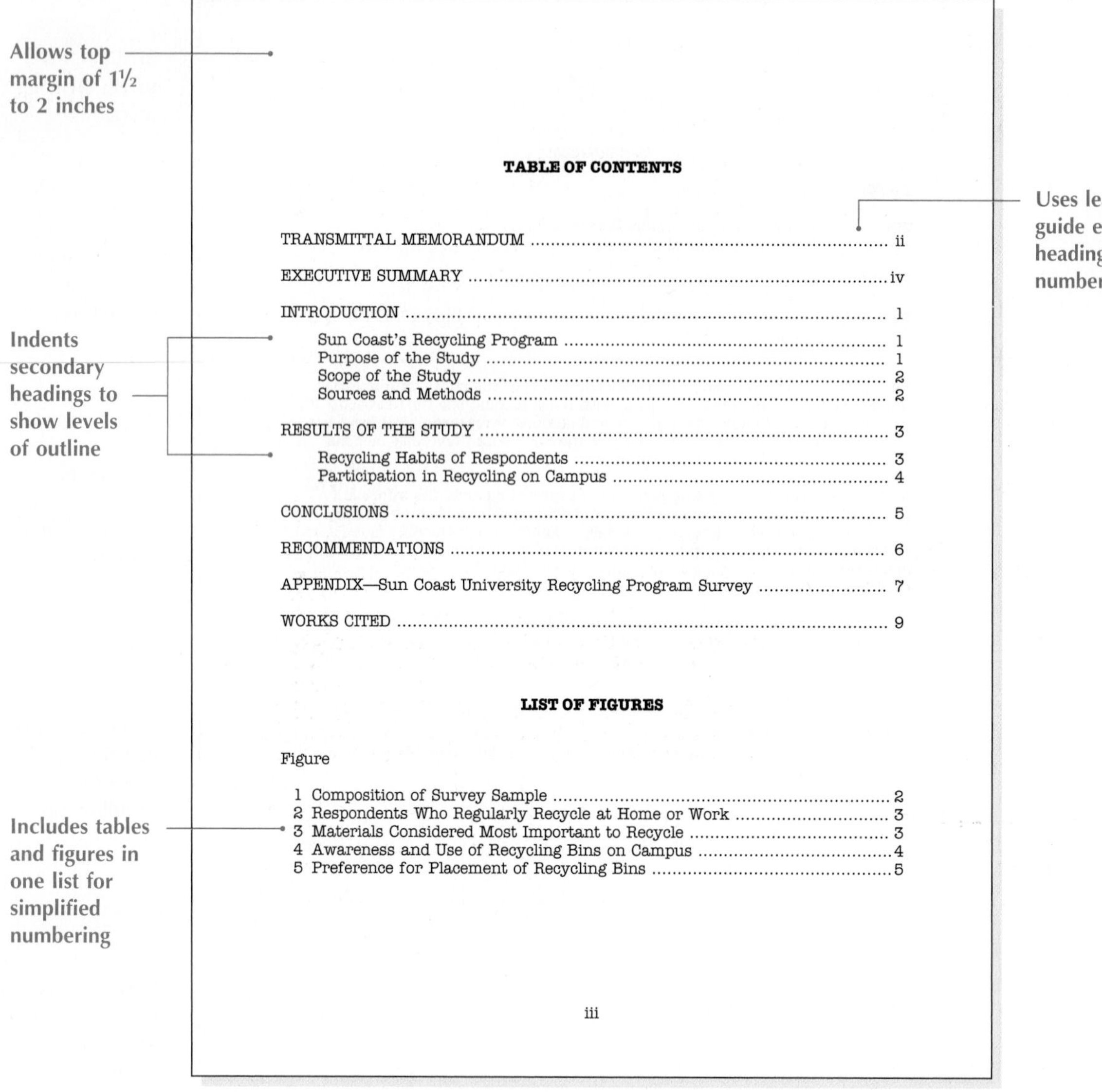

Because Alan's table of contents and list of figures are small, he combines them on one page. Notice that he uses all caps for the titles of major report parts and a combination of upper- and lowercase letters for first-level headings. This duplicates the style within the report.

Advanced word processing capabilities enable you to generate a contents page automatically, including leaders and accurate page numbering—no matter how many times you revise!

FIGURE 14.4 *Continued*

EXECUTIVE SUMMARY

Purposes of the Report

The purposes of this report are to (1) determine the Sun Coast University campus community's awareness of the campus recycling program and (2) recommend ways to increase participation. Sun Coast's recycling program was intended to respond to the increasing problem of waste disposal, to fulfill its social responsibility as an educational institution, and to meet the demands of legislation requiring individuals and organizations to recycle.

A questionnaire survey was conducted to learn about the campus community's recycling habits and to assess participation in the current recycling program. A total of 220 individuals responded to the survey. Since Sun Coast University's recycling program includes only aluminum, glass, paper, and plastic at this time, these were the only materials considered in this study.

Tells purpose of report and briefly describes survey

Recycling at Sun Coast

Most survey respondents recognized the importance of recycling and stated that they do recycle aluminum, glass, paper, and plastic on a regular basis either at home or at work. However, most respondents displayed a low level of awareness and use of the on-campus program. Many of the respondents were unfamiliar with the location of the bins around campus and, therefore, had not participated in the recycling program. Other responses indicated that the bins were not conveniently located.

Summarizes findings of survey

The results of this study show that more effort is needed to increase participation in the campus recycling program.

Draws primary conclusion

Recommendations for Increasing Recycling Participation

Based on the findings from our survey of 220 respondents, the researchers make the following recommendations to increase participation in the Sun Coast University campus recycling program:

1. Relocate the recycling bins for greater visibility
2. Develop incentive programs to gain the participation of individuals and on-campus student groups
3. Train student volunteers to give on-campus presentations explaining the benefits of using the recycling program
4. Increase advertising about the program

Concisely enumerates four recommendations using parallel (balanced) phrasing

iv

Numbers pages that precede the body with lowercase roman numerals

For readers who want a quick picture of the report, the executive summary presents its most important elements. Alan has divided the summary into three sections for increased readability.

Executive summaries focus on the information the reader requires for making a decision related to the issues discussed in the report. The summary may include some or all of the following elements: purpose, scope, research methods, results, conclusions, and recommendations. In jargon-free language, a good executive summary condenses what management needs to know about a problem and its study.

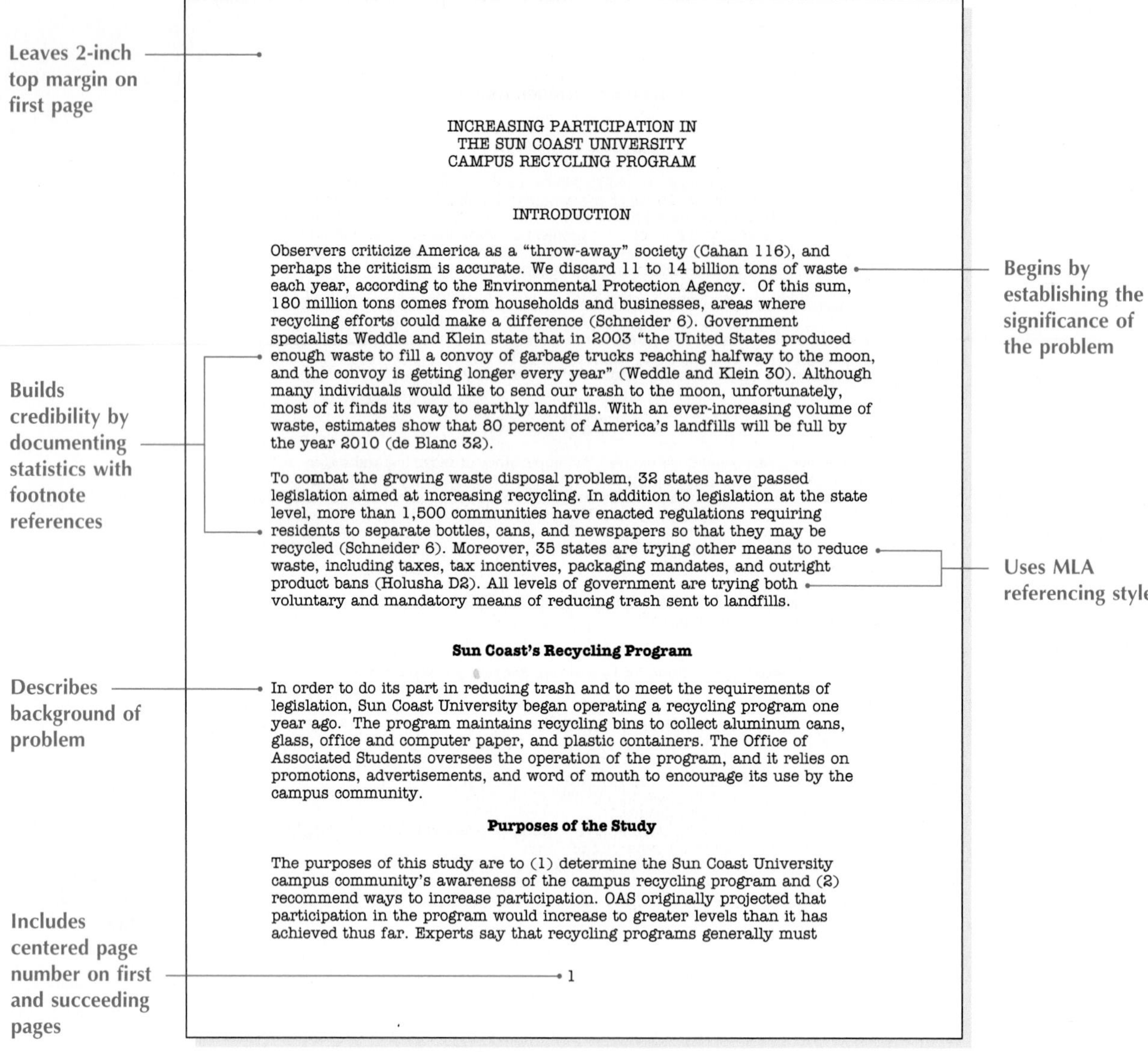

Leaves 2-inch top margin on first page
INCREASING PARTICIPATION IN
THE SUN COAST UNIVERSITY
CAMPUS RECYCLING PROGRAM
INTRODUCTION
Observers criticize America as a "throw-away" society (Cahan 116), and perhaps the criticism is accurate. We discard 11 to 14 billion tons of waste each year, according to the Environmental Protection Agency. Of this sum, 180 million tons comes from households and businesses, areas where recycling efforts could make a difference (Schneider 6). Government specialists Weddle and Klein state that in 2003 "the United States produced enough waste to fill a convoy of garbage trucks reaching halfway to the moon, and the convoy is getting longer every year" (Weddle and Klein 30). Although many individuals would like to send our trash to the moon, unfortunately, most of it finds its way to earthly landfills. With an ever-increasing volume of waste, estimates show that 80 percent of America's landfills will be full by the year 2010 (de Blanc 32).
To combat the growing waste disposal problem, 32 states have passed legislation aimed at increasing recycling. In addition to legislation at the state level, more than 1,500 communities have enacted regulations requiring residents to separate bottles, cans, and newspapers so that they may be recycled (Schneider 6). Moreover, 35 states are trying other means to reduce waste, including taxes, tax incentives, packaging mandates, and outright product bans (Holusha D2). All levels of government are trying both voluntary and mandatory means of reducing trash sent to landfills.
Begins by establishing the significance of the problem
Builds credibility by documenting statistics with footnote references
Uses MLA referencing style
Sun Coast's Recycling Program
Describes background of problem
In order to do its part in reducing trash and to meet the requirements of legislation, Sun Coast University began operating a recycling program one year ago. The program maintains recycling bins to collect aluminum cans, glass, office and computer paper, and plastic containers. The Office of Associated Students oversees the operation of the program, and it relies on promotions, advertisements, and word of mouth to encourage its use by the campus community.
Purposes of the Study
The purposes of this study are to (1) determine the Sun Coast University campus community's awareness of the campus recycling program and (2) recommend ways to increase participation. OAS originally projected that participation in the program would increase to greater levels than it has achieved thus far. Experts say that recycling programs generally must
Includes centered page number on first and succeeding pages
1

The first page of a report generally contains the title printed 2 inches from the top edge. Titles for major parts of a report (such as *Introduction, Results, Conclusion,* and so forth) are centered in all caps. First-level headings are bold and printed with upper- and lowercase letters. Second-level headings begin at the side. For an illustration of heading formats, see Figure 13.5.

Notice that Alan's report is single-spaced. Many businesses prefer this space-saving format. However, some organizations prefer double-spacing, especially for preliminary drafts.

Page numbers may be centered 1 inch from the bottom of the page or placed 1 inch from the upper right corner at the margin.

operate at least a year before results become apparent (de Blanc 33). The OAS program has been in operation one year, yet gains are disappointing. Therefore, OAS authorized this study to determine the campus community's awareness and use of the program. Recommendations for increasing participation in the campus recycling program will be made to the OAS based on the results of this study.

Scope of the Study

Describes what the study includes and excludes

This study investigates potential participants' attitudes toward recycling in general, their awareness of the campus recycling program, their willingness to recycle on campus, and the perceived convenience of the recycling bins. Only aluminum, glass, paper, and plastic are considered in this study, as they are the only materials being recycled on campus at this time. The costs involved in the program were not considered in this study, since a recycling program generally does not begin to pay for itself during the first year. After the first year, the financial benefit is usually realized in reduced disposal costs (Steelman, Desmond, and Johnson 145).

Sources and Methods

Current business periodicals and newspapers were consulted for background information and to learn how other organizations are encouraging use of in-house recycling programs. In addition, a questionnaire survey (shown in the appendix) of administrators, faculty, staff, and students at Sun Coast University campus was conducted to learn about this group's recycling habits. In all, a convenience sample of 220 individuals responded to the self-administered survey. The composition of the sample closely resembles the makeup of the campus population. Figure 1 shows the percentage of students, faculty, staff, and administrators who participated in the survey.

Discusses how the study was conducted

Figure 1

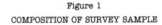

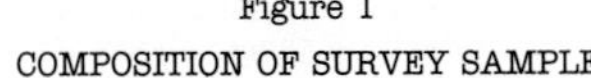
COMPOSITION OF SURVEY SAMPLE

Uses computer-generated pie graph to illustrate makeup of survey

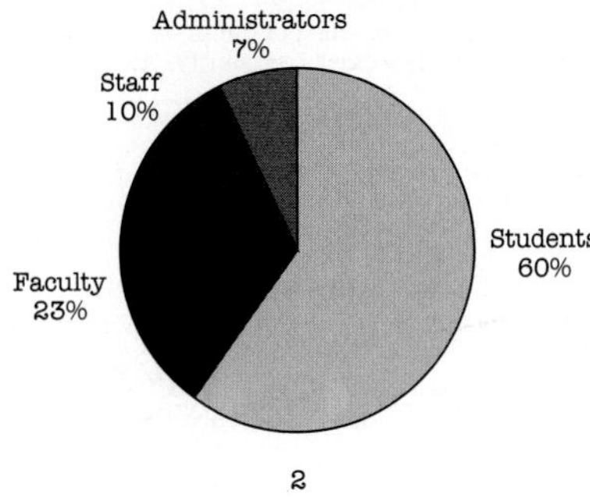

2

Because Alan wants this report to be formal in tone, he avoids *I* and *we.* Notice, too, that he uses present-tense verbs to describe his current writing *(this study investigates),* but past-tense verbs to indicate research completed in the past *(newspapers were consulted).*

If you use figures or tables, be sure to introduce them in the text. Although it's not always possible, try to place them close to the spot where they are first mentioned. If necessary to save space, you can print the title of a figure at its side.

FIGURE 14.4 ***Continued***

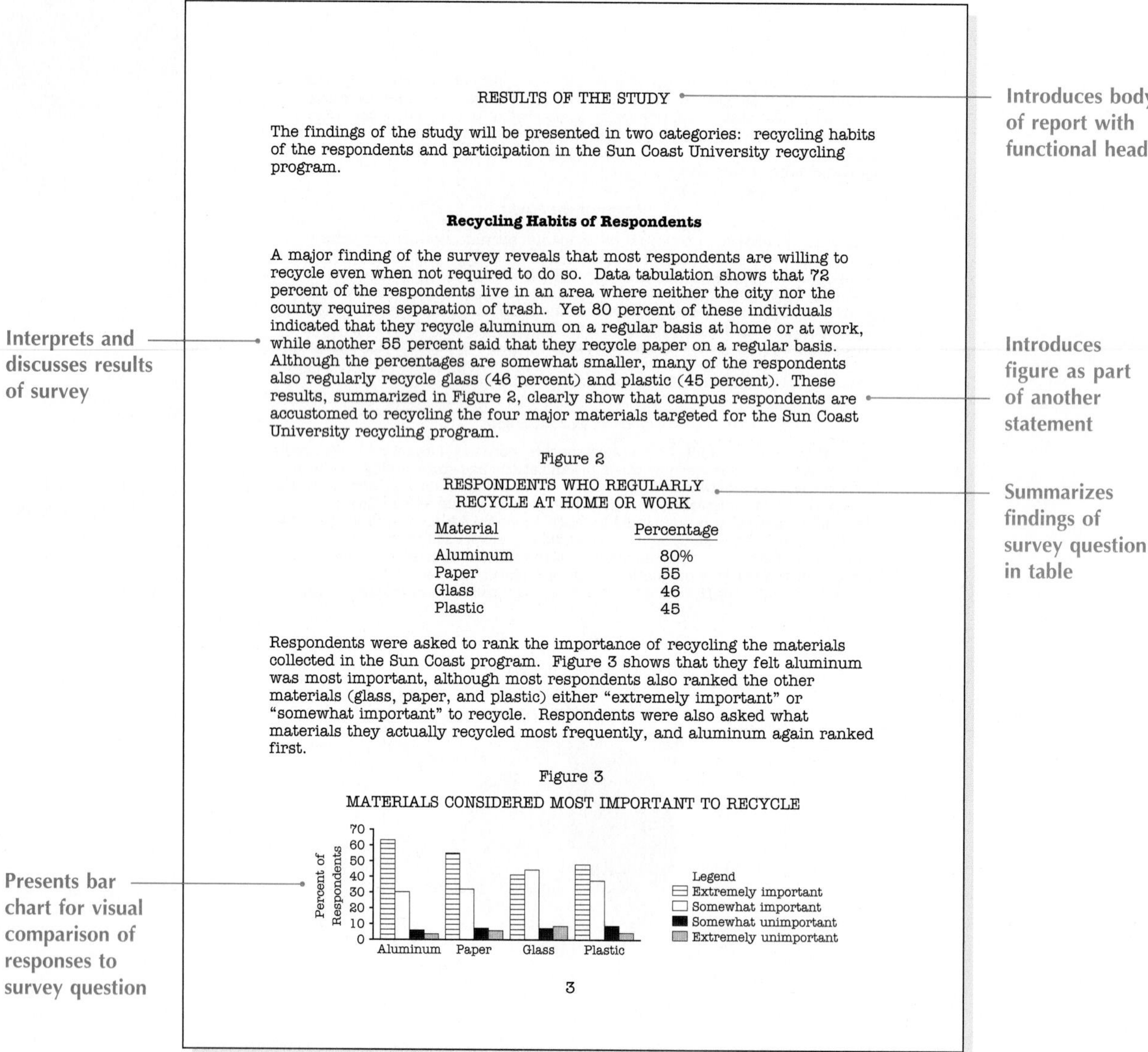

RESULTS OF THE STUDY

The findings of the study will be presented in two categories: recycling habits of the respondents and participation in the Sun Coast University recycling program.

Recycling Habits of Respondents

A major finding of the survey reveals that most respondents are willing to recycle even when not required to do so. Data tabulation shows that 72 percent of the respondents live in an area where neither the city nor the county requires separation of trash. Yet 80 percent of these individuals indicated that they recycle aluminum on a regular basis at home or at work, while another 55 percent said that they recycle paper on a regular basis. Although the percentages are somewhat smaller, many of the respondents also regularly recycle glass (46 percent) and plastic (45 percent). These results, summarized in Figure 2, clearly show that campus respondents are accustomed to recycling the four major materials targeted for the Sun Coast University recycling program.

Figure 2

RESPONDENTS WHO REGULARLY RECYCLE AT HOME OR WORK

Material	Percentage
Aluminum	80%
Paper	55
Glass	46
Plastic	45

Respondents were asked to rank the importance of recycling the materials collected in the Sun Coast program. Figure 3 shows that they felt aluminum was most important, although most respondents also ranked the other materials (glass, paper, and plastic) either "extremely important" or "somewhat important" to recycle. Respondents were also asked what materials they actually recycled most frequently, and aluminum again ranked first.

Figure 3

MATERIALS CONSIDERED MOST IMPORTANT TO RECYCLE

3

Introduces body of report with functional head

Interprets and discusses results of survey

Introduces figure as part of another statement

Summarizes findings of survey question in table

Presents bar chart for visual comparison of responses to survey question

Alan selects the most important survey findings to interpret and discuss for readers. Notice that he continues to use present-tense verbs *(the survey reveals* and *these results clearly show)* to discuss the current report.

Because he has few tables and charts, he labels them all as "Figures." Notice that he numbers them consecutively and places the label above each figure. Report writers with a great many tables, charts, and illustrations may prefer to label and number them separately. Tables are labeled as such; everything else is generally called a figure. When tables and figures are labeled separately, tables may be labeled above the table and figures below the figure.

Adds personal interpretation

When asked how likely they would be to go out of their way to deposit an item in a recycling bin, 29 percent of the respondents said "very likely," and 55 percent said "somewhat likely." Thus, respondents showed a willingness—at least on paper—to recycle even if it means making a special effort to locate a recycling bin.

Participation in Recycling on Campus

For any recycling program to be successful, participants must be aware of the location of recycling centers and must be trained to use them (de Blanc 33). Another important ingredient in thriving programs is convenience to users. If recycling centers are difficult for users to reach, these centers will be unsuccessful. To collect data on these topics, the survey included questions assessing awareness and use of the current bins. The survey also investigated reasons for not participating and the perceived convenience of current bin locations.

Introduces more findings and relates them to the report's purpose

Student Awareness and Use of Bins

Two of the most significant questions in the survey asked whether respondents were aware of the OAS recycling bins on campus and whether they had used the bins. Responses to both questions were disappointing, as Figure 4 illustrates.

Figure 4

AWARENESS AND USE OF RECYCLING BINS ON CAMPUS

Location	Awareness of bins at this location	Use of bins at this location
Social sciences building	38%	21%
Bookstore	29	12
Administration building	28	12
Computer labs	16	11
Library	15	7
Student union	9	5
Department offices	6	3
Campus dormitories	5	3
Unaware of any bins; have not used any bins	20	7

Arranges responses from highest to lowest with "unaware" category placed last

Only 38 percent of the respondents, as shown in Figure 4, were aware of the bins located outside the social sciences building. Even fewer were aware of the bins outside the bookstore (29 percent) and outside the administration building (28 percent). Equally dissatisfying, only 21 percent of the respondents had used the most visible recycling bins outside the social sciences

Clarifies and emphasizes meaning of findings

4

In discussing the results of the survey, Alan highlights those that have significance for the purpose of the report.

As you type a report, avoid widows and orphans (ending a page with the first line of a paragraph or carrying a single line of a paragraph to a new page). Strive to start and end pages with at least two lines of a paragraph, even if a slightly larger bottom margin results.

building. Other recycling bin locations were even less familiar to the survey respondents and, of course, were little used. These responses plainly show that the majority of the respondents in the Sun Coast campus community have a low awareness of the recycling program and an even lower record of participation.

Reasons for Not Participating

Respondents offered several reasons for not participating in the campus recycling program. Forty-five percent said that the bins are not convenient to use. Thirty percent said that they did not know where the bins were located. Another 25 percent said that they are not in the habit of recycling. Although many reasons for not participating were listed, the primary one appears to center on convenience of bin locations.

Discusses results of other survey questions not represented in tables or charts

Location of Recycling Bins

When asked specifically how they would rate the location of the bins currently in use, only 13 percent of the respondents felt that the bins were extremely convenient. Another 35 percent rated the locations as somewhat convenient. Over half the respondents felt that the locations of the bins were either somewhat inconv enient or extremely inconvenient. Recycling bins are currently located outside nearly all the major campus buildings, but respondents clearly considered these locations inconvenient or inadequate.

In indicating where they would like recycling bins placed (see Figure 5), 42 percent of the respondents felt that the most convenient locations would be outside each building on campus. Placing recycling bins near the food service facilities on campus seemed most convenient to another 33 percent of those questioned, while 15 percent stated that they would like to see the bins placed near the vending machines. Ten percent of the individuals responding to the survey did not seem to think that the locations of the bins would matter to them.

Clarifies results of another survey question with textual discussion accompanied by table

Figure 5

PREFERENCE FOR PLACEMENT OF RECYCLING BINS

Outside each building on campus	42%
Near food service facilities	33
Near vending machines	15
Does not matter	10

CONCLUSIONS

Based on the findings of the recycling survey of members of the Sun Coast University campus community, the following conclusions are drawn:

1. Most members of the campus community are already recycling at home or at work without being required to do so.

5

After completing a discussion of the survey results, Alan articulates what he considers the five most important conclusions to be drawn from this survey. Some writers combine the conclusions and recommendations, particularly when they are interrelated. Alan separated them in his study because the survey findings were quite distinct from the recommendations he would make based on them.

Notice that it is unnecessary to start a new page for the conclusions.

Draws conclusions based on survey findings; summarizes previous discussion

2. Over half of the respondents recycle aluminum and paper on a regular basis; most recycle glass and plastic to some degree.
3. Most of the surveyed individuals expressed a willingness to participate in a recycling program. Many, however, seem unwilling to travel very far to participate; 42 percent would like recycling bins to be located outside every campus building.
4. Awareness and use of the current campus recycling program are low. Only a little over one third of the respondents knew of any recycling bin locations on campus, and only one fifth had actually used them.
5. Respondents considered the locations of the campus bins inconvenient. This perceived inconvenience was given as the principal reason for not participating in the campus recycling program.

RECOMMENDATIONS

Supported by the findings and conclusions of this study, the following recommendations are offered in an effort to improve the operations and success of the Sun Coast recycling program:

Lists specific actions to help solve report problem; suggests practical ways to implement recommendations

1. Increase on-campus awareness and visibility by designing an eye-catching logo that represents the campus recycling program for use in promotions.
2. Enhance comprehension of recycling procedures by training users how to recycle. Use posters to explain the recycling program and to inform users of recycling bin locations. Label each bin clearly as to what materials may be deposited.
3. Add bins in several new locations, particularly in the food service and vending machine areas.
4. Recruit student leaders to promote participation in the recycling program by giving educational talks to classes and other campus groups, informing them of the importance of recycling.
5. Develop an incentive program for student organizations. Offer incentives for meeting recycling goals as determined by OAS. On-campus groups—such as fraternities, sororities, and clubs—could compete in recycling drives designed to raise money for the group, the university, or a charity. Money from the proceeds of the recycling program could be used to fund the incentive program.

6

The most important parts of a report are its conclusions and recommendations. To make them especially clear, Alan enumerated each conclusion and recommendation. Notice that each recommendation starts with a verb and is stated in command language for emphasis and readability.

Report recommendations are most helpful to readers when they not only make suggestions to solve the original research problem but also describe specific actions to be taken. Notice that Alan goes beyond merely listing ideas; instead, he provides practical suggestions for ways to implement the recommendations.

Includes copy of survey questionnaire so that report readers can see actual questions

APPENDIX

SUN COAST UNIVERSITY RECYCLING PROGRAM SURVEY

Sun Coast University recently implemented a recycling program on campus. Please take a few minutes to answer the following questions so that we can make this program as convenient and helpful as possible for you to use.

Explains why survey is necessary, emphasizing "you" view

1. Please indicate which items you recycle on a regular basis at home or at work. (Check *all* that apply.)
   - ☐ Aluminum
   - ☐ Glass
   - ☐ Paper
   - ☐ Plastic
2. Do you live in an area where the city/county requires separation of trash?
   ☐ Yes ☐ No
3. How important is it to you to recycle each of the following:

	Extremely Important	Somewhat Important	Somewhat Unimportant	Extremely Unimportant
Aluminum				
Glass				
Paper				
Plastic				

Provides range of answers that will be easy to tabulate

4. How likely would it be for you to go out of your way to put something in a recycling bin?

Very Likely	Somewhat Likely	Somewhat Unlikely	Very Unlikely

5. Which of the following items do you recycle *most* often? (Choose *one* item only.)
   - ☐ Aluminum
   - ☐ Glass
   - ☐ Paper
   - ☐ Plastic
   - ☐ Other
6. The following are locations of the recycling bins on campus. (Check *all* those of which you are aware.)
   - ☐ Administration building
   - ☐ Bookstore
   - ☐ Campus dorms
   - ☐ Computer labs
   - ☐ Engineering building
   - ☐ Library
   - ☐ Social sciences building
   - ☐ Student union
   - ☐ I'm unaware of any of these recycling bins.

7

Alan had space to add the word "Appendix" to the top of the survey questionnaire. If space were not available, he could have typed a separate page with that title on it. If more than one item were included, he would have named them Appendix A, Appendix B, and so on.

Notice that the appendix continues the report pagination.

7. Which of the following recycling bins have you actually used? (Check *all* that you have used.)
   - ☐ Administration building
   - ☐ Bookstore
   - ☐ Campus dorms
   - ☐ Computer labs
   - ☐ Engineering building
   - ☐ Library
   - ☐ Social sciences building
   - ☐ Student union
   - ☐ I've not used any of these recycling bins.

8. If you don't recycle on campus, why don't you participate?
   - ☐ I'm not in the habit of recycling.
   - ☐ I don't know where the bins are.
   - ☐ The bins aren't convenient to me.
   - ☐ Other ______________________

9. How do you rate the convenience of the bins' locations?
   - ☐ Extremely convenient
   - ☐ Somewhat convenient
   - ☐ Somewhat inconvenient
   - ☐ Extremely inconvenient

10. Which of the following possible recycling bin locations would be most convenient for you to use? (Check *one* only.)
    - ☐ Outside each building
    - ☐ Near the food service facilities
    - ☐ Near the vending machines
    - ☐ Does not matter
    - ☐ Other ______________________

11. Please indicate:
    - ☐ Student
    - ☐ Faculty
    - ☐ Administrator
    - ☐ Staff

COMMENTS:

Thank you for your responses! Please return the questionnaire in the enclosed, stamped envelope to Sun Coast University, School of Business, Rm. 321. If you have any questions, please call (555) 450-2391.

8

Anticipates responses but also supplies "Other" category

Uses scale questions to capture degrees of feeling

Requests little demographic data to keep survey short

Offers comment section for explanations and remarks

Concludes with appreciation and instructions

FIGURE 14.4 *Continued*

Works Cited

Cahan, Vicky. "Waste Not, Want Not? Not Necessarily." BusinessWeek 17 July 2004: 116. — Magazine

de Blanc, Susan. "Paper Recycling: How to Make It Effective." The Office Dec. 2003: 32.

Foster, David. "Recycling: A Green Idea Turns to Gold." The Los Angeles Times. 5 Mar. 2005, Bulldog ed. Metro, CyberTimes. Retrieved 7 Mar. 2005 <http://www.times.com/library/cyber/week/y05dat.html>. — Online Newspaper

Freeman, Monique M. Personal interview. 2 Nov. 2005. — Interview

Landsburg, Steven E. "Who Shall Inherit the Earth?" Slate 1 May 2003. Retrieved 2 May 2005 <http://www.slate.com/Economics/03-05-04/Economics.asp>. — Online Magazine

Schneider, Keith. "As Recycling Becomes a Growth Industry, Its Paradoxes Also Multiply." The New York Times, 20 Jan. 2005, sec. 4: 6.

Steelman, James W., Shirley Desmond, and LeGrand Johnson. Facing Global Limitations. New York: Rockford Press, 2003. — Book

Steuteville, Robert. "The State of Garbage in America." Part 1. BioCycle. Apr. 2005. Retrieved 30 Nov. 2005 <http://www.biocycle/recycle/guid.html>. — Online Magazine

"Tips to Reduce, Reuse, and Recycle." Environmental Recycling Hotline. Retrieved 8 July 2005 <http://www.primenet.com/cgi-bin/erh.pl>. — World Wide Web

Weddle, Bruce, and Edward Klein. "A Strategy to Control the Garbage Glut." EPA Journal 12.2 (2004): 28–34. — Journal

9

On this page Alan lists all the references cited in the text as well as others that he examined during his research. (Some authors list only those works cited in the report.) Alan formats his citations following the MLA referencing style. Notice that all entries are arranged alphabetically. He underlines book and periodical titles, but italics could be used. When referring to online items, he shows the full name of the citation and then identifies the URL as well as the date on which he accessed the electronic reference.

Most word processing software today automatically updates citation references within the text and prints a complete list for you. For more information about documentation styles, see Appendix C.

Checklist for Preparing Formal Reports

Report Process

- ✓ **Analyze the report problem and purpose.** Develop a problem question (*How is e-mail affecting productivity and security at MegaTech?*) and a purpose statement (*The purpose of this report is to investigate the use of e-mail at MegaTech and recommend policies and procedures that enhance company productivity and security.*).

- ✓ **Anticipate the audience and issues.** Consider primary and secondary audiences. What do they already know? What do they need to know? Divide the major problem into subproblems for investigation.

- ✓ **Prepare a work plan.** Include problem and purpose statements, as well as a description of the sources and methods of collecting data. Prepare a tentative project outline and a work schedule with anticipated dates of completion for all segments of the project.

- ✓ **Collect data.** Begin by searching secondary sources (electronic databases, books, magazines, journals, newspapers) for information on your topic. Then, if necessary, gather primary data by surveying, interviewing, observing, and experimenting.

- ✓ **Document data sources.** Prepare note cards or separate sheets of paper citing all references (author, date, source, page, and quotation). Select a documentation format and use it consistently.

- ✓ **Interpret and organize the data.** Arrange the collected information in tables, grids, or outlines to help you visualize relationships and interpret meanings. Organize the data into an outline (Chapter 6).

- ✓ **Prepare graphics.** Make tables, charts, graphs, and illustrations—but *only* if they serve a function. Use graphics to help clarify, condense, simplify, or emphasize your data.

- ✓ **Compose the first draft.** At a computer write the first draft from your outline. Use appropriate headings as well as transitional expressions (such as *however, on the contrary*, and *in addition*) to guide the reader through the report.

- ✓ **Revise and proofread.** Revise to eliminate wordiness, ambiguity, and redundancy. Look for ways to improve readability, such as bulleted or numbered lists. Proofread three times for (1) word and content meaning, (2) grammar and mechanical errors, and (3) formatting.

- ✓ **Evaluate the product.** Examine the final report. Will it achieve its purpose? Encourage feedback so that you can learn how to improve future reports.

Report Components

- ✓ **Title page.** Balance the following lines on the title page: (1) name of the report (in all caps); (2) name, title, and organization of the individual receiving the report; (3) author's name, title, and organization; and (4) date submitted.

- ✓ **Letter of transmittal.** Announce the report topic and explain who authorized it. Briefly describe the project and preview the conclusions, if the reader is

PROCESS TO PRODUCT

Applying Your Skills at Hewlett-Packard

IN MANY WAYS proposals are similar to long reports. Both are written to solve a problem, and both require research. Assume that you are part of a group of interns being trained by Mary Piecewicz at Hewlett-Packard. She has developed two problems as part of your program. (1) In the first problem, Piecewicz asks your team to compare and contrast proposal components at HP with what you learned in your business communication class in college. (2) As a second problem, she asks you individually to profile a Fortune 500 company in preparation for an HP proposal to that company. Learn about its sales, major products, competitors, history, corporate strategies, corporate culture, and financial picture. Study recent news releases, relevant newspaper articles, and its annual report.

Your Task

Select one of the two problems previously described. (1) As a team, discuss similarities and differences in proposal components at Hewlett-Packard and component suggestions for letter proposals described in your textbook. Submit an individual or group memo to Mary Piecewicz summarizing your comparison. (2) To profile a Fortune 500 company of your choice, conduct research on the Web and in the library. What information would be necessary to enable Hewlett-Packard to develop a relationship with the targeted company? Submit an individual memo report. ■

http://www.hp.com

case study

supportive. Close by expressing appreciation for the assignment, suggesting follow-up actions, acknowledging the help of others, or offering to answer questions.

- ✓ **Table of contents.** Show the beginning page number where each report heading appears in the report. Connect the page numbers and headings with leaders (spaced dots).
- ✓ **List of illustrations.** Include a list of tables, illustrations, or figures showing the title of the item and its page number. If space permits, put these lists on the same page with the table of contents.
- ✓ **Executive summary.** Summarize the report purpose, findings, conclusions, and recommendations. Gauge the length of the summary by the length of the report and by your organization's practices.
- ✓ **Introduction.** Explain the problem motivating the report; describe its background and significance. Clarify the scope and limitations of the report. Optional items include a review of relevant literature and a description of data sources, methods, and key terms. Close by previewing the report's organization.
- ✓ **Body.** Discuss, analyze, and interpret the research findings or the proposed solution to the problem. Arrange the findings in logical segments following your outline. Use clear, descriptive headings.
- ✓ **Conclusions and recommendations.** Explain what the findings mean in relation to the original problem. If requested, make enumerated recommendations that suggest actions for solving the problem.

✓ **Appendix.** Include items of interest to some, but not all, readers, such as a data questionnaire or computer printouts.

✓ **References and bibliography.** If footnotes are not provided in the text, list all references in a bibliographical section called "Works Cited" or "References."

Summary of Learning Objectives

1 **Discuss the components of informal proposals.** Most informal proposals contain (1) a persuasive introduction that explains the purpose of the proposal and qualifies the writer; (2) background material identifying the problem and project goals; (3) a proposal, plan, or schedule outlining the project; (4) a section describing staff qualifications; (5) a budget showing expected costs; and (6) a request for approval or authorization.

2 **Discuss the special components in formal proposals.** Beyond the six components generally contained in informal proposals, formal proposals may include these additional parts: (1) copy of the RFP (request for proposal), (2) letter of transmittal, (3) executive summary, (4) title page, (5) table of contents, (6) list of illustrations, and (7) appendix.

3 **Discuss the components of typical business plans.** Business plans help entrepreneurs secure start-up funding and also provide a road map to follow as a business develops. Typical business plans include the following: letter of transmittal or executive summary, table of contents, company description, product or service description, market analysis, description of operations and management, financial analysis, and appendixes. For start-up businesses seeking financial backing, the product/service description as well as the operations and management analyses are particularly important. They must promote growth potential and promise a management team capable of implementing the business plan.

4 **Identify formal report components that precede the introduction as well as elements to include in the introduction.** Formal reports may include these beginning components: (a) vinyl or heavy paper cover, (b) title page, (c) letter of transmittal, (d) table of contents, (e) list of illustrations, and (f) executive summary. The introduction to a formal report sets the scene by discussing some or all of the following topics: background material, problem or purpose, significance of the topic, scope and organization of the report, authorization, review of relevant literature, sources and methods, and definitions of key terms.

5 **Describe the formal report components that follow the introduction.** The body of a report discusses, analyzes, interprets, and evaluates the research findings or solution to a problem. The conclusion tells what the findings mean and how they relate to the report's purpose. The recommendations tell how to solve the report problem. The last portions of a formal report are the appendix, references, and bibliography.

6 **Specify tips that aid writers of formal reports.** Before writing, develop a realistic timetable and collect all necessary data. During the writing process, work from a good outline, work in a quiet place, and use a computer. Also, try to write rapidly, revising later. While writing, use verb tenses consistently, and avoid *I* and *we.* A few days after completing the first draft, revise to improve clarity, coherence, and conciseness. Proofread the final copy three times.

chapter review

1. What is a proposal? (Obj. 1)
2. What is the difference between solicited and unsolicited proposals? (Obj. 1)
3. What are the six principal components in an informal letter proposal? (Obj. 1)
4. How is a formal proposal different from an informal proposal? (Obj. 2)
5. Why does an entrepreneur need to write a business plan? (Obj. 3)
6. Discuss eight components of typical business plans. (Obj. 3)
7. What does a mission statement cover, and why is it so important in a business plan? (Obj. 3)
8. Why are formal reports written in business? Give an original example of a business-related formal report. (Obj. 4)
9. What is a table of contents, and when should it be written? (Obj. 4)
10. What should be included in the executive summary of a formal report? (Obj. 4)
11. What should be included in the introduction to a formal report? (Obj. 4)
12. What should the writer strive to do in the body of a formal report? (Obj. 5)
13. What is the purpose of a bibliography? (Obj. 5)
14. In your view, what are six of the most important tips for the writer of a formal report? Explain each of your choices. (Obj. 6)
15. What are first-person pronouns, and why do most writers of formal reports avoid them? (Obj. 6)

critical thinking

1. Why are proposals important to many businesses? (Obj. 1)
2. Compare and contrast proposals and business plans. (Objs. 1–3)
3. How do formal reports differ from informal reports? (Objs. 4–6)
4. Discuss the three phases of the writing process in relation to formal reports. What activities take place in each phase? (Objs. 4–6)
5. **Ethical Issue:** Is it ethical to have someone else proofread a report that you will be turning in for a grade?

THREE GREAT RESOURCES FOR YOU!

1. ***Guffey Student Web Site***
   http://guffey.swlearning.com

   Your companion Web site offers chapter review quizzes, WebThink activities, updated chapter URLs, and many additional resources.

2. ***Guffey XTRA!***
   http://guffeyxtra.swlearning.com

   This online study assistant includes Your Personal Language Trainer, Speak Right!, Spell Right!, bonus online chapters, Documents for Analysis, PowerPoint slides, and much more.

3. ***Student Study Guide***

   Self-checked workbook activities and applications review chapter concepts and develop career skills.

activities

14.1 Proposals: Comparing Real Proposals (Objs. 1 and 2)

WEB

Many new companies with services or products to offer would like to land corporate or government contracts. But they are intimidated by the proposal (RFP) process. You have been asked for help by your friend Destini, who has started her own designer uniform company. Her goal is to offer her colorful yet functional uniforms to hospitals and clinics. Before writing a proposal, however, she wants to see examples and learn more about the process.

Your Task. Use the Web to find at least two examples of business proposals. Don't waste time on sites that want to sell templates or books. Find actual examples. Then prepare a memo to Destini in which you do the following:

a. Identify two sites with sample business proposals.
b. Outline the parts of each proposal.
c. Compare the strengths and weaknesses of each proposal.
d. Draw conclusions. What can Destini learn from these examples?

14.2 Proposals: SportsMed Solicits Your Proposal (Obj. 1)

CRITICAL THINKING | **LISTENING** | **SPEAKING** | **TEAM**

In university towns, sports medicine is increasingly popular. A new medical clinic, SportsMed Institute, is opening its doors in your community. A friend recommended your small business to the administrator of the clinic, and you received a letter asking you to provide information about your service. The new medical clinic specializes in sports medicine, physical therapy, and cardiac rehabilitation services. It is interested in retaining your company, rather than hiring its own employees to perform the service your company offers.

Your Task. Working in teams, first decide what service you will offer. It could be landscaping, uniform supply, laundry of uniforms, general cleaning, computerized no-paper filing systems, online medical supplies, patient transportation, supplemental hospice care, temporary office support, or food service. As a team, develop a letter proposal outlining your plan, staffing, and budget. Use persuasion to show why contracting your services is better than hiring in-house employees. In the proposal letter, request a meeting with the administrative board. In addition to a written proposal, you may be expected to make an oral presentation that includes visual aids and/or handouts. Send your proposal to Dr. Daryl Kerr, Director, SportsMed Institute. Supply a local address.

14.3 Proposal and Grant Writing: Learning From the Nonprofits (Objs. 1 and 2)

INFOTRAC

You'd like to learn more about writing business proposals and especially about writing grants. The latter involve funding supplied by an institution, foundation, or the government. You might one day even decide to become a professional grant/proposal writer. But first you need experience.

Your Task. Volunteer your services for a local nonprofit organization, such as a United Way (**http://national.unitedway.org/**) member agency, an educational institution, or your local church. To learn more about writing grants, complete an InfoTrac subject guide search for *proposal.* Click articles under the categories of *business proposal writing* and *grant proposal writing.* Your instructor may ask you to submit a preliminary memo report outlining ten or more pointers you learn about writing proposals and grants for nonprofit organizations.

14.4 Business Plans: Can Your Team Write a Winning Plan? (Obj. 3)*

CRITICAL THINKING | LISTENING | SPEAKING | TEAM | WEB

Business plans at many schools are more than classroom writing exercises. They have won regional, national, and worldwide prizes. Although some contests are part of MBA programs, other contests are available for undergraduates. One business plan project at the University of California, Santa Barbara, resulted in the development of a portable oxygen concentrator. Three students wrote a proposal that not only won one of the school's business plan writing contests but also attracted venture capital backing of over $500,000. The trio was challenged to come up with a hypothetical business plan. One of the team members suggested making a portable oxygen device to improve the mobility and quality of life for her grandmother. The student trio didn't actually make the device—just outlined the concept. Contest judges recognized the commercial potential and helped bring the device into production.[7]

As part of a business plan project, you and your team are challenged to come up with an idea for a new business or service. For example, you might want to offer a lunch service with fresh sandwiches or salads delivered to office workers' desks. You might propose building a better Web site for an organization. You might want to start a document preparation business that offers production, editing, and printing services. You might have a terrific idea for an existing business to expand with a new product or service.

Your Task. Working in teams, explore entrepreneurial ventures based on your experience and expertise. Conduct team meetings to decide on a product or service, develop a work plan, assign responsibilities, and create a schedule. Your goal is to write a business plan proposal that will convince potential investors (sometimes your own management) that you have an excellent business idea and that you can pull it off. Check out sample business plans on the Web. The two "deliverables" from your project will be your written business plan plus an oral presentation. Your written report should include a cover, transmittal document (letter or memo), title page, table of contents, executive summary, proposal (including introduction, body, and conclusion), appendix items, optional glossary, and sources. In the body of the proposal, be sure to explain your mission and vision, the market, your marketing strategy, operations, and financials. Address your business plan proposal to your instructor.

14.5 Formal Reports: Intercultural Communication (Objs. 4–6)

TEAM

U.S. businesses are expanding into foreign markets with manufacturing plants, sales offices, and branch offices abroad. Most Americans, however, have little knowledge of or experience with people from other cultures. To prepare for participation in the global marketplace, you are to collect information for a report focused on an Asian, Latin American, or European country where English is not regularly spoken. Before selecting the country, though, consult your campus international student program for volunteers who are willing to be interviewed. Your instructor may make advance arrangements with international student volunteers.

Your Task. In teams of three to five, collect information about your target country from the library and other sources.

* A complete instructional module is available for this activity.

Then invite an international student representing your target country to be interviewed by your group. As you conduct primary and secondary research, investigate the topics listed in Figure 14.5. Confirm what you learn in your secondary research by talking with your interviewee. When you complete your research, write a report for the CEO of your company (make up a name and company). Assume that your company plans to expand its operations abroad. Your report should advise the company's executives of the social customs, family life, attitudes, religions, education, and values in the target country. Remember that your company's interests are business oriented; don't dwell on tourist information. Write your report individually or in teams.

14.6 Business Plans: Studying Samples and Selecting the Best (Obj. 3)

WEB

As a member of a group of venture capitalists with money to invest in start-up companies, you must make a choice. Assume your group has received three business plan proposals. ***Your Task.*** Visit either Bplans.com <**www.bplans.com**> or the Small Business Administration site <**http://www.sba.gov/starting_business/**>. Find the total list of 60 free sample plans. Browse the list and select three business plans to study. Analyze all parts of each plan. Then, select one that you will recommend for funding. Prepare a memo to your investor group explaining why you think this start-up business will succeed. Also comment on the organization, format, and writing style of the business plan. What are its strengths and weaknesses? Address your memo to your instructor.

14.7 Proposal, Business Plan, and Report Topics (Objs. 1–6)

A list with nearly 100 report topics is available at **Guffey Xtra!** <**http://guffeyxtra.swlearning.com**>. The topics are divided into the following categories: accounting, finance, personnel/human resources, marketing, information systems, management, and general business/education/campus issues. You can collect information for many of these reports by using InfoTrac and the Web. Your instructor may assign them as individual or team projects. All involve critical thinking in organizing information, drawing conclusions, and making recommendations. The topics include assignments appropriate for proposals, business plans, and formal reports. Check out this list to give you ideas that you can adapt to your interest or to current events.

14.8 Executive Summary: Reviewing Articles (Objs. 5 and 6)

INFOTRAC

Many managers and executives are too rushed to read long journal articles, but they are eager to stay current in their careers. Assume your boss has asked you to help him stay abreast of research in his field. He asks you to submit to him one executive summary every month on an article of interest. ***Your Task.*** In your field of study, select a professional journal, such as the *Journal of Management.* Using InfoTrac, look for articles in your target journal. Select an article that is at least five pages long and is interesting to you. Write an executive summary in a memo format. Include an introduction that might begin with *As you requested, I am submitting this executive summary of* . . . . Identify the author, article name, journal, and date of publication. Explain what the author intended to do in the study or article. Summarize three or four of the most important findings of the study or article. Use descriptive rather than functional headings. Summarize any recommendations made. Your boss would also like a concluding statement indicating your reaction to the article. Address your memo to Matthew R. Ferranto.

14.9 Unsolicited Proposal: Thwarting Dorm Room Thievery (Objs. 1 and 2)

CONSUMER | CRITICAL THINKING | TEAM

As an enterprising college student, you recognized a problem as soon as you arrived on campus. Dorm rooms filled with pricey digital doodads were very attractive to thieves. Some

Figure 14.5 ***Intercultural Interview Topics and Questions***

Social Customs

1. How do people react to strangers? Friendly? Hostile? Reserved?
2. How do people greet each other?
3. What are the appropriate manners when you enter a room? Bow? Nod? Shake hands with everyone?
4. How are names used for introductions? Is it appropriate to inquire about one's occupation or family?
5. What are the attitudes toward touching?
6. How does one express appreciation for an invitation to another's home? Bring a gift? Send flowers? Write a thank-you note? Are any gifts taboo?
7. Are there any customs related to how or where one sits?
8. Are any facial expressions or gestures considered rude?
9. How close do people stand when talking?
10. What is the attitude toward punctuality in social situations? In business situations?
11. What are acceptable eye contact patterns?
12. What gestures indicate agreement? Disagreement?

Family Life

1. What is the basic unit of social organization? Basic family? Extended family?
2. Do women work outside of the home? In what occupations?

Housing, Clothing, and Food

1. Are there differences in the kinds of housing used by different social groups? Differences in location? Differences in furnishings?
2. What occasions require special clothing?
3. Are some types of clothing considered taboo?
4. What is appropriate business attire for men? For women?
5. How many times a day do people eat?
6. What types of places, food, and drink are appropriate for business entertainment? Where is the seat of honor at a table?

Class Structure

1. Into what classes is society organized?
2. Do racial, religious, or economic factors determine social status?
3. Are there any minority groups? What is their social standing?

Political Patterns

1. Are there any immediate threats to the political survival of the country?
2. How is political power manifested?
3. What channels are used for expression of popular opinion?
4. What information media are important?
5. Is it appropriate to talk politics in social situations?

Religion and Folk Beliefs

1. To which religious groups do people belong? Is one predominant?
2. Do religious beliefs influence daily activities?
3. Which places have sacred value? Which objects? Which events?
4. How do religious holidays affect business activities?

Economic Institutions

1. What are the country's principal products?
2. Are workers organized in unions?
3. How are businesses owned? By family units? By large public corporations? By the government?
4. What is the standard work schedule?
5. Is it appropriate to do business by telephone? By computer?
6. How has technology affected business procedures?
7. Is participatory management used?
8. Are there any customs related to exchanging business cards?
9. How is status shown in an organization? Private office? Secretary? Furniture?
10. Are businesspeople expected to socialize before conducting business?

Value Systems

1. Is competitiveness or cooperation more prized?
2. Is thrift or enjoyment of the moment more valued?
3. Is politeness more important than factual honesty?
4. What are the attitudes toward education?
5. Do women own or manage businesses? If so, how are they treated?
6. What are your people's perceptions of Americans? Do Americans offend you? What has been hardest for you to adjust to in America? How could Americans make this adjustment easier for you?

students move in with more than $3,000 in gear, including laptop computers, digital cameras, MP3 players, PDAs, and DVD players. You solved the problem by buying an extra-large steel footlocker to lock away your valuables. But shipping the footlocker was expensive (nearly $100), and you had to wait for it to arrive from a catalog company. Your bright idea is to propose to the Associated Student Organization that it allow you to offer these steel footlockers to students at a reduced price and with campus delivery. Your footlocker, which you found by searching the Web, is extremely durable and works great as a coffee table, nightstand, or card table. It comes with a smooth interior liner and two compartments.

Your Task. Working individually or with a team, imagine that you have made arrangements with a manufacturer to act as a middleman selling footlockers on your campus at a reduced price. Consult the Web for manufacturers and make up your own figures. But how can you get the ASO's permission to proceed? Give that organization a cut? Use your imagination in deciding how this plan might work on a college campus. Then prepare an unsolicited proposal to your ASO. Outline the problem and your goals of protecting students' valuables and providing convenience. Check the Web for statistics regarding on-campus burglaries. Such figures should help you develop one or more persuasive "hooks." Then explain your proposal, project possible sales, discuss a timetable, and describe your staffing. Submit your proposal to Toni Bell, president, Associated Student Organization.

C.L.U.E. review 14

On a separate sheet edit the following sentences to correct faults in grammar, punctuation, spelling, numbers, proofreading, and word use.

1. The format and organization of a proposal is important, if a writer want it to be taken serious.
2. Proposals are writen offers to do the following solve problems, provide services or sell equippment.
3. Our Vice-President and Manager worked to-gether to prepare 2 RFPs, that solicit competitive bids.
4. Just between you and I we work very hard to develop a "hook" to capture a readers attention.
5. If a proposal is to long and it's Budget is vague it will not succede in it's goal.
6. A important item in most Proposals, is the Budget which is a list of project cost.
7. If a proposal is sent to the President or I it should definitly explain the specific credentials and expertise of key personal for the project.
8. Dr Ryan Williams and him wanted to start there own business therefore they wrote a business plan, that included a detailed market analysis.
9. Mary Morley who is a member of our research and development department wondered whether her formal report would be presented at the May 15th meeting?
10. If you're report is complex be sure to proof-read it 3 times.

Rich chapter resources are available on the Web sites.

unit 5

Presentations

chapter 15

Speaking With Confidence

chapter 16

Employment Communication

chapter 15

Speaking With Confidence

objectives

1 Discuss two important first steps in preparing effective oral presentations.

2 Explain the major elements in organizing the content of a presentation, including the introduction, body, and conclusion.

3 Identify techniques for gaining audience rapport, including using effective imagery, providing verbal signposts, and sending appropriate nonverbal messages.

4 Discuss designing and using effective visual aids, handouts, and multimedia presentation materials.

5 Specify delivery techniques for use before, during, and after a presentation.

6 Explain effective techniques for adapting oral presentations to cross-cultural audiences.

7 List techniques for improving telephone, voice mail, and remote conferencing effectiveness.

Walt Disney Imagineering Sells Tokyo Disneyland on Winnie the Pooh

ALTHOUGH MANY NEW Japanese theme parks have failed, Tokyo Disneyland continues to rank as the world's most popular attraction, receiving over 25 million visitors last year.[1] Yet, it has felt the pinch of increasing competition and declining attendance during periods of economic slowdown. Like all theme parks, Tokyo Disneyland understood the need to offer fresh attractions and exciting new rides to keep the crowds coming back year after year. In its search for dynamic new ideas to expand its already popular park, Tokyo Disneyland turned to Walt Disney Imagineering.

Generating and implementing new ideas for the Disney theme parks are tasks of Walt Disney Imagineering. This is the research, design, and engineering subsidiary of Walt Disney Attractions. Although Tokyo Disneyland is a Disney theme park and Disney retains creative control of the park, the park is actually owned and operated by the Oriental Land Company. This company makes all financial and investment decisions. While creative concepts come from Disney Imagineering teams, those ideas are not automatically accepted by theme park owners. Imagineering teams not only had to dream up exciting new concepts for the Tokyo park, but they also had to *sell* the ideas and win the approval of Japanese owners. Millions of dollars in contracts and hundreds of jobs in the United States and in Japan rested on successful presentations to the owners of Tokyo Disneyland.

Jon Georges, former lead show producer for the Tokyo Disneyland Project, was part of a talented Imagineering team that came up with a totally new attraction and restaurant concept for the Disney theme park. Based on Winnie the Pooh and Alice in Wonderland characters, the creative project involved two phases. The first was a theme restaurant called the "Queen of Hearts Banquet Hall." The second was a major ride attraction based on Winnie the Pooh characters. Both concepts required considerable persuasion to win approval.

Oral presentation skills played a big part in persuading Tokyo Disneyland owners to invest in new theme park attractions.

Traditionally, the Japanese park owners had accepted only attractions that had proved technically successful in other theme parks. Naturally, they were reluctant to try a restaurant concept and a ride technology that were both brand new. Selling the Japanese on the new concepts required exceptional oral presentations from Jon Georges and the Imagineering team.[2]

Critical Thinking

- What kinds of oral presentations might you have to make in your chosen career field?
- Why are most people fearful of making presentations?
- How do you think people become effective speakers?

http://www.imagineering.org/

CONTINUED ON PAGE 523

case study

learning objective

1

Many businesspeople must make presentations as part of their careers.

Preparing Effective Oral Presentations

At some point everyone in business has to sell an idea, and such persuasion is often done in person. Like most of us, Jon Georges at Walt Disney Imagineering does not consider himself a professional speaker. He admits that he once was so afraid of public speaking that he started a couple of speech courses as part of his degree program at UCLA but always dropped out. Finally, he took a night class in speaking and began to get over his fears.

Many future businesspeople fail to take advantage of opportunities in college to develop speaking skills. Yet, such skills often play an important role in a successful career. In fact, the No. 1 predictor of success and upward mobility, according to an AT&T and Stanford University study, is how much you enjoy public speaking and how effective you are at it.[3] Speaking skills are useful at every career stage. You might, for example, have to make a sales pitch before customers or speak to a professional gathering. You might need to describe your company's expansion plans to your banker, or you might need to persuade management to support your proposed marketing strategy. This chapter prepares you to use speaking skills in making oral presentations and in using the telephone, voice mail, and conferencing to advantage.

For any presentation, you can reduce your fears and lay the foundation for a professional performance by focusing on five areas: preparation, organization, audience rapport, visual aids, and delivery.

Knowing Your Purpose

Preparing for an oral presentation means identifying the purpose and knowing the audience.

The most important part of your preparation is deciding what you want to accomplish. Do you want to sell a health care program to a prospective client? Do you want to persuade management to increase the marketing budget? Do you want to inform customer service reps of three important ways to prevent miscommunication? Whether your goal is to persuade or to inform, you must have a clear idea of where you are going. At the end of your presentation, what do you want your listeners to remember or do?

Eric Evans, a loan officer at First Fidelity Trust, faced such questions as he planned a talk for a class in small business management. Eric's former business professor had asked him to return to campus and give the class advice about borrowing money from banks in order to start new businesses. Because Eric knew so much about this topic, he found it difficult to extract a specific purpose statement for his presentation. After much thought he narrowed his purpose to this: *To inform potential entrepreneurs about three important factors that loan officers consider before granting start-up loans to launch small businesses.* His entire presentation focused on ensuring that the class members understood and remembered three principal ideas.

Knowing Your Audience

A second key element in preparation is analyzing your audience, anticipating its reactions, and making appropriate adaptations. Audiences may fall into four categories, as summarized in Figure 15.1. By anticipating your audience, you have a better idea of how to organize your presentation. A friendly audience, for example, will respond to humor and personal experiences. A neutral audience requires an even, controlled delivery style. The talk would probably be filled with facts, statistics, and expert opinions. An uninterested audience that is forced to attend requires a brief presentation. Such an audience might respond best to humor, cartoons, colorful visuals, and startling statistics. A hostile audience demands a calm, controlled delivery style with objective data and expert opinion.

Figure 15.1 ***Succeeding With Four Audience Types***

Audience Members	Organizational Pattern	Delivery Style	Supporting Material
Friendly			
They like you and your topic.	Use any pattern. Try something new; involve the audience.	Be warm, pleasant, and open; use lots of eye contact and smiles.	Include humor, personal examples, and experiences.
Neutral			
They are calm, rational; their minds are made up, but they think they are being objective.	Present both sides of the issue. Use pro/con or problem/solution patterns. Save time for audience questions.	Be controlled. Do nothing showy; use confident, small gestures.	Use facts, statistics, expert opinion, comparison, and contrast. Avoid humor, personal stories, and flashy visuals.
Uninterested			
They have short attention spans; they may be there against their will.	Be brief—no more than three points. Avoid topical and pro/con patterns that seem lengthy to the audience.	Be dynamic and entertaining. Move around; use large gestures.	Use humor, cartoons, colorful visuals, powerful quotations, and startling statistics.
	Avoid darkening the room, standing motionless, passing out handouts, using boring visuals, or expecting the audience to participate.		
Hostile			
They want to take charge or to ridicule the speaker; they may be defensive, emotional.	Organize using a noncontroversial pattern such as a topical, chronological, or geographical strategy.	Be calm and controlled. Speak evenly and slowly.	Include objective data and expert opinion. Avoid anecdotes and humor.
	Avoid a question-and-answer period, if possible; otherwise, use a moderator or accept only written questions.		

Other elements, such as age, gender, education, experience, and the size of the audience will affect your style and message content. Analyze the following questions to help you determine your organizational pattern, delivery style, and supporting material.

Audience analysis issues include size, age, gender, experience, attitude, and expectations.

- *How will this topic appeal to this audience?*
- *How can I relate this information to their needs?*
- *How can I earn respect so that they accept my message?*
- *What would be most effective in making my point? Facts? Statistics? Personal experiences? Expert opinion? Humor? Cartoons? Graphic illustrations? Demonstrations? Case histories? Analogies?*
- *What measures must I take to ensure that this audience remembers my main points?*

If you've agreed to speak to an audience with which you are unfamiliar, ask for the names of a half dozen people who will be in the audience. Contact them and learn about their backgrounds and expectations for the presentation. This information can help you answer questions about what they want to hear and how deeply you should explore the subject. You'll want to thank these people when you start your speech. Doing this kind of homework will impress the audience.

learning objective

2

Organizing the Content for a Powerful Impact

Once you have determined your purpose and analyzed the audience, you're ready to collect information and organize it logically. Good organization and conscious repetition are the two most powerful keys to audience comprehension and retention. In fact, many speech experts recommend the following admittedly repetitious, but effective, plan:

- **Step 1:** Tell them what you're going to say.
- **Step 2:** Say it.
- **Step 3:** Tell them what you've just said.

Capturing Attention in the Introduction

How many times have you heard a speaker begin with, *It's a pleasure to be here.* Or, *I'm honored to be asked to speak.* Boring openings such as these get speakers off to a dull start. Avoid such banalities by striving to accomplish three goals in the introduction to your presentation:

- Capture listeners' attention and get them involved.
- Identify yourself and establish your credibility.
- Preview your main points.

Attention-grabbing openers include questions, startling facts, jokes, anecdotes, and quotations.

If you're able to appeal to listeners and involve them in your presentation right from the start, you're more likely to hold their attention until the finish. Consider some of the same techniques that you used to open sales letters: a question, a startling fact, a joke, a story, or a quotation. Some speakers achieve involvement by opening with a question or command that requires audience members to raise their hands or stand up. Additional techniques to gain and keep audience attention are presented in the accompanying Career Coach box.

To establish your credibility, you need to describe your position, knowledge, or experience—whatever qualifies you to speak. Try also to connect with your audience. Listeners are particularly drawn to speakers who reveal something of themselves and identify with them. A consultant addressing office workers might reminisce about how she started as an administrative assistant; a CEO might tell a funny story in which the joke is on himself.

After capturing attention and establishing yourself, you'll want to preview the main points of your topic, perhaps with a visual aid. You may wish to put off actually writing your introduction, however, until after you have organized the rest of the presentation and crystallized your principal ideas.

Take a look at Eric Evans' introduction, shown in Figure 15.2, to see how he integrated all the elements necessary for a good opening.

Organizing the Body

The best oral presentations focus on a few key ideas.

The biggest problem with most oral presentations is a failure to focus on a few principal ideas. Thus, the body of your short presentation (20 or fewer minutes) should include a limited number of main points, say, two to four. Develop each main point with adequate, but not excessive, explanation and details. Too many details can obscure the main message, so keep your presentation simple and logical. Remember, listeners have no pages to leaf back through should they become confused.

When Eric Evans began planning his presentation, he realized immediately that he could talk for hours on his topic. He also knew that listeners are not good at sep-

career coach

Nine Techniques for Gaining and Keeping Audience Attention

Experienced speakers know how to capture the attention of an audience and how to maintain that attention during a presentation. Here are nine proven techniques.

- **A promise.** Begin with a promise that keeps the audience expectant (for example, *By the end of this presentation I will have shown you how you can increase your sales by 50 percent*).
- **Drama.** Open by telling an emotionally moving story or by describing a serious problem that involves the audience. Throughout your talk include other dramatic elements, such as a long pause after a key statement. Change your vocal tone or pitch. Professionals use high-intensity emotions such as anger, joy, sadness, and excitement.
- **Eye contact.** As you begin, command attention by surveying the entire audience to take in all listeners. Take two to five seconds to make eye contact with as many people as possible.
- **Movement.** Leave the lectern area whenever possible. Walk around the conference table or between the aisles of your audience. Try to move toward your audience, especially at the beginning and end of your talk.
- **Questions.** Keep listeners active and involved with rhetorical questions. Ask for a show of hands to get each listener thinking. The response will also give you a quick gauge of audience attention.
- **Demonstrations.** Include a member of the audience in a demonstration (for example, *I'm going to show you exactly how to implement our four-step customer courtesy process, but I need a volunteer from the audience to help me*).
- **Samples/gimmicks.** If you're promoting a product, consider using items to toss out to the audience or to award as prizes to volunteer participants. You can also pass around product samples or promotional literature. Be careful, though, to maintain control.
- **Visuals.** Give your audience something to look at besides yourself. Use a variety of visual aids in a single session. Also consider writing the concerns expressed by your listeners on a flipchart or on the board as you go along.
- **Self-interest.** Review your entire presentation to ensure that it meets the critical *What's-in-it-for-me?* audience test. Remember that people are most interested in things that benefit them.

Career Application

Watch a lecture series speaker on campus, a department store sales presentation, a TV infomercial, or some other speaker. Note and analyze specific techniques used to engage and maintain the listener's attention. Which techniques would be most effective in a classroom presentation? Before your boss or work group?

arating major and minor points. Thus, instead of submerging his listeners in a sea of information, he sorted out a few principal ideas. In the banking industry, loan officers generally ask the following three questions of each applicant for a small business loan: (1) Are you ready to "hit the ground running" in starting your business? (2) Have you done your homework? and (3) Have you made realistic projections of potential sales, cash flow, and equity investment? These questions would become his main points, but Eric wanted to streamline them further so that his audience would be sure to remember them. He capsulized the questions in three words: *experience, preparation,* and *projection.* As you can see in Figure 15.2, Eric prepared a sentence outline showing these three main ideas. Each is supported by examples and explanations.

How to organize and sequence main ideas may not be immediately obvious when you begin working on a presentation. The following methods, which review

FIGURE 15.2 ***Oral Presentation Outline***

1 Prewriting

ANALYZE: The purpose of this report is to inform listeners of three critical elements in securing business loans.

ANTICIPATE: The audience members are aspiring businesspeople who are probably unfamiliar with loan operations.

ADAPT: Because the audience will be receptive but uninformed, explain terms and provide examples. Repeat the main ideas to ensure comprehension.

2 Writing

RESEARCH: Analyze previous loan applications; interview other loan officers. Gather critical data.

ORGANIZE: Group the data into three major categories. Support with statistics, details, and examples. Plan visual aids.

COMPOSE: Prepare a sentence outline. Consider using presentation software to outline your talk.

3 Revising

REVISE: Develop transitions between topics. Prepare note cards or speaker's notes.

PRACTICE: Rehearse the entire talk and time it. Practice enunciating words and projecting your voice. Practice using your visual aids. Develop natural hand motions.

EVALUATE: Tape record or videotape a practice session to evaluate your movements, voice tone, enunciation, and timing.

What Makes a Loan Officer Say "Yes"?

I. INTRODUCTION

A. How many of you expect one day to start your own businesses? How many of you have all the cash available to capitalize that business when you start? *(Captures attention)*

B. Like you, nearly every entrepreneur needs cash to open a business, and I promise you that by the end of this talk you will have inside information on how to make a loan application that will be successful. *(Involves audience)*

C. As a loan officer at First Fidelity Trust, which specializes in small-business loans, I make decisions on requests from entrepreneurs like you applying for start-up money. *(Identifies speaker)*

Transition: Your professor invited me here today to tell you how you can improve your chances of getting a loan from us or from any other lender. I have suggestions in three areas: experience, preparation, and projection. *(Previews three main points)*

II. BODY *(Establishes main point)*

A. First, let's consider experience. You must show that you can hit the ground running.
1. Demonstrate what experience you have in your proposed business.
2. Include your résumé when you submit your business plan.
3. If you have little experience, tell us whom you would hire to supply the skills that you lack.

Transition: In addition to experience, loan officers will want to see that you have researched your venture thoroughly.

B. My second suggestion, then, involves preparation. Have you done your homework?
1. Talk to local businesspeople, especially those in related fields.
2. Conduct traffic counts or other studies to estimate potential sales.
3. Analyze the strengths and weaknesses of the competition.

Transition: Now that we've discussed preparation, we're ready for my final suggestion.

C. My last tip is the most important one. It involves making a realistic projection of your potential sales, cash flow, and equity.
1. Present detailed monthly cash-flow projections for the first year.
2. Describe *What-if* scenarios indicating both good and bad possibilities.
3. Indicate that you intend to supply at least 25 percent of the initial capital yourself.

Transition: The three major points I've just outlined cover critical points in obtaining start-up loans. Let me review them for you.

(Develops coherence with planned transitions)

III. CONCLUSION

A. Loan officers are most likely to say "yes" to your loan application if you do three things: (1) prove that you can hit the ground running when your business opens; (2) demonstrate that you've researched your proposed business seriously; and (3) project a realistic picture of your sales, cash flow, and equity. *(Summarizes main points)*

B. Experience, preparation, and projection, then, are the three keys to launching your business with the necessary start-up capital so that you can concentrate on where your customers, not your funds, are coming from. *(Provides final focus)*

and amplify those discussed in Chapter 13, provide many possible strategies and examples to help you organize a presentation:

Main ideas can be organized according to chronology, geography/space, topic/function/conventional grouping, comparison/contrast, journalism pattern, value/size, importance, problem/solution, simple/complex, and best case/worst case.

- **Chronology.** Example: A presentation describing the history of a problem, organized from the first sign of trouble to the present.
- **Geography/space.** Example: A presentation about the changing diversity of the workforce, organized by regions in the country (East Coast, West Coast, and so forth).
- **Topic/function/conventional grouping.** Example: A report discussing mishandled airline baggage, organized by names of airlines.
- **Comparison/contrast (pro/con).** Example: A report comparing organic farming methods with those of modern industrial farming.
- **Journalism pattern.** Example: A report describing how identity thieves can ruin your good name. Organized by *who, what, when, where, why,* and *how.*
- **Value/size.** Example: A report describing fluctuations in housing costs, organized by prices of homes.
- **Importance.** Example: A report describing five reasons that a company should move its headquarters to a specific city, organized from the most important reason to the least important.
- **Problem/solution.** Example: A company faces a problem such as declining sales. A solution such as reducing the staff is offered.
- **Simple/complex.** Example: A report explaining genetic modification of plants such as corn, organized from simple seed production to complex gene introduction.
- **Best case/worst case.** Example: A report analyzing whether two companies should merge, organized by the best case result (improved market share, profitability, employee morale) opposed to the worse case result (devalued stock, lost market share, employee malaise).

In the presentation shown in Figure 15.2, Eric arranged the main points by importance, placing the most important point last where it had maximum effect. When organizing any presentation, prepare a little more material than you think you will actually need. Savvy speakers always have something useful in reserve such as an extra handout, transparency, or idea—just in case they finish early.

Summarizing in the Conclusion

Nervous speakers often rush to wrap up their presentations because they can't wait to flee the stage. But listeners will remember the conclusion more than any part of a speech. That's why you should spend some time to make it most effective. Strive to achieve two goals:

- Summarize the main themes of the presentation.
- Include a statement that allows you to leave the podium gracefully.

Effective conclusions summarize main points and allow the speaker to exit gracefully.

Some speakers end limply with comments such as, *I guess that's about all I have to say.* This leaves bewildered audience members wondering whether they should continue listening. Skilled speakers alert the audience that they are finishing. They use phrases such as, *In conclusion, As I end this presentation*, or *It's time for me to sum up.* Then they proceed immediately to the conclusion. Audiences become justly irritated with a speaker who announces the conclusion but then digresses with one more story or talks on for ten more minutes.

A straightforward summary should review major points and focus on what you want the listeners to do, think, or remember. You might say, *In bringing my presentation to a close, I will restate my major purpose . . .* Or, *In summary, my major purpose has been to . . . . In support of my purpose, I have presented three major points. They are (1) . . . , (2) . . . , and (3) . . . .* Notice how Eric Evans, in the conclusion shown in Figure 15.2, summarized his three main points and provided a final focus to listeners.

If you are promoting a recommendation, you might end as follows: *In conclusion, I recommend that we retain Matrixx Marketing to conduct a telemarketing campaign beginning September 1 at a cost of X dollars. To complete this recommendation, I suggest that we (1) finance this campaign from our operations budget, (2) develop a persuasive message describing our new product, and (3) name Lisa Beck to oversee the project.*

In your conclusion you might want to use an anecdote, an inspiring quotation, or a statement that ties in the opener and offers a new insight. Whatever you choose, be sure to include a closing thought that indicates you are finished. For example, *This concludes my presentation. After investigating many marketing firms, we are convinced that Matrixx is the best for our purposes. Your authorization of my recommendations will mark the beginning of a very successful campaign for our new product. Thank you.*

learning objective 3

How the Best Speakers Build Audience Rapport

Good speakers are adept at building audience rapport. They form a bond with the audience; they entertain as well as inform. How do they do it? Based on observations of successful and unsuccessful speakers, we learn that the good ones use a number of verbal and nonverbal techniques to connect with the audience. Some of their helpful techniques include providing effective imagery, supplying verbal signposts, and using body language strategically.

Effective Imagery

You'll lose your audience quickly if your talk is filled with abstractions, generalities, and dry facts. To enliven your presentation and enhance comprehension, try using some of these techniques:

Use analogies, metaphors, similes, personal anecdotes, personalized statistics, and worst- and best-case scenarios instead of dry facts.

- **Analogies.** A comparison of similar traits between dissimilar things can be effective in explaining and drawing connections. For example, *Product development is similar to the process of conceiving, carrying, and delivering a baby.* Or, *Downsizing or restructuring is similar to an overweight person undergoing a regimen of dieting, habit changing, and exercise.*
- **Metaphors.** A comparison between otherwise dissimilar things without using the words *like* or *as* results in a metaphor. For example, *Our competitor's CEO is a snake when it comes to negotiating.* Or, *My desk is a garbage dump.*
- **Similes.** A comparison that includes the words *like* or *as* is a simile. For example, *Our critics used our background report like a drunk uses a lamppost—for support rather than for illumination.* Or, *She's as happy as someone who just won the lottery.*
- **Personal anecdotes.** Nothing connects you faster or better with your audience than a good personal story. In a talk about e-mail techniques, you could reveal your own blunders that became painful learning experiences. In a talk to potential investors, the founder of a new ethnic magazine might tell a story about growing up without positive ethnic role models.

- **Personalized statistics.** Although often misused, statistics stay with people—particularly when they relate directly to the audience. A speaker discussing job searching might say, *Look around the room. Only three out of five graduates will find a job immediately after graduation.* If possible, simplify and personalize facts. For example, *The sales of Coca-Cola totaled 2 billion cases last year. That means that six full cases of Coke were consumed by every man, woman, and child in the United States.*
- **Worst- and best-case scenarios.** Hearing the worst that could happen can be effective in driving home a point. For example, *If we do nothing about our computer backup system now, it's just a matter of time before the entire system crashes and we lose all of our customer contact information. Can you imagine starting from scratch in building all of your customer files again? However, if we fix the system now, we can expand our customer files and actually increase sales at the same time.*

spotlight *on communicators*

Patricia F. Russo, CEO of Lucent Technologies, the largest maker of equipment for telephone companies, used an excellent metaphor to suggest her company's troubles. Describing her effort to reduce Lucent's workforce and return to profitability during an economic downturn, she said, "We're trying to fly a 747 in the middle of a storm and change the engines while we're at it." In comparing two dissimilar things, this apt metaphor helps us visualize the difficulty of Lucent's tasks. Metaphors are particularly effective in oral presentations.

Verbal Signposts

Speakers must remember that listeners, unlike readers of a report, cannot control the rate of presentation or flip back through pages to review main points. As a result, listeners get lost easily. Knowledgeable speakers help the audience recognize the organization and main points in an oral message with verbal signposts. They keep listeners on track by including helpful previews, summaries, and transitions, such as these:

Knowledgeable speakers provide verbal signposts to indicate when they are previewing, summarizing, or switching directions.

- **Previewing**

  The next segment of my talk presents three reasons for . . . .

  Let's now consider the causes of . . . .
- **Summarizing**

  Let me review with you the major problems I've just discussed . . . .

  You see, then, that the most significant factors are . . . .
- **Switching directions**

  Thus far we've talked solely about . . . ; now let's move to . . . .

  I've argued that . . . and . . . , but an alternate view holds that . . . .

You can further improve any oral presentation by including appropriate transitional expressions such as *first, second, next, then, therefore, moreover, on the other hand, on the contrary,* and *in conclusion.* These expressions, which you learned about in Figure 6.7 and also in Chapter 13, build coherence, lend emphasis, and tell listeners where you are headed. Notice in Eric Evans' outline, in Figure 15.2, the specific transitional elements designed to help listeners recognize each new principal point.

Nonverbal Messages

Although what you say is most important, the nonverbal messages you send can also have a potent effect on how well your message is received. How you look, how you move, and how you speak can make or break your presentation. The following suggestions focus on nonverbal tips to ensure that your verbal message is well-received.

A speaker's appearance, movement, and speech affect the success of a presentation.

- **Look terrific!** Like it or not, you will be judged by your appearance. For everything but small in-house presentations, be sure you dress professionally. The rule of thumb is that you should dress at least as well as the best-dressed person in the audience.
- **Animate your body.** Be enthusiastic and let your body show it. Emphasize ideas to enhance points about size, number, and direction. Use a variety of gestures, but don't consciously plan them in advance.
- **Punctuate your words.** You can keep your audience interested by varying your tone, volume, pitch, and pace. Use pauses before and after important points. Allow the audience to take in your ideas.
- **Get out from behind the podium.** Avoid being planted to the podium. Movement makes you look natural and comfortable. You might pick a few places in the room to walk to. Even if you must stay close to your visual aids, make a point of leaving them occasionally so that the audience can see your whole body.
- **Vary your facial expression.** Begin with a smile, but change your expressions to correspond with the thoughts you are voicing. You can shake your head to show disagreement, roll your eyes to show disdain, look heavenward for guidance, or wrinkle your brow to show concern or dismay. To see how speakers convey meaning without words, mute the sound on your TV and watch the facial expressions of a talk show personality.

learning objective 4

Planning Visual Aids, Handouts, and Multimedia Presentations

Before you make a business presentation, consider this wise proverb: "Tell me, I forget. Show me, I remember. Involve me, I understand." Your goals as a speaker are to make listeners understand, remember, and act on your ideas. To get them interested and involved, include effective visual aids. Some experts say that we acquire 85 percent of all our knowledge visually. Therefore, an oral presentation that incorporates visual aids is far more likely to be understood and retained than one lacking visual enhancement.

Visual aids clarify points, improve comprehension, and aid retention.

Good visual aids have many purposes. They emphasize and clarify main points, thus improving comprehension and retention. They increase audience interest, and they make the presenter appear more professional, better prepared, and more persuasive. Furthermore, research shows that the use of visual aids actually shortens meetings.[4] Visual aids are particularly helpful for inexperienced speakers because the audience concentrates on the aid rather than on the speaker. Good visuals also serve to jog the memory of a speaker, thus improving self-confidence, poise, and delivery.

Types of Visual Aids

Fortunately for today's speakers, many forms of visual media are available to enhance a presentation. Figure 15.3 describes the pros and cons for a number of visual aids that can guide you in selecting the best visual aid for any speaking occasion. Three of the most popular visuals are multimedia slides, overhead transparencies, and handouts.

Multimedia Slides. With today's excellent software programs—such as Microsoft PowerPoint, Apple Keynote, Lotus Freelance Graphics, Corel Presentations, and Astound Presentation—you can create dynamic, colorful presentations with your PC.

FIGURE 15.3 ***Consider the Pros and Cons for Visual Aid Options***

Medium	Pros	Cons
Multimedia slides	Creates professional appearance with many color, art, graphic, and font options. Easy to use and transport via removable disk, Web download, or e-mail attachment. Inexpensive to update.	Presents potential incompatibility issues. Requires costly projection equipment and practice for smooth delivery. Tempts user to include razzle-dazzle features that may fail to add value.
Transparencies	Gives professional appearance with little practice. Easy to (1) prepare, (2) update and maintain, (3) locate reliable equipment, and (4) limit information shown at one time.	Appears to some as an outdated presentation method. Holds speaker captive to the machine. Provides poor reproduction of photos and some graphics.
Handouts	Encourages audience participation. Easy to maintain and update. Enhances recall because audience keeps reference material.	Increases risk of unauthorized duplication of speaker's material. Can be difficult to transport. May cause speaker to lose audience's attention.
Flipcharts or whiteboards	Provides inexpensive option available at most sites. Easy to (1) create, (2) modify or customize on the spot, (3) record comments from the audience, and (4) combine with more high-tech visuals in the same presentation.	Requires graphics talent. Difficult for larger audiences to see. Prepared flipcharts are cumbersome to transport and easily worn with use.
Video	Gives an accurate representation of the content; strong indication of forethought and preparation.	Creates potential for compatibility issues related to computer video formats. Expensive to create and update.
Objects for demonstration	Offers a realistic reinforcement of message content. Increases audience participation with close observation.	Leads to extra work and expense in transporting and replacing worn objects. Limited use with larger audiences.

The output from these programs is generally shown on a PC monitor, a TV monitor, an LCD (liquid crystal display) panel, or a screen. With a little expertise and advanced equipment, you can create a multimedia presentation that includes stereo sound, videos, and hyperlinks, as described shortly in the discussion of multimedia presentations.

To maintain control, distribute handouts after you finish speaking.

Overhead Transparencies. Student and professional speakers alike still rely on the overhead projector for many reasons. Most meeting areas are equipped with projectors and screens. Moreover, acetate transparencies for the overhead are cheap, easily prepared on a computer or copier, and simple to use. Because rooms need not be darkened, a speaker using transparencies can maintain eye contact with the audience. A word of caution, though: stand to the side of the projector so that you don't obstruct the audience's view.

Handouts. You can enhance and complement your presentations by distributing pictures, outlines, brochures, articles, charts, summaries, or other supplements. Speakers who use computer presentation programs often prepare a set of their slides

To maintain control, distribute handouts after you finish speaking.

along with notes to hand out to viewers. Timing the distribution of any handout, though, is tricky. If given out during a presentation, your handouts tend to distract the audience, causing you to lose control. Thus, it's probably best to discuss most handouts during the presentation but delay distributing them until after you finish.

Designing a Multimedia Presentation

PowerPoint has become the business standard for presenting, defending, and selling ideas.

Whether making a presentation to a dozen people sitting around a conference table or speaking to an audience of 500 in a large auditorium, smart speakers choose to put their key points on-screen to underscore and reinforce them. As a result, computer programs such as PowerPoint have become the business standard for presenting, defending, and selling ideas most effectively. Business speakers use computer presentations because they are economical, flexible, and easy to prepare. Changes can be made right up to the last minute. The medium provides a smorgasbord of visual and auditory enhancements to keep audience attention and to drive home key points. Most important, though, such presentations, when done well, can make even amateurs look like real pros.

Critics say that PowerPoint is too regimented and produces "bullet-pointed morons."

Yet, PowerPoint has its critics. They charge that the program dictates the way information is structured and presented. PowerPoint stifles "the storyteller, the poet, the person whose thoughts cannot be arranged in the shape of an Auto-content slide."[5] PowerPoint, say its detractors, is turning the nation's businesspeople into a "mindless gaggle of bullet-pointed morons."[6] But storytellers and poets are unlikely to be using PowerPoint to express their ideas. Business speakers, on the other hand, use PowerPoint because it increases audience enjoyment, comprehension, and retention. PowerPoint speakers, however, are effective only when they are skillful. To avoid landing in that category of "bullet-pointed morons," you must focus on creating your presentation, building bullet points, and adding multimedia elements.

Creating Your Presentation

All presentation programs require you to (1) select or create a template that will serve as the background for your presentation and (2) make each individual slide by selecting a layout that best conveys your message. You can use one of the templates provided with the program, download one from many Web sites, or create one from scratch.

Novice and even advanced users choose existing templates because they are designed by professionals who know how to combine harmonious colors, borders, and fonts for pleasing visual effects. If you prefer, you can alter existing templates so they better suit your needs. Adding a corporate logo, adjusting the color scheme to better match the colors used on your organization's Web site, or selecting a different font are just some of the ways you can customize existing templates.

Overused templates and clip art produce "visual clichés" that bore audiences.

Be careful, though, of what one expert labels "visual clichés."[7] Overused templates and even clip art that ship with PowerPoint can weary viewers who have seen them repeatedly in presentations. Instead of using a standard template, key in "PowerPoint template" in your favorite search engine. You will see hundreds of template options available as free downloads. Unless your employer requires that presentations all have the same look, your audience will most likely appreciate fresh templates that complement the purpose of your presentation and provide visual variety.

Whether you create your own template or choose one designed by professionals, consider these principles when evaluating color options. Warm colors—reds, oranges, and yellows—are best to highlight important elements. Blue is associated with calmness; yellow signals caution; red can mean stop, financial loss, or danger; and green relates to nature, go, and money.

Background and text colors depend on the lightness of the room.

The color for backgrounds and text depends on where the presentation will be given. Use light text on a dark background for presentations in darkened rooms. Use dark text on a light background for computer presentations in lighted rooms. Avoid using a dark font on a dark background, such as red text on a dark blue background. Likewise, avoid using a light font on a light background, such as white text on a pale blue background. Dark on dark or light on light results in low contrast, making the slides difficult to read.

In selecting the best slide layout for each slide, you again can choose from the layout options that are part of your presentation program, or you can create a layout from scratch by adding your own elements to each slide. Figure 15.4 illustrates some of the many layout options for creating your slides. You can alter layouts by repositioning, resizing, or changing the fonts for the placeholders in which your title, bulleted list, organization chart, video clip, photograph, or other elements appear.

When team members are working together to prepare a slide presentation, be sure that each member is using the same template. That way when they merge their individual sections into one presentation file, no one will be surprised about how the slides look. To maintain a consistent look throughout the presentation, only one team member should be in charge of making color, font, or other global formatting changes to the slide and title masters. Team members should be encouraged to follow the global formatting established by the master slides. In addition, team members should understand that making global changes one time using the master slides is a definite plus. It prevents the hassles associated with changing many individual slides.

Building Bullet Points

Bullet points should be short phrases that are parallel.

When you prepare your slides, translate the major headings in your presentation outline into titles for slides. Then build bullet points using short phrases. In Chap-

FIGURE 15.4 ***Selecting a Slide Layout***

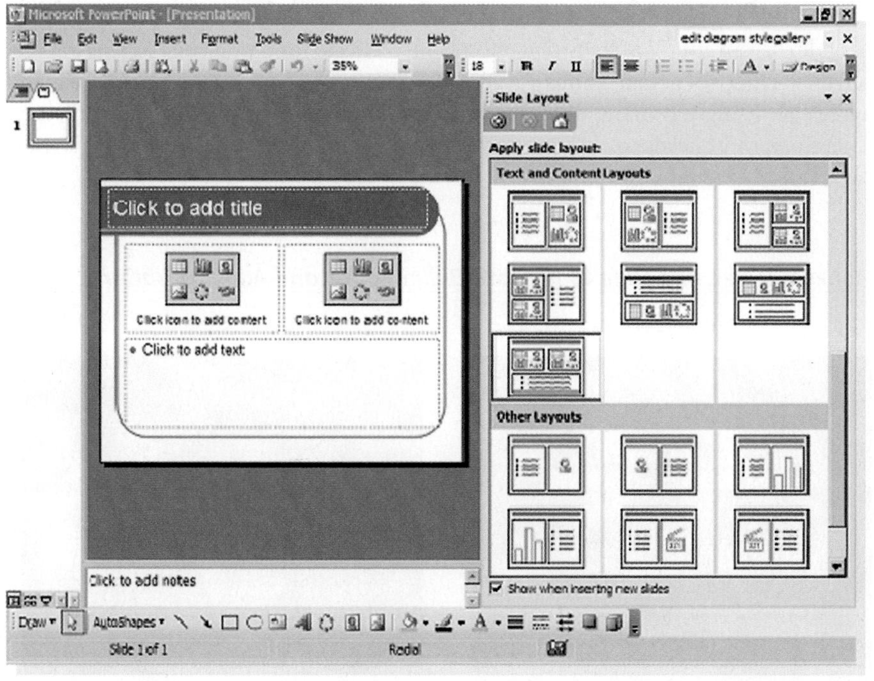

You may choose from a variety of slide layout plans, or you may design your own slide to fit your material.

ter 5 you learned to improve readability by using graphic highlighting techniques, including bullets, numbers, and headings. In preparing a PowerPoint presentation, you will use those same techniques.

Let's say, for example, that Matt wants to persuade the seven trainers in his department to use more audience participation. He has to convince them that trainee feedback describing some sessions as "one-way information dumps" is proof that improvement is needed. Matt wants to emphasize how trainers and trainees can benefit by including audience-involvement techniques. Here is a portion of the text he wrote.

> *Today's audience members interact with cell phones, computers, ATMs, and other communication media. So when they come to one of your training sessions, they often expect you to include two-way dialog and interactivity through audience-involvement techniques. Such techniques include asking the trainees to guess a statistic before revealing it, dividing the trainees into small groups to discuss an issue, and encouraging participation with giveaways. In addition to meeting audience expectations, incorporating interactivity into a presentation also benefits the speaker. Audience-involvement techniques can be used to reinforce key points and to add variety to the presentation by changing the pace and giving audiences a "break" from listening to just one person. Interactivity also helps the speaker build rapport with the audience and encourages audience members to get to know each other.*

Text can be converted to bullet points by experimenting with key phrases that are concise and balanced grammatically.

To convert the preceding text into bullet points, Matt started with a title and then listed the main ideas that related to that title as illustrated in the left slide of Figure 15.5. He worked with the list until all the items were parallel. That meant considerable experimenting with different wording. Matt went through many revisions before creating the revised slide pictured on the right of Figure 15.5. Notice that Matt revised the title to promote reader benefits. Notice also that the bullet points are concise and parallel. They should be key phrases, not complete sentences. Finally, adding a photo illustrates the point and adds interest.

Incremental bullet points enable a speaker to animate the presentation and control the flow of ideas.

PowerPoint's animation feature will allow Matt to focus viewer's attention on each point of this bulleted slide. By choosing from a variety of effects such as "fly" in from the top or "wipe" right, he can time the display of each bullet point to coordinate with his comments on each point. In addition, when Matt moves from slide to slide, he can use *slide transition* effects. Such effects for a new slide appearing onscreen include Venetian blinds or spinning like spokes on a wheel. Most experts agree that using too many different build and transition effects can be distracting. Therefore, Matt needs to choose effects that will help his audience focus on his message, not the technology.

FIGURE 15.5 ***Revising Slide to Improve Bullet Points and Add Illustration***

Before Revision

Reasons to Use Interactivity
• Audience members expect it
• Helps speaker reinforce key points
• Adds variety to the presentation
• Can be used to build rapport with audience
• Encourages audience members to get to know each other

After Revision

Interactivity Enhances Your Presentation
• Meets audience expectations
• Reinforces key points
• Adds variety
• Builds rapport with your audience
• Encourages participants to meet each other

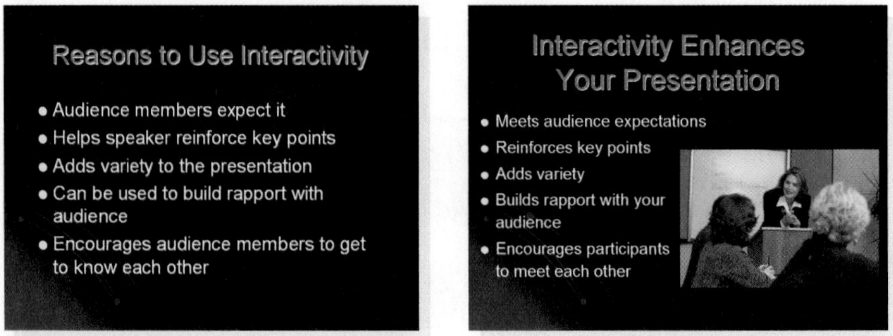

Matt revised the wording on the left slide to achieve the more visually appealing right slide that communicates reader benefit in the title and demonstrates concise and parallel bullet points.

For the most readable slides, apply the Rule of Seven. Each slide should include no more than seven words in a line, no more than seven total lines, and no more than 7 × 7 or 49 total words. If possible, use fewer words. Remember that presentation slides depict an idea graphically or provide an overview; they don't tell the whole story. That's the job of the presenter.

Adding Multimedia Elements

Multimedia elements include sound, animation, video, and other visual elements.

Few approaches are more mind numbing to your audience than displaying endless slides of bulleted lists. Thanks to the multimedia features available on presentation programs, you can include sound, animation, video, and other visual elements to enhance your content. For example, video clips can add excitement and depth to a presentation. You might use video to capture attention in a stimulating introduction, to show the benefits of a product in use, or to bring the personality of a distant expert or satisfied customer right into the meeting room.

Another way to enliven a presentation is with photographic images. These images are easy to obtain thanks to stock photos that can be purchased online and to the prevalence of low-cost scanners and digital cameras. Furthermore, presenting processes, operations, and sequences in an animated flowchart format reflects the information more accurately than the same data presented in a bulleted list.

PowerPoint, for example, has a diagram gallery feature that offers users many interesting options for presenting information. Figure 15.6 illustrates six common diagram types. The accompanying slide shows how Matt chose the radial diagram option to present the bulleted list shown in Figure 15.5. When Matt displays this slide, he will animate the boxes so that the center box appears first. Subsequent boxes will appear timed with his explanation of each.

Use animation to introduce elements of the presentation as they unfold in your spoken remarks.

Numeric information is more easily grasped in charts or graphs than in a listing of numbers. Moreover, in most programs, you can animate your graphs and charts. Say, for instance, you have four columns in your bar chart. You can control the entry of each column by determining in what order and how each column appears on the screen. The goal is to use animation strategically to introduce elements of the presentation as they unfold in your spoken remarks.

Most programs are also capable of generating hyperlinks ("hot" spots on the screen) that allow you to jump instantly to sources outside your presentation. With a click of your mouse, you could take your audience "live" to a Web site that contains up-to-the-minute data related to your presentation. Hyperlinks can enhance

FIGURE 15.6 ***Use a Diagram Gallery Option to Convert the Bulleted List from Figure 15.5 to an Animated Diagram***

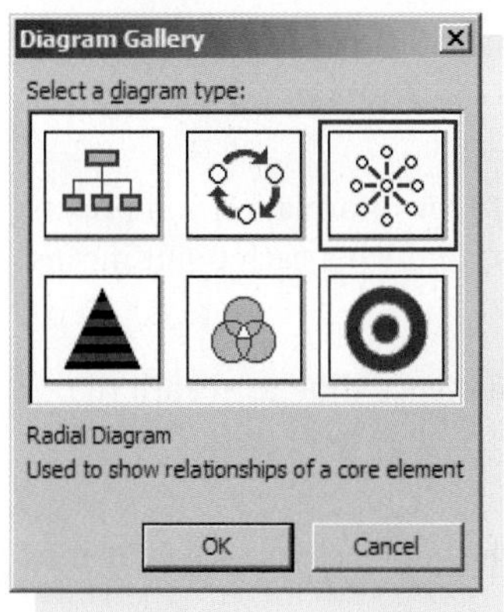

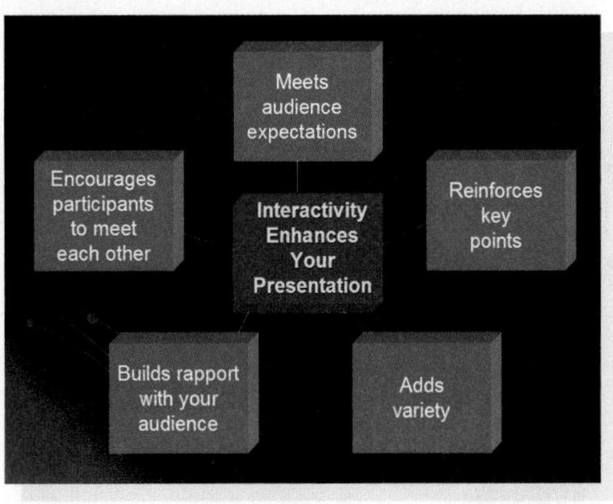

This slide was created using the radial diagram option from the PowerPoint diagram gallery.

interest in your presentation by adding interactive features and a wide variety of multimedia elements.

Be warned, though, that using multimedia effects or visual enhancements just because you can is never a good enough reason to include them. Every multimedia and visual effect you use should enhance your message and engage your audience. Using too many "bells and whistles" is annoying and may cause your audience to remember the entertaining slides rather than the key points.

Producing Speaker's Notes and Handouts

You also have a variety of options for printing hard-copy versions of your presentation. You can, for example, make speaker's notes that are a wonderful aid for practicing your talk. Beneath the miniature image of each slide is space for you to key in your supporting comments for the abbreviated material in your slides. You can also include up to nine miniature versions of your slides per printed page. These miniatures are handy if you want to preview your talk to a sponsoring organization or if you want to supply the audience with a summary of your presentation.

Moving Your Presentation to the Internet

Internet options for slide presentations range from posting slides online to conducting a live Web conference with slides, narration, and speaker control.

You have a range of alternatives, from simple to complex, for moving your multimedia presentation to the Internet. The simplest option is posting your slides online for others to access. Even if you are giving a face-to-face presentation, attendees appreciate these *electronic handouts* because they don't have to lug them home. The most complex option for moving your multimedia presentation to the Internet involves a Web conference or broadcast.

Web presentations with slides, narration, and speaker control have emerged as a way for anyone who has access to the Internet to attend your presentation without leaving the office. For example, you could initiate a meeting via a conference call, narrate using a telephone, and have participants see your slides from the browsers on their computers. If you prefer, you could skip the narration and provide a prerecorded presentation. Web-based presentations have many applications, including providing access to updated training or sales data whenever needed.[8]

Avoiding Being Upstaged by Your Multimedia Presentation

One expert urges speakers to "use their PowerPresence in preference to their PowerPoint."[9] Although multimedia presentations supply terrific sizzle, they cannot replace the steak. In developing a presentation, don't expect your slides to carry the show. Your goal is to avoid letting PowerPoint "steal your thunder." Here are suggestions for keeping control in your slide presentation:

To avoid making PowerPoint the main event, a speaker should look at the audience, not at the screen; leave the lights on; and use other visualization techniques.

- Use your slides primarily to summarize important points, as shown in Figure 15.7. For each slide have one or more paragraphs of narration to present to your audience.
- Remember that your responsibility is to *add value* to the information you present. Explain the analyses leading up to the major points and what each point means.
- Look at the audience, not the screen.
- As you show new elements on a slide, allow the audience time to absorb the information, then paraphrase and elaborate on what they have seen. Do NOT read verbatim from a slide.
- Leave the lights as bright as you can. Make sure the audience can see your face and eyes.

FIGURE 15.7 ***Preparing a PowerPoint Presentation***

Tips for Preparing and Using Slides

- Keep all visuals simple; spotlight major points only.
- Use the same font size and style for similar headings.
- Apply the Rule of Seven: No more than seven words on a line, seven total lines, and 7×7 or 49 total words.
- Be sure that everyone in the audience can see the slides.
- Show a slide, allow the audience to read it, then paraphrase it. Do NOT read from a slide.
- Rehearse by practicing talking to the audience, not to the slides.
- Bring backup transparencies in case of equipment failure.

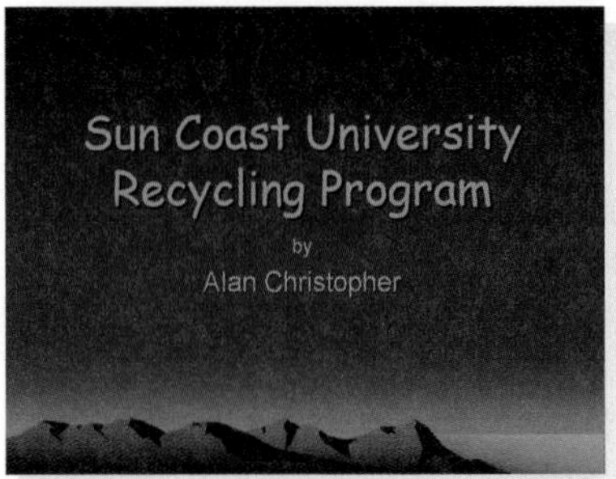

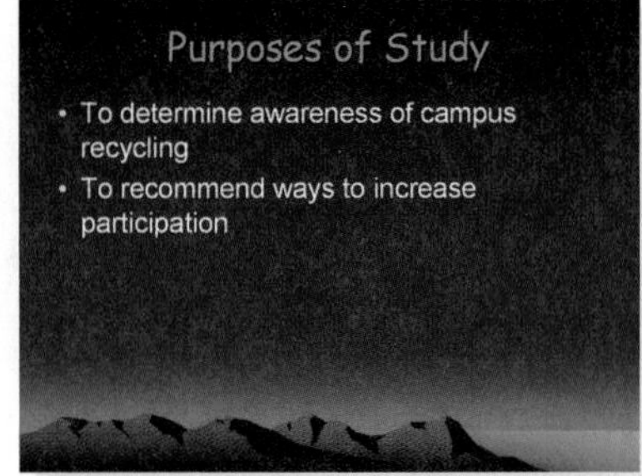

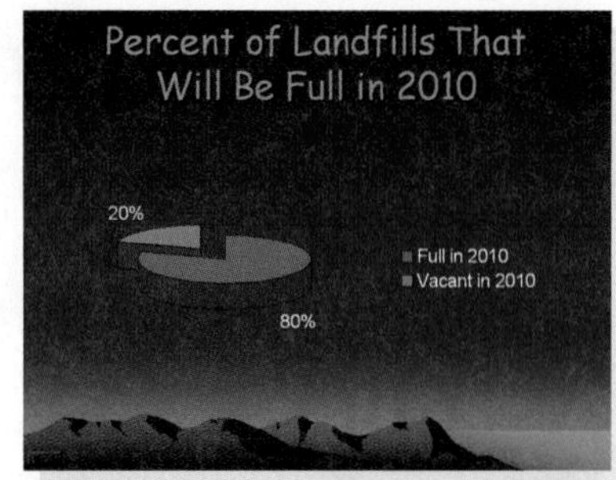

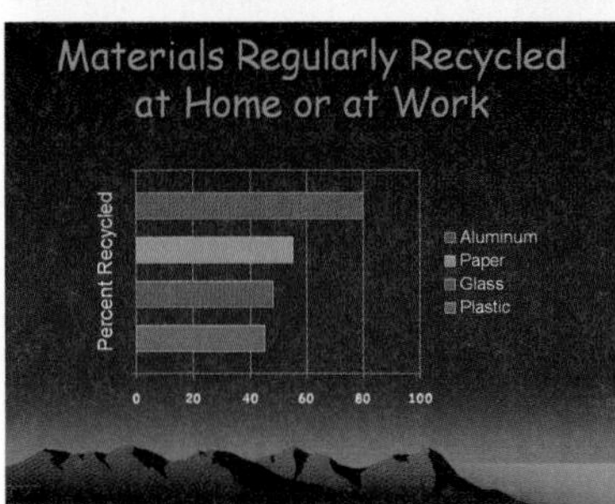

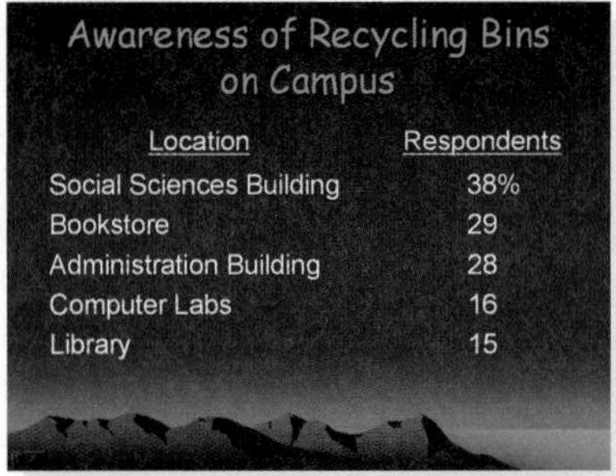

Twin Problems
• Low level of awareness of recycling bins on campus
• Low rate of participation by students and faculty

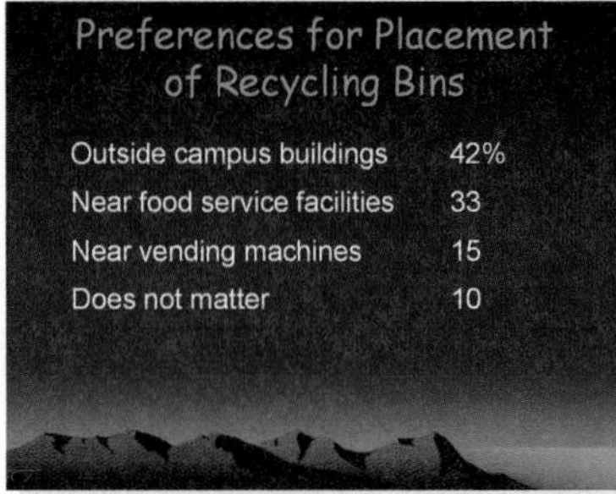

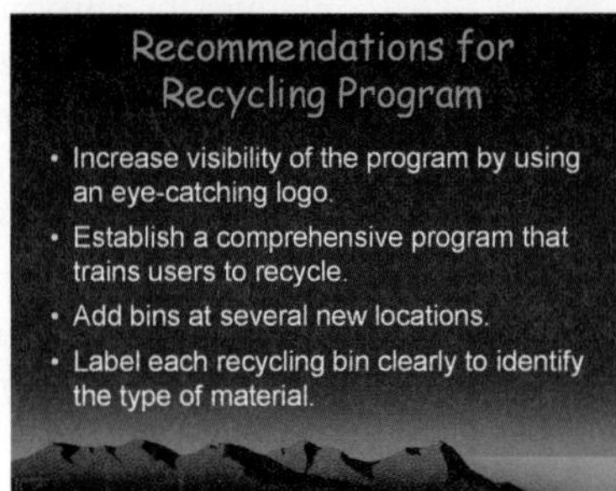

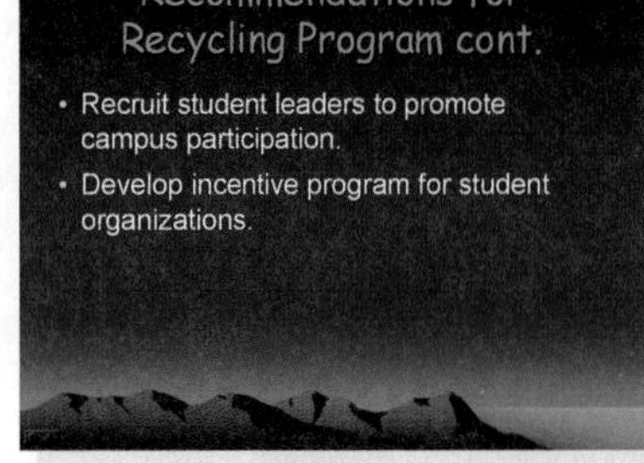

- Use a radio remote control (not infrared) so you can stand near the screen rather than remain tethered to your computer. Radio remotes will allow you to be up to 50 feet away from your laptop.
- Maintain a connection with the audience by using a laser pointer to highlight slide items to discuss.
- Darken the screen while you discuss points, tell a story, give an example, or involve the audience. Strike B on the keyboard to turn on or off the screen image.

- Don't rely totally on PowerPoint. Help the audience visualize your points by using other techniques. Drawing a diagram on a white board or flipchart can be more engaging than showing slide after slide of static drawings. Showing real objects is a welcome relief from slides.
- In case of equipment failure, bring backups of your presentation. Overhead transparencies or handouts of your presentation would provide good substitutes. Transferring your presentation to a CD or a USB flash drive that could run from any available notebook might prove useful as well.

Remember that your slides merely supply a framework for your presentation. Your audience came to see and hear you!

learning objective 5

Polishing Your Delivery and Following Up

Once you've organized your presentation and prepared visuals, you're ready to practice delivering it. You'll feel more confident and appear more professional if you know more about various delivery methods and techniques to use before, during, and after your presentation.

Delivery Methods

The "notes" delivery method results in more convincing presentations than presentations that are memorized or read.

Inexperienced speakers often feel that they must memorize an entire presentation to be effective. Unless you are an experienced performer, however, you will sound wooden and unnatural. What's more, forgetting your place can be disastrous! That's why we don't recommend memorizing an entire oral presentation. However, memorizing significant parts—the introduction, the conclusion, and perhaps a meaningful quotation—can be dramatic and impressive.

If memorizing won't work, is reading your presentation the best plan? Definitely not! Reading to an audience is boring and ineffective. Because reading suggests that you don't know your topic very well, the audience loses confidence in your expertise. Reading also prevents you from maintaining eye contact. You can't see audience reactions; consequently, you can't benefit from feedback.

Neither memorizing nor reading creates very convincing presentations. The best plan, by far, is a *notes* method. Plan your presentation carefully and talk from note cards or an outline containing key sentences and major ideas. By preparing and then practicing with your notes, you can talk to your audience in a conversational manner. Your notes should be neither entire paragraphs nor single words. Instead, they should contain a complete sentence or two to introduce each major idea. Below the topic sentence(s), outline subpoints and illustrations. Note cards will keep you on track and prompt your memory, but only if you have rehearsed the presentation thoroughly.

spotlight on communicators

Novice speakers often speed up their delivery, perhaps out of nervousness or eagerness to sit down. Justice Sandra Day O'Connor, shortly after becoming the first woman on the Supreme Court, revealed a trick she uses when she has important words to speak: "I taught myself early on to speak very slowly—enunciating every word—when I wanted someone's undivided attention."

Photo: © AP/Wide World Photos

Delivery Techniques

Stage fright is both natural and controllable.

Nearly everyone experiences some degree of stage fright when speaking before a group. "If you hear someone say he or she isn't nervous before a speech, you're talking either to a liar or a very boring speaker," says corporate speech consultant Dianna Booher.[10] Being afraid is quite natural and results from actual physiological

career coach

How to Avoid Stage Fright

Ever get nervous before making a presentation? Everyone does! And it's not all in your head, either. When you face something threatening or challenging, your body reacts in what psychologists call the *fight-or-flight response*. This response provides your body with increased energy to deal with threatening situations. It also creates those sensations—dry mouth, sweaty hands, increased heartbeat, and stomach butterflies—that we associate with stage fright. The fight-or-flight response arouses your body for action—in this case, making a presentation.

Because everyone feels some form of apprehension before speaking, it's impossible to eliminate the physiological symptoms altogether. You can, however, reduce their effects with the following techniques:

- **Breathe deeply.** Use deep breathing to ease your fight-or-flight symptoms. Inhale to a count of ten, hold this breath to a count of ten, and exhale to a count of ten. Concentrate on your counting and your breathing; both activities reduce your stress.
- **Convert your fear.** Don't view your sweaty palms and dry mouth as evidence of fear. Interpret them as symptoms of exuberance, excitement, and enthusiasm to share your ideas.
- **Know your topic.** Feel confident about your topic. Select a topic that you know well and that is relevant to your audience.
- **Use positive self-talk.** Remind yourself that you know your topic and are prepared. Tell yourself that the audience is on your side—because it is!
- **Shift the spotlight to your visuals.** At least some of the time the audience will be focusing on your slides, transparencies, handouts, or whatever you have prepared—and not totally on you.
- **Ignore any stumbles.** Don't apologize or confess your nervousness. If you keep going, the audience will forget any mistakes quickly.
- **Feel proud when you finish.** You'll be surprised at how good you feel when you finish. Take pride in what you've accomplished, and your audience will reward you with applause and congratulations. Your body, of course, will call off the fight-or-flight response and return to normal!

Career Application

Interview someone in your field or in another business setting who must make oral presentations. How did he or she develop speaking skills? What advice can this person suggest to reduce stage fright? When you next make a class presentation, try some or all of the techniques described here and note which are most effective for you.

changes occurring in your body. Faced with a frightening situation, your body responds with the fight-or-flight response, discussed more fully in the accompanying Career Coach box. You can learn to control and reduce stage fright, as well as to incorporate techniques for effective speaking, by using the following strategies and techniques before, during, and after your presentation.

Before Your Presentation

- **Prepare thoroughly.** One of the most effective strategies for reducing stage fright is knowing your subject thoroughly. Research your topic diligently and prepare a careful sentence outline. Those who try to "wing it" usually suffer the worst butterflies—and make the worst presentations.
- **Rehearse repeatedly.** When you rehearse, practice your entire presentation, not just the first half. Place your outline sentences on separate cards. You may also wish to include transitional sentences to help you move to the next topic. Use these cards as you practice, and include your visual aids in your rehearsal. Rehearse alone or before friends and family. Also try rehearsing on audio- or videotape so that you can evaluate your effectiveness.

spotlight *on communicators*

To give rhythm and punch to your presentations, says corporate speech consultant Dianna Booher, make ample use of these three techniques: triads *("we are one nation—black, white, brown"; "government of the people, by the people, and for the people": "you must have faith, hope, and charity");* alliteration *("we wish you health, happiness, and hope"); and* rhyme *("American business must automate, emigrate, or evaporate").*

- **Time yourself.** Most audiences tend to get restless during longer talks. Thus, try to complete your presentation in no more than 20 minutes. Set a timer during your rehearsal to measure your speaking time.
- **Request a lectern.** Every beginning speaker needs the security of a high desk or lectern from which to deliver a presentation. It serves as a note holder and a convenient place to rest wandering hands and arms. But don't lean on it.
- **Check the room.** Before you talk, make sure that a lectern has been provided. If you are using a computer, a projector, or sound equipment, be certain they are operational. Check electrical outlets and the position of the viewing screen. Ensure that the seating arrangement is appropriate to your needs.
- **Greet members of the audience.** Try to make contact with a few members of the audience when you enter the room, while you are waiting to be introduced, or when you walk to the podium. Your body language should convey friendliness, confidence, and enjoyment.
- **Practice stress reduction.** If you feel tension and fear while you are waiting your turn to speak, use stress-reduction techniques, such as deep breathing. Additional techniques to help you conquer stage fright are presented in the Career Coach box on page 521.

During Your Presentation

- **Begin with a pause.** When you first approach the audience, take a moment to adjust your notes and make yourself comfortable. Establish your control of the situation.
- **Present your first sentence from memory.** By memorizing your opening, you can immediately establish rapport with the audience through eye contact. You'll also sound confident and knowledgeable.

Eye contact, a moderate tone of voice, and natural movements enhance a presentation.

- **Maintain eye contact.** If the size of the audience overwhelms you, pick out two individuals on the right and two on the left. Talk directly to these people.
- **Control your voice and vocabulary.** This means speaking in moderated tones but loudly enough to be heard. Eliminate verbal static, such as *ah, er, you know,* and *um.* Silence is preferable to meaningless fillers when you are thinking of your next idea.
- **Put the brakes on.** Many novice speakers talk too rapidly, displaying their nervousness and making it very difficult for audience members to understand their ideas. Slow down and listen to what you are saying.
- **Move naturally.** You can use the lectern to hold your notes so that you are free to move about casually and naturally. Avoid fidgeting with your notes, your clothing, or items in your pockets. Learn to use your body to express a point.
- **Use visual aids effectively.** You should discuss and interpret each visual aid for the audience. Move aside as you describe it so that it can be seen fully. Use a pointer if necessary.
- **Avoid digressions.** Stick to your outline and notes. Don't suddenly include clever little anecdotes or digressions that occur to you on the spot. If it's not

Photo: Courtesy of Dianna Booher—Booher Consultants, Inc.

Process in Progress

Walt Disney Imagineering Revisited

JON GEORGES AND a Walt Disney Imagineering design team worked intensively on a new creative concept for one of the world's most-visited theme parks, Tokyo Disneyland. The entire project, however, would come to a screeching halt without a successful presentation before the owners of Tokyo Disneyland. The Imagineering team had to convince the assembled Japanese that new Winnie the Pooh feature attractions, as well as associated merchandise shops and a major restaurant, would be exciting and profitable additions to the existing theme park.

Understanding the audience and anticipating its reaction were integral parts of Jon's preparation for a presentation. For the Tokyo Disneyland project, Jon and the Imagineering team wanted to present their concepts in broad terms to see whether the financiers liked the total idea. But Jon also knew that this audience would be detail oriented. "Japanese businessmen tend to want particulars—like the color of the concrete, the number of restrooms, and the exact location where visitors would exit an attraction."

Other adaptations Jon made for the Tokyo presentation involved choice of language and presentation style. Carefully avoiding Disney and design jargon, he consciously used common words and simple sentences, which the translator had little trouble converting to Japanese. In making his presentation, Jon kept in mind three important elements: organization, visuals, and focus. Although he had thousands of details in mind, he forced himself to keep his presentation logical and simple. He concentrated on one powerful point: convincing his Japanese listeners that the new attractions would enhance the value of Tokyo Disneyland and would draw more visitors through the turnstiles.

Critical Thinking

- What questions should Jon Georges have asked himself in anticipating the audience for the Tokyo Disneyland presentation?
- Why is simplicity important in an oral presentation, and why was it particularly important for the Tokyo Disneyland presentation?
- Why are visual aids critical for both local and international audiences?

CONTINUED ON PAGE 530

case study

part of your rehearsed material, leave it out so that you can finish on time. Remember, too, that your audience may not be as enthralled with your topic as you are.

- **Summarize your main points.** Conclude your presentation by reiterating your main points or by emphasizing what you want the audience to think or do. Once you have announced your conclusion, proceed to it directly.

After Your Presentation

- **Distribute handouts.** If you prepared handouts with data the audience will need, pass them out when you finish.
- **Encourage questions.** If the situation permits a question-and-answer period, announce it at the beginning of your presentation. Then, when you finish, ask for questions. Set a time limit for questions and answers.
- **Repeat questions.** Although the speaker may hear the question, audience members often do not. Begin each answer with a repetition of the question. This also gives you thinking time. Then, direct your answer to the entire audience.

The time to answer questions, distribute handouts, and reiterate main points is after a presentation.

- **Reinforce your main points.** You can use your answers to restate your primary ideas (*I'm glad you brought that up because it gives me a chance to elaborate on . . .*). In answering questions, avoid becoming defensive or debating the questioner.
- **Keep control.** Don't allow one individual to take over. Keep the entire audience involved.
- **Avoid *Yes, but* answers.** The word *but* immediately cancels any preceding message. Try replacing it with *and.* For example, *Yes, X has been tried. And Y works even better because . . . .*
- **End with a summary and appreciation.** To signal the end of the session before you take the last question, say something like, *We have time for just one more question.* As you answer the last question, try to work it into a summary of your main points. Then, express appreciation to the audience for the opportunity to talk with them.

learning objective

6

Adapting to International and Cross-Cultural Audiences

Every good speaker adapts to the audience, and cross-cultural presentations call for special adjustments and sensitivity. When working with an interpreter or speaking before individuals whose English is limited, you'll need to be very careful about your language. For his presentation in Tokyo, Jon Georges spoke slowly, used simple English, avoided jargon and clichés, and used short sentences.

Beyond these basic language adaptations, however, more fundamental sensitivity is often necessary. In organizing a presentation for a cross-cultural audience, think twice about delivering your main idea up front. Many people (notably those in Japanese, Latin American, and Arabic cultures) consider such directness to be brash and inappropriate. Remember that others may not share our cultural emphasis on straightforwardness.[11]

Addressing cross-cultural audiences requires a speaker to consider audience expectations and cultural conventions.

Also consider breaking your presentation into short, discrete segments. In Japan, Jon Georges divided his talk into three distinct topics: theme park attractions, merchandise shops, and food services. He developed each topic separately, encouraging discussion periods after each. Such organization enables participants to ask questions and digest what has been presented. This technique is especially effective in cultures where people communicate in "loops." In the Middle East, for example, Arab speakers "mix circuitous, irrelevant (by American standards) conversations with short dashes of information that go directly to the point." Presenters who are patient, tolerant, and "mature" (in the eyes of the audience) will make the sale or win the contract.[12]

Match your presentation to the expectations of your audience. In Germany, for instance, successful presentations tend to be dense with facts and precise statistics. Americans might say "around 30 percent" while a German presenter might say "30.4271 percent."

Remember, too, that some cultures prefer greater formality than Americans exercise. Writing on a flipchart or transparency seems natural and spontaneous in this country. Abroad, though, such informal techniques may suggest that the speaker does not value the audience enough to prepare proper visual aids in advance.[13]

This caution aside, you'll still want to use visual aids to communicate your message. These visuals should be written in both languages, so that you and your audience understand them. Never use numbers without writing them out for all to see. If possible, say numbers in both languages. Distribute translated handouts, summarizing your important information, when you finish. Finally, be careful of your body language. Looking people in the eye suggests intimacy and self-confidence in this country, but in other cultures such eye contact may be considered disrespectful.

Whether you are speaking to familiar or cross-cultural audiences, your presentation requires attention to content and strategy. The following checklist summarizes suggestions for preparing, organizing, and illustrating an oral presentation.

Checklist for Preparing and Organizing Oral Presentations

Getting Ready to Speak

- ✓ **Identify your purpose.** Decide what you want your audience to believe, remember, or do when you finish. Aim all parts of your talk toward this purpose.

- ✓ **Analyze the audience.** Consider how to adapt your message (its organization, appeals, and examples) to your audience's knowledge and needs.

Organizing the Introduction

- ✓ **Get the audience involved.** Capture the audience's attention by opening with a promise, story, startling fact, question, quote, relevant problem, or self-effacing joke.

- ✓ **Establish yourself.** Demonstrate your credibility by identifying your position, expertise, knowledge, or qualifications.

- ✓ **Preview your main points.** Introduce your topic and summarize its principal parts.

Organizing the Body

- ✓ **Develop two to four main points.** Streamline your topic so that you can concentrate on its major issues.

- ✓ **Arrange the points logically.** Sequence your points chronologically, from most important to least important, by comparison and contrast, or by some other strategy.

- ✓ **Prepare transitions.** Between each major point write "bridge" statements that connect the previous item to the next one. Use transitional expressions as verbal signposts (*first, second, then, however, consequently, on the contrary*, and so forth).

- ✓ **Have extra material ready.** Be prepared with more information and visuals in case you have additional time to fill.

Organizing the Conclusion

- ✓ **Review your main points.** Emphasize your main ideas in your closing so that your audience will remember them.

- ✓ **Provide a final focus.** Tell how your listeners can use this information, why you have spoken, or what you want them to do.

Designing Visual Aids

- ✓ **Select your medium carefully.** Consider the pros and cons of each alternative.
- ✓ **Highlight main ideas.** Use visual aids to illustrate major concepts only. Keep them brief and simple.
- ✓ **Use aids skillfully.** Talk to the audience, not to the visuals. Paraphrase their contents.

Developing Multimedia Presentations

- ✓ **Learn to use your software program.** Study template and slide layout designs to see how you can adapt them to your purposes.
- ✓ **Select colors based on the light level in the room.** Consider how mixing light and dark fonts and backgrounds affects their visibility.
- ✓ **Use bulleted points for major ideas.** Make sure your points are all parallel and observe the Rule of Seven.
- ✓ **Include multimedia options that will help you convey your message.**
- ✓ **Make speaker's notes.** Jot down the narrative supporting each slide and use these notes to practice your presentation.
- ✓ **Maintain control.** Don't let your slides upstage you. Engage your audience by using additional techniques to help them visualize your points.

learning objective

7

Improving Telephone, Voice Mail, and Remote Conferencing Skills

Despite the heavy reliance on e-mail, the telephone is still an extremely important piece of equipment in offices. With the addition of today's wireless technology, it doesn't matter whether you are in or out of the office. You can always be reached by phone. In a Career Coach box in Chapter 1, you learned some specific techniques for being courteous in using cell phones. In this chapter we'll focus on traditional telephone techniques as well as voice mail and remote conferencing efficiency. As a business communicator, you can be more productive, efficient, and professional by following some simple suggestions.

Making Telephone Calls Efficiently

Telephones, voice mail, and remote conferencing should promote goodwill and increase productivity.

Before making a telephone call, decide whether the intended call is really necessary. Could you find the information yourself? If you wait a while, will the problem resolve itself? Perhaps your message could be delivered more efficiently by some other means. Some companies have found that telephone calls are often less important than the work they interrupted. Alternatives to telephone calls include instant messaging, e-mail, memos, or calls to voice mail systems. If you must make a telephone call, consider using the following suggestions to make it fully productive.

- **Plan a mini-agenda.** Have you ever been embarrassed when you had to make a second telephone call because you forgot an important item the first time? Before placing a call, jot down notes regarding all the topics you need to discuss. Following an agenda guarantees not only a complete call but also a quick one.

You'll be less likely to wander from the business at hand while rummaging through your mind trying to remember everything.

- **Use a three-point introduction.** When placing a call, immediately (1) name the person you are calling, (2) identify yourself and your affiliation, and (3) give a brief explanation of your reason for calling. For example: *May I speak to Larry Lopez? This is Hillary Dahl of Sebastian Enterprises, and I'm seeking information about a software program called Power Presentations.* This kind of introduction enables the receiving individual to respond immediately without asking further questions.
- **Be brisk if you are rushed.** For business calls when your time is limited, avoid questions such as *How are you?* Instead, say, *Lisa, I knew you'd be the only one who could answer these two questions for me.* Another efficient strategy is to set a "contract" with the caller: *Look, Lisa, I have only ten minutes, but I really wanted to get back to you.*

spotlight *on communicators*

Instead of commanding telephone callers to "Hold, please," ask politely whether the caller is able to hold, advises Telephone Doctor Nancy Friedman. She helps companies improve their employees' telephone skills. One phrase she prohibits is "I don't know." It's better to say, "I'll find out." She also recommends that people smile before they answer the phone. That prevents "emotional leakage," taking personal frustration out on a caller.

- **Be cheerful and accurate.** Let your voice show the same kind of animation that you radiate when you greet people in person. In your mind try to envision the individual answering the telephone. A smile can certainly affect the tone of your voice, so smile at that person. Keep your voice and throat relaxed by keeping your head straight. Don't squeeze the phone between your shoulder and your ear. Moreover, be accurate about what you say. *Hang on a second; I'll be right back* rarely is true. It's better to say, *It may take me two or three minutes to get that information. Would you prefer to hold or have me call you back?*

Making productive telephone calls means planning an agenda, identifying the purpose, being courteous and cheerful, and avoiding rambling.

- **Bring it to a close.** The responsibility for ending a call lies with the caller. This is sometimes difficult to do if the other person rambles on. You may need to use suggestive closing language, such as the following: (1) *I've certainly enjoyed talking with you,* (2) *I've learned what I needed to know, and now I can proceed with my work,* (3) *Thanks for your help,* (4) *I must go now, but may I call you again in the future if I need . . . ?* or (5) *Should we talk again in a few weeks?*
- **Avoid telephone tag.** If you call someone who's not in, ask when it would be best for you to call again. State that you will call at a specific time—and do it. If you ask a person to call you, give a time when you can be reached—and then be sure you are in at that time.
- **Leave complete voice mail messages.** Remember that there's no rush when you leave a voice mail message. Always enunciate clearly. And be sure to provide a complete message, including your name, telephone number, and the time and date of your call. Explain your purpose so that the receiver can be ready with the required information when returning your call.

Receiving Telephone Calls Professionally

With a little forethought you can project a professional image and make your telephone a productive, efficient work tool. Developing good telephone manners and techniques will also reflect well on you and on your organization.

- **Identify yourself immediately.** In answering your telephone or someone else's, provide your name, title or affiliation, and, possibly, a greeting. For example, *Larry Lopez, Proteus Software. How may I help you?* Force yourself to speak

Photo: Courtesy of Nancy Friedman, President, Telephone Doctor, Customer Service Trainer

clearly and slowly. Remember that the caller may be unfamiliar with what you are saying and fail to recognize slurred syllables.

Receiving productive telephone calls means identifying oneself, acting responsive, being helpful, and taking accurate messages.

- **Be responsive and helpful.** If you are in a support role, be sympathetic to callers' needs. Instead of *I don't know,* try *That's a good question; let me investigate.* Instead of *We can't do that,* try *That's a tough one; let's see what we can do.* Avoid *No* at the beginning of a sentence. It sounds especially abrasive and displeasing because it suggests total rejection.
- **Practice telephone confidentiality.** When answering calls for others, be courteous and helpful, but don't give out confidential information. Better to say, *She's away from her desk* or *He's out of the office* than to report a colleague's exact whereabouts. Also be tight lipped about sharing company information with strangers. Security experts insist that employees answering telephones must become guardians of company information.[14]
- **Take messages carefully.** Few things are as frustrating as receiving a potentially important phone message that is illegible. Repeat the spelling of names and verify telephone numbers. Write messages legibly and record their time and date. Promise to give the messages to intended recipients, but don't guarantee return calls.
- **Explain what you're doing when transferring calls.** Give a reason for transferring, and identify the extension to which you are directing the call in case the caller is disconnected.

Making the Best Use of Voice Mail

Voice mail eliminates telephone tag, inaccurate message-taking, and time-zone barriers; it also allows communicators to focus on essentials.

Because telephone calls can be disruptive, many businesspeople are making extensive use of voice mail to intercept and screen incoming calls. Voice mail links a telephone system to a computer that digitizes and stores incoming messages. Some systems also provide functions such as automated attendant menus, allowing callers to reach any associated extension by pushing specific buttons on a touch-tone telephone.

Voice mail is quite efficient for message storage. Because as many as half of all business calls require no discussion or feedback, the messaging capabilities of voice mail can mean huge savings for businesses. Incoming information is delivered without interrupting potential receivers and without all the niceties that most two-way conversations require. Stripped of superfluous chitchat, voice mail messages allow communicators to focus on essentials. Voice mail also eliminates telephone tag, inaccurate message-taking, and time-zone barriers.

However, voice mail should not be overused. Individuals who screen all incoming calls cause irritation, resentment, and needless telephone tag. Here are some ways to make voice mail work most effectively for you:

- **Announce your voice mail.** If you rely principally on a voice mail message system, identify it on your business stationery and cards. Then, when people call, they will be ready to leave a message.
- **Prepare a warm and informative greeting.** Make your mechanical greeting sound warm and inviting, both in tone and content. Identify yourself and your organization so that callers know they have reached the right number. Thank the caller and briefly explain that you are unavailable. Invite the caller to leave a message or, if appropriate, call back. Here's a typical voice mail greeting: *Hi! This is Larry Lopez of Proteus Software, and I appreciate your call. You've reached my voice mailbox because I'm either working with customers or talking on another line at the moment. Please leave your name, number, and reason for calling so that I can be prepared when I return your call.* Give callers an idea of when you will be available, such as *I'll be back at 2:30* or *I'll be out of my office until*

tech talk

Making Effective Conference Calls

Teleconferencing allows participants to participate in a group telephone call. However, conference calls cannot replicate the experience of meeting in person. Participants, therefore, need to make the most of this communication medium by *capitalizing* on its efficiencies and *compensating* for the lack of face-to-face interactions. The guidelines that follow will help you accomplish both of these goals.

As a conference leader, you should do the following:

- Choose equipment that provides excellent audio quality and user-friendly features.
- Select carefully who should be invited to participate.
- Establish a clear list of desired outcomes.
- Create and distribute an agenda. Include directions for dialing into the call and attach visual aids that are numbered for easy reference during the call.
- Greet participants as they "check in," engaging in small talk those who are waiting until everyone is online.
- Encourage the silent members to participate.
- Poll each member each time a decision point is reached.
- Acknowledge when an issue cannot be resolved during that call or when it may require a second call or a different medium to resolve.
- Review conclusions reached and assignments made, and end the call on a positive note.
- Prepare and send out immediately the to-do list with the deadlines and designees.
- Request feedback on how to improve future conference calls.

As a conference participant, you should do the following:

- Compensate for the shortcomings of this medium by (1) weighing carefully what you say and how you say it and (2) listening with concentration and focus.
- Place your call in a quiet room to minimize the interference of background noise.
- Identify yourself each time you speak.
- Remember that communication is two-way and that this medium requires extra effort to make that happen.

Career Application

Interview two or three professional businesspeople and ask them questions such as the following: How many conference calls, Web conferences, and videoconferences have you participated in during the past year? How effective were these conferences compared with face-to-face meetings? What suggestions do you have for improving conferencing effectiveness? Be prepared to share your interviewees' responses with the rest of your class.

Wednesday, May 20. If you screen your calls as a time-management technique, try this message: *I'm not near my phone right now, but I should be able to return calls after 3:30.*

- **Test your message.** Call your number and assess your message. Does it sound inviting? Sincere? Understandable? Are you pleased with your tone? If not, says one consultant, have someone else, perhaps a professional, record a message for you.

Getting Together Through Remote Conferencing

Tightened airport security and trimmed travel budgets have created a boon for remote conferencing. As you learned in Chapter 2, collaborative technology can take many forms. It typically uses three media alone or in combination: (1) Participants in *teleconferences,* also known as *conference calls,* communicate by telephone. (2) Participants in *Web conferences* are linked by their Web browsers and can view presentations, documents, and live or recorded video. They usually talk to one another by

PROCESS TO PRODUCT

Applying Your Skills at Walt Disney Imagineering

WHEN HE WAS a lead show producer at Walt Disney Imagineering, Jon Georges developed new ideas for theme park attractions. He and other members of Imagineering teams were constantly doing research to gather ideas for new projects or for fleshing out current ideas. Staff members also kept track of what others were doing in the area of themed environments. How are other parks attracting big crowds? What's happening in Las Vegas? What kind of new themed restaurants are opening—and closing? Imagineering teams "benchmark" (compare) their efforts against those of similar developers of entertainment concepts.

Your Task

Jon Georges asks you and other Imagineering interns to research and locate one or two current theme park innovations or trends. Prepare an outline of your findings. Then use the outline as the basis for creating a PowerPoint presentation that you will use to inform Jon of your findings. ■

case study

Many face-to-face meetings are being replaced with remote conferences; options include teleconferences, Web conferences, and videoconferences.

telephone. (3) Participants in *videoconferences* see live images carried over digital telephone networks or the Internet.

Those using these remote conferencing options are quick to point out the benefits and drawbacks of staying at the office instead of traveling. Benefits include saving time and money, increasing productivity, avoiding airport hassles, and having more time at home with families. Drawbacks include untimely technology breakdowns, fewer opportunities to build relationships, and limitations in gauging audience reactions and body language.

Of the three remote-conferencing options, teleconferencing is the most widely used. Two thirds of the conferencing industry's annual revenues of roughly $4 billion are attributed to conference calls.[15] These calls are the easiest to coordinate and require the least expense related to equipment and preparation time. The Tech Talk box on page 529 provides suggestions for helping you be comfortable and effective when you must participate in conference calls.

Summary of Learning Objectives

1 **Discuss two important first steps in preparing effective oral presentations.** First, identify what your purpose is and what you want the audience to believe or do so that you can aim the entire presentation toward your goal. Second, know your audience so that you can adjust your message and style to its knowledge and needs.

2 **Explain the major elements in organizing the content of a presentation, including the introduction, body, and conclusion.** The introduction of a good presentation should capture the listener's attention, identify the speaker, establish credibility, and preview the main points. The body should discuss two to four main points, with appropriate explanations, details, and verbal signposts to guide listeners. The conclusion should review the main points, provide a final focus, and allow the speaker to leave the podium gracefully.

3 **Identify techniques for gaining audience rapport, including using effective imagery, providing verbal signposts, and sending appropriate nonverbal messages.** You can improve audience rapport by using effective imagery including analogies, metaphors, similes, personal anecdotes, statistics, and worst/best-case scenarios. Rapport is also gained by including verbal signposts that tell the audience when you are previewing, summarizing, and switching directions. Nonverbal messages have a powerful effect on the way your message is received. You should look terrific, animate your body, punctuate your words, get out from behind the podium, and vary your facial expressions.

4 **Discuss designing and using effective visual aids, handouts, and multimedia presentation materials.** Use simple, easily understood visual aids to emphasize and clarify main points. Choose multimedia slides, transparencies, flipcharts, or other visuals. Generally, it's best to distribute handouts after a presentation. Speakers employing a program such as PowerPoint use templates, layout designs, and bullet points to produce effective slides. A presentation may be enhanced with slide transitions, sound, animation, video elements, and other multimedia effects. Speaker's notes and handouts may be generated from slides.

5 **Specify delivery techniques for use before, during, and after a presentation.** Before your talk prepare a sentence outline on note cards or speaker's notes and rehearse repeatedly. Check the room, lectern, and equipment. During the presentation consider beginning with a pause and presenting your first sentence from memory. Make eye contact, control your voice, speak and move naturally, and avoid digressions. After your talk distribute handouts and answer questions. End gracefully and express appreciation.

6 **Explain effective techniques for adapting oral presentations to cross-cultural audiences.** In presentations before groups whose English is limited, speak slowly, use simple English, avoid jargon and clichés, and use short sentences. Consider building up to your main idea rather than announcing it immediately. Also consider breaking the presentation into short segments to allow participants to ask questions and digest small parts separately. Beware of appearing too spontaneous and informal. Use visual aids to help communicate your message, but also distribute translated handouts summarizing the most important information.

7 **List techniques for improving telephone, voice mail, and remote conferencing effectiveness.** You can improve your telephone calls by planning a mini-agenda and using a three-point introduction (name, affiliation, and purpose). Be cheerful and responsive, and use closing language to end a conversation. Avoid telephone tag by leaving complete messages. In answering calls, identify yourself immediately, avoid giving out confidential information when answering for others, and take careful messages. In setting up an automated-attendance voice mail menu, limit the number of choices. For your own message prepare a warm and informative greeting. Tell when you will be available. Evaluate your message by calling it yourself. Remote conferencing uses three media alone or in combination: *teleconferencing*, *Web conferencing*, and *videoconferencing*. Teleconferencing is the most widely used remote conferencing option.

chapter review

1. In preparing an oral presentation, you can reduce your fears and lay a foundation for a professional performance by focusing on what five areas? (Obj. 1)
2. In the introduction of an oral presentation, you can establish your credibility by using what two methods? (Obj. 2)
3. For a 20-minute presentation, how many main points should be developed? (Obj. 2)
4. Which part of a speech—the introduction, body, or conclusion—will listeners most remember? (Obj. 2)
5. List six techniques for creating effective imagery in a presentation. Be prepared to discuss each. (Obj. 3)
6. Name three ways for a speaker to use verbal signposts in a presentation. Illustrate each. (Obj. 3)
7. Why are visual aids particularly useful to inexperienced speakers? (Obj. 4)
8. Why are transparencies a favorite visual aid? (Obj. 4)
9. Name specific advantages and disadvantages of multimedia presentation software. (Obj. 4)
10. How is the Rule of Seven applied in preparing bulleted points? (Obj. 4)
11. What delivery method is most effective for speakers? (Obj. 5)
12. Why should speakers deliver the first sentence from memory? (Obj. 5)
13. How might presentations before international or cross-cultural audiences be altered to be most effective? (Obj. 6)
14. What is a three-point introduction for a telephone call? (Obj. 7)
15. Name two benefits and two drawbacks to remote conferencing. (Obj. 7)

critical thinking

1. Why is it necessary to repeat key points in an oral presentation? (Objs. 2 and 5)
2. How can a speaker make the most effective use of visual aids? (Obj. 4)
3. How can speakers prevent multimedia presentation software from stealing their thunder? (Obj. 4)
4. Discuss effective techniques for reducing stage fright. (Obj. 5)
5. **Ethical Issue:** Critics of PowerPoint claim that flashy graphics, sound effects, and animation often conceal thin content. Consider, for example, the findings regarding the space shuttle *Challenger* accident that killed seven astronauts. Report authors charged that NASA scientists had used PowerPoint presentations to make it look as though they had done analyses that they hadn't. Overreliance on presentations instead of analysis may have contributed to the shuttle disaster.[16] What lessons about ethical responsibilities when using PowerPoint can be learned from this catastrophe in communication? (Objs. 1, 2, and 4)

THREE GREAT RESOURCES FOR YOU!

1. ***Guffey Student Web Site***
http://guffey.swlearning.com
Your companion Web site offers chapter review quizzes, WebThink activities, updated chapter URLs, and many additional resources.

2. ***Guffey XTRA!***
http://guffeyxtra.swlearning.com
This online study assistant includes Your Personal Language Trainer, Speak Right!, Spell Right!, bonus online chapters, Documents for Analysis, PowerPoint slides, and much more.

3. ***Student Study Guide***
Self-checked workbook activities and applications review chapter concepts and develop career skills.

activities

15.1 Critiquing a Speech (Objs. 1–4)

Your Task. Search online or your library for a speech that has been delivered by a significant businessperson or a well-known political figure. Write a memo report to your instructor critiquing the speech in terms of the following:

a. Effectiveness of the introduction, body, and conclusion
b. Evidence of effective overall organization
c. Use of verbal signposts to create coherence
d. Emphasis of two to four main points
e. Effectiveness of supporting facts (use of examples, statistics, quotations, and so forth)

15.2 Knowing Your Audience (Objs. 1–2)

Your Task. Select a recent issue of *Fortune, Business 2.0, Fast Company, BusinessWeek,* or another business periodical approved by your instructor. Based on your analysis of your classmates, select an article that will appeal to them and that you can relate to their needs. Submit to your instructor a one-page summary that includes the following: (a) author,

article title, source, issue date, and page reference; (b) one-paragraph article summary; (c) a description of why you believe the article will appeal to your classmates; and (d) a summary of how you can relate the article to their needs.

15.3 Overcoming Stage Fright (Obj. 5)

What makes you most nervous when making a presentation before class? Being tongue-tied? Fearing all eyes on you? Messing up? Forgetting your ideas and looking silly?
Your Task. Discuss the previous questions as a class. Then, in groups of three or four talk about ways to overcome these fears. Your instructor may ask you to write a memo (individual or collective) summarizing your suggestions, or you may break out of your small groups and report your best ideas to the entire class.

15.4 Outlining an Oral Presentation (Objs. 1 and 2)

One of the hardest parts of preparing an oral presentation is developing the outline.
Your Task. Select an oral presentation topic from the list in Activity 15.8 or suggest an original topic. Prepare an outline for your presentation using the following format.

Title	
Purpose	
	I. INTRODUCTION
Gain attention of audience	A.
Involve audience	B.
Establish credibility	C.
Preview main points	D.
Transition	
	II. BODY
Main point	A.
Illustrate, clarify, contrast	1.
	2.
	3.
Transition	
Main point	B.
Illustrate, clarify, contrast	1.
	2.
	3.
Transition	
Main point	C.
Illustrate, clarify, contrast	1.
	2.
	3.
Transition	
	III. CONCLUSION
Summarize main points	A.
Provide final focus	B.
Encourage questions	C.

15.5 Investigating Oral Communication in Your Field (Objs. 1 and 5)

Your Task. Interview one or two individuals in your professional field. How is oral communication important in this profession? Does the need for oral skills change as one advances? What suggestions can these people make to newcomers to the field for developing proficient oral communication skills? Discuss your findings with your class.

15.6. Exploring the New World of Web Conferencing (Obj. 2–5)

INFOTRAC | LISTENING | SPEAKING | WEB

Your boss at the Home Realty Company is interested in learning more about Web conferencing but doesn't have time to do the research herself. She asks you to find out the following:

a. In terms of revenue, how big is the Web conferencing industry?
b. Who are the leading providers of Web conferencing tools?
c. What are the typical costs associated with holding a Web conference?
d. How are other realtors using Web conferencing?

Your Task. Using InfoTrac and the Internet, locate articles and Web sites that will provide the information your boss has outlined. Be prepared to role-play an informal presentation to your boss in which you begin with an introduction, answer the four questions in the body, and present a conclusion.

15.7 Researching *Fortune* List Information (Objs. 1–5)

INFOTRAC

Your Task. Using InfoTrac, perform a search to learn how *Fortune* magazine determines which companies make its annual lists. Research the following lists. Then organize and present a five- to ten-minute informative talk to your class.

a. Fortune 500
b. Global 500
c. 100 Best Companies to Work For
d. America's Most Admired Companies
e. Global Most Admired Companies

15.8 Choosing a Topic for an Oral Presentation (Objs. 1–5)

Your Task. Select a topic from the following list or from the report topics at the end of Chapters 13 and 14. For an expanded list of report topics, look at **Guffey Xtra! <http://guffeyxtra.swlearning.com>**. Prepare a five- to ten-minute oral presentation. Consider yourself an expert who has been called in to explain some aspect of the topic before a group of interested people. Because your time is limited, prepare a concise yet forceful presentation with effective visual aids.

a. What are the top five career opportunities for your college major? Consider job growth, compensation, and benefits. What kind of academic and other experience is typically required to apply for each?
b. What information and tools are available at Web job banks to college students searching for full-time employment after graduation? Consider Monster.com and other job banks.
c. How can attendance be improved in a minor sports field (your choice) at your school?
d. What simple computer security tips can your company employ to avoid problems?
e. What is telecommuting, and for what kinds of workers is it an appropriate work alternative?
f. What criteria should parents use in deciding whether their young child should attend parochial, private, public, or home school?
g. What travel location would you recommend for college students at Christmas or another holiday or in the summer?
h. What is the economic outlook for a given product, such as domestic cars, laptop computers, digital cameras, fitness equipment, or a product of your choice?
i. How can your organization or institution improve its image?
j. What are the Webby Awards, and what criteria do the judges use to evaluate Web sites?
k. What brand and model of computer and printer represent the best buy for college students today?
l. What franchise would offer the best investment opportunity for an entrepreneur in your area?
m. How should a job candidate dress for an interview?
n. What should a guide to proper cell phone use include?
o. Are internships worth the effort?
p. What risks are involved for companies without written rules for e-mail and instant messaging?
q. Where should your organization hold its next convention?
r. What is your opinion of the statement "Advertising steals our time, defaces the landscape, and degrades the dignity of public institutions"?[17]
s. What would you need to know if you were deciding whether to go to the next Olympics?
t. What is the outlook for real estate (commercial or residential) investment in your area?
u. What are the pros and cons of videoconferencing for [name an organization]?
v. What do the personal assistants for celebrities do, and how does one become a personal assistant? (Investigate the Association of Celebrity Personal Assistants.)
w. Can a small or midsized company reduce its telephone costs by using Internet phone service?
x. What scams are on the Federal Trade Commission's List of Top 10 Consumer Scams, and how can consumers avoid falling for them?
y. How are businesses and conservationists working together to protect the world's dwindling tropical forests?
z. Should employees be able to use computers in a work environment for anything other than work-related business?

15.9 Improving Telephone Skills by Role-Playing (Obj. 7)

Your Task. Your instructor will divide the class into pairs. For each scenario take a moment to read and rehearse your role silently. Then play the role with your partner. If time permits, repeat the scenarios, changing roles.

Partner 1

a. You are the personnel manager of Datatronics, Inc. Call Elizabeth Franklin, office manager at Computers Plus. Inquire about a job applicant, Chelsea Chavez, who listed Ms. Franklin as a reference.
b. Call Ms. Franklin again the following day to inquire about the same job applicant, Chelsea Chavez. Ms. Franklin answers today, but she talks on and on, describing the applicant in great detail. Tactfully close the conversation.
c. You are now the receptionist for Tom Wing, of Wing Imports. Answer a call for Mr. Wing, who is working in another office, at Extension 134, where he will accept calls.
d. You are now Tom Wing, owner of Wing Imports. Call your attorney, Michael Murphy, about a legal problem. Leave a brief, incomplete message.
e. Call Mr. Murphy again. Leave a message that will prevent telephone tag.

Partner 2

a. You are the receptionist for Computers Plus. The caller asks for Elizabeth Franklin, who is home sick today. You don't know when she will be able to return. Answer the call appropriately.
b. You are now Ms. Franklin, office manager. Describe Chelsea Chavez, an imaginary employee. Think of someone with whom you've worked. Include many details, such as her ability to work with others, her appearance, her skills at computing, her schooling, her ambition, and so forth.
c. You are now an administrative assistant for attorney Michael Murphy. Call Tom Wing to verify a meeting date Mr. Murphy has with Mr. Wing. Use your own name in identifying yourself.
d. You are now the receptionist for attorney Michael Murphy. Mr. Murphy is skiing in Aspen and will return in two days, but he doesn't want his clients to know where he is. Take a message.
e. Take a message again.

Rich chapter resources are available on the Web sites.

video resources

Video Library 1: *Building Workplace Skills*

Effective On-the-Job Oral Presentations

Watch this video to see how businesspeople apply Guffey's 3-x-3 writing process in developing a persuasive oral presentation.

C.L.U.E. review 15

On a separate sheet edit the following sentences to correct faults in grammar, punctuation, spelling, and word use.

1. Even though he was President of the company Mr Thomas dreaded the 2 or 3 presentations he made everyyear.
2. The companies CPA asked my colleague and I to explain the principle ways we planned to finance it's thirty year mortgage?
3. My team and I are greatful to be able to give a twenty minute presentation however we can emphasize only 3 or 4 major point.
4. The Introduction to a presentation should accomplish 3 goals (a) Capture attention, (b) Establish credibility and (c) Preview main points.
5. Travis wondered whether focusing on what you want the audience to remember, and summarizing you're main points was equally important in the Conclusion?
6. Speakers must remember that there listeners unlike readers' can not controll the rate of presentation, or flip back thorough pages to review main points.
7. Most novice speakers talk to rapidly, however they can learn to speak more slow, and listen to what they are saying.
8. When speakers first approach the audience they should take a moment to adjust there notes, and make yourself comfortable.
9. One West coast company found that, telephone interruptions consumed about eighteen percent of staff members workdays.
10. Good telephone manners reflect on you and you're company however to few employees are trained proper.

15.10 Consumer: Will Maxing Out My Credit Cards Improve My Credit Rating?

CONSUMER | INFOTRAC | WEB

The program chair for the campus business club has asked you to present a talk to the group about consumer credit. He saw a newspaper article saying that only 10 percent of Americans know their credit scores. Many consumers, including students, have dangerous misconceptions about their scores. Not knowing your score could result in denial of credit as well as difficulty obtaining needed services and even a job. ***Your Task.*** Using InfoTrac and the Web, learn more about credit scores and typical misconceptions. For example, is a higher or lower credit score better? Can you improve your credit score by marrying well? If you earn more money, will you improve your score? If you have a low score, is it impossible to raise it? Can you raise your score by maxing out all your credit cards? (One survey reported that 28 percent of consumers believed the latter statement was true!) Prepare an oral presentation appropriate for a student audience. Conclude with appropriate recommendations.

chapter 16

Employment Communication

objectives

1 Prepare for employment by identifying your interests, evaluating your assets, recognizing the changing nature of jobs, choosing a career path, and studying traditional and electronic job-search techniques.

2 Compare and contrast chronological, functional, and combination résumés.

3 Organize, format, and produce a persuasive résumé.

4 Describe techniques that optimize a résumé for today's technologies, including preparing a scannable résumé, an inline résumé, and an e-portfolio.

5 Write a persuasive cover letter to accompany a résumé.

6 Write effective employment follow-up letters and other messages.

7 Evaluate successful job interview strategies.

COMMUNICATION IN PROCESS

Carnival Captures Cruise Market and Job Applicants

CARNIVAL CRUISE LINES, "The Most Popular Cruise Line in the World," just keeps growing and growing. After its debut in 1972 with one ship, Carnival launched increasingly larger and more luxurious ships. It currently has 15 "Fun Ships," many of which entertain up to 3,000 guests. The new "mega-liners" are floating palaces where guests enjoy multidecked glass atriums, marble-topped bars, Venetian-glass sculptures, a variety of dining options, spas, casinos, discos, jazz clubs, Las Vegas style entertainment, video arcades, bountiful buffets, and even Internet cafes with access to e-mail and Web sites.

In recent years Carnival has essentially reinvented all aspects of its Fun Ship cruise experience while continually striving to deliver the best "bang for the buck" in the industry. Firmly rooted in Miami, Carnival is one of the area's largest employers. Just as guests eagerly sign up for cruise vacations, job applicants flock to fill its shoreside staff openings.

Carnival recruiting specialist Bonnie Gesualdi-Chao and her department have examined between 12,000 and 13,000 résumés annually. Most of these résumés are generated by newspaper advertisements or by referrals made by employees, travel and tourism schools, colleges, and universities. Bonnie Gesualdi-Chao's primary task was recruiting employees for positions in the call center, which received thousands of daily telephone inquiries regarding cruise options. Many Carnival managers start in call center positions because these jobs are a good way to get to know the company.

Looking over thousands of résumés taught Bonnie some quick scanning techniques. She read each one-page résumé rapidly looking for education, skills, and experience. She was not interested in job descriptions. She wanted to see results. What did the applicant accomplish in a previous job, internship, or course work? How did those accomplishments equip the candidate for a Carnival job? A well-written résumé tailored to a specific opening immediately caught Bonnie's attention. She was also impressed by applicants who had done their homework and showed that they knew something about Carnival.[1]

The résumés of job applicants at Carnival Cruise Lines must be in ship shape to stand out.

Critical Thinking

- In applying for a job, why must you investigate carefully any company in which you are interested?
- Why do you think recruiters are more interested in an applicant's education, skills, and experience than in job descriptions from previous positions?
- Since recruiters glance over résumés quickly, how can an applicant make a résumé stand out?

http://www.carnival.com

CONTINUED ON PAGE 560

case study

learning objective

1

Finding a satisfying career means learning about oneself, the job market, and the employment process.

Preparing for Employment

One day you may be sending your résumé to a recruiting specialist such as Bonnie Gesualdi-Chao, who reads thousands of such résumés annually. What can you do to make your résumé and cover letter stand out? This chapter provides many tips for writing dynamite résumés and cover letters, as well as suggestions for successful interviewing. But the job-search process actually begins long before you are ready to write a résumé. Whether you are looking for an internship, applying for a full-time position, searching for a part-time job, competing for a promotion, or changing careers, you must invest time and effort preparing yourself. You can't hope to find the position of your dreams without first (1) knowing yourself, (2) knowing the job market, and (3) knowing the employment process.

One of the first things you should do is obtain career information and choose a specific job objective. At the same time, you should be studying the job market and becoming aware of substantial changes in the nature of work. You'll want to understand how to use the latest Internet resources in your job search. Finally, you'll need to design a persuasive résumé and cover letter appropriate for small businesses as well as for larger organizations that may be using résumé-scanning programs. Following these steps, summarized in Figure 16.1 and described in this chapter, gives you a master plan for landing a job you really want.

Identifying Your Interests

The employment process begins with introspection. This means looking inside yourself to analyze what you like and dislike so that you can make good employment choices. Career counselors charge large sums for helping individuals learn about themselves. You can do the same kind of self-examination—without spending a

FIGURE 16.1 ***The Employment Search***

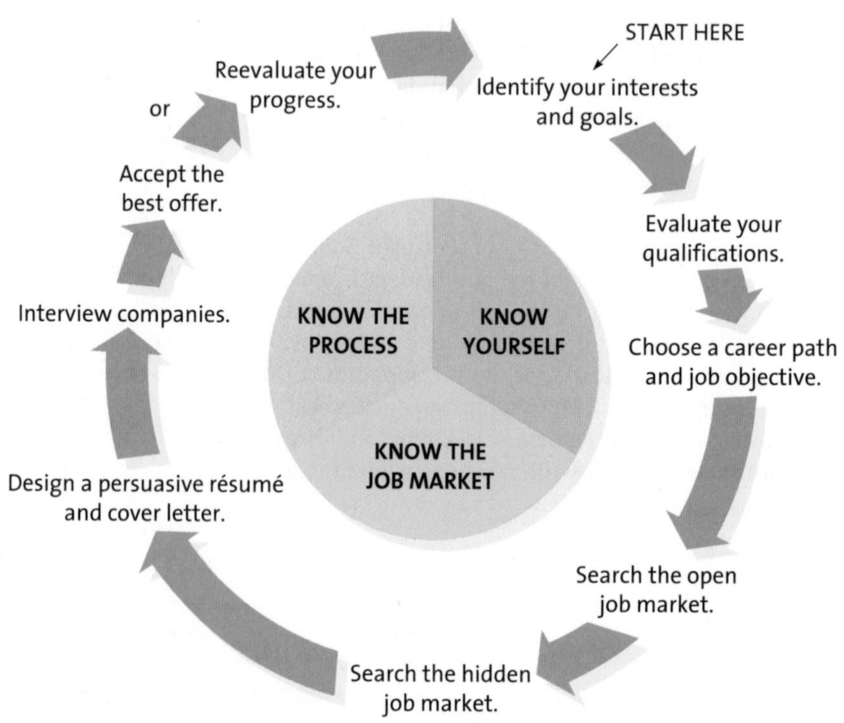

dime. For guidance in choosing a field that eventually proves to be satisfying, answer the following questions. If you have already chosen a field, think carefully about how your answers relate to that choice.

Answer specific questions to help yourself choose a career.

- *Do I enjoy working with people, data, or things?*
- *How important is it to be my own boss?*
- *How important are salary, benefits, technology support, and job stability?*
- *How important are working environment, colleagues, and job stimulation?*
- *Would I rather work for a large or small company?*
- *Must I work in a specific city, geographical area, or climate?*
- *Am I looking for security, travel opportunities, money, power, or prestige?*
- *How would I describe the perfect job, boss, and coworkers?*

Evaluating Your Qualifications

In addition to your interests, assess your qualifications. Employers today want to know what assets you have to offer them. Your responses to the following questions will target your thinking as well as prepare a foundation for your résumé. Remember, though, that employers seek more than empty assurances; they will want proof of your qualifications.

Decide what qualifications you possess and how you can prove them.

- *What computer skills can I offer?* Employers are often interested in specific software programs.
- *What other skills have I acquired in school, on the job, or through activities?* How can you demonstrate these skills?
- *Do I work well with people? Do I enjoy teamwork?* What proof can you offer? Consider extracurricular activities, clubs, class projects, and jobs.
- *Am I a leader, self-starter, or manager?* What evidence can you offer?
- *Do I speak, write, or understand another language?*
- *Do I learn quickly? Am I creative?* How can you demonstrate these characteristics?
- *Do I communicate well in speech and in writing?* How can you verify these talents?

spotlight *on communicators*

Computer mogul Michael Dell says that he learned one lesson early: Don't hire someone based on the company's immediate job needs. Because the nature of jobs is changing constantly, Dell prefers to hire a candidate based on that person's potential to grow and develop. Dell started his computer company in his University of Texas dorm room with $1,000 in capital in 1983. He now oversees a thriving company that currently ranks No. 6 on Fortune *magazine's Global "Most Admired" list. He was the youngest CEO of a company ever to earn a* Fortune *500 ranking.*

Recognizing the Changing Nature of Jobs

As you learned in Chapter 1, the nature of the workplace is changing. One of the most significant changes involves the concept of the "job." Following the downsizing of corporations and the offshoring of jobs in recent years, companies are employing fewer people in permanent positions.

People feel less job security after downsizing and offshoring of jobs.

Other forms of employment are replacing traditional jobs. In many companies teams complete special projects and then disband. Work may also be outsourced to a group that's not even part of an organization. Because new technologies can spring up overnight making today's skills obsolete, employers are less willing to hire people into jobs with narrow descriptions. Instead, they are hiring contingency employees who work temporarily and then leave. What's more, big companies are no longer the main employers. People work for smaller companies, or they are starting their own businesses. By 2020 small, privately owned companies are expected to comprise 25 percent of U.S. businesses.[2]

Photo: © AP/Wide World Photos

"Jobs" are becoming more flexible and less permanent.

What do these changes mean for you? For one thing, you should probably forget about a lifelong career with a single company. Don't count on regular pay raises, promotions, and a comfortable retirement income. You should also become keenly aware that a career that relies on yesterday's skills is headed for trouble. You're going to need updated, marketable skills that serve you well as you move from job to job. Upgrading your skills and retraining yourself constantly is the best career strategy for the twenty-first century. People who learn quickly and adapt to change will always be in demand even in a climate of surging change.[3]

Chosing a Career Path

Career information can be obtained at campus career centers and libraries, from the Internet, in classified ads, and from professional organizations.

The employment picture today is much different from that of a decade or two ago. By the time you are 30, you can expect to have had five to seven jobs. The average employee will have worked at 12 to 15 jobs over the course of a career, staying an average of 3.6 years at each job.[4] Some of you probably have not yet settled on your first career choice; others are returning to college to retrain for a new career. Although you may be changing jobs in the future, you still need to train for a specific career area now. In choosing an area, you'll make the best decisions when you can match your interests and qualifications with the requirements and rewards in specific careers. Where can you find the best career data? Here are some suggestions:

- **Visit your campus career center.** Most have literature, inventories, software programs, and Internet connections that allow you to investigate such fields as accounting, finance, office technology, information systems, hotel management, and so forth.
- **Search the Web.** Many job-search sites on the Web offer career-planning information and resources. You'll learn about some of the best sites in the following discussion.
- **Use your library.** Many print and online resources are especially helpful. Consult *O*NET Occupational Information Network, Dictionary of Occupational Titles, Occupational Outlook Handbook,* and *The Jobs Rated Almanac* for information about career duties, qualifications, salaries, and employment trends.

Summer and part-time jobs and internships are good opportunities to learn about different careers.

- **Take a summer job, internship, or part-time position in your field.** Nothing is better than trying out a career by actually working in it or an allied area. Many companies offer internships and temporary jobs to begin training college students and to develop relationships with them. These relationships sometimes blossom into permanent positions. Jon Georges, spotlighted in Chapter 15, commuted 90 minutes each way to work at Disneyland while in high school and college. That tenacity undoubtedly helped his résumé stand out from the hundreds that Disney Imagineering received.
- **Interview someone in your chosen field.** People are usually flattered when asked to describe their careers. Inquire about needed skills, required courses, financial and other rewards, benefits, working conditions, future trends, and entry requirements.
- **Monitor the classified ads.** Early in your college career, begin monitoring want ads and Web sites of companies in your career area. Check job availability, qualifications sought, duties, and salary range. Don't wait until you're about to graduate to see how the job market looks.
- **Join professional organizations in your field.** Frequently, professional groups offer student membership status and reduced rates. You'll get inside information on issues, career news, and possibly jobs.

Figure 16.2 ***Job Boards Jump Start a Job Search***

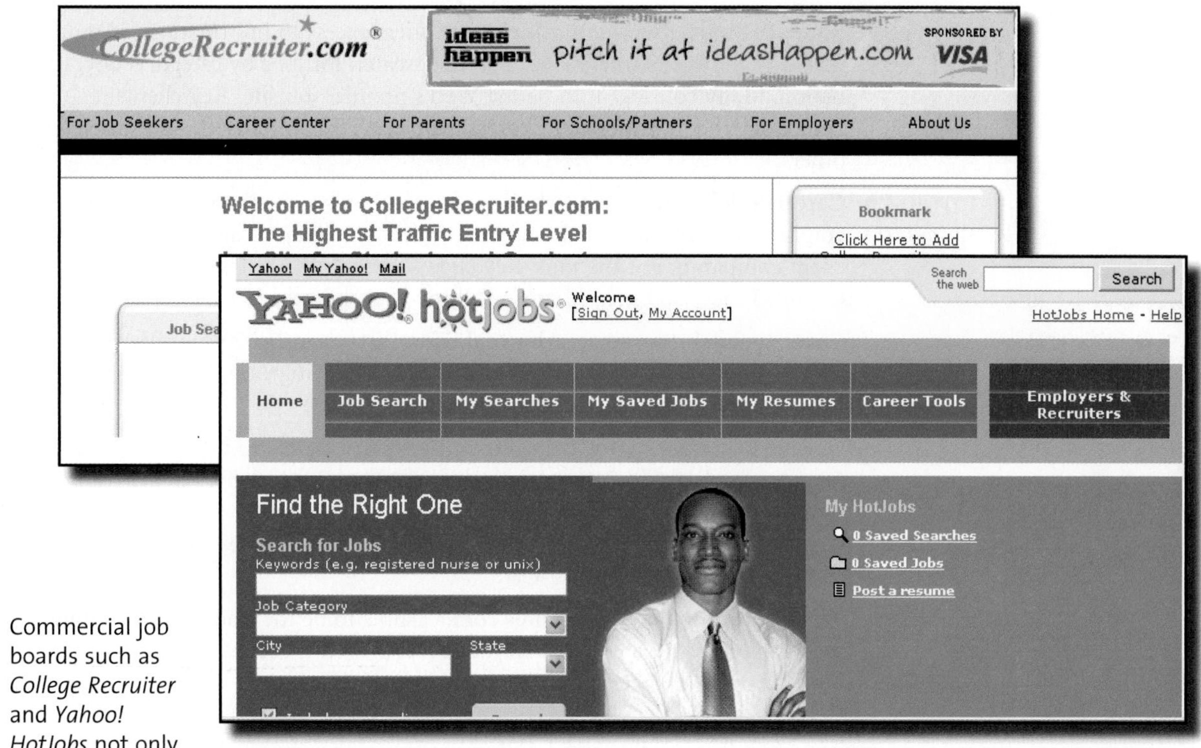

Commercial job boards such as *College Recruiter* and *Yahoo! HotJobs* not only list millions of job openings but also provide excellent tips for conducting job searches, writing résumés, organizing cover letters, and preparing for job interviews.

Searching for a Job Electronically

Job boards list many jobs, but finding a job electronically requires more work than merely clicking a mouse.

Another significant change in the workplace involves the way we find jobs. Searching for a job electronically has become a common, but not always fruitful, approach. With all the publicity given to Internet job boards, you might think that electronic job searching has totally replaced traditional methods. Not so! Although Web sites such as *CollegeRecruiter.com* <**http://www.collegerecruiter.com**> and *Yahoo! HotJobs* <**http://hotjobs.yahoo.com**>, shown in Figure 16.2, list millions of jobs, actually landing a job is much harder than just clicking a mouse.

Job searches conducted solely online may not produce jobs.

Both recruiters and job seekers complain about job boards. Corporate recruiters say that the big job boards bring a flood of candidates, many of whom are not suited for the listed jobs. Job candidates grumble that listings are frequently out-of-date and fail to produce leads. Applicants worry about the privacy of information posted at big boards. Most important, studies have shown that the percentage of hires resulting from job boards is astonishingly low—1.4 percent at Monster.com, 0.39 percent at HotJobs.com, and 0.27 percent at CareerBuilder.[5] The truth is that job hunts conducted solely online rarely produce jobs.[6]

Despite these gloomy prospects, many job seekers use job boards to gather job-search information, such as résumé, interviewing, and salary tips. Job boards serve as a jumping-off point in most searches. And, who knows—you might get lucky and be hired for the job of your dreams from an online site. With over 40,000 job boards

The best-known job boards provide job-search, résumé, interviewing, and salary tips.

and employment Web sites deluging the Internet, it's hard to know where to start. We've listed a few of the best-known online job sites here:[7]

- **Monster Board <www.monster.com>** offers access to information on more than 1 million jobs worldwide. You may search for jobs by category, city, or nation. Many consider it to be the Web's premier job site. Key clients include FedEx, Raytheon, American Express, Apple, AT&T, Microsoft, Starbucks, and others.
- **CareerBuilder <www.careerbuilder.com>** claims to be the nation's largest employment network. At this writing it lists 225,000 jobs and has over 100,000 client companies posting jobs. Key clients include IKEA, U.S. Air Force, Canon, Tenet, Gap Inc., Microsoft, Firestone, and others.
- **CareerJournal <www.careerjournal.com>** lists over 75,000 executive positions from over 10,000 companies. Key clients include Citigroup, UBS, Merrill Lynch, Charles Schwab, Edward Jones, and Allstate.
- **College Recruiter <www.collegerecruiter.com>** claims to be the "highest traffic entry-level job site" for students and graduates. It lists over 60,000 jobs from more than 5,000 client companies such as Air National Guard, Army National Guard, Central Intelligence Agency, Wells Fargo, T-Mobile, RadioShack, U.S. Navy, and Enterprise Rent-a-Car.
- **Yahoo! Hot Jobs <www.hotjobs.com>** claims to be the leader in the online recruiting industry and says that job seekers voted it the "Best General Purpose Job Board for Job Seekers."

Beyond the Big Job Boards. Disillusioned job seekers increasingly turn their backs on job boards but not on electronic job-searching tactics. Savvy candidates know how to use their computers to search for jobs at Web sites such as the following:

Job prospects may be more promising at the Web sites of corporations, professional organizations, employers' organizations, and niche fields.

- **Corporate Web sites.** Probably the best way to find a job online is at a company's own Web site. One poll found that 70 percent of job seekers felt they were more likely to obtain an interview if they posted their résumés on corporate sites. In addition to finding a more direct route to decision makers, job seekers thought that they could keep their job searches more private than at big board sites.[8]
- **Association Web sites.** Online job listings have proved to be the single-most popular feature of many professional organizations such as the National Association of Sales Professionals, the Association for Financial Professionals, and the American Chemical Society. Although you pay a fee, the benefits of joining a professional association in your career field are enormous.
- **DirectEmployers.com.** Several hundred companies now use *DirectEmployers.com* as a gateway to job listings at their own Web sites. This search engine combs over 1,100 corporate sites and links job seekers directly to them, thus bypassing the big commercial job boards. You can enter a job description or job title, and a list of openings pops up. When you click one, you're taken straight to the company's Web site, where you can apply.
- **Niche Web sites.** If you want a job in a specialized field, look for a niche Web site, such as *HealthCareerWeb.com, CareerWomen.com, SixFigureJobs.com*, and so on.

Many jobs are posted on the Internet, but most hiring is still done through personal contact.

Thousands of job boards listing millions of jobs now flood the Internet. The harsh reality, however, is that landing a job still depends largely on personal contacts. One employment expert said, "Online recruiting is a little like computer dating. People may find dates that way, but they don't get married that way."[9] Another professional placement expert said, "If you think just [posting] your résumé will get you a job, you're crazy. [Electronic services are] just a supplement to a core strategy of networking your buns off."[10]

Candidates are doing less pavement pounding and more keyboard pounding in searching for jobs today. Experts say that one third of all new-hires now come through the Internet, and the majority of those leads come from the company's own Web site. Including a referral from a company employee helps to send your résumé to the top of the pile.

Photo: Courtesy of Rubberball Productions/Getty Images

Searching for a Job Using Traditional Techniques

Finding the perfect job requires an early start and a determined effort. Whether you use traditional or online job-search techniques, you should be prepared to launch an aggressive campaign. Moreover, you can't start too early. Some universities now require first- and second-year students to take an employment seminar called "Reality 101." Students are told early on that a college degree alone doesn't guarantee a job. They are cautioned that grade-point averages make a difference to employers. They are also advised of the importance of experience, such as internships. Traditional job-search techniques, such as those described here, continue to be critical in landing jobs.

- **Check classified ads in local and national newspapers.** Be aware, though, that classified ads are only one small source of jobs, as discussed in the Career Coach box on page 544.
- **Check announcements in publications of professional organizations.** If you do not have a student membership, ask your professors to share current copies of professional journals, newsletters, and so on. Your college library is another good source.
- **Contact companies in which you're interested, even if you know of no current opening.** Write an unsolicited letter and include your résumé. Follow up with a telephone call. Check the company's Web site for employment possibilities and procedures.
- **Sign up for campus interviews with visiting company representatives.** Campus recruiters may open your eyes to exciting jobs and locations.
- **Ask for advice from your professors.** They often have contacts and ideas for expanding your job search.
- **Develop your own network of contacts.** Networking still accounts for most of the jobs found by candidates. Therefore, plan to spend a considerable portion of your job-search time developing a personal network. The accompanying Career Coach box gives you step-by-step instructions for traditional networking as well as some ideas for online networking.

The Persuasive Résumé

learning objective

2

Winning an interview is the goal of a persuasive résumé.

After using both online and traditional resources to learn about the employment market and to develop job leads, you'll focus on writing a persuasive résumé. Such a résumé does more than merely list your qualifications. It packages your assets into a convincing advertisement that sells you for a specific job. The goal of a persuasive résumé is winning an interview. Even if you are not in the job market at this moment, preparing a résumé now has advantages. Having a current résumé makes you look well organized and professional should an unexpected employment opportunity arise. Preparing a résumé early also helps you recognize weak qualifications and gives you two or three years in which to bolster them.

career coach

Network Your Way to a Job in the Hidden Market

Although many jobs appear on job boards, even more are not advertised at all. The "hidden" job market accounts for as many as 75 percent of all positions available.[11] Companies don't always announce openings publicly because it's time consuming to interview all the applicants, many of whom aren't qualified. What's more, even when a job is advertised, companies dislike hiring "strangers." They are more comfortable hiring a person they know.

Smart job seekers won't count on the Internet to land a job. *Workforce Management,* along with countless other personnel experts, admitted that "most new hires come by word of mouth and employee referrals."[12] The key to finding a good job, then, is converting yourself from a "stranger" into a known quantity. Probably the best way to become a known quantity is by networking. You can use either traditional methods or online resources.

Traditional Networking

- **Step 1: Develop a List.** Make a list of anyone who would be willing to talk with you about finding a job. List your friends, relatives, former employers, former coworkers, members of your church, people in social and athletic clubs, present and former teachers, neighbors, and friends of your parents. Also consider asking your campus career center for alumni contacts who will talk with students.
- **Step 2: Make Contacts.** Call the people on your list or, even better, try to meet with them in person. To set up a meeting, say *Hi, Aunt Martha! I'm looking for a job and I wonder if you could help me out. When could I come over to talk about it?* During your visit be friendly, well organized, polite, and interested in what your contact has to say. Provide a copy of your résumé, and try to keep the conversation centered on your job-search area. Your goal is to get two or more referrals. In pinpointing your request, ask two questions. *Do you know of anyone who might have an opening for a person with my skills?* If not, *Do you know of anyone else who might know of someone who would?*
- **Step 3: Follow Up on Your Referrals.** Call the people whose names are on your referral list. You might say something like, *Hello. I'm Carlos Ramos, a friend of Connie Cole. She suggested that I call and ask you for help. I'm looking for a position as a marketing trainee, and she thought you might be willing to spare a few minutes and steer me in the right direction.* Don't ask for a job. During your referral interview ask how the individual got started in this line of work, what he or she likes best (or least) about the work, what career paths exist in the field, and what problems must be overcome by a newcomer. Most important, ask how a person with your background and skills might get started in the field. Send an informal thank-you note to anyone who helps you in your job search, and stay in touch with the most promising contacts. Ask whether you may call every three weeks or so during your job search.

Online Networking

As with traditional networking, the goal of online networking is to make connections with people who are advanced in their fields. Ask for their advice about finding a job. Most people like talking about themselves, and asking them about their experiences is an excellent way to begin an online correspondence that might lead to "electronic mentoring," a letter of recommendation from an expert in the field, or information on an internship opportunity. Making online connections with industry professionals is a great way to keep tabs on the latest business trends and potential job leads.

- **Step 1: Choose a Group to Join.** Familiarize yourself with the options available for building your own professional network. Current favorites include *Linkedin.com, Ryze.com, Zerodegrees .com,* and *Itsnotwhatyouknow.com.* Some of these sites are fee-based while others are free.
- **Step 2: Join a Site and Begin Making Connections.** Typically, joining a network requires creating a password, filling in your profile, and adding your business contacts. At some sites, you can specify search criteria to locate and then contact individuals directly. At other sites both parties' e-mail addresses are hidden. The site then acts as an intermediary connecting the people only after they agree to share their contact information. Once you've connected with an individual, the content of your discussions and the follow-up will be similar to that of traditional networking. The medium, however, will center on electronic communication through e-mail and chatroom discussions.

Career Application

Begin developing your network. Conduct at least one referral interview or join one online networking group. Record the results you experienced and the information you learned from the networking option you chose. Report to the class your reactions and findings.

Choosing a Résumé Style

Your qualifications and career goal will help you choose from among three résumé styles: chronological, functional, and combination.

Chronological. The most popular résumé format is the chronological résumé, shown in Figure 16.3. It lists work history job by job, starting with the most recent position. As Bonnie Gesualdi-Chao at Carnival Cruise Lines pointed out, recruiters favor the chronological style because such résumés quickly reveal a candidate's education and experience record. Recruiters are familiar with the chronological résumé, and as many as 85 percent of employers prefer to see a candidate's résumé in this format.[13] But it is less appropriate for people who have changed jobs frequently or who have gaps in their employment records. For college students and others who lack extensive experience, the functional résumé format may be preferable.

Chronological résum[…] focus on job history with most recent positions listed first.

Functional. The functional résumé, shown in Figure 16.4, focuses attention on a candidate's skills rather than on past employment. Like a chronological résumé, the functional résumé begins with the candidate's name, address, telephone number, job objective, and education. Instead of listing jobs, though, the functional résumé groups skills and accomplishments in special categories, such as *Supervisory and Management Skills* or *Retailing and Marketing Experience.* This résumé style highlights accomplishments and can de-emphasize a negative employment history. People who are changing careers or who do not have steady employment histories may prefer the functional résumé. Recent graduates with little employment experience often find the functional résumé useful. Be aware, though, that job boards may insist on chronological format. What's more, some recruiters are suspicious of functional résumés, thinking the candidate is hiding something.

Because functional résumés focus on skills, they may be more advisable for graduates with little experience.

Combination. The combination résumé style, shown in Figure 16.5, draws on the best features of the chronological and functional résumés. Sometimes called the *chrono-functional* résumé, this format emphasizes a candidate's capabilities while also including a complete job history. For recent graduates the combination résumé is a good choice because it enables them to profile what they can do for a prospective employer. If the writer has a specific job in mind, the items should be targeted to that job description.

Combination résumés present capabilities along with a complete job history.

Deciding on Its Length

Experts simply do not agree on how long a résumé should be. Conventional wisdom has always held that recruiters prefer one-page résumés. That's because busy recruiters are said to give no more than 30 seconds to each résumé they peruse. However, a carefully controlled study of 570 recruiters revealed that they *claimed* they preferred one-page résumés. However, the recruiters actually *chose* to interview the applicants with two-page résumés.[14] It should be pointed out, though, that the researchers in this study used hypothetical résumés of graduating seniors with accounting majors who had outstanding credentials. Yet, the fact remains that recruiters who are serious about candidates often prefer a full picture with the kind of details that can be provided in a two-page résumé.

Recruiters may say they prefer one-page résumés, but many choose to interview those with longer résumés.

The entire question may become moot as recruiters increasingly encourage online résumés, which are not restricted by page lengths. Perhaps the best advice is to make your résumé as long as needed to sell your skills. Individuals with more experience will naturally have longer résumés.

1 Prewriting ◀▶ 2 Writing ◀▶ 3 Revising

Analyze: The purpose is to respond to a job advertisement and win an interview.

Anticipate: The reader probably sees many résumés and will skim this one quickly. He or she will be indifferent and must be persuaded to read on.

Adapt: Emphasize the specific skills that the targeted advertisement mentions.

Research: Investigate the targeted company and its needs. Find the name of the person who will be receiving this résumé.

Organize: Make lists of all accomplishments and skills. Select those items most appropriate for the targeted job.

Compose: Experiment with formats to achieve readability, emphasis, and attractiveness.

Revise: Use present-tense verbs to describe current experience. Bullet experience items. Check for parallel phrasing. Adjust spacing for best effect.

Proofread: Be sure to run your spell checker. Read for meaning. Have a friend proofread and critique your draft.

Evaluate: Will this résumé impress a recruiter in 30 seconds? Will it prompt an invitation to an interview?

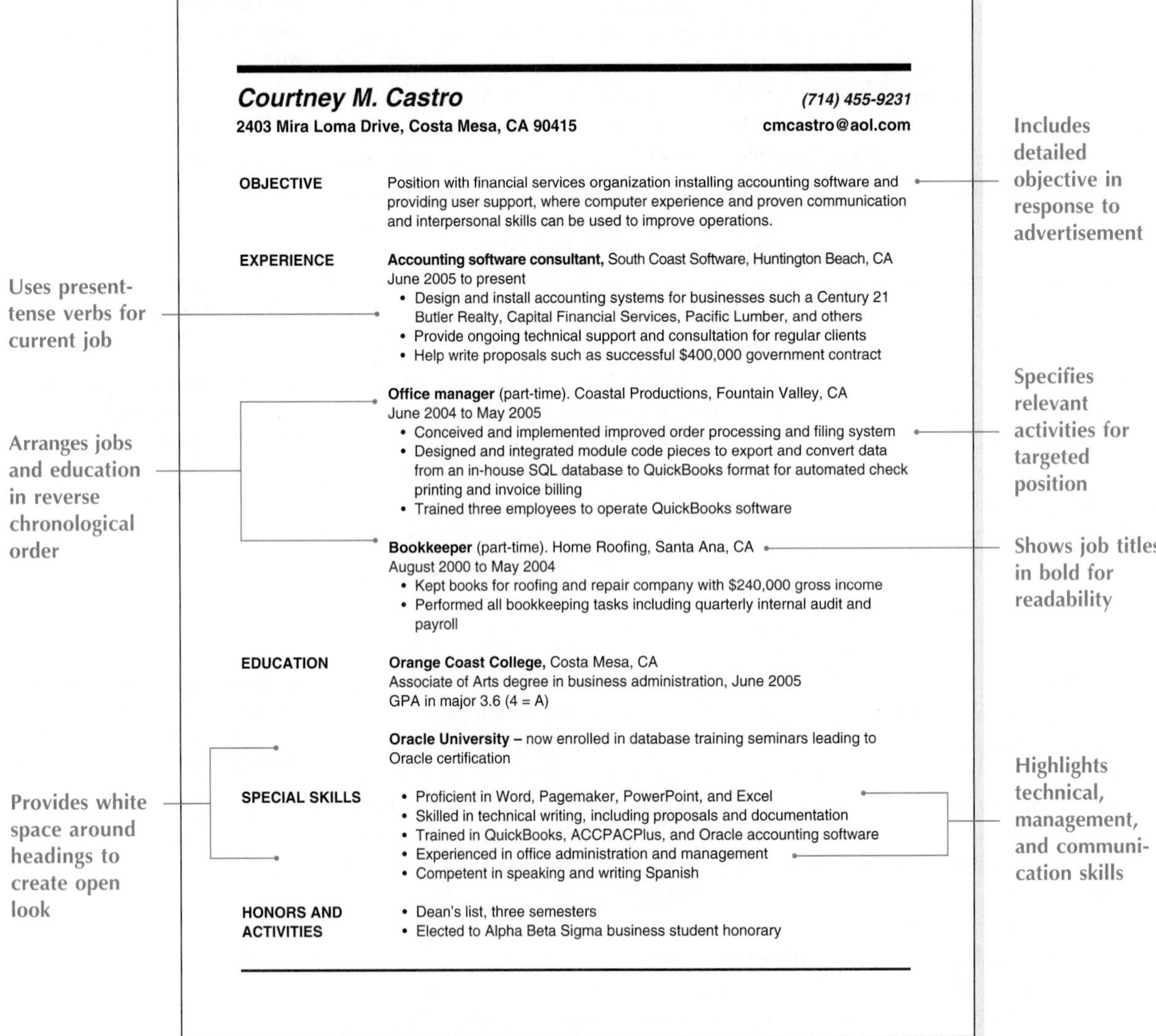

Courtney M. Castro — *(714) 455-9231*

2403 Mira Loma Drive, Costa Mesa, CA 90415 — **cmcastro@aol.com**

OBJECTIVE

Position with financial services organization installing accounting software and providing user support, where computer experience and proven communication and interpersonal skills can be used to improve operations.

EXPERIENCE

Accounting software consultant, South Coast Software, Huntington Beach, CA
June 2005 to present

- Design and install accounting systems for businesses such a Century 21 Butler Realty, Capital Financial Services, Pacific Lumber, and others
- Provide ongoing technical support and consultation for regular clients
- Help write proposals such as successful $400,000 government contract

Office manager (part-time). Coastal Productions, Fountain Valley, CA
June 2004 to May 2005

- Conceived and implemented improved order processing and filing system
- Designed and integrated module code pieces to export and convert data from an in-house SQL database to QuickBooks format for automated check printing and invoice billing
- Trained three employees to operate QuickBooks software

Bookkeeper (part-time). Home Roofing, Santa Ana, CA
August 2000 to May 2004

- Kept books for roofing and repair company with $240,000 gross income
- Performed all bookkeeping tasks including quarterly internal audit and payroll

EDUCATION

Orange Coast College, Costa Mesa, CA
Associate of Arts degree in business administration, June 2005
GPA in major 3.6 (4 = A)

Oracle University – now enrolled in database training seminars leading to Oracle certification

SPECIAL SKILLS

- Proficient in Word, Pagemaker, PowerPoint, and Excel
- Skilled in technical writing, including proposals and documentation
- Trained in QuickBooks, ACCPACPlus, and Oracle accounting software
- Experienced in office administration and management
- Competent in speaking and writing Spanish

HONORS AND ACTIVITIES

- Dean's list, three semesters
- Elected to Alpha Beta Sigma business student honorary

Includes detailed objective in response to advertisement
Uses present-tense verbs for current job
Specifies relevant activities for targeted position
Arranges jobs and education in reverse chronological order
Shows job titles in bold for readability
Highlights technical, management, and communication skills
Provides white space around headings to create open look

FIGURE 16.4 *Functional Résumé*

Recent graduate Kevin Tuohy chose this functional format to de-emphasize his meager work experience and emphasize his potential in sales and marketing. This version of his résumé is more generic than one targeted for a specific position. Yet, it emphasizes his strong points with specific achievements and includes an employment section to satisfy recruiters.

The functional format presents ability-focused topics. It illustrates what the job seeker can do for the employer instead of narrating a history of previous jobs. Although recruiters prefer chronological résumés, the functional format is a good choice for new graduates, career changers, and those with employment gaps.

FIGURE 16.5 C

KEVIN M. TOUHY

P.O. Box 341 Phone: (412) 359-2493
Monroeville, PA 15146 Cell: (412) 555-3201 E-mail: ktouhy@aol.com

OBJECTIVE Position in sales, marketing, or e-marketing with opportunity for advancement

SALES AND MARKETING SKILLS
- Developed people and sales skills by demonstrating lawn-care equipment in central and western Pennsylvania
- Achieved sales amounting to 120 percent of forecast in competitive field
- Personally generated over $30,000 in telephone subscriptions as part of the President's Task Force for the Northeastern University Foundation
- Conducted telephone survey of selected businesses in two counties to discover potential users of farm equipment and to promote company services
- Successfully served 40 or more retail customers daily as clerk in electrical appliance department of national home hardware store

COMMUNICATION AND COMPUTER SKILLS
- Conducted research, analyzed findings, drew conclusions, and helped write 20-page report contending that responsible e-marketing is not spam
- Learned teamwork skills such as cooperation and compromise in team projects
- Delivered PowerPoint talks before selected campus classes and organizations encouraging students to participate in campus voter registration drive
- Earned A's in Interpersonal Communication and Business Communication
- Developed Word, Outlook, Excel, PowerPoint, and Internet Explorer skills
- Commended by instructors for ability to learn computer programs quickly

ORGANIZATIONAL AND MANAGEMENT SKILLS
- Helped conceptualize, organize, and conduct highly effective campus campaign to register student voters
- Scheduled events and arranged weekend student retreat for Marketing Club
- Trained and supervised two counter employees at Pizza Planet
- Organized courses, extracurricular activities, and part-time employment to graduate in seven semesters

EDUCATION
Bachelor of Business Administration, Northeastern University, June, 2005
Major: Business Administration with e-marketing emphasis
GPA: Major, 3.7; overall, 3.3 (A = 4.0)
Related Courses: Marketing Research; Internet Advertising, Sales, and Promotion; and Competitive Strategies for the Information Age
Associate of Arts, Community College of Allegheny County, 2003
Major: Business Administration with marketing emphasis. **GPA**: 3.7

EMPLOYMENT
2004-2005, Pizza Planet, Pittsburgh
Summer, 2004, Bellefonte Manufacturers Representatives, Pittsburgh
Summers, 2001-2003, Home Depot, Inc., Pittsburgh

Includes general objective for all-purpose résumé

Uses functional headings that emphasize necessary skills for sales and e-marketing position

Quantifies achievements with specifics instead of generalities

Employs action verbs and bullet points to describe skills

Calls attention to computer skills

Highlights recent education and contemporary training while de-emphasizing employment

Avoids dense look and improves readability by "chunking" information

...mbination Résumé

Because Casey wanted to highlight her skills and capabilities along with her experience, she combined the best features of functional and traditional résumés. She used the tables feature of her word processing program to help her format. Casey's résumé required part of a second page because she included references, a practice preferred by employers in her region who say it saves time.

For more résumé models, see Figures 16.10–16.14.

Casey J. Jepson
1103 Wood Road
Boscobel, WI 53805

Home: (608) 375-1926 Cell: (608) 778-5195 E-mail: cjepson@tds.net

SKILLS AND CAPABILITIES

- Able to keyboard (65 wpm) and use ten-key calculator (150 kpm)
- Proficient with Microsoft Word, Excel, Access, PowerPoint, FrontPage, and Publisher (passed MOS certification exam)
- Competent in Internet research, written and oral communication, records management, desktop publishing, computer software troubleshooting, and proofreading and editing business documents
- Trained in QuickBooks, Flash, Photoshop, and Dreamweaver

Omits objective to keep all options open

Focuses on skills and aptitudes that employers seek

EXPERIENCE

Administrative Assistant Work Study
SWTC (Southwest Wisconsin Technical College), Fennimore, WI, August 2004 – present

- Create letters, memos, reports, and forms in Microsoft Word
- Develop customized reports and labels using Microsoft Access
- Maintain departmental Microsoft Excel budget

Loan Support Specialist
Community First Bank, Boscobel, WI, May 2002 – July 2004

- Prepared loan documents for consumer, agricultural, and commercial loans
- Ensured compliance with federal, state, and bank regulations
- Originated correspondence (both oral and written) with customers and agencies
- Ordered and interpreted appraisals, titles, and credit reports
- Created and maintained paper and electronic files for customers

Customer Sales Representative
Lands' End, Dodgeville, WI, winter seasons 2002–2004

- Developed customer service skills answering phones, placing orders
- Resolved customers' merchandise questions and problems
- Enjoyed working in teams to achieve company goals

Arranges employment by job title for easy recognition

EDUCATION

Southwest Wisconsin Technical College, Fennimore, WI
Major: Administrative Assistant with Help Desk certificate
AA degree expected May 2006. GPA in major: 3.8 (4.0 = A)

ACTIVITIES AND AWARDS

- Assisted state president and coordinated all activities of the BPA (Business Professionals of America) Torch Awards Program while serving as state vice president
- Placed first in state BPA Administrative Assistant competition
- Earned second place in Bill Wolfe Writing Contest
- Served as SWTC Student Senate Representative for Administrative Assistant program

Combines activities and awards to fill out section

Casey J. Jepson

REFERENCES

Mr. Jeff Schmitz Loan Supervisor Community First Bank 925 Wisconsin Avenue Boscobel, WI 53805 (608) 375-4116	Ms. Sue Winder Work Study Supervisor Southwest Wisconsin Technical College 1800 Bronson Boulevard Fennimore, WI 53809 (608) 822-3622, Ext. 1200	Mrs. Sondra Ostheimer Business/Communication Instructor Southwest Wisconsin Technical College 1800 Bronson Boulevard Fennimore, WI 53809 (608) 822-3622, Ext. 1266

Includes references because local employers expect them (most résumés today omit references)

Arranging the Parts

learni

3

The p... arranged w... tant qualificatio...

Although résumés have standard parts, their arrangement and content should be strategically planned. The most persuasive résumés emphasize skills and achievements aimed at a particular job or company. They show a candidate's most important qualifications first, and they de-emphasize any weaknesses. In arranging the parts, try to create as few headings as possible; more than six generally looks cluttered. No two résumés are ever exactly alike, but most writers consider including all or some of these items: main heading, career objective, education, experience, capabilities and skills, awards and activities, and references.

Main Heading. Your résumé should always begin with your name, address, and telephone number. If possible, include a number where messages may be left for you. Prospective employers tend to call the next applicant when no one answers. Avoid showing both permanent and temporary addresses; some specialists say that dual addresses immediately identify about-to-graduate college students. For your e-mail address, be sure it sounds professional instead of something like *toosexy4you @hotmail.com* or *sixpackguy@yahoo.com*. Keep the main heading as uncluttered and simple as possible. Don't include the word *résumé*; it's like putting the word *letter* above correspondence.

Career objectives are most appropriate for specific, targeted openings, but they may limit a broader job search.

Career Objective. Opinion is divided about the effect of including a career objective on a résumé. Recruiters think such statements indicate that a candidate has made a commitment to a career. Career objectives, of course, make the recruiter's life easier by quickly classifying the résumé. Such declarations, however, can also disqualify a candidate if the stated objective doesn't match a company's job description.[15] Many career advisors think that putting a job objective on a résumé kills more opportunities for candidates than typos do. What should you do?

You have three choices regarding career objectives. The first is to omit the objective, which makes sense if it is an all-purpose résumé. A second possibility involves using a general statement, such as *Objective: Challenging position in urban planning* or *Job Goal: Position in sales/marketing.* The third, and probably the most effective plan, is to write a specific career objective when applying for a targeted position. Match the objective to the job description. For example, *Objective: To work in the health care industry as a human resources trainee with exposure to recruiting, training, and benefit administration.* With today's word processing capabilities, you can easily change the objective for each application. You should write a separate résumé for each job.

Some consultants warn against using the words *entry-level* in your objective, as these words emphasize lack of experience. Because companies generally prefer individuals with experience, it's smart to get all the experience you can while in school. It's also wise to prepare individual résumés that are targeted for each company or position sought.

spotlight *on communicators*

In her many authoritative books, revered résumé guru Yana Parker strongly advocated lean and focused résumés. Skip the clutter of overly precise dates by listing only years, she said. Short periods of unemployment need not be explained, but longer periods should be accounted for in a positive statement telling what you were doing. "Remember," she advised, "that a résumé is a marketing piece, not an historical document or a confessional." She suggested including a specific job objective, perhaps even a job title. Then, recruiters would not have to guess what you're looking for.

Photo: Courtesy of Yana Parker

Education. The next component is your education—if it is more noteworthy than your work experience. In this section you should include the name and location of schools, dates of attendance, major fields of study, and degrees received. Your grade-point average and/or class ranking are important to prospective employers. One way to enhance your GPA is to calculate it in your major courses only (for example, *3.6 in major*). By the way, it is not unethical to showcase your GPA in your major—so long as you clearly indicate what you are doing.

on section shows de- GPA but does not list es a job applicant has

Some applicants want to list all their courses, but such a list makes for very dull reading. It's better to refer to courses only if you can relate them to the position sought. When relevant, include certificates earned, seminars attended, and workshops completed. Because employers are interested in your degree of self-sufficiency, you might wish to indicate the percentage of your education for which you paid. If your education is incomplete, include such statements as *B.S. degree expected 6/07* or *80 units completed in 120-unit program.* Entitle this section *Education, Academic Preparation,* or *Professional Training.*

The work experience section of a résumé should list specifics and quantify achievements.

Work Experience or Employment History. If your work experience is significant and relevant to the position sought, this information should appear before education. List your most recent employment first and work backward, including only those jobs that you think will help you win the targeted position. A job application form may demand a full employment history, but your résumé may be selective. Be aware, though, that time gaps in your employment history will probably be questioned in the interview. For each position show the following:

- Employer's name, city, and state
- Dates of employment
- Most important job title
- Significant duties, activities, accomplishments, and promotions

Describe your employment achievements concisely but concretely. Avoid generalities such as *Worked with customers.* Be more specific, with statements such as *Served 40 or more retail customers a day, Successfully resolved problems about custom stationery orders,* or *Acted as intermediary among customers, printers, and suppliers.* If possible, quantify your accomplishments, such as *Conducted study of equipment needs of 100 small businesses in Phoenix, Personally generated orders for sales of $90,000 annually, Keyboarded all the production models for a 250-page employee procedures manual,* or *Assisted editor in layout, design, and news writing for 12 issues of division newsletter.* One professional recruiter said, "I spend a half hour every day screening 50 résumés or more, and if I don't spot some [quantifiable] results in the first 10 seconds, the résumé is history."[16]

In addition to technical skills, employers seek individuals with communication, management, and interpersonal capabilities. This means you'll want to select work experiences and achievements that illustrate your initiative, dependability, responsibility, resourcefulness, and leadership. Employers also want people who can work together in teams. Thus, include statements like *Collaborated with interdepartmental task force in developing ten-page handbook for temporary workers* and *Headed student government team that conducted most successful voter registration in campus history.*

Statements describing your work experience can be made forceful and persuasive by using action verbs, such as those shown in Figure 16.6 and illustrated in Figure 16.7. You'll also want to include plenty of solid nouns, which we'll present shortly.

Emphasize the skills and aptitudes that recommend you for a specific position.

Capabilities and Skills. Recruiters want to know specifically what you can do for their companies. Therefore, list your special skills, such as *Proficient in preparing federal, state, and local payroll tax returns as well as franchise and personal property tax returns.* Include your ability to use the Internet, computer programs, office equipment, foreign languages, or sign language. Describe proficiencies you have acquired through training and experience, such as *Certified in computer graphics and Web design through an intensive 350-hour classroom program.* Use expressions such as *competent in, skilled in, proficient with, experienced in,* and *ability to.*

FIGURE 16.6 ***Strengthen Your Résumé With Action Verbs***

accelerated	constructed	encouraged	facilitated	organized	resolved	
achieved	converted	engineered	improved	originated	restructu	
analyzed	designed	established	increased	overhauled	reviewec	
collaborated	directed	expanded	introduced	pioneered	revitalize	
conceptualized	enabled	expedited	managed	reduced	screened	transformed

You'll also want to highlight exceptional aptitudes, such as working well under stress, learning computer programs quickly, and interacting with customers. If possible, provide details and evidence that back up your assertions; for example, *Mastered PhotoShop in 25 hours with little instruction.* Search for examples of your writing, speaking, management, organizational, and interpersonal skills—particularly those talents that are relevant to your targeted job. For recent graduates, this section can be used to give recruiters evidence of your potential. Instead of *Capabilities,* the section might be called *Skills and Abilities.*

Awards, honors, and activities are appropriate for résumés; most personal data are not.

Awards, Honors, and Activities. If you have three or more awards or honors, highlight them by listing them under a separate heading. If not, put them with activities. Include awards, scholarships (financial and other), fellowships, honors, recognition, commendations, and certificates. Be sure to identify items clearly. Your reader may be unfamiliar, for example, with Greek organizations, honoraries, and awards; tell what they mean. Instead of saying *Recipient of Star award,* give more details: *Recipient of Star award given by Pepperdine University to outstanding graduates who combine academic excellence and extracurricular activities.*

It's also appropriate to include college, community, and professional activities. High school activities and accomplishments are not generally included. Employers are interested in evidence that you are a well-rounded person. This section provides an opportunity to demonstrate leadership and interpersonal skills. Strive to use action statements. For example, instead of saying *Treasurer of business club,* explain

FIGURE 16.7 ***Use Action Verbs in Statements That Quantify Achievements***

Identified weaknesses in internships and **researched** five alternate programs

Reduced delivery delays by an average of three days per order

Streamlined filing system, thus reducing 400-item backlog to 0

Organized holiday awards program for 1,200 attendees and 140 workers

Designed three pages in HTML for company Web site

Represented 2,500 students on committee involving university policies and procedures

Calculated shipping charges for overseas deliveries and **recommended** most economical rates

Managed 24-station computer network linking data in three departments

Distributed and **explained** voter registration forms to over 500 prospective voters

Praised by top management for enthusiastic teamwork and achievement

Secured national recognition from National Arbor Foundation for tree project

Sample Reference List

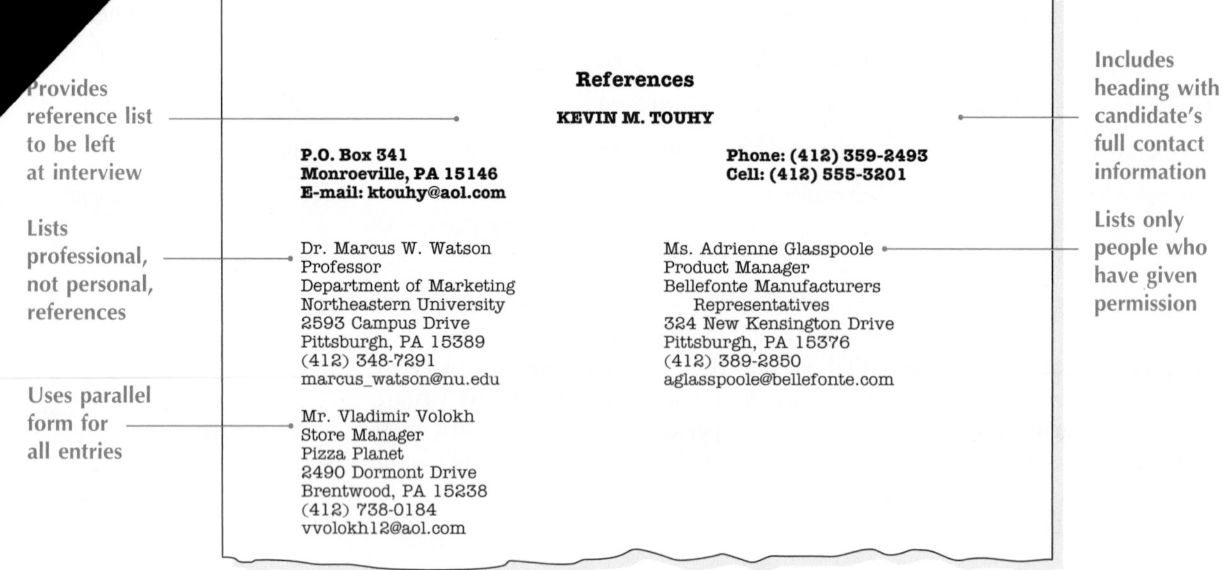

Provides reference list to be left at interview
Lists professional, not personal, references
Uses parallel form for all entries
Includes heading with candidate's full contact information
Lists only people who have given permission

References

KEVIN M. TOUHY

P.O. Box 341
Monroeville, PA 15146
E-mail: ktouhy@aol.com

Phone: (412) 359-2493
Cell: (412) 555-3201

Dr. Marcus W. Watson
Professor
Department of Marketing
Northeastern University
2593 Campus Drive
Pittsburgh, PA 15389
(412) 348-7291
marcus_watson@nu.edu

Ms. Adrienne Glasspoole
Product Manager
Bellefonte Manufacturers Representatives
324 New Kensington Drive
Pittsburgh, PA 15376
(412) 389-2850
aglasspoole@bellefonte.com

Mr. Vladimir Volokh
Store Manager
Pizza Planet
2490 Dormont Drive
Brentwood, PA 15238
(412) 738-0184
vvolokh12@aol.com

more fully: *Collected dues, kept financial records, and paid bills while serving as treasurer of 35-member business management club.*

Omit personal data not related to job qualifications.

Personal Data. Today's résumés omit personal data, such as birth date, marital status, height, weight, and religious affiliation. Such information doesn't relate to genuine occupational qualifications, and recruiters are legally barred from asking for such information. Some job seekers do, however, include hobbies or interests (such as skiing or photography) that might grab the recruiter's attention or serve as conversation starters. Naturally, you wouldn't mention dangerous pastimes (such as bungee jumping or sports car racing) or time-consuming interests. But you should indicate your willingness to travel or to relocate, since many companies will be interested.

References are unnecessary for the résumé, but they should be available for the interview.

References. Listing references on a résumé is favored by some recruiters and opposed by others. Such a list takes up valuable space. Moreover, references are not normally instrumental in securing an interview—few companies check them before the interview. Instead, recruiters prefer that you bring to the interview a list of individuals willing to discuss your qualifications. If you do list them, use parallel form, as shown in Figure 16.8. Include land addresses, telephone numbers, and e-mail addresses.

Whether or not you include references on your résumé, you should have a separate list, such as that in Figure 16.8, available when you begin your job search. Ask three to five instructors or previous employers whether they will be willing to answer inquiries regarding your qualifications for employment. Be sure, however, to provide them with an opportunity to refuse. No reference is better than a negative one. Later in this chapter you'll learn more about how to write a reference request.

Do not include personal or character references, such as friends, family, or neighbors, because recruiters rarely consult them. Companies are more interested in the opinions of objective individuals. One final note: most recruiters see little reason for including the statement *References furnished upon request.* It's like saying the sun comes up every morning.

Optimizing Your Résumé for Today's Technologies

learn

4

Because r ingly becc able data three versions.

Thus far we've aimed our résumé advice at human readers. However, the first reader of your résumé may well be a computer. Hiring organizations today use a variety of methods to process incoming résumés. Some organizations still welcome traditional print-based résumés that may include attractive formatting. Larger organizations, however, must deal with thousands of incoming résumés. Increasingly, they are placing those résumés directly into searchable databases. So that you can optimize your chances, you may need three versions of your résumé: (1) a traditional print-based résumé, (2) a scannable résumé, and (3) an inline résumé for e-mailing. You should also be aware of the significant role of résumé keywords.

Designing a Traditional Print-Based Résumé

A traditional print-based résumé is attractive, readable, and outlined with headings in an orderly, uncluttered format.

Traditional print-based résumés are attractively formatted to maximize readability. You can create a professional-looking résumé by using your word processing program to highlight your qualifications. The examples in this chapter provide ideas for simple layouts that are easily duplicated. You can also examine template résumés for styling ideas. Their inflexibility, however, leads to frustration as you try to force your skills and experience into a predetermined template sequence. What's more, recruiters who read hundreds of résumés can usually spot a template-based résumé. Instead, create your own original résumé that fits your unique qualifications. Your print-based résumé should use an outline format with headings and bulleted points to present information in an orderly, uncluttered format. An attractive print-based résumé is necessary (1) when you are competing for a job that does not require electronic submission, (2) to present in addition to an electronic submission, and (3) to distribute when you are interviewed. Even if a résumé is submitted electronically, nearly every job candidate will want to have an attractive traditional résumé handy for human readers.

Although you may submit a scannable résumé to an organization, you'll want to bring an attractive print résumé with you when you reach the interview stage of hiring.

Photo: Courtesy of Rubberball Productions/Getty Images

Preparing a Scannable Résumé

Applicant-tracking software scans incoming résumés searching for keywords.

To screen incoming résumés, many mid- and large-sized companies use automated applicant-tracking software. These systems scan an incoming résumé with optical character recognition (OCR) looking for keywords. The most sophisticated programs enable recruiters and hiring managers to search for keywords, rank résumés based on the number of "hits," and generate reports. Information from your résumé is stored, usually from six months to a year.

Before sending your résumé, find out whether the recipient uses scanning software. If you can't tell from the job announcement, call the company to ask whether it scans résumés electronically. If you don't get a clear answer and you have even the slightest suspicion that your résumé might be read electronically, you'll be smart to prepare a plain, scannable version.

umés use plain for- ırge font, quality ɜ, and white space.

Tips for Maximizing Scannability. A scannable résumé must sacrifice many of the graphic enhancements you might have used to dress up your traditional print résumé. To maximize scannability:

- **Avoid unusual typefaces, underlining, and italics.** Moreover, don't use boxing, shading, or other graphics to highlight text. These features don't scan well. Most applicant-tracking programs, however, can accurately read bold print, solid bullets, and asterisks.
- **Use 10- to 14-point type.** Because touching letters or unusual fonts are likely to be misread, it's safest to use a large, well-known font, such as 12-point Times Roman or Helvetica. This may mean that your résumé will require two pages. After printing, inspect your résumé to see whether any letters touch—especially in your name.
- **Use smooth white paper, black ink, and quality printing.** Avoid colored or textured paper, and use a good printer.
- **Be sure that your name is the first line on the page.** Don't use fancy layouts that may confuse a scanner.
- **List each phone number on its own line.** Your land and cell phone numbers should appear on separate lines to improve recognition.
- **Provide white space.** To ensure separation of words and categories, leave plenty of white space. For example, instead of using parentheses to enclose a telephone area code, insert blank spaces, such as 212 799-2415. Leave blank lines around headings.
- **Avoid double columns.** When listing job duties, skills, computer programs, and so forth, don't tabulate items into two- or three-column lists. Scanners read across and may convert tables into gobbledygook.
- **Don't fold or staple your résumé.** Send it in a large envelope so that you can avoid folds. Words that appear on folds may not be scanned correctly.

Scanners produce "hits" when they recognize targeted keywords such as nouns describing skills, traits, tasks, and job titles.

Tips for Maximizing "Hits." In addition to paying attention to the physical appearance of your résumé, you must also be concerned with keywords that produce "hits" or recognition by the scanner. To maximize hits:

- **Focus on specific keywords.** Study carefully any advertisements and job descriptions for the position you want. Select keywords that describe skills, traits, tasks, and job titles.
- **Incorporate words from the advertisement or job description.** Describe your experience, education, and qualifications in terms associated with the job advertisement or job description for this position.
- **Use typical headings.** Include expected categories such as Objective, Experience, Employment, Work History, Skills, Summary of Qualifications, and Accomplishments. Scanning software looks for such headings.
- **Use accurate names.** Spell out complete names of schools, degrees, and dates.
- **Be careful of abbreviations.** Minimize unfamiliar abbreviations, but maximize easily recognized abbreviations—especially those within your field, such as CAD, COBRA, or JIT. When in doubt, though, spell out! Computers are less addled by whole words.
- **Describe interpersonal traits and attitudes.** Hiring managers look for keywords and phrases such as *time management skills, dependability, high energy, leadership, sense of responsibility,* and *team player.*

FIGURE 16.9 ***Interpersonal Keywords Most Requested by Employers Using Résumé-Scanning Sof***

Ability to delegate	Creative	Leadership	Self-
Ability to implement	Customer oriented	Multitasking	Self-
Ability to plan	Detail minded	Open communication	Settir
Ability to train	Ethical	Open minded	Supportive
Accurate	Flexible	Oral communication	Takes initiative
Adaptable	Follow instructions	Organizational skills	Team building
Aggressive worker	Follow through	Persuasive	Team player
Analytical ability	Follow up	Problem solving	Tenacious
Assertive	High energy	Public speaking	Willing to travel
Communication skills	Industrious	Results oriented	
Competitive	Innovative	Safety conscious	

*Reported by Resumix, a leading producer of résumé-scanning software.

Source: Joyce Lain Kennedy and Thomas J. Morrow, *Electronic Résumé Revolution* (New York: John Wiley & Sons), 70. Reprinted by permission of John Wiley & Sons, Inc.

- **Use more than one page if necessary.** Computers can easily handle more than one page so include as much as necessary to describe your qualifications and maximize hits.
- **Consider adding a keyword summary.** Some authorities recommend adding a special paragraph loaded with keywords. Others think it is unnecessary and clutters a résumé.

If you decide to include a keyword summary, go through your traditional résumé and mark all relevant nouns. Also try to imagine what eight to ten words an employer might use to describe the job you want. Then select the 25 best words for your summary. Because interpersonal traits are often requested by employers, consult Figure 16.9. It shows the most frequently requested interpersonal traits, as reported by Resumix, one of the leaders in résumé-scanning software. You may entitle your list *Keyword Summary*, *Keyword Profile*, or *Keyword Index*. Here's an example of a possible keyword summary for a junior accountant:

A computer-friendly résumé may contain a keyword summary filled with words (usually nouns) that describe the job or candidate.

KEYWORD SUMMARY

Accountant: Public. Junior. Staff. AA, Delgado Community College—Business Administration. BA, Nicholls State University—Accounting. Payables. Receivables. Payroll Experience. Quarterly Reports. Unemployment Reports. Communication Skills. Computer Skills. Excel. Word. PCs. Mainframes. Internet. Web. Networks. J. D. Edwards Software. Ability to learn software. Accurate. Dean's List. Award of Merit. Team player. Willing to travel. Relocate.

Preparing an Inline Résumé for E-Mailing

An *inline* résumé is one that is stripped of formatting and embedded within an e-mail message. An inline résumé may also be called an *ASCII* résumé, a *plain text* résumé, or an *electronic* résumé. Regardless of its name, this format is increasingly requested because employers worry about viruses and word processing incompatibilities in attachments. Employers don't want to open attachments. They prefer inline résumés

…oyers prefer **inline** *résumés …cause these plain-text documents are immediately searchable and avoid viruses and software incompatibilities.*

that are immediately searchable and avoid the scanning step.[17] Many job boards also require inline résumés. Thus, you should be prepared with an inline résumé that can be imported directly into an e-mail message. To create an inline résumé:

- **Follow all the tips for a scannable résumé.** An inline résumé requires the same attention to content, formatting, and keywords as that recommended for a scannable résumé.
- **Consider reformatting with shorter lines.** Many e-mail programs wrap lines longer than 60 characters. To avoid having your résumé look as if a chain saw attacked it, use a short line length (such as 4 inches).
- **Think about using keyboard characters to enhance format.** In addition to using capital letters and asterisks, you might use spaced equals signs (= = =) and tildes (~ ~ ~) to create separating lines that highlight résumé categories.
- **Move all text to the left.** Do not center items; start all text at the left margin. Remove tabs.
- **Save your résumé in plain text (.txt) or rich text format (.rtf).** After saving it as a text file, send your résumé to yourself and check to see whether any non-ASCII characters appear. They may show up as question marks, square blocks, or other odd characters.

Creating an E-Portfolio

An e-portfolio offers links to examples of a job candidate's performance, talents, and accomplishments in digitized form.

As the workplace becomes increasingly digitized, you have yet another way to display your qualifications to prospective employers—the digitized e-portfolio. Resourceful job candidates in other fields—particularly writers, models, artists, and graphic artists—created print portfolios to illustrate their qualifications and achievements. Now business and professional job candidates are using electronic portfolios to show off their talents.

An *e-portfolio* is a collection of digitized materials that provides viewers with a snapshot of a candidate's performance, talents, and accomplishments. It may include a copy of your résumé, reference letters, special achievements, awards, certificates, work samples, a complete list of your courses, thank-you letters, and anything else that touts your accomplishments. An advanced portfolio might include links to electronic copies of your artwork, film projects, blueprints, and photographs of classwork that might otherwise be difficult to share with potential employers. Moreover, you can include razzle-dazzle effects such as color, animation, sound, and graphics.

Job candidates generally offer e-portfolios at Web sites, but they may also burn them onto a CD.

E-portfolios are generally presented at Web sites, where they are available 24/7 to employers. Some colleges and universities not only make Web site space available for student e-portfolios but also provide instruction and resources for scanning photos, digitizing images, and preparing graphics. E-portfolios may also be burned onto CDs that you mail to prospective employers.

E-portfolios have many advantages. At Web sites they can be viewed whenever convenient for an employer. Let's say you are talking on the phone with an employer in another city who wants to see a copy of your résumé. You can simply refer the employer to the Web address where your résumé resides. E-portfolios can also be seen by many individuals in an organization without circulating a paper copy. But the real reason for preparing an e-portfolio is that it shows off your talents and qualifications more thoroughly than a print résumé.

Applying the Final Touches to Your Résumé

Because your résumé is probably the most important message you will ever write, you'll revise it many times. With so much information in concentrated form and with so much riding on its outcome, your résumé demands careful polishing, proofreading, and critiquing.

In addition to ten, a résumé formatted and proofread.

As you revise, be certain to verify all the facts, particularly those involving your previous employment and education. Don't be caught in a mistake, or worse, distortion of previous jobs and dates of employment. These items likely will be checked. And the consequences of puffing up a résumé with deception or flat-out lies are simply not worth the risk. Other ethical traps you'll want to avoid are described in the Ethical Insights box on page 559.

Polishing. As you continue revising, look for other ways to improve your résumé. For example, consider consolidating headings. By condensing your information into as few headings as possible, you'll produce a clean, professional-looking document. Study other résumés for valuable formatting ideas. Ask yourself what graphics highlighting techniques you can use to improve readability: capitalization, underlining, indenting, and bulleting. Experiment with headings and styles to achieve a pleasing, easy-to-read message. Moreover, look for ways to eliminate wordiness. For example, instead of *Supervised two employees who worked at the counter*, try *Supervised two counter employees.* Review Chapter 6 for more tips.

Above all, make your print-based résumé look professional. Avoid anything humorous or "cute," such as a help-wanted poster with your name or picture inside. Eliminate the personal pronoun *I*. The abbreviated, objective style of a résumé precludes the use of personal pronouns. Use white good-quality paper and a first-rate printer. Be prepared with a résumé for people to read as well as one for a computer to read.

Proofreading. After revising, you must proofread, proofread, and proofread again for spelling, mechanics, content, and format. Then, have a knowledgeable friend or relative proofread it yet again. This is one document that must be perfect.

Because résumés must be perfect, they should be proofread many times.

By now you may be thinking that you'd like to hire someone to write your résumé. Don't! First, you know yourself better than anyone else could know you. Second, you'll end up with either a generic or a one-time résumé. A generic résumé in today's highly competitive job market will lose out to a targeted résumé nine times out of ten. Equally useless is a one-time résumé aimed at a single job. What if you don't get that job? Because you will need to revise your résumé many times as you seek a variety of jobs, be prepared to write (and rewrite) it yourself.

A final word about résumé-writing services. Some tend to produce eye-catching, elaborate documents with lofty language, fancy borders, and fuzzy thinking. Here's an example of empty writing: "Innovative problem solver with business acumen and emotional intelligence required for achieving 21st century business imperatives."[18] Sure! Save your money and buy a good interview suit instead.

Adapting. Nearly everyone writes a résumé by adapting a model, such as those in Figures 16.3 through 16.5 and 16.10 through 16.14. The chronological résumé for Rachel Chowdhry shown in Figure 16.12 is typical of candidates with considerable working experience. Although she describes four positions that span a 14-year period, she manages to fit her résumé on one page. However, two-page résumés are justified for people with long work histories.

As you prepare to write your current résumé, consult the following checklist to review the job-search process and important résumé-writing techniques.

Checklist for Writing a Persuasive Résumé

Preparation

- ✓ **Research the job market.** Learn about available jobs, common qualifications, and potential employers. The best résumés are targeted for specific jobs with specific companies.

- ✓ **Analyze your strengths.** Determine what aspects of your education, experience, and personal characteristics will be assets to prospective employers.

- ✓ **Study models.** Look at other résumés for formatting and element placement ideas. Experiment with headings and styles to achieve an artistic, readable product.

Headings and Objectives

- ✓ **Identify yourself.** List your name, addresses, and telephone numbers.

- ✓ **Include a career objective for a targeted job.** If this résumé is intended for a specific job, include a statement tailored to it (*Objective: Cost accounting position in the petroleum industry*).

Education

- ✓ **Name your degree, date of graduation, and institution.** Emphasize your education if your experience is limited.

- ✓ **List your major and GPA.** Give information about your studies, but don't inventory all your courses.

Work Experience

- ✓ **Itemize your jobs.** Start with your most recent job. Give the employer's name and city, dates of employment (month, year), and most significant job title.

- ✓ **Describe your experience.** Use action verbs to summarize achievements and skills relevant to your targeted job.

- ✓ **Promote your "soft" skills.** Give evidence of communication, management, and interpersonal talents. Employers want more than empty assurances; try to quantify your skills and accomplishments (*Developed teamwork skills while collaborating with six-member task force in producing 20-page mission statement*).

Special Skills, Achievements, and Awards

- ✓ **Highlight your computer skills.** Remember that nearly all employers seek employees who are proficient in using the Internet, e-mail, word processing, databases, spreadsheets, and presentation programs.

- ✓ **Show that you are a well-rounded individual.** List awards, experiences, and extracurricular activities—particularly if they demonstrate leadership, teamwork, reliability, loyalty, industry, initiative, efficiency, and self-sufficiency.

ethical insights

Are Inflated Résumés Worth the Risk?

A résumé is expected to showcase a candidate's strengths and minimize weaknesses. For this reason, recruiters expect a certain degree of self-promotion. Some résumé writers, however, step over the line that separates honest self-marketing from deceptive half-truths and flat-out lies. Distorting facts on a résumé is unethical; lying is illegal. Most important, either practice can destroy a career.

Given the competitive job market, it might be tempting to puff up your résumé. You wouldn't be alone in telling fibs or outright whoppers. One study found that 44 percent of applicants lied about their work histories, 23 percent fabricated licenses or credentials, and 41 percent falsified their educational backgrounds.[19] Although recruiters can't check everything, most will verify previous employment and education before hiring candidates. Over half will require official transcripts.

After hiring, the checking process may continue. If hiring officials find a discrepancy in GPA or prior experience and the error is an honest mistake, they meet with the new-hire to hear an explanation. If the discrepancy wasn't a mistake, they fire the person immediately. No job seeker wants to be in the unhappy position of explaining résumé errors or defending misrepresentation. Avoiding the following common problems can keep you off the hot seat:

- **Inflated education, grades, or honors.** Some job candidates claim degrees from colleges or universities when in fact they merely attended classes. Others increase their grade-point averages or claim fictitious honors. Any such dishonest reporting is grounds for dismissal when discovered.
- **Enhanced job titles.** Wishing to elevate their status, some applicants misrepresent their titles. For example, one technician called himself a "programmer" when he had actually programmed only one project for his boss. A mail clerk who assumed added responsibilities conferred upon herself the title of "supervisor." Even when the description seems accurate, it's unethical to list any title not officially granted.
- **Puffed-up accomplishments.** Some job seekers inflate their employment experience or achievements. One clerk, eager to make her photocopying duties sound more important, said that she assisted the *vice president in communicating and distributing employee directives.* An Ivy League graduate who spent the better part of six months watching rented videos on his VCR described the activity as *Independent Film Study*. The latter statement may have helped win an interview, but it lost him the job. In addition to avoiding puffery, guard against taking sole credit for achievements that required many people. When recruiters suspect dubious claims on résumés, they nail applicants with specific—and often embarrassing—questions during their interviews.[20]
- **Altered employment dates.** Some candidates extend the dates of employment to hide unimpressive jobs or to cover up periods of unemployment and illness. Let's say that several years ago Cindy was unemployed for 14 months between working for Company A and being hired by Company B. To make her employment history look better, she adds seven months to her tenure with Company A and seven months to Company B. Now her employment history has no gaps, but her résumé is dishonest and represents a potential booby trap for her.

The employment process can easily lure you into ethical traps, such as those described in Chapter 1. Beware of these specific temptations:

- **The relative-filth trap:** *A little fudging on my GPA is nothing compared with the degrees that some people buy in degree mills.*
- **The rationalization trap:** *I deserve to call myself "manager" because that's what I really did.*
- **The self-deception trap:** *Giving myself a certificate from the institute is OK because I really intended to finish the program, but I got sick.*

Falling into these ethical traps risks your entire employment future. If your honest qualifications aren't good enough to get you the job you want, start working now to improve them.

Career Application

As a class, discuss the ethics of writing résumés. What's the difference between honest self-marketing and deception? What are some examples from your experience? Where could college students go wrong in preparing their résumés? Is a new employee "home free" if an inflated résumé is not detected in the hiring process? Are job candidates obligated to describe every previous job on a résumé? How can candidates improve an unimpressive résumé without resorting to "puffing it up"?

PROCESS IN PROGRESS

Carnival Cruise Line Revisited

BONNIE Gesualdi-Chao, former recruiting specialist at Carnival Cruise Lines, preferred one-page chronological résumés because they're easy to read and provide a quick history of a candidate. "I'm generally recruiting for entry-level positions; and I want to see their education, internships, summer jobs, and experience lined up in chronological order," said Bonnie. "I'm also very interested in skills and training—such as computer knowledge, a second language, travel and tourism courses, seminars, and symposiums. Because I'm scanning many résumés quickly, the chronological format is best for me."

In regard to experience and training, Bonnie was most interested in achievements that related to Carnival and its job requirements. For example, if a position were open in group sales reservations, she would look for someone who had worked in a travel agency or who had attended travel and tourism school or who had coordinated special events for large groups.

For entry-level positions, Bonnie said, "I'm not expecting a whole lot of experience, but I do look to see whether an applicant's college classes relate to the job and whether the person was interested enough in the field to complete an internship. Since we are the 'Fun Ships' and we're in the vacation industry, we're also looking for people who are enthusiastic, eager, and ready to have fun. But we'd also like them to be hard-working and dedicated."

Critical Thinking

- If job recruiters seem to prefer one-page, chronological résumés, why should candidates use any other format?
- Why not prepare one excellent résumé, and use the same one for all applications?
- How can a candidate with little actual work experience prepare a chronological résumé that doesn't look skimpy?

CONTINUED ON PAGE 579

case study

Final Tips

- ✓ **Look for ways to condense your data.** Omit all street addresses except your own. Consolidate your headings. Study models and experiment with formats to find the most readable and efficient groupings.
- ✓ **Double-check for parallel phrasing.** Be sure that all entries have balanced construction, such as similar verb forms (*Organized files, trained assistants, scheduled events*).
- ✓ **Make your résumé computer friendly.** If there's a chance your résumé will be read by a computer, be sure to remove graphics and emphasize keywords. Be ready with an inline version to embed in e-mail messages.
- ✓ **Consider omitting references.** Have a list of references available for the interview, but don't include them or refer to them unless you have a specific reason to do so.
- ✓ **Project professionalism and quality.** Avoid personal pronouns and humor. Use quality paper and a high-performance printer.
- ✓ **Proofread, proofread, proofread.** Make this document perfect by proofreading at least three times.

FIGURE 16.10 *Chronological Résumé*

Jeffrey used desktop publishing and word processing features to design a chronological traditional print-based résumé that he planned to give to recruiter during an interview. If recruiters or job banks required a scannable or inline résumé, Jeffrey had those versions ready to submit.

Although he had little paid work experience off campus, Jeffrey's résumé lo impressive because of his relevant summer, campus, and extern experiences. He describes specific achievements related to finance, his career goal.

FIGURE 16.11 C

Places honors first for emphasis

Quantifies many experiences

Organizes computer skills into three categories

Shows leadership qualities and well-rounded personality

Jeffrey V. O'Neill

2590 Roxbury Drive
Montpelier, Vermont 05602
(802) 672-5590
joneill@aol.com

Objective

To obtain a challenging position using my financial education and experience.

Education

- Millikin School of Commerce, University of Virginia
  Bachelor of Science in Commerce, May 2006. GPA: 3.8
  Concentrations in Finance and Management Information Systems

Honors

Golden Key National Honor Society — Dean's List 2002–2005
Phi Eta Sigma Freshman Honor Society — Vermont State Scholarship

Experience

Kraft General Foods International, Ryebrook, New York (Summer 2005)
Systems Engineer
- Independently analyzed and documented purchasing system and reengineered procedures to improve efficiency
- Evaluated use of 25 PCs and made recommendations to CIO that would save over $30,000
- Conducted cost-benefit study to update PCs and improve network integration for 150 users

Milliken Computer Lab, Charlottesville, Virginia (Fall 2004 to present)
Lab Consultant
- Provide technical assistance to over 300 students and 25 faculty members in the use of lab hardware and software
- Developed time management, team building, and communication skills while working with instructors and students in computer lab
- Demonstrated ability to accept and respond to criticism, learn job tasks quickly, and solve problems independently

Lehman Brothers, Stamford, Connecticut (March 2004)
Extern
- Gained valuable insights into U.S. capital markets while assisting consultants
- Analyzed equity-options trades to learn about financial securities

Computer Experience

Languages:	C, C++, Java, Perl, HTML
Environments:	VAX/VMS, UNIX, Microsoft Windows
Applications:	Excel, Word, PowerPoint, FrontPage, Dreamweaver

Activities

- Student Council Representative to Admissions Committee, Fall 2005
- Commerce School Rep, Student Council, Spring 2005 to present
- Finance Society, Chairman for Investments Game, Spring 2005
- Intramural soccer and basketball, tennis, guitar

Combination Résumé

Rick's résumé answers an advertisement specifying skills for a staff accountant. He chose a combination format to allow him to highlight the skills his education and limited experience have provided. Responding to the advertisement, he could target his objective and shape his statements to the precise job requirements.

To produce this attractive print-based résumé, he employed italics, bold, and scalable font features from his word processing program. He realized that this résumé might not be scannable and could not be embedded in an e-mail message. That's why he was ready with an inline version that shortened the line length and stripped the fancy formatting in case he had to submit it electronically.

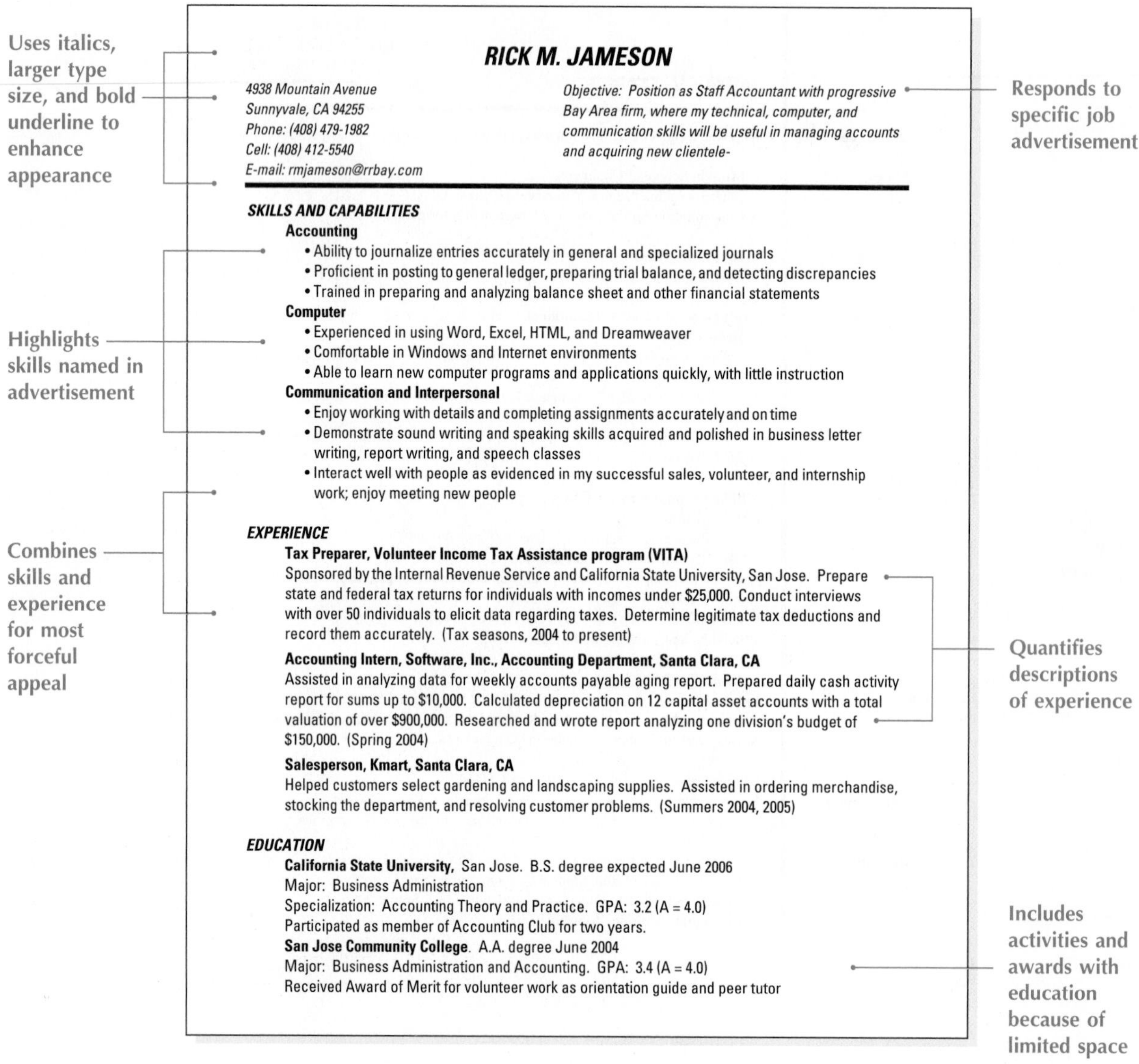

Uses italics, larger type size, and bold underline to enhance appearance
Responds to specific job advertisement
Highlights skills named in advertisement
Combines skills and experience for most forceful appeal
Quantifies descriptions of experience
Includes activities and awards with education because of limited space

RICK M. JAMESON

4938 Mountain Avenue
Sunnyvale, CA 94255
Phone: (408) 479-1982
Cell: (408) 412-5540
E-mail: rmjameson@rrbay.com

Objective: Position as Staff Accountant with progressive Bay Area firm, where my technical, computer, and communication skills will be useful in managing accounts and acquiring new clientele-

SKILLS AND CAPABILITIES

Accounting
- Ability to journalize entries accurately in general and specialized journals
- Proficient in posting to general ledger, preparing trial balance, and detecting discrepancies
- Trained in preparing and analyzing balance sheet and other financial statements

Computer
- Experienced in using Word, Excel, HTML, and Dreamweaver
- Comfortable in Windows and Internet environments
- Able to learn new computer programs and applications quickly, with little instruction

Communication and Interpersonal
- Enjoy working with details and completing assignments accurately and on time
- Demonstrate sound writing and speaking skills acquired and polished in business letter writing, report writing, and speech classes
- Interact well with people as evidenced in my successful sales, volunteer, and internship work; enjoy meeting new people

EXPERIENCE

Tax Preparer, Volunteer Income Tax Assistance program (VITA)
Sponsored by the Internal Revenue Service and California State University, San Jose. Prepare state and federal tax returns for individuals with incomes under $25,000. Conduct interviews with over 50 individuals to elicit data regarding taxes. Determine legitimate tax deductions and record them accurately. (Tax seasons, 2004 to present)

Accounting Intern, Software, Inc., Accounting Department, Santa Clara, CA
Assisted in analyzing data for weekly accounts payable aging report. Prepared daily cash activity report for sums up to $10,000. Calculated depreciation on 12 capital asset accounts with a total valuation of over $900,000. Researched and wrote report analyzing one division's budget of $150,000. (Spring 2004)

Salesperson, Kmart, Santa Clara, CA
Helped customers select gardening and landscaping supplies. Assisted in ordering merchandise, stocking the department, and resolving customer problems. (Summers 2004, 2005)

EDUCATION

California State University, San Jose. B.S. degree expected June 2006
Major: Business Administration
Specialization: Accounting Theory and Practice. GPA: 3.2 (A = 4.0)
Participated as member of Accounting Club for two years.
San Jose Community College. A.A. degree June 2004
Major: Business Administration and Accounting. GPA: 3.4 (A = 4.0)
Received Award of Merit for volunteer work as orientation guide and peer tutor

FIGURE 16.12 *Chronological Résumé for Experienced Candidate*

Because Rachel had many years of experience and seeks executive-level employment, she focuses on her experience. She chose a chronological format to show the steady progression of her career to executive positions, a movement that impresses and assures recruiters.

Although Rachel restricted her résumé to one page, many high-level candidates use two or three pages to fully describe their experience.

RACHEL M. CHOWDHRY
P.O. Box 3310
Thousand Oaks, CA 91359
E-mail: rchowdhry@west.net
(805) 490-3310

OBJECTIVE: SENIOR FINANCIAL MANAGEMENT

PROFESSIONAL HISTORY AND ACHIEVEMENTS

11/02 to 5/06 CONTROLLER

United Plastics, Inc., Newbury Park, CA (extruder of polyethylene film for plastic aprons and gloves)
- Directed all facets of accounting and cash management for 160-employee, $3 billion business
- Supervised inventory and production data processing operations and tax compliance
- Talked owner into reducing sales prices, resulting in doubling first quarter 2005 sales
- Created cost accounting by product and pricing based on gross margin
- Increased line of credit with 12 major suppliers

1/00 to 10/02 CONTROLLER

Burgess Inc., Freeport, IL (major manufacturer of flashlight and lantern batteries)
- Managed all accounting, cash, payroll, credit, and collection operations for 175-employee business
- Implemented a new system for cost accounting, inventory control, and accounts payable, resulting in a $100,000 annual savings in computer operations
- Reduced staff from 10 persons to 5 with no loss in productivity
- Successfully reduced inventory levels from $1.1 million to $600,000
- Helped develop new cash management system that significantly increased cash flow

8/98 to 11/99 TREASURER/CONTROLLER

The Builders of Winter, Winter, WI (manufacturer of modular housing)
- Supervised accounts receivable/payable, cash management, payroll, and insurance
- Directed monthly and year-end closings, banking relations, and product costing
- Refinanced company with long-term loan, ensuring continued operational stability
- Successfully lowered company's insurance premiums by 7 percent

4/94 to 6/98 SUPERVISOR OF GENERAL ACCOUNTING

Levin National Batteries, St. Paul, MN (local manufacturer of flashlight batteries)
- Completed monthly and year-end closing of ledgers for $2 million business
- Audited freight bills, acted as interdepartmental liaison, prepared financial reports

ADDITIONAL INFORMATION

Education: B.S.B.A. degree, University of Minnesota, major in Accounting, 1993

Certification: CPA Review, Academy of Accountancy, Minneapolis, Minnesota

Personal: Will travel and/or relocate

Emphasizes steady employment history by listing dates FIRST

Uses action verbs but includes many good nouns for possible computer scanning

De-emphasizes education because work history is more important for mature candidates

Explains nature of employer's business because it is not immediately recognizable

Describes and quantifies specific achievements

16.13 *Scannable Résumé*

Leticia P. Lopez prepared this "plain Jane" résumé free of graphics and fancy formatting so that it would scan well if read by a computer. Notice that she includes a keyword summary that contains job titles, skills, traits, and other descriptive words. To improve accurate scanning, she avoids bullets, italics, underlining, and columns. A résumé to be scanned need not be restricted to one page.

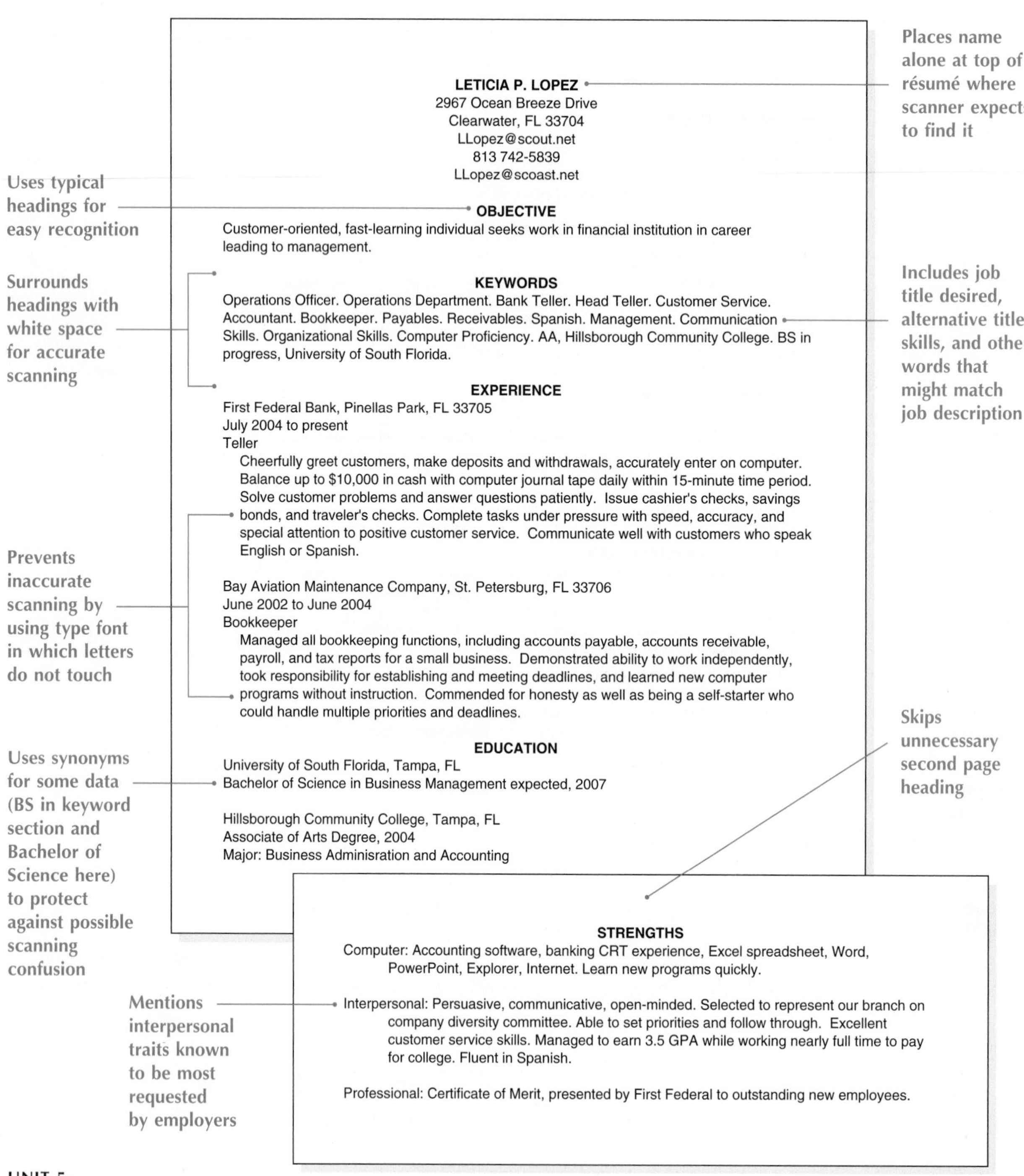

LETICIA P. LOPEZ
2967 Ocean Breeze Drive
Clearwater, FL 33704
LLopez@scout.net
813 742-5839
LLopez@scoast.net

OBJECTIVE

Customer-oriented, fast-learning individual seeks work in financial institution in career leading to management.

KEYWORDS

Operations Officer. Operations Department. Bank Teller. Head Teller. Customer Service. Accountant. Bookkeeper. Payables. Receivables. Spanish. Management. Communication Skills. Organizational Skills. Computer Proficiency. AA, Hillsborough Community College. BS in progress, University of South Florida.

EXPERIENCE

First Federal Bank, Pinellas Park, FL 33705
July 2004 to present
Teller
Cheerfully greet customers, make deposits and withdrawals, accurately enter on computer. Balance up to $10,000 in cash with computer journal tape daily within 15-minute time period. Solve customer problems and answer questions patiently. Issue cashier's checks, savings bonds, and traveler's checks. Complete tasks under pressure with speed, accuracy, and special attention to positive customer service. Communicate well with customers who speak English or Spanish.

Bay Aviation Maintenance Company, St. Petersburg, FL 33706
June 2002 to June 2004
Bookkeeper
Managed all bookkeeping functions, including accounts payable, accounts receivable, payroll, and tax reports for a small business. Demonstrated ability to work independently, took responsibility for establishing and meeting deadlines, and learned new computer programs without instruction. Commended for honesty as well as being a self-starter who could handle multiple priorities and deadlines.

EDUCATION

University of South Florida, Tampa, FL
Bachelor of Science in Business Management expected, 2007

Hillsborough Community College, Tampa, FL
Associate of Arts Degree, 2004
Major: Business Adminisration and Accounting

STRENGTHS

Computer: Accounting software, banking CRT experience, Excel spreadsheet, Word, PowerPoint, Explorer, Internet. Learn new programs quickly.

Interpersonal: Persuasive, communicative, open-minded. Selected to represent our branch on company diversity committee. Able to set priorities and follow through. Excellent customer service skills. Managed to earn 3.5 GPA while working nearly full time to pay for college. Fluent in Spanish.

Professional: Certificate of Merit, presented by First Federal to outstanding new employees.

Places name alone at top of résumé where scanner expects to find it
Uses typical headings for easy recognition
Surrounds headings with white space for accurate scanning
Includes job title desired, alternative titles, skills, and other words that might match job description
Prevents inaccurate scanning by using type font in which letters do not touch
Skips unnecessary second page heading
Uses synonyms for some data (BS in keyword section and Bachelor of Science here) to protect against possible scanning confusion
Mentions interpersonal traits known to be most requested by employers

FIGURE 16.14 ***Inline Résumé***

To be sure it would transmit well when embedded within an e-mail message, Leticia prepared an inline résumé with all lines starting at the left margin. She used a 4-inch line length to avoid awkward line breaks. To set off her major headings, she used the tilde character on her keyboard. She saved the document as a text file (.txt or .rtf) so that it could be read by different computers. At the end she included a statement saying that an attractive, fully formatted hard copy of her résumé was available on request.

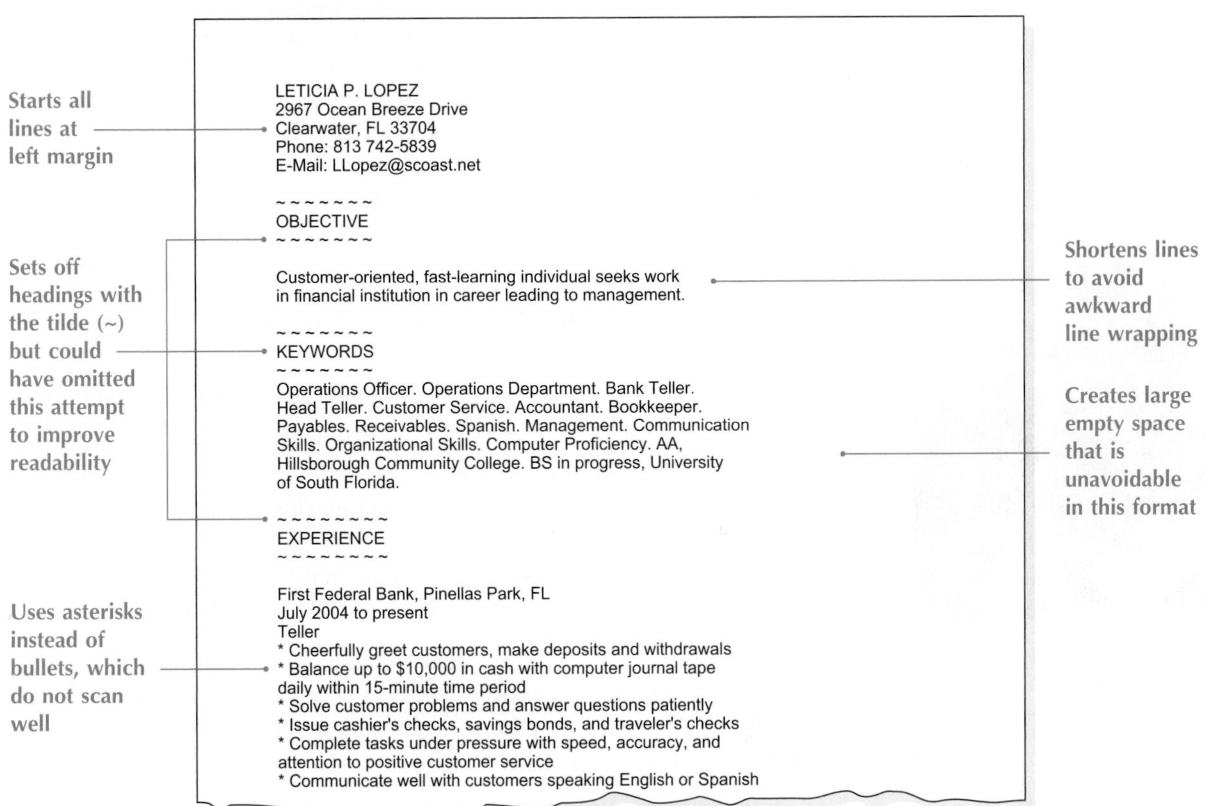

Starts all lines at left margin

Sets off headings with the tilde (~) but could have omitted this attempt to improve readability

Uses asterisks instead of bullets, which do not scan well

Shortens lines to avoid awkward line wrapping

Creates large empty space that is unavoidable in this format

LETICIA P. LOPEZ
2967 Ocean Breeze Drive
Clearwater, FL 33704
Phone: 813 742-5839
E-Mail: LLopez@scoast.net

~ ~ ~ ~ ~ ~ ~
OBJECTIVE
~ ~ ~ ~ ~ ~ ~

Customer-oriented, fast-learning individual seeks work
in financial institution in career leading to management.

~ ~ ~ ~ ~ ~ ~
KEYWORDS
~ ~ ~ ~ ~ ~ ~
Operations Officer. Operations Department. Bank Teller.
Head Teller. Customer Service. Accountant. Bookkeeper.
Payables. Receivables. Spanish. Management. Communication
Skills. Organizational Skills. Computer Proficiency. AA,
Hillsborough Community College. BS in progress, University
of South Florida.

~ ~ ~ ~ ~ ~ ~ ~
EXPERIENCE
~ ~ ~ ~ ~ ~ ~ ~

First Federal Bank, Pinellas Park, FL
July 2004 to present
Teller
* Cheerfully greet customers, make deposits and withdrawals
* Balance up to $10,000 in cash with computer journal tape
daily within 15-minute time period
* Solve customer problems and answer questions patiently
* Issue cashier's checks, savings bonds, and traveler's checks
* Complete tasks under pressure with speed, accuracy, and
attention to positive customer service
* Communicate well with customers speaking English or Spanish

The Persuasive Cover Letter

learning objective

5

Cover letters introduce résumés, relate writer strengths to reader benefits, and seek an interview.

Job candidates often slave over their résumés but treat the cover letter as an afterthought. This critical mistake could sink a job search. Even if an advertisement doesn't request one, be sure to distinguish your application with a persuasive cover letter (also called a *letter of application*). It has three purposes: (1) introducing the résumé, (2) highlighting your strengths in terms of benefits to the reader, and (3) gaining an interview.

Recruiting professionals disagree about how long to make a cover letter. Many prefer short letters with no more than three paragraphs. Others desire longer letters that supply more information, thus giving them a better opportunity to evaluate a candidate's qualifications. These recruiters argue that hiring and training new employees is expensive and time-consuming; therefore, they welcome extra data to guide them in making the best choice the first time. Follow your judgment in writing a brief or a longer cover letter. If you feel, for example, that you need space to explain in more detail what you can do for a prospective employer, do so.

Regardless of its length, a cover letter should have three primary parts: (1) an opening that introduces the message and identifies the position, (2) a body that sells the candidate, and (3) a closing that requests an interview and motivates action.

Introduce Your Message

The opener of a cover letter gains attention by addressing the receiver by name.

Your cover letter will be most appealing if it begins by addressing the reader by name. Rather than sending it to *Human Resources Manager* or *Personnel Department*, take the time to discover the name of the appropriate individual. Make it a rule to call the organization for the correct spelling and the complete address. This personal touch distinguishes your letter and demonstrates your serious interest.

How you open your cover letter depends largely on whether the application is solicited or unsolicited. If an employment position has been announced and applicants are being solicited, you can use a direct approach. If you do not know whether a position is open and you are prospecting for a job, use an indirect approach. Whether direct or indirect, the opening should motivate the receiver to continue reading. Strive for openings that are more imaginative than *Please consider this letter an application for the position of . . . .*

In writing the opening of your cover letter, try to refer to the name of an employee or to the source of your information.

Openings for Solicited Jobs. Here are some of the best techniques to open a cover letter for a job that has been announced:

- **Refer to the name of an employee in the company.** Remember that employers always hope to hire known quantities rather than complete strangers:

  Mitchell Sims, a member of your Customer Service Department, told me that IntriPlex is seeking an experienced customer service representative. The attached summary of my qualifications demonstrates my preparation for this position.

  At the suggestion of Ms. Jennifer Larson of your Human Resources Department, I submit my qualifications for the position of staffing coordinator.

- **Refer to the source of your information precisely.** If you are answering an advertisement, include the exact position advertised and the name and date of the publication. For large organizations it's also wise to mention the section of the newspaper where the ad appeared:

  Your advertisement in Section C-3 of the June 1 *Daily News* for an accounting administrator greatly interests me. With my accounting training and computer experience, I believe I could make a valuable contribution to Quad Graphics.

  From your company's Web site, I learned about your need for a sales representative for the Ohio, Indiana, and Illinois regions. I am very interested in this position and believe that my education and experience are appropriate for the opening.

  Susan Butler, placement director at Sierra University, told me that DataTech has an opening for a technical writer with knowledge of Web design and graphics.

- **Refer to the job title and describe how your qualifications fit the requirements.** Hiring officers are looking for a match between an applicant's credentials and the job needs:

  Will an honors graduate with a degree in recreation and two years of part-time experience organizing social activities for a convalescent hospital qualify for your position of activity director?

  Because of my specialized training in computerized accounting at Boise State University, I feel confident that I have the qualifications you described in your advertisement for a cost accountant trainee.

Photo: Photodisc Red/Getty Images

Openings for Unsolicited Jobs. If you are unsure whether a position actually exists, you may wish to use a more persuasive opening. Since your goal is to convince this person to read on, try one of the following techniques:

Openers for unsolicited jobs show interest in and knowledge of the company, as well as spotlighting reader benefits.

- **Demonstrate interest in and knowledge of the reader's business.** Show the hiring officer that you have done your research and that this organization is more than a mere name to you:

  Because Signa HealthNet, Inc., is organizing a new information management team for its recently established group insurance division, could you use the services of a well-trained information systems graduate who seeks to become a professional systems analyst?

- **Show how your special talents and background will benefit the company.** Personnel directors need to be convinced that you can do something for them:

  Could your rapidly expanding publications division use the services of an editorial assistant who offers exceptional language skills, an honors degree from the University of Maine, and two years' experience in producing a campus literary publication?

In applying for an advertised job, Alysha Cummings wrote the solicited cover letter shown in Figure 16.15. Notice that her opening identifies the position and the newspaper completely so that the reader knows exactly what advertisement Alysha means.

Sell Your Strengths in the Body

The body of a cover letter promotes the candidate's qualifications for the targeted job.

Once you have identified your purpose in the letter opening, you should use the body of the letter to promote your qualifications for this position. If you are responding to an advertisement, you'll want to explain how your preparation and experience fill the stated requirements. If you are prospecting for a job, you may not know the exact requirements. Your employment research and knowledge of your field, however, should give you a reasonably good idea of what is expected for this position.

It's also important to stress reader benefits. In other words, you should describe your strong points in relation to the needs of the employer. Hiring officers want you to tell them what you can do for their organizations. This is more important than telling what courses you took in college or what duties you performed on your previous jobs. Instead of *I have completed courses in business communication, report writing, and technical writing,* try this:

> Courses in business communication, report writing, and technical writing have helped me develop the research and writing skills required of your technical writers.

Choose your strongest qualifications and show how they fit the targeted job. And remember, students with little experience are better off spotlighting their education and its practical applications, as these candidates did:

> Because you seek an architect's apprentice with proven ability, I submit a drawing of mine that won second place in the Sinclair College drafting contest last year.
>
> Composing e-mail messages, business letters, memos, and reports in my communication and microcomputer application courses helped me develop the writing, language, proofreading, and computer skills mentioned in your ad for an administrative assistant.

FIGURE 16.15 ***Solicited Cover Letter***

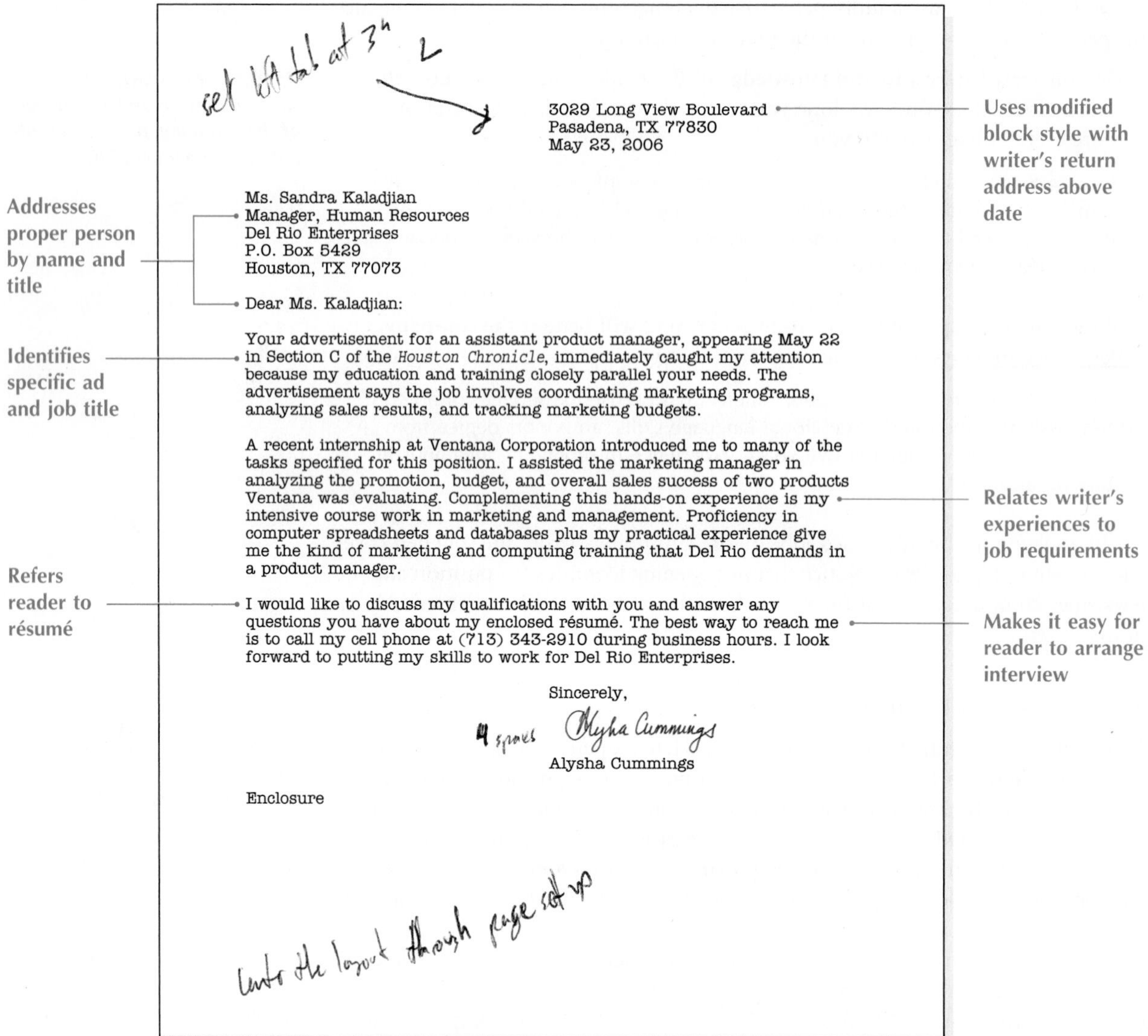

3029 Long View Boulevard
Pasadena, TX 77830
May 23, 2006

Ms. Sandra Kaladjian
Manager, Human Resources
Del Rio Enterprises
P.O. Box 5429
Houston, TX 77073

Dear Ms. Kaladjian:

Your advertisement for an assistant product manager, appearing May 22 in Section C of the *Houston Chronicle*, immediately caught my attention because my education and training closely parallel your needs. The advertisement says the job involves coordinating marketing programs, analyzing sales results, and tracking marketing budgets.

A recent internship at Ventana Corporation introduced me to many of the tasks specified for this position. I assisted the marketing manager in analyzing the promotion, budget, and overall sales success of two products Ventana was evaluating. Complementing this hands-on experience is my intensive course work in marketing and management. Proficiency in computer spreadsheets and databases plus my practical experience give me the kind of marketing and computing training that Del Rio demands in a product manager.

I would like to discuss my qualifications with you and answer any questions you have about my enclosed résumé. The best way to reach me is to call my cell phone at (713) 343-2910 during business hours. I look forward to putting my skills to work for Del Rio Enterprises.

Sincerely,

Alysha Cummings

Enclosure

Uses modified block style with writer's return address above date
Addresses proper person by name and title
Identifies specific ad and job title
Relates writer's experiences to job requirements
Refers reader to résumé
Makes it easy for reader to arrange interview

Employers seek employees who are team players, take responsibility, show initiative, and learn easily.

In the body of your letter, you may choose to discuss relevant personal traits. Employers are looking for candidates who, among other things, are team players, take responsibility, show initiative, and learn easily. Notice how the following paragraph uses action verbs to paint a picture of a promising candidate:

> In addition to developing technical and academic skills at Mid-State University, I have gained interpersonal, leadership, and organizational skills. As vice president of the business students' organization, Gamma Alpha, I helped organize and supervise two successful fund-raising events. These activities involved conceptualizing the tasks, motivating others to help, scheduling work sessions, and coordinating the efforts of 35 diverse students in reaching our goal. I enjoyed my success with these activities and look forward to applying such experience in your management trainee program.

Finally, in this section or the next, you should refer the reader to your résumé. Do so directly or as part of another statement, as shown here:

> As you will notice from my résumé, I will graduate in June with a bachelor's degree in business administration.
>
> Please refer to the attached résumé for additional information regarding my education, experience, and references.

The body of a cover letter can be expanded or contracted depending on how long you want your letter to be. As noted earlier, experts are divided on length. If you prefer a shorter cover letter, reduce the size of the body.

Request an Interview in the Closing

The closing of a cover letter requests an interview and makes it easy to respond.

After presenting your case, you should conclude by asking for an interview. Don't ask for the job. To do so would be presumptuous and naive. In requesting an interview, you might suggest reader benefits or review your strongest points. Sound sincere and appreciative. Remember to make it easy for the reader to agree by supplying your telephone number and the best times to call you. And keep in mind that some hiring officers prefer that you take the initiative to call them. Here are possible endings:

> I hope this brief description of my qualifications and the additional information on my résumé indicate to you my genuine desire to put my skills in accounting to work for you. Please call me at (405) 488-2291 before 10 a.m. or after 3 p.m. to arrange an interview.
>
> To add to your staff an industrious, well-trained administrative assistant with proven word processing and communication skills, call me at (350) 492-1433 to arrange an interview. I can meet with you at any time convenient to your schedule.
>
> I would appreciate the opportunity to discuss my qualifications more fully in an interview. I can be reached on my cell phone at (213) 458-4030.
>
> Next week, after you have examined the attached résumé, I will call you to discuss the possibility of arranging an interview.

Sending Your Cover Letter by E-Mail

Serious job candidates will send a professional cover letter even if a résumé is submitted by e-mail.

It sounds like a "no brainer," but many applicants using the Internet don't include cover letters with their résumés submitted online. A résumé that arrives without a cover letter makes the receiver wonder what it is and why it was sent. Recruiters want you to introduce yourself, and they also are eager to see some evidence that you can write. Because it's only e-mail, some candidates either skip the cover letter or think they can get by with one-line cover letters such as this: *Please see attached résumé, and thanks for your consideration.*

If you are serious about landing the job, take the time to prepare a professional cover letter. You may use the same cover letter you would send by land mail but shorten it a bit. As illustrated in Figure 16.16, don't include an inside address for the e-mail recipient. Also move your return address from the top of the letter to just below your name. Include your e-mail address and phone number. Remove tabs, bullets, underlining, and italics that might be problematic in e-mail messages.

Be careful when sending e-mail cover letters. One widespread goof involves mismerging. Let's say you send the same cover letter to different companies. Unless you're alert, you might send a letter to Fed-Ex that says, "I'm eager to put my skills to work for you at UPS."[21] Also be mindful of the impression your e-mail address makes. Avoid addresses such as *hotbabe@hotmail.com* or *buffedguy@aol.com.* Moreover, don't include anything unbusinesslike, such as your favorite inspirational quotation, in your signature block.

FIGURE 16.16 ***E-Mail Cover Letter***

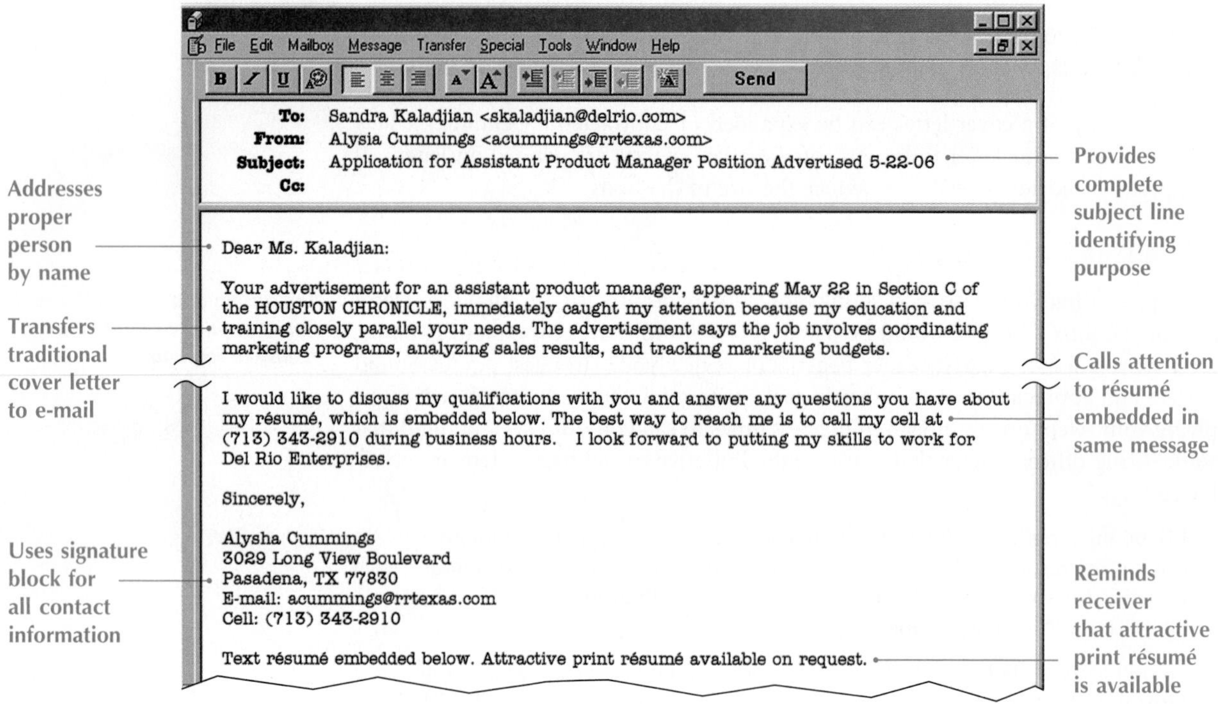
File Edit Mailbox Message Transfer Special Tools Window Help
Send
Addresses proper person by name
Transfers traditional cover letter to e-mail
Uses signature block for all contact information
Provides complete subject line identifying purpose
Calls attention to résumé embedded in same message
Reminds receiver that attractive print résumé is available

To: Sandra Kaladjian <skaladjian@delrio.com>
From: Alysia Cummings <acummings@rrtexas.com>
Subject: Application for Assistant Product Manager Position Advertised 5-22-06
Cc:

Dear Ms. Kaladjian:

Your advertisement for an assistant product manager, appearing May 22 in Section C of the HOUSTON CHRONICLE, immediately caught my attention because my education and training closely parallel your needs. The advertisement says the job involves coordinating marketing programs, analyzing sales results, and tracking marketing budgets.

I would like to discuss my qualifications with you and answer any questions you have about my résumé, which is embedded below. The best way to reach me is to call my cell at (713) 343-2910 during business hours. I look forward to putting my skills to work for Del Rio Enterprises.

Sincerely,

Alysha Cummings
3029 Long View Boulevard
Pasadena, TX 77830
E-mail: acummings@rrtexas.com
Cell: (713) 343-2910

Text résumé embedded below. Attractive print résumé available on request.

Final Tips

Look for ways to reduce the overuse of "I."

As you revise your cover letter, notice how many sentences begin with *I.* Although it's impossible to talk about yourself without using *I,* you can reduce "I" domination with this writing technique. Make activities and outcomes, and not yourself, the subjects of sentences. For example, rather than *I took classes in business communication and computer applications,* say *Classes in business communication and computer applications prepared me to . . . .* Instead of *I enjoyed helping customers,* say *Helping customers was a real pleasure.*

A cover letter should look professional and suggest quality.

Like the résumé, your cover letter must look professional and suggest quality. This means using a traditional letter style, such as block or modified block. Also, be sure to print it on the same quality paper as your résumé. As with your résumé, proofread it several times yourself; then, have a friend read it for content and mechanics. Don't rely on spell check to find all the errors. The following checklist provides a quick summary of suggestions to review when you compose and proofread your cover letter.

Checklist for Writing a Persuasive Cover Letter

Opening

 **Use the receiver's name.** Whenever possible, address the proper individual by name.

 **Identify your information source, if appropriate.** In responding to an advertisement, specify the position advertised as well as the date and publication name. If someone referred you, name that person.

- ✓ **Gain the reader's attention.** Use one of these techniques: (1) tell how your qualifications fit the job specifications, (2) show knowledge of the reader's business, (3) describe how your special talents will be assets to the company, or (4) use an original and relevant expression.

Body

- ✓ **Describe what you can do for the reader.** Demonstrate how your background and training fill the job requirements.

- ✓ **Highlight your strengths.** Summarize your principal assets from education, experience, and special skills. Avoid repeating specific data from your résumé.

- ✓ **Refer to your résumé.** In this section or the closing, direct the reader to the attached résumé. Do so directly or incidentally as part of another statement.

Closing

- ✓ **Ask for an interview.** Also consider reviewing your strongest points or suggesting how your assets will benefit the company.

- ✓ **Make it easy to respond.** Tell when you can be reached during office hours or announce when you will call the reader. Note that some recruiters prefer that you call them.

E-Mailing

- ✓ **Include a cover letter with your résumé.** Send the same letter that might go by land mail except remove the formatting.

- ✓ **Put your contact information in the signature area.** Move your return address from the top of the letter to the signature block. Include your phone number and e-mail address.

Follow-Up Letters and Other Employment Documents

learning objective 6

Although the résumé and cover letter are your major tasks, other important letters and documents are often required during the employment process. You may need to make requests, write follow-up letters, or fill out employment applications. Because each of these tasks reveals something about you and your communication skills, you'll want to put your best foot forward. These documents often subtly influence company officials to extend an interview or offer a job.

Reference Request

To secure good letters of recommendation, find willing people and provide ample data about yourself.

Most employers expect job candidates at some point to submit names of individuals who are willing to discuss the candidates' qualifications. Before you list anyone as a reference, however, be sure to ask permission. Try to do this in person. Ask an instructor, for example, if he or she would be willing and has the time to act as your recommender. If you detect any sign of reluctance, don't force the issue. Your goal is to find willing individuals who think well of you.

A reference request is most effective if it provides a description of the position, its requirements, and the recommendation deadline.

What your recommenders need most is information about you. What should they stress to prospective employers? Let's say you're applying for a specific job that requires a letter of recommendation. Professor Orenstein has already agreed to be a reference for you. To get the best letter of recommendation from Professor Orenstein, help her out. Write a letter telling her about the position, its requirements, and the recommendation deadline. Include a copy of your résumé. You might remind her of a positive experience with you (*You said my report was well-organized*) that she could use in the recommendation. Remember that recommenders need evidence to support generalizations. Give them appropriate ammunition, as the student has done in the following request:

Dear Professor Orenstein:

Identify the target position and company. Tell immediately why you are writing.

Recently I applied for the position of administrative assistant in the Human Resources Department of Host International. Because you kindly agreed to help me, I am now asking you to write a letter of recommendation to Host.

Specify the job requirements so that the recommender knows what to stress in the letter. Also, supply data to jog the memory of the writer.

The position calls for good organizational, interpersonal, and writing skills, as well as computer experience. To help you review my skills and training, I enclose my résumé. As you may recall, I earned an A in your business communication class; and you commended my long report for its clarity and organization.

Provide a stamped, addressed envelope.

Please send your letter before July 1 in the enclosed stamped, addressed envelope. I'm grateful for your support, and I promise to let you know the results of my job search.

Application or Résumé Follow-up Letter

A résumé follow-up letter jogs the recruiter's memory, demonstrates your serious interest, allows you to emphasize your qualifications, and add new information.

If your letter or application or résumé generates no response within a reasonable time, you may decide to send a short follow-up letter like the one shown here. Doing so (1) jogs the memory of the hiring officer, (2) demonstrates your serious interest, and (3) allows you to emphasize your qualifications or add new information.

Dear Ms. Farmer:

Open by reminding the reader of your interest.

Please know I am still interested in becoming an administrative support specialist with Quad, Inc.

Substitute letter *or* résumé *if appropriate. Use this opportunity to review your strengths or to add new qualifications.*

Since I submitted an application [*or* résumé] in May, I have completed my schooling and have been employed as a summer replacement for office workers in several downtown offices. This experience has honed my word processing and communication skills. It has also introduced me to a wide range of office procedures.

Close by looking forward positively; avoid accusations that make the reader defensive.

Please keep my application in your active file and let me know when I may put my formal training, technical skills, and practical experience to work for you.

Interview Follow-Up Letter

Sending a thank-you letter after an interview reveals good manners and enthusiasm for the job.

After a job interview you should always send a brief letter of thanks. This courtesy sets you apart from other applicants, most of whom will not bother. Your letter also reminds the interviewer of your visit as well as suggesting your good manners and genuine enthusiasm for the job. Follow-up letters are most effective if sent immediately after the interview. In your letter refer to the date of the interview, the exact job title for which you were interviewed, and specific topics discussed. Avoid worn-out phrases, such as *Thank you for taking the time to interview me.* Be careful, too, about overusing *I*, especially to begin sentences. Most important, show that you really want the job and that you are qualified for it. Notice how the interview follow-up letter in Figure 16.17 conveys enthusiasm and confidence.

FIGURE 16.17 ***Interview Follow-Up Letter***

3592 Channel Islands Boulevard
Ventura, CA 90630
May 26, 2006

Mr. Eric C. Nielson
Comstock Images & Technology
3201 State Street
Santa Barbara, CA 93104

Dear Mr. Nielson:

Talking with you Thursday, May 25, about the graphic designer position was both informative and interesting.

Thanks for describing the position in such detail and for introducing me to Ms. Ouchi, the senior designer. Her current project designing the annual report in four colors on a Macintosh sounds fascinating as well as quite challenging.

Now that I've learned in greater detail the specific tasks of your graphic designers, I'm more than ever convinced that my computer and creative skills can make a genuine contribution to your graphic productions. My training in Macintosh design and layout suggests that I could be immediately productive on your staff.

You will find me an enthusiastic and hard-working member of any team effort. I'm eager to join the graphics staff at your Santa Barbara headquarters, and I look forward to hearing from you soon.

Cordially,

Christopher D. Wiley

Christopher D. Wiley

Mentions the interview date and specific position

Highlights specific skills for the job

Shows appreciation, good manners, as well as perseverance—traits that recruiters value

Personalizes the message by referring to topics discussed in the interview

Reminds reader of interpersonal skills as well as his enthusiasm and eagerness for this job

Rejection Follow-up Letter

If you didn't get the job and you think it was perfect for you, don't give up. Employment specialists encourage applicants to respond to a rejection. The candidate who was offered the position may decline, or other positions may open up. In a rejection follow-up letter, it's OK to admit you're disappointed. Be sure to add, however, that you're still interested and will contact them again in a month in case a job opens up. Then follow through for a couple of months—but don't overdo it. You should be professional and persistent, but not a pest. Here's an example of an effective rejection follow-up letter:

Following up after a job rejection indicates persistence and may lead to a position.

Dear Mr. O'Neal:

Although I'm disappointed that someone else was selected for your accounting position, I appreciate your promptness and courtesy in notifying me.

Subordinate your disappointment to your appreciation at being notified promptly and courteously.

Emphasize your continuing interest. Express confidence in meeting the job requirements.

Because I firmly believe that I have the technical and interpersonal skills needed to work in your fast-paced environment, I hope you will keep my résumé in your active file. My desire to become a productive member of your Transamerica staff remains strong.

Refer to specifics of your interview. If possible, tell how you are improving your skills.

I enjoyed our interview, and I especially appreciate the time you and Mr. Samson spent describing your company's expansion into international markets. To enhance my qualifications, I've enrolled in a course in International Accounting at CSU.

Take the initiative; tell when you will call for an update.

Should you have an opening for which I am qualified, you may reach me at (818) 719-3901. In the meantime, I will call you in a month to discuss employment possibilities.

Application Forms

Employment application forms, whether on paper or online, require accurate information carefully inserted.

Some organizations require job candidates to fill out job application forms instead of submitting résumés. This practice permits them to gather and store standardized data about each applicant. Whether the application is on paper or online, follow the directions carefully and provide accurate information. The following suggestions can help you be prepared:

- Carry a card summarizing those vital statistics not included on your résumé. If you are asked to fill out an application form in an employer's office, you will need a handy reference to the following data: social security number; graduation dates; beginning and ending dates of all employment; salary history; full names, titles, and present work addresses of former supervisors; and full names, occupational titles, occupational addresses, and telephone numbers of persons who have agreed to serve as references.
- If possible, look over all the questions before starting. Fill out the form neatly, printing if your handwriting is poor.
- Answer all questions. Write *Not applicable (N.A.)* if appropriate.
- Be prepared for salary questions. You may be asked what your previous jobs paid, or you may be asked what salary you expect. Unless you know what comparable employees are earning in the company, the best strategy is to suggest a salary range or to write in *Negotiable* or *Open.*
- Ask whether you may submit your résumé in addition to the application form.

learning objective 7

Interviewing for Employment

Job interviews, for most of us, are intimidating; no one enjoys being judged and, possibly, rejected. You can overcome your fear of the interview process by knowing how it works and how to prepare for it.

Trained recruiters generally structure the interview in three separate activities: (1) establishing a cordial relationship, (2) eliciting information about the candidate, and (3) giving information about the job and company. During the interview its participants have opposing goals. The interviewer tries to uncover any negative information that would eliminate a candidate. The candidate, of course, tries to minimize faults and emphasize strengths to avoid being eliminated. You can become a more skillful player in the interview game if you know what to do before, during, and after the interview.

Before the Interview

Prior to an interview, applicants should research the organization and plan answers to potential questions.

- **Research the organization.** Never enter an interview cold. Visit the library or use your computer to search for information about the target company or its field, service, or product. Visit the company's Web site and read everything. Call the company to request annual reports, catalogs, or brochures. Ask about the organization and possibly the interviewer. Learn something about the company's size, number of employees, competitors, reputation, and strengths and weaknesses.
- **Learn about the position.** Obtain as much specific information as possible. What are the functions of an individual in this position? What is the typical salary range? What career paths are generally open to this individual? What did the last person in this position do right or wrong?
- **Plan to sell yourself.** Identify three to five of your major selling points regarding skills, training, personal characteristics, and specialized experience. Memorize them; then in the interview be certain to find a place to insert them.
- **Prepare answers to possible questions.** Imagine the kinds of questions you may be asked and work out sample answers. Although you can't anticipate precise questions, you can expect to be asked about your education, skills, experience, and availability. The Career Coach box on page 576 shows some of the most common questions and suggests responses.
- **Prepare success stories.** Rehearse two or three incidents that you can relate about your accomplishments. These may focus on problems you have solved, promotions you have earned, or recognition or praise you have received.
- **Arrive early.** Get to the interview five or ten minutes early. If you are unfamiliar with the area where the interview is to be held, you might visit it before the scheduled day. Locate the building, parking facilities, and office. Time yourself.
- **Dress appropriately.** Heed the advice of one expert: "Dress and groom like the interviewer is likely to dress—but cleaner."[22] Don't overdo perfume, jewelry, or after-shave lotion. Avoid loud colors; strive for a coordinated, natural appearance. Favorite "power" colors for interviews are gray and dark blue. It's not a bad idea to check your appearance in a restroom before entering the office.

During the Interview

During an interview, applicants should act confident, focus on their strengths, and sell themselves.

- **Establish the relationship.** Shake hands firmly. Don't be afraid to offer your hand first. Address the interviewer formally (*Hello, Mrs. Jones*). Allow the interviewer to put you at ease with small talk.
- **Act confident but natural.** Establish and maintain eye contact, but don't get into a staring contest. Sit up straight, facing the interviewer. Don't cross your arms and legs at the same time (review body language cues in Chapter 3). Don't manipulate objects, like a pencil or keys, during the interview. Try to remain natural and at ease.
- **Don't criticize.** Avoid making negative comments about previous employers, instructors, or others. Such criticism may be taken to indicate a negative personality. Employers are not eager to hire complainers. Moreover, such criticism may suggest that you would do the same to this organization.
- **Stay focused on your strengths.** Be prepared to answer questions such as those shown in the accompanying Career Coach box. If the interviewer asks

career coach

Looking Good When You Answer Key Interview Questions

Interviewers want to learn about your job experiences, skills, and education so that they can evaluate who you are and decide how you might perform on the job. You can be prepared for the questions in most interviews by studying the following typical questions and strategies for answering them successfully:

- **Why do you want to work for us?** Questions like this illustrate why you must research an organization thoroughly before the interview. Go to the company's Web site, read its annual report, conduct library research, ask friends, and read the company's advertisements and other printed materials to gather data. Describe your desire to work for this organization not only from your perspective but also from its point of view. What have you to offer?
- **Why should we hire you?** This is an opportunity for you to sell your strong points in relation to this specific position. Describe your skills, academic preparation, and relevant experience. If you have little experience, don't apologize—the interviewer has read your résumé. Emphasize strengths as demonstrated in your education, such as initiative and persistence in completing assignments, ability to learn quickly, self-sufficiency, and excellent attendance. One career expert said that the best answer he ever heard to this question was, *I meet deadlines, pay attention to details, can multitask, and always make my boss look good.*
- **What can you tell me about yourself?** Your first response should be to ask what aspect of your job skills and people skills you should focus on. Use this chance to promote yourself. Stick to professional or business-related strengths; avoid personal or humorous references. Be ready with at least three success stories illustrating characteristics important to this job. Demonstrate responsibility you have been given; describe how you contributed as a team player. Focus your answer on an area of your résumé.
- **What are your strongest (or weakest) personal qualities?** Stress your strengths, such as *I believe I am conscientious, reliable, tolerant, patient, and thorough.* Add examples that illustrate these qualities: *My supervisor said that my research was exceptionally thorough.* If pressed for a weakness, you might disguise a strength as a weakness: *Perhaps my greatest fault is being too painstaking with details.* Or, *I am impatient when tasks are not completed on time.* Don't admit weaknesses, not even to sound human. You'll be hired for your strengths, not your weaknesses.
- **Tell me about a time when . . . .** For this behavioral question, be ready to apply the storytelling STAR technique. Describe a **S**ituation or **T**ask, what **A**ction you took, and the **R**esult. For example, *In a team project to develop a business plan, I saw that our group desperately needed a style guide to be able to turn out a professional, coherent, and consistent plan. So I spearheaded group discussions in which we eventually hammered out a style guide resulting in a much-improved final plan.* Practice telling brief, vivid stories that demonstrate learning. Try to relate them to strengths you have mentioned on your résumé.
- **What do you expect to be doing ten years from now?** Formulate a realistic plan with respect to your present age and situation. One possible response is, *Still learning and taking on new challenges.* The important thing is to be prepared for this question.

4-18-07 DUE

a question that does not help you promote your strongest qualifications, answer briefly. Alternatively, try to turn your response into a positive selling point, such as this: *I have not had extensive paid training in that area, but I have completed a 50-hour training program that provided hands-on experience using the latest technology and methods. My recent training taught me to be open to new ideas and showed me how I can continue learning on my own. I was commended for being a quick learner.*

Interviewers tend to ask key questions similar to those in the Career Coach box.

- **Find out about the job early.** Because your time will be short, try to learn all you can about the target job early in the interview. Ask about its responsibili-

- **Do you prefer working with others or by yourself?** This question can be tricky. Provide a middle-of-the-road answer that not only suggests your interpersonal qualities but also reflects an ability to make independent decisions and work without supervision.

- **What kinds of people irritate you?** Avoid letting yourself fall into the trap of sounding overly critical. One possible response is, *I've always gotten along well with others. But I confess that I can be irritated by complainers who don't accept responsibility.*

- **Have you ever changed your major during your education? Why?** Another tricky question. Don't admit weaknesses or failures. In explaining changes, suggest career potential and new aspirations awakened by your expanding education, experience, or maturity.

- **Give me an example of a problem you solved and what your role was.** This is a good time to employ the STAR strategy! Tell a concise story explaining the situation or task, what you did, and the result. For example, *When I was at Ace Products, we continually had a problem of excessive backorders. After analyzing the situation, I discovered that orders went through many unnecessary steps. I suggested that we eliminate much paperwork. As a result, we reduced backorders by 30 percent.* Go on to emphasize what you learned and how you can apply that learning to this job. Practice your success stories in advance so that you will be ready.

- **Tell me about your most rewarding or disappointing work (or school) experiences.** Focus on positive experiences such as technical and interpersonal skills you acquired. Avoid negative or unhappy topics. Never criticize former employers. If you worked for an ungrateful, penny-pinching slave driver in a dead-end position, say that you learned all you could from that job. Move the conversation to the prospective position and what attracts you to it.

- **Have you established any new goals lately?** Watch out here. If you reveal new goals, you may inadvertently admit deficiencies. Instead of *I've resolved to finally learn something about graphics design*, try *Although I'm familiar with simple graphics programs, I decided to get serious about graphics design by mastering Adobe PhotoShop and Illustrator.*

- **What are your long- and short-term goals?** Suggest realistic goals that you have consciously worked out before the interview. Know what you want to do with your future. To admit to an interviewer that you're not sure what you want to do is a sign of immaturity, weakness, and indecision.

- **Tell me about a time when you influenced someone to accept your ideas.** The recruiter is interested in your leadership and teamwork skills. You might respond, *I've learned to appreciate the fact that the way you present an idea is just as important as the idea itself. When trying to influence people, I put myself in their shoes and find some way to frame my idea from their perspective. I remember when I . . . .*

- **Do you have any questions?** Always be ready with questions, such as these: *Why is the position open? What are the initial duties? What training is available? How did you* [the interviewer] *get started with the company? What trends do you see in the company's future?*

Career Application

In teams of two to four, role-play an employment interview. Take turns playing interviewer and interviewee. Answer four to five questions, and then switch. Imagine a company where you'd like to work and answer accordingly.

ties and the kinds of people who have done well in the position before. Inquiring about the company's culture will help you decide if your personality fits with this organization.

- **Prepare for behavioral questions.** Instead of traditional interview questions, you may be asked to tell stories. The interviewer may say, *Describe a time when* or *Give me an example . . .* To respond effectively, learn to use the storytelling or STAR technique. Ask yourself, what the **S**ituation or **T**ask was, what **A**ction you took, and what the **R**esults were.[23] Practice using this method to recall specific examples of your skills and accomplishments. Examples of behavioral

spotlight *on communicators*

Employers today increasingly rely on behavioral interviews to select the right candidate. Instead of traditional questions, you may be asked to "describe a time when . . . ." Career consultant Daisy Wright advises using the storytelling or STAR technique when responding. Ask yourself what the ***S****ituation or* ***T****ask was, what* ***A****ction you took, and what the* ***R****esults were. This method helps you recall specific job-related examples of your skills and accomplishments. Be sure to focus on the successful role you played.*

questions: (1) *Tell me about a problem you solved in a unique way,* (2) *Describe a time when you had to analyze information and make a recommendation,* and (3) *Give me an example of a time when you were under stress to meet several deadlines.* To be fully prepared, develop a coherent and articulate STAR narrative for every bullet point on your résumé.

- **Prepare for salary questions.** Remember that nearly all salaries are negotiable, depending on your qualifications. Knowing the typical salary range for the target position helps. The recruiter can tell you the salary ranges—but you will have to ask. If you've had little experience, you will probably be offered a salary somewhere between the low point and the midpoint in the range. With more experience you can negotiate for a higher figure. A word of caution, though. One personnel manager warns that candidates who emphasize money are suspect because they may leave if offered a few thousand dollars more elsewhere.
- **Be ready for inappropriate questions.** If you are asked a question that you think is illegal, politely ask the interviewer how that question is related to this job. Ask the purpose of the question. Perhaps valid reasons exist that are not obvious.
- **Ask your own questions.** Often, the interviewer concludes an interview with *Do you have any questions about the position?* Inquire about career paths, orientation or training for new employees, or the company's promotion policies. Have a list of relevant questions prepared. If the interview has gone well, ask the recruiter about his or her career in the company.
- **Conclude positively.** Summarize your strongest qualifications, show your enthusiasm for obtaining this position, and thank the interviewer for a constructive interview. Be sure you understand the next step in the employment process.

After the Interview

Keeping notes of the meeting helps candidates remember what happened.

- **Make notes on the interview.** While the events are fresh in your mind, jot down the key points—good and bad.
- **Write a thank-you letter.** Immediately write a letter thanking the interviewer for a pleasant and enlightening discussion. Be sure to spell his or her name correctly.

ALL-TIME FAVORITE INTERVIEW QUESTIONS

Available at **Guffey Xtra! <http://guffeyxtra.swlearning.com>** is a bonus online chapter, "Employment and Other Interviewing." You'll find in-depth information about all kinds of interviewing plus a list of favorite employment interview questions AND strategic answers for many. Additional interviewing tips and questions are in the Study Guide accompanying this book.

Process to Product

Applying Your Skills at Carnival Cruise Lines

AS AN ASSISTANT to Bonnie Gesualdi-Chao at Carnival Cruise Lines, you must help her prepare "before" and "revised" résumé examples. Bonnie was to make a presentation at a nearby college regarding good résumé practices. Her goal was to show students how to improve their résumés so that they were more likely to get them the jobs they sought. You know that in the experience section of a résumé, Bonnie wanted to see specific results and achievements rather than a job title or a list of duties. She showed you one example:

Résumé statement from an applicant for a customer service representative opening:

BEFORE

Responsible for telephones and assisting counselors

REVISED

- Cheerfully answered telephone and in-person questions from parents and students
- Scheduled appointments, greeted visitors, and maintained student files for 12 counselors

Your Task

Based on what you learned in this chapter, use your own experience or your imagination to prepare at least four additional examples of "before" and "revised" examples that Bonnie might use in her presentation. You may use examples from any career area but try to quantify the examples and strive to relate the statements to a targeted career area or actual position, such as accountant, sales representative, product manager, management trainee, or administrative assistant. ■

case study

Summary of Learning Objectives

1 **Prepare for employment by identifying your interests, evaluating your assets, recognizing the changing nature of jobs, choosing a career path, and studying traditional and electronic job-search techniques.** The employment process begins with an analysis of your likes and your qualifications. Because the nature of jobs is changing, your future work may include flexible work assignments, multiple employers, and constant retraining. You can learn more about career opportunities through your campus career center, the Web, your library, internships, part-time jobs, interviews, classified ads, and professional organizations. Traditional job-search techniques range from newspaper ads to developing your own network of friends and relatives. Electronic job-search techniques include visiting Internet job sites and company Web sites.

2 **Compare and contrast chronological, functional, and combination résumés.** Chronological résumés, listing work and education by dates, rank highest with recruiters. Functional résumés, highlighting skills instead of jobs, appeal to people changing careers or those having negative employment histories. Functional résumés are also effective for recent graduates who have little work experience. Combination résumés, including a complete job history along with skill areas, are increasingly popular.

3 **Organize, format, and produce a persuasive résumé.** Target your résumé for a specific job. Study models to arrange most effectively your main heading, career objective (optional), education, work experience, capabilities, awards and activities, personal data (optional), and references (optional). Use action verbs to show how your assets will help the target organization.

4 **Describe techniques that optimize a résumé for today's technologies, including preparing a scannable résumé, an inline résumé, and an e-portfolio.** In addition to a print-based traditional résumé, candidates should consider preparing a scannable résumé that limits formatting and emphasizes keywords. Keywords are nouns that an employer might use to describe a position and its requirements. Inline résumés (also called *ASCII*, *plain text*, or *electronic* résumés) are stripped of all formatting and prepared as a text file so that they may be embedded within e-mail messages. An e-portfolio is a collection of digitized materials that illustrate a candidate's performance, talents, and accomplishments. E-portfolios may be posted at Web sites or burned onto CDs.

5 **Write a persuasive cover letter to accompany a résumé.** Gain attention in the opening by addressing the receiver by name and mentioning the job or a person who referred you. Build interest in the body by stressing your strengths in relation to the stated requirements. Explain what you can do for the targeted company. Refer to your résumé, request an interview, and make it easy for the receiver to reach you. If you send your cover letter by e-mail, shorten it a bit and include complete contact information in the signature block. Remove tabs, bullets, underlining, and italics that could be problematic in e-mail.

6 **Write effective employment follow-up letters and other messages.** Follow up all your employment activities with appropriate messages. After submitting your résumé, after an interview—even after being rejected—follow up with letters that express your appreciation and continuing interest.

7 **Evaluate successful job interview strategies.** Learn about the job and the organization. Prepare answers to possible questions and be ready with success stories. Act confident and natural. Be prepared with STAR narratives so that you can answer behavioral questions. Be ready to ask or answer salary questions. Have a list of your own questions, summarize your key strengths, and stay focused on your strong points. Afterwards, send a thank-you letter.

chapter review

1. Name at least five questions that you should ask yourself to identify your employment qualifications. (Obj. 1)
2. List five sources of career information. (Obj. 1)
3. How are most jobs likely to be found? Internet job boards? Corporate Web sites? Classified ads? Employment agencies? Professional organizations? Networking? (Obj. 1)
4. What is the goal of a résumé? (Obj. 2)
5. What is a chronological résumé, and what are its advantages and disadvantages? (Obj. 2)
6. What is a functional résumé, and what are its advantages and disadvantages? (Obj. 2)
7. Describe three options you have in writing a career objective for your résumé. Which is most appropriate? (Obj. 3)
8. In addition to technical skills, what traits and capabilities are employers seeking? (Obj. 3)
9. To optimize your résumé for today's technologies, how many versions of your résumé should you expect to make? What are they? (Obj. 4)
10. What changes must be made in a typical résumé to make it effective for computer scanning? (Obj. 4)
11. What are the three purposes of a cover letter? (Obj. 5)
12. What information goes in the body of a cover letter? (Obj. 5)
13. Other than a cover letter, what other kinds of documents might you need to write in the employment process? (Obj. 6)
14. What information should a candidate gather in preparing for a job interview? (Obj. 7)
15. How are behavioral interview questions different from traditional questions? Give an example that would be appropriate for your career field. (Obj. 7)

critical thinking

1. How has the concept of the "job" changed, and how will it affect your employment search? (Obj. 1)
2. How is a résumé different from a company employment application? (Objs. 1 and 2)
3. Some job candidates think that applying for unsolicited jobs can be more fruitful than applying for advertised openings. Discuss the advantages and disadvantages of letters that "prospect" for jobs. (Obj. 5)
4. How do the interviewer and interviewee play opposing roles during job interviews? What strategies should the interviewee prepare in advance? (Obj. 7)
5. **Ethical Issue:** Job candidate Karen accepts a position with Company A. One week later she receives a better offer from Company B. She wants very much to accept it. What should she do?

THREE GREAT RESOURCES FOR YOU!

1. Guffey Student Web Site
http://guffey.swlearning.com

Your companion Web site offers chapter review quizzes, WebThink activities, updated chapter URLs, and many additional resources.

2. Guffey XTRA!
http://guffeyxtra.swlearning.com

This online study assistant includes Your Personal Language Trainer, Speak Right!, Spell Right!, bonus online chapters, Documents for Analysis, PowerPoint slides, and much more.

3. Student Study Guide

Self-checked workbook activities and applications review chapter concepts and develop career skills.

activities

16.1 Document for Analysis: Résumé (Objs. 2 and 3)

One effective way to improve your writing skills is to critique and edit the résumé of someone else.

Your Task. Analyze the following poorly organized résumé. Discuss its weaknesses. Your instructor may ask you to revise sections of this résumé before showing you an improved version.

Brenda Ann Trudell
5349 West Plaza Place
Tulsa, OK 74115-3394
Home: (918) 834-4583 Cell: (918) 594-2985
E-mail: supahsnugglykitty@aol.com

Seeking to be hired at Mead Products as an intern in Accounting

SKILLS: Accounting, Internet browsers (Explorer and Netscape), Excel, PowerPoint, QuickBooks, Access, database, spreadsheet.

EDUCATION
Langston University, Tulsa, Oklahoma. Now working on B.B.A. Major: Accounting; GPA in major is 3.5. Expected degree date: June, 2006. Interested in forensic accounting. Took Analysis and Application of Accounting Data as well as Financial Reporting and Concepts.

EXPERIENCE
Assistant Accountant, 2003 to present. Marsh and McLennan, Inc., Bookkeeping/Tax Service, Tulsa. I keep accounting records for several small businesses accurately. I prepare 150 to 200 individual income tax returns each year. At the same time for Overland Truck Lines I keep track of and update A/R records. I make all the payroll records for 16 employees at three other firms. Have to be accurate and work independently. The owner of Marsh and McLennan said I was reliable and painstaking.

Peterson Controls Inc., Tulsa. I held a Data Processing Internship from July to October, 2005. I helped design and maintain spreadsheets and also processed weekly and monthly information for production uptime and downtime. I helped prepare graphs to illustrate uptime and downtime data. I answered calls on the telephone, directed them, and photocopied and collated data and distributed it as needed.

Langston University, Tulsa. I marketed the VITA program to Langston students and organized volunteers and supplies. Official title: Coordinator of Volunteer Income Tax Assistance Project. I did this for three years. I'm proud to be able to help neighborhood people, and I developed people skills.

Community Service: March of Dimes Drive, Central Park High School; All Souls Unitarian Church, assistant director of Children's Choir.

16.2 Document for Analysis: Cover Letter (Obj. 5)

The following cover letter was written by Brenda Trudell to accompany her résumé (see Activity 16.1).

Your Task. Analyze each section of the following cover letter written by Brenda and discuss its weaknesses. Your instructor may ask you to revise this letter before showing you an improved version.

Dear Human Resources Director:

Please consider this letter as an application for the position of intern that I saw at your Web site. Although I am working part time and trying to finish my degree program, I think an internship at your industry-leading firm would be beneficial and would certainly look good on my résumé.

I have been studying accounting at Langston University for four years. I have taken courses in business law, statistics, finance, management, and marketing, but I am most interested in my accounting courses. I am especially interested in forensic accounting.

I have been a student volunteer for VITA, in addition to my course work during the tax season. I liked VITA because it is a project to help individuals in the community prepare their income tax returns, and I learned a lot from this experience. I also worked at Marsh and McLennan learning to keep the books for many small business firms. I should mention that I have had another internship, which was at Peterson Controls. I worked with graphs and spreadsheets, but I am more interested in forensics accounting.

I am a competent, accurate, well-organized person who gets along pretty well with others. I feel that I have a strong foundation in accounting as a result of my course work and my experience. I hope you will agree that, along with my personal qualities and my desire to succeed, I qualify for the internship, which begins March 1, with your company.

Sincerely,

16.3 Identifying Your Employment Interests (Obj. 1)

Your Task. In an e-mail or a memo addressed to your instructor, answer the questions in the section "Identifying Your Interests" at the beginning of the chapter. Draw a conclusion from your answers. What kind of career, company, position, and location seem to fit your self-analysis?

16.4 Evaluating Your Qualifications (Objs. 1, 2, and 3)

Your Task. Prepare four worksheets that inventory your qualifications in these areas: employment, education, capabilities and skills, and honors and activities. Use active verbs when appropriate.

a. **Employment.** Begin with your most recent job or internship. For each position list the following information: employer, job title, dates of employment, and three to five duties, activities, or accomplishments. Emphasize activities related to your job goal. Strive to quantify your achievements.
b. **Education.** List degrees, certificates, and training accomplishments. Include courses, seminars, or skills that are relevant to your job goal. Calculate your grade-point average in your major.
c. **Capabilities and skills.** List all capabilities and skills that recommend you for the job you seek. Use words like *skilled, competent, trained, experienced,* and *ability to.* Also list five or more qualities or interpersonal skills necessary for a successful individual in your chosen field. Write action statements demonstrating that you possess some of these qualities. Empty assurances aren't good enough; try to show evidence (*Developed teamwork skills by working with a committee of eight to produce a . . .*).
d. **Awards, honors, and activities.** Explain any awards so that the reader will understand them. List campus, community, and professional activities that suggest you are a well-rounded individual or possess traits relevant to your target job.

16.5 Choosing a Career Path (Obj. 1)

WEB

Many people know amazingly little about the work done in various occupations and the training requirements.

Your Task. Use the online *Occupational Outlook Handbook* at **http://www.bls.gov/oco**, prepared by the Bureau of Labor Statistics, to learn more about an occupation of your choice. Find the description of a position for which you could apply in two to five years. Learn about what workers do on the job, working conditions, training and education needed, earnings, and expected job prospects. Print the pages from the *Occupational Outlook Handbook* that describe employment in the area in which you are interested. If your instructor directs, attach these copies to the cover letter you will write in Activity 16.10.

16.6 Locating Salary Information (Obj. 1)

WEB

What salary can you expect in your chosen career?

Your Task. Visit *America's Career InfoNet* at **www.acinet.org** and create a detailed salary report. Step through the choices under the "Wages and Trends" link. Base your selections on the kind of employment you are seeking now or will be seeking after you graduate. Bring a printout of your occupation report to class. Be prepared to discuss your report during a class discussion and to submit your printout to your instructor.

16.7 Searching the Job Market (Obj. 1)

Where are the jobs? Even though you may not be in the market at the moment, become familiar with the kinds of available positions because job awareness should become an important part of your education.

Your Task. Clip or print a job advertisement or announcement from (a) the classified section of a newspaper, (b) a job board on the Web, (c) a company Web site, or (d) a professional association listing. Select an advertisement or announcement describing the kind of employment you are seeking now or plan to seek when you graduate. Save this advertisement or announcement to attach to the résumé you will write in Activity 16.9

16.8 Posting a Résumé on the Web (Obj. 4)

WEB

Learn about the procedure for posting résumés at job boards on the Web.

Your Task. Prepare a list of at least three Web sites where you could post your résumé. Describe the procedure involved in posting a résumé and the advantages for each site.

16.9 Writing Your Résumé (Objs. 2 and 3)

Your Task. Using the data you developed in Activity 16.4, write your résumé. Aim it at a full-time job, part-time position, or internship. Attach a job listing for a specific position (from Activity 16.7). Also prepare a list of references. Revise your résumé until it is perfect.

16.10 Preparing Your Cover Letter (Obj. 5)

Your Task. Write a cover letter introducing your résumé. Again, revise until it is perfect.

16.11 Following Up After Submitting Your Résumé (Obj. 6)

Your Task. A month has passed since you sent your résumé and cover letter in response to a job advertisement. Write a follow-up letter that doesn't offend the reader or damage your chances of employment.

16.12 Following Up After an Interview (Obj. 6)

Your Task. Assume you were interviewed for the position you seek. Write a follow-up thank-you letter.

16.13 Requesting a Reference (Obj. 6)

Your Task. Your favorite professor has agreed to recommend you. Write to the professor and request that he or she send a letter of recommendation to a company where you are applying for a job. Provide data about the job description and about yourself so that the professor can target its content.

16.14 Developing Skill With Behavioral Interview Questions (Obj. 7)

LISTENING SPEAKING WEB

Behavioral interview questions are increasingly popular, and they take a little practicing before you can answer them easily.

Your Task. Use your favorite search engine to locate lists of behavioral questions on the Web. Select five skills areas such as communication, teamwork, and decision making. For each skill area find three behavioral questions that you think would be effective in an interview. In pairs of two students, role-play interviewer and interviewee alternating with your listed questions. Your goal is to answer effectively in one or two minutes. Remember to use the STAR method when answering.

16.15 Answering Puffball and Killer Questions in a Virtual Interview (Obj. 7)

WEB

Two Web sites offer excellent interview advice. At **http://interview.monster.com** you can improve your interviewing skills in snappy virtual interviews. You'll find questions, answers, and explanations for interviews in job fields ranging from administrative support to human resources to technology. At **http://www.wetfeet.com/advice/interviewing.asp** you can learn how to answer résumé-based questions, learn how to handle preinterview jitters, and see dozens of articles filled with helpful tips.

Your Task. Visit one or both of the targeted Web sites. If these URLs have been changed, use your favorite search engine to locate "Monster Interviews" and "WetFeet Interviews."

16.16 Creating an Interview Cheat Sheet (Obj. 7)

Even the best-rehearsed applicants sometimes forget to ask the questions they prepared, or they fail to stress their major accomplishments in job interviews. Sometimes applicants are so rattled they even forget the interviewer's name. To help you keep your wits during an interview, make a "cheat sheet." It summarizes key facts, answers, and questions. Use it before the interview and also review it as the interview is ending to be sure you have covered everything that is critical.

Your Task. Prepare a cheat sheet with the following information:

Day and time of interview:

Meeting with: (Name of interviewer, title, company, city, state, zip, telephone, cell, fax, pager, e-mail)

My major accomplishments: (four to six)

My management or work style: (four to six)

Things you need to know about me: (three to four items)

Reason I left my last job:

Answers to difficult questions: (four to five answers)

Questions to ask interviewer:

Things I can do for you:

16.17 Writing a Rejection Follow-Up Letter (Obj. 6)

Assume you didn't get the job. Although someone else was selected, you hope that other jobs may become available.

Your Task. Write a follow-up letter that keeps the door open.

16.18 Finding Special Tips for Today's Résumé Writers (Obj. 4)

INFOTRAC

You graduated last year and landed a terrific job. Now you've been invited back to talk to students about writing résumés.

Your Task. Using InfoTrac, research the topic of employment résumés. Read at least three recent articles. In a memo to your instructor, outline the tips you plan to include in your presentation. List eight or more good tips that are not covered in this chapter. Pay special attention to advice concerning the preparation of online résumés. The subject line of your memo should be "Special Tips for Today's Résumé Writers."

16.19 Swapping Résumés (Obj. 2)

A terrific way to get ideas for improving your résumé is seeing how other students have developed their résumés.

Your Task. Bring your completed résumé to class. Attach a plain sheet with your name at the top. In small groups exchange your résumés. Each reviewer should provide at least two supportive comments and one suggestion for improvement on the cover sheet. Reviewers should sign their names with their comments.

16.20 Evaluating Your Course

Your boss has paid your tuition for this course. As you complete the course, he (or she) asks you for a letter.

Your Task. Write a letter to a boss in a real or imaginary organization explaining how this course made you more valuable to the organization.

16.21 Consumer: Being Wary of Career Advisory Firms With Big Promises and Big Prices (Obj. 1)

CONSUMER | INFOTRAC | WEB

Not long ago employment agencies charged applicants 5 percent of their annual salaries to find jobs. Most agencies have quit this unethical practice, but unscrupulous firms still prey on vulnerable job seekers. Some career-advisory firms claim to be legitimate, but they make puffed-up promises and charge inflated fees—$4,000 is typical.

Your Task. Using InfoTrac and the Web, find examples of current employment scams or danger areas for job seekers. In a presentation to the class or in team discussions, describe three examples of disreputable practices candidates should recognize. Make recommendations to job seekers for avoiding employment scams and disappointment with career-advisory services.

Rich chapter resources are available on the Web sites.

video resources

Video Library 1: Building Workplace Skills Sharpening Your Interview Skills

This video shows you the job interview of Betsy Chin and lets you critique her performance. Based on what you learned in this chapter and your own experiences, what did she do well and what could she improve?

C.L.U.E. review 16

On a separate sheet edit the following sentences to correct faults in grammar, punctuation, numbers, spelling, proofreading, and word use.

1. The employment process begins with introspection which is a word that mean looking inside yourself to analyse what you like and dislike.
2. You cant hope to find the job of your dreams' without first: (1) Knowing yourself; (2) knowing the job market and (3) know the employment process.
3. Candidates complain about Job Boards, because fewer then one point four percent of the candidates are actually hired.
4. With over forty thousand job boards and employment web sites deluging the internet its hard to know where to start looking.
5. Preparing a résumé while you are still in school, help you recognize week qualifications, and give you 2 or 3 years in which to bolster it.
6. Recruiters like to see Career Objectives on résumés, however it may restrict a candidates chances.
7. Todays résumés omit personel data such as birth date, martial status, hite, weigt and religious affiliation.
8. I wonder how many companys now use applicant tracking software to scan candidates résumés and search for keywords?
9. In the latest issue of BusinessWeek did you see the article titled Should you use a career objective on your résumé
10. Before going to a job interview you should research the following, company size, number of employees, competitors, reputation, strengths and weakness.

appendix A

Competent Language Usage Essentials (C.L.U.E.)

A Business Communicator's Guide

In the business world, people are often judged by the way they speak and write. Using the language competently can mean the difference between individual success and failure. Often a speaker sounds accomplished; but when that same individual puts ideas in print, errors in language usage destroy his or her credibility. One student observed, "When I talk, I get by on my personality; but when I write, the flaws in my communication show through. That's why I'm in this class."

What C.L.U.E. Is

This appendix provides a condensed guide to competency in language usage essentials (C.L.U.E.). Fifty guidelines review sentence structure, grammar, usage, punctuation, capitalization, and number style. These guidelines focus on the most frequently used—and abused—language elements. Presented from a business communicator's perspective, the guidelines also include realistic tips for application. Frequent checkpoint exercises enable you to try out your skills immediately. In addition to the 50 language guides in this appendix, you'll find a list of 160 frequently misspelled words plus a quick review of selected confusing words.

The concentrated materials in this guide help novice business communicators focus on the major areas of language use. The guide is not meant to teach or review *all* the principles of English grammar and punctuation. It focuses on a limited number of language guidelines and troublesome words. Your objective should be mastery of these language principles and words, which represent a majority of the problems typically encountered by business writers.

How to Use C.L.U.E.

Your instructor may give you the short C.L.U.E. language diagnostic test (located in the Instructor's Manual) to help you assess your competency. A longer self-administered diagnostic test is available as part of Your Personal Language Trainer with the GuffeyXtra! materials. Either test will give you an idea of your language competence. After taking either diagnostic test, read and work your way through the 50 guidelines. You should also use the self-teaching Trainer exercises, all of which correlate with C.L.U.E. Concentrate on areas where you are weak. Memorize the spelling list and definitions for the confusing words located at the end of this appendix.

Within these C.L.U.E. materials, you will find two kinds of exercises for your practice. (1) *Checkpoints*, located in this appendix, focus on a small group of language guidelines. Use them to test your comprehension as you complete each section. (2) *Review exercises*, located in the text chapters, cover all guidelines, spelling words, and confusing words. Use the review exercises to reinforce your language skills at the same time you are learning about the processes and products of business communication. As you complete the review exercises, you may wish to use the standard proofreading marks shown in Appendix D.

Many students want all the help they can get in improving their language skills. For additional assistance with grammar and language fundamentals, *Business Communication: Process and Product*, 5e, offers you unparalleled interactive and print resources:

- **Your Personal Language Trainer.** This new self-paced learning tool is located at **Guffey Xtra!** Dr. Guffey acts as your personal trainer in helping you pump up your language muscles. Your Personal Language Trainer provides the rules plus hundreds of sentence applications so that you can try out your knowledge and build your skills with immediate feedback and explanations.
- **Speak Right!**, found at **Guffey Xtra!**, reviews frequently mispronounced words. You'll hear correct pronunciations from Dr. Guffey so that you will never be embarrassed by mispronouncing these terms.
- **Spell Right!**, found at **Guffey Xtra!**, presents frequently misspelled words along with exercises to help you improve your skills.
- **Study Guide C.L.U.E. Exercises.** The Student Study Guide accompanying this textbook provides many additional C.L.U.E. review exercises, and the answers are available for immediate checking.
- **Reference Books.** More comprehensive treatment of grammar and punctuation guidelines can be found in Clark and Clark's *A Handbook for Office Workers* and Guffey's *Business English.*

Guidelines: Competent Language Usage Essentials

Sentence Structure

GUIDE 1: Express ideas in complete sentences. You can recognize a complete sentence because it (a) includes a subject (a noun or pronoun that interacts with a verb), (b) includes a verb (a word expressing action or describing a condition), and (c) makes sense (comes to a closure). A complete sentence is an independent clause. One of the most serious errors a writer can make is punctuating a fragment as if it were a complete sentence. A fragment is a broken-off part of a sentence.

Fragment	**Improved**
Because 90 percent of all business transactions involve written messages. Good writing skills are critical.	Because 90 percent of all business transactions involve written messages, good writing skills are critical.
The recruiter requested a writing sample. Even though the candidate seemed to communicate well.	The recruiter requested a writing sample, even though the candidate seemed to communicate well.

Tip. Fragments often can be identified by the words that introduce them—words such as *although, as, because, even, except, for example, if, instead of, since, so, such as,* *that, which,* and *when.* These words introduce dependent clauses. Make sure such clauses are always connected to independent clauses.

DEPENDENT CLAUSE — INDEPENDENT CLAUSE

Since she became supervisor, she had to write more memos and reports.

GUIDE 2: Avoid run-on (fused) sentences. A sentence with two independent clauses must be joined by a coordinating conjunction (*and, or, nor, but*) or by a semicolon (;). Without a conjunction or a semicolon, a run-on sentence results.

Run-on	**Improved**
Robin visited resorts of the rich and the famous he also dropped in on luxury spas.	Robin visited resorts of the rich and famous, and he also dropped in on luxury spas.
	Robin visited resorts of the rich and famous; he also dropped in on luxury spas.

GUIDE 3: Avoid comma-splice sentences. A comma splice results when a writer joins (splices together) two independent clauses—without using a coordinating conjunction (*and, or, nor, but*).

Comma Splice	**Improved**
Disney World operates in Orlando, EuroDisney serves Paris.	Disney World operates in Orlando; EuroDisney serves Paris.
	Disney World operates in Orlando, and EuroDisney serves Paris.
Visitors wanted a resort vacation, however they were disappointed.	Visitors wanted a resort vacation; however, they were disappointed.

Tip. In joining independent clauses, beware of using a comma and words such as *consequently, furthermore, however, therefore, then, thus,* and so on. These conjunctive adverbs require semicolons.

✓ *Checkpoint*

Revise the following to rectify sentence fragments, comma splices, and run-ons.

1. Although it began as a side business for Disney. Destination weddings now represent a major income source.
2. About 2,000 weddings are held yearly. Which is twice the number just ten years ago.
3. Weddings may take place in less than one hour, however the cost may be as much as $5,000.
4. Limousines line up outside Disney's wedding pavilion, they are scheduled in two-hour intervals.
5. Most couples prefer a traditional wedding, others request a fantasy experience.

For all the Checkpoint sentences, compare your responses with the answers at the end of Appendix A beginning on page A-21.

Grammar

Verb Tense

GUIDE 4: Use present tense, past tense, and past participle verb forms correctly.

Present Tense	Past Tense	Past Participle
(Today I _____)	(Yesterday I _____)	(I have _____)
am	was	been
begin	began	begun
break	broke	broken
bring	brought	brought
choose	chose	chosen
come	came	come
do	did	done
give	gave	given
go	went	gone
know	knew	known
pay	paid	paid
see	saw	seen
steal	stole	stolen
take	took	taken
write	wrote	written

The package *came* yesterday, and Kevin *knew* what it contained.

If I *had seen* the shipper's bill, I *would have paid* it immediately.

I *know* the answer now; I wish I *had known* it yesterday.

Tip. Probably the most frequent mistake in tenses results from substituting the past participle form for the past tense. Notice that the past participle tense requires auxiliary verbs such as *has, had, have, would have,* and *could have.*

Faulty	Correct
When he *come* over last night, he *brung* pizza.	When he *came* over last night, he *brought* pizza.
If he *had came* earlier, we *could have saw* the video.	If he *had come* earlier, we *could have seen* the video.

Verb Mood

GUIDE 5: Use the subjunctive mood to express hypothetical (untrue) ideas. The most frequent misuse of the subjunctive mood involves using *was* instead of *were* in clauses introduced by *if* and *as though* or containing *wish.*

If I *were* (not *was*) you, I would take a business writing course.

Sometimes I wish I *were* (not *was*) the manager of this department.

He acts as though he *were* (not *was*) in charge of this department.

Tip. If the statement could possibly be true, use *was.*

If I *was* to blame, I accept the consequences.

✓ Checkpoint

Correct faults in verb tenses and mood.

6. If I was you, I would have went to the ten o'clock meeting.
7. The manager could have wrote a better report if he had began earlier.
8. When the vice president seen the report, he immediately come to my office.
9. I wish the vice president was in your shoes for just one day.
10. If the manager had knew all that we do, I'm sure he would have gave us better reviews.

Verb Voice

For a discussion of active- and passive-voice verbs, see page 177 in Chapter 6.

Verb Agreement

GUIDE 6: Make subjects agree with verbs despite intervening phrases and clauses. Become a detective in locating *true* subjects. Don't be deceived by prepositional phrases and parenthetic words that often disguise the true subject.

Our study of annual budgets, five-year plans, and sales proposals *is* (not *are*) progressing on schedule. (The true subject is *study*.)

The budgeted item, despite additions proposed yesterday, *remains* (not *remain*) as submitted. (The true subject is *item*.)

A vendor's evaluation of the prospects for a sale, together with plans for follow-up action, *is* (not *are*) what we need. (The true subject is *evaluation*.)

Tip. Subjects are nouns or pronouns that control verbs. To find subjects, cross out prepositional phrases beginning with words such as *about, at, by, for, from, of,* and *to.* Subjects of verbs are not found in prepositional phrases. Also, don't be tricked by expressions introduced by *together with, in addition to,* and *along with.*

GUIDE 7: Subjects joined by* and *require plural verbs. Watch for true subjects joined by the conjunction *and.* They require plural verbs.

The CEO and one of his assistants *have* (not *has*) ordered a limo.

Considerable time and money *were* (not *was*) spent on remodeling.

Exercising in the gym and jogging every day *are* (not *is*) how he keeps fit.

GUIDE 8: Subjects joined by* or *or* nor *may require singular or plural verbs. The verb should agree with the closest subject.

Either the software or the printer *is* (not *are*) causing the glitch. (The verb is controlled by the closer subject, *printer*.)

Neither St. Louis nor Chicago *has* (not *have*) a chance of winning. (The verb is controlled by *Chicago*.)

Tip. In joining singular and plural subjects with *or* or *nor*, place the plural subject closer to the verb. Then, the plural verb sounds natural. For example, *Either the manufacturer or the distributors are responsible.*

GUIDE 9: *Use singular verbs for most indefinite pronouns.* The following pronouns all take singular verbs: *anyone, anybody, anything, each, either, every, everyone, everybody, everything, neither, nobody, nothing, someone, somebody,* and *something.*

Everyone in both offices *was* (not *were*) given a bonus.

Each of the employees *is* (not *are*) being interviewed.

GUIDE 10: *Use singular or plural verbs for collective nouns, depending on whether the members of the group are operating as a unit or individually.* Words such as *faculty, administration, class, crowd,* and *committee* are considered *collective* nouns. If the members of the collective are acting as a unit, treat them as singular subjects. If they are acting individually, it's usually better to add the word *members* and use a plural verb.

Correct
The Finance Committee *is* working harmoniously. (*Committee* is singular because its action is unified.)

The Planning Committee *are* having difficulty agreeing. (*Committee* is plural because its members are acting individually.)

Improved
The Planning Committee members *are* having difficulty agreeing. (Add the word *members* if a plural meaning is intended.)

Tip. In the United States collective nouns are generally considered singular. In Britain these collective nouns are generally considered plural.

✓ Checkpoint

Correct the errors in subject–verb agreement.

11. The agency's time and talent was spent trying to develop a blockbuster ad campaign.

12. Your e-mail message, along with both of its attachments, were not delivered to my computer.

13. Each of the Fortune 500 companies are being sent a survey regarding women in management.

14. A full list of names and addresses are necessary before we can begin.

15. Either the judge or the attorney have asked for a recess.

Pronoun Case

GUIDE 11: *Learn the three cases of pronouns and how each is used.* Pronouns are substitutes for nouns. Every business writer must know the following pronoun cases.

Nominative or Subjective Case Used for subjects of verbs and subject complements	**Objective Case** Used for objects of prepositions and objects of verbs	**Possessive Case** Used to show possession
I	me	my, mine
we	us	our, ours
you	you	you, yours
he	him	his
she	her	her, hers
it	it	its
they	them	their, theirs
who, whoever	whom, whomever	whose

GUIDE 12: Use nominative case pronouns as subjects of verbs and as complements. Complements are words that follow linking verbs (such as *am, is, are, was, were, be, being,* and *been*) and rename the words to which they refer.

She and *I* (not *her* and *me*) are looking for entry-level jobs. (Use nominative case pronouns as the subjects of the verb phrase *are looking.*)

We hope that Marci and *he* (not *him*) will be hired. (Use a nominative case pronoun as the subject of the verb phrase *will be hired.*)

It must have been *she* (not *her*) who called last night. (Use a nominative case pronoun as a subject complement.)

Tip. If you feel awkward using nominative pronouns after linking verbs, rephrase the sentence to avoid the dilemma. Instead of *It is she who is the boss,* say *She is the boss.*

GUIDE 13: Use objective case pronouns as objects of prepositions and verbs.

Send the e-mail to *her* and *me* (not *she* and *I*). (The pronouns *her* and *me* are objects of the preposition *to.*)

The CEO appointed Rick and *him* (not *he*) to the committee. (The pronoun *him* is the object of the verb *appointed.*)

Tip. When a pronoun appears in combination with a noun or another pronoun, ignore the extra noun or pronoun and its conjunction. Then, the case of the pronoun becomes more obvious.

Jason asked Jennifer and *me* (not *I*) to lunch. (Ignore *Jennifer and.*)

The waiter brought hamburgers to Jason and *me* (not *I*). (Ignore *Jason and.*)

Tip. Be especially alert to the following prepositions: *except, between, but,* and *like.* Be sure to use objective pronouns as their objects.

Just between you and *me* (not *I*), that mineral water comes from the tap.

Everyone except Robert and *him* (not *he*) responded to the invitation.

GUIDE 14: Use possessive pronouns to show ownership. Possessive pronouns (such as *hers, yours, whose, ours, theirs,* and *its*) require no apostrophes.

All reports except *yours* (not *your's*) have to be rewritten.

The apartment and *its* (not *it's*) contents are *hers* (not *her's*) until June.

Tip. Don't confuse possessive pronouns and contractions. Contractions are shortened forms of subject–verb phrases (such as *it's* for *it is*, *there's* for *there is*, *who's* for *who is*, and *they're* for *they are*).

✓ Checkpoint

Correct errors in pronoun case.

16. My partner and me have looked at many apartments, but your's has the best location.

17. We thought the car was her's, but it's license plate doesn't match.

18. Just between you and I, do you think there printer is working?

19. Theres not much the boss or me can do if its broken, but its condition should have been reported to him or I earlier.

20. We received several applications, but your's and her's were missing

GUIDE 15: Use pronouns ending in self only when they refer to previously mentioned nouns or pronouns.

The president *himself* ate all the M & Ms.

Send the package to Mike or *me* (not *myself*).

Tip. Trying to sound less egocentric, some radio and TV announcers incorrectly substitute *myself* when they should use *I.* For example, "Jerry and *myself* (should be *I*) are cohosting the telethon."

GUIDE 16: Use who or whoever for nominative case constructions and whom or whomever for objective case constructions. In determining the correct choice, it's helpful to substitute *he* for *who* or *whoever* and *him* for *whom* or *whomever.*

For *whom* was this software ordered? (The software was ordered for *him.*)

Who did you say called? (You did say *he* called?)

Give the supplies to *whoever* asked for them. (In this sentence the clause *whoever asked for them* functions as the object of the preposition *to.* Within the clause *whoever* is the subject of the verb *asked.* Again, try substituting *he: he asked for them.*)

✓ Checkpoint

Correct any errors in the use of *self*-ending pronouns and *who/whom.*

21. The boss herself is willing to call whoever we decide to honor.

22. Who have you asked to develop ads for our new products?

23. I have a pizza for whomever placed the telephone order.

24. The meeting is set for Wednesday; however, Matt and myself cannot attend.

25. Incident reports must be submitted by whomever experiences a personnel problem.

Pronoun Reference

GUIDE 17: Make pronouns agree in number and gender with the words to which they refer (their antecedents). When the gender of the antecedent is obvious, pronoun references are simple.

> One of the boys lost *his* (not *their*) new tennis shoes. (The singular pronoun *his* refers to the singular *One*.)
>
> Each of the female nurses was escorted to *her car* (not *their cars*). (The singular pronoun *her* and singular noun *car* are necessary because they refer to the singular subject *Each*.)
>
> Somebody on the girls' team left *her* (not *their*) headlights on.

When the gender of the antecedent could be male or female, sensitive writers today have a number of options.

Faulty

Every employee should receive *their* check Friday. (The plural pronoun *their* does not agree with its singular antecedent *employee*.)

Improved

All employees should receive *their* checks Friday. (Make the subject plural so that the plural pronoun *their* is acceptable. This option is preferred by many writers today.)

All employees should receive checks Friday. (Omit the possessive pronoun entirely.)

Every employee should receive *a* check Friday. (Substitute *a* for a pronoun.)

Every employee should receive *his* or *her* check Friday. (Use the combination *his* or *her*. However, this option is wordy and should be avoided.)

GUIDE 18: Be sure that pronouns such as **it, which, this,** ***and*** **that** ***refer to clear antecedents.*** Vague pronouns confuse the reader because they have no clear single antecedent. The most troublesome are *it, which, this,* and *that.* Replace vague pronouns with concrete nouns, or provide these pronouns with clear antecedents.

Faulty

Our office recycles as much paper as possible because *it* helps the environment. (Does *it* refer to *paper, recycling,* or *office*?)

The disadvantages of local area networks can offset their advantages. That merits further evaluation. (What merits evaluation: advantages, disadvantages, or offsetting of one by the other?)

Improved

Our office recycles as much paper as possible because *such efforts* help the environment. (Replace *it* with *such efforts*.)

The disadvantages of local area networks can offset their advantages. That fact merits further evaluation. (*Fact* supplies a concrete noun for the vague pronoun *that*.)

Faulty	Improved
Negotiators announced an expanded health care plan, reductions in dental coverage, and a proposal of on-site child care facilities. *This* caused employee protests. (What exactly caused employee protests?)	Negotiators announced an expanded health care plan, reductions in dental coverage, and a proposal of on-site child care facilities. *This* reduction in dental coverage caused employee protests. (The pronoun *This* now has a clear reference.)

Tip. Whenever you use the words *this, that, these,* and *those* by themselves, a red flag should pop up. These words are dangerous when they stand alone. Inexperienced writers often use them to refer to an entire previous idea, rather than to a specific antecedent, as shown in the preceding example. You can usually solve the problem by adding another idea to the pronoun (such as *this reduction*).

✓ Checkpoint

Correct the faulty and vague pronoun references in the following sentences. Numerous remedies exist.

26. Every employee must wear their picture identification badge.

27. Flexible working hours may mean slower career advancement, but it appeals to many workers.

28. Any renter must pay his rent by the first of the month.

29. Someone in this office reported that his computer had a virus.

30. Obtaining agreement on job standards, listening to coworkers, and encouraging employee suggestions all helped to open lines of communication. This is particularly important in team projects.

Adjectives and Adverbs

GUIDE 19: Use adverbs, not adjectives, to describe or limit the action of verbs.

Andrew said he did *well* (not *good*) on the exam.

After its tune-up, the engine is running *smoothly* (not *smooth*).

Don't take the manager's criticism *personally* (not *personal*).

She finished her homework *more quickly* (not *quicker*) than expected.

GUIDE 20: Hyphenate two or more adjectives that are joined to create a compound modifier before a noun.

Follow the *step-by-step* instructions to construct the *low-cost* bookshelves.

A *well-designed* keyboard is part of this *state-of-the-art* equipment.

Tip. Don't confuse adverbs ending in *-ly* with compound adjectives: *newly enacted* law and *highly regarded* CEO would not be hyphenated.

✓ Checkpoint

Correct any problems in the use of pronouns, adjectives, and adverbs.

31. My manager and me could not resist the once in a lifetime opportunity.

32. Because John and him finished their task so quick, they made a fast trip to the recently opened snack bar.

33. If I do good on the exam, I qualify for many part time jobs and a few full time positions.

34. The vice president told him and I not to take the announcement personal.

35. In the not too distant future, we may enjoy more practical uses of robots.

Punctuation

GUIDE 21: Use commas to separate three or more items (words, phrases, or short clauses) in a series.

Downward communication delivers job instructions, procedures, and appraisals.

In preparing your résumé, try to keep it brief, make it easy to read, and include only job-related information.

The new ice cream flavors include cookie dough, chocolate raspberry truffle, cappuccino, and almond amaretto.

Tip. Some professional writers omit the comma before *and*. However, most business writers prefer to retain that comma because it prevents misreading the last two items as one item. Notice in the previous example how the final two ice cream flavors could have been misread if the comma had been omitted.

GUIDE 22: Use commas to separate introductory clauses and certain phrases from independent clauses. This guideline describes the comma most often omitted by business writers. Sentences that open with dependent clauses (often introduced by words such as *since, when, if, as, although,* and *because*) require commas to separate them from the main idea. The comma helps readers recognize where the introduction ends and the big idea begins. Introductory phrases of more than five words or phrases containing verbal elements also require commas.

If you recognize introductory clauses, you will have no trouble placing the comma. (A comma separates the introductory dependent clause from the main clause.)

When you have mastered this rule, half the battle with commas will be won.

As expected, additional explanations are necessary. (Use a comma even if the introductory clause omits the understood subject: *As we expected.*)

In the spring of last year, we opened our franchise. (Use a comma after a phrase containing five or more words.)

Having considered several alternatives, we decided to invest. (Use a comma after an introductory verbal phrase.)

To invest, we needed $100,000. (Use a comma after an introductory verbal phrase, regardless of its length.)

Tip. Short introductory prepositional phrases (four or fewer words) require no commas. Don't clutter your writing with unnecessary commas after introductory phrases such as *by 2006, in the fall* or *at this time.*

GUIDE 23: Use a comma before the coordinating conjunction in a compound sentence. The most common coordinating conjunctions are *and, or, nor,* and *but.* Occasionally, *for, yet,* and *so* may also function as coordinating conjunctions. When coordinating conjunctions join two independent clauses, commas are needed.

The investment sounded too good to be true, *and* many investors were dubious. (Use a comma before the coordinating conjunction *and* in a compound sentence.)

Southern California is the financial fraud capital of the world, *but* some investors refuse to heed warning signs.

Tip. Before inserting a comma, test the two clauses. Can each of them stand alone as a complete sentence? If either is incomplete, skip the comma.

Promoters said the investment offer was for a limited time and couldn't be extended even one day. (Omit a comma before *and* because the second part of the sentence is not a complete independent clause.)

Lease payments are based largely on your down payment and on the value of the car at the end of the lease. (Omit a comma before *and* because the second half of the sentence is not a complete clause.)

✓ Checkpoint

Add appropriate commas.

36. Before she enrolled in this class Erin used to sprinkle her writing with commas semicolons and dashes.

37. After studying punctuation she learned to use commas more carefully and to reduce her reliance on dashes.

38. At this time Erin is engaged in a serious yoga program but she also finds time to enlighten her mind.

39. Next fall Erin may enroll in communication and merchandising or she may work for a semester to earn money.

40. When she completes her junior year she plans to apply for an internship in Los Angeles Burbank or Long Beach.

GUIDE 24: Use commas appropriately in dates, addresses, geographical names, degrees, and long numbers.

September 30, 1963, is his birthday. (For dates use commas before and after the year.)

Send the application to James Kirby, 20045 45th Avenue, Lynnwood, WA 98036, as soon as possible. (For addresses use commas to separate all units except the two-letter state abbreviation and the zip code.)

Lisa expects to move from Cupertino, California, to Sonoma, Arizona, next fall. (For geographical areas use commas to enclose the second element.)

Karen Munson, CPA, and Richard B. Larsen, Ph.D., were the speakers. (For professional designations and academic degrees following names, use commas to enclose each item.)

The latest census figures show the city's population to be 342,000. (In figures use commas to separate every three digits, counting from the right.)

GUIDE 25: Use commas to set off internal sentence interrupters. Sentence interrupters may be verbal phrases, dependent clauses, contrasting elements, or parenthetical expressions (also called transitional phrases). These interrupters often provide information that is not grammatically essential.

Harvard researchers, working steadily for 18 months, developed a new cancer therapy. (Use commas to set off an interrupting verbal phrase.)

The new therapy, which applies a genetically engineered virus, raises hopes among cancer specialists. (Use commas to set off nonessential dependent clauses.)

Dr. James C. Morrison, who is one of the researchers, made the announcement. (Use commas to set off nonessential dependent clauses.)

It was Dr. Morrison, not Dr. Arturo, who led the team effort. (Use commas to set off a contrasting element.)

This new therapy, by the way, was developed from a herpes virus. (Use commas to set off a parenthetical expression.)

Tip. Parenthetical (transitional) expressions are helpful words that guide the reader from one thought to the next. Here are typical parenthetical expressions that require commas:

as a matter of fact	in addition	of course
as a result	in the meantime	on the other hand
consequently	nevertheless	therefore
for example		

Tip. Always use *two* commas to set off an interrupter, unless it begins or ends a sentence.

✓ Checkpoint

Insert necessary commas.

41. James listed 1805 Martin Luther King Street San Antonio Texas 78220 as his forwarding address.

42. This report is not however one that must be classified.

43. Employment of paralegals which is expected to increase 32 percent next year is growing rapidly because of the expanding legal services industry.

44. The contract was signed May 15 2003 and remains in effect until May 15 2008.

45. As a matter of fact the average American drinks enough coffee to require 12 pounds of coffee beans annually.

GUIDE 26: Avoid unnecessary commas. Do not use commas between sentence elements that belong together. Don't automatically insert commas before every *and* or at points where your voice might drop if you were saying the sentence out loud.

Faulty
Growth will be spurred by the increasing complexity of business operations, and by large employment gains in trade and services. (A comma unnecessarily precedes *and*.)

Faulty

All students with high grades, are eligible for the honor society. (A comma unnecessarily separates the subject and verb.)

One of the reasons for the success of the business honor society is, that it is very active. (A comma unnecessarily separates the verb and its complement.)

Our honor society has, at this time, over 50 members. (Commas unnecessarily separate a prepositional phrase from the sentence.)

✓ Checkpoint

Remove unnecessary commas. Add necessary ones.

46. Car companies promote leasing because it brings customers back into their showrooms sooner, and gives dealers a steady supply of late-model used cars.

47. When shopping for a car you may be offered a fantastic leasing deal.

48. The trouble with many leases is, that the value of the car at the end of the lease may be less than expected.

49. We think on the other hand, that you should compare the costs of leasing and buying, and that you should talk to a tax adviser.

50. Many American automakers are, at this time, offering intriguing lease deals.

Semicolons, Colons

GUIDE 27: Use a semicolon to join closely related independent clauses. Experienced writers use semicolons to show readers that two thoughts are closely associated. If the ideas are not related, they should be expressed as separate sentences. Often, but not always, the second independent clause contains a conjunctive adverb (such as *however, consequently, therefore,* or *furthermore*) to show the relation between the two clauses.

Learning history is easy; learning its lessons is almost impossible.

He was determined to complete his degree; consequently, he studied diligently.

Serena wanted a luxury apartment located near campus; however, she couldn't afford the rent.

Tip. Don't use a semicolon unless each clause is truly independent. Try the sentence test. Omit the semicolon if each clause could not stand alone as a complete sentence.

Faulty	**Improved**
There's no point in speaking; unless you can improve on silence. (The second half of the sentence is a dependent clause. It could not stand alone as a sentence.)	There's no point in speaking unless you can improve on silence.
Although I cannot change the direction of the wind; I can adjust my sails to reach my destination. (The first clause could not stand alone.)	Although I cannot change the direction of the wind, I can adjust my sails to reach my destination.

GUIDE 28: Use a semicolon to separate items in a series when one or more of the items contains internal commas.

Representatives from as far away as Blue Bell, Pennsylvania; Bowling Green, Ohio; and Phoenix, Arizona, attended the conference.

Stories circulated about Henry Ford, founder, Ford Motor Company; Lee Iacocca, former CEO, Chrysler Motor Company; and Shoichiro Toyoda, chief, Toyota Motor Company.

GUIDE 29: Use a colon after a complete thought that introduces a list of items. Words such as *these, the following,* and *as follows* may introduce the list or they may be implied.

The following cities are on the tour: Louisville, Memphis, and New Orleans.

An alternate tour includes several West Coast cities: Seattle, San Francisco, and San Diego.

Tip. Be sure that the statement before a colon is grammatically complete. An introductory statement that ends with a preposition (such as *by, for, at,* and *to*) or a verb (such as *is, are,* or *were*) is incomplete. The list following a preposition or a verb actually functions as an object or as a complement to finish the sentence.

Faulty	**Improved**
Three Big Macs were ordered by: Pam, Jim, and Lee. (Do not use a colon after an incomplete statement.)	Three Big Macs were ordered by Pam, Jim, and Lee.
Other items that they ordered were: fries, Cokes, and salads. (Do not use a colon after an incomplete statement)	Other items that they ordered were fries, Cokes, and salads.

GUIDE 30: Use a colon after business letter salutations and to introduce long quotations.

Dear Mr. Duran: Dear Lisa:

The Asian consultant bluntly said: "Americans tend to be too blabby, too impatient, and too informal for Asian tastes. To succeed in trade with Pacific Rim countries, Americans must become more willing to adapt to native cultures."

Tip. Use a comma to introduce short quotations. Use a colon to introduce long one-sentence quotations and quotations of two or more sentences.

✓ *Checkpoint*

Add appropriate semicolons and colons.

51. Marco's short-term goal is an entry-level job his long-term goal however is a management position.

52. Speakers included the following professors Rebecca Hilbrink University of Alaska Lora Lindsey Ohio University and Michael Malone Central Florida College.

53. The recruiter was looking for three qualities loyalty initiative and enthusiasm.

54. Microsoft seeks experienced individuals however it will hire recent graduates who are skilled.

55. South Florida is an expanding region therefore many business opportunities are available.

Apostrophe

GUIDE 31: Add an apostrophe plus s *to an ownership word that does not end in an* s *sound.*

We hope to show a profit in one year's time. (Add *'s* because the ownership word *year* does not end in an *s.*)

The company's assets rose in value. (Add *'s* because the ownership word *company* does not end in *s.*)

All the women's votes were counted. (Add *'s* because the ownership word *women* does not end in *s.*)

GUIDE 32: Add only an apostrophe to an ownership word that ends in an s *sound—unless an extra syllable can be pronounced easily.*

Some workers' benefits will cost more. (Add only an apostrophe because the ownership word *workers* ends in an *s.*)

Several months' rent are now due. (Add only an apostrophe because the ownership word *months* ends in an *s.*)

The boss's son got the job. (Add *'s* because an extra syllable can be pronounced easily.)

Tip. To determine whether an ownership word ends in an *'s,* use it in an *of* phrase. For example, *one month's salary* becomes *the salary of one month.* By isolating the ownership word without its apostrophe, you can decide whether it ends in an *s.*

GUIDE 33: Use a possessive pronoun or 's *to make a noun possessive when it precedes a gerund, a verb form used as a noun.*

We all protested *Laura's* (not *Laura*) smoking.

His (not *Him*) talking on his cell phone angered moviegoers.

I appreciate *your* (not *you*) answering the telephone while I was gone.

✓ *Checkpoint*

Correct any problems with possessives.

56. Both companies executives received huge bonuses, even when employees salaries were falling.

57. In just one weeks time we promise to verify all members names and addresses.

58. The manager and I certainly appreciate you bringing this matter to our CPAs attention.

59. All beneficiaries names must be revealed when insurance companies write policies.

60. Is your sister-in-laws job downtown?

Other Punctuation

GUIDE 34: Use one period to end a statement, command, indirect question, or polite request. Never use two periods.

Matt worked at BioTech, Inc. (Statement. Use only one period.)

Deliver it before 5 p.m. (Command. Use only one period.)

Stacy asked whether she could use the car next weekend. (Indirect question)

Will you please send me an employment application. (Polite request)

Tip. Polite requests often sound like questions. To determine the punctuation, apply the action test. If the request prompts an action, use a period. If it prompts a verbal response, use a question mark.

Faulty	**Improved**
Could you please correct the balance on my next statement? (This polite request prompts an action rather than a verbal response.)	Could you please correct the balance on my next statement.

GUIDE 35: Use a question mark after a direct question and after statements with questions appended.

Are they hiring at BioTech, Inc.?

Most of their training is in-house, isn't it?

GUIDE 36: Use a dash to (a) set off parenthetical elements containing internal commas, (b) emphasize a sentence interruption, or (c) separate an introductory list from a summarizing statement. The dash has legitimate uses. However, some writers use it whenever they know that punctuation is necessary, but they're not sure exactly what. The dash can be very effective, if not misused.

Three top students—Gene Engle, Donna Hersh, and Mika Sato—won awards. (Use dashes to set off elements with internal commas.)

Executives at IBM—despite rampant rumors in the stock market—remained quiet regarding dividend earnings. (Use dashes to emphasize a sentence interruption.)

Japan, Taiwan, and Turkey—these were areas hit by recent earthquakes. (Use a dash to separate an introductory list from a summarizing statement.)

GUIDE 37: Use parentheses to set off nonessential sentence elements, such as explanations, directions, questions, or references.

Researchers find that the office grapevine (see Chapter 1 for more discussion) carries surprisingly accurate information.

Only two dates (February 15 and March 1) are suitable for the meeting.

Tip. Careful writers use parentheses to de-emphasize and the dash to emphasize parenthetical information. One expert said, "Dashes shout the news; parentheses whisper it."

GUIDE 38: Use quotation marks to (a) enclose the exact words of a speaker or writer; (b) distinguish words used in a special sense, such as slang; or (c) enclose titles of articles, chapters, or other short works.

"If you make your job important," said the consultant, "it's quite likely to return the favor."

The recruiter said that she was looking for candidates with good communication skills. (Omit quotation marks because the exact words of the speaker are not quoted.)

This office discourages "rad" hair styles and clothing. (Use quotes for slang.)

In *BusinessWeek* I saw an article entitled "Communication for Global Markets." (Use quotation marks around the title of an article; use all caps, underlines, or italics for the name of the publication.)

Tip. Never use quotation marks arbitrarily, as in *Our "spring" sale starts April 1.*

✓ Checkpoint

Add appropriate punctuation.

61. Will you please send your print catalog as soon as possible

62. (Direct quote) Our Super Bowl promotion said the CEO will cost nearly $500,000

63. (De-emphasize) Two kinds of batteries see page 16 of the instruction booklet may be used in this camera

64. Tim wondered whether sentences could end with two periods

65. All computers have virus protection don't they

Capitalization

GUIDE 39: Capitalize proper nouns and proper adjectives. Capitalize the *specific* names of persons, places, institutions, buildings, religions, holidays, months, organizations, laws, races, languages, and so forth. Don't capitalize common nouns that make *general* references.

Proper Nouns	**Common Nouns**
Michelle Deluca	the manufacturer's rep
Everglades National Park	the wilderness park
College of the Redwoods	the community college
Empire State Building	the downtown building
Environmental Protection Agency	the federal agency
Persian, Armenian, Hindi	modern foreign languages

Proper Adjectives	
Hispanic markets	Italian dressing
Xerox copy	Japanese executives
Swiss chocolates	Reagan economics

GUIDE 40: Capitalize only specific academic courses and degrees.

Professor Donna Howard, Ph.D., will teach Accounting 121 next spring.

James Barker, who holds bachelor's and master's degrees, teaches marketing.

Jessica enrolled in classes in management, English, and business law.

GUIDE 41: Capitalize courtesy, professional, religious, government, family, and business titles when they precede names.

Mr. Jameson, Mrs. Alvarez, and Ms. Robinson (Courtesy titles)
Professor Andrews, Dr. Lee (Professional titles)
Rabbi Cohen, Pastor Williams, Pope John (Religious titles)
Senator Tom Harrison, Mayor Jackson (Government titles)
Uncle Edward, Mother Teresa, Cousin Vinney (Family titles)
Vice President Morris, Budget Director Lopez (Business titles)

Do not capitalize a title when it is followed by an appositive (that is, when the title is followed by a noun that renames or explains it).

Only one professor, Jonathan Marcus, favored a tuition hike.

Local candidates counted on their president, George W. Bush, to raise funds.

Do not capitalize titles following names unless they are part of an address:

Mark Yoder, president of Yoder Enterprises, hired all employees.

Paula Beech, director of Human Resources, interviewed all candidates.

Send the package to Amanda Harr, Advertising Manager, Cambridge Publishers, 20 Park Plaza, Boston, MA 02116.

Generally, do not capitalize a title that replaces a person's name.

Only the president, his chief of staff, and one senator made the trip.

The director of marketing and the sales manager will meet at 1 p.m.

Do not capitalize family titles used with possessive pronouns.

my mother, his father, your cousin

GUIDE 42: Capitalize the principal words in the titles of books, magazines, newspapers, articles, movies, plays, songs, poems, Web sites, and reports. Do *not* capitalize articles (*a, an, the*) and prepositions of fewer than four letters (*in, to, by, for*) unless they begin or end the title. The *to* in infinitives (*to run, to say, to write*) is also not capitalized unless it appears as the first word of a title or subtitle.

I enjoyed the book *A Customer Is More Than a Name.*

Did you read the article titled "Companies in Europe Seek Executives With Multinational Skills" that appeared in *Newsweek*?

We liked the article titled "Advice From a Pro: How to Say It With Pictures."

Check the "Advice and Resources" link at the *CareerBuilder* Web site.

(Note that the titles of books are underlined or italicized but the titles of articles are enclosed in quotation marks.)

GUIDE 43: Capitalize north, south, east, west, *and their derivatives only when they represent specific geographical regions.*

from the Pacific Northwest	heading northwest on the highway
living in the East	east of the city
Midwesterners, Southerners	western Oregon, southern Ohio

GUIDE 44: Capitalize the names of departments, divisions, or committees within your own organization. Outside your organization capitalize only* specific *department, division, or committee names.

Attorneys in our Legal Assistance Department met at 2 p.m.

Samsung offers TVs in its Consumer Electronics Division.

We volunteered for the Employee Social Responsibility Committee.

You might send an application to their personnel department.

GUIDE 45: Capitalize product names only when they refer to trademarked items. Don't capitalize the common names following manufacturers' names.

Sony portable television	Skippy peanut butter	NordicTrack treadmill
Eveready Energizer	Norelco razor	Kodak color copier
Coca-Cola	Apple computer	Big Mac sandwich

GUIDE 46: Capitalize most nouns followed by numbers or letters (except in page, paragraph, line, and verse references).

Room 14	Exhibit A	Flight 12, Gate 43
Figure 2.1	Plan No.1	Model Z2010

✓ Checkpoint

Capitalize all appropriate words.

66. vice president moore bought a new nokia cell phone before leaving for the east coast.

67. when you come on tuesday, travel west on highway 5 and exit at mt. mckinley street.

68. The director of our human resources department called a meeting of the company's building security committee.

69. our manager and president are flying on american airlines flight 34 leaving from gate 69 at the las vegas international airport.

70. my father read a businessweek article titled can you build loyalty with bricks and mortar?

Number Usage

GUIDE 47: Use word form to express (a) numbers* ten *and under and (b) numbers beginning sentences. General references to numbers *ten* and under should be expressed in word form. Also use word form for numbers that begin sentences. If the resulting number involves more than two words, however, recast the sentence so that the number does not fall at the beginning.

We answered *six* telephone calls for the *four* sales reps.

Fifteen customers responded to the *three* advertisements today.

A total of 155 cameras were awarded as prizes. (Avoid beginning the sentence with a long number such as *one hundred fifty-five.*)

GUIDE 48: Use figures to express most references to numbers 11 and over.

Over *150* people from *53* companies attended the two-day workshop.

A four-ounce serving of Haagen-Dazs toffee crunch ice cream contains *300* calories and *19* grams of fat.

GUIDE 49: Use figures to express money, dates, clock time, decimals, and percents.

One item cost only *$1.95;* most, however, were priced between *$10* and *$35.* (Omit the decimals and zeros in even sums of money.)

A meeting is scheduled May 12. (Notice that we do *not* write May 12th.)

Deliveries are made at 10:15 a.m. and again at 4 p.m. (Use lowercase *a.m.* and *p.m.*)

All packages must be ready by 4 o'clock. (Do *not* write 4:00 o'clock.)

When U.S. sales dropped *4.7* percent, net income fell *9.8* percent. (Use the word *percent* instead of the symbol %.)

GUIDE 50. Use a combination of words and figures to express sums of 1 million and over. Use words for small fractions.

Orion lost *$62.9 million* in the latest fiscal year on revenues of *$584 million.* (Use a combination of words and figures for sums of 1 million and over.)

Only one half of the registered voters turned out. (Use words for small fractions.)

Tip. To ease your memory load, concentrate on the numbers normally expressed in words: numbers *ten* and under, numbers at the beginning of a sentence, and small fractions. Nearly everything else in business is generally written with figures.

✓ *Checkpoint*

Correct any inappropriate expression of numbers.

71. Although he budgeted fifty dollars, Jake spent 94 dollars and 34 cents for his cell phone.
72. Is the meeting on November 7th or November 14th?
73. We receive UPS deliveries at nine AM and again at four fifteen PM.
74. The company applied for a fifty thousand dollar loan at six%.
75. The United States population is close to 300,000,000, and the world population is estimated to be nearly 6,500,000,000.

Key to C.L.U.E. Checkpoint Exercises in Appendix A

This key shows all corrections. If you marked anything else, double-check the appropriate guideline.

1. Disney, destination
2. yearly, which
3. hour; however,

4. pavilion;
5. wedding;
6. If I *were* you, I would have *gone* . . . .
7. could have *written* . . . had *begun* earlier.
8. vice president *saw* . . . immediately *came*
9. vice president *were*
10. manager had *known* . . . would have *given*
11. talent *were* spent
12. attachments, *was*
13. companies *is*
14. addresses *is*
15. attorney *has*
16. My partner and *I* . . . . , but *yours*
17. was *hers*, but *its*
18. you and *me* . . . *their* printer
19. *There's* not much the boss or *I* can do if *it's* broken, . . . reported to him or *me* earlier.
20. but *yours* and *hers*
21. *whomever*
22. *Whom* have you asked . . . .
23. for *whoever*
24. Matt and *I*
25. by *whoever*
26. Every employee must wear *a* picture identification badge, OR *All employees* must wear picture identification *badges.*
27. slower career advancement, but *flexible scheduling* appeals to many workers. (*Revise to avoid the vague pronoun* it.)
28. Any renter must pay *the* rent . . . . OR *All renters must pay their rent* . . . .
29. reported that *a* computer . . . OR reported that *his or her* computer . . . .
30. communication. *These techniques are* particularly important (*Revise to avoid the vague pronoun* This.)
31. My manager and *I* could not resist the *once-in-a-lifetime* opportunity.
32. John and *he* finished their task so *quickly*
33. do *well* . . . *part-time* jobs and a few *full-time*
34. told him and *me* . . . *personally.*
35. *not-too-distant* future
36. class, Erin . . . with commas, semicolons,
37. studying punctuation,
38. program,

39. merchandising,

40. junior year, . . . in Los Angeles, Burbank,

41. Street, San Antonio, Texas 78220,

42. not, however,

43. paralegals, . . . next year,

44. May 15, 2003, . . . May 15, 2008.

45. fact,

46. sooner [*delete comma*]

47. car,

48. is [*delete comma*]

49. think, on the other hand, . . . buying [*delete comma*]

50. automakers are [*delete comma*] at this time [*delete comma*]

51. entry-level job; his long-term goal, however,

52. professors: Rebecca Hilbrink, University of Alaska; Lora Lindsey, Ohio University; and Michael Malone, Central Florida College.

53. qualities: loyalty, initiative,

54. individuals; however,

55. region; therefore,

56. companies' . . . employees'

57. one week's time, . . . members'

58. appreciate *your* . . . CPA's

59. beneficiaries'

60. sister-in-law's

61. possible.

62. "Our Super Bowl promotion," said the CEO, "will cost nearly $500,000."

63. Two kinds of batteries (see page 16 of the instruction booklet)

64. two periods.

65. protection, don't they?

66. Vice President Moore . . . Nokia . . . East Coast

67. When . . . Tuesday, . . . Highway 5 . . . Mt. McKinley Street.

68. Human Resources Department . . . Building Security Committee

69. Our . . . American Airlines Flight 34 . . . Gate 69 at the Las Vegas International Airport

70. *BusinessWeek* article titled, "Can You Build Loyalty With Bricks and Mortar?"

71. $50 . . . $94.34

72. November 7 or November 14 [*delete "th"*]

73. 9 a.m. . . . 4:15 p.m. (Note only one period at the end of the sentence.)

74. $50,000 . . . 6 percent.

75. 300 million . . . 6.5 billion

Confusing Words

accede: to agree or consent
exceed: over a limit
accept: to receive
except: to exclude; (prep) but
adverse: opposing; antagonistic
averse: unwilling; reluctant
advice: suggestion, opinion
advise: to counsel or recommend
affect: to influence
effect: (n) outcome, result; (v) to bring about, to create
all ready: prepared
already: by this time
all right: satisfactory
alright: unacceptable variant spelling
altar: structure for worship
alter: to change
appraise: to estimate
apprise: to inform
ascent: (n) rising or going up
assent: (v) to agree or consent
assure: to promise
ensure: to make certain
insure: to protect from loss
capital: (n) city that is seat of government; wealth of an individual; (adj) chief
capitol: building that houses state or national lawmakers
cereal: breakfast food
serial: arranged in sequence
cite: to quote; to summon
site: location
sight: a view; to see
coarse: rough texture
course: a route; part of a meal; a unit of learning
complement: that which completes
compliment: (n) praise, flattery; (v) to praise or flatter
conscience: regard for fairness
conscious: aware
council: governing body
counsel: (n) advice, attorney; (v) to give advice
credible: believable
creditable: good enough for praise or esteem; reliable
desert: arid land; to abandon
dessert: sweet food
device: invention or mechanism
devise: to design or arrange
disburse: to pay out
disperse: to scatter widely
elicit: to draw out
illicit: unlawful
envelop: (v) to wrap, surround, or conceal
envelope: (n) a container for a written message
every day: each single day
everyday: ordinary
farther: a greater distance
further: additional
formally: in a formal manner
formerly: in the past
grate: (v) to reduce to small particles; to cause irritation; (n) a frame of crossed bars blocking a passage
great: (adj) large in size; numerous; eminent or distinguished
hole: an opening
whole: complete
imply: to suggest indirectly
infer: to reach a conclusion
lean: (v) to rest against; (adj) not fat
lien: (n) a legal right or claim to property

liable:	legally responsible
libel:	damaging written statement
loose:	not fastened
lose:	to misplace
miner:	person working in a mine
minor:	a lesser item; person under age
patience:	calm perseverance
patients:	people receiving medical treatment
personal:	private, individual
personnel:	employees
plaintiff:	(n) one who initiates a lawsuit
plaintive:	(adj) expressive of suffering or woe
populace:	(n) the masses; population of a place
populous:	(adj) densely populated
precede:	to go before
proceed:	to continue
precedence:	priority
precedents:	events used as an example
principal:	(n) capital sum; school official; (adj) chief
principle:	rule of action
stationary:	immovable
stationery:	writing material
than:	conjunction showing comparison
then:	adverb meaning "at that time"
their:	possessive form of *they*
there:	at that place or point
they're:	contraction of *they are*
to:	a preposition; the sign of the infinitive
too:	an adverb meaning "also" or "to an excessive extent"
two:	a number
waiver:	abandonment of a claim
waver:	to shake or fluctuate

160 Frequently Misspelled Words

absence
accommodate
achieve
acknowledgment
across
adequate
advisable
analyze
annually
appointment
argument
automatically
bankruptcy
becoming
beneficial
budget
business
calendar
canceled
catalog
changeable
column
committee
congratulate
conscience
conscious
consecutive
consensus
consistent
control
convenient
correspondence
courteous
criticize
decision
deductible
defendant
definitely
dependent
describe
desirable
destroy
development
disappoint
dissatisfied
division
efficient
embarrass
emphasis
emphasize
employee
envelope
equipped
especially
evidently
exaggerate
excellent
exempt
existence
extraordinary
familiar
fascinate
feasible
February
fiscal
foreign
forty
fourth
friend
genuine
government
grammar
grateful
guarantee
harass
height
hoping
immediate
incidentally
incredible
independent
indispensable
interrupt
irrelevant
itinerary
judgment
knowledge
legitimate
library
license
maintenance
manageable
manufacturer
mileage
miscellaneous
mortgage
necessary
nevertheless
ninety
ninth
noticeable
occasionally
occurred
offered
omission
omitted
opportunity
opposite
ordinarily
paid
pamphlet
permanent
permitted
pleasant
practical
prevalent
privilege
probably
procedure
profited
prominent
quality
quantity
questionnaire
receipt
receive
recognize
recommendation
referred
regarding
remittance
representative
restaurant
schedule
secretary
separate
similar
sincerely
software
succeed
sufficient
supervisor
surprise
tenant
therefore
thorough
though
through
truly
undoubtedly
unnecessarily
usable
usage
using
usually
valuable
volume
weekday
writing
yield

appendix B

Reference Guide to Document Formats

Business documents carry two kinds of messages. Verbal messages are conveyed by the words chosen to express the writer's ideas. Nonverbal messages are conveyed largely by the appearance of a document. If you compare an assortment of letters and memos from various organizations, you will notice immediately that some look more attractive and more professional than others. The nonverbal message of the professional-looking documents suggests that they were sent by people who are careful, informed, intelligent, and successful. Understandably, you're more likely to take seriously documents that use professional formatting techniques.

Over the years certain practices and conventions have arisen regarding the appearance and formatting of business documents. Although these conventions offer some choices (such as letter and punctuation styles), most business documents follow standardized formats. To ensure that your documents carry favorable nonverbal messages about you and your organization, you'll want to give special attention to the appearance and formatting of your letters, envelopes, e-mail messages, and fax cover sheets.

Spacing and Punctuation

For some time typists left two spaces after end punctuation (periods, question marks, and so forth). This practice was necessary, it was thought, because typewriters did not have proportional spacing and sentences were easier to read if two spaces separated them. Professional typesetters, however, never followed this practice because they used proportional spacing, and readability was not a problem. Fortunately, today's word processors now make available the same fonts used by typesetters.

The question of how many spaces to leave after concluding punctuation is one of the most frequently asked questions at the Modern Language Association Web site (**http://www.mla.org**). MLA experts point out that most publications in this country today have the same spacing after a punctuation mark as between words on the same line. Influenced by the look of typeset publications, many writers now leave only one space after end punctuation. As a practical matter, however, it is not wrong to use two spaces.

Letter Placement

The easiest way to place letters on the page is to use the defaults of your word processing program. These are usually set for side margins of 1 inch or 1¼ inches. Many companies today find these margins acceptable.

If you want to adjust your margins to better balance shorter letters, use the following chart:

Words in Body of Letter	Side Margins	Blank Lines After Date
Under 200	$1\frac{1}{2}$ inches	4 to 10
Over 200	1 inch	2 to 3

Experts say that a "ragged" right margin is easier to read than a justified (even) margin. You might want to turn off the justification feature of your word processing program if it automatically justifies the right margin.

Letter Parts

Professional-looking business letters are arranged in a conventional sequence with standard parts. Following is a discussion of how to use these letter parts properly. Figure B.1 illustrates the parts of a block-style letter. (See Chapter 9 for additional discussion of letters and their parts.)

Letterhead. Most business organizations use $8\frac{1}{2} \times 11$-inch paper printed with a letterhead displaying their official name, street address, Web address, e-mail address, and telephone and fax numbers. The letterhead may also include a logo and an advertising message.

Dateline. On letterhead paper you should place the date two blank lines below the last line of the letterhead or 2 inches from the top edge of the paper (line 13). On plain paper place the date immediately below your return address. Since the date goes on line 13, start the return address an appropriate number of lines above it. The most common dateline format is as follows: *June 9, 2006.* Don't use *th* (or *rd*) when the date is written this way. For European or military correspondence, use the following dateline format: *9 June 2006.* Notice that no commas are used.

Addressee and Delivery Notations. Delivery notations such as *FAX TRANSMISSION, FEDERAL EXPRESS, MESSENGER DELIVERY, CONFIDENTIAL,* or *CERTIFIED MAIL* are typed in all capital letters two blank lines above the inside address.

Inside Address. Type the inside address—that is, the address of the organization or person receiving the letter—single-spaced, starting at the left margin. The number of lines between the dateline and the inside address depends on the size of the letter body, the type size (point or pitch size), and the length of the typing lines. Generally, one to nine blank lines are appropriate.

Be careful to duplicate the exact wording and spelling of the recipient's name and address on your documents. Usually, you can copy this information from the letterhead of the correspondence you are answering. If, for example, you are responding to *Jackson & Perkins Company,* don't address your letter to *Jackson & Perkins Corp.*

Always be sure to include a courtesy title such as *Mr., Ms., Mrs., Dr.,* or *Professor* before a person's name in the inside address—for both the letter and the envelope. Although many women in business today favor *Ms.*, you'll want to use whatever title the addressee prefers.

FIGURE B.1 ***Block and Modified Block Letter Styles***

Block style
Mixed punctuation

Letterhead — **Island Graphics**
893 Dillingham Boulevard
Honolulu, HI 96817-8817
(808)493-2310
http://www.islandgraphics.com

↓ Dateline is 2 inches from the top or 1 blank line below letterhead

Dateline — September 13, 200x

↓ 1 to 9 blank lines

Inside address — Mr. T. M. Wilson, President
Visual Concept Enterprises
1901 Kaumualii Highway
Lihue, HI 96766

↓ 1 blank line

Salutation — Dear Mr. Wilson:

↓ 1 blank line

Subject line — SUBJECT: BLOCK LETTER STYLE

↓ 1 blank line

Body — This letter illustrates block letter style, about which you asked. All typed lines begin at the left margin. The date is usually placed 2 inches from the top edge of the paper or one blank line below the last line of the letterhead, whichever position is lower.

This letter also shows mixed punctuation. A colon follows the salutation, and a comma follows the complimentary close. Open punctuation requires no colon after the salutation and no comma following the close; however, open punctuation is seldom seen today.

If a subject line is included, it appears two lines below the salutation. The word *SUBJECT* is optional. Most readers will recognize a statement in this position as the subject without an identifying label. The complimentary close appears one blank line below the end of the last paragraph.

↓ 1 blank line

Complimentary close — Sincerely,

↓ 3 blank lines

Signature block — Mark H. Wong
Graphics Designer

↓ 1 blank line

Reference initials — MHW:pil

Modified block style,
Mixed punctuation

In the modified block-style letter shown at the left, the date is centered or aligned with the complimentary close and signature block, which start at the center. Mixed punctuation includes a colon after the salutation and a comma after the complimentary close, as shown above and at the left.

Remember that the inside address is not included for readers (who already know who and where they are). It's there to help writers accurately file a copy of the message.

In general, avoid abbreviations such as *Ave.* or *Co.* unless they appear in the printed letterhead of the document being answered.

Attention Line. An attention line allows you to send your message officially to an organization but to direct it to a specific individual, officer, or department. However, if you know an individual's complete name, it's always better to use it as the first line of the inside address and avoid an attention line. Here are two common formats for attention lines:

MultiMedia Enterprises
931 Calkins Road
Rochester, NY 14301

ATTENTION MARKETING DIRECTOR

MultiMedia Enterprises
Attention: Marketing Director
931 Calkins Road
Rochester, NY 14301

Attention lines may be typed in all caps or with upper- and lowercase letters. The colon following *Attention* is optional. Notice that an attention line may be placed two lines below the address block or printed as the second line of the inside address. You'll want to use the latter format if you're composing on a word processor because the address block may be copied to the envelope and the attention line will not interfere with the last-line placement of the zip code. Mail can be sorted more easily if the zip code appears in the last line of a typed address.

Whenever possible, use a person's name as the first line of an address instead of putting that name in an attention line. Some writers use an attention line because they fear that letters addressed to individuals at companies may be considered private. They worry that if the addressee is no longer with the company, the letter may be forwarded or not opened. Actually, unless a letter is marked *Personal* or *Confidential,* it will very likely be opened as business mail.

Salutation. For most letter styles place the letter greeting, or salutation, one blank line below the last line of the inside address or the attention line (if used). If the letter is addressed to an individual, use that person's courtesy title and last name (*Dear Mr. Lanham*). Even if you are on a first-name basis (*Dear Leslie*), be sure to add a colon (not a comma or a semicolon) after the salutation. Do not use an individual's full name in the salutation (not *Dear Mr. Leslie Lanham*) unless you are unsure of gender (*Dear Leslie Lanham*).

For letters with attention lines or those addressed to organizations, the selection of an appropriate salutation has become more difficult. Formerly, writers used *Gentlemen* generically for all organizations. With increasing numbers of women in business management today, however, *Gentlemen* is problematic. Because no universally acceptable salutation has emerged as yet, you could use *Ladies and Gentlemen* or *Gentlemen and Ladies.*

One way to avoid the salutation dilemma is to address a document to a specific person. Another alternative is to use the simplified letter style (shown in Figure B.2), which conveniently omits the salutation (and the complimentary close).

Subject and Reference Lines. Although experts suggest placing the subject line one blank line below the salutation, many businesses actually place it above the salutation. Use whatever style your organization prefers. Reference lines often show policy or file numbers; they generally appear one blank line above the salutation. Use initial capital letters for the main words or all capital letters.

Body. Most business letters and memorandums are single-spaced, with double-spacing between paragraphs. Very short messages may be double-spaced with indented paragraphs.

Complimentary Close. Typed one blank line below the last line of the letter, the complimentary close may be formal (*Very truly yours*) or informal (*Sincerely* or *Cordially*). The simplified letter style omits a complimentary close.

Signature Block. In most letter styles the writer's typed name and optional identification appear three or four blank lines below the complimentary close. The combination of name, title, and organization information should be arranged to achieve a balanced look. The name and title may appear on the same line or on separate lines, depending on the length of each. Use commas to separate categories within the same line, but not to conclude a line.

Sincerely yours,

Jeremy M. Wood

Jeremy M. Wood, Manager
Technical Sales and Services

Cordially yours,

Casandra Baker-Murillo

Casandra Baker-Murillo
Executive Vice President

Courtesy titles (*Ms., Mrs.,* or *Miss*) should be used before names that are not readily distinguishable as male or female. They should also be used before names containing only initials and international names. The title is usually placed in parentheses, but it may appear without them.

Yours truly,

K. C. Tripton

(Ms.) K. C. Tripton
Project Manager

Sincerely,

Leslie Hill

(Mr.) Leslie Hill
Public Policy Department

Some organizations include their names in the signature block. In such cases the organization name appears in all caps one blank line below the complimentary close, as shown here.

Cordially,

LIPTON COMPUTER SERVICES

Shelina A. Simpson

Ms. Shelina A. Simpson
Executive Assistant

Reference Initials. If used, the initials of the typist and writer are typed one blank line below the writer's name and title. Generally, the writer's initials are capitalized and the typist's are lowercased, but this format varies.

Enclosure Notation. When an enclosure or attachment accompanies a document, a notation to that effect appears one blank line below the reference initials. This notation reminds the typist to insert the enclosure in the envelope, and it reminds the recipient to look for the enclosure or attachment. The notation may be spelled out (*Enclosure, Attachment*), or it may be abbreviated (*Enc., Att.*). It may indicate the number of enclosures or attachments, and it may also identify a specific enclosure (*Enclosure: Form 1099*).

Copy Notation. If you make copies of correspondence for other individuals, you may use *cc* to indicate carbon copy, *pc* to indicate photocopy, or merely *c* for any kind of copy. A colon following the initial(s) is optional.

Second-Page Heading. When a letter extends beyond one page, use plain paper of the same quality and color as the first page. Identify the second and succeeding pages with a heading consisting of the name of the addressee, the page number, and the date. Use either of the following two formats:

Ms. Rachel Ruiz	2	May 3, 2006

Ms. Rachel Ruiz
Page 2
May 3, 2006

Both headings appear 1 inch from the top edge of the paper followed by two blank lines to separate them from the continuing text. Avoid using a second page if you have only one line or the complimentary close and signature block to fill that page.

Plain-Paper Return Address. If you prepare a personal or business letter on plain paper, place your address immediately above the date. Do not include your name; you will type (and sign) your name at the end of your letter. If your return address contains two lines, begin typing so that the date appears 2 inches from the top. Avoid abbreviations except for a two-letter state abbreviation.

580 East Leffels Street
Springfield, OH 45501
December 14, 2006

Ms. Ellen Siemens
Escrow Department
TransOhio First Federal
1220 Wooster Boulevard
Columbus, OH 43218-2900

Dear Ms. Siemens:

For letters in the block style, type the return address at the left margin. For modified block-style letters, start the return address at the center to align with the complimentary close.

Letter Styles

Business letters are generally prepared in one of three formats. The most popular is the block style, but the simplified style has much to recommend it.

Block Style. In the block style, shown in Figure B.1, all lines begin at the left margin. This style is a favorite because it is easy to format.

FIGURE B.2 ***Simplified Letter Style***

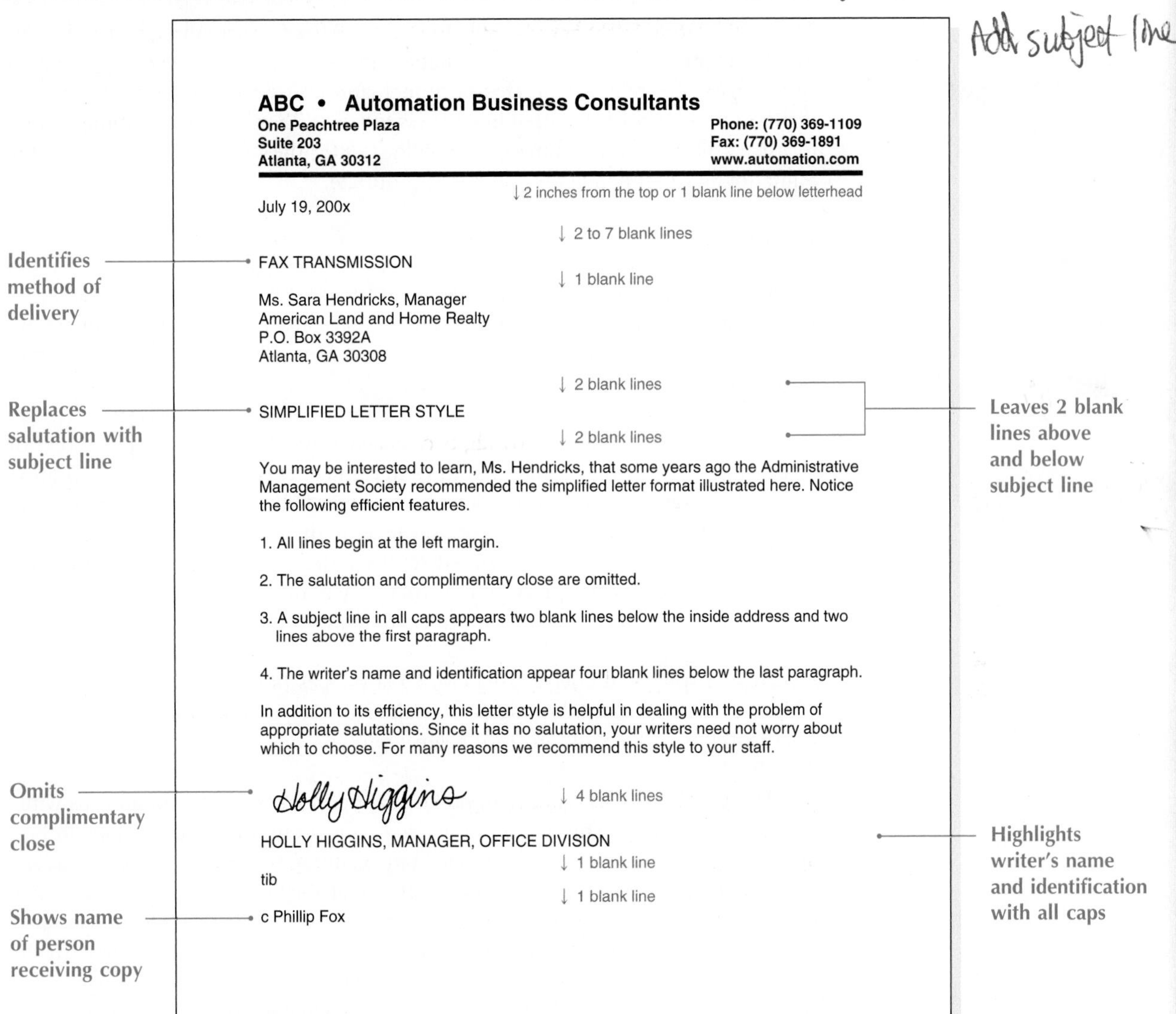

ABC • Automation Business Consultants
One Peachtree Plaza
Suite 203
Atlanta, GA 30312

Phone: (770) 369-1109
Fax: (770) 369-1891
www.automation.com

July 19, 200x

FAX TRANSMISSION

Ms. Sara Hendricks, Manager
American Land and Home Realty
P.O. Box 3392A
Atlanta, GA 30308

SIMPLIFIED LETTER STYLE

You may be interested to learn, Ms. Hendricks, that some years ago the Administrative Management Society recommended the simplified letter format illustrated here. Notice the following efficient features.

1. All lines begin at the left margin.

2. The salutation and complimentary close are omitted.

3. A subject line in all caps appears two blank lines below the inside address and two lines above the first paragraph.

4. The writer's name and identification appear four blank lines below the last paragraph.

In addition to its efficiency, this letter style is helpful in dealing with the problem of appropriate salutations. Since it has no salutation, your writers need not worry about which to choose. For many reasons we recommend this style to your staff.

Holly Higgins

HOLLY HIGGINS, MANAGER, OFFICE DIVISION

tib

c Phillip Fox

Modified Block Style. The modified block style differs from block style in that the date and closing lines appear in the center, as shown at the bottom of Figure B.1. The date may be (1) centered, (2) begun at the center of the page (to align with the closing lines), or (3) backspaced from the right margin. The signature block—including the complimentary close, writer's name and title, or organization identification—begins at the center. The first line of each paragraph may begin at the left margin or may be indented five or ten spaces. All other lines begin at the left margin.

Simplified Style. Introduced by the Administrative Management Society a number of years ago, the simplified letter style, shown in Figure B.2, requires little formatting. Like the block style, all lines begin at the left margin. A subject line appears in all caps two blank lines below the inside address and two blank lines above the first paragraph. The salutation and complimentary close are omitted. The signer's name and identification appear in all caps four blank lines below the last paragraph. This letter style is efficient and avoids the problems of appropriate salutations and courtesy titles.

Punctuation Styles

Two punctuation styles are available for letters. *Mixed* punctuation, shown in Figure B.1, requires a colon after the salutation and a comma after the complimentary close. *Open* punctuation contains no punctuation after the salutation or complimentary close. It is seldom used in business today. With mixed punctuation, be sure to use a colon—not a comma or semicolon—after the salutation. Even when the salutation is a first name, the colon is appropriate.

Envelopes

An envelope should be of the same quality and color of stationery as the letter it carries. Because the envelope introduces your message and makes the first impression, you need to be especially careful in addressing it. Moreover, how you fold the letter is important.

Return Address. The return address is usually printed in the upper left corner of an envelope, as shown in Figure B.3. In large companies some form of identification (the writer's initials, name, or location) may be typed above the company name and address. This identification helps return the letter to the sender in case of nondelivery.

On an envelope without a printed return address, single-space the return address in the upper left corner. Beginning on line 3 on the fourth space ($\frac{1}{2}$ inch) from the left edge, type the writer's name, title, company, and mailing address.

Mailing Address. On legal-sized No. 10 envelopes ($4\frac{1}{8}$ x $9\frac{1}{2}$ inches), begin the address on line 13 about $4\frac{1}{4}$ inches from the left edge, as shown in Figure B.3. For small envelopes ($3\frac{5}{8}$ x $6\frac{1}{2}$ inches), begin typing on line 12 about $2\frac{1}{2}$ inches from the left edge.

The U.S. Postal Service recommends that addresses be typed in all caps without any punctuation. This Postal Service style, shown in the small envelope in Figure B.3, was originally developed to facilitate scanning by optical character readers. Today's OCRs, however, are so sophisticated that they scan upper- and lowercase letters easily. Many companies today do not follow the Postal Service format because they prefer to use the same format for the envelope as for the inside address. If the same format is used, writers can take advantage of word processing programs to "copy" the inside address to the envelope, thus saving keystrokes and reducing errors. Having the same format on both the inside address and the envelope also looks more professional and consistent. For those reasons you may choose to use the familiar upper- and lowercase combination format. But you will want to check with your organization to learn its preference.

In addressing your envelopes for delivery in this country or in Canada, use the two-letter state and province abbreviations shown in Figure B.4. Notice that these abbreviations are in capital letters without periods.

Folding. The way a letter is folded and inserted into an envelope sends additional nonverbal messages about a writer's professionalism and carefulness. Most businesspeople follow the procedures shown here, which produce the least number of creases to distract readers.

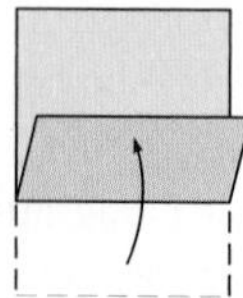
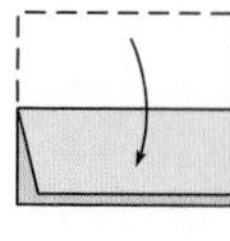
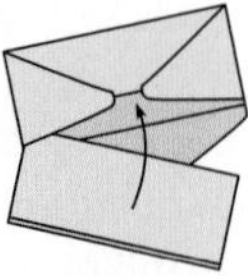

FIGURE B.3 ***Envelope Formats***

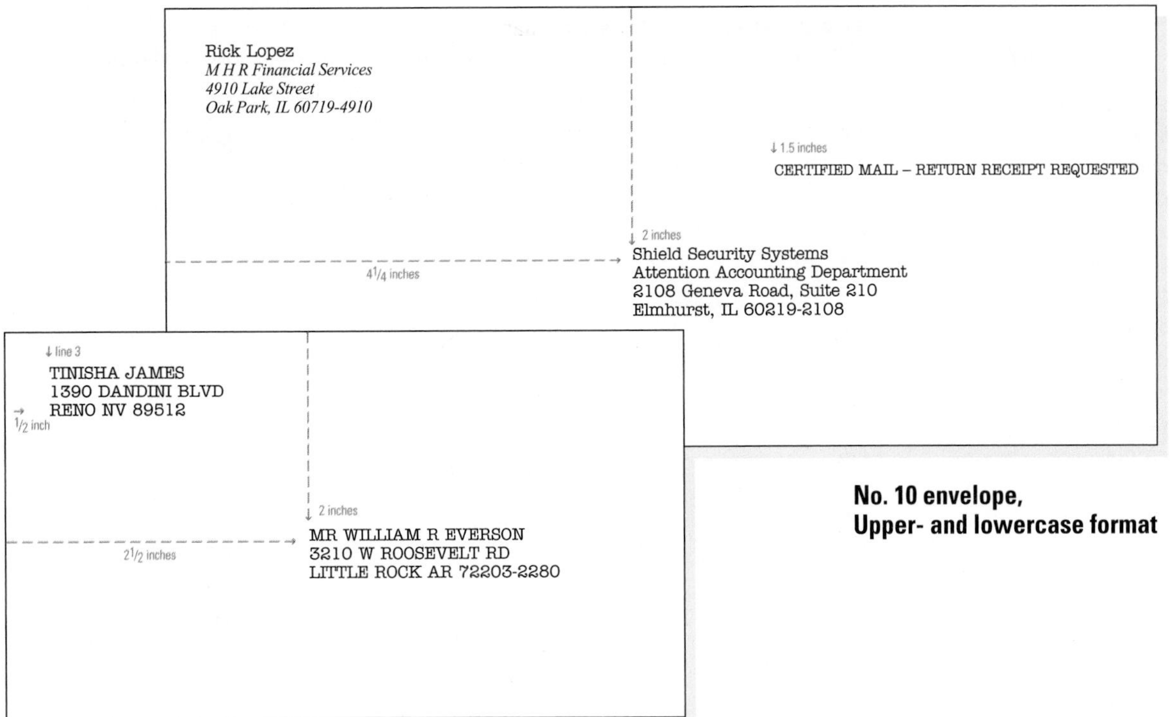

No. 10 envelope, Upper- and lowercase format

No. 6¾ envelope, Postal Service uppercase format

For large No. 10 envelopes, begin with the letter face up. Fold slightly less than one third of the sheet toward the top, as shown in the diagram on page A-34. Then fold down the top third to within ⅓ inch of the bottom fold. Insert the letter into the envelope with the last fold toward the bottom of the envelope.

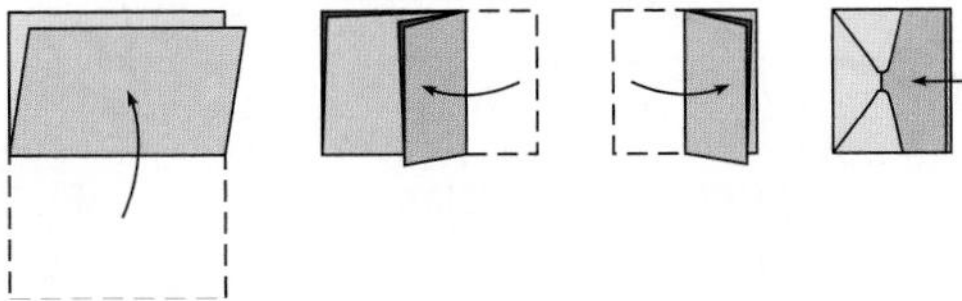

For small No. 6¾ envelopes, begin by folding the bottom up to within ⅓ inch of the top edge. Then fold the right third over to the left. Fold the left third to within ⅓ inch of the last fold. Insert the last fold into the envelope first.

E-Mail Messages

Because e-mail is a developing communication medium, formatting and usage are still fluid. The following suggestions, illustrated in Figure B.5 and also in Figure 8.2 in Chapter 8, may guide you in setting up the parts of any e-mail message. Always check, however, with your organization so that you can follow its practices.

To *Line.* Include the receiver's e-mail address after *To.* If the receiver's address is recorded in your address book, you just have to click on it. Be sure to enter all addresses very carefully since one mistyped letter prevents delivery.

FIGURE B.4 ***Abbreviations of States, Territories, and Provinces***

State or Territory	Two-Letter Abbreviation	State or Territory	Two-Letter Abbreviation
Alabama	AL	North Dakota	ND
Alaska	AK	Ohio	OH
Arizona	AZ	Oklahoma	OK
Arkansas	AR	Oregon	OR
California	CA	Pennsylvania	PA
Canal Zone	CZ	Puerto Rico	PR
Colorado	CO	Rhode Island	RI
Connecticut	CT	South Carolina	SC
Delaware	DE	South Dakota	SD
District of Columbia	DC	Tennessee	TN
Florida	FL	Texas	TX
Georgia	GA	Utah	UT
Guam	GU	Vermont	VT
Hawaii	HI	Virgin Islands	VI
Idaho	ID	Virginia	VA
Illinois	IL	Washington	WA
Indiana	IN	West Virginia	WV
Iowa	IA	Wisconsin	WI
Kansas	KS	Wyoming	WY
Kentucky	KY		
Louisiana	LA		
Maine	ME	**Canadian**	**Two-Letter**
Maryland	MD	**Province**	**Abbreviation**
Massachusetts	MA	Alberta	AB
Michigan	MI	British Columbia	BC
Minnesota	MN	Labrador	LB
Mississippi	MS	Manitoba	MB
Missouri	MO	New Brunswick	NB
Montana	MT	Newfoundland	NF
Nebraska	NE	Northwest Territories	NT
Nevada	NV	Nova Scotia	NS
New Hampshire	NH	Ontario	ON
New Jersey	NJ	Prince Edward Island	PE
New Mexico	NM	Quebec	PQ
New York	NY	Saskatchewan	SK
North Carolina	NC	Yukon Territory	YT

From *Line.* Most mail programs automatically include your name and e-mail address after *From*.

Cc *and* Bcc. Insert the e-mail address of anyone who is to receive a copy of the message. *Cc* stands for carbon copy or courtesy copy. Don't be tempted, though, to send needless copies just because it's so easy. *Bcc* stands for blind carbon copy. Some writers use *bcc* to send a copy of the message without the addressee's knowledge. Writers are also using the *bcc* line for mailing lists. When a message is being sent to a number of people and their e-mail addresses should not be revealed, the *bcc* line works well to conceal the names and addresses of all receivers.

FIGURE B.5 ***E-Mail Message***

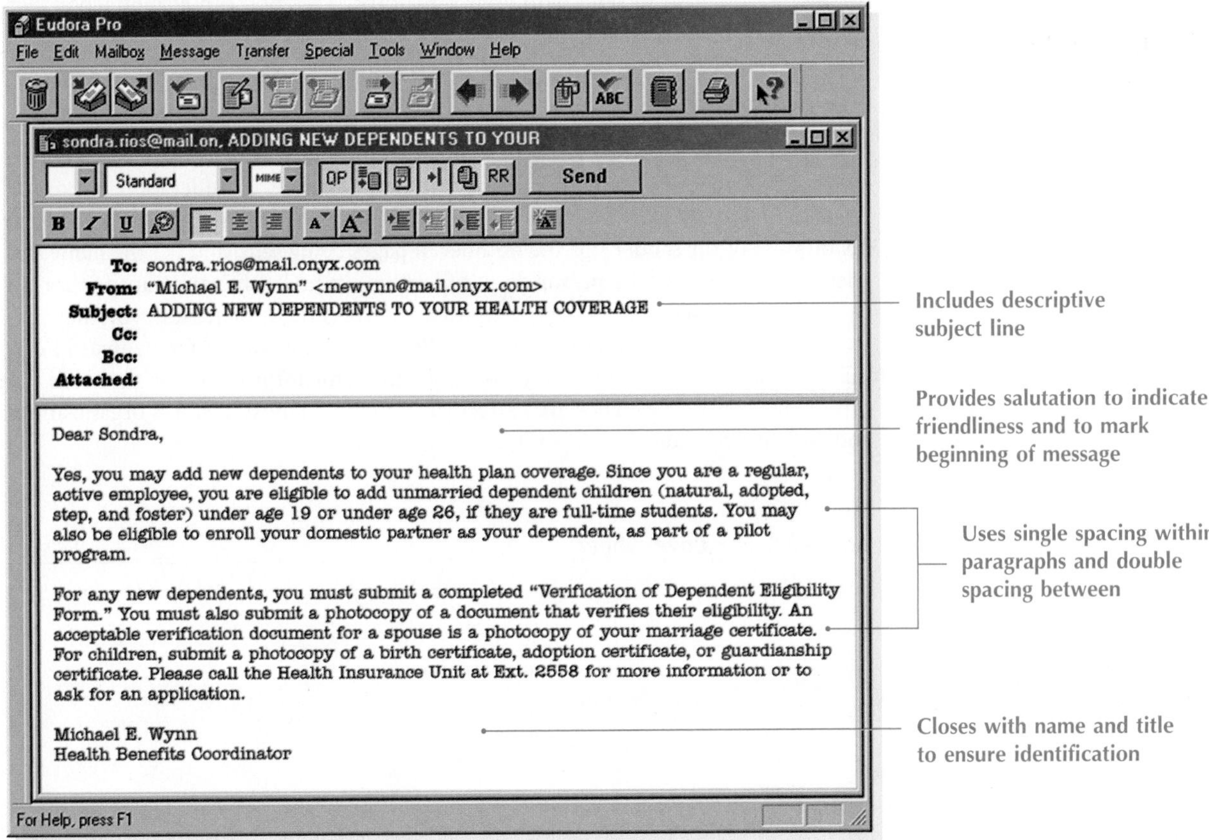
Eudora Pro

sondra.rios@mail.on, ADDING NEW DEPENDENTS TO YOUR

To: sondra.rios@mail.onyx.com
From: "Michael E. Wynn" <mewynn@mail.onyx.com>
Subject: ADDING NEW DEPENDENTS TO YOUR HEALTH COVERAGE
Cc:
Bcc:
Attached:

Dear Sondra,

Yes, you may add new dependents to your health plan coverage. Since you are a regular, active employee, you are eligible to add unmarried dependent children (natural, adopted, step, and foster) under age 19 or under age 26, if they are full-time students. You may also be eligible to enroll your domestic partner as your dependent, as part of a pilot program.

For any new dependents, you must submit a completed "Verification of Dependent Eligibility Form." You must also submit a photocopy of a document that verifies their eligibility. An acceptable verification document for a spouse is a photocopy of your marriage certificate. For children, submit a photocopy of a birth certificate, adoption certificate, or guardianship certificate. Please call the Health Insurance Unit at Ext. 2558 for more information or to ask for an application.

Michael E. Wynn
Health Benefits Coordinator

Subject. Identify the subject of the e-mail message with a brief but descriptive summary of the topic. Be sure to include enough information to be clear and compelling. Capitalize the initial letters of principal words, or capitalize the entire line.

Salutation. Include a brief greeting, if you like. Some writers use a salutation such as *Dear Sondra* followed by a comma or a colon. Others are more informal with *Hi, Sondra!*, or *Good morning* or *Greetings.* Some writers treat an e-mail message like a memo and skip the salutation entirely. See Chapter 8 for a more complete discussion of e-mail salutations.

Message. Cover just one topic in your message, and try to keep your total message under two or three screens in length. Single-space and be sure to use both upper- and lowercase letters. Double-space between paragraphs.

Closing. Conclude an e-mail message, if you like, with *Cheers, Best wishes,* or *Warm regards,* followed by your name and e-mail address (because some programs and routers do not transmit your address automatically). If the recipient is unlikely to know you, it's not a bad idea to include your title and organization. Some veteran e-mail users include a *signature file* with identifying information embellished with keyboard art. Use restraint, however, because signature files take up precious space. Writers of e-mail messages sent within organizations may omit a closing and even skip their names at the ends of messages because receivers recognize them from identification in the opening lines.

Attachment. Use the attachment window or button to select the path and file name of any file you wish to send with your e-mail message. You can also attach a Web page to your message.

Fax Cover Sheet

Documents transmitted by fax are usually introduced by a cover sheet, such as that shown in Figure B.6. As with memos, the format varies considerably. Important items to include are (1) the name and fax number of the receiver, (2) the name and fax number of the sender, (3) the number of pages being sent, and (4) the name and telephone number of the person to notify in case of unsatisfactory transmission.

When the document being transmitted requires little explanation, you may prefer to attach an adhesive note (such as a Post-it fax transmittal form) instead of a full cover sheet. These notes carry essentially the same information as shown in our printed fax cover sheet. They are perfectly acceptable in most business organizations and can save considerable paper and transmission costs.

FIGURE 8.6 ***Fax Cover Sheet***

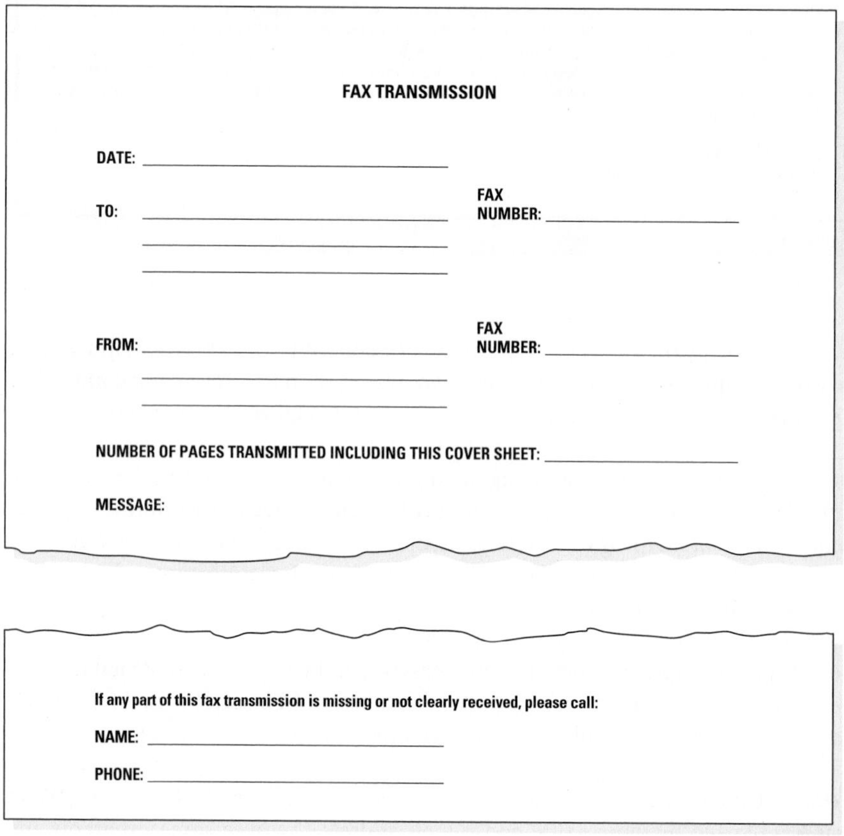

FAX TRANSMISSION

DATE: ______________________

TO: ______________________ **FAX NUMBER:** ______________________

FROM: ______________________ **FAX NUMBER:** ______________________

NUMBER OF PAGES TRANSMITTED INCLUDING THIS COVER SHEET: ______________

MESSAGE:

If any part of this fax transmission is missing or not clearly received, please call:

NAME: ______________________

PHONE: ______________________

appendix C

Documentation Formats

For many reasons business writers are careful to properly document report data. Citing sources strengthens a writer's argument, as you learned in Chapter 12. Acknowledging sources also shields writers from charges of plagiarism. Moreover, good references help readers pursue further research.

Before we discuss specific documentation formats, you must understand the difference between *source* notes and *content* notes. Source notes identify quotations, paraphrased passages, and author references. They lead readers to the sources of cited information, and they must follow a consistent format. Content notes, on the other hand, enable writers to add comments, explain information not directly related to the text, or refer readers to other sections of a report. Because content notes are generally infrequent, most writers identify them in the text with a raised asterisk (*). At the bottom of the page, the asterisk is repeated with the content note following. If two content notes appear on one page, a double asterisk identifies the second reference.

Your real concern will be with source notes. These identify quotations or paraphrased ideas in the text, and they direct readers to a complete list of references (a bibliography) at the end of your report. Researchers have struggled for years to develop the perfect documentation system, one that is efficient for the writer and crystal clear to the reader. As a result, many systems exist, each with its advantages. The important thing for you is to adopt one system and use it consistently.

Students frequently ask, "But what documentation system is most used in business?" Actually, no one method dominates. Many businesses have developed their own hybrid systems. These companies generally supply guidelines illustrating their in-house style to employees. Before starting any research project on the job, you'll want to inquire about your organization's preferred documentation style. You can also look in the files for examples of previous reports.

References are usually cited in two places: (1) a brief citation appears in the text, and (2) a complete citation appears in a bibliography at the end of the report. The two most common formats for citations and bibliographies are those of the Modern Language Association (MLA) and the American Psychological Association (APA). Each has its own style for textual references and bibliography lists. For more discussion and examples of citations for electronic formats, go to your student Web site (**http://guffeyswlearning.com**).

Modern Language Association Format

Writers in the humanities frequently use the MLA format, as illustrated in Figure C.1. In parentheses close to the textual reference appears the author's name and page cited. If no author is known, a shortened version of the source title is used. At the end of the report, the writer lists alphabetically all references in a bibliography called

FIGURE C.1 ***Portions of MLA Text Page and Bibliography***

Peanut butter was first delivered to the world by a St. Louis physician in 1890. As discussed at the Peanut Advisory Board's Web site, peanut butter was originally promoted as a protein substitute for elderly patients ("History," screen 2). However, it was the 1905 Universal Exposition in St. Louis that truly launched peanut butter. Since then, annual peanut butter consumption has zoomed to 3.3 pounds a person in the United States (Barrons 46). America's farmers produce 1.6 million tons of peanuts annually, about half of which is used for oil, nuts, and candy. Lisa Gibbons, executive secretary of the Peanut Advisory Board, says that "peanuts in some form are in the top four candies: Snickers, Reese's Peanut Butter Cups, Peanut M & Ms, and Butterfingers" (Meadows 32).

Works Cited

Barrons, Elizabeth Ruth. "A Comparison of Domestic and International Consumption of Legumes." *Journal of Economic Agriculture* 23 (2004): 45–49.

"History of Peanut Butter." *Peanut Advisory Board.* Retrieved 19 Jan. 2006 <http://www.peanutbutterlovers.com/History/index.html>.

Meadows, Mark Allen. "Peanut Crop Is Anything but Peanuts at Home and Overseas." *Business Monthly*, 30 Sept. 2005, 31–34.

"Works Cited." To see a long report illustrating MLA documentation, turn to Figure 14.4 in Chapter 14. For more information consult Joseph Gibaldi, *MLA Handbook for Writers of Research Papers*, 6e (New York: The Modern Language Association of America, 2003).

MLA In-Text Format. In-text citations generally appear close to the point where the reference is mentioned or at the end of the sentence inside the closing period. Follow these guidelines:

- Include the last name of the author(s) and the page number. Omit a comma, as (Smith 310).
- If the author's name is mentioned in the text, cite only the page number in parentheses. Do not include either the word *page* or the abbreviations *p.* or *pp.*
- If no author is known, refer to the document title or a shortened version of it, as (Facts at Fingertips 102).

MLA Bibliographic Format. The "Works Cited" bibliography lists all references cited in a report. Some writers include all works consulted. A portion of an MLA bibliography is shown in Figure C.1. A more complete list of model references appears in Figure C.2. Following are selected guidelines summarizing important points regarding MLA bibliographic format:

- Use italics or underscores for the titles of books, magazines, newspapers, and journals. Check with your organization or instructor for guidance. Capitalize all important words.

Figure C.2 ***MLA Bibliography Sample References***

Works Cited

American Airlines. *2005 Annual Report.* Fort Worth, TX: AMR Corporation.

Annual report

Berss, Marcia. "Protein Man." *Forbes* 24 Oct. 2004: 65–66.

Magazine article

Connors, H. Lee. "Saturn's Orbit Still High With Consumers." *Marketing News Online.* 31 Aug. 2005. 1 Sept. 2005 <http:// www.marketingnews.com/08-31-05.htm>.

Magazine article, online

"Globalization Often Means That the Fast Track Leads Overseas." *The Washington Post* 17 June 2005: A10.

Newspaper article, no author

Lancaster, Hal. "When Taking a Tip From a Job Network, Proceed With Caution." *The Wall Street Journal* 7 Feb. 2005: B1.

Newspaper article, one author

Markoff, John. "Voluntary Rules Proposed to Help Insure Privacy for Internet Users." *New York Times on the Web* 5 June 2005. 9 June 2005 <http://www.nytimes.com/library/tech/06/05/biztech/ articles/05privacy.html>.

Newspaper article, online

PG.com. 2005. Procter & Gamble home page. 28 Nov. 2005 <http://www.pg.com>.

Entire Internet site

Pinkerton Investigation Services. *The Employer's Guide to Investigation Services,* 3rd ed. Atlanta: Pinkerton Information Center, 2005.

Brochure

Rivera, Francisco. Personal interview. 16 May 2006.

Interview

Rose, Richard C., and Echo Montgomery Garrett. *How to Make a Buck and Still Be a Decent Human Being.* New York: HarperCollins, 2004.

Book, two authors

"Spam: How To Eliminate It From Your Workplace." *SmartPros.* 8 Aug. 2003. 12 Sept. 2005 <http://accounting.smartpros.com/ x10434.xml>.

Internet document, no author

U.S. Dept. of Labor. *Child Care as a Workforce Issue.* Washington, DC. GPO, 2005.

Government publication

"Wendy's International, Inc.," *Hoover's Online.* 2005. Hoover's Inc. 9 Nov. 2005 <http://www.hoovers.com/wendy's-ID_11621-free -co-factsheet.xhtml>.

Article from online database

Wetherbee, James C., Nicholas P. Vitalari, and Andrew Milner. "Key Trends in Systems Development in Europe and North America." *Journal of Global Information Management* 3.2 (2004): 5–20. ["3.2" signifies volume 3, issue 2]

Journal article with volume and issue numbers

Yellen, Mike. <myellen022@yahoo.com> "Managing Managers and Cell Phones." Online posting. 26 June 2005. Technical Writers Listserv. 9 Sept. 2005 <http://www.techwr-l.com/techwhirl/ archives/>.

Online posting (listservs and newsgroups)

Note 1: If a printed document is viewed electronically and you have no reason to believe the electronic version is different from the print version, use the same format as for the print citation. More extensive information about electronic documentation formats can be found at **http://guffeyswlearning.com**.

Note 2: To prevent confusion, you might add the words "Accessed" or "Retrieved" preceding the date you accessed an online source.

- Enclose the titles of magazine, newspaper, and journal articles in quotation marks. Include volume and issue numbers for journals only.
- For Internet citations, include a retrieval date. Although MLA format does not include the words "Retrieved" or "Accessed," such wording helps distinguish the retrieval date from the document date.

American Psychological Association Format

Popular in the social and physical sciences, the American Psychological Association (APA) documentation style uses parenthetic citations. That is, each author reference is shown in parentheses when cited in the text, as shown in Figure C.3. At the end of the report, all references are listed alphabetically in a bibliography called "References." For more information about APA formats, see the *Publication Manual of the American Psychological Association*, 5e (Washington, DC: American Psychological Association, 2001).

APA In-Text Format. Within the text, document each specific textual source with a short description in parentheses. Following are selected guidelines summarizing important elements of APA style:

- Include the last name of the author(s), date of publication, and page number, as (Jones, 2002, p. 36). Use "n.d." if no date is available.
- If no author is known, refer to the first few words of the reference list entry and the year, as (Computer Privacy, 2003, p. 59).

FIGURE C.3 ***Portions of APA Text Page and Bibliography***

Peanut butter was first delivered to the world by a St. Louis physician in 1890. As discussed at the Peanut Advisory Board's Web site, peanut butter was originally promoted as a protein substitute for elderly patients (History, n.d.). However, it was the 1905 Universal Exposition in St. Louis that truly launched peanut butter. Since then, annual peanut butter consumption has zoomed to 3.3 pounds a person in the United States (Barrons, 2004, p. 46). America's farmers produce 1.6 million tons of peanuts annually, about half of which is used for oil, nuts, and candy. Lisa Gibbons, executive secretary of the Peanut Advisory Board, says that "peanuts in some form are in the top four candies: Snickers, Reese's Peanut Butter Cups, Peanut M & Ms, and Butterfingers" (Meadows, 2005, p. 32).

References

Barrons, E. (2004, November). A comparison of domestic and international consumption of legumes. *Journal of Economic Agriculture*, 23 (3), 45–49.

Meadows, M. (2005, September 30). Peanut crop is anything but peanuts at home and overseas. *Business Monthly*, 14, 31–34.

History of peanut butter (n.d.). Peanut Advisory Board. Retrieved January 17, 2006, from http://www.peanutbutterlovers.com/History/index.html

- Omit page numbers for general references, but always include page numbers for direct quotations.

APA Bibliographic Format. List all citations alphabetically in a section called "References." A portion of an APA bibliography is shown in Figure C.3. A more complete list of model references appears in Figure C.4. APA style requires specific capitalization and sequencing guidelines, some of which are summarized here:

- Include an author's name with the last name first followed by initials, such as *Smith, M. A.* First and middle names are not used.

FIGURE C.4 ***Model APA Bibliography Sample References***

References

American Airlines. (2005). *2005 Annual Report.* Fort Worth, TX: AMR Corporation. — Annual report

Atamian, R. M., & Ferranto, M. (2003). *Driving market forces.* New York: HarperCollins. — Book, two authors

Berss, M. (2004, October 24). Protein man. *Forbes*, 154, 65–66. — Magazine article

Cantrell, M. R., & Watson, H. (2004, January 10). Violence in today's workplace [Electronic version]. *Office Review*, 26 (1), 24–29. — Magazine article, viewed electronically

Globalization often means that the fast track leads overseas. (2004, June 16). *The Washington Post*, p. A10. — Newspaper article, no author

Lancaster, H. (2005, February 7). When taking a tip from a job network, proceed with caution. *The Wall Street Journal*, p. B1. — Newspaper article, one author

Lang, R. T. (2004, March 2). Most people fail to identify nonverbal signs. *The New York Times.* Retrieved November 15, 2004, from http://www.nytimes.com — Newspaper article, online

Moon, J. (2002). Solid waste disposal. *Microsoft Encarta 2000* [CD-ROM]. Redmond, WA: Microsoft. — CD-ROM encyclopedia article

Pinkerton Investigation Services. (2005). *The employer's guide to investigation services* (3rd ed.) [Brochure]. Atlanta: Pinkerton Information Center. — Brochure

Wetherbee, J. C., Vitalari, N. P., & Milner, A. (2004, May). Key trends in systems development in Europe and North America. *Journal of Global Information Management, 3* (2), 5–20. ["3 (2) signifies volume 3, series or issue 2] — Journal article with volume and issue numbers

Wilson, G., & Simmons, P. (2004). *Plagiarism: What it is, and how to avoid it.* Retrieved July 4, 2004, from Biology Program Guide 2001/2002 at the University of British Columbia Web site: http://www.zoology.ubc/ca/bpg/plagiarism.htm — World Wide Web document with author and date

WWW user survey reveals consumer trends. (n.d.). Retrieved August 2, 2005, from http://www.cc.gatech.edu/gvu/user_surveys/survey-2004-10/ — World Wide Web document, no author, no date

Yudkin, M. (2004, August 24). The marketing minute: Truth is always in season [Msg. ID:ruf6kt0aiu5eui6523qsrofhu70h21evoj@4ax.com]. Message posted to news://biz.ecommerce — Message to online forum or discussion group

- Show the date of publication in parentheses immediately after the author's name, as *Smith, M. A. (2002).*
- Italicize the titles of books. Use "sentence-style" capitalization. This means that only the first word of a title, proper nouns, and the first word after an internal colon is capitalized.
- Do not italicize or underscore the titles of magazine and journal articles. Use sentence-style capitalization for article titles.
- Italicize the names of magazines and journals. Capitalize the initial letters of all important words.

Citing Electronic Sources

Standards for researchers using electronic sources are still emerging. When citing electronic media, you should hold the same goals as for print sources. That is, you try to give credit to the authors and to allow others to easily locate the same or updated information. However, traditional formats for identifying authors, publication dates, and page numbers become confusing when applied to sources on the Internet. Strive to give correct credit for electronic sources by including the author's name (when available), document title, Web page title, Web address, and retrieval date. Formats for some electronic sources are shown here. More extensive information about electronic documentation formats may be found at **http://guffeyswlearning.com**.

appendix D

Correction Symbols

In marking your papers, your instructor may use the following symbols or abbreviations to indicate writing or formatting weaknesses. You'll find that studying these symbols and suggestions will help you understand your instructor's remarks. Knowing this information can also help you evaluate and improve your own letters, memos, e-mail messages, reports, and other writing. For specific writing guidelines and self-help exercises, see Appendix A, Competent Language Usage Essentials (C.L.U.E.).

Grammar and Mechanics

Act Use active-voice verbs.
Apos Use apostrophe correctly.
Art Use a correct article (*a, an,* or *the*).
Cap Correct capitalization error.
Cm Insert a comma.
CmConj Use a comma before a coordinating conjunction (*and, or, nor, but*) that joins independent clauses.
CmIntro Use a comma after an introductory clause or a long phrase.
CmSer Insert commas to separate items in a series.
CS Correct a comma splice by separating clauses with a period or a semicolon.
DM Correct a misplaced or dangling modifier by moving the modifier closer to the word it describes or by supplying a clear subject.
Exp Eliminate expletives (*there is, there are,* and *it is*)
Frag Revise sentence fragment to express a complete thought.
Num Express numbers in appropriate word or figure form.
ProAgr Make pronoun agree in number with its antecedent.
ProCase Use appropriate nominative, objective, or possessive case.
Ref Correct vague pronoun reference. Avoid pronoun that refers to a phrase, clause, sentence, or paragraph.
RO Revise run-on or fused sentence by adding a period or a semicolon to separate independent clauses.
Sp Correct spelling error.
S/V Make verbs agree with their subjects.
Vb Use correct verb tense.
V/Shift Avoid unnecessary shifts in verb tense.
UnCm Eliminate unnecessary comma.

Content, Organization, and Style

Asgn	Follow assignment instructions.
Awk	Recast to avoid awkward expression.
Ch	Use longer sentences to avoid choppiness. Vary sentence patterns.
Cl	Improve clarity of ideas or expression.
Coh	Develop coherence between ideas. Repeat key ideas, use pronouns, or add transitional expression.
Cop	Avoid copying textbook examples or wording.
DS	Use direct strategy by starting with the main idea.
Exp	Expand or explain an incomplete idea.
IS	Use the indirect strategy by explaining before introducing the main idea.
Log	Reconsider faulty logic.
Neg	Revise negative expression with a more positive view.
Ob	Avoid stating the obvious.
Org	Improve organization by grouping similar ideas.
Par	Express ideas in parallel form.
Redun	Avoid redundant expression.
Tone	Use a conversational, positive tone that promotes goodwill.
WC	Improve word choice.
You	Emphasize the "you" view.

Format

DS	Insert a double space.
F	Choose an appropriate format for this document.
GH	Use graphic highlighting (bullets, lists, indentions, or headings) to enhance readability.
Mar	Improve margins to fit document attractively on the page.
SS	Insert a single space.
TS	Insert a triple space.

Proofreading Marks

Proofreading Mark	Draft Copy	Final Copy
Align horizontally	TO: Rick Munoz	TO: Rick Munoz
Align vertically	166.32 132.45	166.32 132.45
Capitalize	Coca-cola	Coca-Cola
	a Nasa official	a NASA official
Close up space	meeting at 3 p. m.	meeting at 3 p.m.
Center	Recommendations	Recommendations
Delete	in my final judgement	in my judgment
Insert apostrophe	our companys product	our company's product
Insert comma	you will of course	you will, of course,
Insert hyphen	tax free income	tax-free income
Insert period	Ms Holly Hines	Ms. Holly Hines
Insert quotation mark	shareholders receive a bonus.	shareholders receive a "bonus."
Insert space	wordprocessing program	word processing program
Lowercase (remove capitals)	the Vice President	the vice president
	HUMAN RESOURCES	Human Resources
Move to left	I. Labor costs	I. Labor costs
Move to right	A. Findings of study	A. Findings of study
Spell out	aimed at 2 depts	aimed at two departments
Start new paragraph	Keep the screen height of your computer at eye level.	Keep the screen height of your computer at eye level.
Stet (don't delete)	officials talked openly	officials talked openly
Transpose	accounts recievable	accounts receivable
Use boldface	Conclusions bf	**Conclusions**
Use italics	The Perfect Résumé ital	*The Perfect Résumé*

key to C.L.U.E. review exercises

Chapter 1

1. To **succeed** in **today's** high-tech **business world,** you need **highly developed** communication skills.
2. You especially need **writing** and **grammar** skills [delete comma] because employees spend **60 percent** of **their** time processing documents.
3. One organization paid **$3,000** each for **12 employees** to attend a **one-week workshop** in communication training.
4. My coworker and **I were surprised** to learn that more information has been produced in the last **30** years **than** in the previous **5,000** years.
5. If you work in **an** office with open **cubicles, it's** rude to listen to **W**eb **radio,** streaming **audio,** or other multimedia [delete comma] without headphones.
6. When making a **decision,** you should gather **information** [delete comma] and **then** weigh the advantages and **disadvantages** of each alternative.
7. If you are defining ***communication,*** for example, a **principal** element **is** the transmission of information and meaning.
8. **Ms.** Johnson had **three** messages to send **immediately; consequently,** she **chose** e-mail because it was **definitely** the [delete **most**] fastest communication channel.
9. **Five** elements that make up your frame of reference are the **following:** experience, **e**ducation, **c**ulture, **e**xpectations, and **p**ersonality.
10. Just between you and **me,** I'm sure our company **p**resident thinks that honesty and integrity **are** more important **than increased** profits.

Chapter 2

1. Our **company's** management **council** had **already** decided to **appoint an** investigative **team; however, it** acted **too slowly.**
2. **Organizations** are forming teams for at least **three** good **reasons:** better decisions, [delete **more**] faster response **times,** and **increased** productivity.
3. Most teams go through **four** development **phases:** **f**orming, **s**torming, **n**orming, and **p**erforming.
4. Some group members play dysfunctional **roles,** and they disrupt the **group's** progress toward **its** goal.
5. Successful **self-directed** teams are **autonomous; that is,** they can hire, fire, and discipline **their** own **members.**
6. Although we tried to reach a **consensus,** several **m**anagers and even the **v**ice **p**resident opposed the **whole** proposal.
7. At last **month's** staff **meeting,** the CEO and **he complimented** the **team's** efforts and made **warm,** supportive comments.
8. Rather **than** schedule many **face-to-face meetings,** the team decided to investigate a **$3,000 desktop** videoconferencing system.
9. When conflict erupted at our **team's January meeting,** we made a **conscious** effort to confront the **underlying** issues.
10. **Fifty-five** people are expected to attend the **t**raining **s**ession on April **15; consequently, she** and I must find a [delete **more**] larger room.

Chapter 3

1. **Everyone** knows how to **listen,** but many of us listen at only **25 percent efficiency.**
2. **It's** wise to avoid arguing or criticizing [delete comma] when listening to a superior.
3. The **four** stages of listening are [delete colon] **p**erception, **i**nterpretation, **e**valuation, and **a**ction.

4. To improve **retention,** you should take notes [delete comma] and rewrite **them immediately** after listening.
5. While waiting for the **speaker's** next **idea,** you should review what was **already spoken.**
6. **High status** and self-confidence **are** conveyed by erect posture.
7. On May **12** [delete comma] the company **p**resident awarded bonuses to Tyler and **me; however,** we didn't **receive** our checks until June **1.**
8. In a poll of nearly **3,000 employees,** only **one third** felt that **their companies** valued **their** opinions and **suggestions.**
9. The appearance and mannerisms of a speaker **affect** a **listener's** evaluation of a message.
10. A list of suggestions for improving retention of a **speaker's** ideas **is** found in an article titled **"Best** Listening **Habits,"** which appeared in ***Fortune.***

Chapter 4

1. The **p**resident of MainStreet Enterprises, along with other executives of local **companies, is** considering **overseas** sales.
2. International business was **already** common among big **companies; however,** even small **businesses** are now seeking global markets.
3. **Three** different employees asked the **s**upervisor and **me** whether we should give gifts to our **C**hinese business **guests.**
4. Gifts for the children of an Arab are **welcome; however,** gifts for an **Arab's** wife are not **advisable.**
5. In **L**atin **A**merica **knives** are not proper **gifts;** they signify cutting off **a** relationship.
6. When it opened **its $120 million** plant in **Beijing,** Motorola had to offer housing **to** attract **quality** applicants.
7. On May **12 an** article titled **"The Chinese Puzzle,"** which appeared in the magazine ***Workforce Management,*** described the **difficulties** of managing **employees worldwide.**
8. We invited **75** employees to hear the **cross-cultural** talk that begins at **4 p.m.** [Delete one period]
9. The **U.S.** Census **B**ureau reports that **one third** of the **foreign-born** population of the United States **is** from [delete colon] **C**entral **A**merica, the **C**aribbean, and **S**outh **A**merica.
10. By **2050** many groups now considered minorities (**A**frican **A**mericans, **H**ispanics, **A**sians, and **N**ative **A**mericans) are projected to constitute **47** percent of the U.S. population.

Chapter 5

1. In this class my friend and I learned that business writing should be [delete colon] **p**urposeful, **e**conomical, and **r**eader **o**riented.
2. **Five** or **six** members of our team will **probably** attend the **writers' workshop; therefore,** be sure they **receive** notices.
3. If I **were you,** I would learn the following **three** parts of the writing **process: prewriting, writing,** and revising.
4. **Experts** suggest that you spend **25** percent of your time planning, **25** percent writing, **45** percent **revising,** and **5** percent proofreading.
5. Although one of the employees **is** not **available,** we **proceeded** to schedule the meeting at **3** p.m. on **Wednesday,** October **12.**
6. The **v**ice **p**resident was surprised to learn that a **two-day** writing workshop for our **company's** employees would cost **$1,200** each.
7. **We're** not asking the seller to **alter its proposal;** we are asking team members to check the **proposal's** figures.
8. **They're** wondering whether a list of all our **customers'** names and addresses **was** inadvertently **released.**
9. As you begin to **write,** you should **analyze** the task [delete comma] and identify the purpose.
10. By replacing unfamiliar words with **everyday,** familiar ones, you can make your audience comprehend your ideas more **quickly.**

Chapter 6

1. When our **m**arketing **m**anager had to write a **20-page report,** she started by collecting information [delete comma] and organizing it.
2. A business **writer's** biggest problem is usually poor **organization,** according to experts.
3. The company **v**ice **p**resident came to the **p**resident and **me** asking for help with **two** complex but **separate** advertising problems.

4. Because neither of us **was** particularly **creative,** we decided to organize a brainstorming session rather **than** work by **ourselves.**

5. Our **brainstorming** session included [delete colon] Amanda, Rory, **Rashid,** and Cynthia.

6. One of our **principal** goals **was** to create **100** ideas in **30 minutes; however,** we were prepared to meet up to **one** hour.

7. Although we knew the **principles** of **outlining,** we had trouble grouping our ideas into **three** to **five** major headings.

8. Robyn **Clarke's** article titled **"A Better Way to Brainstorm,"** which appeared in the magazine ***Black Enterprise,*** was helpful to the **p**resident and **me.**

9. Frontloading a message saves a **reader's time; therefore, it's** worth making the effort to put the main idea first.

10. By learning to distinguish **phrases** from clauses, **you'll** be better able to avoid **three** basic sentence **faults:** the fragment, the **run-on sentence,** and the comma splice.

Chapter 7

1. My manager **told** my colleague and **me** that we had to be more **conscious** of our proofreading because our reports had **too** many errors.

2. Readers want to scan messages **quickly; therefore,** we should use **everyday** language and be concise.

3. Even in **Europe** and **Canada,** company executives are **disappointed** by messages that are **too** long **and too** difficult to read.

4. One **manager's** report contained so many **redundancies** that **its** main **principles** requesting **state** and **federal** funding **were** lost.

5. **Your** writing will sound [**more fresh** or, preferably, **fresher**] if you eliminate trite business **phrases** such as "pursuant to **your request.**"

6. All **three** of our **company's recruiters**—Angelica Santos, Kirk Adams, and David Toms—**criticized their poorly written** procedures.

7. To help **receivers** anticipate and comprehend ideas **quickly, two** special writing techniques **are helpful: parallelism,** which involves balanced **writing,** and **bulleting,** which **makes** important points more visible.

8. When I **proofread an** important **document,** I **always** work with a **buddy** [delete comma] and read from a printed copy.

9. Read a message once for word **meanings;** read it again for **grammar** and mechanics.

10. **It's almost** impossible to improve **one's** communication skills **alone; therefore, everyone** should take advantage of this educational **opportunity.**

Chapter 8

1. More **than 90** percent of **companies** now use **e-mail; therefore,** employees must become more **knowledgeable** about **its** dangers.

2. Most e-mails and memos **deliver straightforward** information that is not sensitive [delete comma] and **requires** little persuasion.

3. If I **were you,** I would check all **incoming** e-mail and attachments that **were** sent to you and **him.**

4. Memos typically contain **four necessary parts:** subject line, opening, **body,** and action closing.

5. Fear of inappropriate e-mail use [omit comma] and the need to boost productivity [omit comma] **have** spurred **employee-monitoring** programs.

6. When you respond **to an** e-mail **message,** you should not **automatically** return the **sender's** message.

7. **Wasn't** it **Dr.** Rivers and **Ms.** Johnson who **always** wrote **their** e-mails in all **capital letters?**

8. A list of the **names** and **addresses** of e-mail recipients **was** sent using the "bcc" function.

9. Our **Information Technology Department,** which was **formerly** in **Room 35,** has moved **its** offices to **Room** 5.

10. The *Evening News Press,* our local **newspaper,** featured as its **principal** article a story **entitled "Cyber-Slacking Is Killing Productivity!"**

Chapter 9

1. Business letters, despite the enormous popularity of e-**mail,** must still be **written** when a **permanent** record is **necessary.**

2. If you follow a writing **process,** organizing the content and composing the first draft **are** easier.

3. Chelsea acts as if she **were** the only person who ever received a **compliment** about her business **writing.**
4. **Chelsea's letter,** which she sent to the manager and **me**, was distinguished by **three characteristics:** clear content, a goodwill tone, and correct form.
5. Davonne **Jordan, who** I think is our **newly appointed vice president,** wants everyone in the **company** to beware of computer viruses.
6. When the **office manager** writes business letters or **memos,** he **always** ends **them** with the same "Do not hesitate" phrase.
7. The manager and **I** realized an item was missing from the **April 1 shipment; consequently,** we sent a claim letter for **$131**.
8. After our supervisor and **she** returned from their meeting at **2 p.m.**, we were able to sort the **customers'** names and addresses more **quickly**.
9. If you must write an order **letter,** be sure to **include** [delete colon] the **quantity, order number, description, unit price, tax, shipping,** and total costs.
10. Matthew enclosed a check for **$200; however,** he worried that it was insufficient to regain the confidence of the customer.

Chapter 10

1. Persuasion requires learning about **your audience** [omit comma] and **analyzing** why **it** might resist your goal.
2. An **especially** effective **argument** includes **two indispensable elements:** a reasonable **request** [omit comma] and a **well-presented** line of reasoning.
3. If **your** goal is to persuade a lending institution to give you **$50,000,** you would probably use rational **appeals.**
4. Our **president** and **senior sales manager** decided to send a sales letter to all current **customers; therefore,** they analyzed the product, **purpose,** and audience.
5. **Their** sales letter focuses on the following **four parts:** (1) **gaining** the **audience's attention,** (2) **convincing it** that the purpose is **worthy,** (3) **overcoming resistance,** and (4) **motivating** action.
6. Experts agree that one of the biggest mistakes in persuasive **requests is** the failure to **anticipate** [omit comma] and **offset** audience resistance.
7. Because the **manager** and **he built** interest with **easy-to-read** facts and **figures, their** letter will **undoubtedly succeed.**
8. A claim letter is a form of **complaint; consequently, it's** wise to use the indirect strategy.
9. Anger and emotion **are** not effective in **persuasion,** but many writers **cannot control their tempers.**
10. Our latest press **release,** which was written in our **Corporate Communication Department,** announces the opening of **three Canadian offices.**

Chapter 11

1. Bad news is **generally disappointing; however,** the negative feelings can be reduced.
2. **Two** ways to reduce the **disappointment** of bad news **are to** [delete colon] (1) give reasons **first** [delete comma] and (2) reveal the news sensitively.
3. When delivering bad **news, it's** important that you make sure the **receiver** understands and **accepts** it.
4. The indirect pattern consists of **four parts:** buffer, reasons, bad news, and closing.
5. Although the indirect pattern is not **appropriate** for every **situation,** it is **usually** better **than** a blunt announcement of bad news.
6. On June **1** our company **president** and **vice president** revealed a **$4 million** drop in **profits,** which was bad news for **everyone.**
7. Because of declining profits and **rising health costs,** the **director** of our Human Resources Department announced **an** increase in each **employee's** contribution to **health benefits.**
8. Most of us prefer to be let down **gently** [delete comma] when **we're** being refused **something; that's** why the **reasons-before-refusal** pattern is effective.
9. When a **well-known tire** company recalled **hundreds** of thousands of **tires, its president** issued **an** apology to the **public** [delete comma] and all injured **customers.**
10. If I **were you,** I would begin the **bad-news** message with a **compliment,** not a blunt rejection.

Chapter 12

1. Reports are a fact of life in **American business; consequently, business writers** must learn to prepare **them.**
2. Although reports vary in **length, content, form,** and **formality level,** they all have **one** purpose.
3. The primary purpose of reports [delete comma] **is** to answer questions and solve problems **systematically.**
4. Letter reports **usually** have side margins of **1 to 1¼ inches.**
5. The format of a report is determined by **its** [delete colon] **length, topic, audience,** and purpose.
6. The CEO and **manager,** who had **gone** to a conference in the **West,** delivered a report to Jeff and **me** when they returned.
7. If **your** report is authorized by **someone,** be sure to review **its work plan** with **that person** before **proceeding.**
8. Ilia was **offered $500** to finish **Max's report,** but she said it was "**too** little and **too** late."
9. To search the **Internet,** you need a browser such as **Microsoft Internet Explorer.**
10. If you wish to illustrate report **data,** you may **choose** from among the following visual **aids:** tables, charts, **graphs,** and pictures.

Chapter 13

1. When conducting research for a **report,** you may face an **incredible** jumble of data **including** [delete colon] printouts, disk files, note cards, **copies** of articles, **interview** notes, **questionnaire results,** and statistics.
2. The information in tables **is usually** easier to read **than** the same information presented in **paragraphs.**
3. When the company president and **I** use the word ***average,*** we are **referring** to the **mean,** which is the arithmetic average.
4. The following **three** statistical terms frequently describe **data:** mean, median, and mode.
5. Readers of **business** [delete apostrophe] reports often turn **first** to the conclusions and **recommendations; therefore,** these **sections** must be written **very** carefully.
6. Informational reports emphasize **facts;** analytical **reports, however,** emphasize reasoning and conclusions.
7. Report conclusions explain what the problem **is; recommendations** tell how to solve it.
8. Frontloading the **recommendations** works when the topic is **routine** [delete comma] and when the audience is receptive.
9. In writing most business **reports,** you will **generally** organize **your** data using **one** of the following **five methods:** time, component, importance, **criteria,** or convention.
10. The introduction to a report should tell **its** purpose and **significance;** it should also preview the main points.

Chapter 14

1. The format and organization of a proposal **are** important [omit comma] if a writer **wants** it to be taken **seriously.**
2. Proposals are **written** offers to do the **following:** solve problems, provide **services,** or sell **equipment.**
3. Our **vice president** and manager worked **together** to prepare **two** RFPs [omit comma] that solicit competitive bids.
4. Just between you and **me,** we **worked** very hard to develop a "hook" to capture a **reader's** attention.
5. If a proposal is **too** long and **its** budget is **vague,** it will not **succeed** in **its** goal.
6. **An** important item in most proposals [omit comma] is the **budget,** which is a list of project **costs.**
7. If a proposal is sent to the president or **me,** it should **definitely** explain the specific credentials and expertise of key **personnel** for the project.
8. **Dr.** Ryan Williams and **he** wanted to start **their** own **business; therefore,** they wrote a business plan [omit comma] that included a detailed market analysis.
9. Mary **Morley,** who is a member of our Research and Development **Department,** wondered whether her formal report would be presented at the May **15 meeting.**

10. If **your** report is **complex,** be sure to **proofread** it **three** times.

Chapter 15

1. Even though he was **p**resident of the **company, Mr.** Thomas dreaded the **two** or **three** presentations he made **every year**.
2. The **company's** CPA asked my colleague and **me** to explain the **principal** ways we planned to finance **its 30-year mortgage.**
3. My team and I are **grateful** to be able to give a **20-minute presentation; however,** we can emphasize only **three** or **four** major **points**.
4. The **introduction** to a presentation should accomplish **three goals:** (a) capture attention, (b) **es**tablish **credibility,** and (c) **p**review main points.
5. Travis wondered whether focusing on what you want the audience to remember [delete comma] and summarizing **your** main points **were** equally important in the **conclusion.**
6. Speakers must remember that **their listeners,** unlike **readers, cannot control** the rate of presentation [delete comma] or flip back **through** pages to review main points.
7. Most novice speakers talk **too rapidly; however,** they can learn to speak more **slowly** [delete comma] and listen to what they are saying.
8. When speakers first approach the **audience,** they should take a moment to adjust **their** notes [delete comma] and make **themselves** comfortable.
9. One West **C**oast company found that [delete comma] telephone interruptions consumed about **18** percent of staff **members'** workdays.
10. Good telephone manners reflect on you and **your company; however, too** few employees are trained **properly**.

Chapter 16

1. The employment process begins with **introspection,** which is a word that **means** looking inside yourself to **analyze** what you like and dislike.
2. You **can't** hope to find the job of your **dreams** without first [delete colon] (1) knowing **yourself,** (2) knowing the job **market,** and (3) **knowing** the employment process.
3. Candidates complain about **j**ob **b**oards [delete comma] because fewer **than 1.4** percent of the candidates are actually hired.
4. With over **40,000** job boards and employment **W**eb sites deluging the **Internet, it's** hard to know where to start looking.
5. Preparing a résumé while you are still in school [delete comma] **helps** you recognize **weak** qualifications [delete comma] and **gives** you **two** or **three** years in which to bolster **them.**
6. Recruiters like to see **c**areer **o**bjectives on **résumés; however, they** may restrict a **candidate's** chances.
7. **Today's** résumés omit **personal** data such as birth date, **marital** status, **height, weight,** and religious affiliation.
8. I wonder how many **companies** now use **applicant-tracking** software to scan **candidates'** résumés and search for **keywords.**
9. In the latest issue of ***BusinessWeek*** [use italics or underlining], did you see the article titled **"Should** You Use a **C**areer **O**bjective on Your **Résumé?"**
10. Before going to a job **interview,** you should research the **following:** company size, number of employees, competitors, reputation, **strengths,** and **weaknesses.**

notes

Chapter 1

1. Based on Jack Neff, "Q&A with Lafley: It's the Consumer, Stupid," *Advertising Age*, 23 February 2004, 20; "P & G: New and Improved," *BusinessWeek*, 7 July 2003, 52–63; Julian E. Barnes, "Procter & Gamble Reports 4% Sales Drop," *The New York Times*, 31 January 2001, C2; Len Lewis, "Procter's Gambit," *Progressive Grocer*, October 2000, 20–26; Jack Neff, "Does P & G Still Matter?" *Advertising Age*, 25 September 2000, 48; Emily Nelson, "Rallying the Troops at P & G," *The Wall Street Journal*, 31 October 2000, B1; Steve Jarvis, "P & G's Challenge," *Marketing News*, 28 August 2000, 1, 13; Gail Kemp, "How Can P & G Rebuild Its Sliding Reputation?" *Marketing*, 15 June 2000, 17; John Bissell, "What Can We Learn From P & G's Troubles?" *Brandweek*, 10 July 2000, 20–22; Conor Dignam, "Procter & Gamble Wobbled Because It Forgot Its People," *Marketing*, 15 June 2000, 21; and Katrina Brooker, "Can Procter & Gamble Change Its Culture, Protect Its Market Share, and Find the Next Tide?" *Fortune*, 26 April 1999, 146+.
2. Ann Zimmerman and Martin Fackler, "Wal-Mart's Japanese Plans Roil Local Retailers," *The Wall Street Journal*, 19 September 2003, A1.
3. Delroy Alexander, "Two Very Different Chiefs Face Off in Burger Wars," *Knight Ridder/Tribune News Service*, 18 September 2003; Suzanne Bidlake, "Burger King's Euro Push," *Marketing*, 20 February 1992, 2.
4. "Kentucky Fried Chicken Tops International Brands in China, People's Daily Web Site," 26 June 2000 <http://English.peopledaily.com.cn> (Retrieved 20 March 2004).
5. Hal Lancaster, "Learning to Manage in a Global Workplace," *The Wall Street Journal*, 2 June 1998, B1.
6. Barbara Booth, "Beg to Differ," *International Business*, November 1996, 28.
7. Christopher Palmeri, "To Really Be a Player, Mattel Needs Hotter Toys," *BusinessWeek*, 28 July 2003, 64; Faye Rice, "Champions of Communication," *Fortune*, 3 June 1991, 112.
8. Thomas W. Malone, *The Future of Work* (Cambridge: Harvard Business School Press, 2004), 32.
9. Max Messmer, "Enhancing Your Writing Skills," *Strategic Finance*, January 2001, 8, and "The Challenges Facing Workers in the Future," *HR Focus*, August 1999, 6.
10. "Team Player: No More 'Same-Ol'Same-Ol'," *Business Week*, 17 October 1994, 95.
11. Sharon Helldorfer and Michael Daly, "Reengineering Brings Together Units," *Best's Review*, October 1993, 82–85.
12. Dwight Cunningham, "The Downside of Technology," *Chicago Tribune Internet Edition*, 2 January 2000; "Wired to the Desk," *Fortune*, Summer 1999, 164.
13. "Behind the Numbers: E-Mail Beats the Phone in Business Communication," *InformationWeek*, 19 May 2003, 66.
14. Matthew Tartaro, "Best Practices for Supporting Home Users," *Network Computing*, 13 June 2003, 73.
15. Keith Naughton, "Designing Your Next Office," *Newsweek*, 28 April 2003, 46.
16. Deborah Keary, Dyane Holt, and Ruhal Dooley, "Appraising Performance, 'Hoteling,' Volunteering," *HRMagazine*, May 2003, 41.
17. Terry Pristin, "A New Office Can Mean Making Do With Less," *The New York Times*, 26 May 2004, C1.
18. Hal Lancaster, "Hiring a Full Staff May Be the Next Fad in Management," *The Wall Street Journal*, 4 April 1998, B1.
19. Andrew Denka, "New Office Etiquette Dilemmas," *CPA Journal*, August 1996, 13.
20. Susan Thea Posnock, "The Pros and Cons of a Virtual Office," *Folio: The Magazine for Magazine Management*, October 2000, 112.
21. Sharon Nelton, "Nurturing Diversity," *Nation's Business*, June 1995, 25–27.
22. Based on Bureau of Labor statistics appearing in R. W. Judy and C. D'Amico's "Workforce 2020: Work and Workers in the 21st Century" (Indianapolis: Hudson Institute), 1997.
23. Bill Clinton, "Presidential Proclamation 7345—National Older Workers Employment Week, 2000," *Weekly Compilation of Presidential Documents*, 2 October 2000, 2174.
24. Patrick Carnevale, as quoted by Genevieve Capowski, "Managing Diversity," *Management Review*, June 1996, 6.
25. Alvin Toffler, *PowerShift* (New York: Bantam Books, 1990), 238. See also Oren Harari, "Flood Your Organization With Knowledge," *Management Review*, November 1997, 33–37.
26. Peter Drucker, "New Realities, New Ways of Managing," *Business Month*, May 1989, 50–51.
27. Ann Grimes, "Techno Talk," *The Wall Street Journal*, 27 June 2002, B4.
28. Steve Lohr, "New Economy," *The New York Times*, 2 February 2004, C6.
29. David Wessel, "The Future of Jobs: New Ones Arise, Wage Gap

Widens," *The Wall Street Journal*, 2 April 2004, A1.

30. W. Michael Fox, Richard Alm, and Nigel Holmes, "Where the Jobs Are," *The New York Times*, 13 May 2004, A27.
31. G. A. Marken, "New Approach to Moving up the Corporate Ladder," *Public Relations Quarterly*, Winter 1996, 47.
32. Faridah Awang, Marcia A. Anderson, and Clora Mae Baker, "Entry-Level Information Services and Support Personnel: Needed Workplace and Technology Skills," *The Delta Pi Epsilon Journal*, Winter 2003, 48; Janette Moody, Brent Stewart, and Cynthia Bolt-Lee, "Showcasing the Skilled Business Graduate: Expanding the Tool Kit," *Business Communication Quarterly*, March 2002, 21–26; "The Challenges Facing Workers in the Future," *HR Focus*, August 1999, 6.
33. Barrett J. Mandel and Judith Yellen, "Mastering the Memo," *Working Woman*, September 1989, 135.
34. Cheryl Hamilton with Cordell Parker, *Communicating for Results* (Belmont, CA: Wadsworth, 1996), 7.
35. Jerry Sullivan, Naoki Karmeda, and Tatsuo Nobu, "Bypassing in Managerial Communication," *Business Horizons*, January/February 1991, 72.
36. Peter Drucker, *Managing the Non-Profit Organization: Practices and Principles* (New York: Harper-Collins, 1990), 46.
37. Jane Black, "Why Offices Are Now Open Secrets: Wildly Popular Technologies Like Instant Messaging and Wi-Fi Make Workers More Productive," *BusinessWeek Online*, 17 September 2003.
38. Dennis K. Berman, "Online Laundry: Government Posts Enron's E-Mail; Amid Power-Market Minutiae, Many Personal Items," *The Wall Street Journal*, 6 October 2003, A1.
39. Tom Geddie, "Technology: It's About Time," *Communication World*, Special Issue Supplement, March 1998, 26–28.
40. Monica Seeley, "How to Reduce the Stress of E-Mail Overload," *Computer Weekly*, 8 April 2003, 44.
41. Bob Nelson, "How to Energize Everyone in the Company," *Bottom Line/Business*, October 1997, 3.
42. Dignam "Procter & Gamble Wobbled," 21.
43. Brooker, "Can Procter & Gamble Change," 146+.
44. Ronald R. Sims, et al., *The Challenge of Front-Line Management: Flattened Organizations in the New Economy* (Westport, CT: Quorum: 2001), 10.
45. Lisa A. Burke and Jessica Morris Wise, "The Effective Care, Handling, and Pruning of the Office Grapevine," *Business Horizons*, May/June, 2003, 71.
46. Robert L. Dilenschneider, "Cultivating the Corporation Grapevine," *The New York Times*, 2 July 1995, F14.
47. Stephanie Zimmermann, Beverly Davenport, and John W. Haas, "A Communication Metamyth in the Workplace: The Assumption That More Is Better," *Journal of Business Communication*, April 1996, 185–204.
48. Bob Nelson, "How to Energize Everyone in the Company," *Bottom Line/Business*, October 1997, 3.
49. Gary R. Weaver, Linda K. Trevino, and Philip L. Cochran, "Corporate Ethics Practices in the Mid-1990's: An Empirical Study of the Fortune 1000," *Journal of Business Ethics*, February 1999, 283–294.
50. Max M. Thomas, "Classroom Conundrum: Profits + Ethics = ?" *Business Month*, February 1990, 6.
51. Tina Kelley, "Charting a Course to Ethical Profits," *The New York Times*, 8 February 1998, BU1.
52. Phyllis Davis, "Oh, Say It Isn't So!" *The National Public Accountant*, September 2003, 33.
53. Peter Vilbig, "The Great Enron Disappearing Act," *New York Times Upfront*, 22 March 2002, 12.
54. "Executives on Trial: Scandal Scorecard," *The Wall Street Journal*, 3 October 2003, B1.
55. Samuel Greengard, "50 Percent of Your Employees Are Lying, Cheating, and Stealing," *Workforce*, October 1997, 46–47.
56. Martha Groves, "Ethics at Work: Honor System," *Los Angeles Times*, 3 November 1997, Careers sec., 3, 15. See also Alison Boyd, "Employee Traps—Corruption in the Workplace," *Management Review*, September 1997, 9.
57. Mary E. Guy, *Ethical Decision Making in Everyday Work Situations* (New York: Quorum Books, 1990), 3.
58. James Flanigan, "Slipshod Business Ethics a Poor Example for Youth," *The Los Angeles Times*, 30 October 2002, C1; Alison Bell, "What Price Ethics?" *Entrepreneurial Woman*, January/February, 1991, 68.
59. Based on Bell, "What Price Ethics?"
60. Amy Harmon, "On the Office PC, Bosses Opt for All Work, and No Play," *The New York Times*, 22 September 1997, A1, C11.
61. David Stewart, "Deception, Materiality, and Survey Research: Some Lessons From Kraft," *Journal of Public Policy & Marketing*, Spring 1995, 15–28.
62. J. Craig Andrews and Thomas J. Maronick, "Advertising Research Issues From FTC Versus Stouffer Foods Corporation," *Journal of Public Policy & Marketing*, Fall 1995, 301–309.
63. Michael Schroeder, "Get Firm 'Abs' in a Few Hours? Don't Believe It," *The Wall Street Journal*, 18 June 1997, B1.
64. Laurel Delaney, "Escape From Corporate America," *Across the Board*, March/April 2003, 38.
65. "Do Your Reps' Writing Skills Need a Refresher?" *Customer Contact Management Report*, February 2002, 7.
66. "The Wall Street Journal Ethics Quiz," *The Wall Street Journal*, 21 October 1999, B1.
67. Barbara Correa, "Victims of Identity Theft Can Spend Years Trying to Clear Up Damage," *Knight Ridder/Tribune Business News*, 5 October 2003; Ryan J. Foley, "Identity-Theft Bill Is Seen as Feeble; Consumer Advocates Say Losses Outnumber Gains; Free Credit Reports Detailed," *The Wall Street Journal*, 16 September 2003.

Chapter 2

1. Discussion of the Harley-Davidson Motor Company based on Joellen Perry and Marianne Lavelle, "Made in America," *U.S. News & World Report*, 17 May 2004, 52; Joseph Weber, "Hurdles of the Road to Hog Heaven," *BusinessWeek*, 10 November 2003, 96; Michelle Starr, "Harley-Davidson Workers Reflect on Company's Long History in York County, Pa," *Knight Ridder/Tribune Business News*, 18 September 2003; John Helyar, "Will Harley Hit the Wall?" *Fortune*, 12 August 2002;

Joe Singer and Steve Duvall, "High-Performance Partnering by Self-Managed Teams in Manufacturing," *Engineering Management Journal*, December 2000, 9; William J. Holstein, "Rebels With a Cause," *U.S. News & World Report*, 13 November 2000; Stuart F. Brown, "Gearing Up for the Cruiser Wars," *Fortune*, 3 August 1998, 128B–128D; Barbara M. Schmitz, "Computer Simulation Helps Improve Motorcycle Handling," *Computer-Aided Engineering*, September 1998, 8–10; Peter Bradley, "Harley-Davidson Keeps Its Eyes on the Road," *Logistics Management & Distribution Report*, August 1998, 68–73; Tim Minahan, "Harley-Davidson Revs Up Development Process," *Purchasing*, 7 May 1998, 44S18–44S23; Aaron Baar, "Harley-Davidson Aims Younger," *Adweek*, 10 August 1998, 4; Robert J. Bowman, "All That It's Cracked Up to Be?" *World Trade*, July 1998, 75–76; and Clyde Fessler, "Rotating Leadership at Harley-Davidson: From Hierarchy to Interdependence," *Strategy & Leadership*, July-August 1997, 42–43.

2. Patricia Buhler, "Managing in the 90s: Creating Flexibility in Today's Workplace," *Supervision*, January 1996, 24–26.
3. Based on Cheryl Hamilton with Cordell Parker, *Communicating for Results*, 6e (Belmont, CA: Wadsworth, 2000), 279; Barton H. Hamilton, Jack A. Nickerson, and Hideo Owan, "Team Incentives and Worker Heterogeneity: An Empirical Analysis of the Impact of Teams on Productivity and Participation," *Journal of Political Economy*, June 2003, 465; and Harvey Robbins and Michael Finley, *Why Teams Don't Work: What Went Wrong and How to Make It Right* (Princeton, NJ: Peterson's/Pacesetter Books, 1995), 11–12.
4. Steve Ennen, "Red Baron Soars With Teamwork: New Pizza Products Sate Lifestyle Needs," *Food Processing*, April 2003, 40.
5. Frank Mueller, Stephen Procter, David Buchanan, "Teamworking in Its Context(s): Antecedents, Nature and Dimensions," *Human Relations*, November 2000, 1387.
6. James R. DiSanza and Nancy J. Legge, *Business and Professional Communication* (Boston: Allyn and Bacon, 2000), 98.
7. Katzenbach and Smith, *The Wisdom of Teams*, 19.
8. Jessica Lipnack and Jeffrey Stamps, *Virtual Teams: People Working Across Boundaries With Technology*, 2e (New York: John Wiley & Sons, 2000), 18.
9. Jessica Lipnack, "Virtual Teams: The Future Is Now" <http://www.linezine.com/7.2/articles/jlvtfin.htm> (Retrieved 28 October 2003).
10. Christine A. Spring, Paul R. Jackson, Sharon K. Parker, "Production Teamworking: The Importance of Interdependence and Autonomy for Employee Strain and Satisfaction," *Human Relations*, November 2000, 1519.
11. The discussion of Tuckman's model is adapted from Robbins and Finley, *Why Teams Don't Work*, Chapter 22. See also Jane Henderson-Loney, "Tuckman and Tears: Developing Teams During Profound Organizational Change," *Supervision*, May 1996, 3–5.
12. Based on Kenneth D. Benne and Paul Sheats, "Functional Roles of Group Members," *Journal of Social Issues 4*, 1949, 41–49; Hamilton and Parker, *Communicating for Results*, 308–312; and J. Keyton, *Group Communication: Process and Analysis* (Mountain View, CA: Mayfield, 1999).
13. Cheryl Hamilton with Cordell Parker, *Communicating for Success*, 6e (Belmont, CA: Wadsworth, 2001), 100–104.
14. Jean H. Miculka, *Speaking for Success* (Cincinnati: South-Western) 1999, 127.
15. I. L. Janis, *Groupthink: Psychological Studies on Policy Decisions and Fiascoes* (Boston: Houghton Mifflin, 1982). See also Shaila M. Miranda and Carol Saunders, "Group Support Systems: An Organization Development Intervention to Combat Groupthink," *Public Administration Quarterly*, Summer 1995, 193–216.
16. Allen C. Amason, Wayne A. Hochwarter, Kenneth R. Thompson, and Allison W. Harrison, "Conflict: An Important Dimension in Successful Management Teams," *Organizational Dynamics*, Autumn 1995, 1.
17. Charles Parnell, "Teamwork: Not a New Idea, But It's Transforming the Workplace," *Executive Speeches*, December 1997/January 1998, 35–40.
18. Katzennbach and Smith, *Wisdom of Teams*, 45.
19. Joel Makower, "Managing Diversity in the Workplace," *Business and Society Review*, Winter 1995, 48–54.
20. Jennifer Bayot, "Developers Bet on Theaters in Glutted L.A.," *The Wall Street Journal*, Eastern edition, 8 November 2000, C1.
21. Katzenbach and Smith, *Wisdom of Teams*, 50.
22. "Workplace Rudeness Is Common and Costly," *USA Today Magazine*, May 2002, 9.
23. Jon Hanke, "Presenting as a Team," *Presentations*, January 1998, 74–82.
24. Hal Lancaster, "Learning Some Ways to Make Meetings Slightly Less Awful," *The Wall Street Journal*, 26 May 1998, B1.
25. Tom McDonald, "Minimizing Meetings," *Successful Meetings*, June 1996, 24.
26. Clyde Fessler, "Rotating Leadership at Harley-Davidson: From Hierarchy to Interdependence," *Strategy & Leadership*, July/August 1997, 42–43.
27. Lancaster, "Learning Some Ways," B1.
28. John C. Bruening, "There's Good News About Meetings," *Managing Office Technology*, July 1996, 24–25.
29. Christopher Marquis, "Doing Well and Doing Good," *The New York Times*, 13 July 2003, BU 2.
30. Kirsten Schabacker, "A Short, Snappy Guide to Meaningful Meetings," *Working Women*, June 1991, 73.
31. J. Keith Cook, "Try These Eight Guidelines for More Effective Meetings," *Communication Briefings* Bonus Item, April 1995, 8a. See also Morey Stettner, "How to Manage a Corporate Motormouth, *Investor's Business Daily*, 8 October 1998, A1.
32. Hamilton and Parker, *Communicating*, 311–312.
33. Andrew Saunders, "Meetings: Would You Miss Them?" *Management Today*, October 2002, 54.
34. Joseph Weber, "Hurdles on the Road to Hog Heaven," *BusinessWeek*, 10 November 2003, 96.
35. Bob Filipczak, "The Soul of the Hog," *Training*, February 1996, 38–42.
36. Marquis, "Doing Well and Doing Good," BU 2.
37. Angeles Arrien, "Geese Teach Lessons on Teamwork," *Motion Systems Distributor*, March-April

2003, 32; and "Flying Like the Geese," *Design Engineering*, December 2001, 9.

Chapter 3

1. "L. L. Bean," press packet and company brochure, L. L. Bean (Freeport, Maine, 2001), Fact Sheet.
2. Ellen Fowler, interview with Mary Ellen Guffey, 17 April 2001; "HR a Catalyst for Business Change at LL Bean," *Human Resource Management International Digest*, November-December 2002, 4.
3. "HR a Catalyst for Business Change at LL Bean," 4.
4. Aaron Baar, "Bean History Key to M/W's Idea," *Adweek*, 16 October 2001, 9.
5. Harvey Robbins and Michael Finley, *Why Teams Don't Work* (Princeton, NJ: Peterson's/Pacesetter Books, 1995), 123.
6. Jennifer Pellet, "Anatomy of a Turnaround Guru," *Chief Executive*, April 2003, 41; Pamela Mounter, "Global Internal Communication: A Model," *Journal of Communication Management 3*, 2003, 265; Howard Feiertag, "Listening Skills, Enthusiasm Top List of Salespeople's Best Traits," *Hotel and Motel Management*, 15 July 2002, 20; R. P. Ramsey and R. S. Sohi, "Listening to Your Customers: The Impact of Perceived Salesperson Listening Behavior on Relationship Outcomes," *Journal of the Academy of Marketing Science 25* (2), 1997, 127–137; Lynn O. Cooper, "Listening Competency in the Workplace: A Model for Training," *Business Communication Quarterly*, December 1997, 75–84; Valerie P. Goby and Justice H. Lewis, "The Key Role of Listening in Business: A Study of the Singapore Insurance Industry," *Business Communication Quarterly*, June 2000, 41+; and L. E. Penley, E. R. Alexander, I. E. Jerigan, and C. I. Henwood, "Communication Abilities of Managers: The Relationship to Performance," *Journal of Management 17*, 1991, 57–76.
7. Faridah Awang, Marcia A. Anderson, and Clora Mae Baker, "Entry-Level Information Services and Support Personnel: Needed Workplace and Technology Skills," *The Delta Pi Epsilon Journal*, Winter, 2003, 48; and American Management Association, "The Challenges Facing Workers in the Future," *HR Focus*, August 1999, 6.
8. Ko DeRuyter and Martin G. M. Wetzels, "The Impact of Perceived Listening Behavior in Voice-to-Voice Service Encounters," *Journal of Service Research*, February 2000, 276–284.
9. Tom W. Harris, "Listen Carefully," *Nation's Business*, June 1989, 78.
10. L. K. Steil, L. I. Barker, and K. W. Watson, *Effective Listening: Key to Your Success* (Reading, MA: Addison-Wesley, 1983); and J. A. Harris, "Hear What's Really Being Said," *Management-Auckland*, August 1998, 18.
11. Eric H. Nelson and Jan Gypen, "The Subordinate's Predicament," *Harvard Business Review*, September/October 1979, 133.
12. International Listening Association, "Listening Factoids" <http://www.listen.org/pages/factoids.html> (Retrieved 16 January 2004).
13. Patrice M. Johnson and Kittie W. Watson, "Managing Interpersonal and Team Conflict: Listening Strategies," in *Listening in Everyday Life*, eds. Michael Purdy and Deborah Borisoff (Lanham, MD: University Press of America, 1997), 126–129.
14. Michael Render, "Better Listening Makes for a Better Marketing Message," *Marketing News*, 11 September, 2000, 22–23.
15. Stephen Golen, "A Factor Analysis of Barriers to Effective Listening," *The Journal of Business Communication*, Winter 1990, 25–37.
16. International Listening Association, "Listening Factoids" <http://www.listen.org/pages/factoids.html> (Retrieved 16 January 2004).
17. James Butcher, "Dominic O'Brien—Master Mnemonist," *The Lancet*, 2 September 2000, 836.
18. Andrew Wolvin and Carolyn Gwynn Coakley, *Listening*, 5e (New York: McGraw-Hill, 1996), 136–137.
19. "Effective Communication," *Training Tomorrow*, November 1994, 32–33.
20. Julia T. Wolf, *Gendered Lives: Communication, Gender, and Culture*, 5e (Belmont, CA: Wadsworth, 2003); Kristin J. Anderson and Campbell Leaper, "Meta-Analyses of Gender Effects on Conversational Interruption: Who, What, When, Where, and How," *Sex Roles: A Journal of Research*, August 1998, 225+; and M. Booth-Butterfield, "She Hears: What They Hear and Why," *Personnel Journal 44*, 1984, 39.
21. L. P. Stewart and A. D. Stewart, *Communication Between the Sexes: Sex Differences and Sex Role Stereotypes* (Scottsdale, AZ: Gorsuch Scarisbrick, 1990).
22. Jayne Tear, "They Just Don't Understand Gender Dynamics," *The Wall Street Journal*, 20 November 1995, A12; Alan Wolfe, "Talking From 9 to 5: How Women's and Men's Conversational Styles Affect Who Gets Heard, Who Gets Credit and What Gets Done at Work," *New Republic*, 12 December 1994.
23. J. Burgoon, D. Coker, and R. Coker, "Communication Explanations," *Human Communication Research*, 12, 1986, 463–494.
24. Michael Tarsala, "Remec's Ronald Ragland: Drawing Rivals to His Team by Making Their Concerns His," *Investor's Business Daily*, 7 November 1997, A1.
25. Ray Birdwhistel, *Kinesics and Context* (Philadelphia: University of Pennsylvania Press, 1970).
26. "What's A-O.K. in the U.S.A. Is Lewd and Worthless Beyond," *The New York Times*, 18 August 1996, E7.
27. "Body Speak: What Are You Saying?" *Successful Meetings*, October 2000, 49–51.
28. Dorothy Leeds, "Body Language: Actions Speak Louder Than Words," *National Underwriter*, 1 May 1995, 18–19.
29. Helen Wilkie, "Professional Presence," *The Canadian Manager*, Fall 2003, 14; Eva Kaplan-Leiserson, "Casual Dress/Back to Business Attire," *Training & Development*, November 2000, 38–39.
30. Marilyn Moats Kennedy, "Is Business Casual Here to Stay?" *Executive Female*, September-October 1997, 31.
31. Nora Wood, Tina Benitez, "Does the Suit Fit?" *Incentive*, April 2003, 31.
32. Laura Egodigwe, "Here Come the Suits," *Black Enterprise*, March 2003, 59; Kaplan-Leiserson, "Casual Dress," 38; and Christine Summerson, "The Suit Is Back in Business—And Now, It's Sporting More Colors and Patterns," *BusinessWeek*, 18 November 2002, 130.
33. "Future Shop: Sporting Goods & Equipment," *Forbes*, 6 April 1998, 48.

34. Paul Miller, "Ax Falls on 300 L.L. Bean Workers," *Catalog Age*, March 2003, 7.
35. "Not Listening Is an American Thing," *HighGain Inc. Newsletter* <http://www.highgain.com/newsletter/back-issues/e-news/06-00/hg-enews-06-00.html> (Retrieved 17 January 2001).
36. "Adopt 'Active Listening' Skills for Better Cross-Functional Team Communication," *Inventory Reduction Report*, January 2002, 9.
37. Leslie Gross Klaff, "Tough Sell," *Workforce*, November 2003, 48.
38. "What's the Universal Hand Sign for 'I Goofed'?" *Santa Barbara News-Press*, 16 December 1996, D2.
39. Arthur H. Bell, "Using Nonverbal Cues," *Incentive*, September 1999, 162.
40. James Calvert Scott, "Business Casual Dress: Workplace Boon or Boondoggle?" Part 2, *Instructional Strategies*, Delta Pi Epsilon, December 1999, 5.

Chapter 4

1. Ken Belson, "Wal-Mart Hopes It Won't Be Lost In Translation," *The New York Times*, 14 December 2003, Sec. 3, 1.
2. Chester Dawson, Alysha Webb, and Wendy Zellner, "Will Wal-Mart Conquer Japan?," *BusinessWeek Online*, 1 April 2002 <http://www.businessweek.com/magazine/content/02_13/b3776141.htm> (Retrieved 24 January 2004).
3. Ibid.
4. Miriam Jordan, "Penney Blends Two Business Cultures," *The Wall Street Journal*, 5 April 2001, A15.
5. Carol Hymowitz, "European Executives Give Some Advice on Crossing Borders," *The Wall Street Journal*, 2 December 2003, B1; Alecia Swasy, "Don't Sell Thick Diapers in Tokyo," *The New York Times*, 3 October 1993, F9.
6. Stanley Holmes, "The Real Nike News Is Happening Abroad," *BusinessWeek*, 21 July 2003, 30.
7. E. S. Browning, "In Pursuit of the Elusive Euroconsumer," *The Wall Street Journal*, 23 April 1992, B1.
8. Gabriella Stern, "Heinz Aims to Export Taste for Ketchup," *The Wall Street Journal*, 21 November 1992, B1.
9. Shona Crabtree, "Cultural Differences," *Eagle-Tribune* <http://www.eagletribune.com/news/stories/19990530/BU-001.htm> (Retrieved 13 February 2001).
10. Mary O'Hara-Devereaux and Robert Johansen, *GlobalWork: Bridging Distance, Culture and Time* (San Francisco: Jossey-Bass, 1994), 245.
11. Patrick J. Kiger, "The China Puzzle," *Workforce*, December 2003, 30.
12. "Creative Jobs Destruction," *The Wall Street Journal*, 6 January 2004, A18.
13. Jonathan D. Glater, "Offshore Services Grow in Lean Times," *The New York Times*, 3 January 2004, B1.
14. Sari Kalin, "Global Net Knits East to West at Liz Claiborne," *Computerworld*, 9 June 1997, G4–G6.
15. "Futurework: Trends and Challenges for Work in the 21st Century," U.S. Department of Labor <http://www.dol.gov/_sec/gils/records/000187.htm> (Retrieved 20 October 2004).
16. Howard Gleckman, "A Rich Stew in the Melting Pot," *Business Week*, 31 August 1998, 76.
17. "Special Report Overseas Media: Mind Your Language," *Marketing Week*, 19 June 2003, 35; and David Harvey, "Going Global," *Home Office Computing*, October 2000, 87.
18. Steve Alexander, "Learn the Politics of Going Global," *Computerworld*, 1 January 2001, S8–S10.
19. Adam Lincoln, "Lost in Translation," *ECFO*, Spring 2001, 38; Sari Kalin, "The Importance of Being Multiculturally Correct," *Computerworld*, 6 October 1997, G16–G17.
20. Andrew Pollack, "Barbie's Journey in Japan," *The New York Times*, 22 December 1996, E3.
21. Lennie Copeland and Lewis Griggs, *Going International* (New York: Plume Books, 1985), 14.
22. Guo-Ming Chen and William J. Starosta, *Foundations of Intercultural Communication* (Boston: Allyn and Bacon, 1998), 40.
23. Iris Varner and Linda Beamer, *Intercultural Communication in the Global Workplace* (Boston: McGraw-Hill Irwin, 2001), 18.
24. Edward T. Hall and Mildred Reed Hall, *Understanding Cultural Differences* (Yarmouth, ME: Intercultural Press, 1987), 183–184.
25. Kathleen K. Reardon, *Where Minds Meet* (Belmont, CA: Wadsworth, 1987), 199.
26. Vivan C. Sheer and Ling Chen, "Successful Sino-Western Business Negotiation: Participants' Accounts of National and Professional Cultures," *The Journal of Business Communication*, January 2003, 62; and Vivienne Luk, Mumtaz Patel, and Kathryn White, "Personal Attributes of American and Chinese Business Associates," *The Bulletin of the Association for Business Communication*, December 1990, 67.
27. Cynthia Gallois and Victor Callan, *Communication and Culture* (New York: John Wiley Sons, 1997), 24.
28. Susan S. Jarvis, "Preparing Employees to Work South of the Border," *Personnel*, June 1990, 763.
29. Gallois and Callan, *Communication and Culture*, 29.
30. Copeland and Griggs, *Going International*, 94.
31. Ibid., 108.
32. Ibid., 12.
33. Jeff Copeland, "Stare Less, Listen More," *American Way*, American Airlines, 15 December 1990.
34. Howard W. French, "Japan's Neglected Resource: Female Workers: Can Japan Change?" *The New York Times*, 25 July 2003, A3; and Karen DeCrow, "Made in Japan; Outmoded Cultural Biases Regarding Women Are Hard to Sink in the Land of the Rising Sun," *Syracuse New Times*, 20 August 2003, 5.
35. E. S. Browning, "Computer Chip Project Brings Rivals Together, But the Cultures Clash," *The Wall Street Journal*, 3 May 1994, A1, A11.
36. Ann Zimmerman and Martin Fackler, "Wal-Mart's Foray Into Japan Spurs a Retail Upheaval," *The Wall Street Journal*, 13 September 2003, A1.
37. Belson, "Wal-Mart Hopes," Sec. 3, p. 12.
38. Ibid., p. 12.
39. S. Ishii and T. Bruneau, "Silence and Silences in Cross-Cultural Perspective: Japan and the United States." In *Intercultural Communication: A Reader* (Belmont, CA: Wadsworth, 1994), 266.
40. Copeland and Griggs, *Going International*, 111.
41. M. R. Hammer, "Intercultural Communication Competence," in Chen and Starosta, *Foundations of Intercultural Communication*, 247.
42. Lillian H. Chaney and Jeanette S. Martin, *Intercultural Business Communication* (Englewood Cliffs, NJ:

Prentice Hall Career and Technology, 1995), 67.
43. Gretchen Weber, "English Rules," *Workforce Management*, May 2004, 47–50.
44. Roger Axtell, *Do's and Taboos Around the World*, 2e (New York: Wiley, 1990), 71.
45. Robert McGarvey, "Foreign Exchange," *USAir Magazine*, June 1992, 64.
46. Andrew W. Singer, "Ethics: Are Standards Lower Overseas?" *Across the Board*, September 1991, 31–34.
47. Ronald Berenbeim, " Global Ethics," *Executive Excellence*, May 2000, 7.
48. Jennifer Dorroh and Armando Saliba, "Stay Out of the Shadows: Mexican Companies, Government Move to Improve Business Ethics and Values," *Business Mexico*, June 2003, 42.
49. Shang-Jin Wei, "Corruption in Developing Countries," *Global Economics*, 12 March 2003 <http://brookings.edu/views/speeches/wei/20030312.htm> (Retrieved 20 October 2004).
50. Bob Davis, "U.S. Battles Europe to Narrow Global Treaty Banning Corruption," *The Wall Street Journal*, 17 June 2003, A1.
51. Kent Hodgson, "Adapting Ethical Decisions to a Global Marketplace," *Management Review*, May 1992, 56.
52. Paul McDougall, "Where's the Line? CIOs and Other Execs Are Questioning Whether Relationships With Vendors Can Be Too Cozy," *Information Week*, 28 April 2003, 22.
53. Charlene Marmer Solomon, "Put Your Ethics to a Global Test," *Personnel Journal*, January 1996, 66–74. See also Larry R. Smeltzer and Marianne M. Jennings, "Why an International Code of Business Ethics Would Be Good for Business," *Journal of Business Ethics*, January 1998, 57–66.
54. Based on Kent Hodgson, "Adapting Ethical Decisions," 54.
55. Based on 2000 U.S. Census figures, as reported by Jane Sneddon Little and Robert K. Triest, "The Impact of Demographic Change on U.S. Labor Markets," *Seismic Shifts: The Economic Impact of Demographic Change*, Proceedings from the Federal Reserve Bank of Boston Conference Series <http://www.bos.frb.org/economic/conf/conf46e1.pdf> (Retrieved 30 January 2004).
56. Fay Hansen, "Tracing the Value of Diversity Programs," *Workforce*, April 2003, 31.
57. Jack Neff, "Diversity," *Advertising Age*, 16 February 1998, S1.
58. Rae Andre, "Diversity Stress as Morality Stress," *Journal of Business Ethics*, June 1995, 489–496.
59. Julia T. Wood, "Gendered Communication Practices," *Gendered Lives* (Belmont, CA: Wadworth, 2002), 119; Jayne Tear, "They Just Don't Understand Gender Dynamics," *The Wall Street Journal*, 20 November 1995, A12; Anne Roiphe, "Talking Trouble," *Working Woman*, October 1994, 28–31; Cristina Stuart, "Why Can't a Woman Be More Like a Man?" *Training Tomorrow*, February 1994, 22–24; and Alan Wolfe, "Talking From 9 to 5: How Women's and Men's Conversational Styles Affect Who Gets Heard, Who Gets Credit, and What Gets Done at Work," *New Republic*, 12 December 1994.
60. Andre, "Diversity Stress," 489–496.
61. John Schwartz and Matthew L. Wald, "Smart People Working Collectively Can Be Dumber Than the Sum of Their Brains," *The New York Times*, 9 March 2003.
62. Genevieve Capowski, "Managing Diversity," *Management Review*, June 1996, 16.
63. Joel Makower, "Managing Diversity in the Workplace," *Business and Society Review*, Winter 1995, 48–54.
64. George Simons and Darlene Dunham, "Making Inclusion Happen," *Managing Diversity*, December 1995 <http://www.jalmc.org/mk-incl.htm> (Retrieved 9 August 1996).
65. Bill Saporito, "Can Wal-Mart Get Any Bigger?" *Time*, 13 January 2003, 38.
66. Ken Cottrill, "The World According to Hollywood," *Traffic World*, 6 November 2000, 15.
67. "Examples of Cultural Blunders Made by U.S. Businessmen," *Eagle Tribune* <http://www.eagletribune.com/news/stories/19990530/BU _002.htm> (Retrieved 13 February 2001).
68. Somporn Thapanachai, "Awareness Narrows Cross-Cultural Gap in Thai Management Training Courses," *Bangkok Post*, Knight-Ridder/Tribune Business News, 6 October 2003.
69. Michele Wucker, "Keep on Trekking," *Working Woman*, December/January 1998, 32–36.
70. Based on Rose Knotts and Mary S. Thibodeaux, "Verbal Skills in Cross-Culture Managerial Communication," *European Business Review 92* (2), 1992, v–vii.
71. Keith Martin and Sheila M. Walsh, "Beware the Foreign Corrupt Practices Act," *International Commercial Litigation*, October 1996, 25–27.
72. Makower, "Managing Diversity."
73. Cora Daniels, "50 Best Companies for Minorities," *Fortune*, 28 June 2004, 138.

Chapter 5

1. Maria Zate, "FedEx to Buy Kinko's for $2.4 Billion in Cash," *Santa Barbara News-Press*, 31 December 2003, A1; Julie Mitchell, "Documents Read in a Click," *Upside*, March 2001, 48; Andy Cohen, "Copy Cats," *Sales & Marketing*, August 2000, 50–58; and Michael H. Martin, "Kinko's," *Fortune*, 8 July 1996, 102.
2. Ann Marsh, "Kinko's Grows Up—Almost," *Forbes*, 1 December 1997, 270–272.
3. Edwin Powell, "Ten Tips for Better Business Writing," *Office Solutions*, November/December 2003, 36; and Hugh Hay-Roe, "The Secret of Excess," *Executive Excellence*, January 1995, 20.
4. Ronald R. Sims, John G. Veres III, Katherine A. Jackson, and Carolyn L. Facteau, *The Challenge of Front-Line Management* (Westport, CT: Quorum Books, 2001), 89.
5. Vanessa Dean Arnold, "Benjamin Franklin on Writing Well," *Personnel Journal*, August 1986, 17.
6. Mark Bacon, quoted in "Business Writing: One-on-One Speaks Best to the Masses," *Training*, April 1988, 95. See also Elizabeth Danziger, "Communicate Up," *Journal of Accountancy*, February 1998, 67.
7. For more information see Marilyn Schwartz, *Guidelines for Bias-Free Writing* (Bloomington, IN: University Press, 1994).
8. Leslie Matthies, as described in Carl Heyel, "Policy and Procedure Manuals," *The Handbook of Executive Communication* (Homewood, IL: Dow Jones-Irwin, 1986), 212.

9. Victor E. Schwartz, "Continuing Duty to Warn: An Opportunity for Liability Prevention or Exposure," *Journal of Public Policy & Marketing*, Spring 1998, 124.
10. Lisa Jenner, "Develop Communication and Training With Literacy in Mind," *HR Focus*, March 1994, 14.
11. Kristin R. Woolever's "Corporate Language and the Law: Avoiding Liability in Corporate Communications," *IEE Transactions on Professional Communication*, 2 June 1990, 95–98.
12. Ibid., 95.
13. Lisa Jenner, "Employment-at-Will Liability: How Protected Are You?" *HR Focus*, March 1994, 11.
14. Robert J. Walter and Bradley J. Sleeper, "Employee Recruitment and Retention: When Company Inducements Trigger Liability," *Review of Business*, Spring 2002, 17–23.
15. Judy E. Pickens, "Communication: Terms of Equality: A Guide to Bias-Free Language," *Personnel Journal*, August 1985, 5.
16. David Wessel, "Listen Up! The Fed Does Speak English," *The Wall Street Journal Online*, 8 February 2004.
17. Leon Gettler, "Jay Conger: Why Chief Executives Fail" Australian Institute of Management <http://www.aim.com.au/resources/article_jconger.html> (Retrieved 7 July 2004).
18. Jay Conger, "Leading in Challenging Times," keynote address presented at the Annual Meeting of The Commission on Colleges, Nashville, TN, December 2003.

Chapter 6

1. Amy Merrick, "Gap Profit More Than Triples on Improved Goods, Marketing," *The Wall Street Journal*, 22 August 2003, B5; Adrienne Carter, "Down But Not Out," *Money*, September 2002, 43; Amy Merrick, "Gap's Image Is Wearing Out—Tired of Trendiness, Shoppers Perceive Lapses in Quality and Defect to Competitors," *The Wall Street Journal*, 6 December 2001, B1; Louise Lee, "Gap: Missing That Ol' Mickey Magic: Bad Fashion Calls and an Exodus of Execs Have Mickey Drexler's Retail Empire Hurting," *Business Week*, 29 October 2001, 86; Robin Blumenthal, "Dressed for Success," *Barron's*, 21 November 2002, 20; and "Eryn Brown, "Marking Up Gap," *Fortune*, 2 September 2002, 188.
2. Merrick, "Gap's Image Is Wearing Out," B1.
3. Louise Lee, "The Gap Has Reason to Dance Again," *BusinessWeek*, 19 April 2004, 42.
4. Li-Anne Huang, "Old Navy—A Retail Success Story," *The Virtual Reporter*, Stanford Graduate School of Business, 29 October 2001 <http://www.virtualreporter.org/news/2001/10/29/Style/Old-Navy.8211.A.Retail.Success.Story-134837.shtml> (Retrieved 5 November 2004); and T. R. Nothum, "Top Woman," *Future Magazine* <http://www.phoenix.edu/students/future/oldissues/Spring2003/ming.html> (Retrieved 1 March 2004).
5. Amy Merrick and Sarah Ellison, "Too Much of a Good Thing?—Gap Faces Same Dilemma as Other Big Retailers That Grew Beyond Demand," *The Wall Street Journal*, 24 July 2002, B1.
6. Interview with Jenny Ming by James J. Owens, "Profiles in Business," 25 January 2003 *Marshall* [University of Southern California] *Magazine* <http://www.marshall.usc.edu/Web/News.cfm?doc_id=5338> (Retrieved 4 March 2004).
7. "How We Run Our business," Gap Inc. Web site <http://www.gapinc.com/about/ataglance/how_we_body.shtm> (Retrieved 4 March 2004).
8. Adrian Furnham, "The Brainstorming Myth," *Business Strategy Review*, Winter 2000, 21–28.
9. Dean Rieck, "AH HA! Running a Productive Brainstorming Session," *Direct Marketing*, November 1999, 78.
10. Kimberly Paterson, "The Writing Process," *Rough Notes*, April 1998, 59–60.
11. Based on information from <http://www.gapinc.com> (Retrieved 4 March 2004).
12. Johan Rindegard, "Use Clear Writing to Show You Mean Business," *InfoWorld*, 22 November 1999, 78.
13. "Improving Factories, Protecting Rights," Gap Inc. <http://www.gapinc.com/social_resp/ifpr_body.shtm> (Retrieved 5 March 2004).
14. Amy Merrick, "Gap Offers Unusual Look at Factory Conditions," *The Wall Street Journal*, 12 May 2004, A1.
15. Dianna Booher, "Develop the First Draft Quickly," *E-Writing* (New York: Pocket Books, 2001), 126; Andrew Fluegelman and Jeremy Joan Hewes, "The Word Processor and the Writing Process," in *Strategies for Business and Technical Writing*, 4e, Kevin J. Harty, ed. (San Diego: Harcourt Brace Jovanovich, 1989), 43. See also Lynn Quitman Troyka, *Simon & Schuster Handbook for Writers*, 4e (Upper Saddle River, NJ: Prentice Hall, 1996), 49.
16. Robert W. Goddard, "Communication: Use Language Effectively," *Personnel Journal*, April 1989, 32.
17. Frederick Crews, *The Random House Handbook*, 4e (New York: Random House, 1991), 152.
18. Jane Spencer, "The Point of No Return—Stores From Gap to Target Tighten Refund Rules," *The Wall Street Journal*, 14 May 2002, D1.
19. Ibid.
20. Kathy M. Kristof, "More Grads Struggling to Repay Loans," *Los Angeles Times*, 14 September 2003, C3.

Chapter 7

1. "Taco Bell Has Quickly Gone From the Weakest to the Strongest of the Fast-Food Chains Owned by Yum Brands Inc.," *The Food Institute Report*, 28 July 2003, 6.
2. Amy Garber, "Yum! Tastes International Success; Plans Long John's Growth," *Nation's Restaurant News*, 22 December 2003, 5.
3. Nancy Brumback, "Yo Quiero Mexican Food," *Restaurant Business*, 1 September 1998, 43–44.
4. Conor Cunneen, "Recipe for Success: Fast-Food Bigwigs Vary Strategies, Menus to Make It in 2004 Market," *Nation's Restaurant News*, 12 January 2004, 30.
5. Peter Elbow, *Writing With Power: Techniques for Mastering the Writing Process* (Oxford: Oxford University Press, 1998), 30.
6. Richard E. Neff, "CEOs Want Information, Not Just Words," *Communication World*, April/May 1997, 22–25.

7. Claire K. Cook, *Line by Line* (Boston: Houghton Mifflin, 1985), 17.
8. William Power and Michael Siconolfi, "Memo to: Mr. Ball, RE: Your Messages, Sir: They're Weird," *The Wall Street Journal*, 30 November 1990, 1; Ralph Brown, "Add Some Informal Polish to Your Writing," *Management*, March 1998, 12.
9. Dianna Booher, *E-Writing* (New York: Pocket Books, 2001), 148.
10. Louise Lague, *People* Magazine editor, interview with Mary Ellen Guffey, 5 February 1992.

Chapter 8

1. "Business: The Battle for the Magic Kingdom; Disney and Comcast," *The Economist*, 14 February 2004, 70.
2. "Eisner Gets to Keep Salary of $1 Million," *The Wall Street Journal*, 14 May 2004, 1; Debra Lau, "Forbes Faces," *Forbes*, 1 January 2001, 116; and Suzy Wetlaufer, "Common Sense and Conflict: An Interview With Disney's Michael Eisner," *Harvard Business Review*, January 2000, 115.
3. Wetlaufer, "Common Sense and Conflict," 115.
4. Michael D. Eisner, "Enlightened Communication," *Vital Speeches*, 15 July 2000, 593.
5. "Email Explosion Ramps up Data Storage Costs; Worldwide Email Traffic to Reach 35 Billion a Day by 2005," *M2 Presswire*, 3 December 2003.
6. Kevin Maney, "How the Big Names Tame E-Mail," *USA Today*, 24 July 2003, 2A.
7. "E-Mail Becoming Crime's New Smoking Gun," *USA Today Marketplace* <http://www.usatoday.com/tech/news/2002-08-15> (Retrieved 14 July 2004); and Jim Carroll, "What Evil Lurks in E-Mail?" *CA Magazine*, June/July 2003, 16.
8. Randall Smith, "Quattrone Found Guilty on 3 Counts in Big U.S. Win," *The Wall Street Journal*, 4 May 2004, A1.
9. Leslie Helm, "The Digital Smoking Gun," *Los Angeles Times*, 16 June 1994, El.
10. Nicholas Varchaver, "The Perils of E-Mail," *Fortune*, 17 February 2003, 98.
11. Bill Goodwin, "Survey Shows Internet Abuse Is Rife," *Computer Weekly*, 27 January 2004, 4; and Quentin Reade, "Staff Internet Abuse Tops Discipline Table," *Personnel Today*, 3 September 2002, 1.
12. Victoria M. Sharpe, "Internet Abuse in the Workplace," *Technical Communication*, November 2003, 656.
13. Lauren M. Bernardi, "The Internet at Work: An Employment Danger Zone," *Canadian Manager*, Summer 2000, 17–18; Dev Strischek, "E-Mail Communication: Some Rules of the Road for the Information Superhighway," *The Journal of Lending & Credit Risk Management*, July–August, 1999, 38; Alan Cohen, "Worker Watchers," *Fortune*, Summer 2001, 70–80; and Joann Greco, "Privacy: Whose Right Is It Anyhow?" *Journal of Business Strategy*, January/February, 2001, 32–35.
14. Eisner, "Enlightened Communication."
15. Ibid.
16. Ibid.
17. John Fielden, "Clear Writing Is Not Enough," *Management Review*, April 1989, 51.
18. Sandra Swanson, "Beware: Employee Monitoring Is on the Rise," *Information Week*, 20 August 2001, 57.
19. Based on Douglas P. Shuit, "Sound the Retreat," *Workforce Management*, September 2003, 39–40.
20. Based on Lisa M. Bee and Gerald L. Maatman, Jr., "E-Mail Abuse Leaves Firms Exposed," *National Underwriter*, 26 January 2004, 27.
21. Joann S. Lublin, "You Should Negotiate A Severance Package—Even Before Job Starts," *The Wall Street Journal*, 13 March 2001, B1.
22. Gustavo Capdevila, "Information: Summit to Act on Junk E-mail 'Epidemic,'" *Global Information Network*, 7 July 2004, 1.

Chapter 9

1. Based on Ken Brown, "Chilling at Ben & Jerry's: Cleaner, Greener," *The Wall Street Journal*, 15 April 2004, B1; "Ben & Jerry's Homemade Inc.," Hoover's Online Fact Sheet <http://www.hoovers.com> (Retrieved 31 May 2004); Matthew Arnold, "Is Ben & Jerry's Losing Its Bohemian Appeal?" *Marketing*, 3 May 2001, 17; "Unilever to Acquire Ben & Jerry's Homemade Inc. for 1.27 Times Revenue," *Weekly Corporate Growth Report*, 17 April 2000, 10698; Laura Mazur, "The Trouble With Takeovers," *Marketing*, 8 February 2001, 26–27; and Alice Blachly, interview with Mary Ellen Guffey, 12 January 1993.
2. Malcolm Forbes, "How to Write a Business Letter," International Paper Company, reprinted in *Strategies for Business and Technical Writing*, 4e, ed. Kevin Harty (Boston: Allyn and Bacon, 1999), 108.
3. Max Messmer, "Enhancing Your Writing Skills," *Strategic Finance*, January 2001, 8–10.
4. Alice Blachly, interview.
5. Dennis Chambers, *Writing to Get Action* (Bristol, VT: Velocity Business Publishing, 1998), 12.
6. Bill Knapp, "Communication Breakdown," *World Wastes*, February 1998, 16.
7. Robert J. Aalberts and Lorraine A. Krajewski, "Claim and Adjustment Letters: Theory Versus Practice and Legal Implications," *The Bulletin of the Association for Business Communication*, September 1987, 5.
8. Michalle Adams and Jodie Kirshner, "Cancel Me! Really! I Mean It!," *U.S. News & World Report*, 18 August 2003, 58.
9. Geoffrey Brewer, "The Customer Stops Here," *Sales & Marketing Management*, March 1998, 30–36.
10. Robert Klara, 'Press 1 to Gripe," *Restaurant Business*, 15 May 1998, 96–102.
11. "Grove's Internet Apology," *Computer Reseller News*, 5 December 1994, 313.
12. Marcia Mascolini, "Another Look at Teaching the External Negative Message," *The Bulletin of the Association of Business Communication*, June 1994, 46; Robert J. Aalberts and Lorraine A. Krajewski, "Claim and Adjustment Letters," *The Bulletin of the Association for Business Communication*, September 1987, 2.
13. Ameeta Patel and Lamar Reinsch, "Companies *Can* Apologize: Corporate Apologies and Legal Liability," *Business Communication Quarterly*, March 2003, 9.
14. Moshe Davidow, "Organizational Responses to Customer Complaints: What Works and What Doesn't," *Journal of Service*

Research, February 2003, 225+; Elizabeth Blackburn Brockman and Kelly Belanger, "You-Attitude and Positive Emphasis: Testing Received Wisdom in Business Communication," *The Bulletin of the Association for Business Communication*, June 1993, 1–5; C. Goodwin and I. Ross, "Consumer Evaluations of Responses to Complaints: What's Fair and Why," *Journal of Consumer Marketing 7*, 1990, 39–47; Marcia Mascolini, "Another Look at Teaching the External Negative Message," *The Bulletin of the Association for Business Communication*, June 1994, 46.

15. Michael W. Michelson Jr., "Turning Complaints Into Cash," *The American Salesman*, December 2003, 22.
16. Davidow, "Organizational Responses."
17. William C. Martucci and Kevin Mason, "State-by-State Listing of Job-Reference Shield Laws," *Employment Relations Today*, Summer 2002, 75.
18. Pamela Gilbert, "Two Words That Can Help a Business Thrive," *The Wall Street Journal*, 30 December 1996, A12.
19. Saburo Haneda and Hirosuke Shima, "Japanese Communication Behavior as Reflected in Letter Writing," *The Journal of Business Communication 1*, 1982, 29. See also Iris I. Varner and Linda Beamer, *Intercultural Communication* (Chicago: McGraw-Hill Irwin, 2001), 131–132.
20. Zhu Yunxia, "Building Knowledge Structures in Teaching Cross-Cultural Sales Genres," *Business Communication Quarterly*, December 2000, 49.
21. Wolfgang Manekeller, as cited in Iris I. Varner, "Internationalizing Business Communication Courses," *The Bulletin of the Association for Business Communication*, December 1987, 10.
22. Dr. Annette Luciani-Samec, French instructor, and Dr. Pierre Samec, French businessman, interviews with Mary Ellen Guffey, May 1995.
23. Retha H. Kilpatrick, "International Business Communication Practices," *The Journal of Business Communication*, Fall 1984, 42–43.
24. Margaret H. Caddell, "Is Letter Writing Dead?" *OfficePro*, November/December, 2003, 22.
25. Based on "McDonald's USA Introduces New Packaging" <http://www.mcdonalds.com/usa/good/environment/packaging.html> (Retrieved 27 May 2004); Elizabeth Crowley, "EarthShell Saw Big Macs and Big Bucks-Got Big Woes—Environmentally Safe Sandwich Containers for McDonald's Haven't Been Easy to Make," *The Wall Street Journal*, 10 April 2001; Frank Edward Allen, "McDonald's to Reduce Waste in Plan Developed With Environmental Group," *The Wall Street Journal*, 17 April 1991, B1; Martha T. Moore, "McDonald's Trashes Sandwich Boxes," *USA Today*, 2 November 1990, 1; Michael Parrish, "McDonald's to Do Away With Foam Packages," *Los Angeles Times*, 2 November 1990, 1; and Mark Hamstra, "McD Supersizes Efforts to Cut Down on Costs," *Nation's Restaurant News*, 29 June 1998, 1, 60.
26. Based on Mark J. Scarp, "Hotel to Cease Pigeon Poisoning," *Scottsdale Tribune*, 28 October 1995.
27. Elizabeth Olson, "When the Check in the Mail Is a Bill," *The New York Times*, 22 April 2004, C5.

Chapter 10

1. Denise Hamilton, "Amazon.com: It's More Than Just Books (and Always Has Been!)," *Searcher*, June 2004, 42; Katherine Bowers, "Fashion First at Target.com; A Partnership Combines Target's Merchandising Expertise With Amazon's Technical Prowess," *WWD*, 12 May 2004, 18; Russ Banham, "Amazon Finally Clicks; Ten Years Old and Profitable at Last: It Offers a Textbook Lesson on How to be Both Focused and Flexible," *CFO*, Spring 2004, 20; Stewart Alsop, "I'm Betting on Amazon .com," *Fortune*, 30 April 2001, 143; Aaron Goldberg, "The Golden Touch," *Upside*, February 2001, 28; Lee Copeland Gladwin, "Borders Turns to Amazon for Outsourcing," *Computerworld*, 16 April 2001, 8; Jessica Davis, "Amazon's Evolutionary Parnerships Come With Valuable Dot-Com Lessons," *InfoWorld*, 16 April 2001, 104; and Ken Kurson, "Amazon," *Money*, May 2001, 87.
2. Seth Faison, "Trying to Play by the Rules," *The New York Times*, 22 December 1991, sec. 3, 1.
3. Ted Pollock, "How to Sell an Idea," *Supervision*, June 2003, 15.
4. John R. Graham, "Improving Direct Mail," *Agency Sales*, January 2002, 47–50.
5. "Pat Friesen, "Customer Testimonials," *Target Marketing*, October 2003, 137.
6. Elaine Tyson, "Direct Mail Success Strategies," *Circulation Management*, 1 February 2004.
7. Kevin McLaughlin, "Words of Wisdom," *Entrepreneur*, October 1990, 101. See also Linda Wastphal, "Empathy in Sales Letters," *Direct Marketing*, October 2001, 55.
8. Clair Enlow, "Grace, Grandeur and a Whole Lot of Sales," *Seattle Daily Journal of Commerce*, online edition, 25 June 2004; and Edward O. Welles, "The Diva of Retail," *Inc.*, October 1999, 36–40.
9. Based on "PDA-Based Software Allows Realtors to Show Homes 'Practically Anywhere'" <http://www.pdare.com/vertical/articles/article-460.xml> (Retrieved 2 July 2004); Michael Antoniak, "Buyer's Guide: PDA Software," *Realtor Magazine Online*, 1 May 2003; and Frank Nelson, "Real Estate Agents' Best Friend," *Santa Barbara News-Press*, 6 June 2004, F1.
10. Based on Debbie D. DuFrene and Carol M. Lehman, "Persuasive Appeal for Clean Language," *Business Communication Quarterly*, March 2002, 48–55.
11. Susan Campbell, "More Hartford, Conn.-Area Workers Telecommute to Beat Winter Blues," *The Hartford Courant*, 5 February 2004; Samantha Marshall, "Battered Companies Let More Freedom Reign; Downsizing Lessens Office Supervision; Not All Employees Ready or Disciplined," *Crain's New York Business*, 14 July 2003, 13; and Jeffery D. Zbar, "Training to Telework," *Home Office Computing*, March 2001, 72.
12. Anthony Marshall, "Technology Fees, Hidden Surcharges Cost Hotels Goodwill," *Hotel and Motel Management*, 5 July 2004, 8.
13. Laura Johannes, "Globe-Trotting Shutterbug Slaps Kodak With the Bill for a Reshoot," *The Wall Street Journal*, 24 April 1998, B1.

14. “EarthShell Corporation and Hood Packaging Corporation Sign Definitive Agreement for Food Service Wraps,” *Canadian Corporate News*, 10 February 2004.
15. Based on Karen Fritscher-Porter, “Don’t Be Duped by Office Supply Scam Artists,” *OfficePro*, June/July 2003, 9–10.

Chapter 11

1. Cathy C. Dial, manager, Consumer Relations, Pepsi-Cola Company, interview with Mary Ellen Guffey, 11 November 1994 and 5 January 1995. Other information from Chad Terhune, “Pepsi’s Net Income Rises 12% Despite Snack-Food Woes,” *The Wall Street Journal*, 16 July 2004, 11; “Community Information—Associations,” PepsiCo <http://www.pepsiworld.com/help/faqs/faq.php?viewall=yes&category=community_info> (Retrieved 19 November 2004); Chad Terhune, “PepsiCo to Identify, Promote Its More-Healthful Products,” *The Wall Street Journal*, 30 July 2004, B3; Adrienne Mand, “DDB Interactive Creates ‘One’ World for Pepsi,” *Brandweek*, 12 October 1998, 332; and Direct Relief International, “What We Do” <http://www.directrelief.org/sections/our_work/what_we_do.html> (Retrieved 2 September 2004).
2. Mohan R. Limaye, “Further Conceptualization of Explanations in Negative Messages,” *Business Communication Quarterly*, June 1997, 46.
3. “Filene’s Basement Bans 2 Shoppers Who Returned Too Much Stuff,” *USA Today*, 14 July 2003, 7B.
4. “2004 Survey on Workplace E-Mail and IM Reveals Unmanaged Risks,” *The ePolicy Institute* <http://www.epolicyinstitute.com/survey/> (Retrieved 14 July 2004).
5. Sandra Swanson, “Employers Take a Closer Look,” *InformationWeek*, 15 July 2002, 40.
6. Elizabeth A. McCord, “The Business Writer, the Law, and Routine Business Communication: A Legal and Rhetorical Analysis,” *Journal of Business and Technical Communication*, April 1991, 183.
7. Ibid.
8. Douglas P. Shuit, “Do It Right or Risk Getting Burned,” *Workforce Management*, September 2003, 80.
9. “Letters to Lands’ End,” *February 1991 Catalog* (Dodgeville, WI: Lands’ End, 1991), 100.
10. Jeff Mowatt, “Breaking Bad News to Customers,” *Agency Sales*, February 2002, 30; and Elizabeth M. Dorn, “Case Method Instruction in the Business Writing Classroom,” *Business Communication Quarterly*, March 1999, 51–52.
11. James E. Goodwin, Chairman and CEO, United Airlines, letter to Mary Ellen Guffey, 1 September 2000.
12. Malcolm Forbes, “How to Write a Business Letter,” International Paper Company, reprinted in *Strategies for Business and Technical Writing*, 4e, Kevin Harty, ed. (Boston: Allyn and Bacon, 1999), 108.
13. Mimi Browning, “Work Dilemma: Delivering Bad News a Good Way,” *Government Computer News*, 24 November 2003, 41; and Mowatt, “Breaking Bad News to Customers.”
14. Browning, “Work Dilemma”; and Bob Lewis, “To Be an Effective Leader, You Need to Perfect the Art of Delivering Bad News,” *InfoWorld*, 13 September 1999, 124.
15. Jeanette W. Gilsdorf, “Metacommunication Effects on International Business Negotiating in China,” *Business Communication Quarterly*, June 1997, 27.
16. Linda Beamer and Iris Varner, *Intercultural Communication in the Global Workplace* (New York: McGraw Hill Irwin, 200), 141.
17. Lewis, “To Be an Effective Leader.”
18. Based on Gene Sloan, “Under 21? Carnival Says Cruise Is Off,” *USA Today*, 29 November 1996; Jill Jordan Sieder, “Full Steam Ahead: Carnival Cruise Line Makes Boatloads of Money by Selling Fun,” *U.S. News & World Report*, 16 October 1995, 72; and “About Carnival Cruise Line,” <http://www.cruisecritic./reviews/cruiseline.cfm?CruiseLineID=9> (Retrieved 27 July 2004).
19. Laura Johannes, “Globe-Trotting Shutterbug Slaps Kodak With the Bill for a Reshoot,” *The Wall Street Journal*, 24 April 1998, B1.
20. Andrew Ross Sorkin, “J. Crew Web Goof Results in Discount,” *The New York Times*, 11 November 1999, D3.
21. Based on Oren Harari, “The POWER of Complaints,” *Management Review*, July-August, 1999, 31.
22. Based on “SUV Surprise,” *The Wall Street Journal*, 15 June 2004, W7.
23. Andrew Osborn, “New From McDonald’s: The McAfrika Burger (Don’t Tell the 12m Starving),” *The Guardian*, 24 August, 2002.
24. Jordana Mishory, “Don’t Shoot the Messenger: How to Deliver Bad News and Still Keep Customers Satisfied,” *Sales and Marketing Management*, June 2008, 18.
25. Tom Cahill, “Bear Stearns Tells Employees Dress Up—Dot Com Is Over,” Bloomberg News Service, 17 September, 2002; “Bear Stearns Reinstates Formal Dress Code,” Reuters Business Report, 21 September 2002; and “Dress Codes: ‘Business Conservative’ Is Making a Comeback,” *HR Briefing*, 1 March 2003, 7.

Chapter 12

1. Liz Bingham, “Building Buzz: Word of Mouth a Key Benefit of Experiential Marketing,” 1 April 2004 <http://www.jackmorton.com/360/market_focus/march04_mf.asp> (Retrieved 6 May 2004).
2. “Lee® Jeans Helps Women Find Their One True Fit,” news release, 12 June 2003 <http://leejeans.netserious.com/netserious/posting_engine.asp?app_id=5a279a302aee11d6889400b0d0b0ad77&cmd=view&post_id=29e9a988a0df11d7889900b0d0b0ad77&topic_id=> (Retrieved 2 March 2004).
3. Lisa Kovalovich, “The Perfect Jeans for You,” *Ladies Home Journal*, 1 March 2002 <www.lhj.com/lhj/story.jhtml?storyid=/templatedata/lhj/story/data/jeans_03012002.xml> (Retrieved 6 May 2004).
4. Linda Tischler, “What’s the Buzz?” *Fast Company*, May 2004, 76–77.
5. Dave Balter, personal e-mail, 14 June 2004.
6. Dave Balter, CEO, BzzAgent, interview with James M. Dubinsky, 11 June 2004.
7. Dave Balter, “Honesty,” *BzzAgent Welcome Kit*, 2004, 6.
8. Laura Mandaro, “Need to Do Research? Go Further Than Google,” *Investor’s Business Daily*, 7 June 2004, A4.
9. Kimberly A. Killmer and Nicole B. Koppel, “So Much Information, So Little Time: Evaluating Web Resources With Search Engines,” *T.H.E. Journal (Technological Horizons in Education)*, August 2002, 21.

10. Lisa Guernsey, "Mining the 'Deep Web' With Specialized Drills," *The New York Times*, 25 January 2001 <http://www.nytimes.com/2001/01/25/technology/25SEAR.html?ex=1090382400&en=9d85ad17e8811b27&ei=5070&ex=1090123200&en=bn83ce4c971d1b> (Retrieved 16 June 2004).
11. Google Inc., "Google Achieves Search Milestone With Immediate Access to More Than 6 Billion Items," press release, 17 February 2004 <http://www.google.com/press/pressrel/6billion.html> (Retrieved 10 July 2004).
12. Michael K. Bergman, "The Deep Web: Surfacing Hidden Value," *Journal of Electronic Publishing*, August 2001 <http://www.press.umich.edu/jep/07-01/bergman.html> (Retrieved 10 July 2004).
13. Alex Wright, "In Search of the Deep Web," *Salon*, 9 March 2004 <http://www.salon.com/tech/feature/2004/03/09/deep_web/index_np.html> (Retrieved 10 July 2004).
14. Mike Brennan and Judith Holdershaw, "The Effect of Question Tone and Form on Responses to Open-Ended Questions: Further Data." *Marketing Bulletin*, 1999, 57–64.
15. Barton Goldsmith, "The Awesome Power of Asking the Right Questions," *OfficeSolutions*, June 2002, 52; and Gerald W. Bracey, "Research-Question Authority," *Phi Delta Kappan*, November 2001, 191.
16. Daphne A. Jameson, "The Ethics of Plagiarism: How Genre Affects Writers' Use of Source Materials," *The Bulletin of the Association for Business Communication*, June 1993, 18.
17. Jerry Large, "Jayson Blair and Jack Kelley Are Journalism's Unbelievable Problem," *The Seattle Times*, 29 March 2004, K1904; and Gabriel Snyder, "Journalists Devour Their Own in Eager Scrutiny," *Variety*, 19 January 2004, 3.
18. Writing Tutorial Services, Indiana University, "Plagiarism: What It Is and How to Recognize and Avoid It" <http://www.indiana.edu/~wts/pamphlets/plagiarism.shtml> (Retrieved 27 July 2004).
19. BzzAgent Mommyof1, "October BzzReport," December 5, 2003 <http://blog.bzzagent.com/article.php?story=20031205100105912> (Retrieved 15 May 2004).
20. Amanda Spake, "Hey Kids! We've Got Sugar and Toys," *U.S. News & World Report*, 17 November 2003, 62.
21. Edward Iwata, "Blackout Report Faults Ohio Utility," *USA Today*, 20 November 2003, 1A.
22. "On Target, American Retailing; America's Other Wal-Mart," *Economist (U.S.)*, 5 May 2001, 6.
23. Christine Dugas, "Credit Cards: Make Sure Child Knows Basics, Consequences," *USA Today*, 30 July 2004, 3B.

Chapter 13

1. Case study based on Alison Overholt, "Listening to Starbucks," *Fast Company*, July 2004, 53; Andy Serwer, "Hot Starbucks to Go," *Fortune*, 26 January 2004, 68; Ann Brown, "What's Brewing at Starbucks?" *Black Enterprise*, August 2004, 25; and Dina ElBoghdady, "The Starbucks Strategy? Locations, Locations, Locations," *The Washington Post*, 25 August 2002, H1.
2. Charlene Marmer Solomon, "Marriott's Family Matters," *Personnel Journal*, October 1991, 40–42; Jennifer Laabs, "They Want More Support—Inside and Outside of Work," *Workforce*, November 1998, 54–56.
3. "Europe View: Transport a Bear for Russia," *The Journal of Commerce Online*, 21 April 2004, 1; "FedEx Rolls Out Europe LTL," *The Journal of Commerce Online*, 18 December 2002, 1; Chuck Hawkins, "FedEx: Europe Nearly Killed the Messenger," *BusinessWeek*, 25 May 1992, 124–126.
4. Overholt, "Listening to Starbucks," 50–56.
5. Serwer, "Hot Starbucks to Go."
6. Timony Aeppel, "Firestone Recall Fuels Interest in 'Smart' Tires," *The Wall Street Journal*, 20 November 2000, B1.
7. "Boeing Shocks Seattle With Strategic Exit," *Corporation Location*, May/June 2001, 8.
8. Overholt, "Listening to Starbucks," 50–56.
9. "Red Light Camera Reform," *WestWays*, May/June 2003, 19.
10. Alex Berenson, "Federal Reserve Says Banks Can Continue Overdraft Plans," *The New York Times*, 8 June 2004, C1.
11. Based on Brian Witt, "Ensuring 'Bounce-Proof' Overdraft Privilege," *Credit Union Magazine*, May 2003, 84; William Webster, "Race to the Bottom," *Forbes*, 21 July 2003, 74; and Steve Cocheo, "Follow the Bouncing Check," *ABA Banking Journal*, April 2003, 32.

Chapter 14

1. "Business: Losing the HP Way: Hewlett-Packard," *The Economist*, 21 August 2004, 58.
2. Dan Neel and Jack McCarthy, "HP Wrestles With Reinvention," *InfoWorld*, 20 August 2001, 17–18.
3. Mary Piecewicz, proposal manager, Hewlett-Packard, interview with Mary Ellen Guffey, 12 January 1999.
4. Randi Schmelzer, "Honolulu Incumbent Defends Kauai Tourism," *AdWeek*, 2 August 2004.
5. Nancy Rivera Brooks and Jesus Sanchez, "U.S. Firms Map Ways to Profit From the Accord," *Los Angeles Times*, 13 August 1992, D1, D2.
6. Mike Martinez, "Fine-Tune Your Business Plan," *Dallas Business Journal*, 17 August 2001, 31.
7. Frank Nelson, "Device From UCSB Trio Ready to Take Its First Breath," *Santa Barbara News-Press*, 5 September 2004, F1.

Chapter 15

1. Based on combined attendance figures as reported in "Tokyo Disney Profits Dip But Parks Remain Popular As Visitors Flow In," *Amusement Business*, 17 May 2004, 6.
2. Jon Georges, interview with Mary Ellen Guffey, 3 February 1999. Other information from "Keith Bradsher, "Disney Is Tailoring New Park to Fit Hong Kong Sensitivities," *The New York Times*, 12 October 2004, W1; "Tokyo Disneyland, Disneysea Log Record Visitors in FY03," *AsiaPulse News*, 2 April 2004; "Business: Welcome to Bankruptcyland; Theme-Parks in Japan," *The Economist*, 5 April 2003, 69; and Natasha Emmons, "Tokyo Disneyland Offers Tix," *Amusement Business*, 18 July 2001, 23.
3. Catherine M. Petrini, "A Survival Guide to Public Speaking," *Training & Development*, September 1990, 15.
4. Wharton Applied Research Center, "A Study of the Effects of the Use of Overhead Transparencies on

Business Meetings, Final Report" cited in "Short, Snappy Guide to Meaningful Presentations," *Working Woman*, June 1991, 73.

5. Stanford communications professor Clifford Nass quoted in Tad Simons, "When Was the Last Time PowerPoint Made You Sing?" *Presentations*, July 2001, 6. See also Geoffrey Nunberg, "The Trouble with PowerPoint," *Fortune*, 20 December 1999, 330–334.
6. Simons, "When Was the Last Time," 6.
7. "How to Avoid the 7 Deadly Sins of PowerPoint," *Yearbook of Experts News Release Wire*, 30 July 2004 (Retrieved 11 October 2004 from LexisNexis Academic database).
8. Robert J. Boeri, "Fear of Flying? Or the Mail? Try the Web Conferencing Cure," *Emedia Magazine*, March 2002, 49.
9. John Ellwood, "Less PowerPoint, More Powerful Points," *The Times (London)*, 4 August 2004, 6.
10. Dianna Booher, *Speak With Confidence* (New York: McGraw-Hill, 2003), 14; and Dianna Booher, *Executive's Portfolio of Model Speeches for All Occasions* (Englewood Cliffs, NJ: Prentice Hall, 1991), 259.
11. Peter Schneider, "Scenes From a Marriage: Observations on the Daimler-Chrysler Merger From a German Living in America," *The New York Times Magazine*, 12 August 2001, 47.
12. Ronald E. Dulek, John S. Fielden, and John S. Hill, "International Communication: An Executive Primer," *Business Horizons*, January/February 1991, 23. See also Susan J. Marks, "Nurturing Global Workplace Connections," *Workforce*, September 2001, 76+.
13. Dulek, Fielden, and Hill, "International Communication," 22.
14. Joan Burge, "Telephone Safety Protocol for Today," *The National Public Accountant*, June 2002, 35.
15. Barbara De Lollis, "Talking Heads Are Catching on as Web Meetings Take Off," *USA Today*, 7 September 2004, p. 1B.
16. Dan Vergano, "Computers: Scientific Friend or Foe?" *USA Today*, 31 August 2004, D6.
17. Michael Jackson, quoted in "Garbage In, Garbage Out," *Consumer Reports*, December 1992, 755.

Chapter 16

1. Bonnie Gesualdi-Chao, personnel coordinator, Carnival Cruise Lines, interview with Mary Ellen Guffey, 22 February 1999. Other information from Heidi Waldrop Bay, "Seaworthy Rewards," *Incentive*, November 2000, 107–114; and William G. Flanagan, "Thanks for the Subsidies," *Forbes*, 7 July 1997, 120.
2. Julie Jansen, "What's Keeping You From Changing Careers?" <http://www.careerjournal.com/jobhunting/change/20030225-jansen.html> (Retrieved 19 October 2004). Article adapted from Jansen's book, *I Don't Know What I Want, But I Know It's Not This: A Step-by-Step Guide to Finding Gratifying Work* (New York: Penguin Books, 2003).
3. Brian O'Connell, *The Career Survival Guide* (New York: McGraw-Hill, 2003), 11–12.
4. Anne Kates Smith, "Charting Your Own Course," *U.S. News & World Report*, 6 November 2000, 57.
5. Lorraine Farquharson, "Technology Special Report: The Best Way to Find a Job," *The Wall Street Journal*, 15 September 2003, R8.
6. Kris Maher and Rachel Emma Silverman, "Your Career Matters: Online Job Sites Yield Few Jobs, Users Complain," *The Wall Street Journal*, 2 January 2002, A7.
7. "The Hot List: Top Job Boards," *Workforce Management*, June 2004, 28.
8. Farquharson, "Technology Special Report: The Best Way to Find a Job."
9. Professor Mark Granovetter, quoted in Susan J. Wells, "Many Jobs on Web," *The New York Times*, 12 March 1998, A12.
10. George Crosby of the Human Resources Network, as quoted in Hal Lancaster, "When Taking a Tip From a Job Network, Proceed With Caution," *The Wall Street Journal*, 7 February 1995, B1.
11. Cynthia Wright, "Networking the No. 1 Way to Find a Job," *Chattanooga Times Free Press (Tennessee)*, 30 September 2004, E6.
12. "The Hot List: Top Job Boards," *Workforce Management*, 28.
13. "Résumé Styles: Chronological Versus Functional? Best-Selling Author Richard H. Beatty Joins in the Résumé Discussion," *Internet Wire*, 5 November 2002, p. 1008309u4205.
14. Elizabeth Blackburn-Brockman and Kelly Belanger, "One Page or Two?: A National Study of CPA Recruiters' Preferences for Résumé Length," *The Journal of Business Communication*, January 2001, 29–57.
15. Katharine Hansen, "Should You Use a Career Objective on Your Résumé?" *Quintessential Careers* <http://www.quintcareers.com/resume_objectives.html> (Retrieved 5 October 2004); and Robert Half, "Some Résumé Objectives Do More Harm Than Good," *CareerJournal.com* <http://www.careerjournal.com/jobhunting/résumés/19971231-half3.html> (Retrieved 5 October 2004).
16. Tom Washington, "Improve Your Résumé 100 Percent," <http://www.nbew.com/archive/961001-001.html> (Retrieved 27 September 1998).
17. Frequently Asked Questions, "Quintessential Résumés & Cover Letters" <http://www.resumesandcoverletters.com> (Retrieved 8 October 2004).
18. Michelle Conlin, "The Résumé Doctor Is In," *BusinessWeek*, 14 July 1003, 116.
19. Roland E. Kidwell Jr., "'Small' Lies, Big Trouble: The Unfortunate Consequences of Résumé Padding From Janet Cooke to George O'Leary," *Journal of Business Ethics*, May 2004, 175.
20. Joan E. Rigdon, "Deceptive Resumes Can Be Door-Openers but Can Become an Employee's Undoing," *The Wall Street Journal*, 17 June 1992, B1. See also Barbara Solomon, "Too Good to Be True?" *Management Review*, April 1998, 28.
21. Anne Fisher, "How to Ruin an Online Job Hunt," *Fortune*, 28 June 2004, 43.
22. J. Michael Farr, *The Very Quick Job Search* (Indianapolis: JIST Works, 1991), 158.
23. Daisy Wright, "Tell Stories, Get Hired," *OfficePro*, August/September 2004, 32–33.

acknowledgments

Chapter 1

p. 5 Kentucky Fried Chicken photo caption based on Terrence H. Witkowski, Yulong Ma, and Dan Zheng, "Cross-Cultural Influences on Brand Identity Impressions: KFC in China and the United States," *Asia Pacific Journal of Marketing and Logistics 15*, 2003, 74.

p. 7 Photo caption based on Andy Shaw, "An Educated Viewpoint on Unplugged Computing," *Computing Canada*, 11 April 2003, 13.

p. 8 Figure 1.2, Racial and Ethnic Makeup of U.S. Workforce Projected to 2020, based on U.S. Department of Labor statistics compiled by Richard W. Judy and Carol D'Amico, *Workforce 2000: Work and Workers in the 21st Century* (Indianapolis, IN: Hudson Institute), 1997.

p. 9 Spotlight on Oren Harari based on Oren Harari, "Flood Your Organization With Knowledge," *Management Review*, November 1997, 33; Oren Harari, "Bold Visions in the New Century," *Management Review*, March 2000, 25.

p. 14 Spotlight on Elaine Chao based on George F. Will, "The Stiletto's Sharp Idea: Hypocrisy of an Unusual Purity Is on Display as Union Leaders Try to Avoid Disclosing Truthful Financial Information to Their Members," *Newsweek*, 12 May 2003, 68; Rachel Pleasant, "Tampa, Florida, Women's Entrepreneurship Summit Draws 500," *Knight Ridder/Tribune Business News*, 24 September 2003; Peter Mead, "Interview: Chao's Challenge: The New World of Work," *Workforce*, June 2001, 90.

p. 18 Career Coach box based on "Govern Cell Phone Use With This Policy," *Info-Tech Advisor Newsletter*, 4 February 2003; Edwin Powell, "Cell Phone Etiquette," *OfficeSolutions*, March 2001, 13; and Catherine Siskos, "Cell Phone Sanctions," *Kiplinger's Personal Finance Magazine*, November 2000, 27.

p. 20 Tech Talk box based on Susan Kousek, "Writing E-Mail That Saves Your and Recipients' Time," *Writing Techniques*, January 2004, 3; Kevin Maney, "How the Big Names Tame E-Mail," *USA Today*, 24 July 2003, A1; Elizabeth Weinstein, "Help! I'm Drowning in E-Mail!" *The Wall Street Journal*, 10 January 2002, B1; and "Ten Tips for Managing E-Mail," *The Office Professional*, February 2004, 1.

p. 25 Photo caption based on "Witness Testifies Tyco's Chief Tried to Fire General Counsel," *The New York Times*, 27 May 2004, C3; Jennifer Reingold, "Make the Buck, Then Pass It," *Fast Company*, December 2003, 31; and "Tyco In Turmoil," *Contractor*, July 2002, 7.

p. 31 A. G. Lafley photo caption based on Bruce Horovitz, "P & G Rewards CEO in Company Rebound," *USA Today*, 11 April 2002, 3B; Robert Berner, "P & G: New and Improved," *BusinessWeek*, 7 July 2003, 52; Luisa Kroll, "A Fresh Face," *Forbes*, 8 July 2002, 67; and Darrell Rigby and Christoher Zook, "Manager's Journal: The Marketplace of Ideas," *The Wall Street Journal*, 3 December 2002, B2.

Chapter 2

p. 44 Tech Talk box based on Bill Snyder, "Teams That Span Time Zones Face New Work Rules," *Stanford Business Magazine*, Mary 2003; Kathlyn H. Loudin, "Building Bridges: Virtual Teamwork in the 21st Century," *Contract Management*, June 2003, 16; David Armstrong, "Building Teams Across Borders," *Executive Excellence*, March 2000, 10; Deborah S. Kezsbom, "Creating Teamwork in Virtual Teams," *Cost Engineering*, October 2000, 33–36.

p. 44 Discussion of team development based on Tony Kontzer and John Foley, "Team Spirit," *InformationWeek*, 28 July 2003, 18; Jon R. Katzenbach and Douglas K. Smith, *The Wisdom of Teams* (New York: HarperCollins, 1994).

p. 45 Figure 2.1 based on Jon R. Katzenbach and Jason A. Santamaria, "Firing Up the Front Line," *Harvard Business Review*, May/June 1999, 107–117; and Suzanne K. Bishop, "Cross-Functional Project Teams in Functionally Aligned Organizations," *Project Management Journal*, September 1999, 6–12.

p. 46 Discussion of group and team roles based on K. E. Benne and Paul Sheats, "Functional Roles and Group Members," *Journal of Social Issues 4*, 1948, 41–49; Cheryl Hamilton and Cordell Parker, *Communicating for Results* (Belmont, CA: Wadsworth, 2000), 309–311.

p. 46 Figure 2.2. Portions reprinted with permission of Peterson's, a division of International Thomson Publishing, FAX 800-730-2215. Adapted from *Why Teams Don't Work* © 1995 by Harvey A. Robbins and Michael Finley.

p. 47 Discussion of conflict and groupthink based on Peggy L. McNamra, "Conflict Resolution Strategies," *OfficePro*, August/September 2003, 25; W. H. Weiss, "Building and Managing Teams," *SuperVision*, November 2002, 19; Stephanie Reynolds, "Managing

Conflict Through a Team Intervention and Training Strategy," *Employee Relations Today*, Winter 1998, 57–64; Odette Pollar, "Sticking Together," *Successful Meetings*, January 1997, 87–90; Kathleen M. Eisenhardt, "How Management Teams Can Have a Good Fight," *Harvard Business Review*, July/August 1997, 77–85; Erich Brockmann, "Removing the Paradox of Conflict from Group Decisions," *Academy of Management Executives*, May 1996, 61–62.

p. 49 Discussion about reaching group decisions based on Christopher M. Avery, "Method for Making Group Decisions," *Religious Conference Manager*, 1 February 2003; Harvey Robbins and Michael Finley, *Why Teams Don't Work* (Princeton, NJ: Peterson's/Pacesetter Books, 1995), 42–45; and Steven A. Beebe and John T. Masterson, *Communicating in Small Groups* (New York: Longman, 1999), 198–200.

p. 51 Photo caption based on "Bristol-Myers Squibb Announces Grants to Area Robotics Teams," press release <http:www.bms.com/news/press/data/pf_press_release_4348.html> (Retrieved 24 March 2004); and "Getting Involved," First Robotics <http://www.usfirst.org/robotics/gtstart.htm> (Retrieved 24 March 2004).

p. 52 Ethical Insights box based on Gerald L. Wilson, *Groups in Context* (New York: McGraw-Hill, 1996), 24–27; and Harvey Robbins and Michael Finley, *Why Teams Don't Work* (Princeton, NJ: Peterson's/Pacesetter Books, 1995), 88–89.

p. 53 Discussion of team-based presentations based in part on Jon Hanke, "Presenting as a Team," *Presentations*, January 1998, 74–82; Frank Jossi, "Putting It All Together: Creating Presentations as a Team," *Presentations*, July 1996, 18–26; Jon Rosen, "10 Ways to Make Your Next Team Presentation a Winner," *Presentations*, August 1997, 31.

p. 54 Spotlight on Peter Drucker based on "Peter Drucker Sets Us Straight," *Fortune*, 12 January 2004, 115; and Laurence Prusak, Thomas H. Davenport, "Who Are the Gurus' Gurus?" *Harvard Business Review*, December 2003, 14.

p. 55 Discussion on meetings based on Phyllis Davis, "Meeting Know How," *Women in Business*, March/April 2003, 27; Jay Antony, "The Good Meeting," *Harvard Business Review*, April 2003, 126; Hal Lancaster, "Learning Some Ways to Make Meetings Slightly Less Awful," *The Wall Street Journal*, 26 May 1998, B1; and Melinda Ligos, "Why Your Meetings Are a Total Bore," *Sales & Marketing Management*, May 1998, 84.

p. 61 Discussion on collaboration tools based on Jeffrey Schwartz, "New Digital Dashboards Help Drive Decisions," *B to B* (Crain Communications, Inc.), 14 July 2003, 1; "Make Online Meetings in Real-Time a Breeze," *Computing Canada*, 31 October 2003, 27; Tom Patterson, "E-Collaboration Tools: Not Just for the Big Boys Anymore," *Learning & Training Innovations*, April 2003, 38; John Jainschigg, "Audioconferencing Update: Conference Calls Are Still the Meat and Potatoes of Enterprise Collaboration," *Communications Convergence*, May 2003, 22; Tom Smith, "See You Online," *Builder*, September 2003, PS95; Tony Kontzer, "Learning to Share," *InformationWeek*, 5 May 2003, 28; Joby O'Brien, "Collaboration Tools," *E-Doc*, July/August 2002, 26; Tony Kontzer, "Team Spirit," *InformationWeek*, 28 July 2003, 18; John Fontana, "Collaborative Software Ages Slowly," *Network World*, 6 January 2003, 23; and "Meetings Without Tears," *Management Services*, May 2003, 28.

Chapter 3

p. 76 Tips for Workplace Listening based on Tom D. Lewis and Gerald Graham, "7 Tips for Effective Listening," *The Internal Auditor*, August 2003, 23; Liz Hughes, "How to Be a Good Listener," *Women in Business*, September/October 2002, 17; Shari Caudron, "Listen Up!" *Workforce*, August 1999, 25–27; Hal Lancaster, "It's Time to Stop Promoting Yourself and Start Listening," *The Wall Street Journal*, 10 June 1997, B1; "Good Ideas Go Unheard," *Management Review*, February 1998, 7; Morey Stettner, "Angry? Slow Down and Listen to Others," *Investor's Business Daily*, 19 January 1998, A1; and John W. Haas and Christa L. Arnold, "An Examination of the Role of Listening in Judgments of Communication," *Journal of Business Communication*, April 1995, 123–139.

p. 76 Listening to Superiors based on Valerie Priscilla Goby and Justus Helen Lewis, "The Key Role of Listening in Business: A Study of the Singapore Insurance Industry," *Business Communication Quarterly*, June 2000, 41+; Lynn O. Cooper, "Listening Competency in the Workplace: A Model for Training," *Business Communication Quarterly*, December 1997, 75–84; and Michael C. Dennis, "Effective Communication Will Make Your Job Easier, *Business Credit*, June 1995, 45.

p. 76 Listening to Colleagues and Teammates based on Patrice M. Johnson and Kittie W. Watson, "Managing Interpersonal and Team Conflict: Listening Strategies," appearing in *Listening in Everyday Life*, edited by Michael Purdy and Deborah Borisoff (New York: University Press of America, 1997), Chapter 5; Max E. Douglas, "Creating Distress in the Workplace: A Supervisor's Role, *Supervision*, October 1996, 6–9; Robert McGarvey, "Now Hear This: Lend Your Employees an Ear—and Boost Productivity," *Entrepreneur*, June 1996, 87; Brian Tracy, "Effective Communication," *Executive Excellence*, October 1998, 13; Stuart Silverstein, "But Do They Listen? Companies Making an Effort to Build Skill," *Los Angeles Times*, 19 July 1998, D5; and Andrew Wolvin and Carolyn Gwynn Coakley, *Listening*, 5e (New York: McGraw-Hill, 1996), Chapters 5 and 8.

p. 77 Listening to Customers based on Nick Langley, "Looking After the Customers," *Computer Weekly*, 2 November 2000, 100; Jeff Caplan, "Golden Age Customer Service Returns," *Direct Marketing*, July 2000, 60; Rosemary P. Ramsey and Ravipreet S. Sohi, "Listening to Your Customers: The Impact of Perceived Salesperson Listening Behavior on Relationship Outcomes," *Journal of the Academy of Marketing*

Science, Spring 1997, 127–137; Daniel Pedersen, "Dissing Customers: Why the Service Is Missing From America's Service Economy," *Newsweek*, 23 June 1997, 56; Michael Render, "Better Listening Makes for a Better Marketing Message," *Marketing News*, 11 September 2000, 22–23; Lynn Thomas, "Listening: So What's in It for Me?" *Rough Notes*, December 1998, 63+.

p. 78 Figure 3.2 based on Lynn Thomas, "Listening: So What's in It for Me?" *Rough Notes*, December 1998, 63–43.

p. 83 Career Coach box (Listening to Nonnative Speakers) based on Tom Marshall and Jim Vincent, "Improving Listening Skills: Methods, Activities, and Resources," Instructor's Manual, *Business Communication: Process and Product*, 4e; Iris Varner and Linda Beamer, *Intercultural Communication in the Global Workplace* (Boston: Irwin, McGraw-Hill, 1995), 37; and Chris Lee, "How to Deal With the Foreign Accent," *Training*, January 1993, 72, 75.

Chapter 4

p. 102 Cosmo Girl caption based on Otto Pohl, "Western Magazines Go Global at a Fast Pace," *The New York Times*, 13 February 2004, W1.

p. 104 Tech Talk box based on Bob Tedeschi, "To Reach Internet Users Overseas, More American Web Sites Are Speaking Their Language, Even Mandarin," *The New York Times*, 12 January 2004, C6; Martin J. Spethman, "Web Site Globalization," *World Trade*, November 2003, 56; Steve Alexander, "Learn the Politics of Going Global," *Computerworld*, 1 January 2001, S8–S10; Sari Kalin, "The Importance of Being Multiculturally Correct," *Computer World*, 6 October 1997, G16–17; and Laura Morelli, "Writing for a Global Audience on the Web," *Marketing News*, 17 August 1998, 16.

p. 108 Figure 4.2 based on Lillian H. Chaney and Jeanette S. Martin, *Intercultural Business Communication* (Upper Saddle River, NJ, Prentice Hall, 2004), Chapter 5; J. Chung's analysis appearing in Guo-Ming Chen and William J. Starosta, *Foundations of Intercultural Communication* (Boston: Allyn and Bacon, 1998), 51; and Mary O'Hara-Devereaux and Robert Johansen, *Globalwork: Bridging Distance, Culture, and Time* (San Francisco: Jossey-Bass, 1994), 55.

p. 115 Figure 4.3 based on Sondra Ostheimer, "Internationalize Yourself," *Business Education Forum*, February 1995, 45. Reprinted with permission of Sondra Ostheimer, Southwest Wisconsin Technical College.

p. 117 Figure 4.4 based on William Horton, "The Almost Universal Language: Graphics for International Documents," *Technical Communication*, Fourth Quarter, 1993, 690.

p. 119 Figure 4.5 based on "The 2003 Corruption Perceptions Index," Transparency International <http://www.transparency.org/surveys/index.html (Retrieved 26 February 2004).

p. 122 Spotlight (J. T. [Ted] Childs) caption based on Steve Charles, "Look Like Your Customers: IBM's Ted Childs Says Diversity Good for Business," Wabash College, 23 September 2003 <http://www.wabash.edu/news/displaystory.cfm?news_ID=1186> (Retrieved 4 February 2004) and "Ultimately, Promoting Diversity Is Good for Business," *Fast Company*, March 2001.

p. 124 Spotlight (Andrea Jung) caption based on "Avon Lady: Dingdong, Opportunity Calling!" *Cosmo Girl!* October 2003, 108; "Andrea Calling: This Is Definitely Not Your Grandmother's Avon," *Institutional Investor International Edition*, August 2002, 17.

Chapter 5

pp. 135, 148, 154 Kinko's case study based on Claudia H. Deutsch, "FedEx Moves to Expand With Purchase of Kinko's," *The New York Times*, 31 December 2003, C6; Sean Callahan, "FedEx Thinks Small With $2.4 Billion Purchase of Kinko's," *B to B*, 19 January 2004, 27; Chris Woodyard, "FedEx Ponies Up $2.4B for Kinko's," *USA Today*, 13 December 2003, B1; "Accounts in Review/2," *Adweek*, 15 June 1998, 12; "Kinko's Strengthens Office Products Assortment," *Discount Store News*, 17 November 1997, 6, 70; Michele Marchetti, "Getting the Kinks Out," *Sales and Marketing Management*, March 1997, 56–64; and Ann Marsh, "Kinko's Grows Up—Almost," *Forbes*, 1 December 1997, 270–272.

p. 142 Spotlight (Danny O'Neill) caption based on Morey Stettner, "Experts' Tips on Writing Top-Notch Memos," *Investor's Business Daily*, 15 June 2000, A1.

p. 144 Spotlight (Condoleezza Rice) caption based on Pat M. Holt, "Less Bush Translation, More Process, Please, Condi," *The Christian Science Monitor*, 5 February 2004, 11; Sheryl Henderson Blunt, "The Unflappable Condi Rice: Why the World's Most Powerful Woman Asks God for Help," *Christianity Today*, September 2003, 42; and Christopher L. Tyner, "Security Adviser Condoleezza Rice," *Investor's Business Daily*, 26 December 2000, A4.

p. 145 Spotlight (Warren Buffet) caption based on Warren Buffet's remarks appearing in the Preface to *A Plain English Handbook* (Washington, DC: Office of Investor Education and Assistance, U.S. Securities and Exchange Commission, 1997) <http://www.sec.gov/consumer/plaine.htm#A9> (Retrieved 5 November 2004); and Andy Serwer, "How to Play the Falling Dollar: The World's Greatest Investor Is Betting Against the Greenback," *Fortune*, 12 January 2004, 143.

p. 147 Spotlight (John H. Johnnson) caption based on "Johnson, Ford, Ash Cited as Greatest Entrepreneurs in U.S. History," *Ebony*, February 2004, 72; and "Ebony's John H. Johnson: How He Went From a Tin-Roof Shack to the Forbes 400," *Investor's Business Daily*, 26 March 1998, 1.

p. 150 Spotlight [Katie Couric] caption based on Ken Parish Perkins, "Prime-Time Interviews Are All About 'The Get'—Got it?" Knight Ridder/Tribune News Service, 10 November 2003, PK6927; and Judy Flander, "Catching Up With Katie Couric," *The Saturday Evening Post*, September/October 1992, 38–42.

p. 151 Spotlight (Jane Bryant Quinn) caption based on Jane Bryant Quinn, "2004: Off to a Great Start: Every Sector Is Now Expanding at a Rapid Rate," *Newsweek,* 19 January 2004, 40; "Best-Selling Finance Gurus: Whose Book Is Best?" *Consumer Reports,* September 2003, 24; and Jane Bryant Quinn, *Making the Most of Your Money* (New York: Simon & Schuster, 1991).

p. 152 Information on Adapting to Legal Responsibilities based in part on Robert J. Walter and Gradley J. Sleeper, "Employee Recruitment and Retention: When Company Inducements Trigger Liability," *Review of Business,* Spring, 2002, 17; Pamela J. Cordier, "Essentials of Good Safety Communications," *Pulp & Paper,* May 2003, 25; and Kristin R. Woolever's "Corporate Language and the Law: Avoiding Liability in Corporate Communications," *IEE Transactions on Professional Communication,* 2 June 1990, 95–98.

Chapter 6

p. 166 Spotlight (Gerry Laybourne) caption based on Allison Romano, "Oxygen: It Lives! Now Can It Breathe?" *Broadcasting & Cable,* 5 May 2003, 10; Lynette Clemetson, "The Birth of a Network: With Oxygen Media, Oprah Winfrey and Gerry Laybourne Are Trying to Create TV History," *Newsweek,* 15 November 1999, 60; and Jim Cooper, "Laybourne Is Born Again," *Mediaweek,* 1 June 1998, 5.

p. 170 Spotlight (Max Messmer) based on Max Messmer, "Enhancing Your Writing Skills," *Strategic Finance,* January 2001, 8–10; and Max Messmer, "Developing Effective Performance Reviews," *Strategic Finance,* March 2004, 13.

p. 177 Spotlight (Arthur Levitt) based on Arthur Levitt Jr. and Richard C. Breeden, "Our Ethical Erosion," *The Wall Street Journal,* 3 December 2003, 16; Bill Carlino, "Industry Split on Levitt Exit," *Accounting Today,* 8 January 2001, 1; and Office of Investor Education and Assistance, U.S. Securities and Exchange Commission: *A Plain English Handbook,* January 1997.

Chapter 7

pp. 191, 201, 204 Opening case study based on Conor Cunneen, "Recipe for Success: Fast-Food Bigwigs Vary Strategies, Menus to Make It in 2004 Market," *Nation's Restaurant News,* 12 January 2004, 30; Amy Garber, "Taco Bell, Long John Silver's: Neil DePasquale," *Nation's Restaurant News,* 26 January 2004, 182; Kate Macarthur, "Taco Bell: Brands in Demand; After Ditching the Dog, Taco Bell Becomes Yum's Strongest Chain by Focusing on the Food," *Advertising Age,* 24 March 2003, 18; and "Taco Bell Offers Low-Fat Versions," *Restaurant Business,* 1 October 2003, 12.

p. 192 Spotlight (Colin Powell) caption based on "Quotations from Chairman Powell: A Leadership Primer," *Management Review,* December 1996, 36.

p. 197 Spotlight (Sam Walton) caption based on "Sam Walton in His Own Words," *Fortune,* 29 June 1992, 98–106.

p. 200 Spotlight caption based on *Washington Post* column, "Words to the Wise on Students' Speech" as quoted in *Writing Concepts,* April 1998, 3.

p. 201 Spotlight (Susan Schott Karr) caption based on "Business Writing: Tips From a Pro," *Financial Executive,* July 2000, 11.

pp. 212–213 Activity 7.15 based on Paula J. Pomerenke, "Teaching Ethics With Apartment Leases," *Business Communication Quarterly,* December 1998, 119.

Chapter 8

p. 218 Spotlight (Michael Eisner) caption based on Michael D. Eisner, "Enlightened Communication," *Vital Speeches,* 15 July 2000, 593.

p. 219 Spotlight (Marco Scibora) caption based on Elizabeth Weinstein, "Help! I'm Drowning in E-Mail!" *The Wall Street Journal,* 10 January 2002, B1.

p. 225 Using E-Mail Smartly and Safely is based on Mary Munter, Priscilla S. Rogers, and Jone Rymer, "Business E-Mail: Guidelines for Users," *Business Communication Quarterly,* March 2003, 26; "E-Mail Acceptable Use: An Enforceable Policy," *Info-Tech Advisor Newsletter,* 30 September 2003; Kevin Maney, "How the Big Names Tame E-Mail," *USA Today,* 24 July 2003, 1A; "Email: The DNA of Office Crimes," *Electric Perspectives,* September/October, 2003, 4; Liz Hughes, "E-Mail Etiquette: Think Before You Send," *Women in Business,* July/August 2003, 29; Elizabeth Weinstein, "Help! I'm Drowning in E-Mail!" *The Wall Street Journal,* 10 January 2002, B1; Lauren Gibbons Paul, "How to Tame the E-Mail Beast," *CIO,* 15 October 2001, 84; Dale Bowen and Bryan Gold, "Policies and Education Solve E-Mail Woes," *American City & County,* May 2001, 8.

p. 227 Spotlight (Liz Hughes) caption based on Liz Hughes, "E-Mail Etiquette: Think Before You Send," *Women in Business,* July/August, 2003, 29.

p. 229 Spotlight (Barbara Hemphill) caption based on Barbara Hemphill, "Top 10 Tips for Managing E-Mail More Effectively," *Doors and Hardware,* January 2004, 34.

Chapter 9

pp. 261–271 Discussion of claim and adjustment letters based on Moshe Davidow, "Organizational Responses to Customer Complaints: What Works and What Doesn't," *Journal of Service Research,* February 2003, p. 26; Michael W. Michelson Jr., "Turning Complaints Into Cash," *The American Salesman,* December 2003, 22; Jeffrey R. Torp, "In Person, by Phone, by Mail, or Online: Managing Customer Complaints," *ABA Bank Compliance,* March/April 2003, 10; Chulmin Kim, Sounghie Kim, Subin Im, and Shanghoon Shin, "The Effect of Attitude and Perception on Consumer Complaint Intentions," *The Journal of Consumer Marketing 20,* 2003, 352; Michelle Andrews and Jodie Kirshner, "Cancel Me! Really! I Mean It!," *U.S. News & World Report,* 25 August 2003, 58; Kevin Lawrence, "How to Profit From Customer Complaints: Turning Problems Into Opportunities," *Canadian Manager,* Fall 2000, 25; Jeffrey J. Roth, "When the Customer's Got a Beef," *ABA Banking*

Journal, July 1998, 24–29; Geoffrey Brewer, "The Customer Stops Here," *Sales & Marketing Management*, March 1998, 30–36; Bill Knapp, "Communication Breakdown," *World Wastes*, February 1998, 16; and Stephen S. Tax, Stephen W. Brown, and Murali Chandrashekaran, "Customer Evaluations of Service Complaint Experiences: Implications for Relationship Marketing," *Journal of Marketing*, April 1998, 60–76.

p. 267 Spotlight (Peggy Foran) caption based on Arthur Levitt, *Take on the Street* (New York: Pantheon Books, 2002), 226.

p. 268 Picture caption based on Kevin Lawrence, "How to Profit From Customer Complaints: Turning Problems Into Opportunities," *Canadian Manager*, Fall 2000, 25.

p. 273 Ethical Insights box and discussion covering letters of recommendation based on Deborah A. Ballam, "Employment References—Speak No Evil, Hear No Evil: A Proposal for Meaningful Reform," *American Business Law Journal*, Spring 2002, 445; Diane Lacy, "References, Cafeteria Changes, Smokers," *HRMagazine*, April 2003, 37; William C. Martucci and Kevin Mason, "State-by-State Listing of Job-Reference Shield Laws," *Employment Relations Today*, 29; and Ellen Harshman and Denise R. Chachere, "Employee References: Between the Legal Devil and the Ethical Deep Blue Sea," *Journal of Business Ethics*, January 2001, 29–39.

p. 277 Spotlight (Andrew S. Grove) caption based on "The Fine Art of Feedback," *Working Woman*, February 1992, 26.

Chapter 10

p. 306 Ethical Insights box based on Lynn Quitman Troyka, *Simon & Schuster Handbook for Writers*, 7e (Upper Saddle River, NJ: Prentice Hall, 2005), 142–145; Frederick Crews, *The Random House Handbook* (New York: Random House, 1987), 76–78; and Stephen Downes, "Stephen's Guide to the Logical Fallacies" <http://www.datanation.com/fallacies> (Retrieved 7 July 2004).

p. 314 Discussion of e-marketing based on Stephan Spencer, "Email Marketing Tips," *Netconcepts* <http://www.netconcepts.com/bob04.htm> (Retrieved 27 June 2004); Jenny C. McCune, "8 Ways to Maximize E-Mail Marketing," *Bankrate.com* <http://www.bankrate.com/brm/news/biz/biz_ops/20020710a.asp?print=on> (Retrieved 27 June 2004); Pat Friesen, "How to Develop an Effective E-Mail Creative Strategy," *Target Marketing*, February 2002, 46–50; Steven C. Bursten, "E-Mail Marketing: Is It on Your Radar Screen?" *Franchising World*, July/August 2001, 60–61; and Karen Gedney and Joanna Belbey, "What Successful B2B E-Mail Messages Have in Common," *ClickZ Network* <http://www.clickz.com/experts/em_mkt/b2b_em_mkt/article.php/3293531> (Retrieved 7 June 2004).

p. 316 Spotlight (Margaret Whitman) caption based on Chris Taylor, "Meg Whitman," *Time*, 26 April 2004, 74; and Stephen B. Shepard, "A Talk With Meg Whitman," *Business Week*, 19 March 2001, 98–99.

p. 317 Spotlight (Herb Kelleher) caption based on Jeffrey A. Krames, "Performance Culture," *Executive Excellence*, November 2003, 16; and Herb Kelleher, "Beware the Impossible Guarantee," *Inc.*, November 1992, 30.

p. 318 Photo caption [laughing baby] based on Austin Lally as quoted in Geoffrey A. Fowler, "Media & Marketing: The Advertising Report: China: On the Secret of P&G's Success in "Ultra" Competitive Market, *The Wall Street Journal*, 21 January 2004, B7.

p. 319 Spotlight (John W. Thompson) caption based on Dan Verton, "Frontline Defenders," *Computerworld*, 29 March 2004, 23; Brian Grow, "Symantec: Leading the Charge Against Hackers," *BusinessWeek*, 21 June 2004, 85; and Larry Hooper, "John Thompson: Chairman and CEO, Symantec," *CRN*, 17 November 2003, 94.

Chapter 11

p. 339 Spotlight (Estee Lauder) caption based on Peter Krass, "Entrepreneur Estee Lauder," *Investor's Business Daily*, 6 April 1998, A3.

p. 341 Photo (Bora Bora) caption based on Chris Woodyard, "Continental Takes Back Free Miles Given in Error," 15 September 2003, 7B.

p. 343 Spotlight (Malcolm Forbes) caption based on Malcolm Forbes, "How to Write a Business Letter," *Strategies for Business and Technical Writing*, 4e, Kevin J. Harty, ed. (Boston: Allyn and Bacon, 1998), 108.

Chapter 12

p. 388 Spotlight (A. J. Jamal) photo caption based on Tom Ehrenfeld, "Out of the Blue," *Inc.*, July 1995, 70.

p. 389 Spotlight (Peggy Laun) caption based on John Case, "The Best Small Companies to Work for in America," *Inc.*, November 1992, 96.

p. 396 Figure 12-7 based on Danny Sullivan, "ComScore Media Metrix Search Engine Ratings," 28 April 2004, <http://searchenginewatch.com/reports/article.php/2156431> (Retrieved 17 July 2004). AOL Search garners over 16 percent of U.S. searches, but it uses Google's technology (which, in essence, puts Google at over 50 percent). MSN, which previously relied on LookSmart and Inktomi for its data, will rely on Yahoo listings until it finishes developing its own proprietary search technology.

p. 403 Spotlight (Tom Peters) caption based on *Thriving on Chaos* (New York: Knopf, 1991), 230–231.

Chapter 13

p. 428 Photo (Paul DePodesta) caption based on Jon Saraceno, "GM Redefines Dodger Way," *USA Today*, 18 March 2004, C1; and Murray Chass, "Tinkering Dodgers Won't Ever Leave Anything to Chance," *The New York Times*, 8 August 2004, 8.

p. 437 Career Coach box based on Dianna Booher, "E-Writing," *Executive Excellence*, April 2001, 16; Janet Bigham Bernstel and Hollis Thomases, "Writing Words for the Web," *Bank Marketing*, March 2001, 16–21; and Pat R. Graves and

Jack E. Murry, "Enhancing Communication With Effective Page Design and Typography," *Delta Pi Epsilon* Instructional Strategies Series, Summer 1990.

p. 438 Spotlight (Anthony Miranda) caption based on Jill Andresky Fraser, "He Asks to Be Audited—Often," *Inc.*, December 1994.

p. 443 Photo caption based on Ann Zimmerman and Martin Fackler, "Wal-Mart's Foray Into Japan Spurs a Retail Upheaval," *The Wall Street Journal*, 19 September 2003, A1.

Chapter 14

p. 470 Spotlight (Tom Sant) caption based on interview with Mary Ellen Guffey, 16 September 2004. See also "Sant: The Proposal Experts" <http://www.santcorp.com>.

p. 472 Photo (Kim and Scott Holstein) caption based on Jim Hopkins, "Pretzel Makers Shoot for Big Dough," *USA Today*, 23 January 2004, 4B.

p. 499 Figure 14.5 based on Sydel Sokuvitz and Amiso M. George, "Teaching Culture: The Challenges and Opportunities of International Public Relations," *Business Communication Quarterly*, June 2003, 97; Anthony C. Koh, "Teaching Understanding Cultural Differences for Business in an Internet-Based Economy," *Journal of Teaching in International Business, 15* (2), 2003, 27; and Karen S. Sterkel, "Integrating Intercultural Communication and Report Writing in the Communication Class," *The Bulletin of the Association for Business Communication*, September 1988, 14–16.

Chapter 15

p. 505 Figure 15.1 based on Janet G. Elsea, "Strategies for Effective Presentations," *Personnel Journal*, September 1985, 31–33, appearing in Cheryl Hamilton, *Communicating for Results* (Belmont, CA: Wadsworth/Thomson Learning, 2001), 340.

p. 507 Career Coach box based on Dianna Booher, "Selling Your Ideas," *Executive Excellence*, May 2004, 27; Sandra Gittlen, "The Public Side of You," *Network World*, 26 July 2004, 61; Hal Lancaster, "Practice and Coaching Can Help You Improve Um, Y'Know, Speeches," *The Wall Street Journal*, 9 January 1996, B1; and Bert Decker, "Successful Presentations: Simple and Practical," *HR Focus*, February 1992, 19.

p. 510 Discussion of vivid imagery based on Ellyn Spragins, "In a Manner of Speaking," *Fortune Small Business*, June 2003, 18; Jeff Olson, *Giving Great Presentations* (Bristol, VT: Velocity Business Publishing, 1997), 32–37; Kevin Daley, "Using the Right Evidence for Effective Presentations," *Communication Briefings*, April 1997, 8a; and Patricia Calderon, "Anatomy of a Great Presentation," *Windows Magazine*, June 1998, 203+.

p. 511 Spotlight (Patricia F. Russo) caption based on Simon Romero and Riva D. Atlas, "Lucent to Cut 10,000 Jobs as Its Losses Keep Mounting," *The New York Times*, 12 October 2002, B1.

p. 513 Figure 15.3 based on Dianna Booher, *Speak with Confidence* (New York: McGraw-Hill Professional, 2003), pp. 131–143; U.S. Department of Labor, "Presenting Effective Presentations with Visual Aids" <http://www.osha.gov/doc/outreachtraining/htmlfiles/traintec.html> (Retrieved 11 October 2004); and Shay McConnon, *Presenting with Power* (Oxford: How To Books, Ltd., 2002), pp. 38–43.

p. 514 Discussion of multimedia presentations based on Bill Howard, "Showtime Follies: The PowerPoint Road Show Presentation Lives On, Despite Maltreatment of the Art Form by Occasionally Clueless Presenters," *PC Magazine*, 13 July 2004, 81; Stephen Porter, "Punch Up Your PowerPoint," *Staging Rental Operations*, 1 May 2004, 3; Linda Bird, "15 Top PowerPoint Tips," *PC Magazine* (30 December 2003), 71; and Greg Jaffe, "What's Your Points, Lieutenant? Just Cut to the Pie Charts," *The Wall Street Journal*, 26 April 2000, A1.

p. 520 Spotlight (Justice O'Connor) caption based on Patricia O'Brien, "Why Men Don't Listen," *Working Woman*, February 1993, 58.

p. 522 Spotlight (Dianna Booher) caption based on Dianna Booher, *Speak With Confidence* (New York: McGraw-Hill, 2003); and Dianna Booher, *Executive's Portfolio of Model Speeches for All Occasions* (Englewood Cliffs, NJ: Prentice Hall, 1991), 252.

p. 527 Spotlight (Nancy Friedman) caption based on interview with Mary Ellen Guffey, 2 February 1999; and Barbara Marsh, "Oh, It's You, We Were Hoping You'd Call, Please Hold," *The Wall Street Journal*, 9 June 1994.

p. 529 Tech Talk box ("Making Effective Conference Calls") based on *The Office Professional*, June 2003, 8; Bill Quirke, "New Rules Needed as Technology Replaces Face-to-Face Meetings," *Personnel Today*, 11 December 2001, 1; and Susan Fox, "Conference Call Protocol," *Association Management*, January 1999, 93–94.

Chapter 16

p. 539 Spotlight (Michael Dell) caption based on John Batelle and Michael Dell, "Still Giving 'Em Dell Twenty Years In, Michael Dell's Hair Is a Little Grayer—But His Taste for Beating the Competition Remains as Strong as Ever," *Business2.0*, May 2004, 99; and Nick Turner, "Entrepreneur Michael Dell," *Investor's Business Daily*, 1 March 1999, A8.

p. 541 Searching for a Job Electronically based on Lorraine Farquaharson, "Technology (A Special Report); The Best Way To . . . Find a Job," *The Wall Street Journal*, 15 September 2003, R8; Kris Maher and Rachel Emma Silverman, "Your Career Matters: Online Job Sites Yield Few Jobs, Users Complain," *The Wall Street Journal*, 2 January 2002, A7; Elisabeth Goodrich and Michelle George, "Employer-Backed Job Site Lets Companies Avoid Monster," *InformationWeek*, 25 February 2002, 24.

p. 544 Networking Career Coach box based on Jeanette Borzo, "The Job Connection: Using Online Networking, Job Seekers Turn Friendship Into Employment," *The Wall Street Journal*, 13 September 2004, R14; "Business: E-Schmoozing; Business Networking," *The Economist*, 10 April 2004, 58; J. Michael Farr, *The Very Quick Job Search*

(Indianapolis: JIST Works, 1991), 50–52; and Bob Rosner, "What Color Is HR's Parachute?," *Workforce*, September 1998, 50–51.

p. 549 Spotlight (Yana Parker) caption based on a personal interview with Mary Ellen Guffey, 1996. Yana Parker is the author of *Damn Good Résumé* (Berkeley: Ten Speed Press, 1996); and "Hot Tips on Résumé Writing," Damn Good Résumé site <http://www.damngood.com/jobseekers/tips.html> (Retrieved 10 October 2004).

p. 553 Optimizing Your Résumé for Today's Technologies based on Anne Fisher, "How to Ruin an Online Job Hunt," *Fortune*, 28 June 2004, 43; Michelle Conlin, "The Résumé Doctor Is In," *BusinessWeek*, 14 July 2003, 116; Frequently Asked Questions, Quintessential Resumes & Cover Letters <http://www.resumesandcoverletters.com/services_prices.html> (Retrieved 26 September 2004); and "How to Write a Scannable Resume, University of Kentucky Career Center <http:www.uky.edu/CareerCenter/scanhowto.html> (Retrieved 28 September 2004).

p. 578 Spotlight (Daisy Wright) caption based on Daisy Wright, "Tell Stories, Get Hired," *OfficePro*, August/September 2004, 32–33.

index

A

B

C

G

H

I

J

K

L

M

N

O

P

Q

R

U

V

W

Y

Z